DATE DUE

IDEOLOGY AND EXPERIENCE

THE LITTMAN LIBRARY OF JEWISH CIVILIZATION

EDITORS

David Goldstein
Louis Jacobs
Vivian Lipman

This Library is dedicated to
the memory of

JOSEPH AARON LITTMAN

IDEOLOGY AND EXPERIENCE
Antisemitism in France at the Time of the Dreyfus Affair

STEPHEN WILSON

Rutherford•Madison•Teaneck
FAIRLEIGH DICKINSON UNIVERSITY PRESS
London and Toronto:
ASSOCIATED UNIVERSITY PRESSES

©1982 by Stephen Wilson

Associated University Presses, Inc.
4 Cornwall Drive
East Brunswick, New Jersey 08816

Associated University Presses
27 Chancery Lane
London WC2A 1NS, England

Associated University Presses
Toronto M5E 1A7, Canada

Library of Congress Cataloging in Publication Data

Wilson, Stephen, 1941–
   Ideology and experience.

   (The Littman library of Jewish civilization)
   Bibliography: p.
   Includes index.
   1. Antisemitism—France.   2. Dreyfus, Alfred, 1859–
1935.   3. Jews—France—Politics and government.
4. France—Ethnic relations.   I. Title.   II. Series:
Littman library of Jewish civilization.
DS146.F8W54   305.8'924'044   81–65467
ISBN 0–8386–3037–5   AACR2

Printed in the United States of America

For Sophia and Rebecca
For Sharon
"Noi siam venuti al luogo ov' io t'ho detto
che tu vedrai le genti dolorose,
ch' hanno perduto il ben dello intelletto."
(Dante, *Inferno*, Canto III)

CONTENTS

MAPS AND TABLES

Maps

Tables

ACKNOWLEDGMENTS

A book such as this is both a personal statement and a link in a greater chain of scholarship. Its many and obvious debts to other writers are acknowledged in the text and notes. The idea that Drumont might be worth studying seriously was first suggested to me by David Sabean, and its germination was greatly aided by the experience of planning and teaching a seminar on antisemitism in the School of European Studies at the University of East Anglia with Werner Mosse. Robert Rowland and Margo Russell kindly read parts of the book in draft and made valuable comments. Acting on these has, I hope, improved the clarity of the exposition and argument, if nothing else. I would also like to thank Lionel Kochan for his encouragement over a number of years and for his editorial suggestions.

Parts of the book have appeared in slightly different form as articles in the *Wiener Library Bulletin*, the *Historical Journal*, the *Journal of Contemporary History*, the *European Studies Review* (vol. 6, no. 2, April 1976, published by Sage Publications, Ltd), and *Annales* (no. 2 1977), and the permission of the editors and/or publishers of these journals to incorporate such previously published material is gratefully acknowledged.

Documents are quoted from the collections held by the French Bibliothèque Nationale, the Archives Nationales, and the Archives de la Préfecture de Police. My thanks are due to the staff of these institutions, and also to those of the Official Publications Department of Cambridge University Library, and of the Inter-Library Loan Department of the University of East Anglia Library, for all their help. All translations in the text are my own unless otherwise acknowledged. A grant from the Sir Ernest Cassel Educational Trust enabled me to undertake one particular piece of research in Paris, as did the hospitality offered me by Daniel Cribier.

Finally, I must pay more than customary tribute to the forbearance of my wife and daughters with a preoccupied husband and father. All that I can say is that the support as well as the distractions which they provided, though the latter were not always well-received, were an inestimable help that is deeply appreciated, and without which this book would not have been finished. The interest of my parents, my parents-in-law, and other relatives and friends, was also a valuable encouragement in a long labour.

The publication of the book has been delayed for unavoidable reasons, and account is not generally taken therefore of work that has appeared on the subject over the last five years. The most important contributions here have probably been: C. Stewart Doty, *From Cultural Rebellion to Counterrevolution: The Politics of Maurice Barrès* (Athens, Ohio, 1976); Zeev Sternhell, *La Droite Révolutionnaire 1885–1914, Les origines françaises du fascisme* (Paris, 1978); and Nelly Wilson, *Bernard–Lazare: Antisemitism and the Problem of Jewish Identity in Late Nineteenth-Century France* (Cambridge, 1978). I am happy to note that their assessments do not obviously conflict with mine.

University of East Anglia
Norwich, England

INTRODUCTION

Until now I have believed in Reason, I have believed that things and events had some logic, I have even believed in human justice! I found it difficult to comprehend anything that was bizarre or extreme. Alas! how my beliefs have been shattered and my sanity shaken! (Alfred Dreyfus, Diary, 14 April 1895)[1]

For our work is not finished, and your innocence must be fully recognized and proclaimed to save France from the moral catastrophe which nearly destroyed her. So long as one innocent man remains convicted, we no longer exist as an honourable or a just people. (Emile Zola, Letter to Dreyfus, 6 July 1899)[2]

It seems to me that an "opinion" as universal as antisemitism, which has flourished in all places and at all times . . . and in every part of the world where there have been and where there are Jews, cannot be the result of pure fantasy and caprice, and that it must owe its emergence and its permanence to factors that are profound and serious. (Bernard Lazare, 1894)[3]

If Dreyfus and his friends become historians and write text-books, you patriots who read me, and I myself who speak to you, . . . we shall be villains in the eyes of posterity. (Maurice Barrès, 1902)[4]

Antisemitism has been hard to grasp and come to terms with, although a large number of writers and scholars have been engaged in the attempt, and, among them, Marx, Freud and Sartre.[5] The difficulty is manifold. First, after the Nazi genocide, the endemic prejudice of non-Jews against Jews has assumed a monstrously inhuman dimension that has unbalanced the study of it. "History holds no parallel to these horrors . . .", Sir Hartley Shawcross told the Nuremberg Tribunal in 1946: they were "crimes so frightful that the imagination staggers and reels back at their very contemplation . . . Both imagination and intellect [are] . . . shattered by the horror of these things . . .".[6] Emerging from

their benumbed horror to study and to attempt to explain so appalling a
phenomenon, scholars have been unable to maintain a so-called academic
objectivity; they have come to the subject with passion, non-Jews with a deep
sense of guilt,[7] Jews with guilt perhaps and certainly with grief and rage.[8] The
study of antisemitism in recent times has generally been undertaken from this
almost inevitable starting-point in the Third Reich; the extermination camps
have been seen as the culmination of centuries of prejudice and discrimination, and their foreign shadow has been thrown back to darken the past.
Moreover, perhaps in an attempt to contain responsibility for the murder of
so many Jews and to find easily recognizable culprits, emphasis was placed in
the post-war years on antisemitism as a phenomenon of individual psychopathology.[9] This emphasis on the part of scholars who were not historians
together with the preference of historians for studying antisemitism as an
organized or political movement combined to produce a concentration on
antisemitism in and by itself, an "antisemitology", which neglected the complex socio-historical fabric of which antisemitism forms a part, and which
alone can explain its incidence and its functions. A further difficulty confront-
ing the student is the fact, which is to some degree obscured if the Nazi "final
solution" is taken as a model, that, unlike many other forms of ethnic prejudice, antisemitism is not, in post-Emancipation Western Europe, directed by
one clearly demarcated social group against another equally clearly demarcated
social group. Much more than the prejudice of white against black in the
United States of America,[10] for example, or the prejudice of the colonizer
against the colonized,[11] antisemitism has an autonomy, a being distinct from
its declared object of hostility, and serves many functions which are unrelated
to the actual presence of Jews or Jewish communities. This, it seems, is what
Louis Golding meant when he declared in 1938: "The Jewish Problem is in
essence a Gentile Problem."[12]

    This book seeks, in a small way, to try to overcome these difficulties, and
to further the general understanding of antisemitism by offering an explanation of its social function in a particular society at a particular time. The
example of France at the time of the Dreyfus Affair was chosen for three main
reasons, two of which are related to the special difficulties outlined above.
First, nineteenth-century France is sufficiently distant in time and place from
the Third Reich to allow a distancing from it and a reduction of its distorting
influence. Secondly, the important upsurge of antisemitism in France in this
period occurred in a country which had a very small Jewish community, by
Central and East European standards, and the "autonomous" aspect of antisemitism, its general social function as an ideology, is thus more evident. Thirdly,
it is a case that is very well documented. Not only were French antisemites
themselves prolific propagandists, but, since antisemitism became a public
political issue, the police authorities at all levels were alerted to it, and it was
reflected and reported extensively in the newspaper press, leaving the historian
in each case with ample evidence. In addition, a number of valuable secondary
works on various aspects of the subject have been completed, notably those
by Byrnes, Verdès-Leroux, Sorlin and Pierrard; these enormously facilitate the

task of general analysis, and we are greatly indebted to them. Finally, the social history of late nineteenth-century France is, despite important gaps, well enough explored for an attempt to be made to place antisemitism in its proper context.

Here we encounter a further problem still, theoretical and methodological, for what is that "antisemitism" which we wish to locate and thereby explain? And does the historian have access to it via his sources? Ackerman and Jahoda offered this very wide "operational definition" of antisemitism, that it is "any expression of hostility, verbal or behavioural, mild or violent, against the Jews as a group, or against an individual Jew because of his belonging to that group."[13] This definition seems an unpromising one for the would-be historian, for antisemitism only leaves important evidence of itself for him when it ceases to exist as private or cultural hostility, and comes to animate a "movement" with organizations, a press, an explicit ideology, or else takes legal and governmental forms. But the difficulty is more apparent than real, and stems from the undifferentiated and abstract definition. The necessary differentiation was made by Shlomo Bergman writing with great perception in 1943:[14]

> What is today usually called antisemitism consists in reality of two distinct groups of attitudes. The first is a dislike of Jews, which is of varying intensity and is rooted in the mores of the community. Intimate association with them is discountenanced and regarded as detrimental to social status. Nevertheless, they are not considered responsible for the major ills of society. This prejudice is broadly similar to that faced by other minorities . . . The other attitude emanates from a definite center of propaganda and supports a group of "intellectuals" who derive their livelihood from the creation of anti-Jewish myths.

The distinction is too sharply drawn and the connection between the two attitudes is not explained, but otherwise Bergman's observation provides us with a very good approach to a working definition of antisemitism as far as France was concerned.

We can ignore purely private individual prejudice against Jews. For the student of society, past or present, the purely private is a will o' the wisp, and hostility to Jews, or anything else, can only interest him when it is to some degree public, that is social. Hostility to Jews on the social and cultural level can take a variety of forms, ranging from hostile beliefs and stereotypes to discriminatory behaviour, formal and informal. In studying antisemitism at this level, the historian is clearly at a disadvantage compared with the social anthropologist or the sociologist; he cannot observe social phenomena directly; he cannot interview people; he has to rely almost exclusively on written documentary evidence that has survived. He may gain some idea of current stereotypes from popular literature and iconography; some evidence of formal discrimination, such as exclusion from clubs, the ban on intermarriage, may be preserved; but antisemitism on the everyday informal level is, with rare exceptions, a closed book to him. We do not know, we cannot know with much certainty, how non-Jews behaved towards Jews in France in the 1890s, in shops or restaurants, in trains, at work, at school, although we may maintain a legitimate curiosity about this, and we may have occasional glimpses of odd examples of behaviour in this sphere. But, this is less of a disadvantage than might at first be supposed. Jews were not, for one thing, as we have already pointed out, a clearly differentiated social group. Moreover, it is the characteristic of antisemitism in late nineteenth-century France precisely that it had become a structured and intellectualized system of ideas. Largely as a result of the advent of mass literacy and of the popular press, antisemitism as a relatively unstructured set of popular attitudes had become articulated into a coherent ideology; and, as a result of the development of political democracy and mass organizations, this structuring on the ideological level was coupled with the emergence of antisemitic groups and leagues. Antisemitism at this second level depended on the existence of antisemitism at the first level, but it was a new social phenomenon with special functions. It is this new antisemitism which is the main concern of this book, and we shall treat it primarily as a system of belief, an explanatory ideology, though, where necessary and appropriate we shall discuss its manifestations in the realm of action.

The book falls into four parts. The first examines various expressions of antisemitism associated directly with the Dreyfus Affair. The Affair was the main public "event" around which antisemitic opinion crystallized in the 1890s, and an attempt is made to assess the importance and significance of this event among different social groups and in different regions of France as well as chronologically, using police reports together with other material. Police reports have the advantage over newspapers that they were not attempting to create as well as claiming to reflect and survey public opinion. Nevertheless, it should be emphasized that a complete study of the Affair as an ideological event on the widest screen would require a thorough analysis of the provincial and the national press, which a single author could not sensibly undertake. We have been content to rely on sampling and on the few secondary works that exist. Subsequent chapters in Part One examine the antisemitic riots of 1898 and the Henry Subscription. The widespread riots and demonstrations of the first two months of 1898 were the most violent expression of antisemitism in the period and have been curiously neglected by historians. The Henry Subscription was organized by the antisemitic daily *La Libre Parole* at the end of 1898 and the start of 1899. Information and messages by subscribers provide a basis for further analysis of the social and regional complexion of antisemitism, but also allow the historian direct access to antisemitic ideas at the popular level in process of transformation into ideology.

Part Two briefly examines antisemitism in France at the end of the past century as an organized movement. Special studies are made of the Ligue Antisémitique Française and of the antisemitic deputies, and of the nature of the support for both. In addition, a look is taken at the antisemitic movement in Algeria, which provided its metropolitan counterpart with a model of extremism. The central part of the book, Part Three, undertakes a thorough and systematic analysis of antisemitic ideology, paying special attention to the writings of Edouard Drumont. Antisemitic ideology is examined under various headings, economic, social, nationalist, racial, religious and sexual, and, in each case, it is related to its social context in order to suggest its motivation and functions. A final chapter looks more closely at the relationship between antisemitism as a structure of belief or ideology and the social experience which it encountered and sought to explain. It is concluded that antisemitism was only one aspect, though temporarily a dominant one, of a general reaction to "modernization" and the experience of rapid social change. Part Four examines the relationship between antisemitism and French Jews. An analysis of the geography of antisemitism in France confirms the view that it was only in part a reaction to Jewish presence. A study of the declared aims of antisemites suggests that they were fundamentally expressive rather than instrumental, and certainly did not represent a realistic "policy". Nevertheless, antisemitism and its manifestations did affect and threaten Jews, and a final chapter examines their reactions to antisemitism, which appear to have been more positive than has been generally supposed.

NOTES

1 Alfred Dreyfus, *Cinq années de ma vie (1894–1899)* (Paris, 1962), p. 91.
2 Emile Zola, *Correspondance, Oeuvres complètes*, 14 (Paris, 1970), p. 1524.
3 Bernard Lazare, *L'Antisémitisme: Son histoire et ses causes* (Paris, 1894), p. vi.
4 Maurice Barrès, *Scènes et doctrines du nationalisme* (1902) (Paris, 1925), II, p. 105.
5 See Karl Marx, "On the Jewish Question" (1843), *Early Texts* (Oxford, 1972), pp. 85–114; Sigmund Freud, *The Psychopathology of Everyday Life* (1901), English Standard Edition, VI (London, 1960), pp. 9–10 and 92–3; Freud, *Analysis of a Phobia in a Four-Year-Old Boy* (1909), ibid., X (London, 1955), p. 36; Freud, *Leonardo da Vinci and a Memory of His Childhood* (1910), ibid., XI (London, 1964), pp. 95–6; Freud, *Civilization and its Discontents* (1930), ibid., XXI (London, 1961), pp. 114–15 and 120; Freud, *Moses and Monotheism: Three Essays* (1939); and *A Comment on Anti-Semitism* (1938), ibid., XXIII (London, 1964), pp. 3–137 and 287–93; and Jean-Paul Sartre, *Réflexions sur la question juive* (Paris, 1946).
6 Sir Hartley Shawcross, Concluding Speech for the Prosecution, 26–27 July 1946, *The Trial of German Major War Criminals: Proceedings of the International Military Tribunal sitting at Nuremberg, Germany*, Part 19 (London, 1948), pp. 452, 407 and 429; see also Mr Justice Jackson, Concluding Speech, 26 July 1946, ibid., p. 387; R.W.Cooper, *The Nuremberg Trial* (Harmondsworth, 1947), pp. 49 and 144; Albert Camus, *L'Homme Révolté* (Paris, 1951), pp. 14 and 229–30; Erik H. Erikson, *Childhood and Society* (1950 and 1965) (Harmondsworth, 1974), p. 348; Charles Y. Glock and Rodney Stark, *Christian Beliefs and Anti-Semitism* (New York, 1966), pp. xvii and 101–2; and George M. Kren and Leon Rappoport, "Victims: the fallacy of innocence", *Societas*, 4 (1974), pp. 111–29.
7 See, for example, François Mauriac, Préface, Leon Poliakov, *Bréviaire de la haine: Le IIIe Reich et les Juifs* (Paris, 1951); F. Lovsky, *L'Antisémitisme chrétien* (Paris, 1970), p. 372; and Lovsky, *La Déchirure de l'absence: Essai sur les rapports entre l'Eglise du Christ et le peuple d'Israël* (Paris, 1971), pp. 22–3.
8 See, for example, Georges Wellers, *De Drancy à Auschwitz* (Paris, 1946), Centre de Documentation Juive Contemporaine; Isaac Schneersohn, Avant-Propos, Henri Monneray, ed., *La Persécution des Juifs dans les pays de l'Est présentée à Nuremberg* (Paris, 1949), C.D.J.C; and Kren and Rappoport, op. cit., pp. 124–5.

9 See, for example, Sartre, op. cit.; T. W. Adorno *et al.*, *The Authoritarian Personality* (New York, 1950); Nathan W. Ackerman and Marie Jahoda, *Anti-Semitism and Emotional Disorder: A Psychoanalytical Interpretation* (New York, 1950); Rudolph M. Loewenstein, *Christians and Jews: A Psychoanalytic Study* (New York, 1951); and James H. Robb, *Working-Class Anti-Semite: A Psychological Study in a London Borough* (London, 1954); see also the critical comments of George L. Mosse, *The Crisis of German Ideology. Intellectual Origins of the Third Reich* (London, 1966), p. 301; Arthur Hertzberg, *The French Enlightenment and the Jews* (New York, 1968), p. 6; Gertrude J. Selznick and Stephen Steinberg, *The Tenacity of Prejudice: Anti-Semitism in Contemporary America* (New York, 1969), pp. 1, 133 and ff, and 190–1; and Léon Poliakov, *Les Juifs et Notre Histoire* (Paris, 1973), p. 93, among others. Many valuable insights have, of course, been developed in this field, to which we are indebted; it is only the exclusive or excessive emphasis on the psychological approach which seems mistaken and unfruitful.

10 See, for example, John Dollard, *Caste and Class in a Southern Town* (New York, 1973); Gunnar Myrdal, *The American Dilemma: the Negro Problem and Modern Democracy* (New York, 1944); Rayford W. Logan, *The Betrayal of the Negro* (New York, 1965); Winthrop D. Jordan, *White over Black: American Attitudes Toward the Negro, 1550–1812* (Chapel Hill, 1968); and Gilbert Osofsky, *The Burden of Race, A Documentary History of Negro-White Relations in America* (New York, 1968).

11 See O. Mannoni, *Psychologie de la Colonisation* (Paris, 1950); Franz Fanon, *Peau noire, Masques blanches* (Paris, 1952); Sheila Patterson, *Colour and Culture in South Africa* (London, 1953); and Albert Memmi, *Portrait du colonisé* (Paris, 1966).

12 Louis Golding, *The Jewish Problem* (Harmondsworth, 1938), p. 11.

13 Ackerman and Jahoda, op.cit., p. 19.

14 Shlomo Bergman, "Some Methodological Errors in the Study of Antisemitism", *Jewish Social Studies*, V (1943), p. 57.

IDEOLOGY AND EXPERIENCE

PART ONE
THE DREYFUS AFFAIR, PUBLIC OPINION
AND ANTISEMITISM

[Dreyfus] . . . has become a man whose name everyone knows, the most famous name since the death . . . of Napoleon. (Charles Péguy, *Notre Jeunesse* (p. 197)

I was only an artillery officer, whom a tragic error prevented from pursuing his normal career. Dreyfus the symbol . . . is not me. It is you who created that Dreyfus . . . (Dreyfus, Letter to Victor Basch, cit. Maurice Barrès—Charles Maurras, *La République ou le roi*, Guy Dupré, Introduction, p. xxx)

CHAPTER I

THE DREYFUS AFFAIR, PUBLIC OPINION AND ANTISEMITISM: I

I

I T IS APPROPRIATE TO BEGIN A STUDY OF ANTISEMITISM IN FRANCE IN THE 1890s with the Dreyfus Affair in the conventional way, for the Affair gave antisemitism a dramatic scenario and provided its proponents with a powerful and lasting[1] myth of Jewish inassimilability and treason. During the years of the Affair, too, the public expression of antisemitism was encouraged, and it assumed new and sharper ideological form. If one can gauge the extent and nature of the involvement of different sections of French society in the Affair, one has a basis for a more general analysis of antisemitism in France and its motivations and functions. Following an old strategy of social historians of revolutions, taken up more recently by social anthropologists and historians of attitudes, the study of the "dramatic occurrence" can open up an understanding of underlying structures.[2] Such an undertaking is not as easy as might at first sight appear, for, despite the large number of studies of the Affair by historians, more interest has, until recently, been shown in the details of the case itself, which were often obscure to contemporaries, and intellectual historians have tended to restrict the wider dimensions of the Affair to their articulation among intellectuals, to the neglect of its impact and interpretation among ordinary people. This is not to suggest that the intellectuals' schema were unimportant, nor that they were divorced from popular views, but that importance can only be measured, the relationship assessed, when we have a clearer idea of what those popular views were.

There has been a tendency among historians to assume too much in this area, though some of their assumptions are correct. There is no doubt, for example, to take our central consideration, that the Affair was a public manifestation of antisemitism, and that it was perceived as such. "It was because of a Jew that the French lined up against each other seventy-five years ago . . .", writes Lovsky.[3] This truism, however, has sometimes been repeated and amplified rather than tested by historians. Stokes, for example, wrote confidently in 1937: "Until the rise of National Socialism under Adolf Hitler, the condemnation of Dreyfus marked the highest tide of modern anti-Semitism";[4] and, more recently, Juan Comas, in an influential UNESCO publication, has pointed to the Affair as one of the main examples of antisemitism in European history, along with the expulsion of the Jews from Spain in the fifteenth century and the nineteenth-century pogroms of Eastern Europe.[5] Such emphasis on the specifically antisemitic aspect of the Affair, though unsubstantiated by these authors, does actually reflect contemporary views. Luce in Roger Martin du Gard's fictional recreation of the Affair, *Jean Barois*, published in 1913, referred to Dreyfus as: "this little unknown Jew, condemned by seven officers . . ."[6] Emile Zola wrote that the Affair was the history of "the crucifixion of a Jew".[7] Charles Péguy saw Dreyfus as "the symbol of the destiny of Israel offered as a sacrifice for the salvation of the other nations";[8] while Daniel Halévy wrote of him: "the hatred of a whole people weighed on him, he underwent an extreme physical and moral punishment; he was a Jew, his infamy was taken as a symbol; the insult to his person insulted a whole race."[9]

But we are here at the level of intellectuals' myth-making, and the historian must attempt to fathom the reality beneath this and other symbolic representations. There is little doubt, first, that Dreyfus's original arrest and condemnation stemmed from the anti-Jewish prejudice of the officer corps, and its attachment, as Joseph Reinach put it, to "the legend of the Jew as Judas, of the Jews as the race of Iscariot, the race of traitors."[10] Dreyfus, himself, told Commandant Forzinetti after his first trial: "My only crime is that I was born a Jew! . . . My God, why did I ever enter the Ecole de Guerre?"[11] It is clear also that the explosion of the Dreyfus Case into the Dreyfus Affair, provoked in part by those convinced of his innocence or of the illegality of his trial, was largely the responsibility of an organized antisemitic movement and newspaper press. "At the origin of the Affair, one discovers the antisemites", wrote Anatole France in 1904, "who for some time had been trying to stir up a tranquil country."[12] "What triumphed in the Affair", wrote Reinach, "was antisemitism; if the law did not hold good for Dreyfus, it was because he was a Jew. Organized antisemitism committed the first crime, carried on the campaign with calculated violence, unleashed the forces of bestiality."[13] Halévy similarly held responsible "the instigators of antisemitic agitation . . ."[14] Léon Daudet, himself one of those instigators and later a contributor to France's main antisemitic daily, admitted: "For *La Libre Parole* and the opinions it stood for, the Dreyfus Affair came as a confirmation, a godsend . . ."[15] But, as Halévy, Reinach and others pointed out, much more was involved than a fillip given to an extremist minority movement, much more than an opportunity which it knew how to exploit. The antisemites may have led the dance, but they were joined by many others. "The professional antisemites", wrote Reinach, "were not alone in launching their anathema. They had the support of men who called themselves liberal . . ."[16] Both Georges de Lauris and Fernand Gregh, for example, sensitive, rational, humane men, confessed in their autobiographies to having seen the campaign on Dreyfus's behalf as some kind of Jewish conspiracy.[17] Respect for the law, for the army, for authority, combined with latent antisemitism to make such attitudes widespread. What the Affair reveals then is the wide extent and great importance of antisemitic prejudice in France, latent, but ready to manifest itself when circumstances allowed or encouraged it. Beneath the surface drama, which revealed and amplified it, beyond the antisemitic press and the antisemitic organizations, which to some extent expressed it, can we bring further into the light "that antisemitism of the depths . . . from the old hidden bed where it has flowed for so many centuries"?[18]

If we turn now to the Dreyfus Affair in French public opinion, we may be dazzled, however, by the blinding lights of certitude. Of the enormous impact of the Affair on opinion, articulate contemporaries were convinced, and they lent it heroic and revolutionary proportions. For Jacques Bainville, for example: "The Dreyfus Affair . . . amounted to a real revolution . . . This struggle of doctrines, feelings and movements . . . repeated on a smaller scale the great crises of the fourteenth century, of the Wars of Religion, of the Fronde, of the Revolution of 1789 . . ."[19] Zola saw the Affair in the same perspective, referring to it as "the culmination of 1789",[20] and this view assumed the status of a catch-phrase in the title of Georges Sorel's *La Révolution dreyfusienne*, published in 1909. For Martin du Gard's Jean Barois, the Affair was "a historical drama comparable to no other . . . humanity divided into two unequal camps . . . on the one side, authority, unwilling to accept the control of reason; on the other, the critical spirit, proudly disdaining the constraints imposed on it by society."[21] In the same vein, Péguy referred to "the immortal Dreyfus Affair . . . the last manifestation of the republican ideal . . . It was a prominent crisis in three histories . . . It was a prominent crisis in the history of Israel. It was a prominent crisis in the history of France . . . It was above all a prominent crisis in the history of Christianity."[22] And Halévy proclaimed in 1910: "Our great-grandfathers had 1789, 1793, the Wars of Liberation; our grandfathers had 1815 and the Cossacks, 1830, 1848; our fathers had 1848, the Franco-Prussian War and the Commune. We had the Affair, just the Affair . . . A single and formidable crisis has left its mark on us . . ."[23] All this is evidence of the Affair's importance for France's intellectual elite, though it is expressed in near-metaphysical terms which make its social meaning difficult to elucidate. This elucidation is made yet more difficult, and the exploration of more popular attitudes has been discouraged, as we have already remarked, by the fact that historians have very often interpreted the Affair and its impact in the same mythical framework. This was cogently pointed out fifteen years ago by J.-P. Peter,[24] and requires little further illustration here.

Two examples must suffice from books with wide audiences. First, Pierre Miquel in his *L'Affaire Dreyfus*, an admirable concise account of the "events" of the case, which stresses the importance of the newspaper press in creating the Affair, asserts that it was "a crossroads in French life", and claims that "with the Affair the main lines of twentieth-century France take form . . .";[25] while Hannah Arendt wrote in *The Origins of Totalitarianism* that the Affair was "the only episode in which the subterranean forces of the nineteenth

century enter the full light of recorded history . . . [thus offering] a foreglow
of the twentieth century [and its horrors] . . ."[26] But neither writer provides
detailed substantiation of these claims, in which we can read echoes of Bainville, Zola, Péguy and Halévy. Despite such conviction of the importance of
the Affair, reflected in the large volume of literature devoted to it, historians
have been strangely reluctant, until very recently, to justify their verdict with
studies in depth of its social, economic and cultural circumstances. It is still
hard therefore to answer the crucial question: why did the case of Captain
Dreyfus assume such importance in its time, becoming the great Affair? The
encounter on the national level between intellectuals and politicians of different persuasions, championing on the one side the Army, the Nation and
Reasons of State, and on the other, Justice, the Rule of Law and Individual
Rights, has had many chroniclers, but they have not told us why this particular
battle took place in the France of the 1890s. Nor do we know how far it
impinged on the lives of ordinary people, or how far it articulated their
interests and desires. Nor is the role of antisemitism in this debate very clear.
Some historians, it is true, have approached the impact of the Affair on public
opinion in a more concrete way, but they have mainly been content with
impressions, more or less unsubstantiated, and guesses, more or less informed,[27] or they have concentrated on the newspaper press.[28] It is agreed
that the Affair was a reflection in some way of antisemitic opinion, that
"opinion" played an important part in the *dénouement* of the Dreyfus Case
itself, and that protagonists on both sides made great efforts to mobilize
support through the press, through public meetings and through pressure-
groups, but very little attention has been paid to the pattern and detail of these
campaigns, or to the reaction which they evoked. Miquel again proclaims:
"The Dreyfus Affair is above all a phenomenon of opinion . . .";[29] but the
study of attitudes in the Affair, provoked or spontaneous, has in fact been
neglected, or, at least, restricted to the level of formalized intellectual or
political debate, as we have already indicated.[30] The significance of the Affair,
however, lies in these attitudes. As Raoul Girardet has written:[31]

> The meaning of the great drama of French conscience of the end of the
> nineteenth century is falsified if it is kept within a purely judicial framework:
> whether Captain Alfred Dreyfus, condemned to life imprisonment on 22
> December 1894 for handing over to Germany documents involving national
> defence, actually committed or did not commit the crime for which he was
> accused, is of relatively little interest to the historian of public opinion.

An equal falsification, Peter has added, of a social crisis, an equal irrelevance
for the social historian, if indeed he is not the same person.

But here we encounter another gross assumption of the conventional historiography. A great historical turning-point, a metaphysical drama, the Affair
was also a social conflict, "a civil war": "the Affair divided the country into
two indomitable factions."[32] Again, this is a generalization for which much
contemporary evidence can be, though it is not always, provided. Léon Bloy,
for example, referred in 1900 to "the legion of rogues who are agitating about

this affair, for or against . . ."[33] Halévy wrote of 1898: "The split was accomplished in an instant. Inside the Parisian bourgeoisie, alone capable of quickly grasping the import of an affair so complicated in its details, each family was in a few days at its post, its plans worked out, entrenched behind closed doors."[34] Gregh recalled that families, too, "were divided . . . old friendships broken, old enmities repaired . . ."[35] Mme Steinheil gives a fuller version of this familiar picture. From 1897, she writes,[36]

> a bitter war between Dreyfusards and anti-Dreyfusards was waged, and the most scurrilous slanders, the worst insults, became weapons of almost universal use. My salon was neutral ground, but I was soon unable to prevent those impassioned duels of words, in which there showed hardly a sign of tolerance or of human sympathy. And these constant duels took place between men who had been the closest friends all their lives, between brothers, between husband and wife, between father and son . . . the whole French nation was divided into two parties . . .

Against this pattern of "civil war", at least among the Parisian bourgeoisie still apt to identify itself with the nation as in the time of Sieyès, must be set evidence of neutrality or willingness to disagree. Mme Steinheil, herself, was a revisionist, but she remained the confidante of President Faure who opposed revision, and, as she says, her salon was "neutral ground", and she continued to number "staunch Dreyfusards and also staunch anti-Dreyfusards" among her friends.[37] Jules Renard, an ardent and active Dreyfusard, maintained his friendship with Maurice Donnay and Louis Paillard, who were in the opposite camp.[38] Auguste Renoir told his son: "People are either pro- or anti-Dreyfus. I would like to try to be simply a Frenchman", and he remained on good terms both with Degas, who was an extreme antisemite, and with Pissarro, who was a Dreyfusard and a Jew.[39] Romain Rolland, according to the Tharauds, also managed to stay "above the *mêlée*" of the Affair as later of the First World War;[40] while Adrien Hébrard, director of *Le Temps*, which was Dreyfusard, continued to be welcome at the anti-Dreyfusard salon of Mme de Loynes.[41] Of course, there were different varieties of neutrality. Sully Prudhomme, Emile Boutroux, Ernest Lavisse and their friends, who founded the Appel à l'Union in January 1899,[42] were expressing a sense of concern and responsibility very different from the apathy or impatience of those remembered by Georges de Lauris:[43]

> Alongside those who enjoyed the conflict, who had hopes of victory for their party or who had strong feelings which were beyond discussion, there were others who could not take the new climate. They regretted the tranquillity of the past, their quiet occupations and pleasures . . . They would willingly have accepted Dreyfusism, or antisemitism, though less easily (for the sake of that disrupted peace).

Different again was the "neutrality" of Léon Bloy, submitting Zola and the Dreyfusards, but also the military and the antisemitic press, to the torrents of his abuse.[44]

But, if this begins to suggest nuances absent from the grand generalizations, it still does not take us very far. We are still with the intellectuals, or at most the educated bourgeoisie. What must be attempted is an assessment of the extent and nature of "opinion" in a less general, a more detailed sense, introducing distinctions by class and social grouping, and trying to measure in some way the intensity of involvement at any time. To do this, letters, diaries, reminiscences of the articulate few have been massively complemented by reports made and collected by the Ministry of the Interior, and particularly by the Sûreté Générale,[45] concerned above all with "mass opinion" and possible threats to public order. Some explanations are necessary about these source materials and their value. The documentation on the Dreyfus Affair in the General Police archives falls into several categories. First, there are assessments of public opinion in their areas by prefects, sub-prefects, local police and, more often, the *commissaires spéciaux*, attached directly to the Sûreté Générale. Reports of this kind were, it seems, called for by the Ministry of the Interior at each turning-point in the history of the Dreyfus Case, in order to assess likely, and then actual, reactions to court decisions and government moves. Occasionally, assessments of opinion were filed without solicitation, usually by police officers who felt that governmental policy was not firm enough. Indications of public opinion were also directly provided by paid police agents, usually in Paris. Second, reports were made as a matter of course on disturbances and demonstrations, and, third, on public and private meetings of a political nature. Reports on meetings usually give a *résumé* of speeches made and indicate the size of attendance. Reports on public meetings were made by police officers who attended them in their official capacity (with powers to close them if they became too disorderly); reports on other political meetings were made by police agents. These also provided the fourth type of documentation, general reports on the activities of political organizations, often on a day-to-day basis. Most political or semi-political organizations, including the Leagues formed or reformed during the Affair, were infiltrated by police agents. Fifth, reports were made on posters put up in towns and villages, and on other propaganda material sold on the streets, distributed at railway stations, or sent through the post; examples of this material were frequently seized by the police and sent to Paris, and they are preserved in the archives with indications of their provenance. Sixth, and much less important, press telegrams, private telegrams of persons under police surveillance, and occasionally private letters, were intercepted by the police. Seventh, the Sûreté Générale, local police and prefects kept a close watch on the newspaper press, and built up large collections of press cuttings. These are mainly, but not exclusively, restricted to the Parisian press; only in September 1899, it seems, was a systematic monitoring of the provincial press undertaken in expectation of the verdict of the Rennes Court Martial. These press cuttings are obviously no substitute for a complete study of the press during the Affair, but they provide useful guidelines in the absence of such a comprehensive study.[46]

The material in the General Police archives is therefore heterogeneous, and provides objective documentation as well as subjective reporting, while the variety and extent of the latter increases its value as evidence. As Richard

Cobb has indicated for an earlier period,[47] police reporting and action were based on certain assumptions, of which one needs to be aware. But, on the whole the quality of reporting is high, and seems to be based on observation rather than stereotyping, and bias is probably traceable. Police officials, like any others, tended to follow the line set by the government and administration, veering to the Left, for example, from mid-1898, and giving vent to an anticlericalism under the Waldeck-Rousseau and, more so under the Combes, government, that had not been so evident or so overtly expressed earlier. They were also naturally professionally concerned with "public order", and prone to be over-suspicious of anarchists, Socialists and workers. They also looked often for pecuniary motives for political stances, and tended to believe that disorder and protest were the work of troublemakers rather than the spontaneous expression of discontent. But few signs of antisemitism appear in police reporting, and they were as hostile to the Extreme Right and to Catholics as they were to the Extreme Left and its representatives.

In what follows the police reports have been used, complemented by other material where appropriate, in two main ways: first, to establish a chronological account of the evolution of opinion during the Affair, relying mainly on subjective reporting; and, secondly, in the next chapter, to analyse the make-up of this opinion in terms of geographical distribution and relationship to social, professional, religious and political groupings, relying here more on the documentation that is amenable to some form of quantification. Subsequent chapters examine in more detail two more deliberate expressions of antisemitism during the Affair: the antisemitic riots of 1898 and the Subscription for the widow of Colonel Henry.

II

The first hint that an officer had been arrested for espionage came in Drumont's antisemitic daily La Libre Parole on 29 October 1894, and the news was definitively confirmed by the same newspaper on 1 November 1894 with the headline: "High treason. Arrest of the Jewish officer A. Dreyfus."[48] According to Reinach, the subsequent trial of Dreyfus, by court martial in camera, was the object of great public interest: "The whole of France, and Paris above all, waited for the verdict in a state of feverish excitement"; and his conviction was universally welcomed: "The vast majority of people wanted the condemnation and applauded it."[49] In parliament and the press, too, the verdict was universally accepted, though the sentence to military degradation and life imprisonment in a fortified place was sometimes felt to be too lenient. "This morning", wrote Maurice Paléologue on 23 December 1894, "there is, in the whole Parisian press, from the Extreme Right to the Extreme Left, from clerical and Royalist papers to the organs of the most advanced Socialism, only one note in the commentaries on the verdict of the court martial; and that is one of approval, relief, comfort, and joy, a triumphant, vindictive and ferocious joy", and he added that the reaction in the provincial press was the same.[50] At this time, as Halévy pointed out, only a handful of persons, Dreyfus's relatives, his lawyer, his prison governors and a few Jews, believed him to be innocent;[51] but Halévy remembered also a certain unease about certain aspects of the case among the young liberal bourgeoisie of Paris to which he belonged:[52]

What was going on? What did we really know about it? Of the trial, nothing; we only received a mere impression of the brief event: too much hatred, too much secrecy; too much passion in an atmosphere of ignorance. But the matter was serious, which justified the procedure. Dreyfus was condemned. The judges took the responsibility for the verdict; we allowed them to do so and subscribed to the sentence.

Halévy reports also the distaste of a Zola, who still believed Dreyfus guilty, at the pleasure taken by crowds and by journalists like Léon Daudet, in the discovery and punishment of the "traitor".[53] This sadism was most obviously reflected in reaction to the degradation ceremony at the Ecole Militaire on 5 January 1895, which was reported with relish in the press,[54] and which was the occasion also for a direct demonstration of popular hatred. Paléologue recounts: "In front of the railings of the courtyard, on the Place de Fontenoy, a huge crowd, held off with difficulty by the police, danced for joy, seethed with excitement, whistled, shouted cries of hatred: "Death to the Jews! . . . Death to the traitor! . . . Death to Judas!"[55] Similar expressions of hostile popular sentiment occurred when Dreyfus was taken from Paris to the coast to embark for the penal settlement. At La Rochelle, the convoy was surrounded by a noisy crowd, shouting: "Put him to death", and Dreyfus was physically assaulted; and he was jeered at by the fishermen of the Ile de Ré.[56]

The police showed little interest in the Affair at this stage, but the few reports that do exist confirm the impression that intense emotion was aroused. It was reported from the Aisne on 6 January 1895:[57]

the public of Saint-Quentin, essentially patriotic as the events of 1870–1 abundantly demonstrated, has read with horror the accounts in the Paris newspapers today of the degradation ceremony. The terrible ordeal undergone by the traitor does not appear to many people to have been severe enough, and that because of his attitude [i.e. his protestation of his innocence]. In the cafés where people talk about this sad affair, they say quite openly . . . since the law will not allow us to get rid of him, let us send the traitor to the Salut Islands, which are both inaccessible and unhealthy, and where he will find an early death.

In the Meurthe-et-Moselle, the reaction seems to have been much the same:[58]

All day yesterday [6 January], the passengers at the railway stations of Conflans and Batilly rushed to the news stands to buy the Paris papers, mainly *La Libre Parole* and *L'Intransigeant.* Everyone was impatient to know how Dreyfus had behaved at his degradation. His protestation of innocence is widely discussed and is seen here as a provocation . . . People regret that the court martial was unable to condemn him to death . . . Many people are expressing great hostility towards the Jews; but, despite this, all remains calm generally, and in a few days everyone will have forgotten about this affair.

Initial opinion was therefore very hostile to the "traitor", but, as the above report guessed, interest died away, a natural evaporation, encouraged, it seems, by the authorities who were anxious to have the case forgotten.[59]

Through 1895, 1896 and most of 1897, police interest in the Affair was small, reflecting their assessment of public interest. However, news of Dreyfus's alleged escape from Devil's Island, published in the *Daily Chronicle* in September 1896, *L'Eclair*'s allegation the same month that a secret document had decided Dreyfus's conviction, the Castelin *interpellation* in the Chamber of Deputies in November 1896, the publication the same month of Bernard Lazare's *Une Erreur judiciaire* and of a facsimile of the *"bordereau"* in *Le Matin*, all renewed discussion of the case, though only in very limited circles. Halévy remembered that Lazare's pamphlet, "so lively and provoking, produced no effect".[60] Similarly, in Martin du Gard's *Jean Barois*, the first rumours of Dreyfus's innocence began to reach the editors of *Le Semeur* towards the end of 1896, but they refused to believe in the possibility of a miscarriage of justice—all except Woldsmuth, who was a Jew.[61] But public interest, or the interest of newspapers, did revive enough for the police to begin to collect press cuttings on reactions to the Affair. These were in general hostile to any questioning of the 1894 verdict, and reflected the establishment view that the Affair should be forgotten. For example, *Le Matin*, despite its own contribution to the revival of interest, protested on 19 November 1896:

> It is from every point of view distressing that the Chamber [of Deputies] has seen fit to devote two hours of debate to this lamentable Dreyfus Affair. The very thought that any kind of conflict might arise from such a debate is already painful to good Frenchmen; and responsible citizens everywhere deplore the fact . . . that a discussion has been reopened which the verdict of the court martial should (definitively have closed).

In *Le Voltaire*, on the same day, L.-L. Klotz declared: "Dreyfus has been judged and well judged. The traitor has been punished. Those who have undertaken the miserable task of defending him have rightly been condemned by public opinion." However, a few dissenting voices were heard. *L'Eclair*, again on the same day, claimed that public opinion was justly alarmed by the secrecy of the Dreyfus trial, adding: "It is absolutely necessary to bring this deplorable Dreyfus Affair, in its entirety, into the light of day." Henri Turot in *La Petite République*, Paris's main socialist newspaper, went further on 11 November 1896, writing:[62]

> It is absolutely intolerable that French citizens should be treated by their rulers like minors . . . and be obliged to take things on faith instead of being able to arrive at their opinions openly and freely. An act of treason has jeopardized the national defence; a man has been tried and sentenced. And, for fear of alleged diplomatic complications, the public has not been given absolute and irrefutable proof of the traitor's guilt. It is not therefore surprising to see a campaign developing in favour of the innocence of the man condemned.

Controversy had begun, and the involvement of "public opinion" in the Affair was announced; but it was not until a year later in late 1897 that the Affair really imposed itself. By then the public pronouncements by Scheurer-Kestner in November and December 1897 and Mathieu Dreyfus's denunciation of Esterhazy had radically changed the nature of the campaign, whose tentative beginnings Turot had noted. Our memoir writers, the police and their agents all registered the mutation. "At the end of 1897", wrote Gregh, "things began to happen, very quickly . . . the Dreyfus Affair really exploded."[63] "The period of quiet investigations, of private conversions, was closed. The matter was public; it forced itself on our attention" wrote Halévy.[64] "Nothing but Dreyfus", reported a police agent in November 1897. "This affair is taking on enormous proportions . . . Nobody talks about anything else." Though still in general hostile to Dreyfus, Parisian opinion in all classes was concerned and alarmed, as further police agent reports indicate:[65]

> The campaign of calumny aimed at exonerating Dreyfus has aroused general indignation, and even profound disgust, especially in the mass of the people . . . this disgust soon gave way to feelings of irritation and then of exasperation directed against the supporters of the traitor . . . and it is frightening to imagine what the future may hold. The situation is considered everywhere and by everyone to be very dangerous. Excitement mounts in the streets at the time when the evening newspapers appear, and is increased by the sensational news which they spread among the public . . . The special editions of the papers are bought out in no time. One finds the same animation, the same feverish excitement in bars and cafés at *apéritif* time, when everyone meets to discuss the events of the day. But it is mainly in working-class *quartiers* that people are most worried . . . For two days also there has been a lot of talk about agitation in the Latin Quarter. If this effervescence among students, which is still superficial at the moment, continues, it will take on a more serious character and will spread to other *quartiers*. We will then see a general popular movement.

In different terms, the same impression of embryonic popular revolt is found in the bourgeois novelist, Martin du Gard: "An irresistible outburst of passions shook the nocturnal heart of Paris."[66] But, after an increase in excitement in the last week of November—"The Dreyfus Affair is assuming an extraordinary intensity with the arrival of Colonel Picquart . . .", a police agent reported—there was a lull in mid-December: "People have calmed down on the subject of the Dreyfus Affair. The declarations made to the Senate have had a good effect . . ." As yet, the Sûreté Générale showed little curiosity about provincial opinion, although a report is preserved from Epinal: "The newspaper articles announcing the intervention of M. Scheurer-Kestner in favour of ex-Captain Dreyfus have made a certain impression on the public . . . the Alsatians have great confidence in M. Scheurer-Kestner, and are inclined to think as he does . . . but the majority remain convinced of Dreyfus's guilt."[67]

From January 1898, with the trial and acquittal of Esterhazy, the arrest of Picquart, and, above all, the publication on 13 January of Zola's *"J'accuse"* in *L'Aurore,* any such temporary calm was entirely dissipated. When Esterhazy was released from prison after his acquittal, he was, according to Paléologue, "acclaimed by a delirious crowd, shouting: "Long live the army! . . . Long live Esterhazy! . . . Death to the Jews!'"[68] and this heralded a new intensity of concern over the Affair which spread generally to the provinces. "That year of 1898 . . . certainly marked us for life . . .", proclaimed Halévy in 1910.[69] "People talked only about the Affair", wrote Reinach. "It now preoccupied everyone."[70] And, referring particularly to "J'accuse", Edouard Herriot recalled: "From then on it was impossible not to take sides. Zola's open letter forced us to rise up, either against an outrageous slanderer, or against an unspeakable ruling clique."[71] Such, of course, had been Zola's intention. "J'accuse" had been deliberately planned by its author as a means of provoking the authorities to prosecute him, and thus provide "an occasion to bring the whole affair out in to the open."[72] The more moderate Dreyfusards were afraid of such a "revolutionary" procedure, fearing a hostile backlash, which in fact occurred: "Zola's action frightened the middle classes and the peasants, made them more angry, threw them more surely into the arms of the military, upholder of the social order." But, on the other hand, "it also stirred the urban proletariat, the students; it did not win them over overnight to the cause of revision; but it appealed to their imagination, it prepared them for the advent of Justice."[73] Reinach here shows an optimism given by hindsight, and betrays also a simplistic class analysis as we shall see, but his main point about the backlash is right. Its most obvious manifestation immediately was the outbreak of antisemitic riots and disturbances all over France in the first two months of 1898. Sixty-nine places in metropolitan France experienced such disturbances, which often involved crowds of thousands and inflicted damage to persons and property. In Algiers a full-scale pogrom took place under the complaisant eye of the military. We will return to a detailed analysis of these disturbances in a later chapter. As a result of them, the police put a close and systematic watch on opinion in the provinces as well as Paris, and for the next two years, general assessments of reactions to the Affair were gathered from all over the country, as well as reports on Dreyfusard and anti-Dreyfusard activity.

The authorities sought to minimize the impact of Zola's accusations and of his subsequent trial by prosecuting him on the minor charge of defamation of a court martial, which removed his right to try to prove the truth of his major allegations against the army chiefs;[74] but this did little to dampen passions inside or outside the court. The trial, which opened in Paris on 7 February 1898 was punctuated by various commotions in the court-room,[75] and was accompanied by violent street demonstrations in the vicinity of the Palais de Justice,[76] while interest in its episodes and its outcome was intense in the capital and in France as a whole. In the words of the Dreyfusard publisher Stock: "public opinion was inflamed to an unbelievable degree; the newspapers, whether favourable or not to the cause of revision, produced a complete unleashing of passions; a general fever reigned . . ."[77] The police reported on 8 February: "Everyone in Paris is interested in the Affair . . .", and on the 15th: "it is hard to imagine the passionate disputes that break out

in cafés and restaurants over the Zola affair."[78] Public demonstrations outside
the Palais de Justice had tended to decline by the second week of the trial,
but on the 17 February they reached a new pitch. On that date, General de
Pellieux's reference to a secret dossier establishing Dreyfus's guilt, set off
scenes of violence in the courtroom, while outside afterwards a crowd, chanting: "Kill them", tried to attack Zola, Leblois, his lawyer, and Reinach, who
reported: "One sensed the taste for blood . . ."[79] Next day, the Paris police
noted: "The agitation is increasing rather than decreasing . . ." The provinces,
too, reflected the agitation of the capital. From Narbonne, the police reported:
"the start of the Zola trial has provoked a lively state of excitement in the
region, which is increasing daily . . ."; and from Saint-Dié: "If only by looking
at the sale of newspapers, one can see that this trial has excited public opinion
to the highest degree." At Béziers, "Interest in the trial was enormous . . .
over 90 per cent of the population followed it closely and a crowd, avid for
news, waited every evening for the telegrams to arrive [from Paris]." Similarly,
in the Haute-Savoie, "the decision of the jury was awaited with impatience,
in the more lively atmosphere of our *chefs-lieux de canton . . .*" Only a few
reports convey a different impression. At Armentières, again according to the
police, "the famous Zola trial has not really aroused the interest of the population . . ." But, save for this one example of an industrial town, it seems that
it was only in remoter rural areas that opinion remained relatively indifferent.
From Château-Gontier in the Mayenne, it was reported that "the public has
followed the various stages of the Zola trial with coolness . . ."; similarly at
Guéret in the Creuse, the eventual verdict "provoked no unusual animation,
because Dreyfusards are rare here."[80] In the Deux-Sèvres, the situation seems
to have been much the same. A primary school teacher from the department
remembered that "when the Dreyfus Affair broke out, after Zola's *"J'accuse"*,
Dreyfusards were rare. Teachers, for whom ideas of the Nation and of the
Republic were at this time inseparable, could not at first imagine that the
Army could be capable of such odious behaviour."[81]

Dreyfusard opinion continued to be rare for some time, but hostility towards it was usually more obviously, even vigorously, expressed. Zola's condemnation to one year's imprisonment and a fine of 3,000 francs was greeted,
according to the police, with nearly unanimous approval all over France. In
many cases this approval was manifested with great public enthusiasm: French
and Russian flags were flown, patriotic demonstrations were held, people
embraced each other in the streets. "There was no distinction between Paris
and the provinces," wrote Reinach. "When the verdict was known, joy was
universal. Military clubs hoisted their flags, as if for a victory in the field."[82]
"France is like a drunken woman", Martin du Gard's Luce noted with distress.[83] The police reports provide a detailed picture of this public reaction.
At Halluin in the Nord, for example, the verdict was received "with the
greatest satisfaction"; at Saint-Malo, with "outward expressions of joy"; at
Saint-Dié, "our patriotic population of the Vosges" welcomed the verdict with
open pleasure, while expressing its thorough disapproval of "the scandalous
and criminal activities" of Dreyfus's supporters, which had earned them the

reprobation of all France. At Le Mans, "the organizers of this odious campaign against the French army" were said to be "the objects of unanimous hostility". The police reports also give some idea of what motivated such reactions. Some emphasis was laid on the psychological tensions created by the long trial itself. At Clermont-Ferrand, the population was said to have been "enervated, over-excited by this long trial"; reports from Epinal referred to "the great sense of relief" provided by the verdict; at Grenoble, "a malaise, obvious to every observer, had weighed on people's minds from the time that the trial opened"; at Amiens, "everyone felt delivered from a nightmare"; but, perhaps more importance was attached by the police to the material interests involved, many reports pointing to the deleterious effect that the trial and its accompanying agitation had had on business. At Charleville, where "the verdict was very favourably received, people are hoping that, with the end of this unfortunate trial, there will be a return to calm, and that business affairs that have suffered as a result of the trial, will resume their normal course." At Tourcoing, it was reported similarly, that "people think that this verdict will bring to an end the commercial crisis that has worsened since the opening of the trial"; at Châlons-sur-Marne, that "the Zola trial has caused a marked halt in commercial transactions, but there is reason to suppose that the verdict rendered will restore confidence, and that very shortly business will return to normal." This commercial crisis, whose exact dimensions have yet to be charted by economic historians, seems to have affected rural areas in the South as well as industrial towns in the North and the East. From Valence, the police reported that people in the countryside as well as in the towns of the region were relieved by the verdict, adding: "People want to hear no more of this wretched affair which has had such a bad effect on everything . . ." At Perpignan, the verdict was similarly welcomed, "for, since the start of this sad affair, the malaise, caused by the poor way that wine is selling, had deteriorated further, and threatened to paralyse trade altogether."[84] This is only one example, as we shall see, of the way in which the Dreyfus Affair and reactions to it were enmeshed in the wider atmosphere of economic depression.

Although, after the irruption of violence and passion in January and February 1898, there seems therefore to have ensued a period of calm, it was, however, an uneasy one, and not unbroken. Demonstrations against Jews recurred in Lorraine, and at Angers and Paris.[85] A report from Epinal in March spoke of the population's still being "troubled and upset", and said that "rumours of all kinds are circulating, some people even believing in the imminence of a war with Germany." The judgment of the Cour de Cassation on 2 April 1898, setting aside Zola's conviction on procedural grounds, exacerbated this state of uneasiness, and dashed people's hopes of seeing a rapid end to the affair. From Saint-Quentin, the police reported that the judgment had made a "very gloomy impression", while at Fécamp and at Saint-Dié, the population was said to be "stupefied". News on 11 April 1898 that Zola was to be tried again did little to allay suspicions that the government was trying to let Zola off, and that the courts were partial.[86] In fact, it appears that the weight of opinion among barristers was firmly against Zola and Dreyfus at this time. Addresses of support and sympathy for the army were voted in March 1898 by the bars *(barreaux)* of Besançon, Dinan, Chambéry, Tours, Le Mans, Pontoise, Orléans, Nice, Saint-Brieuc, Grenoble, Rennes and Toulon.[87] Against this, a few reports began to come in, however, of doubts about Dreyfus's guilt, and of support for reopening his case, from "respectable" sections of society. From Veynes in the Hautes-Alpes, it was pointed out that, beneath the apparent unanimity with which the condemnation of Zola had been greeted, there lay serious divergences of opinion: "In the decent section of the population, among railway employees, for example, there are men with a certain education, and very definitely patriotic, who are beginning to ask whether Emile Zola may not, up to a point, be right." From Epinal, it was reported that "several rich industrialists and rentiers, who are not Jewish, have become revisionist"; and these included the mayor Mieg, of the important firm of Dollfuss, Mieg et Cie, and Kampmann, former president of the Tribunal of Commerce.[88]

It was in this atmosphere of continuing alarm and the beginnings of a shift in opinion that the campaign began for the General Elections of May 1898. It has often been asserted that the absence of obvious reference to the Affair in the election campaign demonstrates lack of public concern about it, at least in the provinces. François Goguel, for example, in a standard work, wrote that the Affair "played almost no role in the elections of spring 1898."[89] Such a judgment lacks plausibility, and is almost certainly wrong, although only a systematic study of the campaign at the local level will be able to establish exactly what the role of the Affair was here. There are many indications, however, that it was far from negligible. Reinach stated that most Republican candidates "made no allusion to the Affair in their official programmes, reserving it for public meetings where their rousing words could evaporate into thin air."[90] Clemenceau corroborated this, when he declared in *L'Aurore* on 5 May, a few days before the first ballot, that there had been no public meeting during the campaign at which candidates had not been asked: "What line will you take in the Dreyfus Affair?", and where protests were not forthcoming if candidates refused to declare themselves.[91] Anatole France wrote, with more emphasis still, in 1904: "The elections were fought nearly everywhere around the Affair, in an unprecedented atmosphere of threats and invective . . ."[92] President Faure, finally, told Mme Steinheil after the election results were known: "Thank Heaven, the elections have shown that the Republican majority was against Dreyfus and his supporters . . ."[93] Some evidence in detail also exists that candidates' views about the Affair played a part in their campaigns and might be decisive in the results. Maurice Lebon, deputy for the 4th Rouen constituency since 1891, declared in March 1898 in an open letter to his constituents that he would not be standing in the May elections, because of his conviction that the Dreyfus case should be reopened.[94] Easier to interpret are the examples of those who did stand. At least two important politicians who were declared Dreyfusards lost their seats, Jaurès at Carmaux and Reinach at Digne.[95] On the other side, Jules Baron in the 1st Cholet constituency set himself in his official programme against "the coalition of international Jewish financiers"; while Léon Borie in the Corrèze promised in his to "silence this gang of cosmopolitan Jews who, for six months, have been attacking the French nation, slandering the army and causing trouble in the country generally."[96] Klotz, a Jew, who stood at Montdidier, felt it necessary to announce in his programme that he was opposed to revision.[97] Cavaignac made the Affair a central issue in his campaign in the Sarthe.[98] All these men were elected, as were three other leading anti-Dreyfusards, Déroulède, leader of the Ligue des Patriotes in Angoulême, Millevoye in the 16th *arrondissement* of Paris and Edouard Drumont in Algiers. Baron, Borie, Millevoye and Drumont were only 4 of 22 successful candidates who were declared antisemites, and who formed an official antisemitic parliamentary group in the Chamber of Deputies. Several of these antisemites ousted well-established sitting deputies.[99]

Some kind of global picture may be obtained, moreover, from studying the programmes or "*professions de foi*" of successful candidates, which were published after the election.[100] Of these, just over 20% referred directly or indirectly to the Affair, direct reference being slightly less common than indirect reference. As an example of the first, Desfarges, an Independent Socialist Republican at Bourganeuf (Creuse) declared: "I have categorically pronounced my opposition to those financiers and cosmopolitan Jews who have used their money to unleash on the country a disturbing campaign to save the traitor Dreyfus who was rightly condemned by his fellow-officers"; while indirect reference usually took the form of defending the army: Dr Clament, a Republican re-elected in the second constituency of Bergerac (Dordogne) declared: "I am among those who want a severe repression of the abominable manoeuvres—against which I have consistently voted—that fail to show an absolute respect for our dear and valiant army . . . the strength and safeguard of the nation!" But, as Reinach suggested, the number of candidates referring to the Affair in campaign speeches but not in their official programmes would raise this figure considerably. Several prominent anti-Dreyfusards and antisemites did not mention the Affair in their programmes, even indirectly, for example Castelin (Laon), Gervaize (Nancy), and Roux who defeated Reinach at Digne. In Paris, where reference to the Affair in official programmes conformed to the national rate of about 20%, the reports of the Prefect of Police on electoral meetings indicate that it was in fact a much more important issue. For example, in the first constituency of the 16th *arrondissement* a meeting of 400 people on 2 May 1898 lapsed into a brawl between rival supporters, when all candidates on the platform were asked to state whether they were for or against reopening the Dreyfus Case; when the trouble had subsided, regret was expressed from the chair "that the Dreyfus question was being brought up in every meeting". In the 2nd constituency of the same *arrondissement* a meeting of 800 on 30 April in support of Millevoye passed a resolution "condemning cosmopolitan Jewry and the traitors allied to Zola"; while another meeting of 400 on 20 May in support of the same candidate passed a similar resolution "condemning the Dreyfusards". In the 2nd constituency of the 18th *arrondissement*, the sitting deputy, Rouanet, a moderate

Socialist, who was eventually re-elected, was greeted at a meeting on 3 May with shouts of "Down with the internationalist! Down with the man who dares to insult the army and defend the Jews", and fighting again broke out between supporters of rival candidates. As we shall see, Rouanet was one of the very few deputies elected or re-elected in 1898 to make a profession of Dreyfusism in his programme. In at least 12 other Paris constituencies, as well as the 1st constituency of Saint-Denis, the Affair was an issue in the elections, according to the police, which would raise their proportion to about 40%.

A further indication of the impact of the Affair in the elections is provided by the electoral policy adopted by antisemitic and anti-Dreyfusard organizations. Confident of the popularity of their views, some of them launched into the electoral arena. Déroulède was only one of five or more members of the Ligue des Patriotes elected in 1898. Jules Guérin, leader of the Ligue Antisémitique Française, told his followers on 3 March 1898 that "recent events . . . have favoured our ideas, and we must now transport them into the forum of the electoral struggle", a view which he expressed to a wider audience the following day at a public meeting at the Salle Wagram in Paris, called specifically to debate: "The General Elections of 1898 and Antisemitism".[101] As we have seen, several antisemitic candidates were elected, and many of these had the sponsorship and support of Guérin's or of other organizations. The more traditional Right seems also to have attempted, in some constituencies, to use anti-Dreyfusism as a means of attracting popular support, a strategy previously employed with Boulangism.[102] In the Haute-Saône, for example, such a strategy, coinciding with a split among the Radicals, seems to have won the Right two seats, while a similar manoeuvre was unsuccessful at Besançon.[103] In contrast, many candidates of the Left, and particularly the Extreme Left, were put in a considerable embarrassment by the Affair. A few, such as Mesureur in the 2nd *arrondissement* of Paris or Gallot at Avallon (Yonne), called for army reforms involving the stricter subordination of the military to civil authority, without mentioning the Affair, but more, while attacking the government, sought to demonstrate their patriotism by condemning the Dreyfusards, for example, Chenavaz, a Democratic Republican at Saint-Marcellin (Isère), who declared: "An odious Dreyfus Affair has taken on threatening proportions, thanks to the weakness, the indecision and the duplicity even of the Government, which has been far too indulgent towards the leaders of this anti-patriotic campaign[104] . . .". The hesitant attitude of most Socialists at this stage, too, owed as much to a sense of its electoral importance and to the knowledge that Dreyfusism was not at all popular, as to "Marxist" scruples about participating in an internecine "bourgeois" conflict, though this was a natural ideological screen to use as shelter. Not all Socialists did use it or anything else to hide behind, notably Rouanet, Jaurès, Guesde and Gérault-Richard, but all but the first lost their seats, almost certainly as a result of their frankness in admitting doubts about Dreyfus's guilt or the legality of his trial.[105]

All of this is reflected in the official programmes of successful candidates. Of those referring to the Affair directly or indirectly, only two could be taken as professions of Dreyfusism, and they were guarded or indirect. Rouanet in Paris declared: "on the Dreyfus question and the military question, I want the truth and the same justice for everyone, at the top as well as at the bottom. I want the affair brought into the open, and I censure those who oppose the cry of 'Long live the army!' to that of 'Long live the Republic!' ";[106] while another Socialist, Zévaès in the 2nd constituency of Grenoble, attacked those who had fomented antisemitic riots earlier in the year. All the rest expressed support for the army, and condemned attacks on it, usually in the strongest terms. Moreover, of those in this category, who mentioned the Affair indirectly, 20 were conservatives, 29 were moderate Republicans, and only 6 were Radicals or Left-wing Republicans; while, of those who mentioned it directly, 19 were conservatives or Right-wingers, 17 were moderate Republicans, and only 9 were Left-wing Republicans. Thus, reference to the Affair was very much a phenomenon of the Centre or the Right; and our view is confirmed that candidates of the Left tended to avoid committing themselves if they could, or else were not elected if they espoused the wrong side. The importance of the Affair in electoral terms can also be gauged by looking at the geographical distribution of constituencies whose deputies mentioned it in their programmes (see Map 4). Constituencies in 54 departments fall into this category, and the bulk of departments concerned are remote from the capital, with the East well-represented, but more so the West and the Massif Central. The Affair was mentioned by deputies in 5 constituencies in the Charente and the Ille-et-Vilaine and by deputies in 3 constituencies in the Loire, the Loire-Inférieure, the Maine-et-Loire, the Orne, the Seine-Inférieure, the Deux-Sèvres and the Vendée. By contrast, deputies from a ring of departments around Paris and from most Mediterranean departments made no mention of it.[107] This suggests that far from being something which concerned only the population of the capital, the Affair was of particular interest and hostility towards the Dreyfusards was particularly strong in the most "backward" provinces, though its impact should not be overemphasized. Dulau, the successful Progressist candidate at Saint-Sever (Landes) declared in his programme: "A certain question has thoroughly upset the commercial transactions of our rural population," but the question he was referring to was not that of Dreyfus but "that of bovine tuberculosis".[108]

Two final indications of the electoral importance of the Affair and of antisemitism in the spring of 1898 are afforded from the local political level. Two weeks before the General Elections, one third of the departmental councils (conseils généraux) of France passed resolutions "relative to the Dreyfus Affair", 11 of which specifically attacked the Dreyfusards, and all of which supported the army.[109] The significance of this is increased, as far as the General Elections are concerned, by the very close links that existed in France between politics at the national and the local level, most deputies and senators being also conseillers généraux. Among influential pressure-groups, too, there seems to have been influence on candidates over this matter, and interest in their attitude towards the Affair. Reinach cited the example of the Agricultural Association of the Est, which resolved: "We will only cast our votes for those candidates who pledge themselves to propose, support and vote for a law disenfranchising the Jews and banning them from public office, civil or military."[110]

What the 1898 General Elections indicate, therefore, is not public indifference towards the Affair, but rather a strong current of opinion against reopening it, which led many candidates and most parties to try to avoid the issue. In the words of a report drawn up for the Premier on the political situation in 1898: "The Dreyfus Affair was in everyone's mind, and underlay all personal polemics, although it was not explicitly in the programme of any party."[111] This current of opinion usually ensured the defeat of known Dreyfusards, and the victory of those squarely in the opposite camp. That the Affair did not emerge as a stronger overt national issue reflects simply the nature of most General Elections of this period in France. "The 1898 elections", Léon Blum explained on the eve of the 1902 elections, which were of a very but uniquely different kind, "were fought during the most confused period of the Dreyfus Affair, and managed by a government that was on its last legs and uncertain of its future policy; they therefore provoked, in the end, only local struggles."[112] In these circumstances, the degree to which the Affair does seem to have been an issue is all the more significant.

A second indicator of opinion in mid-1898 is provided by the police reports on the distribution of the poster, "Des Réponses à Mr Cavaignac", put out by the newly-formed Ligue des Droits de l'Homme in the late summer. Both Méline's speech in the Chamber of Deputies in February 1898, declaring that there was no Dreyfus Affair, and Cavaignac's speech as Minister of War of 7 July, in which he produced the Henry forgery *("faux Henry")*, had been voted to be posted up in every commune in France.[113] This poster of the Ligue des Droits de l'Homme was the first riposte to governmental attempts to stifle the Affair, as well as the first important action of the Dreyfusard league. The police reported that the poster had been put up in 70 towns. In some places, posting was prevented by the authorities, in others, it was merely delayed so as not "to excite the public". Reactions to the poster were mixed. At Le Puy, "nobody noticed the presence of these posters on the walls of the town"; at Laon, they produced "a certain impression of disgust in the public"; at Montbéliard, they "excited the public enormously . . . and drew even army officers out of their normal reserve . . . It is a matter of great regret that the present state of legislation does not permit the repression of such agitation"; at Toulouse and several other places, the posters were ripped down or defaced.[114]

The revisionist campaign had moved from the level of individualist gestures to that of collective action, but a further personal drama was to set it definitively in motion, and September 1898, contemporaries and historians agree, marked a real turning-point.[115] On 31 August 1898 Colonel Henry committed suicide in his cell at the Mont-Valérien prison, after having confessed to forging at least one of the secret documents which had decided Dreyfus's conviction. Henry was celebrated as a hero, the first fatal casualty of the Affair, by the Nationalist press, and particularly by the young Charles Maurras in

La Gazette de France.[116] *La Libre Parole* later raised a considerable sum of money for his widow by subscription, an enterprise to which we will return in a subsequent chapter. But despite these efforts of the anti-Dreyfusards, faith in the army had been severely, irrevocably, shaken. Even President Faure, a staunch opponent of revision, apparently began to have his doubts, and thought of resigning;[117] while among the Dreyfusards, now growing in numbers, worry about the secrecy and apparent illegality of the original court martial began to give way to the conviction that Dreyfus was in fact innocent.[118] Moderate opinion also began to see revision as the only way out of the impasse of the Affair: "the business world, as well as a number of ordinary people who had not known up till then what to think, breathed a sigh of relief, hoping that the crisis that had dragged on so long, was finally moving towards a solution."[119] Moreover, in response to this new climate of opinion, revisionist meetings were organized all over the country from September 1898, primarily by the Ligue des Droits de l'Homme.[120] The Socialists, too, became involved, and, alarmed by anti-Dreyfusard street action in the capital, formed a *Comité de Vigilance* in early October. Demonstrations became frequent, particularly in Paris. The Ligue des Patriotes, the Ligue Antisémitique Française and a Revolutionary Coalition organized large-scale demonstrations in the Place de la Concorde on 25 October on the occasion of the reopening of the Chamber of Deputies. Rival groups clashed, violence occurred and a large number of arrests were made.[121] As Mme Steinheil noted in her diary at the time: "The Dreyfus dispute waxes hotter than ever."[122]

The police reports allow one a more detailed perspective on this movement of opinion, particularly in the provinces, and they also illustrate how it was affected, channelled, by organizations and by the newspaper press. From Cette, it was reported at the end of October: "Nobody is talking of anything but the judgment of the Cour de Cassation in the Dreyfus Affair. [On 29 October, the court had declared Mme Dreyfus's request for a revision of her husband's trial to be admissible.] The liveliest discussions are held in public places all the time, between Dreyfusards and anti-Dreyfusards. Nevertheless the majority of the population is more calm, and does not indulge in noisy manifestations of opinion on this subject." The public in the Ain were said to be "very preoccupied by the agitation now occurring in Paris about the Dreyfus Affair, and people are worried by what may result from it . . . The predominant opinion is, however, still in favour of reopening the case, which is seen as the only means of bringing the present agitation to an end . . . The Dreyfus and Picquart Affairs are the object of discussions all over the region." (Picquart was put on trial in September for leaking confidential information, and sent before a court martial in November.) A report from Limoges was more specific, pointing out that the impression produced by the Affair and by attacks on the army chiefs was "absolutely different in the town and in the country". In Limoges, itself, most workers followed

very closely the line taken by their favourite newspapers, *Le Rappel du Centre* and *La Bataille Sociale.* In other words, they share the "revisionist" point of view of these organs . . . Where workers are grouped together, therefore, in factories or workshops, it is not rare to hear them express fairly strong criticism . . . of any leaders . . . But in the countryside, things are not so bad. Those living in remote places and busy with peaceful agricultural work have often never even heard of the Affair.

The report concludes by pointing out that the Affair "is having a bad effect on trade, and on business in general, and people are thus very anxious to see it come to an end."[123] As we have seen, this was a view that appears frequently in police reports, and it suggests an important underlying factor in attitudes to the Affair. The Prefect of the Nord, for example, had noted earlier in the year: "Although no demonstrations are likely at Roubaix, the Dreyfus Affair and the various incidents that have stemmed from it are beginning to paralyse business transactions causing serious concern among the public."[124]

In addition to the report from the Ain, quoted above, another from Montauban confirms that the shift of opinion in the autumn of 1898 was a provincial as well as a Parisian phenomenon.

I must point out to you [wrote the *commissaire spécial*], that a radical change in public opinion about the revision of the 1894 trial has taken place. Before I went on leave, the population of the department of the Tarn-et-Garonne, almost without exception, was absolutely hostile to Dreyfus and opposed to any proposal to reopen his case . . . all that has taken place since, and particularly the forgery of Colonel Henry, and his suicide when it was discovered, has caused people to change their minds . . . The revision of the Dreyfus Case, without being positively wished for, is today accepted by most people as perhaps the only means of getting out of the inextricable position we seem to have been in for the last year.

The report goes on to mention the anger of army officers stationed in the town at the attacks on their leaders; by contrast, "the civilian population is less irritated by such attacks. However, the gross insults so often thrown at members of the Government by certain newspapers . . . are having a deplorable effect", and many Republicans were said to be accusing the government of weakness. However, as the report from Limoges suggests, some places remained untouched by the emotions aroused by the Affair, and these were not necessarily remote rural backwaters. At Montereau in the Seine-et-Marne, people were said to be "indifferent and sceptical";[125] while from Toulouse, the Prefect reported that a revisionist meeting, which had led to street demonstrations, had left the mass of the population "indifferent": "this is its usual attitude each time that the Dreyfus question is raised."[126]

The "Réponses à Mr Cavaignac" poster marked the opening, as we have indicated, of an intensive campaign, mounted by the Dreyfusard press and the Ligue des Droits de l'Homme, aided by Radical, Socialist and anarchist groups, in favour of the reopening of the Dreyfus Case. A police agent reported in November: "An attempt is being made just now in Paris and the provinces, to organize in support of ex-Colonel Picquart . . . an important movement of agitation, which, it is hoped, will prove much more serious than the whole campaign mounted so far by *L'Aurore* . . ."[127] Mme Steinheil wrote about the same time: "The attention of France is entirely focused . . . on the Picquart trial."[128] Reinach reported that, during the Picquart trial, protests by the thousand were received by Dreyfusard newspapers, while flowers and letters of sympathy also poured in, and he evoked the atmosphere in Paris that November in these terms:[129]

> Every evening there were public meetings. People crowded in, in an electric atmosphere, to applaud the speeches that expressed in sonorous or violent words what they all felt, workers and bourgeois, working women . . . and society ladies . . . Afterwards, groups in which one could recognize members of the Institut and professors of the Sorbonne, converged on the Cherche-Midi prison, chanting: "Long live Picquart!"

But this is only one Parisian aspect of a much larger movement that reached all over France, and on which the police reports provide valuable information. Francis de Pressensé, Jaurès, Octave Mirbeau, Pierre Quillard, Sébastien Faure and others made speech tours from September onwards, and their campaign reached its height in December. In that month 24 revisionist meetings were reported in Paris and its suburbs, and 20 in other towns. It is probable that this number would have been considerably larger had Dreyfusards not encountered difficulties in hiring halls. A police agent reported in October 1898 that "it is impossible to organize a meeting in favour of Dreyfus at Bourges, Nevers, Fourchambault, Dijon, Auxerre or Troyes. The owners of halls and rooms will not let them at any price, and do not conceal the fact that the only reason for their refusal lies in their fear of getting into trouble with the police or other authorities."[130] Simple fear of incurring unpopularity with other clients and of having their property damaged, was probably equally important as a motive. In bigger towns, revisionist meetings often drew audiences of over a thousand. It has been suggested that people sometimes attended through simple curiosity, attracted by famous names.[131] There may be some truth in this, though Reinach gives a very different picture for Paris, and in many instances, meetings triggered off demonstrations and counter-demonstrations, in the capital, but also at Lyon, Nice, Montpellier, Toulouse and Marseille. Though played down by the Prefect, the disturbances at Toulouse involved a crowd estimated at 12,000–15,000; Pressensé, Mirbeau and Quillard were attacked with clubs and missiles; and 15 arrests were made.[132] Nor were the people of Marseille simply "curious" about the Affair. The photographer Nadar, who had his studio there at the time, wrote in a letter: "The Dreyfus Affair has brought everything to a standstill, and has ousted all other topics from the newspaper columns . . ."[133] Beyond these counter-demonstrations, organized anti-Dreyfusard response to the revisionist campaign in the last months of 1898 seems to have been very weak, judging from police reports, though Dardenne quotes reports in the press of "nationalist" demonstrations in "all French towns" on the occasion of the return of troops from manoeuvres in September and October.[134] Lack of public response on any large scale to the violent demonstrations of early 1898, and the quickly hostile attitude of the authorities towards disorderly behaviour whatever the pretext, seem to have inhibited anti-Dreyfusard activity to some degree. "On the practical side", wrote Maurice Barrès to Maurras on 1 November 1898, "we have suffered an uninterrupted succession of defeats."[135] Only ten meetings, organized by "nationalist" and antisemitic groups on the subject of the Affair were reported by the police for the whole three-month period from 1 December 1898 to the end of February, three of which were in Paris.[136]

1899 was a year of continuous interest in the Affair and of extreme manifestations of opinion on both sides, articulated in step with its dramatic unfolding. In January the Chambre Criminelle of the Cour de Cassation began its hearings to decide whether the Dreyfus Case should be reopened, provoking renewed controversy and disturbances in Paris, which pressured the government into accepting a Nationalist proposal to transfer responsibility for this decision to the Cour de Cassation as a whole. The *loi de dessaisissement* was passed on 1 March. In February, President Faure died and was replaced by Emile Loubet, who was known to be unopposed to the revision of the Dreyfus Case. Loubet's election on 18 and Faure's funeral on 23 February were the occasions for large-scale demonstrations in Paris, and for an attempted *coup* by Déroulède, and his followers. On 3 June, the revision of the case was ordered, and next day Loubet was the object of an important hostile demonstration at Auteuil. The President was struck with a cane by Baron Christiani on his arrival at the racecourse, and was pelted with rotten eggs on his departure; 100 arrests were made.[137] On 22 June the Waldeck-Rousseau government was formed, a government of Republican defence, determined to liquidate the Affair. Through August and the first half of September, Dreyfus's second trial took place in Rennes, culminating in his second condemnation on 9 September. On 19 September he was pardoned by the President of the Republic. The police and other reports reflect public reaction to these various developments.

In January and February 1899 the revisionist campaign continued; in these two months, 10 revisionist meetings were reported by the police in Paris, and 17 in the provinces. These meetings, like earlier ones, seem to have aroused great interest, and to have had some influence in shaking people's convictions. From Toulouse, the Prefect wrote in mid-January: "The announcement of another meeting . . . on the Dreyfus Affair has been badly received in general, but has caused real concern." However, in a neighbouring department, a revisionist meeting seems to have won adherents to the Dreyfusard cause: "The population of Moissac . . . cannot believe that it is only a few shady individuals and noisy youths who are provoking the demonstrations in favour of the prisoner on Devil's Island."[138] As during the elections the previous May, wider political conflicts and disagreements were incorporating themselves with or expressing themselves through the Affair. "The great struggle", wrote Mme Steinheil in February, "is no longer between Dreyfusards and anti-Dreyfusards, but between the Republic and the enemies of the Republic, between Radicals and Socialists on the one hand, Royalists and 'anti-Semites' on the other."[139] This wider dimension, always latently present, can be seen in the renewed violence of the first half of 1899. Demonstrations were reported in January in Clermont-Ferrand, Orléans and Paris, and on 5 February six people were wounded and 31 arrested in troubles in Marseille after a Ligue des Patriotes meeting. The anti-Dreyfusard demonstrations in Paris, following the death of Faure in February, were among the most serious during the whole Affair. After his election at Versailles on 18 February, Loubet was booed and jeered at all the way from the Gare Saint Lazare to the Elysée Palace. On 19 February 128 arrests were made in the capital, and on 23 February, the day of the funeral, 257, mainly for refusal to circulate, seditious cries, insulting and attacking the police, and "rebellion".[140] Déroulède's attempt to persuade General Roget to lead his troops to the Elysée Palace was not immediately taken very seriously either by the police or the newspapers. *Le Matin* referred on 29 February to "a poet's *coup d'état*"; *Le Journal du Peuple,* on the same day, to "the grotesque attempt". However, it was an indication of the lengths to which the anti-Dreyfusards were prepared to go, and it increased the impatience of the public and the authorities with the leagues, and particularly with the violent action of their members on the streets. Further demonstrations were reported in April and May at Avignon, Marseille, Troyes, Paris and in Algeria.[141] Police raids on league headquarters began at this time, and prosecution of their leaders was prepared. This movement of exasperation, directed now against the anti-Dreyfusards, was strengthened by the events of June 1899, the decision to retry the Dreyfus Case at Rennes, and the attacks on President Loubet, though neither event as yet brought any pacification. Rather, as Reinach reported: "The agitation in the streets, the plotting in the salons picked up and intensified . . ."[142]

There were, according to the police, various reactions to the moves which culminated in the judgment of the Cour de Cassation of 3 June. From Montauban, it was reported in March that the law laying down that the decision about the Dreyfus Case should be made by the Court as a whole, and not just by its Criminal Chamber as was usual, had been "well received", but stress was laid on the fact that "public opinion is desperately anxious to see the end of the Dreyfus Affair, and is becoming tired of the slowness of the procedure."[143] The eventual judgment of the Cour de Cassation, calling for a retrial, was ordered to be posted in all communes in France, which enables one to gauge reactions. In a fair number of communes, mayors refused to allow the judgment to be posted, and were suspended from their functions as a result. Elsewhere, the notices were often quickly covered over or defaced. From the Maine-et-Loire, for example, it was reported that "in many communes . . . the notices were torn as soon as they were put up, or else they were covered with slogans, as they were at Angers"; from the Manche, that "nearly all the notices reproducing the text of the judgment of the Cour de Cassation that were put up at Cherbourg have been covered over with bands of paper with the following inscriptions: Long live France! Long live the army!" On the whole, where the notices were not the objects of hostile reaction of this kind, the police seem not to have filed a report. From Cette, however, it was noted that the judgment posted up had been "well received";[144] while from

Nice, it was reported: "In this region, the Dreyfus question has always been regarded as relatively unimportant and has not excited the population. The local press retails the various phases of the Affair, but without adding any comments that would allow one to class it in one camp rather than the other." The judgment of the Court was thus greeted "rather coldly", although it was said to have "upset some people's ideas . . . and helped to increase the number of those believing in the possibility of a miscarriage of justice."[145]

Opinion was much more clearly expressed, and on a wider scale, in imitation of or in reaction against the anti-Dreyfusard demonstrations at Auteuil on 4 June. Demonstrations, often of a violent nature, were reported in June from 28 places in France. At Lyon disturbances occurred on four successive days in the second week in June; at Le Havre a crowd of several hundred stoned the windows of a department store in a manner reminiscent of the riots of January and February 1898.[146] But the contrary movement seems to have enjoyed much more support, the attacks on the Republic's titular head, evoking the kind of public shock and indignation that the assassination of President Carnot had aroused in 1894.[147] Pro-Loubet demonstrations were organized in Paris in the week following 4 June.[148] Many organizations and municipalities sent addresses of sympathy to Loubet, for example, the council of Saint-Quentin, where "the grave incidents which took place on Sunday . . . have aroused great indignation in the population"; and that of Marseille, from where the police reported: "The movement of sympathy for the President of the Republic, provoked by the incidents at Auteuil, has become general in the department of the Bouches-du-Rhône . . . This is so obvious that the antisemites and 'nationalists' who had intended to demonstrate, have abandoned the idea . . ." At Cette, the news from Auteuil produced "a general explosion of sympathy for the Head of State". In the Lot-et-Garonne, the effect of the news was similarly great,[149]

> particularly since it came at the time of the big annual fair held at Agen, which attracts 20,000 people from this and neighbouring departments, for the purposes of trade and agriculture. This reactionary demonstration is thoroughly condemned by everyone, even by most of the conservatives of the region . . . In the face of the gravity of the situation, the Republicans of Agen, from Socialists to Moderates, feel that united action is necessary, and addresses have been sent by all these groups to assure the President of their full support and sympathy.

The movement towards Republican unity and defence, reflected on the national level by the formation of the Waldeck-Rousseau government on 22 June, was noted elsewhere. As Halévy commented, with some exaggeration: "It was a question of determining whether the Republic would succeed in forming one last government that would save it, or whether it would give up, and leave the way open to Déroulède."[150] The police at Montauban wrote that "the Auteuil incident has done more to bring republican factions together than any campaign organized for the purpose could have done"; and the same report stressed public exasperation at such incidents: "The public in general is getting very tired of these scandalous occurrences that take place nearly every day . . .". At Epinal, the police forecast that: "The minority which supports the 'nationalist' movement will soon be regarded as seditious, if it continues to foment disorder . . ." These two reports, and others from at least 8 places, indicate that people expected repressive measures to be taken against such troublemakers. From Dieppe, another report suggested something of what motivated this swing of opinion against the anti-Dreyfusards, economic interests that had earlier predisposed people against the revisionists: "People are very worried and upset by all these incidents, and are afraid that foreign visitors will be apprehensive about coming to France in these circumstances, which would do a lot of harm in our town."[151] This echoes previous reports of the disadvantageous effect of the Affair on business, and foreshadows the general "truce" occasioned by the 1900 *Exposition.*

Many reports were made more generally in June 1899 of a new growth of interest in the Affair as the Rennes trial approached. Simultaneously, revisionist opinion continued to spread. This is reflected in the pattern of public meetings devoted to the Affair at this time. In the five months, March to July 1899, 40 important revisionist meetings were reported outside Paris. From June to August 1899, however, only 8 anti-Dreyfusard meetings were reported, 3 in Rennes itself in July. From Rouen, the police wrote in June: "The Dreyfus question and the mustering of Socialist forces for the defence of the Republic are the order of the day."[152] From the Finistère, the Prefect reported, in anticipation of Dreyfus's arrival in France:

> In previous reports . . . I expressed the view that the people of Brest, indifferent by temperament, would not mark the arrival of Dreyfus by demonstrations in one sense or the other, but I also warned that this tranquillity might be upset by the presence of troublemakers from outside. These troublemakers have arrived . . . Nevertheless, it is fair to add . . . that, beyond the agitation which these people are beginning to stir up, the curiosity of the population has been fanned to fever heat by the newspapers, most of which have special correspondents here . . .

From Rennes itself, the police wrote that: "Most of the population used to be anti-Dreyfusard, although, after the judgment of the Cour de Cassation, some people have begun to waver",[153] This was a familiar reaction, as we have seen, and was more confidently reported from Nantes:[154]

> In different reports I have indicated the progress of revisionist ideas in different circles; the Socialist meeting held yesterday confirms this impression once again, and one feels, from mixing with different groups and listening to general conversations, that a profound change has taken place in all unprejudiced minds both on the subject of the Dreyfus Affair and with regard to antisemitism.

Through July and August, the police continued to be most attentive to public opinion, especially in the region around Rennes, where anti-Dreyfusard and antisemitic demonstrations, sometimes violent, occurred, and where further trouble was expected. The Head of the Sûreté Générale reported to Waldeck-Rousseau on 6 July:[155]

> Before the discovery of the Henry forgery, all but a few inhabitants of Rennes were openly anti-revisionist. Since then, several university professors, the Ligue pour la Défense des Droits de l'Homme et du Citoyen, the Cercle des Études Sociales, etc. . . . have organized various public meetings, which have had the result of convincing two to three thousand people of the innocence of Captain Dreyfus. The rest of the population remains convinced of his guilt. Two camps exist, therefore, and, despite their numerical inequality, they are resolved, it is said, to carry out noisy and dangerous demonstrations once the trial opens. They will only require a little encouragement from outside agitators, from Paris and elsewhere.

A police agent reported from Rennes the same day: "Certain industrialists are trying to prevent demonstrations by workers. Yesterday, Mr Oberthire [Oberthur], the big printer of the Faubourg de Paris, had his machines stopped, called together his employees, and told them that anyone getting involved in politics at the present moment would be dismissed without a qualm, even if he were the oldest worker in the place." From near-by Dinan, however, it was reported: "The town . . . and the surrounding region are very calm. No demonstrations are planned, although the main element in this constituency is clerical and anti-Dreyfusard."[156]

Once the trial had opened in August, disturbances broke out repeatedly in Rennes itself, despite employers' threats and despite the massive presence of troops, *gendarmerie* and police;[157] and they also occurred in Paris and in 13 other towns in France.[158] An experienced police agent wrote in mid-August of Paris: "Spirits have really been aroused on one side and the other, and the nationalist propaganda in the press, through songs and in the streets, carried on even by members of the clergy, is bearing its fruit. The masses no longer conceal their aversion to the present Government and their sympathy for Guérin and his companions."[159] Guérin, leader of the Ligue Antisémitique Française, had barricaded himself in the league's headquarters in the rue Chabrol in Paris, known as a result as "Fort Chabrol", originally to evade arrest by the police, but then in an attempt to provoke some kind of popular movement.[160] Although they themselves seem not to have taken the "Fort Chabrol" affair very seriously, the police and their agents reported a fair amount of interest in it, many people apparently regarding it as a government-inspired attempt to divert attention from events in Rennes. One agent reported, for example, that agitation was rife among the workers in the *ateliers* of the Chemins de Fer du Nord, who thought that Guérin was a government stooge, adding that "people are beginning to get really worked up over the inertia of the government."[161] It was reported at the same time that news of the arrest of Déroulède, for complicity in a plot against the régime along with Guérin and the Royalists, "had produced real public emotion, above all on the *grandes boulevards . . .*".[162] In Marseille, the Socialists staged a demonstration against General Mercier on 15 August, and the police commented: "A very lively atmosphere, provoked by what is happening at Rennes and intensified by the traditional *fête* of 15 August, has reigned all evening in the city centre . . . Many disputes have broken out between antisemites and other demonstrators . . ."[163] From Chitry-les-Mines in the Nièvre, Jules Renard wrote to a friend on 11 September: "the trial has gripped me to such an extent that I have lost interest in everything else . . . those people throw me into a rage . . . that Lemaître . . . that Barrès!"[164]

Outside the biggest cities, however, and away from the vicinity of the trial, opinion in general seems to have been more detached, and signs of boredom were growing. Among educated people at this time, Halévy wrote: "Everyone cursed the very existence of the Affair, and wanted to see it finally settled . . . It was urgent to free the country from a scandal that had got out of all proportion."[165] A police report from Nice stated:[166]

> The events going on at Rennes, as well as the arrests made in connection with the plot . . . against the régime, seem to evoke in this district only simple curiosity. It is true that the population of Nice is following the different phases of the Dreyfus trial and of the Orleanist conspiracy attentively, but it is following them without passion, and merely reads the newspapers . . . the Dreyfus Affair itself bores rather than excites people in the coastal region, and things have gone no further than a mild demonstration by a few young people, whom no one has ever heard of. They are trying to attract attention today by means of an message of congratulation to M. Déroulède, repeating what they tried to do a few weeks ago, when they greeted the military tattoo with shouts of 'Long live the army!' People laugh at them, and thus prevent anyone from taking such goings-on at all seriously.

Similar reports came from other parts of France; from the Isère, where the Prefect noted on 1 September 1899 that "the [Dreyfus] question does not greatly interest the members of the departmental council or the population as a whole . . .";[167] from the Nièvre, where, Renard notwithstanding,

> the agitation which has developed in several other departments has not been in evidence here . . . [But, though] the Guérin, Dreyfus and related affairs have not greatly excited people . . . a certain uneasiness is strongly felt, and people are afraid that serious trouble may break out in Paris and the big cities. Whatever happens, however, the verdict of the Rennes court martial will be accepted without discussion by the majority of the population.

In Charleville, the police wrote that opinion was divided, but contained:

> On the one hand, the iron and steel workers, mostly revolutionary Socialists, seem, after attending meetings addressed by Jaurès, to doubt Dreyfus's guilt; on the other hand, the agricultural workers and the bourgeois tend to believe that he is guilty. The impression produced by these conflicting ideas upsets people, without, however, leading to any serious clashes between them. Decent people, who have been following the course of the trial closely and who earnestly desire the end of this sad affair, will accept the

verdict of the court, whatever it is, but they will also expect the Government to take strong action against those who may try to cause trouble.

From Cette came the same view that the Rennes verdict would be accepted with relief, whichever way it went, with the explanation: "Our town is . . . essentially a business centre, and people are therefore practical. The Dreyfus trial interests them, but they do not get passionate about it. There are no reactionaries here, or militant 'nationalists' . . ."[168] Martin du Gard assessed public opinion during the Rennes trial in a similar way, and related public lack of enthusiasm to Dreyfus's actual performance. His stoic behaviour represented "a kind of heroism that excluded sympathy and was alien to the popular mentality. He might perhaps have won over the crowd had he adopted a more theatrical attitude; but that self-control, the fruit of such effort, was seen as passivity, indifference, and even those who had campaigned on his behalf for four years responded unfavourably."[169] As this suggests, however, the low key was not universally approved or accepted, and, in Paris, at least one police agent did not view the approach of the Rennes verdict with the same equanimity as the provincial police: "The political situation in Paris is getting worse and worse, and the ranks of the antisemites and of the enemies of the President of the Republic and of the Government are growing every day . . ."[170]

In the event such a view proved alarmist, although an accurate forecast of the development of organized opinion in the capital, when Dreyfus's second condemnation was known. "The evening of the judgment of the Rennes court, and the next day," wrote Raphaël Viau of *La Libre Parole*, "the *boulevards* were the scene for what can only be called riots. All the leagues together celebrated their triumph there, and this led to regular brawls between Dreyfusards and anti-Dreyfusards."[171] Police reports, which were collected on public reaction to the Rennes verdict from all departments, indicate, however, that such violence was rare. Dreyfusard protest meetings were held in five departments, at Charleville, Besançon, Le Havre, Lille and in Paris, but from only eleven departments was any disturbance reported, the most serious being in Paris again, at Alais in the Gard and at Rennes itself. At Belfort, the windows of the house of Dreyfus's brother were broken. At Bar-le-Duc and at Saint-Dié, which had both experienced serious antisemitic riots in 1898, further trouble was feared, but did not materialize. From Saint-Dié, it was reported: "The antisemitic demonstration expected on the occasion of the announcement of the Rennes verdict, and in anticipation of which the sub-prefect had requested aid from the military authorities, has not in fact led to any disorder . . ." Interest in the verdict, however, was enormous. At Montauban, large queues formed every evening at the railway station during the last week of the trial to wait for the evening papers. At Troyes, "the judgment of the court martial attracted a large crowd outside the offices of the Crédit Lyonnais. Some shouts of 'Down with Dreyfus!' or 'Long live Dreyfus!' were heard . . ." From Ajaccio, it was reported: "The news of the condemnation of the ex-captain . . . has produced a profound impression in Corsica . . ."; from Toulouse: "big crowds in the streets . . . the impression produced is great . . ."; from Remiremont: "The condemnation of Dreyfus, learned here last Saturday at seven in the evening, is the object of all conversations. Many groups gather in the streets and the cafés are very busy." One restaurant owner in the town hoisted the tricolour. At Dieppe, it was reported a little later that "the Dreyfus and Picquart Affairs are all that anyone is talking about." These reports refer in general to towns, and the reaction, or lack of reaction, of rural populations is harder to gauge, although, from the Lot, the Prefect wrote:[172]

> In general, away from the important centres, the population has remained almost indifferent . . . Moreover, in the countryside people have only very vague and often erroneous ideas [about the Rennes trial and the Affair]. Thus the verdict . . . could only have produced a very slight impression on the mass of the inhabitants, which is in fact the situation.

But, if, in general, reaction was calm, it was none the less, in the towns at least, puzzled. A minority of fanatics might be able to see the verdict as a "triumph", but its ambiguity was more evident to a much larger number of people. For Mme Steinheil, it was "fantastic";[173] while Léon Bloy wrote: "Yet again Dreyfus was condemned in a manner that completely dishonoured his judges, and in circumstances where it was so necessary to do nothing to aggravate the unspeakable shame of our military command."[174] Reinach related the "stupor" of the Dreyfusards at "the reconviction in the absence of proofs of innocence, at what was perhaps the most extraordinary verdict in history, extenuating circumstances for treason . . .", and concluded that it represented "a disguised verdict of acquittal".[175] The police reports indicate that these feelings of bewilderment were quite widespread. In the territory of Belfort, for example, the verdict was accepted calmly.

> The dozen Jewish families of the locality [Delle] have behaved as if they were not interested, and no demonstrations have occurred in the rest of the population. This verdict, however, is diversely appreciated . . . The majority of electors see it as justified; but a strong minority, who find rightly or wrongly, that the proofs of Dreyfus's guilt were not certain enough, would have preferred an acquittal, which alone, according to them, could have restored a state of calm.

The same dissatisfaction with the verdict, but diffused more widely, was reported from Marseille, where it was said to have

> produced surprise and astonishment, among "Nationalists" as well as revisionists. The former do not understand the admission of extenuating circumstances, and do not dare to demonstrate their approval of the condemnation too loudly. The latter, who expected an acquittal . . . or the confirmation of the 1894 judgment, are somewhat disorientated by this very unexpected verdict.

At Cette, "what emerges . . . from most of the soundings of opinion that have been made, is that people consider the punishment inflicted . . . to be too much or too little . . ." At Nantes, where the verdict produced "a profound emotion in the public . . . people had followed the course of the trial very closely, and in the face of the weakness of the prosecution's case, fully expected an acquittal . . . The actual verdict was received with stupor, and seems to satisfy no one . . ." At Cahors, "people expected either a simple condemnation or an acquittal, but not a verdict of guilty mitigated by extenuating circumstances." From Agen, it was reported that the Masonic Lodge had voted the Rennes verdict "an offence against reason"; while at Châlons-sur-Marne, "the Rennes verdict is seen in democratic circles as a condemnation of courts martial . . ."[176] Moreover, many of those disturbed by the verdict expressed their concern to its victim. "During the few days following the Rennes verdict," wrote Dreyfus himself, "I received thousands of telegrams and letters from every corner of France . . . indignant protests from honest citizens against this disgraceful piece of injustice."[177]

From most reports, it emerges that people had looked to the Rennes verdict to settle the Affair, once and for all, and allow a return to normality, but were doubtful whether this would in fact be the outcome. From the Indre, for example, the police noted: "People want to see this Affair over and done with, but they are reluctant to believe that this has been achieved; and from Châlons-sur-Marne, it was reported that

> for most people the verdict merits the respect due to a case that has been judged . . . They think that the Affair belongs to the judicial sphere and should remain there, that politics should not be brought into it, because this would be bad for the country . . . Most people think that up till now the bitterness of the struggle could be explained by very natural emotions, but that these emotions no longer have any justification. The partisans of justice should pursue their ends with calm and dignity, and work, above all, to give the country the rest and quiet it so badly needs.

The same desire for tranquillity was noted in many other places, for example, at Longwy, where the verdict was welcomed "with a great feeling of relief (and where) . . . people are in general pleased to see the end of an affair that has troubled our country for so long." Similarly in the Nièvre, where the verdict was taken "calmly . . . the only fact worth pointing out is the overtly-expressed wish to see this affair finally wound up, so that trade is no longer upset by it, and business can return to normal." At Montauban, again, "it would be difficult to emulate the degree of public exasperation and indignation that was reached during the revisionist campaign . . . the dominant sentiment now is one of extreme lassitude and of an earnest desire that the Affair be terminated."

However, as the reports of bewilderment at the contradictory nature of the Rennes verdict indicate, in many areas, it was felt that the end of the Dreyfus Affair had not yet arrived. At Bar-le-Duc, the police reported that "the Republicans realize that this solution may only be provisional"; while the Prefect of the Lot, again, wrote that most of the urban population "have seen in the verdict of the court martial simply another reason to increase their doubts about Dreyfus's guilt. This view is expressed in conversations all the time."

This feeling, he considered, could only grow, particularly since it was shared by *La Dépêche de Toulouse*, a newspaper, "with a wide circulation in the department and throughout the whole of the Midi, and one which has a great influence on people's opinions."[178] Another Toulouse paper, *Le Télégramme*, summed up the situation on 10 September 1899 in these terms: "People counted on the Rennes verdict to put an end to the unhealthy agitation which has troubled the country for the past two years. Unfortunately, it seems unlikely to have this effect. We are afraid that the judgment of the court martial will not have the necessary authority, and that the country will not understand it."[179] On the whole, these fears proved unjustified. The desire for "tranquillity" and reconciliation, for a return to normality, so clearly expressed in the police reports, overrode the demands of judicial consistency, so clearly offended by the Rennes verdict, by Dreyfus's subsequent pardon on 19 September and by the law of amnesty of December 1900. On the other hand, the Republican journalist was right in sensing the massive feeling of anger directed at those who were seen as responsible for upsetting that "tranquillity", for dividing the country, and for disturbing the normal tenor of life, a feeling that expressed itself in the large Radical swing in the 1902 General Elections, and in the anticlerical, and, to a lesser extent, the anti-militarist, movement, which accompanied and followed them.

Immediately, governmental reaction to the Rennes verdict, in the shape of Dreyfus's pardon, made the situation even more ambiguous. Integral Dreyfusards, like Péguy,[180] were bitterly disappointed that Dreyfus accepted the pardon, but, in general, the act of clemency seems to have been well received. At Bourg-Madame in the Pyrénées-Orientales, at Perpignan and at Privas, the police reported favourable reaction. At Montauban, "although expected for several days now, the news of Dreyfus's pardon produced a great effect here. In general . . . it is welcomed, and most people see in it a sign of the reduction of tension and of the pacification, which everyone wants. [Even army officers] . . . seem not unpleased with this way of ending the Affair." At Lille, it was noted that "trade and industry seem to have recovered confidence [as a result of the pardon]".[181] Following this, the last three months of 1899 seem to have been quiet on the whole, although demonstrations were reported from seven places, of which the most serious and violent was at Albi on 15 October. Preparations were also in hand for the municipal elections of 1900, which were the occasion for a renewal of agitation, particularly in Paris.[182] However, despite this brief reversion, historians[183] and contemporaries seem agreed that 1900 was a year of "truce" as far as the Affair was concerned, deliberately encouraged for the 1900 *Exposition*, which opened in mid-April. "The Universal *Exposition*", wrote Léon Daudet," . . . marked a suspension of hostilities in the political conflicts of the day . . ."[184] "There were clouds on the horizon", wrote Maurice Waleffe similarly. "Fashoda, the Dreyfus Affair . . . but the blue sky of the *Exposition* drove them away."[185] As Auguste Lalance had told Dreyfus in September 1899: "In your interest, and above all in the highest interest of France, it would be well for the agitation that surrounds your name to cease for a while. There should be a truce of at least one year . . . We must wait until the *Exposition* is over before we can usefully take up the campaign for vindication once more."[186] The same feeling is discernible in the press. A typical headline, from *L'Eclair* on 22 May 1900, declared: "We have had enough of the Dreyfus Affair."[187] And the truce extended to Dreyfus's opponents, as a police agent report from Paris in February makes clear: "Even the nationalists have decided to observe the 'truce' of the *Exposition . . .*", adding, however, "and they will take advantage of it to reconstitute their organizations on a serious basis."[188] A factor of some importance, of course, behind this "truce", at least in Paris, must have been the economic benefits that the *Exposition* promised, and that people did not want to see jeopardized. "1900 was the year of the *Exposition,*" commented Simon Arbellot. ". . . the streets of Paris were full of rich foreigners and business was thriving."[189] The enactment of a general act of amnesty in December 1900 for all those involved in the Affair was opposed by most leading Dreyfusards,[190] but general opinion was not behind them. "From the start", wrote Reinach, "public opinion welcomed the promise of an amnesty in an extremely favourable way. It applauded the announcement that the government would oppose any reinvestigation of the trials, that it wanted to silence the Affair."[191] And, for some, perhaps most, this was the end. According to Julien Benda: "Dreyfus's pardon, then the amnesty law. The Affair was finished."[192] A schoolmaster from the Deux-Sèvres recalled that except for a few people, "the Dreyfus Affair came to an end around me in a certain atmosphere of indifference: the pardon had been granted, rehabilitation would follow, the forces of reason had won."[193]

But for others this was not the final ragged act, and not all had such faith in "the forces of reason"; nor was 1900 a period of unbroken calm. We have already referred to the municipal elections, but the police reports provide a guide to reactions to two further events, more directly related to the Affair. First, reactions were monitored to the verdict of the Haute Cour in January 1900, condemning Déroulède, Buffet, Guérin and Habert to severe penalties for their supposed conspiracy against the Republic.[194] These men were regarded as the leaders of the anti-Dreyfusard cause, and evoked sympathy as such from their supporters, and it was feared that the harsh sentences imposed on them might lead to further conflict. From Montbéliard, for example, the police wrote that

> the verdict of the Haute Cour is being discussed in the different political circles, where it has created some impression . . . Among Republicans, from Radicals to Socialists, it is generally approved and welcomed. But moderate Republicans consider the penalties too serious, and already envisage, well before the *Exposition,* a Presidential pardon for the offenders, as a gesture of political conciliation. In the army, the condemnations . . . are generally disapproved, as they are in the reactionary party, which seems to have no intention, up to the present, of disarming.

Similar reports were filed from Bordeaux, Nantes, Fourmies and Montauban, where the police claimed that the severe sentences had had a salutary effect in checking the tendency among the public to expect attacks on the government to go unanswered, adding an old refrain: "public opinion is on edge and worried still, and wants only one thing, the end of all these discussions as soon as possible." At Epinal also, the police volunteered the opinion that a general amnesty would be well received. Elsewhere diminishing interest in the Affair and its ramifications was noted. At Chalandray in the Aisne, the Haute Cour judgment aroused little interest; in the Nord, "the verdict . . . has not made much impression . . . although the public followed the different phases of the trial, it tended to lose interest"; at Epinal, again, "the average person . . . was at first opposed to the trial, but soon became indifferent";[195] at Toulouse, "the bulk of the population" was said to be "quite unmoved" by the demonstrations of protest organized against the verdict. However, as this last report indicates, some people did react very strongly to the Haute Cour judgment. Protest meetings were staged up and down the country, and other demonstrations of support for the condemned "nationalist" leaders were reported. For example, ninety electors from Corsica sent a telegram to Drumont, editor of La Libre Parole, protesting "with indignation against the verdict", and adding, "Down with the Jews!"[196]

A further indication of the continuation of anti-Dreyfusard propaganda in the provinces, in the face of waning public interest, is provided by reports on the distribution of a poster, giving the text of the letter of resignation of General Jamont. Jamont was Vice-President of the Conseil Supérieur de la Guerre, and resigned because he claimed that the reorganization of the army leadership, following the Affair, was putting national defence in jeopardy.[197] The poster, sponsored by the "nationalist" press and the Leagues was put up during July 1900 in at least 52 departments, in many cases in every town, although the authorities in several places prevented its posting, or else quickly had it covered over or removed. But such precautions were unnecessary, for reaction to this attack on the government was almost nil. As the police reported, typically, from Saint-Quentin: "This poster has hardly been noticed by the public." Only one case of a more positive response was reported, from Montbéliard, where the posters were covered with anticlerical stickers.[198]

Little to do with the Affair appears in police reports for 1901. "Nationalist" propaganda continued to refer to it, but with little apparent impact. More important, the whole atmosphere of acrimonious debates and violent demonstrations seems to have been generally repudiated. For example, the police reported on the occasion of the regional Agricultural Show at Epinal in June 1901: "the population of Epinal, true to its localism and as a rule apathetic, is not at all interested in the programme of the 'nationalist' committee here, and will not participate in the agitation which that committee is trying to create." Similarly, the Prefect of the Seine-et-Oise commented on a meeting of the Ligue de la Patrie Française at Saint-Germain-en-Laye in March 1901: "Because of the violent language used by the platform speakers, this meeting has gone down very badly."[199] Interest in the Affair did not really resume again until the end of 1902. The death of Zola in September revived speculation, and his funeral on 5 October became a Dreyfusard demonstration attended by 20,000 people.[200] Already on 6 August 1902 *L'Intransigeant* had announced "The Resumption of the Affair",[201] and newspapers generally began to discuss it again. Judging by the amount of space devoted to the Affair in the press cuttings of the Sûreté Générale; this interest reached a peak in March–April 1903, and again from December 1903 to March 1904, when the Cour de Cassation accepted a new request for the reopening of the Dreyfus Case. But despite this wide press coverage, and the efforts of Right-wing politicians to revive the old struggle,[202] the public seems to have remained uninterested. "In spite of all the noise being made by the Ligue de la Patrie Française, in spite of the banquets, meetings and manifestoes . . . on the subject of the reopening of the Dreyfus Affair," wrote one Paris police agent in December 1903, "there is really nothing behind it all . . ."; and, according to the Paris correspondant of the Italian newspaper *Tribuna*, although the Affair filled the papers again, "the feverish impetuosity of before is so far missing among the public, although the 'nationalists' are trying to stir up agitation of that kind." In the provinces, things were not very different. From Bellegarde in the Ain, the police reported: "the decision to reopen the Dreyfus Affair has been received in the region without emotion . . ."; although the same reporter noted in March 1904: "The examination by the Cour de Cassation of the revision of the Dreyfus Case, without provoking the same agitation as in 1899, has nevertheless made a profound impression on people here." At Issoudun, also, it was reported that the reopening of the Affair had "produced real excitement in some circles."[203] It seems that as the provinces had been slow to follow Paris in becoming interested in the Affair in the first place, so provincial opinion may have lagged behind that of the capital in becoming bored with it. However, by 1904, the Affair very much took second place to other issues and talking-points, particularly the government's attack on the Church,[204] and the final stages of the Dreyfus Affair were played out in an atmosphere of general indifference. As a police agent reported from Paris at the end of 1903: "Not again! people are saying [of the Affair]; let's finish with it as soon as possible and find something else to talk about."[205]

The end of the Affair did not come, of course, until July 1906, when Dreyfus was finally exonerated, reintegrated into the army with promotion, and made a *chévalier* of the Legion of Honour; and this final act was the occasion for appropriate demonstrations, favourable and hostile. Telegrams of congratulation poured in.[206] At Bordeaux, the Ligue des Droits de l'Homme organized a peaceful demonstration and procession to the grave of its founder Trarieux, which was followed by 2,500–3,000 people, including the Prefect of the Gironde. The Action Française put up posters in several towns protesting against the rehabilitation of the "traitor". The new Royalist organization had "celebrated" the twelfth anniversary of Dreyfus's first court martial by staging two large public meetings in Paris in January 1906, and it presented General Mercier in June 1907 with a gold medal paid for by a subscription.[207] In general, however, reaction was more passive, and the usual feeling one of relief. According to Reinach, the final exoneration of Dreyfus "surprised no one . . . Nevertheless it was welcomed with joy by his supporters, and with satisfaction by the immense majority of the public . . ."[208] At Granville, the police reported: "the reintegration of Dreyfus into the army . . . and also his decoration have had a good effect in the region . . . The advanced Republicans have demonstrated their joy, while the reactionaries have not dared, as before, to criticize the decisions openly." At Château-Thierry, "most of the rural population was in the town for the market [when the final verdict became known], and the papers were read avidly"; the decision was much discussed and widely welcomed. At Nantes, the police reported that "the expected rehabilitation . . . seems not to have preoccupied the mass of the population very much. But the Republicans are overjoyed; and emotions are even stronger in reactionary circles, where a further trial had been hoped for, which might have provided a new period of agitation." A perceptive police agent in Paris summed up the situation:[209]

> Apart from a few journalists like Judet . . . no one is seriously opposed to the expected rehabilitation . . . It is generally agreed, in opposition circles, that the Affair is finally over. Among the people, the same sentiment predominates. I would go further: indifference has replaced the bitter conflict of a few years ago, and the legal solution of this Affair, which was so serious, which divided so many people, which aroused so much passion, has been accepted without a murmur by most of the population. This phenomenon cannot be explained . . . unless one takes account of the way in which the public was overtaxed and tired by the length and slowness of the latter stages of the Affair, and overwhelmed by the sheer volume of printed material which they produced.

Legally and in terms of popular involvement the Affair was over, though one more ritual, one more violence were still to come, the translation of Zola's ashes to the Panthéon in June 1908, an apotheosis of the writer who had symbolized the Dreyfusard conscience, and an official ceremony at which Dreyfus was shot in the arm by a journalist.[210] After this, the Affair moved completely on to the level of mythology, where we have already encountered it, at the beginning of this chapter. It was incorporated into the ideology of the Right, particularly by the Action Française; it lived on in a certain liberalism of the Left, where it was inspired by a more enduring literature; it lived on, too, as a component, a new patterning of that antisemitism which it so clearly and yet so confusedly articulated.

NOTES

1 For the persistence of the mythology of the Dreyfus Affair into the 1930s, the 1940s and beyond, see Paul Nizan, *Les Chiens de garde* (1932) (Paris, 1974), p. 118; *Le Procès de Charles Maurras; Compte rendu sténographique* (Paris, 1946), p. 371; Julien Benda, "L'Eternelle Affaire", *L'Ordre*, 15 January 1948, in *Les Cahiers d'un clerc (1936–49)* (Paris, 1949), pp. 156–9; J.-P. Peter, "Dimensions de l'Affaire Dreyfus", *Annales*, 16 (1961), pp. 1141–67; and Jean-François Revel, "Etre de gauche" (16 December 1968), *Les Idées de notre Temps, Chroniques de "L'Express", 1966–71* (Paris, 1972), p. 214.

2 The enormous emphasis of modern French historiography on the periods of the Revolution, the Second Republic and the Paris Commune is implicitly or explic-

itly justified as exemplifying this strategy. For its use by social anthropologists, see Ronald Frankenberg, "British Community Studies: Problems of Synthesis", in Michael Banton, ed., *The Social Anthropology of Complex Societies* (London, 1966), pp. 142–8; and, for a brilliant pioneer study in the history of attitudes, see Michel de Certeau, *La Possession de Loudun* (Paris, 1970); see also Edgar Morin *et al., La Rumeur d'Orléans* (Paris, 1969), pp. 101–3.

3 Lovsky, *La Déchirure de l'absence*, p. 7.

4 Richard L. Stokes, *Léon Blum from Poet to Premier* (London, 1937), p. 57.

5 Juan Comas, "Racial Myths", in *Race and Science*, UNESCO (1951) (New York, 1969), p. 33; see also Arnold Rose, "The Roots of Prejudice" in ibid., p. 403.

6 Roger Martin du Gard, *Jean Barois* (1913) (Paris, 1965), p. 274.

7 Cit. Henri Guillemin, *Zola: Légende et vérité* (Paris, 1971), p. 27.

8 Jérôme and Jean Tharaud, *Notre cher Péguy* (Paris, 1926), I, p. 187.

9 Daniel Halévy, *Apologie pour notre passé* (1907–10), in *Luttes et problèmes* (Paris, 1911), p. 21.

10 Joseph Reinach, *Histoire de l'Affaire Dreyfus*, VI, *La Révision* (Paris, 1908), p. 457; see also Maurice Paléologue, *Journal de l'Affaire Dreyfus, 1894–9; L'Affaire Dreyfus et le Quai d'Orsay* (Paris, 1955), pp. 7, 35–6, 38 and 157; and chapter XII, pp. 391–2 below.

11 Cit. Jean-Louis Lévy, "La Vie du capitaine Dreyfus", in Dreyfus, *Cinq années de ma vie*, p. 260.

12 Anatole France, *L'Eglise et la République* (1904) (Paris, 1964), p. 49.

13 Reinach, *Histoire de l'Affaire Dreyfus*, III, *La Crise: Procès Esterhazy-Procès Zola* (Paris, 1903), p. 481.

14 Halévy, op. cit., p. 47.

15 Léon Daudet, *Au Temps de Judas* (Paris, 1933), p. 14.

16 Reinach, *Histoire de l'Affaire Dreyfus*, I, *Le Procès de 1894* (Paris, 1901), p. 469.

17 Georges de Lauris, *Souvenirs d'une belle époque* (Paris, 1948), p. 94; Fernand Gregh, *L'Age d'or* (Paris, 1947), p. 286.

18 Reinach, op. cit., I, p. 468.

19 Jacques Bainville, *Histoire de France* (Paris, 1924), pp. 535–6.

20 Emile Zola, "Justice", *L'Aurore*, 5 June 1899, in Zola, *L'Affaire Dreyfus; La Vérité en marche* (Paris, 1969), p. 154.

21 Martin du Gard, op. cit., p. 292.

22 Péguy, *Notre Jeunesse* (hereafter *NJ*), pp. 14, 51 and 54.

23 Halévy, op. cit., pp. 13–14. See also Georges Guy-Grand, *La Philosophie nationaliste* (Paris, 1911), p. 13: "L'histoire des idées ne saura trop insister à l'avenir sur le coup de fouet intellectuel que fut la fameuse Affaire; elle eut non seulement dans les coeurs, mais aussi dans les cerveaux, une vibration profonde, dont l'effet n'est pas encore épuisé."

24 The most significant contributions since then towards a more objective account have been: Pierre Sorlin, *Waldeck-Rousseau* (Paris, 1966); Sorlin, *"La Croix" et les Juifs (1880–99): Contribution à l'histoire de l'antisémitisme contemporain* (Paris, 1967); Michael R. Marrus, *The Politics of Assimilation: A Study of the French Jewish Community at the time of the Dreyfus Affair* (London, 1971); and Janine Ponty, "La Presse quotidienne et l'Affaire Dreyfus en 1898–1899: Essai de typologie", *Revue d'Histoire Moderne et Contemporaine*, 21 (1974), pp. 193–220.

25 Pierre Miquel, *L'Affaire Dreyfus* (Paris, 1968), p. 126.

26 Hannah Arendt, *The Origins of Totalitarianism* (Cleveland, 1962), pp. 120 and 93.

27 Viz. the misleading titles of Nicholas Halasz, *Captain Dreyfus: The Story of a Mass Hysteria* (New York, 1955); H. R. Kedward, *The Dreyfus Affair, Catalyst for Tensions in French Society* (London, 1965); and Douglas Johnson, *France and the Dreyfus Affair* (London, 1966). Kedward, however, writes (p. 119): "One needs to know how deeply the conflicts penetrated into the provinces:

how for example, the provincial meetings of the Ligue des Droits de l'Homme were received." Johnson is less careful, stating (p. 212): "There were periods of indifference, as the 1898 and 1902 elections show; there were areas of indifference, as most of the provinces show . . ."; the first statement needs important qualification, as we shall see, while the second is made without evidence to support it. French historians, brought up in a stricter school, are, on the whole, but not always, more prudent; see François Goguel, *La Politique des partis sous la Troisième République* (Paris, 1958), p. 100; Robert Gauthier, ed., *"Dreyfusards!"; Souvenirs de Mathieu Dreyfus et autres inédits* (Paris, 1965), p. 270; Miquel, op. cit., p. 47; and Pierre Sorlin, *La Société française, 1840–1914* (Paris, 1969), pp. 246–7.

28 In addition to Ponty, and Sorlin's study of *La Croix*, see P. Boussel, *L'Affaire Dreyfus et la Presse* (Paris, 1966).

29 Miquel, op. cit., p. 7.

30 See C. Delhorbe, *L'Affaire Dreyfus et les écrivains français* (Paris, 1932); Jacques Madaule, *Le Nationalisme de Maurice Barrès* (Marseille, 1943); Léon S. Roudiez, *Maurras jusqu'à l'Action Française* (Paris, 1957); Claude Digeon, *La Crise allemande de la penseé française (1870–1914)* (Paris, 1959); J.-J. Fiechter, *Le Socialisme français: De l'Affaire Dreyfus à la Grande Guerre* (Geneva, 1965); Marie-Claire Bancquart, *Anatole France polémiste* (Paris, 1962); Alain Silvera, *Daniel Halévy and his times* (Ithaca, 1966); and Zeev Sternhell, *Maurice Barrès et le nationalisme français* (Paris, 1972).

31 Raoul Girardet, *La Société militaire dans la France contemporaine (1815–1939)* (Paris, 1953), p. 235.

32 J.-L. Lévy, op. cit., p. 262; and Jacqueline Morand, *Les Idées politiques de Louis-Ferdinand Céline* (Paris, 1972), p. 48.

33 Léon Bloy, *Je m'accuse* (1900), *Oeuvres*, IV (Paris, 1965), p. 176; see also Paléologue, op. cit., p. 141 (26 September 1898).

34 Halévy, op. cit., pp. 49–50.

35 Gregh, op. cit., p. 288; see also Péguy, *Cahiers de la Quinzaine*, 23 January 1906, in Péguy, *Souvenirs* (Paris, 1939), pp. 72–3.

36 Marguerite Steinheil, *My Memoirs* (London, 1912), pp. 84 and 77.

37 Ibid., pp. 77 and 89–91.

38 Jules Renard, Letters to Maurice Donnay (19 December 1898) and to Louis Paillard (14 August and 5 September 1899), in Renard, *Correspondance* (Paris, 1953), pp. 197–8 and 205.

39 Jean Renoir, *Renoir My Father* (London, 1965), pp. 242–3.

40 Tharaud, op. cit., II, p. 33.

41 Léon Daudet, *Salons et journaux: Souvenirs des milieux littéraires, politiques, artistiques et médicaux de 1880 à 1908*, Quatrième série (Paris, 1917), p. 35.

42 See Halévy, op. cit., p. 73. A similar attitude was expressed by Lyautey, then a lieutenant-colonel, who wrote to Paul Desjardins from Madagascar on 2 February 1899: "Je ne pardonne ni 'à vos amis' ni aux 'autres' d'avoir de nouveau, par leurs violences réciproques, coupé la France en deux. Et je cherche en vain l'esprit de notre chère 'Union' du début . . ." (referring to the Union pour l'Action Morale founded by Desjardins in 1891); Lyautey, *Choix de lettres 1882–1919* (Paris, 1947), p. 169.

43 Lauris, op. cit., p. 99.

44 Bloy, op. cit., pp. 209–10 and *passim.*

45 Archives Nationales, Police Générale: F7 12449–12481; F7 12717–12720; F7 12842–12843; F7 12854; F7 12870–12873; and F7 12921–12926, of which further particulars are provided below. The Archives de la Préfecture de Police have also been used.

46 See n. 28.

47 Richard Cobb, *The Police and the People: French Popular Protest 1789–1820* (London, 1972), pp. 3–45.

48 Reinach, op. cit., I, pp. 191–2 and 205. It seems that *La Libre Parole* had a tip-off from the War Ministry.
49 Ibid., pp. 462 and 467; see also Paléologue, op. cit., p. 21.
50 Paléologue, op. cit., p. 30; see also Boussel, op. cit., pp. 35–70; and Ponty, op. cit., p. 201.
51 Halévy, op. cit., p. 27.
52 Ibid., p. 25.
53 Ibid., pp. 26–7.
54 See Léon Daudet, "Le Châtiment", *Le Figaro*, 6 January 1895, cited *in extenso* in Boussel, op. cit., pp. 70–5; and Maurice Barrès, "La Parade de Judas", January 1895, in Barrès, *Scènes et doctrines du nationalisme*, I, pp. 142–5.
55 Paléologue, op. cit., p. 37.
56 Reinach, op. cit., I, pp. 565–6; Halévy, op. cit., p. 30.
57 Report, Commissaire spécial, Saint-Quentin (Aisne), 6 January 1895. AN F⁷ 12464, "Affaire Dreyfus".
58 Report, Commissaire spécial, Conflans-Jarny (Meurthe-et-Moselle), 7 January 1895. Ibid.
59 Halévy suggests that the antisemitic press dropped the case under pressure from the military; op. cit., p. 30.
60 Ibid., p. 37.
61 Martin du Gard, op. cit., pp. 209–10.
62 *Le Matin*, 19 November 1896; *Le Voltaire*, 19 November 1896; *L'Eclair*, 19 November 1896; *La Petite République*, 11 November 1896.
63 Gregh, op. cit., p. 286.
64 Halévy, op. cit., p. 42; see also Paléologue, op. cit., pp. 60–1.
65 Reports, Police agents, Paris, 17, 19 and 20 November 1897. AN F⁷ 12473, "Affaire Dreyfus".
66 Martin du Gard, op. cit., p. 242.
67 Reports, Police agents, Paris, 26 November and 9 December 1897; and Commissaire spécial, Epinal (Vosges), 4 November 1897. AN F⁷ 12473. The reports refer to Scheurer-Kestner's intervention in the Senate on Dreyfus's behalf, and to the government's reassurances on that occasion. Scheurer-Kestner represented the Vosges.
68 Paléologue, op. cit., p. 87 (11 January 1898).
69 Halévy, op. cit., p. 13.
70 Reinach, op. cit., III, p. 249.
71 Edouard Herriot, *Jadis, Avant la première guerre mondiale* (Paris, 1948), pp. 133–4.
72 Zola, "Impressions d'audience", cit. Henri Mitterand, *Zola journaliste de l'affaire Manet à l'affaire Dreyfus* (Paris, 1962), p. 240.
73 Reinach, op. cit., III, pp. 240 and 242.
74 See Léon Blum, "Le Procès", *La Revue Blanche*, 15 March 1898, *L'Oeuvre de Léon Blum 1891–1905* (Paris, 1954), pp. 343–58.
75 See *Le Procès Zola devant la Cour d'Assises de la Seine et la Cour de Cassation (7 février–23 février—31 mars–2 avril 1898), Compte-rendu sténographique "in-extenso"* (Paris, 1898), 2 vols; and Paléologue, op. cit., pp. 112–13 and 116 (16, 17 and 23 February 1898).
76 See various police reports, AN F⁷ 12464 "Affaire Dreyfus, Procès Zola"; also Paléologue, op. cit., pp. 108–9 (7 and 8 February 1898); and Reinach, op. cit., III, pp. 341–2.
77 P.-V. Stock, *Mémorandum d'un éditeur, Troisième série, L'Affaire Dreyfus anecdotique* (Paris, 1938), p. 49.
78 Reports, Police agents, 8 and 15 February 1898. AN F⁷ 12464.
79 Reinach, op. cit., III, pp. 441–2.
80 Reports, Police agent, Paris, 18 February 1898; Commissaire spécial, Narbonne (Aude), 19 February 1898; Commissaire spécial, Saint-Dié (Vosges), 19 Febru-

ary 1898; Commissaire spécial, Béziers (Hérault), 24 February 1898; Commissaire spécial, Saint-Julien-en-Genevois (Haute-Savoie), 25 February 1898; Commissaire spécial, Armentières (Nord), 25 February 1898; Commissaire spécial, Château-Gontier (Mayenne), 24 February 1898; and Commissaire de police, Guéret (Creuse), 24 February 1898. AN F7 12474.

81 Jacques Ozouf, *Nous les maîtres d'école, Autobiographies d'instituteurs de la belle époque* (Paris, 1967), p. 23.
82 Reinach, op. cit., III, p. 480.
83 Martin du Gard, op. cit., p. 281.
84 Reports, Commissaire de police, Halluin (Nord); Commissaire spécial, Saint-Malo (Ille-et-Vilaine); Commissaire spécial, Saint-Dié; Commissaire spécial, Le Mans (Sarthe); Commissaire spécial, Royat (Puy-de-Dôme); Commissaire spécial, Epinal; Commissaire spécial, Grenoble (Isère); Commissaire de police, Amiens (Somme); Commissaire de police, Charleville (Ardennes); Commissaire spécial, Tourcoing (Nord); Commissaire spécial, Châlons-sur-Marne (Marne); Commissaire spécial, Valence (Drôme); and Commissaire central, Perpignan (Pyrénées-Orientales); 24 and 25 February 1898. AN F7 12474.
85 Reinach, op. cit., III, p. 539.
86 Reports, Commissaire spécial, Epinal, 2 March 1898; Commissaire spécial, Saint-Quentin, 4 April 1898; Commissaire spécial, Fécamp (Seine-Inférieure), 4 April 1898; and Commissaire spécial, Saint-Dié, 5 April 1898. AN F7 12474.
87 See various reports, ibid.
88 Reports, Commissaire spécial, Veynes (Hautes-Alpes), 28 February 1898; and Commissaire spécial, Epinal, 24 February 1898. Ibid.
89 Goguel, op. cit., p. 90; see also Johnson, op. cit., pp. 130–3; and J.-B. Duroselle, "L'Antisémitisme en France de 1886 à 1914", *Cahiers Paul Claudel, 7, La Figure d'Israël* (Paris, 1968), p. 67.
90 Reinach, op. cit., III, p. 581.
91 Cit. Henriette Dardenne, *Godefroy Cavaignac: Un républicain du progrès aux débuts de la 3e République* (Paris, 1969), p. 490.
92 France, op. cit., p. 55.
93 Steinheil, op. cit., pp. 75–6; see also Jacques de Lacretelle, *Silbermann* (1922) (Paris, 1950), pp. 73–4.
94 See Reinach, op. cit., III, p. 582; and Jean Jolly, ed., *Dictionnaire des parlementaires français: Notices biographiques sur les ministres, députés et sénateurs français de 1889 à 1940* (Paris, 1960—), *passim.*
95 Reinach, op. cit., III, pp. 582–6; and Harvey Goldberg, *The Life of Jean Jaurès* (Madison, 1962), pp. 228–31.
96 Cit. Jolly, ed., op. cit., pp. 468 and 672.
97 Reinach, op. cit., III, p. 581.
98 Dardenne, op. cit., pp. 490–8.
99 See chapter VIII for a full analysis of the antisemitic parliamentary group.
100 *Journal Officiel de la République Française, Chambre des Députés, Documents parlementaires, Annexes de la Chambre des Députés, Projets de Loi, Propositions et Rapports, 7e législature, Session ordinaire de 1900,* Annexe no. 1321, pp. 838–1050; pp. 883 and 885 quoted.
101 Daily Reports, Prefect of Police, 3, 1, 21 and 4 May; and 4 and 5 March 1898. Archives de la Préfecture de Police, Ba 106.
102 See Adrien Dansette, *Le Boulangisme* (Paris, 1946), chapter VII; Jacques Néré, *Le Boulangisme et la Presse* (Paris, 1964), pp. 167–202; and Frederic H. Seager, *The Boulanger Affair: Political Crossroad of France 1886–1889* (Ithaca, 1969), pp. 80–4 and *passim.*
103 See Henri Carel, "Les Forces politiques en Haute-Saône de 1870 à 1914"; and R. Marlin, "La Droite à Besançon de 1870 à 1914", in *Recherches sur les forces politiques de la France de l'Est*, Journées d'études de Strasbourg organisées au Palais universitaire sous les auspices de l'Association Interuniversitaire de l'Est

par l'Institut d'Études Politiques et la Faculté des Lettres et Sciences Humaines de Strasbourg, December 1964 (no place or date of publication), pp. 244–5 and 230.
104 *Journal Officiel,* etc., p. 918.
105 See Reinach, op. cit., III, p. 587; and chapter II, pp. 66–70 below, for further discussion of Socialist attitudes.
106 *Journal Officiel,* etc., p. 1001.
107 The full list of departments, with numbers of constituencies concerned, if more than one, is as follows: Ain, Basses-Alpes, Ardèche (2), Ariège, Aude, Aveyron (2), Bouches-du-Rhône, Calvados (2), Cantal (2), Charente (5), Charente-Inféri-eure (2), Corrèze (2), Côte-d'Or, Côtes-du-Nord, Creuse, Dordogne, Eure, Finistère, Gers, Gironde (2), Ille-et-Vilaine (5), Indre, Isère (2), Loire (3), Haute-Loire, Loire-Inférieure (3), Lozère, Maine-et-Loire (3), Manche, Mayenne (2), Meurthe-et-Moselle, Meuse (2), Morbihan (2), Nord (2), Orne (3), Pas-de-Calais, Puy-de-Dôme, Hautes-Pyrénées, Belfort, Haute-Saône (2), Saône-et-Loire, Sarthe (2), Savoie, Seine (10), Seine-Inférieure (3), Seine-et-Marne (2), Seine-et-Oise (4), Deux-Sèvres (3), Somme (2), Tarn, Vendée (3), Vienne, Haute-Vienne (2), Vosges; and Algerian departments (2).
108 *Journal Officiel,* etc., p. 922.
109 Dardenne, op. cit., p. 490.
110 Cit. Reinach, op. cit., III, p. 540.
111 "Situation générale des Partis politiques en 1898". AN F⁷ 12719, "Nationalistes 1898–1910".
112 Blum, "Les Elections de 1902" (April 1902), *L'Oeuvre de Léon Blum 1891–1905,* p. 493. Dardenne's conflicting view, that the 1898 elections represented an ideological conflict on the national level, remains unconvincing; see Dardenne, op. cit., p. 489.
113 See Dardenne, op. cit., pp. 504 and 772–5, which gives the text of Cavaignac's speech; and Paléologue, op. cit., pp. 126–7.
114 Reports, Prefect, Haute-Loire, 23 July 1898; Commissaire de police, Laon (Aisne), 24 July 1898; and Commissaire spécial, Montbéliard (Doubs), 29 July 1898. AN F⁷ 12467, "Affaire Dreyfus", Dossier: "Des Réponses à Mr Cavaignac".
115 E.g. Martin du Gard, op. cit., p. 292; and Maurice Larkin, *Church and State after the Dreyfus Affair, The Separation Issue in France* (London, 1974), p. 71.
116 See Barrès-Maurras, op. cit., pp. 649–50, for the text of this article.
117 Steinheil, op. cit., pp. 89–91 and 101.
118 See Péguy, *NJ,* p. 119.
119 Reinach, op. cit., IV, *Cavaignac et Félix Faure* (Paris, 1904), p. 270.
120 Ibid., pp. 271–3, 296–7 and 413.
121 Ibid., pp. 329–34; Steinheil, op. cit., p. 98; and various reports, AN F⁷ 12461 and F⁷ 12466, "Affaire Dreyfus".
122 Steinheil, op. cit., p 94.
123 Reports, Commissaire spécial, Cette (Hérault), 31 October 1898; Commissaire spécial, Ambérieu (Ain), 4 October and 12 December 1898; and Commissaire spécial, Limoges (Haute-Vienne), 18 November 1898. AN F⁷ 12466.
124 Report, Prefect, Nord, 20 January 1898. AN F⁷ 12467.
125 Reports, Commissaire spécial, Montauban (Tarn-et-Garonne), 30 September 1898; and Commissaire de police, Montereau (Seine-et-Marne), 8 October 1898. AN F⁷ 12466.
126 Report, Prefect, Haute-Garonne, 24 December 1898. AN F⁷ 12465, "Affaire Dreyfus".
127 Report, Police agent, 25 November 1898. Ibid.
128 Steinheil, op. cit., p. 100.

129 Reinach, op. cit., IV, pp. 390–5; see also "Adresses au colonel Picquart à l'occasion du Ier janvier 1899". AN F⁷ 12465.

130 Report, Police agent, 1 October 1898. This attitude persisted in some places into 1899 and beyond. Halls were refused for meetings to be addressed by Jaurès and Pressensé in January 1899 at Toulouse at the request of the Prefect, and in April 1899 at Albi on the advice of the mayor; see Reports, Prefect, Haute-Garonne, 17 January 1899; and Commissaire spécial, Albi (Tarn), 20 April 1899. AN F⁷ 12466; see also Dardenne, op. cit., pp. 512–13.

131 E.g. by Roland Andréani, "L'Antimilitarisme en Languedoc méditerranéen avant la Première Guerre Mondiale", Revue d'Histoire Moderne et Contemporaine, 20 (1973), p. 106, of meetings addressed by the anarchists Faure and Henri Dhorr in the Gard and the Hérault.

132 Reinach, op. cit., IV, p. 426; and Reports, Commissaire spécial, Toulouse (Haute-Garonne), 23 and 28 December 1898. AN F⁷ 12465. A further meeting in Toulouse in January 1899, addressed by Jaurès, Pressensé and Gérault-Richard again led to violent demonstrations, and 20 arrests were made; see Report, Commissaire spécial, Toulouse, 23 February 1899. AN F⁷ 12466.

133 Nadar, Letter, 12 December 1898, cit. Jean Prinet et Antoinette Dilasser, Nadar (Paris, 1966), p. 217. Pressensé addressed a crowd of 4,000 at the Alhambra in Marseille on 8 December; the meeting caused great excitement, and fighting broke out during it; see Reports, Commissaire spécial, Marseille, 8 and 9 December 1898. AN F⁷ 12465.

134 Dardenne, op. cit., p 513.

135 Letter, 1 November 1898, Barrès-Maurras, op. cit., p 192.

136 In addition to the police reports, see Reinach, op. cit., IV, pp. 426–8.

137 Reinach, op. cit., V, Rennes (Paris, 1905), pp. 111–17.

138 Reports, Prefect, Haute-Garonne, 17 January 1899; and Commissaire spécial, Moissac (Lot), 24 January 1899. AN F⁷ 12466.

139 Steinheil, op. cit., p. 102.

140 See Paléologue, op. cit., p. 173; Reports, Prefect of Police, 20 and 25 February 1899. AN F⁷ 12449, "Ligue des Patriotes 1882–1906"; and Reinach, op. cit., IV, pp. 570–601.

141 See, in addition to various police reports, Reinach, op. cit., V, p. 74; and Raphaël Viau, Vingt ans d'antisémitisme 1889–1909 (Paris, 1910), p. 189.

142 Reinach, op. cit., V, pp. 110–11.

143 Report, Commissaire spécial, Montauban, 6 March 1899. AN F⁷ 12466.

144 Reports, Commissaire spécial, Angers (Maine-et-Loire), 23 June 1899; Prefect, Manche, 24 June 1899; and Commissaire spécial, Cette, 5 June 1899. AN F⁷ 12465.

145 Report, Commissaire spécial, Nice (Alpes-Maritimes), 6 June 1899. AN F⁷ 12487, "Ligue des Droits de l'Homme 1898–1908".

146 See various reports, Dossier "Manifestations politiques provoquées par les partis hostiles au Gouvernement après les troubles des courses d'Auteuil, 4 Juin 1899". AN F⁷ 12458, "Surveillance des nationalistes, 1899".

147 See Jacques Chastenet, La République triomphante 1893–1906 (Paris, 1955), p. 62. (I believe that there exists an article on reactions to Carnot's assassination, which I am unable to trace.)

148 See Police report, 11 June 1899. AN F⁷ 12458; and Halévy, op. cit., pp. 78–9.

149 Reports, Commissaire spécial, Saint-Quentin, 6 June 1899; Commissaire spécial, Marseille, 9 June 1899; Commissaire spécial, Cette, 6 June 1899; and Commissaire spécial, Agen (Lot-et-Garonne), 6 June 1899. AN F⁷ 12458.

150 Halévy, op. cit., p. 85.

151 Reports, Commissaire spécial, Montauban, 7 June 1899; Commissaire spécial,

Epinal, 5 June 1899; and Commissaire spécial, Dieppe (Seine-Inférieure), 5 June 1899. AN F⁷ 12458.

152 Report, Commissaire spécial, Rouen (Seine-Inférieure) 5 June 1899. AN F⁷ 12465.

153 Reports, Prefect, Finistère, 25 June 1899; and Police, Rennes (Ille-et-Vilaine), 21 June 1899. AN F⁷ 12464, "Affaire Dreyfus".

154 Report, Commissaire spécial, Nantes (Loire-Inférieure), 30 June 1899. AN F⁷ 12465.

155 "Note pour Monsieur le Président du Conseil" from Directeur de la Sûreté Générale, 6 June 1899. AN F⁷ 12464; see also Paléologue, op. cit., p. 192 (6 August 1899), reporting a conversation with the Prefect. (Paléologue attended the trial as the official representative of the Quai d'Orsay.)

156 Reports, Police agent, Rennes, 6 July 1899; and Police, Rennes, 5 July 1899. AN F⁷ 12464.

157 Twenty-two infantry companies, 6 squads of mounted gendarmes and nearly 300 gendarmerie à pied were in Rennes for the trial. Note, Minister of the Interior to Minister of War, 3 July 1899. AN F⁷ 12464. See also, in addition to various police reports, Paléologue, op. cit., pp. 211–12 and 251.

158 In addition to police reports, see Reinach, op. cit., V, pp. 425–6.

159 Report, Police agent, Paris, 21 August 1899. AN F⁷ 12923, "Affaire Dreyfus".

160 On "Fort Chabrol", see Police reports, Dossier: "Affaire de la rue Chabrol". AN F⁷ 12462, "Mouvement antisémite, 1899"; Police agent reports, dossier 2. AN F⁷ 12882, "Ligue Antisémitique, 1899"; and Reinach, op. cit., V, pp. 425–6. For further discussion, see chapter VI, pp. 184–5 below.

161 Report, Police agent, Paris, 18 August 1899. AN F⁷ 12464.

162 Report, Police, Paris, 12 August 1899. AN F⁷ 12449.

163 Report, Commissaire spécial, Marseille, 15 August 1899. AN F⁷ 12458.

164 Renard, Letter to Maurice Pottecher, 11 September 1899, Correspondance, pp. 206–7.

165 Halévy, op. cit., p. 68.

166 Report, Commissaire spécial, Nice, 15 August 1899. AN F⁷ 12449.

167 Reports, Prefect, Isère, 1 and 10 September 1899. Archives Départementales, 51 M2⁶, cit. P. Barral, Le Département de l'Isère sous la Troisième République: Histoire sociale et politique (Paris, 1962), p. 364.

168 Reports, Commissaire spécial, Nevers, 30 August 1899; Commissaire spécial, Charleville, 30 August 1899; and Commissaire spécial, Cette, 7 September 1899. AN F⁷ 12465.

169 Martin du Gard, op. cit., p. 311; see also Paléologue, op. cit., pp. 194–5, 198 and 210–11, on Dreyfus's unappealing performance at Rennes. Contrast this with Reinach's appreciation of the impact of Zola's "J'accuse".

170 Report, Police agent, Paris, 2 September 1899. AN F⁷ 12466.

171 Viau, op. cit., pp. 218–21.

172 Reports, Gendarmerie, Saint-Dié, 10 September 1899; Police des chemins de fer, Troyes (Aube), 11 September 1899; Commissaire spécial, Ajaccio, 11 September 1899; Telegram, Prefect, Haute-Garonne, 10 September 1899; Reports, Commissaire spécial, Remiremont (Vosges), 11 September 1899; Commissaire spécial, Dieppe, 30 November 1899; and Prefect, Lot, 14 September 1899. AN F⁷ 12465, Dossier: "État de l'opinion publique et manifestations après le jugement de Rennes, 9 septembre 1899". See also Paléologue, op. cit., pp. 261 and 264, on the immediate reaction to the verdict at Rennes. The crowd outside the court-room received the verdict in silence, but, later: "La foule, qui a envahi la gare, est dans un tel paroxysme de passion délirante ou furieuse qu'on nous fait entrer par une porte dérobée."

173 Steinheil, op. cit., p. 103.

174 Bloy, Je m'accuse, Oeuvres, IV, p. 208.

175 Reinach, op. cit., V, pp. 535–6.

176 Reports, Commissaire spécial, Delle (Belfort), 10 September 1899; Commissaire spécial, Marseille, 11 September 1899; Commissaire spécial, Cette, 10 September 1899; Commissaire spécial, Nantes, 10 September 1899; Prefect, Lot, 14 September 1899; Telegram to *Le Petit Parisien* from Agen, 13 September 1899; and Report, Commissaire special, Châlons-sur-Marne, 14 September 1899. AN F⁷ 12465.
177 *Memoirs of Captain Dreyfus 1899–1906,* Pierre Dreyfus, *Dreyfus: His Life and Letters* (London, 1937), p. 225.
178 Reports, Municipal police, Le Blanc (Indre), 10 September 1899; Commissaire de police, Châlons-sur-Marne, 14 September 1899; Commissaire spécial, Longwy (Meurthe-et-Moselle), 12 September 1899; Prefect, Nièvre, 12 September 1899; Commissaire spécial, Montauban, 13 September 1899; Commissaire spécial, Bar-le-Duc (Meuse), 11 September 1899; and Prefect, Lot, 14 September 1899. AN F⁷ 12465.
179 *Le Télégramme de Toulouse,* 10 September 1899.
180 See Tharaud, op. cit., I, pp. 188–9.
181 Reports, Commissaire spécial, Montauban, 22 September 1899; and Commissaire spécial, Lille (Nord), 23 September 1899. AN F⁷ 12467.
182 See Report, Police agent, Paris, 31 January 1903. AN F⁷ 12870, "Ligue des Patriotes, 1898–1906", Dossier no. 5; also D. R. Watson, "The Nationalist Movement in Paris, 1900–1906", in David Shapiro, ed., *The Right in France 1890–1919,* St Antony's Papers, no. 13 (London, 1962), pp. 66–76.
183 See R. D. Mandell, "The Affair and the Fair: Some Observations on the Closing Stages of the Dreyfus Case", *Journal of Modern History,* 39 (1967), pp. 253–65; also Goguel, op. cit., p. 98; and Sorlin, *Waldeck-Rousseau,* pp. 419–20.
184 Daudet, *Salons et journaux,* p. 198.
185 Maurice de Waleffe, *Quand Paris était un paradis: Mémoires 1900–39* (Paris, 1947), p. 154.
186 Auguste Lalance, Letter to Dreyfus, 27 September 1899, cit., Pierre Dreyfus, op. cit., p. 219; see also Steinheil, op. cit., p. 128; J. J. Jusserand, *What Me Befell. The Reminiscences of* (London, 1933), p. 212; Abel Combarieu, *Sept ans à l'Elysée avec le Président Emile Loubet* (Paris, 1932), pp. 57–9; and Gauthier, ed., op. cit., pp. 241–4.
187 *L'Eclair,* 22 May 1900. The paper added: "Les élections municipales . . . dans toute la France, se sont faites sur ce terrain: *l'affaire Dreyfus ne sera pas rouverte.*"
188 Report, Police agent, Paris, 14 February 1900. AN F⁷ 12719, "Nationalistes 1898–1910". A later police report made the same point, though taking a different view of the effect of the "truce" on Nationalist fortunes: "La période de paix obligatoire, créée par l'Exposition . . . a aidé beaucoup au refroidissement des adversaires de la République, qui, endormis maintenant, auront peine à s'éveiller . . .", Police report, 20 January 1901, "Résumé générale de la Situation en décembre 1900". AN F⁷ 12870.
189 Simon Arbellot, *La Fin du boulevard* (Paris, 1965), p. 23.
190 See Pierre Dreyfus, op. cit., pp. 229–31, 238, 247 and 258.
191 Reinach, op. cit., VI, p. 22.
192 Julien Benda, *La Jeunesse d'un clerc* (Paris, 1936), p. 214.
193 Ozouf, op. cit., p. 24.
194 Déroulède and Buffet were sentenced to 10 years' banishment; Guérin to 10 years' detention; and Habert to 5 years' banishment. Reinach, op. cit., VI, pp. 59–65; see also Barrès, *Scènes et doctrines,* I, pp. 263–74.
195 Reports, Commissaire spécial, Montbéliard, 6 January 1900; Commissaire spécial, Montauban, 16 December 1899; Commissaire spécial, Lille, 5 January 1900; and Commissaire spécial, Epinal, 8 January 1900. AN F⁷ 12453, "Haute

Cour, 1899'', Dossier: "Impression produite par le jugement de la Haute Cour".

196 Report, Prefect, Haute-Garonne, 22 January 1900; and Telegram, 7 January 1900. AN F⁷ 12455, "Surveillance des nationalistes".

197 See David B. Ralston, *The Army of the Republic: The Place of the Military in the Political Evolution of France, 1871–1914* (Cambridge, Mass., 1967), pp. 288–91. Jamont's charge became a common theme of the "Nationalist" Right at the time and later; see, for example, Charles Maurras, *Vingt-cinq ans de monarchisme* (1924), *Oeuvres capitales* (Paris, 1954), II, pp. 444–5.

198 Report, Commissaire de police, Saint-Quentin, 22 July 1900. AN F⁷ 12453–12454, "Surveillance des nationalistes".

199 Reports, Commissaire spécial, Epinal, 14 June 1901; and Prefect, Seine-et-Oise, 13 March 1901. AN F⁷ 12457, "Surveillance des nationalistes".

200 Halévy, op. cit., pp. 104–6; Pierre Dreyfus, op. cit., pp. 280–1.

201 *L'Intransigeant*, 6 August 1902.

202 For "Nationalist" attempts to revive anti-Dreyfusism in 1904, see Daudet, *Au Temps de Judas*, chapters 7 and 8.

203 Reports, Police agent, Paris, 5 December 1903; Police agent, Paris, no date; Commissaire spécial, Bellegarde (Ain), 26 December 1903 and 5 March 1904; and Commissaire de police, Issoudun (Indre), 2 December 1903. AN F⁷ 12470, "Affaire Dreyfus".

204 For the emotion aroused by this in the provinces, see, for example, Jean-Marie Mayeur, "Géographie de la résistance aux Inventaires (février-mars 1906)", *Annales*, 21 (1966), pp. 1259–72.

205 Report, Police agent, Paris, 1 December 1903. AN F⁷ 12470.

206 Pierre Dreyfus, op. cit., pp. 357–63.

207 See Barrès-Maurras, op. cit., pp. 464 and 479.

208 Reinach, op. cit., VI, p. 477.

209 Reports, Commissaire spécial, Granville (Manche), no date; Commissaire de police, Château-Thierry (Aisne), 13 July 1906; Commissaire spécial, Nantes, 16 July 1906; and Police agent, Paris, 21 July 1906. AN F⁷ 12472, "Affaire Dreyfus". Associated with the Ligue de la Patrie Française, Judet was editor of *Le Petit Journal* until 1904, when he became director of *L'Éclair*. He was involved in pro-German activities during the First World War, it seems, fled to Switzerland in 1917, and was accused and found guilty of treason, in his absence, in 1919; see Claude Bellanger, Jacques Godechot, Pierre Guiral and Fernand Terrou, eds., *Histoire générale de la presse française*, III, *De 1871 à 1940* (Paris, 1972), pp. 303, 345–6, 435 and 545; Daudet, *Salons et journaux*, pp. 84–94; and Ernest Judet, *Ma Politique 1905–1917* (Paris, 1923).

210 See Pierre Dreyfus, op. cit., p. 368; and Barrès-Maurras, op. cit., p. 483, n.

CHAPTER II
THE DREYFUS AFFAIR, PUBLIC OPINION AND
ANTISEMITISM: II

I

So far the account of opinion during the Dreyfus affair has been chronological, giving some indication of how it developed, spread and changed during the decade after 1895. But, with some exceptions, reference has been to general "public opinion", to the attitudes of the "population" of one place or another, schematic global categories that must be further broken down, if we are to understand what the Affair meant as a social phenomenon. In this chapter an attempt will be made to analyse the extent and the nature of public interest and involvement in the Affair, in geographical, political and social terms, that will make that significance clearer. It is not enough to know that the Affair was the occasion for public excitement and agitation in the provinces as well as in Paris, and that this agitation and excitement reached a height in the years 1898 and 1899, quickly subsiding afterwards. We need to know, as far as possible, where the excitement was most intense, and among what social groups. Only then will we be in a position to suggest why it erupted at all.

Something can be gleaned in answer to the first question about the geography of opinion, from the police reports on disturbances during the Affair, on Dreyfusard and anti-Dreyfusard meetings, and on the distribution of sections of the various Leagues created or recreated on one side or the other. For the years 1898 and 1899, the police kept a very close watch on all three, and their reports almost certainly give a fair idea of the geographical distribution of each. Slightly over 100 disturbances or incidents related to the Affair, were reported between December 1898 and December 1899. (Disturbances in 1898 will be considered in the next chapter.) These ranged from serious riots, which we have already encountered, such as those in Paris and Marseille in February 1899, to minor public expressions of opinion of a collective nature, often on the occasion of military parades, or public meetings. Forty-nine places experienced these disturbances, and some pattern is discernible in their distribution (see Map 1).[1] As will be seen in the case of the distribution of revisionist meetings and of sections of the Ligue des Droits de l'Homme, there was a heavy concentration in the South, 14 of the towns concerned being south of a line drawn between Bordeaux and Valence. Eleven places were in the Eastern frontier departments, and 14 in the North-Western quarter of France, with an important concentration in Brittany. The last two regions were ones of Right-wing electoral strength.[2] This pattern of disturbances repeats that of the antisemitic riots of January and February 1898, 29 places experiencing disturbances in both periods.[3] Again, as might be expected, it was, on the whole, the more important towns, in 30 cases the *chefs-lieux de département*, which experienced trouble. The most serious disturbances at both times were generally in the big cities.

The pattern of distribution of meetings occasioned by the Affair is similar. Between October 1898 and December 1899, 138 revisionist meetings were reported in 64 places; of these 21 were in Languedoc or Provence, 9 were in the Lyon region, and 23 in the North-Eastern quarter of France. The rest were scattered[4] (see Map 2). Eighteen places had more than one meeting, and there were over 40 in Paris and its suburbs. Here there is evidently some correlation with Left-wing electoral strength,[5] and also an indication of the influence of France's three biggest cities, one in each region; this impression is supported by the fact that where speakers' names were reported, they were in 52 cases outsiders, usually national figures like Jaurès and Pressensé, or in the Lyon region, notables of the local capital like Dr Augagneur. In only 18 cases was it actually reported that the speaker was local, though where no names are recorded, it is likely that speakers were local men. The correlation with the distribution of sections of the Ligue des Droits de l'Homme is again expectedly close; 28 meetings occurred where sections existed or were to be founded.[6] Similarly, 22 meetings were held in places that had experienced antisemitic riots in 1898. Again it was mainly larger towns that were involved, 29 *chefs-lieux de département*, including Paris; although in the Midi and the North, meetings were common in much smaller places. Reports on anti-Dreyfusard meetings over the same period are much thinner. Whether this is an archival accident, or whether it reflects a real slackening of anti-Dreyfusard effort, once the Leagues became the objects of official disapproval, or whether they never felt it necessary to mount a campaign on the same scale as the revisionists, is not clear, though the last factor was probably decisive until late 1898: anti-Dreyfusism was the prevailing opinion, which it was not necessary to campaign for in most places. Between March 1898 and December 1899, only 23 anti-Dreyfusard meetings were reported outside Paris, from 17 places, of which 11 were *chefs-lieux de département*[7] (see Map 3). Including Paris, 15 of these places experienced disturbances in 1898 or 1899, 10 had revisionist meetings, 11 had sections of the Ligue des Droits de l'Homme, and 6 had anti-Dreyfusard organizations. At anti-Dreyfusard meetings the reliance on outside speakers was even greater than in the case of Dreyfusard ones. At 15 meetings, the speaker was reported to be an outsider, nearly always from Paris, and usually either Guérin, Lemaître, Déroulède or Syveton, all leaders of the

MAP 1 DISTURBANCES CONNECTED WITH THE DREYFUS AFFAIR (DECEMBER 1898-DECEMBER 1899.

Number of disturbances reported per department

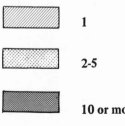

1

2-5

10 or more

MAP 2 REVISIONIST MEETINGS (1898-1899)

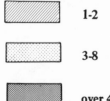

Number of Revisionist meetings reported per department between September 1898 and the end of 1899.

	1-2
	3-8
	over 40.

MAP 3 ANTI-DREYFUSARD MEETINGS (MARCH 1898-DECEMBER 1899)

Departments in which anti-Dreyfusard meetings reported (1 to 3 per department) Paris and Seine not included:

MAP 4 DISTRIBUTION BY DEPARTMENT OF CONSTITUENCIES WHOSE DEPUTIES REFERRED TO THE DREYFUS AFFAIR IN THEIR ELECTORAL PROGRAMMES (MAY 1898).

1 constituency per department

2 or more constituencies per department

anti-Dreyfusard leagues; in only 3 cases was the speaker reported to have been local. All of this suggests that militant opinion in the Affair was found mainly in the bigger towns, and particularly the large cities; that these towns were well-distributed through the country, but that initiative tended to come from Paris, and to a lesser degree from local capitals like Lyon, Marseille or Nantes. This fits in with the usual view of the pattern of the distribution of news and ideas in France. The analysis also suggests that militancy on one side stimulated militancy on the other, towns with active Dreyfusards also having active anti-Dreyfusards. Again, this is what one would expect in a conflict, but it does show that the conflict, though played out on the national level, was also articulated on the local level. Nevertheless, it is clear as well that Dreyfusard opinion was particularly evident and vocal in the South, while anti-Dreyfusard opinion was most important in the Eastern frontier zone, in the West and in parts of the North. Here, a further indicator of the distribution of opinion about the Affair, which we discussed in the previous chapter, is of interest, and that is the incidence by department of references to the Affair in the programmes of successful candidates in the May 1898 General Elections, which, we have seen, were nearly universally anti-Dreyfusard (see Map 4). Such declarations of anti-Dreyfusism were particularly evident in the East and more so in the West and the Massif Central, and were absent in a ring of departments around the capital and in many Southern Departments. Map 4 in effect is almost a mirror image of Map 2 of revisionist meetings. But the anti-Dreyfusism which it reflects is very much a reaction in remote rural areas to news of disturbances and threats to order and authority in the capital and other cities, something different from, though it may have underpinned, more militant expressions of opinion.

The analysis of opinion during the Affair can be taken a stage further by considering information provided by police reports on the Leagues. These were the characteristic organizations of the crisis—"All kinds of leagues are springing up", wrote Mme Steinheil in February 1898[8]—and their members can fairly be regarded as the chief militants on either side in the conflict. The oldest of the Leagues was the Ligue des Patriotes, originally founded in 1882 "to develop the moral and physical strength of the nation by means of propaganda and the organization of military and patriotic education", with the ultimate aim of revising the Treaty of Frankfurt and restoring Alsace-Lorraine to France.[9] Its first president was the historian Henri Martin, and both Hugo and Gambetta acted as its patrons. "There is thus no doubt at all", Sternhell has commented, "that, in its early days, sponsored by the great personalities of the régime, subsidized by the public authorities, its members honoured and decorated, the Ligue des Patriotes conformed to the strictest Republican orthodoxy."[10] By the mid-1880s, it had sections (comités) in every department, and in every arrondissement of Paris. However, it became actively engaged in the Boulangist assault on the Opportunist Republic in the late 1880s, and was legally dissolved in April 1889.[11] The League survived, however, in semi-clandestinity. An attempt was made to reconstitute it formally in 1894, but, although a central committee was re-established in March 1897, the effective reorganization of the League did not come until September or October 1898.[12] Its declared aim in 1899 was "to group all Frenchmen without distinction of party, religion or caste, in a common cause: the reconstitution and perfecting of our army",[13] but it did not hide its complete opposition to the Republic in its existing form, advocating a thorough revision of the Constitution, the strengthening of the executive, and the replacement of parliamentary by plebiscitary democracy. Anti-Dreyfusism subsumed and gave coherence to these themes.

The organization of the Ligue des Patriotes, like that of the other Leagues, remained loose, and revolved closely around its flamboyant leader, the poet Paul Déroulède, who had been in control since 1885.[14] After his arrest and banishment from France, a police agent commented: "The Ligue des Patriotes without Paul Déroulède is rather like a train without driver or fireman . . ."; and another added: "Déroulède's exile has markedly slowed down the spread, and cut down the activities of the League."[15] Nevertheless, the League did not rely for its effectiveness simply on the charisma of its leader. It published a newspaper, Le Drapeau, and put out anti-Dreyfusard and other propaganda in the form of posters, brochures, almanacs, songs and postcards. It also held public meetings in Paris and the provinces, and was particularly active in the staging of demonstrations. In February 1899, the police estimated that the total membership of the League was 600,000. At this time, its leaders were certainly thinking in terms of hundreds of thousands, since they ordered 300,000 membership forms from a printer in Versailles. Such figures should certainly be viewed with some scepticism, though Rutkoff's suggestion of a total membership of about 40,000 at the height of the Affair is probably too conservative. League-sponsored public meetings in Paris in 1899 and 1900 were attended by audiences of 5,000, though provincial audiences were much lower. Support seems to have fallen off considerably after this, as already indicated, since a police estimate in December 1902 put the Paris membership at only 21,000, of which only 500 were said to be real militants, available for street demonstrations. However, 100,000 people turned out to welcome Déroulède on his return from exile in November 1905.

Some indications exist of the geographical distribution and social make-up of this membership. Exhaustive enquiries made by the Ministry of the Interior in March 1897 revealed that no provincial sections of the League existed at that date; and in October 1901 the police noted that: "If the organization of the Ligue des Patriotes is fairly strong in Paris, it barely exists in the provinces . . . Déroulède has always believed that Paris leads France, and that a movement which succeeds in Paris, will certainly by that fact win over the provinces; so he and his friends have never bothered about provincial organization."[16] Déroulède probably never forgot that he had been temporarily ousted from the leadership of the League in 1887 by a revolt of provincial members, hostile to its evolution from moderate Republicanism, with a strong tendency towards non-involvement in party politics, to active involvement in the Boulangist movement,[17] and there are signs that this divergence between Parisian leadership and provincial rank-and-file survived in the reconstituted League of

MAP 5 THE LIGUE DES PATRIOTES, PROVINCIAL SECTIONS (1899-1905).

Sections per department

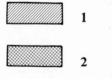

1

2

the late-1890s. The police comment should be seen in this context, and it does ignore the considerable propaganda effort made by the League in the provinces, and its search for members there, if only to procure funds. At the General Assembly of the League held in November 1901, delegates from 20 departments, including the Seine, were present, and for the period 1899–1905 police reports were filed on the activities of 15 provincial sections[18] (Map 5). Of these 8 were in towns which experienced an antisemitic riot in 1898; and 10 were in towns that also had a section of the Ligue des Droits de l'Homme. A police report in March 1899 stated that 250,000 membership forms had been intercepted on their way to Marseille, the Côte-d'Or and the Nord, "regions where *Le Drapeau* . . . has most subscribers".[19] No other areas of particular strength are obvious outside the capital, though it is interesting that the League seems to have been absent from both the West and from the East. In Paris, the League was reported to be fairly strong in all but the 4th, 10th, 14th, 15th and 20th *arrondissements*, and very strong in the 17th, which was a mainly working-class or petty-bourgeois district. Actual membership figures exist for some *arrondissements* in 1901; these range from 100 to 200 and hardly substantiate the claims for total membership, referred to above, unless this fell off very rapidly. There is some evidence that this may have been the case; many police reports after 1899 suggest that the League was on the decline and that it was losing members to other organizations. The League at this time was still split between Republicans and anti-Republicans, and swung in the former direction after Déroulède's flirtation with the Right had proved so disastrous. The Haute Cour prosecutions also deprived it of vital Catholic and Royalist funds.[20]

The diverse social complexion of League membership may be reflected in this political division. It was reported in June 1899 of the Marseille section, the largest outside Paris, with 4,000 members: "It should be noted that the League has recruited supporters most easily in the rich *quartiers;* its militants are nearly all members of Catholic clubs or else Bonapartists of the Corsican colony."[21] A similar bias is suggested by membership in some Paris *arrondissements*, although, by contrast, analysis of that of the 7th *arrondissement*, the only one for which detailed information is available, reveals a predominance of petty-bourgeois. Professions are given for 51 out of a total membership of 215; of this sample, 19 were clerks or white-collar workers *(employés)*, 10 were artisans or shopkeepers, 9 belonged to the liberal professions, 6 were in business, 4 worked in hotels, 1 was a cab-driver and 1 a retired army officer. Involvement in business was also reported of members at Troyes, where the president of the local section was a wholesale trader *(négociant)* and Treasurer of the Chamber of Commerce; at Dijon, where the League was led by an industrialist; and at Nevers, where 200 members in 1904 were said to be businessmen. At Lyon, the section committee included a travelling salesman and a dealer in artificial flowers and feathers; at Nice, two small businessmen and a clerk.[22] In March 1900, the committee of the Syndicat des Voyageurs de Commerce complained that some of its members had been seduced by the "nationalists", to the extent of going to visit Déroulède at San Sebastian.[23]

Finally, a police agent reported in December 1902: "The petitions in favour of the revision of the Constitution, which are flowing into the Ligue des Patriotes, usually bear only the signatures of workers, shop clerks, small businessmen and small farmers, except from Nice where some lawyers have signed."[24] An incomplete list of League members in 1899, discovered by Girardet, confirms this evidence. He found that members fell into two clear social groups: travelling salesmen, small traders and shopkeepers, on the one hand; and, on the other, retired military men, though he does not specify whether these were officers or NCOs.[25] The police reports suggest perhaps more heterogeneity, and a stronger civilian element among the upper bourgeoisie. Taken together, the sources provide only impressions, and conclusions based on them must be tentative, but they do confirm the view, found in the previous chapter, that short- and long-term crises in the business world may often have provoked "nationalist" and anti-Dreyfusard attitudes, and that the agitation in France during the Affair had a certain socio-economic motivation.

This idea is reinforced by information available on the second largest anti-Dreyfusard League, the Ligue de la Patrie Française. The initiative for the formation of this organization came from a group of writers and intellectuals centred on the fashionable Right-wing salon of the Comtesse de Loynes. This had been one of the most important literary salons in Paris for over a generation.[26] Waleffe relates that Mme de Loynes came to Paris as a washerwoman and graduated through the demi-monde to aristocratic respectability,[27] but, whatever her origins, she was by the turn of the century extremely wealthy and an important source of finance for Right-wing movements.[28] The founders of the Ligue de la Patrie Francaise included the poet François Coppée, the critic Jules Lemaître, Charles Maurras, Henri Vaugeois, Louis Dausset and Gabriel Syveton.[29] They published an appeal in Le Soleil, a Royalist daily, on 31 December 1898, with a first list of adherents, which included 23 members of the French Academy and 16 of the Institut.[30] The committee of the League, set up next month, included Ferdinand Brunetière, editor of the Revue des Deux Mondes, the historians Albert Vandal, Petit de Julleville and Albert Rambaud, Maurice Barrès, the cartoonist Forain and the poet Mistral, with Lemaître as President. The adherence of Cavaignac, after his resignation as Minister of War in September 1899, gave the League its only important political figure.[31] Literary, academic, aristocratic therefore, in contrast to the Ligue des Patriotes, which "was primarily interested in street agitation and demonstrations",[32] the Ligue de la Patrie Française was more restrained in its activities, contenting itself in general with propaganda through posters, pamphlets, newspapers and public meetings. It was "above all a moral force", declared its President in February 1900, "a movement of opinion";[33] and Reinach commented: "Its propaganda was carried on, legally, through the press and through meetings. Its leaders left the dirty work of the streets to Guérin, the risks of a coup to Déroulède."[34] With this moderate face, the League seems to have had the support of wealthy conservatives in many areas, particularly Catholics—"Catholics enrolled en masse", Reinach claimed[35]—and this financial and social weight gave it a very important, perhaps dominant, role in the anti-Dreyfusard camp. After the League's unsuccessful foray into electoral politics in 1902,[36] such conservatives began to switch their support elsewhere, principally to the Catholic Action Libérale, but also to the Action Française,[37] and by 1905 the Ligue de la Patrie Française had virtually ceased to exist.

At the height of its influence in the years 1898 to 1901, the League claimed at least 40,000 members in Paris and the provinces, and had at least 20 provincial sections.[38] Lemaître claimed early in 1899 that the sections in Saint-Etienne, Marseille and Nancy had 3000 members each.[39] The police reported that the Lyon group had 1500 members in September 1901, and membership was also strong, according to them, in the department of the Nord, and in Eastern France. The League, like similar organizations, apparently adopted a policy of not stating the professions of members on their membership cards, and it did not keep regular lists of members; nevertheless, something can be gleaned from police reports about the social complexion of those members. First, in the Loire and the Nord, both industrial departments, the League had the financial support of industrialists and important business interests. The police reported in March 1904 that the League was still strong in Saint-Etienne, where it "received . . . large subsidies from the main business interests of the town", and where its leadership was provided by one of the largest ribbon manufacturers.[40] This patronage may well have brought in captive working-class support, though Lemaître's claim to a total working-class membership of 15,000 in 1899 seems excessive.[41] Business interests were also prominent in the League at Epinal, and at Lyon, where the committee in 1904 included, however, two journalists and two retired army officers in addition to two silk merchants. A report from Rouen, dated April 1901, confirms and amplifies these impressions, giving an indication of how the League sought to use existing networks. Its main concern in forming a local section, it was claimed,[42] was

> to search out and instal as its agents in the provinces men with some standing in business or industry, retired civil servants or army officers, with relations in many different circles, in the same way that the leadership of antisemitic and patriotic groups was given to workers and small traders, to forestall opposition, and attract these elements to the movement. The initial support (for the League, however) came from the reactionary party and from young men attending Church schools.

In Lille, similarly, the section, founded in August 1899, was recruited mainly among Catholic students.[43]

If the Ligue de la Patrie Française existed and operated within established conservative networks, the third of the large anti-Dreyfusard organizations, the Ligue Antisémitique Française had more autonomy, a stronger group identity of its own. Founded by Jules Guérin in 1897, it was more extreme, more prepared to use physical violence even than the Ligue des Patriotes, and, with an ambiguously "socialist" programme, it seems also to have been more interested in attracting mass support. Police estimates of total membership

range from 11,000 in July 1898 to 5,000 in August 1899, figures which tally
with other information, and which suggest that the League was at the height
of its power in 1898. Membership was mainly Parisian, although 20 provincial
branches existed, the largest at Lyon, Nantes, Nancy, Marseille, Lille and
Rodez. Distribution of the membership within Paris, as well as information
on the professions of militants, suggest that, although the League may have
had an important measure of support from workers and artisans as well as from
small traders and lower white-collar workers, its leadership was almost exclusively bourgeois, with a high proportion engaged in some kind of business. This
emphasis was reflected in the economic nature of the League's antisemitism,
directed very often against large department stores, and is a feature of anti-
Dreyfusard opinion that we have already several times encountered. The life
of the Ligue Antisémitique was even shorter than that of the Ligue de la Patrie
Française, and it does not seem really to have survived the removal of its leader
at the end of 1899. We will return in a later chapter to a more detailed analysis
of its structure and activities.

On the Dreyfusard side, only one League of any importance emerged, the
Ligue de Défense des Droits de l'Homme et du Citoyen, founded in February
1898, and usually known as the Ligue des Droits de l'Homme. The League
had a precedent in La Société des Droits de l'Homme et du Citoyen, founded
by Joffrin, Clemenceau and Ranc in 1888 to counter Boulangism,[44] yet another indication of the way in which the Dreyfus Affair resumed that earlier
conflict. According to its initiator and first President, Ludovic Trarieux, Senator for the Gironde and Minister of Justice in the Ribot government of 1895,
"the promoters of the League were the main defence witnesses at the Zola
trial of February 1898", and its foundation was a direct response to the
antisemitic and "nationalist" riots of the first two months of that year. The
League's charter was based on the Declaration of the Rights of Man of 1789,
and its declared aim, according to its statutes, was "to combat all forms of
intolerance and arbitrary rule", and, in particular, to bring about the revision
of the Dreyfus case.[45] As we have seen, the League took the lead in the
revisionist campaign of 1898–9, arranging public meetings, distributing posters and leaflets, and creating its own provincial sections. From early on, it
received support from existing Left-wing organizations, Anarchist, Socialist
and Radical, and also from Masonic lodges. The League evolved from being
the principal Dreyfusard pressure-group into being a semi-political organization with a wider programme, which included, by 1905, job security for civil
servants and their right to form trade unions, national health and welfare
schemes, the abolition of the death penalty, the end of arbitrary administrative
control of prostitution, as well as action on behalf of individual French citizens, whose civil rights had been infringed upon, protests against Tsarist
repression and against the brutalities of the French colonial administration,
and a plan for international disarmament. In addition to espousing such
humanitarian causes, the League had also become, by 1902, if not before, one
of the most vigorous supporters of governmental anticlericalism. Reinach
referred in 1904 to "its markedly anticlerical character".[46] The Nantes section

voted, typically, in October 1902, a resolution congratulating Combes on the policies of his government vis-à-vis the Church, and encouraging him to apply the law against the religious orders "absolutely without exceptions."[47] The militant anticlericalism of the League gave it some importance in local and also in national electoral politics, particularly in 1902.

The League is of interest as an indicator of opinion in two main ways. As the first and most important Dreyfusard organization, its complexion, social and political, provides a direct guide to the complexion of militant Dreyfusard opinion. Further, the extent of League membership in France, and, particularly, the distribution of and attendance at League meetings gives some idea of how widespread and intense was interest in revision, at a more general level. First, the social complexion of the League. Its founders were university intellectuals, such as Charles Seignobos, Louis Havet, Emile Duclaux, director of the Institut Pasteur, and politicians, such as Joseph Reinach, Yves Guyot, Arthur Ranc and Scheurer-Kestner. This pattern was still evident in the membership of the central committee in June 1902: of its 31 members, 7 were politicians, 4 were journalists, and 16 were university teachers. The same pattern is found also in the provincial leadership, with less emphasis on university teachers. The professions of committee members are given in police reports between 1898 and 1906 for 29 sections (200 sections were represented at the 1903 Congress of the League). Analysis of this sample gives 12 university or *lycée* teachers, 5 primary school teachers, 11 lawyers, 5 medical men, 2 pharmacists, 6 businessmen, 5 journalists, 4 civil servants, 2 magistrates, 1 architect, 1 engineer, 2 rentiers, 1 locksmith, 1 antique dealer, 1 café owner, 1 trade union secretary, and 5 Protestant clergy. Moreover, the leadership seems to have been representative of the membership as a whole. The police reported from Saint-Etienne in January 1899, for example, that "the bulk of the membership belongs to the liberal professions";[48] and Herriot remembered that the Lyon section had comprised doctors, professors and barristers.[49] By contrast, there is little evidence of lower-class support for the League on any scale. A League meeting at La Rochelle in December 1900 was attended by all classes, according to the police; meetings at Blois and Nîmes in 1901 were held in the local Bourses du Travail; and the vice-president of the Dunkerque section in 1905 was the secretary of the Syndicat des Ouvriers du Port. But, to set against this, a meeting organized by the section of Rochefort in January 1902 was broken up by workers protesting against the refusal of the municipal council to vote a subsidy for the Bourse du Travail. Two minorities do seem to have been important among League members, at least in some sections. In 1899 the police reported that Jewish membership of the League was important at Marseille and at Nice, and both sections had Jewish presidents. A police report from Paris in 1903, moreover, referred to "a fairly numerous Jewish group which constitutes the advanced wing of the League".[50] We have noted the presence of Protestant clergy on section committees, and there are indications that this minority was particularly in evidence in the Tarn and the Tarn-et-Garonne.[51]

The presence of these minorities, however, does not alter the impression that League members were, on the whole, respectable and moderate bourgeois; as Herriot said of those of Lyon, they were "men of standing . . ."[52] Nevertheless, police reports do indicate the existence of political divisions within the League, and, particularly, the swift emergence of a Left-wing faction. From the start, we have seen, the League received the support of existing Left-wing bodies. For example, the police reported from Marseille early in 1899 that "most of the militant anarchists . . . have joined", and following further anti-Dreyfusard action: "The incidents on Sunday have led several Socialist groups to join the League . . ." Similarly, a League meeting at Montbéliard in March 1900 was said to have had "a completely Socialist character". At Saint-Etienne, on the other hand, the members were said to be "people known up till now for their moderate views."[53] Many police reports, in fact, refer directly to Left-wing and moderate factions within the League, the latter usually holding control. Over the first decade of its existence, the impression is that the League evolved away from "radicalism". This evolution can be seen in the growing number of mayors and municipal councillors found among committee members. Gradual acceptance by the "establishment", development even into a new political establishment, can also be gauged from the police reports. In August 1899 at Nice, for example, the police commented on the fact "that nobody has heard of the people who are trying to organize the League here . . ." A year later, the leaders of the local section in a neighbouring department were said to "enjoy an excellent reputation". A note of scorn or condescension in the reporting gives way sometimes to one of somewhat artificial and conformist enthusiasm, which is well illustrated by a report from Nantes in 1906. "The League has played an important role in Nantes and in the whole of France in the last few years . . .", it states.[54]

> Born of the Dreyfus Affair, it served as the first rallying point for Dreyfusards at a time when it was dangerous to declare oneself a Dreyfusard. It grouped together all those who realized that the Army Command, in the hands of the Jesuits, was framing an unfortunate Jew, and who sensed the immense danger to France and to democracy represented by the Society of Jesus. It rallied all intelligent Republicans, in other words all anticlericals.

The changing status of the League and the corresponding change in attitudes towards it reflects the general shift of opinion towards the Dreyfusards that we have charted in the previous chapter; but both, the tone of the Nantes police officer reminds us, were examples also of the corruption of the original Dreyfusard idealism into political opportunism, so eloquently denounced by Péguy.[55]

The same evolution can be seen in the increasing size of League membership. At the first General Assembly in December 1898, a total membership of 6000 was claimed, and delegates from Le Havre, Lyon, Rouen, Rennes, Marseille, Nancy, Saint-Etienne and Orléans were present. Total membership was estimated by the police at 74,000 in December 1906 and at 83,000 in December 1907. Figures are not available to give an accurate idea of the growth of membership figures in the intervening period, but something can

MAP 6 THE LIGUE DES DROITS DE L'HOMME, PROVINCIAL SECTIONS, (1899-1906).

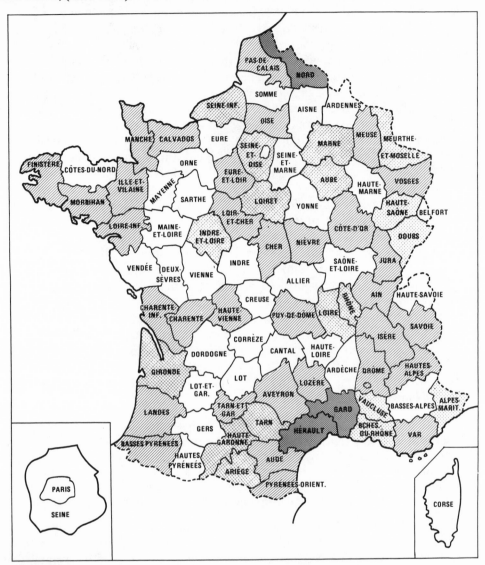

Departments with 2-3 sections by the end of 1899

Departments with 1 section by the end of 1899

Departments with sections founded 1900-1906

By 1906, the Nord had 6 sections; the Gard, the Doubs, the Hérault and the Basses-Pyrénées at least 4; and the Marne, the Charente, the Charente-Inferieure and the Pyrenees-Orientales had 3.

be made of information on the number of local sections and on the membership figures that are given for some of these. The League claimed to have 320 local sections in May 1902, and 200 were represented at the 1903 Congress. Membership of these local sections seems to have been around 50 in smaller places, and 200 to 400 in big cities, although Marseille had 4,000 in January 1899. Putting these two sets of figures together would provide a total membership of around 20,000 for 1902–3. A comment on these figures is appropriate here. The Leagues were hardly mass organizations by the standards of today, but in contemporary terms they were, and as such they were a novelty, and represented an unprecedented mobilization of opinion and support. As a point of comparison, the first mass political party in France, the Socialist SFIO, had 35,000 members in 1905, a figure which had risen to only 73,000 by 1914.[56]

More important, however, for our purpose than total membership is its distribution in time and space. Details are available on 103 sections for the whole period 1898–1906. Of this sample, only 9 had been formed in the first year of the League's existence, and 21 by the end of 1899, that is, by the end of the "heroic" period of the Affair. Police surveillance of the League at this time was very close, and the figures for this period are probably fairly complete.[57] A further 17 sections were formed in 1900, a further 24 in 1901–3, creations which may be assumed to have had an electoral motive. Twenty-two more sections were created in 1904–6 (see Map 6). Since Dreyfus was not finally rehabilitated until 1906, it is fair to connect these latter-day sections of the League with the Affair, although in many cases the connection must have been tenuous. It seems clear from all this that the implantation of the Ligue des Droits de l'Homme in the provinces was much stronger than that of the anti-Dreyfusard Leagues, and that its provincial base was very much more solid. Of the whole sample of 103, sections existed in 60 departments, with high concentrations in the North, the East and particularly the South. The departments of the Nord and the Pas-de-Calais together had 10 sections, and the 11 easternmost departments of France had 18. However, 65 sections were found on or south of the Loire, and 38 were south of Valence. The Midi Congress of the League in March 1904 was attended by delegates from 32 sections. This Southern emphasis is also pronounced if the sections formed before the end of 1899 alone are considered; 11 of the 21 were south of Lyon. There is an obvious correlation here with the well-known pattern of French electoral opinion. The Mediterranean departments where the League was particularly important were strongholds of the Extreme Left.[58] Another correlation is equally important. Thirty-seven League sections were created in towns that experienced antisemitic disturbances in January and February 1898, including 13 of the 21 formed before the end of 1899. This suggests that the spread of the League in the provinces was motivated by the same revulsion against antisemitic violence that had inspired its founders in Paris. Of course both kinds of political activity or reaction were most likely to occur in the same bigger towns and cities, where political life generally was more intense. It is worth reiterating, however, that anti-Dreyfusard activity seems to have directly stimulated Dreyfusard activity and vice versa. If one can subscribe to the traditional assertion that French opinion was divided by the Affair, it is with the proviso that it was not simply a matter of individuals, with different cultural preconceptions, considering the pros and cons and then making a choice. Opinion was collectively formed, through the press, but also through organizations and the dialectic of their encounters. A related problem in the assessment of the geography of opinion should also be broached here. It is arguable that areas where one or the other attitude was dominant might have no reason or occasion to express that attitude, and that the absence of reports of manifestations of opinion cannot therefore be taken as an infallible indicator of apathy. Not infallible certainly, but two factors reduce the fallibility to a minimum. One is the necessary element of conflict that we have just discussed. The Affair was a conflict between Dreyfusards and anti-Dreyfusards. The second factor is the large number of different indicators of opinion, subjective and objective, that we have used. So, only in the case of the 1898 elections have we found an apparent absence of interest in the Affair to be misleading, and there is every reason to think that this was exceptional.

II

We turn now to the involvement or non-involvement in the Affair of existing political groups. The fact that the crisis produced its own special organizations, the Leagues, is already significant here; in general, established groups were reluctant or slow to engage themselves. There is an important difference, too, between the mode of involvement of the Left and of the Right. This is partly a question of visibility. Conservatives and reactionaries tended to operate through ad hoc groupings and social networks, while political parties of the "cadre" or mass membership type, existing autonomously and continuously, were a phenomenon, and a novel phenomenon, of the Left and the Extreme Left.[59] This means that to study the involvement of parties in the Affair is mainly to study the involvement of parties of the Left. Not of course that conservatives, the dynastic Rights, ex-Boulangists were not involved in the Affair; we have already seen that they were; but in organizational terms they were much more closely enmeshed with the anti-Dreyfusard Leagues, themselves in one sense representing a general movement towards, a quest for Right-wing forms of a more popular kind,[60] than were the parties of the Left even with the Ligue des Droits de l'Homme. It is appropriate, therefore, to leave discussion of the traditional Right and the Affair until later, and to concentrate here on the behaviour of the more independent organizations of the Left.

The participation of groupings of the Extreme Left in the Dreyfusard campaign alongside the Ligue des Droits de l'Homme has been noted earlier. Of the 64 revisionist meetings reported between September 1898 and the end of 1899, Socialists were involved as principal organizers or as speakers in 37, and anarchists in 23. The figures for the last four months of 1898 alone are 14 and 10 respectively. By contrast, more moderate Republicans were notably absent from the Dreyfusard movement. Their fear of involvement was very evident, we have seen, in the 1898 elections, and was reflected in the policy of the governments in which they predominated. Not until mid-1899 was revision adopted as a definite governmental policy, and even then Waldeck-Rousseau was motivated more by considerations of "law and order" than by those of "justice".[61] As Reinach wrote, moderate Republicans seem to have been motivated by a fear of "rocking the boat", of stimulating further disturbances: "it was the violence of the passions that the Affair provoked that above all frightened ministers";[62] and for a long time they followed Méline's line of denying that the Affair existed.[63] Certainly, several of them, including Ribot, Bourgeois and Casimir-Périer had doubts about Dreyfus's guilt and about the legality of his trial, as early as 1897, but they took little or no action in the matter.[64] "Why", asked Halévy, "why did not the Ribot, the Poincaré, the Aynard, try to make their party accept the revision that was in line with their principles, and which, moreover, they judged to be necessary?" The answer which he provided can serve as a guide in the interpretation of the whole problem of political involvement in the Affair:[65]

> Doubtless they were most reluctant to arm the revolutionaries, by themselves exposing the crimes of which certain army leaders were guilty. This is understandable; but such reluctance should have been overcome. Through fear of an uproar that their stand on principle would have well authorized them to stop, these liberals in fact permitted a revolutionary movement to develop against which they were powerless, since they were discredited by their failure to act.

Of course, there were exceptions to this abstentionism among moderate Republicans, of which the most notable example was that of Scheurer-Kestner. He was one of the first Dreyfusards, raising his doubts about the case in the Senate in July 1897, as we have seen, and taking an active part in the revisionist campaign, publicly and behind the scenes.[66] A weightier, but less active, convert was Louis Barthou, a minister in the Dupuy cabinet (May 1894–January 1895), and in that of Méline from 1896 to 1898, and President of the Progressist parliamentary group. Opposed to revision, while in the government, out of respect for the judicial process *("la chose jugée")*, he became a Dreyfusard after the discovery of the Henry forgery, voting, for example, against the *loi de dessaisissement* in 1899, and for Loubet in the Congress of the same year. But his attitude was untypical of his party,[67] and Halévy's analysis was in essence correct. It was the Left, the Extreme Left, that made the running in the Dreyfusard cause, and which reaped the political benefits. It is important to remember here the fear that the Extreme Left still inspired in bourgeois politicians and in the bourgeoisie generally. Georges de Lauris, for example, pointed out the novelty which political action in the revisionist campaign alongside the Extreme Left represented for young men of his class and generation: "We found it odd to be mixing with Radicals and Socialists. In shaking hands with them, we had the impression that we were escaping from the prejudices of our families, breaking from our backgrounds. We also felt an agreeable sense of personal security. They were not so terrible after all, and even paid us compliments."[68]

The involvement of the Radicals in the Affair was less obvious than Lauris might seem to suggest, and the impression from other sources is that most of them avoided any commitment that might be politically risky until well into 1899 or later. "The main consideration of the Radicals", commented Reinach, "was always to keep in step with popular attitudes . . . to swim with the current . . .";[69] while Halévy remarked that Arthur Ranc, a Dreyfusard as early as 1895 was unique, "the only Radical in the party of that name . . ."[70] Clemenceau, often thought of as one of the most important and earliest Dreyfusards, did not, in fact, become converted until the end of October 1898.[71] The daily, Le Radical, joined the Dreyfusard cause right at the start of 1898, but La Dépêche de Toulouse did not come over until July 1899.[72] Two examples from the police reports on the electoral campaign of 1898 in Paris illustrate the opportunism, mixed also with a certain patriotism, of Radicals of even an extreme persuasion. Camille Pelletan, at an electoral meeting in his constituency of Neuilly-Boulogne-Billancourt in March 1898, violently attacked "the financial powers, the Haute Banque, the big industrialists and international big business, which gravitated around the Méline government", including, however, the leaders of the armed forces in this anti-Dreyfusards' rogues' gallery; he then affirmed his patriotism, declared that Dreyfus ought to have been shot, and expressed his regret that some of his political friends had become involved in the Dreyfusard campaign.[73] Pelletan later lauded Cavaignac's speech of July 1898 in La Lanterne, though he did change camp after the Henry suicide.[74] René Goblet, another Left-wing Radical with a Paris constituency, and well-known for his staunch opposition to Boulanger,[75] was more obviously hedging at a meeting in the 1st arrondissement in May 1898. Questioned about his attitude to the Affair, he declared his horror of treason, a crime of which he thought Dreyfus was certainly guilty, "being unable to imagine that French officers could possibly have condemned him otherwise"; he then expressed the familiar view that revision of the case was a matter for the courts, and had nothing to do with politics. He concluded, however, by expressing his admiration for the Dreyfusard stance taken by the Socialist leader, Jaurès.[76]

But how typical was Jaurès? Jean Steens, in 1902, summed up the attitude of the Socialists during the Affair in the following unflattering terms: "Opposed to involvement at the start, then sitting on the fence, then enthusiastic Dreyfusards, they followed their party through the whole spectrum of opinion."[77] We have seen that at the time of the 1898 elections only a few Socialist leaders, Jaurès, Guesde, Grousset, Chauvin, Gérault-Richard, supported the cause of revision; "the party men, with Millerand and Viviani, aligned themselves with Cavaignac".[78] Reinach, whose judgment this is, suggested that the majority leaders were motivated here by jealousy of Jaurès, and by fear of losing electoral support, if they adopted an unpopular policy, motives often masked by Marxist rhetoric about avoiding embroilment in a purely bourgeois conflict. Only in the Autumn of 1898 did Socialist leaders change course and begin to play an important part in the Dreyfusard campaign.[79] Daniel Ligou, Claude Willard, J.-J. Fiechter, Janine Ponty and Robert Wistrich have added details and nuances to this contemporary view, without altering its general lines.[80] Ponty, for example, has indicated that only one Socialist daily was revisionist by January 1898, *Le Réveil du Nord*, a Guesdiste organ, and that the most important Socialist daily, doctrinally eclectic, *La Petite République*, did not commit itself to Dreyfusism until the middle of the same year.[81] The police reports on Socialist activity during the Affair confirm and illustrate the same interpretation.

Not until January 1898 do reports begin to indicate that Socialists were seriously concerned about the Affair, and about the attitude that they should take towards it. This was a question which became more pressing as the General Elections of 1898 approached. A report of April 1898 pointed out the dilemma of Socialist candidates and their supporters:

> Opinions are very divided, it appears, on this matter, which is worrying them a great deal on the eve of the elections. It is felt that the Affair constitutes a ready-made weapon against Socialists and that their opponents will not hesitate to exploit this to the full. In effect, either Socialists must opt for Zola and thus for Dreyfus, and then their electoral chances in many constituencies become very doubtful; or they must opt against Dreyfus, but such an adoption of patriotic and pro-military socialism will alienate the revolutionary and internationalist wing of their supporters.

Some Socialists did opt clearly in the Spring of 1898 for one side or the other, along the lines suggested here. For example, the La Chapelle group of the Parti Ouvrier Socialiste Révolutionnaire passed a resolution in January 1898 calling on all groups of the party to show their support for Zola "after his bold action, which has stripped off the mask from the political clowns who are running the country in alliance with the sabre-rattlers and the holy-water boys . . ."[82] A meeting of the Comité Central Socialiste Révolutionnaire (rue Quincampoix), in February 1898, also called for active Socialist intervention in the Affair, "from which a revolutionary movement could well emerge". Some Socialist groups seem to have heeded this call for action. At the demonstration in May 1898 on the occasion of Drumont's arrival at the Gare de Lyon after his successful election in Algiers, the police reported that "a fairly serious affray took place between antisemites and Socialists . . ." But such open espousal of the Dreyfusard cause seems to have been unpopular in many places. At an electoral meeting in the first constituency of the 16th *arrondissement* of Paris in May, "Maurice Charnay explained the position of the Socialists on the Dreyfus Affair, and said that they were not fighting on behalf of an individual, but for a principle. He pointed out that the Dreyfus Affair and those of Zola and Esterhazy were all linked, but, at this point, the audience protested violently, and the speaker was shouted down with insults." To avoid such incidents, and to avoid losing votes as a result, many Socialists took refuge at this time in an alleged neutrality, which, although opportunistically motivated, could be justified in terms of strict Socialist doctrine. For example, the Groupe Central de la Jeunesse Blanquiste, at a meeting called in January 1898 to discuss its attitude to the Affair, voted to campaign "against militarism and clericalism, and against the Jews." A speaker told a meeting of the Union des Groupes Socialistes et Révolutionnaires of the 8th *arrondissement* in February: "We Socialists ought not to take sides for the antisemites or for Zola; these people who are fighting each other today, will soon make it up when it is a question of exploiting us . . . The Zola Affair, like Boulangism before it, is aimed at diverting Socialism from its true course." A candidate of the Comité Central Socialiste Révolutionnaire in the 11th *arrondissement,* where antisemitism had some following, told a party meeting in April 1898 "that he did not want to commit himself on the Dreyfus Affair, believing that Socialists had no business in getting involved in it, and that Catholics and Jews should be left to tear each other apart."[83] Candidates of the Parti Ouvrier Français and the Comité Central in the 14th, 17th and 18th *arrondissements* took up similar positions.

The line is often hard to draw between such opportunism, deriving from an acute awareness that antisemitism and "nationalism" were deep-rooted popular attitudes that it would be politically imprudent to meet head on, and a more positive commitment to such attitudes themselves. Both antisemitism and chauvinistic patriotism were of course well-established political stances on the Extreme Left,[84] which makes it difficult for the historian, as it was presumably difficult for contemporaries, to distinguish clearly between "orthodox" Socialist groups which retained "nationalist" and antisemitic leanings, and "unorthodox" socialistic groups, such as those led by Rochefort and by Guérin, for whom "nationalism" and antisemitism were central issues. At a meeting of the "orthodox" Fédération Socialiste Nantaise in December 1897, for example, "a certain Mangin, a member of the Fédération, protested violently against the apology for the Jews which had been made by Benjamin Dreyfus, declaring that Socialists everywhere had no worse enemy than the Jews."[85] Nor were such sentiments confined to the rank-and-file of "orthodox" Socialists. Aristide Briand, at a debate, organized in Nantes in December 1898 by the local antisemitic group, protested that workers were as patriotic as anyone, and stated: "We agree that Jews have proved that they are particularly rapacious. But if you get rid of them without modifying the capitalist system, they will simply be replaced by non-Jews, and you will be back to square one."[86] Even taking account of its circumstances, this speech represented a very large concession to antisemitic arguments. Even Jaurès, in mid-1898, spoke in the same vein, telling an audience of 6,000 at the Salle du Tivoli-Vauxhall in June that the main danger for Socialism lay in the fact that reactionaries were taking the name of Socialist, but accompanying this warning against antisemitism and "nationalism" with the assertion that "the Jewish race, concentrated and clever, always devoured by the drive to make a profit, manipulates the capitalist system with great skill . . ."[87] Nor is this a solitary example. In *La Petite République* in December 1898, Jaurès rehearsed the old themes of Socialist antisemitism, familiar from the writings of Fourier, Toussenel and Proudhon, referring to "the social behaviour of the Jews, which is founded on the idea of dealing", to "the Jews, conditioned by centuries of speculation to practising close solidarity, and fashioned over the ages for the

manipulation of liquid wealth, who exercise in our society such a disproportionate and redoubtable influence . . ."[88] Moreover, similar remarks, sometimes more extreme can be found coming from Guesde, and from "independent" Socialists like Benoît Malon of *La Revue Socialiste* and Clovis
Hugues.[89] The same ambivalence is evident vis-à-vis the "nationalism" of the
anti-Dreyfusards. The Prefect of the Bouches-du-Rhône, for example, commented on the attitude of local Socialists towards the arrival of the "nationalists" ' hero, Marchand, in Marseille in May 1899:[90]

> far from being hostile to the organization of patriotic demonstrations for
> this occasion, the Socialists . . . are competing with the "Nationalists" for
> the honour of celebrating the event. It is true that the anarchists and a few
> intransigeant revolutionaries are opposed to this attitude, but the Socialist
> party is not influenced by what they think, and they will not attempt to go
> against the crowd.

As this, and the reports from Nantes, indicate, the police reports do provide
some idea of Socialist attitudes outside the capital. In the Spring of 1898, the
pattern in Paris seems to have been echoed in the provinces. In some places,
Socialists were reported to have expressed dismay at Zola's condemnation in
February, for example at Vierzon (Cher) and at Douai, while elsewhere they
were said to be indifferent towards the Affair, for example at Armentières.[91]
The wide geographical scattering of Socialist-inspired revisionist meetings
later in 1898 and in 1899 is evidence of a considerable eventual interest in the
Affair among provincial militants, although this interest seems sometimes to
have been prompted from above or outside. It was reported, for example, in
December 1898, from Anor (Nord): "The Socialist party of the region, which
till now has not been interested in the Affair, has, on an invitation from the
federal committee, begun to circulate a petition in favour of Picquart."[92] It
is probable that the relative strength in different regions of the different
Socialist parties or schools played some part in deciding local attitudes to the
Affair and the way which they evolved. The relatively late espousal of the
Dreyfusard cause in the Nord, must presumably be related to the predominance there of the Guesdiste Parti Ouvrier Français, for example.[93] The police
reports single out, too, the Allemaniste Parti Ouvrier Socialiste Révolutionnaire, both as the most militant revolutionary Socialist group in France, and
as the earliest and most sincerely involved in the revisionist campaign.[94]
Whether this equation is objectively true, or more an example of police
assumptions, it is of great interest, not least because Lucien Herr, who did so
much to spread Dreyfusard opinion in university and Socialist circles, belonged to the Parti Ouvrier Socialiste Révolutionnaire.[95] On the other hand,
police reporting indicates, too, that the lines between the various Socialist
groupings were not always very clearly drawn in the provinces; the police
reports themselves often refers simply to the *"Socialistes"*, without qualification.[96]

The police reports provide some indications, too, of the nature and motivation of Socialist commitment to the Dreyfusard cause in the provinces as well

as in Paris. Examples are given of idealistic, sentimental Dreyfusism, far removed from the atmosphere of political calculation that seems to have dominated in the capital. *L'Ouvrier du Finistère*, for example, a somewhat severe and "purist" weekly on normal occasions, in its issue for 24 June 1899, carried a banner headline: "Welcome to the Martyr"; while a poster put up by the Socialists of Rennes in June 1899 called for fidelity to "the sacred cause of Justice . . ."[97] On the local level, as indeed on the national, this rhetoric was attached, by this time, to very real fears. We have seen that a Socialist "Comité de Vigilance" was set up in Paris in October 1898. Local Socialists seem to have experienced the same alarm, some prompted from outside, others led to opt for revisionism through fear of local antisemites and "nationalists", and the feeling that they must organize to prevent these enemies from dominating the streets. This was certainly the case at Nantes.[98] On the national and the local levels, too, Socialists became afraid of a reactionary *coup;* hence their stress on the theme of the Republic in danger. A poster put out by the Rennes Socialists in June 1899 was headed: "The Republic in Danger", and claimed with pride: "It was the Socialist party which first launched that cry."[99] But if the Affair was the occasion for Socialist rallying to the Republican regime which they had previously attacked,[100] it must be remembered also that the situation in France in 1898 and 1899 was seen by the Right, but also by the Extreme Left, as one of revolutionary potential. For example, a speaker told the Comité Plebiscitaire of the 14th *arrondissement* of Paris in June 1898 that "the Zola Affair would stir up a lot of trouble, and that soon the People would overthrow the existing government"; while an anarchist meeting in the rue de Charenton in February was told that the clergy and the military were inciting the "mob" in the direction of another massacre on the scale of the Commune.[101] At Marseille in December 1898, François de Pressensé, who was converted to Socialism via the Affair, explained, according to the police, "why he and his friends were making an appeal to the people; it was that they no longer had any confidence in their elected representatives"; and this feeling was also expressed in a resolution passed at another big revisionist meeting at Saint-Etienne, the same month, by which those present placed "all their hopes in popular action".[102] Allowances made, therefore, for the strong tradition of verbal violence on Right and Left in France, Jules Guesde was not indulging in pure rhetoric, when he called Zola's *"J'accuse"* "the most revolutionary act of the century".[103] The revisionist campaign by its nature, by the fact that it questioned "authority" and attacked the authorities, had a revolutionary dimension.[104]

This was perceived sooner and welcomed more wholeheartedly by the Anarchists than by the Socialists. As early as January 1898, the police reported that the *Le Libertaire* group was planning a Dreyfusard protest meeting,[105] and six such meetings are reported to have taken place in Paris in the first two months of 1898. The first was held at the Tivoli-Vauxhall on 15 January, to protest against the Esterhazy court martial's being held *in camera.* One of the speakers was Louise Michel, who, while declaring that she was not for or against Dreyfus or Esterhazy, "stated that it was the duty of Anarchists to unearth iniquities everywhere, and, in the present circumstances, to protest against the attempt to stifle truth and justice." She pointed out that Anarchists had been and could again become the victims of similar abuses of justice, and appealed: "Prepare yourselves for a great movement of protest against established society . . ." In further meetings Parisian Anarchists became more clearly Dreyfusard. For example, a speaker told an audience of 150 at a meeting called by the Parti d'Action Révolutionnaire Communiste in February 1898: "Until recently Dreyfus was an officer and therefore our enemy; now he has fallen victim to the society which we are fighting, and he is therefore one of us." This became a favourite theme among Anarchists, along with the argument that the Affair provided an ideal occasion to expose the evils of the existing social order. So, an Anarchist speaker at a Socialist meeting in February 1898 praised Zola for "unveiling the monstrous crimes committed in the name . . . of militarism and patriotism"; while Sébastien Faure told an audience of 1500 at the Salle Chaynes in January: "We think that we ought to exploit the present crisis fully in order to propagate our ideas, since it is a crisis which reveals to the proletariat the complete corruption of bourgeois society." Another speaker made the same point more baldly in April: "If we announce a meeting on the subject of Anarchism . . . we will get an audience of about 150, while if we announce one on the revision of the Dreyfus Affair, we can expect 2,000",[106] a view borne out by police estimates of attendance at meetings of these different kinds. Anarchists were also involved in revisionist demonstrations in Paris as early as February and April 1898, and a police agent reported, rather wearily, at the end of the year that another Anarchist group had been formed, this time at Marseille, "to organize agitation over the Dreyfus-Picquart Affair".[107] All of this qualifies somewhat Jean Maitron's view that Anarchists did not become involved in the Affair until late 1898, when their participation became, in his words, "active and almost general".[108] It seems that the impression of increased Anarchist involvement in the Affair in 1899—for example in the pro-Loubet demonstrations in June 1899 or in Rennes during the second Dreyfus trial, when they provided a bodyguard for the Dreyfusard leaders[109]—reflects more the fact that, by then, the revisionist campaign had finally taken off and become important, rather than any real increase in the specifically Anarchist contribution to the cause. That contribution had been significant from early in 1898, and there is no evidence that it grew in relative terms in the following year, as that of the Socialists undoubtedly did. The Anarchist contribution is difficult to gauge, however, at any stage, because of the tendency in police and press to associate Anarchists instinctively with any subversive movement or any disturbance. If trouble or protest occurred, Anarchists were expected to be involved. So, it was reported, as we have seen, by the police from Nevers, for example, during the Rennes trial: "the agitation which has broken out in several departments has not manifested itself in the Nièvre, where we have very few Anarchists."[110] Save for a few reports of demonstrations and of revisionist meetings addressed by

Anarchists, nearly all in the South, this is incidentally, one of the very few references to Anarchists in provincial police reporting about the Affair. Moreover, these speakers, like the Rennes bodyguard, came from Paris. The Dreyfusism of the Anarchists was thus essentially a phenomenon of the capital.

This does not mean that all Anarchists did become Dreyfusards. Perhaps the main inhibiting factor here was antisemitism, which seems to have lingered on longer and more strongly in the non-doctrinal atmosphere of popular protest fostered by Anarchism, than it did in "orthodox" Socialist circles. During the Anarchist "bombings" of 1892–3, Drumont had stuck his neck out by showing some sympathy for the authors of what were generally regarded as "outrages", portraying their authors as men driven to desperation by a heartless society;[111] and Séverine was, at this time, a contributor to *La Libre Parole.*[112] In the late 1890s, the tradition symbolized by this sympathy, this association, survived. At a meeting of the Club d'Art Social in Paris in January 1898, an Anarchist speaker claimed that antisemitism was the fault of the Jews; while Paule Mink, at a meeting of "freethinkers and antisemites" in the 20th *arrondissement* in March 1898, delivered an attack on "the Jews and all capitalists in general".[113] The *Almanach du Père Peinard,* one of the more popular Anarchist publications, was heavily tinged with antisemitism. A cartoon in its 1899 issue carried a slogan in the same vein: "Down with all Capitalists, Jews and Papists!"[114] Moreover, as we shall see, links existed between some Anarchists and the Ligue Antisémitique Française.[115]

Our investigation of organized political opinion and its involvement in the Affair confirms the established view that Dreyfusism was a phenomenon of the Left and anti-Dreyfusism of the Right, but the evidence imposes certain qualifications. First, the Affair produced its own organizations, and existing political groupings were to a large extent by-passed, at least in the early stages. This relates to the fact that most Republican and Left-wing parties tried hard, until mid-1899, not to become involved. For groups in power, it was a question of stifling criticism of the established authorities which they represented; for opposition groups, of fear of running counter to popular views, as well as of their own attachment to a nationalism and an antisemitism that their explicit ideology frequently rejected. The initiative in breaking with this neutrality came clearly from the Extreme Left, from the Anarchists and the revolutionary Allemanistes. Anxious not to allow them to make all the running, and seriously alarmed by the degree of support for militant anti-Dreyfusism and its exploitation by Right-wing forces aiming, more or less seriously, to overthrow the Republican regime, the Socialists as a whole, in a new movement of unity, the Radicals, and many moderate Republicans, later joined the cause, forming a loose coalition of Republican defence under the leadership of Waldeck-Rousseau from 1899 to 1902. As Péguy lamented, this politicization of the Affair represented a fundamental change of style in Dreyfusism, and a mutation, perhaps, in the significance of the Affair. A popular movement of an inchoate kind was directed into familiar, established channels; emotions, passions, that had briefly erupted into the public arena were tamed, pushed back into the private world, or that of small groups. We will return later to the general problem of the way in which "opinion" was articulated through political groups and other institutional forms. Before we do, can we learn anything of interest about this "opinion" by examining among which social groups it was most prevalent?

III

We saw in the previous chapter that the rural population seems in general to have been indifferent to the Affair. In the towns and cities, indifference existed, too, but was not the rule, either among bourgeois or workers. The police reports yield evidence of antisemitism and "nationalism" among workers, and it is known that the anti-Dreyfusard Leagues tried, with partial success, to recruit them. Reinach, despite hopes to the contrary, also reported considerable hostility, or indifference to the Dreyfusard cause, among urban workers.[116] On the other side, there is some evidence in the police reports, some already quoted, that workers in some areas did respond fairly readily to the revisionist campaign. The petitions, organized on behalf of Picquart by *Le Rappel,* were signed by workers and artisans as often as by bourgeois; and reports on revisionist meetings at Mâcon and Sotteville-les-Rouen, for example, mentioned a high proportion of workers in the audience. More generally, there was an expectation that any agitation to do with the Affair would involve workers. A police agent reported during the Zola trial in Paris, for example: "It is above all the workers, many of whom are out of work, who are manifesting their discontent at this time . . ."[117] Such reports of course reflect, to some degree, a general assumption that any disturbances would be likely to involve workers, which suggests caution in relying on them too far as a guide to actual working-class involvement in this particular conflict. However, other evidence, pointing in the same direction, exists. Halévy was in no doubt that the massive Dreyfusard demonstration in the capital in July 1899 was a working-class demonstration. Organized by the Socialists, it had a spontaneity reminiscent of the Commune of 1871:

> The workers came in vast numbers. The little red roses, that were to remain popular for several years, and which gave the sombre Socialist masses an air of grace and gaiety, were then worn for the first time . . . Secure in their numbers and in the feeling that their enemies were scattered before them, from the Place de la Concorde to the grandstand of Longchamps, the workers occupied, happily and in orderly fashion, that Paris of wealth and elegance, which usually they entered so seldom. They came and went, and walked about, covering the streets and walks; they were enjoying themselves, and made everyone share in their pleasure.

And, again in the Autumn of 1899, after Dreyfus's liberation, "there was dancing in the streets of Paris for several evenings in honour of our victory, and 200,000 workers, (on 19 November) bearing their red flags, which had been banned until then, marched to the Place du Trône to salute Dalou's statue of the triumphant Republic."[118]

Trade unions *(syndicats),* as this reference to red flags indicates,[119] played a prominent part in the November 1899 demonstration, but they were very much latter-day converts to the Dreyfusard cause. Police reports indicate that syndicalists, like Anarchists and Socialists, were earlier divided over the Affair, but with the weight of opinion being very much against becoming involved. Only one case is reported of a *syndicat* sharing in the organization of a revisionist meeting—at Besançon in June 1899—though, as we have seen, a few revisionist meetings were held in Bourses du Travail; and the President of the Chambre Syndicale des Tisseurs spoke on behalf of Dreyfus at an anti-Dreyfusard meeting at Cours (Rhône) in December 1898.[120] There is otherwise little evidence in the police reports of syndicalist participation in the Dreyfusard movement at this stage, although the Ninth National Congress of the Travailleurs des Chemins de Fer in April 1898, took a relevant stand on principle, voting decisively to reject a proposal of its Algiers branch to exclude Jews from membership, "on the grounds that among workers questions of race are of no consequence."[121] The attitude of the Confédération Générale du Travail can be gauged from a pamphlet very widely distributed in the spring of 1898 (at least 25,000 copies were printed). This stated: "Workers! We are the ones who are eternally exploited, and we should not take sides in this conflict between Jews and Christians, who are both as bad as each other." However, it continued: "The Republic, which is the indispensable condition of future social emancipation, is in peril . . . and revolutionaries, Socialists and all sincere Republicans must unite in solidarity to defend it and to oppose an insurmountable barrier to both Jesuit and Jewish speculators and exploiters." Inspired by this fear, the Council of the CGT sat in permanent session during the Zola trial, "with instructions to make an appeal to the working class, if necessary . . ."[122] There are echoes here of the similar reaction of the Anarchists, who were, of course, influential in the syndicalist movement, but the CGT and its member unions seem not to have followed the Anarchists into further commitment until the virtual liquidation of the Affair at the end of 1899. Even then, tactical considerations remained uppermost, as a report made four years later reveals:[123]

> The CGT is preoccupied with the attitude that workers should adopt towards the reopening of the Dreyfus Affair. The members of the Committee, in complete accord here with the rank and file, are agreed that the CGT should have nothing to do with the campaign which has begun. They consider that . . . through their action [in this Affair] in the past, they have simply drawn the chestnuts from the fire for the benefit of a few politicians, who have picked up seats as deputies in the battle . . . and even ministerial portfolios, while the proletariat has gained nothing. Not even the reform of courts martial that was formally promised. Ordinary soldiers continue to be condemned without mercy, while officers are acquitted. In these circumstances, workers should abstain; and, if the partisans of Dreyfus want supporters, let them look elsewhere.

This exemplifies a disillusionment over the political exploitation of the Affair, which, as we have seen, was not peculiar to syndicalist circles, although there it had special significance, since it led to the declaration of independence from

Socialism in the Charter of Amiens of 1906, and, more generally, informed the new militancy of unions in the decade before 1914. Evident also in the 1903 report, is the strong anti-militarist motivation behind the temporary involvement of syndicalism in the Affair, a motivation that was alien to many middle-class Dreyfusards.

If we turn now to the involvement of the middle and upper classes in the Affair, we find that several groups, professional and confessional, stand out: students and university teachers, the officer corps, Catholic clergy and laity, Protestants and Jews. The last three categories are not, of course, exclusively middle- or upper-class, but militancy among them does seem to have been mainly a phenomenon of the elite. The important role of students in the agitation of the years 1898 to 1900 is one of its obvious features. A police agent, writing in November 1897, prophesied correctly: "The Dreyfus Affair will have a big impact in the Latin Quarter . . ."[124] "Politics", wrote Georges de Lauris, "recovered its attraction for young people in the movement of the Affair, which offered us the opportunity of immediate action. It seemed that one could plunge straight in, and how it generated endless talk and conversations!" He remembered, moreover, that "beyond a certain age, it was rare for people to be revisionist, as one said."[125] Other evidence exists to support this suggestion that it was young people, in particular, who became Dreyfusards. Fernand Gregh, another example himself, told Anatole France at the end of 1897 that "all young people" were Dreyfusards.[126] The Tharaud brothers recounted that they and their peers at the Ecole Normale Supérieure were nearly all of the same persuasion, applying "the famous critical method" to the documents of the Dreyfus Case, and then abandoning their books and their studies "to throw into the struggle . . . the resources of a young intellectual élite".[127] And they described the way in which the young Péguy mobilized students in Dreyfusard demonstrations in and around the Sorbonne.[128] Halévy, who also took part in these demonstrations, indicated, too, the general strength and enthusiasm of student Dreyfusism.[129] Some examples of Dreyfusard student groups, moreover, are reported by the police, of which the most important was the Ligue Démocratique des Ecoles in Paris; others existed at Montpellier and Lille. But Reinach, while agreeing that student involvement was intense, presents a rather different picture. Referring to early 1898, he wrote[130] that

> students were divided, roughly along the same lines as their teachers. The Comité des Etudiants having protested against Zola, other students, belonging to the same organization, repudiated this action, and sent the writer their congratulations. In the provinces, wherever there were Catholic Faculties, the split was quite clear. At Lille, the students of the independent academic establishments burned Zola in effigy, while those of the State Faculties replied with counter-demonstrations.

The weight of evidence, indeed, suggests that student opinion and demonstrations were much more frequently anti-Dreyfusard than they were Dreyfusard. Zola deplored this fact in his brochure, *Lettre à la Jeunesse* of December 1897, in which he castigated the antisemitism and "nationalism" of students of the capital.[131] And this bias seems to have been even stronger in the provinces. Students were the initiators in many cases of the antisemitic riots of early 1898, as we shall see in the next chapter, and they played a noticeable part in subsequent disturbances. For example, the students of the Ecole Supérieure de Commerce at Lyon staged an anti-Picquart demonstration in December 1898, those of the Faculté des Sciences et des Lettres at Bordeaux a "tumultuous" antisemitic demonstration in January 1899, and students of Lille a "nationalist" demonstration in December 1899.[132] Such behaviour, indeed, came to be expected. A police agent reported in May 1898 that a new series of student demonstrations was very likely in Paris, if Zola's original condemnation was not confirmed, adding: "In the provincial universities, the attitude will be the same . . .";[133] while from Rennes, it was noted as a matter of course: "The students of Rennes . . . will doubtless demonstrate in favour of the army . . ."[134] And, on a lower level of action, it was reported from Montpellier in December 1898 that the majority of students had positively refused to sign a petition circulating in favour of Picquart. Finally, it is clear that students were well represented in the various anti-Dreyfusard organizations, both in the Leagues themselves, and and in the auxiliary and other youth movements associated with them, for example, the Jeunesse Royaliste, the Jeunesse Antisémite, the Comité d'Etudiants Antisémites Catholiques, the Union des Jeunes Patriotes de Lille, and the Jeunesse de l'Union Nationale.[135]

How are we to explain this emphasis on youth, which seems to be characteristic, particularly of the anti-Dreyfusard movement? What was the attraction of "nationalism" and antisemitism to young people? We shall return to this question in detail in another chapter, but the beginnings of an answer can be made here. It is significant, first, that student anti-Dreyfusism often contrasted or conflicted with the Dreyfusism of their professors. We have seen that the Ligue des Droits de l'Homme was mainly founded by university teachers, and, as Reinach pointed out, teachers in higher education had become prominent in the revisionist movement by 1898. He also suggested that secondary teachers, though publicly reticent through fear of administrative reprisals, generally shared these Dreyfusard convictions,[136] convictions which may have been evident to their pupils. Thus, although in many institutions, Catholic Faculties, for example, or the Ecole Normale Supérieure,[137] teachers and students seem to have shared the same anti-Dreyfusard or Dreyfusard opinions, in many others, perhaps more, there was a situation of latent, and often manifest, conflict. And this is not pure hypothesis, for many cases are reported of student demonstrations directed against Dreyfusard teachers within their Faculties, for example, at Toulouse and Montpellier in December 1898, at Lyon in June 1899 and at Clermont-Ferrand in February 1900. In Algiers in December 1898, according to a press telegram: "Students of écoles supérieures meeting this evening have decided to go on strike if Professor Moreau who signed Picquart petition continues in his post. They plan to prevent his course taking place tomorrow and to force him to resign."[138] This was a familiar enough occurrence for Martin du Gard to incorporate it in Jean Barois, in which, in

June 1898, Luce is forced to abandon his course at the Collège de France as a result of incessant barracking.[139] This divergence of opinion runs along the same lines as the underlying class distinction in French higher and secondary education, between upper-class students and teachers of more modest social origins, but it may also be a sign of other tensions in university Faculties.[140] One must take account, too, of traditional student hooliganism that any crisis would raise to a new pitch. Finally, the overcrowding of the liberal professions, the more intense competition to enter these and the service of the State, seem to have created pressures and fears that took antisemitic form, particularly in the Faculties of Law and of Medicine, which most students attended, an idea which we will explore further later.

The position of army officers was rather different, since, like Jews, they were involved in the Affair willy nilly. Their collective honour was directly impugned by any questioning of the High Command or of court martial procedures, and it was around the army that "nationalist", anti-Dreyfusard sentiment naturally coalesced. This, in its turn, reflected a certain view of the social order for which the military was paradigmatic, and a much wider patriotism that found it hard to accept criticism of the instrument of national defence. François Mauriac wrote that the anti-Dreyfusism of his family was largely based on an unshakeable belief that army officers could do no wrong;[141] while Reinach attributed popular opposition to revision mainly to the feeling that, in the interests of national defence, the actions of the army should not be questioned.[142] The average Frenchman in the 1890s, declared Gabriel Monod, had lost his faith in God, but still believed in "the infallibility of the military".[143] The force and importance of such sentiments can be gauged from the fact that so many Dreyfusards either found it very difficult to break with them, or else continued to express them in a different form. Herriot, the son of an army officer, related how he only became a Dreyfusard after great heart-searching.[144] The revisionist paper, Le Temps, declared on 1 September after Henry's suicide: "Our respect and affection for the army remains intact."[145] Péguy, similarly, did not allow his ardent Dreyfusism to diminish his "enthusiasm for military matters" and his love of military order.[146] Reinach expressed a common Dreyfusard argument, when he told Barrès later: "It was we who defended the real and permanent interests of the army by refusing to separate them from the cause of justice";[147] while Georges de Lauris revealed that patriotism was not the only consideration that inhibited bourgeois partisans of revision in the crisis: "The army was our protection against foreign enemies, but was it not also our protection against the internal agents of disorder?"[148] Of course, the whole Affair put in question and weakened these assumptions. L'Indépendance du Franche-Comté, for example, commented after the publication of "J'accuse":[149]

Until now the army was regarded as the living rampart of the nation. People of whatever political persuasion had confidence in the leaders who tomorrow perhaps might have the responsibility of conducting the national defence. The Dreyfus syndicate and M. Zola have changed all that. According to them, it suffices to be an officer in order to be a traitor. It suffices to belong to the High Command in order to be a thug.

However, this is testimony, rather, of anti-Dreyfusard perceptions, than of Dreyfusard reality, as our earlier quotations indicate. Antimilitarism, fostered by bourgeois experience of the asperities of barracks life now that military service had become universal, and by Socialist and Anarchist opposition to the army's internal policing functions, was boosted by the Affair, but still remained confined to a small minority of extremists.[150] Army officers were thus the objects of respect, or more; "the army had never been more popular", wrote Reinach, "nor more adulated . . ."[151] On the one side, they were courted— we have seen that many anti-Dreyfusard demonstrations took place on military occasions or outside military clubs—on the other side, care was taken to focus criticism on a few heads and to spare the susceptibilities of officers as a whole, though the notion of collective honour militated against the success of such a manoeuvre.

Two other related factors need to be borne in mind in considering the attitude of army officers to the Affair and their inevitable involvement in it. The first is that the officer corps had acquired by the end of the nineteenth century an aristocratic tone that it had lacked before; "the old nobility and the Catholics, driven out of civilian public employment by the triumph of democracy, had directed their sons into the military career."[152] This meant that many officers came from and moved in a social milieu where Right-wing hostility to the Republican regime was common; and this hostility was exacerbated by the Affair. Reinach again noted that anti-Dreyfusism was predominant among the aristocracy, a natural corollary of its Catholicism and its Royalism: "the nobility and the clergy were at once unanimously opposed to revision . . . The Faubourg Saint-Germain took advantage of the occasion to break with the few Jews who had managed to force an entry . . ."[153] The Pretender, the Duc d'Orléans, was a convinced antisemite and anti-Dreyfusard, and he and his supporters attempted, as we have seen, to use the Affair to revive the declining fortunes of his cause in France.[154] Only a small handful of old-style liberal Orleanists seem to have leaned in the other direction, but, as Halévy pointed out, their influence was also small.[155] Against this pull towards commitment to Right-wing anti-Dreyfusism there stood the French army's long-standing tradition of political neutrality,[156] but the increased popularity of the army, its own changed complexion, its cultivation by Right-wing movements, and the very nature of the Affair, were eroding that tradition, giving rise to new fears and temptations and suggesting that the existing modus vivendi between the civil power and the military might be coming to an end.[157] Symbolic of this was the prevalence in the years 1898 to 1900 of rumours of a military *coup* in the offing. A police report in December 1898, for example, noted that belief in the imminence of a military *coup* was strong at *L'Aurore* and among Dreyfusards in general, a view confirmed by P.-V. Stock.[158] Mme Steinheil wrote in February 1899: "There are constant rumours of military plots . . .";[159] while Charles Brunellière, the Socialist leader in Nantes, told a friend in August 1899: "There has been, there still is a danger of a military pronunciamento", adding that he had good inside information on the subject.[160] Nor was it just a matter of Dreyfusard suspicions; the idea of a *coup* had its positive supporters. Reinach wrote of the situation at the end of 1898: "Such a state of disorder played into the hands of the Caesarists, especially in Paris, among the small shopkeepers, small traders and small rentiers. These peaceful people were once again seduced by the idea of restoring peace by the sword."[161] Moreover, as we have seen, various political leaders were involved, more or less seriously, in planning *coups*, which, it was hoped, would involve the military. These included Rochefort, Déroulède, Drumont, Guérin and the Royalists, but also apparently President Faure.[162] Léon Blum, writing in 1902, refused to take such plotting seriously: "The famous *coup* . . . would have meant a revolution, and, among the moderate or nationalist leaders, none save M. Rochefort, seems to be exactly animated by the revolutionary spirit . . . All the leaders of that party are by nature conservatives, and conservatives are, above all, enemies of *coups d'etat*, of sudden adventures whose outcome is unsure."[163] The police and governments, however, took the possibility of a *coup* very seriously, finally prosecuting several "Nationalist" and Royalist leaders for conspiring against the regime, as we have seen; and a close watch was kept on army officers by the police. Their reports, together with other sources, enable one to gauge the attitude of officers to the idea of a *coup*, and to the various stages of the Affair.

Approaches were made to some officers, both by the Nationalists and by the Royalists, but with little success. The police reported in December 1898 that the Duc d'Orléans could "not find a single high-ranking officer who was willing to forswear his duty in order to promote a restoration."[164] Those who took part in such discussions—and a few officers probably became further involved than Ralston suggests—[165] seem not to have been impressed by their would-be partners in revolution. Viau, for example, described a reception attended by Drumont at the Cercle Militaire in Paris in 1899, at which the journalist's evocation of "the Providential Soldier" fell on deaf ears, while his bad table manners and sartorial vulgarity made an even worse impression.[166] Other officers rebuffed advances or disappointed anti-Dreyfusard hopes. Marchand, for example, whom the anti-Dreyfusards fêted as a hero, proved a solid Republican.[167] This does not mean that army officers did not express passionate reactions to the Affair, nor did some of them conceal their hostility to the Republic. Members of the armed forces were involved in the 1898 riots, and occasionally in later disturbances. In the disorders of June 1899 they were among the demonstrators in three cases reported, and, at Nice, two officers were arrested, one for uttering seditious cries, the other for striking a policeman.[168] A large number of officers on active service contributed to the Henry Subscription, which they had been forbidden to do by the Minister of War;[169] and, as we have seen, retired officers played a role of some significance in the anti-Dreyfusard Leagues. Most officers on active service, however, seem to have avoided the public expression of their opinion about the Affair. From Montbéliard, it will be remembered, the police reported that the "Réponses à Mr Cavaignac" posters in July 1898 "drew even army officers out of their usual reserve."[170] The police assumed that behind this reserve lay firm anti-Republican and anti-Dreyfusard opinions, an assumption which they could sometimes substantiate, directly or indirectly. The Prefect of Police reported in February 1898 that Lieutenant-colonel du Halgouët, deputy for the Ille-et-Vilaine had told a meeting of the Jeunesse Royaliste in Paris that, although "in his opinion . . . the army should not get involved in politics, he knew how most officers felt; above all else, they respected God and the King"; and he added that "the army will only obtain the respect which is due to it, if the King returns to France."[171] A report on the Dinan garrison of two cavalry regiments in July 1899 indicated that the commander of one of them, a Colonel Brescey, was an "averred anti-Republican", who had publicly demonstrated this opinion when President Faure had visited the town. And the same report went on to highlight the clericalism and the isolation of the garrison:

> about 18 months ago abbé Duprès formed a military club in the town where NCO's and men gather in the evenings. The club is encouraged by the officers . . . and attempts are made there to influence the men's opinions . . . It is, in fact, a "clerical" organization . . . There exist no real links between the garrison and the civilian population. Officers mix only with the important English colony here.

At Rennes, also, the familiar connection between Army and Church was stressed by the police, who noted that the officers of the garrison sent their sons to the "Saint Vincent boarding school, run by priests".[172] Another report, from Valence in February 1898, made some important distinctions about opinion in different branches of the military: "Army officers are evidently overexcited, above all retired officers, of which there are a great number at Valence . . . The artillery is relatively calm, while the hussars are most agitated." Officers were said to be very hostile towards the government, including the Minister of War, "whom they call General Politician. Cavalry officers are incensed by the favourable testimony of their former chief, General de Galliffet, in favour of Picquart."[173] These qualifications are of interest, even if they are unsurprising.

Unlike civilian opinion, therefore, army opinion on the Affair was virtually unanimous. Ralston does mention a few cases of high-ranking officers who had doubts about the legality of Dreyfus's trial and his guilt fairly early on, for example General Hagron, a member of President Faure's staff, but he stressed the agonizing dilemma that such men found themselves in, torn between such doubts and collective loyalty and honour. He also noted that Adolphe Messimy, a captain in the Chasseurs Alpins, who became converted to revisionism after Henry's suicide, left the army in the face of the universal hostility which he encountered.[174] But army opinion, nevertheless evolved in much the same way as civilian opinion, indignation becoming exhausted as the legal processes dragged on. At Chalandray, for example, it was reported in June 1899, some officers "expressed their views with violence, (while others) . . . maintained a prudent silence . . ." However, the same report claimed that even moderate officers, at this time, "were very angry about the decision of the Cour de Cassation over the Dreyfus Case . . . [and] are very ready to believe that the whole of the court was bought with Jewish money." This reporter also thought that most officers in mid-1899 were generally favourable to the idea of a *coup d'état*, without having any clear perception of what its outcome might be: "they can see no further than the actual *coup*, which would, in their words, get rid of the lawyers who are running the country . . ."[175] But this does not represent any serious qualification of our previous remarks on the subject. As Reinach commented, "the anger [of army officers], their scorn for the Republic evaporated in chat".[176] At Perpignan in June 1899 the police had a different impression and reported a more positive shift of opinion, relating the views of at least one officer, who had abandoned his original belief in Dreyfus's guilt and had been shocked by the attacks on President Loubet. However, at Rennes, on the eve of the announcement of the verdict, Paléologue reported that "the garrison, officers and men, talks only of throwing the Dreyfusards in the river Vilaine . . .";[177] and military reaction generally to the Rennes verdict seems to have been unanimous again. At Le Blanc (Indre), news of Dreyfus's second condemnation was received with applause at the café frequented by the officer corps; at Cherbourg, it was reported that "the verdict has produced a good impression . . . among the military".[178] After this, the police reports indicate a gradual acceptance, more or less reluctant, of the reversal of the 1894 verdict. At Montauban, in September 1899, it was said that officers were not opposed to Dreyfus's pardon, hoping that it would mean the end of the Affair. No reaction was reported to the reopening of the case in 1903, and the officer corps seems to have accepted Dreyfus's reintegration in their midst in 1906 without protest, and even, in some cases, with enthusiasm. Pierre Dreyfus recounted that "colleagues received him with joy, and every mark of respect. As early as 28 July [1906], a banquet was given in his honour at the Cercle Militaire by artillery officers of the First Division of Cavalry . . ."[179]

No further professional or age group seems to have been involved in the Affair to the same extent as were army officers, university teachers and students, with the exception of small traders, to whom we shall return in the next chapter.[180] However, religious groups were closely involved in a conflict, which soon developed into another stage of the Third Republic's endemic struggle against clericalism.[181] Although it is difficult to say what proportion of each group was actually committed, it is clear that Protestants and Jews, both small minorities in France, ranged themselves in the Dreyfusard camp, while Catholics were on the opposite side. It is probably fair to distinguish between militant practising Catholics, who were much more actively engaged in the conflict, and the conformist majority who were much more lukewarm, though there is much evidence to suggest that Catholic engagement was both intense and widespread. Mauriac has described his family's rabid anti-Dreyfusism as typical, "the intoxication of a family of the provincial Catholic bourgeoisie . . ."[182] Jules Dessaint declared in 1904 that, for Catholics generally, "Dreyfus's guilt is a dogma to add to rest of their *credo.*" Charles Maurras explained in *La Gazette de France*, in January 1906: "the immense majority of French Catholics, the people as well as the élites, the lower and the higher clergy as well as intellectuals, took a stand against the anarchy of the Dreyfusards, which, in threatening the national interest, threatened, indirectly, but just as surely, the interest and security of the Church."[183] And Péguy, from the other side, agreed: "All the political forces of the Church were against Dreyfusism."[184] Among the clergy, anti-Dreyfusism seems to have been particularly strong among the religious orders. Pierre Pierrard recalled the Fathers of the Christian Schools, whom he encountered as a child: "They had lived through those years of passionate polemics. For them, belief in Dreyfus's guilt was an intangible dogma, of the same order as their belief in the divine mission of the Church of Rome; and their conviction resisted all arguments and all proofs."[185] We have seen that anti-Dreyfusism was strong among Catholic students and in Catholic schools, often run by the religious orders. The Catholic press, too, led by *La Croix* of the Assumptionists, was overwhelmingly anti-Dreyfusard.[186] "When the Dreyfus Affair erupted", wrote Pierrard, "Catholic newspapers triumphed . . ."[187] Moreover, Catholic organizations took a leading part in the anti-Dreyfusard campaign, notably the Union Nationale of abbé Garnier.[188] We will discuss the whole problem of Catholic antisemitism in a later chapter, but, to anticipate, there is much evidence of overt antisemitism among the parish clergy which must have involved them in the Affair. The episcopate was much less openly engaged, since bishops were more exposed to administrative reprisals and disciplinary action if they departed from political neutrality. Nevertheless, some bishops did declare themselves unmistakeably.[189] As Pierrard and others have pointed out, there were some Dreyfusards among the Catholic clergy and laity, for example, abbés Brugerette, Serres, Pichot, Vignot and Louis Birot, Père Vincent Maumus, Anatole Leroy-Beaulieu, Léon Chaine, Paléologue, Picquart, Dreyfus's lawyer Demange, and Paul Viollet who founded a Comité Catholique pour la Défense du Droit in February 1899. But the Comité had only 100–200 members at its height, and such men formed a very small and uninfluential minority in the Church, honoured, singled out for notice only by posterity.[190] As Maurras, again, pointed out, many of "these Catholic Dreyfusards belonged to that ancient but tiny sect of liberal Catholics";[191] while others were attached to groups even further to the Left and thus even more marginal.[192] Of course, many were unattached individuals; and by no means all Left-wing Catholics were Dreyfusards. As we shall see, for example, the Christian Democratic movement in France at this time was strongly marked with antisemitism.

We have seen that Protestants were prominent in the Ligue des Droits de l'Homme, but their presence in Dreyfusard ranks was noted in other ways by the police. As early as February 1898, there is evidence that Protestant communities in the East of France inclined towards revisionism. From Montbéliard, the police reported after Zola's first condemnation that: "In the Protestant community, people remain in favour of the revision of the Dreyfus Case"; at Belfort, those who did not share in the general enthusiasm with which this verdict was greeted, included Jews and "some Protestant notables"; while at Epinal, several Protestant industrialists, including Mieg of Dollfuss, Mieg et Cie, were said to be partisans of revision at the same date.[193] Some further indications of Protestant involvement can be given. According to Michel Arnod, most Protestants in Nancy were Dreyfusard, a lead being given to them in this respect by their minister, Nyegaard.[194] At Montbéliard, similarly, the petition in support of Picquart of December 1898 was circulated by "the Protestant minister Jaulmes".[195] Again, Mme Dreyfus was rented a house in Rennes for the period of the trial of her husband, by a Protestant widow.[196] Protestant Dreyfusism doubtless stemmed from a tradition of independence and of questioning authority, though this tradition was stronger in the Calvinist communities of the South on which our evidence is silent.[197] But it was also in part a movement of self-defence, for Protestants were included in "Nationalist" and anti-Dreyfusard attacks on alleged foreign elements in French society, along with Jews and Freemasons.[198] It reflects, too, the traditional politico-religious division, very important in some areas, between Republican Protestants and anti-Republican or Right-wing Catholics.[199]

Is it fair to categorize French Jews as a religious group? In some ways, yes, although we shall return to this problem of definition and identity in the last part of this book. The reaction of Jews to the Affair is, of course, central to our concern, and will, again, be considered further later, in the context of Jewish reaction to antisemitism generally. Immediately, one can say that Jews were the main victims of anti-Dreyfusard propaganda and violence, and that many felt implicated in the Affair as Jews, and reacted accordingly. We have seen that Jews took an active part in the Ligue des Droits de l'Homme, and some of the Alsace-Lorraine societies, which organized revisionist meetings, seem to have been primarily Jewish associations.[200] A police agent reported in Paris in October 1897 that "this [Dreyfus] Affair remains of passionate concern among Jewish circles in general"; and the police noted the following month that Jews in Epinal were broadcasting their conviction that Dreyfus was innocent.[201] Further reports in February and March 1898 indicate that the revisionist press and the revisionist campaign in general were receiving Jewish financial support.[202] Other testimony confirms this view, suggesting indeed that the Jewish contribution to the Dreyfusard campaign was crucial. Its initiators included, alongside Dreyfus's immediate family, Joseph Reinach, probably the leading Jewish politician of the day, and Bernard Lazare. Many Jewish intellectuals and notables quickly joined the cause, including Arthur Lévy, Daniel Halévy, Léon Say, Julien Benda, Edmond Fleg, Marcel Proust, Marcel Schwob, Léon Blum, Sarah Bernhardt and the society hostess Mme Emile Straus and her husband.[203] *La Revue Blanche*, directed by the Natanson brothers, and to which Blum, Benda and others contributed, was a centre of Dreyfusard opinion,[204] and began the publication of Reinach's revisionist history of the Affair in 1901. Jews were also prominent, as E. M. Lévy noted, among the clientèle of Péguy's *Cahiers de la Quinzaine*, which upheld the cause of an idealistic Dreyfusism from 1900: "many belonged to more or less assimilated circles (the Reinachs and a number of university people), but one could cite also several rabbis, strictly orthodox Jews of French origin, and foreign Jews, practising and Zionist."[205] For many Jews, moreover, the Affair represented a turning-point, a political awakening, the occasion for a new assessment of their identity as Jews. "The Dreyfus Affair played a decisive role in my spiritual life", wrote Benda. "It became a sort of mould into which I cast the other great moral conflicts of which I was a witness . . . The Dreyfus Affair turned me into a publicist. It changed me from a pure intellectual into an intellectual in action. I abandoned the realm of thought which remains distant and aloof, for that which is willing to descend into the streets."[206] Léon Blum, similarly, ceased to be a non-committed intellectual and became a Socialist, while Bernard Lazare was prompted on the road to Zionism by his experience of the Affair.[207]

Not all Jews, of course, did react in this positive way to the Affair. As Blum recalled:[208]

> A great misfortune had befallen Israel. One suffered it in silence, waiting patiently for that silence and for time to efface its effects. Most Jews indeed greeted the start of the campaign for revision with great circumspection and with suspicion. The dominant feeling could be expressed like this: "It's something in which Jews should not get involved . . ." . . . above all, they did not want, by coming to the defence of a fellow-Jew, to lend any encouragement to the antisemitism that was then rife.

Reinach also pointed out that in the spring of 1898, "certain Jews allowed themselves to be intimidated, made themselves inconspicuous", and he quoted a letter printed in Le Gaulois on 22 January 1898 from a Fernand Ratisbonne, in which he "strongly criticized this sterile campaign, which was throwing discredit on the army in which he had had the honour to serve in 1870".[209] Arthur Meyer, the editor of Le Gaulois, was, of course an anti-Dreyfusard, as were a few other prominent Jews, for example, the Radical politician Klotz.[210] But the importance of such examples should not be exaggerated, as it was by abbé Pichot, who declared in 1899 that "it was difficult not to notice that almost no Jews were favourable to Dreyfus."[211] Other contemporaries, on both sides, were simply more observant. A "Jew-finder", like Léon Daudet, presented a picture very similar to that which emerges from the sources taken together: "Too many Jews, moved by ethnic emotion, threw themselves into the Dreyfusard movement. Others hesitated. Others, through calculation or some secret instinct, became partisans of France."[212] Barrès, too, in an article in Le Figaro in February 1898, remarked on the high incidence of Jews among the Dreyfusards.[213] On the other side, Reinach reported that from the Autumn of 1898, "most Jews . . . had committed themselves to the struggle, out of a sense of justice or a feeling of solidarity."[214] Moreover, as we shall argue at greater length in a later chapter, the passivity of many Jews, referred to by Blum, the exaggerated patriotism, even antisemitism of others, require very careful interpretation. All reflected an intense awareness of a pervading antisemitism, that reached new levels of violence at the time of the Affair; and Jewish reactions to both must be considered in this context of uncertainty and threat. The importance of specific kinds of Jewish reaction, in particular, whether positive or negative, can only be fairly measured, if account is taken of the barriers of habit, prudence and fear that it had to overcome. If this is done, the Jewish involvement in the Dreyfusard movement becomes even more impressive. To conclude, both Reinach and Blum noted certain class differences among Jews here, the wealthy being much less willing to commit themselves in case such commitment should prejudice their successful progress towards assimilation or social acceptance by non-Jews. Reinach pointed out that the Rothschilds did not "intervene in the struggle", although they did "refuse to disavow the defenders of Dreyfus".[215] Blum stressed[216] that it was, above all,

> rich Jews, middle-class Jews, Jews in the civil service (who) were afraid of the struggle undertaken on behalf of Dreyfus . . . Jews of Dreyfus's generation, who belonged to the same social class, who, like him, had got through difficult competitive examinations, and had become staff officers or had entered one of the great departments of State, were exasperated by the idea that hostile prejudice might cut short their irreproachable careers. So, having abandoned the traitor to his fate, they repudiated the embarrassing zeal of his advocates.

And, even those who did have tender consciences relieved them often with discretion, preferring others to take the limelight, if Reinach is to be believed: "while the big Jewish financiers, thanks to the few bank notes that we obtained from them, always in the greatest secrecy, were really just extras in the Affair, small Jews gave very much more, not in cash, but of themselves . . ."[217]

IV

The student of "opinion" and of popular disturbances is always conscious of the fact that the one may be manipulated, and the other engineered. The Dreyfus Affair would have been impossible, or at least vastly different, without the intervention of the Leagues and their propaganda, and of the newspaper press. But if the Affair was, in a sense, produced by them, their role must be seen as a function of society at large, different, but not distinct in kind from the patterning of responses according to social class, professional grouping or religious affiliation, that we have already considered. This is borne out by the police reports and our other sources, although they do point to a significant development of the role of "opinion" makers.

As far as demonstrations and disturbances are concerned, it is clear that there were groups and organizations, such as the Ligue Antisémitique Française, which deliberately set out to foment disorder, and to commit and provoke acts of violence, and that their role in the 1898 riots and in subsequent disturbances was considerable. The Prefect of the Haute-Garonne reported in January 1898 that the Royalists of Toulouse had announced that they would prevent a projected revisionist meeting from taking place: "with this aim in mind, they organized a real armed gang, openly recruiting among elements prepared for anything, calling on people to provide themselves with weapons, and facilitating their purchase, and giving everyone detailed instructions for the attack planned on the meeting hall. On the Socialist side, similar organization and recruiting also took place, but on a much more limited scale."[218] A police agent reported that demonstrators were being recruited in a similar way on the occasion of the second Zola trial at Versailles in July 1898. P.-V. Stock recounted an example of Dreyfusard self-protection, against such procedures, or simple crowd violence, that, however, employed the same methods. During the Rennes trial, he wrote, he brought in Anarchists to protect the defence witnesses: "At my request, Dreyfusard Anarchists agreed to come to Rennes, and, among them . . . my friends, Delesalle and Dubois-Desaulle, who had agreed to recruit them, and to organize them for the job. This job consisted of mounting guard at strategic points along the route that we had to take to get to the Lycée [where the trial took place]."[219] On the whole, such deliberate, even crude, procedures seem to have been very rare, and they were usually quickly countered by the police, obviating the need for organized self-protection. More discreet fomenting of disorder was occasionally reported, and may have been more widespread. A police agent claimed that many of the demonstrators outside the Palais de Justice during the first Zola trial, in February 1898, were agitators "dressed up as workers". There were rumours that money was being widely distributed in the West to finance demonstrations during the period of the Rennes trial. The police discounted these, but believed that the disturbances in Marseille in May 1899 were attributable to the financial incentives provided by reactionary local business interests.[220] It is well to stress here that, although some national organizations might have liked to orchestrate opinion more widely, their influence and resources were strictly limited, and initiative, in the provinces, was largely in local hands. The Ligue des Droits de l'Homme seems here to have made a virtue of necessity. We have seen that it played an important part in the revisionist campaign throughout France, but Reinach emphasized that "the League . . . , at no time, sought to centralize the movement of resistance, or to conduct its operations."[221]

The problem of determining how far disturbances, in particular, were spontaneous, is rendered more difficult by the fact that the police and their informers shared the common upper- and middle-class belief, referred to earlier, that any kind of disturbance or trouble, while involving workers and criminal elements, must be the work of agitators or *"meneurs"*. This conviction was easily coupled with the belief in a Jewish conspiracy to form the myth of the "Jewish syndicate" of anti-Dreyfusard propaganda. We shall consider this myth further in a later chapter, but it is of interest here on two related counts. The idea that "the Dreyfus Affair [was] . . . an immense plot hatched by the Jews"[222] was acceptable, attractive, seemed reasonable to a large number of contemporaries.[223] Even the police, for a time, appear to have entertained it, taking serious notice, for example, of a police agent who commented on the conversion to revisionism of the Anarchist *Le Libertaire*, which had coincided with its emergence from chronic financial difficulties: "Surely this is further proof of the support they are getting from the Syndicate."[224] This is a valuable reminder of the widespread proclivity towards irrational social explanations, often antisemitic, in French society in the 1890s. In its exaggeration, it also reveals clearly to us the screen of contemporary perceptions that we can never neglect, but which we must always try to penetrate. The overall impression left by the police and other reports on this whole question of the relationship between opinion and organizations is that the latter were vehicles as much as prime movers. Of crucial significance here is the fact that the Affair overtook existing organizations, and itself produced new ones. As far as actual disturbances are concerned, the Leagues and other formal groups undoubtedly played a role as initiators and leaders, but there was also an important element of spontaneity present, or at least a widespread willingness to be persuaded or guided into more or less violent public demonstrations of opinion, something that we shall explore further in the next chapter. The most striking confirmation, perhaps, of this impression is provided by the fact that although attempts to foment demonstrations continued after the end of 1899, demonstrations themselves became rare, and formal and informal support for the Leagues in general declined. But, to obtain a complete picture, we need to take account of other aspects of the problem, and, notably, of the role of the newspaper press.

We have already encountered many references among the police reports to the role of the press in the Affair, and its role has been stressed by other contemporaries and by historians. Henri Vaugeois in 1909 referred to "the enormous power of the press that was revealed to us in the Dreyfus Affair . . ."[225] Reinach, similarly, noted its "decisive role";[226] and the same observation was made by Harbaroux in Martin du Gard's *Jean Barois:* "It is the nationalist press that is the cause of everything. Those people never let the public draw breath, or collect their wits!"[227] Among historians, Boussel and Miquel have come to the same conclusion,[228] while J.-L. Lévy has written that the press played "a sort of double role, giving information but also distorting it, mixing revelation and calumny in a way that drove people crazy . . ."[229] In order to understand what Reinach called the "intoxication" of opinion by the press,[230] it is important to realize not only that the mass-circulation newspaper press was the only form of mass-media apart from posters and speeches, but also that it was a relative novelty. Cheap dailies with large circulations date from the 1880s,[231] and in the last decade of the century journalists were experimenting in sensationalism on a naive audience. As Drumont, later editor of *La Libre Parole* and one of the main practitioners of sensational journalism in the period wrote, with the disingenuous appearance of concern, in 1891: "French people don't think any more; they have no time to think, they have forgotten how to think; they let their newspaper do their thinking for them . . ."[232] The anti-Dreyfusards seem to have been much more successful at this new style of journalism, and to have had fewer scruples about using it, than their opponents, despite the enormous impact of Zola's *"J'accuse"* in *L'Aurore.* It is characteristic that Zola, himself, expressed the utmost contempt for what he called "the prostituted press",[233] and that his open letter was not originally planned for newspaper publication.[234] Reinach related, too, the distaste which Scheurer-Kestner, himself director of *La*

République Française, expressed for the suggestion that he might try to
engage support for the Dreyfusard cause in the press in 1897: "This old
Republican, this grand bourgeois despised most journalists; and out of fear lest
he be accused of trying to corrupt the press, he ignored it."[235]

The weight, too, of journalistic opinion was, in the crucial years 1897–9,
against revision. "Against the mass of newspapers which proclaimed the certainty of Dreyfus's guilt", wrote Reinach, "there was no countervailing voice,
or only the weakest! . . . The great liberal organs took refuge in an alleged
neutrality that was sad to see; they reported all the lies [of the other side], and
thus contributed to their dissemination."[236] Only recently has a comprehensive quantitative study been made of the press during the Affair, by Janine
Ponty, and it confirms Reinach's view. In January and February 1898, she
concludes, "anti-Dreyfusism largely predominated in the Parisian press, while
in the provincial press it had a virtual monopoly",[237] and she sees respect for
"the due judicial process" and simple conservatism as the main reasons for
this. Only seven dailies, of which six were Parisian, had broken with this
conformity: *Le Réveil du Nord, Le Radical, Le Rappel, L'Aurore, Les Droits
de l'Homme, Le Siècle* and *La Fronde.* Only the last four were wholeheartedly
Dreyfusard, and the circulation of all seven made up only 3.7% of the total
circulation of French dailies. All but *Le Siècle* were Left-wing. *La Petite
République* became revisionist in the summer of 1898, and a few others began
to express doubts after Henry's suicide. By the end of 1898, only 8 dailies,
however, were Dreyfusard, with only 8% of the total circulation. By the end
of 1899, important organs, such as *Le Figaro* and *La Dépêche de Toulouse,*
had joined the Dreyfusard camp, but still only 11 Parisian and 6 provincial
dailies were Dreyfusard, with between 10% and 15% only of total circulation.[238]

This, in itself, says something about the relationship between opinion and
the press, for revisionism eventually triumphed in the face of the odds. As
Herriot commented, more generally: "When one thinks about it, it is amazing
that the truth managed to break through the barriers that were so systematically set against it."[239] Most contemporaries, however, were convinced that
the press both influenced and reflected opinion. Which role was more important, and whether they were mutually exclusive, do not seem to be questions
that much bothered them. Drumont, for example, in 1898, happily equated
"the organization of the Press" with "the functioning of thought and opinion
in France";[240] and there is a trend in the police reports towards the substitu-
tion of cuttings from the press for an official's own assessment of opinion in
his area. As surely as typewritten reports begin to replace the old longhand
ones, so, during the period of the Affair, the spread and development of the
newspaper press, can be read in the archives of General Police, and particularly
the progress of the assumption that press and public opinion could be equated.
But, paradoxically, at the same time, police officials accused the press of
exploiting opinion, and of exaggeration, motivated by pecuniary interest. For
example, it was reported from Chalandray in June 1899 that "public opinion
. . . is being worked on here by the reactionary press which represents the

country as being on the verge of ruin, and which is ready to broadcast any kind of lie";[241] and the Prefect of the Finistère accused the press of deliberately over-emphasizing the importance of disturbances and agitation: "It is regrettable that newspapers should be exaggerating everything just now, in order to increase their circulations."[242] Moreover, there is certainly some substance to this accusation. Figures of those attending meetings or participating in demonstrations were usually higher in the newspapers than they were in the administrative reports. The circulation of papers, too, seems to have been connected with the way in which they sensationalized news to do with the Affair. Abel Combarieu wrote that "the Dreyfus Affair for two years brought in big profits for the Nationalist newspapers. Their circulation and their sales were very greatly increased by this drama, which was given a new turn nearly every day . . .";[243] and commercial competition here cut across ideological boundaries, papers which took the same side in the conflict competing vigorously for readers by vying in sensational disclosures and claims.[244] The press, then, was able to excite a relatively unarmed readership; it articulated and legitimized popular views and fears, popular prejudice; driven by a crude commercialism, unfettered by legal restraints, it purveyed a heady rhetoric of principle and struggle; its power to influence and shape opinion was thus very great. But it should not be confounded with that opinion itself,[245] though the inter-relation between the two had undoubtedly become, precisely by means of the Affair, both closer and more complex.

There is another important way in which the police reports suggest refinements to the crude concept of public opinion. We have seen how national political organizations reacted to the Affair, but the reports indicate how the Affair, albeit an influence from outside, was absorbed and became a function of local politics. At Cette, for example, it was reported in October 1898, that the Socialist municipal council, which "even included some internationalists . . . is taking great pleasure in attacking the court martial, the army High Command, as well as the army in general." At Toulouse, the revolutionary Socialists, "persons without influence or mandate", according to the Prefect, tried to monopolize the organization of meetings for the important revisionist speakers, thus putting the Radical-Socialists, the parliamentary representatives of the region and *La Dépêche de Toulouse,* out of countenance.[246] Elsewhere, and perhaps as the Dreyfusard cause gathered support, such political ambitions, showed themselves more transparently, on the local, as we have already argued they did on the national, level. For example, a revisionist and anti-Nationalist meeting was held at Morlaix (Finistère) in June 1899; but the "partisans of the group in control of the municipal council" refused to attend —unsurprisingly, since at the meeting both the Sub-prefect and the municipal council came under attack. On the occasion of the disorders at Alais in September 1899, the Prefect commented: "The Dreyfus Affair is actually only a pretext, and the agitation is . . . really just one more episode in the struggle between M.M. Derèze and de Ramel, between the reactionaries and the Republicans, who wish to win back the control of the city hall, which they lost three years ago as a result of their internal divisions."[247] Similarly, in a way that seems to have been repeated on a wide scale later, the Ligue des Droits de l'Homme, functioned at Lille, as early as July 1899, according to the police, as "a unifying link between Radicals and Socialists . . . People even think that this League may replace Freemasonry in the Nord, and that it will play an important part in the forthcoming municipal elections."[248] At Nantes, it was reported a little later, that the reactionaries were grouping their forces for the coming municipal elections behind the mask of "Nationalism". Unlikely to win control of the municipality with a straightforward anti-Republican programme, the police remarked, "they have hypocritically placed their flag in their pockets for a while, and are preparing an equivocal and dishonest campaign, based on the exploitation of the Dreyfus Affair, on support for the army of which they claim to be the sole defenders, and, of course, on the Jewish question."[249]

V

A lot more work needs to be done on the local level, of the kind undertaken by Barral, Dupeux and others,[250] before such impressions can become more than impressions. But they have their value in pointing to the areas where the social meaning of the Affair must be sought: in the rivalry of local political factions and cliques, in the development of the press and of national organizations, in reactions to economic and social transformations that threatened the status of certain groups and undermined their view of the world and of themselves. The Affair marks, too, a significant step in the process by which literacy and universal suffrage fundamentally altered the framework of popular attitudes, creating for the first time a relatively integrated "public opinion". Those previously outside political and national life were brought into a national socio-psychological crisis, through the action of objective social factors that we can outline, but also impelled by less palpable forces of want and fear, bewilderment and envy, exasperation and hope, which we can only grasp indirectly. Even perceptive and observant contemporaries felt this sense of bafflement. Halévy, for example, who watched the Dreyfusard demonstration in Paris on 19 November 1899, with Paul Desjardins, wrote of it: "We read the words written on the banners: Liberty, Equality, Labour, Solidarity. We heard the shouting, which alternated with chants of: Long live the Social Republic! Paul Desjardins . . . observed: When these men read or pronounce these words, which we read or hear, what do they mean to them? It should be possible to know, but we do not know."[251] And Desjardins's remark could be extended to cover all the slogans of the time, and particularly those of antisemitism.

But if we are only beginning to write the social history of the Dreyfus Affair, certain conclusions can, nevertheless, be drawn at this stage. First, the Affair aroused passionate interest in the provinces as well as in Paris; meetings were held; demonstrations, sometimes riots, took place; people joined Dreyfusard and anti-Dreyfusard organizations, in towns throughout France. The Affair filled the newspapers, produced posters, books and pamphlets by the hundred, stimulated also the large-scale production of artefacts, perhaps even more characteristic of popular involvement: prints, postcards, figures in plaster, cardboard and wood, even cigarette-papers reproducing the famous *"bordereau"*.[252] Exactly who became involved in this agitation and why, is not so clear, although, in the big cities certainly and very likely in smaller towns also, it was not merely the well-educated and the articulate. The Affair was accompanied by, perhaps it occasioned, a short-term business crisis, but in looking for economic reasons for anxiety and disturbance, longer-term changes must also be taken into account, particularly, it seems, in the tertiary sector. The Affair also seems to have had a special significance for young people, for a generation that was coming of age at the opening of a new century, symbolic perhaps of entry into a changed and alarming world. We know enough about nineteenth-century society to realize that when a contemporary writes that "everyone" was interested in the Affair, this probably means everyone whom he considered to be important, everyone like himself, bourgeois and literate,[253] and it seems that the mass of the rural population, at least, was relatively untouched by the Affair, as it was relatively untouched by any other political issue of the same kind. The impact of social change, the pattern of national integration was uneven, and, as Pierrard reminds us, the 1890s was still "an epoch in which the provinces had retained—despite the railways— much of their ancient impenetrability . . ."[254] Geographically remote, poorly educated, preoccupied with their work, peasants and country people in many places, simply did not or could not understand what the Affair was about. Roger Thabault wrote of his village in the West: "The Dreyfus Affair which aroused so much passion throughout France left Mazières practically unmoved. It was too complicated and confusing and too many matters unknown in this corner of the land were involved for even the most enlightened to become really excited."[255] And there is much other evidence of this lack of comprehension, not only on the part of peasants. A level-crossing keeper, interviewed by *Le Figaro* in July 1899, confessed that he had never heard of Dreyfus: "We don't have money to spare to buy newspapers . . . As a family, we keep to ourselves. If I've any spare time, I spend it looking after the chickens, or doing the garden."[256] J.-R. Bloch described a travelling salesman about the same time, who "had heard of the Affair, but only what was said about it in the dining-rooms of commercial hotels or the corridors of railway trains, and he did not attach much importance to it".[257] Again Péguy received a letter from a Catholic friend at the height of the Affair, which explained: "This Affair is news to me. I live in the depth of the provinces, and I've enough to do just to earn my living."[258] From another angle, Combarieu commented that, on a visit with President Loubet to Dijon in May 1899, he realized that "the people of the provinces had not been affected by the Nationalist press of Paris, whose range of influence did not appear to extend very far beyond the perimeter of the *grands boulevards.*"[259]

But we must not go too far in playing down the Affair's impact on provincial and popular opinion. Geographical remoteness by itself was no guarantee of indifference. An attempt to map the distribution of antisemitic opinion systematically must be left to a later chapter, but we have already accumulated some information under this heading, and have a rough idea of the geographical incidence of interest in the Affair itself. Its epicentre, to use J.-L. Lévy's term,[260] was in Paris, but other large urban centres, Marseille, Lyon, Lille, Rouen, Nantes, for example, were secondary centres of involvement, and this involvement extended into their rural hinterlands. Moreover, the West, the South, and the East, participated, in different ways, to a peculiar degree. Lorraine, for example, seems to have been a centre of patriotic anti-Dreyfusism. As Barrès wrote to Maurras in 1904: "you won't find more than one Lorrainer who was a Dreyfusard."[261] Moreover, relative indifference seems often to have gone along with an underlying antipathy towards the Dreyfusards. These were intellectuals, members of the liberal bourgeoisie, in the main. Although the minority of politically-conscious workers rallied behind Dreyfusard Socialist leadership, as Halévy insisted, "Dreyfus's cause . . . was never popular among ordinary people . . ."[262] It seems, indeed, that in so far as lower-class opinion was involved in the Affair, it was very largely in support of the army, for the authorities, and against the Jews, which puts antisemitism again at the centre of the crisis.

Something can be concluded, secondly, about the chronological pattern of interest in the Affair. Only in the two years 1898 and 1899 was this interest intense and widespread, and, within this period, the two months of January and February 1898, the month of December 1898, and the four months from June to September 1899, were high-points of agitation. It is much more difficult to plot the evolution of opinion for or against Dreyfus than to trace simple interest in the Affair. As we have seen, there are reasons to believe that revisionism never became entirely popular, that revision was accepted *faute de mieux*. Nevertheless, there does here seem to have been a swing of some significance towards the Dreyfusards, coinciding with the revisionist campaign of December 1898, but only becoming decisive in June 1899. This view, derived mainly from the police reports, accords with Péguy's assessment[263] of

> the *graph of public belief in the innocence of Dreyfus* . . . Starting from just about *zero* in 1894 (with the exception of his family and a very small number of other individuals), one can say that it rose . . . continuously until the day when the ship, which returned Dreyfus to France, introduced amongst us the person at the heart of the whole debate. From then on, in spite of appearances to the contrary, despite an apparent plateau, in reality it began slowly, regularly, to fall.

However, acknowledging the poor impression made by Dreyfus, himself, as we have done, and, aware of the considerations of expediency that overtook the revisionist cause, we can only record those appearances, which were of increasing Dreyfusard support through till the end of 1899 and the pardon. But it is true that the Dreyfusard cause seems then to have been helped much more by the extremist activities of its opponents, and particularly the attacks on President Loubet, than by its own positive propaganda, or by any general awakening of till then dormant liberal consciences. Once the Dreyfusard campaign, in effect, ceased being the work simply of an awkward minority, and became identified with Republican defence, it became a bandwagon, rallying the forces of conformity to its side.

This introduces the third conclusion. As J.-P. Peter has pointed out,[264] a feature of the Affair, on both sides, was, paradoxically, the search for unity. The call to unite against the enemy, internal and external, the appeal of belonging, were central characteristics of the "nationalist", anti-Dreyfusard movement, one of whose component organizations actually called itself the Union Nationale. A poster put up in Lyon in August 1899 illustrated this concern very well. "If you believe in the danger of a cosmopolitan invasion," it declared, "if the mysterious and frightening power of the masonic Lodges worries you; if the weakness of our foreign policy alarms you; if you believe in the need for energetic action against the anti-French tendencies of the Syndicate that is ruling the country, then GROUP TOGETHER, UNITE TO DEFEND YOURSELVES!"[265] This quest for unity was equally present on the other side. For example, Article Three of the statutes of the Ligue des Droits de l'Homme "appeals to all those, without distinction of religious belief or political opinion, who want a sincere union of all Frenchmen"; while the League's manifesto of July 1898 argued that antisemitism threatened "the Unity of the Nation which our fathers have passed on to us."[266] And the same concern is found again among those who sought to maintain a positive neutrality in the Affair, like Sully Prudhomme, Emile Boutroux and Ernest Lavisse, who launched an "Appeal for Unity" in January 1899.[267] This search for unity was above all a search for identity, characteristic perhaps of industrializing societies at a certain stage in their development, a reaction to that process of social disintegration so acutely observed and analysed at the time by Emile Durkheim,[268] and, at the same time, an attempt to find and to provide a system of values to suit the new and larger social forms that were emerging. These considerations are of the utmost importance in explaining the passionate nature of the commitment on both sides in the Dreyfus Affair, and the fundamentalist, sometimes metaphysical, dimension lent to it. Péguy, while all too aware of the political exploitation of the Affair, realized, emphasized this profounder ideological aspect. "Our Dreyfusism", he wrote in 1910, "was a religion . . . [the Affair was] a religious outburst, a religious crisis . . ."[269] The truth of this affirmation can perhaps be gauged, the tone of this religion perceived, from two examples, one of public rhetoric, the other of private ritual. B. Guinaudéad wrote of Dreyfus in L'Aurore on 10 September 1899: "His children must learn how much he has suffered, and how great he is. They must know that he has a halo about his head for all time, and that from one end of Europe to the other, from one end of the civilized world to the other, men solemnly uncover their heads at the sound of his name, which is the name of the noblest of martyrs."[270] And Mme Steinheil related that her acquaintance Mme R. "wore deep mourning during all the time Dreyfus was a prisoner, and appeared in a gaudy blue gown on the day of his liberation."[271]

What concerns us, however, is the "religion" of the anti-Dreyfusards, for whom Dreyfus was not a martyr but a traitor, a religion centred very much on antisemitism; and two particular phenomena, episodes in the Affair, allow us to penetrate further in our investigation of that antisemitism and its social meaning. These are the antisemitic riots of 1898 and the Henry Subscription, which form the subjects of the next two chapters.

NOTES

1 In December 1898, in Paris, Lyon, Marseille, Nice, Toulouse and Montpellier; in January 1899, in Paris(2), Orléans, Clermont-Ferrand and Toulouse; in February 1899, in Paris(3), Marseille and Rouen; in April 1899, in Avignon; in May 1899, in Paris, Marseille and Troyes; in June 1899, in Rennes, Brest(2), Nantes(2), Bourg, Besançon, Vierzon, Marseille, Belfort, Nice(3), Valenciennes, Lille, Armentières, Lorient(3), Poligny, Lons-le-Saunier, Chinon, Tours, Bordeaux, Toulouse, Paris, Poitiers, Epinal, Castres, Le Havre, Rouen, Versailles and Lyon(3); in July and August 1899, in Rennes(7), Bellegarde, Nîmes, Paris, Besançon, Saint-Brieuc, Marseille, Charleville, Nice, Vannes, Béziers, Montpellier, Avignon(3), Saint-Jean-de-Luz and Saint-Pol; in September 1899, in Belfort, Bourges, Sartène, Alais, Vienne, Bar-le-Duc, Perpignan and Rennes; in October 1899, in Albi and Aubervilliers; in November 1899, in Paris, Rennes and Blois; in December 1899, in Paris(2), Saint-Brieuc and Lille.
2 See François Goguel, *Géographie des élections françaises sous la Troisième et la Quatrième République* (Paris, 1970), pp. 32–9.
3 See Map 7.
4 Revisionist meetings were reported, in September 1898, in Paris(2), Reims, Sotteville-les-Rouen, Montpellier, Saint-Etienne and Marseille; in October 1898, in Paris(2), Montereau, Cette and Tours; in December 1898, in Montpellier(2), Nice, Troyes, Marseille, Toulouse, Saint-Etienne, Béziers, Feignies, Hautcourt, Le Havre, Lille, Villefranche, Lyon, Mâcon(2), Auxerre, Nantes, Alais, Nancy and Paris with its suburbs(24); in January 1899, in Paris(6), Saint-Denis(2), Orléans, Moissac, Clermont-Ferrand, Toulouse, Sotteville-les-Rouen and Saint-Chamond; in February 1899, in Paris(3), Lyon, Mâcon, Rouen, Saint-Quentin, Saint-Etienne, Roanne, Marseille(2), Ay and Besançon; in March 1899, in Valentigney, Seloncourt and Montbéliard; in April 1899, in Nantes, Avignon, Roanne, La Ciotat, Tarascon, Saint-Hippolyte, Saint-Jean-du-Gard, Andeye, Ledéguey, Nîmes(2), Alais and Vauvert; in May 1899, in Marseille, Paris, Amiens, Rouen, Cette, Grenoble and Rive-de-Gier; in June 1899, in Besançon, Morlaix, Brest(2), Nîmes(2), Nantes(2), Saint-Florentin, Paris(2), Mende, Armentières and Montauban; and in the rest of 1899, in Albi, Le Mans, Lille(3), Rennes, Lyon, Charleville, Besançon, Nantes, Le Havre, Aubervilliers, Saint-Brieuc, Toulouse, Ax-les-Thermes, Roubaix, Paris and Montpellier. (Andeye—possibly Andé (Eure)—and Ledéguey—possibly Ledergues (Aveyron)—do not figure as such in *Dictionnaire des Communes* (Paris, 1971) and have not been included in Map 2).
5 See Goguel, *Géographie des élections françaises*, pp. 66–71.
6 See pp. 62–3 below.
7 Anti-Dreyfusard meetings were reported in this period at Dijon, Toulouse(2), Caen, Nantes(2), Cours, Marseille(3), Troyes, Valenciennes, Nancy, Rennes(3), Saint-Cloud, Sedan, Lyon, Avignon, Angers and Saint-Nicolas.
8 Steinheil, *My Memoirs*, p. 102.
9 Article 11 of Statutes, cit. Raoul Girardet, "La Ligue des Patriotes dans l'histoire du nationalisme français, 1882–1888", *Bulletin de la Société d'Histoire Moderne*, Douzième série, no. 6 (1958), p. 4.
10 Sternhell, *Maurice Barrès et le nationalisme français*, pp. 67–8.
11 Alexandre Zévaès, *Au Temps du Boulangisme* (Paris, 1930), pp. 155–7.
12 See various police reports, AN F[7] 12449 and 12450, "Ligue des Patriotes".

Information on the subsequent history of the League is taken mainly from these reports, and from those in AN F⁷ 12451, and AN F⁷ 12870–12873, "Ligue des Patriotes"; see also Peter M. Rutkoff, "The Ligue des Patriotes: The Nature of the Radical Right and the Dreyfus Affair", *French Historical Studies*, 8 (1973–4), pp. 585–603, which I saw only after writing this chapter.

13 Speech by Marcel Habert at public meeting in the 11th *arrondissement* of Paris. Daily Report, Prefect of Police, 21 January 1898. APP Ba 106. Habert, a deputy, was Vice-President of the League.

14 Zévaès, *Au Temps du Boulangisme*, p 155.

15 Reports, Police agents, Paris, 9 December 1902, AN F⁷ 12870; and AN F⁷ 12451. On Déroulède's charisma, see also Charles Maurras, *Au Signe de Flore. Souvenirs de vie politique. L'Affaire Dreyfus, La fondation de l'Action Française 1898–1900* (Paris, 1931), p. 97.

16 Report, Police, 13 October 1901. AN F⁷ 12451.

17 See Girardet, "La Ligue des Patriotes", p. 4.

18 These were at Nice, Dijon, Alise-Sainte-Reine, Bordeaux, Lille, Lyon, Chalon-sur-Saône, Montceau-les-Mines, Maisons-Laffitte, Marseille, Valenciennes, Limoges, Troyes, Nantes and Lens.

19 Report, Commissaire de police, Pithiviers (Loiret), 6 March 1899. AN F⁷ 12449.

20 See Reports by Police agents, Paris, 6 December 1898. AN F⁷ 12451; and 2 September 1899. AN F⁷ 12453; also Reports, AN F⁷ 12870; and AN F⁷ 12455–12457, "Surveillance des nationalistes, 1899".

21 Report, Commissaire spécial, Marseille, 13 June 1899. AN F⁷ 12449.

22 See Report, Prefect, Aube, 22 July 1899; AN F⁷ 12449; Reports, Police and Police agents, Paris, 29 April and 16 November 1901; and 24 May 1904. AN F⁷ 12451; Report, Commissaire spécial, Nice, 7 February 1902. AN F⁷ 12455; and Report, Police, 14 March 1904. AN F⁷ 12719.

23 Report, Police agent, Paris, 8 March 1900. AN F⁷ 12870.

24 Report, Police agent, Paris, 5 December 1902. AN F⁷ 12719.

25 Girardet, "La Ligue des Patriotes", p. 5.

26 See Daudet, *Salons et journaux*, chapters 1–3; and Gregh, *L'Age d'or*, p. 263.

27 Waleffe, *Quand Paris était un paradis*, pp. 17 and 126; see also *The Confessions of Arsène Houssaye, Man about Paris* (London, 1972), p. 281, on the less respectable portion of her career.

28 The daily, *L'Action Française*, was founded in 1908, with money left to Mme Léon Daudet by Mme de Loynes. Eugen Weber, *Action Française, Royalism and Reaction in Twentieth-Century France* (Stanford, 1962), pp. 47–8.

29 Reinach, *Histoire de l'Affaire Dreyfus*, IV, pp. 499–505; Daudet, *Au Temps de Judas*, pp. 144–5; Barrès-Maurras, *La République ou le roi*, pp. 201–24.

30 Sternhell, *Maurice Barrès*, p. 338.

31 Barrès-Maurras, op. cit., p. 195.

32 Police report, "Situation générale des Partis politiques en 1898", 9 February 1904, AN F⁷ 12719.

33 Cit. Sternhell, *Maurice Barrès*, pp. 338–9.

34 Reinach, op. cit., IV, p. 505; see also Daudet, *Au Temps de Judas*, p. 152; and Maurras, *Au Signe de Flore*, pp. 102–4.

35 Reinach, op. cit., IV, p. 503.

36 See Daudet, *Salons et journaux*, p. 99; and Pierre Pierrard, *Juifs et catholiques français: De Drumont à Jules Isaac (1886–1945)* (Paris, 1970), p. 136.

37 See various police reports, 1902–05. AN F⁷ 12719.

38 The police specify the location of only half of these: at Grenoble, Saint-Etienne, Nancy, Lille, Toulon, Limoges, Saint-Dié, Nice, Belfort, Lyon, Marseille and Rouen.

39 Reinach, op. cit., IV, p. 503.

40 Reports, Police, 19 March 1904; and Prefect, Loire, 9 April 1904. AN F⁷ 12456.

41 Reinach, op. cit., IV, p. 503.

42 Report, Commissaire spécial, Rouen, 24 April 1901. AN F⁷ 12457, "Surveillance des nationalistes".

43 Pierrard, op. cit., pp. 134–5.

44 Zévaès, *Au Temps du Boulangisme,* p. 106.

45 See testimony of Trarieux at the trial of Duclaux, prosecuted for belonging to an unauthorized association, reported in *Le Siècle,* 19 April 1899.

46 Reinach, op. cit., IV, p. 413. See also, on the League generally, though mainly for a later period, Jean and Monica Charlot, "Un Rassemblement d'Intellectuels, La Ligue des Droits de l'Homme", *Revue Française de Science Politique,* 9 (1959), pp. 995–1028; and, on its link with Freemasonry, Mildred J. Headings, *French Freemasonry under the Third Republic* (Baltimore, 1949), pp. 98–9 and 131–2.

47 Report, Commissaire spécial, Nantes, 12 October 1902. AN F⁷ 12487, "Ligue des Droits de l'Homme, 1898–1908". This file is the main source of information on the League.

48 Report, Commissaire spécial, Saint-Etienne, 19 January 1899. AN F⁷ 12487.

49 Herriot, *Jadis, Avant la première guerre mondiale,* pp. 138–9.

50 Report, Police, Paris, 31 December 1903. AN F⁷ 12487.

51 The attraction to the League of Protestants and Jews was also noted by Reinach, op. cit., IV, p. 414; see also Pierrard, op. cit., pp. 133–4.

52 Herriot, op. cit., pp. 138–9.

53 Reports, Commissaire spécial, Marseille, 19 January and 7 February 1899; Commissaire spécial, Montbéliard, 11 March 1900; and Commissaire spécial, Saint-Etienne, 19 January 1899. AN F⁷ 12487.

54 Reports, Commissaire spécial, Nice, 2 August 1899; Commissaire spécial, Gap (Hautes-Alpes), 7 August 1900; and Commissaire central, Nantes, 20 September 1906. AN F⁷ 12487.

55 Péguy, *Notre Jeunesse, passim.*

56 Daniel Ligou, *Histoire du socialisme en France (1871–1961)* (Paris, 1962), p. 183.

57 Sections reported before the end of 1899 were at Nice, Ax-les-Thermes, Marseille, Saint-Etienne, Valentigney, Héricourt, Nîmes, Saint-Hippolyte-du-Fort, Vauvert, Toulouse, Bordeaux, Béziers, Cette, Reims, Lyon, Rouen, Albi, Orléans, Nancy, Tourcoing, and Lille. Montpellier, Avignon, Saint-Germain-en-Laye, Tours and Montbéliard probably also had sections before 1900.

58 Goguel, *Géographie des élections françaises,* pp. 68–9.

59 See Maurice Duverger, *Political Parties, Their Organization and Activity in the Modern State* (London, 1954), particularly Book I, chapter 1, "Party Organization".

60 See René Rémond, *La Droite en France de la Première Restauration à la Ve République* (Paris, 1963), pp. 157–77.

61 Sorlin, *Waldeck-Rousseau,* pp. 410–11.

62 Reinach, op. cit., III, p. 35.

63 Méline, then Premier, told the Chamber of Deputies on 24 February 1898, in a speech that was posted all over France: "Il n'y a plus ni procès Zola, ni procès Esterhazy, ni procès Dreyfus", cit. Colette Becker, "Chronologie de l'Affaire Dreyfus", in Zola, *L'Affaire Dreyfus,* p. 18. This reiterated an earlier statement to the Chamber on 4 December 1897 to the effect that: "Il n'y a pas d'affaire Dreyfus", cit. Paléologue, *Journal de l'Affaire Dreyfus,* p. 82.

64 Reinach, op. cit., III, pp. 34–5. According to Paléologue, Casimir-Périer, President of the Republic at the time of the original Dreyfus trial, was worried by the start of 1898 by his knowledge that secret documents had been communicated to the judges, but, called as a witness in the first Zola trial, he decided not to divulge this information to the court, for fear of stirring up trouble and violence, but hoping that he would be able to do so at a later date. Paléologue, op. cit., pp. 100–2 (29 January 1898). Again, Delcassé put aside any doubts and concentrated on minimizing the political repercussions of the Affair: "il espère que la lenteur,

la méthode, la complication et le galimatias des procédures finiront par enlever
à l'odieuse affaire ce qu'elle a de plus irritant", ibid., p. 141 (26 September 1898).
65 Halévy, *Apologie pour notre passé*, p. 69. A minister in 1894, Poincaré avoided
   discussion of the Affair publicly until November 1898, when, in a speech in the
   Chamber, he attacked the abuses committed by the *Etat-Major* and the attempts
   to cover them up. He explained his earlier silence by reference to respect for the
   proper judicial process, and said that he was now freeing his conscience of a great
   burden; see Paléologue, op. cit., pp. 147–8 (28 November 1898).
66 See Zola, "M. Scheurer-Kestner", *Le Figaro*, 25 November 1897, in Zola, op. cit.,
   pp. 67–71; and Gauthier, ed., *"Dreyfusards!"*, pp. 94–116 and *passim*.
67 Jean Bousquet-Mélou, *Louis Barthou et la circonscription d'Oloron (1889–1914)*
   (Paris, 1972), pp. 99–101 and 111–15. The *loi de dessaisissement*, as we have seen,
   removed the right to adjudicate the plea for a revision of the Dreyfus case from
   the Chambre criminelle of the Cour de Cassation, and gave it to the whole court
   in plenary session, a change that was generally considered to disadvantage the case
   for revision.
68 Lauris, *Souvenirs d'une belle époque*, pp. 91–2.
69 Reinach, op. cit., III, p. 570.
70 Halévy, op. cit., p. 28.
71 See Daudet, *Au Temps de Judas*, p. 61; Halévy, op. cit., p. 60; Ponty, "La Presse
   quotidienne et l'Affaire Dreyfus", p. 207; and D.R. Watson, *Georges Clemenceau: A Political Biography* (London, 1974), pp. 145–55.
72 Ponty, op. cit., pp. 206 and 216.
73 Daily Report, Prefect of Police, 19 March 1898. APP Ba 106.
74 Herriot, op. cit., p. 192; Reinach, op. cit., III, p. 34.
75 René Goblet (1828–1905) was earlier deputy for the Somme. Boulanger was
   Minister of War in his government of 1886–7, but Goblet soon became his
   political opponent, serving in the anti-Boulangist government of Charles Floquet,
   1888–1889, as Minister for Foreign Affairs; see Zévaès, *Au Temps du Boulangisme*, pp. 46–53 and 95–6.
76 Daily Report, Prefect of Police, 13 May 1898. APP Ba 106.
77 Jean Steens, "Souvenirs d'un Dreyfusard: les Socialistes", *Le Siècle*, 22 March
   1902.
78 Reinach, op. cit., III, pp. 33–4; see also Pierre Dreyfus, *Dreyfus*, pp. 176–7.
79 Reinach, op. cit., IV, pp. 329–31.
80 Ligou, op. cit., pp. 134–56; Claude Willard, *Le Mouvement socialiste en France
   (1893–1905): Les Guesdistes* (Paris, 1965), pp. 410–21; Fiechter, *Le Socialisme
   français*, pp. 47–57; Ponty, op. cit., *passim*; Robert S. Wistrich, "French Socialism and the Dreyfus Affair", *Wiener Library Bulletin*, 28, nos 35–6 (1975). (I read
   Wistrich's valuable article, based mainly on the press, only after writing this
   chapter.)
81 Ponty, op. cit., pp. 210–11 and 215; Daudet, *Au Temps de Judas*, p. 29.
82 Police report, "Les socialistes et la question Zola-Dreyfus", 9 April 1898; and
   Report, Police agent, Paris, 24 January 1898. AN F7 12474.
83 Daily Reports, Prefect of Police, 9 February, 31 and 18 May, 23 January, 18
   February, and 5 April 1898. APP Ba 106.
84 For Socialist antisemitism, see Edmund Silberner, "Charles Fourier on the Jewish
   Question", *Jewish Social Studies*, 8 (1946), pp. 245–66; Zosa Szajkowski, "The
   Jewish Saint-Simonians and Socialist Antisemites in France", *Jewish Social Studies*, 9 (1947), pp. 33–60; Silberner, "Proudhon's Judeophobia", *Historia Judaica*,
   10 (1948), pp. 61–80; Robert F. Byrnes, *Antisemitism in Modern France* (New
   Brunswick, 1950), pp. 114–25; Jeannine Verdès-Leroux, *Scandale financier et
   antisémitisme catholique: Le krach de l'Union Générale* (Paris, 1969), pp. 105–8;
   and chapter XI, pp. 333–8 below. The chauvinism of the Extreme Left was, of
   course, evident in the Paris Commune of 1871; see, for example, Aimé Dupuy,
   1870–1871, La Guerre, la Commune et la presse (Paris, 1959), pp. 102–36; and

Susan Lambert, *The Franco-Prussian War and the Commune in Caricature 1870–71* (London, 1971), Victoria and Albert Museum; see also Michel Winock, "Socialisme et Patriotisme en France (1891–4)", *Revue d'Histoire Moderne et Contemporaine*, 20 (1973), pp. 376–423.

85 Report, Commissaire spécial, Nantes, 23 December 1897. AN F⁷ 12460, "Mouvement antisémite".

86 Report, Commissaire spécial, Nantes, 13 December 1898. AN F⁷ 12465. Guesdistes also appeared in debates with antisemites, and, although they usually made their opposition to antisemitism clear, the conditions in which they did so suggested, and suggest, a certain ambivalence; see Willard, *Les Guesdistes*, pp. 410–11; and Verdès-Leroux, op. cit., p. 155.

87 Daily Report, Prefect of Police, 8 June 1898. APP Ba 106.

88 *La Petite République*, 13 December 1898, cit. Verdès-Leroux, op. cit., p. 159; see also the testimony of Marc Jarblum, "Démocratie, question nationale et sionisme en Europe centrale: qu'en pensait Jaurès? Deux témoignages. I. Marc Jarblum évoque ses rencontres avec Jaurès", *Le Mouvement Social*, no. 52 (1965), pp. 85–93.

89 See François Bournand, *Les Juifs et nos contemporains (L'Antisémitisme et la question juive)* (Paris, 1898), pp. 61–5; Silberner, "French Socialism and the Jewish Question 1865–1914", *Historia Judaica*, 16 (1954), pp. 3–38; and Verdès-Leroux, op. cit., pp. 152–61.

90 Report, Prefect, Bouches-du-Rhône, 4 May 1899. AN F⁷ 12465.

91 Reports, Commissaires spéciaux, Vierzon (Cher), Douai (Nord), and Armentières (Nord), 25 February 1898. AN F⁷ 12474.

92 Report, Commissaire special, Anor (Nord), 9 December 1898. AN F⁷ 12465.

93 See Willard, *Les Guesdistes*, pp. 222–59. Deville, Guesdiste deputy for the 4th *arrondissement* of Paris, made no bones about declaring his belief in Dreyfus's guilt at an adoption meeting in March 1898; see Daily Report, Prefect of Police, 20 March 1898. APP Ba 106.

94 See, for example, Report, Police agent, Paris, 3 July 1899. AN F⁷ 12458; Reports, Police agents, Paris, 28 November 1898, and 11 September 1899. AN F⁷ 12465; and Daily Reports, Prefect of Police, 31 January, 20 February, and 20 May 1898. APP Ba 106. On the militant nature of the POSR, see Michel Winock, "La Naissance du Parti 'Allemaniste' (1890–1)", *Le Mouvement Social*, no. 75 (1971), pp. 33–62.

95 See Charles Andler, *Vie de Lucien Herr (1864–1926)* (Paris, 1932), pp. 94–5 and 114–51; and Léon Blum, *Souvenirs sur l'Affaire* (Paris, 1935), pp. 27–33 and 150.

96 The same impression emerges very clearly from the letters of the Nantes Socialist leader, Charles Brunellière; see Claude Willard, ed., *La Correspondance de Charles Brunellière (1880–1917)* (Paris, 1968).

97 *L'Ouvrier du Finistère*, 24 June 1899; and Report, Prefect, Ille-et-Vilaine, 11 June 1899. AN F⁷ 12465.

98 See Report, Commissaire spécial, Nantes, 10 September 1899. AN F⁷ 12465; and Letter, Brunellière to Lagardelle, 31 August 1898, Willard, ed., op. cit., pp. 155–6.

99 Poster, "La République en péril. Appel aux Travailleurs", enclosed with Report, Prefect, Ille-et-Vilaine, 11 June 1899. AN F⁷ 12465.

100 In addition to Fiechter, op. cit., pp. 47–117, see Jacques Pinsot, "Quelques problèmes du socialisme en France vers 1900", *Revue d'Histoire Economique et Sociale*, 36 (1958), pp. 332–68; L. Derfler, " 'Le Cas Millerand': Une nouvelle interprétation", *Revue d'Histoire Moderne et Contemporaine*, 10 (1963), pp. 81–104; and Derfler, "Réformisme and Jules Guesde: 1891–1904", *International Review of Social History*, 12 (1967), pp. 66–80.

101 Daily Reports, Prefect of Police, 7 June, and 21 February 1898. APP Ba 106.

102 Reports, Commissaire spécial, Marseille, 8 December 1898; and Commissaire central, Saint-Etienne, 4 December 1898. AN F⁷ 12465.

103 Cit. Willard, *Les Guesdistes*, p. 411.
104 Luce, in Martin du Gard's *Jean Barois*, pp. 237–8, stressed the very radical implications of publicly questioning the verdict against Dreyfus and of working to vindicate him; it would be to unleash "le scandale, et délibérément, comme un révolutionnaire, assaillir de front cet ensemble sacré: l'ordre constitué de la nation!"
105 Report, Police agent, Paris, 11 January 1898. AN F⁷ 12473.
106 Daily Reports, Prefect of Police, 16 January, 12 and 13 February, 23 January, and 11 April 1898. APP Ba 106.
107 Report, Police agent, Paris, 17 December 1898. AN F⁷ 12465.
108 Jean Maitron, *Histoire du mouvement anarchiste en France (1880–1914)* (Paris, 1955), p. 318.
109 See Police Report, 11 June 1899. AN F⁷ 12458; and Stock, *Mémorandum d'un éditeur*, Troisième série, p. 105.
110 Report, Commissaire spécial, Nevers, 30 August 1899. AN F⁷ 12465.
111 See Edouard Drumont, *De l'Or, de la boue, du sang, du Panama à l'anarchie* (Paris, 1896), pp. 99–244. The book is dedicated to Séverine.
112 See Viau, *Vingt ans d'antisémitisme*, pp. 71–9.
113 Daily Report, Prefect of Police, 11 March 1898. APP Ba 106.
114 "Sus à tous les Capitalos Tant Juifs que Crétins". Two "populos" are conversing. The first says: "Tel que vous me voyez, mossieu, j'ai travaillé cinquante ans chez ces sales youpins!"; to which the other replies: "Eh moi, mossieu, tel que vous me voyez, j'ai bûché un demi-siècle pour ces bons catholiques!" *Almanach du Père Peinard* (1899).
115 See chapter VI, p. 180 below.
116 Reinach, op. cit., III, p. 253.
117 Report, Police agent, Paris, 15 February 1898. AN F⁷ 12474.
118 Halévy, op. cit., pp. 78–9 and 92. See also Péguy's remarkable evocation of the same *"journée"* of 19 November: "La Triomphe de la République", *Cahiers de la Quinzaine*, January 1900, in Péguy, *Oeuvres en prose 1898–1908* (Paris, 1959), pp. 103–22.
119 On the importance of this emblem in the Syndicalist movement, see Sylvain Humbert, *Le Mouvement syndical* (Paris, 1912), p. 18; and, generally, Gabriel Perreux, *Les Origines du drapeau rouge en France* (Paris, 1930); Annie Kriegel, *Le Pain et les roses: Jalons pour une histoire des socialismes* (Paris, 1973), pp. 238–9; and Robert Brécy, "Le Drapeau Rouge", *Revue d'Histoire Moderne et Contemporaine*, 22 (1975), pp. 262–8.
120 Reports, Commissaire central, Besançon (Doubs), 25 June 1899; and Commissaire de police, Cours (Rhône), 10 December 1898. AN F⁷ 12465.
121 Daily Report, Prefect of Police, 30 April 1898. APP Ba 106.
122 Appeal of the CGT, "Au Peuple, à l'Armée!", February 1898, with Police report, 26 February 1898. AN F⁷ 12474; and Report on meeting of Conseil National of the CGT, Daily Report, Prefect of Police, 5 February 1898. APP Ba 106.
123 Report, Police agent, Paris, 11 December 1903, "Les ouvriers et l'Affaire Dreyfus". AN F⁷ 12470.
124 Report, Police agent, Paris, 20 November 1897. AN F⁷ 12473.
125 Lauris, op. cit., pp. 90 and 98.
126 Gregh, op. cit., p. 291.
127 Tharaud, *Notre cher Péguy*, I, pp. 133–4; also ibid., pp. 149–50; Tharaud, *Mes années chez Barrès* (Paris, 1928), pp. 25–6; and Robert J. Smith, "L'Atmosphère politique à l'Ecole Normale Supérieure à la fin du XIXe siècle", *Revue d'Histoire Moderne et Contemporaine*, 20 (1973), pp. 255–8.
128 Tharaud, *Notre cher Péguy*, I, pp. 162–8; also Daniel Halévy, *Péguy and Les Cahiers de la Quinzaine* (London, 1946), pp. 43–4.
129 Halévy, *Apologie*, pp. 59–60.
130 Reinach, op. cit., III, pp. 248–9. Pierrard, op. cit., pp. 94–5, says that the Lille

students of the State Faculties demonstrated *against* Zola and Dreyfus in January 1898.

131 Zola, "Lettre à la Jeunesse" (December 1897), in Zola, op. cit., pp. 89–98.
132 See Telegram, Prefect, Rhône, 17 December 1898. AN F⁷ 12465; *La France du Sud-Ouest*, 11 January 1899; and Report, Commissaire spécial, Lille, 29 December. AN F⁷ 12456.
133 Report on students' meeting, Police agent, 11 May 1898. AN F⁷ 12474.
134 Police report, Rennes, 21 June 1899. AN F⁷ 12464.
135 See, for example, Daily Report, Prefect of Police, 26 January 1898. APP Ba 106; and Report, Commissaire spécial, Lille, 10 July 1900. AN F⁷ 12456.
136 See Reinach, op. cit., III, pp. 245 and 247–8; see also Dardenne, *Godefroy Cavaignac*, p. 551; and Pierre Dreyfus, op. cit., pp. 192–3, 197–200 and 206–15.
137 On the Dreyfusism of both staff and students at the ENS, see Smith, op. cit., pp. 249–51.
138 Press agency telegram, Algiers, 8 December 1898. AN F⁷ 12465.
139 Martin du Gard, op. cit., pp. 283–4.
140 See Paul Gerbod, *La Condition universitaire en France au XIXe siècle* (Paris, 1965); and P. H. Stock, "Students versus the University in Pre-World War Paris", *French Historical Studies*, 7 (1971), pp. 93–110.
141 François Mauriac, "L'Affaire Dreyfus vue par un enfant", in Dreyfus, *Cinq années de ma vie* (Paris, 1962), p. 13.
142 Reinach, op. cit., III, pp. 26–9.
143 Cit. Henri Guillemin, "L'Affaire", in *Zola* (Paris, 1969), Collection Génies et Réalités, chapter VIII, p. 243.
144 Herriot, op. cit., pp. 129 and 133; see also Martin du Gard, op. cit., pp. 209 and 273.
145 Cit. Ponty, op. cit., p. 213.
146 Tharaud, *Notre cher Péguy*, I, p. 156; see also Péguy, *NJ*, p. 56.
147 Maurice Barrès, *Mes Cahiers* (Paris, 1936), X, p. 244. Even Urbain Gohier, whose tone was much more hostile, claimed that his target was the corrupt High Command and the officer corps and not the national army. He wrote in 1898: "Zola n'a pas insulté l'armée: il a dénoncé les pires ennemis de l'armée, les ramassis d'intrigants, de menteurs, de faussaires, de factieux qui la déshonorent et qui la perdront avec la patrie." Gohier, *L'Armée contre la nation* (Paris, 1899), p. 334 and *passim;* see also Zola, Letter to Dreyfus, 6 July 1899, Zola, *Oeuvres complètes*, 14, p. 1524.
148 Lauris, op. cit., p. 93; see also Martin du Gard, op. cit., pp. 209 and 273.
149 *L'Indépendance du Franche-Comté*, 26 February 1898, cit. Marlin, "La Droite à Besançon", p. 230.
150 See Maurras, *Au Signe de Flore*, pp. 53–4; Maurice Donnay, *Des Souvenirs . . .* (Paris, 1933), pp. 232–60; Girardet, *La Société militaire*, pp. 213–35; Ralston, *The Army of the Republic*, p. 221; and Andréani, "L'Antimilitarisme en Languedoc", pp. 107–8.
151 Reinach, op. cit., III, pp. 556–7.
152 Ibid., p. 555; see also Girardet, op. cit., pp. 77–86 and *passim;* and Pierre Chalmin, *L'Officier français de 1815 à 1870* (Paris, 1957).
153 Reinach, op. cit., III, pp. 265 and 273. The same point is made by Proust; see Marcel Proust, *A la Recherche du temps perdu*, English Uniform Edition (London, 1957), VII, pp. 109, 111 and 204. On the antisemitism of the aristocracy in general, see chapter X, pp. 271–9 below.
154 See Reinach, op. cit., III, p. 274; IV, pp. 299–312, 427, 559–63; V, pp. 181–4; Maurras, *Au Signe de Flore*, p. 141; Samuel M. Osgood, *French Royalism under the Third and Fourth Republics* (The Hague, 1960), p. 71; and Ralston, op. cit., p. 224.
155 Reinach, op. cit., III, pp. 272–3; Halévy, *Apologie*, p. 61.
156 See Girardet, op. cit., pp. 117–58.

157 See Ralston, op. cit., particularly chapter 5.
158 Police report, 2 December 1898, Dossier: "Coup d'état de 1898", AN F⁷ 12717, "Tentative de coup d'état militaire 1898–9"; and P.-V. Stock, op. cit., pp. 139–41.
159 Steinheil, op. cit., p. 102.
160 Brunellière, Letter to Hamon, 1 August 1899, Willard, ed., op. cit., p. 166; see also Gohier, op. cit., pp. viii, xvii, 137 and 142.
161 Reinach, op. cit., IV, p. 426.
162 In addition to many police reports, see Reinach, op. cit., IV, pp. 299–322, 427, 559–63, 571–615; and V, pp. 181–4, 257–8 and 308–13; Barrès-Maurras, op. cit., pp. 249, 286–7, 295, 315, 371 and 444; Halévy, Apologie, p. 91; and Steinheil, op. cit., pp. 95 and 143.
163 Blum, "Les Elections de 1902" (April 1902), L'Oeuvre de Léon Blum 1891–1905, pp. 499–500.
164 Police report, 9 December 1898. AN F⁷ 12434, "Agissements royalistes", cit. Ralston, op. cit., p. 224.
165 Ibid., pp. 222–6; but see Reinach, op. cit., IV, pp. 306–7; Daudet, Au Temps de Judas, pp. 235–6; and Report, Police agent, 6 August 1900, AN F⁷ 12870, claiming to have evidence that two particular regiments were ready to follow Déroulède in February 1899.
166 Viau, op. cit., pp. 208–15; see also Edouard Drumont, La Dernière Bataille, Nouvelle étude psychologique et sociale (Paris, 1890), p. 186.
167 See Viau, op. cit., pp. 215–16; Daudet, Au Temps de Judas, pp. 133–4 and 229; Barrès-Maurras, op. cit., p. 314; and Barrès, Scènes et doctrines, II, pp. 91–105.
168 Report, Commissaire central, Nice, 11 June 1899. AN F⁷ 12458. The other cases were at Lorient (Morbihan), and Poligny (Jura), also in June 1899.
169 See chapter IV, pp. 137–8 below.
170 Report, Commissaire spécial, Montbéliard, 29 July 1898. AN F⁷ 12467.
171 Daily Report, Prefect of Police, 26 February 1898. APP Ba 106.
172 Police reports, Rennes, 5 and 15 July 1899. AN F⁷ 12464. The pupils of this school had just demonstrated outside the barracks.
173 Report, Commissaire spécial, Valence, 20 February 1898. AN F⁷ 12474. Sorlin, Waldeck-Rousseau, pp. 406–10, notes that Galliffet reciprocated this feeling, showing great contempt for his military colleagues, when he became Minister of War in June 1899.
174 Ralston, op. cit., pp. 220–1. Paléologue mentioned also that a former "sous-chef du Service des Renseignements", Lieutenant-Colonel Cordier, who had been a close collaborator with Colonel Sandherr, became a Dreyfusard at the same time (August 1899), "ce qui déchaîne sur lui les fureurs de l'Etat-major." Paléologue, op. cit., p. 235. A better-known figure, who voiced his doubts about the role of the état-major in the Affair, was Lyautey, but he did so privately, and, as a colonial officer, he was an outsider; see Lyautey, Letter to vicomte É.-M. de Vogüé, 3 January 1899. Choix de lettres, p. 166.
175 Report, Commissaire spécial, Chalandray (Aisne), 6 June 1899. AN F⁷ 12458.
176 Reinach, op. cit., IV, p. 307.
177 Paléologue, op. cit., p. 251 (5 September 1899).
178 Telegram, Commissaire spécial, Cherbourg (Manche), 10 September 1899. AN F⁷ 12465.
179 Pierre Dreyfus, op. cit., p. 367.
180 An unusual indication of the anti-Dreyfusard opinions of small traders was noted by Barrès: small traders at Rennes called pieces of foreign money "dreyfusardes". Barrès, Scènes et doctrines, I, p. 214.
181 The most recent accounts of anticlericalism in this period are: Sorlin, Waldeck-Rousseau, pp. 423–49; Malcolm O. Partin, Waldeck-Rousseau, Combes and the Church: The Politics of Anticlericalism (Durham, N.C., 1969); and Larkin, Church and State after the Dreyfus Affair.
182 Mauriac, op. cit., p. 11; see also, generally, abbé Henri de Saint-Poli (abbé J.

Brugerette), *L'Affaire Dreyfus et la mentalité catholique en France* (Paris, 1904), which suggests that such an attitude was typical; but also Jacques Piou, *Le Comte Albert de Mun, Sa vie publique* (Paris, 1919?), which suggests that more passive attitudes prevailed: "Les catholiques s'efforçaient . . . de ne pas mêler de question confessionnelle à l'affaire Dreyfus, et de parler seulement du respect de la chose jugée et de l'honneur militaire; leur religion leur recommandait d'ailleurs la prudence, car elle espère voir un jour les Israélites reprendre leur place dans la famille chrétienne. Quand ils prenaient part au débat, ce qui était rare, c'était surtout pour repousser les outrages faits à leur foi ou à l'armée" (p. 190).

183 Jules Dessaint, *L'Alliance Républicaine Démocratique*, March 1904; Charles Maurras, *La Gazette de France*, 28 January 1906, cit. Pierrard, op. cit., pp. 186 and 209.

184 Péguy, *NJ*, p. 115; also ibid., p. 126, quoting Jaurès.

185 Pierrard, op. cit., p. 88; see also Anatole France, *L'Eglise et la République*, pp. 49–62.

186 See Sorlin, *"La Croix" et les Juifs*, pp. 110–20; Ponty, op. cit.; France, op. cit., p. 53; and Pierrard, op. cit., p. 94, citing *La Croix du Nord*, 13 January 1898: "A bas les juifs! oui! parce que le traître, le vrai traître est juif . . ."

187 Pierrard, op. cit., p. 92.

188 See Louis Divry (abbé Rosat), *L'abbé Garnier aux temps héroïques de l'apostolat des classes ouvrières* (Paris, 1936); and my "Catholic Populism in France at the Time of the Dreyfus Affair: the *Union Nationale*", *Journal of Contemporary History*, 10 (1975), pp. 667–705.

189 See Pierrard, op. cit., p. 82; and Alexandre Zévaès, *L'Affaire Dreyfus* (Paris, 1931), p. 209. Paléologue, who visited Rome in March 1898 and in March 1899, noted that the Vatican took Dreyfus's guilt for granted in 1898, but not in the following year, and attributed the change of view to Leo XIII personally; Paléologue, op. cit., pp. 117 and 178–9.

190 Saint-Poli, op. cit., pp. 177–99 and 205–13; Pierre Dreyfus, op. cit., pp. 204–5, 211 and 239; Paléologue, op. cit., p. 35; Pierrard, op. cit., pp. 186–212; Reinach, op. cit., IV, p. 420; Duroselle, "L'Antisémitisme en France", p. 64; Lévy, "La Vie du capitaine Dreyfus", pp. 263–4.

191 Maurras, December 1900, cit. Pierrard, op. cit., p. 209.

192 For example, the group that later crystallized as Le Sillon; see Barrès-Maurras, op. cit., p. 504; and chapter XIV, p. 533 below.

193 Reports, Commissaire spécial, Montbéliard, 24 February 1898; and Commissaire spécial, Belfort, 25 February 1898; also Report, Commissaire spécial, Epinal, 24 February 1898. AN F⁷ 12474.

194 Michel Arnod, "Un aspect du Protestantisme à Nancy de 1850 à 1914. Paroisse et Cité", *Recherches sur les forces politiques de la France de l'Est*, p. 209.

195 Telegram, Commissaire spécial, Montbéliard, 5 December 1898. AN F⁷ 12465.

196 Police report, Rennes, 23 June 1899. AN F⁷ 12464. On the other side, Cavaignac had a Protestant mother, but had been brought up as a Catholic; Dardenne, op. cit., p. 25.

197 See André Gide, *If it die . . .* (1920) (Harmondsworth, 1957), pp. 35–9; André Chamson, *A Time to Keep* (London, 1957), pp. 56–9 and *passim;* and Samuel Mours et Daniel Robert, *Le Protestantisme en France du XVIIIe siècle à nos jours (1685–1970)* (Paris, 1972).

198 For example, a pamphlet, *Le Complôt protestant* was put out by *La Croix*, and distributed in places as far apart as Perpignan, Avignon, Laval and Amiens (Police reports, April 1898. AN F⁷ 12463); and, at Montpellier, in December 1898, an anti-Protestant poster was put up by "un groupe d'ouvriers Socialistes indépendants" on the occasion of a speech to be made by Pressensé (Report, Commissaire spécial, Montpellier, December 1898. AN F⁷ 12465).

199 See André Siegfried, *Géographie électorale de l'Ardèche sous la Troisième République* (Paris, 1949), pp. 54–66; and René Rémond, ed., *Forces religieuses et attitudes politiques dans la France contemporaine* (Paris, 1965).

200 In addition to inference from police reports, see Edouard Drumont, *La France juive, Essai d'histoire contemporaine* (1886) (Paris, no date), I, pp. 422–5.

201 Report, Police agent, Paris, 3 October 1897; also Report, Commissaire spécial, Epinal, 4 November 1897. AN F⁷ 12473.

202 Report, Police agent, Paris, 12 February 1898. AN F⁷ 12474; and Report, Police agent, Paris, 28 March 1898. AN F⁷ 12473.

203 Halévy, *Apologie*, pp. 27, 29 and *passim;* Benda, *La Jeunesse d'un clerc*, pp. 196–205; Pierrard, op. cit., p. 227; Gregh, op. cit., p. 290; Daudet, *Au Temps de Judas*, pp. 98 and 173; Gilbert Ziebura, *Léon Blum et le parti socialiste 1872–1934* (Paris, 1967), pp. 35–6; Joanna Richardson, *Sarah Bernhardt* (London, 1959), pp. 125–6; Paléologue, op. cit., p. 104; E. de Clermont-Tonnerre, *Mémoires*, I, *Au Temps des équipages* (Paris, 1928), pp. 198–203.

204 Benda, op. cit., pp. 207–9; Tharaud, *Mes années chez Barrès*, pp. 27–31; Daudet, op. cit., pp. 111–12; Ziebura, op. cit., pp. 18–23, 37; A.B. Jackson, *La Revue Blanche (1889–1903); Origine, influence, bibliographie* (Paris, 1960), pp. 100–32.

205 E.M. Lévy, Letter, 8 September 1960, cit. Lazare Prajs, "Péguy et le peuple juif", *Cahiers Paul Claudel*, 7, p. 401; see also Jules Isaac, "Les amitiés juives de Péguy", *Expériences de ma vie*, I, *Péguy* (Paris, 1960), pp. 304–11.

206 Benda, *La Jeunesse d'un clerc*, pp. 203–4.

207 Ziebura, op. cit., pp. 35–6; Marrus, *The Politics of Assimilation*, pp. 164–95.

208 Blum, *Souvenirs sur l'Affaire*, pp. 25–6.

209 Reinach, op. cit., III, p. 335.

210 Daudet, *Au Temps de Judas* pp. 148–9; Reinach, op. cit., III, p. 581. Gohier's claim that "les journaux les plus ardents à repousser la révision de la sentence qui a frappé Dreyfus ont des juifs pour directeurs" is an exaggeration, though he is able to cite *Le Gaulois, Le Voltaire* (Klotz), and *Le Soir* (Pollonais); Gohier, op. cit., pp. 175, 247 and 266–7.

211 Abbé Pichot, *La Conscience chrétienne et l'affaire Dreyfus* (Paris, 1899), p 27, cit. Johnson, *France and the Dreyfus Affair*, p. 213 n. Johnson appears to lend far too much weight to this observation, failing to allow for the fact that it and similar disclaimers were intended to counter theories of wide-scale Jewish conspiracy.

212 Daudet, *Au Temps de Judas*, p. 89.

213 Barrès-Maurras, op. cit., pp. 644–5.

214 Reinach, op. cit., IV, p. 414.

215 Ibid., III, pp. 273–4.

216 Blum, *Souvenirs sur l'Affaire*, pp. 25–6.

217 Reinach, op. cit., IV, pp. 444–5.

218 Report, Prefect, Haute-Garonne, 17 January 1899. AN F⁷ 12466.

219 P.-V. Stock, op. cit., p. 105.

220 Report, Police agent, Paris, 12 February 1898. AN F⁷ 12474; also various prefects' reports, June 1899. AN F⁷ 12464; and Report, Commissaire spécial, Marseille, 9 May 1899. AN F⁷ 12465.

221 Reinach, op. cit., IV, p. 49.

222 Martin du Gard, op. cit., p. 284.

223 See, for example, Mauriac, op. cit., pp. 13–14; Daudet, *Au Temps de Judas*, p. 26; Reinach, op. cit., III, pp. 19–21; IV, p. 50; Dardenne, op. cit., p. 539; and Paléologue, op. cit., pp. 31 (23 December 1894), 82–3 (4 December 1897), citing de Mun's speech in the Chamber, and 84 (13 December 1897), citing Vogüé.

224 Report, Police agent, Paris, 11 January 1898. AN F⁷ 12473.

225 Charles Maurras, *Enquête sur la monarchie* (Paris, 1909), p. 167.

226 Reinach, op. cit., III, p. 16.
227 Martin du Gard, op. cit., p. 284; see also Daudet, *Au Temps de Judas*, pp. 29–50.
228 Miquel, *L'Affaire Dreyfus*, pp. 7–9 and 52–3; Boussel, *L'Affaire Dreyfus et la presse, passim.*
229 Lévy, "La Vie du capitaine Dreyfus", pp. 265–6.
230 Reinach, op. cit., III, pp. 155–6.
231 See Bellanger *et al.*, eds., *Histoire générale de la presse française*, III, pp. 137–8 and *passim.*
232 Edouard Drumont, *Le Testament d'un antisémite* (Paris, 1891), p. 58. A similar view was expressed by Emile Durkheim in his inaugural Lecture in the Faculty of Letters at Bordeaux in 1888; see Steven Lukes,*Emile Durkheim, His Life and Work: A Historical and Critical Study* (London, 1973), p. 102.
233 Zola, "Procès-Verbal", *Le Figaro*, 5 December 1897, in Zola, *L'Affaire Dreyfus*, p. 84; see also ibid., pp. 70, 77, 104 and 107.
234 Zévaès, *L'Affaire Dreyfus*, pp. 87–9. But, as an old journalist, he quickly realized that newspaper publication would have maximum impact, and force a prosecution; see Mitterand, *Zola journaliste*, p. 240.
235 Reinach, op. cit., III, p. 16; see also Herriot, op. cit., p. 131.
236 Reinach, op. cit., III, pp. 16–17. A police report noted in February 1898: "*L'Aurore* est le seul journal Dreyfusard qui se vend. Les autres ne portent pas." Report, Police agent, Paris, 12 February 1898. AN F⁷ 12474.
237 Ponty, op. cit., p. 201.
238 Ibid., pp. 206–20.
239 Herriot, op. cit., p. 134.
240 Drumont, *Le Testament d'un antisémite*, p. 58.
241 Report, Commissaire spécial, Chalandray, 6 June 1899 (referring in particular to *Le Petit Journal* and *Le Nouvelliste de Lyon*). AN F⁷ 12458.
242 Telegram, Prefect, Finistère, 27 June 1899. AN F⁷ 12465.
243 Combarieu, *Sept Ans à l'Élysée*, p. 3; see also Miquel, op. cit., pp. 52–3; Gauthier, ed., op. cit., pp. 33–5; Jean Variot, *Propos de Georges Sorel* (Paris, 1935), pp. 130–1. On the other hand, the anti-Dreyfusard commitment of its editor, Judet, seems to have cut the circulation of *Le Petit Journal;* see Raymond Manévy, *La Presse de la IIIe République* (Paris, 1955), p. 102.
244 See Sorlin, *"La Croix" et les Juifs*, pp. 196–203 and *passim;* Bellanger *et al.* eds., op. cit., III, pp. 342–5; and Report, Police agent, Paris, 12 February 1898. AN F⁷ 12474.
245 A point made by Thibaudet in 1924, but not sufficiently considered by many historians of newspaper opinion: "Il y a une puissance qui s'appelle l'opinion, et qu'il ne faut pas confondre avec la presse." Albert Thibaudet, *Les Princes lorrains* (Paris, 1924), p. xv.
246 Reports, Commissaire spécial, Cette, 2 October 1898; and Prefect, Haute-Garonne, 17 January 1899. AN F⁷ 12466.
247 Report, Prefect, Finistère, 26 June 1899; and Telegram, Prefect, Gard, 13 September 1899. AN F⁷ 12465.
248 Report, Commissaire spécial, Lille, 31 July 1899. AN F⁷ 12487.
249 Report, Commissaire spécial, Nantes, 14 February 1900. AN F⁷ 12456.
250 See Barral, *L'Isère sous la Troisième République*, particularly pp. 402–16; Georges Dupeux, *Aspects de l'histoire sociale et politique du Loir-et-Cher, 1848–1914* (Paris, 1962), particularly pp. 534–50; L. Desgraves et G. Dupeux, eds., *Bordeaux au XIXe siècle* (Bordeaux, 1969), particularly pp 330–5; and various contributions, already cited, to *Recherches sur les forces politiques de la France de l'Est.*
251 Halévy, *Apologie*, pp. 92–3. For a slightly different, and later, version, see Halévy, *Péguy and Les Cahiers de la Quinzaine*, p. 47.
252 See P.-V. Stock, op. cit., pp. 243–4; and various examples in the General Police archives, for example AN F⁷ 12921, "Affaire Dreyfus".
253 For example, Maurice Vauthier, *La France et l'Affaire Dreyfus* (Paris, 1899), pp.

23–28; or even Charles Seignobos, *L'Evolution de la IIIe République (1875–1914)* (Paris, 1921), p. 197.

254 Pierrard, op. cit., p. 83.
255 Roger Thabault, *Education and Change in a Village Community: Mazières-en-Gâtine, 1848–1914* (London, 1971), p. 167.
256 *Le Figaro*, 2 July 1899, cit. Reinach, op. cit., V, p. 199.
257 Jean-Richard Bloch, *Lévy: Premier livre de contes* (Paris, 1925), p. 30.
258 Péguy, *NJ*, p. 208.
259 Combarieu, op. cit., p. 14.
260 Lévy, "La Vie du capitaine Dreyfus", p. 259.
261 Barrès, Letter to Maurras, 7 October 1904, in Barrès-Maurras, op. cit., p. 428.
262 Halévy, *Apologie*, p. 78; see also Halévy, Diary entry, 14 November 1897, *Degas parle . . .* (Paris, 1960), pp. 121–2.
263 Péguy, *NJ*, p. 117.
264 Peter, "Dimensions de l'Affaire Dreyfus", pp. 1163–6.
265 Poster, "Appel aux Patriotes", put out by *L'Avenir,* Report, Prefect, Rhône, 17 August 1899. AN F⁷ 12465.
266 See Dossier, "Le Procès des ligues, avril 1899". AN F⁷ 12487.
267 Halévy, *Apologie*, p. 73.
268 Notably in Emile Durkheim, *Le Suicide: Etude de sociologie* (Paris, 1897).
269 Péguy, *NJ*, p. 113; see also Paléologue, op. cit., p. 146 (23 November 1898), referring to "la crise morale que traverse la France et qui ressemble sous tant de rapports à une crise religieuse . . ."
270 Cit. Bloy, *Je m'accuse, Oeuvres,* IV, p. 207; see also the religious imagery used in Zola's "Lettre à Madame Alfred Dreyfus", published in *L'Aurore,* 29 September 1899, Zola, *L'Affaire Dreyfus*, pp. 167–77.
271 Steinheil, op. cit., p. 85.

CHAPTER III
THE ANTISEMITIC RIOTS OF 1898

T HE ANTISEMITIC RIOTS OF 1898 HAVE BEEN MENTIONED IN CHAPTER I, BUT they warrant further consideration and analysis, particularly since, with the exception of Reinach, and recently of Sorlin and Pierrard,[1] historians of the Dreyfus Affair have passed them over in complete or relative silence, thus ignoring what was probably the high-point of popular involvement in the Affair, and certainly the main manifestation of hostility to Jews in the period. Seignobos merely stated: "In several towns, the crowd shouted: "Death to the Jews!" and manhandled some of them", though he did say a little more about the riots in Algeria.[2] Zévaès went further, referring to "trouble in the streets, acts of violence, pillaging, assaults . . . in many towns . . .", but he mentioned disturbances only in Nantes, Rennes, Rouen, Nancy, Marseille, Clermont-Ferrand, Saint-Malo, Bar-le-Duc and Algeria.[3] Kayser also paid more attention to the riots, but mentioned only those in Algeria, Paris, Rennes, Lyon, Grenoble and Saint-Malo.[4] Chastenet noted the occurrence of "antisemitic riots" early in 1898, but referring to Paris and Algeria only, and apparently not realizing that the worst riots in France took place before the Zola trial.[5] More recently, Miquel mentions troubles in Algeria, Paris, Bordeaux, Rennes, Lyon, Aix and Toulouse, and adds that "riots or brawls are reported from all towns of any size", going into no further detail;[6] while Dardenne refers to "patriotic demonstrations . . . in all the big towns in France", which gives a very misleading impression.[7] Among non-French historians, Hannah Arendt is exceptional in her appreciation of the significance of the 1898 riots, but, though she instinctively senses their scope and importance, she produces no supporting evidence for her conclusions.[8] For French Jews, by contrast, 1898 was not a date to forget. J.-R. Bloch evoked in 1913, in *Lévy*, the terror of Jewish families in a small town in the West, the object of daily insults, but also of larger-scale assaults on their houses by gangs of youths and hostile crowds. Ten years later, the non-Jewish narrator returned to the town, and was greeted by a now prosperous and influential Lévy, who exclaimed: "What an enormous difference from 1898 . . . !"[9] Similarly, the historian Jules Isaac, himself the son of a Jewish army officer like Dreyfus, recollected in old age: "France seemed to have returned to the time of the Religious Wars; the possibility of another Saint Bartholomew's massacre—of Jews and Protestants who were, willy-nilly, associated in the conflagration—was not excluded";[10] while Drault commented in 1935: "The Jews made no mistake on this score. They remembered the antisemitic campaigns of 1898 much better than the conservatives and the Catholics"; and he recounted that a French Jew had told him, with reference to the Nazi persecution of 1933: "We were only a hair's breadth from that in France [in 1898] . . ."[11]

From administrative and police reports,[12] it is possible to redress the balance against the weight of historians' neglect, and to show that such fears, while exaggerated, had something very real to feed on, to show that Jewish memories were not mistaken. This evidence establishes that the 1898 riots were both serious and widespread, as well as providing a good idea of what provoked them. They can thus be placed in the wider perspective, not simply of French antisemitism, but of popular disturbances in general in nineteenth-century France, for the two had traditionally gone together. Certainly, anti-Jewish riots were no novelty in modern France. Jews had been among the victims of the White Terror in Provence in the 1790s,[13] and violence against Jews was common in the East. Szajkowski has observed: "Anti-Jewish riots became a kind of tradition which the Alsatian people observed upon the outbreak of any revolution in France", and serious disturbances were reported there in 1789, 1830–2 and 1848. In 1832, 2 people were killed and 20 wounded in antisemitic riots at Bergheim (Haut-Rhin).[14] In 1848, in the worst of a series of over 50 outbreaks, half-a-dozen Jewish residences at Brumath were broken into and looted.[15] While clearly owing much to such historical precedents, the riots of 1898 were a phenomenon on an altogether wider scale, though they were, with a few exceptions, less violent. The Ministry of the Interior received reports from its agents and officials of riots and disturbances of a specifically antisemitic nature during January and February 1898 in 55 places in metropolitan France, including Paris. Chronologically, these occurred in three waves: the first wave of 23 in the week up to and including 23 January, a Sunday; the second wave of 19 in the week following and including 23 January; the third wave of four in the period 23–28 February. Seven occurred on 23 January only, and two on 6 February. Riots occurred in Paris during the third week of January, and off and on during the first Zola trial, which opened on 7 February. Press telegrams retained by the Ministry of the Interior, and other sources, indicate riots in a further 14 places, of which at least 7 occurred before 23 January. In addition to these 69 riots or disturbances in January and February 1898,[16] a few isolated outbreaks are reported for the remaining months of 1898 and for 1899.[17] As we have seen, the most important of these, though less exclusively antisemitic, was the demonstration in the Place de la Concorde on 25 October 1898.[18] In Algeria, antisemitic riots took place during the same period, the most serious being that in Algiers from 18 to 25 January 1898.[19]

The more serious riots in metropolitan France occurred in the first wave.

Paris experienced riots from 14 to 20 January; Marseille from 16th to 20th; Bordeaux from 15th to 20th; Nantes from 17th to 20th; Rouen from 17th to 22nd; Chalon-sur-Saône from 18th to 23rd; Lyon from 17th to 19th; Perpignan from 18th to 22nd; Nancy from 17th to 20th; and Angers from 19th to 23rd. By 23 January, when much of the population was free from work and available to demonstrate in the streets, the authorities had the situation in hand. Thirteen places reported riots on Sunday 23 January, but most were minor, and half were one-day affairs, probably in imitation of the bigger riots of the week before, However, in Dijon, the Sunday demonstration began a series which lasted until 27 January and other places, mainly in the East, experienced the second wave of riots, of which the most serious were at Saint-Dié from 28 to 30 January; at Epinal from 26th to 31st; and at Ligny (Meuse) from 26th to 28th. The small third wave included two serious riots, at Bar-le-Duc from 23rd to 25th; and at Dieppe from 24 to 26 February. The pattern which seems to emerge is of riots in large urban centres in the week before 23 January, with Paris taking the lead in time. These had some echoes in smaller towns, in particular on Sunday 23 January. In the week after and later in February, further riots developed in smaller towns, particularly in the East.

The East stands out also when the geographical distribution of the riots is analysed (see Map 7).[20] Riots occurred in most of France's big cities and in towns in many departments, but there were clear areas of high incidence, and the highest incidence was in the East. Twenty-three occurred in the sector formed by lines drawn from Calais to Paris and from Paris to Geneva; of these, 12 occurred in the departments of the Vosges, the Meurthe-et-Moselle, the Meuse, the Doubs, and in the territory of Belfort. The second area of high incidence was the Mediterranean coastal region and the Rhône valley, where there were 16.[21] The third area of high incidence was the West, north of the Loire, where 14 riots occurred, six of them in Normandy.[22] There is obviously some correlation here with the familiar political geography of France. The East and the West were Right-wing electoral strongholds, where antisemitism also might be expected to be strong. The Mediterranean coastal region and the Rhône valley were electorally Left-wing, where again, in an atmosphere of intense political conflict, Right-wing extremism and antisemitism might be expected. We will return to a discussion of the electoral aspects of antisemitism in a later chapter. The "nationalist" aspect of the 1898 riots, also, is suggested by their distribution. They frequently occurred on or near frontiers, particularly in the East, but also in the North, the South-West and the West, where seven riots took place in ports. This patriotic element, moreover, was quite explicit in many cases, demonstrations being specifically made in favour of the army and against Zola, its supposed detractor. Many of the riots were accompanied by shouts of "Vive l'armée". At Dijon, Toulouse, Béziers, Saint-Malo, Perpignan, Marseille, Nantes, Vannes, Bar-le-Duc and probably Besançon, demonstrations took place outside the military club, and at Angers outside the barracks. At eight places conscripts led or took part in the demonstrations, which coincided with the annual drawing of lots for military

MAP 7 ANTISEMITIC RIOTS (1898) BY DEPARTMENT.

Number of riots or demonstrations per department

None

1

2

3 or more

service.[23] At Cherbourg and Epinal, members of the armed forces themselves instigated antisemitic demonstrations; at Lunéville, the army was reported to have behaved sympathetically towards the demonstrators; at Nantes, the local army commander was very reluctant to let troops be used to quell the disturbances. The only demonstration reported involving veterans of the Franco-Prussian War was at Bar-le-Duc in November 1898, but many veterans' associations sent patriotic addresses to the army in March 1898.[24] We shall come across further indications of the nationalism and militarism that informed the 1898 riots, but, more striking than these positive characteristics was the fact that they were directed against Jews.

The size and gravity of the riots varied enormously, from a handful of drunken conscripts shouting anti-Jewish slogans, as at Montbéliard on 17 January, or a dozen students throwing stones at the house of a Jewish professor, as at Tournon on 23 January, to full-scale riots lasting several days and involving several thousand people. Including those reported only by press telegram and which the authorities did not presumably take very seriously, about forty demonstrations can be classed as minor, involving 50 or fewer demonstrators usually, occurring on one day only, and occasioning little actual damage to persons or property. The other thirty odd were more serious. Of these, twelve involved crowds of 500 or more demonstrators; 4,000 were reported at Angers and Marseille; 3,000 at Nantes; 2,000 at Rouen; and between 1,000 and 1,500 at Saint-Dié, Bar-le-Duc and Saint-Malo. The demonstrators gathered in force in important squares and thoroughfares, chanting slogans, throwing stones, attacking Jewish property and sometimes Jewish people, and insulting and resisting the police who tried to disperse them. In 17 places, such riots occurred on three or more successive days: for three, at Dieppe, Bar-le-Duc, Nancy, Lunéville, Ligny, Lyon, Perpignan, Saint-Dié and Epinal; for four, at Chalon-sur-Saône, Nantes and Dijon; for five, at Angers, Bordeaux and Marseille; for six, at Rouen; for seven or more, in Paris. At Dieppe, Lunéville, Nantes, Saint-Die, Bar-le-Duc, Bordeaux and Marseille, mayors published official appeals for a return to calm. Troops were called in to help the police and *gendarmerie* at Angers, Lunéville, Nantes, Saint-Dié, Rouen and Paris, and cavalry charges were made against the rioters. Damage to property was reported in 15 towns, mainly windows broken and shop fronts smashed, but at Angers, Marseille and several places in Lorraine shops were pillaged, while looting was only prevented at Bordeaux, Nantes and Chalon-sur-Saône through strenuous efforts by the police. In some cases, synagogues, rabbis' houses and other residences were attacked. Injuries were reported in 9 towns. Arrests were made in twenty towns, mainly for refusal to circulate, occasionally for *"rebellion"* and assaulting the police. Over 20 people were arrested at Dieppe, Angers, Nancy, Rouen, Nantes and Saint-Etienne; 39 at Lunéville; 61 at Lyon; 103 at Bordeaux; 108 in Marseille and over 200 in Paris.[25]

The histories that mention them suggest that the 1898 riots were a fairly spontaneous reaction to the publication of Zola's *"J'accuse"* in *L'Aurore* on 13 January and to the subsequent Zola trial. Reinach, for example, wrote: "In the week that followed Zola's letter . . . tumultuous demonstrations broke out nearly every day . . ."[26] And the chronology of the riots, backed up, by the administrative reports lends support to this thesis. The Prefect of the Côte-d'Or wrote on 29 January 1898: "Like most big towns, Dijon has experienced its demonstrations provoked by the campaign undertaken in favour of ex-Captain Dreyfus and above all by the intervention of M. Zola and by his attacks on the army". The police reported from Lunéville that "the agitation which is being made about the Dreyfus Affair, and Zola's letter, have stirred up a violent wave of antisemitism"; and from Charmes (Vosges) that "the proceedings of the Zola trial seem to have aroused the antisemitic demonstrations".[27] In Paris, as we have seen, continuous disturbances surrounded the Zola trial, and, describing the scene outside the Palais de Justice after sentence had been given, Martin du Gard made very clear how the revisionist campaign of L'Aurore triggered off a generalized antisemitic response: "Individuals with Jewish features were grabbed, surrounded and roughed up by delirious youths who danced round them, brandishing flaming torches, made from rolled-up copies of L'Aurore . . ."[28] Reports from all over France on public reaction to Zola's first sentence agreed that opinion had been exasperated by his intervention, and that it welcomed the verdict of the jury against him; they also testified to the enormous interest aroused by the Zola affair, which was reflected in increased newspaper sales. For example, the police reported from Béziers: "Interest in the Zola trial was enormous; nine out of ten people followed it, and a crowd, avid for news, waited impatiently every evening for the press telegrams to arrive"; while at Veynes (Hautes-Alpes), "an unprecedented sale of newspapers" was remarked.[29] In 9 of the 1898 riots, the shouting of anti-Zola slogans was reported, and at Alais on 23 January a Zola guy was paraded through the streets, while elsewhere the author was burnt in effigy.[30]

But if "J'accuse" and the Zola trial provided an occasion for the expression of outraged patriotic opinion, and brought to the surface certain primitive forms of ritual aggression, the reaction was only to a certain extent spontaneous. There were those to suggest what forms this expression might take and against whom the aggression should be directed. At Le Havre, Troyes, Charmes, Vannes, Saint-Dié, Nantes, Epinal, Reims, Lille, Bar-le Duc and Saint-Etienne, riots followed the appearance of antisemitic posters in the town. At Saint-Etienne, the posters read: "Imitate your brothers of Paris, Lyon, Marseille, Nantes, Toulouse . . . join with them in demonstrating against the underhand attacks being made on the Nation."[31] In at least five cases, riots followed antisemitic meetings or speeches: at Caen, a meeting organized by the Comité de Défense Religieuse et Sociale; in Toulouse, an anti-Dreyfusard meeting; in Poitiers, an antisemitic address by the editor of the Royalist newspaper, Le Réveil du Poitou; in Nevers, a speech by abbé Garnier; in Marseille, a speech by the deputy Hugues.[32] At Reims, riots occurred after an address given by Benoît Lévy at a meeting organized by the Ligue de l'Enseignement, an important anticlerical pressure-group. In at least eleven cases Catholic organizations were explicitly reported to be responsible for the disturbances, which confirms Reinach's view that "the demonstrations were organized by Catholic clubs", and that their ring-leaders were "monks or nobles".[33] From Moulins, the police reported, on 26 January, that "for some days now the militant members of the Catholic Club have been inciting the young people of the town to demonstrate against the Jews, so far without success". Of the demonstration at Alais, the Prefect reported that "these young people belong to the Royalist youth organization, and the younger ones to the schools of the religious orders". At Vannes, the posters inviting the population to demonstrate were put up by young "clericals"; at Lille by students of the Catholic Faculty. At Saint-Etienne, "the majority of the demonstrators were pupils or ex-pupils of certain establishments run by the religious orders, and the young clientèle of the Ligue Sociale Catholique, from where the posters emanated . . ." At Nîmes, the demonstrators were described as Royalist and Catholic. The troubles at Arras, Angers, Chalon-sur-Saône, as well as at Moulins and Lunéville, were laid at the door of the Catholic Club. From Rouen, the Prefect reported: "On the one hand, instructions and encouragement are received here from Paris; on the other hand, the movement appears to be directed by a certain number of people belonging to the militant clerical reactionary party . . ."; similarly, at Lunéville, "the clerical opposition" was said to be fomenting the troubles.[34]

Only in three cases were disturbances linked by the authorities to the intervention of a specific antisemitic organization. In Paris, the Ligue Antisémitique Française clearly stimulated the riots, and its militants were active in the streets.[35] At Marseille, the police reported an appeal by the League on 20 January, but this came on the fifth day of the disturbances, and they attributed little effect to it. Similarly, it was reported from Poitiers on 22 January that the League, "in collaboration with M.de Coursac, the reactionary candidate in the forthcoming General Elections and one of its most zealous members, was very actively trying to aggravate the antisemitic disturbances . . ."[36] But there are indications that antisemitic groups and organizations were active in many places before January 1898, and their activity cannot have been unconnected with the outbreak of the riots later, even if they did not directly instigate them through posters, the press, word of mouth or direct example. Antisemitic addresses had been given by the Marquis de Morès at Clermont-Ferrand and at Dijon in 1895, and Lille antisemites attended a mass in his memory in 1897.[37] An antisemitic group was reported at Saint-Etienne in May 1896, and a section of the Ligue Antisémitique Française at Bordeaux in March 1897. The League, the most violently-inclined antisemitic organization in France, had been founded in January 1897, and claimed to have correspondents in 52 departments in April 1898; and it seems that the riots of January and February 1898 in the provinces, as in the capital, owed something to its organization. The riots certainly seem to have given a boost to its membership, and by June 1898 provincial sections of the League were known to exist at Lille, Perpignan, Roanne, Montpellier, Lunéville, Rouen, Bordeaux, Poitiers, Toulouse, Grenoble, Marseille, Nancy, Nantes, Rennes, and probably Auxerre.[38] With the exception of Roanne, all these places experienced riots in January or February. Again, when police searches were made at the headquarters of Royalist and antisemitic organizations in September 1899, groups in 18 of the riot towns were thought important enough to raid.[39] The participation in the riots of anarchists was reported at Marseille, Dijon and Chalon-sur-Saône, but no initiatives were attributed to them.

The responsibility of the local press was invoked in a few reports. At Chalon-sur-Saône, two local papers were said to have been the instigators of the riots, along with the Catholic Club. Similarly, at Rouen, the leading role in inspiring the troubles was attributed to the editor of *Le Patriote de Normandie*, and, at Nantes, the demonstrations were announced in the Royalist *L'Espérance du Peuple*. Although not saddled with responsibility elsewhere, the role of the press must have been considerable in most places. It is known that Poitiers, Nantes, Perpignan, Moulins, Lyon and Saint-Dié had a local antisemitic press before the riots, and the provincial circulation of *La Libre Parole* and *La Croix*, the main national antisemitic newspapers, was important. In addition, by 1895 *La Croix* had over 80 provincial editions.[40] At Agen, Lille, Lyon and Perpignan demonstrations took place against local newspapers hostile to antisemitism. All in all, the riots seem to have been deliberately provoked by political or semi-political groups in more cases than not, though such provocation would obviously not have succeeded, nor would demonstrations have escalated into large-scale riots, without a large measure of active support.[41] Some initiative came from Paris, and there seems to have been a trend for smaller centres to imitate larger ones, spontaneously or not, but, within this context, the troubles seem, more often than not, to have had local promptings. Events in Paris provided the occasion for the riots, but they were a function of local economic, social and political circumstances.

So the question of the political inspiration behind the 1898 riots leads to that of their social complexion. The administrative reports are far from comprehensive on this subject, but they give a rough picture of the age, class and professions of demonstrators, and occasionally a more precise breakdown of those arrested. In 23 cases, the demonstrators were mainly students. In ten or so more, reference is simply made to young people, often in their teens. This was also the impression of Reinach, who referred to "gangs of youths, students or self-styled students . . ."[42] As we have seen, eight involved young conscripts. As in this case, a ritual element may have been present, gang warfare between different groups of students, or between students and other youths.[43] Evidence of more general participation is given for 16 towns. At Marseille, the riots were set off by students, who "were joined in great numbers by the usual trouble-makers", and, later, rioters were said to belong to "all classes of society".[44] This accords with Reinach's view that the Marseille rioters were made up of "the vagrant population of the port . . . led by bright young men . . ."[45] Those arrested on 17 January are listed as three labourers, two clerks, two plumbers, two cooks, two artisans, a packer and a student. At Troyes, the thirty or so demonstrators were clerks and shop-assistants. At Dijon, 400 workers and white-collar workers were involved in the disturbances of 26 January, and, according to the Prefect, most of the population gave them their tacit support. At Sedan, demonstrators were young people of "the working class", according to a report by the *gendarmerie*.[46] At Bordeaux, clerks and artisans figured among those arrested, and the Prefect reported that no students took part in the disturbances on 18 January. According to the Agence Havas, rioters at Rouen included workers, clerks and students. At Saint-Dié and Ligny, workers were among the rioters, but at Nancy and Cette student demonstrators' hopes that workers would join them were disappointed. According to a press telegram, the Nantes disturbances of 18 January were the work of criminal elements, but Reinach reported that port workers and students were involved.[47] The only complete breakdown of those arrested, outside Paris, is that for Lyon, where of 60 arrested, 25 were students, 7 white-collar workers *(employés de commerce)*, 4 without profession, 1 a travelling salesman, 1 an engraver, 2 working jewellers, 1 a draughtsman, 1 a confectioner, 1 a chemist, 1 a jeweller, 1 a mechanic, 1 a cabinet-maker, 2 dyers, 1 a plasterer, 1 a packing-case manufacturer, 1 a grocer, 1 an architect, 1 a domestic servant, 1 a waiter, 1 a shop assistant, 1 a butcher's assistant and 1 a textile finisher.[48] In Paris, "the disturbances of 18 and 19 January seem to have been relatively unimportant, being localized in the Latin Quarter, and having little following among workers",[49] but on 15 January students had been joined by "butcher boys, pastrycooks and young vagabonds" and also by "ordinary people sitting at cafés".[50] The breakdown of the 83 arrested in Paris between 14 and 18 January gives 29 students or schoolboys, 5 without profession, 5 clerks, 4 printing workers, 4 draughtsmen, 2 butcher's assistants, 3 waiters, 2 cooks, 2 servants, 1 dentist, 2 sculptors, 1 artist, 1 actor, 1 salesman, 3 shop assistants, 1 wine merchant, 1 watchmaker, 1 turner, 1 tailor, 1 pastrycook, 1 rubber worker, 1 gilder, 1 tapestry-weaver, 3 building workers, 1 housepainter, 1 glass-blower, 1 rentier, 1 barber, 1 labourer and 2 hawkers.[51] In nearly all cases reported students seem to have started the demonstrations; in about half, however, they were soon joined by young workers and white-collar workers, and by criminal elements. According to Reinach again: "Everywhere malefactors were involved, taking advantage of the upset to carry out their work."[52] But, as the Paris, Marseille, Bordeaux and Lyon reports indicate, in the big towns at least, the 1898 riots were not merely examples of youthful effervescence and hooliganism, but involved adult artisans, workers and shopkeepers, and even bourgeois. As the police reported from Lunéville on 24 January: "Even in the bourgeoisie and among Republicans of the first water, people are very worked up against the Jews."[53]

What was the nature of this antisemitism, and what prompted it, beyond the simple pretext afforded by the Dreyfus Affair? First, there is a fair correlation between the existence of a Jewish community in a town and the outbreak of an antisemitic riot. According to Marrus, the largest Jewish communities in France in the 1890s were in Paris, Marseille, Bordeaux, Nancy, Bayonne, Besançon, Lille and Reims, and Jewish population remained important in Lorraine and in the environs of Avignon.[54] Riots occurred in all these places in 1898, save Bayonne. The administrative reports confirm the impression that antisemitic behaviour here was a reaction to a Jewish presence. The Prefect of the Ardèche expressed some surprise at the disturbance in Tournon, because there were few Jews in the region. At Cette, the police did not take the demonstrations seriously, reporting: "Moreover, there are very few Jews here. Those there are are held in a certain esteem and keep up very cordial relations in all political circles." By contrast, in Lorraine, the authorities saw the existence of large Jewish communities as an obvious explanation of the antisemitic outbreaks and as a gauge of their gravity. Although at Sedan, the police reported that "there is . . . no animosity against the Jews here", the story was different at Saint-Dié, Bar-le-Duc, Epinal and Lunéville, where "it is undeniable that the vast majority of the population, ordinarily so peaceful and undemonstrative, was only too ready to lend a complaisant ear to the provocations of these ringleaders [the Catholic instigators of the disturbances] . . . The situation was rendered even more tense by the fact that the Jewish colony at Lunéville is very important and very wealthy."[55] This is confirmed by Reinach who noted: "All over Lorraine, at Lunéville, at Epinal, at Bar-le-Duc, in the smallest villages, Jews were jeered at, beaten up, and had mud thrown at them; they retorted by throwing stones . . ."[56] At Dijon, too, where there was also a Jewish community, the riots grew out of old hatreds: "Antisemitic prejudice exists in a non-violent, but latent state in the old society of Dijon, and also among the ordinary people and in the world of commerce."[57]

This correlation between antisemitic riots and Jewish presence is worth establishing, since it is a connection that some writers either assume or discount a priori. Byrnes, for example, is inclined to see little relation between antisemitism and real Jews in France around 1890, save in the East.[58] This is a problem that we shall return to, but the phenomenon of the 1898 riots does underline one of its crucial aspects. In general, it seems to be true that antisemitism in France was not prompted by real grievances against Jews, by the experience of coexistence; on the other hand, it was directed against real Jews. To put it crudely, Jews did not "cause" antisemitism, but they were its inevitable victims. So, the 1898 riots were often, as we have seen, expressions of patriotic sentiment, of support for the army and of opposition to Zola, but their main targets were Jews, and Jews were attacked in a material way. Sometimes demonstrators merely shouted: "Down with the Jews! Kill the Jews!"[59] Occasionally, Jews were physically assaulted. In eight cases, synagogues or rabbis' houses were attacked and damaged; and in twelve or more cases, demonstrations occurred outside the private houses of Jews, with threats and throwing of stones; for example on 11 February in Paris, "about a thousand people attacked the Dreyfus house on the Boulevard Sebastapol".[60] But by far the most frequent form of antisemitic demonstration in the first two months of 1898 was an attack on Jewish shops or businesses. In thirty towns these were the focus of the crowd's hostility. For example, at Saint-Malo, "the demonstrators concentrated their attention on the Cristal Palace store"; at Granville, the crowd gathered "outside the Belle Jardinière department store, owned by M. Cerf". At Ligny there was a demonstration outside the house of a Jewish draper. In many places shop fronts and windows were broken, and at Angers, Marseille and elsewhere, as we have seen, shops were pillaged. In most cases hostility was directed against big stores owned or supposed to be owned by Jews, but at Vincey (Vosges) a protest occurred against a more traditional form of Jewish economic activity: a group of young people demonstrated "on the occasion of an auction of land . . . on behalf of certain Jews from this locality, and in particular of M. Isidore Marx, a general agent"; Marx and his lawyer were assaulted by the crowd.[61]

Although shops are an obvious target for the most casual trouble-maker, the attacks on Jewish shops were not fortuitous; in many cases they seem to have been part of a long-sustained campaign against Jewish business and commerce, mounted by antisemitic organizations. In Paris, the campaign was ruthlessly led by the Ligue Antisémitique Française; a police agent reported on 14 January 1898 that the antisemites were preparing "a riot that will be much more serious than the last one . . . it will have one clear aim: the pillage of Jewish shops".[62] In December 1897, the police in Nantes had reported "Death to the Jews" slogans being stamped on advertisements put out by Jewish shops and businesses; and they reported on 25 January 1898:

> the business interests of Nantes intend to try to set up an antisemitic league. Several important traders in the town have been thinking along these lines for some time, believing that they could not compete with the Jews, given the very low tax assessment made on the latter, which they claim bears no relation to the wide range of goods that the Jews in practice sell. Their proposal has obtained a lot of support, and these people want to take advantage of current events and of the present widespread feeling of hostility towards the Jews to found in Nantes an association to defend their interests against the Jews, and to press their views on the authorities.

Jews were said, in addition, to be dishonest traders, making huge profits at the expense of consumers and "honest traders".[63] As early as 1896, Poitiers had such an association, a Ligue Antisémitique du Commerce Poitevin, to which 200 shopkeepers belonged, and which put out propaganda, addressed especially to "the ladies of Poitiers", and urging them: "For the honour and the salvation of France, buy nothing from the Jews."[64] The Prefect of the Marne, moreover, reported on 22 June 1896 that "for some time now, stickers have been appearing on walls [in Reims] every day, bearing these words: 'Never buy from a Jew. Keep France for the French. Drive out the Jews from France . . .' "[65]

At the Ecclesiastical Congress held at Reims in August 1896, similar, if more guarded, opinions were expressed, one delegate saying: "We know only too well about the merciless war waged on small traders by big department stores, those immense bazaars selling the produce of the whole world under one roof."[66] The Lyon Congress of Christian Democracy in 1897 passed a resolution denouncing the influence of "monopolistic department stores and big Jewish credit organizations".[67] At Epinal, the police reported in February 1898, "many traders and customers of the Catholic religion have felt obliged to boycott all Jewish establishments . . ."[68] In May 1897, at Bordeaux, 600 people attended a meeting at which Jules Guérin, leader of the Ligue Antisémitique Française, delivered an attack on Jewish business and monopolies.

A month later another antisemitic speaker called on the population of Montpellier to defend "local commerce against the Jewish system", a call that was echoed by leading articles in two local newspapers, one of which, *Le Réveil Commercial Industriel et Agricole,* called for a campaign of resistance against the spread of department stores and for a special tax on them.[69] Propaganda campaigns of a similar nature were reported from Nantes, Marseille, Dijon, Lille, Roubaix, Vesoul, Bar-le-Duc, Grenoble, Toulouse and Caen. At Caen, a poster, "Réflexions d'un petit commerçant caennais", claimed that, as a result of unfair competition from Jewish shops, small traders were being forced out of business; customers were upbraided for abandoning their local small shops, seduced by lower prices that were only obtained through fraudulent means and by holding down wages. In at least three departments in 1898, Directories of Jews *(Indicateurs des Juifs)* were circulating; these publications gave a full list of Jews in the department with addresses and professions, and provided the means, it was hoped, for an effective boycott of Jewish enterprises.[70] Police searches at Caen in August 1899 at the Groupe d'Action Française discovered stickers, with the familiar slogan: "For the honour and the salvation of France, buy nothing from the Jews."[71] As *Le Petit Phare* of Nantes commented in December 1898: "There seems to be a group of people . . . who have undertaken to elevate patriotism to the heights of 'the corner-shop question', and who make no attempt to conceal this."[72]

From the administrative reports and elsewhere, it is possible to begin to explain this phenomenon. First, there is considerable evidence, as we have seen, of a business recession in the winter of 1897–98. In Paris during February 1898 many reports came in of serious reductions in business and employment, particularly in the sensitive clothing and fashion trades. "Business interests are getting worried and impatient", it was reported on 17 February; "work in some trades, like fashions, has come to a halt"; and on the same day: "in Belleville, Ménilmontant, Charonne and Bagnolet, the domestic workers are seriously short of work. The entrepreneurs (who usually supply them with work) have none to give, claiming that the department stores and the mills have reduced, and in some cases completely suspended, their orders. This crisis affects particularly ready-made clothing for men, and thus shirt- and waistcoat-makers, and also shoe-makers." Another report, dated 23 February, and entitled "The present commercial situation in Paris" stated: "Since the Zola trial, the costume feathers trade has been in a state of crisis"; firms had little or no business: "Abroad people are exaggerating what is happening in France, and it is this which explains this stoppage in business transactions."[73] In the provinces, too, reports from thirteen towns, eight of which had riots, refer to some kind of commercial and business slump in the first two months of 1898, which most attributed to the commotion and uncertainty caused by the revisionist campaign. For example, the police reported on 24 February from Besançon: "Everyone is talking today of this unfortunate affair and the general opinion is that preoccupation with it should cease . . . so that business, which has suffered a lot since the start of the trial, may recover."

Reaction to the business crisis could take a directly nationalist and antisemitic turn, as at Nancy, where "businessmen and industrialists are complaining about the prolongation of the crisis which threatens to bring business to a halt. They are demanding that financial interests be protected against cosmopolitan speculators, and are calling for a vigorous national policy at home and abroad."[74] The antisemitic organizations tried hard to push opinion in this direction; and it is not surprising therefore to find those most exposed to economic and social pressures, grasping at "the Jewish plot"[75] as an explanation for their difficulties and their sufferings, and even taking the antisemites' promises of social justice at their face value. A perceptive police agent commented that, given "the clever way in which antisemitism has been presented", one could understand its appeal for the deprived and the discontented, and even "excuse such people for having thought that Drumont was a Socialist".[76] One can see, too, how they and others, particularly small traders, might vent their despair on the new big shops, with their arrogant displays of goods, for the department stores seem to have aroused a peculiar degree of hostility. The heroine of a novel, published in 1894, confessed: "when I saw so many of the old-fashioned shops closing . . . when I heard tell of such and such a trader going bankrupt . . . I boiled over with rage against these enormous shops that are crushing the tiny ones . . . and often, in the evening, saying my prayers, I shouted out to the good God what a good idea he would have if one night he swept them all away . . ."[77] This seems an authentic testimony and not an isolated one, of the kind of violent emotion that lay behind "the corner-shop question", a resurgence of the age-old hatred of the hoarder, the monopolist, though much more needs to be known about the business situation in Paris and the provinces in the 1890s, and particularly about the situation of retail trade, before such impressions can be definitively confirmed.

Another related factor, evoked by the police agent quoted above, which seems central to explaining the appeal of antisemitism and its development into violence in this period is the state of bewilderment in which large numbers of people found themselves. The orchestration of the riots by political organizations ran parallel with, and indeed depended on, a high degree of popular disorientation, which, as we have seen, was socio-economic as well as political and cultural. So the Prefect of the Seine-Inférieure, while reporting that the riots in Rouen were instigated by the local Right-wing press, reported also that many demonstrators "did not seem to know why they were demonstrating".[78] In circumstances of uncertainty and insecurity, irrational behaviour, rumours and panics were natural. The police reported, for example, from Epinal in March 1898 that the Zola affair had "sown trouble and panic among our people here in the East. Rumours of all kinds have been circulating, and it has even been affirmed that a war with Germany is imminent."[79] An antisemitic poster: "The Nation in Danger" ("La Patrie en Danger"), put up in twenty-five towns all over France, most of which had riots in January or February, caused considerable alarm in September 1898. At Laval, it occasioned "an enormous panic among the peasants in for the market", who thought there was a war, and 1,000 hectolitres of wheat were left unsold.[80]

A similar incident was reported from Delle on the Eastern frontier in February; the mayor reported to the police *commissaire:* "The peasants of the surrounding region, in town for the market, have asked me if it is true that there has been a revolution in Paris. Have you received news of this?"[81] *Le Peuple* of Lyon declared on 19 January 1898: "We are in an extremely disturbed situation. Days like this have not been seen since 1871."[82] As one commentator pointed out, the movements of January 1898 were the more disturbing and dangerous in that their aims and motives were uncertain and vague; such movements, even on the smallest scale were "not something to be ignored", wrote the editor of *L'Indépendant des Pyrénées-Orientales:*[83]

> It was thus, with the action of youths and apprentices, so much sung and joked about, that Boulangism began. One cannot deny that at the present time France is in such a state of nervousness and over-excitement that all such stupidities are to be feared . . . Nothing is so dangerous, so serious, as these popular movements that have no absolutely precise cause, and can thus produce the most diverse effects.

All of this serves as a reminder that the France of the 1890s, despite the spread of modern communications and of popular education, was not so far away, in other ways, from the France of the Grande Peur of 1789.[84]

According to the testimony of Léon Blum—writing in the perspective of the 1930s, it must be remembered—the French antisemitic movement during the Dreyfus Affair "was not an antisemitism of pogroms, of violent or bloody demonstrations . . ."[85] The evidence presented in this chapter does not altogether confirm this view. There were "violent or bloody demonstrations" in 1898 in about thirty French towns. If little serious damage to persons or property was actually done, the Jewish population was terrorized, and the public authorities, local and national, were extremely alarmed. The Minister of the Interior instructed all Prefects "to make concerted arrangements with the military authorities in order to maintain order",[86] and after mid-January 1898 even minor manifestations of antisemitic sentiment were reported and repressed. For all too often a seemingly minor demonstration of high spirits by "our young people"[87] had developed into an outbreak of violent rioting, involving artisans, shopworkers and bourgeois, and lasting several days. Moreover, in Algeria, closely linked at that time to France, there were pogroms, on a scale unknown in the metropolitan territory. Trouble began in Algiers on 18 January 1898 with students burning Zola in effigy. The demonstration escalated, and, for several days, from 20 to 25 January, an antisemitic mob rampaged in the city, encouraged by the local authorities, and tolerated by the military. Whole streets of shops in the Jewish quarter were sacked, looted and burned. In all, 158 shops were destroyed in this way. At least 6 Jews were assaulted by the crowd, 2 with fatal results; 9 rioters, 47 police and an unknown, but probably large, number of Jews were seriously injured; and 1 demonstrator was killed. Over 500 arrests were ultimately made. Riots on a lesser scale occurred elsewhere in the colony, at Mustapha, Mostaganem, Saint-Eugène, La Maison Carré, Boufarik, Blida, Sétif, and at Constantine

and Oran, where the synagogues were desecrated.[88] These incidents, moreover, were only the most serious in a series of demonstrations against Jews that
recurred in Algeria over a period of years. For example, the campaign against
Jewish shops reached an intensity unknown in France during the "reign" of
Max Régis as mayor of Algiers. Jewish shopkeepers were discriminated against
in by-laws, and vigilante brigades were organized to photograph and denounce
non-Jews who patronized Jewish shops.[89] We will examine the context of this
virulent antisemitism in a later chapter,[90] but it may be emphasized here that
although the pogrom of Algiers had no real counterpart in France itself, it
served as a powerful example there.

The riots of 1898, then, are an indication of the very real strength of
antisemitism in France, and show that large numbers of people were prepared
to make the step from holding antisemitic opinions to taking antisemitic
action. The outbreaks were frequently provoked by political or semi-political
groups, clerical, Royalist, or more purely antisemitic, but this is of less significance than the fact that such initiatives evoked a positive response on a fairly
wide scale. In the big cities, in particular, and in smaller places in the East,[91]
the riots seem to have had important support, active and passive, from members of all classes. Normally peaceful towns, like Bar-le-Duc, described in 1900
as "a placid little city, white and clean, and as bourgeois as can be",[92] wit-
nessed ugly scenes of disorder and mob hysteria. This willingness to participate
in or to condone collective violence can be explained, we have suggested, by
the circumstances of political uncertainty and economic depression of the
years 1897 and 1898. But much further light can be cast on the motivation
of antisemitism at this time and on its social complexion by analysis of the
nation-wide Henry Subscription, which forms the subject of the next chapter.

NOTES

1 For Reinach, see various references below; for Pierrard, see *Juifs et catholiques
   français*, pp. 94–102. Sorlin, *"La Croix" et les Juifs*, p. 221, provides a map, but
   it is unfortunately incomplete.
2 Seignobos, *L'Evolution de la IIIe République*, p. 196.
3 Zévaès, *L'Affaire Dreyfus*, pp. 109–10.
4 Jacques Kayser, *L'Affaire Dreyfus* (Paris, 1946), pp. 142–44.
5 Chastenet, *La République triomphante*, p. 119.
6 Miquel, *L'Affaire Dreyfus*, pp. 50–1. Incidentally, there is no mention of a disturbance in Aix-en-Provence in the police reports.
7 Dardenne, *Godefroy Cavaignac*, pp. 483–86.
8 Arendt, *The Origins of Totalitarianism*, pp. 107 and 111.
9 Bloch, *Lévy*, pp. 76 and 39–58.
10 Isaac, *Expériences de ma vie*, I, p. 131. The police reports mention no riots against
   Protestants, but there were minor overt expressions of anti-Protestantism; see
   chapter II, p. 83 and n. 198 above; and chapter XII, pp. 415–16 below.
11 Jean Drault, *Drumont, La France juive et La Libre Parole* (Paris, 1935), p. 241.
12 Mainly AN F[7] 12460, F[7] 12461, F[7] 12467 and F[7] 12474, but other sources have
   been used as indicated.
13 See Cobb, *The Police and the People*, p. 145.
14 Zosa Szajkowski, "French Jews during the Revolution of 1830 and the July Monar-

chy", *Historia Judaica*, 22 (1961), pp. 116–20; Szajkowski, *Jews and the French Revolutions of 1789, 1830 and 1848* (New York, 1970), pp. xxix–xxx; Bernhard Blumenkranz, ed., *Histoire des Juifs en France* (Toulouse, 1972), pp. 279 and 284–5.

15 See M. Ginsburger, "Les Troubles contre les Juifs d'Alsace en 1848", *Revue des Etudes Juives*, 62 (1912), pp. 110–11; Szajkowski, *Jews and the French Revolutions*, pp. xxx and 924; Blumenkranz, ed., op. cit., p. 319; Drumont, *La France juive*, I, p. 367.

16 At Agen (Lot-et-Garonne); Alais (Gard); Angers (Maine-et-Loire); Angoulême (Charente); Arras (Pas-de-Calais); Auxerre (Yonne); Avignon (Vaucluse); Bar-le-Duc (Meuse); Belfort; Besançon (Doubs); Béziers (Hérault); Bordeaux (Gironde); Caen (Calvados); Cette (Hérault); Chalon-sur-Saône (Saône-et-Loire); Charmes (Vosges); Cherbourg (Manche); Clermont-Ferrand (Puy-de-Dôme); Dieppe (Seine-Inférieure); Dijon (Côte-d'Or); Epernay (Marne); Epinal (Vosges); Granville (Manche); Grenoble (Isère); Le Havre (Seine-Inférieure); Ligny (Meuse); Lille (Nord); Limoges (Haute-Vienne); Lunéville (Meurthe-et-Moselle); Lyon (Rhône); Marmande (Lot-et-Garonne); Marseille (Bouches-du-Rhône); Montbéliard (Doubs); Montluçon (Allier); Montmorillon (Vienne); Montpellier (Hérault); Moulins (Allier); Nancy (Meurthe-et-Moselle); Nantes (Loire-Inférieure); Nevers (Nièvre); Nîmes (Gard); Niort (Deux-Sèvres); Orléans (Loiret); Paris (Seine); Périgueux (Dordogne); Perpignan (Pyrénées-Orientales); Poitiers (Vienne); Privas (Ardèche); Reims (Marne); Rennes (Ille-et-Vilaine); Rodez (Aveyron); Rouen (Seine-Inférieure); Saint-Brieuc (Côtes-du-Nord); Saint-Dié (Vosges); Saint-Etienne (Loire); Saint-Jean-de-Maurienne (Savoie); Saint-Malo (Ille-et-Vilaine); Sedan (Ardennes); Senones (Vosges); Sens (Yonne); Tarbes (Hautes-Pyrénées); Toulouse (Haute-Garonne); Tournon (Ardèche); Tours (Indre-et-Loire); Troyes (Aube); Valence (Drôme); Vannes (Morbihan); Versailles (Seine-et-Oise); and Vincey (Vosges). See Map 7.

17 These occurred in Avignon, Paris and various places in Lorraine in March and April 1898; at Vesoul (Haute-Saône) in August 1898; at Grenoble in January 1899 on the occasion of the Régis trial there; at Versailles and Epinal in June 1899; and at Rennes in September 1899, after the announcement of the verdict. See Report, Commissaire spécial, Vesoul, 15 August 1898. AN F⁷ 12461; Report, Commissaire central, Grenoble, 12 January 1899. AN F⁷ 12459; Telegrams, Prefects, Vosges and Seine-et-Oise, 25 June 1899. AN F⁷ 12458; Police Report, Rennes, 11 September 1899. AN F⁷ 12923; and Reinach, *Histoire de l'Affaire Dreyfus*, III, p. 539.

18 *Le Journal des Débats* reported a crowd of 2,000–3,000 on this occasion and 120 arrests; other papers reported a much higher number of demonstrators. Prefects and police occasionally accused the press of exaggeration here, as more generally in reporting on reactions to the Affair. As far as the riots are concerned, this seems to have applied only to the antisemitic press, which had an interest in inflating their importance. The fact that the police and other officials were on their guard against exaggeration makes their assessment of the importance of the riots the more trustworthy.

19 See pp. 119–20 below.

20 For a full comparison with maps of opinion during the Affair, and of other expressions of antisemitism, see chapter XVII, pp. 655 and ff. below.

21 Eight riots occurred along the PLM railway line, which may be significant.

22 This area was chosen for a big recruiting campaign by the Ligue Antisémitique Française later in 1898. Police report, 30 August 1898. AN F⁷ 12460.

23 Demonstrations by conscripts were usual on the occasion of the *"tirage"*; see, for example, Report, Prefect, Drôme, 31 January 1898. AN F⁷ 12467; and Vallès, "Prends ton sac!", *L'Evénement*, 1 March 1866, in Jules Vallès, *Oeuvres complètes, La Rue* (Paris, 1969), pp. 110–11.

24 Various reports. AN F⁷ 12474.
25 In addition to police and other reports cited above, see Reinach, op. cit., III, pp. 275–6.
26 Ibid., III, p. 275; also p. 244.
27 Reports, Prefect, Côte-d'Or, 29 January 1898; Commissaire spécial, Lunéville, 24 January 1898; and Commissaire spécial, Charmes, 19 February 1898. AN F⁷ 12467.
28 Martin du Gard, *Jean Barois*, pp. 278–80; see also Guillemin, *Zola légende et vérité*, pp. 161–2.
29 Reports, Commissaire spécial, Béziers, 24 February 1898; and Commissaire spécial, Veynes, 28 February 1898. AN F⁷ 12474.
30 The parading and/or burning of Dreyfus and Zola guys, reported from several places, was often an adaptation of traditional customs as at Saint-Jean-de-Maurienne, where the customary burning of the guy assumed a topical antisemitic form; Report, Commissaire spécial, 23 February 1898. AN F⁷ 12461. At Bar-le-Duc, a guy representing the local rabbi was carried through the streets, burned, and the remains thrown in the river Ornain; see Bournand, *Les Juifs et nos contemporains*, pp. 136–7.
31 Report, Commissaire spécial, Saint-Etienne, 22 January 1898. AN F⁷ 12467.
32 Was this the Vicomte d'Hugues, conservative deputy for the Basses-Alpes (1893–8), or, as seems more likely, Clovis Hugues, the poet, Socialist, ex-Boulangist, and deputy for Marseille and then Paris (1881–9 and 1893–1906), of whose antisemitism at this time we have other evidence; see chapter XI, p. 336 below.
33 Reinach, op. cit., III, pp. 244 and 274.
34 Reports, Commissaire spécial, Moulins, 26 January 1898; Prefect, Gard, 24 January 1898; Prefect, Loire, 25 January 1898; Prefect, Seine-Inférieure, 21 January 1898; and Commissaire spécial, Lunéville, 24 January 1898. AN F⁷ 12467.
35 See, for example, Police reports, 18 February 1898. AN F⁷ 12474.
36 Report, Prefect, Vienne, 22 January 1898. AN F⁷ 12467.
37 Morès was one of the first important antisemitic activists in France; see Byrnes, *Antisemitism in Modern France*, pp. 225–50; and chapter V, pp. 172–3 below.
38 See various reports. AN F⁷ 12459; and chapter VI, pp. 183–4, 192 below.
39 See various reports. AN F⁷ 12462, "Mouvement antisémite".
40 See various reports, AN F⁷ 12467; Boussel, *L'Affaire Dreyfus et la presse*, pp. 91–2; Sorlin, *"La Croix" et les Juifs*, pp. 25–55; Pierrard, op. cit., pp. 92–102; and J.-M. Mayeur, "Les Congrès nationaux de la 'Démocratie Chrétienne' à Lyon (1896–1897–1898)", *Revue d'Histoire Moderne et Contemporaine*, 9 (1962), pp. 173–5.
41 This lends some support to Ginsberg's thesis that: "Anti-Jewish risings are in general deliberately planned and organized and are in no sense 'spontaneous'." [Morris Ginsberg, "Antisemitism" (1943), *Essays in Sociology and Social Philosophy* (Harmondsworth, 1968), p. 202]; but suggests that such a thesis plays down too much the 'spontaneous' element, or, at least, the need for active participation by large numbers of people, who are not simply being forced or manipulated. Writing of collective violence in general, Terry Ann Knopf seems to err in the other direction [Knopf, "Sniping—a new pattern of violence?" (1969), in Stanley Cohen and Jock Young, *The Manufacture of News: Deviance, Social Problems and the Mass Media* (London, 1973), pp. 210–25]; though the warning that observers and the media can overstructure violent events, finding patterns where none exist, or existed, is to be heeded.
42 Reinach, op. cit., III, p. 244.
43 Zola referred in 1882 to "la vieille haine qui mettait souvent aux prises la jeunesse des écoles et les employés de commerce . . ." in Paris. Emile Zola, *Au Bonheur des Dames* (1882) (Paris, 1968), p. 170.
44 Report, Commissaire spécial, Marseille, 18 January 1898. AN F⁷ 12467.
45 Reinach, op. cit. III, p. 276.
46 Report, Gendarmerie, Sedan, 26 January 1898. AN F⁷ 12467.

47 Reinach, op. cit., III, p. 275.
48 See Reports, Prefect, Rhône, 19 and 20 January 1898. AN F⁷ 12467.
49 Report, Prefect of Police, 19 January 1898. AN F⁷ 12467.
50 Report, Commissaire de police, chef de la 3e Brigade, Paris, 15 January 1898. APP Ba 1043.
51 Report on arrests, 14–18 January 1898. Ibid.
52 Reinach, op. cit., III, p. 276.
53 Report, Commissaire spécial, Lunéville, 24 January 1898. AN F⁷ 12467.
54 Marrus, *The Politics of Assimilation*, pp. 31–2; see also Zosa Szajkowski, "The Growth of the Jewish Population of France", *Jewish Social Studies*, 8 (1946), pp. 179–96 and 297–318.
55 Reports, Commissaires spéciaux, Cette, 25 January; Sedan, 26 January; and Lunéville, 24 January 1898. AN F⁷ 12467.
56 Reinach, op. cit., III, p. 276.
57 Report, Prefect, Côte-d'Or, 29 January 1898. AN F⁷ 12467.
58 Byrnes, op. cit., pp. 252–61.
59 "A bas les Juifs!"; "Conspuez les Juifs!"; "Mort aux Juifs!"
60 Police telegram, cit. Guillemin, *Zola légende et vérité*, p. 161.
61 Reports, Gendarmerie, Saint-Malo, 24 January 1898; Commissaire spécial, Granville, 25 January 1898; Commissaire spécial, Charmes, 10 February 1898. AN F⁷ 12467.
62 Police report, 14 January 1898. APP Ba 1043.
63 Reports, Commissaire spécial, Nantes, 22 December 1897, and 25 January 1898. AN F⁷ 12460.
64 AN F⁷ 12461.
65 Report, Prefect, Marne, 22 June 1896. AN F⁷ 12460.
66 Cit. René Rémond, *Les Deux Congrès écclésiastiques de Reims et de Bourges 1896–1900: Un témoignage sur l'Eglise de France* (Paris, 1964), p. 72.
67 Mayeur, "Les Congrès nationaux", p. 204; Maurice Montuclard, *Conscience religieuse et démocratie: La deuxième démocratie chrétienne en France 1891–1902* (Paris, 1965), p. 125.
68 Report, Commissaire spécial, Epinal, 19 February 1898. AN F⁷ 12474.
69 Report, Commissaire spécial, Montpellier, 26 January 1898. AN F⁷ 12460.
70 Poster, 24 June 1899, and other items. AN F⁷ 12463; see also chapter X, p. 283 below.
71 Police report, August 1899. AN F⁷ 12462.
72 See Report, Commissaire spécial, Nantes, 13 December 1898. AN F⁷ 12460.
73 Administrative report, 17 February 1898; Reports, Police agent, Paris, 17 February 1898; and Police agent, 23 February 1898, "La Situation actuelle du commerce à Paris". AN F⁷ 12474.
74 Reports, Commissaires spéciaux, Besançon, 24 February; and Nancy, 27 February 1898. AN F⁷ 12474.
75 A pamphlet entitled *Le Complôt juif* was distributed by *La Croix* in April 1898 in several towns in different parts of the country; see AN F⁷ 12463. For further discussion of the "Jewish conspiracy" idea, see chapter XII, pp. 409 and ff. below.
76 Report, Police agent, no date, "Boulangisme et Antisémitisme". AN F⁷ 12459. For discussion of the "socialism" of Drumont and other antisemites, see chapter XI.
77 Gyp, *Le Mariage de Chiffon* (1894) (Paris, no date—Nelson edition), p 110.
78 Report, Prefect, Seine-Inférieure, 20 January 1898. AN F⁷ 12467.
79 Report, Commissaire spécial, Epinal, 2 March 1898. AN F⁷ 12474.
80 Report, Police, Laval (Mayenne), 17 September 1898. AN F⁷ 12463.
81 Report, Commissaire spécial, Delle (Belfort), 23 February 1898. AN F⁷ 12474.
82 *Le Peuple*, 19 January 1898.
83 *L'Indépendant des Pyrénées-Orientales*, 20 January 1898.
84 On this wide-scale collective panic, see Georges Lefebvre, *La Grande Peur de 1789* (Paris, 1932). For a modern resurgence of the same kind of phenomenon, with

specifically antisemitic connotations, see Morin *et al.*, *La Rumeur d'Orléans.*
85 Blum, *Souvenirs sur l'Affaire*, pp. 62–3.
86 Circular, Minister of the Interior to prefects, 22 January 1898. AN F[7] 12467.
87 The expression was used by a *Le Temps* correspondent of the demonstrations at Rodez. Report, 27 January 1898. AN F[7] 12460.
88 See Report, Procureur-Général, Algiers, 11 February 1898, and other reports. AN F[80] 1688; also Reinach, op. cit., III, pp. 277–82 and 539–40; Pierrard, op. cit., pp. 144–5; L'Hermite, *L'Anti-Pape, Drumont-Démon* (Issoudun, 1899), pp. xx–xxi. There were also riots in March 1898 at Tunis, where antisemitism was, however, in general less virulent; see Pierre Soumille, "L'Idée de Race chez les Européens de Tunisie dans les années 1890–1910", Paper given at Colloque sur l'Idée de Race dans la pensée politique française, Aix and Marseille, March 1975, pp. 3–4.
89 See Dossier, "Vexations municipales contre les Juifs, 1898–9". AN F[80] 1688.
90 See chapter IX, pp. 230–4 below.
91 In addition to evidence already cited, see Reports, Commissaires spéciaux, Senones, 9 February 1898. AN F[7] 12467; and Vesoul, 15 August 1898. AN F[7] 12461.
92 Ardouin-Dumazet, *Voyage en France, 21e série, Haute-Champagne—Basse-Lorraine* (Paris and Nancy, 1900), pp. 258–9.

CHAPTER IV
THE HENRY SUBSCRIPTION 1898–9

O N 31 AUGUST 1898 LIEUTENANT-COLONEL HENRY, DETAINED IN THE
Mont-Valérien prison, on suspicion of having fabricated evidence to incrimi-
nate Dreyfus, cut his throat with a razor. His suicide was the sensational
prelude to the decision of the Cour de Cassation in October to accept an
appeal for the revision of the Dreyfus Case. In November and December
1898, Joseph Reinach, France's most prominent Jewish politician, suggested,
in a series of articles in *Le Siècle,* that Henry had been not only a forger but
also an accomplice in treason of Esterhazy. Henry's widow protested to Reinach about these allegations and threatened to sue him for libel. On 14
December 1898, *La Libre Parole,* the main antisemitic daily in France,
opened a public subscription to pay the costs of her case. The balcony of the
newspaper's offices in Paris carried a banner which read: "For the widow and
the orphan of Colonel Henry against the Jew Reinach".[1] The subscription
brought in 131,000 francs before it closed on 15 January 1899. The subscription list, which the newspaper published, provides a unique sample of antisemitic and anti-Dreyfusard opinion. "In the history of antisemitism", wrote
Raphaël Viau, who worked on the editorial staff of *La Libre Parole,* "the 'red
lists', as the Dreyfusards have called them, remain a document that paints far
better than any simple account, the state of mind of the 'opposition' of that
time . . ."[2] 25,000 subscriptions were received.[3] About half the subscribers
indicated their place of residence; about half gave their professions; while a
large number sent messages with their donations. This allows one to undertake
a quantitative as well as qualitative analysis of the antisemitic attitudes which
they expressed along geographical, socio-professional and socio-psychological
lines.[4]

The interpretation of the subscription list raises again the problem of
spontaneity. How far can it be taken as a genuine expression of popular
attitudes? How far was it a simple propaganda exercise on the part of *La
Libre Parole?* Here the way in which subscriptions were organized is impor-

tant. Most entries were from individuals, usually but not always anonymous; sometimes they came from couples or families. A good number, however, were sent in the name of groups. These were sometimes *ad hoc* groupings, for example: "Collection among patriotic clerks"; or "Collection taken among the true Frenchmen of Cogolin (Var)".[5] Occasionally loose professional groupings contributed, for example: "A workshop of seamstresses at Saumur . . ."; or "A group of servants from the *entresol* of the rue Saint-Dominique [i.e. the Ministry of War]".[6] More rare were contributions from formal professional groups, such as "Collection taken by the Union of watchmakers and jewellers of Agen at the banquet of Saint Eloi".[7] Contributions from political groups were more common, but not numerically very important, for example: "a meeting of the Republican Club of Fraize (Vosges) . . ."; or "Union Nationale, Roanne".[8] In all, therefore, the degree of organization of the subscription list by political or other formal groups seems to have been small, while the intervention of informal groupings is itself a sign of collective "spontaneity", affirming the existence of a social as well as an individual or family dimension to popular antisemitism.[9] Here a more decisive "distorting" or mediating factor must be discussed. The subscription list may be a reflection of popular attitudes, but these attitudes were channelled through the columns of a Parisian daily. Subscribers were thus inevitably people who read and who wrote to newspapers; they tended to be urban and educated, therefore, rather than rural and uneducated. Though they were not necessarily regular readers of *La Libre Parole*—only a small proportion actually declared that they were—their messages must to some extent have echoed the paper's opinions and style of expression.[10] But this is a particular illustration of the general problem of the relationship of "opinion" and press, which we discussed in an earlier chapter. The latter impinged on the former, but did not completely reflect it or create it. Thus the state of symbiosis between subscriber and newspaper does not simply call into question the value of the subscription list as an expression of "spontaneous" opinion. It accurately reflects what was a fundamental characteristic of antisemitism, and of other sets of attitudes, in this period. Antisemitism was becoming more structured, and found its most developed expression in the press and in books, which were the agents of the transformation of scattered popular attitudes into a more coherent body of ideas. The subscription list illustrates a significant stage in this process, and is valuable as such. It should be pointed out, moreover, that a significant gap still remained between antisemitic ideology, as expressed in the press and in books, and the more directly "popular" expression of opinion in the subscription list, for the latter was both less explicitly coherent and its tone was often considerably more extreme than that of *La Libre Parole*'s editorial and news copy.

It might be asked also to what extent the subscription list was primarily an expression of antisemitism, rather than of support for the army and for the anti-Dreyfusard cause in general. We have seen that these causes necessarily had antisemitic implications. Moreover, the sponsorship of the subscription, the way in which the appeal was framed "against the Jew Reinach", and the content of subscribers' messages, as we shall see, leave little doubt that it was mainly an expression of antisemitism. But it was not exclusively so. This in effect represents its essential value for the student of antisemitism, for it shows how antisemitism was part of a wider set of values and attitudes, and acted as the focus for a variety of discontents.

I

The subscription list provides an indication of the geographical incidence of antisemitism in France to set beside those obtained from the examination of other phenomena: reactions to the Affair, the 1898 riots, and so on.[11] This is not only of interest in its own right, but it points the way towards wider sociological explanations. Of the total number of subscribers, 44.5% gave place or department of residence. Including those who gave only general region of residence or origin, the geographical location of 48.5% of subscribers is known. Table I provides a breakdown of the distribution of subscribers by size of place of residence, compared with the distribution of France's total population in the categories of agglomeration chosen.

The categories chosen here are somewhat arbitrary, but the conclusion emerges clearly. There was a high incidence of subscribers, and thus of overt and articulate antisemites, in urban centres, large and medium-size, and a low incidence in rural areas. This corroborates the expected bias of the sample. Antisemitism of the kind portrayed in the subscription list was an urban phenomenon, though not especially characteristic of big cities. It was not, with rare exceptions a rural phenomenon, to be associated with "backwardness", illiteracy and lack of education.[12]

The distribution of subscribers by department yields similar, but more detailed, results, if it is compared also with the distribution of total population by department. In Table II, illustrated by Map 8, departments are listed first in order of total population, and then in order of number of subscribers, noting the discrepancy, if any, in units of 10 places.

Fifteen departments occupy the same position on both lists. A further 30 show a discrepancy of plus or minus 1, but, given the crudity of the device

TABLE I: Henry Subscription—subscribers by place of residence

	Distribution of subscribers(%)	Distribution of total population in 1901(%)[13]
Cities of over 50,000 inhabitants	42	17.5
Towns and cities of 5,000 to 50,000 inhabitants	46	18
Towns, villages, etc. of under 5,000 inhabitants	12	64.5

TABLE II: Henry Subscription—subscribers by department

Departments listed in order of population[14] in thousands (1886)	Departments in order of number of subscribers	Discrepancy in units of 10 places, plus or minus
1 Seine 2961	1	
2 Nord 1670	2	
3 Pas de Calais 854	22	−2
4 Seine-Inférieure 833	10	+1
5 Gironde 776	9	
6 Rhône 773	7	
7 Finistère 708	26	−2
8 Loire-Inférieure 643	29	−2
9 Côtes-du-Nord 628	59	−5
10 Saône-et-Loire 626	15	
11 Ille-et-Vilaine 621	16	
12 Seine-et-Oise 618	5	+1
13 Bouches-du-Rhône 605	3	+1
14 Loire 603	21	−1
15 Isère 582	47	−3
16 Puy-de-Dôme 570	50	−3
17 Aisne 556	35	−2
18 Somme 549	36	−2
19 Morbihan 535	38	−2
20 Maine-et-Loire 528	25	
21 Manche 521	27	+1
22 Dordogne 492	28	+1
23 Haute-Garonne 481	33	−1
24 Charente-Inférieure 463	52	−3
25 Hérault 439	32	−1
26 Calvados 437	14	+1
27 Vendée 435	57	−3
28 Basses-Pyrénées 433	46	−2
29 Meurthe-et-Moselle 432	8	+2
30 Marne 429	19	+1
31 Sarthe 426	24	+1
32 Allier 425	49	−2
33 Gard 417	30	
34 Aveyron 416	69	−3
35 Vosges 413	18	+2
36 Oise 403	56	−2
37 Côte d'Or 381	12	+2
38 Ardèche 375	76	−4
39 Loiret 374	13	+3
40 Orne 367	54	−1
41 Charente 366	48	−1
42 Ain 364	70	−3
43 Haute-Vienne 363	53	−1
44 Eure 359	55	−1
45 Tarn 359	75	−3

46	Yonne 355	62	−2
47	Cher 355	68	−2
48	Seine-et-Marne 355	31	+2
49	Deux-Sèvres 354	72	−2
50	Nièvre 348	66	−2
51	Vienne 343	6	+4
52	Indre-et-Loire 341	45	+1
53	Mayenne 340	40	+1
54	Ardennes 333	41	+1
55	Aude 332	61	−1
56	Corrèze 326	80	−2
57	Haute-Loire 320	85	−3
58	Drôme 315	4	+5
59	Doubs 311	42	+2
60	Lot-et-Garonne 307	51	+1
61	Landes 302	77	−1
62	Indre 296	43	+2
63	Meuse 291	17	+5
64	Haute-Saône 291	39	+2
65	Creuse 285	79	−1
66	Eure-et-Loir 284	63	
67	Var 284	11	+6
68	Jura 281	73	
69	Loir-et-Cher 279	65	
70	Corse 278	60	+1
71	Haute-Savoie 275	74	
72	Gers 274	86	−1
73	Lot 272	87	−1
74	Savoie 267	44	+3
75	Aube 257	64	+1
76	Haute-Marne 248	82	−1
77	Vaucluse 242	23	+5
78	Cantal 242	83	
79	Alpes-Maritimes 238	23	+6
80	Ariège 238	84	
81	Hautes-Pyrénées 235	67	+1
82	Tarn-et-Garonne 214	71	+1
83	Pyrénées-Orientales 211	58	+2
84	Lozère 141	81	
85	Basses-Alpes 129	34	+5
86	Hautes-Alpes 123	78	+1
87	Belfort (Territoire) 80	37	+5

being used, these may also be regarded as at par. Twenty-four departments have minus scores of 2 or more; and 18 departments have plus scores of 2 or more. These scores can be taken as indicators of a low and of a high incidence of antisemitism, respectively.

With the exception of 4 relatively industrialized departments of the North (Pas-de-Calais, Aisne, Somme and Oise), and 3 other departments, remote but with some industry (Loire-Inférieure, Allier and Tarn), the 24 departments with high minus scores are geographically remote, often mountain, rural departments of both high and low population. This becomes particularly clear, if those with scores of minus 3 or less are isolated (Isère, Puy-de-Dôme, Charente-Inférieure, Vendée, Aveyron, Ain, Tarn, Haute-Loire, all with minus 3; Ardèche with minus 4; and Côtes-du-Nord with minus 5). This confirms the finding from Table I. Of particular interest here is the low incidence of subscriptions from Brittany and the West. Here the predominance of Right-wing political attitudes[15] and the high incidence of religious observance,[16] both often associated with antisemitism, might have led one to expect a high incidence. The low incidence is probably to be explained mainly by the fact that literate expressions of antisemitism, of the kind afforded by the subscription list, would be unlikely even among the urban populations of these largely "backward" and rural departments. It does not, of course, mean that other expressions and forms of antisemitism were absent, at least in the towns, as we have seen in considering the 1898 riots. The Right-wing electoral stance of Breton and other departments of the West and South-West was still very much the reflection of a hierarchical social order, where the mass of the population was only passively involved in politics, and followed the electoral lead provided by the clergy and the landed aristocracy.[17] It is significant, in this context, that 9 departments on or below par elected deputies in 1898, who joined the antisemitic group in the Chamber of Deputies (Landes(2); Gers(3); Aveyron(1); Lozère(1); Gard(1); Gironde(2); Deux-Sèvres(1); Loire-Inférieure(1); and Seine(2)). Antisemitic deputies here were sitting in the main for rural "pocket boroughs", where antisemitism was another face of an old-style conservatism of notables, and not the reflection of popular attitudes as such.[18] This impression is further confirmed by the fact that of the 47 departments from which national or local politicians sent subscriptions, 34 were on or below par.[19] It is likely also that the low incidence of antisemitic subscriptions in the West and in other conservative departments is related to the fact that Jewish minorities were unimportant or unknown there, suggesting that on the popular level Jewish presence may have been more important in motivating or arousing antisemitism than it was among the middle and upper classes.

The 18 departments with high plus scores fall into three main groups. First, there are the departments of the East, many frontier departments (Meurthe-et-Moselle, Vosges, Meuse, Haute-Saône,[20] Belfort, Côte-d'Or[21] and Doubs[22]). This group, centered on Lorraine, was a region with a long-standing tradition of popular antisemitism, linked to a large-scale Jewish presence.[23] The riots of 1898 here, as we have seen, renewed patterns of violence that had expressed themselves in the Revolutionary period, in the 1830s and in 1848. "I have a horror of yids [*youpins*]", wrote one Alsatian subscriber, "like all my compatriots."[24] The East was also a region where proximity to the German frontier and the lost provinces seems to have stimulated a high degree of loyalty to army and nation. It had traditionally provided a large contingent of army recruits, before the introduction of universal conscription,[25] and it was

MAP 8 THE HENRY SUBSCRIPTION.

Minus 2 or less

At par or minus or plus 1

Plus 2 and plus 3

Plus 4, 5, and 6

from the East that many leading figures in the "nationalist" movement came, notably Maurice Barrès.[26] Electoral choices here, in contrast to the West, often reflected an antisemitism with popular roots. The Meuse and the Meurthe-et-Moselle elected antisemitic deputies in 1898, and politicians from the Meurthe-et-Moselle, the Vosges, the Marne, the Haute-Saône and the Côte-d'Or contributed to the Henry Subscription. The second group of plus-scoring departments, in or to the South of the Paris basin (Seine-et-Marne,[27] Loiret, Indre and Vienne) is more heterogeneous. Of the four, only the Vienne was markedly Right-wing in electoral terms. In general, however, antisemitism seems in these departments to have accompanied political and social conservatism. It seems not to have been "popular", and was not linked to an experience of coexistence with Jewish communities, though in the Paris region it was possibly related to the presence there of large estates, owned by prominent Jews, something to which Drumont and others drew attention.[28] The emergence of the Loiret as a department of high incidence is interesting in view of the recent eruption of antisemitism in the city of Orléans, and it seems very likely that, then as later, antisemitism in such a milieu was an attitude par excellence of a threatened but inadaptive provincial bourgeoisie.[29]

The third group of plus-scoring departments is located in the South (Drôme, Var, Savoie, Vaucluse, Alpes-Maritimes and Basses-Alpes in the South-East; and Pyrénées-Orientales in the South-West). All but two had scores of plus 5 or plus 6, which suggests a very large departure from the norm of low incidence in geographically isolated rural departments. How is this overt antisemitism in the South-East in particular to be explained? First, there was the presence in the region of historic Jewish communities. Although these had greatly diminished by the end of the nineteenth century, there were still sizeable communities in the Vaucluse and the Alpes-Maritimes.[30] The South-Eastern Mediterranean and Alpine departments, moreover, suffered in a particularly severe way in the years of agricultural depression, rural exodus, phylloxera, and the demise of traditional industrial crops such as madder, which coincided in France with the rise of organized antisemitism.[31] This would have affected urban populations dependent on the marketing and processing of agricultural products as well as rural populations themselves. As Henri Baudrillart reminds us, in the case of Digne (Basses-Alpes), the chief town of such a department "has an eminently rural aspect. The yokes of oxen that passed through it all the time struck us more than its streets and monuments."[32] In four departments, thirdly, peculiar political factors provided a link between regional economic crisis and the expression of antisemitism. Joseph Reinach, himself, the main butt of the Henry Subscription—"I was, with Zola, the most insulted of Dreyfus's defenders"[33]—had been deputy for Digne, where he lost his seat in 1898 in a campaign, marked by the expression of much hostility towards him personally. Boni de Castellane, a candidate in a neighbouring constituency, recalled that: "On the day of the elections, he came to Castellane, but was sent on his way with whistles by threats of violence from my supporters, fleeing in a coupé with his friends."[34] His name is mentioned or referred to by several hundred subscribers, many from the department of the Basses-Alpes and 55 specifically from Digne, for example: "A former elector of Joe the Swine, from Digne".[35] Reinach also had political ambitions, it seems, in Savoie, which is reflected in such entries as: "Natives of Savoie very sorry to see Reinach getting a footing in their region"; or: "A native of Savoie against the German Jew Reinach".[36] Reinach had political associations, too, with the Alpes-Maritimes, where another Jewish politician, the banker R.-L. Bischoffsheim, had been a deputy since 1889. Bischoffsheim's election then had been invalidated on grounds of corruption, but he was re-elected, and retained his seat in 1893 and 1898.[37]

In the Var, similarly, the large number of subscribers reflects hostility directed against a particular figure, this time Clemenceau, the politician mentioned most often in the subscription list after Reinach, and again, by the end of 1898, a prominent Dreyfusard. Clemenceau had lost his seat in the Var in 1893 after a noisy campaign against him mounted by ex-Boulangists and Nationalists.[38] Something of this feeling against Clemenceau, deriving from the time of the Panama scandal, which itself had antisemitic associations, obviously remained at the local level, and was exacerbated by his involvement in the Affair. Two typical entries read: "A group of patriots from Salernes (Var), ashamed of having had a Clemenceau for deputy . . . "; and "A little offering from five electors of Clemenceau in the Var, sickened by the role adopted by their former deputy".[39] It seems likely that in these South-Eastern departments the connection with prominent Dreyfusard and Jewish politicians provided the opportunity for the expression of general grievances in antisemitic form, grievances which had their origins in economic difficulties and in forced social and economic transformation. It is also possible to see here an embryonic regional revolt against national government and administration, which seemed to be doing little or nothing for the victims of the agricultural crisis, a revolt directed symbolically against national political figures, who had claimed to represent the region. This suggestion is lent force by the fact that many constituencies in this area of France tended to select non-local but nationally important men to represent them in parliament, precisely on the grounds that this was the means of procuring maximum benefits for themselves from the "spoils" system.[40] They must therefore have been peculiarly disappointed. Though there are some grounds, then, for thinking that antisemitism in this region was in some sense a popular protest against established politicians and their system, it had other dimensions. Of the three antisemites elected as deputies here in 1898, one was an ex-*communard*, but the other two were Right-wingers, sitting for "pocket-boroughs". Was antisemitism here also a reaction to the precocious development of Socialism in the area, a Right-wing substitute for this popular cause? Subscriptions to the list from local and national politicians, moreover, came from the Var, the Vaucluse and the Basses-Alpes, all departments in which the Extreme Left was strong.[41]

A small number of places in France provided an unusually large number of subscribers. These included, beyond Digne already discussed: Maureilhan (Hérault) 21; Bonneville-la-Louvet (Calvados) 56; Longchamp près Genlis

(Côte-d'Or) 42; Cambrai (Nord) 66; Sarlat (Dordogne) 41; and Levallois (greater Paris) 138. Here no overall pattern seems discernible, and these examples of high incidence merely illustrate the diversity of the social context of antisemitism. Maureilhan was a small village in a large-scale wine-producing area near Béziers. Here antisemitism may have been related to general difficulties suffered by viticulture in the post-phylloxera period, or to particular features of large-scale wine production. Some of the same factors may have operated at Longchamp.[42] Bonneville was another small village, near the fashionable resort of Trouville. The Calvados was a department where "Nationalism" was comparatively strong.[43] It is also possible to speculate that antisemitism in Bonneville may have been related to the proximity of the resort, and to its expansion at the expense of its environs. Cambrai was a city of over 20,000 inhabitants, the seat of an archbishopric and a centre of linen cloth or cambric manufacture. Here a special commitment to Catholicism and difficulties in the basic industry may have been linked to the expression of antisemitism. Levallois, a North-Western suburb of Paris, was experiencing the strains of rapid urban growth and economic transformation, and from other sources it is known that antisemitism proved attractive in such marginal areas of the capital.[44] Sarlat was a small town and a *chef-lieu d'arrondissement;* no particular reasons for an antisemitic penchant here can be suggested.

In all, the geographical break-down of the subscription list leads to three main conclusions. First, the antisemitism of the sample was mainly urban, but it was by no means restricted to big cities, being found on an important scale and in idiosyncratic form in many small provincial towns. Second, antisemitism was strong in the East where it had traditional popular roots and was related to a particular form of coexistence with Jewish communities, but it was also strong in an area like the South-East, where local grievances were not directly related to a local Jewish presence but took an antisemitic form by projection on to national figures with local connections. Here it is possible to see both the metamorphosis of antisemitism into an ideology which operated on the national level, primarily via the newspaper press, and the expression of local and regional hostility to intrusion by outsiders, of resistance to the creation in all spheres, but mainly the economic, the political, the educational, of a national society. Third, in areas like the West and the South-West, although antisemitism existed on the electoral level, it did not there serve as a channel for popular grievances to any extent, but was merely a new variant of the prevailing conservatism of the reigning political élites. Its populist connotations suggest, however, that antisemitism in these circumstances may have been the means chosen by cadre-type political oligarchies in order to meet the democratic threat to their position, which they felt, rightly or wrongly, to be imminent in an era of general electoral shifts to the Left and the rise of the Socialist vote. There is some evidence that Boulangism had been adopted as a label by conservatives for the same reasons some years earlier, as we have seen,[45] and Viau provided such an interpretation of electoral antisemitism in the provinces in its early days in 1893.[46]

II

Out of a total of over 25,000 subscribers, professions are listed for 15,755, that is 61%. Table III gives a breakdown of the subscribers by profession, together with a breakdown of France's total active population using roughly the same categories. The percentages of subscribers by profession must be read with caution, given the unmeasurable potential bias of the sample, but their comparison with the proportion of such professional categories in the working population as a whole yields interesting, if often tentative, results. Divergence up or down from an assumed even distribution of antisemitism throughout all categories can be taken as some indication of a high or a low incidence of antisemitism in those categories. It will be seen that there was a high incidence among workers and artisans, among the military, among students, among the liberal professions and among the Catholic clergy; and a low incidence among white-collar workers, servants, industrialists and rural professions. By this index, antisemitism was of normal incidence, if it may be put that way, among shopkeepers and small traders, a finding that is out of line with information from other sources, as is the low incidence among white-collar workers. Other-

TABLE III: Henry Subscription—subscribers by profession

Professions	Incidence in the subscription (%)	Incidence in total active population (1896) (%)[47]
Workers and artisans	39.25	20.2
Military	28.6	3.0
Students in higher and secondary education	8.6	0.6 (of total pop. active and non-active)
Liberal Professions	8.25	2.6
White-collar workers	6.9	13.1
Catholic clergy	3.1	0.2
Shopkeepers and small traders	2.1	3.0 (*patrons* in commerce)
Domestic and other servants	1.8	4.7
Industralists and business cadres	0.9	3.5 (*patrons* in industry)
Rural occupations	0.5 (including aristocracy)	44.4

Note: The categories are not always exactly equivalent, as will be seen, and the second column does not total 100%, because it takes into account categories not relevant in the subscription list.

wise there are no surprises. These two discrepancies may derive from the nature of the index. Shopkeepers, in particular, though prepared to participate in collective manifestations of antisemitism of other kinds may have felt that entries to the subscription would have somehow exposed them to reprisals from their clientèle. They may therefore have abstained, or subscribed without giving their professions. One should remember also that the distribution of antisemitism among professional groups in the total population need not have coincided exactly with the professional complexion of declared antisemites, although one would expect a fair degree of concordance, which we in fact have.

Prominent among workers and artisans were those employed in the clothing industry, including, for example, working tailors, hatters, seamstresses, shirt-makers, embroiderers and dressmakers. This was an industry traditionally associated with Jews, and an industry where the introduction of ready-made clothing, sold usually in big stores, was cutting out the independent artisan, while the introduction of the sewing-machine permitted the survival of a semi-artisanal domestic sweating-system.[48] The entries by clothing workers seem to reflect a sense of frustration and exploitation created by this situation, for example: "A little seamstress from Montmartre, to make a robe for the president of the High Court out of the skin of Reinach"; or "A needlewoman from Melun who spits in the odious face of the contemptible Reinach and of all Jews to express her total disgust".[49] In some cases this feeling was directly related to exploitation by a Jewish employer, for example: "Three embroider-ers of Bains-les-Bains (Vosges), who, working for a Jew, earn 14 sous in 15 hours."[50]

Although not of high incidence—there would be special reasons inhibiting entries from this category: lack of education and opportunity, fear of reprisals —the entries from servants provide valuable insights into the motivation and function of lower-class antisemitism. Many of the servants who contributed were servants of Jews, for example: "A yid's valet"; "A janitor with Jewish employers, disgusted by the yids"; or "Jeanne, ex-maid of some yids . . ."[51] Waiters with specific grievances against Jews can also be put in this category, for example: "A waiter, victim of the suppression of tipping by the Jews at Le Mans"; "A waiter at the Porte Maillot, insulted in a gross and cowardly manner by a filthy Yid by the name of Dreyfus"; or "H.S. A waiter in a hotel at Nancy, who will not grow rich on the tips he gets from Jews."[52] But such direct links between servants' antisemitism and service for Jews were not always present, and it seems likely that servants and waiters were here express-ing a revolt against their situation as servants, but a revolt that would not involve them in any real consequences or retribution. They dared not attack, probably they would not have thought of attacking, employers and masters as such, but they could safely vent their resentments against Jews, and Jewish employers; for this attack did not fundamentally confront or undermine the institution of service, but merely allowed those resentments, which it necessar-ily generated, to express themselves in a harmless way.[53] Several employers of servants seem to have sensed this, and thus associated their servants, paternalistically, with their own contributions. So there are entries from "my cook", from "my servant Martin for the expulsion of the Jews", from "a *Parisienne* who does not fancy those who are circumcised", and from "her maid",[54] while a major in the engineers, included his assistants, his batman and another servant in his entry. This mechanism is only one example of antisemitism's general function of providing an illusory criticism of the social system. This wider function is exemplified in the entries from self-declared socialists, such as: "A revolutionary socialist, former member of the community centre of the Impasse Pers, who declares: Down with the Jews and the representatives of the people who sell themselves to the Jewish capitalist exploiters."[55] Another example of such misdirected and thus essentially ineffective social criticism or protest is provided by an entry from "four patriotic Breton workers opposed to the so-called nobles of Rennes who continue to be the best customers of Jewish businesses",[56] a protest which carries the implication that "real" nobles would not do such a thing, and which thus makes no fundamental attack on the nobility as such. To lend support to this view there is an entry from a Comte de B., making the same kind of criticism of his own class: "Shame on the nobility for hobnobbing with the Jews."[57] We will take this interpretation of lower-class and socialistic antisemitism further in a later chapter.

The highest incidence by profession in the list is found in the military, which also provided the largest single professional grouping. 4,500 members of the armed forces subscribed. Of these just under 3,000 were officers, of whom at least 1,700 were on active service. They included 5 generals and 9 colonels or lieutenant-colonels on active service, and 30 generals and 55 colonels or lieutenant-colonels from the reserve. Though not perhaps too surprising, given the nature of the subscription and its appeal to a feeling of solidarity with a fellow-officer (not, be it noted, mobilized on behalf of Dreyfus), this participation of army officers in a public cause of a semi-political kind marked a radical departure, as we noted in chapter II, from the tradition of military non-involvement in civilian affairs well established in France by the end of the nineteenth century. This was made even more striking, as we have also noted, by the fact that the Minister of War, Freycinet, had issued a circular specifically enjoining members of the armed forces not to contribute to the Henry Subscription. Several officers drew attention, indeed, to the fact that they were flouting this ban, for example: "An artillery captain, who had already subscribed, to say 'Go to blazes!' to Freycinet who is prohibiting all participation in the Henry Subscription"; "An infantry captain from Saint-Etienne reprimands M.de Freycinet for the circular forbidding officers to subscribe"; "An officer who does not recognize any right of the English Jew Freycinet to prevent him from coming to the aid of the orphan of a French officer"; and "A group of officers at the Ecole de Guerre sends its modest offering, and regrets that its members cannot sign their names, for silence and abstention weigh very heavily today on the heart of France's Great Silent Army [*la Grande Muette*]."[58] As suggested here, most officers retained their anonymity, although a significant number did give their names. Another, more cautious, way of getting round the ban was taken by the large number of officers who subscribed through their wives. A typical entry of this kind read: "The wife of an officer, to defend the honour of the army against Reinach Ltd . . . Let Freycinet come and find me."[59]

Three main themes emerge in the entries from members of the military. First, there is simple defence of the professional institution attacked or felt to be attacked by the Dreyfusards, for example: "Comte Jean de Castellane, former lieutenant in the 29th Dragoons, to protest against the insulters of the army".[60] The most common expression of this *esprit de corps* was via solidarity with Colonel Henry himself, who was presented as a victimized comrade, or superior, for example: "An ex-sergeant-major of the military justice department, in memory of Colonel Henry, who died for his country"; or "An ex-NCO who once served in one of late Lieutenant-colonel Henry's regiments".[61] Second, officers gave expression through antisemitism and complaints of Jewish "invasion" of the army, to frustrations over advancement and promotion, for example: "From a soldier belonging to a frontier regiment commanded by a colonel who is a Freemason and a lieutenant who is a Jew . . ."; "A small officers' mess which is unfortunate enough to have to eat with a Jew"; or "An artillery lieutenant ashamed to see so many Jews in his arm".[62] In this context, it should be pointed out that the subscription list provides no clear evidence that antisemitism was more or less prevalent in any single branch of the military. Third, a fair number of army officers pressed their abandonment of the tradition of non-involvement to its logical conclusion, and evoked direct military intervention as the only solution to what they regarded as an intolerable social and political crisis, for example: "A captain who hates the Jews calls for a Morny and a Saint-Arnaud to save the Nation . . ."; "A sub-lieutenant of the reserve . . . Where are you, my general? and when will it be, the clean sweep that will save us?"; or "A cavalry captain who begs General X . . . the only saviour possible, to put an end to the agony of France."[63] These entries confirm the view expressed in chapter II that a minority of officers were thinking, albeit vaguely, of a *coup* in the years 1898 and 1899.

The significance of the military's contribution to the subscription list goes far beyond the confines of the profession. Not only did those who had at some time served in the armed forces identify with them and continue to reflect their attitudes, for example: "an ex-army surgeon with the army of Africa, former mayor of Biarritz, and a fanatical supporter of the army still"; or "Dérigon P., radical Republican and patriotic Catholic; ex-NCO with the 46th regiment of foot with the army of the Loire, ready to march when called upon against the anti-French coalition . . .";[64] but the army served as a paradigm for the whole antisemitic-nationalist system of thought, to be analysed below.

In contrast to that of the military, the high percentage of students in the subscription list might appear surprising, had not previous chapters forewarned us. Would one not expect prejudice to diminish as the level of education increased?[65] Is youth not usually attracted to more generous political opinions? Both assumptions in this case appear to be wrong, for individuals and groups from Faculties, schools and *lycées* from all over France sent contributions. As we have seen, one of the reasons for student espousal of antisemitism seems to be a concern over worsening student career prospects. Secondary and higher education were the gateways to careers in the state service and in the liberal professions, the preferred employment of the bourgeoisie and the aspiring bourgeoisie. For a variety of reasons these careers were becoming more competitive at the end of the nineteenth century, and the simultaneous emergence of Jews in these careers provided the justification for an antisemitic explanation of the phenomenon.[66] A second factor, which again we have already encountered, that helps to explain antisemitism among students is the fact that, in adopting such an attitude, they were frequently consciously setting themselves against the views of their teachers. Typical student entries include: "Five antisemitic students angered by the Dreyfusism of the professors of the Sorbonne"; "Five medical students sickened by the attitude of their teachers"; "A student at the Ecole des Chartes, sickened by the conduct of some of his professors"; while an entry from an adult "protests against the university professors . . ."[67] One can detect here a certain anti-intellectualism, which we will discuss further below. Moreover, as has been suggested elsewhere, this conflict of opinion between teachers and students probably reflects significant class differences between the two groups, as well as structural tensions within the higher education system in France, which, for example, was excessively examination-orientated.[68] Account must also be taken of the probable attraction for young people of extremism as a means of self-assertion, as well as of the fact that antisemitism could appear in the guise of a socialistic anti-bourgeois cause to be associated with a wider revulsion against the rationalism of the academic establishment.[69]

Antisemitism in the liberal professions is closely related to that of students, since, as we have mentioned, higher education was for many a preparation for these prestige careers. The high incidence of antisemitism in this category is the more significant in that one would expect the liberal professions, with their high level of education and vocational rationality, to be comparatively immune to the attractions of the irrational mode of social explanation afforded by antisemitism. This suggests that the force of any countervailing factors must have been considerable. Among the liberal professions, the medical and legal careers provided the largest number of subscribers, followed by writers and publicists, by politicians, and by teachers of all grades. Law and medicine were perhaps the most favoured of these professions, and both, moreover, were overcrowded and competitive. The contribution of journalists to antisemitism in the 1890s has already been stressed, and the connection with a crisis in the publishing business has been established by Byrnes.[70] Twenty-eight archivists *(archivistes-paléographes)* subscribed, a surprisingly large number in a presumably small profession. The reason for this seems to lie in the specifically paleographic aspect of the Dreyfus Case, and also in the fact that the Ecole des Chartes, where archivists were trained, seems mainly to have attracted men from conservative milieus. For them, the fact that Paul Meyer, the Ecole's director was a Jew and a leading Dreyfusard was a special provocation.

We have seen a reference to this in a student entry, and an archivist typically declared himself "not an intellectual, I know Paul Meyer too well . . ."[71] Antisemitic teachers were, it seems, a small minority in their profession, but their presence in the list is a reminder that not all of them conformed to the anti-Dreyfusard stereotype of them. Very few higher civil servants subscribed, presumably in part a reflection of adherence to the civil service tradition of non-involvement in politics, a tradition, as we have seen, that many army officers had abandoned.

The low incidence of subscribers among white-collar workers and those engaged in small-scale commerce does not match what other sources indicate of the incidence of antisemitism in these groups, as we have pointed out. However, certain sub-categories do fit the expected pattern, for example that of travelling salesmen, 123 of whom subscribed. The list, moreover, does provide a good idea of what motivated antisemitism among these categories, taken as a whole: the alleged "invasion" of the professions by Jews, and complaints of "unfair" Jewish competition. Many small traders, as well as clerks, shop-workers and other groups, saw themselves as, in one way or another, the victims of the economic activity of Jews, for example, "Feutrier, photographic dealer and antisemite, victim of the Jews".[72] We will return to this general theme of victimization below.

Immediately, the theme of a Jewish "invasion" of certain professions and of "unfair" Jewish competition is worth considering further, since it was found among many professional groups, where, it seems, access, promotion or success were becoming more difficult, and where this mode of explanation had an obvious appeal. An artillery captain from Versailles declared that he was "not only indignant that there were still any Jewish officers in the army, but outraged by the fact that they were never the last to receive decorations and promotion".[73] "A group of candidates for the Ecole Polytechnique" wrote "to protest against the Jewish invasion",[74] a theme repeated, explicitly or implicitly, in many of the entries from students at lycées, working for a coveted place in one of the great vocational Schools of the tertiary level, for example: "The pupils of the Saint-Cyr class at the Lycée Henri IV". Further up the ladder, a doctor wrote in the same vein "to pull down a peg or two the Jews who suck up to anyone at the Faculty"; while "a group of true Frenchmen" hoped to see "Jews excluded from all public employment".[75] The same motivation, as we have suggested, underlay the antisemitism of small traders, businessmen and white-collar workers. A chemist, for example, subscribed, "out of hatred of the big Jewish chemist shops"; a wine retailer subscribed "to oppose the Jews, the oppressors of small traders"; a commercial traveller wished that "all Jewish employees be fired from Catholic shops"; another declared himself "in favour of the expulsion of the Jews from all trading Exchanges"; while "the chief cashier at the Grand Bazar at Verdun [wished to see] all the Yids at the bottom of the Meuse."[76]

In the context of business and trade, and particularly of retail trade, this fear of Jewish competition overlaps with two further related themes, which we have already encountered. First, there was the attack on big department stores.

A subscriber from Nevers wrote "to protest against the condemnation of a humble employee of a big Jewish store, on the testimony of its Jewish director." "An employee of the Bon Marché", subscribed, he said, "in spite of the prohibition of his cowardly management, afraid of displeasing the yids"; while another entry simply voiced this imprecation: "For the ruin of a department store".[77] Linked to such complaints about departments stores, which were thought to be ruining small traders, and which were identified with Jews, was the call to boycott Jewish shops and businesses, a call, we have seen, that was raised to the level of a concerted campaign in the years 1898 and 1899 by antisemitic newspapers and organizations. A fair number of entries expressed support for this campaign. For example, an artillery captain from Nancy declared that neither he nor his family "ever set foot in a Jewish shop". "J.C., a Frenchwoman from Lorraine" appealed: "French patriots, never buy from the Jews . . ." An "anti-Jew" described herself as "never buying from the yids"; and a "Norman" as one who "never buys from the Jews at any price"; while another entry asked: "When will the women of France understand that they ought to buy nothing from the children of Israel?"[78] The appearance of this theme in the subscription list, unprompted it seems, as well as the general impact of the campaign, suggest that it echoed popular attitudes. In the same general sense was an atavistic voice, reflecting popular obsession with dearth: "A poor old couple to stop the Jewish invasion of the markets, which is causing us to die of hunger"; and what can be seen as an updated version of the same fear from "a fanatical protectionist . . ."[79]

Among rural professions, reference was made in more than one entry to phylloxera, but no other theme emerges strongly in this under-represented category, unless it is the very general one of hostility to capitalism and to money, and of attachment to the land and to the more stable social system that went with it. One entry read: "Be bold, men of the land, in face of the traitor and the plunderer!"[80] As we shall see below, such "rural" values were very generally espoused by antisemites, and were by no means confined to those living and working in the countryside. Another rural entry is of interest, because it, too, came from a winegrower, but also because it directed against the Jews a protest, which, like that of antisemitic servants, might alternatively have been directed against the rich in general, as consumers of the surplus produced by the poor: "Henri Loubeau, a small winegrower, enraged by the thought that the yids can drink the excellent Montreuil-Bellay wine, which he produces."[81] Two other categories, the clergy and the nobility, had close links with rural society, though only the latter have been placed, somewhat arbitrarily, under the heading of rural professions. The high incidence of antisemitism among the Catholic clergy is well established from other sources, and we will discuss the Catholic dimension of antisemitism further below. From 366 titled nobles, and 433 with the particle attached to their names, came contributions. Not only is this testimony to the enduring vitality of the nobility as a social group, whose conservative mentality embraced antisemitism, and presumably lent it a reflection of its own high status, but the large sums donated by the nobility indicate also that it remained economically powerful, and, in particular, that it was probably the main source of finance for organized antisemitism. Among the usual contributions of a few francs, stand out 39 noble contributions of 100 francs each, and 5 of over 100 francs. This does not, of course, rule out the possibility that noble antisemitism was also in part motivated by relative poverty and loss of status. Indeed, as we shall see, some entries suggest that it was.[82] The relative prominence of the nobility in the list contrasts with the relative absence of industrialists, for whom antisemitism seems to have held no particular attraction.

Finally, the contribution of a non-professional category, that of women, should be mentioned. Of the total number of subscribers, a known 10% were women. At a time when women had no political rights, and little opportunity or inclination to involve themselves in public life, this becomes a significant proportion. Women had always, of course, been prominent in the past in popular movements concerned with the availability and price of food, and, as we have seen, antisemitism, with its claim that Jews were responsible for economic difficulties and its call to boycott Jewish shops, had some of the characteristics of age-old popular movements against food-hoarders and monopolists.[83] As we have seen, also, wives of army officers had special reasons to contribute. The subscription list for Henry's widow also attracted support from a large number of fellow-widows. Moreover, antisemitism seems, in a way to be examined below, to have had special sexual connotations, especially for unmarried women; in addition, at least one group of "patriotic feminists"[84] sent a contribution.

III

A large proportion of the entries to the subscription list are accompanied by short messages. In combination with the geographical and professional break-downs, these provide material for an analysis of the make-up and function of antisemitism as a socio-psychological attitude.[85] The main characteristics of this attitude are threefold. It provided an explanation of and a compensation for failure and deprivation of various kinds, that exculpated the ego by laying blame clearly elsewhere. It affirmed a set of absolute and unchanging values in a world of flux. It projected on to the Jew and his associates everything that threatened or contradicted this static view of the world and society; the Jew was an agent of change, disruption and revolution, in this perspective, and, more particularly, an unclean polluting element which had to be expelled from the city, or exterminated.

Many subscribers made a special declaration of their unfortunate social and economic circumstances, for example: "A working woman earning her living by the sweat of her brow"; "Three Christian Democrats, not at all well off . . ."; "An unemployed worker".[86] Others made the same point by explaining that their contributions represented a sacrifice on their part, for example: "From the savings of a modest lady patriot"; "A month's coffee [given up] for the little Henry boy . . ."; "An inmate of La Salpêtrière ["an asylum for aged and insane women" in Paris][87] who will go without her wine"; or "M., a poor old janitor, an ex-NCO: To defend the flag, two days' pay".[88] In this connection, subscribers presented themselves again and again as the victims of the Jews, for example: "The household of a lieutenant-colonel on active service ruined by a Jew after six months of marriage"; "The orphan of a high-ranking officer, whose husband, victim of the bad faith of the Jews, has been without work for two years"; or "A noble lady ruined by the Jews, which has caused the death of her husband".[89] Subscriptions were sometimes addressed to Mme Henry, as from one victim to another, for example: "To the victim of the big Jews, from another of their victims".[90] It is significantly difficult to classify these complaints clearly, but they seem to spread between two definite poles. First, complaints were made about specific actions by Jews, for example: "An Alsatian robbed several times by the Jews"; "In memory of what the Jews have made me lose on my hops"; "A curate [*vicaire*] of La Villette, from whom the only Jew he knows stole 200 francs".[91] In some cases, Jews were actually named in such entries; for example: "I was robbed by Bernheim"; "A trader from Rennes and his family, to express their hatred of the yids Ober, Jubé, Weill, Sexer, Albert and Hurstel. Long live France!"; or "A neighbour of the Jews Borg and Lévy, rabbit-skin merchants at Bordeaux".[92] Other entries refer to specific Jewish communities in Besancon, Le Mans and Paris, for example. There are also many references to financial investments that proved disastrous, and where that disaster can be blamed, directly or indirectly, on the Jews, for example: "G. . . . ex-civil servant, financial and administrative victim of the Jews and the Freemasons"; or "F.-H. Chappez, former prisoner in the Sainte-Pélagie, reduced to starvation, victim of the Jews of the Northern [Railway] Company . . ."[93] Here the Panama scandal and the crash of the Union Générale bank are frequently evoked by their "victims".[94] At the other pole, subscribers express various discontents, laying blame implicitly or explicitly on Jews, but providing no rationale for this ascription. Subscriptions in this category include such entries as: "A gentleman who regrets his having been exiled to Montluçon"; "a patriot hit by phylloxera, at Bergerac"; "a civil servant removed from his post in 1889"; "a sub-prefect of the Second Empire, now ruined"; and also arguably "an angry bachelor",[95] and the fathers of large families who drew attention to themselves by this fact alone, though the fiscal reforms probably envisaged by each were mutually contradictory.[96] Entries of this kind which placed the blame for misfortune more explicitly on Jews include: "The disabled father of a family. Out of hatred for the Jews"; "A father of seven who detests the Jews"; "A miserable commercial traveller, enemy of all Jews and foreigners."[97] Although antisemitic reaction was sometimes related to actual unfavourable encounters with Jews, more often, blame was cast on "the Jews" as an abstract entity, an impersonal agency of all kinds of ill fortune.

Venting hatred against the Jews in this way was presumably an outlet for personal and professional frustration, and a way of explaining failure that did not pin responsibility on the ego. Antisemitism could thus fulfil in some way a need of the unsuccessful, of the sad and lonely, like the subscriber who signed herself: "Victim of a cruel and unjust world".[98] But the antisemitism of the subscription list did more than simply provide people with an explanation of their situation of real or imagined misfortune and with a means of expressing their sense of persecution. It actually offered them relief of an immediate kind. Not only were they able, by contributing to the Subscription, to join in some form of collective ritual which itself provided an alleviation of their frustrations, but antisemitism gave them a direct compensation for feelings of deprivation. This can be seen in entries which contrast the real poverty of subscribers with the "wealth" bestowed on them by their adoption or declaration of antisemitism. "Four inhabitants of the Carentan" wrote that they "were not well off, but they were anti-Jewish". "Lydia M., aged twenty" declared that she was "rich only in her hatred of the yids". "A landowner from the Beuvron valley" wrote that he was "rich in antisemitic sentiments". "Two Alsatian sisters" stated that "their hearts were fuller of patriotism than their purses were of money". Stressing the value of the collective involvement provided by the Subscription, "a family from the Auvergne, suffering from cold and hunger . . . nevertheless wishes to join with all true French people to express its hatred of the Jewish and Dreyfusard blackguards."[99] In this perspective, the money subscribed to the fund by some contributors ceased to be money at all. It was "the little sou of France opposed to the Jewish millions"; or, as another entry put it: "My 10 sous are worth far more than the 100,000 francs of the Rothschilds."[100] This introduces the general theme of the identification of the Jews with money, which we will consider further below.

First, we must complete our examination of antisemitism as a means of explaining misfortune, and, in particular, social derogation. A number of subscribers made declarations of poverty, which implied a reduction in status, for example: a colonel who wrote that "he could smoke only cheap cigars"; "a high-ranking officer, retired, with a family to support, obliged to work after forty years of active service . . ."; "a true Royalist, aged 80, reduced by thievery to the Hospice Galliéra [an old people's home] . . ."; or the aristocrat who stated: "Although Marquise du Goujon, having been swindled by a certain by a manager of a bank in the rue de la Banque . . . I have no more than 1 franc to give to the widow and the orphan."[101] Here antisemitism as an explanation of personal misfortune is lent a social dimension by reference to a normative static social hierarchy, according to whose rules such derogation should not have occurred. Social change is thus registered, deplored and explained in terms of Jewish intervention. In one entry, it is even measured in terms of the incidence of Jews in society: "An old inhabitant of Epernay, who knew his dear town when it had only 3 Jewish families. Alas . . . there are 53 today."[102] This view is found in complementary form among those whose social circumstances have not altered, who often indeed take a certain relish in emphasizing their low social station, but who accept that station in the context of a social hierarchy where it is or ought to be secure, and where that security is affirmed or sought in opposition to the Jews. We have already encountered this mechanism in the case of servants. It probably also informed the attitude of the many subscribers who described themselves as "small" or "little" people, for example: "A little mayor from the Orne"; "A small industrialist ruined by the Jews"; "A little soldier in the African Light Cavalry, who cannot stand the

Jews"; or "Just a little country priest";[103] as well as the many who sent their "modest offering" *("modeste obole")*. This attitude of submissive social deference was frequently evoked in connection with the Dreyfus Affair itself, where indignation was expressed at the way in which Dreyfusards were questioning the military hierarchy. So "a group of NCOs is outraged by seeing their leaders insulted"; abbé Marchand was "indignant that such odious accusations against the army chiefs should be tolerated"; while "D.T., a modest clerk", proclaimed: "Long live the army! Down with the Jews!"[104] Such deliberate affirmation of the social and moral order, or a certain conception of it, is found also in more general terms, in such entries as: "Albert Bouy and René Piprot, a subscription with the sole aim of defending Mme Henry against people with no respect for law or religion"; "A Frenchwoman who grieves to see the Jews destroying all our traditions"; "A widow and an orphan who believe that the time has come for all good people to take comfort and for the wicked to tremble"; "A lieutenant in the Marines. For the confounding of the Jews and the triumph of all honest men"; or the possibly facetious: "The last bourgeois of Périgueux".[105]

Jews, together with Protestants, Freemasons, intellectuals and politicians, were seen as the agents of social change; they were symbols of confusion and alteration. Against them, to be safe from the threat which they posed, antisemites affirmed and invoked a stable social order, stable moral values, immutable and absolute categories.[106] This was done in a number of ways. In opposition to the foreign quality of the Jew, his non-Frenchness, the quintessential Frenchness of the antisemite could be proclaimed, as in such entries as: "A group of true Frenchmen [*vrais Français*] . . ."; "A group of friends, true Frenchmen, and true patriots . . ."; or "Let us oppose Jewish solidarity with French solidarity".[107] The antisemitism of the antisemite itself could also be given an absolute quality, for example: "From a convinced antisemite"; "An antisemite from Orléans, propagandist for truth"; or "L.M., the authentic antisemitic café-owner",[108] probably another facetious entry, but which only emphasizes a characteristic of *bona fide* entries, like a caricature. This absolutist affirmation was also very easily cast in racial terms, race being an innate and absolute quality. "Why want the Jews to be French?", asked one subscriber: "Negroes aren't white"; while another posited simply: "The Jew is not French".[109] References to the Jewish "race" are common in the subscription list, and the terminology was also used the other way. One subscriber signed herself: "A pure-blooded Frenchwoman"; another: "A Frenchwoman by race"; a third: "a pure-blooded Norman".[110]

The affirmation of a stable social order is found further in the attachment of subscribers to certain institutions: family and kin, region and nation, army and Church. The proclamation of French race was already a proclamation of ancestry, but this was found also in its own right. Many subscriptions were sent, we have seen, from "a family" rather than from an individual. Moreover, many subscribers defined themselves in terms of pedigree, for example: "A really French Frenchman, the descendant of officers and senior magistrates, brother of a Marine officer killed in action . . ."; "the grandson of an officer of the First Empire"; "The daughter of an ex-NCO, wounded on the field of battle"; "A man from the Vendée, who would be only too pleased to get down the arms of his ancestors of 1793 and take a few pot-shots at the yids who are poisoning the country"; or "A descendant of Jacques d'Arc, the brother of Joan, ruined by Rothschild".[111] As the example from the Vendée indicates, this attachment to kin and ancestry was related to attachment to historical region or province. The latter attachment was evinced in 850 entries. Seventeen subscribers declared themselves from Berry; 16 from Franche-Comté; 19 from Gascony; 19 from Burgundy; 10 from Périgord; 26 from Normandy; 8 from Picardy; 9 from Dauphiné; 42 from the Auvergne; 129 from Champagne; 90 from Brittany; 116 from Alsace; 56 from Lorraine; and 138 from the East generally. Two messages were delivered in Provençal. Three sentiments seem to inform this regionalism. First, there was an attachment to the historical province of "old France", as against the modern department. One entry reads: "Two natives of Berry ashamed to say that they come from the Cher".[112] Second, there are those who have had to move from their native region for one reason or another, and who express regret or resentment over this unwelcome migration. It was fairly common for subscribers writing from one place to point out that they really belonged to another. For example, two subscribers from Tarbes and from Algiers referred to themselves as *Limousins*, a subscriber from Lyon said that he was a native of Dauphiné, while another declared himself: "A Breton from La Chèze, exiled in Normandy".[113] This reference to migration is most common in the case of Alsatians and Lorrainers, who had additional and special reasons for drawing attention to their origins, and for holding to them. This brings us to the third point, the proclamation of regional attachments that were seen as more "national" than others. Alsace-Lorraine, in particular, was symbolic of France as a whole, of the Nation and the cult of the Nation, of opposition to the enemy, external and internal. An officer declared: "Let Alsace-Lorraine maintain its confidence in us!"[114] But this ultra-patriotism was not only associated with the lost provinces, but was attached also to other frontier provinces, notably in the West. One entry came from "a patriot of the Western frontier".[115] This preoccupation with frontiers, encountered elsewhere in the subscription list also, is of great significance in the general explanation of antisemitism. Frontiers were not only to be defended against external enemies, but also against Jews living in France. One subscriber described himself as a "defender of the nation and the frontier against the Jews".[116] Here again we encounter an affirmation of absolute categories. The antisemite constructs a world of extreme order and clear definitions, and one of his fundamental concerns is to draw a line, a frontier, around this world, to mark it off and save it from the world of confusion, marginality and ambiguity represented by the Jew.

"Long live the Church, the army and France".[117] These were the pillars of the antisemite's static cosmos. We have already encountered attachment to the nation with the concept of the "true Frenchman" and the cult of the frontier province. "Nationalist" was also, of course, as we have seen, the chosen epithet of the political movement which ran its course, intermingled and in harness, with organized antisemitism in the period 1895–1905.[118] Nation, Church and army are in the subscription list interdependent concepts, as the entry just cited and others make clear, for example that from "a group of pupils of a religious school in the provinces, the future defenders of the Nation, antisemites in their souls", who refer to the army as "the emblem of the Nation".[119] The strict connection between the army and the Nation can be seen, moreover, from the involvement of outsiders in each of the main themes expressed by members of the military themselves. First, subscribers outside the army included themselves in its *esprit de corps* and felt that the "honour" of the army was something which concerned them, for example, "an antisemitic lady, in honour of the Army". Another subscriber expressed the same sense of solidarity in the most personal way: "A young lady who desires to have the great honour of marrying an officer".[120] Similarly, Colonel Henry was not only a victimized colleague for the military, but also a hero and a martyr for all those who identified with the army. "In memory of our dear martyr", read one entry. "In admiration of the colonel for his patriotic death", read another.[121] Second, non-military subscribers shared the concern of the military over the presence of Jews in the armed forces and advocated their expulsion from the profession, for example: "For the elimination of the Jews from the army"; "For the expulsion of the Jewish officers who are dishonouring the army"; or "For a law to ban Jews from commissions in the Army."[122] The Jew was set in specific contrast to the army: "For the army against the Jews"; "Long live the army! Down with the Jews!"; "Long live the army! Death to the Jews!"[123] As the army was the emblem of the Nation and of the values which it represented, so the Jew was given opposite characteristics. The Jews were anti-French, "people without a country", "the cosmopolitan gang", "bought by foreigners", "the race of traitors", "the enemy of the Interior".[124] It is as if the army and the Nation, and the values which they stand for, could only be given consistency and strength by a reiterated denial of the opposites which defined, but also threatened, them. We will return to a general consideration of this mechanism below. Meanwhile, and third, non-military subscribers gave their support to the idea of a *coup d'état.* This was sometimes expressed in terms of a specifically Royalist or Bonapartist restoration,[125] for example: "Comte de Paris, where are you?"; or "A family of shoemakers who demand a Napoleon"; sometimes in more general terms: "For the flag! A *coup d'état* to save us"; sometimes with the implication of a consequent expulsion of the Jews: "When will it happen, the *coup d'état* that will rid us of the whole dirty lot of Jews and their friends!".[126] But a *coup* was very often envisaged in terms of an explicit military intervention also, for example: "V.M. from Charenton. To arm the avenging hand"; "One who cries out: Long live the army! Long live the sword that will get rid of all the vermin for us!"; "A patriot who is waiting for the avenging sword"; or "Are the generals waiting for the people to polish their swords?"[127] Support for military intervention in the form of a *coup* is, moreover, only one aspect of an attitude which took the army as a model for the kind of stable and hierarchical society that antisemites yearned for. In this perspective, the respect of NCOs and men for their officers, the military habit of obedience, became a paradigm for a general pattern of social deference, which was reflected in many of the entries already considered.

The Catholic Church performed the same function in the antisemitic mentality, although this is made less explicit in the subscription list. About 350 members of the Catholic clergy, and 200 declared members of the laity, subscribed to the list. Of significance in terms of attachment to hierarchy is the concern expressed by several subscribers that bishops were absent from the list, for example: "A poor priest, sickened to realize that no bishop in France has sent in his offering"; or "M . . . heartbroken to see that not a single bishop has participated in the subscription".[128] Many subscribers made a simple affirmation of their Catholicism, for example: "28 members of a Catholic working-men's club in Paris, after having fulfilled their religious duties at midnight mass"; or: "A Catholic antisemite . . ."[129] Others linked attachment to the Church with attachment to family, Nation and army, for example: "A. Krumenacker, soldier of Christ"; "The G.R. family, for God and the Nation"; "A Christian family, united and patriotic"; or "For God, the Nation and the extermination of the Jews".[130] This last entry indicates how the same dichotomy found in the militarist-nationalist complex of ideas between the absolute fixed world of the antisemite, and the confusion represented by the Jew, which must be eliminated, was present also in the related Catholic mentality; and how the same frontier was drawn, though in different terminology, between the two. "The goodness of God ends where the Jew begins", declared one entry.[131] So Christian eschatological terminology was employed to call for the expulsion or the extermination of the Jews in order that Catholic order might be restored, for example: "The Misses Moy, Marie and Thérèse, who call for a new Joan of Arc to drive the Jew out of France"; "Christ! Lend us your whip to drive the Jewish moneychangers from the temple of France"; and "A Christian woman. Noël! Noël! Cry of old France. For restoration through Our Lord Jesus Christ."[132] The reference to "old France" made in this last entry was, as we have seen, a general point of reference in antisemitic thinking, but it also represented a view prevailing in the Church in France that society had been and should remain integrally Christian. Such a non-pluralist view, of course, left no room for Jews, Protestants or freethinkers, and it was a view which hardened among Catholics, and into which the faithful tended to retreat more and more as dechristianization progressed in society at large.[133] We will discuss this aspect of Catholic antisemitism in chapter XIV below.

The expulsion/extermination call was accompanied in Catholic thinking by reference to Jewish responsibility for the crucifixion of Christ, for example: "Sacred Heart of Jesus, hasten the promised miracle which will proclaim the triumph of your Church and deliver the Catholic nations from the shameful yoke of those who crucified you.[134] Other references to this traditional postulate of Catholic antisemitism include: "A little Gentile, out of hatred of the deicide Jew, the cause of all our misfortunes"; and, less directly: "An inmate of La Salpêtrière, who wants to see all the Jews crucified"; and "Judas Iscariot will be the next one to be rehabilitated".[135] Another Christian feature echoed in the list, which evoked the whole complex antisemitic dichotomy in another form, was the old identification of the Jew with the Devil.[136] This was sometimes reflected unconsciously in stock phrases, as when subscribers wished "that all the Jews and their friends may go to the devil"; or: "To the devil with the unspeakable Reinach . . ."[137] Also present were the Romantic trappings of black magic, as when Jews are referred to as "vampires".[138] But one entry is clear and explicit: "Satan reigns. Arouse yourselves!"[139] In passing, a further feature of Christian antisemitism, as manifested in the subscription list, should be mentioned: the particular connection, well known in other manifestations, that is suggested between Christian Democracy and hostility towards Jews.[140] Two entries are sent specifically from "Christian Democrats",[141] and there are at least four contributions from sections of the Union Nationale of abbé Garnier. There is a suggestion here of the same kind of "populism" manifested in "socialist" entries, coupled interestingly, as we have seen, with a special penchant towards antisemitism among the lower clergy. The association of antisemitism with Catholicism did not exclude the expression of anticlerical or anti-Christian antisemitism, for example: "A freethinker, who is as opposed to Jewish or Protestant clericalism as to any other"; or "Hélène, atheist, Socialist and antisemite".[142] This serves as a reminder that anticlericalism was in many ways similar in structure and function to antisemitism,[143] and could overlap with it, though another entry suggests which was likely to be the dominant factor in such a partnership: "A freethinker whom the Jews will turn into a church-goer".[144]

Having examined the main features of the antisemite's world of absolutes, we must return now to the opposing world of confusion represented by the Jew. A very clear example of the dualism is the opposition which is established between honour and money. In contrast to honour, which is embodied in the army and the family, the Jew is identified with money, which is liquid and unstable, and associated with social change, uncertainty and possible disaster. So "a Frenchwoman calls on God to rescue France from the golden calf"; while another entry declared: "Down with money that is impure and corrupting".[145] A traditional way of making this identification was by evoking the name of Rothschild, which, as we have seen, several contributors did. Another entry referred to "the Jew and his brother-in-law the banker".[146] Against the uncertainty and the polluting power of money are set the values of social order and hierarchy, symbolized in the concept of honour, for example: "Honour against money"; "French honour against Jewish gold"; "For honour and for France"; or "Two daughters of a magistrate dismissed (for his principles), the sisters of officers. In this family, our word, our arms are not for sale."[147] Another entry protested in the name of honour and the values of a land-based society against the alleged capture of the latter by Jews and the consequent reversal of values: "Someone who wishes that some of the subscription money be used to buy a villa near the castle of the anti-patriotic yid, so that passers-by can read on the castle: 'Swindling and shame!' and on the villa: 'Honour and loyalty!' "[148]

The identification of the Jew with money is just one example of the characterization of the Jew in the antisemitic mentality, as amorphous, Protean and ultimately indefinable. This finds expression in a familiar way in the subscription list in the association of Jews with a host of allied enemies, Protestants, Freemasons, politicians, intellectuals and "Jew-lovers" ("judaïsants"), for example: "May Christ confound the plans of his enemies, Jews, Freemasons and fellow-travellers of the Jews"; "For France, against the triple alliance of Freemasons, Jews and Protestants"; or "[against] the anti-French coalition of anarchists, intellectuals, Jews, Freemasons and Protestants."[149] Anti-Protestantism is a specific feature of Catholic entries, for example: "A French Catholic out of hatred for the Jews and the Protestants, enemies of France"; "Someone who is beginning to sympathize with the massacre of Saint Bartholomew, in face of the anti-patriotic attitude of the Protestants"; or "Down with the Huguenots, who are as dangerous, as low as the Jews".[150] Another group included in the "bloc" of enemies was that of magistrates, accused of collusion with Dreyfus and the Jews, for example: "Protest against the intrigues of the senior magistrates of France"; or "For the sword that will cut in pieces the criminal judges of the Cour de Cassation".[151] In all 156 "insults addressed to the Cour de Cassation and the Magistrature" were received.[152] Republican politicians and foreigners also figured. We have seen examples of attacks on Republican politicians, in the cases of Reinach and Clemenceau. The Republic itself was also identified with the Jews, for example: "A group of patriotic small farmers of Coutances against the Republic of the Jews and the Freemasons who are dishonouring France".[153] Foreigners indicted were the Germans, but, more often, the English. A "French captain" declared himself the "victim of the English and the Jews"; Clemenceau and other politicians were branded "the lackeys of the Jews and the English"; while stock reference was made to "perfidious Albion".[154]

Various features of this creation of a galaxy of opponents bear further examination. First is the Protean nature of the enemy, continuing the indefinable and thereby ultra-threatening characteristics attached particularly to the Jew himself. This function of the proliferation of enemies can be seen clearly in the case of the concept of the "enjuivé", the "judaïsant", "the Jews, Jew-like and their consorts . . ."[155] This concept greatly extends the danger and threat represented by the Jews, objectively a small and presumably relatively powerless minority, and allows them to be built up by the antisemite into a vast and overwhelming conspiracy. So subscribers could refer to "the Syndicat of treason", to "the Jewish and Masonic tyrants", and to "the horrible spider which is sucking all the blood of our country!"; and it could be claimed that "France . . . is dying under its Jews".[156] The whole form of the subscription list fits into this view of things. Subscribers were not attacking a defenceless Jewish minority, but, on the contrary, they were defending a helpless widow and an orphan against brutal attack, for example: "Eleven captains of the Marines, defenders of the widow and the orphan against the abominable Reinach"; "To defend the unfortunate widow and the orphan against an all-too-easy attack of the strong against the weak"; "disgust and scorn for Reinach, the cowardly insulter of a defenceless woman"; or "To help to defend a four-year old orphan attacked in dastardly fashion by the whole of Israel".[157] We have seen, in this context, how antisemites characterized themselves as "victims". In these different ways, a weak minority is paradoxically credited with near-total power, and is erected into a massive threat against which antisemites need to defend themselves.

Before broaching an explanation of this paradox, we must consider three further features of the antisemite's galaxy of enemies. The first is the inclusion in it of intellectuals. Anti-intellectualism was expressed in simple statements of hostility or dissociation, for example: "A non-intellectual"; or "A barber from Bourg, a patriot, but not an intellectual . . ."[158] Intellectuals, moreover, were explicitly associated with Jews, for example: "G. Delafargue, ex-captain in the Territorials, at Plougonver. Out of France with the yids and with their pimps, the intellectuals"; or, in a more innate way: "To muzzle all pedants and Jews, who are all the same under the skin".[159] As we saw in the professional breakdown, many subscribers were in "intellectual" occupations and some of these "intellectuals" actually proclaimed their anti-intellectualism, for example: "Doctor L.F., disgusted by these eunuchs called Intellectuals"; "M. Pelloux, medical student, but not an intellectual"; "A non-intellectual teacher"; "The pupils of the Philosophy and Rhetoric class of a Catholic college in Nantes, with the exception of one Intellectual poseur"; or "an archivist who is not an intellectual . . ."[160] This apparent contradiction is explained by other entries which make clear the connotations of the term: "Intellectual means incoherent, unbalanced"; "The Intellectuals are cowards"; "The Intellectuals are consultant-professors in anarchism";[161] and, as mentioned above, intellectuals are eunuchs. They thus have the same characteristics of confusion and ambiguity as the Jew. Moreover, a clear distinction was made by subscribers between being an intellectual and being intelligent. "Against the intellectuals who have lost their reason", affirmed one subscriber; while others announced themselves as "a student who is too intelligent to be an intellectual"; or as "an intelligent intellectual".[162] Emphasis on this distinction allowed those who possessed no officially-sanctioned status as persons of superior intelligence to turn the tables on those "intellectuals" who did, and who by so possessing this status in a newly-literate society made them feel inferior, envious and inadequate. "A rural mayor" declared himself "sickened by the clique that runs the University and which would crawl lower than anyone in front of a dictator, if France . . . gave herself one". Subscriptions were sent: "Out of hatred for the University pedants"; and "Out of hatred for the Homais, the so-called Intellectuals"; also from "a member of the intellectual proletariat"; and from "a university teacher, victim of the intellectuals".[163] Thus, one can argue that antisemitism, particularly in the intellectualized form in which it was developed in books, pamphlets and the newspaper press in the last decades of the nineteenth century, not only reflected the fact that society had become generally literate, but that it also performed an important function in salving the wounded pride of those disadvantaged in a society where intelligence as officially defined and sanctioned, and especially the passing of examinations, were becoming increasingly important as marks of status and as the means of rising and succeeding, and, more crucial, of not falling, in the social scale. We have seen that antisemites expressed fear and refusal in in the face of a competitive and meritocratic society, that they measured status by ascription and not by achievement, and anti-intellectualism, like anti-capitalism, derived from these related attitudes. More, antisemitism provided a short-cut to intelligence, to knowledge, as it were; it was a lore that was outside and beyond the normative lore of the "intellectuals", with roots in an older, instinctive, non-rational view of the world, connected with the past, the race, the historical region, the family, and with religion. So "a corporal of the 15th Dragoons" boasted that he was "a Frenchman who learned his history in [Drumont's] *La France juive*, which means that he knows a lot more about it than the intellectuals."[164] Related to this attitude is the claim laid to empirical knowledge, which "intellectuals" with their theories do not possess, for example: "An engineer who has seen the Jews at first hand".[165] The same attempt to resist a change in values probably informs the related views expressed by subscribers on the subject of education, which was in the 1890s making the majority of French children literate, and probably socializing them in a way alien to many parents. "It would not be surprising", wrote one subscriber wishfully, "if the State schools lost their pupils. Fathers of families want their children to receive an education that is more French."[166] This conflict over the function and aims of education in France was, of course, also an explicit conflict between Catholics and anticlerical Republicans.[167] The whole syndrome about intellectuals and education is also a factor that must be considered in any explanation of the predilection of students for antisemitism, that we have already discussed.

The second feature of the antisemite's *bloc* of enemies to merit further consideration is the fact that its very Protean nature made it difficult, if not impossible, for the objects of hostility to exculpate themselves in rational ways. The subscription list provides many examples of Freemasons, Protestants and Jews reacting to the witch-hunt mounted against them in the only way which it allowed them, by joining it. So there are entries from "a Freemason too old now to protest against the Jews who have invaded and who are dishonouring Freemasonry"; from "a Protestant who takes *La Libre Parole*"; from "a Protestant officer, who has no wish to see his co-religionists confused with a rabble of immigrants claiming to belong to the Reformed Church"; from "a Protestant who resents being associated with the Jews"; and from "two Protestants outraged by the attitude of certain of their co-religionists . . ."[168] Here the objects of antisemitic hostility attempt either to dissociate themselves from the prevailing conception posited of the group to which they belong, or they try to deflect opprobrium from their group on to another in the complex, usually the Jews. Within the terms set by the antisemite, attempts at rational self-defence or the refutation of blanket accusations and condemnations are ruled out. This is made very clear in the half-dozen entries from Jews attempting the same pathetic and self-defeating exercise in self-exculpation. This could be done only by virtually denying that one was a Jew, for example: "A Jewess deceived by the Yids who has given her heart to an Aryan"; "An

Israelite disgusted by the Jews"; or "A Jewess who denies her origin".[169] The fundamental contradiction in this espousal of antisemitism by Jews was that antisemitism did not allow such a denial of Jewishness. Third, it should be reiterated that the antisemite's constellation of enemies gave him an ever-renewed and ever-renewable negative self-definition. As "a Breton lieutenant in the reserve" wrote, if he was nothing else, he was always "anti-Jewish, anti-Huguenot and anti-Freemason".[170] Thus the antisemite created and discovered personal and social identity by setting himself in opposition to the Jew and his many associates. The force of this mechanism and its implications will become clearer if we consider the pervasive claim in the subscription list that the Jew was an agent of pollution.

In entry after entry Jews were referred to as animals, for example: "I hold a Jew in less esteem than the lowest of the animals that I have on my farm"; or "Jew, in other words a stinking and dangerous beast . . ."[171] In particular, Jews were called chimpanzees, orang-outangs, monkeys and pigs. This identification of Jews with animals is a form of the expression of Jewish otherness which received pseudo-scientific formulation in racialist terminology, but it was a mode of characterization which opens up wider avenues of explanation. The identification of a group of human beings with the non-human is already the expression of a profound feeling of ambiguity about them, and this view is further strengthened by the fact that the particular animals chosen are those which themselves have semi-human characteristics: apes, monkeys and hairless pigs. The ambiguity and the confusion of categories are reinforced again when the identification is extended to lower orders in the animal kingdom, for Jews were additionally referred to as "Jewish vermin", "the Jewish plague", "these centipedes", "the Jewish microbe", "these mites", "the cancer", "these bugs", "the horrible spider", and "Synagogue lice"; while Reinach is called "toad, reptile, amphibian . . ."[172] The Jew was thus identified with the ill-defined and dirty category of insect or reptile, with the unseen cause of disease, nebulous again and associated with dirt. Such, Mary Douglas has argued, are the characteristics of the polluting agent, and the reasons for the danger he represents; he does not fit into established classificatory categories, and thus threatens and disturbs any ordered view of the world.[173] The polluting, and thus dangerous, quality of the Jew was indicated in other, more direct terms, for example: "Down with the stinking Jews"; "The Jews are people who are not clean"; "Someone whose stomach is turned by the sight of a Jew"; "An enemy of a régime which lets the Jews foul the flag"; "A sewage worker who would not dare to touch Reinach for fear of being polluted"; or "Someone who blocks his nostrils every time that he passes rue Laffitte, for fear of breathing in Jewish microbes".[174] The polluting, threatening quality of the Jew lies in the fact that he is hard to define; he is ambiguous, marginal, interstitial. He is not properly French; he is associated with commercial professions and with the fluidity of financial transactions. In more obviously symbolic fashion, he is identified with the semi-human ape or monkey, with the amphibian, with the dirty insect or the inchoate microbe. This last identification, parallel to ancient accusations of well-poisoning, provides a telling metaphor, in addition, of the all-powerful secret role attributed to the Jewish minority in socio-economic life. Around the Jew in fact are clustered all the qualities of vagueness, uncertainty and change, which are the opposites of the values of certainty and absoluteness which the antisemite proclaims and adheres to: pedigree, race, family, region, Nation, Church, army and tradition—values that can be summed up as those of order and hierarchy.

A further ingredient in the conception of the Jew as a polluting agent, and one which gave it special personal intensity, was the projection on to the Jew of a fear of sex. This is found in various forms. First, there was the obsession of some subscribers with the fact that Jews are circumcised, for example: "Three of the uncircumcised. For the little goy"; "Down with those who are baptized with the pruning-shears!"; or "I am impatiently awaiting the the disappearance of the circumcised."[175] Circumcision, here, presumably evoked a fear of castration in men, as Freud suggested,[176] although women, too, expressed a horror of the practice. Then there were a large number of entries expressing an anxiety about sex by a rejection of sexuality. There were entries from women wishing to be men, for example: "A young Frenchwoman who would like to wear trousers and march under the orders of Déroulède"; or "A young lady who deplores the fact that she is not a man. Long live the army!"[177] Invocations of the transvestite Joan of Arc could also be placed in this category. There were entries also from those proclaiming their celibacy, for example: "A group of celibate ladies".[178] Associating the Jew more explicitly with sex as something strange and frightening were the large number of entries from girls and unmarried women, which expressed a horror of male Jews and the wish to have no contact with them, for example: "A.D., a *Parisienne* who cannot stand a Jew"; "A beautiful girl from Clermont-Ferrand, upset by the fact that her parents force her to mix socially with abominable yids [*youpins*]"; "A young woman whom the sight of a yid [*youtre*] sickens"; or "A lady who would hate to embrace von Reinach".[179] This feeling was often expressed in terms of rejecting a possible marriage with a Jew, for example: "Four girls of marriageable age who do not want Jewish husbands"; "A not-so-young lady, who will remain a spinster rather than marry a Jew"; or "a poor girl who would not marry a Jew for all the gold in the world".[180] These entries can be seen as straightforward condemnations of intermarriage, especially if set beside entries which make this consideration more obvious, such as: "Shame on the dastardly officer who has just taken a Jewish wife!";[181] but it should be remembered also that for most women of the time sexual relations would be thought of exclusively in terms of marriage, and the straightforward explanation of such entries would leave unexplained the need to reject what was not usually being offered or proposed, what was even culturally proscribed. Further support is lent to the suggestion that what is being rejected is sexuality itself, identified with the Jew, by the entries which referred to predatory sexual behaviour on the part of Jewish men, for example: "A poor schoolteacher deceived by rich Yids"; "A working girl seduced by her Jewish employer"; "A woman kidnapped by the Jews"; or "To put Christian women on their guard against Jews".[182] The subscription itself on behalf of a French woman attacked by a Jew fits into the same scheme, as one entry makes very plain: "A man from Roubaix who wants to contribute his modest share in rescuing a Frenchwoman from the hands of a Jew".[183] Underlying this attribution of special and frightening sexual power to the Jew, an attribution encountered in the case of other ethnic minorities,[184] was perhaps the anxiety of one group that its womenfolk would be captured by another. This was certainly one of the structural features of the Orléans rumour of 1969.[185] Confirmation of this suggestion is provided by the fact that, as in relations between Whites and Blacks in the Southern United States, women were often excluded from attack. The Jewess, in France, was associated with sexuality, but with a sexuality that was at least partially controlled and primarily the province, via prostitution, of the non-Jewish male.[186] Jewish women were sexually available to non-Jewish men, in a context where they were clearly inferiors and could be regarded as objects. Sexual relations with the Jewess therefore posed little threat to the antisemite's hierarchical universe, and could even create or strengthen his feeling of superiority. But, given this unilateral trespass across the boundaries, the Jewish male came more than ever to pose a threat, not only to the non-Jewish woman, as the embodiment of sex itself, but to non-Jewish men also, as a deprived but potent rival.

But we must return to the theme of the Jew as a polluting agent, a theme of which the fear of sex was but one aspect, and particularly to its teleological implications. Since the Jew was unclean, it was necessary to exclude or eliminate him for the health of the city. Thus one subscriber contributed "to disinfect us from the Jewish plague"; while another, already quoted, stated: "Jew, that is to say stinking and and dangerous beast: destruction is necessary".[187] It is in fact the characterization of the Jews as a polluting agents, threatening the good order and well-being of society, which explains the endless calls for their expulsion and extermination. As we have seen, many subscribers called for the exclusion of Jews from certain professions, and particularly from the army and the Civil Service. Some sought to restrict Jewish rights even further. One entry called for a blanket withdrawal of civil rights: "Outlaw the Jews!"; another proposed: "It should be forbidden for any Jew to travel on French soil without a yellow robe distinguishing him from French citizens",[188] thus attempting to restore the legal cantonment and sumptuary discrimination of the pre-emancipation period. Another example of proposed legal discrimination is provided by an entry which called for the confiscation of Jewish property: "A citizen in favour of the confiscation by the State of all property stolen by the Jews".[189] More frequent were appeals for the expulsion of Jews from France, for example: "When will the Jews be expelled?"; "For the expulsion of the race of traitors"; or "Out of France with the Jews!"[190] Moreover, expulsion was advocated on the explicit grounds that Jews were polluting, for example: "For the repatriation of the dirty Jews in Israel"; "Treat the Jews as if they had the plague and send them off to Palestine . . ."; or "If you want to avoid the bubonic plague, send the yids to Panama . . ."[191]

One finds the same justification used in the more extreme calls for extermination. Such entries include typically: "A lieutenant in the Marines for the end of the Jews"; "A group of officers who want the Jews to be exterminated"; "for the complete extermination of the Jewish race"; or simply the often repeated: "Death to the Jews!"[192] The link with pollution was made in many such entries, for example: "For the destruction of Jewry, really a human phylloxera"; "Get rid of the Jewish plague"; "We don't need lice-powder but gun-powder to destroy these pests"; "Partisans of the destruction of Jewish vermin"; "The flood of insults against the Army will be washed away in rivers of blood"; or "A history graduate who thinks that the Inquisition was an institution of public welfare, and the massacre of Saint Bartholomew an act of national cleansing".[193] On occasion, the need to remove the polluting agent had explicitly genocidal connotations, for example: "For the radical circumcision of the yids, the plague of the universe"; or "To prevent the multiplication of the evil race of yids".[194] Subscribers were not content either with the advocacy of extermination in general terms. Entry after entry betrayed a personal sadistic involvement in detailed tortures and cruel deaths wished on Jews, for example: "A military doctor . . . who wishes that vivisecetion were practised on Jews rather than on harmless rabbits"; "A group of officers on active service. To buy nails to crucify the Jews"; "A lady schoolteacher who calls for the return of the *noyades* of Nantes"; "Berthe, a cook, to roast the Jews"; "to make a dog's meal by boiling up certain noses"; "J.C., a patriot from the Isère, would like to see all Jews nailed to the wall"; "R.G., anti-Dreyfusard from Le Mans, would like all Jews to have their eyes put out"; "A coachman from Savoie who would like to have the Jews crushed to pulp with bludgeons"; "An inhabitant of Baccarat who would like to see all the yids, yiddesses and their brats in the locality burned in the glass furnaces here"; "Break the Jews on the wheel"; "All yids should be burned at the stake . . ."; "To turn all the yids into mincemeat"; "Someone who is in favour of bringing back torture to soften up the carcases of these good yids"; or: "To give Jew-ball [*Reinach*] an acid bath for a New Year present".[195] This dismal catalogue leaves little doubt that antisemitism provided an important outlet for repressed violence, aggression and feelings of inferiority. Moreover, the conception of Jews as sub-human animals allowed wishes for their elimination to be easily couched in the language of butchery. In allowing its adherents to vent their sadistic feelings in this extreme way, antisemitism was also presenting them with an immediate compensation. They were given a false sense of self-importance by their clear attachment to the high cause of army, Nation and the forces of order and hierarchy. Participation in the collective call for the suppression of the main enemy of that cause, the Jews, gave that attachment a new degree of commitment, and made it more obvious and binding. Verbal extremism was a step towards the level of action, and the implementation of a duty. So "J.O." boasted that he would not remain "inactive when the alarm rings for the massacre of the Jews"; and "Simon, victim of Panama" declared that he desired "to do his duty in the suppression of the Jews".[196] The relief provided by participation in extreme antisemitism and the simulation of action can perhaps be detected also in those entries where subscribers showed a very high degree of involvement in the wish to wound and kill, for example: "A cavalry officer in the reserve, profoundly anti-Dreyfusard, who would love to massacre the dirty yids with his own hands"; "A Corsican medical student . . . would like to dissect all the yids in France"; "P.G. . . . who would love to circumcise some Jews"; "A bookbinder who would like to bind antisemitic books with the skin of Jews"; "Someone who would like to eat some Jew, so that he could defecate it"; or "abbé Cros, ex-lieutenant, for a bedside rug made with Yid skins, so that he could tread on it night and morning".[197] Before discussing the function and implications of this verbal sadism further, it should be set beside the apparently contrasting sentimentality that also characterizes the subscription list.

The note of sentimentality and self-pity is evident in the constant reference to victimization, already encountered, but it is inherent in the whole conception of the subscription, a subscription for a widow and an orphan launched in the Christmas season. Some entries make this particularly clear, for example: "for the valiant widow . . ."; "to the unfortunate widow and her dear child"; "For Mme Henry and her dear child"; or: "A kiss for the little cherub".[198] A further degree of sentimentality is achieved in entries sent in the name of children, for example: "G., Charles and H. Aubry. All the pennies from their money-box with a big kiss for their friend, the little Henry boy"; "A group of young antisemitic children, aged from four to eleven, just before they open their presents round the Christmas tree . . ."; or an entry from "two children in the hope that the child Jesus won't forget their unfortunate little friend on Christmas Eve".[199] Such sentimentality was by no means incidental to antisemitism, but is simply another reflection of its essential refusal of reality. It was linked, moreover, through childhood to the same extreme exclusions encountered above. Several subscribers boasted of inculcating antisemitic sentiments in their children, for example: "A father who brings up his children to hate the Jews"; or "J. Cochet who is teaching his son to tie knots to hang the Jews with"[200]; and the same boast was made by a "state schoolteacher from the Jura who never fails to tell his pupils that the Jews and their friends are the vampires of France".[201] Jews here are set in the line of the traditional bogeymen of the fairy- and folk-tale; antisemitism, indeed, can, up to a point, be seen as the extension of these, the prolongation of childhood's phobias into adult and social life.[202] It can thus be at once something kept fondly alive within families, associated with money-boxes and Christmas, and, at the same time, the deliberate expression of hatred and the advocacy of physical violence and extermination.

This brings us back to the problem of the intention and implications of such verbal extremism, and raises the question of whether or how far the subscription list represents the real and serious advocacy of wholesale destruction. The entries in the list do give support to the idea of a logic of extermination being inherent in antisemitic attitudes and opinions, however apparently "moderate".[203] Expulsion would be a sufficient aim, if antisemites were concerned simply with a real and definable minority. In fact, as we have indicated, the Jew of the antisemites is largely a mythical construct, essentially indefinable, and defence against his vague power requires more radical measures. This essential lack of definition, the association of the Jew with a host of fellow-travellers and *"judaïsants"* makes him ineradicable in practice, and so formulae of malediction escalate against him. As he looms more Protean, more threatening and more powerful, the gestures necessary to exorcize his power have to become more and more extreme, until they end in the invocation of genocide. From another perspective, the antisemite's world of absolutes leaves no room for half-measures. The Jew must be totally eradicated from it. As one subscriber put it, she was "for the triumph of the truth and the extermination of the Jews",[204] and the one necessarily implied the other. But, despite the occurrence of actual physical violence directed against real Jews in the period of the Dreyfus Affair, one must be careful to point out that this logic of extermination remained on the level of ritual gesture and psychological compensation. There is a parallel here with the violent revolutionary rhetoric, calling for the destruction of the bourgeois world, which contemporary Socialists continued to employ, while pursuing reformist policies in practice.[205] Antisemites were, of course, even less integrated into the established political system than the Socialists, and it is arguable that their ideology would therefore be likely to have an even higher mythical content. Antisemitism, in this perspective, can be seen as a magical reaction to the process of social change, a magical conception of that process, and an expressive rather than an instrumental means of coping with it and with the strains which it imposed. As with similar ritualistic reactions to social change in simpler societies, such as the cargo cults of Melanesia, it was a blend of the traditional and the modern,[206] or rather an attempt to reassert what were seen as traditional values by necessarily modern means, since the traditional world was changed, changing or under threat of change. And thus, to an extent, the espousal of antisemitic attitudes and the deliberate expression of antisemitic opinions were, as we have suggested above, ends in themselves, which did not require further fulfilment in action. The antisemite found his means of explaining and thus of coming to terms with social change, when he identified the Jew as responsible for that change, and when he was able to define himself and his own situation in contrast to the Jew. This solution was ritualized in the accusation of pollution and the call for expulsion and extermination, and received public, semi-liturgical display in the newspaper press, in attendance at meetings and demonstrations, and in participation in public subscriptions. But the translation of such a "final solution" into practice was not necessarily implied or intended. Indeed, as Sartre perceived,[207] the antisemite needed the Jew, and required his continued existence in order to define himself, and it is only with the hindsight provided by the Nazi "holocaust" that one can imagine a different teleology. Although antisemitism as a system of ideas always contained potential justification for practical genocide, the reasons for the transformation of this antisemitism from a system of ideas and beliefs that was virtually closed into an ongoing system of action cannot be found in analysis of the structure or the function of the former, but must lie rather in its general social context; and in France of the 1890s such a transformation was out of the question. But this should not lead us to neglect the fact that, though antisemitism created its own mythical concept of the Jew, it was also directed inevitably against real Jews, and we will consider the implications of this in the last part of this book.

Analysis of the Henry Subscription has allowed us to penetrate attitudes to the Dreyfus Affair and the antisemitism which it aroused or exposed, to some depth, an analysis which we will pursue further and on a wider front in Part Three. Meanwhile, in order to substantiate the assertion as to the mainly non-political and non-activist nature of antisemitism in the 1890s, and to provide further information about it, we will now turn to an examination of the organized antisemitic movement in France in the period.

NOTES

1 Reinach, *Histoire de l'Affaire Dreyfus*, IV, pp. 431–9; see also Paléologue, *Journal de l'Affaire Dreyfus*, pp. 132–3.
2 Viau, *Vingt ans d'antisémitisme*, p. 181.
3 *La Libre Parole* organized similar subscriptions on other occasions, notably in November and December 1901 to launch the Comité National Antijuif, but the number of subscribers was small compared with the Henry Subscription. In calculating the total number of subscribers to the latter, groups have been counted as 10 units, although they were frequently larger.
4 The task of analysing the Henry Subscription is greatly facilitated by the existence of Pierre Quillard, *Le Monument Henry: Listes des souscripteurs classés mé-thodiquement et selon l'ordre alphabétique* (Paris, 1899), referred to hereafter as Q.
5 Q, p. 613.
6 Q, pp. 452 and 370.
7 Q, p. 366.
8 Q, pp. 588 and 401.
9 The same pattern of expression of opinion by professional and other groups is found interestingly in another contemporary instance. After her acquittal from the charge of murdering her mother and her husband, Mme Steinheil received a large number of letters from families, from groups of army officers and NCOs, from "classes" of students and from groups of employees at banks and factories. Steinheil, *My Memoirs*, p. 454. Did the parallel in forms of expression extend also to what was being expressed? Was there a connection between an interest in crime and anti-Jewish prejudice, a common sadism at the basis of both, as the Dreyfu-sard Octave Mirbeau suggested in *Le Journal d'une femme de chambre* (1900) (Paris, 1964), pp. 338–47 and *passim?* For some confirmation of this hypothesis, see pp. 156–7 below.
10 As Waleffe commented in another context: "Toute campagne de presse un peu vive excite les fous". *Quand Paris était un paradis*, p. 422. In fact, however, very few entries could be said to reflect individual lunacy, but see n. 105 below.
11 See chapter XVII, pp. 655 and ff. below; and Sorlin, *"La Croix" et les Juifs*, pp. 220–2.
12 This runs counter to findings for the contemporary United States; see Selznick and Steinberg, *The Tenacity of Prejudice*, pp. 73–7 and 93, where education is said to be "the crucial factor in predicting anti-Semitic prejudice".
13 These figures are taken from J.-C. Toutain, *La Population de la France de 1700 à 1959, Cahiers de l'Institut de Science Economique Appliquée*, Supplément no. 133 (Série AF, no. 3) (Paris, 1963), Table 16, pp. 60–1.
14 These figures are taken, for convenience, from A.de Foville, *La France écono-mique, Statistique raisonnée et comparative* (Paris, 1890), p. 12.

15 See André Siegfried, *Tableau politique de la France de l'Ouest sous la Troisième République* (Paris, 1913); Goguel, *Géographie des élections françaises*, pp. 32–9.

16 See Jacques Gadille, *La Pensée et l'action politiques des évêques français au début de la IIIe République 1870–1883* (Paris, 1967), I, maps between pp. 152 and 153, "La Vitalité religieuse des diocèses de France en 1877".

17 See Siegfried, op. cit.; Maurice Bordes, "L'évolution politique du Gers sous la IIIe République", *Information Historique* (1961), pp. 19–22.

18 On the whole question of electoral antisemitism, see chapter VIII.

19 Of these, the Finistère (-2) was represented by subscriptions from 2 national and 2 local politicians; the Morbihan (-2), from 2 national; the Loire-Inférieure (-2), from 4 national and 2 local; the Deux-Sèvres (-2), from 2 national and 1 local; the Vendée (-3), from 2 national; the Aveyron (-3), from 1 national; and the Côtes-du-Nord (-5), from 1 national.

20 The Haute-Saône experienced an intense political conflict during the period of the Affair; see Carel, "Les Forces politiques en Haute-Saône".

21 Raymond Long, *Les Elections législatives en Côte-d'Or depuis 1870: Essai d'interprétation sociologique* (Paris, 1958), however, finds no evidence of antisemitism at a political level in this department.

22 Marlin suggests that overt antisemitism among the Right in the Doubs was a comparatively recent phenomenon, and relates its emergence to the experience of a militantly Republican Jewish Prefect, Isaïe Levaillant from 1883 to 1885; see Marlin, "La Droite à Besançon", pp. 229–31. Levaillant was later Prefect of the Haute-Saône; see Drumont, *La France juive*, II, pp. 419–20.

23 See Paul Leuilliot, *L'Alsace au début du XIXe siècle: Essais d'histoire politique, économique et religieuse (1815–1830)* (Paris, 1960), III, pp. 231–46; Hertzberg, *The French Enlightenment and the Jews*, pp. 121, 257 and 366–7; see also chapter III, pp. 107 and 115 above; and chapter XVII, pp. 663–5 below.

24 Q, p. 444.

25 See Chalmin, *L'Officier français*, p. 197; Girardet, *La Société militaire*, p. 282.

26 See Thibaudet, *Les Princes lorrains;* Madaule, *Le Nationalisme de Maurice Barrès*, chapter III; Sternhell, *Maurice Barrès*, pp. 285–90 and 322–36.

27 Philippe Bernard, *Economie et Sociologie de la Seine-et-Marne, 1850–1950* (Paris, 1953), provides no evidence of antisemitism in this department.

28 See Drumont, *La France juive*, II, p. 82; Drumont, *La Dernière Bataille*, pp. 12–14; Viau, op. cit., pp. 112–18.

29 See Morin *et al.*, *La Rumeur d'Orléans*.

30 See Z. Szajkowski, "The Decline and Fall of Provençal Jewry", *Jewish Social Studies*, 6 (1944), pp. 31–54; Marrus, *The Politics of Assimilation*, pp. 31–2.

31 See Henri Baudrillart, *Les Populations agricoles de la France*, 3e série, *Les Populations du Midi* (Paris, 1893), pp. 196, 231 and *passim;* Placide Rambaud et Monique Vincienne, *Les Transformations d'une société rurale, La Maurienne (1561–1962)* (Paris, 1964); Jacques Basso, *Les Elections législatives dans le département des Alpes-Maritimes de 1860 à 1939, Eléments de sociologie électorale* (Paris, 1968), pp. 209–11; Pierre Rollet, *La Vie quotidienne en Provence au temps de Mistral* (Paris, 1972), chapters VII and VIII.

32 Baudrillart, op. cit., p. 190.

33 Reinach, op. cit., III, p. 586.

34 Boni de Castellane, *L'Art d'être pauvre* (Paris, 1926), p. 164; see also Dardenne, *Godefroy Cavaignac*, p. 490.

35 "Yousouf-Crapule". Q, p. 538.

36 Q, p. 552.

37 See Marrus, op. cit., p. 226; Basso, op. cit., pp. 190–1; Zévaès, *L'Affaire Dreyfus*, p. 122; A.S. Grenier, *Nos Députés, 1898–1902* (Paris, no date), p. 32.

38 See Gaston Monnerville, *Clemenceau* (Paris, 1968), pp. 192–210.

39 Q, pp. 541 and 538.

40 See Louis Andrieux, *A travers la République, Mémoires* (Paris, 1926), chapter VII, "Comment je devins Bas-Alpin", pp. 343–58; Pierre Barral, "Géographie de l'opinion sous la Troisième République", *Information Historique* (1962), p. 154.
41 See Goguel, *Géographie des élections françaises*, pp. 62–9; Roger Pierre, *Les Origines du syndicalisme et du socialisme dans le Drôme (1850–1920)* (Paris, 1973); and n. 46 below.
42 On the winegrowers of the Côte-d'Or in this period, see Robert Laurent, *Les Vignerons de la "Côte-d'Or"* (Paris, 1957), I, pp. 325–62; and II, pp. 15–16 and 113–18; also, more generally, Germain Martin and Paul Martenot, *La Côte d'Or (Etude d'économie rurale)* (Dijon and Paris, 1909).
43 See Siegfried, op. cit. (1964 edition), pp. 485–95. Abbé Garnier, leader of the antisemitic Union Nationale, came from this department and retained support there; see Divry, *L'Abbé Garnier*, pp. 16–22 and 64–6.
44 See Jean Bastié, *La Croissance de la banlieue parisienne* (Paris, 1964); and chapter VI, p. 189 below. The municipal council of Levallois-Perret was dominated by the Union Nationale in the late 1890s, according to Divry, op. cit., p. 29.
45 See chapter I, p. 18 and n. 102 above.
46 See Viau, op. cit., p. 60; and chapter VIII, pp. 222–6 below.
47 Figures here are taken from Toutain, op. cit., Tables 60–90, pp. 162 and ff.; and from Foville, op. cit., p. 62, for the clergy. Not all the figures relate to 1896, but this is not for our purposes too important.
48 See Paul Boyaval, *Lutte contre le sweating-system* (Paris, 1911); Charles Benoist, *Les Ouvrières de l'aiguille à Paris* (Paris, 1895); M. Rouff, "Une industrie motrice: La haute couture parisienne et son évolution", *Annales*, I (1946), pp. 116–33; Henriette Vanier, *La Mode et ses métiers; Frivolités et luttes des classes 1830–1870* (Paris, 1960).
49 Q, pp. 528 and 519.
50 Q, p. 454.
51 Q, pp. 504, 453 and 284.
52 Q, pp. 470 and 436.
53 Among many examples of latent conflict in the master-servant relationship portrayed in literature of the time, see Mirbeau, op. cit.; Proust, *A la Recherche du temps perdu*, English uniform Edition, V, pp. 12–15 and 27; VII, pp. 260–9; and VIII, p. 268. For further discussion, see my "Proust's *A la Recherche du temps perdu* as a Document of Social History", *Journal of European Studies*, 1 (1971), pp. 224–7.
54 Q, pp. 529, 461 and 485.
55 Q, p. 499.
56 Q, p. 623.
57 Q, p. 111.
58 Q, pp. 25, 28, 58 and 52.
59 Q, p. 533. Such entries are not included in the total of 4,500 given above.
60 Q, p. 17.
61 Q, pp. 68 and 70.
62 Q, pp. 87, 59 and 33.
63 Q, pp. 25, 38 and 27. Morny and Saint-Arnaud were the authors of the successful *coup* of 2 December 1851.
64 Q, pp. 159 and 419.
65 Such, with qualifications, is the prediction proffered by Selznick and Steinberg, op. cit., pp. 80–3.
66 See Marrus, op. cit., pp. 40–5.
67 Q, pp. 188, 186, 183 and 519–20.
68 See the critique of Hippolyte Taine, *Les Origines de la France contemporaine*, XI, *Le Régime moderne*, Tome troisième (1899) (Paris, 1947), pp. 333–58.
69 Drumont's writings, for example, as we have noted, had a strong socialistic or populist flavour; see chapter XI. For student anti-rationalism, the vogue of Barrès

among the young is significant; see also, for a slightly later period, "Agathon" (Henri Massis et Alfred de Tarde), *Les Jeunes Gens d'aujourd'hui* (Paris, 1913).

70 See Byrnes, *Antisemitism in Modern France,* pp. 140–55 and 280–90; Byrnes, "The French Publishing Industry and its Crisis in the 1890s", *Journal of Modern History,* 23 (1951), pp. 232–42.

71 Q, p. 524.

72 Q, p. 420.

73 Q, p. 26.

74 Q, p. 186.

75 Q, pp. 189, 159 and 469.

76 Q, pp. 162, 416, 497, 481, and 420.

77 Q, pp. 121, 531 and 492.

78 Q, pp. 26, 436, 448, 481 and 495.

79 Q, pp. 485 and 212.

80 Q, p. 431.

81 Q, p. 424.

82 See also chapter X, pp. 275–7 below.

83 See Yves-Marie Bercé, *Croquants et nu-pieds: Les soulèvements paysans en France du XVIe au XIXe siècle* (Paris, 1974); Paule-Marie Duhet, *Les Femmes et la Révolution 1789–1794* (Paris, 1971); Olwen Hufton, "Women in Revolution 1789–1796", *Past and Present,* 53 (1971), pp. 90–108; Cobb, *The Police and the People,* pp. 232–9 and *passim;* Edith Thomas, *Les Pétroleuses* (Paris, 1963).

84 Q, p. 615.

85 As Girardet has pointed out: "Les souscripteurs ayant généralement accompagné leurs envois de commentaires divers, il n'est guère de document idéologique qui se prêterait davantage à une étude approfondie de psychologie sociale." Raoul Girardet, *Le Nationalisme français 1871–1914* (Paris, 1966), p. 178.

86 Q, pp. 378, 369 and 392.

87 Karl Baedeker, *Paris and its Environs, Handbook for Travellers* (Leipzig, 1900), p. 267.

88 Q, pp. 608, 480, 505 and 610.

89 Q, pp. 20, 482 and 694.

90 Q, p. 444.

91 Q, pp. 444, 463 and 104.

92 Q, pp. 474, 613 and 505.

93 Q, pp. 126–7 and 508.

94 For the importance of the latter in antisemitic mythology, see Verdès-Leroux, *Scandale financier et antisémitisme catholique.* It is interesting that the theme of "victimization" was also important in German rhetoric in the early twentieth century; see J.P. Stern, *Hitler, The Führer and the People* (London, 1975), pp. 29–34.

95 Q, pp. 389, 391, 513, 400 and 365.

96 Fiscal relief for large families was part of the platform of organized antisemitism; see chapter X, p. 293 below.

97 Q, pp. 486 and 487.

98 Q, p. 404.

99 Q, pp. 438, 434, 225 and 465.

100 Q, pp. 500 and 540.

101 Q, pp. 57 and 106.

102 Q, p. 472.

103 Q, pp. 133, 474, 84 and 100.

104 Q, pp. 74, 96 and 432.

105 Q, pp. 417, 469, 404, 37 and 363. Like others of its genre, the Henry Subscription invited a fair number of facetious entries; Quillard list 272 in this category, pp. 405–14.

106 This interpretation owes a great deal to Sartre, *Réflexions sur la question juive.*

107 Q, pp. 469, 612 and 443–4.
108 Q, pp. 448, 449 and 438.
109 Q, pp. 490 and 475.
110 Q, pp. 466, 619 and 390.
111 Q, pp. 468, 395, 378, 504 and 530.
112 Q, p. 362.
113 Q, p. 363.
114 Q, p. 46.
115 Q, p. 627.
116 Q, p. 437.
117 Q, p. 633.
118 See Girardet, *Le Nationalisme français;* Sternhell, *Maurice Barrès;* Barrès, *Scènes et doctrines du nationalisme.*
119 Q, p. 191.
120 Q, pp. 450 and 598.
121 Q, pp. 577 and 574.
122 Q, pp. 492, 493 and 494.
123 Q, pp. 438, 432 and 421.
124 Q, pp. 488, 417, 418, 465 and 475. It is interesting to note in this context that Jews were identified, with minor objective justification, with the organization of insurance against conscription in the nineteenth century; as providers of replacements for the sons of the bourgeoisie selected for military service, they were "marchands d'hommes", and could serve as targets for the projection of any feelings of guilt that this evasion of patriotic duty may have occasioned, at the time or retrospectively; see N. Sales de Bohigo, " 'Marchands d'Hommes' et Sociétés d'Assurances contre le service militaire au XIXe siècle", *Revue d'Histoire Economique et Sociale,* 46 (1968), pp. 339–80. The buying of substitutes was abolished in 1872, but those with higher educational qualifications were exempted from the full period of military service until 1905, something which, as Ralston points out, helped to swell the ranks of French students; see Ralston, *The Army of the Republic,* pp. 47 and 302–5.
125 The list included 97 entries from declared Royalists and 63 from declared Bonapartists.
126 Q, pp. 221, 223, 220 and 452 ("toute la fripouille juive et judaïsante").
127 Q, pp. 220, 230, 227 and 228.
128 Q, pp. 103 and 220.
129 Q, pp. 222 and 436.
130 Q, pp. 218, 219 and 138.
131 Q, p. 453.
132 Q, pp. 425, 456 and 613.
133 See Gadille, op. cit., particularly I, pp. 46–108; Michel Denis, *L'Eglise et la République en Mayenne, 1896–1906* (Paris, 1967); Sorlin, *"La Croix" et les Juifs;* and chapter XIV, pp. 556–9 below.
134 Q, p. 498.
135 Q, pp. 471, 505 and 523.
136 See Joshua Trachtenberg, *The Devil and the Jews* (New Haven, 1943); Léon Poliakov, "Le Diable et les Juifs, La 'Diabolisation' des Juifs en Occident", in M. Milner, ed., *Entretiens sur l'homme et le diable* (Paris, 1965), pp. 189–212; Freddy Raphaël, "Le Juif et le Diable dans la civilisation de l'Occident", *Social Compass,* 19 (1972), pp. 549–66.
137 Q, pp. 434 and 514.
138 Q, pp. 149 and 477.
139 Q, p. 498.
140 See chapter XIV, pp. 527–32 below.
141 Q, p. 369.
142 Q, pp. 538 and 422.

143 See Anatole Leroy-Beaulieu, *Les Doctrines de haine: L'antisémitisme, L'anti-protestantisme, L'anticléricalisme* (Paris, 1902).
144 Q, p. 477.
145 Q, pp. 469 and 441.
146 Q, p. 469.
147 Q, pp. 57, 472, 59 and 536.
148 Q, p. 503.
149 Q, pp. 495, 436 and 419.
150 Q, pp. 431, 432 and 441.
151 Q, pp. 46 and 230.
152 Q, pp. 558–65.
153 Q, p. 222.
154 Q, pp. 23, 527 and 220.
155 Q, p. 476.
156 Q, pp. 458, 483 and 434.
157 Q, pp. 29, 424, 520 and 487.
158 Q, pp. 635 and 613.
159 Q, pp. 13 and 489.
160 Q, pp. 158, 180, 637, 190 and 524.
161 Q, pp. 635–6. The term and the concept of the "intellectual" originated in France at this time of course; for further discussion, see chapter XVI, pp. 606–12 below.
162 Q, pp. 635–6 and 193.
163 Q, pp. 34, 463, 635, 398 and 152.
164 Q, p. 82.
165 Q, p. 146.
166 Q, p. 482.
167 See Mona Ozouf, *L'Ecole, l'Eglise et la République 1871–1914* (Paris, 1963).
168 Q, pp. 470, 212, 49, 435 and 494.
169 Q, pp. 410, 432 and 476. (The term *"israélite"* was that used by French Jews and in polite usage of them, in distinction to *"juif"* which had pejorative connotations; see chapter V, p. 169 and n. 5; and chapter X, p. 262 and n. 165 below.)
170 Q, p. 37.
171 Q, pp. 422 and 455.
172 Q, pp. 416, 485, 419, 437, 457, 528, 452, 461, 483, 491 and 551.
173 Mary Douglas, *Purity and Danger: An Analysis of Concepts of Pollution and Taboo* (London, 1966).
174 Q, pp. 428, 475, 502, 463, 557 and 474.
175 Q, pp. 580, 442 and 475.
176 "The castration complex is the deepest unconscious root of antisemitism; for even in the nursery little boys hear that a Jew has something cut off his penis—a piece of his penis, they think—and this gives them a right to despise Jews." Sigmund Freud, *Analysis of a Phobia in a Five-Year-Old Boy* (1909); and "The conclusion strikes me as inescapable that here we may also trace one of the roots of the antisemitism which appears with such elemental force and finds such irrational expression among the nations of the West. Circumcision is unconsciously equated with castration." *Leonardo da Vinci and a Memory of his Childhood* (1910). Freud, English Standard Edition, X, p. 36, and XI, pp. 95–6 n.
177 Q, pp. 642–3 and 598.
178 Q, p. 378.
179 Q, pp. 430, 456, 466 and 529.
180 Q, pp. 467, 466 and 405.
181 Q, p. 434.
182 Q, pp. 149, 483, 486 and 489.
183 Q, pp. 497–8.
184 See, for example, John Dollard, *Caste and Class in a Southern Town* (New York, 3rd ed., 1957), chapter VII; Calvin C. Hernton, *Sex and Racism* (London, 1969).

185 The rumour, occurring in other French towns also, consisted of the belief that young girls were being abducted for the "white slave trade" from changing cubicles of dress shops or boutiques, owned by Jews; originating among adolescent girls, it spread to many other sections of the community, and especially adult women; see Morin *et al.*, op. cit.

186 See Sartre, op. cit., (1954 edition), pp. 56–7; Luce A. Klein, *Portrait de la Juive dans la littérature française* (Paris, 1970); and chapter XV, pp. 590–6 below.

187 Q, pp. 419 and 455.

188 Q, pp. 476 and 473.

189 Q, p. 456.

190 Q, pp. 418, 465 and 476.

191 Q, pp. 492, 495 and 502.

192 Q, pp. 36, 59, 416 and 500.

193 Q, pp. 430, 435, 452, 485, 501 and 150.

194 Q, pp. 80 and 489.

195 Q, pp. 39, 59, 149, 417, 435, 436, 439, 456, 472, 475, 501, 491, 503 and 517–18. ("Boule-de-Juif" was a nickname for Reinach, coined by Rochefort or Déroulède; see chapter XI, n. 90; and chapter XII, n. 68).

196 Q, pp. 436 and 427.

197 Q, pp. 55, 186, 439, 496, 503 and 95.

198 Q, pp. 448, 54, 489 and 568.

199 Q, pp. 566, 471 and 22.

200 Q, pp. 486 and 418.

201 Q, p. 422.

202 This suggestion confirms the general interpretation of antisemitism made by Norman Cohn, *Warrant for Genocide: The Myth of the Jewish World-Conspiracy and the Protocols of the Elders of Zion* (London, 1967), pp. 251–68.

203 See Adorno *et al.*, *The Authoritarian Personality*, p. 633; and Albert Memmi, *Portrait d'un Juif* (Paris, 1969), pp. 203–4; also the comments of Mosse, *The Crisis of German Ideology*, pp. 138–9.

204 Q, p. 424.

205 See M. Perrot and A. Kriegel, *Le Socialisme français et le pouvoir* (Paris, 1966), pp. 9–83.

206 See, for example, John Beattie, *Other Cultures: Aims, Methods and Achievements of Social Anthropology* (London, 1964), pp. 71–2, 204–7 and 260–4; Peter Worsley, *The Trumpet Shall Sound: A Study of "Cargo" Cults in Melanesia* (London, 1957).

207 Sartre, op. cit., p. 14.

PART TWO
THE ANTISEMITIC MOVEMENT IN FRANCE
AT THE END OF THE NINETEENTH
CENTURY

CHAPTER V
DRUMONT, *LA FRANCE JUIVE* AND *LA LIBRE PAROLE*

T HE JEWISH SYSTEM HAS NEVER BEEN MORE THREATENED", PRO-claimed Edouard Drumont in 1891; "never has the Jew been the object of such justified hatred, of such unanimous cursing, never has the desire to put an end to his evil exploitation burned so strongly in everyone."[1] "Today, the Christian has only to listen, on every side he hears a cry go up of reprobation against the Jew, for whom the liberal of 1830 had such tender feelings."[2] The research of Byrnes, Verdès-Leroux, Sorlin, Pierrard and others[3] has shown that these boasts by the main apostle of French antisemitism were not vain. Hostility towards Jews was not, of course, new in nineteenth-century France. The Emancipation of 1791 had been won in the face of considerable opposition, and had been partially reversed by Napoleon I. The discriminatory legislation of the First Empire did not lapse until 1818, and full legal equality was not secured until the formal abolition of the oath *more judaico* in 1846.[4] The removal of central governmental authority during the Revolutionary period and in 1848 had, moreover, revealed the existence of a strong current of popular hostility in some areas, particularly in the East. This revealed itself also in popular usage—the word *"juif"* being a current term of abuse[5]—and in popular literature, which had a well-developed hostile stereotype of the Jewish banker and usurer.[6] This popular cultural antisemitism was maintained to some extent in the teaching and the practice of the Catholic Church,[7] and was lent a certain novel impetus in the writings of early Socialists like Fourier, Toussenel and Proudhon.[8] However, it is not until the 1880s and 1890s that one can speak of an antisemitic movement in France, a movement that translated ancient prejudices into an ideology of modern idiom, and which expressed itself in an extensive literature in periodical and book form, as well as in specifically antisemitic organizations. Only then did antisemitism become an issue of prime importance, "the ethnographical and social problem, which for some time, rightly or wrongly, has preoccupied so many decent people".[9] The Dreyfus Affair only intensified and extended the scope of an agitation which had begun a decade before, and in the Affair itself, as we have seen, susceptible opinion was orchestrated by militant journalists and activists. "For several years, antisemitism was to rage without serious opposition", a contemporary wrote in 1902.[10] The general nature of antisemitic ideology and the reasons for its success will be discussed in the third part of this book, but first the history and make-up of the organized movement that took the lead in its promulgation must be outlined.

As French antisemites were well aware,[11] they were participating in a phenomenon, which had European dimensions, but French antisemitism has also its own particular internal history. Its mutation into an organized movement and ideology can be dated fairly precisely from the early 1880s. According to Jules Isaac, "around 1880, antisemitism had still made little headway in French society. I did not yet suspect that, in the eyes of other French people, it would be an indelible defect simply to be a Jew"[12]; and Charles Gide told Dagan in 1899 that "only a decade ago no one would have been able to predict that antisemitism would become acclimatized in France . . ."[13] As Verdès-Leroux has emphasized,[14] the crash of the Union Générale Bank in 1882 played an important part in changing this state of affairs, and heralded a new kind of antisemitic movement and argumentation. Symbolizing in retrospect the start of the "Great Depression", and fitting easily with the popular association of the Jews with the mysteries of high finance, points to which we shall return, the crash deserves something of the status of a founding event, not least on the subjective level. Widely interpreted in the press as the result of deliberate action against the Catholic finance house by its Jewish rivals, led by Rothschild, the crash directly affected many small savers and indirectly worried many more. "Crash?", remembered Maurice Donnay. "It was the first time that I had heard that word uttered. I was totally ignorant of anything to do with the Stock Exchange, but they explained to me that the Union Générale was a Catholic bank that Jewish High Finance had had it in for, and that a lot of people had been ruined."[15] "Historically", wrote Léon Daudet later, Drumont was to reap the harvest of "the justified irritation produced by the engineering of the Union Générale crash";[16] and already in 1885, the *Revue Bleue* noted: "It cannot escape the attentive observer, that for a few years now a current of antisemitism has grown up, even in Paris."[17]

But the popularization of antisemitism as an ideology providing a total and detailed system of social explanation came a year later in 1886 with the publication of Drumont's *La France juive.* In his *Testament d'un antisémite* (1891), Drumont claimed that he had been "the initiator of a great movement in France",[18] and this was a claim with which friends and enemies concurred. "Antisemitism was merely a slightly shameful tradition of the Ancien Régime", wrote Maurice Barrès in *Le Figaro* in February 1890, "when, in the spring of 1886, Drumont revived it with a slogan that caused a great stir."[19] "It was only with the appearance of *La France juive*", wrote François Bournand in 1898, "that an antisemitic movement made itself apparent and acquired cohesion";[20] while Raphaël Viau agreed that "antisemitism in France dates from *La France juive,* for Toussenel had been forgotten . . ."[21] Another antisemitic writer, the Comtesse de Martel, who wrote a series of popular novels under the pseudonym of "Gyp," expressed the same view: "Until the time of *La France juive*, we detested the Jews, of course, but it was of little consequence . . ."[22] "One cannot deny", admitted a critic, "that from the day on which he launched *La France juive* on the country, M. Drumont has exercised a considerable influence over a large part of the nation . . ."[23]

Edouard Drumont (1844–1917)[24] was a man of modest origins, the son of college *répétiteur,* who later worked as a minor civil servant at the Hôtel de Ville in Paris. His family's only claim to fame was Edouard's maternal uncle, the historian Alexandre Buchon, whom he probably attempted to emulate. After passing the *baccalauréat,* Drumont followed his father into the municipal civil service, but soon left this employment for journalism, impelled by youthful literary ambitions. His early adult years were, in his own words, "bitter",[25] but the degree of his "failure" before 1886 has been exaggerated.[26] By the 1870s, he had achieved a certain position in the competitive newspaper world, writing for *Le Bien Public, La Liberté* and *Le Monde;* he had a book about Paris published in 1878, and two novels in 1879 and 1885, and his play: *Je déjeune à midi* was put on in Paris in 1874.[27] Drumont was a Catholic, reconverted after a youthful loss of faith, and, despite a certain indulgence for the Second Empire and for the monarchy of the Ancien Régime, a political Republican.[28] *La France juive,* published only on the recommendation of Alphonse Daudet, a personal friend,[29] was an almost instant success, as the quotations above have suggested. The book had sold over 100,000 copies by the end of the first year of its publication, and the popular edition of 1888 went through 10 impressions in ten years; by 1912, it had run through 200 impressions, and had been translated into six languages.[30] Almost at once, Drumont became relatively wealthy, and famous: "an unknown writer before [from 1886] . . . he was a celebrity . . .";[31] and his subsequent books were also best-sellers,[32] though none was to repeat the achievement of *La France juive.* The success of this large two-volume work, running to over 1,000 pages, rambling, repetitive, derivative, surprised contemporaries, and has surprised historians, who have seen it as simply "a conglomeration of stupidities and untruths", or "a collection of scandalous or obscene anecdotes".[33] As such, its appeal testifies to the strength of the demand which it satisfied, though, as we shall see in Part Three, the ideology which it represents had a powerful inner coherence, and clearly reflected in its peculiar way an aspect of popular mentality that readers could at once recognize. As Drumont, himself put it, his "only merit had been to put into print what everyone was thinking".[34]

On the level of organization, as opposed to ideology or propaganda alone, the French antisemitic movement began to take clear form with the foundation in September 1889, by Drumont, Jacques de Biez, Albert Millot and the Marquis de Morès, of La Ligue Nationale Antisémitique de France.[35] The aim of this organization, according to its statutes was "to combat by the propaganda of truth, in the open and by legal means, the pernicious influences of the Jewish-Financial Oligarchy . . ."[36] The first important manifestation of the Ligue's activities was a public meeting at Neuilly in January 1890 in aid of the re-election of Francis Laur to the Chamber of Deputies. Its organizers used the occasion to elaborate general antisemitic views and policies; Drumont attacked the Rothschilds in what had become traditional fashion, while Morès called for the lynching of the Jewish population.[37] All this made some impact on public opinion, and the Chief Rabbi of France, Zadoc Kahn, protested in a letter to *Le Temps:* "Things have gone too far when a hundred years after the Revolution of 1789, such provocations can be made in public meetings against a whole category of citizens who are as good Frenchmen and Frenchwomen as anyone else . . . "[38] The Ligue's statutes declared that it was open to all political and religious opinions, and the general complexion of its founders and spokesmen was extremely heterogeneous. Biez was a Radical; Laur a Boulangist; and Morès a Catholic aristocrat and a Royalist. The Neuilly gathering reflected this diversity, Socialists and Anarchists rubbing shoulders with members of the Jockey Club, under the presidency of a Boulangist.[39] However, the impact of the Ligue was short lived, and, as the Chief Rabbi's intervention suggests, much reaction to it was hostile. Drumont admitted that the Ligue's posters were torn down almost as soon as they were put up; and Biez related bitterly in 1891 that the antisemites enjoyed little public support, and claimed that newspaper editors and printers were boycotting their writings.[40] The Ligue itself never really got off the ground as an organization, and was formally wound up in October 1890.[41]

A less ambitious antisemitic organization, but one that was more novel in style, remained in being under the aegis of the Marquis de Morès. Morès (1858–96) was an ex-army officer and an aristocrat of Spanish descent. "Antonio-Amédeu-Maria-Vincenzo Manca, Marquis de Morès, son of the Duke of Vallombrosa, was just the man", commented Arnoulin ironically, "to give back France to the French." ("La France aux Français" was one of the main slogans of the antisemitic movement, as we shall see.)[42] Very wealthy after his marriage to a German-American heiress in 1882, Morès returned to France in 1889, after unsuccessful ventures in large-scale ranching in North Dakota and in railway promotion in Indo-China.[43] One of the promoters, as we have seen, of the Ligue Nationale Antisémitique, for which he apparently provided most of the finance,[44] Morès also founded a body known as Morès et ses Amis. In contrast to the Ligue, dedicated to peaceful, if provocative, propaganda, this body was bent on causing disturbance by violent means.[45]

> He has his troops, his devoted comrades, [Henry de Bruchard wrote] who are well regimented and always ready: old revolutionaries, socialists who had seen the Commune, young men just out of the army, all that the people, the lower bourgeoisie of Paris regards as unyielding and independent, the "eternal Boulangists", cadres that always re-form themselves for street demonstrations. Morès always marches at the head, pays out of his own pocket, multiplies audacious enterprises and truly imposes himself on the people.

Viau noted that Morès found an especially fertile recruiting ground for his "Friends" among the butchers of the La Villette abattoirs, among whom he "enjoyed an enormous popularity."[46] The group was active in noisy demonstrations, and engaged in actual violence against Jewish persons and property; its hooliganism was accompanied by a kind of "national socialist" rhetoric.[47] In addition to his popular following in Paris in the early 1890s, Morès also had enthusiastic support among the Catholic upper class in the capital and in the provinces, where he made frequent speeches. Having quarrelled publicly with Drumont in 1893, and having run through his wife's fortune, Morès left France in 1896 for what seems to have been a semi-suicidal expedition to Tunisia. He was killed there by native tribesmen the same year.[48] After his death, which was blamed on the English and the Jews, Morès was revered as a hero and a martyr by French antisemites, and the anniversary of his death was piously celebrated. His organization continued on a more formal footing as Les Amis de Morès,[49] and was still in existence in 1898–9, though by then it seems to have become an auxiliary of the Ligue Antisémitique in Paris, and in Marseille of the Ligue des Patriotes.[50]

Meanwhile, the antisemitic movement had consolidated its influence in another direction with the foundation in 1892 of an independent antisemitic daily, La Libre Parole,[51] edited by Drumont. As we shall see, La Libre Parole was not the first antisemitic newspaper in France, nor even the first antisemitic daily. La Croix, run by the Assumptionists, had adopted an antisemitic line from the mid-1880s,[52] and some other Catholic papers had, more tentatively, followed suit. But La Libre Parole was distinctive for its exclusive devotion to the cause of antisemitism and for its deliberately sensational exploitation of it. In May 1892, Drumont, in an editorial, accused the Minister of Public Works, Burdeau, of taking bribes from Rothschild in return for supporting the renewal of the "privilège" of the Banque de France. Burdeau successfully sued Drumont for libel the following month, which earned the latter a three-month prison sentence; but the circulation of La Libre Parole doubled. In the same initial year, the newspaper began a systematic attack on Jewish army officers, which resulted in a much-reported duel between its editor and a Jewish officer, Crémieu-Foa, and another in which the Marquis de Morès killed Armand Mayer.[53] La Libre Parole also played a leading part in launching the Panama scandal in 1892, an affair, like that of the Union Générale, which capitalized on popular prejudice against "Jewish Finance" and political corruption.[54] As Viau wrote: "It was Panama that definitively marked the arrival of La Libre Parole."[55] Two years later, as we have seen, it was La Libre Parole, which was first to report the arrest and then trial of Dreyfus.[56] By this time it had achieved a circulation of 200,000,[57] which was considerable by the standards of the day. By this time also, it was much more than a sensational newspaper. It was, in the words of Léon Daudet, a journalist who worked for it from 1900 to 1908, the "official organ . . . of French antisemitism", and served as a kind of headquarters for what had become an organized movement.[58] Daudet recalled that "beyond the established staff of the paper, a large number of colleagues and politicians came in and out of the offices of La Libre Parole . . ."; and, especially during the period of the Dreyfus Affair, its premises on the Boulevard Montmartre were the centre of constant popular agitation and demonstrations.[59] The organization of the Henry Subscription was only part of a wider political activity.

By the mid-1890s, therefore, Drumont was the generally recognized leader of an antisemitic movement of some importance, "the accepted head of antisemitism".[60] But, though he enjoyed an "immense popularity"[61] with the public at large, or a section of it, he was a curious and inneffective political leader. A widower by 1885,[62] he was of a shy, retiring disposition. Daudet who knew him well wrote: "He was excessively introspective . . . He was not at all expansive, he was set in his ways, very old-fashioned, rather eccentric, a man of habit and contemplation . . . He was scholarly, a kind of secular monk . . .";[63] while Jacques Piou referred to him as "a man of sombre character, believing fervently in his mission . . ."[64] His eccentricities included a belief in palmistry, in ghosts and in spiritualism.[65] He tended to shun public occasions, and had little administrative ability or political skill. Daudet, again, wrote that "his political sense was not on a level with his erudition or his talent for polemic . . ."; and claimed that *La Libre Parole* would not have survived without its business manager Charles Devos . . .", who made up for Drumont's deficiency in this sphere.[66] Drumont was characteristically ineffective as a deputy, both on the constituency level and in the Chamber. Elected for Algiers with a huge majority in 1898, he was surprised to lose his seat in 1902. "He did not realize", explained Daudet, "that the Algerians had sent him to the Chamber with hopes that he had disappointed."[67] He disliked electioneering, was a poor public speaker, and intervened very little in the debates of the Chamber, where his presence "passed almost unnoticed . . ."[68] Drumont's influence, in effect, came through the written word, and not as "a man of action".[69] He was the leader of a school, the master of most of the antisemitic writers and activists of the time,[70] but, more perhaps than any of them, "a master journalist",[71] a consummate manipulator of the new mass medium of the press.

Drumont's prestige and influence were at their height during the Dreyfus Affair. "In those agitated times," wrote Piou, "his paper and his books articulated the passions of a body of public opinion . . . His influence reached its apogee when the Dreyfus Affair appeared to the crowd as the justification of his doctrines and the realization of his prophecies."[72] The Affair, we have seen, projected antisemitism on to the screen of general opinion, giving it an unprecedented national audience and dimension. Moreover, with the Affair, the movement moved again on to the level of political organization, this time successfully. Duroselle has pointed out that in the early 1890s, "antisemitism had not gone beyond the stage of a movement of opinion, relatively formless, and not at all organized . . ."[73] The Tharaud brothers also noted that before the Affair, "Drumont and his *Libre Parole* did not make a great impact, beyond a fairly restricted circle. In the optimist atmosphere of the time, antisemitism seemed an attitude that belonged to a previous age, something archaic and obsolete."[74] Viau similarly commented on the huge increase in Drumont's popularity between the early and the late 1890s.[75] The latter years saw the creation of antisemitic clubs and associations all over France, the revival of the antisemitic league, the proliferation of the antisemitic press, and the entry of antisemites into national electoral politics, and it is to these developments that we now turn.

NOTES

1 Drumont, *Le Testament d'un antisémite* (hereafter *TA*), p. 3.
2 Drumont, *La Dernière Bataille*, (hereafter *DB*), p. 504.
3 Byrnes, *Antisemitism in Modern France;* Sorlin, *"La Croix" et les Juifs;* Verdès-Leroux, *Scandale financier et antisémitisme catholique;* Pierrard, *Juifs et catholiques français*, pp. 19–30; Duroselle, "L'Antisémitisme en France"; François Delpech, in Blumenkranz, ed., *Histoire des Juifs en France*, Part 3, chapters 1 and 2.
4 See Delpech, op. cit., pp. 265–82, 286–99 and 306; Hertzberg, *The French Enlightenment and the Jews*, pp. 338–68.
5 "JUIF . . . Fig. et familièrement. Celui qui prête à l'usure ou qui vend exorbitamment cher, et, en général, quiconque cherche à gagner de l'argent avec âpreté." E. Littré, *Dictionnaire de la langue française* (Paris, 1878), III, p. 212. For examples of this usage, see Jules Vallès, *Le Bachélier* (1881) (Paris, 1972), p. 202: "L'usurier est là . . . Il faut bien se contenter de paroles quand on n'a pas d'argent! grogne le juif"; and Georges Courteline, *Les Petites Nouvelles Quotidiennes*, 6 April 1885, *Chroniques, Oeuvres complètes* (Paris, 1927), p. 286: (of Esau) "un Juif indigne de l'être et je serais bien surpris si M.de Rothschild ne le désavouait pas pour parent. Au surplus, s'il n'était point Juif dans le mauvais sens du mot, son frère Jacob l'était pour lui . . ." See also chapter X, p. 262 and no. 165; and chapter XIX, p. 717 below.
6 See Earle Stanley Randall, *The Jewish Character in the French Novel, 1870–1914* (Evanston, Ill., 1941); Byrnes, op. cit., pp. 104–10; C. Lehrmann, *L'Elément juif dans la littérature française* (Paris, 1960).
7 See chapter XIV, pp. 512–17 and ff. below.
8 See Byrnes, op. cit., pp. 114–25; chapter II, p. 68 above; and chapter XI, pp. 332–4, below.
9 Paul Arène, *Le Journal*, 11 February 1895, cit. Patrick Dumont, *La Petite Bourgeoisie vue à travers les contes quotidiens du "Journal" (1894–1895): Etude de mentalité* (Paris, 1973), p. 45.
10 Jacques Prolo, *La Caverne antisémite* (Paris, 1902), p. 35.
11 E.g. Drumont, *La France juive* (hereafter *FJ*), I, pp. 131 and 137; Drumont, *DB*, pp. 146–8; Drumont, *TA*, pp. 136 and 140–67, "La Question Juive à l'Etranger"; Bournand, *Les Juifs et nos contemporains*, pp. 258–65, "Les Opinions étrangers". There were no French delegates at the International Anti-Jewish Congress held at Dresden in 1882, but Lueger was later in contact with Drumont, and it was hoped that he might attend the Lyon Antisemitic Congress of 1896; see Verdès-Leroux, op. cit., p. 118; Bournand, op. cit., pp. 262–5.
12 Isaac, *Expériences de ma vie*, I, p. 20; see also Delpech, op. cit., p. 305.
13 Henri Dagan, *Enquête sur l'antisémitisme* (Paris, 1899), p. 59.
14 Verdès-Leroux, op. cit., p. 12 and *passim.*
15 Donnay, *Des Souvenirs*, p. 273. Durkheim wrote that the consequences of the crash "were felt not only in Paris but throughout France", and attributed the perceptible rise in the suicide rate in 1882 to it; see *Suicide* (1897) (London, 1970 edition), pp. 241–2. Zola's *L'Argent* (1891) was based largely on the Union Générale crash, and similarly testifies to its impact; see Henri Guillemin, *Présentation des Rougon-Macquart* (Paris, 1964), pp. 353 and 357–8. On the crash itself, see Jean Bouvier, *Le Krach de l'Union Générale (1878–1885)* (Paris, 1960).
16 Léon Daudet, *Paris vécu*, ler série (Paris, 1929), pp. 30–1.

17 *La Revue Politique et Littéraire (Revue Bleue)*, 1885, cit. Verdès-Leroux, op. cit., p. 121. On the origin of the term *"antisémitisme"*, see chapter XIII, pp. 456–7 below.

18 Drumont, *TA*, p. 3.

19 Barrès, "La Formule anti-juive", *Le Figaro*, 22 February 1890, cit. Barrès-Maurras, *La République ou le Roi*, pp. 626–27.

20 Bournand, op. cit., p. 27.

21 Viau, *Vingt ans d'antisémitisme*, p. 5.

22 Cit. Bournand, op. cit., p. 135.

23 Stéphane Arnoulin, *M. Édouard Drumont et les Jésuites* (Paris, 1902), p. 6; see also Zola, in Dagan, op. cit., pp. 18–19.

24 The main sources for Drumont's biography before 1886 are his own writings, which historians have in general been content to follow; see particularly *DB*, pp. 232, 243, 249–50 and 267–90; also Bournand, op. cit., p. 30; Byrnes, op. cit., chapter III; E. Beau de Loménie, *Edouard Drumont ou l'anticapitalisme national* (Paris, 1968), pp. 72 and 91. The claim by Joseph Aron, *Mon pauvre Drumont* (Paris, 1896), pp. 3 and 16; L'Hermite, *L'Antipape*, p. 227; Prolo, op. cit., p. 13, and others, that Drumont was himself of Jewish descent, can be taken no more seriously than most of their speculations about his career, though Reinach gives it some credence; see Reinach, *Histoire de l'Affaire Dreyfus*, I, pp. 216–17.

25 Drumont, *DB*, p. viii.

26 Particularly by Byrnes, op. cit., p. 142; through Drumont undoubtedly had a sense of having failed before 1886.

27 See Arnoulin, op. cit., pp. 17–23, 59–65 and 72–98; Pierrard, op. cit., p. 32; entry in Jolly, ed., *Dictionnaire des parlementaires français;* Drault, *Drumont, La France juive et La Libre Parole*, pp. 8 and 28, who says that Drumont was chief editor of *Le Monde*.

28 Drumont, *DB*, pp. 221–6 and 283–5; Drumont, *TA*, p. 389; Prolo, op. cit., pp. 5–12; Arnoulin, op. cit., *passim;* Duroselle, op. cit., pp. 51–2; Pierrard, op. cit., pp. 49–51; see also chapter VIII, p. 217; and chapter XI, p. 348 below.

29 See Drumont, *DB*, pp. 201, 211 and 309–11; Drumont, *TA*, pp. 232–3; Bournand, op. cit., p. 30; Léon Daudet, *Les Oeuvres dans les hommes* (Paris, 1922), pp. 145–8, 154 and 161; Byrnes, op. cit., pp. 148–52. Drumont was also a friend of the photographer, cartoonist and aeronaut Nadar; Prinet and Dilasser, *Nadar*, p. 249. The fact that two leading figures of the day esteemed him highly gives some idea of his contemporary standing, though Nadar made it clear that he did not share his antisemitic opinions.

30 See Drumont, *TA*, pp. 318 and 417–18; Arnoulin, op. cit., p. 122; Byrnes, op. cit., pp. 148–55; Duroselle, op. cit., p. 49; Verdès-Leroux, op. cit., p. 125; Pierrard, op. cit., pp. 17 and 31–2.

31 Drumont, *DB*, p. xvii.

32 *La Fin d'un monde* (1888) sold 70,000 copies; *La Dernière Bataille* (1890) sold 80,000.

33 Pierrard, op. cit., p. 38; Sartre, *Réflexions sur la question juive*, p. 53; see also Arnoulin, op. cit., pp. 123–34 and 143–9.

34 Drumont, *FJ*, II, Nouvelles notes rectificatives (no pagination).

35 See Viau, op. cit., pp. 7–14; Verdès-Leroux, op. cit., pp. 170–1; Pierrard, op. cit., pp. 137–40; Drault, op. cit., pp. 39–41 and 46–8.

36 Statutes, Article 6, cit. Viau, op. cit., p. 8.

37 Viau, op. cit., pp. 15–16; Byrnes, op. cit., pp. 235–6.

38 *Le Temps*, 20 January 1890, cit. Viau, op. cit., pp. 17–18; see also Drumont, *DB*, p. 38; and *TA*, p. 59.

39 See Viau, op. cit., p. 14.

40 Drumont, *TA*, p. 368; Jacques de Biez, *Les Rothschild et le péril juif: Réponse à M.le Commandant Blanc, Rédacteur-en-chef du "Petit Caporal"* (Paris, 1891), pp. 3–5.

41 Pierrard, op. cit., pp. 138–9.
42 Arnoulin, op. cit., p. 167. According to Drault, op. cit., p. 55, Morès was also a descendant of the French Ducs des Cars.
43 See Steven S. Schwarzschild, "The Marquis de Morès: The Story of a Failure", *Jewish Social Studies*, 22 (1960), pp. 4–15; Byrnes, op. cit., pp. 227–32; Pierrard, op. cit., p. 138; Drault, op. cit., pp. 55–60.
44 Pierrard, op. cit., p. 137.
45 Henry de Bruchard, "Le Marquis de Morès: Un héros de l'Antisémitisme", *Revue Critique des Idées et des Livres*, 8 (1911), p. 279, cit. Schwarzschild, op. cit., p. 17; see also Byrnes, op. cit., pp. 242–3; Pierrard, op. cit., pp. 138–9.
46 Viau, op. cit., p. 44.
47 Ibid., pp. 44–5; Byrnes, op. cit., pp. 237–9; Schwarzschild, op. cit., p. 17.
48 Viau, op. cit., pp. 69–71; Jules Guérin, *Les Trafiquants de l'antisémitisme: La Maison Drumond and Co.* (Paris, 1905), pp. 69–96; Drault, op. cit., pp. 193–6; Byrnes, op. cit., pp. 246–50; Pierrard, op. cit., pp. 138–9. The Archbishop of Tunis, Mgr Combes, officiated at his funeral; see Soumille, "L'Idée de Race chez les Européens de Tunisie".
49 See Guérin, op. cit., pp. 97–101; Barrès, *Scènes et doctrines*, II, pp. 50–91; Stern-hell, *Maurice Barrès*, p. 144; Pierrard, op. cit., pp. 138–40; Drault, op. cit., pp. 65–6.
50 Reports, Police agent, Paris, 14 February 1898. AN F⁷12474; and Commissaire spécial, Marseille, 6 June 1899. AN F⁷12449.
51 Another paper of this name, edited by Tony Moilon, appeared between 1868 and 1869, but seems to have had no connection with that of Drumont; see Alexandre Zévaès, *Henri Rochefort, Le Pamphlétaire* (Paris, 1946), p. 58.
52 See Sorlin, *"La Croix" et les Juifs*, p. 92; Drumont, *FJ*, II, p. 123.
53 See Drault, op. cit., pp. 113–22; Marrus, *The Politics of Assimilation* pp. 197–200.
54 See Adrien Dansette, *Les Affaires de Panama* (Paris, 1934); Jean Bouvier, *Les Deux Scandales de Panama* (Paris, 1964), pp. 140–58 and *passim*; J.-M. Mayeur, *Les Débuts de la IIIe République 1871–1898* (Paris, 1973), pp. 205–7.
55 Viau, op. cit., p. 49; see also Drault, op. cit., pp. 127–62.
56 See chapter I, p. 9 above; on all these and other campaigns of *La Libre Parole* see also Viau, op. cit., pp. 20–6 and 57–8; Arnoulin, op. cit., p. 195; Barrès-Maurras, op. cit., p. 173; Pierrard, op. cit., pp. 33–4; Beau de Loménie, op. cit., pp. 103–5 and 391–415.
57 Viau, op. cit., p. 50; Duroselle, op. cit., p. 69.
58 Daudet, *Paris vécu*, Ier série, p. 26; see also ibid., pp. 28–30; Daudet, *Au Temps de Judas*, pp. 14–15; Daudet, *Les Oeuvres dans les hommes*, pp. 171–5; Daudet, *Salons et journaux*, pp. 275–85.
59 Daudet, *Salons et journaux*, p. 280 (Daudet mentioned "le malingre Firmin Faure, le bavard Thiébaud, le sérieux Congy, le rouge Barillieu" and Charles Bernard); see also ibid., pp. 285–6; Daudet, *Paris vécu*, Ier série, p. 30; Viau, op. cit., pp. 36–8.
60 Daudet, *Les Oeuvres dans les hommes*, p. 178; see also Fore-Fauré, *Face aux Juifs! (Essai de psychologie sociale contemporaine)* (Paris, 1891), Dédication; Arnoulin, op. cit., p. 8; Dagan, op. cit., pp. 19–23 and 46; and Arthur Meyer, *Ce que mes yeux ont vu* (Paris, 1912), p. 122.
61 Daudet, *Les Oeuvres dans les hommes*, p. 155.
62 Drumont married in 1882, but his wife died in 1884. He married again, secretly, in 1910; see Arnoulin, op. cit., pp. 106–7; Drault, op. cit., pp. 300–1 and 309.
63 Daudet, *Salons et journaux*, p. 271; *Paris vécu*, Ier série, p. 27.
64 Piou, *Le Comte Albert de Mun*, p. 192.
65 See Drumont, *DB*, pp. 218, 227 and 517; Viau, op. cit., p. 281; Daudet, *Les Oeuvres dans les hommes*, p. 184; Daudet, *Salons et journaux*, p. 271; and Drault, op. cit., p. 221.
66 Daudet, *Au Temps de Judas*, p. 13; and *Paris vécu*, Ier série, pp. 28–9; see also Viau, op. cit., pp. 45–8, and Daudet, *Salons et journaux*, p. 277.

67 Daudet, *Les Oeuvres dans les hommes*, p. 188. For the context of Drumont's election and for electoral antisemitism generally, see chapters VIII and IX below.
68 Daudet, *Salons et journaux*, pp. 224–5; see also Viau, op. cit., p. 32.
69 Piou, op. cit., p. 192; and Reinach, op. cit., IV, p. 303.
70 See Pierrard, op. cit., p. 71; Verdès-Leroux, op. cit., pp. 145–6.
71 Daudet, *Salons et journaux*, p. 272.
72 Piou, op. cit., p. 192.
73 Duroselle, op. cit., pp. 61–2.
74 Jérôme and Jean Tharaud, *Petite Histoire des Juifs* (Paris, 1927), p. 235; see also Byrnes, op. cit., pp. 335–8.
75 Viau, op. cit., pp. 57 and 97–102.

CHAPTER VI
THE LIGUE ANTISEMITIQUE FRANÇAISE

D RUMONT REMAINED THE UNOFFICIAL LEADER OF THE ANTISEMITIC movement in France, but that movement became increasingly diverse, and his prestige within it was rivalled by that of others. Of these perhaps the most important in the crucial period 1898–1899 was Jules Guérin, the man of action in contrast to the writer. With the Ligue Antisémitique Française, founded in February 1897, Guérin seemed to have organized the body of militants, ready for action, that the circumstances of the Affair required. As the Prefect of Police, Lépine, testified at Guérin's trial in 1899: with the Ligue, "the antisemitic movement acquired its own sections . . . more firmly constituted and more strictly disciplined even than those of the Ligue des Patriotes and the Royalists. The practical flair . . . of M. Jules Guérin had made of them a fighting force that the police had to reckon with."[1] And the Ligue's several thousand members in Paris and the provinces played a leading part in the agitation, "direct action" and street-fighting of these years. This activist role, as well as the Ligue's "socialism", its anticlericalism and the cynicism of its leaders represented also a significant new trend in antisemitism that can fairly be labelled proto-fascist.

Reviving the moribund Ligue Antisémitique de France of 1889,[2] the Ligue Antisémitique Française began life under the wing of Drumont's *Libre Parole*. The newspaper supported the Ligue in its columns and inserted its communications; and Drumont agreed to be its honorary president. Guérin acted as Drumont's electoral agent and henchman in Algiers in May 1898, but disagreements between the two men, of such different temperament, came to a head after the successful campaign. Drumont seems to have been jealous of Guérin's growing influence. Ligue news was no longer published in *La Libre Parole*, and Drumont refused, in particular, to support a recruitment campaign with publicity or funds. Guérin's answer was to break completely with Drumont, and to turn the Ligue's house bulletin into a rival newspaper, the illustrated weekly, *L'Antijuif*, in August 1898.[3] "The practical support he [Drumont] gave us was practically nil", wrote Guérin in 1905, "that is, when he was not seeking positively to counteract what we were doing . . .";[4] and relations between the two leaders deteriorated into a running exchange of insults and accusations of turpitude.[5] However, other *Libre Parole* editors and members of the original Ligue Antisémitique de France continued to be heavily represented on the Paris committee of Guérin's Ligue, and some contributed to his weekly.[6]

Guérin seems to have nursed two apparently contradictory ambitions: to become a kind of overlord and directing agent for all the political groups supporting antisemitism—he tried, for example, to infiltrate the Ligue des Patriotes[7]—and to win exclusive popular support for his own organization by an uncompromising and violent attack on Jews, with clearly radical implications. Day-to-day circumstances, personal jealousies, opportunism and chance decided which line the Ligue actually followed at any time; as a report of the Ministry of the Interior put it: "the policy . . . of Jules Guérin was always a hybrid one, incoherent, short-term, always dictated by self-interest and modified from day to day . . .".[8] Although Guérin eventually ended up in the arms of the Royalists, who were simply those with most money to spend backing political hooliganism, only rarely, as in the May 1898 elections, did the Ligue co-operate closely with other groups. Usually, it pursued an independent line, or, at least, tried to dissociate itself from the antisemitic establishment. A police report made the point in January 1899:[9]

> As happens with all "parties" once they reach a certain size, opposing factions were clearly developing within the antisemitic movement, and one could begin to talk about a Right and a Left. Drumont's influence was complete over the Right-wing antisemites, who belonged to the reactionary "parties"; but those of the Left, who, like M. Morinaud, deputy for Algeria, were ready to make declarations of anticlericalism, were less willing to recognize the authority of *La Libre Parole*. It was the latter, above all, that Guérin sought to rally round him.

The Ligue thus presented itself as a radical Left-wing organization, at least in the first two years of its existence. At a meeting in February 1898, Guérin asserted that: "Antisemitism is essentially socialist . . .";[10] and candidates supported by the Ligue in Paris in the 1898 elections declared themselves to be socialists and launched attacks on the Jews as the exploiters of "the working class". Supporters of the ex-*communard* Rochefort, editor of *L'Intransigeant*, worked in alliance with the Ligue Antisémitique at this time, as did certain sections of the Jeunesse Blanquiste. Guérin had moved in Blanquiste-Boulangist circles, as had Millevoye, the only Ligue-supported candidate elected in Paris in May 1898. Guérin set out to win the support of extreme Left-wing groups, and gained that of the Anarchists associated with *Le Révolutionnaire*, which was printed on the same presses as *L'Antijuif*. Viau, moreover, remarked on the presence of "former Anarchists" at the Ligue's headquarters.[11] As Reinach pointed out, Guérin's later prestige with the Royalists derived from their belief that he might be able to bring "*syndicats*" and working-class organizations into the cause.[12] The "socialism" of the Ligue must, however,

be seen in its nineteenth-century context, when, as Roche, another unorthodox socialist put it, socialism was not "the monopoly of any particular sect".[13]
As we have seen in considering attitudes towards the Affair, the Socialist
antisemitic tradition was still strong in France in the late 1890s, when even
Jaurès bowed to it.[14] Many orthodox Socialists had antisemitic leanings,
through opportunism if not conviction, and the distinction between a Left-
wing Socialism with antisemitic leanings and a Right-wing antisemitic movement with socialistic trappings was not then as clear-cut as historians have
subsequently made it. Those classes whose support each tried to capture were
probably equally ready to accept either the Jewish *"accapareurs"* (monopolists), or the class struggle as explanations of economic difficulties and social
inequality. Similarly, it was not easy, presumably, to judge between the respec-
tive arguments, either that orthodox Socialists, and particularly Collectivists,
were duping the "people" at the behest of Jewish capitalists, or that antisemitism was the catspaw of clerical reaction. Another important factor here was
the increasing fear of socialism among the bourgeoisie, generated by the steady
growth of the socialist poll, a fear that did not encourage the drawing of fine
distinctions but tended to lump all critics of the social order under the same
generic heading. Guérin's type of anti-Jewish socialism was doubtless spontaneously accepted by some, but it was certainly also encouraged and promoted as a substitute for orthodox Socialism by those perspicacious enough
to see that it did not represent a serious danger to the holders of power and
property. In the words of a critic of antisemitism in June 1898: "the secret
aim of its leaders is to stir up the masses against Jewish capitalism, in order
precisely to protect Christian capitalism . . ."[15] We shall discuss such socialistic antisemitism more generally in chapter XI; but some idea of its character
can be gained from the programme of the Ligue Antisémitique.

This was mainly economic in emphasis. The short-term economic malaise
occasioned by the uncertainties of the Dreyfus Affair, as well as longer-term
structural changes in the French economy, notably in retail distribution and
food production, all gave economic antisemitism a ready audience. According
to Guérin, "cosmopolitan speculators, hand-in-glove with unscrupulous and
ambitious politicians, have become all-powerful in France, thanks to the gold
they have piled up by robbing small savers, by cruelly exploiting producers, and
by imposing on all consumers, for products that are basic essentials, the highest
prices, fixed by rings and cartels . . ."[16] These speculators were, of course, Jews:
"The three mainsprings of the economy: money, credit and the transport
system, are in the hands of the Jews", Guérin told an audience in February
1898. His solution was to bring the Banque de France under democratic
control, to keep Jews out of government administration, and to introduce
reforms in the organization of the railways, reducing fares and even nationaliz-
ing the network. However, in general the Ligue was critical of any trend
towards state socialism and welfare, with its accompanying corruption, bureaucratization and increased taxation; and indeed called for extensive tax reductions, for "a real alleviation of the fiscal burden that is crushing the taxpayer".
Guérin also called for "a curb on ill-gotten fortunes" by fiscal means,[17] though

the Ligue does not seem to have joined those few antisemites who supported proposals for a graduated income tax; Millevoye supported the tax in principle in 1898, but believed it to be impractical. A call was made, however, for a less controversial tax on foreign workers, and the Ligue supported the maintenance of protectionism, and even advocated higher tariffs. In August 1898, Guérin was planning the creation of a "national association for the mutual protection of labour", which would also act as "a kind of Bourse du Travail destined to combat collectivist and Allemaniste conceptions in the economic, political and social sphere";[18] and an attempt was made to give the Ligue headquarters some of the features of a Bourse du Travail: a public library and reading-room, free medical consultations and cheap legal advice.

But perhaps the main plank in the Ligue's economic platform was its campaign against big department stores. Hostility towards these had been, we have seen, an important motive in the antisemitic riots of January and February 1898, and it became an important issue, too, in the general election campaign in Paris in May. After a discussion of "department stores and co-operative societies: their harmful effects from the point of view of small traders and all workers", the Ligue's electoral committee of the 17th *arrondissement* set up a special working party to plan the fight against them. This involved physical attacks on Jewish shops by Ligue militants, and a boycott of Jewish shops and businesses, for which a special appeal was made to women supporters and sympathizers.[19] The Ligue also had a bureau to look after the interests of travelling salesmen. All in all, its economic programme was a catalogue of grievances against paying taxes, against high prices, against "unfair" competition, against new wealth, rather than a constructive policy, and it was clearly aimed, rhetoric apart, at small traders, petty businessmen and artisans rather than at the industrial working class.

Another feature of the Ligue's radical approach to antisemitism was its determination to stay clear of any close association with "clericalism". This ostensibly marks it off from Christian Democratic organizations, such as the Union Nationale, which otherwise had a similar programme, and, of course, from *La Libre Parole*, which had a predominantly Catholic clientèle. A speaker at a Ligue Antisémitique meeting in April 1898 said that in order to obtain popular support, antisemites should emphasize their independence of any confessional alignment, and another speaker in May "warned the antisemites against the intrusion of the clergy in their ranks", adding: "we must at all costs avoid the charge made by our enemies that the antisemites are, if not the defenders, at least the allies, of the clericals."[20] As this quotation suggests, the reason for the Ligue's anticlericalism was not, in general, ideological, but stemmed from an appreciation of the lack of popular sympathy for the Church, which at that time was still associated in France with political reaction. And the same opportunism meant that in practice the Ligue could not avoid a considerable dependence on Catholic membership and support. "On the one hand", reported the police in August 1899, "it is allied with the Union Nationale of the abbé Garnier, and on the other, it welcomes antisemites who are freethinkers . . ."[21] In 1905, Guérin claimed that he had always been "respectful of religious beliefs",[22] and several section leaders in Paris were militant Catholics. The links with the Church were even stronger in the provinces. At Rennes, for example, the local Ligue section maintained close relations with *La Croix*, while at Roanne the local section was actually founded by members of the Union Nationale.[23] In 1901, moreover, effective leadership of Guérin's expiring organization passed into the hands of a priest, the abbé Duvaux.[24]

The long-term aims of the Ligue, given its opportunism, were necessarily uncertain. Its speakers called for Jews to be deprived of French citizenship, to be banned from public positions, and to be expelled from France. The "suppression" of Jews and a "Jewish massacre of Saint Bartholomew" were also advocated at meetings, and, in February 1898, Guérin invited French peasants to imitate those of Galicia who were supposed to have burnt a Jewish family alive. "He spoke only of beatings, of pillage and of massacre . . .", commented Reinach.[25] However, for Guérin and the Ligue a large element in all this was fantasy rather than policy; and, in their "ceaseless and merciless fight against the Jews",[26] they showed some awareness of the limits beyond which violence became counter-productive. Nevertheless, there was no mistaking that the immediate policy of the Ligue was openly and deliberately violent. According to a report of August 1899, already cited: "Jules Guérin intended to make of the Ligue, not an instrument of peaceful propaganda aimed at spreading antisemitic ideas through free discussion, but rather a means of revolutionary agitation . . ."[27] As Bernanos put it, Guérin was a "veritable entrepreneur of disturbances",[28] and he was known familiarly as "Strong Arm".[29] The Ligue had a special "demonstrations committee",[30] and became notorious for attacks on Jewish property, for breaking up rival meetings, and for the organization of street demonstrations. We have seen that the Ligue played a leading part in the riots of January and February 1898, particularly in Paris. In January 1898, wrote Reinach, "Guérin exercised his troops, sometimes in the Latin Quarter, sometimes on the boulevards", and his *ligueurs* were in the forefront of the demonstrations outside the Palais de Justice during the first Zola trial. In March and April of the same year, Reinach again commented that "Guérin's brawlers and bully-boys still overawed the streets of the capital . . ."[31] As Drumont's electoral agent in May 1898, Guérin was instrumental also in organizing noisy and violent street demonstrations in Algiers.[32] The Ligue issued a manifesto in October inviting the public to demonstrate on the occasion of the reopening of the Chamber of Deputies after the summer recess, and Guérin and his men were again among the more vociferous and active participants in the riot which took place in the Place de la Concorde on the 25th of the same month. In mid-December, the Ligue was again involved in disturbances in Paris and Nantes; and it took the lead, alongside the Ligue des Patriotes, in the renewed disturbances that attended the funeral of President Faure on 23 February 1899.[33] Guérin and some of his associates were prosecuted for their violent activities. Guérin was accused of beating up a policeman during the 25 October demonstration, but was convicted only of carrying illegal weapons. In January 1899 he was accused of complicity in the attempted murder of a rival journalist, but was again acquitted; while in April 1899 he was sentenced to eight days' imprisonment for violent behaviour in Algiers.[34]

Guérin had been an associate of the Marquis de Morès, and, emulating him, recruited a uniformed bodyguard of about fifty men, mainly from among the butcher boys of La Villette, who acted as the Ligue's shock troops. "One never saw him", wrote Reinach, "without his entourage of La Villette butchers, armed with clubs, iron bars in wooden sheaths, weighing at least a kilo. They would have died for him. His popularity . . . depended on the fear that he inspired. People believed him capable of anything."[35] At the Ligue's headquarters, the members, including this bodyguard, were trained in boxing, shooting and fencing, as well as in the use of the weighted clubs. As already mentioned, it is hard to judge how far the violence was intended to go, though there is no doubt that Guérin was deeply involved in plans for some kind of *coup* against the Republican regime in 1899. He visited the Royalist Pretender, the Duc d'Orléans, at Marienbad in July 1898, and received funds and encouragement; and Reinach suggested that Guérin had plans to invade the Palais-Bourbon during the October 1898 demonstration, on Royalist prompting.[36] As we have seen, rumours of *coups* were in the air all through 1898 and 1899, and the seriousness of Guérin's insurrectionary intentions remains problematical, as does the scope of the conspiracy in which he was involved. The Bonapartists were apparently very anxious not to be implicated with Guérin,[37] and it seems that he was not directly involved either in Déroulède's schemes for a military takeover, although the Ligue Antisémitique and the Ligue des Patriotes were working in close collaboration in 1899.[38] The parallel conspiracies of Guérin and the Royalists and of the Ligue des Patriotes seem to have come to a head in mid-1899, but their importance was exaggerated by the government as a means of disarming the Leagues. Moves were made in early August to arrest the leaders of the Royalist movement, of the Ligue des Patriotes and of the Ligue Antisémitique Française.[39] To escape arrest, and "to protest against the abuse of power by the authorities", Guérin, with a few supporters, barricaded himself in the Ligue's headquarters at 51 rue de Chabrol, whose doors and windows were armour-plated, and withstood a police siege for forty days.[40] It was suggested at the time within the antisemitic movement and elsewhere, as we have noted earlier, that this siege of "Fort Chabrol" was a planned diversion from the Dreyfus trial at Rennes, and that Guérin was acting as a government stooge, a charge which he hotly, and probably honestly, denied.[41] The evidence certainly suggests that Guérin was acting independently and in a way that both dismayed his political allies and worried the police. Police agents expressed some alarm at what one called "the rebellion of the antisemites", and reported that Guérin enjoyed the support of a section of the population of the capital, including the Gardes de Paris.[42] However, the authorities, though very aware of Guérin's potential for causing trouble and anxious to get him out of the way, seem ultimately to have shared the conviction of the public and the press that the "Fort Chabrol" affair was more a joke than a threat to public order, let alone the régime. Léon Daudet later expressed this feeling by referring to it as an "absurd initiative", while Mme Steinheil called it a "farce".[43] Guérin was prosecuted later in the year in the Haute Cour, together with Déroulède, Habert and the Royalist leaders, and was convicted of conspiring against the Republic. He was sentenced to ten years' imprisonment. This was commuted to exile in July 1901, when he moved to Brussels. After the proclamation of an amnesty in 1907, he returned to France, and died in 1909.[44]

But to return to the Ligue before this *dénouement*. Its periods of action alternated with periods of caution and observance of legal methods. Reinach pointed out that Guérin "in addition to a very lively understanding of how to manage brutal and direct action, also possessed political finesse, and, if need were, prudence".[45] He was well aware, in the words of Charles Maurras, that "Leaded canes . . . are frightening . . .",[46] and he knew how to exploit gentler means of persuasion. He had, in fact, a real flair for propaganda. Besides *L'Antijuif*, which had an illustrated supplement, the Ligue published a large amount of other material, including songs, confetti with antisemitic slogans, posters, and photographs of Guérin. Guérin and others toured the provinces several times, using motor-cars to distribute leaflets as well as making speeches. The Ligue, moreover, had its own special emblem, an oak-leaf and an ear of corn. At first averse to electoral politics, Guérin decided in March 1898 that "recent events . . . have favoured antisemitic ideas and they must now be carried over into the electoral struggle."[47] In the General Elections in May, therefore, the Ligue sponsored certain candidates and tried to obtain guarantees of antisemitism as the price for supporting others. In all, it supported eight candidates in Paris, only one of whom was elected, as we have seen. Of the 22 deputies belonging to the antisemitic parliamentary group in the 1898 Chamber, at least nine had connections with the Ligue, although most of them seem later to have dissociated themselves from it. This apparently disillusioned Guérin a little, although, recovering his self-confidence, he later claimed part of the credit for the very good showing of the antisemites in the 1900 municipal elections in France.[48]

Whether engaged in electoral politics or in direct action, pure opportunism seems to have guided the policy of the Ligue's leaders. Lacour pointed out in June 1898 that there were two levels in antisemitic action and propaganda, "the first which involves the leaders who direct the movement according to secret aims, and the second, which is addressed to the public at large . . ."[49] The secret aims of Guérin and his cronies were apparently quite mundane. Apart from seeking some kind of compensation for previous personal failures, they were, to put it crudely, in antisemitism for the money. Guérin, himself, came to the movement with a career of shady business, fraud and bankruptcy behind him, which had, in fact barred his access to Radical party politics. He had been involved in two petroleum companies which went bankrupt in 1888 and 1891. In 1888 he was convicted of theft and industrial espionage, and, after a fire in his offices in the same year, the insurance company claimed fraud and successfully refused to pay for the alleged damage.[50] The Ligue was built up in large part in order to obtain funds, first of all from members in the shape of subscriptions, and then from opposition parties to whom Guérin offered his services against finance. Viau commented that, in the Spring of 1899, "the Ligue had never been doing better . . . that is to say, never had it been more prosperous."[51] Predictably, most of the Ligue's extraordinary funds seem to have come from Royalist sources, whose political intentions were ostensibly far removed from those of Guérin. Maurras wrote later that "a good half of France's antisemites had been committed to the cause of the Pretender by Jules Guérin",[52] though most of them probably did not realize it. Leading Royalists spoke at Ligue meetings, but Guérin had always stressed that the Ligue was open to all comers, and he was naturally careful to conceal his financial dependence on the Royalists from the mass of his supporters, which makes it difficult to assess its extent. Reinach claimed, almost certainly correctly, that Guérin obtained 15,000–25,000 francs a month from the Duc d'Orléans from August 1898, in addition to receiving various lump sums. He also claimed that Guérin was subsidized by the army, which seems less likely, but not implausible. Guérin later admitted receiving 10,000 francs from Boni de Castellane, though whether this was a personal gift or a subsidy from the Royalist movement is obscure. Guérin also denied receiving money from the government, and, significantly, limited a similar denial of direct Royalist funding to the period after his imprisonment and exile.[53]

By 1899 certainly, the Ligue was well provided, from whatever sources. Viau again noted the generally sumptuous nature of the installations at the rue de Chabrol headquarters; there was an internal telephone system—something of a novelty for the time—and L'Antijuif was printed on the premises with the most up-to-date equipment, which included two Marinoni presses. Between 15 and 20 printing workers were employed on this "extravagant plant", and, although they were not fully occupied, they were very handsomely paid.[54] Generous towards their staff, Guérin and his associates also diverted a good proportion of the Ligue's funds to their own personal use, Guérin, notably, having a luxurious apartment fitted out at the rue de Chabrol. The Ligue's campaign against Jewish business, moreover, was intended to further their own business interests; for example, Guérin, Max Régis, the mayor of Algiers, and others planned to float a company to buy up Jewish firms ruined as a result of the January 1898 pogrom in Algiers, which the same men had helped to foment and carry out.[55] The links between the Ligue and the antisemitic movement in Algeria were, one should point out, very close, another indication of its radical image and its extremism. At a meeting in May 1898, Guérin "extolled the energy of the antisemites of Algeria, and offered them as an example to be followed by those of metropolitan France."[56] Viau noted the presence at the rue de Chabrol of "Algerians brought to Paris by Max Régis and left in the lurch by him"; and Guérin himself pointed to this hospitality in order to score off Drumont: "the Algerians would be the first to recognize that they met with a much warmer welcome [with us] . . . and obtained much more practical help than they ever found at their deputy's."[57]

On the organization of the Ligue, which reflected the opportunism already referred to, one cannot do better than quote from the report drawn up for the government by the police in August 1899: "The Ligue is the completely personal creation of M.Jules Guérin. There are no policy-forming meetings and no general constitutive assembly." In Paris, sections were not established on a formal footing until mid-1898 and, even then,

> this organization remained something of an improvisation and never really meant anything, since the sections at no time had any independence or freedom of action . . . The Ligue has no Board of Directors or Executive Committee. With the title of General Secretary, M.Guérin is its absolute master; he alone opens all the correspondence, he receives the funds and spends them as he sees fit, without having to render any account of his actions. A certain number of militants meet together from time to time, at more or less regular intervals, depending on circumstances, and hold small meetings at the Ligue's headquarters under the chairmanship of Guérin. But these meetings, open in principle to all members, but attended in practice only by a variable but small number of militants, only deliberate on topics submitted to them by Guérin.

In fact, the meetings of the Ligue seem to have been rather more regular and important than this suggests. Fifty to a hundred militants attended weekly meetings at the Ligue's headquarters, according to police agent reports, and its public meetings attracted much greater numbers. A meeting protesting against the "Dreyfus Syndicate" in Paris in January 1898, for example, was attended by 500; a "patriotic meeting" at Suresnes in February 1898 by 1,000 people; and electoral meetings in aid of the Ligue's candidates in the 16th and 18th *arrondissements* of Paris, about the same time, drew audiences of 700 to 800. However, there is no doubt about the flimsiness of the Ligue's organizational structure and its dependence on Guérin's personal leadership. As the August 1899 report stated: "M.Guérin's authority derives much more from his personal influence over Ligue members than from its actual constitution. He is really the heart of the organization. If he is absent . . . or ill . . . the Ligue suspends its activities."[58] Other reports corroborate this; for example, when Guérin was ill in June 1898, attendance at meetings dwindled, subscriptions ceased to flow, and the Ligue began to disintegrate; similarly, after his arrest in September 1899, an agent reported: "disorganization is total . . ."[59] The corollary of this strict dependence on the leader was the latter's considerable charisma, which was attested by friends and enemies. *Le Nouvelliste de l'Ouest* proclaimed on the occasion of Guérin's visit to Nantes in December 1898: "Everyone has heard of the Secretary General of the Ligue Antisémite de France, the "good giant", as Drumont has called him; everyone has heard of his legendary battles against the Dreyfusards . . ."[60] On the other side, Stéphane Arnoulin wrote in 1902 that Guérin still had "determined men completely devoted to his person in all the *quartiers* [of Paris]".[61]

When his failure to have the Ligue officially registered led to a successful prosecution, Guérin turned it in April 1899 into the "Grand Occident de France", arguing that masonic lodges had never been obliged to seek such authorization. The change of name, for it was nothing else, brought a revival of interest for a while. Weekly meetings of the Grand Occident with attendances of up to 400, and even one of 1,500, are reported for 1900, but, by then, Guérin's links with the organization had become virtually non-existent. It was reported also that members were switching their allegiance to the Ligue de la Patrie Française, a course that the latter's President, Jules Lemaître, tried to encourage.[62] As a police agent reported in December 1899: "the Ligue finished with Guérin . . . and he will not be able to reconstitute it . . . the confidence that people had in him has not been transferred to anyone else."[63] The Grand Occident continued to exist for a few years, under clerical leadership, as we have seen, and in 1902 Guérin, still in exile, attempted a come-back by founding a new periodical, *La Tribune Française*. This was not a success, and by the end of 1902, Viau related: "The Grand Occident . . . had virtually disappeared. Terrorized by the Haute Cour, the important members in Paris and in the provinces had ceased to send in reports and, naturally, their subscriptions remained unpaid. Of all the participants in the feverish agitation and the violence that emanated from the rue de Chabrol, only a handful of hotheads remained . . ."[64] From Lyon, three years later, a police agent reported in the same sense: "The Lyonnais section of the Grand Occident de France, which was very strong at one time, has shared in the débâcle suffered by the main rue de Chabrol establishment."[65] Before discussing this sudden eclipse further, some analysis of Ligue membership must be attempted, for whatever the venality of its leaders and the relatively ephemeral nature of its organization, what is most significant about the Ligue is the fact that it mobilized large numbers of people into active antisemitism. How many were they? and where did they come from, geographically and in terms of class and profession?

Police estimates of the total membership of the Ligue varied from 11,000 in July 1898 to 5,000 in August 1899. Guérin at one time claimed 54,000, of whom 10,000 were said to be in Paris, but, as the police pointed out, it was decidedly in his interest to exaggerate the number of his adherents. The Ligue's weekly, *L'Antijuif*, was printed in editions of 40,000; apparently, however, up to half of these were not sold, but were distributed as free propaganda. A membership of between 5,000 and 10,000 would seem likely, with a larger number of sympathizers, especially in the provinces, where only local leaders were officially members of the Ligue, and where the niceties of internecine rivalries between the various antisemitic groupings in Paris were probably not always appreciated.[66] Two lists of members of the Ligue have been preserved, one in the Archives Nationales, the other in the Archives de la Préfecture de Police.[67] The first is a list of 393 names, provided by a police agent within the Ligue in April 1898; the other list of 409 names was taken from a notebook found on Guérin when he was arrested, probably in April 1899. Only the names on the first list and 71 of those on the second can positively be identified as actual members of the Ligue, although the police believed that the second list as a whole was made up of Guérin's supporters. Very few names appear on both lists, and it is fair to guess that they are complementary. The second list is in rough alphabetical order from C to S inclusive, and is obviously incomplete. In view of the fact that the poor organization of the Ligue militated against exact membership records, that many members did not pay their dues, and that Guérin was always changing membership cards and numbers in an attempt to prevent police infiltration,[68] it would in any case be foolish to look to these lists as a guide to the accuracy of the membership estimates given above, although they do provide a concrete 800 in Paris. The value of the lists lies rather in the light which they throw on the geographical distribution and social milieu of Ligue membership in the capital, since in nearly all cases they provide the addresses of members.

By far the largest contingent came from the 11th *arrondissement* (154), followed by the 17th (94), the 9th (81), the 18th (65) and the 10th (56). The 2nd, 5th, 6th, 8th and 16th *arrondissements* had between 30 and 40 members each; membership in other districts was insignificant. Not surprisingly, this pattern of distribution matches that of the organization of the Ligue. There were sections in the 2nd, 4th, 9th, 10th, 11th, 16th, 17th and 18th *arrondissements*, those in the 18th and, above all, the 11th being particularly active; a police agent commented in September 1898 that "the Ligue Antisémitique has a large following . . . in the 11th *arrondissement*",[69] for example. The Ligue's headquarters, moreover, were successively in the 9th, the 18th and the 10th. Two further comparisons are more revealing. First, the *arrondissements* with the highest proportion of the membership sample were precisely those with large Jewish populations. According to the 1942 statistics, the 11th had the highest proportion of Jews of all the Paris *arrondissements*, followed by the 18th, the 20th, the 10th, the 3rd, the 4th and the 19th.[70] For three *arrondissements*, the correlation is close, and this suggests that Ligue membership may very well have been directly connected with Jewish presence and competition, a hypothesis that we will return to in a more general context in chapter XVII. Second, the *arrondissements* with a high proportion of the membership sample were predominantly districts of "popular" or lower-class residence. Support in the 7th, 8th and 16th *arrondissements*, if typical of the general population there, was probably upper and middle class; that in the 5th and 6th *arrondissements* (the Latin Quarter) may well have come mainly from students; but, in all these cases, the proportion of the membership sample was small; and it seems that the Ligue's main support came from the 11th, the 18th, the 10th and the 17th, which were, in decreasing order of density, working-class *arrondissements*.[71] A sprinkling of Ligue members was found, too, in working-class suburbs further from the centre, such as Montrouge, Courbevoie and Charenton. Too much should not be made of a sample that may not be entirely representative, and it is hazardous to assume that members in a predominantly working-class district were necessarily themselves working-class. But, taken with the Ligue's "radicalism", this evidence suggests that it may well have succeeded in attracting a measure of support from artisans and workers, as well as from small traders, lower white-collar workers and middle-class people.

Direct evidence of the social complexion of Ligue membership is unfortunately scanty. The professions of only 99 Paris members can be established from the membership lists and other sources. These were people whose job was presumably "important" enough to record, and they cannot be taken as typical of the total membership, though they probably are representative of the militants. 30 (of the 99) were in business or commerce; 20 were involved in politics or journalism; 18 were in the liberal professions; 13 were ex-army officers; 6 industrialists; 6 ecclesiastics; and 6 artisans. Ligue militants, therefore, seem to have been almost exclusively bourgeois or lower middle-class, with a high proportion engaged in some kind of business. Evidence from other sources indicates that Ligue meetings were attended by "businessmen . . . butchers . . . white-collar and a few other workers . . ."; Paris cab-drivers and travelling salesmen were two other professional groups said to be particularly attracted, to which Reinach added "street-porters . . . rag-pickers and criminals of all kinds."[72] The only objective source available for the professions of rank and file antisemites is that provided by the lists of those arrested in the anti-Jewish riots, which the Ligue did more than any other group to instigate. Of these the most important probably took place in January 1898, as we saw in chapter III; of the 83 then arrested in Paris, 29 were students, 23 artisans or workers, 16 white-collar workers, waiters or servants, 5 in the liberal professions, 4 small traders, and 6 without profession. Not too much should be made, again, of so small and so indirect a sample, but it does complement and confirm the other evidence.

It is interesting that women, not usually involved in political organizations in nineteenth-century France, seem to have been involved to a considerable extent in the activities of the Ligue, as we have seen that they were in the Henry Subscription. The Ligue's campaign against Jewish shops was largely aimed at women, as we have already pointed out, but they are also reported to have attended Ligue meetings and apparently became members. Viau related that special *"fêtes-concerts"* were organized at the rue de Chabrol for women members and their children, and explained the special sexual attraction which the violence of the Ligue had for upper-class women in particular: "Many society ladies went to the public meetings, and the details which they heard there [about the brutality of the *ligueurs*], thrilled them deliciously. They asked to be presented to these good fellows, and joyfully placed their little hands in their suede gloves in the great hairy paws that were so good at delivering blows . . ."[73] However, as this indicates, women remained strictly auxiliaries, and Guérin was particularly hostile to feminism, or any departure by women from their traditional subservient role in society.[74]

Comparison of the two membership lists yields one interesting result. The first list seems to be much more "working class" than the second; it shows addresses in the 11th and 17th *arrondissements* outnumbering those in all the other *arrondissements* put together; whereas in the second list the distribution of membership over all Paris is much more even. In addition, the second list contains at least 30 aristocratic names, and the first only 7. This suggests one of two things: either (which seems unlikely) that the lists are different in kind, the first being a list of rank-and-file membership and the second of leaders; or (more probably) that, within a year, the social complexion of the Ligue altered, that it lost much of its popular support, leaning as a result more heavily on an upper-class, and incidentally Catholic, clientèle.

MAP 9 BRANCHES OF THE LIGUE ANTISÉMITIQUE FRANCAISE.

Although the Ligue was primarily a Parisian organization, it had, as we have seen, important links with the antisemitic movement in Algeria and in the French provinces. Guérin and others toured France making speeches, and the Ligue claimed to have correspondents in 52 departments. It also had branches or sections in 20 or more places, although police agents sometimes referred to 100 or more. It can be established that there were branches at Rouen, Nancy, Vesoul, Marseille, Bordeaux, Nantes, Nevers, Yvetot, Poitiers, Valenciennes, Lille, Toulouse, Perpignan, Montpellier, Rennes, Lyon, Roanne, Grenoble, Rodez, Epernay, Noisy-le-Sec(Seine), and in the Yonne and the Dordogne (see Map 9). These were all places where antisemitism is known, from other evidence, to have been important. Local membership was usually estimated at about 50 or 60 per branch, although in mid-1898 Lille had 110 members, Nantes 300, Marseille 126, and Rodez about 200. The Nancy branch was put at 2,800, while Lyon boasted two branches of over 1,000 strong.[75] The social composition of provincial rank-and-file membership is impossible to gauge from the few lists that survive, but something can be made of the scattered information concerning 75 provincial committee members; 18 of these were in politics or journalism; 15 were in the liberal professions; 13 were ex-army officers; 12 were in business or commerce; 5 were property-owners *(propriétaires)* or rentiers; 5 were white-collar workers or servants; 4 were industrialists; 2 were artisans; and 1 was a priest. An additional 25 had aristocratic names. The mixture is much the same as in Paris, although the proportion of business men is smaller, and the absence of the clergy more striking. Pierrard's independent researches, however, indicate that the Ligue's links with provincial Catholicism were closer than this suggests, at least in some places. For example, the secretary of the Bordeaux branch was a manufacturer of church ornaments; the organizer of the Nantes branch was a Catholic bookseller; while Catholics, often students, were prominent at Toulouse, Nancy, Nevers, Yvetot and Poitiers. There were close relations also between some branches and the local Catholic press and Catholic organizations.[76]

In conclusion to this chapter, four points can be made. First, the Ligue Antisémitique Française, with its "socialist" pretensions had some success among the lower-class districts of Paris, particularly where the presence of a large and visible Jewish community could plausibly be related to economic difficulties. Second, for its leader, the Ligue was, in large part, a means of procuring his own financial benefit, while its programme, so far as it existed, was opportunistically, not to say cynically, conceived. But, third, despite this lack of real ideological fervour at the top, Guérin attracted a devoted following, foreshadowing later exponents of the *Führerprinzip*. Despite its somewhat ramshackle structure, the Ligue was an organization operating on a national level with some degree of effectiveness for three years, and, particularly in the capital, it established antisemitic violence as a frequent and organized occurrence. With a membership of thousands, its activities were tolerated, at least temporarily, by many more. With Guérin and his Ligue, in effect, in contrast to Drumont and *La Libre Parole* antisemitism in France moved from the level of a movement of opinion to the level of organization and action. However, lastly, the Ligue Antisémitique lacked many of the qualities of an effective political organization, and, in contrast to his Viennese counterpart and contemporary, Lueger,[77] Guérin was ultimately a political failure. This was partly through reasons of temperament; for all his cynicism, Guérin had romantic delusions and poor judgment of events, as the "Fort Chabrol" incident indicates. Moreover, since in Paris, unlike Vienna, there was no elected mayoralty to capture, there was little incentive for the antisemitic and "Nationalist" factions in the city to overcome their divisions and work together for a real political prize. They had done this in Algeria, as we shall see, but had discovered that the implementation of antisemitism at municipal level quickly encountered opposition from the central government.[78] A relatively concerted effort was made also in the municipal elections in Paris in 1900, but though successful, it, too, led nowhere.[79] The municipal council of the city was a body with very limited powers, and whatever the support for it within the council, antisemitism could never enter into its practice. The political climate in France had only been temporarily favourable to the Ligue and to organized antisemitism in general, and from mid-1899, with the advent of Waldeck-Rousseau to power, this climate changed, as we shall see. But first we must explore further the antisemitic movement as a whole at the height of its development.

NOTES

1 Cit. Guérin, *Les Trafiquants de l'antisémitisme*, p. 139.
2 Some people continued to refer to it under the old name.
3 L'Hermite, *L'Anti-Pape*, pp. 130–3; Guérin, op. cit., pp. 101–19; Viau, *Vingt ans d'antisémitisme*, pp. 192 and 195; Drault, *Drumont, La France juive et La Libre Parole*, p. 246; Pierrard, *Juifs et catholiques français*, pp. 143–6.
4 Guérin, op. cit., p. 109.
5 See ibid., chapters VIII–XI and *passim*.
6 Viau, op. cit., pp. 192 and 313–14; Pierrard, op. cit., pp. 143–4.
7 Reinach, *Histoire de l'Affaire Dreyfus*, IV, p. 304.
8 Report on the Ligue Antisémitique Française, Ministry of the Interior, August 1899. AN F⁷ 12459, "Mouvement Antisémitique". Unless otherwise stated, information is taken from AN F⁷ 12459 and from other police reports: AN F⁷ 12882–12883, "Ligue Antisémitique"; APP Ba 106, "Rapports quotidiens"; and Ba 1103, "Jules Guérin".
9 Police report, January 1899. APP Ba 1103.
10 Daily Report, Prefect of Police, 1 March 1898. APP Ba 106.
11 Viau, op. cit., p. 193.
12 Reinach, op. cit., IV, pp. 303–4.
13 Daily Report, Prefect of Police, 21 April 1898. APP Ba 106.
14 See chapter II, pp. 68–9.
15 L. Lacour, Speech, Salle des Sociétés Savantes, Paris. Daily Report, Prefect of Police, 29 June 1898. APP Ba 106.
16 Guérin, op. cit., p. 140.
17 Daily Report, Prefect of Police, 12 February 1898. APP Ba 106; see also the "constitution" of the *Grand Occident de France*. AN F⁷ 12882, Dossier III, Pièce 55.
18 Report, Police agent, 10 August 1898. AN F⁷ 12882, Dossier I, Pièce 40.

19 Daily Report, Prefect of Police, 31 March 1898. APP Ba 106; see also Report, Police agent, 12 February 1898. AN F⁷ 12474.

20 Daily Reports, Prefect of Police, 2 April and 11 May. APP Ba 106.

21 Police report, August 1899. AN F⁷ 12459.

22 Guérin, op. cit., p. 138.

23 Reports, Police, Rennes, 1 July and 2 September 1899. AN F⁷ 12464; and Commissaire spécial, Roanne, 28 April 1899. AN F⁷ 12480.

24 Pierrard, op. cit., pp. 144 and 150.

25 Reinach, op. cit., IV, p. 304.

26 Report, Police agent, 10 September 1898. AN F⁷ 12882, Dossier I, Pièce 43.

27 Report, Ministry of the Interior, August 1899. AN F⁷ 12459.

28 Georges Bernanos, *La Grande Peur des bien-pensants: Edouard Drumont* (Paris, 1931), pp. 346–7.

29 "le Bras". L'Hermite, op. cit., pp. 130–3.

30 Daily Report, Prefect of Police, 22 January 1898. APP Ba 106.

31 Reinach, op. cit., III, pp. 277, 341–2 and 539.

32 See particularly L'Hermite, op. cit., pp. 130–3 and 143–57. The book is prefaced by Paul Vibert, who stood against Drumont as a Radical, and who presumably supplied the author with information, if he did not in fact write the book himself.

33 Reinach, op. cit., IV, pp. 330–2, 426–8 and 601; Pierrard, op. cit., p. 144; Report, Police agent, 29 April 1899. AN F⁷ 12464.

34 L'Hermite, op. cit., p. 165; Arnoulin, *M. Edouard Drumont*, pp. 178–9; Police reports. APP Ba 1103.

35 Reinach, op. cit., IV, p. 304; see also Arnoulin, op. cit., p. 178; Bernanos, op. cit., p. 347; Daudet, *Les Oeuvres dans les hommes*, p. 171.

36 Report, Police agent, 30 August 1899. AN F⁷ 12452; Halévy, *Apologie*, p. 91; Reinach, op. cit., IV, pp. 302–4 and 331–2.

37 Report, Police agent, 19 August 1899. AN F⁷ 12464; and Reinach, op. cit., IV, p. 306.

38 Reports, Police agents, 29 April 1899. AN F⁷ 12464; 17 August 1899, and 18 October 1900. AN F⁷ 12870; Viau, op. cit., p 199; Guérin, op. cit., pp. 200–15; Reinach, op. cit., IV, pp. 590–2 and 601.

39 Viau, op. cit., pp. 190–1; Reinach, op. cit., V, pp. 181–4 and 257–8.

40 Guérin, op. cit., p. 194. On "Fort Chabrol", see ibid., chapter VI; Police Reports. AN F⁷ 12462; AN F⁷ 12464; AN F⁷ 12466; and AN F⁷ 12882, Dossier II; Reinach, op. cit., V, pp. 313 and 422–7; Viau, op. cit., pp. 192–3; Bernanos, op. cit., pp. 350–5; Drault, op. cit., pp. 258–69.

41 Report, Police agent, 18 August 1899. AN F⁷ 12464; Stock, *Mémorandum d'un éditeur*, 3e série, pp. 129–34; Viau, op. cit., pp. 302–5; Guérin, op. cit., pp. 159, 171–7 and 191–2.

42 Reports, Police agents, 16 and 21 August and 2 September 1899. AN F⁷ 12923. That the episode did catch the popular imagination is indicated by the fact that "Le Fort Chabrol" was used as the name of a café as far away as Belfort (Report, Commissaire spécial, Belfort, 29 November 1904. AN F⁷ 12455); it was also referred to in soap advertisements.

43 Daudet, *Au Temps de Judas*, p. 13; Steinheil, *My Memoirs*, p. 128; see also Stock, op. cit., pp. 112 and 129: "cette comédie . . . cette bouffonnerie du Fort Chabrol . . ."

44 Viau, op. cit., p. 285; Guérin, op. cit., chapter VII; Drault, op. cit., p. 274; Pierrard, op. cit., p. 149.

45 Reinach, op. cit., IV, p. 304.

46 Maurras, Letter to Barrès, March 1899. Barrès-Maurras, op. cit., pp. 224–5.

47 Guérin, Speech. Daily Report, Prefect of Police, 4 March 1898. APP Ba 106.

48 Police agents' reports refer to the election of 14 antisemitic mayors in France and of over 100 municipal councils in which antisemites had the majority or were well represented, but it has not been possible to check these extravagant-sounding

claims. However, the antisemites certainly did well in Paris; see chapter VIII, p. 214 and n. 6 below.

49 Daily Report, Prefect of Police, 29 June 1898. APP Ba 106.
50 L'Hermite, op. cit., pp. 165–82; Arnoulin, op. cit., pp. 176–9; Stock, op. cit., pp. 132–5; Police Reports. APP 1103.
51 Viau, op. cit., p. 190.
52 Maurras, *Au Signe de Flore*, p. 97.
53 Reinach, op. cit., III, p. 342, and IV, pp. 303–4 and 587; Guérin, op. cit., pp. 192 and 484–6; see also Viau, op. cit., p. 191; Police Reports, AN F⁷ 12882, Dossiers I and II.
54 Viau, op. cit., pp. 192–3.
55 See particularly AN F⁷ 12882, Dossier I, Pièces 26, 65 and 71.
56 Daily Report, Prefect of Police, 1 June 1898. APP Ba 106.
57 Viau, op. cit., p. 193; Guérin, op. cit., p. 128.
58 Report, Ministry of the Interior, August 1899. AN F⁷ 12459.
59 Report, Police agent, 13 September 1899. AN F⁷ 12882, Dossier II, Pièce 78.
60 *Le Nouvelliste de l'Ouest*, 12–13 December 1898; see also Report, Commissaire spécial, Nantes, 13 December 1898. AN F⁷ 12465.
61 Arnoulin, op. cit., p. 178.
62 See AN F⁷ 12882, Dossier III; Viau, op. cit., pp. 286–7; Guérin, op. cit., p. 280.
63 Report, Police agent, 13 December 1899. AN F⁷ 12882, Dossier II, Pièce 98.
64 Viau, op. cit., pp. 313–15.
65 Report, Police agent, 3 April 1905. AN F⁷ 12457; see also Report, Prefect, Rhône, 15 February 1901. Ibid.
66 George L. Mosse, "The French Right and the Working Classes: Les Jaunes", *Journal of Contemporary History*, 7, nos 3–4 (1972), p. 189, seriously underestimates both the size and the importance of the Ligue Antisémitique.
67 AN F⁷ 12882, Dossier I, Pièce 7; APP Ba 1103.
68 Guérin even suggested, op. cit., p. 169, that no membership records at all were kept, which is evidently not true. A lot of the Ligue's papers were deliberately destroyed during the Fort Chabrol siege. The success of the police in infiltrating the Ligue and other similar organizations is amply demonstrated by the reports on which this study has so much relied; and leaders were well aware of it. Syveton declared that "La Patrie Française, comme toute ligue d'opposition qui se respecte, entretient une demi-douzaine de policiers", cit. Daudet, *Au Temps de Judas*, p. 231. Péguy was so suspicious of police infiltration that he listed subscribers to the *Cahiers de la Quinzaine* by their initials only and not their full names; see Tharaud, *Notre cher Péguy*, I, p. 120. See also Reinach, op. cit., IV, p. 570.
69 Report, Police agent, 1 September 1898. AN F⁷ 12480.
70 See M. Roblin, *Les Juifs de Paris* (Paris, 1952), chapter V. Religious affiliation was omitted from French censuses after 1872, and thus no official count of Jewish population or its distribution is available for the period being studied. Despite their provenance, the 1942 statistics have been preferred to earlier ones, because they take account of the important influx of East European Jews into Paris in the last quarter of the nineteenth century. It is perhaps relevant here, as Drumont noted, that the 9th *arrondissement* had at least two Jewish municipal councillors in the 1880s; see Drumont, *La Dernière Bataille*, p. 139; and *Le Testament d'un antisémite*, p. 86. See also, on the migration of Jews to the suburbs, Drumont, *DB*, p. 107; and, on the Jewish population of the 4th *arrondissement*, Clermont-Tonnerre, *Mémoires*, I, p. 222.
71 See Jacques Rougerie, *Paris libre 1871* (Paris, 1971), p. 18; Watson, "The Nationalist Movement in Paris", pp. 50–3; Louis Chevalier, *Les Parisiens* (Paris, 1967).
72 Report, Police agent, 12 May 1899. AN F⁷ 12882, Dossier II, Pièce 52; and Reinach, op. cit., III, p. 342.

73 Viau, op. cit., pp. 191 and 194.
74 See Report, Police agent, 6 July 1898. AN F⁷ 12882, Dossier I, Pièce 35, on Guérin's hostile reaction to Max Régis's association with Séverine.
75 In addition to police reports, see Pierrard, op. cit., p. 148.
76 Ibid., pp. 147–8; see also Report, Commissaire spécial, Rennes, 2 September 1899. AN F⁷ 12464, on links between the local Ligue secretary and *La Croix.*
77 See P.G.J. Pulzer, *The Rise of Political Anti-Semitism in Germany and Austria* (New York, 1964), pp. 162–206.
78 See chapter IX, p. 233.
79 Jewish schools were secularized in the 9th and 10th *arrondissements*, but that was as far as "municipal" antisemitism went in Paris, and even this could be construed as a primarily anticlerical action and the implementation of governmental policy in education; see Pierrard, op. cit., p 150.

CHAPTER VII
THE ANTISEMITIC MOVEMENT: MISCELLANEOUS
ORGANIZATIONS, GENERAL CHARACTERISTICS
AND THE PRESS

THE LIGUE ANTISEMITIQUE FRANÇAISE WAS ONLY THE MOST IMPORTANT OF a large number of antisemitic organizations that sprang up in France at the time of the Dreyfus Affair. Many political groups then competed to exploit what seemed a promising means of obtaining popular support, and, as we saw in discussing the Affair itself, politicians and publicists across the whole political spectrum, from freethinking Anarchists and members of the Parti Ouvrier Français to Catholic Royalists, openly espoused antisemitism. We shall consider this all-pervasiveness of antisemitism and its combination with other political and social causes in the next part of this book, confining our attention here to those who dubbed themselves, or were known, as "the professional antisemites",[1] that is to formal groupings and organs whose main declared raison d'être was ideological hostility to Jews, though the distinction between these and less committed organizations is, of course, not absolute or always easy to make.

Besides Les Amis de Morès, which seems to have faded away, except in the provinces by the late 1890s, and the Ligue Antisémitique, the only organizations, operating on a national level, which fall clearly into the former category, were La Jeunesse Antisémite et Nationaliste and the Fédération Nationale Antijuive. The first apparently originated as La Ligue Antisémite des Etudiants de Paris, founded under Drumont's auspices in 1894.[2] It was put on a more formal footing in March 1898 under the leadership of a young lawyer, Edouard Dubuc, with Drumont as honorary president, and a loose federation of provincial sections was formed.[3] By 1900, according to Pierrard, these existed at Toulouse, Bordeaux, Saint-Etienne, Dijon, Langres, Vesoul, Lille, Le Havre, Caen, Issoudun and Nice, and another was reported in 1901 at Saint-Germain-en-Laye.[4] In the same year, the police reported that 80 delegates attended a congress in Paris.[5] La Jeunesse Antisémitique was very closely associated with the Royalist movement; members frequently belonged both to it, and to La Jeunesse Royaliste; at Le Havre one man was the secretary of both organizations. At Caen the local Jeunesse Antisémitique was also known in 1899 as the Groupe d'Action Francaise, and must have been one of the first such groups in the provinces.[6] The Royalism of La Jeunesse Antisémite also implied close connections with the Church. The organizer of the Caen group was abbé Masselin, director of *La Croix du Calvados*.[7] Moreover, most members seem to have been Catholic students. A Cercle Antisémitique d'Etudes Sociales, which functioned in Paris, was apparently an offshoot of La Jeunesse Antisémite.[8] Few estimates of membership figures are available, though the Lyon section was reported to have 200 members in 1901, when the group was already on the decline,[9] and there were several groups in Paris of comparable size. Guérin related that, at the end of 1899, La Jeunesse Antisémite "wanted to extend its organization and to try to widen the scope of its action and propaganda";[10] and Dubuc and Cailly created a new body, Le Parti National Antijuif, with this end in view, whose weekly organ, *Le Précurseur*, lasted until at least 1903.[11] But La Jeunesse Antisémite, like the Grand Occident, felt the effect of governmental repression at this time—some of its leaders were arrested alongside Guérin and the Royalist leaders, and its premises were searched by the police—and, instead of expansion, it underwent a decline. Yet another avatar of the group, Les Volontiers de la Liberté, had only 150 members in 1903, and these had dwindled to 5 by 1904.[12]

Drumont had been involved in the original Ligue Antisémitique of 1889, in Guérin's Ligue in its early days, and in La Jeunesse Antisémite, but in a strictly honorary capacity. La Fédération Nationale Antijuive was more properly his organization, or at least that of *La Libre Parole*. It originated as Le Comité National Antijuif, founded by Drumont and Devos at the end of 1901, to fight the 1902 General Elections. A subscription launched by the newspaper, on the same lines as the Henry Subscription, was relatively successful, bringing in 30,000 francs by January 1902.[13] But the Comité failed to obtain the support of all antisemites, let alone the "Nationalist" opposition as a whole, even in the electoral period. Moreover, the antisemites' showing in the 1902 elections marked a big fall from that of 1898.[14] The Comité was nevertheless turned in 1903 into a permanent organization, the Fédération Nationale Antijuive, whose aim was to regroup all the forces of antisemitism under one umbrella. It again failed in its task, and a big rally organized in April 1905 with the "Syndicats Jaunes" was attended by only 280 people.[15]

In addition to these national organizations, there were a fair number of purely local antisemitic groups, which had only tenuous links, if any, with the centrally-organized movement. As we have seen, for example, Poitiers had a Ligue Antisémitique du Commerce Poitevin in 1896, to which 200 shopkeepers belonged;[16] Rennes had a Groupe Antisémitique Nationaliste Rennais in July 1899;[17] and Nantes had a Ligue Patriotique Antisémite de Nantes, with 270 members in 1898–99. More important was the Ligue Anti-Juive d'Alger, founded in 1892, and also known as the Ligue Socialiste Anti-Juive, which had 750 members in 1895;[18] but we will discuss the antisemitic movement in Algeria more fully in chapter IX. Mention should also be made of the ephemeral and, it seems, exclusively Parisian Ligue Radicale Antisémitique, founded in 1892 by Fernand Grégoire, with Drumont and Morès as honorary presidents, to act as a liaison organization between the antisemites and ex-Boulangists.[19]

Immediately, we must provide some analysis of the general characteristics of organized antisemitism in France. We have referred so far to an antisemitic movement in the singular, but we have also demonstrated that it lacked formal unity. "What all these good people lack", Drumont told Viau, "is good leadership, direction by one leader."[20] Not only did most antisemites belong to different schools or organizations, but these groups, while co-operating to some degree in demonstrations, propaganda and election campaigns, also spent a great deal of energy in quarrelling among themselves. We have seen that relations between *La Libre Parole* and the Ligue Antisémitique Française were inimical, but the Ligue and La Jeunesse Antisémite were similarly hostile to each other.[21] Drault, a journalist on *La Libre Parole*, wrote: "Grand Occident, Patrie Française, Jeunesse Antisémite, Ligue des Patriotes united only for demonstrations [like those directed against Loubet in 1899]. In general, they were all very jealous of each other, and they were not, of course, all fighting for the same political régime . . ."[22] But genuine political disagreements merged with pure rivalry between the different leaders, and with clashes of personality. Drumont, in particular, despite his professed disapproval of disputes, was notoriously quarrelsome and difficult to work with,[23] and the history of his relations with the other antisemitic leaders is one of continual disagreements and conflicts. Having dedicated *La Dernière Bataille* to Morès in 1890, for example, and having co-operated closely with him in the first Ligue Antisémitique, Drumont broke with him publicly in 1893, as we have mentioned. Drumont had apparently intervened on Morès's behalf in order to secure for him a substantial loan from the Jewish banker Cornélius Herz. When Morès revealed the master's departure from antisemitic principle in the press, Drumont riposted with a savage article in *La Libre Parole*, and had nothing more to do with Morès until he attended his funeral.[24] Drumont also quarrelled with Jacques de Biez, and was on bad terms with Lemaître, leader of the Ligue de la Patrie Francaise, with Rochefort and with Barrès, and in all cases the dislike was mutual.[25] Within the antisemitic schools or groups, such quarrelling seems also to have been endemic. Léon Daudet, for example, relates that Devos, the business manager of *La Libre Parole*, and Gaston Méry, one of its chief editors, were bitter and active enemies.[26] Such conflicts must have seriously reduced the effectiveness of the antisemitic movement, while bringing it also into public disrepute. Viau commented on the open polemic engaged in by Drumont and Guérin in 1903 that it "threw each day more and more discredit on the editors of the two antisemitic newspapers . . ."[27]

All organizations have their share of internal conflict and suffer from the effects of clashes of personality. The French Socialist movement at this time, for example, still comprised a number of warring sects, that were only slowly and with difficulty moving towards the unification of 1905.[28] But, as has been suggested for American movements of a similar kind,[29] the tendencies towards disunity, organizational disorder and quarrelling among leaders were peculiarly strong in the French antisemitic movement. They were exacerbated by several characteristic and structural features in particular: the leadership cult and the difficulty of finding funds, and, related to these and pulling in opposite directions: the almost religious fanaticism of members, and the very large element of pure opportunism that seems to have motivated and guided those at the top. We have already come across these characteristics in connection with the Ligue Antisémitique Française, but they were by no means peculiar to it.

We have earlier noted the adulation that Morès and Guérin received from their followers, and Drumont and others enjoyed the same devotion.[30] Viau wrote that members of the first Ligue Antisémitique "would—out of political passion—have committed the worst excesses, at the slightest indication from Drumont or from Morès, from Morès especially, whose redoubtable strength impressed them much more than his intelligence, and who appeared, in their eyes . . . as a legendary hero, a kind of d'Artagnan."[31] Those who worked on *La Libre Parole,* he related again, regarded themselves, not as ordinary journalists working for a salary, "but rather as Drumont's disciples . . . every remark of M. Drumont had for us the significance of Holy Writ."[32] The young Max Régis, leader of the movement in Algeria, was the object of what can only be called a religious cult. Among the hundreds of fan-letters which followed him from Algeria on his visit to Paris in 1898, one addressed him as "Our Jesus".[33] Such flattery can only have fed the natural egotism of these men, and the status of petty Messiahs, conveyed on them, encouraged them to try to extend their own influence over the whole antisemitic movement rather than to accept co-operation with other leaders as equals.

The struggle to recruit members and to raise funds acted in the same direction. Initially, the various antisemitic groups financed themselves almost exclusively by subscription. Drumont wrote of the first Ligue Antisémitique: "The cost of its antisemitic propaganda was never very great, thanks to the individual devotion of the members of the committee. Expenses were all covered by the small subscription fees paid by members of the Ligue. These were usually 3 francs, but a few, a very few, were of 20 to 50 francs."[34] As we have seen, *La Libre Parole* maintained this traditional way of raising funds, but the later antisemitic organizations, and in particular, Guérin's Ligue Antisémitique relied on it to a much lesser extent. As Drumont pointed out in 1891, subscriptions did not normally bring in a great deal of money: "We are not the ones to be embarrassed by the question: Where does the money come from? With us, the money just doesn't come."[35] But, as this suggests, once organized antisemitism was established, more important resources became available to it in the form of subsidies from the old opposition "parties". They saw in the circumstances of the Affair an opportunity to extend their influence, if not to bring down the régime, and they were anxious to buy the popular support and the militancy that the antisemites seemed able to offer. "Thanks to the Affair", wrote Anatole Leroy-Beaulieu in 1902, "antisemitism became a power to reckon with, and, like all such powers, it was courted".[36] For the different antisemitic (and "Nationalist") groups, it then became a question of trying to convince the mainly Royalist and Catholic providers of funds that they had a membership large and important enough to justify subsidization, and then subsidization on a more generous scale than their rivals, if not exclusive financial support. Thus, wrote Viau, there developed "among the leaders, an underhand struggle, a fierce mutual disparagement, with the intention of attracting as much money as possible into the till of their own particular league . . ."[37] A police agent reported, similarly, in 1903 that the other "Nationalist" groups were regarded "in the worst possible light . . . at *La Libre Parole* . . . because of the resources with which they are supplied by their supporters. The antisemites believe that these resources should come to *La Libre Parole*, and this is the determining factor in the policy which they pursue."[38] The antisemitic and "Nationalist" groups, according to another police report, dated 1901, were "closed sects which had no intention of surrendering one jot of their autonomy; far from consenting to allow themselves to be submerged in a united party, each one was only trying to recruit supporters at the expense of the others . . ."[39]

This brings us to the apparent polarity in the antisemitic movement between near-religious fanaticism on the one hand, and the pursuit of material interest on the other. There is no doubt that the various antisemitic groups were characterized by the sectarianism referred to in the police report just quoted. As Piou remarked, Drumont was a man "with a mission",[40] and antisemites represented a band of the faithful. "I was an antisemite", wrote Viau, "I believed . . ."[41] Each grouping, the movement as a whole, was the context for this faith, providing individual members with the intense feeling of belonging, of losing themselves, that Sartre has seen as an essential feature of antisemitism.[42] Drumont, characteristically, wrote of *Le Testament d'un antisémite*, whose title itself is significant: "This book is above all a book for friends, a book that is written for those who love us."[43] We will examine this socio-psychological function of antisemitism further in the next part of this book, but it is important to stress here the strength of the sense of being an antisemite, of belonging to the movement, of being, precisely, among friends. For it was this feeling, and the commitment to an ideology that went with it, that actually made and kept in being an antisemitic movement as such, that made it more than a simple collection of rival groups. But accepting antisemitic ideas and opinions was frequently not enough of itself; commitment to the ideology also involved joining the movement, belonging to it, whether one actually paid up membership dues to a specific organization or not. Antisemitism here showed itself to be both more and less than a political party;[44] it was not a rational political option, or a movement conceived as a means to an end, but rather a movement that was an end in itself. And it is this aspect, the depth of the need to believe and belong, which probably explains the opportunism which was another main characteristic of organized antisemitism. It was not simply, as Sartre argues, that antisemitism could have no genuine programme, and was thus forced to be opportunistic, though this is doubtless true—a point again that we will examine later; but also that the gratuitousness of the antisemites' need to believe, its absence of real content, of contact with social reality, gave it an excessive quality that lent itself easily and obviously to exploitation. Another point worth making in this connection is that the cynicism of some antisemitic leaders and their manipulation of their following in no way renders antisemitism an artificial social and political phenomenon. Quite the opposite, for such leaders could not have succeeded unless they were able to count on the pre-existence in society at large of antisemitic values and beliefs, and, indeed, the ideological utterances of the most cynical, devoid of all personal commitment and distortion, could very well be the most authentic testimony of real popular attitudes.[45]

But out and out cynics were rare, if they existed at all. There are obviously degrees of exploitation, too, and a fair amount of apparently cynical behaviour on the part of antisemitic leaders could co-exist with a genuine belief in the message that they were conveying. This is certainly the case with Drumont himself, despite charges to the contrary. For L'Hermite and Arnoulin, Drumont was simply a tool of the religious orders, and notably the Jesuits, using antisemitism in the interests of "clericalism".[46] Guérin claimed that Drumont's interests were more mundane, accusing him of being simply a "merchant of antisemitism", and writing that, for its editor and his associates, "La Libre Parole was a business enterprise and nothing else".[47] To substantiate the charge, Guérin claimed, in particular, that La Libre Parole blackmailed Le Crédit Foncier and other firms, threatening to publish bad news about their shares unless they paid to prevent it; also that, while campaigning against department stores, La Libre Parole accepted advertisements from them, as well as from other Jewish businesses.[48] The commercial exploitation of antisemitism also involved La Libre Parole in fraudulent lotteries and in the marketing of patent medicines and other goods. Again, according to Guérin, Devos and Drumont were actively engaged in the manufacture and sale of "Le Traitement du Chartreux", a worthless cure-all advertised in the columns of their daily at 9 francs a bottle, which had nothing to do with the monks of La Chartreuse as was implied by its name.[49] Others made similar claims and cast similar doubts on the purity of Drumont's motives. The novelist Georges Darien, for example, in L'Ogre (1891) painted a picture of the antisemitic leader as a pure opportunist;[50] and the anarchist Elie Murmain told a meeting in February 1898 that Drumont was simply expoiting antisemitism for the money.[51] This agreement suggests that Guérin was not indulging in complete fantasy in his denigration of his rival. In Le Testament d'un antisémite, Drumont felt it necessary to point out that he had not made a fortune from La France juive, and that he was only the tenant and not the owner of his country house; and the same defensiveness is found in Léon Daudet's later apologia.[52] Drumont clearly did make a great deal of money from his best-selling books,[53] but it seems likely that he was not directly involved in the grosser forms of financial exploitation of credulity associated with La Libre Parole, though, of course, he was ultimately responsible for everything that the paper published. Here, in fact, lay the real venality of Drumont and his enterprise, for La Libre Parole thrived on calumny and insinuation, and depended on acquiring a daily supply of poisonous information or gossip. "Throughout every evening", recalled Viau of the time of the Panama scandal, "we saw shifty-looking people arriving, coming mysteriously to bring us the 'latest tips'. They were mostly former tools, ex-cronies [of Republican politicians] . . . They furnished the paper with most of its sensational articles, and they did it, not even for thirty pieces of silver . . . [but] for the simple pleasure of stabbing unarmed opponents in the back, cravenly and, above all, with impunity . . ."[54]

The antisemitic movement, in effect, as the accounts of Viau and Guérin well convey, was a milieu especially attractive to men on the make, unscrupulous and mutually suspicious and competitive. As Verdès-Leroux has observed, "antisemitism was not only a passion, it was a career";[55] and, whatever the truth of Guérin's allegations about Drumont, there is considerable evidence of the cynical exploitation of popular credulity by antisemites for their own material advantage, as we have seen in the case of Guérin himself. Marketing frauds using the antisemitic ploy included the sale of a "Chartreuse antijuive", an imitation of the real liqueur, and a more extensive racket involving postal sales organized by *La Croisade Française*.[56] The same calculating use of antisemitism was found also in the movement's recruitment and fund-raising itself, as we have already suggested. A particularly blatant example of this is provided by the report of a police agent on a committee meeting of the Fédération Nationale Antijuive in March 1904, at which it was decided to launch a propaganda campaign in the provinces, rather than in Paris, "because, to use the academic expression of Devos, it is in the sticks that you get the best suckers, and the Master [Drumont] and his intendant . . . are counting on provincial gullibility to replenish their coffers . . ."[57] Antisemitism could be used, too, to further political careers, and to sell newspapers. Maurice Barrès, who had written a pro-Jewish article in *Le Voltaire* in January 1888, opened a violently antisemitic campaign as a parliamentary candidate in Nancy twelve months later that won him the seat, a conversion that can at the least be dubbed convenient;[58] and a number of other politicians made the same conversion in 1898, as we shall see in the next chapter. According to Arnoulin, J.-B.Gérin, the chief financial backer of *La Libre Parole* in 1892, had undergone the same profitable reversal of opinions as Barrès, since, two years earlier, he had tried to establish another newspaper, to represent Jewish interests.[59] Many others then tried to get a share of the successful journalistic vein opened up by *La Libre Parole*, often quite opportunistically. Viau wrote, for example that Thiébaud, an ex-Boulangist, "exploited the Jew in *L'Eclair* for his own private advantage".[60] The rivalry of different antisemitic groups, of different interests, here became merged in commercial competition, in a sales-war. Sorlin has demonstrated, in particular, that the antisemitism of *La Croix* was deliberately espoused and fostered in order to increase sales, and that *La Croix* and *La Libre Parole* competed for readers via the medium of antisemitism, a competition rendered more intense by the fact that they catered for roughly the same clientèle.[61] The last word on opportunistic antisemitism should, perhaps, be left to Drumont's most vigorous and reactionary critic, Léon Bloy:[62]

things were going very well, editions multiplied and royalties piled up with Rothschildean precision, which excited the slobbering concupiscence of a whole tribe of envious scribblers of the same kidney who had not been blessed with his bountiful brain-wave, but they resolved at once to devote themselves to the same exploits. They all . . . understood admirably that the battle against the Jews could be—for those in the know—the most excellent dodge to repair many a disaster or to buck up many an ailing enterprise.

The role of the press as an instrument for exploiting popular credulity has been referred to more than once, and implied in much of the analysis in this and preceding chapters, and this crucial aspect of the antisemitic movement requires further description and discussion. Like the wider "Nationalist" movement, organized antisemitism was a movement of leagues and of newspapers, and, quantitatively, the second were more important than the first, for the leagues and other groupings involved only relatively small numbers, while the antisemitic press reached a vast public. Bernard Lazare, writing in 1894, before the eruption of the Affair, saw the development of an antisemitic press as a relative mitigation: "anti-Jewishness changed, it became purely literary, purely an affair of opinion . . ."[63] If this observation had some validity in pointing a contrast between the situation before and after Emancipation and between antisemitism in Eastern and Western Europe at the time, it proved too sanguine as far as France was concerned, and seriously underestimated the power of the newspaper to revive and remodel old prejudices. Others were more awake, as Lazare himself was to prove later,[64] to the potentialities of the new mass media. Le Journal des Débats, for example, commented in January 1893 that journalism had become "a very lucrative commodity and a very redoubtable weapon . . . Our need of tittle-tattle has grown and multiplied through the very satisfaction which it receives every day. On rising every morning, we address this mental prayer to the fetishes of publicity, the only divinities in whom we still have a relic of faith: Give us this day our daily scandal."[65] And Emile Zola, himself a journalist and a beneficiary of the new literacy, pointed in 1898 to the power of "that abominable Parisian press, so harsh towards the weak and little, so fond of insulting those who have none to defend them, so eager to coin money out of misfortune, and ready to spread insanity on all sides, simply to increase sales!"[66] The antisemites, we have seen, were quick to realize and exploit this propaganda power. In creating La Libre Parole in 1892, Drumont was simply acting on his conviction, expressed in the previous year, as we have seen, that: "French people don't think for themselves any more, they don't have time to, they no longer know how to; they let their newspaper do their thinking for them; their brains are made out of paper."[67]

If the antisemites were not altogether successful as the organizers of a political movement, they displayed much more talent as writers and propagandists. "Propaganda! Propaganda! we were crying already . . .", remembered Maurras;[68] and La Libre Parole, in particular, was a pioneer of modern techniques in this field.[69] As Drumont, himself, wrote in 1896: "The Antisemites had the sense of the mentality, of the state of mind of their readers, as a rider has the sense, through the bridle, of the temperament of a horse; he knows that he must not pull it up too sharply and, that in exciting it too violently, he risks driving it crazy rather than guiding it."[70] Léon Daudet, later of *L'Action Française*, acknowledged his debt to Drumont in these terms: "Drumont was a master journalist; he inculcated in me certain principles whose efficacy I have long recognized, notably the principle of repetition: 'The simplest idea [he told me] will not get into their heads, unless it is gone over again and again.' "[71] We have already seen how successful the antisemitic press was in exciting public opinion at the time of the Affair. "It is the duty of historians", wrote a Dreyfusard pamphleteer in 1898, "to show how a certain section of the press . . . built up over a long period the state of mind which rendered such criminal aberrations possible. This press created an atmosphere of suspicion around the Jews in general, and around Jews in the army, in particular; it managed to persuade part of the public . . . that Jewish officers were perpetual candidates for treason."[72] Leroy-Beaulieu wrote similarly in 1902 that "the anti-Jewish press exercised a veritable reign of terror over certain groups in the population . . ."[73] The same view was shared by the police; one agent reported in February 1898 at the time of the riots: "People are over-excited and the provocations of the antisemitic newspapers are bearing their fruit."[74] "Without Drumont and *La Libre Parole*", concluded Jules Isaac, "without the excesses of the press, there would have been no Dreyfus Affair . . . Exploited, inflamed by the many voices of a mass circulation press, the anti-Jewish sentiments, so deeply embedded in Christian society, acquired an irresistible force."[75]

What, more precisely, were the scope and physiognomy of this antisemitic press? How many were its voices? A distinction should be made, as with antisemitic organizations, between newspapers which specialized in antisemitism,[76] and those which used it only incidentally. A specialized antisemitic press began in France in the early 1880s. A weekly, *L'Anti-juif, Organe de Défense Sociale*, published three issues at the end of 1881; another, *L'Antisémitisme: Le Juif voilà l'Ennemi!*, edited by abbé Chabauty, appeared at Montdidier in 1882; while a third, *L'Anti-Sémitique*, was launched in 1883, becoming a daily, under the name *Le Péril Social*, in 1884. Another weekly, *L'Anti-Youtre*, ran for five issues in 1891.[77] But these were ephemeral and small-scale publications, and an antisemitic press of some size and importance was not established till some years later. France's leading antisemitic daily, through the 1890s and 1900s was *La Libre Parole*, whose history we have already encountered. Founded in 1892, it soon became, in the words of Henri Dagan, "the official organ of Antisemitism",[78] reaching the height of its influence around the turn of the century. By 1905, it had fallen into relative eclipse, and was amalgamated in 1910 with *Le Peuple Français*, formerly the organ of the Union Nationale; and control of the paper passed from the hands of Drumont into those of a liberal Catholic editorial team.[79] *La Libre Parole* had a circulation of 200,000 in 1893, a figure that must have increased considerably during the height of the Affair before falling to 47,000 in 1910.[80] Its readership seems to have been mainly, but not exclusively, petty bourgeois and Catholic. Dagan wrote in 1899 that it was read by "an important section of the small clerical bourgeoisie", but that "it also had the ear of Catholic financiers and of some freethinkers . . ."[81] According to Drault, it was "read by *curés* and *communards*".[82] The second large-circulation daily devoted to the antisemitic cause, though less exclusively so than La Libre Parole, was La Croix. Founded in 1883 by the Assumptionists, La Croix went through two periods of intense antisemitism, from 1889 to 1892 and from 1898 to 1899. Its clientèle seems to have been much the same as that of its rival, but its circulation was larger. Its national edition sold 170,000 copies in 1895 and 140,000 in 1910; but, in addition, it had 73 weekly, 7 bi-weekly and 6 daily regional editions.[83] To these two national dailies must be added L'Intransigeant of Henri Rochefort, which was violently antisemitic during the Affair, although Drumont, who, as we have seen, disliked Rochefort, sometimes claimed that his paper was not sufficiently committed to the cause.[84] The circulation of L'Intransigeant was 70,000 in 1910, but was almost certainly three times this in the late 1890s.[85] Its clientèle was rather different from that of the two preceding dailies: "a Voltairean petty bourgeoisie, prudent, uncertain, hesitating on the brink of revolutionary politics, and a section of the working class seduced by the rhetoric of nationalism and patriotism . . .", according to Dagan.[86] The antisemitism of L'Intransigeant continued, though in lower key, after the paper was taken over by Léon Bailby in 1908.[87] Dagan also categorized the Royalist Gazette de France and Le Peuple Français as specialist antisemitic dailies in 1899.[88] La Gazette de France published Maurras's famous apologia for Colonel Henry: "Le Premier Sang" in September 1898; and one of its former editors, Goudezki, became chief editor of L'Antijuif.[89] Le Peuple Français was founded in 1893 by abbé Garnier, who had worked for La Croix, and antisemitism was an important ingredient in its brand of Catholic populism.[90]

In addition to such national or Parisian dailies, there were also specialist antisemitic newspapers in the provinces, and a specialist weekly or fortnightly press in the capital. Among the former, the most prominent, were the various regional editions of La Croix, already mentioned, Le Lillois and Le Nord, and, above all, Le Nouvelliste de l'Ouest, edited in Nantes, and La France Libre of Lyon. According to the police, Le Nouvelliste was very much under the influence of Guérin.[91] La France Libre, founded in 1893 by Mouthon, became a daily two years later, and reached a circulation of 40,000 by 1898, which was quite substantial for the provinces.[92] On an altogether different scale from the provincial antisemitic press in France, was that in Algeria, which boasted four important dailies, as well as several weeklies. Of the former, the oldest was Le Petit Colon, edited by Marchal, who became a deputy in 1898; the other three were Le Télégramme d'Alger, founded in 1896, L'Express d'Alger, and Le Républicain de Constantin, edited by Morinaud, who also became a deputy.[93] Of the metropolitan weeklies the more important were Guérin's L'Antijuif, founded in 1898 and still going strong in 1900;[94] La Libre Parole Illustrée, which ran from 1893 to 1897;[95] and Le Précurseur, official organ of Le Parti National Antijuif.[96] To these should be added, *L'Espérance*, a fortnightly, founded in 1896, whose editors had close links with *La Libre Parole*;[97] the Jesuit fortnightly, *La Cività Cattolica*, which was influential in French Catholic circles;[98] the very successful weekly run by the Assumptionists, *Le Pèlerin*;[99] and a variety of diocesan bulletins.[100]

Antisemitism was so wide-spread in the French press at the time of the Affair, as we saw in chapter II, that it is hard to make a definitive categorization of papers that were incidentally antisemitic in the period. What is significant is that so large a number of papers can be so designated. Among the more prominent, in terms of size or commitment, were *L'Autorité*, *Le Monde*,[101] *L'Echo de Paris*, *L'Eclair*,[102] *Le Gaulois*, *Le Journal*, *Le Petit Journal*, *L'Univers* and *La Dépêche de Toulouse*,[103] which together covered a readership of the most varied political and social complexion. For example, *L'Autorité* was a Bonapartist paper, edited by Paul de Cassagnac, who expressed doubts about Dreyfus's guilt as early as 1897. His paper had earned Drumont's criticism well before this, but he joined the antisemitic group in the Chamber of Deputies in 1898, and *L'Autorité* was generally regarded as a supporter of the antisemitic cause; its circulation was 20,000 in 1910.[104] *L'Echo de Paris* was described by Léon Daudet as "the favourite paper of army officers, devoted to anti-Dreyfusism in the style of the *Patrie Française*".[105] *Le Gaulois* was the paper of Parisian high society and its hangers-on, and had a Jewish editor, Arthur Meyer.[106] *L'Univers* was the intransigent Catholic daily, founded in 1833 and edited by Louis Veuillot from 1842 to 1880; in relative eclipse by the 1890s, it was one of the few papers of the day, beside his own, to earn Drumont's praise. In its turn, *L'Univers* recommended *La France juive* to its readers, and supported Drumont in 1909, when he tried to get elected to the Academy.[107] In 1913 it gave credence to the supposed ritual murder in Kiev. These were all papers with fairly modest circulations, appealing to a mainly middle- or upper-class readership. *Le Journal* and *Le Petit Journal* were representative of the popular press. *Le Journal*, founded in 1892 by Fernand Xau, had a circulation of 300,000 by the mid-1890s. Eclectically Republican in politics, its clientèle was predominantly petty bourgeois. Antisemitism of a Left-wing anti-capitalist variety was present in the serials which it ran in the mid-1890s, and became more general and nationalist in tone at the time of the Affair.[108] *Le Petit Journal*, dating from 1863, edited by the Catholic Judet and owned by Marinoni, inventor of the rotary press, was one of the largest Parisian dailies, with a circulation of a million in 1898. Its antisemitism was the more significant in that it adopted an ostensible stance of political neutrality. In March 1892, it gave away free copies of an illustrated edition of *La France juive*, and it was later ardently anti-Dreyfusard.[109]

In addition to periodicals, antisemitism was also propagated via a large number of other publications: books, pamphlets, posters and stickers, to which we have often referred. *La Libre Parole* sponsored a "Librairie Antisémite,"[110] and itself put out posters and pamphlets. Four thousand copies of one of these, *Le Péril juif*, for example, were distributed in Rennes in July 1899; and the same pamphlet was again being broadcast by the Comité National Antijuif during the 1902 General Election campaign.[111] *La Croix* had a more substantial auxiliary publishing concern, "La Bonne Presse", and put out pamphlets, such as *Le Complôt juif*.[112] Mention should also be made of Savine's collection, "Bibliothèque Antisémite", which included works by Drumont, Fore-Fauré, Chirac, Bontoux and Desportes. Other genres were also exploited. Directories or *Indicateurs des Juifs* were published in several departments, as we have seen.[113] Songs, such as "La Marseillaise antijuive" and "Le Marche antisémite", also appeared, and seem to have been particularly successful in Algeria, where, according to the deputy Firmin Faure: "the antisemitic campaign began with songs . . ."[114] The antisemites also had the advantage of having the active support of France's three leading cartoonists, Forain, Willette and Caran d'Ache, who provided posters, newspaper and other cartoons, and who ran a very successful satirical weekly, *Psst!* during the Affair.[115] The pictorial representation of Jewish stereotypes by these and other artists must have been one of the most powerful and effective weapons of antisemitic propaganda, and, to judge by the persistence of such images into the mid-twentieth century,[116] they were an authentic reflection of popular antisemitism at the profoundest level.

NOTES

1 Biez, *Les Rothschild et le péril juif*, p. 3; Péguy, *Notre Jeunesse*, p. 187.
2 AN F⁷ 12720, Dossier: "La Jeunesse Antisémite et Nationaliste"; Duroselle, "L'Antisémitisme en France", p. 62.
3 Viau, *Vingt ans d'antisémitisme*, p. 98. Pierrard, *Juifs et catholiques français*, p. 140, says that Dubuc was an engineer. See also Drault, *Drumont, La France juive et La Libre Parole*, p. 229.
4 Pierrard, op. cit., pp. 140–2; Report, Commissaire de police, Saint-Germain-en-Laye, 21 April 1901. AN F⁷ 12457.
5 AN F⁷ 12720.
6 Police report, Caen, August 1899. AN F⁷ 12462.
7 Pierrard, op. cit., p. 142.
8 See, for example, Daily Report, Prefect of Police, 4 June 1898. APP Ba 106.
9 Report, Police agent, 5 September 1901. AN F⁷ 12457.
10 Guérin, *Les Trafiquants de l'antisémitisme*, p. 122.
11 Ibid., p. 124; AN F⁷ 12483; Report, Prefect, Rhône, 7 July 1903. AN F⁷ 12457
12 Viau, op. cit., pp. 319–20.
13 Ibid., pp. 287–90; *La Libre Parole*, November 1901–April 1902.
14 See chapter VIII, p. 216.
15 On this and the Fédération generally, see AN F⁷ 12720, Dossier: "Comité National Antijuif"; Police report, 31 December 1903. AN F⁷ 12458; Reports, Police agents, 7 April and 5 June 1903. AN F⁷ 12719; Pierrard, op. cit., pp. 150–1.
16 AN F⁷ 12461; see chapter III, p. 116.
17 Police reports, July 1899. AN F⁷ 12464; AN F⁷ 12923.
18 Police reports. AN F⁷ 12459.
19 Police report, 13 August 1892. Ibid..
20 Viau, op. cit., p. 204.
21 See Guérin, op. cit., p. 122.
22 Drault, op. cit., pp. 251–2.
23 See Daudet, *Salons et journaux*, p. 277; and, particularly, Viau, op. cit., pp. 62–9, the testimony of someone who worked for a time as Drumont's secretary.
24 Viau, op. cit., pp. 69–71; Guérin, op. cit., pp. 69–96; Drault, op. cit., pp. 193–6.

25 See Daudet, *Au Temps de Judas*, p. 83; Barrès, Letter, 9 November 1897, Barrès-Maurras, *La République ou le roi*, p. 146; Drault, op. cit., pp. 33–50 and 85–7.

26 Daudet, *Paris vécu*, Ier série, p. 29; Daudet, *Salons et journaux*, p. 277; see also Viau, op. cit., p. 96; and Drault, op. cit., pp. 84–5, who casts doubt on the sincerity of Méry's antisemitism.

27 Viau, op. cit., p. 321.

28 See Pinsot, "Quelques problèmes du socialisme en France"; Georges Lefranc, *Le Mouvement socialiste sous la Troisième République (1875–1940)* (Paris, 1963), pp. 48–133; Fiechter, *Le Socialisme français*, pp. 77–117.

29 See Edward A. Shils, "Authoritarianism: 'Right' and 'Left'," in Richard Christie and Marie Jahoda, eds., *Studies in the Scope and Method of "The Authoritarian Personality"*, Continuities in Social Research (Chicago, Ill., 1954), pp. 45–8, on American nativist movements.

30 E.g. Déroulède; see Maurras, *Au Signe de Flore*, p. 97; and Police Report, 9 December 1902. AN F⁷ 12870, "Ligue des Patriotes", Dossier no. 4; and Marchand; see Barrès, *Scènes et doctrines*, II, pp. 91–105.

31 Viau, op. cit., pp. 44–5; see also Bernanos, *La Grande Peur des bien-pensants*, pp. 315–19.

32 Viau, op. cit., pp. 96 and 118.

33 "Notre Jésus-Régis." Ibid., pp. 178–9.

34 Drumont, *Le Testament d'un antisémite*, p. 41.

35 Ibid., p. 40.

36 Leroy-Beaulieu, *Les Doctrines de haine*, pp. 10–11; see also Reinach, *Histoire de l'Affaire Dreyfus*, IV, pp. 49–50, and V, p. 135; Barrès-Maurras, op. cit., p. 235.

37 Viau, op. cit., p. 203.

38 Report, Police agent, 7 April 1903. AN F⁷ 12719.

39 Police report, 20 January 1901, "Résumé général de la situation en décembre 1900". AN F⁷ 12870.

40 Piou, *Le Comte Albert de Mun*, p. 192.

41 Viau, op. cit., p. 120.

42 Sartre, *Réflexions sur la question juive*, pp. 36–7.

43 Drumont, *TA*, p. 3.

44 See the observations of Mac Rae and Wiles on populist movements in general in Ghita Ionescu and Ernest Gellner, eds, *Populism: Its Meanings and National Characteristics* (London, 1969), pp. 156–7 and 167.

45 See the more general argument of my forthcoming article: "Late Nineteenth-Century Nationalism and Imperialism in Europe: A Critique of the Manipulative Model".

46 See L'Hermite, *L'Anti-Pape;* Arnoulin, *M. Edouard Drumont;* also Drault, op. cit., p. 27.

47 Guérin, op. cit., p. 44.

48 Ibid., pp. 47–52, 60–2, 340–3 and 370–89.

49 Ibid., pp. 363–7, 386–7 and 456–63.

50 See Auriant, "Autour de Georges Darien: Edouard Drumont jugé par Léon Bloy", *Mercure de France*, 242, 15 March 1933, pp. 760–2.

51 Speech, Meeting of "groupe d'études économiques et sociales", Salle des Mille Colonnes, Paris. Daily Report, Prefect of Police, 24 February 1898. APP Ba 106.

52 Drumont, *TA*, pp. 415–19; Daudet, *Les Oeuvres dans les hommes*, pp. 180–3.

53 Daudet, *Les Oeuvres dans les hommes*, p. 156.

54 Viau, op. cit., p. 48.

55 Verdès-Leroux, *Scandale financier et antisémitisme catholique*, pp. 121–2.

56 Barral, *L'Isère sous la IIIe République*, p. 248; AN F⁷ 12842, Dossier no. 24: "La Croisade Française".

57 Report, Police agent, 10 March 1904. AN F⁷ 12719.

58 Sternhell, *Maurice Barrès*, pp. 34–5.

59 Arnoulin, op. cit., pp. 163–5; Drault, op. cit., p 89.

60 Viau, op. cit., p. 272.

61 Sorlin, *"La Croix" et les Juifs*, pp. 59, 110–14 and 206–7; see also Guérin, op. cit., p. 362.

62 Léon Bloy, *Le Salut par les Juifs* (1892), *Oeuvres*, IX (Paris, 1969), p. 24; see also Zola, in Dagan, *Enquête sur l'antisémitisme*, p. 20.

63 Lazare, *L'Antisémitisme*, p 205.

64 Lazare's role as a Dreyfusard propagandist has been referred to in chapter II; see also Péguy, *Notre Jeunesse*, pp. 66 and 74–89; Gauthier, ed., *"Dreyfusards!"*, pp. 80–100; Marrus, *The Politics of Assimilation*, pp. 164–95; and chapter XIX, pp. 695 and ff. below.

65 *Le Journal des Débats*, 27 January 1893, cit. Verdès-Leroux, op. cit., p. 190; see also chapter II, pp. 87–9 above.

66 Emile Zola, *Paris* (1898) (London, 1898 edition), p. 187.

67 Drumont, *TA*, p. 58.

68 Maurras, *Au Signe de Flore*, p. 293.

69 Later antisemites in France and Germany showed surprisingly little advance here, despite the introduction of the new technology of radio and film; see particularly Z.A.B. Zeman, *Nazi Propaganda* (London, 1964), pp. 11–13, 21 and *passim*.

70 Drumont, *De l'Or, de la boue, du sang* (hereafter *OBS*), p. 69; see also Drumont, *La Dernière Bataille*, p. 317.

71 Daudet, *Salons et journaux*, pp. 272–3. Daudet and Maurras had tried to buy *La Libre Parole* for the Action Française in 1906–7, and their own daily *L'Action Française* owed much to Drumont's in style and techniques; see Daudet, *Les Oeuvres dans les hommes*, p. 186.

72 "L'Archiviste" (S. Reinach), *Drumont et Dreyfus; Etudes sur La Libre Parole de 1894 à 1895* (Paris, 1898), p. 7.

73 Leroy-Beaulieu, *Les Doctrines de haine*, p. 277.

74 Report, Police agent, 10 February 1898. AN F⁷ 12474.

75 Isaac, *Expériences de ma vie*, I, p. 116; see also Lacretelle, *Silbermann*, pp. 107–10.

76 Dagan, op. cit., p. 81.

77 Drumont, *La France juive*, I, p. 131; Drault, op. cit., pp. 67–79; Verdès-Leroux, op. cit., p. 118; Pierrard, op. cit., p. 28.

78 Dagan, op. cit., p. 89.

79 See Arbellot, *La Fin du boulevard*, pp. 147–8; Duroselle, op. cit., p. 69; Bernanos, op. cit., pp. 393–4; Bellanger *et al.*, eds, *Histoire générale de la presse française*, III, pp. 343–5; Emile Poulat, *Intégrisme et Catholicisme intégral: Un Réseau secret international antimoderniste: La Sapinière (1909–1921)* (Paris, 1969), pp. 238–9.

80 Duroselle, op. cit., p. 69; "Tirage des journaux quotidiens à la date du ler novembre 1910". AN F⁷ 12843, Dossier no. 14.

81 Dagan, op. cit., p. 92.

82 Drault, op. cit., p. 88; also Arbellot, op. cit., p. 147 (both citing an anonymous opinion of the time).

83 Sorlin, *"La Croix" et les Juifs*, pp. 41–55 and 107–28.

84 Dagan, op. cit., pp. 90–1; Bournand, op. cit., pp. 51–2; Gohier, *L'Armée contre la nation*, p. 266; AN F⁷ 12471 (Press cuttings); Drumont, *FJ*, II, p. 219; Drumont, *TA*, pp. 82–3.

85 "Tirage des journaux quotidiens . . .". AN F⁷ 12843.

86 Dagan, op. cit., p. 93; see also Verdès-Leroux, op. cit., p. 40; Zévaès, *Au Temps du Boulangisme*, pp. 55–8 and 232; and Bellanger *et al.*, eds, op. cit., III, pp. 341–2.

87 Daudet, *Salons et journaux*, p. 102; Waleffe, *Quand Paris était un paradis*, pp. 311–12.

88 Dagan, op. cit., p. 89.

89 See Barrès-Maurras, op. cit., pp. 649–50; Police report, 1 June 1900. AN F⁷ 12719; and Bellanger et al., eds, op. cit., III, p. 320.

90 See my "Catholic Populism in France at the time of the Dreyfus Affair"; and chapter XIV, pp. 529–32.

91 Reports, Commissaire spécial, Nantes, 13 December 1898. AN F⁷ 12465; and 8 January 1900. AN F⁷ 12453.

92 Viau, op. cit., p. 62; Henri Rollet, L'Action sociale des catholiques en France 1871–1914 (Paris, 1948–58), I, p. 417; Mayeur, "Les Congrès nationaux", pp. 173–5.

93 See L'Hermite, op. cit., p. 372; AN F⁷ 12842, Dossier no. 15 (Le Télégramme d'Alger); and Jolly, ed., Dictionnaire des parlementaires français (Marchal and Morinaud entries).

94 See Police report, 1 June 1900. AN F⁷ 12719. L'Antijuif ceased publication in December 1902.

95 Bellanger et al., eds, op. cit., III, p. 345.

96 See Viau, op. cit., p. 228.

97 Police report, 18 December 1908. AN F⁷ 12842, Dossier no. 16.

98 Pierrard, op. cit., p. 28; see also Charlotte Klein, "Damascus to Kiev: Civiltà Cattolica on Ritual Murder", Wiener Library Bulletin, 27 (1974), new series no. 32, pp. 18–25.

99 Le Pèlerin had a circulation of 140,000 in 1897; see Sorlin, "La Croix" et les Juifs, pp. 26–30.

100 See Verdès-Leroux, op. cit., pp. 210–28, "L'antisémitisme dans les Semaines Religieuses (1892)".

101 See Arnoulin, op. cit., pp. 155–8; Pierrard, op. cit., pp. 61–3.

102 L'Eclair had a circulation of about 60,000 in 1903; see Bellanger et al., eds, op. cit., III, pp. 345–6; and Daudet, Salons et journaux, p. 89.

103 See Bournand, op. cit., pp. 82–5; Bousquet-Mélou, Louis Barthou, p. 115; and Bellanger et al., eds, op. cit., III, pp. 342–3.

104 See Pierre Dreyfus, Dreyfus, p. 87; Bellanger et al., eds, op. cit., III, pp. 317–18; Drumont, TA, pp. 81 and 294.

105 Daudet, Au Temps de Judas, p. 39; see also Daudet, Salons et journaux, pp. 45–50; and Bellanger et al., eds, op. cit., III, pp. 346–7.

106 See Meyer, Ce que mes yeux ont vu; Daudet, Au Temps de Judas, p. 44; Bellanger et al., eds, op. cit., III, pp. 322–3.

107 See Drumont, TA, pp. 145 and 293; Arnoulin, op. cit., pp. 72–3 and 155–8; Bournand, op. cit., p. 124; Pierrard, op. cit., pp. 21–6, 61–4 and 161–4; Poulat, op. cit., pp. 362–4; Bellanger et al., eds, op. cit., II, pp. 128, 267–9 and passim; and III, pp. 184–6, 328–9 and passim; also C. Lecigne, Louis Veuillot (Paris, 1913); Philip Spencer, Politics of Belief in Nineteenth Century France: Lacordaire; Michon; Veuillot (London, 1954).

108 Dumont, La Petite Bourgeoisie à travers les contes du "Journal", pp. 5, 7 and 44–7. However, Barrès wrote to Maurras in January 1898 that he had omitted explicit reference to the Jews in "La Protestation des Intellectuels", so that Fernand Xau would agree to publish it in Le Journal; see Barrès-Maurras, op. cit., pp. 167–8.

109 Bellanger et al., eds, op. cit., III, pp. 300–4; Sorlin, La Société française, I, pp. 241–3; Arbellot, op. cit., p. 156; Daudet, Salons et journaux, pp. 85–9; Daudet, Au Temps de Judas, pp. 41–2; Eugen Weber, Satan franc-maçon: La mystification de Léo Taxil (Paris, 1964), p. 15.

110 See AN F⁷ 12456; Guérin, op. cit., pp. 456–63.

111 Police report, 4 July 1899. AN F⁷ 12464; Pierrard, op. cit., p. 150.

112 Sorlin, "La Croix" et les Juifs, chapter 1; Police report, March 1898. AN F⁷ 12463.

113 AN F⁷ 12463; and see chapter III, p. 117 above.

114 Daily Report, Prefect of Police, 4 June 1898. APP Ba 106; also Viau, op. cit., p. 178. "La Marseillaise antijuive", popularized by Régis, included the verse:

"Ya trop longtemps qu' nous sommes dans la misère,/Chassons l'Etranger,/ Ça f'ra travailler./Ce qu'il nous faut c'est un meilleur salaire,/Chassons du pays/Tout' cette bande de Youddis!" "La Marche antisémite" began: "A mort les juifs! A mort les juifs!/Il faut les pendre/Sans plus attendre . . ."

115 See Jacques Lethève, *La Caricature et la presse sous la IIIe République* (Paris, 1961), pp. 53–107; Gérard Blanchard, *Histoire de la bande dessinée* (Paris, 1974), pp. 150–3; Bournand, op. cit., pp. 139–42; Daudet, *Au Temps de Judas*, pp. 48–50; Robert F. Byrnes, "Jean-Louis Forain: Antisemitism in French Art", *Jewish Social Studies*, 12 (1950), pp. 247–56.

116 Compare illustrations in Lethève, op. cit.; Sorlin, *"La Croix" et les Juifs* and *La Libre Parole Illustrée*, 26 August 1893, reproduced in Zola, *Oeuvres complètes*, VII, p. 1201, with those in Marcel Ophuls, *The Sorrow and the Pity* (London, 1975), p. 216, for example.

CHAPTER VIII
ANTISEMITISM IN FRENCH POLITICS: THE ANTISEMITIC GROUP IN THE CHAMBER OF DEPUTIES 1898–1906

W E HAVE DESCRIBED THE IMPACT OF THE DREYFUS AFFAIR ON OPINION in France, and we have seen that antisemitism generated serious riots there in 1898. We have seen also that there existed, by the late 1890s, a small but enthusiastic antisemitic movement, enjoying a large measure of tolerance, if not support, and having at its disposal an impressive propaganda apparatus. We have argued that this movement had serious organizational weaknesses, and that its aims and function were not primarily political; but it did enter the arena of formal politics with some degree of success. We have already seen that the Dreyfus Affair figured more prominently in the General Elections of May 1898 than historians have usually allowed. What, more generally, was the significance of antisemitism in political terms? Was the antisemitic movement regarded as a legitimate political organization? How far was it an electoral and parliamentary force?

Antisemitism seems to have appeared as an electoral platform in metropolitan France for the first time in 1889 (it began earlier in Algeria[1]). According to Byrnes, the first Frenchman to stand for public office specifically as an antisemite was the cartoonist Willette, who stood unsuccessfully for election to the Chamber of Deputies in the 9th *arrondissement* of Paris in the General Elections of 1889.[2] But he was not alone and he may not have been the first. In the same elections, two Boulangist candidates were elected, after running largely antisemitic campaigns, the young Maurice Barrès in Nancy, which had a strong local tradition of hostility to Jews, and Francis Laur in Saint-Denis. Laur's election was invalidated, but he was re-elected in 1890 with the sponsorship, as we have seen, of the Ligue Nationale Antisémitique.[3] Two other Boulangists elected in 1889, Jules Delahaye and Gauthier de Clagny, were also known to hold antisemitic opinions, while four more, Chiché, Castelin, Paulin-Méry and Millevoye, later joined the cause. In addition, the Royalist Comte du Breil de Pontbriand, who also entered the Chamber of Deputies in 1889, soon established a reputation as a militant antisemite.[4] In 1890, antisemites made a showing, too, in the municipal elections in Paris in April; but, of the ten candidates standing, who included Drumont and Morès, only one, a Blanquiste Boulangist in Belleville, obtained a serious proportion of the vote.[5] Antisemites were to continue to contest the municipal elections in the capital over the next decade, but achieved little success until the short-lived break-through of 1900, when they formed part of the "Nationalist" alliance which won control of the city council.[6]

On the national level, the General Elections of 1893 marked a stand-still in the fortunes of the antisemites. Barrès, Chiché, Delahaye and Millevoye lost their seats, but Castelin, Gauthier de Clagny, Laur, Paulin-Méry and Pontbriand were re-elected. A few newcomers also joined their ranks, for example, the Vicomte d'Hugues, a conservative elected in the Basses-Alpes, and the Royalist Georges Berry, elected in the Seine, a "notorious antisemite", according to Reinach.[7] It should be noted that most, if not all, these deputies were elected on platforms which coupled antisemitism with other political causes, usually Boulangism or conservatism of various kinds. Two prominent antisemites, moreover, had stood for the first time in 1893 and failed to get elected. Abbé Garnier of the Union Nationale stood at Clignancourt, where he reached the second ballot, a partial success repeated two years later in a by-election at Cherbourg.[8] Drumont stood in 1893 at Amiens, a constituency that Millevoye had represented in the previous legislature, but the antisemitic leader received only a very small proportion of the vote. Viau commented, with reason: "This failure shows that if, at that time, antisemitism had been adopted in the provinces, as an excellent weapon by conservative, Royalist, Bonapartist and clerical groups, it had not yet penetrated to the popular level, to the mass of electors."[9] But the small nucleus of antisemitic deputies who were elected at this time were, however, responsible for the introduction of antisemitic issues into the discussions of the Chamber, where, indeed, they seem to have been able to count on wider support. In November 1891, for example, 30 deputies supported a call for the expulsion of the Rothschild family from France.[10] A Bill put down by Pontbriand in January 1893 represented a more comprehensive, though implicit, attack on Jews. It would have excluded from public employment all who could not prove three generations of forebears born in France. This forerunner of the antisemitic legislation of Vichy, couched in the language of the aristocratic reaction of the 1780s, received the support of 158 deputies.[11] According to Raphaël Viau, again, the "Jewish question" was openly debated for the first time in the Chamber in May 1895, when four deputies declared themselves disciples of Drumont.[12]

However, although antisemitism seems thus to have maintained a political presence in the legislature through the 1890s, 1898 marks a mutation in its fortunes. In January of that year Pontbriand revived his 1893 Bill, and it again received over 150 votes. In February, nearly 200 deputies supported an *interpellation* by Denis, asking the government "what measures it intended to take to end the predominance of Jews in the various branches of the administration".[13] But most significant was the success in the May General Elections of a substantial contingent of 22 declared antisemites. Although only 6 of them formally stood under the label *"antisémite"* or *"anti-juif"*, the platforms of all of them seem to have been unmistakably antisemitic, and to have been much more explicitly and exclusively so than had been the case previously; and they formed, for the first time, an antisemitic parliamentary group.[14] This group, moreover, represented only a hard core, and, as in the two previous legislatures, a much larger number of deputies supported proposals for legislation of an antisemitic nature. The most important of these was a Bill put down in February 1899 that sought to abrogate the political clauses of the Crémieux decree of 1870, and thus to disenfranchise the Jewish population of Algeria. Sixty-five deputies sponsored this proposal.[15] Despite this measure of support, however, and despite the fact that some antisemites, for example Millevoye, Habert and Daudé-Gleize made a reputation in the Chamber (Drumont, by contrast, disappointed his followers by his lack of oratorical skill and parliamentary acumen[16]), antisemitism was never a force of any great importance within the established political system, nor did it constitute a united and coherent party.[17] The opposition to revision of the Dreyfus Case within the Chamber and within government, though it may have rested on an unconscious bedrock of anti-Jewish prejudice, was more obviously motivated by fear of upsetting political and legal order than by any deliberate antisemitism.[18] But analysis of the parliamentary group and its fellow-travellers does not merely reveal its lack of real political significance. It provides a valuable insight into the way in which, in a crisis, antisemitism could find a place, albeit marginal, in the political spectrum in France, providing old causes with a new and popular face, as well as reflecting new resentments and grievances. It is thus worth while to examine the antisemitic deputies as a group in some detail, and to scrutinize their electoral base, to try to determine how far they were representative and of what.[19]

First, we will consider those who belonged to the antisemitic parliamentary group, that is the hard-core of militants. The pattern of their parliamentary careers confirms the impression that the scope of electoral antisemitism in 1898 was a novelty and a comparatively short-lived one, though it was not a mere flash in the pan. We have seen that a handful of antisemites entered the Chamber in 1889 and 1893. In fact the most experienced member of the 1898 parliamentary group, the Bonapartist Paul de Cassagnac, was first elected in the Gers in 1876, though there is no evidence of his antisemitism at this date. Three members of the group began their parliamentary careers in 1889 (Chiché, Pontbriand and Millevoye), and 2 in 1893 (Habert and Denis); but the other 16 were all elected for the first time in 1898. In eleven cases they ousted the sitting deputy, which again suggests the introduction of a novel force at constituency level. Table IV shows through how many legislatures members of the 1898 group sat.

Half, therefore, were elected only once or twice, but half had longer political careers, and in addition, three went on to the Senate (Pontbriand, Daudé-

TABLE IV: Antisemitic Deputies—parliamentary careers

No. of legislatures sat through	No. of deputies of the 1898 antisemitic group
1	5
2	6
3	3
4	4
5	2
6	2

Gleize and Massabuau). The 1898–1902 legislature was, however, the climax of their fortunes as a group. The 1902 elections marked a sudden fall, which was followed by a steady decline. Nine of the group lost their seats in 1902, and Firmin Faure only ensured his re-election by switching from Oran to the Seine (Saint-Denis). (Charles Bernard's move from Bordeaux to the 18th *arrondissement* of Paris did not have the same successful outcome.) Pontbriand moved to the Senate in 1901, and Habert was disqualified in the same year, after being convicted of plotting against the régime. Thus the original 1898 group could only muster half its forces in the 1902 legislature. In 1906, three more lost their seats, and Daudé-Gleize moved to the Senate, reducing the contingent to seven.[20] Of these, Denis died in 1908, while Jacquey, Ferrette and Lasies were not returned in 1910, leaving Massabuau and Millevoye as the only representatives of the original group in the 1910 legislature. Lasies returned in the 1914 legislature, and Habert, Ferrette and Morinaud were re-elected in 1919, the last holding his old Constantine seat until 1942. But well before the First World War, the decline in numbers of antisemitic deputies had been accompanied by the progressive abandonment of antisemitism as a main political programme. As early as the end of 1899, Cavaignac, the "Nationalist" leader, in a private note on the political persuasion of potential supporters in the Chamber, listed only six as *"antisémites"*, designating other members of the group as "Nationalists" or *"patriotes"*, though he almost certainly excluded the anti-Republicans.[21] More significant, in 1906 the antisemitic parliamentary group was wound up,[22] and antisemitism among deputies became again purely a matter of personal conviction.

But let us return to the make-up of the group in its heyday. Its members were comparatively young, as the large number of débutants among them would lead one to expect. Ferrette was only twenty-nine in 1898; nine others were in their thirties; six in their forties; four in their fifties; and two in their sixties—the oldest, General Jacquey, was only sixty-four. The mean age was 41.5, and the median age 40. The social complexion of the group was mixed: four were aristocrats, four of "popular" origin, the rest bourgeois. By profession, most were barristers or *"avocats"* (12), or journalists (11), often combining the two occupations; in addition, 5 were ex-army officers, 1 a pharmacist, 1 an estate manager and 7 were landowners (in five cases in combination with other professions). The high incidence of lawyers was a phenomenon common to politicians as a whole, whatever their opinions, but that of journalists, though also a phenomenon found among all politicians, can also be read as a reflection of the fact that, as we have seen, antisemitism, and particularly organized antisemitism, was to a large extent a creation of the newspaper press. The political complexion of the group was also mixed. Membership of the group did not exclude belonging to other parliamentary groups, and members gave indications of their general political persuasions in writings, speeches and votes, as well as through the formal political labels which they adopted in elections. (Only Drumont stood in 1898 as an unqualified *"anti-Juif"*, but he nevertheless made it known that he was a Republican.) Of the 22, 1 was a Blanquiste Socialist (Bernard); 5 were Radicals or Radical-Socialists (Abel-Bernard, Denis, Ferrette, Morinaud and Marchal); and 6 called themselves Republicans or Independent Republicans (Pascal, Jacquey, Daudé-Gleize, Massabuau, Gervaize and Drumont). This category was by no means homogeneous, however. Daudé-Gleize, Ferrette and Jacquey were "Nationalists", standing as Nationalist Republicans in 1902. Pascal was a Progressist; and Massabuau's label of *"Républicain Rallié"*, did not prevent him from joining the Monarchist group in the Chamber. We have already discussed Drumont's peculiar brand of Republicanism, which allowed him to express sympathies both with the two dynastic tendencies of the Right and with the Collectivists and the Anarchists. In addition, four of the antisemitic group referred to themselves as *"Conservateurs"* or members of the *"Droite"* (Delpech-Cantaloup, Cassagnac, Maussabré, and Pontbriand), labels that barely concealed the Bonapartism of the first two, and the Royalism of the others. A further two were openly Bonapartist or *"Plébiscitaire"* (Lasies and Aulan). The remaining four were ex-Boulangists or *"Révisionnistes"*. Of these, Chiché called himself a Socialist, and of the other three (Millevoye, Habert and Faure), only Faure was overtly Right-wing. Thus although the group as a whole sat on the Right of the Chamber, at least half, and probably more, stood for programmes of a Left-wing, if Populist, tendency, and only six were clearly associated with the traditional dynastic parties of the Right. Seven, however, were Catholics or represented Catholic interests.

If we turn now to those who joined the antisemitic group in sponsoring the Bill of 1899 to disenfranchise the Jews of Algeria—a token of serious political antisemitism—some interesting comparisons and contrasts emerge. Forty-five additional deputies are concerned (two of the antisemitic group did not sponsor the Bill). Table V shows the pattern of the parliamentary careers of these deputies, and its divergence from that of members of the official parliamentary group. All in all, the patterns are contrasting, and it is characteristic that only 15 (33%) of the Disenfranchisement Bill sponsors were débutants in 1898, as against 16 (72%) of the antisemitic parliamentary group. The latter were mainly newcomers, who irrupted on to the parliamentary scene in 1898, and stayed there through one or two legislatures, but rarely more. They were not professional politicians. Those who gave them their support over the Disenfranchisement issue included a much smaller proportion of newcomers,

TABLE V: Antisemitic Deputies—parliamentary careers

No. of legis-latures sat through	No. of Disenfranch-isement Bill sponsors[23]	Percentage of Disenfranchisement Bill sponsors	Percentage of antisemitic group
1	6	15	22.7
2	2	5	27.3
3	8	20	13.6
4	8	20	18.2
5	6	15	9.0
6 or more	10	25	9.0

and 1898 was not a particularly significant date in the history of the sample. The 45, moreover, were, in the main, deputies who enjoyed a long parliamentary career; they were professionals in effect, though some would have resented the label. Two of them, to take the extreme examples, sat through nine legislatures: Galpin, who was deputy for the Sarthe from 1885 until 1923, and the Baron de Grandmaison, who represented the Maine-et-Loire as deputy, and then as senator, from 1893 until 1943. At least 8 (18.9%) of the Disenfranchisement Bill sponsors became senators, the normal culmination of a successful parliamentary career, as against 3 (13.6%) of the antisemitic group. Also significant is the fact that of the antisemitic parliamentary group only 10 (45.5%) entered parliamentary politics via the usual apprenticeship in local and departmental politics. Eight were conseillers-généraux in 1898 and 4 were mayors. By contrast 34 (75.6%) of the additional sponsors of the Disenfranchisement Bill served an apprenticeship in local politics before entering the Chamber, 22 as conseillers-généraux and 17 as mayors (the functions were often combined). All of this goes to indicate that the additional 45 were much more closely enmeshed in the established political system than were the members of the antisemitic group. The latter were militants, fanatics, outsiders, representing a political option of an alien and not altogether acceptable kind, at least in undiluted form. The 45 who supported them over the Disenfranchisement Bill were more "moderate", not wholeheartedly or exclusively committed to antisemitism as a political cause. They were insiders, professionals, taking the opportunity to voice their prejudice, or to curry favour with the electorate, an opportunity created by a movement outside the Chamber. However, what is perhaps most significant is the fact that these career politicians were prepared, for a while, to take political antisemitism seriously, and to ally themselves with its direct representatives in the Chamber. In so doing they lent it some legitimacy, and what motivated such men, always anxious to ensure their re-election, must have been a sense of the potential electoral strength of antisemitism, a sense, too, probably of its force as a vote of protest directed against themselves and the parliamentary system of which they were the beneficiaries.

This contrast between the antisemitic group and the 45 additional sponsors of the Disenfranchisement Bill is reinforced if the factors of age, status and profession and political affiliation are considered. The additional sponsors were older than the members of the antisemitic group, though still perhaps comparatively young. Grandmaison began his parliamentary career in 1893 as the youngest deputy in France, aged twenty-eight. In 1898, 12 of the group were in their thirties; 14 in their forties; 15 in their fifties; 2 in their sixties; and 1 was seventy-five. The mean age was 46, and the median age 44–45.[24] It would be interesting to compare these figures with those for other parliamentary groups and for the Chamber of Deputies as a whole, to confirm or disprove the impression that antisemitic deputies as a whole were younger than average, an indication again of the novelty of political antisemitism in France, and another illustration of its association with youth. The social and/or professional status of 38 of the additional sponsors is known. The largest category was that of landowners *(propriétaires),* of whom there were 19 (50%), but this professional category was frequently combined with others, and does not necessarily denote owners of large estates. Twelve of the group were lawyers (31.5%), in contrast to 54.5% among the antisemitic group. Thirteen were aristocrats; and 9 (23.3%) were ex-army officers. In addition, there were 3 doctors, 4 industrialists, 4 miscellaneous liberal professions, 1 ecclesiastic and 4 journalists. The additional sponsors thus shared with the antisemitic group that high incidence of lawyers that characterized French politics, but it did not have its very strong association with the press. The professional base of the additional sponsors was much broader than that of the antisemitic group, but it was very much slanted towards rural traditional society. The same bias is evident in the political complexion of the additional sponsors. Though still heterogeneous, this was much more heavily weighted to the Right than that of the antisemitic group. Only 9 of the 45 were Socialists, Radical-Socialists or Radical Republicans (including one ex-*communard*). Six were ex-Boulangists or *"Révisionnistes"*, two of whom belonged to the Ligue des Patriotes and called themselves Socialists. Five were moderate Republicans or Progressists. Seven stood as Independents or as Independent, Liberal or Catholic Republicans. By contrast, 18 stood as *"Conservateurs"*, most of whom were Catholic monarchists, though some called themselves *"Ralliés"*,[25] and one was an overt Bonapartist. Thus only about 15, or one-third at the outside, belonged to the Left or were even *bona fide* Republicans, and of these perhaps half a dozen belonged to the extreme Left. The other two-thirds, many under the familiar guise of Independent, Liberal or unqualified Republican, belonged firmly to the traditional Right. This becomes even clearer, if one looks at the geographical distribution of the constituencies which the antisemitic deputies of both groups represented (see Maps 10 and 11).

Of the 22 members of the antisemitic parliamentary group, one stood for Paris (16th *arrondissement*); one for a seat in the Paris region (Rambouillet); two for Bordeaux; one for Nancy; and one for Bar-le-Duc. Four represented Algerian constituencies. The rest, with two exceptions, represented rural constituencies in the South or the South-West. The departments of the Landes

MAP 10 ANTISEMITIC DEPUTIES (1898).

● Deputies belonging to the parliamentary group.

⊗ Deputies not belonging to the parliamentary group who supported
the Pontbriand Bill.

ALGERIA:

Algiers: ●●
Constantine: ●
Oran: ●

MAP 11 ANTISEMITIC DEPUTIES BY DEPARTMENT (1898).

Deputies belonging to the parliamentary group plus those who supported the Pontbriand Bill:

1 per department

2-3 per department

4 and more per department

and the Gers alone returned five. Thus, although 10 members of the antisemitic group represented urban centres or constituencies with large Jewish populations and strong currents of popular antisemitism, as many stood for rural constitiencies where the pressure of local-level antisemitism cannot have been important. The pattern changes further in this direction, if the sponsors of the Disenfranchisement Bill are added. The representation of Paris and the Seine leaps from one to seven, and the department of the Vosges is added in the East; but the main additions come elsewhere. The Var, the Alpes-Maritimes and the Hautes-Pyrénées are added to the Gard, the Drôme, the Vaucluse, the Lozère, the Aveyron, the Landes, the Gers and the Gironde, in the South and the South-West. The Dordogne and the Corrèze (with four seats) are also now represented in the Centre of France. But the bulk of the additional group represented constituencies in the West, the stronghold of the traditional anti-Republican Right. While only 2 members of the antisemitic group represented a Western constituency, Maussabré (Parthenay) and Pontbriand (Chateaubriant), 23 of the additional sponsors did so, including 2 from the Côtes-du-Nord, 2 from the Maine-et-Loire, 3 from the Ille-et-Vilaine, and 4 from the Loire-Inférieure.

Having noted this difference of emphasis in their electoral base, if the two groups are compared, we must note also that it is not very great, and it is reasonable therefore to pursue the analysis for both groups together. Taking all 67 antisemitic deputies about whom information is available, that is 63, excluding those from Algeria, 36, or well over half, represented departments, in which, according to Goguel, the Right obtained a majority in the 1898 elections.[26] Only 2 represented departments in which the Right obtained all the seats, but another 19 represented departments in which the Right won all the seats but one. On the departmental level, therefore, the correlation between electoral antisemitism and the traditional Right seems to be fairly close, although ten deputies from these Right-wing departments were certainly not Royalists or Bonapartists. Habert and Gauthier de Clagny in the Seine-et-Oise were ex-Boulangists and members of the still Republican Ligue des Patriotes. Daudé-Gleize in the Lozère was a "Nationalist", who later joined the Union Républicaine. Poullan in the Alpes-Maritimes was a Progressist. Le Hérissé in the Ille-et-Vilaine was another ex-Boulangist, who later joined the Gauche Démocratique. Denis in the Landes, Decker-David in the Gers and Pédébidou in the Hautes-Pyrénées called themselves Radical Republicans; while Ferrette in the Meuse and Gervaize in the Meurthe-et-Moselle were elected on "Populist" Republican platforms. However, this leaves 26, who did belong to the traditional Right. For some of them, sitting for pocket-boroughs, where deputies were only in a very tenuous sense representative of their constituents, the espousal of political antisemitism seems to have been almost gratuitous. This was the case for a number of deputies from constituencies in the West. The Baron de Grandmaison, for example, kept the same seat of Saumur in the Maine-et-Loire for 40 years; the Vicomte de Montfort was re-elected for Yvetot in the Seine-Inférieure for the third time in 1898 and was unopposed. The Comte de Pontbriand also sat for a pocket-borough, that of Chateaubriant in the Loire-Inférieure. He too was elected unopposed in 1898, and on his transfer to the Senate in 1901, handed on his seat to his nephew the Comte Ginoux de Fermon, who, again, was elected without opposition. At Dinan in the Côtes du Nord, similarly, Rioust de Largentaye had inherited the seat from his father, and was returned unopposed in 1898. Savary de Beauregard at Bressuire in the Deux-Sèvres and abbé Gayraud at Brest in the Finistère were also elected in 1898 without opposition. Antisemites occupied pocket-boroughs in other areas, too, not all of them in Right-wing departments. The Comte d'Aulan, for example, succeeded to his father's seat of Nyons in the Drôme in 1898,[27] and Desjardins had succeeded his brother as deputy for Saint-Quentin in the Aisne in 1893. The Comte d'Alsace at Neufchateau in the Vosges, and Gauthier de Clagny at Versailles in the Seine-et-Oise were elected unopposed in 1898. The bulk of antisemitic deputies were, in this connection, natives of the department, and often of the constituency, which they represented, though this was probably a common characteristic among all deputies.

If the antisemitism of deputies for such constituencies, nearly all of which were bastions of the traditional Right, cannot be explained in terms of their electoral base, except in so far as it left a free rein to political eccentricity, in other similar cases it can. There is some evidence that constituencies that had been pocket-boroughs were ceasing to be so, and that the traditional predominance of the Right in such seats was thus under serious threat. In such circumstances, antisemitism seems in some cases to have been adopted to replace or combine with Boulangism in giving the Right a new, attractive and popular face. In this context, it is perhaps significant that antisemitism was relatively unimportant among deputies in departments where the Right won all the seats in 1898, and most important among those in departments where it won all but one of the seats, but where, in six cases, it had lost ground between 1893 and 1898.[28] The example of the Gers is instructive here.[29] Traditionally Bonapartist, the department fell to the Republicans in 1892–3, when they gained control of the majority of municipal councils and of the Conseil Général, as well as winning all five seats in the Chamber. Lectoure elected an independent Socialist. Moreover, in 1897 the Republicans also won the senatorial elections in the department. The 1898 elections for the Chamber marked a come-back for the Bonapartists and their Boulangist allies, who regained three of the seats, using antisemitic platforms to do so. The Radical Decker-David, presumably influenced by the nature of local campaigning, also took up the antisemitic cause. The constituencies of the Gers had not only traditionally belonged to the Right; they were also pocket-boroughs. The Cassagnac family had represented the department in almost unbroken succession since the Second Empire, sitting mainly for Condom, which Lasies, closely associated with them, took over in 1898. Paul de Cassagnac was then elected for Mirande, and his lieutenant Delpech-Cantaloup for Lectoure. Decker-David, moreover, owed his seat at Auch to his having married the daughter of its former deputy and mayor, Jean David. The 1898 come-back was partial and shortlived, however. Cassagnac lost his seat in 1902 to a

Radical, and Delpech-Cantaloup lost his to a Radical-Socialist; while Lasies in Condom was vigorously opposed by another Radical-Socialist. A similar situation of antisemitism being used in an attempt to stave off threats from the Left was present in other areas, too, as the defeats of many antisemitic deputies in 1902 indicates. The Comte d'Aulan lost his family seat of Nyons to a Radical; Pascal was beaten at Uzès in the Gard by a Radical-Socialist; and Roy de Loulay at St-Jean-d'Angély in the Charente-Inférieure was defeated by a Radical.

It is interesting that, among departments of Right-wing predominance, electoral antisemitism was more prevalent in the West and the South-West than in the East, where popular antisemitism was more in evidence and was related to the presence of well-established Jewish communities.[30] This can be explained perhaps by the fact that the predominance of the Right was a fairly recent phenomenon in the East, and that it did not involve the anti-Republicanism which characterized the traditional Right in the West.[31] This suggests that antisemitism coupled fairly easily with anti-Republicanism of the traditional and Catholic variety, but that authentic Republicanism, even of an extremely conservative kind might be an obstacle to its use and acceptance in electoral politics, even if local hostility to Jews was strong. It suggests also that the conservative Republicans of the East felt much more secure electorally and/or took a much more realistic approach to politics than their traditionalist counterparts in the West and South-West. The relatively poor correlation between the distribution of antisemitic deputies in 1898 and that of antisemitic riots in the same year lends support to this idea. Eight departments experienced riots in two or more places, but elected no antisemitic deputies. Four of these departments were firmly Republican, electing no deputies of the Right at all in 1898, and 2 were in the East. By contrast, 12 departments, mainly in the West and the South-West elected antisemitic deputies in 1898, but apparently experienced no antisemitic riots.

Twenty-six antisemitic deputies represented departments which were predominantly Left-wing in 1898, and two represented departments where Left and Right were evenly balanced electorally. Here the traditional Right was not much in evidence, as might be expected, though de Ramel at Alais (Gard) and Roy de Loulay at St-Jean d'Angély (Charente-Inférieure) were "Conservateurs"; and Saint-Martin at La Châtre (Indre) belonged to the "Droite". Aulan in the Drôme was also a Right-winger, standing as a Plebiscitary Nationalist. The Independent label assumed by Pain at Civray (Vienne) and by Fouquet at Bernay (Eure) can probably be read in the same sense; while Lerolle was elected in the 7th arrondissement of Paris as a conservative Catholic. More certainly, Georges Berry, also elected for the Seine—as a "Conservateur Rallié"—but owning estates in the Haute-Vienne, had been a traditional Royalist until 1893; and Napoléon Magne, scion of a Bonapartist dynasty, was elected as such in the Dordogne. Desjardins stood in the Aisne as a Liberal Republican, which suggests conservative inclinations; while Millevoye (16th arrondissement of Paris), Paulin-Méry (13th arrondissement of Paris), Castelin (Aisne), and Borie (Corrèze) were ex-Boulangists. However,

Millevoye and Paulin-Méry were both of Left-wing tendency, and the remaining twelve deputies in this category also claimed in one way or another to be of the Left. Gabiat (Haute-Vienne) and Pascal (Gard) were Progressists; Lachaud and Delmas, both from the Corrèze were Radicals; Abel-Bernard (Vaucluse) and Saba (Aude) were Radical-Socialists. Cluseret in the Var was a Socialist Republican, one of the original members of the Ligue des Patriotes and an ex-*communard*. Ferrand was sponsored in Saint-Denis by a Comité Radical-Socialiste Anticollectiviste. Charles Bernard (Bordeaux) was a Blanquiste, and stood as a Socialist, and later, in Paris, as a *"Socialiste Patriote"*. His Boulangist colleague Chiché (Bordeaux) also called himself a Socialist, as did Paul Bernard (13th *arrondissement* of Paris). Finally, Goussot (Saint-Denis), a member of the Ligue des Patriotes, was elected in 1893 as a Socialist and in 1898 as a *"Socialiste Nationaliste"*. There is evidence here that electoral antisemitism was aimed with some success at lower-class voters, in the capital and its suburbs, as well as in Bordeaux and possibly in the Midi. In the Seine, the Seine-et-Oise, the Gironde, the Gard and the Vaucluse, there is also a correlation between this electoral appeal of antisemitism and the existence of a sizable Jewish population, although, by 1898, this had become, in the last two departments, more a historical memory than a contemporary fact.[32] The presence of four antisemitic deputies in the Corrèze, of whom three were Radicals or Radical-Socialists, is very difficult to explain, though it possibly had some function in a local feud between different Radical factions. Léon Vacher, mayor of Tulle and its deputy with one interruption since 1876, was defeated in that constituency in 1902 by another Radical-Socialist. There is a certain similarity here, and in Left-wing antisemitic constituencies generally, with the situation in the Algerian constituencies. In both electoral antisemitism was a genuinely Left-wing phenomenon, and at Constantine and Algiers, as at Tulle, antisemitic Radicals, Morinaud and Marchal, were elected in 1898, and defeated in 1902 by fellow-Radicals.

Overall it seems clear that, although electoral antisemitism probably began and certainly had a real importance in some urban constituencies, it was in the main a characteristic of rural ones, many of which were held by the old Catholic Right. Here it was a symptom of incipient or on-going change in the political structure. There are indications that it served, like Boulangism before it, as a platform intended to halt an actual or expected decline in the traditional Right-wing vote, and it may also have served as a convenient mask with which erstwhile Royalists covered their effective *"ralliement"* to the Republican Right, represented from 1896 to 1898 by the government of Méline. Baron (Maine-et-Loire), the Baron d'Elva (Mayenne) and the Comte de Lévis-Mirepoix (Orne), for example, had all belonged to Méline's majority, which represented an abandonment of Catholic and Royalist principle that may not have gone down well among the notables in their constituencies. Antisemitism may also have served to mark a certain distance between former Royalists, who "rallied" more overtly to the Republican régime, and established Republican conservatives, acting as a sign to the more politically aware voters, like Catholicism which it usually accompanied, but without its profound potential for conflict, that there still was a real difference between them. This interpretation is lent further force by the fact that, as we have seen, in the East at least, Right-wing Republicanism tended to be inimical to antisemitism, despite its local attractions. Nevertheless, antisemitism was not, on the whole, a major element in Right-wing politics in the West and the South, though it was unmistakably present, encouraged by Catholicism, ready to be emphasized when circumstances warranted. Moreover, it remained a minor theme in electioneering on the traditional Right up to the time of the First World War and beyond. Jacques Piou, for example, referred to the "Judeo-Masonic conspiracy" in his campaign in the Lozère in 1913.[33]

In Paris, and a few other urban centres, electoral antisemitism had a different face. Linked with the Boulangist heritage in several cases, as it was in some Right-wing rural areas, it had something of Boulangism's popular emotional appeal. But here it was not simply a remodelled facet of an old-world political establishment, but a new type of protest movement, Populist, even pseudo-Socialist. It was not the product of a manipulated electoral system, but, to a greater or lesser extent, the reflection of popular aspirations, fears and resentments, channelled often against real Jewish communities, but generated by experience of and reactions to thoroughgoing social and economic change. Its meaning was not conservative, but ambiguously democratic. It was an intruder on the normal political scene, critical of the parliamentary system which it temporarily invaded. It cut across established political boundaries and allegiances, and announced from the world of the press, of the mass media, a new style of mass politics, pointing forward, in some ways, to the structures characteristic of Fascism. This is most clear, perhaps, in Algeria, where all four antisemitic candidates ousted sitting Republican deputies with platforms of varying degrees of radicalism and campaigns of rare violence. As we have seen, the typical manifestation of political antisemitism was the League and not the political party, and many of the more militant deputies belonged to or were associated with one or other of the anti-Dreyfusard Leagues. But, ultimately, antisemitism in France in the 1890s and 1900s proved as ineffective a vehicle for political protest and change as Boulangism had been. Including adherents from all parts of the political spectrum, it was too heterogeneous to formulate a common policy, let alone to undertake concerted and coherent political action. The accession of antisemites to the Chamber of Deputies brought the movement some prestige, and probably tended in the short-run to legitimize antisemitism as a political option. But the antisemites in the Chamber remained a small and powerless minority. Their numbers fell quickly, as we have seen, after the success of 1898, as the antisemitic movement declined in force in the country at large, and by 1906, if not before, antisemitism as a main electoral platform and as a force of any kind in Parliament in France was dead.

NOTES

1 See Z. Szajkowski, "Socialists and Radicals in the Development of Antisemitism in Algeria (1884–1900)," *Jewish Social Studies*, 10 (1948), p. 261.

2 Byrnes, *Antisemitism in Modern France*, p. 292.
3 See Sternhell, *Maurice Barrès*, pp. 90 and 232; Verdès-Leroux, *Scandale financier et antisémitisme catholique*, pp. 122 and 169; also Drumont, *La Dernière Bataille*, p. 194; and *Le Testament d'un antisémite*, pp. 110–15.
4 See Mayeur, "Les Congrès nationaux" p. 182; Duroselle, "L'Antisémitisme en France de 1886 à 1914", p. 62; Reinach, *Histoire de l'Affaire Dreyfus*, I, p. 206; Zévaès, *Au Temps du Boulangisme*, pp. 182–3; and Jean Jolly, ed., *Dictionnaire des parlementaires français, passim.* Antisemitism was not in general characteristic of Boulangism, though it became more important among Boulangists as the movement declined.
5 See Verdès-Leroux, op. cit., p. 169; and Drumont, "Une Election municipale en 1890", *TA*, Book V.
6 See Drault, *Drumont, La France juive et La Libre Parole*, p. 280; Zévaès, *L'Affaire Dreyfus*, pp. 189–90; Divry, *L'Abbé Garnier*, p. 29; and Watson, "The Nationalist Movement in Paris," pp. 49–84.
7 Reinach, op. cit., III, p. 581; see also Jolly, op. cit.
8 See Divry, op. cit., pp. 55–62.
9 Viau, *Vingt ans d'antisémitisme*, p. 60.
10 "L'Archiviste", *Drumont et Dreyfus*, p. 22.
11 Ibid.; and Weber, *Satan franc-maçon* pp. 16–17, who seems to have got his figures wrong.
12 Viau, op. cit., pp. 102–3.
13 Cit. Sternhell, op. cit., p. 238.
14 See AN F⁷ 12459; and Police report, 4 June 1898. APP Ba 106. Viau, op. cit., p. 179; and Verdès-Leroux, op. cit., p. 170, unaccountably put the number at 19 only; while Duroselle, op. cit., lists only 11. The full list is as follows, with the constituencies which the deputies represented:
ABEL-BERNARD, Emile—Apt (Vaucluse).
AULAN, Marie, Comte de Suarès d'—Nyons (Drôme).
BERNARD, Charles—Bordeaux, *2e circonscription* (Gironde).
CASSAGNAC, Paul de Granier de—Mirande (Gers).
CHICHÉ, Albert—Bordeaux, *1er circonscription* (Gironde).
DAUDÉ-GLEIZE, Paulin—Mende (Lozère).
DELPECH-CANTALOUP, Jules—Lectoure (Gers).
DENIS, Théodore—Dax, *1er circonscription* (Landes).
DRUMONT, Edouard—Alger, *1er circonscription.*
FAURE, Firmin—Oran, *1er circonscription.*
FERRETTE, Paul—Bar-le-Duc (Meuse).
GERVAIZE, Ludovic—Nancy, *3e circonscription* (Meurthe-et-Moselle).
HABERT, Marcel—Rambouillet (Seine-et-Oise).
JACQUEY, Général Armand—Mont-de-Marsan (Landes).
LASIES, Joseph—Condom (Gers).
MARCHAL, Charles—Alger, *2e circonscription.*
MASSABUAU, Joseph—Espalion (Aveyron).
MAUSSABRÉ-BEUFVIER, Gilbert, Marquis de—Parthenay (Deux-Sèvres).
MILLEVOYE, Lucien—16th *arrondissement* of Paris, *2e circonscription* (Seine).
MORINAUD, Jean—Constantine, *1er circonscription.*
PASCAL, Léonce—Uzès (Gard).
PONTBRIAND, Fernand, Comte du Breil de—Chateaubriant (Loire-Inférieure).
    It is not clear how many antisemitic candidates this leaves who did *not* get elected, but who obtained a substantial proportion of the vote. We know, for example, that the Royalist Sabran-Pontevès stood on an antisemitic platform in the 19th *arrondissement* of Paris, and Monniot as an antisemite pure and simple in the Somme, neither making much impact (Grenier, *Nos Députés, 1898–1902*, pp. 464 and 516), but they may not be typical, and further research would be worthwhile.
15 "Proposition de loi (annexe au procès-verbal de la séance du 9 février 1899) tendant

à abroger, dans ses effets politiques, les dispositions du décret du 24 octobre 1870 (dit décret Crémieux)". AN F^{80} 1688. Other legislation proposed by the antisemitic group included an amnesty for those involved in public disturbances and administrative irregularities in Algeria, and a bill giving the colony financial autonomy; see Viau, op. cit., p. 274. The deputies who joined those of the antisemitic group in sponsoring the above bill were:

ALSACE, Thierry, Comte d'—Neufchâteau (Vosges).

ANTHIME-MÉNARD—Saint-Nazaire, *1er circonscription* (Loire-Inférieure).

BARON, Jules—Cholet, *1er circonscription* (Maine-et-Loire).

BERNARD, Paul—13th *arrondissement,* Paris, *1er circonscription* (Seine).

BERRY, Georges—9th *arrondissement,* Paris, *1er circonscription* (Seine).

BORIE, Léon—Tulle, *1er circonscription* (Corrèze).

CASTELIN, André—Laon, *2e circonscription* (Aisne).

CLUSERET, Gustave—Toulon, *2e circonscription* (Var).

DECKER-DAVID, Paul-Henry—Auch (Gers).

DELMAS, Arthur-Vincent—Ussel (Corrèze).

DERRIEN, Henri—Lannion, *1er circonscription* (Côtes-du-Nord).

DESJARDINS, Pierre-Jules—Saint-Quentin, *2e circonscription* (Aisne).

ELVA, Christian, Comte d'—Laval, *1er circonscription* (Mayenne).

ESTOURBEILLON DE LA GARNACHE, Régis, Marquis de L'—Vannes, *1er circonscription* (Morbihan).

FERRAND, Stanislas—Saint-Denis, *5e circonscription* (Seine).

FOUQUET, Camille—Bernay (Eure).

GABIAT, Camille—Bellac (Haute-Vienne).

GALOT, Jules—Paimboeuf (Loire-Inférieure).

GALPIN, Gaston—Le Mans, *2e circonscription* (Sarthe).

GAUTHIER DE CLAGNY, Albert—Versailles, *2e circonscription* (Seine-et-Oise).

GAUTRET, Jean—Sables-d'Olonne, *1er circonscription* (Vendée).

GAYRAUD, Hippolyte—Brest, *3e circonscription* (Finistère).

GOUSSOT, Emile—Saint-Denis, *1er circonscription* (Seine).

GRANDMAISON, Georges, Baron Millin de—Saumur (Maine-et-Loire).

HALGOUËT, Joseph de Poulpiquet du—Redon (Ille-et-Vilaine).

LACHAUD, Jean—Brive, *1er circonscription* (Corrèze).

LA FERRONNAYS, Henri, Marquis de—Ancénis (Loire-Inférieure).

LARGENTAYE, Rioust de—Dinan, *2e circonscription* (Côtes-du-Nord).

LE HÉRISSÉ, René—Rennes, *1er circonscription* (Ille-et-Vilaine).

LEROLLE, Paul—7th *arrondissement,* Paris (Seine).

LÉVIS-MIREPOIX, Marie, Comte de—Alençon (Orne).

MAGNE, Napoléon—Périgueux, *2e circonscription* (Dordogne).

MONTAIGU, Joseph, Comte de—Saint-Nazaire, *2e circonscription* (Loire-Inférieure).

MONTFORT, Louis, Vicomte de—Yvetot, *2e circonscription* (Seine-Inférieure).

PAIN, Maurice—Civray (Vienne).

PAULIN-MERY—13th *arrondissement,* Paris, *2e circonscription* (Seine).

PÉDÉBIDOU, Adolphe—Tarbes, *1er circonscription* (Hautes-Pyrénées).

POULLAN, Félix—Nice, *2e circonscription* (Alpes-Maritimes).

RAMEL, Augustin de—Alais, *2e circonscription* (Gard).

ROY DE LOULAY, Louis—Saint-Jean d'Angély (Charente-Inférieure).

SABA, Edmond—Castelnaudary (Aude).

SAINT-MARTIN-VALOGNE, Marie-Aimé—La Châtre (Indre).

SAVARY DE BEAUREGARD, Henri—Bressuire (Deux-Sèvres).

SURCOUF, Robert—Saint-Malo, *2e circonscription* (Ille-et-Vilaine).

VACHER, Léon—Tulle, *2e circonscription* (Corrèze).

    This list does not exhaust the number of deputies sympathetic to antisemitism, it should be noted; it does not, for example, include Boni de Castellane, deputy for the Basses-Alpes, 1898–1910; see Boni de Castellane, *L'Art d'être pauvre,* pp. 107–8.

16 See Daudet, *Les Oeuvres dans les hommes*, p 188; and Daudet, *Salons et journaux*, pp 274–275.
17 As Drault wrote: "Il y eut . . . des députés antisémites de tous les partis, mais il n'y eut jamais de parti antisémite"; op. cit., p. 78.
18 See Halévy, *Apologie*, p. 69; Sorlin, *Waldeck-Rousseau*, pp. 391–422; and chapter I, pp. 16–20 above.
19 Information for this analysis is taken mainly from Jolly, op. cit. and from Grenier, *Nos Députés, 1898–1902* and *Nos Députés, 1902–1906* (Paris, no date).
20 Chiché and Charles Bernard stood and were defeated in both 1902 and 1906. Seven other antisemitic candidates, débutants, who had not belonged to the antisemitic group of 1898, also stood in 1902: Ménard, Jousselin, Thiébaud, Boisandré, Papillaud, Monniot and Congy, of whom only the last was elected, for the 11th *arrondissement* of Paris. Viau, op. cit., pp. 294–302. Barrès, again not a member of the 1898 group, returned to the Chamber in 1906 as deputy for the 1st *arrondissement* of Paris, which he represented until his death in 1923. See Barrès-Maurras, *La République ou le Roi*, p. 302, note by Guy Dupré.
21 Dardenne, *Godefroy de Cavaignac*, p. 668.
22 See Bernanos, *La Grande Peur des bien-pensants*, pp. 367 and 385.
23 Information is not available for the whole parliamentary career of 5 sponsors, who have therefore been omitted here.
24 The date of birth of one in the sample is not available. Incidentally Jolly's dates of birth are often at variance with those given by Grenier, but not enough to be significant.
25 That is Catholic Royalists who followed the papal injunction of 1892 to "rally" to the Republican régime.
26 Goguel, *Géographie des elections françaises*, pp. 36–7. As indicated, deputies sat at this time for single member constituencies, but analysis by departments is simpler and follows current practice among French historians, thus permitting such comparisons and correlations.
27 Boni de Castellane, too, in the Basses-Alpes, sat for a seat which his father had represented in the National Assembly 1871–1875; Boni de Castellane, op. cit., pp. 233–5.
28 Goguel, *Géographie des elections françaises*, pp. 30–5.
29 See Bordes, "L'Evolution politique du Gers sous la IIIe République", pp. 19–22.
30 See Szajkowski, "The Growth of the Jewish Population of France".
31 See Barral, "Géographie de l'opinion sous la Troisième République", p. 152.
32 See Szajkowski, "The Decline and Fall of Provençal Jewry"; and Marrus, *The Politics of Assimilation*, pp. 31–2.
33 Patrice L.-R. Higonnet, *Pont-de-Montvert, Social Structure and Politics in a French Village, 1700–1914* (Cambridge, Mass., 1971), p. 129.

CHAPTER IX
THE ANTISEMITIC MOVEMENT IN ALGERIA:
FRENCH ANTISEMITISM IN DECLINE

BEFORE WE CONSIDER THE DECLINE OF THE ANTISEMITIC MOVEMENT IN France in more detail, we should examine further the parallel movement in Algeria. This, we have seen, was more extreme than its metropolitan counterpart, and acted as a model and a pace-setter for the latter. "It is via Algeria", Drumont anticipated in 1886, "that the antisemitic campaign in France will begin".[1] Close links existed, moreover, between the two movements by the 1890s. Drumont was elected deputy for Algiers in 1898; Guérin maintained particularly friendly relations with Max Régis, Morinaud and other Algerian antisemitic leaders, both in Paris and on his visits to the colony;[2] while Morès was credited with being "the initiator of the movement in Algeria."[3] However, the "movement in Algeria" had its own distinct make-up and *raison d' être*, which explain its peculiar success and virulence. It had its own political organization in the Ligue Anti-Juive d'Alger, founded in 1892, and led by Morinaud and Régis.[4] A local antisemitic press had existed from the early 1880s, and most of the colony's newspapers had joined the cause by the mid- or late-1890's. Of these the most violent was Régis's daily, *L'Antijuif Algérien*, which had a circulation of 20,000 in 1898, and "by comparison with which", according to Sorlin, "*La Croix* and *La Libre Parole* seem almost conciliatory".[5] Physical, as well as verbal, violence against Jews was also an Algerian tradition by the end of the century, and the "pogroms" of the late 1890s were only a repetition or an escalation of similar demonstrations in the 1880s.[6] Moreover, as we have seen also, 4 of the colony's 6 deputies and at least 1 of its 3 senators in 1898 were declared antisemites;[7] and, in addition, the antisemites captured political power at the municipal level in Algiers and elsewhere at the same time.

The extraordinary development of antisemitism in Algeria can be explained by a combination of factors: the presence of an old and important Jewish community in a territory with a corrupt political system, a large European immigrant population, a recently conquered native population, and a lopsided "colonial" economy. The Jews of Algeria were a large, little assimilated minority group, well-established before the French occupation of 1830,[8] and numbering some 50,700 in 1898. Their population had doubled since 1850, and was about one-sixth the size of the French *colon* population.[9] Like North African Jewry as a whole, most Algerian Jews lived in poverty or near-poverty, and were engaged in artisanal occupations, though a small proportion were engaged in business on a larger scale and in money-lending; and there had been some progress towards assimilation and some further social ascension in the last decades of the nineteenth century.[10] However, naturalized only in 1870,[11] Algerian Jews were still the object of traditional hatreds in a land-based economy dependent on usurious credit,[12] to which were added new hostilities deriving from the colonial situation. One of the features of this situation was a peculiar political system, which gave the colony a degree of local self-government, while allowing it full representation in the two French Assemblies. Local political office in Algeria was very lucrative by French standards; official salaries were high and "the illegitimate perquisites" of office could be enormous, besides which the positions of law officials *(les offices ministériels)* were not venal, as in France, but the objects of a spoils system. The prizes in the political contest were therefore considerable. Elections, in addition, were outrageously corrupt; votes were bought and sold; voters and candidates were intimidated; and, since the Jews formed a significant minority (nearly 10% of the electorate) and tended to vote as a bloc, "it is by the Jewish vote that one triumphs or is defeated".[13] Paul Vibert, who stood against Drumont in 1898, saw this last claim as something of an exaggeration, but, nevertheless, testified to the fact that Drumont's victory depended to a large extent on the full exploitation of Algerian electoral *moeurs.* [14] In these circumstances, antisemitism was an obvious platform for the political opposition to choose in order to unseat the "Opportunist" establishment. "Politically", wrote Viau, the movement was directed against M.M. Etienne, deputy for Oran, and Thomson, deputy for Constantine";[15] and, as we have seen, this aim was largely accomplished in 1898. The disturbances in that year had been instigated for this purpose, but agitation continued in the hopes of consolidating the electoral victory by forcing the French government to repeal the Crémieux decree of 1870, which had naturalized and enfranchised the Jews of Algeria.[16]

The Algerian antisemitic movement was therefore of definite Left-wing complexion; its leaders were Radicals and Socialists, and they were also anticlerical.[17] The Catholic Right apparently provided them with some finance, in the hope, perhaps, of bringing about a restoration of military rule in the colony, but its influence remained mainly covert and was of little importance, at least in political terms.[18] The fact that Drumont sat on the Right in the Chamber of Deputies was very adversely commented upon.[19] The mass-appeal of political antisemitism in Algeria was clearly related to its pseudo-revolutionary use of violence in action and rhetoric, and to its crude anti-capitalist platform. Posters in Oran in 1882 declared: "All means are good and must be employed in the destruction of the Jews by the Europeans."[20] Régis called on a crowd in Algiers in January 1898 "to water the tree of liberty with Jewish blood";[21] and we have seen that in his campaigns he used antisemitic songs, which presented the expulsion of the Jews as a solution to working-class poverty and low wages.[22] In the towns, antisemitism seems to have been very much a vehicle by which *colons* aimed to eliminate Jewish business competition. The economist Molinari told Henri Dagan in 1899 that it was "a question of competition on the part of *colons* from France, who emigrate to Algeria with the idea of quickly making their fortunes . . . but, who find that the field is already occupied by Jewish traders and businessmen . . .".[23] Hence the particular appeal and success of the boycotting of Jewish shops and businesses organized by *L'Antijuif*. Shops, cafés and businesses displayed signs reading: "Anti-Jewish establishment", or "Catholic establishment"; the names of those patronizing Jewish concerns were published; and cases were reported of physical attacks being made on such people, and of firms' dismissing Jewish employees.[24] In the countryside, where many *colons*, particularly those engaged in wine production, had become indebted in the 1890s, the antisemites raised the old familiar cry of Jewish usury with similar effect.[25]

Another element in the appeal of antisemitism was the fact that much of the *colon* population was of non-French origin. Antisemitism was particularly strong in this recently naturalized milieu. Vibert referred to it as forming "the main contingent of M. Drumont's electors";[26] and Régis, himself, was of Italian origin. Antisemitism here ran parallel to a movement against all foreigners, which helps to explain its function,[27] for it allowed naturalized *colons* to assert their Frenchness or their Algerian identity through opposition to the Jews, whose naturalization, on the contrary, was claimed to be a legal trick that must be reversed. This operation both relieved their anxieties about their own national identity, and deflected hostility against them, on the part of French-born *colons*, on to a third and convenient party. The Catholic origins of these Spanish, Italian and Maltese *colons* also predisposed them to antisemitism. When Vibert asked one why he hated the Jews, he received the reply: "How do you expect us not to have it in for the Jews? They killed Jesus."[28] It is interesting, in this context, that the positive accompaniment of antisemitism among *colons* was often an assertion of French or Algerian identity, via the wider concept of Latinity, which of course included Italians and Spaniards, while clearly excluding both Jews and the Arab-Berber native population. Latinity also established a claim to the territory of Algeria that predated the Islamic conquest.[29] A further and related ideological peculiarity of Algerian antisemitism was the fact that, of necessity, it tended to eschew the specifically racial mode of expression that was becoming quite common in metropolitan France. Since it needed to make a distinction between Arabs and Jews, it could not employ the dualistic terminology of Aryan and Semite, since the latter term included both. As Leroy-Beaulieu commented: "in the face of the Arabs and of Islam, the antisemite has to discard his pretentious scientific disguise, and show himself as simply and vulgarly anti-Jewish."[30]

Three features of the Algerian antisemitic movement caused the metropolitan government particular concern, and led to a reaction against it. The first is related to the point which we have just made. The antisemites attempted to exploit and encourage Arab hostility towards the Jews.[31] They contrasted

Arab loyalty to France and nobility of character with Jewish treachery and self-seeking, claiming that the naturalization of the Jews was unfair to the Arabs, and that the Crémieux decree had been the main cause of the Arab insurrection of 1871.[32] This last charge cannot be substantiated,[33] but it may have raised hopes in some quarters; and the rebellion which broke out in Marguerite in April 1901 was attributed, at least in part and with some justification, to the state of unrest brought about by antisemitic agitation over a period of years.[34] Second, there was present in the antisemitic movement a strong current of hostility to the metropolitan government, and the beginnings of an autonomist trend,[35] that no central government could tolerate. Third, the antisemites, as we have seen, won control of the municipal councils in all the major towns of the colony, and proceeded to apply legal discrimination against Jews. Jewish municipal employees and teachers were sacked; Jews were excluded from public assistance and from hospitals; licences were withdrawn from Jewish traders and cab-drivers; ritual slaughtering facilities were removed from abattoirs; and Jewish café-owners were refused leave to place tables on the pavements outside their premises. At Constantine, it was even proposed to exclude Jewish children from primary schools.[36] With a certain delay, attributable to prudence and the desire to give no encouragement to claims that it treated the colony high-handedly, the metropolitan government took firm measures to bring the situation under control, reversing an earlier policy of *laissez-faire.*[37] It was aided in this by the internal divisions and incompetent leadership that characterized the Algerian antisemitic movement,[38] like its French counterpart, and by the efforts of local Radical politicians and of a section of the local Republican press, notably *La Revanche* and *La Vigie Algérienne.*[39] Government policy was also assisted by the obviously bad effects of the antisemitic disturbances on the economy, for example on the tourist trade, and by the good wine harvest of 1901, which dissipated the grievances of many rural *colons.*[40] Most important, perhaps, was the spectre of Arab revolt that the antisemites seemed to have raised that same year. The policy was thus implemented without difficulty. Antisemitic mayors, and notably Max Régis, were dismissed for abuse of their authority from mid-1899; and it was made quite clear that discrimination against French citizens by municipalities would not be tolerated. The colony was granted a degree of financial and administrative independence in 1900, which deflated "autonomist" tendencies, while *colons* were reminded of the advantages of their dependent status by a threat to apply the two-year conscription law in Algeria.[41] Success, in a sense, had spelt the downfall of the antisemitic movement in Algeria, at least politically and for some time to come;[42] and this was confirmed by the electoral *débâcle* of 1902, in which all four of the seats held by antisemites were lost, including Drumont's.[43] But, more important to the historian of French antisemitism, the success of the Algerian movement alerted government and opinion in metropolitan France to the dangers implicit in the antisemitic movement in France itself.

But before we leave North Africa, a few lines must be devoted to antisemitism in Tunisia. Like Algeria, Tunisia had a large and ancient Jewish community, numbering about 60,000 by the end of the nineteenth century.[44] It also had an immigrant European population of various national origins and of Catholic faith. But antisemitism was much less important there than in Algeria. It was present in the local press from the late 1880s, but intermittently and in relatively low key. There were antisemitic riots in Tunis in the spring of 1898, but they had few past precedents locally, at least, since the French Protectorate had been established in 1881, and seem to have been largely influenced by events in Algeria. The expression of hostility to Jews on the part of Europeans was, moreover, mainly religious rather than political or economic in form. The old custom of Christian children beating Jewish children in Holy Week had not entirely disappeared by 1900, for example; and *La Dépêche Tunisienne* reported in April 1901 that a representation of the Passion by an Italian troupe had been greeted with shouts of "Death to the Jews" from audiences. The explanation for the more traditional tone of antisemitism in Tunisia, and for its general lack of development, seems to lie in the territory's status as a Protectorate. Jews were not French citizens or electors, and were not involved in political conflict. The *colon* population was small, and European presence less dominant. The economic and social structure of Tunisia, in effect, was far less affected by "colonization" than was that of Algeria, and the co-existence of different ethnic communities was more readily tolerated.[45] This confirms the observation of Cohen-Hadria that the virulence of antisemitism in North Africa varied according to the degree of French or European penetration;[46] and lends support to the more general argument that links the emergence of racialism directly to European colonialism.[47]

We have seen that the antisemitic movement in France began in the early 1880s and reached its apogee in the period 1898–1900. Riots in over 50 towns, the election of 22 deputies, the success of an antisemitic daily press, and the existence of more than one antisemitic organization, all proclaimed its importance. Many contemporaries became justifiably alarmed. "The antisemitic movement", wrote Henri Dagan in 1899, "has become more widespread than ever, and asserts itself with new force and boldness . . . it has shocked many people and thrown them into confusion . . ."[48] "The anti-Jewish passion seemed to have suddenly seized three-quarters of the French population", agreed the Tharaud brothers.[49] President Loubet's secretary, Abel Combarieu, referred to "the antisemitic agitation, from which arose sometimes the whiff of civil war . . ."; and the police, too evoked the same threat.[50] And, as late as 1902, Péguy warned:[51]

> The individual quarrels of the antisemitic and the "Nationalist" leaders should not obscure from us the danger inherent in antisemitism and in "Nationalism". On the contrary, if "parties", so badly led by rival leaders, have obtained everywhere the results that we have seen, it is clear that they must have behind them the substantial passions of a substantial part of the population. Movements as widespread, as profound, as durable, are not fabricated by stratagem or by artifice.

The antisemites themselves, too, as we have seen, felt the wind in their sails. As early as 1892, for example, Edmond Picard welcomed "the recrudescence of antisemitism which at the moment is in a state of ferment everywhere in Europe".[52] Viau wrote that in 1897: "The anti-Jewish agitation . . . revived . . . on a vast scale";[53] while Drumont himself proclaimed: "The whole of Paris, workers and bourgeois . . . was shouting with one voice: Long live Drumont! Down with the Jews!"[54] But those observers who took a less sanguine view of the prospects of organized antisemitism were proved right, at least as far as France was concerned, and for the short and medium term. The Radical leader, René Goblet, for example, dismissed antisemitism in 1898 as "a fairly superficial effervescence"; while the journalist A. Servanine, declared similarly: "I don't believe that antisemitism has a future in a country with an ironic sense of humour like France, where, sooner or later, people will come to see the ridiculous aspects of such views; for they are absurd rather than really odious."[55] And several of the contributors to Henri Dagan's *Enquête* expressed the same opinion.[56]

A detailed analysis of the social complexion of French antisemites must wait until a later chapter; but it is probably true to say that the Dreyfus Affair revealed the existence in France of a very general tolerance of the expression of antisemitic opinion, and even of violence against Jews. Antisemitism, in effect, was latent in French culture. "Let us not forget", declared General de Galliffet, Minister of War in the Waldeck-Rousseau government, "that in France, the vast majority of people is antisemitic";[57] and Jules Isaac pointed to "the strength, the extent and the virulence of anti-Jewish prejudice" as a basic feature of French society at the turn of this century.[58] Some examples will illustrate what Isaac was referring to, beyond the militant antisemitic movement as such. Take the attitude of the Catholic editor of the influential *Revue des Deux Mondes,* Ferdinand Brunetière. He wrote a hostile review of *La France juive* in 1886, but, in the course of it, declared that he did not personally like Jews. In 1898, he wrote a more general article on antisemitism, in which he was very critical of its racial formulations, but agreed that Jews, Freemasons and Protestants collectively were too powerful, and saw the antisemitic movement as, to some extent, a justifiable reaction against this situation. He later played a prominent part in the foundation of the anti-Dreyfusard Ligue de la Patrie Française, but then resigned from it because he felt that it was *too* antisemitic.[59] There was a similar ambiguity in the attitude of the career diplomat, Maurice Paléologue. Professionally concerned with the diplomatic aspects of the Affair, he was early convinced that a deliberate miscarriage of justice had occurred, but did little or nothing about it. He wrote later: "Instinctively, I dislike the Jews; but I find antisemitism deeply repugnant, having seen at too close quarters its iniquity, aberrations and baseness."[60] It is significant here that the opponents of antisemitism, as we shall see,[61] very rarely countered it as a movement directed specifically against Jews, but rather as a threat to the Republic and to public order; and that the expression of antisemitism of a "mild" or unthinking kind, was not uncommon among the ranks of the Dreyfusards and the critics of the "Nationalist" and antisemitic

movement. The Journals of André Gide, for example, a Protestant by upbringing, a writer with a large number of Jewish acquaintances, who directed his
satire against Barrès and the "Nationalists", are sprinkled with antisemitic
remarks.[62] Jules Renard, an active Dreyfusard, who again had a large number
of Jewish acquaintances, and who was a close friend of Thadée and Alfred
Natanson, of Léon Blum and of Tristan Bernard, could refer to his publishers
as "yids", and tell Bernard: "There is one fault with which I have often to
reproach men of your race, and that is indiscretion."[63] Other Dreyfusards who
shared these antisemitic prejudices included Jaurès,[64] Urbain Gohier,[65] Clemenceau,[66] Octave Mirbeau[67] and Picquart.[68] Around the hard core of antisemitic militants, therefore, there was a much wider body of disarmed opponents and neutral opinion, even of large numbers of potential sympathizers,
ready to follow the band-waggon of organized antisemitism. Léon Daudet
recalled that "around . . . La Libre Parole were grouped, not only the doctrinaire antisemites . . . , but also many good people, ordinary French people,
of no particular political persuasion . . ."[69] As Selznick and Steinberg have
shown for the United States in the 1960s,[70] the success of organized antisemitism depended as much on the tacit support, even on the indifference and
apathy, of such a majority, as it did on the activity of a minority of militants.
But, of equal and related importance in determining the vicissitudes of the
antisemitic movement was the attitude of the public authorities, for they had
an important role in helping to establish norms for behaviour and expression
in this, as in other spheres, and they could and did, mobilize the forces of law
and order to sustain those norms.

Although anti-Jewish prejudice seems to have been widespread and well
established among the French élite, and probably among the population at
large, its translation into policy was always, in the period under discussion,
inhibited by an attachment to the egalitarian ideology of the French Revolution, though this itself was related to the emergence of racial ideology, as we
shall see.[71] The only instance of legalized discrimination against Jews in
metropolitan France was the secularization of Jewish schools in the 9th and
10th arrondissements of Paris in 1900–2, at the behest of antisemitic municipal councillors, to which we have already referred.[72] Moreover, as was indicated in chapter VIII, political antisemitism was very much a characteristic
of the anti-Republican Right, which must further have predisposed the Republican authorities against it. There is, accordingly, very little evidence of
support for antisemitism among the civilian authorities in France, and, even
in the army, its public expression was unusual, outside the context of the
Affair. The Gardes de Paris were said, as we have seen, to be favourable to
Guérin during the siege of "Fort Chabrol", but the agent, who related this,
also related the anger of the police officers of the Sûreté over this supposed
sympathy.[73] Two Lyon police chiefs were reported to be antisemites in 1904,
by another agent,[74] but this is one of the very few reports of its kind, and the
police, on the whole, seem to have regarded the antisemites with neutrality
or hostility, as potential or actual trouble-makers to be kept under close
surveillance. Anti-Dreyfusard leanings are occasionally detectable in police

reporting, particularly during the early years of the Affair, but antisemitic leanings of a more general kind are almost never present. It is significant that a Reims officer *(commissaire)*, who placed a *"La France aux Français"* sticker on his vehicle was immediately reprimanded as early as 1896.[75] Hannah Arendt's assertion that "the complicity of the police was everywhere patent" in the 1898 riots is totally unsubstantiated,[76] although Reinach does relate that, when the riots began, "the police, at first, let things happen . . .", and that, in their later stages, "the forces of law and order, harassed and outnumbered, lost patience and let fly at everyone, Christians and Jews",[77] which gives rather a different picture. From limited evidence, it seems that the French courts maintained the same neutrality. This can be seen, even in the laborious process of the Dreyfus Affair itself, in which the partiality of the courts-martial in both Dreyfus's trials, and of the Cour d'Assises in Zola's first trial in particular, contrasted with the detachment of the Cour de Cassation, and notably its Chambre Criminelle.[78] Away from the Affair, a big exception it is true, antisemitic bias in the courts seems to have been very rare. Some local *tribunaux de commerce* may have been intimidated by the prevailing mood of antisemitism, like that of Montbéliard in December 1898;[79] and Reinach suggested that antisemitic demonstrators were treated leniently by the courts, in contrast to anarchists and those guilty of offences against the State who received very heavy sentences. There is probably some truth in this, though Reinach himself mentioned the case of Baron Christiani who received a four-year prison sentence for striking President Loubet at Auteuil in June 1899, an offence against the Head of State, but one that was committed in the context of a basically antisemitic demonstration.[80] In general, moreover, the courts seem to have readily entertained suits for defamation brought against the antisemitic press. Drumont's *La France juive devant l'opinion*, for example, was seized and its further diffusion halted by court order, following a private complaint against it; and *La Libre Parole* was more than once successfully sued for libel.[81] Indeed, Drumont and others repeatedly claimed that the courts were completely under Jewish influence.[82]

But what was decisive here was the attitude of governments. It was the claim of Drumont and other antisemites, again, that the governments of the Third Republic were entirely favourable to, if not dominated by, the Jews, and that they were therefore always and actively hostile to antisemitism and the antisemitic movement.[83] There is an element of truth, at least in the latter part of such claims, but they ignore two factors, which, in practice, made the position of governments less clear-cut. One was that leading politicians were often not themselves free of the prevailing antisemitic prejudice, and did not regard antisemitic organizations and an antisemitic press as *ipso facto* dangerous or socially undesirable. The second was that the circumstances of the Affair temporarily paralysed governmental action. Until revision of the case became governmental policy in mid-1899, it was difficult if not impossible to act to restrain the antisemites, who were among the leading defenders of respect for the legal decision *("la chose jugée")*. At that time, as we have seen, it was the Dreyfusards and the opponents of antisemitism, who, in the perspective of governmental policy and public opinion, were posing a threat to the established order. A small indication of this conviction on the part of the authorities is provided by the fact that the French consul at Ghent was relieved of his position in April 1898, for having signed a petition in support of Zola.[84] As the Radical journalist, Henry Maret, put it, more strongly, the antisemitic campaign of the late 1890s "was able to affect the country profoundly, thanks to the cowardice of the government and of the two Chambers".[85] From mid-1899, however, the attitude of government changed decisively. Loubet replaced Faure, who had been an opponent of revision, as President of the Republic in February. The revision of the Dreyfus Case was accepted in June, and the Affair was "liquidated" by the end of the year by the Waldeck-Rousseau government. Simultaneously, the government took action against the anti-Dreyfusard Leagues, playing up the danger which they represented to the régime, but also genuinely concerned by the way in which organized antisemitism had been so readily exploited by the opponents of the Republic. Another factor that must have carried a great deal of weight on the governmental level was the serious danger represented by the success of the antisemitic movement in Algeria.

The Waldeck-Rousseau government was riding and leading a movement of opinion against organized antisemitism that had begun in the spring of 1898, when the antisemites had raised the spectre of civil commotion. After the 1898 riots, much of the population came to realize the futility and the danger of such disturbances, both economically and politically. Economic crisis may have created a following for antisemitism when it could be blamed on the Jews, a point to which we shall return in the next chapter; but its prolongation was increasingly blamed on the antisemites themselves. Already in February 1898, non-Jewish employees of several Jewish firms in Paris, laid off temporarily because of the disturbances, were reported to be "very annoyed with Drumont and his gang."[86] What the commercial community, what the community at large wanted above all was a return to calm and normality, as the administrative reports, quoted in chapter I, repeatedly and emphatically stressed. What hurt Jewish business hurt business in general, and what threatened Jews threatened the political order in France, as a certain M. Dufour, of the firm of *Sildart et Dufour* reminded the Prefect of Police in October 1898:[87]

> I am not a Jew, but I do quite a lot of business with Jews . . . So, when our friends the antisemites start shouting: "Down with the Jews" and "Death to the Jews", and when they set up a boycott of Jewish firms . . . they are doing me a commercial injury . . . Our public buildings bear the slogan "Liberty, Equality, Fraternity", so I hope that one has the right to expect that anyone living in France will not be put on some black list to have his livelihood taken away and then his property pillaged . . .

Most were less generous and less perspicacious than this, appreciating simply the end of a period of uncertainty and confusion. As J.-P. Peter has pointed out, the Affair repeated the pattern of disturbances and returns to "order" that had punctuated the history of nineteenth-century France, proving yet again that "the dominant classes, even if they are divided and struggling among themselves for power, detest disorder and the country in revolt".[88] But the "reaction" had a much wider base than this suggests, as the unusually decisive elections of 1902 indicated.[89] What is significant for our purposes is that a "strong" government of Republican defence took action against antisemitism as an organized movement, albeit not because it was antisemitic, and also, by pardoning Dreyfus, helped to establish new limits to the expression of antisemitism as an opinion, at least for those who recognized the legitimacy of the government.

So, as we have seen in examining its various manifestations, the antisemitic movement in France entered after 1900 into a decline. Beset by internal rivalries, only superficially united politically and lacking a solid organizational base, it was poorly equipped to face the combination of governmental repression and the evaporation of popular support. Indeed, adversity exacerbated its weaknesses, and destroyed most of its constituent parts. In 1900, Viau noted that "violence was now confined to newspaper articles";[90] but even verbal expressions of antisemitism were becoming rarer, and only thirteen antisemitic meetings are reported in Paris for the two years 1900 and 1901.[91] Activity revived during the 1902 General Election campaign, but the overwhelming defeat of the antisemites and of the "Nationalist" opposition as a whole led to an even more marked withdrawal.[92] At the same time, antisemitism was relinquished by the "Nationalist" movement, that had made such use of it in its hey-day. Significant, for example, was the refusal of several leading "Nationalists", including Coppée and Barrès, to attend the 11th annual banquet of La Libre Parole in 1903.[93] Antisemitism had failed to provide the unifying element for a successful popular opposition movement, and merely compounded the already serious divisions within it over the constitutional and the "clerical" issues.[94] By 1904, the Jeunesse Antisémitique and the Fédération Nationale Antijuive were almost without members, and the Grand Occident de France had virtually disappeared. The antisemitic parliamentary group, after losing half its members in 1902, was wound up in 1906. By 1910, the circulation of La Libre Parole had dwindled to one quarter of its level at the time of the Affair. The last edition of La France juive to be published before the Second World War came out in 1912.[95] Meanwhile, the antisemitic leaders had abandoned the struggle. Max Régis gave up antisemitic politics in 1902, discouraged, as he said, by "the dismal indifference", which it was encountering.[96] Guérin died in 1909. Drumont went into virtual retirement some years earlier, relinquishing his connection with La Libre Parole in 1910, and dying in obscurity in 1917.[97] As Viau admitted in 1910: "It is now an established fact that antisemitism is undergoing a period of contraction."[98] In fact, the only organization in the decade before 1914, which attempted to continue antisemitic agitation in the old style was the Action Française. Beyond propaganda in its daily and in book-form, it organized street demonstrations in 1907, 1908 and 1911; but it was never able to mobilize popular support of the kind that Guérin and Drumont had enjoyed.[99]

The "Union Sacrée" of 1914 brought even this manifestation of political antisemitism virtually to an end;[100] and Léon Daudet, one of the leaders of the Action Française, concluded in 1922 that the French antisemitic movement "remained a *rendezvous*, where people of every opinion could meet, but which had and never could have any practical effectiveness".[101] This marks the distance between the movement of the 1890s and the 1900s and the revival of legal antisemitism and official persecution by the Vichy State and the occupying powers in the 1940's.[102] But, whatever their effects, both, as well as the movement of the inter-war years which links them chronologically,[103] depended on the existence of antisemitism in the bed-rock of French culture. As Péguy argued at the time of the Affair, and as Poliakov and Ophuls have shown for the legislation and the persecution of Vichy,[104] the success of organized antisemitism requires at least passive assent from the majority of the population. Historical factors determine the degree to which antisemitism in a society is expressed on the public and organized level or on the level of social or "private" prejudice, but the interaction of both levels is necessary. In turning now from the history of the antisemitic movement to an analysis of antisemitic ideology and its functions, we are moving towards the second level, though we may never finally reach it. The ideology, rather, mediated between the two levels, articulating popular attitudes in particular circumstances, assuming, revealing, reflecting them, but, at one remove, thus using and changing them also.

NOTES

1 Drumont, *La France juive*, II, p. 47.
2 See Guérin, *Les Trafiquants de l'antisémitisme*, pp. 128–30; and Daily Report, Prefect of Police, 1 June 1898. APP Ba 106.
3 Daily Report, Prefect of Police, 4 June 1898. APP Ba 106; see also Schwarzschild, "The Marquis de Morès", pp. 24–5.
4 Police reports. AN F⁷ 12459; Bournand, *Les Juifs et nos contemporains*, p. 249; and Szajkowski, "Socialists and Radicals in the Development of Antisemitism in Algeria" pp. 266–70.
5 Sorlin, *"La Croix" et les Juifs*, p. 115; see also Drumont, *La France juive*, II, pp. 51–3; Viau, *Vingt ans d'antisémitisme*, p. 176; Bournand, op. cit., p. 249; and chapter VII, p. 206 above.
6 See Drumont, *FJ*, II, pp. 48–9; and chapter III, pp. 119–20 above. 42 Jews, moreover, had been killed in a pogrom in Algiers in 1805 before French rule of Algeria began; see Claude Martin, *Histoire de l'Algérie française 1830–1962* (Paris, no date), p 225.
7 Viau, op. cit., p 179; Bournand, op. cit., pp. 255–6; François Dagen, "Courrier d'Algérie, Considérations sur les causes de la grandeur et de la décadence de l'antisémitisme en Algérie", *Cahiers de la Quinzaine*, 13th cahier, 4th série, February 1903, pp. 43–4; Pierrard, *Juifs et catholiques français*, p. 146; L'Hermite, *L'Anti-Pape*, pp. 277–9; and chapter VIII, pp. 216 and ff. above.
8 See Szajkowski, "French Jews during the Revolution of 1830 and the July Monarchy", p. 121.
9 Reinach, *Histoire de l'Affaire Dreyfus*, III, p. 278; Blumenkranz, ed., *Histoire des Juifs en France*, p. 333.
10 See Louis Durieu, "Le Prolétariat Juif en Algérie", *La Revue Socialiste*, XXIX (1899), pp. 513–33; and Blumenkranz, ed., op. cit., p. 333; see also Victor Hugo,

Choses vues, Souvenirs, Journaux, Cahiers 1830–1846 (Paris, 1972), p. 463; Eugène Aubin, *Morocco of Today* (London, 1906), chapter XVI and *passim;* and Joy Collier, *Algerian Adventure* (London, 1944), pp. 56, 117 and 120, on Morocco; and Memmi, *Portrait d'un Juif,* pp. 155–7 and *passim;* and E. Cohen-Hadria, "Souvenirs. Les milieux juifs de Tunisie avant 1914 vus par un témoin", *Le Mouvement Social,* no. 60 (1967), pp. 89–107, on Tunisia.

11 See Louis Forest, *La Naturalisation des Juifs algériens et l'insurrection de 1871, Etude historique* (Paris, no date), pp. 3–20; and Z. Szajkowski, "The Struggle for Jewish Emancipation in Algeria after the French occupation", in Szajkowski, *Jews and the French Revolutions of 1789, 1830 and 1848,* pp. 1119–32.

12 For the more benevolent attitude towards Jews traditional in Islamic society, see Léon Poliakov, "La Condition juive dans l'Empire des Califes", in Poliakov, *Les Juifs et notre histoire* pp. 34–53; but see also the more pessimistic view of David Littman, "Jews under Muslim Rule in the late Nineteenth Century", *Wiener Library Bulletin,* 28, nos 35–6 (1975), pp. 65–76.

13 Report, Procureur-Général, Algiers, 11 February 1898. AN F^{80} 1688; also Durieu, op. cit., p. 527; F. Dagen, op. cit., pp. 49, 61–2 and 70; Drumont, *FJ,* II, pp. 31–5; Bournand, op. cit., pp. 72–4; Reinach, op. cit., III, p. 277; L'Hermite, op. cit., pp. xxi–xxii, 126–33, 270–4 and 290–3; Bernanos, *La Grande Peur des bienpensants,* p. 343; Speech, Firmin Faure, Daily Report, Prefect of Police, 9 June 1898. APP Ba 106; C.-R. Ageron, *Les Algériens musulmanes et la France (1871–1919)* (Paris, 1968), I, pp. 584–5.

14 Vibert, Préface, L'Hermite, op. cit., p. vi; see also n. 13 above.

15 Viau, op. cit., p. 174; see also Durieu, op. cit., p. 514; F. Dagen, op. cit., pp. 48–9; and Andrieux, *A Travers la République,* pp. 347–8. Eugène-Napoléon Etienne (1844–1921), deputy for Oran 1881–1920 was Sous-Sécrétaire d'Etat for the Colonies in 1887 and 1889–90; Vice-President of the Chamber of Deputies 1892–5, 1902–5 and 1906–14; Minister of the Interior 1905; and Minister of War 1906. He was also the founder and leader of the Colonial Group in the Chamber. Gaston Thomson was deputy for Constantine, then for other Algerian constituencies, for over 50 years; Minister for the Navy 1905–8; and for Commerce 1914. Both men were protégés of Gambetta, members of the Gauche Démocratique, and then of the Alliance Républicaine Démocratique. Neither was unseated by the antisemites in 1898, though Morinaud defeated Thomson in 1919. See *Dictionnaire de biographie française,* Fascicule LXXIII (Paris, 1971), pp. 206–7; Jolly, ed., *Dictionnaires des parlementaires français;* Georges Bonnefous, *Histoire Politique de la Troisième République* (Paris, 1956–1957), I, pp. 407–8 and 412; and II, p. 447; Jacques Chastenet, *Histoire de la Troisième République* (Paris, 1954–1957), II, pp. 142 and 265; III, pp. 217–18, 277–8 and 297; and IV, pp. 21, 66 and 171; Henri Brunschwig, *Mythes et réalités de l'impérialisme colonial français 1871–1914* (Paris, 1960), p. 112; J.P.T. Bury, *Gambetta and the Making of the Third Republic* (London, 1973), p. 58; Martin, op. cit., p. 282.

16 Szajkowski, "Socialists and Radicals in the Development of Antisemitism in Algeria", pp. 262–4.

17 Ibid., *passim;* Bournand, op. cit., pp. 250–4; F. Dagen, op. cit., pp. 47–51.

18 Police report, 30 November 1896. AN F^7 12842; Bournand, op. cit., p. 119; F. Dagen, op. cit., pp. 45–7; L'Hermite, op. cit., pp. 1–4; Sorlin, *"La Croix" et les Juifs,* pp. 115–16 and 171–2.

19 F. Dagen, op. cit., pp. 63–4.

20 Cit. Drumont, *FJ,* II, p. 48.

21 Cit. Reinach, op. cit., III, p. 280; see also Viau, op. cit., p. 177; and Speech, Guérin, Daily Report, Prefect of Police, 1 June 1898. APP Ba 106.

22 See chapter VII n. 114.

23 Dagan, *Enquête sur l'antisémitisme,* pp. 45–6; see also Durieu, op. cit., p. 514; and F. Dagen, op. cit., pp. 51–5.

24 "Maison anti-sémite", "Maison Catholique". L'Hermite, op. cit., pp. 31–48. L'Hermite even noted one shop called "L'Ombrelle Antijuive".

25 Drumont, *FJ*, II, pp. 13–16; Bournand, op. cit., pp. 34–5, 170–1, 221 and 254; F. Dagen, op. cit., pp. 51–5; and Sorlin, *"La Croix" et les Juifs*, p. 115.

26 Vibert, Préface, L'Hermite, op. cit., p. xiv; also ibid., p.x.

27 Reinach, op. cit., III, p. 280; F. Dagen, op. cit., pp. 55–61; Szajkowski, "Socialists and Radicals in the Development of Antisemitism in Algeria", pp. 275–8; R. Goutalier, "Musulmanes et Juifs au Maghreb", Paper given at Colloque sur l'Idée de Race dans la pensée politique française, Aix-Marseille, March 1975, p.6.

28 "ils ont fait mourir *Jésou*"; Vibert, Préface, L'Hermite, op. cit., p. xiv.

29 See Martine Astier Loutfi, *Littérature et colonialisme: L'Expansion coloniale vue dans la littérature romanesque française 1871–1914* (Paris and The Hague, 1971), pp. 76–8; Annie Rouquier and Pierre Soumille, "La Notion de Race chez les Français d'Algérie à la fin du 19e siècle", Paper given at Colloque sur l'Idée de Race, 1975, pp. 1–3; and my "The 'Action Française' in French Intellectual Life", *Historical Journal*, 12 (1969), p. 345.

30 Leroy-Beaulieu, *Les Doctrines de haine*, p. 12; see also Rouquier and Soumille, "La Notion de Race chez les Français d'Algérie", p. 4; and chapter XIII, pp. 456–7 below.

31 For an example of Arab hostility to Jews, see André Gide, *The Journals of André Gide*, Volume I: *1889–1913* (New York, 1955), p. 61 (1896).

32 See Drumont, *FJ*, II, pp 11–13, 17, 20–7, 38–41 and 47; Bournand, op. cit., pp. 35, 72–4, 120, 152 and 170–3; Bernanos, op. cit., pp. 340–2; and Rouquier and Soumille, "La Notion de Race chez les Français d'Algérie", pp. 9–13, who point out that hostile stereotyping of the Arab was still, nevertheless, present.

33 Forest, op. cit., pp. 21–55 (based on the Parliamentary Commission of Enquiry of 1871–2); Charles-André Julien, *Histoire de l'Algérie contemporaine: La Conquête et les débuts de la colonisation (1827–1871)* (Paris, 1964), pp. 452–500.

34 Szajkowski, "Socialists and Radicals in the Development of Antisemitism in Algeria", pp. 264–5; and Ageron, op. cit., I, pp. 600–6.

35 Ageron, op. cit., I, pp. 569–77 and 595–9.

36 "Vexations municipales contre des Juifs". AN F⁸⁰ 1688; Durieu, op. cit., pp. 531–3; and Pierrard, op. cit., pp. 144–6.

37 See Daily Report, Prefect of Police, 11 May 1898. APP Ba 106.

38 F. Dagen, op. cit., pp. 63–7; and Daudet, *Au Temps de Judas*, p. 13.

39 See AN F⁸⁰ 1688; and Viau, op. cit., pp. 307–3. The "Opportunists" had, of course, been the victims of antisemitism in Algeria, and not all Radicals had espoused the cause, as the example of Vibert illustrates. In 1902, all four of the seats gained by the Antisemites in 1898, were taken by Radicals; see Grenier, *Nos Députés, 1902–1906*, pp. 576–80.

40 F. Dagen, op. cit., pp. 69 and 74–5; but, see Ageron, op. cit., I, pp. 590–1, who points out that the connection made by contemporaries between antisemitism and difficulties in the wine trade ignores the fact that the years 1895–1899 were good ones for Algerian viticulture; see also H. Isnard, "Vigne et Colonisation en Algérie 1880–1947", *Annales*, II, (1947), pp 288–300.

41 See AN F⁸⁰ 1688; AN F⁸⁰ 1689; F. Dagen, op. cit., pp. 73 and 75–6; Ageron, op. cit., I, p. 598; and II, pp. 982–9; and, on this and generally, Martin, op. cit., Part 3, chapter II, pp. 225–43.

42 Algeria again experienced antisemitic riots in 1936, when a Right-wing antisemite, Enjalbert, was elected deputy for Oran; see Francis Koerner, "L'Extrême Droite en Oranie (1936–1940)", *Revue d'Histoire Moderne et Contemporaine*, 20 (1973), pp. 574–5.

43 See n. 39 above; also F. Dagen, op. cit., pp. 43–4; and Blumenkranz, ed., op. cit., p. 366.

44 The figure of 150,000, given by Rouquier and Soumille, "Différences et Ressemblances constatées dans l'étude comparative de la notion de races chez les

Français d'Algérie et de Tunisie entre 1890 et 1910", Colloque sur l'Idée de Race, 1975, was revised in discussion by Carol Iancu.
45 Soumille, "L'Idée de Race chez les Européens de Tunisie", pp. 2–4; but see Littman, op. cit., pp. 67–8, for examples of anti-Jewish violence in Tunisia before 1881.
46 Cohen-Hadria, op. cit., p. 97.
47 See Arendt, *The Origins of Totalitarianism*, pp. 185–221; Pierre L. van den Berghe, *Race and Racism: A Comparative Perspective* (New York, 1967), pp. 16–17; Memmi, *Portrait du colonisé*; Christine Bolt, *Victorian Attitudes to Race* (London, 1971), pp. 208–18 and *passim*; Peter Worsley, "Colonialism and Categories", in Paul Baxter and Basil Sansom, eds., *Race and Social Difference: Selected Readings* (Harmondsworth, 1972), pp. 98–101; and Pierre J. Simon, "Portraits Coloniaux des Vietnamiens (1858–1914); and Jean-Pierre Chrétien, "Les Deux Visages de Cham", Colloque sur l'Idée de Race, 1975.
48 Henri Dagan, op. cit., p v.
49 Tharaud, *Petite Histoire des Juifs*, p. 237.
50 Combarieu, *Sept ans à l'Elysée*, pp. v–vi; and, e.g., Report, Police agent, 16 August 1899. AN F⁷ 12923.
51 Péguy, "Les Elections", 24 May 1902, *Oeuvres en prose 1898–1908*, p. 1311.
52 Edmond Picard, *Synthèse de l'antisémitisme* (Paris and Brussels, 1892), p. 40.
53 Viau, op. cit., pp. 142–3.
54 Cit. Bernanos, op. cit., p. 36.
55 Bournand, op. cit., pp. 123–4.
56 E.g. Georges Renard and Elisée Reclus, Henri Dagan, op. cit., pp. 25–6.
57 Cit. Zévaès, *L'Affaire Dreyfus*, p. 182.
58 Isaac, *Expériences de ma vie*, I, p. 116.
59 F. Brunetière, "Revue Littéraire, La France juive", *Revue des Deux Mondes*, 1 June 1886, pp. 693–704; Brunetière, "Après le Procès", ibid., 15 March 1898, pp. 428–30; and Maurras, *Au Signe de Flore*, p. 103.
60 Paléologue,*Journal de l'Affaire Dreyfus*, pp. 105–6, note, no date; and *passim*.
61 See chapter XIX, pp. 703–6 below.
62 See Gide, *The Journals*, I, pp. 89–91, 108, 110, 128, 154, 202, 234–5, 287 and 292.
63 "youtres". Renard, Letters to his sister, August 1886; and to Tristan Bernard, 3 June 1908, *Correpondance*, pp. 60 and 356; see also ibid., pp. 104, 107, 113–17, 190, 192–208, 260, 264, 351 and 370; and Stokes, *Léon Blum*, p. 49.
64 See chapter II, pp. 68–9 above.
65 See Gohier, "Enjuivés", 17 June 1898, *L'Armée contre la nation*, pp. 263–8; and Arbellot, *La Fin du boulevard*, pp. 41–2.
66 See Bournand, op. cit., pp. 65–71; and Benda, *La Jeunesse d'un clerc*, p. 161.
67 See Daudet, *Au Temps de Judas*, p. 67.
68 See Barrès-Maurras, *La République ou le roi*, p. 246 n.
69 Daudet, *Au Temps de Judas*, p. 13.
70 Selznick and Steinberg, *The Tenacity of Prejudice*, pp. 65–6.
71 See Chapter XIII, pp. 483–4 below.
72 Pierrard, op. cit., p. 150; and chapter VI, n. 79 above.
73 Report, Police agent, 2 September 1899. AN F⁷ 12923.
74 Report, Police agent, 14 March 1904. AN F⁷ 12719.
75 Report, Prefect, Marne, 20 January 1896. AN F⁷ 12460.
76 Arendt, op. cit., p. 111.
77 Reinach, op. cit., III, pp. 244 and 276–7.
78 See particularly Paléologue, op. cit., pp. 155–88.
79 See *L'Aurore*, 8 December 1898; and Chapter XIX, pp. 700–1 below.
80 Reinach, op. cit., V, p. 135.
81 See Drumont, *La Dernière Bataille*, p. 412; and chapter XIX, p. 717 below.
82 E.g. Drumont, *Le Testament d'un antisémite*, pp. 74, 208–9 and 222–4; and *DB*, pp. 18–19 and 409.

83 E.g. Drumont, *DB*, pp. 121–4; and Biez, *Les Rothschild et le péril juif*, pp. 3–5; see also chapter XI, pp. 348–50; and chapter XII, p. 399 below.
84 Report, Police agent, 23 April 1898. AN F⁷ 12474.
85 Bournand, op. cit., p. 79.
86 Report, Police agent, 12 February 1898. AN F⁷ 12474.
87 Letter from Dufour to Prefect of Police, no date. APP Ba 1103.
88 Peter, "Dimensions de l'Affaire Dreyfus", pp. 1163–64.
89 See Goguel, *La Politique des partis sous la Troisième République*, p. 117. The novelty in the situation, in contrast to the "reactions" which followed the Revolution of 1848 and that of 1871, was the assumption of the mantle of defender of the social order by "radical" governments, an apparent contradiction marked by the entry of Millerand, a Socialist, into the Waldeck-Rousseau ministry, alongside General de Galliffet, notorious in the labour movement for his part in the suppression of the Paris Commune, which itself foreshadowed the advent to power of Clemenceau and Briand, erstwhile rebels turned strike-breakers in office.
90 Viau, op. cit., p. 266.
91 Reports, Prefect of Police, 1900–1901. AN F⁷ 12458.
92 See Blum, "Les Elections de 1902", *L'Oeuvre de Léon Blum 1891–1905*, pp. 493–507.
93 Viau, op. cit., pp. 316–18.
94 See my "L'Action Française et le mouvement nationaliste français des années 1890 et 1900", Paper given at 4th Colloque Maurras, Aix-en-Provence, March 1974, published in *Etudes Maurrassiennes*, 4 (1980).
95 Pierrard, op. cit., pp. 31–2.
96 Viau, op. cit., p. 307.
97 Drault, *Drumont, La France juive et La Libre Parole*, pp. 295–9 and 310; Pierrard, op. cit., p. 151; Blumenkranz, ed., op. cit., p. 366.
98 Viau, op. cit., p. 344. Marcel Sembat wrote, however, in *L'Humanité* on 26 April 1911 that: "L'antisémitisme est fort à la mode . . .", cit. Eugen Weber, *The Nationalist Revival in France, 1905–1914* (Berkeley, 1959), p. 176, n. 13.
99 Pierrard, op. cit., p. 223; Blumenkranz, ed., op. cit., p. 365; my "L'Action Française et le mouvement nationaliste"; and see Chapter XII, pp. 388–9 below.
100 See Blumenkranz ed., op. cit., p. 366; and Weber, *Action Française*, pp. 89–112. When *La Libre Parole* accused Durkheim in January 1916 of being a German agent, a charge taken up by a senator, Gaudin de Vilaine, Painlevé, the Minister of Public Instruction, vigorously protested, and forced the charge to be withdrawn; see Lukes, *Emile Durkheim*, p. 557.
101 Daudet, *Les Oeuvres dans les hommes*, p. 170; also Pierrard, op. cit., p. 136.
102 See *Les Juifs sous l'Occupation*, Centre de Documentation Juive Contemporaine (Paris, 1945); Robert Aron, *Histoire de Vichy 1940–1944* (Paris, 1954), pp. 218–33, 419–20, 526–8 and 630–1; J. Billig, "La Question Juive", in *La France sous l'Occupation* (Paris, 1959), pp. 145–60; Gérard Walter, *La Vie à Paris sous l'Occupation 1940–1944* (Paris, 1960), pp. 175–93; Henri Amouroux, *La Vie des Français sous l'Occupation* (Paris, 1961), chapter XIV; Olga Wormser-Migot, "De 1939 à 1945", in Blumenkranz, ed., op. cit., pp. 389–421; Poliakov, "Les Juifs à l'heure de Vichy", *Les Juifs et notre histoire*, pp. 166–83. For further brief discussion of antisemitism in the period of the Second World War, see chapter XX below.
103 See Wladimir Rabi, "De 1906 à 1939", in Blumenkranz, ed., op. cit., pp. 380–3; Pierrard, op. cit., pp. 229–86; and Morand, *Les Idées politiques de Louis-Ferdinand Céline*, chapter II, for example.
104 Léon Poliakov, "An Opinion Poll on Anti-Jewish Measures in Vichy France", *Jewish Social Studies*, 15 (1953), pp. 135–50; Ophuls, *The Sorrow and the Pity*, pp. 60–1, 73–83, 137–44 and 147–9.

PART THREE
TYPES OF ANTISEMITISM

CHAPTER X
ECONOMIC ANTISEMITISM

I. "THE JEWISH-FINANCIAL OLIGARCHY"

I N AN ARTICLE IN *LE FIGARO* IN DECEMBER 1897, EMILE ZOLA EXPRESSED HIS sense of bewilderment at the spectacle of a revival of antisemitism:[1]

> The idea of returning to the wars of religion, of reviving religious persecutions, of wishing people to exterminate each other because they belong to one race or another, seems so nonsensical, in our century of emancipation, that such an enterprise seems to me just stupid . . . I cannot believe . . . that such a movement can ever achieve any real significance in France, in this country where the critical spirit, fraternal feelings and the exercise of reason are esteemed.

Other contemporaries shared Zola's inability to accept the apparent irrationality of antisemitism, and many of them therefore explained it as a primarily economic phenomenon, as a means by which rational economic interests were defended or pursued. Such was the opinion of the majority of the academics and journalists who contributed to Henri Dagan's *Enquête sur l'antisémitisme* in 1899. According to Professor Achille Loria:[2]

> At the basis of the doctrinaire antisemitism of today, lies the same essentially economic cause, which engendered the legislative antisemitism of the past. It was the rivalry of Christian capital against Jewish capital which provoked the persecutions of the Jews in the Middle Ages, and their exclusion from the ownership of land, and from places of honour and influence. In the same way, today, it is Christian capitalists and landowners, in competition with Jews, who are agitating for the re-establishment of the old barbarous proscriptions.

The economist E. Levasseur expressed the view that "It is the very difficult economic situation which has revived these religious passions . . .";[3] while Charles Gide, another economist, wrote that antisemitism was "exclusively economic in its causes. It is not an opinion, but the expression of an interest."[4]

Henri Maret, director of *Le Radical*, put forward much the same kind of explanation, saying that the characteristics of contemporary antisemitism were "incontestably economic. People do not detest the Jews because they belong to a different race or to a different religion, but quite simply because it is believed that they are accumulating wealth, and this is coveted."[5] Although placing less emphasis on this economic interpretation, Bernard Lazare, in his study of antisemitism published in 1894, also saw it as an instrument of economic competition, writing that this type of antisemitism was "the most violent . . . the most bitter, and the most basic, since it represented the defence of immediate and selfish interests."[6] Again, Anatole Leroy-Beaulieu, while stressing other aspects of antisemitism as well, concluded that it was a form of "anti-capitalism".[7]

Many features of the antisemitism of the period confirm the validity of this economic interpretation.[8] Antisemites very often directed their attacks against Jews as the agents of capitalism, as bankers, speculators and monopolists, *"accapareurs"* and *"agioteurs"*, the authors of financial crashes and the inspirers and beneficiaries of the impersonal rule of Money. Antisemitism was also closely associated, in particular, with the grievances of small traders and shopkeepers against big department stores and co-operatives, as we have seen; with the reactions of landowners, often noble, to the agricultural depression of the 1880s and 1890s; and with the movement against foreign influence in the French economy, which found expression in Protectionism and in the call to control the influx of immigrant labour. More generally, "Jewish domination" was held to be responsible for the general economic crisis of the later decades of the nineteenth century, and for long-term changes in economic structure. Despite all this, however, analysis of antisemitic ideology and action suggests that it was a reaction to economic phenomena of a less rational kind than the simplistic psychology of some contemporary observers assumed.

But, first, there is no doubt that antisemitism was conceived in economic terms by its creators and supporters. For example, the statutes of the Ligue Nationale Antisémitique de France, founded in 1889, stated that the aim of the organization was to combat "the pernicious influences of the Jewish-financial Oligarchy, whose secret and merciless conspiracy threatens each day more and more the Prosperity, the Honour and the Security of France".[9] Drumont wrote that with F. Laur's attack on Jewish control of the Banque de France in January 1890: "Antisemitism . . . at last showed itself in its real character, in the economic and social sphere."[10] In 1898, he declared that antisemitism was "the natural and logical grouping of all the forces of the nation united against the common enemy: the parasite, the speculator and the traitor.[11]" Such claims were reflected in antisemitic propaganda which made the Jews responsible for short-term economic and financial crises, and also maintained that many of the basic features of the capitalist economy were specifically Jewish.

We have already noted the role of the crash of the Union Générale Bank in the history of French antisemitism. According to I. Levaillant, writing in 1907: "One can affirm with near-certainty that it was at the precise moment that the Union Générale failed, that there germinated the idea that has been the mainstay of antisemitic propaganda, and which has allowed the Jews as a bloc to be held responsible for all public disasters."[12] The journalist Mermeix wrote similarly in 1892: "in 1882 there occurred the crash of the Union Générale, and it is really from that financial catastrophe that one can date the start of the antisemitic Fronde in France."[13] As Verdès-Leroux has shown, the crash was frequently attributed at the time to Jewish influence. *Le Pays*, for example, in February 1882, claimed that it was the work of "this gang of Jews which has invaded the country, which has us in its stranglehold, and which is crowding us out . . ."[14] More important, it was taken as a point of reference by antisemites, and set the pattern for the explanation of subsequent financial and business crises. Gaston Méry, for example, wrote in *La Libre Parole* in November 1902 that the Union Générale crash could be seen "as the last phase of a gigantic struggle between two different worlds, between two societies, between two rival powers . . . It marked the definitive triumph of the Jews in France".[15] Thus, both Drumont and *La Croix* presented the Panama scandal in 1892 as a Jewish affair, as they had attributed the failures of the Comptoir des Métaux and the difficulties of the Comptoir d'Escompte in 1889, to Jewish influence. *La Croix* declared in March 1889:[16]

> The Union Générale was assassinated, because it was competing successfully with the Jews, because its directors were leading Catholics . . . The Panama Company is left to die because it tried to get along without placing itself under the tutelage of Jewish financiers . . . The Comptoir d'Escompte is being rescued, because its capital belongs more to the big financiers than to the people . . .

Drumont had never regarded the Panama Company in this friendly light, and, of course, *La Libre Parole* was instrumental in launching the scandal itself,[17] and in exposing another Jewish speculative swindle, this time with more serious elements of political corruption. Drumont warned in November 1892:[18]

> Jewish Finance will crush yet more unfortunate people . . . one will learn that even companies that one believed to be indestructible, like the Comptoir d'Escompte, are unable to resist a run on them . . . the Jews will have kept up the price of shares up to the last moment; then they will exchange them for gold, surreptitiously, so as not to raise the alarm, and the unfortunate *goyim* will be left with bits of paper worth just as much as those shares with the pictures of Panama on them.

Zola commented with reason in 1897: "We have the antisemites to thank for the dangerous virulence which the Panama scandals exhibited."[19]

This attribution of business scandals and crises to Jewish influence continued into the later 1890s, and seems to have echoed or influenced popular attitudes. The police reported, for example, from Saint-Quentin in January 1895: "The Southern Railways affair is producing a very bad impression here, and people are talking a lot about M. Reinach, who is involved in it. Every time, they say, that some shady business is exposed to the light of day, we see the name of Reinach appear . . ."[20] Joseph Reinach, here referred to, was the nephew of Baron Jacques de Reinach, who committed suicide as a result, it seems, of his alleged implication in the Panama scandal.[21] Moreover, as we have seen, the business crisis of early 1898 was widely blamed on the supposedly Jewish-inspired campaign to reopen the Dreyfus Case. A speaker at a Union Nationale meeting in Paris in February 1898 referred to "this Jewish campaign . . . which is doing so much damage to the business affairs of the country";[22] and, at another Union Nationale meeting in Paris two months later, another speaker claimed that the Jews and the Freemasons were "the cause of the industrial and commercial crisis that France is suffering at the moment".[23] The police sent in reports of the same claim being made in over a dozen provincial towns in the first half of 1898; for example, at Nancy: "Businessmen and industrialists, complaining over the prolongation of the crisis which threatens to stop business altogether, are demanding that their interests be protected against cosmopolitan speculators . . ."[24] In January 1898, in Paris again, Guérin spoke of the intention of Jewish financiers to ruin all rival enterprises, while a speaker at a meeting of the Comité de la Jeunesse Royaliste of the 3rd and 4th *arrondissements* attacked "the Jews whom one finds behind all financial scandals".[25]

This antisemitic interpretation of financial and business crises and scandals must be related to certain structural features of nineteenth-century capitalism in France. As Jean Bouvier has indicated, in this context, the financial scandal was normal rather than abnormal, the natural corollary of a system which combined a high level of state economic patronage with political corruption and a strong penchant for speculative rather than "safe" financial dealings.[26] Such a system needed and attracted small investors, but ruined many of them. The Socialist Zévaès referred to "a middle class, a petty bourgeoisie, which was the victim of the combination of financial centralization and of the swindling of High Finance . . . of vast financial piracies, of huge speculative operations that devastated the money market . . ."[27] Such victims, small investors who saw their savings disappear, rentiers who saw quick fortunes made by others, sought, if not redress, then explanation, and were ready to heed those who claimed to discern behind the apparent chaos of Stock Exchange and credit operations, the unseen hand of the Jew. Drumont wrote that the companies and businesses "that one believed to be indestructible" turned out to be "built of cardboard . . .";[28] he referred to the world of finance as "this world of incoherence . . . of unprecedented disorder . . ."; and declared: "In order to understand the Panama affair, one must imagine Chaos . . ."[29] But, having thus evoked the inherent flux and instability of capitalist finance, Drumont and other antisemites went on to claim that all this was mere appearance. They offered a key to the mysteries of High Finance, by postulating that its vagaries in fact followed a clear plan, and resulted from the deliberate policies of the Jews.[30] Moving closer to reality, antisemites sensed too that the financial scandal, the Stock Exchange gamble, were more than accidental aspects of the capitalist system, and, from their commentary on its crises, they went on to develop a critique of what they conceived to be the essential features of the system itself.

Thus, in the words of Leroy-Beaulieu, antisemites held the Jews responsible for an economic system characterized by "the predominance of material interests, the preponderance of industry, trade and finance . . . the reign of money, the tyranny of gold . . ."[31] "M. Edouard Drumont, in his books", wrote François Bournand in 1898, "has proved that the time has arrived when money dominates everything, corrupts everything, is capable of everything . . . Money is the God of our time . . ."[32] Fifteen years earlier, the Comte de Mun had similarly qualified his time as "the century of Usury".[33] La Croix proclaimed in January 1886: "King Capital, with his court of speculators, stock-brokers, and industrialists, Capital freed from all restraints, from all control . . . there is the seat of corruption!"[34] The antisemitic congress of Christian Democracy at Lyon in November 1896 voted a resolution "totally rejecting capitalism, the modern form of Usura Vorax",[35] a theme developed by a pamphlet published in Roubaix in 1898, which denounced "Usury, that is to say making profits without working for them"; and asked, rhetorically, "Who can deny that the country has been turned into a vast field for usury, a prey to shameful appetites, or that Paris, a city once so French, the capital of civilization, has become today a cosmopolitan centre for the most shameless speculation and exploitation?"[36] At a Union Nationale meeting in Paris in January of the same year, the police reported: "Billiet denounced Capital as the cause of poverty . . . These words provoked applause and sustained shouts of 'Long live the army! Down with the Jews!' "[37] This dimension of the critique of capitalism had been emphasized by Drumont in La France juive. "Today, thanks to the Jew, money, to which the Christian world attached only secondary importance and assigned only a subordinate role has become all-powerful. The power of capitalism concentrated in a small number of hands governs as it pleases the economic life of whole peoples, enslaving its workforce and glutting itself on profits acquired without labour."[38] Capitalism was compared unfavourably with pre-capitalism:[39]

St Louis demonstrated his genius for political economy by placing the producer and the consumer in a direct relationship; he put the two representatives of labour face to face, relegating the middle-man and the parasite to a much humbler position. Being Jewish, today's economic organization is naturally the complete opposite of the Christian organization of St. Louis . . . The Jewish system destroys all guarantees of the integrity of the individual trader and the collective guarantee that had been provided by the guilds, substituting for all this the vague anonymity of the modern firm.

Another element of stability in the old economy had been its basis in landed property, but this, too, had gone, or was under threat. The San Remo Manifesto of the Royalist Pretender, the Duc d'Orléans, declared in 1899 that the causes of the Jewish question "dated back to the time when property in land was outstripped, to a fantastic degree, by other forms of wealth . . ."[40]

As these quotations begin to indicate, what antisemites were objecting to in their critique of capitalism was the supposedly radical change in social relationships which it occasioned, and they were reacting also to a process of rapid and seemingly total social change, over which they felt they had no control. We will discuss their reaction to, or their refusal of, social change, in more detail in Chapter XVI, confining ourselves immediately to aspects that were cast in a specifically anti-capitalist mould. Essential here was the characterization of nineteenth-century society as one dominated by money, a characterization that pointed both to the impersonal and exploitative nature of social relationships, and to the mystery, the vagueness, of the economic process. As we have seen, this characterization was a cliché in antisemitic writing. To mention only a few further examples, Drumont wrote in *La France juive* that "wealth is the only power left";[41] Thiébaud denounced "the dictatorship of money";[42] and an anonymous Catholic theologian told Bournand that antisemitism was "the natural reaction to the way in which the Jews have abused the power of money".[43] For Catholics and for intellectuals, in particular, the dominance of money was seen also as the sign of the dominance of materialism. "Money always has the last word in our time", wrote Drumont; "it bars the way to the development of ideas . . ."[44] Edmond de Goncourt, referred similarly, in an interview published in *La Libre Parole* in February 1897, to "this nineteenth century in which faith in things of the spirit has been lost", in which the Jews "have made money the ruling factor in government, in social life, in war, in everything . . ."[45] As Goncourt suggests, a society in which the things of the spirit, intellectual values, were esteemed was also one with an established hierarchy. "Every intellectual or social Authority is powerless", wrote Drumont again, "corrupted, unable to serve the community. The domination of money is absolute."[46] "When the basis of society is money," commented Edmond Picard, "power rests not with the most intelligent, but with those best equipped to make money, and the talent for making money requires all the vices";[47] and, as a member of the liberal professions, burdened also presumably with a virtuous nature, he referred to "the humiliating yoke of money".[48]

Here, as in their general critique of capitalism, antisemites were giving a particular slant to an analysis that had much wider currency, and of which Marxism was only one sophisticated variant. Many writers in nineteenth-century France shared their dislike of a society increasingly dominated by the cash nexus, and pointed to the deleterious social effects of such a dominance, without necessarily seeing the phenomenon as in any way Jewish. The Genevois Amiel wrote in his *Journal* in 1866, for example:[49]

In our epoch of individualism and of "each man for himself . . .", the movements of the public funds are all that now represent to us the beat of the common heart . . . We feel ourselves bound up with and compromised in all the world's affairs, and we must interest ourselves whether we will or no in the terrible machine whose wheels may crush us at any moment. Credit produces a restless society, trembling perpetually for the security of its artificial basis.

Ferdinand Brunetière, in a critical review of *La France juive* in 1886, to which we have referred, conceded that: "In our modern societies, it is absolutely true that the only criterion for distinguishing among men is money, and that nothing else counts—not birth, education, achievement, even genius—unless a few millions are attached to them".[50] More savagely, and this time with an anti-American slant, Léon Bloy referred, in a letter to René Martineau in 1904, to the fire at the Iroquois Theatre in Chicago as "this consoling carbonization of property-owners and worshippers of the stupid Golden Calf . . ."[51] More significant perhaps, because it came from an arch-critic of antisemitism, was Péguy's comment in 1910, so similar to that of Drumont: "in this modern world wholly preoccupied with money, wholly bound up with money, Christianity is contaminated by money, and sacrifices its faith and its customs for the sake of economic and social peace . . . Money is everything, money dominates the modern world."[52] The triumph of money, the presence of new forms of wealth, was not merely, either, the pretext for rhetorical denunciations. It posed real dilemmas of conscience, especially for wealthy Catholics. Louis Martin, for example, the father of St Thérèse of Lisieux, was a successful jeweller and clock-maker in Alençon. He deliberately avoided any investments that involved the Stock Exchange, and wrote to his daughter Céline: "I feel that I could easily become very interested in the skilful management of my fortune. But the slope is slippery, and I do not wish to go too near this evaluation of perishable riches."[53] That the preoccupation with money-making prevailed at large in society, and had permeated all classes is suggested by contemporary fiction, too. According to Célestine, the lady's maid in Octave Mirbeau's *Journal d'une femme de chambre* (1900): "Worshipping a million! . . . It's a low sentiment, common not only among the bourgeois, but among most of us, small folk, the humble, penniless ones of this world."[54] Similarly, Zola depicted the salesmen and salesgirls of *Au Bonheur des Dames* (1883), "thinking only of money, competing with each other for money, from Monday till Saturday . . ."[55]

Antisemitic writers were therefore responding to a phenomenon that was very generally felt and resented; they simply, in effect, added a new explanatory element to a conventional response, and one that was fairly often present anyway in some form. Péguy was sure that, in a society dominated by money, "the horizontal social distinction between rich and poor has become infinitely more important, more rigid, more absolute . . . than any vertical racial separation of Jews and Christians";[56] but Brunetière did more than echo or refute antisemitic claims in this sphere. Jews, he admitted, had not created modern capitalism, but they seemed to profit inordinately from it.[57] Other writers, while welcoming or admiring the Jewish contribution to the creation of a money economy, also lent support to the idea that it was specifically Jewish. Maupassant, for example, referred in *Mont-Oriol* (1887) to the Jews as destroying "a rural, small-scale economy to replace it with a collective and urban economy", but saw their role as necessary to social and economic progress.[58] A similar stance was adopted by the Dominican Père Didon, who agreed that Jews might be in positions of dominance in modern society through their financial influence, but added that this was simply a sign of their adaptability, which non-Jews should emulate, instead of complaining.[59] It is possible, too, that an antisemitic explanation of capitalism became more attractive as the impact of the money economy increased in the later part of the nineteenth century, both in intensity and in geographical spread, penetrating even rural areas with new ways and values. All those who castigated the power of money were implicitly or explicitly, attacking a relative novelty. Zola, for example, contrasted the money-mindedness of the employees of his giant department store, with the more disinterested attitude of those working for more traditional establishments. In this context, Herriot recalled the attitude of an "old bourgeois family" from the Aube in the late 1880s: "No one ever gave lectures about honesty, but honesty in all forms was exemplified all the time. Nor did one ever hear people talking about money."[60] All of this makes it easier to understand the appeal of this aspect of antisemitism at the time. As Lyautey wrote to a friend from Madagascar in June 1901: "Ah! the day that you discover a formula which attacks speculation and shady finance, I shall applaud with both hands, since I see very well what both consume and spoil, but I do not see what they fertilize and produce, nor what moral and social needs they fulfil."[61] For Lyautey, himself, antisemitism may not have been that formula, but for many others it was.

Beyond the cash nexus itself, two features of the capitalist economy in particular were singled out by antisemites as the special and crucial areas of Jewish activity and responsibility: its tendency towards concentration and monopolism; and its dependence on credit. As Guérin told a gathering of Les Amis de Morès in July 1896: "the present economic order . . . is the work of monopolists and speculators . . ."[62] The theme of Jewish monopolism was a constant feature of antisemitic propaganda of the 1880s and 1890s. It figured in an important way in Barrès's Nancy campaign of 1889.[63] A brochure, entitled *Justice, Egalité!*, put out in the 1890s, called for "legal action against the Jewish monopolists."[64] A poster, put up in May 1898 in Charleville, Perpignan and other towns, asked: "Where are the monopolists?", and replied: "in the Jewish community."[65] *Le Complôt juif*, a broadsheet published in 1898, presented an alleged programme for the Jewish domination of France, which involved cornering whole sections of the economy: "Trade and speculation, both particularly profitable sectors, must never be allowed to slip from Jewish hands, and first of all, the trade in alcohol, in butter, in bread and in wine must be monopolized . . ."[66] Guérin again, in a talk given at Bordeaux in May 1897, spoke of the Jewish "monopolization" of the French economy,[67] and, more specifically, he told a meeting of the Cercle Antisémitique d'Etudes Sociales in Paris in February 1898: "The Jews have taken over the three mainsprings of the economy: money, credit and transport."[68] *La Croix*, in 1894, denounced the Jewish monopoly of mines and petroleum.[69] The most extended development of this theme was found in the writings of Drumont. "Wherever you turn", he wrote in 1891, "you will find a syndicate of monopolists, who in order to realize yet higher profits, do not hesitate to put the existence of the nation itself in jeopardy."[70] In a long chapter in *La Fin d'un monde* (1889), entitled "Les Monopoles", he exposed what he called "the odious monopoly, the monopoly that will end by arousing popular anger against the Jews and their friends . . . the monopoly exercised over all the basic necessities, not only of industry, but of life itself"; and he instanced the supposed Jewish monopolies over the markets in wheat, sugar, coffee and copper, and also over the newspaper press, the book-trade, and big department stores.[71] As *Le Complôt juif* indicates, the theme of Jewish monopoly was related to that of Jewish domination and of the supposed Jewish world conspiracy, which we will discuss in chapter XII. Drumont claimed, for example, that the Jews were planning "to crush France completely, to make it a colony in the hands of the financiers of Israel, and to expropriate the French in favour of all the Jews in the world."[72] Similarly, according to a Union Nationale broadsheet put out in November 1897: "The Jews control everything, big business and industry, and have turned the French into a herd of milch cows."[73] This lent the theme a perennial quality, made explicit, for example by the Jesuit Père Constant, who wrote in 1897 that "The Jews had been the monopolizers of wealth in every century . . .";[74] but it also had a topicality, which helps to explain its appeal at the end of the century. Père Constant, like other antisemites, claimed that monopolization was intensifying, and here, as with the critique of the money economy generally, antisemitic analysis was part of a wider debate related to real structural changes in the economy. Socialists, in particular, pointed to the trend towards the concentration of the means of production in larger units and fewer hands, and denounced private monopolies.[75] The socialistic note on which Drumont concluded his discussion in *La Fin d'un monde* would thus have special resonance: "The great banking house, the big factory backed up by a Jewish syndicate, the department store, all cast their shadow on the horizon like the feudal castle of the past, and small firms, like the small dwellings of old, are afraid of their terrible neighbours."[76]

Antisemitic attacks on speculative finance, on the Haute Banque and the Jewish banker were similar in kind, projecting fears of the mysterious workings of the economy on to fantasy figures of giant stature and power, and reflecting in this way very general anxieties;[77] but the convention here was more exclusively antisemitic, and was almost certainly much older and better-established. A development of the traditional association of the Jews with usury and money-lending, the theme of the "Jewish bank" was common by the time of the July Monarchy. Pierre Leroux, for example, explained in *L'Encyclopédie Nouvelle* in January 1846, that by "the Jewish spirit" he meant "the profit principle, the interest in lucre, in gain, the spirit of business and speculation; in a word, the spirit of the banker."[78] The same association was maintained in such works as J.-B. Capefigue's *Histoire des grandes opérations financières* (1855–60),[79] reappearing as a central theme of late nineteenth-century antisemitism. The General Assembly of the Oeuvre des Cercles d'Ouvriers called in 1889 to celebrate the "Counter-Centenary of the French Revolution" appealed to the government "to withdraw from Jewish banks all influence over financial operations".[80] Drumont asserted that the Jews were "the absolute masters of the Banque de France";[81] and, as we have seen, the first campaign of *La Libre Parole* in 1892 was against the renewal of the privileged status of the Bank. Drumont boasted: "The days of the cosmopolitan Haute Banque are now counted. Thanks to us, the names of the plutocrats who incarnate monopolistic and scheming Jewry are engraved on the minds of the people from which nothing can efface them."[82] Jacques de Biez wrote about the same time that: "Our country is the prey of the German Jewish bank. Its life is being gambled away by a few Barons of Usury, dragged up from the ghettos of Germany . . ."[83] To this nationalistic note, Picard added the element of increasing concentration: "The attack on the Haute-Banque, on the Stock Exchange, on the Jews, it is all the same thing . . . Almost unaided the Jew controls the Haute Banque, and is grabbing hold of small local banks. In most towns of any importance, credit depends entirely on the Jew."[84] The same themes occurred in propaganda of the late 1890s. After an attack on Jews and Freemasons, a speaker at a Union Nationale meeting in Paris in February 1898 called for the suppression of the Haute Banque and of "organizations that engaged in speculation under the cover of anonymity".[85] During the election campaign of 1898 in Paris, candidates claimed that "the Banque de France is . . . in Jewish hands", and denounced "Jewish financiers . . ."[86] More generally, Léon Daudet, who wrote articles attacking Jewish financiers for *La Libre Parole* in the early 1900s, declared that "the nineteenth century has been the century par excellence of banks and of finance, that is the Jewish century . . ."[87] And the deputy abbé Gayraud told Bournand in 1898: "The Haute Banque means the Jews, led by Rothschild . . . and the title of Toussenel's book is just as topical as it was fifty years ago: the Jews are still and more than ever, the rulers of our epoch."[88]

As this reminds us again, the antisemites were working in a well-worn tradition. The Jewish banker and financier, for example, was one of the stereotypes of nineteenth-century French fiction, from Baron Nucingen in Balzac's *La Maison Nucingen* (1838), to Justus Steinberger in Zola's *Paris* (1898) and Ali Habenichts in Claudel's *Le Pain dur* (1918).[89] Maupassant's Walter in *Bel-Ami* (1885) was a typical example: "He had become, in a few days, one of the masters of the world, more powerful than kings, one of those men who make others bow their heads and tremble, who bring out in others all that is low in the human heart, every cowardice and envy. He was no longer Walter the Jew, the boss of a disreputable bank . . . He was Monsieur Walter the Jewish millionnaire."[90] This stereotype was probably an accurate reflection of popular attitudes, and certainly reflected popular usage. Toussenel explained his use of the word *"Juif"*: "this word is used in its popular sense: *Juif,* banker, money dealer".[91] Drumont claimed that the eighteenth-century financier Law, who figured in school-book historiography, was a Jew, adducing the etymology: "Law (Lewis, Levy)",[92] possibly another reflection of a popular stereotype. Whatever the truth of this, the fictional stereotype was adopted and continued by numerous antisemitic novels of the 1890s and 1900s, including Ohnet's *Nemrod et Cie* (1892), Bourget's *Cosmopolis* (1893), Vogüé's

Les Morts qui parlent (1899), Paul Adam's *Le Mystère des foules* (1895), Champsaur's *Lulu* (1900), and J.-H. Rosny (aîné)'s *La Juive* (1907).[93]

The villain in Champsaur's novel was Baron Alphonse de Mothschild, tribute to the fact that the most powerful symbol of Jewish financial power, the Jewish banker par excellence remained at the start of this century what it had been earlier in the nineteenth century for Toussenel, Proudhon and their contemporaries:[94] Rothschild. And there is no doubt that this was an authentic popular symbolization; "as rich as the Rothschilds" was apparently a common figure of speech by the 1840s, if not before,[95] and attacks on the Rothschilds were an ingredient of early French socialist propaganda, seeking popular support. Antisemites of the 1880s and 1890s made full use of the theme. Drumont made continual references to the power of the Rothschilds and continually attacked them. He referred in *La France juive* to "the preponderant role played by the house of Rothschild under the July Monarchy".[96] But the Rothschild influence did not end there. In 1890, he declared: "Rothschild is the Grand Vizier of France, as he was, in the last elections, the Great Elector";[97] and, in 1891, he wrote that the Third Republic was "no longer the Republic of the French, but the Kingdom of Rothschild . . ."[98], a charge reiterated in 1894: Rothschild, whose grandfather had entered Paris at the heels of Blücher, is now "our king and master."[99] Such claims were a commonplace of antisemitic writing. Jules Guérin made repeated references to "the omnipotence of the Rothschilds".[100] Biez wrote a book, *Les Rothschild et le péril juif* (1891); Rochefort an article, entitled "Haroun al Rothschild", in 1898.[101] Picard referred in 1892 to "the Rothschilds, these superJews, who are so marvellously the incarnation of their race and its all-powerful type".[102] Jewish pride in the Rothschilds—*L'Univers Israélite* boasted in April 1889 that they were "the greatest financial power of our time"[103]—only increased their suitability as a general target for abuse in the press and public meetings. Significantly, such ritual attacks on the Rothschilds were not confined to the specifically antisemitic press and antisemitic meetings. The failure of the Union Générale and other financial disasters were blamed on Rothschild by Socialists and by antisemites.[104] Attacks occurred later in *La Petite République*[105] as well as *La Croix* and *La Libre Parole*[106] and, during the first six months of 1898 in Paris, were made by speakers at meetings organized by antisemitic groups, for example at a meeting of "the antisemites of Montmartre" in March, but also at a gathering of La Jeunesse Révolutionnaire Internationaliste, and by Jaurès at a big rally in June.[107] This simply confirms, as Memmi has written, that "The economic symbol of the Rothschilds formed part of the objective language and was common to everyone."[108] However, the antisemites extended the attack on the Rothschilds from the sphere of verbal cliché to that of action. F. Laur denounced Rothschild's alleged control of the Banque de France in the Chamber of Deputies in January 1890; and in November 1891, as we have seen, 30 deputies supported a motion calling for the expulsion of the Rothschild family from France. In May 1892, Morès organized a hostile demonstration at a Rothschild wedding.[109] In 1893, Morès and Vallée concocted a plan to kidnap Alphonse de Rothschild; while in 1896, after gamekeepers on one of the Rothschild estates near Paris had shot a poacher, Drumont sent down reporters from *La Libre Parole* in an attempt to stir up trouble among the tenants.[110] Viau, Drumont and Guérin made several attempts also to provoke members of the Rothschild family to fight duels with them, notably through a campaign of abuse against Henri de Rothschild in *La Libre Parole* in 1900. This campaign, aimed at reviving the flagging circulation of the newspaper backfired, at least in financial terms, since Henri de Rothschild sued Viau and Drumont for defamation, and was awarded 20,000 francs in damages.[111]

The function of the Rothschild myth was clearly summarized by Barrès in an article in *Le Figaro* in 1892, that is worth quoting at length:[112]

All these banking and financial influences are resumed in a single influence that has finally become dominant, partly via the businesses which it owns itself, much more by the way in which it has been able to bring to catastrophe all those who have tried to set up a rival power in face of it. This influence, notorious in the popular imagination, is the influence of Rothschild. Everything ends up each morning on the desk of such a man. First, there are the concerns held directly in his name: mines, factories, railways, banks. Then there are thousands of miles of railway network, over which, under his authority, passes ceaselessly to and fro, in a tumult of iron and steam, the movement of men and goods which creates the economic life of an immense area of the country. There are also mining regions scattered over the North and the South of France. There, whole populations live at his mercy; the ground is excavated, scooped out in every direction by his workings, right under the foundations of the houses and the roots of the crops. But, elsewhere too, where his power is not apparent, it is probably just as great. In those great credit establishments, seemingly independent, where so many small fortunes are brought together, in that huge and feverish market of the Stock Exchange where all wealth is made and unmade from one moment to the next, none is strong enough not to feel always the pressure of such a supremacy, not constantly to worry about what its next move might be. There seems indeed no limit to what Rothschild can do, since the finances of several of the great European Powers are completely dependent on him!

Rothschild was thus the manipulator, the master of the apparently chaotic economic world. This world was alien, threatening, about to undermine all that seemed most stable, hearth and land, constantly in flux, but the idea that it had a master, albeit an evil one, perhaps the Evil One, was more comfortable than a blunt confrontation of unregulated anarchy.[113]

Also to be noted here is the obvious connection made between money and power. In capitalist society, the economic sphere was no longer subordinate, nor even distinct. "Money is the governing power", wrote Picard, "because money buys everything else."[114] So, as we have seen, Rothschild, the Jews, were not only masters of the economy, but of the State, and the formal governmental apparatus, though they exercised this power indirectly through political corruption. "At the present time, no politician, be his Christian sentiments never so sincere, is invulnerable to the terrible power of money . . .", wrote Drumont in 1886.[115] "Jewish finance", echoed Léon Daudet, "by enslaving and dominating successive democratic politicians, became the real ruler of the democratic Republic. The Republic is the reign of money . . ."[116] Abbé Lémann claimed unsurprisingly therefore that the Jews had originally bought their Emancipation in the first National Assembly;[117] and from this first step they had gone on to achieve a position as tyrants. Daudet, again, referred to "the financial tyranny of the Semites";[118] and Goncourt in 1897 evoked a kind of parody of the Ancien Régime, with "the money-lords of France set over a population of poor Catholics held in slavery".[119] As we have seen, the Dreyfusard campaign was generally seen by antisemites as a prime example of Jewish finance-based political power. Daudet, for example, wrote that "The anti-national profligacy of the powers of money was the instigator of the Dreyfus Affair. These powers fed the press, and corrupted Parliament and public opinion",[120] an interpretation that was not entirely consistent with the idea that the Republic was an entirely Jewish instrument. More important, however, than this typical ambiguity, was the role played by the latter assertion in arguments for Right-wing political remedies, as we shall see later.[121]

In the economic sphere, again, antisemites directed their attacks against specific institutions and called for specific reforms, though they characteristically had no very clear or consistent programme. As we have seen, Guérin and others called for a reform of the constitution of the Banque de France. Guérin also proposed a reform of the way in which French railways were financed and operated: "Fares should be proportional to the quantities of goods transported, and shareholders' dividends would then cease to be subsidized to the present excessive extent",[122] a reference to the fact that railway companies offered proportional fare reductions for long-distance movement of goods, and that the government guaranteed a certain return on capital invested in what were still private companies.[123] On another tack, Poccaton, at a meeting of the Cercle Antisémitique d'Etudes Sociales in Paris in June 1898, called on the antisemitic deputies to work for the reduction of the National Debt, which was said to be "entirely in the hands of the Jews"; and, in March the same year, a speaker at a meeting of La Jeunesse Antisémite et Nationaliste made a more common plea for "Protectionism, and roundly criticized Free Trade, calling for a reform of import tariffs".[124] Drumont had complained of "unfair foreign competition" in French markets in La France juive;[125] and Protectionism was supported by most antisemitic deputies, as it was, of course by the majority of Republican politicians.[126] Calls were also made, as we shall see, for raising the patente tax paid by department stores, and for the restriction and control of immigrant labour; and Drumont demanded a reform of the legislation dealing with large companies, which he saw were acquiring "a governmental character".[127]

However, the impression left by the economically-orientated propaganda of late nineteenth-century French antisemitism is not of a programme of specific reforms based on a rational analysis of the structure of the economy, perceived in realistic terms, but rather of a floundering attempt to come to terms with

phenomena that were barely understood, and, for that reason, feared. Antisemites were right in thinking that banks made excessive profits, and losses,
through speculating with funds entrusted to them for long-term investment,[128] for example; they were right in thinking that the holders of railway
stock were being subsidized at the expense of taxpayers; but they were clearly
wrong in their ascription of these and other features of the economic system
to the machinations of the Jews. To understand the mis-direction of their
analysis, it is necessary to remember the presence of what Memmi has called
"the morbidity of the economic situation of the Jew".[129] Like other minorities
in pre-industrial societies, the Jews fulfilled certain specialist functions in the
economies of European societies, trading, peddling, making clothes, money-
lending.[130] The Christian prohibition of usury, and the reluctance of societies
based on kinship ties to engage in exchanges involving cash save through
"foreigners",[131] had rendered definitive the association of Jews with dealings
involving money, and thus with capitalist activity, though Jews, of course, had
no monopoly in this sphere. Jewish segregation in Christian society had moreover perpetuated and accentuated their specialization both in capitalist and
in marginal economic roles, since it was here alone, until Emancipation and
beyond, that Jews over the generations built up expertise and networks.[132]
The antisemitic interpretation of capitalism must also have owed its appeal
to its very simplicity, and here one must remember that many essential aspects
of the capitalist economy were still in late nineteenth-century France novelties
for most people and thus things remote and mysterious. Zola, who was ignorant of the world of finance until he came to prepare *L'Argent* (1891), referred
in the first chapter of the novel to "the mystery of financial operations into
which very few French intellects penetrate".[133] Drumont, himself, in an
unguarded moment admitted his relative ignorance, too, of "financial matters".[134] But it was not simply "high finance" that was unfamiliar. By 1914,
more than half the French population was still rural, and only 15% of it lived
in big cities of over 100,000 inhabitants.[135] Direct experience of the urban
market economy was thus limited, and its intrusion into the agricultural sector
was a recent phenomenon in many areas.[136] Popular experience of banks, in
the form of deposit banks was still in its infancy;[137] paper money was often
regarded with a suspicion that Drumont, like other "populists" was able to
voice.[138] Fear of investing in anything but land, mortgages, or, perhaps,
government stock, was still strong.[139] Popular knowledge of economics, of
course, was virtually non-existent.[140] Moreover, linking a traditional and hated
Jewish specialism,[141] still the butt of antisemitic attack,[142] with the comparatively "late" modernization of the French economy, usury was still a social
reality, not only in the countryside, but also in the capital. Georges de Lauris
remembered that in the 1890s: "The usurer was not yet outmoded", being
much used by young men with expectations.[143] Where the usurer was not a
familiar figure, where he was not a Jew, the stereotype of the Jewish usurer
was kept alive via fiction, notably that of Balzac.[144] It is not surprising
therefore that antisemites misunderstood the real role of Jews in French

economic life, and that they transposed that role from the real and historical, to the mythical level.

Various contemporary critics of antisemitism pointed out this basic misunderstanding. As early as 1846, Leroux had argued: "It is in part the persecutions of which they have been the victims from the beginning of their history that have caused that spirit of lucre and speculation which still makes the Jews odious to so many of the peoples among whom they live . . ."[145] Leroy-Beaulieu explained that Jews had come to exercise the intermediary commercial professions and to act as financiers, not through "any innate vocation, resulting from their semitic origin", as the antisemites supposed, but because "over many generations, all other professions have been systematically closed to them", and because Christians had been officially banned from practising usury.[146] Several of the contributors to Dagan's *Enquête* made the same socio-historical observation, for example Levasseur, who declared:[147]

> It is incontestable that the Jews have a genius for financial and commercial affairs; the experience of their ancestors, who were placed in very particular conditions of existence, seem to have been handed on to them today. Thanks to their extraordinary activity, to their obstinate hard work, and to the constant application of their minds to business, they have attained positions of exceptional wealth which have aroused jealousy and envy. If they have profited from the economic situation, it is because they had been prepared to do so over a long period.

Bernard Lazare also stressed that the connection between the Jews and capitalist activity had a concrete historical explanation: "Jewish Emancipation was connected with the history of the preponderance of industrial and speculative capital . . ."[148] Both these quotations betray a tendency in their authors towards attributing a certain role in the development of capitalism to an essential "Jewishness", belying their historical environmentalism, a tendency that is obvious in the work of their contemporary Werner Sombart.[149] This is mentioned only to indicate the enormous appeal of such essentialist explanations even for scholarly historians, and thus to place in context the much more pronounced flight from historical relativism on the part of antisemites.

They sometimes admitted that the preponderance of Jewish capital had a historical dimension, but they attributed it, nevertheless, to basically ahistorical Jewish characteristics. Picard, for example, referred to "the Jews' dominating faculty, the faculty for enriching themselves";[150] and told Dagan that "the Jew acts in Aryan civilization like his congenerate the Saracen when he scoured the Mediterranean with his piratical corsairs"; it was simply "the form of the pillage that had changed, becoming intellectual, expressing itself in Stock Exchange forays"; "the character of the struggle of Aryan and Semite", he maintained, ". . . is first and foremost ETHNIC in origin . . ."[151] Drumont in *La France juive* asserted that Semites lacked all creativity and were essentially parasitic, and wrote of Paul Bert that "his legendary rapacity . . . proved his racial origin"[152] Goncourt, again, in 1897, referred to the Jews as "that race, which has, without a doubt, a special aptitude for acquiring capital . . ."[153] Although the formulation of this idea in such explicitly racial terms was not all that common, it was frequently expressed through the claim that Jewish economic success stemmed from the exercise of particularly Jewish moral qualities,[154] and, more particularly, that it could be attributed to Jewish cupidity, dishonesty, malpractices and fraud. Proudhon wrote of the Jew in *Césarisme et Christianisme* (1883): "He is an intermediary, always fraudulent and parasitic, who operates, in trade as in philosophy, by means of falsification, counterfeiting [and] horsedealing . . ."[155] Another Socialist, Jules Vallès, in 1881, evoked "Shylock the self-interested, the miser, the Jew, the man after his pound of flesh!"[156] Chirac, in *Les Rois de la République* (1888), referred to Jewish "intrigues", and to an inherent Jewish inclination towards swindling and theft.[157] In a different tradition, Léon Bloy in *Le Salut par les Juifs* (1892), presented Abraham's bargaining with God over the fate of Sodom and Gomorrah as "the first Jewish speculation", and referred to "the notorious Jewish cupidity . . . that instinct for profiteering and double-dealing . . ."[158] The Royalist satirical magazine, *Le Triboulet*, expressed the same commonplace in November 1894: "The Jew is just a mixture of a robber and a ruffian . . .";[159] while a play performed at a soirée given by the Union Nationale of Roanne in December 1898, according to the police, showed the Jew as "a crook taking every opportunity to deceive those with whom he does business".[160] At a higher level of sophistication, Léon Daudet wrote in 1896 that "the Jew is in a class of his own. Love, hatred, joy and sorrow are with him displaced, distorted, unrecognizable . . . The Jew has no pride, no tact, no sense of honour, no pity, no capacity for anger. He is thus able to insinuate himself into the confidence of Christians and set them against each other . . ."[161] According to Drumont, too, the Jew was similarly "lacking in all moral sense, without scruples, convinced that other people are of no account, and that he need not bother about hurting them . . ."[162] It was "the theory of Rothschild that a promise made to a non-Jew did not engage a Jew".[163] Moreover, the whole Jewish financial system "reposed on a vast imposture . . ."[164]

As we shall see, this kind of accusation was made use of in the antisemitic campaign against Jewish stores, and, as the quotation from Picard indicates, it was related also to a more developed racialism. It also again reflected a view of the Jew that was deeply embedded in the popular mentality, and expressed in common parlance. According to the *Dictionnaire de l'Académie* in the middle of the nineteenth century: "*Juif* [is] used familiarly of all who show a great avidity for money and keenness to obtain it . . . This merchant is a real Jew."[165] Many examples of this or similar usage can be cited from literature through the century, and a few must suffice from high fiction. The miller in George Sand's *Le Meunier d'Angibault* (1852) utters the semi-proverbial: "Be a fighter in war, and a Jew with the Jews!"[166] The money-lender Lheureux in Flaubert's *Madame Bovary* (1857) tells Emma that she may repay him when she wishes, explaining: "we are not Jews!"[167] Saint-Potin in Maupassant's *Bel-Ami* says of Walter: "The boss? Now there's a real Jew! We won't ever change them. What a race!" And he went on to cite instances of "an astonishing avarice, of that avarice peculiar to the Children of Israel, penny-pinching, hagglings worthy of a housewife, shameful reductions and discounts begged for and obtained, all expressive of the life style of a usurer and a pawnbroker."[168] Examples of a prejudice perennial in Christian society, such clichés probably served, by the end of the nineteenth century, to label and explain changes in business practice inherent in the process of economic concentration, and particularly in the retail sector. Drumont saw credit sales as a form of Jewish usury;[169] and Léon Daudet lamented in 1911 that "business and industrial transactions used to be conducted with an openness and a probity that are only found now in the very few firms that have still escaped the foreign yoke."[170]

The same appeal to absolute essences to explain contingent realities, evident in the idea of innate Jewish economic qualities, can be seen in the quasi-metaphysical identification of the Jew with Money or Gold as such. As we have seen, antisemites presented the money economy as something specifically Jewish. Drumont said of La France juive that "it attacked . . . the formidable power of money".[171] The Belgian Socialist Vandervelde told a meeting of Collectivist students in Paris in February 1898 that Marx had wanted modern society to free itself from "Jewry, that is to say from the régime of money."[172] "The Jews are the money-people!", declared Goncourt in 1897;[173] and Maurras wrote about the same time: "People think that the Jews just have the money, but Money has delivered everything else into their hands . . ."[174] But there was more to this identification than simply a misguided economic argument. The Jew was quite literally identified with the substance and the symbol in whose manipulation he was supposed to be adept. According to Drumont, "Money was incarnated in the Jew";[175] and Jacques Piou wrote that, for the antisemitic leader, "the Jews personified the accursed Mammon . . ."[176] These religious connotations can also be seen in Balzac's assertion that Money was the "God of the Jews";[177] and are developed in Bloy's Le Salut par les Juifs.[178] As Memmi reminds us, "Judas betrayed his master for money".[179]

The abstract entity, Money, a symbol of much more than economic significance, was lent further, magical, power and meaning, when it was evoked in the form of Gold. Arthur Meyer, the Jewish editor of Le Gaulois, who made no secret of his having a certain sympathy for antisemitism wrote: "A merciless war must be waged against Money . . . We must break the Golden Calf";[180] and the incidental or the deliberate identification of the Jew with gold in this way was a commonplace of antisemitic writing. Balzac's Genestas in Le Médecin de campagne (1833), for example, related of a Jew whom he met in Poland on the retreat from Moscow: "The frost had not so stiffened the old father Jew's fingers but that he could count gold fast enough; he had thriven uncommonly during our reverses. That sort of gentry lives in squalor and dies in gold."[181] An old admirer of the actress Rachel told Mme. Steinheil that: "Rachel loved love and loved gold."[182] While obviously related to such semi-traditional associations, with their sexual connotations, similar statements by antisemites at the end of the century were usually more deliberate, and formed

some kind of comment on the capitalist economy as such. Paul Adam wrote
of the Jews in his novel *L'Essence du Soleil* (1890): "The priests of the Golden
Calf have made a religion of the idolatrous worship of monetary symbols
. . ."[183] For abbé Lémann, "gold had always been the great power of this
people", but was the instrument in particular of their "preponderance" in
modern society.[184] *Le Peuple Ardennais* announced in November 1899 that
its programme was "to free the country from the Jewish doctrine that upholds
the cult of gold in commercial and industrial matters to the detriment of the
independence of the citizen and of human dignity."[185] But gold as a symbol
lost nothing of its resonance, in antisemitic propaganda, for being used in an
economic argument. Drumont, who entitled a collection of his articles, published in 1896, *De l'Or, de la boue, du sang,* wrote of Rembrandt in *La France
juive:* "His work is Jewish in colour, it is yellow, that warm and burning yellow,
like a mediaeval Jew's badge reflected in gold . . ."[186] A pamphlet, *La Fin de
la France,* seized by the police in August 1899, declared, in ritual fashion, that
the main weapon of the Jews was "Gold, Gold, Gold!"[187] Harnessing the
symbol in a piece of socio-economic analysis, Maurras wrote in 1905:[188]

> From the authority of princes of our race, we have passed under the rod
> of the merchants of gold . . . This Gold certainly represents a powerful
> Force, but a force with no signature, no identifying mark; Gold escapes
> responsibility and thus vengeance. It is hard, impersonal, but volatile. Its
> reign can be either that of a friend or that of an enemy, that of a compatriot
> or that of a foreigner. It can serve, without one knowing, Paris, Berlin or
> Jerusalem. This domination, the most absolute, yet the least responsible, is
> nevertheless that which prevails in the countries which call themselves
> advanced . . . Gold, infinitely divisible, is also the great divider . . .

And, in the same vein, *Le Complôt juif* presented the alleged programme of
the Jews in these terms: "When we have become the sole possessors of all the
world's gold, real power will be finally ours . . . for gold is the greatest power
in the world . . . gold is the driving force, the recompense, the instrument of
all that man fears and desires . . . this is the real mystery, the key to the
universe, to the future!"[189]

Here we have a prime example of the irrational mode of economic explanation adopted by the antisemites, but also a clear indication of the mechanism
of that explanation. What alarmed them about the economic system, what
they tried in some way to come to terms with and to exorcize was its threatening mystery, "that mysterious power of finance which one cannot resist", as
Drumont put it,[190] "the Minotaur which is about to devour us", in the more
colourful expression of Picard.[191] This power was undefined, characterized by
"anonymous organizations engaged in speculation", by "anonymous and irre-
sponsible companies",[192] by Money, itself, whose essence was "its fluidity
. . . its mobility . . ."[193] As such, it was uncontrollable, being based, moreover,
on "the floating debt" and on "capital freed from all restraints, from all control
. . ." By positing a secret manipulation of the economy by the Jews, antisemites
could both express its lack of definition and controllability, for so it must seem

to non-Jews until they were enlightened, and, at the same time, counter and exorcize that lack, that chaotic void, by providing the key to its apparent mysteries.

A further development of this defining function of antisemitism can be seen in the distinction drawn between "good" and "bad" money, "good" and "bad" capital. This can be seen at the simplest level in a letter published in *Le Lillois* in January 1891 from a trader "indignant that the money of Catholics ends up in Jewish purses . . ."[194] But the distinction involved a much wider condemnation of non-productive wealth. According to Drumont: "With the Semite, everything starts and ends with the Stock Exchange; his economic activity is purely a speculation."[195] "The huge fortunes of the Jews", he wrote in *La France juive*, ". . . are not the fruit of real work . . . the Rothschild family . . . never discovered a mine, or brought new land into cultivation . . . Jewish wealth . . . is essentially parasitical and usurious, it is not the fruit of labours built up over generations, but the result of speculation and theft . . . Although he extracts all the profit from it, the Jew scorns manual labour, the labour of workshops and fields; he only admires the broker, the middleman . . ."[196] Elsewhere, he contrasted money gained through speculation with "money well earned", and opposed "money-capital" to "intellectual capital".[197] And in a letter, read at a public meeting in Paris in March 1898, he declared: "On the one hand, there is France, a France which is hard-working, active, creative, productive, whose children wish only to live honestly by their labour; on the other, there is a handful of Jews, cosmopolitans and money merchants who want to live in opulence and luxury at the expense of those who produce."[198] The same point was made by other antisemites. Chirac provided this definition of "Jewry" in 1883: "Consumption without production, that is to say living at the expense of others, constitutes *parasitism*. Elevated to a system and exercised by means of the monopolization of the symbols of exchange, this constitutes *Jewry*."[199] From 1891, *La Croix*, while continuing its attacks on High Finance and the Stock Exchange, contrasted the speculation associated with both, and which was bad, with serious business investment, which was good, and made Jewish involvement the criterion for distinguishing the former.[200] Picard explained to Dagan that his opposition to "the formation of monstrous Jewish fortunes" lay in the fact that they represented "the accumulation of wealth simply for the purpose of speculation, with nothing socially useful to show for it . . ."[201] A speaker at a Union Nationale meeting in Vincennes in January 1898 again made the distinction between Jewish capital, which was liquid and could, at any moment, be taken out of the country, and Catholic capital which served society and nation.[202] The poster, "Les Accapareurs où sont-ils?", put up in various towns in 1898 drew a similar contrast between Jewish and Catholic wealth, this time the wealth of the religious orders:[203]

The wealth of the religious orders comes from the family or personal wealth of their members, or from donations and gifts freely given them. The Money of the religious orders is used to build many religious houses—which provides employment for workers—it serves also to provide a refuge for the poor, for the sick, for orphans and for old people . . . The Money of the Jew, however, derives more often than not from sinful dealings on the Stock Exchange, from criminal speculations, from financial intrigues and the most ignoble swindling. The Money of the Jew becomes foreign money—it serves purely selfish interests; it is used to strangle trade, to acquire monopolies, to destroy our industry; it is the instrument of voracious usury and of treason.

This contrast so firmly drawn in antisemitic ideology demonstrates an attachment to the older economic values of self-sufficiency and work, which the development of capitalism tended to render archaic or subsidiary.[204] It also reflected dismay at what was seen as the over-extension of the "parasitic" tertiary sector.[205] But, most important, it served to ensure that the anticapitalism of the antisemites did not become an all-out attack on wealth as such, and its unequal distribution. As Memmi has pointed out, what antisemites objected to was "parvenu money"; "their virtuous indignation was not at all intended to do away with privilege . . ."[206] La Croix, therefore, emphasized, in 1894, that the Socialists were attacking the wrong target in attacking capitalism itself, and that, without the Jews, "capital would again become an instrument of labour and not of speculation".[207] In the same sense, Drumont stressed that Jewish capital was accumulated at the expense of ordinary people and used to their disadvantage. Not only did "monopolies and speculations crush small traders and manufacturers",[208] but the Jews had ruined "thousands of workers with their speculations",[209] and caused "an increase in the cost of living that primarily affected the poor".[210] But "this huge diversion of wealth really earned by the workers"[211] was presented less as an inherent feature of capitalism, as it was in Socialist theory, and more as some kind of foreign tribute levied by the Jews. This was a considerable and unavowed retreat from the assertion that capitalism was Jewish, and represented a fundamental, but very significant, misunderstanding of the real function of money in the economy, as can be seen from Drumont's assumption that since Jewish immigrants "had nothing when they arrived here, they must have taken their money from somewhere . . ."[212] The same ultimate defence of capitalism, while criticizing its parts,[213] is evident with Picard. He attacked "sterile speculation, conceded that "abnormal concentrations of wealth were not limited to Jews"; but emphasized that "the Jewish question is a question of the abuse of capital, but of capital concentrated in the hands of a foreign race"; and pointed to "the mistake that the revolutionary socialists currently make in attributing social evils to the excesses of large-scale industry".[214] Another variant of the same argument was the suggestion that the interests of employers and workers were basically the same and that the Jew was inimical to both. Pierre Veuillot wrote in L'Univers, for example, in January 1890, that; "One fact stares everyone in the face: while industrialists, businessmen, farmers, workers and artists . . . are getting poorer in this time of crises which we are suffering, the Jews alone, who are always the richest to start with, have continued to get richer . . ."[215] This is an example, too, of a much more basic assumption of the antisemites, that again served to deflect hostility from the rich in general, the assumption that Jews were always wealthy. "This is a claim that makes one smile", commented Péguy sadly.[216] We will return to the "conservative" implications of this theme in our discussion of socialistic antisemitism in the next chapter. What is relevant here is not so much that, nor its obvious lack of accord with social reality, with the fact of Jewish poverty, but rather its explanatory role. It was part of the wider attempt that we have described to introduce meaning into the apparent anarchy of the money economy, to find some order to hold on to in a world of seeming chaos. The same sense of order was maintained or constructed through an attachment to the "non-capitalist" rural sector of the economy and its values.

II. "THE JEW DOES NOT PLANT . . ."

The corollary of the identification of the Jew with money and with urban capitalism, however qualified, was to oppose the Jew to the land and to rural society. For antisemites, Jews were essentially foreign to the land and to agriculture. Drumont contrasted the "landless" Jew with "the man who is French, born and bred, whose fathers have colonized and tilled the soil . . ."[217] The San Remo Manifesto of 1899 asked who alone could profit from the preponderance of "wealth in stocks and shares . . . if not the Jews, who, not only do not love the land, but are quite proof against any attachment to it?"[218] Jacques Bainville, of the Action Française, declared in 1905: "The Jew does not plant, because he himself has no roots . . . What would he need with leaves and flowers?"[219] H. Jarzel's *Petit Catéchisme nationaliste* of 1901 described the Jews as "the only people that does not love to cultivate the earth", adding; "there are no Jewish peasants in France . . ."[220] From this it followed that even if Jews did acquire land, they could not be its real owners; "in the eyes of M. Edouard Drumont," wrote Viau, "even if M. Henri de Rothschild had paid ten times their actual value for his estates, he was still not their real owner, simply because he was a Jew."[221]

Antisemites, nevertheless, accused the Jews of taking over the rural as well as the urban economy. *La Croix* claimed that the Jews were ruining French agriculture and exploiting both peasants and big landowners. They were said to be encouraging the excessive division of holdings, and to be keeping down agricultural prices deliberately, hoping by both means to acquire land for themselves.[222] A more conspiratorial dimension was lent to this thesis in a pamphlet published by Jules Ménard in Rennes in 1887, whose title well summarized its argument: *Le Cultivateur ruiné par la Juiverie Internationale sous le couvert de la Société dite La Graineterie Française.* According to Ménard, the monopoly of military grain supplies accorded to the company by the Ministry of War not only represented a threat to national security, but was one of the main causes of agricultural depression. Ménard's theme was taken up by Drumont in *La Fin d'un monde* in 1889: "*La Graineterie Francaise,* which . . . is entirely in the hands of German Jews, has taken French agriculture for its domain . . . The Republican Freemasons, who really control the Ministry of War are helping . . . cosmopolitan Jewry to ruin our agriculture, so that when a war with Germany comes, it will be German Jews who control all our supplies."[223] This thesis was elaborated at length later in Léon Daudet's *L'Avant-Guerre* (1911).

Other charges were made more specifically on behalf of the working rural population. Drumont claimed that Jews were harsh landlords, reviving the evils of the Ancien Régime, such as indiscriminate hunting over agricultural land: "the Jewish owners of *latifundia*", he wrote; "the Jewish millionnaires are squeezing the little French peasant in a vice."[224] Antisemites also played on the traditional rural hostility towards middlemen and merchants, which could, in the East in particular, be fastened on to real Jews. "In Alsace", wrote Drumont in *La France juive*, "a peasant cannot sell his cow without having recourse to a Jew as middleman . . ."[225] The old charge of usury was also used here, and given new development. A broadsheet of the Union Nationale claimed in November 1897 that the Jews "are no longer content with battening on the people of the towns, they are swarming over the countryside and devouring it with their usury, so that its ruin is almost complete."[226] "Who exploits the peasant?", asked a poster put up in Senones, in February 1898, in the same context: "The Jew!"[227] The Jewish usurer had been a familiar and hated figure in several rural areas earlier in the century, notably in the East,[228] and antisemitic violence had been directed against Jews on this pretext in 1848, both there and in the Alpine region.[229] The creation of new kinds of credit organization from the time of the Second Empire had reduced, but not eliminated, peasant reliance on usurers,[230] and the stereotype of the Jewish usurer seems to have remained alive in popular mythology. It continued to figure, for example, in the popular "Images d'Epinal".[231] Fear of the usurer seems probably to have motivated also the considerable suspicion of any form of agricultural credit found even among members of agricultural associations in the 1880s.[232] The antisemites claimed that peasants had every right to be suspicious, since so many of them had fallen victim to Jewish speculative enterprises.

> Lévy, speculating in wheat, deprived the peasant of his livelihood, and the peasant then turned to Jacob, who was already waiting for him, and who offered him stock and shares in finance companies . . . The amount of fantastic shares of this kind, bought by peasants, cannot be imagined unless one has actually lived in the countryside. Certain departments have been ravaged by brokers; while notaries acted as centralizing agents to bring in subscriptions to the Panama company.[233]

There is some evidence from other sources to confirm that peasant investment in the Panama company and other such enterprises was considerable and often disastrous. Zévaès wrote that "many peasants" in the 1880s "were the victims of large-scale embezzlements."[234] Henri Baudrillart, in his careful enquiry into rural society, referred in 1893 to "this deadly drain of small savings that has been established in the countryside by the most shameless speculative organizations". Here he had the Haute-Garonne particularly in mind, but he found the same phenomenon elsewhere, for example in the Ardèche, where "several sinister financiers had been active, and had got away with over 4 million francs, taken mainly from peasants."[235] As Drumont commented, peasants may well have wished to keep quiet about such losses: "The peasant is too secretive to complain; he would be afraid of diminishing his credit, and above all of attracting ridicule by exposing his stupidity . . ."[236] But it is likely that grievances so generated and repressed may have found expression in antisemitism, in hostility to the Jew as the symbol of speculation, of finance and of alien urban exploitation.

All of this should be set in the context of the agricultural crisis suffered by France in the last decades of the nineteenth century. Occasioned by the opening-up of the semi-closed rural economy to national and world markets, and exacerbated by the outbreaks of phylloxera which decimated French vines from the 1860s and of silkworm disease, the crisis was marked by declining prices for agricultural products, by declining rents and land values, by the collapse in many areas of traditional industrial crops, such as hemp, linen and madder, as well as by general rural depopulation. The crisis was felt unevenly by different regions, and by different sectors of the rural economy. Cereal producers, representative often of the most traditional sector, were among the hardest hit, but so were the always market-orientated winegrowers. Tenant-farmers and their landlords were more affected than small peasant proprietors, more geared to self-sufficiency, or able to revert to it. Moreover, while rents and prices fell, agricultural wages remained stable or rose, as the rural labour force declined.[237] Contemporaries, whether victims or not, thus had an economic disaster with radical social implications to explain, and one which threatened a whole set of values centred on the land and on the peasant. It was easy, in these circumstances, to blame modern economic forms and/or the Republican régime. Imbart de la Tour wrote in 1900 that: "At the present moment, French farmers and peasants have no more formidable enemy than the speculators and the politicians."[238] Lyautey claimed in a letter written in June 1901: "I know the provinces very well and I can confirm from having seen it for myself that medium- and small-scale property is being crushed; the peasant and the agricultural worker, at Châteaudun, at Nancy, at Dôle, is living simply from day to day. In ruining us all, the present régime has gratuitously deprived itself of support and good-will, and has destroyed one of the best elements in our social capital."[239] Such an interpretation could very well expand to include one that was more specifically antisemitic. Achille Loria expressed the view in 1899 that "the fundamentally economic *raison d'être* of antisemitic agitation explains why it has become particularly acute in the period of dispossession that agricultural capital and property are undergoing today . . ."[240] Lazare, similarly, made the point in 1894 that: "Landed capital, in its struggle with industrial capital, has become antisemitic, because the Jew is, for the landed proprietor, the most typical representative of commercial and industrial capitalism", referring to the commercialization of French agriculture that the crisis reflected and occasioned.[241] We saw in our discussion of the Henry Subscription that the geographical incidence of expressions of antisemitism can plausibly be related to the incidence of the agricultural crisis, for example in the South-East.[242] Antisemitic writers, too, as we have seen, related rural economic difficulties directly and indirectly to Jewish influence. Drumont, for example, commented on the crisis and its attendant rural depopulation in *La France juive*: "While our workers crowd into the towns, looking for jobs that are becoming rarer and rarer, agriculture is abandoned . . . the land has lost three-quarters of its value."[243] The Marquis de Vogüé, in *Les Morts qui parlent* (1899), a novel serialized in *La Revue des Deux Mondes*, portrayed a provincial deputy, "a small farmer, ruined by the fall in wheat, and very acrimonious as a result. This man of the land was looking for signatures to a bill on the naturalization of foreigners; he proposed to restrict this; what he was really aiming at were the Jews"[244]—a not uncommon reaction that we will return to in a later section of this chapter.

There is, however, expectedly little direct evidence of the expression of antisemitic opinion on the part of the rural population itself, less articulate than its urban counterpart, more recently literate, more preoccupied with the concrete problems of getting a living. Some inferences can be drawn, none the less, from such sources as the Henry Subscription, from scattered references in other literature, and from what we know of the make-up of antisemitism in general. As we shall discover in chapter XIV, French antisemitism was very frequently Catholic in inspiration and tone, and Catholicism was stronger in rural than in urban areas, and particularly strong in certain isolated regions, such as the West, where organized antisemitism was also important.[245] We have seen also that antisemitic deputies were frequently elected in rural constituencies, and, though we have stressed that their electoral base was usually far from democratic, antisemitic deputies made a point of defending agricultural interests in the Chamber. More particularly, Anthime-Ménard, the Comte de Lévis-Mirepoix, Lasies and Firmin Faure championed viticultural interests, and upheld the privilege of home-distillers, while Poullan from the Alpes-Maritimes was a member of the Chamber's Agricultural Commission, that had been set up on a permanent basis in 1898 on the initiative of Déroulède.[246] There is evidence, too, of agricultural organizations expressing hostility to Jews, though these were not of course very representative of peasants. The Agricultural Association of the Est issued a declaration in March 1898, as we have seen, announcing that it would only support candidates (in the forthcoming General Election) who pledged themselves to sponsor a law depriving Jews of the franchise and banning them from positions in the civil service and the armed forces.[247] According to Pierrard, abbé Vial was congratulated for his prize-winning antisemitic essay in the *Libre Parole* competition of 1895 by the President of the Société des Agriculteurs de France.[248] Antisemitic propaganda, moreover, was directed at peasants, and distributed among them. Stickers of the Ligue Antisémitique Française found at Vesoul in August 1898 addressed "Peasants, farmers, patriots";[249] Mirbeau's Joseph in *Le Journal d'une femme de chambre* is described as distributing antisemitic material in rural Normandy;[250] a Catholic peasant from

Ygrande (Allier), visited by Daniel Halévy in 1910, possessed a copy of one of Drumont's works, one of the very few books that he had.[251] It is very difficult to assess how far such propaganda could count on the existence of a traditional antisemitism among rural populations, though there is some evidence that it could. An entry to the *Libre Parole* subscription of 1901–2 came from "a practising Catholic who sucked in a hatred of the Jew with the milk of his peasant mother".[252] Leaving aside the interesting psychological dimensions of such a statement, and the fact that an antisemite might very well have believed that such ought to have been the source of his obsessive conviction, we can note that a general hostility towards Jews probably did form an ingredient of peasant socialization and culture, as there is abundant evidence that it did of middle-class urban culture. And we can sometimes glimpse that it may have been of a peculiar and archaic kind. Baudrillart recounted that in the Ardèche: "Certain peasants still believe that doctors attach a great value to the *fat of a Christian*, and, until very recently, when a dead man with any degree of *embonpoint* had been buried, his relatives and friends would mount guard at night in the cemetery, with their guns ready to shoot at any miscreant who might have dared to disinter him."[253] Given the frequent identification of the doctor with the Jew,[254] this custom may be seen as a vestige of popular antisemitic belief, related to that in ritual murder. A similar instance occurs in a story published by Maupassant in *Le Gaulois* in February 1883, entitled "Le Père Judas". More an anecdote than a story, it describes two beggars, a man and a woman, living in a remote rural area. He is supposed by the local population to be Judas or the Wandering Jew, and the couple are known as "Le Père Judas" and "La Juive". Neither went to church or made the sign of the cross by wayside crucifixes. The old man refused to let the *curé* in to administer the last sacraments to the old woman. Moreover, he had magical curing powers. When he died, it was on Good Friday, and his body was eaten by pigs, confirmation to the peasants that he was indeed the Wandering Jew.[255] A nice compendium of traditional antisemitic beliefs that has an air of authenticity about it. We will, in a later chapter, consider how such beliefs were articulated by antisemitic writers into a more modern ideology, a process that we have already seen at work in detail. What we cannot do is to show how ancient prejudices were harnessed to explain novel phenomena within peasant thinking itself, or indeed that of most other social groups, though there are the strongest indications that this is what happened, as we have repeatedly suggested. A final possible motive for peasant antisemitism may be mentioned, before we leave the subject, and that was the relationship that existed in some areas between a malingering rural domestic industry and the big Parisian department stores, that were widely regarded as Jewish concerns. Halévy was told that the women of Domérat (Allier) "sew for the big Paris stores", and their conditions of work and remuneration were deteriorating by the early years of this century.[256]

One social group that was, at least in part, rural, escaped from the rule of inarticulacy, and that was the landed aristocracy. We have already seen that the agricultural crisis hit landlords particularly hard, and that antisemites claimed that the Jews were splitting up large estates. It is not surprising, therefore, to find considerable evidence that antisemitism of various kinds was strong among aristocrats. To take organized antisemitism first, aristocrats were well-represented among the leaders and propagandists of the movement. These included Gougenot des Mousseaux, author of *Le Juif, le Judaïsme et la Judaïsation des peuples chrétiens* (1869), republished in 1886, and an important influence on Drumont and others;[257] Morès; Rochefort; Boni de Castellane, one of Guérin's main backers;[258] and the Comtesse de Martel, who wrote a series of successful novels under the pseudonym, "Gyp", who contributed to *La Libre Parole,* and who belonged to the inner circle of antisemitic leaders at the time of the Affair.[259] The first big antisemitic rally in France, held in Paris in January 1890 was attended by members of the Jockey Club and the aristocracy generally, according to its sponsors. Drumont listed among them, the Prince de Tarente, the Duc de Luynes, the Duc d'Uzès, the Comte de Gontaut-Biron, the Comte de Dion, the Vicomte de Kervégan, the Marquis de Saulty, the Baron de Meyronnet, the Vicomte de Bréteuil and Prince Poniatowsky.[260] 800 members of the aristocracy subscribed to the Henry Subscription;[261] and a high proportion of the antisemitic deputies were aristocrats, as we have seen.[262] Moreover, active anti-Dreyfusism was common in the same milieu. To give only one indication of this, at least 25 members of the aristocracy were arrested during the demonstrations at Auteuil in June 1899.[263] In addition, most Royalist organizations, which were at this time largely aristocratic in complexion, were also antisemitic, for example, La Jeunesse Royaliste.[264] The Comte de Sabran-Pontevès, member of the princely aristocracy, stood as an antisemitic Royalist candidate for the 19th *arrondissement* of Paris in 1898;[265] and Morès was a Royalist of sorts.[266] We have already quoted from the antisemitic San Remo Manifesto of the Royalist Pretender, who was notoriously anti-Dreyfusard.[267] The tradition of Royalist antisemitism was to be continued after the Affair by the Action Française.[268] Royalist antisemitism was, furthermore, explicitly related to rural problems and to an idealization of aristocratic landlordism. André Buffet declared in his reply to Maurras's *Enquête sur la monarchie* in 1909:[269]

> Monsieur le Duc d'Orléans is particularly resolved to defend rural interests . . . to encourage our agricultural producers in a thousand ways, and to punish parasitical speculators severely . . . Agricultural associations [*syndicats*], agricultural credit schemes will obtain the energetic protection of the King of France. But the Jews who are engaged in a scandalous traffic in landed property will be stopped in their pillaging by strict legislation. The land of France will be fixed in the hands of families with real roots in the soil. Working the land, today so precarious and risky, will again become a stable occupation . . . New habits will prevent the absenteeism of landowners, and this will re-establish the old community of interests between landowner and worker . . . The rural exodus towards the towns will then cease . . .

Aristocratic espousal of organized antisemitism was underpinned by what one might call a social antisemitism, a dislike of mixing socially with Jews. This is difficult to assess, partly for lack of evidence, partly because aristocratic society was in essence exclusive of Jews and anyone else who was not an aristocrat. What strikes one at first, in fact, is the degree to which French aristocratic society did receive Jews if they were of sufficiently high status, or had some special interest. The actress Rachel was received in the salons of the Faubourg Saint-Germain in the 1840s,[270] as Proust's Swann was esteemed there half a century later.[271] Boni de Castellane, despite his antisemitic commitment, mixed socially with the Rothschilds, tried desperately hard to persuade Sarah Bernhardt to dine with him, and acted as a second to Arthur Meyer in his duel with Drumont.[272] As this reminds us, the main "society" newspaper of the day, Le Gaulois, was edited by a Jew who married a Turenne.[273] Georges de Lauris wrote that what worried many of his fellow aristocratic socialites about the Affair was that it "might cause pain to the Rothschilds".[274] This selective admittance of Jews into the highest social circles received a great deal of adverse comment from antisemites. Drumont, for example, wrote that the Duc de Bisaccia "had lost, through keeping bad company, through keeping company with Jews, that flower of gentlemanly courtesy that used to characterize the French nobility"; and he expressed his horror at the fact that the Duchesse de Chartres, "a woman with royal blood in her veins", should have paid a call on the wife of a Jewish prefect.[275] However, such intercourse shocked, one suspects, because it was unusual, and, as we have seen, there is plenty of evidence of aristocratic anti-Jewish prejudice. The Marquis de Montfanon, in Bourget's Cosmopolis (1893), cannot have been untypical in his instinctive dislike for Baron Justus Hafner and his daughter: "They are the quintessence of what I dislike most, people like them! They are the incarnation of all that is most detestable in the modern world, these cosmopolitan adventurers, playing at being grands seigneurs with millions filched on the Stock Exchange. They have no country . . . They have no religion. Their name, their faces, proclaim them to be Jews . . ."[276] There is some evidence, too, that aristocratic circles became more hostile towards Jews at the time of the Affair, despite Lauris's observation. According to Reinach:[277]

> The Faubourg Saint-Germain took advantage of the occasion to break with the few Jews who had forced their way across its threshold . . . Only those were kept on, whose daughters with their vast dowries had revitalized and bailed out the mortgaged estates of the aristocracy. People kept their distance from the Rothschilds, who without intervening directly in the struggle, yet refused to disavow the defenders of Dreyfus.

And Proust recorded a similar impression.[278]

Two areas, in particular, reveal the depth and permanence of aristocratic hostility to Jews: their exclusion from clubs, and the rarity of intermarriage. Members of the Jewish aristocracy had been admitted to French aristocratic clubs from the middle of the century. Alphonse de Rothschild, and his brother Gustave, for example, joined the Jockey Club in the early 1850s, and members of the family later belonged to the Cercle de l'Union.[279] But they were exceptions. Gregh, wrote of Charles Haas, one of the models for Proust's Swann, that: "He was said to be the only Jewish member of the Jockey Club . . . he was a member although he was a Jew."[280] Indeed, it seems that by the end of the century, a more consistent policy of exclusion was in operation, possibly in reaction to greater pressure from Jews to join, and younger members were said to be ostracizing existing Jewish members.[281] The marriage patterns of the higher aristocracy, at least, also betray an antisemitic bias. During the half-century up to the First World War, the French princely aristocracy maintained a high degree of endogamy, which was broken, if at all, it seems, for financial reasons, as Reinach suggests. The 1913 edition of the *Almanach de Gotha* lists 14 cases of the marriage of princes, dukes and their close relatives to American women, but only 6 cases of marriage to Jewish co-nationals and fellow-aristocrats.[282] Such marriages seem to have been nearly universally disapproved. According to his daughter, Agénor de Gramont's second marriage to Marguerite de Rothschild was opposed by her father, and frowned on by the Faubourg Saint-Germain, which regarded him as an eccentric anyway because he was a Republican.[283] In Zola's *Paris* (1898), while Duthil regards the marriage of Gérard de Quinsac and Camille Duvillard, whose mother is a Jew, as "quite the thing", the Comtesse de Quinsac tells her old friend the Marquis de Morigny, "how abominable such a marriage must be. It will be the end of our race and our honour!"[284] This reveals an ambiguity of attitude that is significant. Marriage to a Jewish heiress was often presented as the only way out of financial difficulties, but it was also a misalliance. In Maupassant's *Bel-Ami* Walter's two daughters are expected to marry aristocrats because they are so wealthy, but the author stresses that Mme Walter herself suffered personally and socially "from having married a Jew".[285] In Guinon's play *Décadence*, Jeannine de Barfleur at first refuses to consider marrying Nathan de Strohmann because he is a Jew, but agrees when it becomes the condition for paying the Duc, her father's, extensive debts; and the marriage is, again, for her a personal disaster. So, though aristocrats may have eschewed Jewish marriages on the whole, they may have felt an additional resentment towards Jews, for having done so. Had the potential matches not been Jews, everything would have been all right. Here it is interesting to note that both Morès and Boni de Castellane married American heiresses from financial motives,[286] and that Drumont claimed that most American heiresses were in fact Jewish.[287] In this very complicated area, three further points are relevant. First, as Ledrain pointed out, intermarriage between non-Jewish men and Jewish women was much more acceptable than that between Jewish men and non-Jewish women, a point to which we will return in chapter XV. When the Duc de Barfleur, in Guinon's play, tells his daughter that many other French aristocrats have married Jews, she points out that these were Frenchmen marrying Jewish women: "That a man of my race should marry a girl of that race, one can accept that! By marrying her, he elevates her to his level! But, for myself, if I married a Jew, I would not lift him to my level, he would bring me down to his! I would cease to be a Barfleur and would become a Strohmann!"[288] Secondly, in using the incidence of intermarriage as an indicator of antisemitism, one must remember, as the Gramont example shows, that there was hostility on both sides. If the French aristocracy had a preference for endogamy, so did Jewish families.[289] Thirdly, hostility towards marriage with Jews was by no means confined to the aristocracy,[290] although it was probably more conspicuous there.

Contemporary observers of antisemitism noted its prevalence among the aristocracy, and suggested reasons for this, which confirm our general interpretation. Yves Guyot, director of *Le Siècle*, told Dagan that antisemitism represented "the revenge . . . of the old landed aristocracy against finance, industry and trade"; while Henry Maret, director of *Le Radical*, argued: "Landowners who are good Christians, but just as much exploiters as bankers, have an interest in making the poor believe that all their sufferings are caused by Jewish financial speculators."[291] Urbain Gohier referred to "members of the gentry who call themselves antisemites, hoping one of these days to do away with their Jewish creditors".[292] Dagan, himself, lent the antisemitism of the landed aristocracy another dimension still, attributing it to economic rivalry, but also to "rivalries of rank, status and honour. A kind of silent envy makes it detest the class of financial plutocrats, whose opulence and luxurious life-style offend its vanity, and overshadow its own armorial bearings and the memory of its past glory . . ." The same suggestion was made by Guyot, again, who said that "the ladies of the Faubourg Saint-Germain . . . can never pardon Jewish ladies for having boxes at the Opera, for having diamonds, carriages and fine mansions . . ."; and Dagan explained Gyp's antisemitism by referring to her "bitterness in the face of parvenus with hooked noses".[293]

This view of a declining aristocracy, often in debt, losing its status and influence, and even its land, and turning to antisemitism both as explanation and as policy, is probably substantially correct, although we lack quantitative evidence of the pace and the extent of that decline. Drumont certainly believed that in "its resolve to break with the Jews . . . the healthy, the French part of the aristocracy . . . was not only obeying its generous and noble sentiments, it was acting in defence of its very existence."[294] He also referred, as we have seen, to the fact that the aristocracy had been very hard hit by the agricultural depression. "Society people are very hard up . . . Tenants are not paying their rents and land is hard to sell."[295] Whether aristocratic estates were in fact being sold up at an unusual rate is hard to guess without statistics, but enough were sold, particularly in areas of traditional aristocratic dominance, such as the West,[296] to give an impression of a very important transfer. The theme was fairly common in fiction, where it could also be given an antisemitic twist. When the ancestral home of the Galart family is finally put up for sale in La Varende's *Pays d'Ouche*, the announcement is made in the press: "Apply to Monsieur Moïse Lévy, 34 avenue des Champs-Elysées, Paris."[297] One should not forget in all this, that the connection of the aristocracy, and particularly the aristocracy à la Proust, with the land, was often remote,[298] and, that like its English counterpart, the French aristocracy was deeply involved in industrial ownership, management and investment, although the real extent of this involvement still requires study.[299] This indicates that aristocratic antisemitism may not necessarily or exclusively have reflected a reaction of landed against industrial and commercial interests. Nevertheless aristocrats were prominent in the defense of landed interests;[300] and, some aristocratic ventures into new forms of investment proved disastrous, and here failure was often blamed on Jews. A significant sector of the aristocracy, for example, was ruined or suffered considerable loss in the Union Générale Affair, which provoked or confirmed a current of antisemitism there.[301]

If one cannot get a very complete picture of the economic position of the aristocracy at the end of the nineteenth century, enough is clear to begin to explain its attraction as a class to antisemitism. Such explanation is aided further by the more certain knowledge that, though it had maintained a certain social prestige, the aristocracy had progressively lost all but local political power and influence from the 1880's, while, at the same time, being ousted from the magistrature and from most branches of the civil service. Georges Fonsegrive, editor of the Catholic review, *La Quinzaine*, observed in 1900:[302]

> Most landowners can think of nothing better to do than go idly to ruination
> . . . At election time, they emerge from their apathy to order their "subjects"
> to vote in such and such a way, and the "subjects" hurry to do exactly the
> opposite . . . They still believe that they are a "ruling class". In fact, they
> rule nothing, and are themselves ruled by the newspapers which they read.

We have referred throughout this discussion to the aristocracy as though it were a homogeneous class or social group, while giving many indications that it was not always so. In a sense the vagueness is to the point, since the aristocracy under the Republic had lost many of its proper internal hierarchies, and its ranks had been inflated by the creations of earlier nineteenth-century régimes and by a host of the self-enobled. This was resented by genuine noble families—another reason perhaps for their dislike for the "barons of Finance" —but most people were less well trained in social distinctions. A significant gulf did, however, remain between the higher aristocracy, vestige of that of the court, and the lesser nobles or gentry; and each produced its own type of antisemitism. Representative of the first was perhaps the Marquis de Morès, despite his lack of the right pedigree, for he combined a Parisian dandyism with a taste for adventure and the talent for squandering a fortune. But more typical was Boni de Castellane (1867–1932). He came of an old Provençal aristocratic family, which had been raised to the peerage, and had achieved renown in the nineteenth century in the person of the Maréchal de Castellane, Boni's great-grandfather. His father, however, had gambled away the family fortune. After a period in the army, Boni repaired his financial position temporarily by marrying Anna Gould, and became one of the leaders of the Parisian society of his day, dazzling his contemporaries with the magnificence of his receptions, and also financing the anti-Dreyfusard Leagues. Like his father and his grandfather before him, he became a deputy in 1898, sitting for the "family" seat of Castellane in the Basses-Alpes, but he was not a serious politician, even as an amateur. By the early 1900s, he was heavily in debt again;

in 1906 he divorced his American wife; and he sank to becoming an antique dealer. He was characteristically inarticulate about the nature of his antisemitism, but can it not be related to the fact, that like the class he came from, he had no social role to play in modern democratic society, and that his birth and upbringing had given him values that were no longer current?[303] His peculiar failure to adapt was extreme, but his disorientation must have been shared by many others, and, like that of many others, sought some remedy in blaming the Jews. No such equivalent type can be obviously chosen to represent the petty aristocracy, closer to the land, closer to the agricultural crisis, and to the passing of the social and political influence of the "notables", but an approximation can be found, at one remove as it were, in Simone de Beauvoir's picture of her father. He was an ardent anti-Dreyfusard, an admirer of Déroulède and later of the Action Française, who "detested foreigners, and was indignant that Jews should be allowed to take part in the government of the country". He laid claim to being an aristocrat, but lacked the means to live up to it. Above all, he never found a social role, and was characteristically most fulfilled in acting. "Half-way between the aristocracy and the bourgeoisie, between the landed gentry and the office worker, respecting but not practising the Catholic religion, he felt himself neither completely integrated with society nor burdened with any serious responsibilities . . ."[304] At a different social level, here is the same aristocratic anomie that we found in Boni de Castellane.

In a broader perspective, it should be remembered that the connection between antisemitism and rural society, between antisemitism and the aristocracy, did not exist only on the level of a real espousal of antisemitism by rural social groups. It formed also, and perhaps more importantly, a crucial component of the ideology of antisemites who were neither country dwellers nor noble. For them, the rural world with its roots in the past, its relative resistance to change, signified a set of stable values posited in the face of an urbanized world of confusion and flux. This idealization of rural society was a theme of very general provenance,[305] and was lent new strength by the agricultural depression. A speech in the Chamber of Deputies in July 1897 by the Republican leader Deschanel, celebrating "our dear French peasant", was voted to be posted in all French communes.[306] Premier Méline was an advocate of "the return to the land".[307] But the theme enjoyed particular favour on the political Right. Charles Jacquier, for example, declared at celebrations to mark the 25th anniversary of the foundation of the Union du Sud-Est des Syndicats Agricoles in the 1880s: "The land tempers the soul and is the great preserver of the race."[308] Imbart de la Tour made the familiar claim in 1900 that "the interests of our country are essentially agricultural . . .", adding: "We must never say: The land is subject to fluctuation like any other merchandise. The land is more than that; it is our soil, our nation: if the land were simply a merchandise, we would not be inconsolable over the loss of Alsace and Lorraine." In this perspective, the depression was "a struggle between living nature and the morbid element that assails it . . . At the moment we are the prey of all manner of disease: politics lacks foundation and direction; everything is collapsing; social relations are over-stretched and threaten to break; new and subversive theories are spawning in the realm of political economy."[309] All of this was the stock-in-trade, as it were, of antisemitism,[310] which added only one extra ingredient to it, but one that had a vital explanatory function. Drumont, for example, celebrated "landed France", lamented the disappearance of the peasant,[311] and made the same contrast between "landed property, which used to be almost unchanging", and its present tendency to become simply a marketable commodity.[312]

The old hereditary aristocracy had an important place in this rustic mythology in its antisemitic version. Morès described the growing Jewish influence in society in these terms: "Castles and forests are passing into the hands of financiers, children of Israel, whose hands are not always pure. The proletariat and the old aristocracy, equally unfortunate, [are being] dispossessed of the soil of France, and between these two classes a parasitic growth [is] extending its tentacles monstrously everywhere."[313] The idealization of the old paternalist aristocracy, and the contrast drawn between it and the new aristocracy of money, were common themes in antisemitic literature in France from the time of Toussenel, who declared in *Les Juifs rois de l'époque* (1847): "The motto of the old aristocracy is this: *Noblesse oblige*. That of the financial aristocracy is: *Every man for himself.*"[314] The readers of Gyp and of the many other novels of aristocratic life produced for general consumption in the later nineteenth century,[315] had the consolation of knowing that in the realm of fiction at least the traditional social hierarchy was maintained, despite threats to it. The aristocrat in this fiction was implicitly or explicitly the opposite of the Jew, the symbol of the old and stable order which the Jew and his money were undermining and threatened to destroy. There could therefore be no more telling depiction of the disorder of modern society, which neo-traditionalist antisemitism sought to repair and overcome, than to see the Jew in the place of the aristocrat. Thus Drumont, like Morès, objected with passion to the Jew as a usurper,[316] to the fact that "Jews, vomited from all the ghettos of Europe, are now installed as the masters in historic houses that evoke the most glorious memories of ancient France . . . the Rothschilds everywhere: at Ferrières and at Les Vaux-de-Cernay, in the abbey founded by Blanche of Castille . . . Hirsch, at Marly, in the place of Louis XIV; Ephrussi, at Fontainebleau, in the place of Francis I; the guano king, Dreyfus, at Pont-Chartrain."[317] Similarly, Guérin wrote: "The Revolution was made against the great *seigneurs*, but their *châteaux* remain, and they are inhabited by our Jewish financiers and their friends, new *seigneurs*, insolent and without pity . . ."[318] When Drumont did attack the aristocracy of his day, which was not infrequently, it was for failing to fulfil its traditional role in society. What he condemned was "the modernized nobility, avid for money, very involved in Stock Exchange speculations, and thus very 'Jewish' ".[319] This nobility lacked all qualities of leadership, political, intellectual and cultural,[320] and mingled and identified with "the Jews, the bankers and the exploiters", instead of protecting and supporting "small landowners who had been ruined, small manufacturers fallen back into the class of wage-earners . . ."[321] What he admired was "the old nobility which made France what it was, who over the centuries, claimed, as the first of its privileges, the right to shed its blood for the nation and did so to profusion . . . the grandeur of the provincial gentry, so honourable in its proud poverty, imbued with no other ideal than that of devotion to the service of the king."[322] As we have seen, this dichotomy reflected a crisis of identity within the aristocracy itself; and we will discuss some of the wider implications of the nostalgia for hierarchy involved in it in a later chapter. Immediately, we must now turn to some other aspects of economic antisemitism.

III."AN ISSUE FOR SHOPKEEPERS"

A special place was occupied in the antisemitism of the later nineteenth century in France by the grievances and claims of small traders and shopkeepers.[323] These were more clearly articulated than the other grievances which we have considered so far, and they were attached to a specific programme of organization and action. So much so that the Socialist Paul Lafargue could refer to antisemitism in general in 1898 as "an issue for shopkeepers".[324]

The special involvement of small traders in antisemitism was noted by many other contemporaries. It was remarked on, for example, by Lazare.[325] E. Duclaux, in Dagan's *Enquête,* said: "Small traders and industrialists have perhaps more direct reasons for complaining of Jewish competition . . ."[326] Zévaès wrote that, at the turn of the century, "Drumont's antisemitism and Rochefort's demagogy always found fertile ground . . . in Paris—a milieu of artisans and small shopkeepers, suffering from the effects of the slump and from the competition of big stores, of a petty middle class that was often the victim of high financial speculations . . ."[327] Police reports and the press tell the same story. According to the Prefect of Police, many antisemitic candidates during the 1898 election campaign in Paris sought and obtained the support of small traders.[328] The Caen police referred in December 1898 to the local "anti-Jewish league, behind which some of our traders are trying to shelter . . ."[329] The police from Roanne reported that the foundation of a "Ligue Antisémite" (a section of the Ligue Antisémitique, in effect), was marked by a public meeting "to which the small traders of the town are invited."[330] From Rennes, during the Dreyfus court martial, it was reported that L. Vial's brochure, *Le Juif Roi,* had been sent through the post unsolicited to many small traders in the town.[331] In April 1902 *La Petite République* referred to "the retail trade so odiously committed to Nationalism", a term that included the antisemitic movement as we shall see.[332] There is objective evidence, too, to indicate that small traders were an important element in the readership of both *La Croix* and *La Libre Parole,*[333] and in the membership of the Ligue Antisémitique Française and of the Union Nationale,[334] and we have encountered them among the subscribers to the Henry Subscription.

Antisemitic propaganda makes clear the reasons for this espousal of antisemitism by traders and shopkeepers. There was a general fear of being run out of business by the Jews. Drumont, whose maternal grandfather had been a grocer, evoked the plight, in *La France juive*, of shopkeepers, "whose business was coveted by a Jew and against whom the whole Jewish trading community conspired, driving them, little by little, to bankruptcy"; "shopkeepers today", he added, "are letting themselves be pushed out to make way for the invaders . . ."[335] Later, in *La Dernière Bataille*, he presented the same picture but indicated the development of a more aggressive attitude towards it: " 'those cursed Yids!', businessmen are exclaiming; 'they have ruined a trade that we used to pursue in honourable fashion.' 'They are destroying our livelihood!', declare small shopkeepers at the doors of their deserted shops. 'They are squeezing us out with their syndicates and their coalitions! If only someone would get rid of them for us!' "[336] In the same vein, Guérin claimed in 1898, in a speech made in the 2nd *arrondissement* of Paris, which had a large Jewish population, that all business there was in the hands of the Jews.[337] In a pamphlet, published in Roubaix in 1898, the president of the Union Commerciale de Roubaix et de ses Cantons, E. Wicart, protested against "the multiplication of public companies and of co-operatives that has coincided with the destruction of small business", and called on his fellow "small traders, reduced to our own devices, abandoned by everyone else", to act together to defend themselves:[338]

> You have worked for forty years to create a little business that will feed your small family; you pay your taxes, you contribute to the prosperity and well-being of the town; you live happy, respected and free; then, suddenly, on the prompting of doctrinaires, capitalists from every country under the sun set up co-operatives that are privileged in various ways and pay no taxes, and you are completely ruined; the business you were so proud of is worth nothing; and you are thrown on to public assistance.

The difficulties, the ousting of small traders, were also felt, however, by those who were not directly involved in it. Maurras, for example, recounted that on his arrival in Paris as a young man in 1885, "I was struck, moved, almost wounded by the sight of these fine streets, these great boulevards decked from street-level to the roofs by foreign signs, covered with names including K and W and Z, letters which our printing workers so wittily call the Jewish letters. *Were the French at home in their own country?* Anyone who raised that question from then on awoke in me a confused feeling of approval."[339]

As the Roubaix pamphlet illustrates, the Jewish threat to small traders was seen sometimes in the form of the co-operative, but much more stress was laid on the competition of department stores. Drumont wrote that the antisemites were campaigning on behalf of "small traders ruined by the big stores . . ."[340] Particular reference was made to the fairly recent development of department stores in provincial towns. A pamphlet, put out by *La Croix* in April 1898, declared: "The emporia and the big stores created in all provincial towns are ruining local business. One sees some Lévy or other set up in a place, and, by means that the Jew alone knows how to employ, he very soon forces local business to founder in face of the competition which it is impossible to withstand."[341] A poster of December 1898, entitled "Reflections of a small trader of Caen", elaborated on the same theme, and is worth quoting at length:[342]

> The Monopolist, with his big store, where he carries on a hundred branches of commerce under one roof without paying the *patente* for each, enjoys an unfair advantage. *He crushes and ruins small business*, by a competition which knows no bounds and is often dishonest, and this should be of concern to everyone! . . . So many interests are threatened by this! So many people are persuaded to buy things that are next to useless! Don't be misled by the label that reads *"Bargain"*. To produce these so-called bargains, any number of tricks are employed, any number of sharp practices are invented daily to stretch and expand the material. All kinds of ingredients, gum, lead salts, have been used to give it weight, and lend it the right feel and appearance. But look at the shoddy stuff, after it has been in a shower, or to the laundry, or even after a short exposure to sunlight, and you will see that it has shrunk, lost its shape, split open. The purchaser of such a garment is left with nothing of any value, while the till of the Jewish department store has been filled. *Workers!* Remember that such "bargains" can also be obtained by pushing down your wages. *Patriots!* You ought to know that all these emporia are usually financed by cosmopolitan and anti-French capital . . . and that their profits will enrich a few Jewish financiers to the detriment of other traders who cannot compete against them. *Landlords, Rentiers!* What will happen to your property, when the traders in our towns are forced to close their shops, which you have failed to patronize?

Le Réveil Commercial, Industriel et Agricole of Montpellier carried a leading article on "Department Stores" in much the same vein in September 1897, as did *La Croix Meusienne* in February 1898, to give only two further examples of such propaganda from the provinces.[343]

But similar attacks were made in Paris, where the department store was a much more familiar institution. They figured prominently, for example, in the 1898 election campaign in the capital. At a Ligue Antisémitique meeting in March in the 18th *arrondissement*, according to the police, "a participant called on the antisemites to attack the co-operative societies and the big stores which are exploiting the workers and ruining small traders".[344] A meeting of the Comité National et Antisémite of the 1st constituency of the 18th *arrondissement*, in the same month, discussed "The Big Stores and the Co-operative Societies: their disastrous implications for small traders and for all workers",[345] apparently in response to this demand. Chauvière, a candidate in the 2nd constituency of the 15th *arrondissement*, called in his programme for the abolition of the *patente* for small traders, and the imposition of a special tax on department stores; and Bichebois, a candidate in the 3rd *arrondissement*, told a meeting in May that his candidature represented "a formidable protest against monopolists and department stores . . ."[346] But such attacks on department stores were not confined to declared antisemites. Charles Benoist, then a moderate Republican and sitting deputy for the 1st constituency of the 6th *arrondissement*, called for the payment of a multiple *patente* by department stores;[347] while a speaker, introducing the candidate of the Parti Ouvrier Français to a public meeting organized by the Comité Electoral Socialiste of the 2nd constituency of the 10th *arrondissement* in March, "attacked the bourgeoisie and the capitalists for their increasing exploitation of the proletariat, and said that the big stores, the Bon Marché and Félix Potin among others, were ruining small businesses. He then appealed to all Socialists to unite in the fight against this scourge which he called Capitalism."[348] As this indicates, the issue of the department stores had become too important and had too much popular support, for non-antisemitic candidates to ignore it, particularly in constituencies where organized antisemitism was strong. It also reveals the extent to which department stores, like banks, had come to symbolize capitalism itself. This symbolization can be seen very clearly, too, in Zola's novel, *Au Bonheur des Dames* (1883), which ambiguously presents the department store as a progressive institution bringing a whole new range of products within the reach of consumers, but also as the heartless destroyer of older types of retail trading and their personnel.[349] It is significant, in addition, that Zola described Mouret, the owner of his department store, who was not a Jew as "essentially more Jewish than all the Jews in the world . . ."[350] The issue of the department store was raised again in the General Election campaign of 1902 in Paris. This time, it seems, several Left-wing newspapers mounted an attack on small traders, which, according to the police, assisted the electioneering of "Nationalist" candidates.[351]

Further indications of the importance of this issue for antisemitism are provided by the clerical congresses of the period. As we have seen, both the Ecclesiastical Congress of Reims in 1896 and the Congress of Christian Democracy at Lyon in 1897 passed resolutions condemning department stores, which were seen as specifically Jewish institutions.[352] The importance of the issue is also reflected by the fact that it was used by antisemitic leaders as the mark of true devotion to the cause. We have seen that Guérin, in attacking Drumont, made much of the allegedly equivocal attitude of *La Libre Parole* towards department stores, pointing out that the newspaper carried advertisements for the Galéries Lafayette, and had published an article in praise of "the big stores" in 1892.[353]

Department stores were also attacked through campaigns on behalf of their employees. Drumont inveighed in *La France juive* against the exploitation practised by the stores, indirectly through their dealing in cheap goods produced by sweated labour, directly vis-à-vis their sales staff, and especially "those poor sales-girls, on their feet, when a sale is on, for ten or twelve hours at a stretch, and whose wages are pitilessly docked if they sit down at all, outside meal-times."[354] Antisemitic organizations, moreover, made overtures to shop workers, many of whom, as we have seen, in fact joined them. The police reported in 1900 of Gaston Méry: "When friends in Marseille, Lyon, Avignon or Bordeaux point out to him the exploitation being practised by the Jews who own the big shops and who tyrannize their employees, he tells them: Get them to join the Grand Occident de France."[355] The movement of independent trade unions or "Syndicats Jaunes", which began in 1901, and which had an avowed antisemitic colouring, enjoyed a particular following, it seems, among white-collar and shop workers; and, although it encouraged the development of co-operatives among its members, its 1904 Congress passed a resolution which stipulated that these co-operatives "must not be set up . . . in competition with small traders, and must avoid attracting their hostility . . ."³⁵⁶ In this field, of course, antisemites were vying with the orthodox Labour movement, and it is interesting to see how closely their programmes compared. For example, the Parti Ouvrier Français held a meeting for shop workers of the 17th *arrondissement* of Paris in April 1898, and offered a programme of reforms, which included compulsory insurance against accidents at work, to be paid by the employers, one day off per week with pay, and the closing of all shops on Sunday afternoons, concrete proposals that the antisemites did not emulate. However, in May 1898, Marcel Sembat addressed a meeting of shop-workers from department stores and advised them to form a union, but told them also: "to avoid at all costs creating any antagonism between themselves and the small traders, whose cause is also a just one."³⁵⁷

But antisemites did not simply issue propaganda against department stores. As we have seen, they tried to organize a boycott of them, and of Jewish businesses in general. Léon Harmel's Union Fraternelle du Commerce et de l'Industrie, founded in 1891, was probably the first organization to call for such a boycott.³⁵⁸ The call was echoed by *La Semaine Religieuse de Limoges* in September 1892,³⁵⁹ and, by the mid and late 1890s, it had become very general. The Prefect of the Marne reported in June 1896 that for some time stickers had been put up daily on the walls of Reims, which read: "Never buy from a Jew, Keep France for the French . . ."³⁶⁰ The same year a brochure put out by the Ligue Antisémitique du Commerce Poitevine appealed to "the ladies of Poitiers . . . for the sake of the honour and salvation of France, never buy from the Jews", and provided a list of 200 traders and shopkeepers, belonging to the Ligue, to whom they were asked to address their custom.³⁶¹ At Marseille in February 1898, the police reported that, despite calls for more vigorous action from some younger members, the Jeunesse Catholique was contenting itself with "propaganda through posters and the press and placing Jewish shops on its index."³⁶² A Ligue Antisémitique sticker calling on people not to patronize Jewish shops was reported from Vesoul in August 1898,³⁶³ and similar action was noted at Lille.³⁶⁴ The "Reflections of a small trader of Caen" poster appealed, similarly: "Everyone, workers, traders, rentiers, employees, in your own interest, buy nothing at the *big monopolistic department stores!* BUY NOTHING FROM THE JEWS!"³⁶⁵ In 1898, too, *"Indicateurs"*, or Directories of Jews, were circulating in at least three departments, the Loire, the Saône-et-Loire and the Seine-Inférieure.³⁶⁶ At a Jeunesse Antisémite meeting in Paris in June 1898, "two travelling salesmen provided . . . statistics of all shops owned by Jews in Brittany and in Normandy", which were to be sent to "friends" in these areas.³⁶⁷ The organizer of the Ligue Antisémitique in Nantes was successfully sued in 1903 for displaying such a list in his shop window.³⁶⁸ This campaign, which bears all the marks of having been well orchestrated and coordinated, continued into 1899 and beyond. At Toulouse, in March 1899, a brochure attacking the Jewish-owned A la Maison de Paris, put out by the local section of the Ligue Antisémitique, was being distributed in the street outside the shop.[369] A police raid in August 1899 on the premises of the Caen Groupe d'Action Française found stickers with the familiar slogan: "For the sake of the honour and the salvation of France, never buy from the Jews."[370] In December 1899, the police intercepted a telegram sent to L'Antijuif in Paris from Remiremont, ordering 3,000 stickers with roughly the same slogan.[371] Earlier in the year, at Grenoble, the word "Juif" was daubed in red paint on shops and pavements outside shops belonging or supposed to belong to Jews, and small "Never buy from the Jews" stickers were placed on walls and urinals.[372]

A feature of this campaign was its special appeal to women. The material put out at Poitiers and Vesoul was specifically aimed at women. A speech made by the Comte de Sabran-Pontevès in Paris in April 1898 was addressed particularly to women.[373] The "Reflections of a small trader of Caen" declared: "Women of France! since it is you who usually do the shopping, the arm to combat the Monopolist—the Jew—is in your hands . . ."[374] As we have seen, in examining the Henry Subscription, antisemitism anyway had a special appeal for women. Nantes boasted a Groupe des Dames Antisémites[375] and, during the siege of "Fort-Chabrol", at least two demonstrations were made on Guérin's behalf by women, once by the women of "La Halle" or the central markets.[376] This appeal to women, in the context of the attack on department stores, must be related to the fact that their appeal rested in the same quarter. It was not for nothing that Zola called his story Au Bonheur des Dames, and in fact the Toulouse section of the Ligue Antisémitique staged a demonstration in March 1898 outside a shop called Le Paradis des Dames.[377] Zola, indeed, insisted on the sexual attraction of the big store, seducing women by the thousand, and described Mouret as having "the brutality of a Jew selling the flesh of women by the pound . . ."[378] The way in which the attraction of the Jewish store co-existed with fantasy fears of being kidnapped there, of suffering some kind of sexual assault, has been highlighted by Edgar Morin in his study of the rumour of Orléans,[379] and the same elements may well have been present in this variant of antisemitism in the 1890s, as Zola's novel suggests.

As we have seen in the first part of this book, Jewish shops and businesses were also attacked in more material ways, sometimes simply by putting antisemitic notices on Jewish shops and houses, and elsewhere. For example, in Nantes, in December 1897, slogans reading "Death to the Jews" were placed with rubber stamps on posters carrying advertisements for Jewish shops.[380] At Epinal, in January 1898, handwritten placards were put up on the houses of Jewish businessmen;[381] and, at Nice, in April 1900, antisemitic stickers were placed on shop windows.[382] Moreover, as we saw in chapter III, the riots of early 1898 were often directed against Jewish shops. In many towns, Jewish shops were physically attacked by angry crowds, and, in some cases, they were broken into and pillaged. In June 1899, Le Nouvelliste de l'Ouest was still calling on the local population "to demolish the Jewish shops".[383]

This whole campaign against department stores and in support of small traders was in part orchestrated by the antisemitic press and organizations, but organizations of small traders and shopkeepers themselves were also active in it, an indication of the real support which it enjoyed. Small traders and their supporters began, from the early 1890s, if not before, to form special organizations to protect their interests, mainly against department stores and co-operatives. As already mentioned, Léon Harmel, the Social Catholic leader, founded L'Union Fraternelle du Commerce et de l'Industrie in the Nord in 1891, specifically to defend Catholic shopkeepers against Jewish competition. The Union Fraternelle sent a report to the Reims Ecclesiastical Congress of 1896, stating that its aims were "to improve the position of small trade and industry, and to allow them to compete against speculation and monopolies."[384] In 1891 also, abbé Garnier, leader of the Union Nationale, founded the Comité du Commerce Parisien for small traders.[385] By the end of the decade, similar organizations existed in several *arrondissements* of Paris,[386] and in many provincial towns, including Roubaix, Poitiers and Nantes. One of the most transparently antisemitic of these was the Ligue Républicain Catholique pour Lutter contre le Commerce Juif, founded in Paris in 1898.[387] On the creation of the Nantes organization, the police reported in January 1898 as we have seen,: "Several important businessmen in the town have for some time now wanted to do this, believing that they cannot otherwise stand up to Jewish competition . . ."[388] By 1903, a national Union du Commerce et de l'Industrie representing small business had been formed, and was said by the police to have the support of a lobby of 25 deputies and 5 senators.[389]

Closely related to the interests of small traders were those of travelling salesmen. As we have seen, they, too, occupied a special place in the antisemitic movement. The police reported from Valence, for example, in February 1898, that the majority of travelling salesmen "is against the Jews".[390] Also in February 1898, 40 travelling salesmen from Brest sent a petition to General de Boisdeffre, calling for the expulsion of the Jews from France.[391] Travelling salesmen also organized under antisemitic auspices to defend their professional interests. In April 1898, for example, the police at Vienne collected the prospectus of a Union des Voyageurs Français Antisémites pour la Défense du Commerce et de l'Industrie, whose headquarters were said to be in Dijon.[392]

As in the case of agricultural interests, there is no doubt that the antisemitism of small traders was the reflection of real grievances, nor that in directing their attention against department stores and co-operatives, small shopkeepers had identified real enemies, whose lower prices and wide range of goods were enticing away their clientèle. Zévaès wrote of the 1880s: "In the towns, small businesses were suffering from the competition of the department stores, which had recently developed considerably. Many medium-sized shops, with established reputations—Le Coin de Rue, Le Pauvre Diable, Les Deux Magots, La Ville de Paris, Les Villes de France, Le Grand Condé, Le Prophète, La Dame Blanche, and so on—disappeared at this time"; and he gave examples of the involvement of small shopkeepers in Boulangism,[393] so similar to antisemitism in many ways. There is the testimony also of Zola, to which we have already referred. The novelist had personal experience of working for Hachette's giant publishing concern,[394] and he well represented the wonder and the fear which which the department store, the big shop, inspired in his contemporaries. In *Au Bonheur des Dames*, he certainly presented a picture of small traders being ruined by their new rival. Baudu, owner of a small shop, tells his niece that "each time Le Bonheur des Dames created a new department, a new collapse occurred among the small shopkeepers in the neighbourhood. The disaster spread outwards in waves, and even the oldest firms were cracking up."[395] In the provinces, the process occurred later, and may have been more of a shock in smaller places, where it came after a period of intense development of local retail trade. Thabault relates that there was a big increase in trading and in the number of shops in Mazières-en-Gâtine between 1870 and 1900: "But they were to suffer; after 1905, as far as their customers in the town were concerned, there was competition from the big Paris stores," trading by mail-order catalogues, as well as from the shops in Parthenay.[396] From tax documents, moreover, Daumard has demonstrated that the share of small trade and industry, in French trade and industry as a whole, fell significantly during the nineteenth century, which meant not only a relative decline in the wealth of those engaged in this sector, but also increased competition among them. She concludes that contemporaries' impression that there was a grave crisis among small traders was therefore fully justified.[397] At least one contemporary who studied the problem, the Vicomte d'Avenel, was a little more skeptical. He pointed out in 1902 that only 10% of the retail trade in clothing and furniture was in the hands of the department stores. What the department stores did, he argued, was not to drive small traders automatically out of business, but to force them to cut their profit margins: "Small shopkeepers are still able to sell things; but, since they can no longer sell them at the prices they would like, they shout out that they are being ruined." But this, in itself, must have involved a cut in living standards, and must have spelled ruin for some traders. The real trouble, according to d'Avenel, finally, was simply that there were too many small shopkeepers in France. In Paris, in particular, he claimed that their number had increased faster than had the total population of the capital. The retail trade was thus overcrowded, but blame was cast by shopkeepers, not on this structural feature itself, but more often on the department stores.[398] In the absence of further research, all one can say is that the argument seems convincing, particularly taken in conjunction with two further factors. The first is the impressionistic evidence of the lack of adaptability of French retailers, clinging to old ways that were inefficient, by modern economic standards, but which probably fulfilled a function of sociability. Maurice Donnay described retailers in the 1880s in these terms: "At that time, shopkeepers took forty years to acquire enough capital to allow them to retire at around 60 to live on the income from it. While they were still in business, they would never let a single opportunity of making a sale escape them, and, it was not uncommon to see a solitary shopkeeper waiting for the odd late customer up to 10 or 11 at night."[399] The second related factor is the survival of such retailers well beyond the 1890s, to stand, for foreign observers as something characteristically French,[400] and to inform later populist movements, such as Poujadism.[401] Shopkeepers, as a class, may have been in difficulties in the 1880s and 1890s, and may have felt deeply threatened, but they were not, as a class, being ruined.

Fears of co-operatives, as of department stores, were similarly exaggerated. There was a considerable expansion of consumer co-operatives, precisely in the period around the turn of the century. Numbers rose from 1,490 in 1900 to 2,148 in 1906, but their development was limited in France compared with that in England. This does not rule out the considerable impact on small retail traders that some of the larger co-operatives must have had, for example La Moissonneuse in the Faubourg Saint-Antoine, which had 15,000 members in 1902.[402] This impact, real or imagined, is reflected in the special discount scheme that the Union Nationale was able to offer its members. As its regulations explained: "Afraid of the institution of co-operatives that will take away their trade and anxious to attract a clientèle paying cash on the nail, shopkeepers will often agree to give discounts of 5, 6, 7 or even 10 per cent [to members]."[403]

Another claim made by antisemites on behalf of small shopkeepers is relevant here, and that is the claim that the interests of small traders, and of workers and petty bourgeois, coincided. Barrès told the electors of Nancy in 1898: "In effect, it is working people who provide small traders with their livelihood, for the bourgeoisie goes to the department stores."[404] Catholic spokesmen complained, similarly, that the Catholic upper-class, and even the religious orders, were patronizing Jewish shops rather than Catholic ones. Mgr Tilloy, for example, deplored the fact in 1897 that "the Jews of the boulevard are the preferred purveyors to the aristocracy and the upper bourgeoisie of Paris, while Christian tradesmen . . . although as skilful, and more honest . . . are generally neglected."[405] Drumont claimed that the Catholics of Nantes and Lille provided Jewish traders with their clientèle, and appealed to Catholics in La France juive "to patronize the tradesmen who shared their religious convictions, or at least did not attack them."[406] There does seem to be some truth in the claim that the clientèle of department stores was upper- and middle-class, though not exclusively so, if Zola's picture is anything to go by.[407] Concomitantly, it also seems to be true that small traders depended very much on working-class custom. When the Manufacture des Tabacs du Gros-Caillou in Paris was threatened with closure in 1898, a representative of the union of tobacco workers appealed at a public protest meeting for the support of the small traders of the quartier, with the argument that "it won't be the bourgeois who will keep them in business [when we have gone]; that sort doesn't do its shopping at the little shops."[408] This may explain, in part, why antisemites were less hostile to co-operatives than to department stores. Objectively less of a threat, the former also served a predominantly working-class clientèle, which, with their populist pretentions, the antisemites did not wish to antagonize.

In his claim that Catholics were patronizing Jewish traders, Mgr Tilloy made special reference to Jewish tailors and dressmakers. Drumont, too, claimed in *La France juive* that *"couturiers* and *couturières* are nearly all of Jewish origin", and saw this fact as responsible for the perversion in contemporary French fashion.[409] Jewish speciality in the cloth trade had traditionally been remarked upon,[410] though quantitative demonstration of it is available only for later in this century.[411] However, antisemitic claims probably had some objective basis in the later nineteenth century also. Léon Blum's father, for example, was the founder of a leading silk accessory firm in Paris, which invented the collapsible silk hat, apparently known as a "Blum" at the time.[412] The family firm of André Maurois, Fraenkel-Blin, had moved from Bischwiller to Elbeuf in 1871, and by the 1890s was one of the biggest woollen manufacturers in that city, employing over 1,000 people.[413] Besides resisting unwelcome competition in this sphere, antisemites, as Drumont shows, were also resisting changes in fashion; and change here was not only particularly rapid, its implications were social and sexual as well as economic. The growing uniformity of dress, which the expansion of ready-made clothing allowed, tended to obliterate social distinctions that had previously been marked by distinctions in costume;[414] while changes in female fashion in particular signified a threat to the traditional image of women, to which, we have seen, antisemites were especially attached.[415] Did some of these fears, mixed with an aristocratic disdain for trade, inspire the objection raised by the antisemitic deputy, the Comte d'Aulan, in 1900, to the very idea of admitting a Paris *couturier* to the Légion d'Honneur?[416]

If the association of Jews with the cloth trade had some basis in fact, their identification, by antisemites, with the big department stores was very wide of the mark. Of the well-known Paris stores, dating mainly from the 1850s and the 1860s, the Bon Marché, the Louvre, the Belle Jardinière, the Printemps and the Samaritaine, none was founded or run by a Jew. The financiers Pereire and Fould had given the Louvre some backing to begin with, but they remained minority share-holders. The founder of the Samaritaine, Cognacq, was a militant Catholic, and financed the Prix Cognacq to encourage large families.[417] Jews probably did own a proportion of later and smaller stores in Paris and the provinces, but there is no evidence, beyond that provided by the antisemites, to suggest that they were particularly prominent here. Department stores were, of course, largely concerned with the retailing of clothes and furnishings, and thus depended, to some extent, on Jewish suppliers.[418] However, large grocery chains, the other important novelty in the distribution sector—we have come across Félix Potin, probably the biggest[419]—almost certainly had no Jewish connection at all, since this would have offended dietary taboos, which even emancipated Jews continued to respect. But, even if the claim that department stores were Jewish had been true, it would have been irrelevant in any explanation of their success, which derived rather from superior organization, economies of scale and the lowering of profit margins. Again, the Jew was introduced by antisemites into economic explanation to fill a gap in comprehension, and also because Jewish influence provided a kind of explanation which relieved those who adopted it of any responsibility for their own failure. The attacks on department stores stressed that their procedures were unfair, and that competition against them was hopeless. The reaction was negative, and the remedies suggested did not entail the adoption of the more effective commercial methods which they practised, but appealed for aid to forces outside the market-place altogether, to the coercive apparatus of the State and to patriotic sentiment. Conversely, as *Le Petit Phare* (of Nantes) wrote in December 1898, echoing Lafargue, there seemed to be a group of people who had undertaken to elevate patriotism to the heights of the interests of shopkeepers.[420]

As the Nantes journalist indicates, there was a considerable element of interested manipulation of public opinion in this brand of antisemitism. Dagan asserted in 1899 that "the leaders of the antisemitic movement are ruined businessmen and financiers or those on the verge of being ruined", and claimed that *La Libre Parole* was simply the organ of non-Jewish business interests using antisemitism to ward off Jewish competition.[421] Guérin made the same accusation against Drumont and his newspaper;[422] but, of course, Guérin, himself, as we have seen, had exactly this kind of commercial interest in antisemitism, and his campaigns against Jewish business in Paris and in Algeria were not unconnected with his own business concerns.[423] Such charges are probably unfair in Drumont's case, although his protest on behalf of "modest provincial bookshops" against Hachette's monopoly of railway station bookstalls, was related to the fact that Hachette apparently refused to stock his own books.[424] Several other antisemitic leaders approximate to Dagan's description of them. Millot, secretary of the Ligue Antisémitique de France in 1890, was an ex-jeweller, who claimed that he had been ruined by fraudulent Jewish competition.[425] Captain Mégé, one of the leaders of the antisemitic and Nationalist movement in Lyon, worked, according to a police agent, as "the representative of a Czech meat processing company".[426] Libaros, the leader of the Nantes section of the Ligue Antisémitique was a Catholic bookseller;[427] while the antisemitic deputy Pascal had himself worked as a sales assistant in the Bon Marché.[428]

The interests of small industrialists were linked in antisemitic writing with those of small traders. Drumont claimed that his readership included the industrialist alongside the trader;[429] and in *La Fin d'un monde*, after describing the plight of "small manufacturers, crushed beneath excessive taxation and unable to struggle any longer against the concerted efforts of large-scale capital", he wrote:

It is among these people that the movement of protest against Semitism has found the most supporters. They are not passive like the poor, who are disciplined to suffering and bow their shoulders so that burdens can be more easily attached to their backs; they have known better days and they remember them; they can appreciate the ravages of the Jew better than proletarians: for they have seen the Jew at work; they know what low means this unscrupulous enemy will stoop to, how underhanded he always is in business and everywhere else. These victims from the Bourgeoisie will soon provide the avant-garde of the army of Socialism

—a term which he used here to describe antisemitism.[430] There is little evidence to support such a claim, such a hope. Small industrialists do not seem to have been prominent in the antisemitic movement; and the small industrial unit remained predominant in France until long after Drumont's time. However, its role in the economy was on the decline by the end of the nineteenth century,[431] and some small industrialists are bound to have suffered difficulties or failures, and may have been tempted to blame the Jews. The antisemitism of the playwright Maurice Donnay may have stemmed from such a source, from his experience of working as a young man in his father's small and unsuccessful engineering works in Paris. He remembered being sent to beg for the renewal of a loan at 20 per cent from "a little financier . . . whose name ended in 'er' . . . and who had a strong German accent".[432] Zola pointed out, moreover, that manufacturers had their own grievances against the department stores. The silk manufacturer Gaujean in *Au Bonheur des Dames* "accused the department stores of ruining French manufacturers; three or four of them imposed their own terms and dominated the market; and he let it be known that the only way to fight back against them was to give every support to small traders . . ."[433]

IV. "WHY ARE FOREIGNERS COMING TO LIVE IN FRANCE?"

We have referred to the patriotic colouring lent to shopkeepers', as well as to rural antisemitism; and economic antisemitism in general had a nationalist dimension. It was a movement to free the French economy from foreign domination, or, in the words of Barrès, "the struggle of the land and the race against a financial feudalism",[434] that was not French. This nationalist element was nowhere more obvious than in the opposition to immigration. Large numbers of Alsatian Jews had come to settle in France after the cession of Alsace to the German Empire in 1871, and about 10,000 Jewish immigrants from Eastern Europe followed them in the next three decades. The second wave, in particular, Yiddish speaking, Orthodox in custom and dress, concentrating in certain *quartiers* of the capital, fitting the antisemitic stereotype much better than older assimilated communities,[435] aroused direct hostility and alarm.[436] But antisemitic hostility to immigration was not exclusively aimed at Jews. It involved a call to limit the entry into France of foreign entrepreneurs and workers generally, and for much tighter control of naturalization; while underlying both was a deep-seated anxiety about France's lack of demographic vitality.

As we have seen, in the eyes of antisemites, even French Jews were foreigners, cosmopolitans, "the cosmopolitans who control big business and industry and seek to belittle France", in the words of a speaker in Paris in April 1898.[437] But this meant that the categories of Jew and foreigner became frequently interchangeable, and that people could nourish their anti-Jewish feelings on the spectacle of the "invasion" of France by foreigners, who were not in the main, it might be admitted, Jewish. Quoting Jacques de Biez, Drumont wrote in 1891 that "the real plague of France are the foreigners who invade her, who abuse her hospitality, and who carve her up like a conquered province."[438] Barrès complained in 1893 of "these thirteen hundred thousand foreigners who are invading all our jobs, and even the liberal professions . . ."[439] Wicart, in the pamphlet already cited, wrote: "Our town of Roubaix has been penetrated by foreigners to such an extent that, before the recent mass naturalizations, three-quarters of the population was exotic. Most big towns have been taken by assault by the international element in the same way, which lives there as if in a country which it has conquered, treating its generous hosts with the greatest scorn."[440] Maurras mounted a campaign in *La Cocarde* in 1895 "against resident foreigners to whom I gave the name of 'metics' after the Metics of ancient Athens . . . "[441] He explained later that he had been motivated here in large part by having seen his native Provence invaded by foreign residents. In 1865, he wrote, the Riviera had been still unspoiled: "The compatriots of Lord Brougham, and our other invaders from Europe, Asia and America, had not yet had time to wreak their havoc there, and the landscape still retained its savage charm . . ."; but thirty years later it had become "a pell-mell of Moorish villas, Gothic castles and German barracks, their ugly shapes all clashing with each other . . . it was Cosmopolis."[442] This irruption was the more shocking in that, for Maurras, Provence had a symbolic significance as the concrete historical region which linked France to the classical order of the Ancient World, in the face of the chaotic forces of Northern barbarism and the Semitic East.[443] It is ironic that his Provençal compatriot, Victor Gelu, had made much the same lament 40 years earlier in 1857, again attributing the modernization of the environment to foreign and Jewish influence.[444]

The Nationalist and antisemitic campaign against "metics" and the "foreign invasion" of France centred on a demand for two specific reforms: the limitation of Naturalization, and a strict control over the employment of foreign labour. Drumont argued in *La France juive* that the Jewish "invasion" of France was greatly aided by "the facility with which naturalization could be obtained";[445] and, in 1889, he referred to "naturalized citizens, the masters of our secrets and the representatives of international Finance, just waiting for us to be defeated so that they can start dealing in our ransom money".[446] Barrès called, in the 1890s, for "a prudent law on naturalization" which would grant full civil rights only to second-generation immigrants, explaining: "It is in vain that a foreigner, when he becomes naturalized, swears to think and to live like a Frenchman; it is in vain that he joins his interests with ours; for the blood obstinately continues to follow its natural course against such oaths, against the laws."[447] Naturalization was a "legal fiction . . . which could never make the blood of a Levantine take on the quality of the blood of a French peasant or a Parisian worker."[448] Implicitly for the same reasons, Forain expressed the view in 1898 that full naturalization should wait until the fourth generation after immigration to France.[449] Léon Daudet, similarly, accused Republican governments of "fabricating false Frenchmen . . . The number of naturalizations [he claimed] has increased in an alarming manner, particularly since 1896." Naturalized citizens, he added, cornered the best jobs, and kept out natives; they were, moreover, responsible for the "low tone" of the French press, for the lowering of ethical standards in business, and for the rise of antimilitarism, besides being potential spies.[450] In *Le Problème de la dépopulation*, published in 1897 and which represented the programme of the recently-founded L'Alliance Nationale pour l'Accroissement de la Population Française, the statistician Jacques Bertillon, brother of the anti-Dreyfusard criminologist Alphonse Bertillon, expressed the same view, and pointed to the fears that underlay it. Naturalization, he said, was seen by some people as a solution to the problem of France's stagnant population, but, in fact, it was no solution: "One can give a certain number of foreigners false French noses, and rights to go with them, but it is more difficult to inculcate in them a love of France, and the desire to fulfil their duty towards her . . ." Frenchmen, in effect, for Bertillon as for Barrès and Daudet, were born and not made, and the naturalized Frenchman would always remain "the foreigner, that is to say the rival, the enemy, and, in the hour of danger, the spy".[451]

Bertillon pointed out that France's resident foreign population, including those who had been naturalized, had risen from just under 400,000 in 1851 to over 1,300,000 in 1891, the figure cited by Barrès. This dramatic increase was, he insisted, the consequence of the slow growth-rate of France's own population. Here, Bertillon brought into the open one of the basic fears underlying Nationalist and antisemitic feeling in the 1880s, 1890s and 1900s: the sense that France's demographic vitality had been lost, and, in particular, the realization that France's population was on the decline relative to that of Britain and Germany, her two main economic rivals, and her potential enemies in war. Bertillon stressed that the sluggish French birth-rate was responsible for France's decline in terms of international prestige and economic prosperity, linking a collective feeling of impotence to a collective feeling of loss of status. Such anxiety, expressed with different emphases, was very general at the time. For example, it informed Zola's populationist novel *Fécondité* (1899), and it inspired the Catholic campaign against depopulation, led by the bishops in the decade before 1914.[452] As so often, the antisemites only gave a special slant to a common theme, and articulated worries that were widespread. In *La France juive*, Drumont pointed to the relative decline of the French population in Europe since the time of the Revolution, and commented: "One feels like a star that is entering its glacial period."[453] Again in 1891, he referred to "the quite legitimate emotion produced by these desolating statistics which confirm, with the help of figures that are beyond dispute, the fact that the birth-rate in France continues to fall, that the French people is voluntarily infertile, producing four times fewer children than its neighbours . . ."[454] For this state of affairs, he blamed the inheritance laws enshrined in the Napoleonic Code, Malthusian practices, the decline of religious and moral standards, and the pressure of public welfare organizations, all of which, of course, came under the general umbrella of Jewish influence.[455] Léon Daudet in 1911 also drew attention to "the progressive fall in the French birth-rate . . . to this fatal crisis in the birth-rate"; and asked: "Are we then finished as a people . . .?"[456] In February of the same year, Daniel

Halévy quoted a passage from *Libre Entretien* in his diary: "In a few years from now, France will have lost the right to monopolize all the land within its frontiers, and its families of sterile landowners will have been expropriated by more prolific nations"; and he commented:[457]

> This is what lies at the root of everything, but which tends to be hushed up. People declaim against this decline or that . . . But only one is irremediable, and it is the cause of the others. It doesn't get mentioned, people say, because it is irremediable. But, in that case, don't let's mention the others. I don't wish to deny the moral and social disorder that we are experiencing. But, then, order never was a French characteristic. A nation is saved by the vitality of its people, the warmth of their characters, the abundance of individual talents. France is threatened today not by disorder, which has always been with us, but by physiological paucity, by a shortage of men. A robust country can support the dead weight of a bureaucracy (Russia), or a body of corrupt politicians (USA, Italy), but when such a bureaucracy, such a body of politicians, is battening on a country whose life itself is ebbing away, then things look very serious . . . This sad conviction explains a great deal: the anger of a Maurras, the despair of a Degas.

Less despairing, other antisemites suggested, like Drumont, that depopulation stemmed from causes that might be reversed, and seem to have believed in the possibility of encouraging French couples to have more children. Wicart, for example, inveighed against Malthusian practices, which, he said, were being propagated in France through English instigation.[458] Léon Daudet also claimed that "Malthusian theories" were being openly and deliberately propagated, with the connivance of Republican governments, and cited the divorce law of 1884 sponsored by "the Jew Naquet".[459] The denunciation of divorce as "an absolutely Jewish idea"[460] was common in antisemitic writing, coupled with an idealization of the Family. Drumont referred to "the Mosaic law to legitimize divorce which the Jew Naquet has succeeded in imposing by force on a country which has for so long owed its moral stature to its respect for the indissolubility of marriage."[461] The antisemite Massabuau, deputy for the Aveyron from 1898 to 1914, was the founder of a review, *La Famille Française.*[462] The Union Nationale, according to one of its candidates in the 1898 elections, was dedicated to "love of the Family".[463] Drumont, in 1891, celebrated "the notion of patrimony, which, born of labour, partakes of its sacred character . . ."[464] A corollary of this cult of the Family, as we saw in discussing the Henry Subscription, was the attempt to make antisemitism a family-based movement. In a talk, given in Paris in April 1898, for example, the Comte de Sabran-Pontevès traced the role of "the Christian woman . . . pilloried the Jews and the Freemasons and called on the women present to teach their children to hate them."[465] More constructively, Christian Democrats and Social Catholics put forward various proposals to encourage larger families, for example, by family allowances, by special fiscal relief, and by legislation to preserve viable family holdings in agriculture.[466] This was all part of a much wider movement among Catholics in favour of the Family.[467] The correlation between Catholic belief and larger families was, moreover, noted by antisemites. Drumont referred ironically in 1891 to "the primitive departments, that is to say, those in which some relic of the old beliefs remains, some vestige of moral sense . . ."[468] Indirectly, a solution was sought for France's demographic crisis in the expansion and development of the colonial Empire. Though some continued to see this as a diversion from the pursuit of revenge against Germany in Europe, others believed, not only that the Empire had repaired France's international standing and prestige, but that it also made up for the mother country's population deficiency in military terms, by providing a supply of native colonial troops.[469]

Antisemitism, then, reflected an anxiety about France's demographic situation in a general way, but it is difficult to establish any correlation between the incidence of antisemitism and the local movement of population. Both were most important in the capital; but, while in the Lyon region the incidence of antisemitism was high and the birth-rate particularly low,[470] at Nancy antisemitism was important, but the demographic situation was relatively favourable.[471] The reason for this seems to be quite obvious. People were aware of the general demographic crisis, and even that the birth-rate had kept up better in Catholic areas, but, in general, the regional and local pattern of the crisis had not impinged on public consciousness. Demographic analysis, after all, was in its infancy, and Bertillon was one of its pioneers.[472]

Though often a theme that ran parallel to antisemitism, the call to limit naturalization was also given an explicitly anti-Jewish colouring. As we saw, Vogüé's deputy, who proposed a law to restrict naturalization, "was really aiming at the Jews". In his Nancy Programme of 1898, Barrès declared that restriction of naturalization was "the best way to get at the Jew . . . It is through this fissure that the worst Jews and a lot of bad Frenchmen have come";[473] and he wrote in 1899 that "Dreyfus is a battlefield on which a Frenchman born of the land and of his ancestors must take up the challenge of the foreigners and the naturalized."[474] The Royalist leader, André Buffet, also presented the strict control of naturalization as a contribution towards the solution of the "Jewish question".[475] Moreover, as we have seen, the call to limit, to prevent or to reverse naturalization was directed very specifically against the Jewish population of Algeria, and nearly 70 deputies sponsored a bill to repeal the Crémieux decree in 1899.[476] In this connection, Daudet claimed in L'Avant-Guerre that the French government's naturalization procedures were supervised by a Jewish civil servant.[477]

A second consequence of the slow rate of demographic growth in France in the second half of the century had been the recourse on a large scale to foreign labour, mainly Belgian and Italian. In La France juive, Drumont referred to France as a country "where the number of births is lower than that in other countries, and which is now obliged to call in foreign workers on to its soil".[478] Bertillon's figures here are correct, and indicate that about 3 per cent of France's recorded population in the 1890s was foreign. The greater number of these immigrants were agricultural and industrial workers, though they were found also in other sectors, for example the liberal professions and retail trade.[479] Although French workers were not very prone to antisemitism, they were frequently hostile to immigrants. E. Duclaux, of the Académie de Sciences, remarked in 1899 that "if the workers complain very little about Jewish influence, one does hear recrimination sometimes against Italian workers and in general against employers' taking on foreign workers. Evidently, there is some justification in this: we know that foreign workers will often work for low wages, which obviously provokes protests, resentments and fighting on the part of French workers."[480] It is well known that violence in the crisis of the late 1840s was sometimes directed against foreign workers,[481] and hostility remained endemic as their numbers increased later in the century. Thabault relates that the railway navvies, many of whom were foreign, who built the Niort-Parthenay railway in the 1880s frightened and shocked the local population.[482] And xenophobic reaction of this kind was not uncommon in France at this time, and indeed often took more extreme forms. Michelle Perrot reports 58 serious collective incidents against foreign workers in France between 1882 and 1889, mainly against Italians; and between 1881 and 1893 at least 30 Italians were killed in such incidents. Violence was less frequent in the 1890s, but feelings still ran high in many places.[483] Such hostility was shown towards the Italian workers of Commercy (Meuse), for example, after the assassination of President Carnot by an Italian anarchist in 1894, that extra police had to be drafted into the region; while Ardouin-Dumazet attributed "the troubles" in Armentières about the same time to the presence of Belgian workers, who made up nearly half the population.[484] It is fair to add that as often immigrant labour seems to have been assimilated without difficulty. Raymond Poignant states that the assimilation of the mainly Belgian immigrants in the Pas-de-Calais presented no problems before 1914;[485] while Robert Louis Stevenson reported this remark from an innkeeper's wife from near Gien in the 1870s: "We have many Italians . . . and they do very well; they do not complain of the people hereabouts."[486]

However, there is some evidence to suggest that hostility towards immigrant workers, whether on the part of French workers or other social classes, could find expression in antisemitic terms. The two themes were coupled by Proudhon, perhaps the most "popular" Socialist theorist in the late nineteenth century.[487] A verse of "La Marseillaise antijuive", which we have quoted in another context, ran: "Go home, foreigners,/That'll give us some work/And put up our wages./Chase out of the country/The whole gang of Yids!"[488] The pattern of distribution of the 1898 riots and of support for the Henry Subscription, as well as other indicators, also suggest a correlation between the presence of immigrant labour and the overt manifestation of antisemitism. This is true of the Lyon region; by the 1870s the Rhône had the second highest proportion of immigrants of all French departments and Lyon had an immigrant population of 15,500 by 1886.[489] It is also true of the East, where the importance of Italian immigration into the new industrial region of Briey, for example, was reflected by the appearance there of four Italian language newspapers in the decade before 1914.[490] We have mentioned hostility towards Italians at Commercy in the 1890s, and here the correlation seems clear, since the town was in a constituency that elected an antisemitic deputy in 1898. So, of course

did Nancy, which, although its birth-rate was relatively buoyant, experienced
a rapid expansion in the last few decades of the century, partly as a result of
foreign immigration. By the turn of the century, 7.5% of the town's population was foreign.[491] But, perhaps, the correlation is most telling for the
South-East, which had experienced the worst of the xenophobic incidents of
the 1880s, where 13% of the population of the Bouches-du-Rhône and 17%
of that of the Alpes-Maritimes were foreign by 1890,[492] and where the high
incidence of antisemitism is otherwise very difficult to explain. Given Thabault's reference to the hostile reception given to foreign workers in the
Parthenay region, it is interesting to note that its deputy, the Marquis de
Maussabré, was a member of the antisemitic parliamentary group. One must
allow here for popular failure to distinguish between the "foreigner", who
simply did not come from the district, and the "foreigner" who was actually
not French, either of whom might be a Jew, and we have seen, that, to an
extent, such confusions were fostered by the antisemites. One suspects, too,
that antisemites, eager for working-class support, fastened on to popular hostility towards foreign workers in the hope of channelling it into their own
movement.

Certainly, the control of immigrant labour was a common theme in their
propaganda. Drumont declared in *La France juive:* "Our French workers
cannot find work, for 400,000 German workers and 200,000 Italians are facing
them . . . with the most formidable competition", aided and encouraged by
the Jews.[493] In the 1898 election campaign, antisemitic candidates in Paris
frequently alluded to the same problem, and offered solutions to it in their
programmes. Lacabane, in the 14th *arrondissement,* referred to "the need to
prevent foreign workers from competing unfairly with French ones"; a candidate in another constituency in the same *arrondissement* called for a ban on
the engagement of foreign workers at rates below those normally paid to
French workers; in the 3rd *arrondissement,* a candidate promised "a tax on
foreign workers"; while in the 16th, another wanted a tax on their employers.[494] A more elaborate policy in this area was presented by Barrès in three
articles in *Le Figaro,* republished as a brochure during the 1893 election
campaign, under the title: "Against the Foreigners: A study for the protection
of French workers". Barrès pointed out that the employment of foreign
workers at low wage-rates not only threatened the wage-rates of French workers, but allowed employers of foreign labour to compete unfairly against their
more patriotic rivals. He therefore proposed a tax on employers of foreign
labour of 10% of their wage bill. In addition, he advocated a tax on foreign
workers, and on foreign residents generally, in lieu of military service (the fact
that foreigners were not liable for military service, and thus did not require
leave of absence on that account, was said to encourage their employment);
the exclusion of foreign workers from any employment related to national
defence; and the expulsion from France of all foreigners who became destitute
and a charge on public assistance. More tentatively, Barrès proposed also a ban
on French employers' going abroad to hire labour, and a ban on the employment of foreigners in any State service or industry.[495] The importance of this

policy for Barrès is indicated by the fact that he returned to it in his articles for *La Cocarde* in 1894,[496] and that it reappeared, in modified form, in his Nancy Programme of 1898.[497] The control and limitation of the influx of immigrant labour also figured in the political programme of the Christian Democratic movement,[498] and in that of Déroulède;[499] while two Left-wing members of the antisemitic parliamentary group, Chiché and Charles Bernard, sponsored unsuccessful Bills to limit the number of foreign workers in France, in 1898 and in 1901.[500]

To conclude this chapter, some other dimensions of what one might call "demographic antisemitism" should be mentioned. First, immigrants and, in particular, Jews were alleged to be unusually prolific in contrast to native French people.[501] We have seen evidence of this in the Henry Subscription, and it is again reflected in the over-estimation of the size of the French Jewish population by antisemites.[502] Paradoxically, "the infertile and destructive character of Jewish civilization"[503] was stressed at the same time. The explanation for this would seem to be that the alleged Jewish fertility was a symbol of Jewish power and sexuality (themes to which we will return in later chapters), and also served as a warning to the French that they had better procreate or be overrun. The assertion of the Jewishness of birth-control and divorce, on the other hand, served to deny that either reflected any real change in French values or cultural practice. And, in each case, the essential difference between the Jews and the French was maintained. The Jews were actually prolific, while the French were temporarily sterile; but, while the Jews favoured and promoted Malthusianism, the French underwent it against their real wishes. A kind of ideal scheme of separate patterns of reproductive behaviour was thus established, a guard perhaps against much feared inter-racial promiscuity.

Second, antisemitism represented a reaction to the shift of population from the countryside to the towns. Laments over "the rural exodus" were, we have seen, a commonplace of Nationalist and antisemitic literature.[504] Drumont pointed out that the urban population of France had risen from 6 millions in 1831 to 13 millions in 1881, and evoked rural emigration in these emotive terms:[505]

These peasants have struggled for many years; so many roots link them to this land, which has so often proved harsh to them, but on which their ancestors have lived; they continue to hope for the ray of sunlight that will recompense them for their labours, but suddenly everything collapses. They owe more than they can repay, they must resign themselves to leaving, sell the big oxen, sell the plough. They put their few belongings on a cart; on the rise, they cast a last look at their native fields; then go off towards the nearest town, towards the factory . . .

More matter of fact, Léon Daudet complained that the government "was attracting to the urban centres, to the factories, all the vital forces of the countryside".[506] As we have seen, the Jew symbolized the wicked city and urban capitalism, against which were set simple and stable rural values; but, beyond opposing urbanization, antisemites seem also to have objected to the mobility of population as such, to the uncontrolled and free movement of people across, but also within, national boundaries. Their ideal was a fixed and rooted population, rooted, as Barrès expressed it, in "the land and the dead". This ideal was constructed in face of a social and economic situation in which people were "uprooted",[507] and the archetypal symbol of the "uprooted" was the Jew, the Wandering Jew.

The myth of the Wandering Jew derived from early Christian legend. Ahasuerus, who had refused to let Christ rest on the way to Calvary, was supposed to have been condemned in punishment to deathless wandering over the earth.[508] This powerful symbolization of the Diaspora[509] remained current down to modern times, and was well established in nineteenth-century France, where it figured in popular prints and literature.[510] It was by no means necessarily a hostile myth, as its classical expression in Eugène Sue's Le Juif errant (1845) shows. Sue's Jew is a defender of the innocent, a compassionate Prometheus, and the reluctant instrument of divine vengeance. Antisemites later in the century could thus take the currency of the myth for granted, but, in exploiting and updating it, they lent it a universally hostile tone. Abbé Desportes, for example, exclaimed: "how many little yids are born in railway trucks!"[511] Drumont referred in La France juive to "the eternally nomadic Semite";[512] and wrote, in qualification, in La Dernière Bataille: "The Jew is . . . no longer the eternal wanderer, whose arrival in the old days upset a peaceful town, he has become master of the caravan, and multitudes follow him without knowing where they are going."[513] Again, in 1892, he described the Jews in these terms: "They arrive from who knows where, they live in a mystery, a question mark stands over their death . . . They do not rise in the world gradually, they jump up suddenly dazzling everyone with huge fortunes whose origin is obscure; they don't die, they disappear again as suddenly like characters in a play . . ."[514] What is this, if not the description of the situation of the urbanized population itself, in which fortunes are quickly made and lost, in which people come and go, or live side by side, anonymously, without attachments, without neighbours, in anomie?[515] The projection of this situation on to the Jew, who is ostracized, expelled from the community on whose boundaries he lives, can be seen as an attempt to overcome it, and to return thereby to the supposed "real" community of village life. Here it is significant that so much opprobrium was directed against Zola, who was not only the author of "J'accuse", but of La Terre (1887), which exploded this rustic myth.[516]

An interesting chronological parallel to antisemitism, in this context, is provided by the contemporaneous resentment against France's properly nomadic population of gypsies. Gypsies or vagabonds and Jews were not uncommonly associated. Jules Vallès, in the 1860s, wrote that strolling players "were all called Jacob or Fritz!"; and referred to the fact that Rachel came of a family of pedlars, and had earned her living as a child as a street singer in Lyon.[517]

Lacretelle's Silbermann declared his ambition "to break with the nomadic life, to free myself from the hereditary destiny that has made most of us vagabonds"; and the narrator in the novel describes his mother's emotion, when she showed him the Jew's House at Nîmes: "I felt in her the same impression of mystery, the same movement of distrust, as when, avoiding a little further on, at the gates of the town, an area, all rutted and disfigured with piles of ashes, she told me: 'That is the place where the gypsies camp.' [518] An echo of the same association can be heard in Maurras's justification of Vichy's antisemitic laws: "a balance must be struck between the Nomad and the Citizen . . ."[519] Attention was focused on gypsies in the French press around the turn of the century, by the arrest of two nomadic criminal gangs in 1898 and in 1902. They aroused something of the same panic, and were charged with the same evil intentions, the same omnipotence, the same omnipresence as Jews. *Le Petit Journal,* wrote, for example, of the first gang, known as *"les vernisseurs"*: "Nearly all the crimes that have ravaged the department of the Eure in recent times can be attributed to this band of malefactors."[520] Gypsies excited the fears of the settled population, for whom vagabondage itself was regarded as a threat and associated with crime, but the fact that these fears prompted action to put an end to nomadic life altogether, suggests that it was a spectacle that aroused still profounder fears, posing a threat to the whole pattern of sedentary life and its values, stimulating an overpowering envy that was too dangerous to be tolerated, the envy of the free by the unfree.[521] A circular issued by the Prefect of the Yonne in April 1895 stated: "The number of vagabonds, foreign nomads and other vagrants, circulating in groups or individually, is increasing all the time. The people engage habitually in begging, and only manage to subsist by means of the alms which they obtain, most often by intimidation, or even by violence." The Prefect thus ordered a strict surveillance of all gypsies and nomads in the department, a ban on camping on all public roads, and the arrest and prosecution for vagabondage of all persons unable to produce evidence of fixed residence or remunerative employment.[522] Thus the representative of the censused, taxed and conscripted population of the 1890s struck out against the survivors of an earlier, more loosely-knit type of social organization. But, though vagabondage had been a structural feature of traditional society, beyond certain limits, it had been a sign of crisis, and the object of severe repression.[523] The nineteenth-century Prefect's response could thus be said to be traditional, and the antisemites' hostility to population movement could be set in the same framework. But, from another point of view, the two responses were related, but different, almost mirror-images. For rather than rejecting, in favour of an urbanized immobile present, a vestige of the traditional society which they sought ostensibly to defend, antisemites sought to freeze the fluidity of modern populations into the supposed solidity of a rural past. While attacking the Wandering Jew, therefore, and opposing the rural exodus, Drumont actually took the part of French paupers threatened by proposed stricter legislation on vagabondage. But he did so on the grounds that they were French, with authentic roots in the country, and that they were being threatened with total uprooting in the form of expulsion from the territory.[524] Here, too, he was assuming the antisemite's role of defender of the poor, which leads us to the subject of the next chapter.

NOTES

1 Zola, "Procès-Verbal", *Le Figaro,* 5 December 1897, in Zola, *L'Affaire Dreyfus,* p. 85.
2 Dagan, *Enquête sur l'antisémitisme,* p. 15.
3 Ibid., p. 9.
4 Ibid., p. 57.
5 Ibid., p. 64.
6 Lazare, *L'Antisémitisme,* p. 385; see also ibid., pp. 225, 227, 238–9 and chapter XIV.
7 Anatole Leroy-Beaulieu, *L'Antisémitisme* (Paris, 1897), pp. 58–9. A Liberal Catholic, Anatole was the brother of Paul Leroy-Beaulieu, the well-known and influential economist; see Roger-H. Guerrand, *Les Origines du logement social en France* (Paris, 1967), pp. 261–81.
8 The interpretation is also valid for certain aspects of antisemitism in the more distant past; for example, there seems to be some correlation between persecutions of the Jews in mediaeval and early modern Europe and times of economic crisis; see Fernand Braudel, *The Mediterranean and the Mediterranean World in the Age of Philip II* (London, 1973), II, pp. 820–22 and 899.
9 Cit. Viau, *Vingt ans d'antisémitisme,* p. 8.
10 Drumont, *Le Testament d'un antisémite,* pp. 132–4.
11 Cit. Bournand, *Les Juifs et nos contemporains,* p. 44.
12 I. Levaillant, "La Genèse de l'antisémitisme sous la Troisième République", *Revue des Etudes Juives,* 53 (1907), cit. Jeannine Verdès, "La Presse devant le krach d'une banque catholique: l'Union Générale—1882", *Archives de Sociologie des Religions,* 19 (1965), p. 127.
13 Mermeix, *Les Antisémites en France: Notice sur un fait contemporain* (Paris, 1892), p 22, cit. Verdès, op. cit., p 126.
14 *Le Pays,* 16 February 1882, cit., ibid., p. 145; see also Verdès-Leroux, *Scandale financier et antisémitisme catholique,* pp. 49–60.
15 *La Libre Parole,* 24 November 1902, cit. Verdès-Leroux, op. cit., p. 73; see also ibid., pp. 13, 69–72, 97 and 117; Daudet, *Au Temps de Judas,* pp. 197–8.
16 *La Croix,* 12 March 1899, cit. Sorlin, *"La Croix" et les Juifs,* p. 90.
17 See chapter V, p. 173 above.
18 Drumont, "La Suprême Entrevue", 21 November 1892, *De l'Or, de la boue, du sang,* p. 73; see also Drumont, *La Dernière Bataille,* pp. 20, 27–30 and Part III; Drumont, *TA,* pp 194–9; Verdès-Leroux, op. cit., pp. 72–3 and 122.
19 Zola, "Procès-Verbal", loc. cit.
20 Report, Commissaire spécial, Saint-Quentin, 6 January 1895. AN F⁷ 12464.
21 See Marrus, *The Politics of Assimilation,* pp. 136–40; Dansette, *Les Affaires de Panama,* chapters IV and V; see also Barrès's fictionalized version of the suicide in *Leurs Figures* (Paris, 1911).
22 Daily Report, Prefect of Police, 15 February 1898. APP Ba 106.
23 Daily Report, Prefect of Police, 17 April 1898. APP Ba 106.
24 Report, Commissaire spécial, Nancy, 27 February 1898. AN F⁷ 12474; see also chapter I, pp. 15, 22, 27 and 32–4; and chapter III, pp. 117–18 above.
25 Daily Reports, Prefect of Police, 29 and 14 January 1898. APP Ba 106.
26 See Bouvier, *Les Deux Scandales de Panama,* pp. 7–13, 199–204 and *passim;* also Bouvier, *Le Krach de l'Union Générale;* Bouvier, *Naissance d'une banque: le Crédit Lyonnais* (Paris, 1968); Verdès-Leroux, "Un prototype des scandales politi-

co-financiers: le krach de l'Union Générale (1882)", *Le Mouvement Social*, no. 66 (1969), pp. 89–103; Duroselle, "L'Antisémitisme en France", pp. 54–5.

27 Zévaès, *Au Temps du Boulangisme*, pp. 21–2.
28 Drumont, "La Suprême Entrevue", loc. cit.
29 Drumont, *DB*, pp. 367 and 347.
30 See, for example, ibid., pp. 385–6.
31 Leroy-Beaulieu, *Les Doctrines de haine*, p. 138.
32 Bournand, op. cit., pp. 31 and 140.
33 Cit. Rollet, *L'Action sociale des catholiques*, I, p. 122.
34 *La Croix*, 22 January 1886, cit. Sorlin, *"La Croix" et les Juifs*, p. 61.
35 Mayeur, "Les Congrès nationaux", p. 202.
36 E. Wicart, *Les Deux Causes de la décadence du pays* (Roubaix, 1898), p. 7.
37 Daily Report, Prefect of Police, 26 January 1898. APP Ba 106.
38 Drumont, *La France juive*, I, pp. xiv–xv.
39 Ibid., II, p. 291.
40 Cit. L. de Gérin-Ricard and L. Truc, *Histoire de l'Action Française* (Paris, 1949), p. 35.
41 Drumont, *FJ*, II, p. 120.
42 Bournand, op. cit., p. 45.
43 Cit. ibid., pp. 203–4.
44 Drumont, *TA*, p. 91.
45 Cit. Bournand, op. cit., pp. 182–3.
46 Drumont, *TA*, p. 225.
47 Picard, *Synthèse de l'antisémitisme*, p. 88.
48 Ibid., p. 102. Picard was an "avocat à la Cour de Cassation de Belgique".
49 Henri-Frédéric Amiel, *Journal intime* (1882) (London, 1906), p. 119.
50 Brunetière, "Revue Littéraire, La France juive", loc. cit., p. 698.
51 Léon Bloy, Letter, 2 January 1904, *Lettres à René Martineau: 1901–1917* (Paris, 1933), p. 216.
52 Péguy, *Notre Jeunesse*, pp. 146 and 184.
53 S.-J. Piat, *The Story of a Family: The Home of the Little Flower* (Dublin, 1954), pp. 257–8.
54 Mirbeau, *Le Journal d'une femme de chambre*, pp. 32–3.
55 Zola, *Au Bonheur des Dames*, p. 115.
56 Péguy, *NJ*, p. 184.
57 Brunetière, op. cit., pp. 696–702.
58 Cit. A.-M. Schmidt, *Maupassant par lui-même* (Paris, 1965), p. 118.
59 Bournand, op. cit., pp. 188–90.
60 Herriot, *Jadis*, I, pp. 52–3.
61 Lyautey, Letter to Max Leclerc, 3 June 1901, *Choix de lettres*, p. 190.
62 Guérin, *Les Trafiquants de l'antisémitisme*, pp. 99–100; see also Fore-Fauré, *Face aux Juifs!*, chapter IV.
63 See Sternhell, *Maurice Barrès*, p. 233.
64 AN F⁷ 12480.
65 AN F⁷ 12463.
66 *Le Complôt juif*. AN F⁷ 12463. This broadsheet, issued by La Bonne Presse, it seems, reproduces "The Rabbi's Speech" fabricated by Goedsche; see Cohn, *Warrant for Genocide*, pp. 34–40 and 269–74; and, for further discussion, chapter XII, p. 409; and chapter XVI, pp. 603–4 below.
67 Report, Commissaire spécial, Bordeaux, 10 May 1897. AN F⁷ 12459.
68 Daily Report, Prefect of Police, 12 February 1898. APP Ba 106.
69 See Sorlin, *"La Croix" et les Juifs*, pp. 108–9.
70 Drumont, *TA*, pp. 115–16; see also ibid., pp. 118 and 129; Drumont, *FJ*, I, pp. 81–2 and 357; Bournand, op. cit., pp. 42–3.
71 Drumont, *La Fin d'un monde: Étude psychologique et sociale* (Paris, 1889) (hereafter *FM*), p. 56; also Book III *passim*. Much the same claims were reiter-

ated by Léon Daudet, *L'Avant-Guerre: Etudes et documents sur l'espionnage juif-allemand en France depuis l'affaire Dreyfus* (Paris, 1911).

72 Drumont, *DB*, p. 197; also ibid., p. xvi.
73 Broadsheet, "UN", November 1897. AN F⁷ 12480.
74 R.P. Constant, *Les Juifs devant l'Eglise et devant l'histoire* (Paris, 1897), cit. Arnoulin, *M. Edouard Drumont*, p. 138.
75 There was a divergence of opinion as to whether state monopolies paved the way to Socialism or not; for this, and more generally, see, for example, Fiechter, *Le Socialisme français*, pp. 154–5; Willard, *Les Guesdistes*, pp. 174–8 and 183; Blum, "Les Monopoles", *La Petite République*, December 1902-January 1903, *L'Oeuvre de Léon Blum 1891–1905*, pp. 509–36.
76 Drumont, *FM*, p. 81.
77 See, for example, the attacks on speculation and on "gold" in the work of Jules Verne discussed by Jean Chesneaux, "Critique sociale et thèmes anarchistes chez Jules Verne", *Le Mouvement Social*, no. 56 (1966), pp. 36–41.
78 Cit. Jacques Viard, "*L'Encyclopédie nouvelle* de Pierre Leroux et l'idée de race", Paper given at Colloque sur l'Idée de Race, 1975, p. 2.
79 See Verdès-Leroux, *Scandale financier*, pp. 93–4 and 109–10.
80 Rollet, op. cit., I, p. 134.
81 Drumont, *TA*, p. 135.
82 See Viau, op. cit., pp. 23–4; Beau de Loménie, *Edouard Drumont*, pp. 391–415; Drumont, *TA*, p. ix.
83 Biez, *Les Rothschild et le péril juif*, p. 7; also ibid., pp. 9–10 and *passim*.
84 Picard, op. cit., pp. 117 and 84.
85 Daily Report, Prefect of Police, 2 February 1898. APP Ba 106.
86 Daily Reports, Prefect of Police, 5 and 17 April 1898. APP Ba 106.
87 Léon Daudet, *Le Stupide Dix-neuvième Siècle* (Paris, 1929), p. 43.
88 Cit. Bournand, op. cit., p. 200. On Toussenel, see chapter XI, pp. 333–4 below.
89 See J.-H. Donnard, *Les Réalités économiques et sociales dans La Comédie Humaine* (Paris, 1961), pp. 297–331; Lehrmann, *L'Elément juif dans la littérature française*, II, pp. 44–52; Randall, *The Jewish Character in the French Novel*, pp. 25–53; Jean Bouvier, "Le Monde des Affaires", in *Zola* (Paris, 1969), pp. 171–91; Guillemin, *Présentation des Rougon-Macquart*, pp. 349–67; Denise R. Gamzon, "Claudel rencontre Israël (1905–1920), *Cahiers Paul Claudel*, 7 (1968), pp. 90–1; see also Drumont, "L'Argent dans l'oeuvre de Balzac", in Beau de Loménie, op. cit., pp. 472–80. Not all financiers in popular or bourgeois fiction were Jews, of course; in E. Sue's *Le Juif errant* (1845), for example, the wicked financier, Baron Tripeau, is not a Jew, while the Samuel family are shown as skilful managers of the Rennepont fortune, but honest, and serving a higher cause than money. The stereotype of the Jewish financier is also obvious in other national literatures; see, for example, Melmotte in Anthony Trollope, *The Way We Live Now* (1875); and the examples in Ernest K. Bramsted, *Aristocracy and the Middle-Classes in Germany, Social Types in German Literature 1830–1900* (Chicago, 1964), pp. 123–4 and 163–4.
90 Guy de Maupassant, *Bel-Ami* (Paris, 1973), pp. 370–1.
91 Cit. Viard, op. cit., p. 2.
92 Drumont, *FJ*, I, p. 259.
93 See Randall, op. cit., pp. 173 and 182–5; Duroselle, op. cit., p. 56; Byrnes, *Antisemitism in Modern France*, pp. 104–10.
94 See Drumont, *FJ*, I, pp. 354–5; Byrnes, op. cit., pp. 115–24; Verdès-Leroux, *Scandale financier*, pp. 58–9, 93–4, 108–9 and 114–16.
95 See, for example, H. de Balzac, *La Muse du Département* (1843) (Paris, 1956, Nelson edition), pp. 252–3.
96 Drumont, *FJ*, I, p. 341.
97 Drumont, *DB*, pp. 20–1.
98 Drumont, *TA*, p. vi.

99 Drumont, "Waterloo", 15 November 1894, *OBS*, p. 305; see also *DB*, pp. 34, 187 and 191–4; *TA*, pp. 15, 29, 34–5, 89, 103, 131, 136–8 and 217–18; *FM*, pp. 51–5.

100 Guérin, op. cit., p. 141.

101 Cit. Bournand, op. cit., pp. 52–5.

102 Picard, op. cit., p. 45.

103 *L'Univers Israélite*, 1 April 1889, cit. Verdès-Leroux, *Scandale financier*, pp. 93–4.

104 See Verdès, "La Presse devant le krach d'une banque catholique", pp. 145–8; Verdès-Leroux, *Scandale financier*, pp. 56–7; Drumont, *DB*, p. 32; Drumont, *TA*, pp. 131 and 337.

105 E.g. *La Petite République*, 9 November 1896.

106 See Sorlin, *"La Croix" et les Juifs*, pp. 173–5; Drault, *Drumont, La France juive et La Libre Parole*, pp. 101–2.

107 Daily Reports, Prefect of Police, 21 January, 31 March, 5 April and 8 June 1898. APP Ba 106.

108 Memmi, *Portrait d'un Juif*, p. 148. For the Rothschild myth in England, see Edgar Rosenberg, *From Shylock to Svengali: Jewish Stereotypes in English Fiction* (London, 1961), pp. 273–4; and in the United States, Rudolf Glanz, "The Rothschild Legend in America", *Jewish Social Studies*, 19 (1957), pp. 3–28, and Richard Hofstadter, *The Paranoid Style in American Politics and other essays* (London, 1966), pp. 293–302.

109 See Drumont, *TA*, p. 132; "L'Archiviste", *Drumont et Dreyfus*, pp. 10–11.

110 Viau, op. cit., pp. 51–4, 112 and 118.

111 Ibid., pp. 272–4.

112 Barrès, *Scènes et doctrines*, II, p. 183. For the real economic and financial power of the Rothschilds, which Barrès and others reflected in exaggerated and distorted fashion, see Jean Bouvier, *Les Rothschild* (Paris, 1967), and Bertrand Gille, *Histoire de la Maison Rothschild* (Geneva, 1965 and 1967), 2 vols.

113 For the continuing association of the Jews with the Devil by modern antisemites, already referred to, see chapter XIV, pp. 543–50 below.

114 Picard, op. cit., p. 80.

115 Drumont, *FJ*, I, p. 430.

116 Daudet, *Les Oeuvres dans les hommes*, p. 195.

117 Abbé Joseph Lémann, *La Préponderance juive*, I, *Ses origines (1789–1791)* (Paris, 1889), pp. 182–4.

118 Daudet, *Les Oeuvres dans les hommes*, p. 149.

119 Cit. Bournand, op. cit., p. 183.

120 Daudet, *Au Temps de Judas*, p. 199.

121 See, for example, chapter XI, pp. 347–8 below.

122 Daily Report, Prefect of Police, 17 March 1898. APP Ba 106.

123 See, for example, Louis Girard, *La Politique des Travaux publics du Second Empire* (Paris, 1952), pp. 396–8 and *passim*; L.-M. Jouffroy, *L'Ere du rail* (Paris, 1953), p. 119; François Caron, *Histoire de l'exploitation d'un grand réseau: La Compagnie du Chemin de Fer du Nord 1846–1937* (Paris, 1973).

124 Daily Reports, Prefect of Police, 4 June and 17 March 1898. APP Ba 106.

125 Drumont, *FJ*, II, pp. 280–4.

126 Apparently only one antisemitic deputy was an overt Free-Trader, Beauregard, who sat for an urban constituency in Saint-Denis; Jolly, ed., *Dictionnaire des parlementaires français*. On Protectionism generally, see É. O. Golob, *The Méline Tariff: French Agriculture and Nationalist Economic Policy* (New York, 1944 and 1968).

127 Drumont, *TA*, pp. 74–75.

128 See, for example, Jean Bouvier, *Le Crédit Lyonnais de 1863 à 1882, Les années de formation d'une banque de dépôts* (Paris, 1961), particularly Part 5.

129 Memmi, op. cit., p. 184.

304IDEOLOGY AND EXPERIENCE

130 See Braudel, op. cit., II, pp. 811–20; Memmi, op. cit., pp. 172–6; Salo Wittmayer Baron, *A Social and Religious History of the Jews*, IV (New York and London, 1957), chapter XXII; and ibid., XII (1967), chapters LI–LIII; and Léon Poliakov, *The History of Anti-Semitism*, II, *From Mohammed to the Marranos* (London, 1974), pp. 319–20.

131 See Lucy Mair, *An Introduction to Social Anthropology* (Oxford, 1965), pp. 158–9 and 181; Burton Benedict, "Sociological Characteristics of Small Territories and their Implications for Economic Development", in M. Banton, ed., *The Social Anthropology of Complex Societies*, pp. 29–30; and Memmi, op. cit., pp. 176–9.

132 See Memmi, op. cit., pp. 180–6; Selznick and Steinberg, *The Tenacity of Prejudice*, p. 187.

133 Cit. Guillemin, *Présentation des Rougon-Macquart*, pp. 352–3.

134 Drumont, *TA*, p. 135.

135 See Toutain, *La Population de la France*, Tables 15 and 16, pp. 54–5.

136 See, for example, Thabault, *Education and Change in a Village Community;* and Daniel Fabre and Jacques Lacroix, *La Vie quotidienne des paysans de Languedoc au XIXe siècle* (Paris, 1973), chapter II; and, for traditional hostility towards trading and the trader, Geneviève Bollême, *La Bibliothèque Bleue: La littérature populaire en France du XVIe au XIXe siècle* (Paris, 1971), p. 140.

137 See Foville, *La France économique*, chapter 23; Vicomte G. d'Avenel, *Le Mécanisme de la vie moderne*, Ier série (Paris, 1898 and 1902), chapter 4; E. Levasseur, *Questions ouvrières et industrielles en France sous la Troisième République* (Paris, 1907), pp. 215–24; Bertrand Gille, *La Banque et le crédit en France de 1815 à 1848* (Paris, 1959); Bouvier, *Le Crédit Lyonnais;* Bouvier, "The Banking Mechanism in France in the late 19th century" (1955), in Rondo Cameron, ed., *Essays in French Economic History* (Georgetown, Ontario, 1970), pp. 341–69.

138 See Drumont, *TA*, pp. 262–3. For the more extreme attitude on this subject of American Populists, see Hofstadter, "Free Silver and the Mind of 'Coin' Harvey", *The Paranoid Style*, pp. 238–315; Hofstadter, "North America", in Ionescu and Gellner, eds, *Populism*, pp. 10 and 19.

139 In Erckmann-Chatrian, *L'Ami Fritz* (Paris, 1865), for example, the misogynist hero warns himself to be prudent: "Et surtout, évite ces trois choses: de devenir trop gras, de prendre des actions industrielles et de de marier" (p. 2). More generally, see Adeline Daumard, "La Fortune mobilière en France selon les milieux sociaux (XIXe–XXe siècles)", *Revue d'Histoire Economique et Sociale*, 44 (1966), pp. 364–92; C. E. Freedeman, "The Growth of the French Securities Market, 1815–1870", in C. K. Warner, ed., *From the Ancien Régime to the Popular Front, Essays in the History of Modern France in Honor of Shepard B. Clough* (New York, 1969), pp. 75–92.

140 See, for example, David I. Kulstein, "Economics Instruction for Workers during the Second Empire", *French Historical Studies*, 1 (1959), pp. 225–34; J. Bouvier, "Mouvement ouvrier et conjonctures économiques", *Le Mouvement Social*, 48 (1964), pp. 4–5 and 20–8.

141 For the traditional attack on Jewish usury, see Rosenberg, op. cit., pp. 27–33; Poliakov, *Les Juifs et notre histoire*, p. 18; Lovsky, *L'Antisémitisme chrétien*, pp. 323–48; Lazare Landau, "Aspects et problèmes spécifiques de l'histoire des Juifs en France", *Revue de l'Histoire de l'Eglise de France*, 59 (1973), pp. 233–4.

142 E.g. Drumont, *FJ*, I, pp. 278–9, 285 and 314–15; and II, p. 304.

143 Lauris, *Souvenirs d'une belle époque*, p. 60.

144 E.g. Balzac, *Gobseck* (1840), and *Le Père Goriot* (1834) (Paris, 1948), pp. 521 and 575; see also Donnard, op. cit., pp. 279–95; and George Sand, *Le Marquis de Villemer* (1864), p. 122, cit. Pierre Guiral et al., *La Société française 1815–1914 vue par les romanciers* (Paris, 1969), p. 119. It is significant that, for Balzac, the word *"capitaliste"* still meant usurer, and such a connotation clearly lingered

on into the later nineteenth century; see note by Albert Prioult, Balzac, *Le Père Goriot*, p. 627.

145 Cit. Viard, op. cit., p. 17.
146 Leroy-Beaulieu, *L'Antisémitisme*, pp. 43–4. See here the similar arguments of Memmi, op. cit., pp. 185–7; and Loewenstein, *Christians and Jews*, pp. 79–87 and 124–6.
147 Dagan, op. cit., p. 9; see also the contributions by Letourneau and Molinari, ibid., pp. 12–14 and 43–4.
148 Lazare, op. cit., p. 225.
149 Werner Sombart, *The Jews and Modern Capitalism* (1911) (New York, 1962), particularly chapters 12 and 13.
150 Picard, op. cit., p. 88.
151 Dagan, op. cit., p. 2.
152 Drumont, *FJ*, II, p. 436; also ibid., I, p. 10; and II, p. 13.
153 Cit. Bournand, op. cit., p. 182.
154 On this claim generally, see Sombart, op. cit., chapter 12; Memmi, op. cit., pp. 161–2; Verdès-Leroux, *Scandale financier*, p. 94.
155 P.-J. Proudhon, *Césarisme et Christianisme* (Paris, 1883), I, p. 139, cit. Silberner, "Proudhon's Judeophobia", p. 67.
156 Vallès, *Le Bachélier*, p. 94.
157 See Silberner, "French Socialism and the Jewish Question", p. 9.
158 Bloy, *Le Salut par les Juifs*, pp. 64–5, 62 and 69.
159 *Le Triboulet*, 11 November 1894, cit. Zévaès, *L'Affaire Dreyfus*, p. 30.
160 Report, Commissaire spécial, Roanne, 12 December 1898. AN F⁷12480. For other examples of such stock claims, see Rouquier and Soumille, "La Notion de Race chez les Français d'Algérie", p. 5, on *L'Antijuif Algérien;* and Boni de Castellane, *Vingt ans de Paris*, Les Oeuvres libres, 52 (Paris, 1925), on Jewish antique dealers. Clemenceau is supposed to have said of Klotz, whom he chose as Minister of Finance in 1918: "Les finances vont mal? donnons-les à un juif! Il sera plus malin qu'un chrétien." Waleffe, *Quand Paris était un paradis*, p. 385.
161 Léon Daudet, *Le Voyage de Shakespeare* (Paris, 1896), p. 187, cit. Randall, op. cit., p. 94. Reissued by Gallimard in 1929, this novel has again been republished by them (Collection Folio, no. 538, 1974).
162 Drumont, "Le Drame juif", 24 November 1892, *OBS*, p. 79.
163 Drumont, *FJ*, I, p. 265; also ibid., I, pp. 77–8.
164 Drumont, *DB*, p. 536. Drumont also detected the Jewish propensity to fraud in their faking of works of art; *FJ*, II, pp. 141–7.
165 Cit. Viard, op. cit., p. 2. As we have seen, the polite form was *"israélite"*.
166 George Sand, *Le Meunier d'Angibault* (Paris, no date), p. 217.
167 Gustave Flaubert, *Madame Bovary, Moeurs de province* (Paris, 1928), p. 114.
168 Maupassant, *Bel-Ami*, p. 76.
169 Drumont, *FJ*, II, p. 304.
170 Daudet, *L'Avant-Guerre*, p. 6.
171 Cit. Bernanos, *La Grande Peur des bien-pensants*, p. 183.
172 Daily Report, Prefect of Police, 16 February 1898. APP Ba 106.
173 Cit. Bournand, op. cit., p. 181.
174 Maurras, *Au Signe de Flore*, p. 54; see also Léon de Montesquiou, *Les Raisons du nationalisme* (Paris, 1905), pp. 122–3.
175 Drumont, *TA*, p. 336.
176 Piou, *Le Comte Albert de Mun*, p. 192.
177 Balzac, *La Cousine Bette* (1846) (New York, no date, Lupton edition), p. 305.
178 Bloy, *Le Salut par les Juifs*, pp. 31–3.
179 Memmi, op. cit., p. 144.
180 Meyer, *Ce que mes yeux ont vu*, p. 131; see also Marquis de Castellane, *Hommes et choses de mon temps* (Paris, 1909), p. 287: "La France de l'avenir m'apparaît ainsi: Au sommet un veau, le veau d'or!"

181 Balzac, *The Country Doctor* (London, 1923, Everyman edition), p. 255.
182 Steinheil, *My Memoirs*, p. 40.
183 Paul Adam, *L'Essence du soleil* (Paris, 1890), cit. Randall, op. cit., p. 75; see also Klein, *Portrait de la Juive*, pp. 130 and 187.
184 Lémann, op. cit., I, p. 182.
185 See Report, Commissaire spécial, Sedan, 6 November 1899. AN F⁷ 12455.
186 Drumont, *FJ*, I, pp. 202–3.
187 See Report, Commissaire spécial, Paris, 16 August 1899. AN F⁷ 12465.
188 Charles Maurras, *L'Avenir de l'intelligence* (Paris, 1905), pp. 12 and 15.
189 *Le Complôt juif*. AN F⁷ 12463.
190 Drumont, *FJ*, I, p. 327.
191 Picard, op. cit., p. 107.
192 Daily Reports, Prefect of Police, 2 February and 22 March 1898 (on meetings of the Union Nationale and of the Ligue Antisémitique). APP Ba 106.
193 Montesquiou, op. cit., p. 122.
194 *Le Lillois*, 25 January 1891, cit. Drumont, *TA*, p. 335.
195 Drumont, *FJ*, I, p. 516; see also *TA*, p. 343.
196 Drumont, *FJ*, I, pp. vi–vii and 523; and II, p. 282.
197 Drumont, *DB*, pp. 247–8 and 317.
198 Cit. Bournand, op. cit., p. 44.
199 *"juiverie"*. Auguste Chirac, *Les Rois de la République* (Paris, 1883), cit. Lovsky, *L'Antisémitisme chrétien*, p. 341.
200 See Sorlin, *"La Croix" et les Juifs*, pp. 62–4 and 89–94.
201 Dagan, op. cit., p. 2.
202 Daily Report, Prefect of Police, 30 January 1898. APP Ba 106.
203 "Les Accapareurs où sont-ils?". AN F⁷ 12463.
204 The same attachment to honourable work and to craftsmanship was central to Péguy's reaction against industrial society [see Péguy, *L'Argent* (1913); *A nos amis, à nos abonnés* (1909), *Souvenirs*, pp. 30–1 and 88; Tharaud, *Notre cher Péguy*, I, pp. 242–8]; and was, of course, quite common generally; see, for example, Asa Briggs, ed., William Morris, *Selected Writings and Designs* (Harmondsworth, 1968); and Thorstein Veblen, *The Instinct of Workmanship and the State of the Industrial Arts* (1914) (New York, 1964).
205 On the growth of the tertiary sector, see Georges Dupeux, *La Société française 1789–1970* (Paris, 1972), pp. 30–1. This sector was, of course, particularly associated with Jewish enterprise; see Loewenstein, op. cit., pp. 86–7; and prejudice against it is not yet extinct: "Apparently in some official circles it is thought that manufacturing is virtuous and distribution is parasitic." Sir Marcus Sieff, *The Observer*, 9 June 1974, "Sayings of the Week".
206 Memmi, op. cit., pp. 191 and 188–9.
207 *La Croix*, 22 November 1894, cit. Sorlin, *"La Croix" et les Juifs*, pp. 109–10.
208 Cit. Bournand, op. cit., p. 44.
209 Drumont, *DB*, p. xvii.
210 Drumont, *FJ*, I, p. 81; also ibid., pp. vii–viii, 3⁄0 and 523; and *DB*, p. 73.
211 Drumont, *FJ*, I, p. xi.
212 Drumont, *TA*, p. 139.
213 On this common ideological device, see Roland Barthes, "Operation Margarine", *Mythologies* (London, 1973), pp. 41–2.
214 Picard, op. cit., pp. 119–20, 43 and 116–17.
215 *L'Univers*, 22 July 1890, cit. Pierrard, *Juifs et catholiques français*, p. 58.
216 Péguy, *Notre Jeunesse*, p. 175. Even a critique of antisemitism, like Lacretelle's *Silbermann*, presented Jews as exclusively wealthy (see pp. 43–4 and 136–7 in particular). On the facts of Jewish poverty, particularly in Eastern Europe and North Africa, there is abundant evidence; see, for example, Durieu, "Le Prolétariat Juif en Algérie"; Tharaud, *Petite Histoire des Juifs*, pp. 199–203; Memmi, op. cit., pp. 170 and *passim*; Alfred Kazin, *A Walker in the City* (New York, 1951),

pp. 38–9 and *passim*. In France, at the end of the July Monarchy, only 1.3% of the Jewish population was wealthy enough to have the vote. In 1857, at the other end of the scale, *Les Archives Israélites* estimated that one-sixth of the Jewish population of Paris was being supported by charity; and 15% of the Jewish population of the Bas-Rhin was classed as "indigent poor" in 1858. These indications, to which many others could be added, demonstrate that French Jews as a whole were certainly no richer and perhaps even poorer than their Gentile co-citizens; see Verdès-Leroux, *Scandale financier*, pp. 116 and 135; Szajkowski, "Poverty and Social Welfare among French Jews (1800–1880)"; "Jewish Poverty in the Lower Rhine in the '50s"; and "Some Statistics on Jewish Poverty in Paris", Szajkowski, *Jews and the French Revolutions*, pp. 1133–61; and Blumenkranz, ed., *Histoire des Juifs en France*, pp. 312–14; also Bloy, Journal, 2 January 1910, cit. Jacques Petit, Introduction, *Le Salut par les Juifs*, p. 14; Prolo, *La Caverne antisémite*, pp. 23–32; L'Hermite, *L'Antipape*, pp. ix–x and 279–80; Clermont-Tonnerre, *Mémoires*, I, p. 222.

217 Drumont, *DB*, p. 134; and *FJ*, I, p. 389; see also *TA*, pp. 152–3.
218 Cit. Gérin-Ricard and Truc, op. cit., p. 35.
219 Jacques Bainville, *Journal 1901–1918* (Paris, 1948), p. 24 (14 August 1905).
220 Henry Jarzel, *Petit Catéchisme nationaliste* (Paris, 1901), p. 3.
221 Viau, op. cit., p. 118.
222 See Sorlin, *"La Croix" et les Juifs*, pp. 108 and 179. *Le Complôt juif* declared: "Nous devons . . . autant que possible, pousser au fractionnement de ces grandes propriétés, afin de nous rendre l'acquisition plus prompte et plus facile"; see also Drumont, *DB*, pp. 11–14.
223 Drumont, *FM*, pp. 57–9.
224 Drumont, *DB*, p. 25; *TA*, pp. 31–2.
225 Drumont, *FJ*, II, p. 141. On Jewish horse and cattle dealers in the East in the pre-1870 period, and popular suspicion of them, see Erckmann-Chatrian, *L'Ami Fritz*, pp. 201–16; Sjazkowski, "French Jews during the Revolution of 1830 and the July Monarchy", p. 127.
226 Broadsheet, "UN", November 1897.
227 Report, Commissaire spécial, Senones (Vosges), 9 February 1898. AN F⁷ 12467; see also Drumont, *FJ*, I, pp. 278–9 and 282.
228 See Leuilliot, *L'Alsace au début du XIXe siècle*, II (Paris, 1959), pp. 176–93.
229 See Sjazkowski, *Jews and the French Revolutions*, pp. 924, 938 and 944–7; Philippe Vigier, *La Seconde République dans la région alpine: Etude politique et sociale* (Paris, 1963), II, pp. 252–65 and 319–37.
230 See n. 137; and Blumenkranz, ed., op. cit., pp. 319–20.
231 See Sjazkowski, *Jews and the French Revolutions*, pp. 924 and 970, for examples from the 1850s.
232 See Pierre Barral, *Les Agrariens français de Méline à Pisani* (Paris, 1968), p. 90.
233 Drumont, *DB*, pp. 534–5; also ibid., p. 438.
234 Zévaès, *Au Temps du Boulangisme*, p. 20.
235 Baudrillart, *Les Populations agricoles de la France*, III, pp. 402 and 554.
236 Drumont, *DB*, p. 535.
237 See D. Zolla, *La Crise agricole dans ses rapports avec la baisse des prix et la question monétaire* (Paris, 1903); Golob, op. cit., chapter 2; Michel Augé-Laribé, *La Politique agricole de la France de 1880 à 1940* (Paris, 1950), Part I, "La Grande Crise agricole".
238 Comte J. Imbart de la Tour, *La Crise agricole en France et à l'étranger: Etude de causes techniques, économiques, politiques et sociales et de leurs remèdes* (Nevers(?), 1900), p. 64; see also Barral, *Les Agrariens français*, pp. 73 and 100–1.
239 Lyautey, Letter to Max Leclerc, 3 June 1901, op. cit., p. 190.
240 Dagan, op. cit., pp. 15–16.
241 Lazare, op. cit., p. 99.
242 See chapter IV, pp. 132–3 above.

243 Drumont, *FJ*, II, p. 285; see also Fore-Fauré, *Face aux Juifs!*, pp. 52–105.
244 E.-M. de Vogüé, *Les Morts qui parlent* (1899) (Paris, no date, Nelson edition), p. 421; *Revue des Deux Mondes*, 1 February–15 April 1899. The Marquis de Vogüé was himself a big landowner and a president of the *Société des Agriculteurs de France*; see Barral, *Les Agrariens français*, pp. 79–80.
245 Glock and Stark found a higher incidence of antisemitism in the United States in the 1960s in rural and religious areas; *Christian Beliefs and Anti-Semitism*, pp. 178–81.
246 See Jolly, ed., *Dictionnaire des parlementaires français;* Barral, *Les Agrariens français*, pp. 81, 100 and 119. Other deputies noticed for their support of agricultural interests were Pontbriand, Delpech-Cantaloup, Denis, Decker-David and Castelin.
247 See chapter I, n. 110.
248 Pierrard, op. cit., p. 68.
249 Report, Commissaire spécial, Vesoul, 15 August 1898. AN F⁷ 12461.
250 Mirbeau, op. cit., pp. 160–1.
251 Daniel Halévy, *Visites aux paysans du Centre* (Paris, 1921), p. 42.
252 Cit. Pierrard, op. cit., p. 56.
253 Baudrillart, op. cit., III, p. 527.
254 See Braudel, op. cit., II, p. 811; Baron, op. cit., VIII (1958), chapter XXXVI; and XII, pp. 80–90; Poliakov, *The History of Anti-Semitism, II, pp. 126–7.*
255 Maupassant, "Le Père Judas", *Oeuvres complètes de Guy de Maupassant: Toine, Le Père Judas* (Paris, 1947), pp. 273–9.
256 Halévy, *Visites aux paysans du Centre*, pp. 50–1.
257 See Byrnes, *Antisemitism in Modern France*, pp. 113–14; Blumenkranz, ed., op. cit., p. 340.
258 See Guérin, op. cit., pp. 191–3; Reinach, op. cit., IV, pp. 589–92; Boni de Castellance, *L'Art d'être pauvre*, pp. 42 and 162. Another aristocratic supporter of Guérin was the Comte de Balincourt; see Sternhell, *Maurice Barrès*, p. 138; see also Drault, op. cit., p. 38, on the Comte de Douville-Maillefeu.
259 See Randall, op. cit., pp. 96–112; Drumont, *FJ*, II, p. 190; Drumont, *DB*, p. 16; Bournand, op. cit., pp. 131–8; Drault, op. cit., pp. 91 and 162; Barrès-Maurras, *La République ou le roi*, pp. 416 and 428; Daudet, *Au Temps de Judas*, pp. 47–8; Halévy, *Apologie*, p. 77: "Madame Gyp était puissante alors. Elle inspirait Lemaître et Guérin."
260 Drumont, *DB*, pp. 39 and 153; Viau, op. cit., p. 14.
261 Quillard, *Le Monument Henry*, pp. 105–28.
262 See chapter VIII, pp. 216, 219 above ; and Clermont-Tonnerre, *Mémoires*, I, pp. 46 and 60–1, for Gontaut and La Ferronays.
263 See Reinach, op. cit., V, pp. 111–17; also ibid., III, pp. 265 and 272–3.
264 See, for example, Daily Reports, Prefect of Police, 14 and 31 January, 6, 17 and 19 March, 14 and 17 April, and 21 June 1898. APP Ba 106.
265 Daily Report, Prefect of Police, 23 March 1898. APP Ba 106.
266 Schwarzschild, "The Marquis de Morès", p. 15.
267 See Steinheil, op. cit., pp. 88 and 103; Daudet, *Au Temps de Judas*, pp. 196–8.
268 See chapter XII, pp. 388–9 below.
269 Maurras, *Enquête sur la monarchie*, pp. 33–4. Despite their basic similarities of approach, Drumont was very hostile to contemporary political Royalism, mainly for reasons of jealousy and wounded class susceptibility; see Drumont, *FJ*, I, pp. 276, 336–8, 341, 359, 407–8, 435–9, 442–4 and 470; ibid., II, pp. 119 and 193–4; and *DB*, pp. 10, 39, 149, 182, 186 and 231.
270 Joanna Richardson, *Rachel* (London, 1956), p. 33.
271 Proust, *A la Recherche du temps perdu*, English Uniform Edition, II (1913); III (1918); VII (1921), pp. 95–6 and *passim.*
272 Castellane, *L'Art d'être pauvre*, pp. 137–41 and 172; Castellane, *Vingt ans de Paris*, pp. 69–72 and 89; Waleffe, op. cit. pp. 274–5.

273 See Drumont, *FJ*, II, p. 182; Daudet, *Salons et journaux*, pp. 147–9; Arbellot, *La Fin du boulevard*, p. 134.

274 Lauris, op. cit., pp. 99–100.

275 Drumont, *FJ*, II, pp. 188–9 and 419; see also ibid., I, pp. xi, 435 and 525–6; and II, pp. 85–93, 97, 102 and 120; Drumont, *DB*, pp. 21, 35–8, 138, 141 and 247; Drumont, *TA*, pp. 36–7, 45, 47, 102–3, 181–2, 219–20 and 245–7; Bournand, op. cit., pp. 52–3 (Rochefort); and Gohier, *L'Armée contre la nation*, p. 5.

276 Paul Bourget, *Cosmopolis* (Paris, 1894), p. 20; see also Henri Lavedan, *Le Prince d'Aurec: Comédie en trois actes* (Paris, 1894), a popular play on the conflict between the aristocracy and the Jews; and Albert Guinon, *Décadence: Comédie en quatre actes* (Paris, 1901), a more extreme version of the same theme.

277 Reinach, op. cit., III, pp. 273–4.

278 See particularly Proust, op. cit., III, p. 125; V, pp. 338–41; VII, pp. 109, 111, 125–6, 145 and 204.

279 See Sir Edward Blount, *Memoirs* (London, 1902), pp. 241–3; Arbellot, op. cit., p. 93; J.-A. Roy, *Histoire du Jockey Club de Paris* (Paris, 1958).

280 Gregh, *L'Age d'or*, p. 160.

281 Arbellot, op. cit., p. 27; see also Drumont, *DB*, pp. 40–1 and 151; and *TA*, pp. 41–4. There are no Jews at the Duc de Barfleur's club in Guinon's *Décadence;* see p. 63. On "social club discrimination" in the United States in the 1960s, which seems to be a similar phenomenon, see Selznick and Steinberg, op. cit., pp. 45–7.

282 The 3rd Duc de Decazes married Isabelle-Blanche Singer in 1888 (p. 347); the 11th Duc de Gramont married Alexandrine de Rothschild, as his second wife, in 1878 (p. 369); the 3rd Prince de Lucinge married Raphaëla Cahen in 1891, and Juliette-Emilie Ephrussi in 1901 (p. 409); Prince Alphonse de Polignac married Jeanne-Emilie Mirès in 1860 (p. 469); and Elzéer-Guillaume de Sabran-Pontevès married Anna Pereira Pinto in 1911 (p. 510). The following members of the higher aristocracy all married Americans: the nephew of the 6th Duc de Broglie in 1907 (p. 310); the Duc de La Rochefoucauld in 1892 (p. 386); the brother of the Prince de Lucinge in 1902 (p. 410); the 9th Duc de Chaulnes et de Picquigny in 1908 (p. 411); Prince Edmond-Melchior de Polignac in 1893 (p. 470); the 6th Duc de Praslin in 1874 (p. 476); the 7th Duc de Praslin in 1910 (p. 475); Comte Horace de Praslin in 1889 (p. 476); the Duc de Richelieu in 1875 (p. 486); the 4th Prince de Chimay in 1890 (p. 490); the Comte Guy de Chabot in 1888 (p. 496); the 5th Duc de Talleyrand in 1908 (p. 528); his brother, the Duc de Valençay, in 1901 (p. 529); and the 4th Duc de Dino in 1887 (p. 529). (All references above to *Almanach de Gotha* (Gotha, 1913)).

Boni de Castellane commented, after his divorce from Anna Gould: "Il est curieux de constater que l'énorme richesse de certaines Américaines leur donne une allure spéciale, et même une faculté de nous impressionner." Castellane, *Vingt ans de Paris*, p. 79. See also Drumont, *FJ*, II, p. 254, for hostile comment on the American wives chosen by French aristocrats: "Elles ont contribué à donner à la société parisienne la physionomie incohérente et bizarre qu'elle a prise depuis quelques années."

Only two instances have been found of marriages in this milieu to non-Jewish commoners or *anoblis:* the 11th Duc de La Trémoïlle with Hélène-Marie Pillet-Will in 1892; and the Marquis Melchior de Polignac to Louise Pommery in 1879; *Almanach de Gotha*, pp. 390 and 470; and Waleffe, op. cit., p. 295.

On the well-established Jewish aristocracy, see Marrus, op. cit., pp. 36–9. It is interesting to note that the *Almanach de Gotha* includes a Jewish calendar.

283 Clermont-Tonnerre, op. cit., pp. 42–3 and 137–8; see also Drumont, *FJ*, I, p. 119.

284 Zola, *Paris* (English edition), pp. 411 and 214; also ibid., pp. 262 and 404–5.

285 Maupassant, *Bel-Ami*, p. 284; also ibid., p. 395 Mme Silbermann's second husband, in Lacretelle's novel, was a French aristocrat; see *Silbermann*, p. 174.

286 Schwarzschild, op. cit., p. 6; Castellane, *Vingt ans de Paris*, p. 35; Castellane,

L'Art d'être pauvre, pp. 88 and 212–13; Clermont-Tonnerre, op. cit., pp. 150–1; Waleffe, op. cit., pp. 138–48. It would be interesting, in this context, to know more about the Sabran-Pontevès marriage referred to in n. 282.

287 Drumont, *FJ*, II, pp. 252–3.

288 Bournand, op. cit., p. 146; Guinon, op. cit., p. 76. The preferred one-way exogamy which is implied here, was, one suspects, characteristic of European upper classes generally to a significant degree. On wife-giving and wife-taking generally, see Mair, *An Introduction to Social Anthropology*, p. 80; and Mair, *Marriage* (Harmondsworth, 1971).

289 In Guinon's *Décadence*, again, old Mme Strohmann is very opposed to her son's marrying a Gentile.

290 The young Jewish man thwarted in his wish to marry a Gentile girl, usually by her family's refusal to accept him, is a common situation in French Jewish novels and autobiographies; see, for example, J.-R. Bloch, . . . *et Cie* (Paris, 1918) (English edition, London, 1930), Part II; Edmond Fleg, *L'Enfant prophète* (Paris, 1928), p. 39; Pierre Hirsch, *De Moïse à Jésus: Confession d'un Juif* (Paris, 1929), pp. 106–42; Emmanuel Berl, *Sylvia* (Paris, 1952), pp. 164–5. More generally, see Stendhal, *Mémoires d'un touriste* (Paris, 1953), I, p. 156, for bourgeois hostility to the idea of a non-Jew marrying a Jewish girl in the early nineteenth century; and Waleffe, op. cit., pp. 59–60, for Jewish hostility to exogamy later.

291 Dagan, op. cit., pp. 30–1 and 64.

292 Gohier, op. cit., p. 5.

293 Dagan, op. cit., pp. 94 and 30–1.

294 Drumont, *DB*, p. 153.

295 Drumont, *FM*, p. 385.

296 See Thabault, op. cit., pp. 148–50, on the sale of the Tusseau estate at Mazières-en-Gâtine in the 1880s; but this and other examples should be set against the remarkable endurance of aristocratic landholding in this region; see Siegfried, *Tableau politique de la France de l'Ouest, passim*. For the relative decline globally of the large estate in France between 1862 and 1908, see Michel Augé-Laribé, *L'Evolution de la France agricole* (Paris, 1912), pp. 103–6, and chapter III, *passim*. It may be significant that Gyp sold the château of Mirabeau in Provence on the eve of the First World War—to Barrès; see Tharaud, *Mes années chez Barrès*, pp. 234–50.

297 Jean de La Varende, *Pays d'Ouche, 1740–1933* (1936) (Paris, 1965), p. 255; see also Georges Ohnet, *La Grande Marnière* (Paris, 1885); René Bazin, *La Terre qui meurt* (Paris, 1899).

298 See, for example, Proust, op. cit., V, pp. 278, 292 and 377; and IX, pp. 35 and 39.

299 Evidence for this is more readily available for the period before 1870, but one would have expected the involvement to have been even greater in the later period; see, for example, Félix Rivet, *La Navigation à vapeur sur la Saône et le Rhône (1783–1863)* (Paris, 1962), p. 310; Jean Vial, *L'Industrialisation de la sidérurgie française, 1814–1864* (Paris, 1967), pp. 194–8 and 374–6; G. Richard, "La Noblesse dans l'industrie textile en Haute-Normandie dans la première moitié du XIXe siècle", *Revue d'Histoire Economique et Sociale*, 46 (1968), pp. 305–38.

300 The first three presidents of the Société des Agriculteurs de France were aristocrats, and two of these were big landowners; see Barral, *Les Agrariens Français*, pp. 79–80.

301 See Drumont, *DB*, p. 40; Guinon, op. cit., pp. 15–25, 43 and 272; Verdès-Leroux, *Scandale financier*, pp. 11–12; Proust, op. cit., III, pp. 118–19.

302 Cit. Robert Cornilleau, *De Waldeck-Rousseau à Poincaré: Chronique d'une génération (1898–1924)* (Paris, 1927), p. 76. On the general decline of aristocratic political power, see Daniel Halévy, *La Fin des notables* (Paris, 1930–7), 2 vols; J. Gouault, *Comment la France est devenue Républicaine: Les élections générales et partielles à l'Assemblée Nationale, 1870–1875* (Paris, 1954).

303 See *Journal du Maréchal de Castellane 1804–1862* (Paris, 1895–1897), I, p. 2 and n.; and I–V, *passim; Dictionnaire de Biographie française*, VII (Paris, 1956), pp. 1359–66; Reinach, op. cit., IV, pp. 589–92; Grenier, *Nos Députés, 1898–1902*, p. 22; Castellane, *L'Art d'être pauvre*, pp. 107–8 and 223–5; Castellane, *Vingt ans de Paris*, pp. 35–41, 51–9 and 84–110; Waleffe, op. cit., pp. 96, 138–43 and 146; Arbellot, op. cit., pp. 9, 17, 19, 31, 56, 84, 88 and 154.

304 Simone de Beauvoir, *Memoirs of a Dutiful Daughter* (1958) (Harmondsworth, 1973), pp. 35 and 32–3.

305 See Marc Bloch, *L'Etrange Défaite, témoignage écrit en 1940* (Paris, 1957), pp. 189–91; Barral, *Les Agrariens français, passim.*

306 Cit. Barral, *Les Agrariens français*, pp. 165–6.

307 See J. Méline, *Le Retour à la terre et la surproduction industrielle* (Paris, 1905); also Barral, *Les Agrariens français*, pp. 83–92; and Augé-Laribé, *La Politique agricole*, pp. 69–71.

308 Cit. Louis de Vaucelles, *"Le Nouvelliste de Lyon" et la défense religieuse (1879–1889)* (Paris, 1971), p. 145; see also Paul Déroulède, *Chants du paysan* (Paris, 1894).

309 Imbart de la Tour, op. cit., pp. 10, 128, and 7–8.

310 The same idealization of the rural world has been noted in contemporary German conservatism, in Nazism, and in Populism generally; see, for example, Mosse, *The Crisis of German Ideology*, pp. 23–6; Kenneth D. Barkin, "Conflict and Concord in Wilhelmian Social Thought", *Central European History*, 5 (1972), pp. 55–71; Stern, *Hitler*, pp. 53–4; Ionescu and Gellner, eds, op. cit., pp. 155–6 and 187–90.

311 Drumont, *FJ*, I, p. 567; also ibid., I, p. 431; *DB*, pp. 1–8, 533, and Book I *passim.*

312 Drumont, *DB*, p. 534.

313 Cit. Schwarzschild, op. cit., p. 17.

314 Cit. Randall, op. cit., pp. 65–6; see also the very similar remark by abbé Lémann, op. cit., I, p. 99.

315 Besides the work of Gyp, Ohnet and Bazin already mentioned, see, for example, Ludovic Halévy, *L'Abbé Constantin* (1882); Jules Clarétie, *Noris* (1883); Jean de La Brète, *Mon Oncle et mon curé* (1897); and Ernest Daudet, *Au Galop de la vie* (1908). On the parallel "silver fork" school of fiction in Britain, see W. R. Burn, *The Age of Equipoise* (London, 1968), p. 60.

316 See chapter XVI, p. 629 below; for the concept of usurpation in Populist thought generally, see Donald MacRae, "Populism as Ideology", Ionescu and Gellner, eds, op. cit., chapter 6, p. 158.

317 Drumont, *OBS*, p. vii; see also ibid., pp. 86–8; Bernanos, op. cit., pp. 163–4.

318 Guérin, op. cit., p. 95.

319 Drumont, *FJ*, I, p. 431.

320 Ibid., II, pp. 72–9, 145 and 173–9.

321 Drumont, *FM*, p. 416; see also ibid., pp. 382–3 and 399–411.

322 Ibid., p. 403. The same condemnation of the defects of the aristocracy, coupled with a profound "belief in the aristocracy as it ought to be", is found among contemporary German antisemites, e.g. in Polenz's *Die Grabenhäger* (1898); see Bramsted, op. cit., pp. 240–1.

323 The special involvement of small traders in Populist and Fascist movements has often been noted; see, for example, William Kornhauser, *The Politics of Mass Society* (London, 1960), pp. 201–7.

324 *Le Socialiste*, 24 July 1898, cit. Silberner, "French Socialism and the Jewish Question", p. 21: "une question de boutique".

325 Lazare, op. cit., p. 385.

326 Dagan, op. cit., p. 54; see also ibid., p. 24 (Georges Renard).

327 Zévaès, *L'Affaire Dreyfus*, p. 110.

328 E.g. Daily Reports, Prefect of Police, 1 and 5 May 1898. APP Ba 106.

329 Report, Commissaire spécial, Caen, 28 December 1898. AN F⁷ 12466.

330 Report, Commissaire spécial, Roanne, 28 April 1899. AN F⁷ 12480.

331 Police report, Rennes, 21 July 1899. AN F⁷ 12464.

332 See pamphlet, *Le Collectivisme, voilà l'ennemi!* AN F⁷ 12872. On Nationalism and Antisemitism, see chapter XII below.

333 See Sorlin, *"La Croix" et les Juifs*, pp. 211–13; and chapter IV, pp. 135–6 above.

334 See chapter VI, pp. 190–2 above; and my "Catholic Populism at the time of the Dreyfus Affair", pp. 672–3.

335 Drumont, *FJ*, I, pp. 53–4 and 232.

336 Drumont, *DB*, pp. 504–5; also ibid., pp. 108 and 230.

337 Daily Reports, Prefect of Police, 10 and 28 June 1898. APP Ba 106.

338 Wicart, op. cit., pp. 2, 19 and 20.

339 Maurras, *Au Signe de Flore*, p. 31.

340 Drumont, *TA*, p. x; also ibid., pp. 165–6 and 336.

341 Cit. Sorlin, *"La Croix" et les Juifs*, p. 213; see also ibid., p. 64.

342 "Réflexions d'un petit commerçant caennais". AN F⁷ 12463.

343 *Le Réveil Commercial, Industriel et Agricole* (Montpellier), 23 September 1897; and *La Croix Meusienne*, 13 February 1898. In Orléans in the 1960s, the term to shop "chez les juifs" was in common usage to describe shopping at cheap department stores; see Morin *et al.*, *La Rumeur d'Orléans*, pp. 160 and 162.

344 Daily Report, Prefect of Police, 22 March 1898. APP Ba 106.

345 Daily Report, Prefect of Police, 31 March 1898. APP Ba 106.

346 Daily Report, Prefect of Police, 6 May 1898; also ibid., 16 March and 16 April 1898. APP Ba 106.

347 Daily Report, Prefect of Police, 6 April 1898. APP Ba 106. After a fairly distinguished political and diplomatic career, Benoist joined the Action Française in 1928; see my "The *Action Française* in French Intellectual Life", p. 349.

348 Daily Report, Prefect of Police, 16 March 1898. APP Ba 106.

349 See the remarks of Guillemin, *Présentation des Rougon-Macquart*, pp. 210–11; Bouvier, "Le Monde des Affaires", *Zola*, p. 174.

350 Zola, *Au Bonheur des Dames*, p. 43; also ibid., p. 92.

351 *L'Aurore*, 29 April 1902, for example, attacked "Tous les vendeurs à faux poids et fausses mesures, tous les falsificateurs de denrées, tous les filous trichant sur la monnaie à vendre, tous les logeurs proxénètes se disputant la clientèle des filles publiques, tous les laitiers empoisonneurs, toute la bande des épiciers, boulangers, bouchers, mastroquets, charcutiers, merciers . . . toute la boutiquaille voleuse embusquée . . .", who were said to provide the "Nationalists" with their main support; see Dossier, "Ligue des Patriotes, 1901–1916". AN F⁷ 12872.

352 See chapter III, p. 116 above.

353 Guérin, op. cit., pp. 40, 60–2 and 374–80.

354 Drumont, *FJ*, II, pp. 165–6. Zola presents a similar picture in *Au Bonheur des Dames*, pp. 182–3 and *passim*, which may, in fact, be the source of Drumont's observation.

355 Police report, 1 June 1900. AN F⁷ 12719.

356 Pierre Biétry, *Le Socialisme et les Jaunes* (Paris, 1906), p. 292; see also ibid., *passim;* Mosse, "The French Right and the Working Classes", pp. 185–208.

357 Daily Reports, Prefect of Police, 21 April and 22 May 1898. APP Ba 106; see also the appeal made to small shopkeepers by Jaurès in 1897: "Le Socialisme et le Petit Commerce", *La Dépêche de Toulouse*, October-December 1897, *Oeuvres de Jean Jaurès*, VI, *Études socialistes*, II, *1897–1901* (Paris, 1933), pp. 37–61.

358 See Sorlin, *"La Croix" et les Juifs*, pp. 212–13.

359 See Verdès-Leroux, *Scandale financier*, p. 213.

360 See chapter III, n. 65.

361 AN F⁷ 12461.

362 Report, Commissaire spécial, Marseille, 25 February 1898. AN F⁷ 12459.

363 Report, Commissaire spécial, Vesoul, 15 August 1898. AN F⁷ 12461.

364 See Pierrard, op. cit., p. 67.

365 "Réflexions d'un petit commerçant caennais".
366 AN F⁷ 12463; and Reinach, op. cit., III, p. 540.
367 Daily Report, Prefect of Police, 23 June 1898. APP Ba 106.
368 See Pierrard, op. cit., p. 148.
369 Report, Commissaire spécial, Toulouse, 30 March 1899. AN F⁷ 12460.
370 Police report, August 1899. AN F⁷ 12462.
371 Report, Prefect of Police, 18 December 1899. AN F⁷ 12453–12454.
372 Report, Commissaire central, Grenoble, 12 January 1899. AN F⁷ 12459.
373 Daily Report, Prefect of Police, 14 April 1898. APP Ba 106.
374 "Réflexions d'un petit commerçant caennais".
375 Report, Commissaire spécial, Nantes, 19 December 1898. AN F⁷ 12460.
376 Police reports, 25 and 31 August 1899. AN F⁷ 12462.
377 See Pierrard, op. cit., p. 148.
378 Zola, Au Bonheur des Dames, p. 92.
379 Morin et al., op. cit., pp. 17–19, 24–5 and 39–52.
380 Report, Commissaire spécial, Nantes, 22 December 1897. AN F⁷ 12460.
381 Report, Commissaire spécial, Epinal, 20 January 1898. AN F⁷ 12474.
382 Report, Commissaire central, Nice, 11 April 1900. AN F⁷ 12453–12454.
383 See Report, Commissaire central, Nantes, 30 June 1899. AN F⁷ 12465.
384 Cit. Rémond, Les Deux Congrès ecclésiastiques, p. 72.
385 Sorlin, "La Croix" et les Juifs, p. 64.
386 See Daily Reports, Prefect of Police, 10 March and 5 May 1898. APP Ba 106.
387 See Pierrard, op. cit., p. 147.
388 See chapter III, n. 63.
389 Police report, 30 June 1903. AN F⁷ 12720.
390 Report, Commissaire spécial, Valence, 20 February 1898. AN F⁷ 12474.
391 See Reinach, op. cit., III, p. 540; Zévaès, L'Affaire Dreyfus, p. 110.
392 Report, Commissaire spécial, Vienne, 29 April 1898. AN F⁷ 12459.
393 Zévaès, Au Temps du Boulangisme, p. 20; also ibid., p. 65.
394 Mitterand, Zola journaliste, pp. 11–19.
395 Zola, Au Bonheur des Dames, p. 258; also ibid., pp. 23–32, 90, 100, 104, 228–33, 259–61 and 429–50.
396 Thabault, op. cit., pp. 153 and 158.
397 A. Daumard, "L'évolution des structures sociales en France à l'époque de l'industrialisation (1815–1914)", Revue Historique, 247 (II), (1972), pp. 327 and 345.
398 Avenel, op. cit., I (1902), pp. 89–90; see also Jaurès, "Le Socialisme et le Petit Commerce", p. 39.
399 Donnay, Des Souvenirs, p. 275.
400 See, for example, Ford Madox Ford, A Mirror to France (London, 1926), pp. 222–3.
401 See, for example, Stanley Hoffmann, Le Mouvement Poujade (Paris, 1956), pp. 314–22.
402 See Levasseur, Questions ouvrières et industrielles, pp. 760–70; Avenel, op. cit., I, pp. 210–11; M. Bourguin, Les Systèmes socialistes et l'évolution économique (1907) (Paris, 1925), pp. 454–60; F. Boudot, "Quelques aspects originaux de l'histoire de la coopération en France", Revue d'Histoire Economique et Sociale, 33 (1955), pp. 5–18.
403 Union Nationale de France, Règlement Général (Paris, 1897), pp. 31–2.
404 Barrès, "Le Programme de Nancy" (1898), Scènes et doctrines, II, p. 163.
405 Cit. Pierrard, op. cit., p. 67.
406 Drumont, FJ, I, p. 168; TA, pp. 333–6.
407 See Zola, Au Bonheur des Dames, pp. 50, 75, 88, 94, 100, 104–5 and passim; also Jaurès, "Le Socialisme et le Petit Commerce", pp. 46–7.
408 Daily Report, Prefect of Police, 25 January 1898. APP Ba 106. On the function of the "corner shop" in another contemporary working-class milieu that cannot have been too dissimilar, see Robert Roberts, The Classic Slum, Salford Life in

the First Quarter of the Century (Harmondsworth, 1973); of particular importance was its being nearby, when even local travel was expensive, and its provision of short-term credit.

409 Drumont, *FJ*, II, p. 159; and ibid., II, pp. 160–4.
410 See, for example, Balzac, *La Rabouilleuse* (1842) (London, 1951, under title *A Bachelors' Establishment*), p. 133.
411 See Morin *et al.*, op. cit., p. 49.
412 Stokes, *Léon Blum*, p. 23.
413 André Maurois, *Mémoires*, I, *Les Années d'apprentissage* (New York, 1942), pp. 15, 32 and 159–67.
414 See the remarks of Proust, op. cit., VII, p. 267; and IX, pp. 188–9.
415 See Morin's analysis of the role of this factor in the "rumeur d'Orléans". Morin *et al.*, op. cit., pp. 56–9; see also chapter XV, pp. 594–6 below.
416 Jolly, ed., op. cit..
417 See Avenel, op. cit., I, chapter 1; Waleffe, op. cit., pp. 284 and 287–8.
418 See Maurois, op. cit., p. 122, for example.
419 See Avenel, op. cit., I, chapter III, pp. 168–208, on Félix Potin.
420 *Le Petit Phare*, 13 December 1898.
421 Dagan, op. cit., p. 93.
422 Guérin, op. cit., chapter XI, "La maison Drumond and Co", and *passim*.
423 See Daily Report, Prefect of Police, 10 June 1898. APP Ba 106; and chapter VI, pp. 185–6 above.
424 Drumont, *TA*, p. 130; also *FM*, pp. 85–98; Drault, op. cit., pp. 17–18.
425 Bernanos, op. cit., pp. 212–13.
426 Report, Police agent, Paris, 5 September 1901. AN F[7] 12457. Another link between antisemitism and the meat trade can be seen in the special following which Morès and Guérin enjoyed among the butchers of La Villette, to which we have already referred.
427 See Pierrard, op. cit., p. 148.
428 Jolly, ed., op. cit.
429 Drumont, *DB*, p. 200.
430 Drumont, *FM*, pp. 40 and 43–4.
431 In 1906, 2,132,800 establishments employed from 1 to 5 workers, and only 151,756 employed over 5 workers; see Dupeux, *La Société française*, p. 204. Markovitch, however, indicates that small-scale industry did begin to lose ground to large-scale from the last third of the nineteenth century; see T. J. Markovitch, *L'Industrie française de 1789 à 1964, Conclusions générales, Cahiers de l'ISEA*, no. 179 (Paris, 1966), pp. 205–12.
432 Donnay, op. cit., pp. 171 and 270–71.
433 Zola, *Au Bonheur des Dames*, p. 23.
434 Barrès, *Scènes et doctrines*, II, p. 180.
435 See Blumenkranz, ed., op. cit., pp. 324–5 and 347–9; Pierrard, op. cit., pp. 25–6; Memmi, op. cit., p. 54; Marrus, op. cit., pp. 33–4.
436 See, for example, Drumont, *FJ*, I, p. 99; and II, pp. 204, 216 and 278.
437 Daily Report, Prefect of Police, 5 April 1898. APP Ba 106, on meeting of the Comité d'Union Républicaine démocrate et anticollectiviste of the 5th *arrondissement*.
438 Drumont, *TA*, p. 155.
439 Barrès, "Contre les étrangers" (1893), *Scènes et doctrines*, II, p. 190.
440 Wicart, op. cit., p. 16.
441 Maurras, *Au Signe de Flore*, p. 37. The word "métèque" does not have this wider meaning in Littré (1878). Waleffe, op. cit., p. 427, claims that it was launched into common parlance by Binet-Valmer's novel, *Les Métèques: Roman des moeurs parisiennes* (Paris, 1907), rather than by Maurras. Binet-Valmer was himself Swiss, and apparently did not intend the word to have a pejorative connotation.

442 Maurras, *Au Signe de Flore*, pp. 41–2.
443 Maurras, "L'Etang de Marthe et les hauteurs d'Aristarché", *Anthinéa* (1901) (Paris, 1920), pp. 217–45.
444 See Victor Gelu, *Marseille au XIXe siècle*, ed. Pierre Guiral (Paris, 1971), pp. 398–403.
445 Drumont, *FJ*, I, p. 422.
446 Drumont, *FM*, p. xxx; also *DB*, p. 73.
447 Barrès, *Scènes et doctrines*, I, p. 96; and II, p. 162.
448 Barrès, *La Cocarde*, 23 October 1894, cit. Sternhell, "Le déterminisme physiologique et racial à la base du nationalisme de Maurice Barrès et de Jules Soury", Paper given at Colloque sur l'Idée de Race, 1975, p. 2.
449 Bournand, op. cit., p. 142.
450 Daudet, *L'Avant-Guerre*, pp. xiii and 5–7.
451 Jacques Bertillon, *Le Problème de la dépopulation* (Paris, 1897), p. 20. Jacques Bertillon was, however, a Dreyfusard, and his wife was part-Jewish; see H. T. Rhodes, *Alphonse Bertillon* (London, 1956), pp. 183–4.
452 See Rollet, op. cit., II, pp. 105–10. Catholic feeling and action was, of course, also prompted by theological objection to contraception; see Jean-Louis Flandrin, *L'Eglise et le contrôle des naissances* (Paris, 1970).
453 Drumont, *FJ*, I, p. 495.
454 Drumont, *TA*, p. 427.
455 Drumont, *FJ*, I, p. xiii; *TA*, pp. 28, 186–8 and 374.
456 Daudet, *L'Avant-Guerre*, pp. viii and x–xi.
457 Halévy, Diary, 15 February 1911, *Degas parle*, pp. 137–8. Degas was an outspoken antisemite.
458 Wicart, op. cit., p. 11.
459 Daudet, *L'Avant-Guerre*, p. xi. Ironically, Daudet's first marriage to Jeanne Hugo was dissolved; see Paul Dresse, *Léon Daudet vivant* (Paris, 1947), pp. 157–63.
460 Drumont, *FJ*, I, p. 114.
461 Ibid., I, p. 116; see also Pierrard, op. cit., p. 69, citing abbé Puig, *Solution de la Question juive* (1897); Evelyn Martha Acomb, *The French Laic Laws (1879–1889): The First Anti-Clerical Campaign of the Third French Republic* (1941) (New York, 1967), pp. 193–202; Drault, op. cit., pp. 45–6.
462 Jolly, ed., op. cit.
463 Daily Report, Prefect of Police, 1 April 1898. APP Ba 106; also *Union Nationale de France, Règlement Général*, p. 3.
464 Drumont, *TA*, p. 191; see also *DB*, p. 257; and chapter XVI, pp. 623–6 below.
465 Daily Report, Prefect of Police, 14 April 1898. APP Ba 106, on meeting of La Jeunesse Royaliste, 1st and 2nd *arrondissements*.
466 See D. V. Glass, *Population Policies and Movements in Europe* (1940) (London, 1967), p. 100; Rollet, op. cit., I, pp. 472–8; Imbart de la Tour, op. cit., pp. 266–70; J.-M. Mayeur, *Un Prêtre démocrate: L'abbé Lemire, 1853–1928* (Paris, 1968), pp. 197–205.
467 See Rollet, op. cit., II, Book III, "La Famille".
468 Drumont, *TA*, p. 188; see also Vaucelles, op. cit., p. 145.
469 See Barrès, "Discours sur le cerceuil de Morès pour demander vengeance" (1896); "Le commandant Marchand et ses rapports avec le Parlement"; and "Le Général Galliéni", *Scènes et doctrines*, II, Book 4; Jacques Paugam, *L'Age d'or du Maurrassisme* (Paris, 1971), pp. 75–7; Raoul Girardet, *L'Idée coloniale en France de 1871 à 1962* (Paris, 1972), chapters IV and V.
470 Vaucelles, op. cit., p. 3.
471 Pierre Clemendot, "Population de Nancy (1815–1938)", *Hommage à Marcel Reinhard: Sur la population française au XVIIIe et au XIXe siècles* (Paris, 1973), p. 122.
472 See, for example, Frank Lorimer, "The Development of Demography"; and

Alfred Sauvy, "Development and Perspectives of Demographic Research in France", in Philip M. Hauser and Otis Dudley Duncan, eds, *The Study of Population, An Inventory and Appraisal* (Chicago, 1959), pp. 124–89.

473 Barrès, *Scènes et doctrines*, II, pp. 161 and 166.

474 Ibid., I, p. 167.

475 Maurras, *Enquête sur la monarchie*, p. 43.

476 See chapter VIII, n. 15.

477 Daudet, *L'Avant-Guerre*, pp. 3–7.

478 Drumont, *FJ*, I, p. 495.

479 Bertillon, *Le Problème de la dépopulation*, p. 18; Foville, op. cit., pp. 52–3; André Armengaud, *La Population française au XIXe siècle* (Paris, 1971), pp. 93–106; see also Barrès, *Scènes et doctrines*, II, p. 189.

480 Dagan, op. cit., p. 54.

481 See A. Chanut, F.-P. Codaccioni, M. Gillet, F. Lentacker, L. Machu, "Aspects industrielles de la crise: le département du Nord", *Aspects de la crise et de la dépression de l'économie française au milieu du XIXe siècle 1846–1851: Etudes sous la direction de E. Labrousse, Bibliothèque de la Révolution de 1848*, XIX (La Roche-sur-Yon, 1956), pp. 102–3 and 130–3; and P. Guiral, "Le cas d'un grand port de commerce, Marseille", ibid., p. 224, referring also to incidents in Paris and at Rouen.

482 Thabault, op. cit., pp. 134 and 255, n. 2.

483 Michelle Perrot, *Les Ouvriers en grève, France 1871–1890* (Paris and The Hague, 1974), pp. 170–1; also pp. 164–179 *passim*.

484 See Claude Lévy, "La Presse de la Meuse devant les attentats anarchistes et les lois de répression (décembre 1893—juin-août 1894)", *Recherches sur les forces politiques de la France de l'Est*, p. 259; Ardouin-Dumazet, *Voyage en France*, 18e série, *Région du Nord*, I, *Flandre et Littoral du Nord* (Paris and Nancy, 1899), pp. 168–9.

485 Raymond Poignant, "Etude sur l'assimilation de l'immigration polonaise dans le Pas-de-Calais", *Population*, 4 (1949), p. 157.

486 Robert Louis Stevenson, *An Inland Voyage* (London, 1924, Tusitala Edition, XVII), pp. 114–15.

487 See Silberner, "Proudhon's Judeophobia", p. 458; Kriegel, "Le Syndicalisme Révolutionnaire et Proudhon", *Le Pain et les Roses*, pp. 69–104.

488 See chapter VII, n. 114. Though apparently originating in Algeria, this song also circulated in France itself.

489 See Vaucelles, op. cit., pp. 3–4.

490 Serge Bonnet, Charles Santini, Hubert Barthélémy, "La Presse du Pays-Haut de 1870 à 1914", *Annales de l'Est*, 17 (1965), pp. 68–9.

491 Clemendot, op. cit., p. 132.

492 See Perrot, op. cit., p. 171; Baudrillart, op. cit., III, pp. 124 and 160; Armengaud, op. cit., pp. 97–9; Pierre Merlin, *L'Exode rural*, Institut National d'Études Démographiques. Travaux et documents, Cahier no. 59 (Paris, 1971), p. 115.

493 Drumont, *FJ*, I, p. 117. Drumont used this opportunity to sing the praises of the "livret", much disliked by workers: "ce livret qui est une garantie pour l'ouvrier français comme pour le patron, qui permet à tout directeur d'établissment de se rendre compte de la nationalité, de l'origine, des antécédents du travailleur"; and he thus claimed that it was the Jews who were seeking its abolition. The "livret ouvrier", or record book for non-agricultural workers, had been created by a law of 1803, which was modified in 1854. The legal requirement to possess one, which gave considerable advantage to employers, was widely ignored by the end of the nineteenth century, and was abrogated in 1890; see E. Levasseur, *Histoire des classes ouvrières et de l'industrie en France de 1789 à 1870* (Paris, 1904), II, pp. 504–7; J.-M. Jeanneney et Marguerite Perrot, *Textes de Droit économique et social français 1789–1957* (Paris, 1957), pp. 191 and 263.

494 Daily Reports, Prefect of Police, 29 April, and 1, 3, 5 May 1898. APP Ba 106.

Much the same proposals were put forward by Firmin Faure in Saint-Denis in 1902; see Jolly, ed., op. cit..

495 Barrès, "Contre les étrangers, Etude pour la protection des ouvriers français" (1893); see *Scènes et doctrines*, II, pp. 186–207.

496 Barrès, "La Concurrence des étrangers"; and "Les employeurs d'étrangers", *La Cocarde*, 7 and 19 November 1894; see Victor Nguyen, "Un essai de pouvoir intellectuel au début de la Troisième République: *La Cocarde* de Maurice Barrès (5 septembre 1894–7 mars 1895)", *Etudes Maurrassiennes*, I (1972), p. 150; also Barrès-Maurras, op. cit., p. 267.

497 See Barrès, *Scenes et doctrines*, II, pp. 157–68.

498 See Rollet, op. cit., I, p. 393.

499 See Sternhell, "Paul Déroulède and the Origins of Modern French Nationalism", *Journal of Contemporary History*, 6, no. 4 (1971), p. 54.

500 See Jolly, ed., op. cit.. The French government did have the right to expel individual aliens by a law of 1849, though even this power was disputed by liberal opinion, and seems to have been little used. It was, of course, a precautionary measure against political subversion, and not an "immigration law" in the modern sense; see Arthur Desjardins, "La loi de 1849 et l'expulsion des Étrangers", *Revue des Deux Mondes*, 2 (1882), pp. 657–80.

501 E.g. Drumont, *FJ*, I, p. 102. Little study has been undertaken of comparative Jewish and non-Jewish demographic trends in France, in great part because of the difficulty of locating Jews in the official statistics. Szajkowski, "The Growth of the Jewish Population of France", is thus mainly concerned with the size and geographical location of Jewish population, but does indicate "a considerably higher rate of natural increase" in the 1860s (p. 194). Jacques Houdaille, "La population de Boulay (Moselle) avant 1850", *Population*, 22 (1967), pp. 1077–84, found the Jewish population to be more fecund than the non-Jewish, because of earlier age at marriage. Erckmann-Chatrian presents the same picture, contrasting, in *L'Ami Fritz* (1865), the late-marrying Kobus with the populationist rabbi, David Sichel. Similar correlation between demographic reality and antisemitic fears has not been found for the later nineteenth century; but see Landau, op. cit., p. 239. Assimilated Jews certainly seem to have adopted French middle-class behaviour in this sphere. Lacretelle's Silbermann was an only child, not the only example in fiction and autobiography.

502 See chapter XII, pp. 414–5 below.

503 Drumont, *FJ*, II, p. 164.

504 E.g. Bazin, *La Terre qui meurt;* Imbart de la Tour, op. cit., p. 129; Vaucelles, op. cit., pp. 145–6; also Merlin, op. cit., pp. xi–xii.

505 Drumont, *FM*, p. 167.

506 Daudet, *L'Avant-Guerre*, p. xi.

507 "la terre et les morts" and "déracinés"; see Barrès, *Les Déracinés* (Paris, 1897); and, for discussion of these appealing slogans, Albert Thibaudet, *Trente Ans de vie française*, II, *La Vie de Maurice Barrès* (Paris, 1921), pp. 107–15 and *passim;* and Robert Soucy, *French Fascism: The Case of Maurice Barrès* (Berkeley, 1972), chapter 3. Incidentally, the use of the term "Fascism" to describe Barrès and his thought is highly tendentious.

508 See James K. Hosmer, *The Jews in Ancient, Mediaeval and Modern Times* (London, 1886), pp. 208–14; Louis Wirth, *The Ghetto* (1928) (Chicago, 1969), p. 13; Rosenberg, op. cit., chapter VIII; Lowenstein, op. cit., p. 45; Baron, op. cit., XI, pp. 177–82.

509 Memmi, op. cit., pp. 135, 184 and 286–9, has pointed to the way in which the myth expresses objective features of the Jewish condition. Kafka referred in the 1920s to "the eternal Jew, being senselessly drawn, wandering senselessly through a senselessly obscene world"; Franz Kafka, *Letters to Milena* (New York, 1953), p. 164; see also Hosmer, op. cit., p. 214.

510 See, for the currency of the myth in France and elsewhere up to the nineteenth

century: J. W. Goethe, *Italian Journey (1786–1788)*, (Harmondsworth, 1970), p. 126; Charles Nisard, *Histoire des livres populaires ou de la littérature du colportage* (Paris, 1864), I, pp. 477–96; Bollême, *La Bibliothèque bleue*, pp. 183–9, for example. For nineteenth-century France, in addition to Sue's novel referred to, see, for example, Hugo, *Choses vues 1830–1846*, p. 280 (1844); Claude Tillier, *Mon Oncle Benjamin* (1843) (Paris, 1963), pp. 79–82; Vallès, *La Rue*, p. 61 (1866); Paul Féval, *La Fille du Juif-errant* (Paris, 1879); J.-K. Huysmans, "L'Image d'Épinal", *Croquis Parisiens* (1880) (Paris, 1905), pp. 141–4; *The Confessions of Arsène Houssaye*, p. 145; Drumont, *FJ*, I, p. 203; Léon Cladel, *La Juive errante* (Paris, 1897); and Guillaume Apollinaire, "Le Passant de Prague", *La Revue Blanche*, 1 June 1902, Apollinaire, *Oeuvres complètes*, I, (Paris, 1965), pp. 105–13; and also Dumont, *La Petite Bourgeoisie vue à travers les contes du "Journal"*, pp. 46–7; Randall, op. cit., pp. 10–12 and Bibliography; Klein, *Portrait de la Juive*, pp. 77–85; Jacques Petit, *Bernanos, Bloy, Claudel, Péguy: Quatre écrivains catholiques face à Israël. Images et mythes* (Paris, 1972), pp. 197–224; and *French Popular Imagery, Five Centuries of Prints*. Arts Council of Great Britain (London, 1974), pp. 46, 128 and 135.

511 Cit. Pierrard, op. cit., p. 25.
512 Drumont, *FJ*, I, p. 58; see also ibid., I, pp. 263, 291 and 530; and II, p. 3; and *DB*, pp. 28 and 192–3.
513 Drumont, *DB*, p. 93.
514 Drumont, "Le Drame juif", *OBS*, pp. 77–8; see also the illustration of the wandering Jews from *Le Pèlerin* in Sorlin, *"La Croix" et les Juifs*, between pp. 90 and 91.
515 The concept of "anomie" was, of course developed by Durkheim at this time, notably in *Le Suicide* (1897); see Lukes, *Émile Durkheim*, chapter 9.
516 On the reception of *La Terre*, see Léon Bloy, "L'Art vertueux", *Inédits de Léon Bloy* (Montreal, 1945), pp. 131–51; Maurice Le Blond, *La Publication de La Terre* (Paris, 1937); Guillemin, *Présentation des Rougon-Macquart*, pp. 287–308. Of relevance here also is the development around the turn of the century of what one might call the "neo-rustic" novel, notably by René Bazin. The two genres were not, of course, ever absolutely distinct, as is demonstrated by the autobiographical fiction of Charles-Louis Philippe, and by a novel such as Marguerite Audoux's *Marie-Claire* (Paris, 1911), or, later, Raymonde Vincent's *Campagne* (Paris, 1937); for some discussion, see Barral, *Les Agrariens français*, pp. 132–5.
517 Vallès, *La Rue*, pp. 131 and 175; see also Richardson, *Rachel*, pp. 13–15.
518 Lacretelle, *Silbermann*, pp. 56–7 and 67.
519 Cit. Pierrard, op. cit., p. 175.
520 *Le Petit Journal*, 29 April 1898.
521 See M. N. Bourguet, "Une Race d'administrés, Les Français de l'An IX vus par leurs préfets", Paper given at Colloque sur l'Idée de Race, 1975, p. 14; Vallès, *La Rue*, p. 73; and Alain-Fournier, *Le Grand Meaulnes* (1913) (Paris, 1966), pp. 91–3, 103, 110–13, 121–3 and 137, for further examples of attitudes towards the nomadic population; for a general interpretation of similar attitudes, see Judith Okely, BBC Radio Talk, London, 9 September 1973.
522 Circular, Prefect, Yonne, 8 April 1895. AN F⁷ 12926, Dossier no. 3, "Vernisseurs (Bande dit des), Vols et assassinats, 1898–1903".
523 See Pierre Guillaume and Jean-Pierre Poussou, *Démographie historique* (Paris, 1970), pp. 213–18.
524 Drumont, *FJ*, II, p. 278.

CHAPTER XI

SOCIAL ANTISEMITISM: "A KIND OF SOCIALISM"

ANTISEMITISM, WE HAVE SEEN, WAS A KIND OF "ANTI-CAPITALISM", AND represented a reaction to important economic changes in France. It was also a protest against a social system, and the expression of social tension and conflict. "The most important cause [of antisemitism]", according to Lombroso in 1899, was "the antagonism between the poor and the rich".[1] And antisemites frequently claimed that their movement was socialist. However, although it did have features that justified the label in the context of the 1890s, and although it clearly reflected social unrest, the function of antisemitism, based as it was on a mistaken and "irrational" social diagnosis, and having a fundamentally conservative aim, was rather to mask class conflict and to divert resentments into a channel that did not threaten the existing social system. In the words of Leroy-Beaulieu, it was "a kind of socialism *sui generis*, a socialism of the Right . . ."[2]

I

There is no doubt that many antisemites saw themselves as engaged in a movement of social protest, a protest of the poor against the rich, as Lombroso suggested, and also of the individual against the system. The example of Drumont, by far the most popular exponent of antisemitism in the period, is instructive. In *Le Testament d'un antisémite,* he declared that "following the example of Jesus, my divine Master, I took up the defence of the oppressed against robbers and against the exploiters of the poor . . . I was the man most interested in reform, the most advanced, the most concerned with social justice that you could find in France . . ."[3] Later he wrote: "On every occasion, we [antisemites] valiantly supported the cause of the persecuted, of the deprived, of the oppressed, of the exploited, of the humble, of the suffering . . .";[4] and again: "I was guided only by the hatred of oppression which was the core of my being."[5] Antisemitism was thus presented as the fruit of compassion and social conscience, and as an attack on the establishment and against tyranny. "I have seen nothing that made me so indignant", wrote

Drumont in 1889, "as the spectacle of miserable French workers, dressed in worn-out, patched-up overalls, their shoes in holes, their faces gaunt with hunger, watching the German Yids pass by on their horses, on the way to the Bois de Boulogne for a canter to work up an appetite before lunch."[6] And in 1890: "When the Jews were all-powerful and no one dared to attack them, I spoke up against them as one must speak to implacable oppressors . . . I have only ever attacked the strong, the powerful and the rich . . ."[7] In 1895, he declared: "Love Liberty! that is the precept that I would like to leave with you . . ."[8]; and the name chosen for his daily, *La Libre Parole*, in 1892, of course, expressed the same pretension. More generally, he claimed that "antisemitism was born from the anger of the dispossessed and the victims [of the Jews]"[9]; and, in all this, he was expressing a widespread feeling "of disgust at the iniquities of our time, a moral revolt against the corruption of politicians and against the provocative display of wealth",[10] that Leroy-Beaulieu agreed was one of the prime motivations of antisemitism in his day. In the same vein, for example, *La France Libre* (the name again is significant) wrote in October 1896 that the Lyon Antisemitic Congress "would allow to be heard the groans of the people condemned to revolt through hunger . . .";[11] and Guérin described the "Fort Chabrol" incident as "the only really energetic action taken in France for years against the abuse of power . . ."[12]

Drumont placed the antisemitic movement of social protest in the context of a conflict between Bourgeoisie and People, familiar in the writings of nineteenth-century French Socialists.[13] In his version, a calculating Bourgeoisie duped and abused a well-intentioned but gullible People:[14]

> The role of the revolutionary Bourgeois . . . has always been that of a blackguard. He excites the People with fine phrases, seduces them from the workshop, makes them drunk with rhetoric, and destroys all their faith and beliefs. Then, when the self-seekers and hangers-on of the Bourgeoisie have obtained all they wanted, they join forces with the Pharisees of the Right . . . to butcher the proletariat at their convenience, as they did in the June Days and in those of May.

Drumont claimed that the democratic bourgeois ideology of the French Revolution "placed those who had nothing at the mercy of those who had something", removing the real right of association that had existed earlier, and replacing it with purely theoretical rights. Duped by this ideology, and "showing a remarkable blindness, the proletariat works with its own hands to assure for the Bourgeoisie that political power, in all its plentitude, which the Bourgeoisie immediately uses against those who gave it to them."[15] But, if the People remained often unaware of it, "the Reign of the Bourgeoisie"[16] represented none the less its objective exploitation. On the occasion of the election of Casimir-Périer, scion of a well-established political and industrial dynasty,[17] to the Presidency of the Third Republic in 1894, Drumont commented: "The mansion that Casimir-Périer inhabits, the princely luxury which surrounds him, the carriage in which he travels, all these he owes to those unfortunate miners who have passed their bleak, hard lives in the black depths of mines, under the perpetual threat of pit-gas."[18] Pointing to the role of the Jews in this scheme, he wrote in *La France juive* that "the Republicans in power seem to have one aim in view: to drive the proletariat into the hands of the Jew so that he can exploit them more easily";[19] and elsewhere he concluded, with a different emphasis: "The Bourgeoisie exploiting the People and dispossessed in its turn by the Jew, this sums up . . . the economic history of the century."[20] Moreover, Drumont envisaged the reign of the Bourgeoisie as inherently unstable and doomed to imminent collapse, though he drew this conclusion less from a conviction of its economic contradictions, or even its injustice, and more from a sense of its profound moral decadence. "The Bourgeoisie", he wrote, "means the predominance of the lowest appetites . . .";[21] "the bourgeois soul [is] incapable of any honest or noble sentiment . . ."[22] Under the significant title of *La Fin d'un monde,* he drew a scathing picture of Parisian High Society and of the French ruling class as a whole. The Bourgeoisie, and the renegade Aristocracy that had amalgamated with it, were mediocre, cowardly, cruel, callous, greedy and corrupt. "What we are witnessing", he concluded, "is the final stages of one phase of social organization; we are approaching the end of the road . . ."[23]

In contrast to the vices of the Bourgeoisie, Drumont celebrated the virtues of the People: "It is only among the People that you will still find a certain feeling for Justice in the abstract, a certain power of indignation that is completely extinct among the representatives of the upper classes . . .", he wrote in 1891; and, referring to his election campaign in Paris in 1890: "I never found myself in the presence of someone belonging to the real People without encountering charm and sincerity."[24] It was among the People, moreover, that genuine religious feeling was preserved. "The real People was profoundly attached to the religion of its ancestors",[25] Drumont wrote of the time of the French Revolution; and he insisted that reaction to the anticlerical "persecution" of the Third Republic came again from the People.

> How moving [he wrote] to watch these simple, humble people struggling against the formidable governmental machine set in motion against them by the wicked men who are in control of it! . . . What acts of courage one finds among the People, in the provinces, and even in Paris! . . . Men have not yet thought of gathering together the names of all these good people who have resisted all to defend their faith, inscribing them in what would be a *golden book* of small folk; but God has already written their names in the book of his justice. They are more than courageous, they are heroic.

And he celebrated, in particular, as typical of "the peasants with hearts of gold", that valiant plebeian of Montaure (Eure), sentenced to 22 days in prison for not sending her children to the state school, "this peasant woman who has borne seven children in her womb and has been thrown into a dungeon in contempt of all justice . . ."[26] In the same way, it was among the People that true patriotic sentiment was to be found. Referring to popular reaction to the news of the disaster at Lang-Son, Drumont wrote:[27]

It is at times of crisis like this . . . that one sees how far the People has retained its splendid qualities. The People has a sudden intuition of where the real responsibilities lie . . . So, spontaneously . . . groups formed . . . shouts were heard of "To the Rothschilds! to the Rothschilds!" . . . What a fund of patriotism still exists among the People . . . How these proletarians really commune and sympathize with our poor soldiers abandoned thousands of miles away, surrounded by numberless hordes . . .

Moreover, as we have seen, the People not only had fine feelings, but expressed them to some purpose, resisting anticlericalism, rejecting Republican politicians, and, of course, supporting antisemitism: "Among so much abject acquiescence and shameful passivity, the People has retained a spark of indignation, and the capacity for generous anger."[28]

But the virtue of the People was probably most typically exemplified, for Drumont, in its role as victim of an evil social system, a role with which he sentimentally sympathized.[29] For example, in *La France juive*, he evoked the fate of a cobbler whom he had known as a child: "With his life savings, he had, through a Jewish money-changer, and without the knowledge of his wife, bought a few Crédit Mobilier shares. He had lost everything, and hanged himself with the cords from his work-table."[30] Again, referring to a wedding at the fashionable church of Saint Philippe-du-Roule in Paris, he wrote: "All that lace had been paid for by the lives of poor people, of those who had killed themselves because they saw ruin staring them in the face";[31] and he commented, more generally: "How often have I said how cruel it was to think that some men possess fortunes running into millions while whole families asphyxiate themselves because they don't have enough to eat?"[32] He extended his sympathy, moreover, to include those whom poverty and injustice had embittered and turned to violence, like the Anarchist Auguste Vaillant executed in 1894 for throwing a bomb in the Chamber of Deputies. Drumont evoked with feeling "the life, the existence of this worker, aged just 32: the miseries of his childhood as a bastard, the convictions for trivial offences . . . the books that worried and then corrupted him . . . the hatred that took possession of his heart, and the temptation to crime which followed on its heels . . ."[33] And here, Drumont was particularly critical of the class-bias of the penal system. It was "a monstrous iniquity" that those convicted of large-scale financial frauds should get off with light fines, while those convicted of petty theft should receive prison sentences: "Three months in prison for a crippled child who travels on the train without paying, but a fine of 3,000 francs for a big financier, an adult and intelligent person, who abuses the trust placed in him by presenting false accounts to his clients! Is this right?"[34] Worse, he pointed out that de Lesseps had never been prosecuted for his part in the vast Panama swindle, whereas "the poor devil who breaks a pane of glass to pinch a loaf of bread is at once locked away, marched from the police station to the magistrate, and from the magistrate to the criminal court."[35] During his stay in the Sainte-Pélagie prison in 1892, moreover, he evoked the wretched lot of the common, as opposed to the political, prisoners, pointing out also that recidivism was in part socially determined:[36]

Poor people! How much, in these fatal destinies, is due to hereditary influences, to bad examples, to bad luck! . . . O Lord! O Lord! They are men even so, and your divine Son, too, was a man. Will you not take pity on these damned of the earth, will you not save some of them, here and now, from the terrible fate that awaits them? While so many clever criminals parade their insolent luxury in Paris, must these men who are not fully responsible for what they do, go on from gaol to gaol until they are finally transported to a penal colony?

In the same vein, Drumont protested, as we have seen, against proposals for tougher measures against vagrancy, which he said was "a purely relative offence, the mark of being poor, of having parents who were too honest to get rich, simply a matter of sleeping rough in a wood or on a bench in a town instead of in a bed . . ."[37] He also championed the cause of the rag-men of Paris, whose livelihood was threatened by Poubelle's modern methods of refuse collection.[38]

In this situation of conflict between Bourgeoisie and People, and of exploitation of the latter by the former, Drumont clearly declared his solidarity with the People. Unlike the bourgeois liberals who duped the People, he wrote: "Our whole enterprise is different. We love the People tenderly; we know what workers suffer, because we can remember being poorer than the poorest among them, but we don't flatter them either . . . I have certainly been one of those who . . . has loved the People most profoundly, who has been in tune with the soul of the People."[39] This claim to possess some special affinity with the People, a special identity with them, and a special right to speak for them, was of crucial importance to Drumont, and one which he repeatedly made.[40] He wrote, for example, of the Duc de Broglie: "What could he know of the Paris of today? He had probably never set foot either in a workshop, or a café, or a brothel; he had never chatted, eye to eye, with workers, raving on after their day's work, or with street-corner orators . . . or with whores who live and die from the corruption of cities."[41] By contrast, Drumont referred to "men like myself", who had done all these things, and "who do not have to go far back in their ancestry to discover good Christian workers . . ."[42] Unlike the distant duke, or any established Republican politician, for that matter, Drumont was of the People and remained in contact with them. So, he could get along with his curé because, "we have a popular side to us, which brings us together . . .";[43] and he could reject the idea of saving as "the social panacea", because he knew how hard it was for poor people to save anything.[44] Here he evoked his own upbringing in decent poverty, but surrounded by a milieu in which crime and misery flourished: "it was there that I learned what a 100-sou piece was worth, what it meant for a poor family . . ."[45] He thus professed that La France juive and his other writings possessed a peculiar, if not unique, existential authority, since they derived "from generations of poor people who have lived their own small lives . . . who have arrived at old age without having taken a penny from anyone else . . . and who have been content with their little place. It is in the name of these humble people, whose voice the world has never heard, that I have spoken . . ."[46]

Drumont's "populism" was widely shared by antisemites, and was expressed in a variety of ways. A. Gabriel claimed, in *Le Courrier de l'Est* in October 1889, that "a usurious Jewish coalition . . . wishes to annihilate the principles of equality and liberty in France."[47] Léon Daudet characterized Jules Lemaître, of the Ligue de la Patrie Française, as "the friend of the small people, suspicious of the respectable and well-to-do . . ."[48] A concern to improve the lot of working people informed the different branches of the Christian Democratic movement[49] and the Assumptionists who ran *La Croix*, [50] and the same concern was manifested in a great deal of antisemitic propaganda, emanating from these and other sources. One of the aims of the Union Nationale, according to its *Règlement Général* of 1897, was "to put an end to the undeserved poverty and misfortune in which so many workers find themselves";[51] and, linking this aim with his antisemitism, abbé Garnier asserted at a meeting in Courbevoie in June 1898, that Jews came to France "to carry off workers' savings . . ."[52] A leaflet, *"Justice! Egalité!"*, put out in the late 1890s, probably by *La Croix*, called for "the just punishment of Jewish speculators and monopolists. Let them be convicted and sentenced in the same way as the poor worker who has stolen a few potatoes or a five franc piece!"[53] Placards posted in Le Mans, in February 1898, declared: "Down with the Jews. Worker, your only enemy is the Jew. Let's hang him on the nearest lamp-post."[54] The idea that the Jews were ultimately responsible for the exploitation of the working classes was, moreover, a commonplace of this propaganda. Drumont, we have seen, referred to the Jews as "implacable oppressors", and claimed that the anticlerical legislation of the Third Republic was a "Jewish persecution" that "fell almost exclusively on the poor".[55] He claimed also that the French worker "worked to enrich the Jews", who then exploited him further through wineshops and pawnbrokers, both of which they owned or controlled.[56] More generally both Drumont and Léon Bloy asserted that the Jews were consumed by "a hatred of the poor".[57] Similarly, a Catholic speaker at a public meeting in Paris in February 1898 referred to the Jews as "a race which oppresses the worker".[58] Barrès characterized the Jew as a "vulture",[59] which was a symbol among workers of the exploiting landlord,[60] and, in an article in 1897, he claimed that "French exploiters . . . were following the example set by Jews".[61]

As this reminds us, many antisemites were vigorous critics of "capitalism" precisely on the grounds that it was an exploitative economic system, that had disastrous social consequences, particularly for workers. Quoting Toussenel, Drumont wrote in *La France juive* that it was "both oppressive and anarchic . . . being based on cupidity, on insatiable cupidity."[62] And he pointed out elsewhere that it was a system of "property without duties or responsibilities",[63] which therefore "provoked labour" to unrest and revolt.[64]

Despite its paternalism and its Catholic attachments, therefore, the antisemitism of Drumont and many of his contemporaries, with its concern for social justice, its identification with the People against the Bourgeoisie, its general pattern of socio-historical analysis, coupled as it was with an overt attack on "capitalism", the occasional expression of revolutionary intentions, and a sense of impending, even necessary, social collapse, deserves to have its claim to be "a kind of socialism" seriously considered. If it was not that "terribly lucid critique of a social system", that Bernanos later supposed it to be,[65] he was reflecting a body of contemporary opinion in his misapprehension, and not simply antisemitic opinion itself, as we have seen. As a perceptive police agent reported in the late 1890s: "The clever way in which antisemitism has been presented explains why it has been able to recruit a certain number of partisans among those, too numerous in the existing social order, who are ignorant of the past, discontented with the present which crushes them, and who drift into the future, oblivious of what surrounds them, men and things. One can excuse such people for having thought that Drumont was a socialist."[66]

The claim to be "socialist" was made by antisemites with varying degrees of commitment and sincerity. It was sometimes present merely in the insistence that the Socialists were saying something that ought to be heeded. La Croix, for example, on May Day 1890, declared that the "social question" would "lead to serious trouble and cause bloodshed. Woe betide those who imagine that they need not bother about it. There is much that is true and legitimate in the demands of the Socialists, and the fact that they must be condemned for their extremism is no reason not to study very seriously what is just in those demands."[67] Drumont's attitude was similar, though he was less ready to condemn extremism out of hand. Working-class resentment and revolts, according to him, were a natural reaction to a social system, which, in contrast to that of the Ancien Régime, despised and exploited workers, while a new corrupt ruling class set them the worst of examples. In the past, he wrote, "the Church gave workers the saints of heaven as comrades; the Jewish and masonic press today regards them all as convicts."[68] And again: "I realize from what they say how much hatred is sown in the hearts of the People by the way in which the ruling classes flout, outrage and destroy those instincts of integrity and fairness that used to prevail in our country."[69] Thus the Paris Commune, though exploited by the Jews, was an understandable, even a "courageous" protest, and its repression an act of barbaric savagery.[70] Drumont also expressed considerable sympathy for the working-class movement generally, and regarded it as completely legitimate:[71]

> It has taken fifty years of struggle for the workers to break the chains so well forged by the triumphant Bourgeoisie in 1789, and by which they were bound hand and foot so that the Bourgeoisie could exercise its industrial exploitation more freely; as far as the right of association is concerned, they are hardly further on today [1891] than they were on the eve of the Revolution.

Socialism was also a movement justified by objective features of the capitalist system. In La France juive, Drumont stressed the inevitability of its appeal, and argued that to debate its rights and wrongs was academic:[72]

> For the worker, the social revolution is an absolute necessity. Convinced from now on that there is nothing beyond this life, bent double beneath

the weight of an exploitation that the demands of capital render more and
more cruel, he sees that he has nothing in this life; he wants to gain
possession of the factories and industrial plant in the same way that the
peasant, before 1789, wanted to gain possession of the land; he calls for the
socialization, for the expropriation to his profit, of the means of production.
All the arguments that one tries to oppose to these claims, which have force
to back them up, may be excellent in themselves, but their value, alas, is
entirely literary or philosophical.

In 1889 Drumont was less cautious and more approving:[73]

Those who, witnessing the terrifying disorder which prevails everywhere
today, are preoccupied with reorganizing society on a new, more rational
and juster, basis, are not . . . enemies of the peace, to be kept at arm's length
. . . Doubtless, there are among them crack-pots and those who are simply
consumed by envy, but the end pursued by Socialists of good faith is very
noble and their entreprise is very necessary . . . collectivist and anarchist
theories . . . are the outcome and the logical result of essential features of
society which the Jewish system has created, with the support and the
approval of the Bourgeoisie . . . this unholy alliance of speculators . . .
conspiring against the worker legitimizes the theories of the collectivists.

In the eyes of many bourgeois, terrified by the "socialist menace", such
statements must have appeared as real professions of faith in socialism. Mag-
nard, for example, the editor of Le Figaro, wrote fairly typically in November
1892: "I call on people to recognize, with me, that antisemitism is the most
dangerous form of socialism, that it is, in reality and above all, a campaign
against the moneyed classes."[74]

Other antisemites expressed views similar to those of Drumont, or even
went a stage further and actually called themselves "Socialists". For example,
the first Ligue Antisémitique, at a meeting in February 1890, passed a resolution in support of the "Socialist" parliamentary candidate Francis Laur that
declared "that society is in danger as a result of the Jewish financial coalition,
and that millionnaires cannot be allowed to exist in the same State where
others are dying of hunger . . ."[75] One of the first antisemitic newspapers in
France, L'Anti-Youtre, which appeared in Paris in 1891, was a self-declared
Socialist weekly.[76] Despite his Royalism, the Marquis de Morès was also
regarded by his admirers as a Socialist. Speaking at his funeral in Paris in July
1896, Barrès declared: "Morès was a Socialist; he accepted the need and
wished for the economic transformation of our society, and a change in its
ruling personnel . . ."[77] On the same occasion, Jules Guérin, who saw himself
as Morès's political heir, described the nature of his Socialism in more detail:[78]

He affirmed the necessity of modifying the process of government, so that
the representatives of the people, who work and produce, would be obliged
to legislate in their favour instead of always serving the interests of the
bankers and the international speculators . . . He knew that all the so-called
attempts, made within the existing economic order, to improve the lot of
the producer and the consumer, were so many misleading and fraudulent
manoeuvres aimed at maintaining the wage-earner in a state of servitude

... The economic theories, defended by Morès, were those, which alone can emancipate Labour and the workers and loose them from an eternal bondage ... and these were theories that involved the decentralization of finance ... It was, finally, in the service of the workers, for whom he dreamed of opening up new markets through trade with central Africa, monopolized by the English, that he met his glorious death ...

Though the argument is forced, the rhetorical framework into which it is forced is clear and very significant.

Both Guérin and Barrès, themselves, moreover, professed to be Socialists. Guérin maintained in 1898, as we have seen, that "antisemitism is essentially Socialist";[79] while Barrès, in the course of his political evolution from Left-wing Boulangism to anti-Dreyfusard Nationalism, adopted a Socialism of a much more developed and well articulated type. "Socialism is the word in which France has placed its hope . . .", he declared in November 1889, "let us therefore be Socialists!";[80] and, in his programme as deputy for Nancy in 1890, he presented the social insurance legislation of Germany as a model for France to follow. Besides advocating this degree of State Socialism, he also at this time called for the nationalization of mines, railways and banks, supported international action on the part of workers, and envisaged a violent revolution, initiated perhaps by a general strike.[81] Although more vague and marking a considerable retreat from these earlier policies, his Nancy Programme of 1898 still proclaimed: "the vital energy, which it is too true that France lacks, she will find within her own frontiers, by encouraging the promotion of her poorest and least favoured citizens, by raising them to new prosperity and to new levels of training. One can see here how nationalism necessarily engenders Socialism. And we define Socialism as 'the moral and material improvement of the most numerous and the poorest class' . . ."[82] Here the influence of Drumont combined with that of Saint-Simon.

Mention should also be made here of Henri Rochefort, almost certainly the most popular of the Nationalist leaders at the time of the Dreyfus Affair, and who combined patriotic Socialism with a strong dose of antisemitism. His popularity dated from the time of his vigorous critique of the Second Empire in *La Lanterne* in the late 1860s.[83] He later became a member of the Government of National Defence, and then a supporter of the Paris Commune, for which he was sentenced to deportation for life. However, he escaped from his prison in New Caledonia,[84] and returned to France in 1880, after the amnesty for the *communards* had been declared. At once, he launched the immediately successful Socialist daily, *L'Intransigeant*, [85] and went on to become "the most popular Boulangist leader".[86] On his return from London after being exiled as a result of this involvement, he was greeted, in February 1895, by a demonstration of 100,000 well-wishers at the Gare du Nord, which was only one indication of his charismatic appeal. Despite his increasing identification with Nationalism, he maintained friendly relations with more orthodox Socialists until the time of the Affair, and retained his fidelity to the Commune.[87] At the same time, he was closely associated with the antisemitic movement, though his relations with Drumont and other antisemites were stormy,[88] and, as we have seen, he lent the cause support in *L'Intransigeant.* [89] According to Léon Daudet, for example, it was Rochefort who coined the nickname *"Boule de Juif"* for Reinach;[90] while Bournand gave him this good reference in 1898: "M. Rochefort has stood up, with the verve and the energy that characterize him, against the power of Israel."[91]

The same combination of socialism and antisemitism also occurs in many of the programmes of candidates in the 1898 General Election in Paris. For example, Poccaton stood in the 1st constituency of the 20th *arrondissement* as an "antisemitic and Republican Socialist candidate". Dr Légué stood in the 2nd constituency of the 18th *arrondissement* as an "anti-Jewish, patriotic and Republican Socialist", and told an electoral meeting "that he had worked for the department of Public Assistance for 17 years and thus knew at first hand the misery suffered by the People; he thus had the right to call himself a Socialist . . ." Tournade, in the 1st constituency of the 16th, "presented himself as an antisemitic Socialist candidate", explaining "that he was standing only in order to combat the Jews who were grinding the faces of the working class"; and Admiral Mathieu, in the 2nd constituency of the 15th, declared that he was "the friend of the poor" and an advocate of "legislation to help workers".[92] Some antisemites who were elected to parliament at this time, and earlier, fulfilled their pledges by sponsoring or supporting Socialist measures in the Chamber of Deputies. Ferrand, for example, supported Bills to introduce progressive income tax and old-age pensions, while Charles Bernard himself introduced Bills on the inspection of work and for the abolition of the press laws of 1894 which sought to censor and control the expression of anarchist and Socialist opinion. Another antisemitic deputy, Abel-Bernard, became a member of the Conseil Supérieur du Travail.[93]

The socialism of antisemites was proclaimed in other ways. The Ligue Anti-Juive d'Alger, founded in 1892, changed its name later in the decade to the Ligue Socialiste Anti-Juive,[94] and we have seen that the socialist strain in Algerian antisemitism was particularly pronounced. In France again, Viau related that he had come to antisemitism in 1887 via "a vague and idealistic Socialism".[95] In February 1899, Maurras referred to the embryonic Action Française group, meeting at the Café Voltaire, as "Nationalist in nuance, with certain Socialist tendencies . . ."[96] A poster sent to the provinces to announce the success of the antisemites and Nationalists in the 1900 municipal elections in Paris proclaimed: "Paris, the Socialist city, the most Republican city in France has just . . . emancipated itself from the Jewish and Dreyfusard yoke."[97] In 1902, Biétry, an antisemite, and later leader of the Syndicats Jaunes movement of "free" trade unions, founded a Parti Socialiste National.[98]

A socialist orientation was also implicit in the antisemites' use of the same revolutionary rhetoric that was still employed by orthodox Socialists of the time. In *La France juive*, Drumont evoked the "Revolution that would be carried out "against the Jews;[99] and, sybil-like in 1891, he proclaimed: "The hour of uprising is not far off!"[100] The Ligue Antisémitique Française was associated in January 1898 with the formation of an "antisemitic Revolutionary committee".[101] At a "patriotic meeting" in Suresnes in February 1898, Thiébaud and Millevoye both made declarations of antisemitic revolutionary Socialism, claiming that "all the principles of 1789 are threatened by the Jewish conspiracy", which, like Drumont, they blamed for the "massacre of Fourmies" and the repression of "the insurgent People" in 1871.[102] More specifically, abbé Duvaux urged one Paris section of the Union Nationale, the same year, to counter governmental anticlericalism by "taking over political power", which meant "taking to the streets . . ."[103] Picard warned Dagan in 1899: "The masses will end by acting in a revolutionary way . . .";[104] while a speaker at a Jeunesse Antisémite meeting in Paris in January 1900 called for the recommencement of street action on the part of antisemites, saying: "It needs only a spark . . . to set everything alight and unleash the revolution . . ."[105] A new antisemitic group, reported by the Belfort police in December 1901, called themselves "the sons of the Revolution".[106] Finally, the "official organ" of the Parti National Antijuif of 1902, Le Précurseur, made the same commitment to the cause of the Revolution, in a different rhetorical way, by using the revolutionary calendar to date its numbers.[107]

To explain the significance of this "socialist" antisemitism, it is necessary to place it in its general historical context, and to relate it to other features of antisemitic ideology. It will have become clear already that not all antisemites were Socialists; indeed, as we shall see, many of them explicitly repudiated Socialism. Antisemitism had its own Left-and Right wings. It is obvious also that many antisemites went through a socialist phase, like Barrès, either through personal conviction, or political opportunism, or a mixture of the two. As Barrès said: "Socialism is the word in which France has placed its hope . . . let us therefore be Socialists!" Leroy-Beaulieu pointed out in 1897 that antisemitism and Socialism represented the same "amalgam of generous aspirations and sheer covetousness", so that their parallel diffusion and success was therefore unsurprising.[108] Picard, writing in 1892, indicated that the Socialist label, besides offering a guarantee of the right moral sentiment, also lent antisemitism a "scientific" status: "Socialism is no longer a bogey but a vast scientific enterprise in which are joined and work those minds from all classes that thirst for justice; Socialism and antisemitism are the same thing."[109] When the general climate of opinion changed, when the supporters of antisemitism realised that Socialism was a dangerous weapon that might turn against their own interests, they betrayed the real nature of their commitment to it by abandoning it, or by reaffirming their distance from it. As Lazare observed in 1894, there was an irony in the fact that[110]

antisemitism, which was professed above all by conservatives, by those who reproached the Jews with having been the auxiliaries of the Jacobins of 1789, of the liberals and of the revolutionaries, had become the ally of these same revolutionaries . . . Antisemitism stirred up the lower middle class, the petty bourgeois, and sometimes the peasant, against the Jewish capitalists, but, in so doing, . . . it encouraged them to hate all capitalists . . .

Several of the contributors to Dagan's *Enquête* pointed to the same paradox. Henry Maret, for example, emphasized: "the more it is demonstrated that the Jews control wealth and credit, the more clear it becomes that it is impossible to destroy the Jews without, at the same time, destroying the basis of our whole social organization. Personally, I would welcome this, but the conservative antisemites ought to know that, by their own efforts, they are advancing the hour of the final catastrophe."[111] Maret, here, tends towards taking rhetoric too much at its face value, though he was surely right to stress that it could be so taken. With such qualification, however, his observation was rightly applied to antisemitism, whether it called itself Socialist or not, and the paradox which he revealed, moreover, had an important positive function. But in order to explain it, we must first situate the term "Socialism".

II

As Sternhell has shown for the early 1890s,[112] and as other evidence indicates for the later part of the decade, the term "socialism" had not then achieved the clarity of definition that historians, often themselves Socialists of a more modern type, have usually lent it in retrospect.[113] The term still covered all those who were concerned with the "social question", with the lot of the working classes, or with the reorganization of society. In the words of Roche, a candidate in the 1898 elections in Paris which we have already quoted: "Socialism is not . . . the monopoly of any particular sect."[114] Lacking doctrinal or organizational unity, the Socialist movement, loosely defined, included Radical-Socialists such as Clemenceau and Pelletan,[115] Nationalists such as Rochefort and Barrès, as well as the various schools of "orthodox" Socialism, grouped around their leaders Brousse, Allemane, Vaillant and Guesde, "independents" such as Millerand and Jaurès, and also anarchists. Barrès commented in 1896, maliciously but with insight:[116]

> Having discovered how far internationalist revolutionary collectivist Socialists leave all these causes on one side in their electoral propaganda, I ask myself whether we are not, in our earnest discussion of such words, the dupes of our own taste for philosophical labels, and whether it would not be better to say simply: "The candidates of the party which has cheap newspapers."

Fashionable Socialism certainly was among intellectuals and would-be intellectuals, but this was no guarantee of a basis in theory, however lax, and the adoption of the label was often just the expression of sentimental feeling for the poor, such as we have encountered in Drumont. The poet, François Coppée, for example, later a member of the Ligue de la Patrie Française, defined himself, not without irony, in December 1894 as "a kind of sentimental Socialist, something of a sceptic, basically rather reactionary, a partisan of the good Lord and of the flag, a man who does not at all believe that all liberties are necessarily good, an admirer of the Little Corporal [Napoleon], but who could accommodate himself to the reign of the King of Yvetot or even of a less paternal tyrant provided that he was really French."[117] Perhaps closer to Drumont in its seriousness, though the two men were completely antagonistic politically and as far as antisemitism was concerned, was the Socialism of Péguy, which the Tharauds described in these terms:[118]

> Péguy's Socialism was much closer to that of St Francis than to that of Karl Marx. It was a disposition of the heart, a religious concept that derived from the experience of his childhood, from the life which he led until he was 15 or 16, at Orléans . . . among small folk still living in the past, serious, honest, devoted to their craft . . . [it was] a long meditation on that state of poverty by which he was surrounded . . .

For yet another intellectual, Socialism had yet other connotations. For Durkheim, it involved the same moral regeneration as for Péguy, but also a rational reorganization of society along lines suggested by rigorous sociological research, while excluding any strict connection with the working-class movement, class conflict or political action.[119]

However, during the 1880s and more so the 1890s and early 1900s, a process of decantation was taking place, which reduced the range of acceptable variety within Socialism, and demarcations were emerging which made the omnibus term less and less applicable. Anarchists and "orthodox" Socialists parted company at the Congress of Paris in 1881, although relations were not entirely severed.[120] At the other end of the political spectrum, the Radical and Radical-Socialist party was created as a formal organization in 1901, and Radical-Socialists became clearly differentiated from their Socialist allies, who, by 1906, were their electoral rivals.[121] The "orthodox" Socialist groups, after breaking apart in the 1880s, strengthened their doctrinal cohesion, and began to move together again from 1893, achieving unification in 1905 on the basis of a common collectivist programme.[122] Finally, and most significant for our purposes, the political ramifications of the Dreyfus Affair drew a clear line between the "orthodox" Socialists, who, after some hesitation, became Dreyfusard and supported Republican governments in this period against the Right,[123] and the nationalist and antisemitic socialists who took the other side. However, in the period that we are considering, this process had not yet worked itself out completely, and attitudes lagged behind political behaviour. The old vague omnibus term, therefore, still held some meaning, and antisemites were able to take advantage of its ambiguity. For example, La Cocarde, a newspaper edited by Barrès, Maurras, Pelletan, Fernand Pelloutier (secretary of the Fédération des Bourses du Travail) and others, was still seeking in 1894 and 1895 to build some kind of socialist unity with the heterogeneous elements that these names represent.[124] Barrès claimed in the paper: "Nationalists with a concern for justice, like Drumont, Socialists, such as those of La Petite République group, are agreed on the most pressing parts of our programme, which is to get hold of excessive wealth and then to distribute it more fairly."[125] Moreover, once the Affair had broken out, links between antisemites and orthodox Socialists still remained, in fact or in project.

Albert Réville, professor at the Collège de France, told Dagan in 1899: "Accusing the Jews of draining off the national capital for their own profit, and proposing, more or less openly, to take this wealth from them, antisemitism has encountered allies in the Socialist parties of collectivist tendency."[126] As we have seen, Drumont expressed sympathies for the oppositional stance and revolutionary aims of the "orthodox" Socialists. He paid particular tribute in *La France juive* and elsewhere to earlier Socialists who had expressed hostility to the Jews. Toussenel's *Les Juifs rois de l'époque* (1845) was "an imperishable masterpiece", to which he often referred.[127] Proudhon was one of "the great minds" of the nineteenth century,[128] to whom he confessed that he owed "a profound intellectual debt."[129] But he expressed equal regard for contemporary Socialists, whether they were antisemitic or not. "Without the Socialists," he wrote in *La Libre Parole* in August 1896, "one would think that France had become deaf and dumb; they are the only party that really acts as an opposition, that demonstrates, in this age of general apathy, any character, energy or initiative."[130] He expressed scorn for those whom he saw as mere opportunistic Socialist politicians, like Brousse,[131] but real admiration for other leaders, like Lafargue, Benoît Malon and Guesde, whom he regarded as genuine revolutionaries and "men of real stature".[132] Of Guesde, he wrote in 1889: "He is not a political intriguer, but a man of faith and passion . . . The men that he has grouped around him are men of real worth."[133] Drumont had met Guesde around this time, and he claimed also to have been "on friendly and cordial terms" with Benoît Malon.[134] It is not surprising, therefore, to find Maurras writing to Barrès in February 1890 that Drumont "will end up by joining the Popular Socialist party . . ."[135] Moreoever, it seems that such a conversion would have been welcomed in some "orthodox" Socialist circles at this time, given the apparent appeal of Drumont's version of anti-capitalism.[136] There is evidence to suggest, too, that a decade later this fellow-feeling survived strongly enough to form the basis for plans for some kind of active collaboration. The police reported in June 1898: "For a long time now . . . Drumont has been trying to reach some kind of understanding with the Socialists and the radicals. He has been involved in lengthy discussions with Pelletan and with Rouanet; but nothing has come of all this, and it is very unlikely that anything will." Nevertheless, the police again reported talk of a rapprochement between antisemites and Guesdistes a year later;[137] and Reinach, stressing motives of political expediency, claimed that the Socialists, for their part, "wished [in mid-1898] to reach an agreement with Drumont; the antisemites were a real threat to them, and were winning away their support."[138] Whatever the reliability of such reports, they indicate that the police and other contemporaries did not think that co-operation between antisemites and "orthodox" Socialists was out of the question.

Among the latter, the greatest affinity with the antisemites was almost certainly among the patriotic wing of the Blanquistes, and links here are a little better documented. Drumont again expressed sympathy with this group in print, though this time it was the antisemitism, as well as the revolutionary stance, of the Blanquistes that earned his praise. "Alone among the revolutionaries", he wrote, "the Blanquistes have had the courage to stress the fact that they belong to the Aryan race and to affirm that race's superiority . . ."[139] He also referred with approval to the antisemitic publications of Regnard and Tridon, whose *Du Molochisme juif* he particularly recommended. Tridon, he wrote, was "the only revolutionary who had dared to attack the Semites ..."[140] This sympathy, moreover, was reciprocated, and a number of Blanquistes, including Regnard, Granger, Cluseret, Da Costa and, for a time, Roche, belonged loosely to the *Libre Parole* milieu, often coming to it via Boulangism. A Ligue Radicale Antisémite had even been founded in 1892 by Grégoire, with Drumont and Morès as honorary presidents, to act as an organ of liaison between antisemites and former Left-wing Boulangists.[141] As we have seen, too, the Ligue Antisémitique Française had connections, not only with anarchist groups, but also with the Blanquistes.[142] Alfred Gabriel in an article in *Le Turco* in 1901, entitled "Revolutionary Antisemitism", recollected that "It was at the Comité Central Socialiste Révolutionnaire, the last bastion of those Blanquistes who remained faithful to patriotism and the tradition of the master, that I first met Jules Guérin ...", adding that, in the eyes of the Blanquistes, Guérin and Morès "were working ... for Socialism".[143] The Ligue Antisémitique Française seems also, like Drumont, to have made overtures to the Guesdistes, since one of its sections put out a poster in February 1898, addressed specifically: "To the Socialists of Roanne", a town where the Guesdistes were strong.[144]

In his study of Anatole France, Levaillant has pointed to another, dynamic, link between antisemitism and Socialism. In the mid-1890s, he wrote, the antisemitism of Drumont and Gyp served "as a liaison agent" between more conservative attitudes and "the socialist line of attack ... Between the aristocratic temper of [Anatole] France and the Socialists, Drumont was able to act, for a certain time, as a stimulating intermediary ..."[145] It seems likely that antisemitism may have fulfilled this mediating function on a wider scale. Urbain Gohier, for example, believed that it had, writing in 1899 that: "Before the present battle was engaged [the Dreyfus Affair], antisemitism was performing a useful role. In denouncing the big Jewish monopolizers of capital, in attacking the vast fortunes of the Jews, it accustomed timid spirits to the idea that certain things needed investigating and that certain reforms were necessary. It thus prepared the way for the Revolution in the most refractory circles."[146] The path to or towards Socialism via populist antisemitism was rendered easier by the fact that antisemitic attitudes persisted among "orthodox" Socialists in the 1890s, as the example of the Blanquistes illustrates.[147]

It has been well demonstrated by a succession of historians that French antisemitism, in its articulate form, was associated in the century or so before the Affair, perhaps primarily with the political Left. It was present among the writers of the Enlightenment, notably Voltaire, and among the Left in the National Assembly which debated the Emancipation issue in the first years of the Revolution.[148] Antisemitism was again an important feature in the writings of the Utopian Socialists of the first half of the nineteenth century, and particularly of Fourier and his disciples.[149] The most important single antisemitic work of this period, which we have already referred to, was *Les Juifs rois de l'époque: Histoire de la féodalité financière*, by the Fourierist Toussenel.

First published in 1845, it was reissued in 1847, 1863, 1886 and 1887.[150] Both Pierre Leroux and Blanqui also gave an antisemitic slant to their different varieties of Socialism.[151] In the middle of the century, the same tradition was continued by Proudhon and by Vallès,[152] who were both admirers of Toussenel. Proudhon, for example, in notes for an article, written in 1847, described the Jews as "that race which poisons everything, by pushing in everywhere, without ever really mixing with any other people"; and went on:[153]

We must demand their expulsion from France, unless they are married to Frenchwomen; and synagogues must be abolished . . . It is not for nothing that Christians have called them deicides. The Jew is the enemy of humanity. This race must be sent back to Asia, or exterminated. H. Heine, A. Weil and others are secret spies . . . What the people of the Middle Ages hated by instinct, I hate quite wittingly, and irrevocably.

Moreover, as Szajkowski has indicated, in the early years of the Third Republic, "the most important anti-semitic publications were those written by Socialists"; and he instanced the writings of Regnard, Tridon and Chirac.[154] Chirac was the author of *Les Rois de la République: Histoire des Juiveries* (1883–9), a work much admired by Drumont, and he continued to propagate his Socialist antisemitism in the next decade.[155] Another significant figure, though neglected in his day, was Vacher de La Pouge, who combined professing a course on racialism at the University of Montpellier in 1889–90, with an engagement in local Socialist politics.[156] In addition, Silberner has shown that the *Revue Socialiste*, edited from 1885 to 1893 by Benoît Malon, whom Drumont knew and admired, as we have seen,[157] published a considerable amount of antisemitic material by Malon himself, as well as by Regnard, Rouanet and Chirac.[158] He also pointed out that many Socialists "flirted" with antisemitism during the Dreyfus Affair, as we have already noted in a previous chapter; and that Myrens and Méric, both Socialists, "acquired some fame as anti-Semites" in the years just prior to 1914, when antisemitism had some following, too, among revolutionary syndicalists. He reminds us, furthermore, that such an opponent of antisemitism as Jaurès was not averse to making unflattering remarks about the Jews.[159]

It is possible to add something to Silberner's picture, for the 1880s and the 1890s, although its outlines remain substantially correct. *La Revue Socialiste*, for example, did give expression to anti-capitalist antisemitism, but it was usually critical of Drumont and his supporters, and it also published attacks on antisemitism.[160] Nor was the attitude of the Guesdistes towards antisemitism quite as simple, as consistently hostile, as Silberner suggests. In *Le Citoyen*, in 1882, for example, Guesde cast the blame for the crash of the Union Générale squarely on the Rothschilds, whom the periodical continually attacked in this period as the symbol of capitalism.[161] Though by 1892, Guesde was denouncing "Drumontism" as "essentially reactionary",[162] as we have seen, such attacks were prompted by political rivalry as much as, if not more than, by an opposition of principle. It is interesting here to note the close similarity in the rhetoric employed by antisemites and by the Guesdistes, particularly in propaganda addressed to rural voters. The *Programme agricole du Parti Ouvrier Français* of 1895, written by Lafargue, declared: "It is not by starving part of the population for the sake of a handful of speculators that the agricultural crisis will be overcome." Similarly, Compère-Morel, another Guesdiste and the first real peasant political militant in France, denounced, in his *La Vérité aux paysans par un campagnard* (1897), the "monopolization of property in the hands of a rapacious and pitiless handful of men who already control credit, industry, commerce, the railways and the mines."[163] This is not to suggest that the Guesdistes were out and out antisemites, although some of them were, but rather to indicate the extent of common ground that Socialism and antisemitism occupied, for historical reasons, and which made it difficult for Socialists, even when they wanted, to disentangle themselves altogether from attitudes that were built in to their tradition. During the Affair, anti-capitalist antisemitism was still a force among "orthodox" Socialists, therefore, and one must conclude that their reluctance to support the Dreyfusard cause, although in part tactical, as we have seen, represented considerably more than a "flirtation" with antisemitism.[164]

The evidence in support of such a view is considerable, both for Paris and the provinces. For example, a philosemitic talk given by Benjamin Dreyfus at a meeting of the Fédération Socialiste Nantaise in December 1897 was interrupted by "a gentleman, called Mangin, a member of the Fédération, who protested vigorously against the apologia for the Jews presented by Dreyfus, declaring that Socialists of all countries had no worse enemies than the Jews."[165] That this was not merely an eccentric private opinion is indicated not only by the fact that Mangin's interruption went apparently unchecked, but also by the fact that a month later, and a week after serious antisemitic disturbances had occurred in Nantes, Charles Brunellière, secretary of the Fédération Nantaise, wrote to a friend that "it was a good idea to let the Jews and the Jesuits scratch each other's eyes out."[166] For some time, indeed, as we have seen again, Brunellière's view represented the "official" view of "orthodox" Socialists on the Affair, as represented in a manifesto, signed by 32 Socialist deputies, and put out on 20 January 1898. This attacked the antisemites, but called for Socialist neutrality in the Dreyfus Affair itself, which was interpreted as a conflict between two sections of the bourgeoisie. On the one side were the clericals trying to win political power;"[167]

> on the other, the Jewish capitalists, after all the scandals which have discredited them, need, if they are to keep their share of the booty, to rehabilitate themselves a little. If they can show that one of their number has been the victim of a miscarriage of justice, through the pressure of public prejudice, they will seek, through the direct rehabilitation of this individual of their class . . . the indirect rehabilitation of all the Jews and Jew-lovers and the Panama men. They will try to wash away all the filth of Israel in this fountain.

As a statement made during a period of antisemitic rioting in France, the neutral status of such a document seems questionable.[168]

Although the election manifesto of the Parti Ouvrier Français, drawn up by Guesde and Zévaès later in 1898, repudiated violent antisemitism,[169] and marked a significant change of attitude among "orthodox" Socialists, antisemitism continued to be manifest in Socialist meetings in Paris during the General Election campaign, and the period running up to it. A public meeting organized by the Comités d'Union Socialiste in the Batignolles-Epinettes district in January 1898 was not untypical. One speaker said that Socialists should not defend the traitor Dreyfus; he was a bourgeois Jew and probably guilty; moreover, his defenders were enemies of the proletariat. "Numerous shouts of 'Down with the Jews!' greeted these words." A second speaker then attacked the Jews in general and Reinach in particular, while a third praised Rochefort. In the same month, Leroy-Beaulieu was greeted at another public meeting with shouts of "Down with the Jews! Long live the Revolution!" from Socialist hecklers. At a meeting in February organized by "collectivist students", the Belgian Socialist leader Vandervelde declared: "Karl Marx was a Jew, but he wanted society to free itself from Jewry, that is from the régime of money." The Jeunesse Blanquiste, although one of its sections decided to demonstrate against the antisemites in February, maintained in general an attitude of strict "neutrality" vis-à-vis the Affair, and resolved to combat "militarism, clericalism and the Jews". The attitude of members of the Guesdiste Parti Ouvrier Français was generally more guarded, but, like the Blanquistes, they, too, still engaged in attacks on the Jews. Zévaès, for example, spoke at a public debate at Suresnes in February 1898, arranged by the Ligue Antisémitique Française: "He expressed his satisfaction with the sudden conversion of the antisemites to the cause of the Revolution", with some irony, but, although he stressed that the main objective of Socialists was to fight against capitalism "without distinction of race, caste or religion", he did go on to declare "his opposition to Jewish and Jewish-style capitalist power . . ."[170]

Antisemitism was probably most marked in this period among "independent" Socialists, as the involvement of La Revue Socialiste earlier would lead one to expect. The poet and deputy, Clovis Hugues, for example, though an opponent of controlling immigration, and though denying that he was "a professional antisemite", yet contributed to La Libre Parole. Interviewed by Bournand in 1898, he made the same point about the contribution of the antisemites to the diffusion of Socialism as Gohier was to do: "I believe that Drumont and his early followers have rendered a great service to the cause of the social Revolution, because, in creating antisemites, they created Socialists in a religious milieu where any other form of propaganda in this direction would have failed."[171] In a similar category was the self-styled "well-known revolutionary", Léon Cladel, who declared in 1891: "if you are talking about the Jews from the point of view of monopolies and of capital, then I hate them and I believe that antisemitism has a lot to recommend it!"[172] Mention should also be made of the Belgian Socialist Léon Hennebicq, who wrote an open letter to Le Peuple in February 1898, expressing support for a thorough-going racial antisemitism, a stance that Barrès later commended.[173] Less eccentric, more in the main-stream of French Socialism, was the Possibilist Gustave Rouanet. To judge from his speeches and writings, he had been an overt antisemite until the early 1890s, and, as such, he earned Drumont's praise.[174] By the late 1890s, he had become an opponent of antisemitism, and again an active one, defending the Crémieux decree, for example, in the Chamber of Deputies in May 1899.[175] As we have suggested, such an evolution characterized many Socialists. But the example of Rouanet also points to the obstacles that such a course could encounter, and the compromises that it might involve. As sitting deputy for the 2nd constituency of the 18th *arrondissement* of Paris, Rouanet made speeches in the 1898 campaign, on separate occasions, attacking the antisemites, and then attacking the Jews. Given his stance on other occasions in this period, it seems likely that the second speech was a sop to his electors, for at a third meeting, in May, as we have seen, he was greeted with shouts of "Down with the anti-patriot! the insulter of the army, the defender of the Jews!"[176]

Rouanet's case points to one of the important motives for the maintenance of antisemitic attitudes among Socialists, beyond personal conviction and force of habit, and one, we have seen, that Reinach stressed: it was risky, especially at election time, to try to run counter to popular prejudice. The 1898 campaign in Paris furnishes ample evidence of this. At the monthly meeting of the Agglomération Parisienne in March 1898, one speaker called on Socialists to take a positive stand against antisemitism, but others protested: "They said that this was just a trap set on the eve of the elections, and that Socialists should keep well out of the bourgeois and capitalist wrangle." With presumably the same considerations in mind, Chassaing, a sitting deputy in the 4th *arrondissement*, "denounced the campaign of defamation being conducted against him by his opponent . . . and energetically denied that he was a supporter of the Jews." Méline, he told his audience, at a meeting of the Comité de l'Union des Républicains Socialistes, had prevaricated over the Dreyfus Affair "so as not to upset the Jews". More courageously, Gérault-Richard, sitting deputy in the 13th *arrondissement*, explained to a meeting in Les Lilas in February: "When you hear people shouting: 'Down with the Jews', just reply 'Death to the capitalists!' and 'Long live the social revolution!'"[177] Gérault-Richard, like several other prominent Socialist Dreyfusards, Vaillant and Jaurès included, lost his seat.[178] But even such Socialists, who did become involved early in the Dreyfusard campaign, felt obliged on occasions to make their obeisance to antisemitic feeling. At an Allemaniste meeting in the 17th *arrondissement* of Paris in February 1898, in a speech attacking the anti-Dreyfusards, "general-councillor Dacquemin denounced the Jewish capitalists as much as the capitalists of any religion . . ." Drawing on the same strain of traditional Socialist rhetoric, Jaurès, in a speech at a meeting in the Salle du Tivoli-Vauxhall in June, to which we have referred, attacked the antisemites for misleading the people as to their real enemy, which was capitalism and not the Jews; but claimed also that "the Jewish race (was) always devoured by the drive to make a profit," and that it "manipulated the capitalist system with great skill . . ."[179] Again Briand, speaking as the

Socialist representative at a debate in Nantes in December 1898 arranged by the local antisemites, pointed out also that capitalism as such was the enemy, but admitted: "We recognize . . . that the Jews have exhibited a quite unusual rapacity . . ."[180] The fact that Briand, like Zévaès, took part in public debates with organized antisemites is, of course, in itself significant, indicating that, for Socialists in the late 1890s, if antisemitism was disappearing or had disappeared from their own programmes, it was still not outside the field of political discussion.

The same area for debate, and sometimes of ambiguous overlap, existed between antisemitism and anarchism, which itself was never entirely distinct from the Socialist movement. Drumont, in fact, characteristically expressed more sympathy with the individualistic gestures of the Anarchists than he did for the more organized opposition of the "orthodox" Socialists. "French anarchism", he wrote in 1889, "is a violent and bitter cry of protest against the present régime, which is based on the glorification of theft, of sophisticated, respectable, well-dressed theft. It is the savage negation of a civilization in which the Bischoffsheim, the Erlanger, the Hirsch are held in honour . . . and cynically flaunt the luxury which they have acquired by plunder."[181] In 1891, he admitted: "I am no enemy of the Nihilists. I admire their intrepid coolness, their abnegation, the heroic patience with which they endure the most horrible privations."[182] And he told the editorial team of the newly-founded Libre Parole the following year: "we must be in some way 'Catholic Anarchists'. We are destroyers, revolutionaries."[183] At the time of the anarchists' "terrorist" campaign of 1892–4, in which a bomb was thrown in the Chamber of Deputies and President Carnot was assassinated, Drumont's continued adherence to such a sympathetic attitude took on a new significance. In an article entitled "La Bombe du Palais-Bourbon" in December 1893, he wrote:[184]

The man in us will always react in horror and shudder at such spectacles. But the thinker is bound to recognize that a society which, deliberately and out of prejudice, commits the nameless crime of depriving the deprived of all belief and all hope, must logically reap the infernal harvest which it has sown. The authors of this crime are those who have demoralized and corrupted the country by cynically selling their votes to all the Jewish bankers . . .

Not only did Drumont suggest that the deputies deserved the bomb that was thrown at them, but, in subsequent articles, he extended the responsibility for anarchist acts of terrorism to bourgeois society as a whole. "The revolutionary Bourgeois", he argued, "who has made the Republic his property, who has corrupted the People so as the better to exploit them, is confronted by the Anarchist who expresses himself exactly as the Bourgeois did in 1789. Of course the Anarchists are very blameworthy; but what examples has society given them?" He pointed out, too, developing this idea, that although Auguste Vaillant might be "an enemy of society", he was also "a child of that society, engendered, formed, or rather deformed, by it, impregnated by it with all the sophistry and spouting that had been in the air for a century, depraved and demoralized by the spectacle of the impunity of the really guilty ones, disorientated by seeing victorious and acclaimed on one day those who, the day before, were being hounded and shot against the walls."[185] Once Vaillant had been executed, Drumont and *La Libre Parole* "adopted" his daughter Sidonie, exhibiting her in public and raising money on her behalf.[186] In the atmosphere of panic and hostility set off in parliament, government and press by the anarchist outrages, the expression of such sentiments, such sentimentality, was revolutionary, and placed Drumont to the Left of most "orthodox" Socialists.[187]

Nor was Drumont alone among antisemites in expressing sympathy for the Anarchists at this time. The attitude of both Morès[188] and Barrès[189] was very similar, though more moderately presented. Abbé Garnier, too, in *Le Peuple Français*, evinced a well-meaning sympathy for and attempt to understand the exasperation of the terrorists.[190] One must remember here also the vague appeal of anarchism in the most general sense to that same generation of young people who found antisemitism so exciting. Both Barrès and Maurras, for example, went through an "anarchist" phase on their road to nationalism.[191]

If, in the words of Leroy-Beaulieu in 1897, "certain antisemites went so far as to adopt a kind of anarchism",[192] this common feeling, expressed with *éclat* by Drumont, also took the form of direct links between the antisemitic and anarchist movements, albeit of a rather tenuous kind. For example, at the time of the outrages, Séverine joined *La Libre Parole*. "She brought with her a reputation as a popular journalist, which could only benefit *La Libre Parole*, making it more attractive to lower-class readers", commented Viau;[193] what he does not add is that she was also a Socialist with strong anarchist sympathies, who had taken over the editorship of *Le Cri du Peuple* in 1885 from Jules Vallès.[194] Significantly, moreover, Drumont's collection of articles, which included those favourable to the Anarchists, *De l'Or, de la boue, du sang* (1896), was dedicated to her.[195] Another female Anarchist, Paule Mink, was on friendly terms with Barrès and Maurras.[196] As we have seen also, the Ligue Antisémitique Française was closely associated with *Le Révolutionnaire*.[197] In certain intellectual milieus, in effect, and at the lowest levels of political adventurism,[198] antisemitism and anarchism overlapped in their appeal, their convenience. Anarchists, we have seen, were prominent among the early Dreyfusards, and often opposed the antisemites. Abbé Garnier's sympathetic, if patronizing approach in *Le Peuple Français*, was significantly met with threats, and one actual attempt, to assassinate him.[199] But the expression of antisemitic sentiment was to be found, too, among Anarchists, who had nothing to do with the antisemitic movement, though they were probably less prone to it than their Socialist counterparts. In *La France juive*, for example, Drumont was able to quote Reclus in support of the claim that the Jews of Algeria were unpatriotic and should not have been naturalized in 1871;[200] and, as we have seen, he could claim Proudhon as his intellectual "mentor". Mention should also be made of Bakunin who had some influence in France, and whose hostility to Jews was openly expressed.[201] And similar instances, from less distinguished sources, can be cited for the period of the Affair itself. For example, a speaker at an anarchist meeting in Paris in January 1898, at the time of the antisemitic riots, claimed that "the present antisemitic agitation [is being] stirred up by the Jews";[202] while the 1899 *Almanach du Père Peinard*, as we have seen, repeated the old refrain: "Down with all Capitalists, Jews and Papists."[203]

However, as Viau related, the pro-Anarchist line of *La Libre Parole* changed in the course of 1894: "Several subscribers had complained, with some bitterness, at seeing their paper singing the praises of anarchism nearly every day, and Drumont had gradually to put a damper on this, to prevent circulation from dropping by several thousand."[204] Abbé Garnier backed down in *Le Peuple Francais*, for the same reason.[205] Moreover, much the same retreat was beaten generally on the "Socialist" front by the antisemites, though more subtly. The lesson, which Barrès had read antisemites in 1890, on the socially disruptive potential of antisemitism and on the threat which Socialism represented, was sinking in: "Listen to the crowds that shout: 'Down with the Jews!' in public meetings", he had told them. "It is: 'Down with social injustice!' that they are really saying! The 80,000 Jews of France do not really concern them. Their anger is directed against the formidable capitalist organization which dominates them. Your anti-Jewish formula will not satisfy them as a programme, though they have latched on to it as a temporary rallying-cry."[206] Such considerations explain why, if, in the words of Bebel, antisemitism was "the socialism of blockheads;" it was also "the anti-socialism of blockheads".[207]

III

Fear of Socialism had always gone hand in hand, among French antisemites of the later nineteenth century, with its espousal. Indeed, as we shall see, the one was a means of allaying the other. Some antisemites had always been opponents of Socialism; others expressed reserves, or gave their own "socialism" a distinct definition, setting it off from that of the "orthodox", and particularly the revolutionary, Socialists. *La Croix* made it very clear from 1894 that its economic antisemitism was also anti-Socialist.[208] Similarly, according to Mayeur, "anticapitalism and anti-Socialism were the two constants of Christian Democracy."[209] According to abbé Garnier in 1896, for example, the Union Nationale was "a league to combat the revolutionaries who are pushing France towards catastrophe",[210] and the denunciation of "the Socialist peril" and "Socialist delusions" occupied a large place in its propaganda.[211] Even Drumont accused the Socialists, in *La France juive*, of "pursuing seductive and dangerous Utopias",[212] though his own alternative to revolution was in the classic "Utopian" tradition. A Socialist working-class revolution, he argued, would very probably succeed in Paris, but not in the rest of France, and would therefore be repressed with great bloodshed. Revolutionary Socialism, seeking to achieve its ends by violent means, was thus misguided, but[213] could not the same ends, which the workers are pursuing, and quite rightly, be achieved by peaceful means? Could not a Christian prince, a leader of resolution and vision be persuaded . . . to confiscate all Jewish property? Then, with the resources thus created, he could allow the workers to experiment with their theories on the direct and collective running of factories and other industrial establishments. Most of the [non-Jewish] owners of industrial plant would readily agree to be expropriated in this friendly fashion, if they received suitable indemnities.

Barrès was a more realistic politician and came much closer than Drumont to the "orthodox" Socialist point of view. Nevertheless, in *La Cocarde*, he expressed his total opposition to Marxism;[214] and, in his speech at Morès's funeral in July 1896, he indicated his disagreement with "certain Socialists [who] . . . show themselves to be very attached to Internationalism, which they regard as a consequence of the Revolution. This is a conception which this Socialist fraction has inherited from Radicalism, and it is a complete negation of historical reality."[215] Barrès had been opposed by a Socialist, when he stood in a by-election in Neuilly-Boulogne in 1896.[216] This is indicative of his own evolution away from Socialism, and of the general divergence between Socialism and antisemitism that was becoming more marked by that date. With and after the Affair, the "socialism" of Barrès became clearly secondary to his antisemitic nationalism. In an article entitled "Socialism and Nationalism" in *La Patrie* in 1903, he referred, for example, to Internationalism and Collectivism as "unverifiable fictions which derive from the imaginations of a few Messianic Jews".[217]

By 1898, this anti-Socialist emphasis, whether directed against Socialism *en bloc*, or merely against "certain Socialists", was a well-established theme in antisemitic propaganda in the capital. A meeting of La Jeunesse Antisémite, for example, in January 1898, declared "war on the Collectivists and the Internationalists".[218] In a speech in February, Georges Thiébaud maintained that antisemitism was in the tradition of the French Revolution and of "peasant revolutions in general", in that it was "a first effort of the French native to reconquer his own land"; but, at the same time, it had nothing at all to do with "the German theories that the Socialists peddle among the workers, without even managing to excite their envy"; such Socialism, he concluded, was "Jewish in conception".[219] Developing this idea a little further at a meeting of "the antisemites of Montmartre" in March, Millevoye accused "the Socialists of upsetting the internal peace of France in order to prepare the way for the Germans". One of the main aims of the Union du Commerce et de l'Industrie, it was asserted in the same month, was "to combat Socialism". Also in March 1898, Jules Guérin, while declaring that "antisemitism is essentially socialist", affirmed that "it was the mortal enemy of the Collectivists who are Internationalists and the defenders of Jewish capital". The Rochefortiste candidate of the Comité Central Socialiste Révolutionnaire in the 1st constituency of the 11th *arrondissement* claimed, in April, that his principal aim was the defeat the Allemanistes and the Collectivists who "aim to sell Socialism into the arms of Germany". At a meeting of the Union des

Républicains Socialistes et Révisionnistes de France, in June, Millevoye again attacked German-inspired Collectivism and State Socialism; while, at a banquet organized by the Socialistes Révisionnistes the same month, the antisemitic leader Paulin-Méry "held up to public scorn the Socialists who saw fit to attack a libertarian, a defender of the poor and humble like Rochefort"; and Marcel Habert of the Ligue des Patriotes attacked "those who betrayed Socialism by misleading the proletariat and by joining the pay-roll of the defenders of traitors".[220]

Again, in the 1902 election campaign in Paris, a candidate, sponsored by the Ligue des Patriotes in the 4th *arrondissement*, put out a leaflet entitled "Collectivism is the enemy!", which claimed that Collectivism meant "the abolition of all property, of the family home, of the army, of the Nation, and also of individual liberty"; and asked rhetorically: "Surely you will not allow the disciple of that German Jew Karl Marx [i.e. the Collectivist candidate] to try to realize in Paris those unhealthy schemes hatched on the other side of the Rhine?"[221] The same antagonism towards Socialism on the part of antisemites was frequently expressed in such electoral rivalry, and particularly in 1898 and 1902. For example, Paul Bernard, an antisemitic "Independent Republican Socialist", beat Gérault-Richard in the 13th *arrondissement* in 1898. In 1902, Firmin Faure beat the sitting deputy for the 4th constituency of Saint-Denis, the Socialist Réau. In the 18th *arrondissement*, Charles Bernard, at one time member of the antisemitic parliamentary group, stood four times against Rouanet, from 1902, finally beating him in 1914. Nor was this phenomenon confined to the capital. Delpech-Cantaloup beat the sitting Republican Socialist at Lectoure in 1898.[222]

It will have become clear that what antisemites objected to in "orthodox" Socialism was its advocacy of collectivism, which was represented as a thorough-going attack on all forms of private property, its non-libertarian attitude towards the State (an objection which they shared with the Anarchists), its internationalism, and also the fact that it was a successful rival in the struggle for popular support, and indeed claimed to represent "socialism" exclusively. These objections were brought out clearly and more systematically in *Le Socialisme et les Jaunes*, a book published in 1906 by Biétry, the antisemitic leader of the Syndicats Jaunes movement. The aim of this movement, he declared, was to "destroy Socialism, [which] . . . is not a philosophical system, nor a humanitarian inclination, nor a science, nor a policy, but a microbe, which creates nothing, which decomposes everything."[223] The parallel with conceptualizations of the Jew, for example in the Henry Subscription, is striking. Socialists, moreover, Biétry claimed, wished to prevent workers from becoming property-owners: "These people who pretend to be fighting monopolies and monopolization in fact wish to create a single monopoly for their own benefit. They want to control all the means of production and exchange themselves, and they find poor fools to applaud this outrage against civilization and human independence."[224] Again the parallel with the function of the Jew in antisemitic ideology is obvious. "Socialist thinking", Biétry continued, "has only two aims in view: atheist materialism and the communal ownership of everything."[225] In contrast, he said, quoting the first issue of *Le Jaune*, of January 1904: "We workers demand THE RIGHT TO PROPERTY. We want to transform the status of wage-earners, not in the direction of Collectivism, but in the direction of the extension of individual property."[226] The main means envisaged for bringing about this "transformation" was the introduction of profit-sharing for workers. Here one can probably see reflected the petty-bourgeois interests, and preconceptions, that organized antisemitism represented, though the appeal of such a programme to the propertyless should not be discounted. It is relevant, in this context, that the Union Nationale made the same manifest appeal to the working class, but, in its programmes, offered concrete policies that can have interested only small property-owners, such as fiscal reform and the reduction of the costs of litigation.[227]

One feature of this emasculated anti-Socialist "socialism" is worth considering further here. Along with its threat to private property, and its internationalism which we will examine in the next chapter, "orthodox" Socialism represented, for Biétry and other antisemites, the extension of the power of the State. Hostility to the increased and increasing power of the State in the nineteenth century was an important ingredient of antisemitism, and another theme through which antisemites gave particular voice to a very general grievance. It therefore lent special force and popularity to their anti-Socialism. Drumont complained in 1890 that "the State intervenes all the time in the life of citizens in the most annoying, stupid and odious way; it is always on your back . . . everyone is dependent more or less on the State . . ."[228] "Two monopolies are invading the world", wrote *La Croix* in February 1891, "that of the State and that of the Jew".[229]

Three themes stand out in the antisemites' protest against increased state power and intervention. First, there was the expression of an age-old hostility to the fisc, traditionally associated with the Jews,[230] a claim that taxation had increased and a call to reduce it. "I know how much anguish a new tax can cause the woman of the people", Drumont claimed in 1890, "and I quite frankly hate . . . these Republican crooks who have, in peacetime, in a few years, increased the tax-burden of the country by twelve hundred millions a year."[231] Though such a complaint followed in a well-worn tradition of popular protest, it was seen as reaction to innovation; "the modern régime has created . . . a special human type, the taxpayer", wrote Drumont again.[232] Much the same point was made by Guérin, who told a meeting of the Cercle Antisémitique d'Etudes Sociales in February 1898 that Jewish control of the State and the economy had occasioned "an increase in taxation", and called for "a reduction of the burden that is crushing the taxpayer".[233] More specifically, the *Règlement Général* of 1897 of the Union Nationale demanded the abolition of the *octroi* and of all taxes on basic necessities, and a lowering of taxes on agriculture and "small scale business and industry"; it also opposed the idea of a progressive income tax, which would require "arbitrary and tyrannical methods" for its collection.[234] Similar demands were made by several Nationalist and antisemitic candidates in the 1898 election campaign in Paris; they occasionally expressed support for the introduction of a graduated income tax, in contrast to moderate Republican opponents, but put more emphasis on the need to abolish the *octroi* and other taxes on consumables.[235] The agricultural crisis, moreover, was frequently (and mistakenly) explained by antisemites and others by reference to high taxation.[236] It is undoubtedly true that levels of taxation increased in France over the nineteenth century, and particularly after 1870.[237] But perhaps more important in the generation of grievances was the fact that France's tax structure did not change over the course of the century since the Revolution, and that the old structure not only distributed the tax burden unevenly in geographical and regional terms, but also, with its emphasis on indirect taxation, placed a disproportionate burden on the less well-off. Advocates of tax reform, and particularly of the progressive income tax, sought to mitigate this inequality, but encountered formidable opposition from the beneficiaries of the old system, and from all those who resented the idea of having to reveal their financial circumstances to public officials. Though progressive income tax was adopted earlier by the Chamber of Deputies, it was blocked by the Senate until the First World War.[238] The antisemites seem characteristically to have been expressing and articulating in this area both the grievances of those genuinely disadvantaged by the old inegalitarian system, and the fears of those who felt threatened by attempts to reform it.

The second theme, related to the first, centred on the increase in the scope of state action and in the size of its personnel. Drumont complained in 1889 that[239]

> The Bourgeoisie . . . had passed over to society collectively responsibility for everything that had been paid for previously with the revenue from the property which it had acquired for a few scraps of paper. The payment of the clergy, public assistance, primary education, all those services which had been financed by the property sold during the Revolution fell on the shoulders of the whole population. Those who bought "national property", or their heirs, still had it, while the State, for its part, took on all the obligations once connected with it, that is to say, it placed them on the backs of all the citizens.

This was not only unfair; it was inefficient. Public Assistance, for example, had been well administered by private and ecclesiastical charities; "but the State took over these foundations on the pretext of running them better; instead, it spends so much on paper-work and on the salaries of officials, that it has nothing left to assist anyone."[240] Similarly, the secularization and the extension of public education, primary and secondary, had led "to a lowering of standards, as everyone agrees".[241] Not only this, but the State had become the prey, the source of spoils for a corrupt ruling class:[242]

> For the Bourgeoisie, there is only one creature that can be exploited with absolute security, for it is reborn every day, with the taxpayers' money; and that is the State. What they are after is a post in the civil service, to be elected a deputy, or to get a place as a magistrate, with all the attendant profits, oiling of palms and bribery. All this constitutes a régime, a system,

which is essentially the same whether it is called Opportunism or Radicalism; for both mean the parliamentary and administrative Republic, milch-cow of the Bourgeoisie . . . thoroughly venal government.

The increase in the scope of state action was the condition for this political corruption, the spoils system, against which Drumont and other antisemites directed so much of their invective. In *La France juive*, for example, Drumont declared: "we know that our Republicans are all schemers, our magistrates dishonest, our civil servants familiar with every crime . . . our statesmen all cheats and the beneficiaries of state concessions . . ."[243] And elsewhere he claimed that the Panama scandal was characteristic of the Third Republic, "this régime of bribes, shady deals, . . . and of waste on the largest scale",[244] a view that was shared by Léon Bloy, Barrès, Jules Soury and abbé Garnier, among others.[245] They all tended to see the increase of state power and action less in terms of the objective extension of the State's roles and responsibilities than in terms of the proliferation, in their perspective largely gratuitous, of a parasitical State personnel. According to the *Règlement Général* of the Union Nationale: "The most urgent requirement now is to make economies [in government spending]. The total budget has almost doubled, just to maintain the partisans and friends of a political clique that thinks it can treat France like a conquered country, to procure jobs for them and assure them big salaries and generous pensions"; and it complained also that there were too many deputies.[246] "The root of the trouble", wrote Drumont again, "is the obstinacy shown by hundreds of thousands of parasites who want to live at the expense of a country that is not rich enough to support them."[247] Similarly, Billiet, in a speech at Roanne in May 1898, called for a large reduction in the number of paid civil servants and state employees."[248] "The State and its creeping bureaucracy" were also attacked by Biétry, who claimed that the latter caused unemployment among workers.[249] His attack, as we have seen, was directly related to an attack on State Socialism. Here, as in the area of taxation, antisemites were clearly registering reaction to an important social and political phenomenon; the civil service did expand in the last third of the nineteenth century, and corruption was a feature of the politics and administration of the Third Republic.[250] They typically saw both as aspects of the same conspiracy, and, as moralists, emphasized the motive force of the latter. Moreover, civil servants and state employees were conceived of as money-making parasites in exactly the same way as the Jews.

The third theme in antisemitic hostility to the State was the threat which the increase in its power represented to individual and local liberties. Biétry, again, wrote that his newspaper, *Le Jaune*, "points out the danger which the State poses for individual liberty and emancipation, by, itself, acquiring a monopoly of the means of production, transport and exchange"; and, quoting a colleague, Poizat, he contrasted the aims of State Socialism and of the Syndicats Jaunes:

Socialism says: "Everything for the State." We say: "Keep the role of the State to a minimum." Socialism works to increase central authority; it wants

more regulations and regimentation, more inquisitorial methods and interference; we, on the other hand, are fighting to increase the rights of the
individual, by conferring on him what is the basis of real independence,
property . . .

The achievement of the welfare State, the "providential" State, in the words
of Japy, would be the equivalent of slavery.[251] Such attacks on centralization
and the urging of "decentralization as the means of social transformation"[252]
occupied an important place in the programmes of Nationalists and antisemites. Drumont protested, in La France juive, that: "The authoritarian régime,
that all-powerful centralization, already such a burden when the governmental
machine was run by men who had some spark of conscience, who had some
attachment, at least, to French traditions, has become a terrible instrument
of oppression in the hands of erstwhile vagabonds, newly naturalized foreigners and vindictive Jews, full of hatred."[253] Again, referring to the Tunisian
expedition of 1881, he wrote: "The whole thing was decided by the Jews, and
the life of thousands of people from Berry, from Brittany, from Poitou, from
Burgundy, was gambled away on a map, in some back shop near the Stock
Exchange . . ."[254] Less melodramatic was Fore-Fauré's lament over the erosion of genuine local government: "Before the Jews, the central power did not
intervene directly in the countryside. It acted, of course, on the main towns
of cantons through officials, such as the justice of the peace, the gendarme,
the tax-collector; but at village level it was obliged to act through and come
to terms with the mayor, who could be obstructive, if he wanted, but who,
most of the time, was simply indifferent."[255] Barrès, in 1895, called for the
liberation of regions and communes from "the uniform discipline of the
State",[256] a theme developed at length in his journalism and his fiction,
notably in Les Déracinés of 1897.[257] He was one of the founders, moreover,
of the Ligue Nationale de la Décentralisation.[258] Maurras was another supporter of the same cause. He saw the State as the agent of Money, and a serious
threat to individual freedom and local self-government: "the State has grown
at the expense of private persons . . . The French State is uniform and
centralized; since its bureaucracy extends to the last school desks of the
furthest hamlet, such a State is perfectly equipped to prevent the development
of any serious opposition, not only to itself, but also to the plutocracy which
it represents." The only guard against the all-pervading power of the "Money-
State"[259] lay in the revival of regional government and local liberties: the
Frenchman would then cease to be "a vague subject" and would become "a
real citizen".[260] To some extent this programme reflected the fact that the
only real political power still held in Republican France by the Right was at
the local departmental or communal level. It is significant, for example, that
the Marquis de l'Estourbeillon de la Garnache, Right-wing deputy for the
Morbihan from 1898 to 1919, combined sitting for a "pocket borough" with
antisemitism and Breton regionalism.[261]

In countering the "socialistic" tendencies of the State, antisemites were
thus reflecting widespread suspicion of growing state intervention in society
and the economy. These suspicions were strengthened, especially among

Catholics, by the resumption at the turn of the century, by the governments of Waldeck-Rousseau and Combes, of the secularization policy of the State in the field of education, and of the strict application of the Concordat and of subsequent legislation against the religious orders in France, which led to the separation of Church and State in 1905–6.[262] As early as 1890, Drumont had presented its anticlericalism as one of the most "tyrannical" features of the French State: "It forbids parents to bring up their children as they wish; and it does not allow French people, who are adults and in possession of all their rights, to group together to take their meals in common and worship God."[263] As we have seen, both Maurras and Fore-Fauré pointed to state education as one of the main instruments of state power. Hostility to the State also increased in reaction to interventionist industrial legislation and the first beginnings of state welfare legislation in France introduced by the Waldeck-Rousseau ministry of 1899. These amounted to three Bills only, one instituting a system of compulsory arbitration in industrial disputes, and another on workers' pensions, neither of which reached the statute book, and a third establishing new maximum hours of work for women and children, which did become law in 1900.[264] But the fact that their author was Millerand, the first Socialist minister in France since 1848, and that they seemed harbingers for the future, caused alarm, which we have seen reflected by Biétry.[265] A final factor motivating antisemitic objections to the increase of state personnel in particular, and which we have already encountered, was that such objections obliquely expressed the fact that entry to the favoured career of state service, at least at higher levels, was becoming increasingly competitive, and was no longer the privilege of a small élite.[266] Paradoxically here, interested antisemites seem to have been reacting against reforms which seemed to militate against them, although such reforms (entry by competitive examination, formal career structures) were precisely designed to counter the forces of patronage and "corruption", of which the antisemites also complained.

It should also be pointed out that the antisemites' general hostility to the State was less clear cut, more ambiguous, than might first appear. As Sartre observed, "in a democracy, antisemitism is a subtle form of what is known as the fight of the citizen against the authorities", but, while formally attacking the State, the antisemite also wanted "a strong power which would take from him the crushing responsibility of thinking for himself".[267] Antisemites also tended to be selective as well as ambivalent in their criticism of the State. They wanted the State to control others, but not themselves; and the object of their attacks was usually the democratic State, and not all States as such. In this context, the antisemites of the 1890s and 1900s in France were characteristically hostile to parliamentary democracy. According to Drumont, political corruption was "the consequence of the parliamentary régime";[268] "Our French Assemblies serve only the interest of the Jew."[269] Abbé Garnier, in 1899, described the parliamentary system as "the régime of Jews, Protestants and Freemasons".[270] In the view of such men, elections were a fraud, if not deliberately rigged;[271] and democracy was a cruel facade, which duped those whom it most exploited, and concealed the real power of the Jews.[272] The

Republican State was thus in a sense attacked because it was not strong enough, because through naïveté or guile it allowed France to be controlled in effect by a superior foreign influence. While attacking the parliamentary Republic, therefore, Drumont and others evoked military *coups*, government by strong men, restorations, all of which would be able and willing to deal firmly with the Jews, besides re-establishing authority in a general manner.

Some antisemites attacked the Third Republic, and the democratic State, from traditional Right-wing or conservative stances, thus presumably mainly from archaism of attitude or interest, or both. Of more significance, in the context of "socialistic" antisemitism, is the attitude of those like Drumont who arrived at conservative stances as a result of disillusionment with the Republic, whose attitude changed, thus providing a dynamic element of explanation. There is little doubt that Drumont was a genuinely disappointed Republican, subscribing, he wrote in 1890, to "the ideals of austerity that the word Republic by itself used once to evoke", contrasting such Republican ideals "of justice, disinterestedness and liberty", current in the days of his father with the present "Republic of thieves, profiteers, crooks, speculators and Jews"; the one resembled the other, he concluded "as much as a virgin resembles a whore".[273] Addressing Jacques de Biez, the following year, he reiterated the same point in much the same words: "The Republic which you loved was the French Republic and not the Jewish Republic; the Republic represented for you what it had represented for your father and for mine: an ideal of disinterestedness, of fraternity and of justice, and you have turned away in scorn from the present regime of ignominy."[274] Such disappointed idealism lies behind the involvement of many Left-wingers in the Boulangist protest against Opportunism,[275] and many antisemites, of course, were ex-Boulangists. Hopes placed in the Third Republic, in its early years, as in the Second in 1848, were too high, as Maurice Donnay conveys. In 1871, he wrote, quoting Jules Simon, people felt that " 'the reign of the thieves and prostitutes was over!' . . . My mind was made up: we had escaped from an epoch of corruption and all citizens were now going to be virtuous . . ." In the early 1880s still, "we were Republicans and the Republic still retained its aura under Gambetta . . . The words, corruption and intrigue were not yet in everyone's mouth . . ."[276] The same Republican ideal was upheld by Péguy in the early years of this century, but it was used as a stick to beat those who had used the Dreyfus Affair for their own low political ends, as a critique of the new Republican establishment; and was anyway regarded as wildly anachronistic.[277]

All of this helps to situate the oppositional stance of Drumont and other antisemites. They had a particular historical political experience, which led them from expecting too much from democratic politics towards a rejection of them altogether. Their disillusionment with the régime was widely shared by their contemporaries, as was their whole moralistic approach to politics, and here is one of the keys to the popularity that organized antisemitism for a time enjoyed. But, however gratifying attacks on corruption and on "the baseness of soul of Republican deputies" proved,[278] their appeal was ultimately limited, as Drumont and others failed to realize. For most people, probably, such attacks could happily co-exist with a real attachment to the Republican régime, and the knowledge that what, from one point of view might be called its "corruption", was, from another, a system of reciprocal exchange of favours which actually worked tolerably well.[279] Much as they disliked this fact, many antisemites must have been aware of it, at some level. It is significant, for example, that many, like Drumont, refused to declare themselves clearly anti-Republican. This brings us back to the anti-Socialist "socialism" of the antisemites, which more explicitly and deliberately reflected and exploited ambivalent attitudes towards the political and social order. But, before examining this problem further in its general aspects, we must look at the specifically antisemitic strand in their anti-Socialism.

<h1 style="text-align:center">IV</h1>

We have noted certain parallels between the function of the Socialist and of the Jew in antisemitic thinking. But the dissociation of the antisemitic movement from Socialism, to which the attack on state power contributed, was made manifest in the claim that Socialism actually was Jewish, in essence or in practice.

The former claim derived in part from a thesis put into currency by certain Left-wing Jewish writers, such as James Darmesteter (1849–94), Bernard Lazare (1865–1903), and, later, Léon Blum, according to which the spirit of the Revolution was identified with Judaism and the Jews.[280] This in turn was related to much older associations of the Jews with resistance to the civil and religious authorities,[281] and to the idea, taken up by several nineteenth-century liberal historians, that modern democratic principles originated with the Prophets. Ernest Renan, for example, declared in 1883, that "The spirit of the prophets is the spirit of Israel itself . . . it heralds the universal religion, the reign of justice."[282] Lazare, too, placed modern movements for social justice in the tradition of the Hebrew Prophets, and argued, in a narrower perspective, that "The emancipated Jew, no longer held back by the faith of his ancestors, having no attachment to the old forms of a society, in whose midst he had lived as a pariah, became, in modern communities, the ideal agent of revolutionary ferment."[283] Taking his cue from Lazare, Maurras, in Anthinéa (1901), evoked "Semitism and its train of mountebanks, necromancers and prophets, disturbed and disturbers, agitators with no country of their own", and wrote of the witch Marthe, symbol of Semitism: "Marthe must have conspired to bring about that revival of the Jewish spirit and of unclean Biblical hysteria which we ironically call the Reformation . . . Was she not in the eighteenth century the soul of the Revolution?"[284] Again, in 1902, he made this disclaimer: "The democratic spirit is Protestant or Jewish, Semitic or German; it does not come from us";[285] and he celebrated Colonel Henry as a valiant combatant "against the Jewish Revolution".[286]

Such association of the Jews with sedition, disruption and Revolution had long been a commonplace of antisemitic writing. For Drumont, the Jew was "the most powerful agent of disorder that the world has ever seen . . .

Wherever the Jews appear, ruin and disorder follow in their wake . . . The Semites excel in the politics of dissolution . . ."[287]; and he referred to "this need that the Jew has to reduce everything to the lowest level, to level everything . . ."[288] Similarly, Fore-Fauré described the Jew as "the artisan of ruin and death".[289] More particularly, the Jews were claimed to have been the artisans and the sole beneficiaries of the Revolution of 1789. Having dreamed of "a universal revolution" from the time of the Middle Ages, according to Drumont again,[290] the Jews provoked the French Revolution, out of self-interest: "the terrible events which took place at the end of the eighteenth century allowed Israel to emerge from its tomb"; moreover, "France fell into dissolution, as a result of the principles of 1789, skilfully exploited by the Jews", and thus became their prey.[291] The Jew, he concluded, "now appears as the sole heir, the unique beneficiary of that Revolution which cost so much blood . . .";[292] and the centenary of the Revolution, celebrated in 1889, was "the centenary of the Jew. M. Zadoc Khan [sic] commemorated the great date with an oration . . . while the *Archives Israélites*, for which 1789 was 'a new Passover', maintained that the French Revolution had very pronounced Jewish characteristics . . ."[293] Many other antisemites made the same general point, with different emphases. Abbé Chabauty wrote in *Les Juifs nos maîtres* (1882): "At the present time, the Revolution in all its reality is the Jewish nation, working and acting throughout the entire world, under the orders of its leaders, . . . against Catholic and Christian society . . ."[294] Writing in a similar vein to that of Drumont, on the centenary of 1789, abbé Lémann claimed that "Jewish preponderance . . . stems from the French Revolution . . . the Rights of Man and the dechristianization of France . . ."; and that the Declaration of the Rights of Man, in particular, was "a weapon of war in the hands of the Jews".[295] Similarly, *La Croix* in May 1889 referred again to the centenary of the Revolution as "the Semitic centenary", and maintained that the Jews had been the instigators of the Revolution, by means of which they had gained, not only their own emancipation, but control of France.[296] And, later, Léon Daudet asserted that the Revolution was "essentially Semitic".[297]

In so far as antisemites identified the revolutionary spirit with the Third Republic, claims that it was a Jewish régime made the same point. "French Monarchy or the Jewish Republic!", proclaimed an Action Française poster of around 1910.[298] Moreover, as we have discovered repeatedly, antisemitic opinion here was a reflection, a refraction of more general opinion. Arthur Meyer, for example, was able to "explain" the appeal of antisemitism in these terms: "The Republic has governed in the interest of the Jews . . . It is, in effect, the Republic, which by raising Jewish power to new heights . . . has stirred up wishes for revenge . . . and has thus fortified and justified antisemitism in the eyes of many French people."[299] In this context, a passage in the *Mémoires* of Joseph Caillaux provides a valuable indication of the extent to which the association of Jews with revolutionary ideas and tyrannical revolutionary government was diffused in educated circles in France in the early years of this century. The example is the more telling in that Caillaux was an established Radical politician, who first achieved political office in Waldeck-Rousseau's ministry of 1899, and who was later Premier (1911–12), a progressive, hostile to Nationalism, the main advocate of a graduated income tax in France, and not otherwise noted for his antisemitism. Yet he wrote, as if it were almost axiomatic, that the Jews were "possessed by millenarian dreams inherited from the depths of ancient Asia", that "in whatever sphere he works, the Jew carries within him the taste for destruction, the thirst to dominate, the need to pursue an ideal, whether precise or confused . . ."[300]

The identification of Socialism itself directly with the Jews was an extension of this essential identification of the Jews with the revolutionary and the subversive. Léon Daudet, for example, wrote that Léon Blum "went in for Socialism, like many of his compatriots, as a result of a hereditary messianic deviant tendency . . ."[301] Jacques de Biez, an early opponent of Socialism, claimed, in 1886, that it was a Jewish theory, and even maintained that "the strike is a Jewish idea . . ."[302] Similarly, for Biétry, materialist socialism was "the Semitic idea par excellence", and he pointed out that it was propagated by Marx, Engels and, in revised form, by Bernstein, all of whom were Jews.[303] In the same way, Drumont asserted in *La France juive:* "The Jew . . . is very clever; to destroy the old society which rejected him, he placed himself at the head of the democratic movement. The Karl Marxes, the Lassalles, the principal Nihilists, all the leaders of the cosmopolitan Revolution are Jews."[304] Again, though the Paris Commune had a generous "French face", it also had "another, Jewish face, self-interested, covetous, ready to loot, and full of low cunning . . . It was the Jewish *communards* who pillaged and murdered, and then set fire to Paris to cover up their crimes."[305] Here we encounter again the distinction drawn between "good" and "bad" socialism, or between some socialisms that were better than others, the criterion of Jewishness always being a mark of the latter. So abbé Delassus attributed Collectivism, in particular, to the Jews.[306] Morès contrasted his own National socialism with international "Jewish" socialism;[307] and Drumont castigated "German Socialism inaugurated by the Jews Lassalle and Marx and continued by Singer . . . the exploitative and lying Socialism of the Jews, so different from real Socialism."[308]

As this implies, antisemites claimed that the Jews were in practice manipulating the Socialist movement for their own capitalist ends. As Drumont put it in 1886, the Jew "invented Socialism, Internationalism, Nihilism; he then launched, against the society that had welcomed him with open arms, revolutionaries and sophists like Herzen, Goldeberg, Karl Marx, Lassalle, Gambetta and Crémieux; he set whole countries alight to further the interests of a few bankers . . ."[309] And he went on to characterize "Jewish policy" in these terms: "One invariably finds a grand display of pompous principles, liberty, equality, fraternity, a programme of progress which is never adhered to . . . clap-trap about emancipation and improvement which turn out to mean the most intolerable persecution and the extortion of large sums of money. Jewish quack socialists and bankers work together."[310] A circular issued to members of the Social Catholic Oeuvre des Cercles d'Ouvriers in June 1890 made the same point: "Who are those who are always talking to the people? The agitators, the seducers, the Freemasons and the Jews, either themselves or through their tools. It is they who are always shouting: 'Long live the People, all power to the People!' Honest folk stay at home and mind their own business."[311] Again Drumont claimed in 1890 that popular "disturbances" and "popular movements" in France were being organized by the Jews;[312] and Daudet asserted later that Jewish bankers "have acted as the financial backers in France of the Reds and of Marxism", instancing the case of L'Humanité, allegedly launched in 1904 by Jewish capitalists.[313] In this context, Biétry made the curious claim that Jews and Socialists were acting in collusion to degrade the status of labour: "Behind what the Jews write and what the Socialists say, one discovers again and again this dominant preoccupation: the attempt to make workers believe that work itself is degrading, debasing, and that all social exploitation rests on human labour", a statement which can be read both as an affirmation of the values of artisanal workmanship, to which, we have seen, antisemites were particularly attached, in the face of those of the factory and its workers, to which Marxists gave most of their attention, and as an attempt to deflect the force of Marx's theory of exploitation. Biétry also illustrated the collusion of Socialists and Jews by arguing that: "By the institution of common ownership of property (preached by the Socialists), the sedentary, *rooted* races would be at the mercy of the wandering races, the races without a homeland, that is to say the Jews, who treat all uncircumcised Gentiles as 'the seed of cattle' . . ."[314]

Many other antisemites of various political persuasions claimed that Jews and Socialists were working together, or that the Jews were using the Socialist movement. Barrès, in *La Cocarde*, made the common observation that Marxist socialism was Jewish.[315] Rochefort and the Comte de Lamase both attacked Socialists as Jewish or in the pay of Jews.[316] The Comte de Sabran-Pontevès told a meeting in Paris in 1898 "that the Socialists were playing the Jews' game".[317] An antisemitic brochure of 1899 referred to "the Jewish gang, the false socialists".[318] Jules Guérin declared in June 1898 that the Anarchists were "in the pay of the Jews"; and wrote in 1905 that "The Jews . . . were trying to control the Socialist movement . . ."[319]

The charge that Revolution and Socialism were Jewish arises naturally from within antisemitic ideology, but did it have any objective justification? It can be argued, with Lazare, that emancipated Jews might be expected to incline towards Left-wing rather than Right-wing politics.[320] Jews were disadvantaged in Christian or post-Christian societies, and Left-wing politics, and especially Socialism, claimed to represent the disadvantaged, and, moreover, did so within a framework of universalism. As a French journalist, Steens, wrote in *Le Siècle* in 1902: "Jews and revolutionaries were made to get on together. Since Socialist doctrines do not admit any racial differences among mankind, there can be no distrust between Jews and Socialists."[321] It is true, as Drumont claimed, furthermore, that French Jews owed their emancipation to the Revolution, and acknowledged this fact with gratitude; also that they were attached to the régime of the Third Republic.[322] Once Emancipation had been achieved, however, Jews played very little part in the French Revolution;[323] nor were Jews prominent in Republican, let alone revolutionary, politics in the later nineteenth century. Adolphe Crémieux, Jules Simon, Reinach and Naquet were the exceptions that prove this rule, and of these only Naquet belonged to the Extreme Left.[324] Again, though Drumont and others could point to a few prominent Jews in the Socialist movement outside France, they could cite hardly any at home. The only instance of Jews being numerically and generally important in a Socialist organization in France was that of the Saint-Simonian movement early in the century, and this may have helped to form future preconceptions, as Szajkowski suggested.[325] Otherwise there are only isolated examples which only disprove the antisemites' contentions; for example, Ennery, elected Socialist deputy for the Lower-Rhine in 1848;[326] or Gaston Crémieux, president of the Commission Départementale at Marseille in 1871, and later shot for this involvement in the local Commune;[327] or the young Daniel Halévy and the young Léon Blum, both converted to Socialism at the time of the Affair;[328] all, at the time, minor figures and unrepresentative of the Jewish community. Here, the prevalence of antisemitism in the Socialist movement itself should be recalled, and attention paid also to the fact that, with its very universalism, and its emphasis on class, as a term of analysis and as a basis for action, orthodox Socialism, as Memmi has argued, failed to take account of the peculiar position of the Jews as a social group with special problems.[329]

V

It is not possible to point to a precise date at which organized antisemitism began to express more hostility than sympathy towards socialism, for we are dealing with a heterogeneous movement, and one in which the ambiguities of socialist rhetoric were exploited with some skill; but there is a definite contrast between the early and the late 1890s in this respect. This reflected a more general crystallization of ideologies on the political level at the time of the Affair. "Nationalism", with which organized antisemitism was intermeshed, became increasingly a Right-wing conservative movement,[330] while "orthodox" Socialism became more precisely defined, as we have seen. The contrast is also attributable to the very success of the antisemitic movement, and to the disturbing and threatening prospect of its violence. Leroy-Beaulieu pointed to the danger in 1897:[331]

> We have seen the antisemitic press provoking the anger of the mob and directing its attention to the mansions of the Jews . . . I am not so naive as to believe that, when the day comes . . . for the antisemitic agitators to lead the people to attack the houses of Jewish bankers, it will be sufficient for good Christian bourgeois to place a figure of Christ or of the Virgin on their doors, in order to protect their own property.

After the 1898 riots, this argument carried very much more weight, and to fears of disorder and violence were added fears for the safety of the régime. L.-J. Lanessan wrote in *Le Rappel* in January 1898 that "the public now realizes that the war on the Jews, and also on the Protestants and the Freemasons, is only a mask, behind which all the enemies of the Republic and of liberty are hiding . . ."[332] Another Left-wing journalist, Henry Maret, agreed: "One has deliberately to close one's eyes, if one is not to see that hatred of the Jew is simply a pretext and that the aim of these people is to destroy the Republic and democracy, by discrediting and ruining true democrats and the most sincere Republicans."[333] It is not clear here whether Maret is simply referring to the antisemites' vilification of Republican leaders, or whether he is making a more interesting comment on the involvement of "sincere Republicans" in the antisemitic movement.

Similar expressions of concern, not for the Republic, but for property, and over the threat to the public peace which antisemitic violence represented, came even from those friendly to the movement. "Leaded canes" were frightening people, Maurras wrote to Barrès in March 1899.[334] "Can we be sure", asked Arthur Meyer in 1911, echoing Leroy-Beaulieu, "that the revolutionaries, whom we have incited to plunder the Jews, will confine their activity within the limits that we have drawn for them? Isn't it likely rather that, having acquired a taste for pillaging and expropriation, they will go on to attack Catholic and Protestant property, both large and small?"[335] The same fear is reflected in the attitude adopted towards the "Fort Chabrol" affair among social groups that might have been expected to have lent at least moral support to such a gesture of defiance against the "Dreyfusard" government on the part of antisemites. But, on the contrary, the police reported in August 1899, "high-ranking retired officers and businessmen . . . are scandalized by the weakness of the government, which is being successfully challenged in the middle of Paris by a small group of rebels . . . Traders and bourgeois generally accuse the government of cowardice or complicity."[336] The affair was used as a stick to beat the government, but Guérin and his supporters earned little or no sympathy in return. Even "orthodox" Socialists at this time expressed concern, whether real or feigned, over the threat to social order posed by the antisemites. Brunellière, for example, complained, at a meeting of the Fédération Socialiste Nantaise in June 1899, that *Le Nouvelliste de l'Ouest* was stirring up civil strife.[337]

All of this reflected a general feeling that the commotion occasioned by the Dreyfus Affair represented a threat to "order", a feeling which facilitated the "liquidation" of the Affair by the Waldeck-Rousseau government in 1899;[338] but it reflected also the growing realization among antisemites themselves that socialistic anti-capitalism was a dangerous as well as a convenient political rhetoric. *Le Nouvelliste de Lyon* had warned in 1896 that antisemitism must not develop into an attack on property as such: "antisemitism must not become the ally of Socialist covetousness . . ."[339] A decade later, as we have seen, Biétry tried to construct a barrier against such "covetousness" with an anti-Socialist trade-unionism, whose main platform was the defence of private property through promising its extension to all. Here we can begin to see the function performed by "socialist" antisemitism as a response to the social fear of the French bourgeoisie in the 1890s.

The call for "order" which aided Waldeck-Rousseau's "liquidation" of the Dreyfus Affair was only one instance of the general social fear, which haunted the French bourgeoisie throughout the century, a fear of the "dangerous classes",[340] of popular violence and revolt, and of revolution that would mean dispossession and death. Added to memories, enshrined in historical mythology, of the first French Revolution, the popular uprisings of 1848 and 1871 had at once justified and exacerbated such fears. The savage repression of the Parisian revolts, in particular, was the culmination of an accumulated obsession, and, in turn, gave rise to new fears of reprisals. The development of trade unions, before and after the granting of legal status to them in 1884, and of strike action, and the electoral success of Socialists, revived alarm in the 1880s and 1890s.[341] In 1889, around 15 Socialist deputies were elected; in 1893, the figure rose to 50.[342] Fears were increased by the anarchist outrages of 1893–4, to which the government responded with new repressive press laws, the *"lois scélérates"*, "laws of terror against all political opposition", in the words of Léon Blum in 1898.[343] In the Chamber of Deputies in December 1894, Jaurès referred to "those, who for two years now . . . have felt threatened by the growing Socialist movement", and was, significantly, ruled out of order by the President.[344] Socialist electoral advance continued in 1898, and the President of the Republic, Faure, commented: "The Socialists had polled an extraordinary number of votes . . . Anarchy was rampant . . . The Chamber was an incoherent assembly . . ."[345] The same fears can be seen projected in the fiction of the time, and particularly in the myth of *"le grand soir"* elaborated, for example, in Claudel's *La Ville* (1892) and Zola's *Paris* (1898).[346] More perceptive, but no less apocalyptic in its implications, was an observation made by Cardinal Mathieu, then Bishop of Angers and a liberal academic prelate, in 1894. "What is novel and significant", he wrote, "is the embittered way in which the masses are now making their demands; they are angry because they realize that socially they are still powerless, while constitutionally the means to achieve political power have been placed in their hands."[347] It was felt by men like Mathieu that the establishment of political democracy, in effect, far from satisfying popular demands, had in fact removed a cause that had centred them on a relatively innocuous objective. At the same time, of course, the fact that Socialists had entered the Palais-Bourbon itself caused alarm among many more people, and the realization that this might represent a real weakening of revolutionary resolve on the part of Socialists, might mean their integration into the political system at least, was largely prevented by their maintenance of a rhetoric which evoked violent revolution,[348] a rhetoric which many still took at its face value. As we have seen, many antisemites went so far as to imitate it, in apparent good faith.

Antisemitism of this kind, as we have also seen, contributed incidentally to the general social fear of the possessing classes; but, as well as feeding this fear, antisemitism also fed upon it, which is more significant. Georges Renard of *La Petite République* observed in 1899: "The antisemitic agitation . . . seems to me to be an episode in the 'clerical' reaction which began in the early 1880s, and which seduced the rich bourgeoisie terrified by the prospect of social reforms . . .",[349] a view borne out by the timing of the success of Drumont's *La France juive*,[350] and, more generally, by the emphasis in antisemitic propaganda on themes of order and hierarchy, which we will examine in detail later.[351] Immediately, it is relevant that this propaganda made an explicit issue of the theme of social defence. An ephemeral antisemitic periodical of 1884 was called *Le Péril Social*,[352] and more than one of the organizations associated with antisemitism in the 1890s placed itself under the same banner, for example the Union du Commerce et de l'Industrie pour la Défense Sociale.[353]

In this situation of social conflict or potential social conflict, in which political groups claiming to represent the working classes, preached political and social revolution aimed at ousting the existing élites, removing disparities of wealth, and socializing the means of production, organized antisemitism, which proposed a similar but alternative remedy, assumed a special function. Antisemitism had real or potential popular support; while often claiming to be socialist, it attacked the "orthodox" and really dangerous Socialists; its social reforms were not directed against private property or the social hierarchy; and it directed resentments and criticisms of the existing social and economic system against one selected target, the Jews. In *La France juive*, Drumont insisted that France could escape "total collapse . . . if all the oppressed agreed to direct their hostility against their one common enemy, the Jew";[354] and he was at pains to point out that his own scheme for the expropriation of Jewish wealth, and the partial socialization of the means of production, "would be accomplished smoothly and without bloodshed, without plunging the country into one of those crises that only benefit our enemies . . ."[355] He also evoked the advent of "a man of the people, a socialist leader", who would have "the magnificent ambition of attaching his name to the peaceful solution of the question of the proletariat", which would involve convincing the "millions" that their real enemy was the Jew.[356] In the same vein, Thiébaud declared at a meeting in Paris in February 1898 that whereas "German Socialism threatened . . . all property . . . and "respectable" capital alongside suspect capital", antisemitism threatened no one but the Jews.[357] It provided, in effect, an ideal diversionary movement, which allowed opposition to the system to express itself in a relatively harmless way. As Sartre observed: "It represented thus a safety valve for the possessing classes who encouraged it, and thereby substituted for a dangerous hostility against a whole system, an innocuous hatred for a group of individuals."[358] Moreover, as several modern commentators have argued, such a diversionary revolt probably suited would-be rebels as much as the potential objects of genuine rebellion. However socialistic, antisemites were fanatics for order, respecters of authority. Afraid of attacking the really powerful, they could attack the Jews with impunity.[359]

The interpretation of antisemitism as a diversion, as a substitute for Socialism was very common in the 1890s, particularly among Jews and among "orthodox" Socialists. Lazare claimed that antisemitism had always had a diversionary function: "It was a distraction and, from time to time, kings, nobles or bourgeois offered their slaves a holocaust of Jews."[360] Looking at his own day in the same perspective, Herzl wrote, in *La Nouvelle Revue Internationale* in January 1898, that "The Christian bourgeoisie seems quite disposed to throw us to the socialist wolves."[361] Among Socialists, Jaurès, in an editorial in *La Dépêche de Toulouse* entitled "False Socialists" in February 1890, described antisemitism as "the socialism of the big house and the sacristy";[362] while Guesde claimed in *Le Socialiste* in 1892 that it was a diversionary movement, aimed at duping people.[363] In January 1895, Maurice Charnay in *Le Parti Ouvrier* suggested similarly, but more particularly, that the government might have invented Dreyfus's treason "in order to stimulate chauvinistic feeling and create a useful diversion at a time when Socialism is beginning to penetrate the army . . ."[364] Fernand Pelloutier told a public meeting in Paris in June 1898 organized by L'Idée Nouvelle that antisemitism was essentially a religious phenomenon; it was the means by which "the bourgeoisie, faced by the rising tide of socialism, attempted to lead the people back to religious beliefs."[365] Jaurès again told another meeting, also in Paris in June 1898, that antisemites wanted "to stir up the crowds against Jewish capitalism", but cried: "Don't touch Christian capitalism!", a mechanism more fully explained by Lacour. "According to him", the police reported, "the leaders of the antisemitic movement have a secret aim, which is to launch the mob against Jewish capitalism in order to save Christian capitalism"; antisemitism thus "addressed itself to the popular classes, boasted of being socialist, appealed to the proletariat", but did so in bad faith.[366] Sébastien Faure expressed a similar view at an anarchist meeting in Paris earlier the same year. "Antisemitism", he said, "is not the struggle against Capital; it is an economic battle against capital belonging to members of a different race; it aims [not to abolish capitalism, but simply] to shift it from one set of hands to another."[367] The following year, Gérault-Richard told a public meeting in Grenoble: "Those who shout so loudly against the Jews are exploiting the worker as much as these ever did; they have only created the antisemitic movement in an attempt to divert from its course the working-class movement, which frightens them."[368]

Such views were not confined to Socialists and those involved in the working-class movement, who had an interest in propagating them. Henry Maret, for example, director of *Le Radical,* also detected a diversionary intention in the antisemitism of the 1890s: "Public opinion had to be diverted. In their attempt to capture the Republic, the clericals had every interest in sending the people off on a false trail. They deliberately exploited the unpopularity of the Jews . . ."[369] Moreover, Leroy-Beaulieu, who was perhaps the most perceptive student and critic of antisemitism in his day, who had no anticlerical axe to grind, and who was also a firm opponent of Socialism, shared the same general view. "In attacking the Jew", he wrote in 1902, "in denouncing him, in presenting him as an object for the suspicions and the anger of the mob, the bourgeois does not compromise his own security; he thereby turns against a third party the resentments of the masses, while at the same time satisfying his own grudges, his own envies. Antisemitism is thus a way of taming social conflict."[370] It is in the nature of socio-historical analysis that such a thesis cannot be proved, but the concordance of informed contemporary opinion with the historian's assessment of the evidence is exact. This does not mean, of course, that antisemitic leaders were entirely cynical, or that their followers were merely dupes. A certain element of manipulation was doubtless present, but one can posit that, in its social and political context, antisemitism had a clearly diversionary function, without necessarily implying that this function was consciously perceived by those involved in it. Indeed too great a degree of self-consciousness here would not only be sociologically incredible, it would logically destroy the function itself. Beyond a critical point, the perception of functions is reserved to outsiders.[371]

From the idea that antisemitism was a diversion from social conflict it follows that it could only be a false socialism, aimed not at fundamental change, but serving, consciously or unconsciously, to maintain the existing social system. In 1897 Leroy-Beaulieu seems to have thought unconsciously, for he wrote that antisemitism was "a naive socialism, a socialism lacking in self-consciousness, the socialism . . . of those who do not see where their ideas are leading . . ."[372] By 1902, as we have seen, he detected more calculation in the "socialism" of the antisemites:[373]

> in effect, antisemitism is only the socialism of the salons, of the clubmen and the gentry, the upper-class socialism of all those whose [unearned] income falls behind their appetites or their ambitions, the bourgeois socialism of life's failures and those with a grudge against fate. This socialism . . . which lacks all futile scientific pretensions . . . has the advantage over the other kind, that it only attacks a definite social group, that is claimed to be alien. This means that, in baying with the antisemites against the crimes of the monopolists or the abuses of capitalism, the Parisian bourgeois and the provincial gentleman do not risk drawing upon themselves, and becoming the first victims of the popular anger stirred up by their declamations.

In his article "Pour les Juifs" in *Le Figaro* in 1896, Zola put forward much the same assessment: "The exploitation of popular revolts by using them to serve a religious passion, the offering-up of the Jew in particular as the prey for the resentments of the have-nots to feed on, with the suggestion that he alone represents wealth, this is a hypocritical and lying socialism that must be denounced, that must be thoroughly discredited."[374]

Such assessments are further supported by the fact that antisemitism, as we have seen in examining its various manifestations, did enjoy a large measure of explicit popular support in the 1890s. Organized antisemitism articulated a prejudice present in all classes, and gave expression to widespread discontents in many different social milieus. As we have seen again, Drumont could boast with justification: "there was a time when the whole of Paris, the Paris of the workers and the Paris of the bourgeois, revolutionary Paris, patriotic Paris was shouting with one voice: Long live Drumont! Down with the Jews!"[375] Nor was this support confined to the capital, as the evidence presented in preceding chapters has amply demonstrated. "For the first time", declared Thiébaud in the late 1890s, "antisemitism has established itself, has taken flight beyond the narrow confines of thinkers and educated people."[376] "The people are instinctively marching with the antisemites . . .", agreed the Socialist *L'Humanité Nouvelle* about the same time in 1898,[377] and Maurras proclaimed in *La Gazette de France* in 1901 that antisemitism had proved to be "the first counter-revolutionary idea . . ." to enjoy real popularity in France in the last hundred years.[378]

But if Maurras here again exposes the conservative aims of populist antisemitism, neither he nor other antisemites could produce a lot of evidence of the positive working-class, as against bourgeois and petty-bourgeois, support which they sometimes claimed and which their propaganda aimed to capture. Drumont, for example, stated that he was writing for "intelligent workers", and claimed that he was read by "workers of Gallic stock" and artisans.[379] A speaker at the Cercle Antisémitique d'Etudes Sociales in Paris in April 1898 "expressed the hope that antisemites would address their message above all to the masses", and, anticipating anti-Catholic resistance in this quarter, added that "they should assure the workers that they were independent of any religious confession."[380] Clearly pursuing such a policy, the antisemites of Grenoble issued an appeal to workers during the Max Régis trial there in January 1899.[381] Similarly, but on a wider scale, *La Croix* and *Le Peuple Français* sought working-class readers;[382] while the Union Nationale and the Ligue Antisémitique Française looked for working-class members.[383] Picard claimed in 1892 that antisemitism "began among the populace", deriving from "popular Aryan instinct"; "the bourgeoisie . . . still hesitates, but the masses do not, and, with a unanimous impulse, demand that Jewish opulence and arrogance be curbed."[384] When he broached the subject later, in Dagan's *Enquête,* however, he was more defensive: "It is a mistake to think that the wage-earners are not interested in the antisemitic movement . . . This is what their leaders say, but they provide no proof of it"; but he referred to working-class support as potential rather than actual: "It is my belief that if the true elements of the Jewish problem got through to the working masses, they also would very quickly join the antisemitic movement . . ."[385] This back-tracking is significant, and reflects the fact that antisemites failed to attract the working-class support for which they had hoped and worked.

There is some evidence, of a mainly impressionistic kind, however, that working-class antisemitism did exist in the period. We have referred to Drumont's general claim to a working-class audience. More convincing is his particular allegation that "the honest workers" of the Gros-Caillou *quartier,* where he stood for election to the municipal council of Paris in 1890, "are all antisemites, and showed their sympathy for me on every occasion", though this did not ensure his election.[386] The movement against immigrant workers, which was orchestrated by antisemites and given an antisemitic colouring, as we have seen, probably made some impact among workers in some areas, although support for the campaign did not come exclusively from this class by any means.[387] Lazare referred to a certain amount of working-class antisemitism, directed specifically against Jewish workers;[388] but other contempo-

raries, such as the economist Charles Gide, while agreeing with the theoretical
assumption that working-class antisemitism would be stimulated by the existence of Jewish workers, pointed out that the latter were too few in France
to produce the expected effect.[389] Using another indicator, Georges Suarez
remembered that, in the 1890s, "hatred of the Jews . . . belonged to the
mystique of the Left, [and] was an anti-capitalist stimulus that was very
common among workers."[390] As we have seen, the persistence of this Left-
wing antisemitism in "orthodox" Socialist ranks during the 1898 election
campaign was largely a concession to the rank-and-file and to potential voters.
That antisemites were able, in some circumstances, to appeal successfully to
this prejudice among workers is indicated by the report of a police agent on
the agitation in the capital in the first months of 1898: "Instead of diminishing, the agitation is, on the contrary, becoming very worrying as a result of
the unemployment that is beginning to be felt now in the working-class and
outlying *quartiers* . . . the antisemites with their meetings are getting people
worked up, and it is dreadful to contemplate to what extremes the already
excited masses may be induced to go."[391] The police reported other occasional
instances of working-class support for antisemitism outside the capital, particularly in the East. In Besançon, in Feburary 1899, for example, an anarchist
meeting held to protest against antisemitism was interrupted by a worker who
claimed that the Jews and not the antisemites had been responsible for the
riots in Algeria, where he had done his military service, and shouted: "Down
with the Jesuits and with the Jews! Let's support the Social Republic and
nothing else!"[392] In January 1900, the police reported that "there were many
readers of *La Libre Parole* (and of other Nationalist papers) among the
workers and employees of the Eastern Railway Company";[393] and an antisemitic talk organized by the Ligue de la Patrie Française at Senones in November 1900 was attended mainly by workers.[394] In this context, *La Croix* did,
to some extent, gain the working-class readership that it sought, though this
seems to have fallen off by the mid and late 1890s.[395]

Antisemitism also found expression in certain workers' organizations. Various Christian Democratic and Social Catholic organizations, like Garnier's
Union Nationale, combined a working-class with an antisemitic orientation.[396] The Catholic workers of de Mun's L'Oeuvre des Cercles Catholiques
d'Ouvriers were, on the whole, hostile towards the Lyon Antisemitic Congress
of 1896, but the Reims group, under the influence of Léon Harmel, participated, and voted an extreme antisemitic resolution the previous year, which
called for the exclusion of Jews from French citizenship.[397] Another antisemitic organization of workers was the Union des Travailleurs Libres founded
in Paris in 1905 by Conty, a member of the Fédération Nationale Antijuive,
and enthusiastically supported, according to Daudet, by Drumont and *La
Libre Parole*. The Union, which ran co-operatives, provided free medical care,
free legal advice, educational courses and a free employment exchange, seems
to have had some success; within a year it had 9 sections in Paris, and had
found jobs for 1,000 workers, although in what professions is not clear.[398] The
Syndicats Jaunes movement, which we have already encountered, and which

had close links with the Union des Travailleurs Libres, provides another example of a workers' organization that used or expressed popular antisemitism, and with some success, since it was estimated to have perhaps 100,000 members in 1906.[399]

However, none of this quite meets the claims of some antisemites to have won the support and be speaking on behalf of the workers. Leroy-Beaulieu commented, in 1897, on "how little hold antisemitism has in the lower depths of the nation, below the middle class and the petty bourgeoisie, among the workers who work with their hands"; and explained: "The reason for this is simple; it is that for the French worker, for the proletarian, the parasite is not the Jew, but the bourgeois, every bourgeois."[400] The same view was shared by several of the contributors to Dagan's *Enquête*. Loria, for example, declared: "Once one realizes that antisemitism is essentially capitalist in its basis, then, one should not be surprised to see that this moral cholera, which sweeps through the rich and powerful classes, hardly exists at all among the workers, the out of work, the really poor."[401] In the same year, Léon Blum observed similarly that, by origin, French antisemitism "is not popular, but upper-class. It was born in the smart clubs and on the race-courses . . . The urban workers will not easily allow themselves to be fanaticized by such absurd myths; moreover, they are much more suspicious of the antisemites than they are of the Jews."[402] This was certainly true of many Socialist militants, as we have seen, and evidence can be found of a very positive hostility to antisemitism on the part of working-class unions. For example, the 9th National Congress of the Union of Railway Workers, held in Paris in April 1898, vigorously rejected a proposal from its Algiers section to exclude Jews from membership of the union, on the grounds that racial questions had no place "among workers".[403]

Some workers obviously were and remained antisemites; others may have expressed a temporary enthusiasm; but for most, it seems, the issue was either irrelevant, or, at most, a vestigial prejudice. For lack of evidence, it is difficult if not impossible to assess the importance of hostility to Jews in the mentality of workers, but, it is clear that, on the level of social or political action and conscious ideology, antisemitism had little meaning for them, and could not compete with syndicalism or "orthodox" Socialism as a means by which they could conceive, come to terms with and possibly change social reality. As Georges Renard told Dagan in 1899: "Workers have not been attracted to antisemitism because Socialism offers them a much wider and much more generous ideal."[404] Sartre has argued that antisemitism was "a snobbery of the poor", providing the sense of belonging to some kind of élite for those without status or the hope of achieving it.[405] If this is so, it would certainly help to explain why lower-class antisemitism was less prevalent among the industrial working class, who were to some extent secure in their own culture, and more prevalent among groups who either lived in close contact with the middle and upper classes, like servants, or who sought to imitate higher class norms, and perhaps penetrate the ranks of the bourgeoisie, like white-collar workers. And the evidence does suggest that antisemitism did have a special appeal among these latter status-conscious groups. Drumont wrote of the milieu of shop-workers, clerks and minor civil servants from which he came: "All these little people, honest and hard-working folk, are with us in spirit, though frightened to show it, frightened by their bosses who are hand in glove with the shady financiers."[406] We have discussed the special motivation for antisemitism among servants in connection with the Henry Subscription, but one comes across it elsewhere, and notably in Octave Mirbeau's *Le Journal d'une femme de chambre* (1900), with its classic evocation of the authoritarian servant in Joseph, who combines being a model gardener and coachman with being a militant antisemite, a sadist and a petty thief.[407] Most of the other servants in the novel also profess an antisemitism, into which there enters a large element of snobbery, as Célestine explains: "I am for the army, for the Nation, for religion and against the Jews . . . There was no one among us servants who didn't hold these smart views . . ."[408]

It is significant here that the workers' organizations that did espouse antisem-itism were organizations *for* workers rather than organizations *of* workers, and organizations, too, whose declared aim was to preserve them from corrup-tion by the Socialist and syndicalist movements, and also very often to rechris-tianize them. This is very much the case with the Union Nationale, which sought to solve "the social problem" with a mixture of paternalism, and proselytism. It provided a wide range of welfare facilities: crèches, dispensaries, community centres and so on, which indeed it helped to pioneer in France, but these were conceived very much as "charities". There were few workers among the actual members of the organization, let alone its leadership; and workers were generally accommodated in a separate Union Nationale Ouv-rière. Moreover, Garnier and other leaders were suspicious of, if not hostile towards trade unions that were genuine working-class organizations, preferring mixed unions of workers and employers.[409] The same paternalism was built in to antisemitic ideology, even when it was trying to be revolutionary. This can be seen very clearly in the writings of Drumont, for whom the People was child-like, good but gullible, in need of protection against the wicked Bour-geoisie and the Jews. Antisemites, he wrote in 1891, were people "whom a certain commiseration for the People" had led "to take up the fight . . . against the Jewish Plutocracy . . ."[410] Workers, for Drumont, were thus "poor folk", "not really responsible for themselves"; Vaillant was "a child". The same patronizing attitude can be detected also in his praise for the Socialist Benoît Malon: "What a good and sympathetic figure he is! He is a man of the People such as only the good old soil of France can produce . . ."[411] This attitude was revealed again, more cynically, by Viau, who pointed out that Drumont always took care to have a "real" worker on the staff of *La Libre Parole*, so that he could appear on platforms as the living embodiment of "The French Worker fleeced by Israel", or "The People exploited by the Jew".[412] Such paternalism was equally, if less surprisingly, present in the attitude of more conservative antisemites. *La Croix Meusienne* complained, for example, in February 1898, that the local Jews were exploiting "our little peasants".[413] The sympathy of antisemites was extended in this way to the People, to the working classes, so long as they were "suffering", "exploited" or "unfortunate", so long as they remained passive, dependent, in need of help. The occasional autodidact, like Benoît Malon, might be singled out for praise as an example of what personal effort might achieve, but, on the whole, workers were not expected to seek their own emancipation or betterment.

This task was undertaken by the antisemites on their behalf, and its accomplishment involved the exercise of perhaps the most important role that antisemites gave themselves. They were not ultimately revolutionaries or socialists, but denouncers and righters of wrongs, "justiciars". Like Proudhon,[414] Drumont insisted that "Justice is the first need of peoples"; and he saw the satisfaction of this need as the basic reason for the success and the popularity of both the Revolution and the Monarchy of the Ancien Régime: "The French Monarchy . . . exercised its function of rendering justice in a virile and Christian manner; it had gibbets for financiers . . . What is the image of the king that has survived most strongly among the people? it is that of a judge dispensing justice under an oak tree."[415] In the same vein, he wrote in connection with the Panama scandal that "at times of profound crisis, there is a kind of deficiency of justice";[416] and he evoked "the thunderbolts of justice" against the Jews.[417] A critic like Arnoulin testified to the success of Drumont's projection of this self-image. With La France juive, he wrote in 1902, Drumont "spoke out as a justiciar"; "the mass of the populace" saw his campaign against the Jews as "an outburst of virtuous indignation"; he was "a man, who like the prophets of old, set himself up as the guide of the People, and who judged the leaders and the counsellors of the nation . . ."[418] Similarly, Bernanos wrote later that the role of La Libre Parole was essentially that of a "justiciar".[419] Leroy-Beaulieu pointed out that the antisemitic press called again and again for "justice by and for the people",[420] a preoccupation that was reflected in the titles of several antisemitic papers and periodicals, for example the Christian Democratic La Justice Sociale. Zola wrote in 1897 that the leaders of antisemitism acted "as avengers and justiciars";[421] and it is true that many of them shared Drumont's image of their role. Léon Daudet referred to both General Mercier and to Syveton, one of the leaders of the Ligue de la Patrie Française who struck General André in the Chamber of Deputies, as "justiciars";[422] and Viau related that in launching a campaign against the Rothschilds in La Libre Parole, "I was going to act as a justiciar".[423] Such a role evidently had great potential appeal, since it related to a powerful stereotype in popular mentality, as Drumont indicated, a stereotype exemplified in the justiciar heroes of popular fiction and, later, of comic strips.[424]

But justice was conceived here by antisemites in its Platonic sense, as a principle of order, of hierarchy. Workers should not be exploited, as small shopkeepers should not have to compete with department stores, and Jews should not live in châteaux. Fore-Fauré, for example, characteristically coupled an emphasis on the charitable aim of the antisemites to provide "bread for all", with a vigorous rejection of a social system based on competition, mobility or the "Jewish" "struggle for life".[425] In this perspective, workers, the People, could not be regarded as equals, for egalitarianism was the very opposite of the hierarchical social order that was the antisemites' point of reference.[426] Here Drumont's description of his own attitude towards the social hierarchy is relevant. "What predominates with me", he wrote in 1890, "is the desire not to be oppressed . . . [But] I am not a Jacobin; that is to say that envy is not one of my vices; I am not jealous of those who have more than I have, and I would agree with Veuillot, when he said: 'I want to reestablish the aristocracy, but not to belong to it.'[427] Moreover, Drumont made a virtue of the socially heterogeneous nature of the support which antisemitism enjoyed. It was, in his view, a movement directed against class conflict and antagonism, and once the Jews were removed, social harmony would ensue. Thus, he wrote of the Neuilly meeting of the first Ligue Antisémitique in 1889:[428]

One could see there, fraternally mixing with the workers, brought together with labouring men by an impulse of patriotism and justice, gentlemen of old family whose names evoke the most glorious pages of our history . . . the representatives of the aristocracy were brought to realize how ready all French people would be to embrace each other as friends, if only the Jew, in the pay of Germany, was not always there, to stir up discord, to envenom misunderstandings, and to encourage us constantly to fight among ourselves.

Antisemitic "socialism" should thus be seen more properly as a populism, as an ideology that expressed concern for the People in an emotive rhetoric, and that claimed to represent and to serve its interests, but that did so from the outside, from above, charitably, paternalistically, within a framework of reference that did not question, that sought, rather, to perpetuate, to revitalize, the social hierarchy by this means. Henri Desprez of the Action Française, made this point neatly when he wrote that "Their formula could be summed up as 'The Revolution for the sake of order'."[429] Such a "revolution" did not work for, but feared social change, and projected this fear on to the Jews.

NOTES

1 Dagan, *Enquête sur l'antisémitisme*, p. 47.
2 Leroy-Beaulieu, *L'Antisémitisme*, p. 61.
3 Drumont, *Le Testament d'un antisémite*, pp. 1–2 and 5.
4 Drumont, "Sur un escalier", 3 November 1892, *De l'Or, de la boue, du sang*, p. 40; see also *La Dernière Bataille*, p. 204.
5 Cit. Bernanos, *La Grande Peur des bien-pensants*, p. 179.
6 Drumont, *La Fin d'un monde*, pp. 510–11.
7 Drumont, *DB*, pp. xix and 3.
8 Drumont, "Revenons . . .", 4 February 1895, *OBS*, p. 317; see also Bernanos, op. cit., pp. 49, 151 and 171–8.
9 Drumont, *DB*, p. xiii; see also Beau de Loménie, *Edouard Drumont*, p. 116.
10 Leroy-Beaulieu, *Les Doctrines de haine*, p. 14.
11 *La France Libre*, 21 October 1896, cit. Mayeur, "Les Congrès nationaux", p. 176.
12 Guérin, *Les Trafiquants de l'antisémitisme*, p. 194.
13 See, for example, P.-J. Proudhon, *De la Capacité politique des classes ouvrières*

(Paris, 1873), pp. 43–52; Maurice Dommanget, *Les Idées politiques et sociales d'Auguste Blanqui* (Paris, 1957), pp. 232–8; Leo A. Loubère, *Louis Blanc; His life and his contribution to the rise of French Jacobin-Socialism* (Buffalo, 1965), pp. 24, 50 and 151; Jules Vallès, *Le Cri du Peuple* (Paris, 1953); Rougerie, *Paris libre 1871*, pp. 79, 121–123 and *passim*.

14 Drumont, "Les Humains", 6 February 1894, *OBS*, pp. 173–4.

15 Drumont, *FM*, pp. 25–6.

16 Ibid., title of Book 2.

17 See Pierre Barral, *Les Périer dans l'Isère au XIXe siècle d'après leur correspondance familiale* (Paris, 1964).

18 Drumont, "Au Congrès", 27 June 1894, *OBS*, p. 233.

19 Drumont, *La France juive*, II, p. 301.

20 Drumont, *FM*, p. 38.

21 Drumont, *DB*, p. 51; also ibid., pp. 71, 76–7 and 217.

22 Drumont, *TA*, p. 283.

23 Drumont, *FM*, p. 380 and *passim*. For the general significance of this emphasis on decadence, see chapter XII, pp. 428–31 below.

24 Drumont, *TA*, pp. 209 and 396.

25 Drumont, *FJ*, I, p. 298.

26 Ibid., II, pp. 518, 521, 526, 522–3 and 530. It is interesting to note that in this context gold is used as a symbol of excellence.

27 Ibid., I, p. 508.

28 Ibid., I, pp. 555–6.

29 This seems to have been a common, indeed perhaps the essential and defining characteristic, of populist movements and ideologies: "populism worshipped the *people*. But the people the populists worshipped were the meek and the miserable, and the populists worshipped them because they were miserable and because they were persecuted by the conspirators." Ionescu and Gellner, eds. *Populism*, p. 4; see also Adorno *et al.*, *The Authoritarian Personality*, p. 237; and Stern, *Hitler*, pp. 18 and 112.

30 Drumont, *FJ*, I, pp. 350–1.

31 Drumont, *TA*, p. 343.

32 Ibid., p. 363. For other examples of Drumont's sentimental evocation of poverty and death, see "La Petite Sidonie", *OBS*, pp. 137–43; and *Le Secret de Fourmies* (Paris, 1892), pp. 33–4, cit. E. Weber, "Nationalism, Socialism and National-Socialism in France", *French Historical Studies*, 2 (1961–2), pp. 299–300.

33 Drumont, *OBS*, p. 142.

34 Drumont, *TA*, pp. 213–15; also ibid., pp. 210–11 and 216–18.

35 Drumont, *DB*, pp. 325–6; also ibid., p. 451. He also waxed indignant in 1893 over the case of "La Mère aux chats", who was sent to prison for a week for stealing food for her many cats, who ate each other while she was away; Drumont, *OBS*, pp. 93–8.

36 Drumont, "Un Dimanche à Sainte-Pélagie", 14 November 1892, *OBS*, p. 66.

37 Drumont, *FJ*, II, p. 278.

38 See ibid., II, pp. 298–301.

39 Drumont, *OBS*, pp. 173–4 and viii.

40 Hitler made a very similar claim; see Stern, *Hitler*, pp. 18 and 112.

41 Drumont, *FJ*, I, p. 417.

42 Ibid., II, p. 435.

43 Drumont, *TA*, p. 390; also ibid., pp. 106 and 109.

44 Drumont, *DB*, p. 230.

45 Ibid., p. 247; also pp. 212–13.

46 Ibid., p. 229.

47 *Le Courrier de l'Est*, 27 October 1889, cit. Sternhell, *Maurice Barrès*, p. 241.

48 Daudet, *Au Temps de Judas*, p. 75.

49 See Montuclard, *Conscience religieuse et démocratie*, chapter 2; and Rollet, *L'Action sociale des catholiques*, I, chapters XI and XII.

50 *L'Assomption et ses oeuvres* (Paris, no date, c. 1895), Part VI, "Les Oeuvres sociales".

51 *Union Nationale de France, Règlement Général*, p. 3.

52 Daily Report, Prefect of Police, 7 June 1898. APP Ba 106.

53 AN F[7] 12480.

54 Telegram to *Le Petit Journal*, 22 February 1898. AN F[7] 12474.

55 Drumont, *FJ*, II, p. 529; also ibid., II, p. 537.

56 Ibid., II, pp. 538 and 303.

57 Bloy, *Le Salut par les Juifs*, p. 35; Drumont, *FJ*, II, pp. 327–8.

58 Daily Report, Prefect of Police, 13 February 1898. APP Ba 106.

59 Barrès, *Scènes et doctrines*, II, p. 143.

60 See Guerrand, *Les Origines du logement social*, pp. 233–6.

61 Barrès, *Scènes et doctrines*, II, p. 183.

62 Drumont, *FJ*, I, p. 345.

63 Drumont, *TA*, p. 32.

64 Drumont, *DB*, p. 29.

65 Bernanos, op. cit., p. 204.

66 Report, Police agent, no date, "Boulangisme et Antisémitisme: L'Affaire Dreyfus". AN F[7] 12459.

67 *La Croix*, 1 May 1890, cit. Sorlin, *"La Croix" et les Juifs*, p. 63.

68 Drumont, *FJ*, I, pp. 282–3.

69 Drumont, *TA*, p. 209; also *DB*, p. 152.

70 See Drumont, *FJ*, I, pp. 401 and 414–16.

71 Drumont, *TA*, pp. 252–3; also *FJ*, II, pp. 324–5.

72 Drumont, *FJ*, I, pp. 517–18.

73 Drumont, *FM*, pp. 2–3, 165–6 and 170; see also Daudet, *Les Oeuvres dans les hommes*, p. 155.

74 *Le Figaro*, 23 November 1892, cit. Verdès-Leroux, *Scandale financier*, p. 152.

75 Cit. ibid., pp. 136–7.

76 See Drault, *Drumont, La France juive et La Libre Parole*, p. 76.

77 Barrès, "Discours sur le cercueil de Morès" (19 July 1896), *Scènes et doctrines*, II, p. 52; see also Drumont, *DB*, p.v; and Schwarzschild, "The Marquis de Morès", pp. 16–17.

78 Guérin, op. cit., pp. 99–100. This passage is also of interest as a rare example of French "Social Imperialism"; for British parallels, see Bernard Semmel, *Imperialism and Social Reform, English Social-Imperial Thought 1895–1914* (London, 1960).

79 Daily Report, Prefect of Police, 1 March 1898. APP Ba 106.

80 Barrès, *Le Courrier de l'Est*, 24 November 1889, cit. Sternhell, "Barrès et la Gauche: du Boulangisme à *La Cocarde* (1889–1895)", *Le Mouvement Social*, no. 75 (1971), p. 89.

81 See ibid., pp. 94–119; also Soucy, *The Case of Maurice Barrès*, chapter 7.

82 Barrès, *Scènes et doctrines*, II, p. 162; see also Sternhell, *Maurice Barrès*, pp. 153–8, 221–31 and 239–41.

83 See Alphonse Daudet, "Henri Rochefort" (1879), *Thirty Years of Paris and of my Literary Life* (London, 1893), pp. 198–223; Zévaès, *Henri Rochefort*, pp. 18–60, 76–84 and 101–4; and Roger L. Williams, "Henri Rochefort's *Lanterne*", *French Historical Studies*, I (1958–60), pp. 319–34.

84 See Jules Vallès, *L'Insurgé* (Paris, 1962), pp. 130–1; Zévaès, *Rochefort*, pp. 107 and 112–46; and Maurice Choury, ed., *Les Poètes de la Commune* (Paris, 1970), pp. 182–3 and 201–2.

85 See Daudet, *Au Temps de Judas*, p. 27; Zévaès, *Rochefort*, pp. 155–61, 167, 177, 204 and 253–7; Arbellot, *La Fin du boulevard*, pp. 140–1; and Verdès-Leroux, *Scandale financier*, p. 40.

86 Sternhell, *Maurice Barrès*, p. 86; see also Mermeix, *Les Coulisses du Boulangisme* (Paris, 1890), p. 375 and *passim;* Zévaès, *Au Temps du Boulangisme,* pp. 55–6, 58, 75, 170–1 and 180–2; and Zévaès, *Rochefort,* pp. 183–95.

87 Zévaès, *Au Temps du Boulangisme,* pp. 231–3; Zévaès, *Rochefort,* pp. 208–20; Daudet, *Salons et journaux,* p. 33; and Arbellot, op. cit., p. 75.

88 The "Faux Norton", produced in the Chamber of Deputies in June 1893 by Millevoye, incriminated Rochefort, who reacted by lampooning the deputy in his characteristic style. In 1896, Rochefort was involved in a personalized polemic with Séverine, then of *La Libre Parole,* in which she was supported by Drumont. Interestingly, Rochefort had worked for a while under Drumont's father at the Hôtel de Ville of Paris in the 1850s. See Zévaès, *Rochefort,* pp. 205–7, 221–3 and 16–17; Drumont, *FJ,* I, pp. 551–4; *TA,* pp. 196–7; and *DB,* p. 261; Beau de Loménie, op. cit., pp. 27–9; see also chapter VII, p. 199 above.

89 See Gohier, *L'Armée contre la nation,* p. 266; Dagan, op. cit., pp. 90–3; and Arbellot, op. cit., p. 27.

90 Daudet, *Au Temps de Judas,* p. 30; also Daudet, *Salons et journaux,* p. 31; and Zévaès, *Rochefort,* pp. 237–40 and 264. According to Drault, op. cit., p. 141, however, the author of the offensive pun was Déroulède.

91 Bournand, *Les Juifs et nos contemporains,* pp. 51–2; also ibid., p. 55.

92 Daily Reports, Prefect of Police, 1 May, 3 May, 21 April, and 5 May 1898. APP Ba 106.

93 See Jolly, ed., *Dictionnaire des parlementaires français;* and Drumont, *TA,* p. 128.

94 See Police reports. AN F⁷ 12459.

95 Viau, *Vingt ans d'antisémitisme,* p. 2.

96 Maurras, Letter to Barrès, 3 February 1899. Barrès-Maurras, *La République ou le roi,* pp. 206–7.

97 Report, Commissaire spécial, Nantes, 18 May 1900. AN F⁷ 12456.

98 Biétry, *Le Socialisme et les Jaunes,* pp. 99–101.

99 Drumont, *FJ,* I, p. 363.

100 Drumont, *TA,* p. 30.

101 Daily Report, Prefect of Police, 20 January 1898. APP Ba 106.

102 Daily Report, Prefect of Police, 16 February 1898. APP Ba 106.

103 Speech at meeting of Union Nationale, La Roquette and Ste Marguerite section, Daily Report, Prefect of Police, 1 February 1898. APP Ba 106. As Georges de Lauris noted in another context, many of those who called for "des révoltes populaires" during the Affair were simply indulging in rhetoric, and had no serious socialist or revolutionary intentions, a point which we will return to later; see Lauris, *Souvenirs d'une belle époque,* pp. 93–4.

104 Dagan, op. cit., pp. 6–7.

105 Report, Prefect of Police, 26 January 1900. AN F⁷ 12458.

106 "Fils de la Révolution". Report, Commissaire spécial, Belfort, 25 December 1901. AN F⁷ 12455.

107 See AN F⁷ 12843.

108 Leroy-Beaulieu, *L'Antisémitisme,* p. 5.

109 Picard, *Synthèse de l'antisémitisme,* p. 119.

110 Lazare, *L'Antisémitisme,* pp. 407–8.

111 Dagan, op. cit., p. 65.

112 See Sternhell, "Barrès et la Gauche"; also, for example, Mitterand, *Zola journaliste,* p. 87; and Pinsot, "Quelques problèmes du Socialisme en France vers 1900".

113 E.g. Paul Louis, *Histoire du socialisme en France* (Paris, 1950); Ligou, *Histoire du socialisme* (1962); Lefranc, *Le Mouvement socialiste sous la IIIe République* (1963).

114 See chapter VI n. 13. Roche was a Blanquiste Boulangist, who later became a Dreyfusard, see p. 333. and n. 141 below.

115 See A. Charpentier, *Le Parti radical et radical-socialiste à travers des congrès*

(1901–1911) (Paris, 1913); Jacques Kayser, *Les Grandes Batailles du radicalisme des origines aux portes du pouvoir, 1820–1901* (Paris, 1962); and L.A. Loubère, "The French Left-wing Radicals: Their Economic and Social Programme since 1870", *American Journal of Economics and Sociology,* 26 (1967), pp. 189–203.

116 Barrès, *Mes Cahiers* (Paris, 1929), I, 1896–1898, p. 65.

117 *Le Journal,* 20 December 1894, cit. Dumont, *La Petite Bourgeoisie à travers les contes quotidiens du "Journal,"* p. 36. See also Gyp, *Le Mariage de Chiffon,* pp. 194 and *passim,* in which both the aristocratic Uncle Max and the prince claim to be "socialists". Coppée's reference to one of Béranger's songs is significant, suggesting that this broad "socialism" reflected a very old popular attitude, expressed with great success by Béranger in the early nineteenth century, and also evident in "sans-culottisme" in the Revolutionary period. Perhaps one could suggest indeed that it was a survival of "sans-culottisme", more authentically "popular" than more modern "ideological" versions of socialism, or at least the ground from which the latter sprang, and in which they found their nourishment? See Jean Touchard, *La Gloire de Béranger* (Paris, 1968), I, pp. 226–8 and *passim;* and Cobb, *The Police and the People,* pp. 314–24 and *passim.*

118 Tharaud, *Notre cher Péguy,* I, pp. 19 and 241; see also ibid., I, pp. 21–2, 26, 75–6 and 123–5; and Péguy, *Notre Jeunesse,* pp. 130–3. Péguy was characteristically unable later to accept the disciplined Socialism of the SFIO; see Halévy, *Péguy and Les Cahiers de la Quinzaine,* pp. 92–8 and 225–6.

119 See Lukes, *Emile Durkheim,* pp. 246–50 and 320–7.

120 See Maitron, *Histoire du mouvement anarchiste,* p. 107.

121 See Kayser, *Les Grandes Batailles du radicalisme,* pp. 290–310; Daniel Bardonnet, *Evolution de la structure du parti radical* (Paris, 1960); and Robert Vandenbussche, "Aspects de l'histoire politique du radicalisme dans le département du Nord (1870–1905)", *Revue du Nord,* 47 (1965), pp. 223–68.

122 See Ligou, *Histoire du socialisme,* pp. 37–175.

123 See Fiechter, *Le Socialisme français,* chapters 1–3.

124 See Maurras, "Ce que fut la 'Cocarde' " (1895), in Barrès, *Scènes et doctrines,* II, pp. 207–13; Sternhell, "Barrès et la Gauche", pp. 103–30; J. Julliard, "Fernand Pelloutier", *Le Mouvement Social,* no. 75 (1971), p. 11; and Nguyen, "Un essai de pouvoir intellectuel au début de la Troisième République".

125 Cit. Beau de Loménie, op. cit., p. 108.

126 Dagan, op. cit., p. 35. A Dreyfusard, Albert Réville published an interesting testimony of a university professor's reaction to the Affair, day by day: *Les Etapes d'un intellectuel: A propos de l'Affaire Dreyfus* (Paris, 1898). Allegedly the diary of a friend, the book is probably autobiographical.

127 Drumont, *FJ,* I, p. 342; also ibid., I, pp. 232, 240, 344–6, 358–9 and 368.

128 Ibid., II, p. 310; also I, pp. 371 and 503.

129 Drumont, *Figures de bronze ou statues de neige* (Paris, 1900), p. 319, cit. Silberner, "Proudhon's Judeophobia", p. 80.

130 *La Libre Parole,* 5 August 1896, cit. Jean Levaillant, *Essai sur l'évolution intellectuelle d'Anatole France* (Paris, 1965), p. 483.

131 Drumont, *DB,* p. 468.

132 Ibid., p. 191.

133 Drumont, *FM,* pp. 155 and 159; also Book IV, *passim.*

134 Drumont, *TA,* p. 436.

135 Maurras, Letter to Barrès, 22 February 1890. Barrès-Maurras, op. cit., pp. 31–2.

136 See Verdès-Leroux, *Scandale financier,* pp. 160–1.

137 Police reports, 4 June 1898, and 26 April 1899. AN F⁷ 12459.

138 Reinach, *Histoire de l'Affaire Dreyfus,* III, p. 586.

139 Drumont, *FM,* p. 185.

140 Drumont, *FJ,* I, p. 13; also *FM,* p. 185.

141 See Maurice Paz, "La notion de Race chez Blanqui et les révolutionnaires de son temps", Paper given at Colloque sur l'Idée de Race, 1975, p. 3; Sternhell, *Maurice*

Barrès, pp. 243–4; Zévaès, *Au Temps du Boulangisme*, pp. 132 and 183; Bournand, op. cit., p. 123; Reinach, op. cit., III, p. 388; and Police report, 13 August 1892. AN F⁷ 12459. As we have mentioned, Roche later became a Dreyfusard.

142 See chapter VI, p. 180 above.

143 Alfred Gabriel, "L'Antisémitisme révolutionnaire", *Le Turco*, 17 May 1901. (AN F⁷ 12843).

144 "Aux Socialistes Roannais". AN F⁷ 12459; and see Willard, *Les Guesdistes*, pp. 270–1.

145 Levaillant, op. cit., pp. 486–7.

146 Gohier, op. cit., p. vi. There is a parallel here with the way in which some Italian Socialists just after the First World War regarded the Christian Democratic "Popular Party" as preparing the way for Socialism proper among the rural population; see Richard A. Webster, *Christian Democracy in Italy 1860–1960* (London, 1961), pp. 61 and 197.

147 The phenomenon of Socialist or socialistic antisemitism was not, of course, peculiar to France at this time, but was found in Germany, Britain and elsewhere; see, for example, Semmel, op. cit., pp. 39–44 and 222–33; Mosse, *The Crisis of German Ideology*, p. 131; Horace B. Davis, *Nationalism and Socialism; Marxist and Labor Theories of Nationalism to 1917* (New York, 1973), pp. 71–2 and *passim*. The parallel between Drumont and Robert Blatchford seems particularly close.

148 See Hertzberg, *The French Enlightenment and the Jews*, chapters IX and X.

149 See Silberner, "Charles Fourier on the Jewish Question", *Jewish Social Studies*, 8 (1946); Silberner, "The Attitude of the Fourierist School towards the Jews", ibid., 9 (1947), pp. 339–62; Byrnes, *Antisemitism in Modern France*, pp. 114–25.

150 On Toussenel, there exists a hagiographic volume by a Nazi-sympathizer: Louis Thomas, *Alphonse Toussenel: Socialiste National antisémite (1803–1885)* (Paris, 1941); see also Szajkowski, "The Jewish Saint-Simonians and Socialist Antisemites in France", p. 47; Verdès-Leroux, *Scandale financier*, pp. 105–7.

151 See Silberner, "Pierre Leroux's Ideas on the Jewish People", *Jewish Social Studies*, 12 (1950), pp. 367–84; Viard, "L'*Encyclopédie nouvelle* de Pierre Leroux", pp. 3 and 17; Paz, op. cit., pp. 4–5; Verdès-Leroux, op. cit., p. 105.

152 On Vallès, see Vallès, *L'Insurgé*, pp. 51 and 59–60; Vallès, *Correspondance avec Hector Malot* (préface et notes de Marie-Claire Bancquart) (Paris, 1968), p. 317; Duroselle, "L'Antisémitisme en France", p. 58; Richard Cobb, "Céline, Traveller to the End of the Night", *Times Literary Supplement*, 25 July 1975, p. 818.

153 Proudhon, Carnets, 24 December 1847, cit. Verdès-Leroux, *Scandale financier*, p. 105; see also Silberner, "Proudhon's Judeophobia".

154 Szajkowski, "The Jewish Saint-Simonians and Socialist Antisemites", p. 58.

155 See Drumont, *FJ*, I, p. 335; *DB*, p. 406; *TA*, pp. 111 and 135–6; and Bournand, op. cit., pp. 227–33.

156 See G. Vacher de Lapouge, *L'Aryen, son rôle social, Cours libre de science politique professé à l'Université de Montpellier 1889–1890* (Paris, 1898); and Guy Thuillier, "Un anarchiste positiviste: Georges Vacher de Lapouge, Paper given at Colloque sur l'Idée de Race, 1975.

157 Picard was also an admirer of Benoît Malon; see Picard, *Synthèse de l'antisémitisme*, pp. 122–3.

158 Silberner, "French Socialism and the Jewish Question 1865–1914", pp. 7–11; see also Sternhell, *Maurice Barrès*, p. 244.

159 Silberner, "French Socialism and the Jewish Question", pp. 11–27; and Silberner, "Anti-Jewish Trends in French Revolutionary Syndicalism", *Jewish Social Studies*, 15 (1953), pp. 195–202. Was this tradition an element in the hostility shown later towards Léon Blum by the French Communist Party? See Kriegel, "Un Phénomène de haine fratricide: Léon Blum vu par les Communistes", *Le Pain et les roses*, pp. 418–424.

160 See Verdès-Leroux, *Scandale financier*, pp. 158–9.

161 See Verdès, "La Presse devant le krach d'une banque catholique", pp. 146–7.
162 *Le Socialiste*, 26 June 1892, cit. Verdès-Leroux, *Scandale financier*, pp. 153–4;
     see also Guesde's speech, "Antisémitisme et Socialisme" (September 1898), in
     Bournand, op. cit., pp. 233–37.
163 Cit. Barral, *Les Agrariens français*, pp. 155 and 161.
164 See Fiechter, op. cit., chapter 1; Péguy, "Demi-réponse à M. Cyprien Lantier",
     16 November 1900, *Oeuvres en prose, 1898–1908*, pp. 282–300; also chapter II,
     pp. 66–70 above.
165 Report, Commissaire spécial, Nantes, 23 December 1897. AN F⁷ 12459.
166 Brunellière, Letter to Codet, 27 January 1898, Willard, ed., *La Correspondance
     de Charles Brunellière*, p. 155.
167 Cit. Zévaès, *L'Affaire Dreyfus*, p. 114; see also Bournand, op. cit., pp. 209–12;
     Fiechter, op. cit., pp. 49–50.
168 Silberner, "French Socialism and the Jewish Question", pp. 13–14, makes this
     point, but less strongly.
169 See Zévaès, *L'Affaire Dreyfus*, p. 122; and Willard, *Les Guesdistes*, pp. 410–21.
170 Daily Reports, Prefect of Police, 15, 23 and 27 January, and 16 and 18 February
     1898. APP Ba 106.
171 Bournand, op. cit., p. 61; and ibid., pp. 62–5; see also Desjardins, "La Loi de 1849
     et l'expulsion des étrangers", pp. 657–8. Hugues was elected as deputy for the 1st
     constituency of the 19th *arrondissement* of Paris in 1898, where he stood against
     Sabran-Pontevès, the candidate supported by the Ligue Antisémitique.
172 Cit. Bournand, op. cit., p. 174.
173 Barrès-Maurras, op. cit., p. 171 n.; Bournand, op. cit., pp. 273–5; Barrès, *Scènes
     et doctrines*, II, pp. 174–7.
174 See Silberner, "French Socialism and the Jewish Question", pp. 10 and 24;
     Drumont, *DB*, p. 430; and *TA*, pp. 116–17 and 136; Drault, op. cit., p. 78.
175 See Rouanet, article in *La Lanterne*, 20 January 1898, cit. Bournand, op. cit., pp.
     222–6; Jolly, ed., op. cit.
176 Daily Reports, Prefect of Police, 28 January, 25 February and 4 May 1898. APP
     Ba 106.
177 Daily Reports, Prefect of Police, 3 March, 24 and 7 February 1898. APP Ba 106.
178 Johnson, *France and the Dreyfus Affair*, p. 133.
179 Daily Reports, Prefect of Police, 20 February and 7 June 1898. APP Ba 106. On
     Jaurès, see also chapter II, n. 88 above; and Bournand, op. cit., pp. 95–102.
180 Reported in *Le Nouvelliste de l'Ouest*, 12–13 December 1898.
181 Drumont, *FM*, p. 172.
182 Drumont, *TA*, p. 157; also p. 68.
183 Drault, op. cit., p. 95.
184 Drumont, "La Bombe du Palais-Bourbon", 10 December 1893, *OBS*, pp. 102–3.
185 Drumont, "Un anarchiste d'autrefois", 11 December 1893, *OBS*, pp. 114–15.
186 See Drumont, "La Petite Sidonie", *OBS*, pp. 137–43; and Viau, op. cit., pp.
     75–6.
187 See, for example, Lévy, "La Presse de la Meuse devant les attentats anarchistes",
     loc. cit.; Jacques Kayser, "La Presse de Dordogne devant les attentats anarchistes
     et les lois de répression, Décembre 1893—Juin-Août 1894", in Kayser, ed., *La
     Presse de province sous la Troisième République* (Paris, 1958), pp. 137–59; also
     Drault, op. cit., pp. 197 and 202–4; Maitron, op. cit., pp. 195–246. Maitron
     mentions Drumont in this context, but fails to bring out his real sympathy with
     the Anarchists.
188 See Morès, *Rothschild, Ravachol et Cie* (Paris, 1892); and Drault, op. cit., p. 100.
189 See Barrès, article in *Le Journal*, 12 January 1894, in Barrès-Maurras, op. cit., pp.
     634–5.
190 See abbé Garnier, "Appel aux anarchistes", *Le Peuple Français*, 17 April 1894,
     cit. Divry, *L'Abbé Garnier*, pp. 110–12.
191 See, for example, Barrès's trilogy, *Le Culte du moi* (Paris, 1888–91); and Madaule,

Le Nationalisme de Maurice Barrès, Part I, "De l'Egotisme au nationalisme"; and, for Maurras, Roudiez, *Maurras jusqu'à l'Action Française,* pp. 161–180 and *passim.*
192 Leroy-Beaulieu, *L'Antisémitisme,* pp. 58–9.
193 Viau, op. cit., p. 72; see also Drumont, *TA,* pp. 88–90 and 214; Bournand, op. cit., p. 175; Drault, op. cit., pp. 211–15 and 223–4; Pierrard, *Juifs et catholiques français,* p. 52.
194 See Maitron, op. cit., pp. 181–223; Byrnes, *Antisemitism in Modern France,* p. 168; Noël Richard, *Le Mouvement décadent* (Paris, 1968), pp. 62–3; and Choury, op. cit., p. 277. Séverine's real name was Caroline Rémy.
195 Mosse is quite mistaken therefore in saying that Séverine was "hardly a friend of his [Drumont's]", "The French Right and the Working Classes", p. 186; though the two did quarrel later, and Séverine became a Dreyfusard; see Benda, *La Jeunesse d'un clerc,* p. 207; and Beau de Loménie, op. cit., p. 138. Séverine was also a friend of Barrès; see Barrès-Maurras, op. cit., p. 92.
196 Barrès-Maurras, op. cit., pp. 328–9.
197 See chapter VI, p. 180 above.
198 For an evocation of these Anarchist milieus, see Victor Serge, *Memoirs of a Revolutionary 1901–1941* (Oxford, 1967), pp. 16–44.
199 See Divry, op. cit., pp. 110–12.
200 Drumont, *FJ,* I, p. 16.
201 On Bakunin, see Verdès-Leroux, *Scandale financier,* pp. 161–2; Anthony Masters, *Bakunin, The Father of Anarchism* (London, 1974), pp. 62, 85 and 182. (I am indebted for this last reference, and for general orientation on Bakunin, to John Biggart.)
202 Daily Report, Prefect of Police, 26 January 1898. APP Ba 106.
203 See chapter II, n. 114; also Verdès-Leroux, *Scandale financier,* pp. 161–2.
204 Viau, op. cit., p. 79.
205 See Divry, op. cit., pp. 110–12.
206 Barrès, article in *Le Figaro,* cit. Georges Suarez, *Briand; Sa vie, son oeuvre* (Paris, 1938), I, p. 160.
207 Ginsberg, "Antisemitism", loc. cit., p. 202.
208 See Sorlin, *"La Croix" et les Juifs,* pp. 107–10.
209 Mayeur, "Les Congrès nationaux", p. 205.
210 Garnier, Speech at Union Nationale regional Congress, Beaujeu, Report, Prefect, Rhône, 22 August 1896. AN F⁷ 12480.
211 "Le Péril Socialiste", talk given to La Jeunesse de l'Union Nationale, Paris, July 1898; also miscellaneous pamphlets. AN F⁷ 12480.
212 Drumont, *FJ,* II, p. 327.
213 Ibid., I, pp. 519–20.
214 See Sternhell, "Barrès et la Gauche", p. 121.
215 Barrès, *Scènes et doctrines,* II, p. 52.
216 See Barrès-Maurras, op. cit., pp. 118 and 136–7.
217 Barrès, "Socialisme et Nationalisme", *La Patrie,* 27 February 1903, cit. Sternhell, *Maurice Barrès,* p. 227.
218 Daily Report, Prefect of Police, 12 January 1898. APP Ba 106.
219 Cit. Bournand, op. cit., p. 49.
220 Daily Reports, Prefect of Police, 10 and 31 March, 6 April, 10 and 12 June 1898. APP Ba 106. "Révisionniste" here implied revision of the Constitution of the Third Republic, an old Boulangist platform, and not revision of the Dreyfus case; on the links between Boulangism and the Nationalist-antisemitic movement of the late 1890s, see chapter XII, pp. 383–5 below.
221 "Le Collectivisme, voilà l'ennemi!" AN F⁷ 12872.
222 See Jolly, ed., op. cit.
223 Biétry, op. cit., p. 1.
224 Ibid., p. 2.

225 Ibid., p. 42.

226 Ibid., p. 115; and also pp. 91 and 118–21.

227 See my "Catholic Populism in France at the time of the Dreyfus Affair", pp. 674–8.

228 Drumont, *DB*, pp. 328 and 495; see also *TA*, p. 12.

229 *La Croix*, 25 February 1891, cit. Sorlin, *"La Croix" et les Juifs*, p. 101.

230 On traditional anti-fiscal revolts in France, see Roland Mousnier, *Peasant Uprisings in Seventeenth-Century France, Russia and China* (London, 1971), pp. 38–40, 46–52, 57–8 and *passim;* Emmanuel Le Roy Ladurie, *Les Paysans de Languedoc* (Paris, 1969), p. 325; Bercé, *Croquants et nu-pieds*, pp. 20–2, 33–5, 94–105, 116–18 and *passim*. On the association of the fisc with the Jews, see Wirth, *The Ghetto*, p. 17.

231 Drumont, *DB*, p. 247.

232 Drumont, *TA*, p. 175; also pp. 24–5 and 29.

233 Daily Report, Prefect of Police, 12 February 1898. APP Ba 106.

234 *Union Nationale de France, Règlement Général*, pp. 57–8 and 54.

235 See Daily Reports, Prefect of Police, 1 and 5 May 1898. APP Ba 106.

236 See Zolla, *La Crise agricole*, pp. 16–17 and *passim*.

237 See Foville, *La France économique*, pp. 425, 444–53 and 492; Levasseur, *Questions ouvrières et industrielles en France sous la Troisième République*, pp. 632–40; Jean Bouvier, "Le système fiscal français du XIXe siècle: Étude critique d'un immobilisme", in Jean Bouvier and Jacques Wolff, eds, *Deux Siècles de fiscalité française XIXe–XXe siècle, Histoire, économie, politique* (Paris and The Hague, 1973), pp. 235 and 240–1.

238 See Foville, op. cit., chapters 27 and 28; *Les Impôts en France, Traité technique* (Paris, 1904), 2 vols, Préface de J. Caillaux; Joseph Caillaux, *Mes Mémoires* (Paris, 1942), I, pp. 237 and 249–57; Robert Schnerb, "La Politique fiscale de Thiers", *Revue Historique*, (1949), in Bouvier and Wolff, eds., op. cit., pp. 158–220; Bouvier, "Le système fiscal français", in ibid., pp. 226–62.

239 Drumont, *FM*, p. 28.

240 Drumont, *FJ*, II, pp. 41–2.

241 Fore-Fauré, *Face aux Juifs!*, p. 136.

242 Drumont, *FM*, p. 47.

243 Drumont, *FJ*, II, pp. 517 and 535–6; see also ibid., I, p. 412.

244 Drumont, *DB*, p. 163; see also ibid., pp. 42–9, 55–69 and *passim;* and *TA*, pp. v, 45 and 75–7.

245 See Léon Bloy, "La République des Vaincus" (1885), *Le Pal, Oeuvres*, IV (Paris, 1965), pp. 68–73; Barrès, *Leurs Figures;* Barrès, *Dans la Cloaque* (Paris, 1914); Jules Soury, *Campagne nationaliste* (Paris, 1902), pp. 223 and *passim*, cit. Sternhell, "Le Déterminisme physiologique et racial", p. 5; and Garnier, speech, Union Nationale Congress, Roanne, 1898, Police agent reports, 13 and 14 February 1898. AN F7 12480.

246 *Union Nationale de France, Règlement Général*, pp. 59–60.

247 Drumont, *FM*, p. 306.

248 Report, Police agent, 1 May 1898. AN F7 12480.

249 Biétry, op. cit., p. 166.

250 Neither phenomenon has yet been adequately studied, but see, on the growth of the civil service, Henri Chardon, *L'Administration de la France, Les fonctionnaires* (Paris, 1908), pp. 135–53 and *passim;* Georges Cahen, *Les Fonctionnaires* (Paris, 1911), pp. 24–7 and *passim;* Eugene N. Anderson and Pauline Anderson, *Political Institutions and Social Change in Continental Europe in the Nineteenth Century* (Berkeley, 1967), pp. 167, 203 and 233; and, on "corruption", Bouvier, *Les Deux Scandales de Panama;* Cahen, op. cit., p. 19; Pierre Legendre, *L'Administration du XVIIIe siècle à nos jours* (Paris, 1969), pp. 203–4 and 208–19; Theodore Zeldin, *France 1848–1945, I, Ambition, Love and Politics* (Oxford, 1973), chapter 19.

251 "L'Etat . . . Bon Dieu . . .". Biétry, op. cit., pp. 164, 171 and 162.
252 Barrès, "Notes sur les idées fédéralistes" (1895), *Scènes et doctrines*, II, p. 229.
253 Drumont, *FJ*, II, p. 476.
254 Ibid., I, p. 483.
255 Fore-Fauré, op. cit., pp. 51–2.
256 Barrès, "Notes sur les idées fédéralistes", loc. cit., p. 223.
257 See Soucy, *The Case of Maurice Barrès*, chapter 3; and Sternhell, *Maurice Barrès*, pp. 324–31.
258 See René Jouveau, "L'Itinéraire félibréen de Charles Maurras avant l'Action Française", *Etudes Maurrassiennes*, 1 (1972), p. 86.
259 Maurras, *L'Avenir de l'intelligence*, pp. 83 and 85; see also Fore-Fauré's very similar thesis on the role of the state school as an instrument of state power; Fore-Fauré, op. cit., pp. 52–105.
260 Maurras, *Enquête sur la monarchie*, p. 323, cit. Henri Morel, "Charles Maurras et l'idée de décentralisation", *Etudes Maurrassiennes*, 1 (1972), p. 121; see also J. Paul-Boncour and Charles Maurras, *Un Débat nouveau sur la République et la décentralisation* (Toulouse, 1905); Maurras, *Dictateur et roi* (1899), *Petit Manuel de l'Enquête sur la monarchie* (Versailles, 1928), pp. 206–8; Maurras, "La Monarchie fédéraliste", *L'Etang de Berre* (Paris, 1928), pp. 147–55; Morel, op. cit., passim.
261 Jolly, ed., op. cit.
262 See Adrien Dansette, *Histoire religieuse de la France contemporaine* (Paris, 1965), pp. 563–641; Partin, *Waldeck-Rousseau, Combes and the Church*; Larkin, *Church and State after the Dreyfus Affair*.
263 Drumont, *DB*, p. 328.
264 See A. Lavy, *L'Oeuvre de Millerand, un ministre socialiste; Faits et documents* (Paris, 1902); Edouard Campagnole, *L'Assistance obligatoire aux vieillards, aux infirmes et aux incurables. Commentaire de la loi du 14 juillet 1905* (Paris, 1908), pp. 1–50 and passim; Levasseur, *Questions ouvrières et industrielles*, pp. 437–48 and 498–514; Jeanneney and Perrot, *Textes du Droit économique et social français*, pp. 265–307; Sorlin, *Waldeck-Rousseau*, pp. 477–9.
265 See Campagnole, op. cit., p. vii; Raoul Persil, *Alexandre Millerand (1859–1943)* (Paris, 1949), pp. 43–4; Sorlin, *Waldeck-Rousseau*, p. 470.
266 Crucial here was the replacement of recruitment by patronage with recruitment by competitive examination, though effective introduction of the latter seems to have lagged considerably behind its formal introduction. Pascal Durand-Bartez, *Histoire des structures du Ministère de la Justice 1789–1945* (Paris, 1973), for example, suggests that effective recruitment by open examination in this Ministry dated from 1909; see also in this little-researched field, Anderson and Anderson, op. cit., p. 204; and Jean-André Tournerie, *Le Ministère du Travail (Origines et premiers développements)* (Paris, 1971), pp. 205–6.
267 Sartre, *Réflexions sur la question juive*, pp. 35–6; see also the remarks by Wiles in Ionescu and Gellner, eds, op. cit., p. 170.
268 Drumont, *DB*, p. 163.
269 Drumont, *FJ*, II, p. 27.
270 Garnier, speech, Troyes. Report, Commissaire central, Troyes, 20 February 1899. AN F⁷ 12466.
271 E.g. Drumont, *DB*, p. 68. Barrès claimed that he had been defeated in the 1902 elections in Paris through electoral fraud and bloc-voting against him by Jews and Freemasons. Barrès-Maurras, op. cit., p. 666.
272 E.g. Drumont, *FJ*, II, pp. 296 and 301; also pp. 209–10, 275, 298, 493–4 and 510–14.
273 Drumont, *DB*, pp. 42 and 221–2.
274 Drumont, *TA*, p. vi.
275 See Zévaès, *Au Temps du Boulangisme*, chapter 1 and passim; Néré, *Le Boulangisme et la presse*, chapter 3; Sternhell, *Maurice Barrès*, chapter 2.

276 Donnay, *Des Souvenirs*, pp. 100–1 and 182–3.
277 See Péguy, *NJ;* and Tharaud, *Notre cher Péguy*, I, p. 39.
278 Drumont, *FJ*, II, p. 296.
279 See Sternhell, *Maurice Barrès*, p. 80; and Dumont, *La Petite Bourgeoisie à travers les contes du "Journal"*, pp. 38–44.
280 See Marrus, *The Politics of Assimilation*, pp. 100–13 and chapter 7; Barrès referred to Darmesteter's *Les Prophètes d'Israël* (1896), in *Mes Cahiers*, I, p. 134; and Maurras referred to Darmesteter also in *Quand les Français ne s'aimaient pas; Chronique d'une renaissance, 1895–1905* (1916) (Paris, 1926), p. 265, in a piece written in 1903. For Blum, see *Nouvelles Conversations de Goethe avec Eckermann* (1901), *L'Oeuvre de Léon Blum 1891–1905*, pp. 264–7; Stokes, *Léon Blum*, pp. 30–1 and 99; and Ziebura, *Léon Blum*, pp. 91–4. For another expression of the same idea, see Benda, *Les Cahiers d'un clerc*, pp. 70–1 and 88–90.
281 See Lovsky, *L'Antisémitisme chrétien*, pp. 290–2.
282 Ernest Renan, "De l'Identité originelle et de la séparation éventuelle du Judaïsme et du Christianisme" (1893), *Oeuvres complètes*, I (Paris, 1947), pp. 912–13. On the espousal of the same idea by Leroux and by Michelet, see Viard, op. cit., p. 25.
283 Lazare, *L'Antisémitisme*, p. 359; see also ibid., chapter XII: "L'Esprit révolutionnaire dans le Judaïsme".
284 Maurras, *Anthinéa*, pp. 237 and 242; see also Maurras, *Jeanne d'Arc, Louis XIV, Napoléon* (Paris, 1937), pp. 224–7, where Lazare is cited in support of such a view; the passage is omitted in the reprint of this work in Maurras, *Oeuvres capitales*, II.
285 Maurras, "Une Revue Latine" (March 1902), *Quand les Francais*, p. 124.
286 Maurras, Préface, *Les Vergers sur la mer* (Paris, 1937), cit. Dupré, Introduction, Barrès-Maurras, op. cit., p. xxxix.
287 Drumont, *FJ*, I, p. 317; and II, pp. 241 and 321.
288 Ibid., II, p. 442.
289 Fore-Fauré, op. cit., p. 8; see also Vogüé, *Les Morts qui parlent*, p. 423, where a character refers to "le ferment juif . . . un agent de décomposition . . . dissolvant des sociétés . . ."
290 Drumont, *FJ*, I, p. 174.
291 Ibid., I, pp. 193 and 16; see also ibid., I, p. 51; II, pp. 434–5; *DB*, pp. 506–7.
292 Drumont, *DB*, p. 96; also ibid., p. 545; and *FJ*, I, p. vi.
293 Drumont, *DB*, p. 95. Zadoc Kahn was France's Chief Rabbi.
294 Cit. Verdès-Leroux, *Scandale financier*, p. 137.
295 Abbé Lémann, *La Préponderance juive*, I, pp. v, ix and 62.
296 Sorlin, *"La Croix" et les Juifs*, pp. 92 and 164–7.
297 Daudet, *Les Oeuvres dans les hommes*, p. 192.
298 AN F⁷ 12854.
299 Meyer, *Ce que mes yeux ont vu*, pp. 130 and 128.
300 Caillaux, *Mes Mémoires* (1942), I, p. 130. The date of publication is clearly significant here, but only perhaps in so far as the ambiance of the early 1940s encouraged Caillaux to express in public prejudices that a Radical politician might have been more likely to have kept quiet about at the start of the century, though contrary instances can and have been cited.
301 Daudet, *Au Temps de Judas*, p. 113.
302 Biez, *La Question juive* (1886), cit. Verdès-Leroux, *Scandale financier*, pp. 143–4.
303 Biétry, op. cit., pp. 5, 12 and 25.
304 Drumont, *FJ*, I, p. 524.
305 Ibid., I, p. 401.
306 See Pierrard, op. cit., p. 116.
307 See Schwarzschild, op. cit., pp. 16–17 and 22.
308 Drumont, *TA*, p. 143.
309 Drumont, *FJ*, I, p. 201.

310 Ibid., II, p. 3.
311 Cit. Rollet, *L'Action sociale des catholiques*, I, p. 350.
312 Drumont, *DB*, p. 105.
313 Daudet, *Au Temps de Judas*, p. 114. On Jewish involvement in *L'Humanité*, see chapter XIX, p. 717 below.
314 Biétry, op. cit., pp. 6 and 42.
315 See Sternhell, "Barrès et la Gauche", p. 121. Picard made the same observation; see Dagan, op. cit., p. 4.
316 See Bournand, op. cit., pp. 55 and 227–8.
317 Daily Report, Prefect of Police, 28 April 1898. APP Ba 106.
318 "La Bande Juive, Les Faux Socialistes". AN F⁷ 12463.
319 Daily Report, Prefect of Police, 1 June 1898. APP Ba 106; and Guérin, op. cit., pp. 10–11.
320 See, for example, Wirth, op. cit., pp. 106–7; Memmi, *Portrait d'un Juif*, pp. 258–76; and Chaim Bermant, "Six Portraits that tell the Anglo-Jewish Story", *Weekend Telegraph*, 1 April 1966, p. 25.
321 J. Steens, "Souvenirs d'un Dreyfusard: Les Socialistes", *Le Siècle*, 22 March 1902.
322 See Benda, *La Jeunesse d'un clerc*, pp. 36–51, 94 and 151–5; Mauriac, "L'Affaire Dreyfus", pp. 16–17; Marrus, op. cit., Part 2.
323 See Blumenkranz, ed., *Histoire des Juifs en France*, p. 282.
324 See S. Posener, *Adolphe Crémieux; A Biography* (Philadelphia, 1940); and Marrus, op. cit., Part 2. Naquet was a Radical Boulangist, and, interestingly, similar in political formation and orientation to many leading antisemites. A few other names could be added to this short list, but they are only minor figures, e.g. Camille Dreyfus, director of *La Nation*, and deputy for the Seine, a Radical; and Klotz, another Radical, whom we have already encountered. The claim made by Drumont and others (e.g. Drumont, *FJ*, I, pp. 527 and ff.; and Hosmer, *The Jews*, pp. 298–304) that Gambetta was Jewish (in addition to having an Italian father) is not supported by any of his biographers; see P.B. Gheusi, *Gambetta, Life and Letters* (London, 1910); Paul Deschanel, *Gambetta* (Paris, 1919); Harold Stannard, *Gambetta and the Foundation of the Third Republic* (London, 1921); and, particularly, J.P.T. Bury, *Gambetta and the National Defence: A Republican Dictatorship in France* (London, 1936), pp. 288–9, Appendix III.
325 See Szajkowski, "The Jewish Saint-Simonians and Socialist Antisemites in France", pp. 37–8 and *passim;* and Drumont, *FJ*, I, pp. 346–53.
326 See Szajkowski, "French Jews during the Revolution of 1830 and the July Monarchy", p. 120.
327 See Choury, op. cit., p. 107.
328 See Daniel Halévy, *Essais sur le mouvement ouvrier en France* (Paris, 1901); Halévy, *Pays Parisiens* (Paris, 1932), pp. 155–204; Ziebura, op. cit., pp. 9–44.
329 Memmi, op. cit., pp. 262–3; see also Kriegel, op. cit., pp. 422–4.
330 See Rémond, *La Droite en France*, chapter VI; and Girardet, *Le Nationalisme français.* Sternhell, *Maurice Barrès*, p. 344, puts special emphasis here on the role of the Ligue de la Patrie Française "[qui] contribue largement à faire basculer le nationalisme vers la droite conservatrice." While descriptively true, this observation, by itself, lacks explanatory force.
331 Leroy-Beaulieu, *L'Antisémitisme*, pp. 59–60.
332 Cit. Bournand, op. cit., p. 122.
333 Cit. ibid., p. 79.
334 See chapter VI, n. 46.
335 Meyer, op. cit., p. 127.
336 Report, Police agent, Paris, 16 August 1899. AN F⁷ 12923.
337 Report, Commissaire central, Nantes, 30 June 1899. AN F⁷ 12465.
338 See Sorlin, *Waldeck-Rousseau*, pp. 410–22; and chapter I, pp. 24–34 above.
339 Cit. Mayeur, "Les Congrès nationaux", p. 204.

340 See Louis Chevalier, *Classes laborieuses et classes dangereuses à Paris pendant la première moitié du XIXe siècle* (Paris, 1958).
341 On the attitude which accompanied the repression of the Paris Commune, see, for example, Paul Lidsky, *Les Ecrivains contre la Commune* (Paris, 1970); on the development of trade unions, see Paul Louis, *Histoire du mouvement syndical en France 1789–1910* (Paris, 1920), chapters VIII and IX and *passim;* on the development of strike action, see Perrot, *Les Ouvriers en grève;* and Edward Shorter and Charles Tilly, *Strikes in France, 1830–1968* (Cambridge, 1974); see also generally, Sorlin, *Waldeck-Rousseau,* pp. 252–5 and 375–6.
342 See Ligou, *Histoire du socialisme,* pp. 108–11 and 122–4.
343 Blum, "Les Lois scélérates", *La Revue Blanche,* 15 June 1898, *L'Oeuvre de Léon Blum 1891–1905,* p. 364; see also Maitron, op. cit., pp. 224 and 237–8.
344 *Journal Officiel, Chambre des Députés,* 24 December 1894, cit. Zévaès, *L'Affaire Dreyfus,* p. 40.
345 Steinheil, *My Memoirs,* p. 75.
346 See Mitterand, *Zola journaliste,* p. 232; and D. Steenhuyse, "Quelques jalons pour l'étude du thème du 'Grand Soir' jusqu'en 1900", *Le Mouvement Social,* no. 75 (1971), pp. 63–76.
347 Edmond Renard, *Le Cardinal Mathieu, 1839–1908* (Paris, 1925), p. 312.
348 See Perrot and Kriegel, *Le Socialisme français et le pouvoir,* pp. 13–30; and Steenhuyse, op. cit.
349 Dagan, op. cit., p. 22.
350 See Byrnes, *Antisemitism in Modern France,* chapter 3, section 3, "The Publication of *La France juive".*
351 See chapter XVI, pp. 632–5 below.
352 See Byrnes, op. cit., p. 135.
353 See Daily Report, Prefect of Police, 10 March 1898. APP Ba 106.
354 Drumont, *FJ,* I, p. 516.
355 Ibid., I, pp. 522–3.
356 Drumont, *TA,* pp. x–xi; and *FJ,* I, p. 526; see also *DB,* p. 120; and Revel, "Une source de l'idée de participation, Édouard Drumont", (April 1968), *Les Idées de notre temps,* p. 192.
357 Cit. Bournand, op. cit., p. 50.
358 Sartre, op. cit., p. 51.
359 See, for example, Loewenstein, *Christians and Jews,* p. 19; and Ackerman and Jahoda, *Anti-Semitism and Emotional Disorder,* p. 66.
360 Lazare, *L'Antisémitisme,* p. 120.
361 Herzl, *La Nouvelle Revue Internationale,* January 1898, cit. Bournand, op. cit., p. 299.
362 Jaurès, *La Dépêche de Toulouse,* 5 February 1890, cit. Verdès-Leroux, *Scandale financier,* pp. 159–60.
363 See ibid., pp. 153–4; and Bournand, op. cit., p. 234.
364 *Le Parti Ouvrier,* 7–8 January 1895, cit. Zévaès, *L'Affaire Dreyfus,* p. 48.
365 Daily Report, Prefect of Police, 29 June 1898. APP Ba 106. On religious antisemitism generally, see chapter XIV.
366 Daily Reports, Prefect of Police, 8 and 29 June 1898. APP Ba 106.
367 Daily Report, Prefect of Police, 16 January 1898. APP Ba 106; see also Bournand, op. cit., p. 231.
368 Report, Commissaire central Grenoble, 11 May 1899. AN F⁷ 12466.
369 Dagan, op. cit., p. 64.
370 Leroy-Beaulieu, *Les Doctrines de haine,* p. 17.
371 See my "Late-Nineteenth-Century Nationalism".
372 Leroy-Beaulieu, *L'Antisémitisme,* pp. 58–9.
373 Leroy-Beaulieu, *Les Doctrines de haine,* p. 16.
374 Zola, "Pour les Juifs", *Le Figaro,* 16 May 1896, *L'Affaire Dreyfus, La Vérité en marche,* p. 62.

375 See chapter IX, n. 54.
376 Cit. Bournand, op. cit., p. 46.
377 *L'Humanité Nouvelle,* III (1898), cit. Byrnes, op. cit., p. 117.
378 *La Gazette de France,* 11 February 1901, in Maurras, *Dictionnaire politique et critique* (Paris, 1932–4), II, p. 360.
379 Drumont, *TA,* pp. 117, 365 and 394–5.
380 Daily Report, Prefect of Police, 2 April 1898. APP Ba 106.
381 Report, Commissaire central, Grenoble, 12 January 1899. AN F7 12459; see also Drault, op. cit., pp. 249–50.
382 See Sorlin, *"La Croix" et les Juifs,* pp. 64 and 69; and Divry, op. cit., pp. 64–6.
383 See chapter VI, pp. 180–2 above; and my "Catholic Populism in France at the time of the Dreyfus Affair", pp. 674–6.
384 Picard, *Synthèse de l'antisémitisme,* pp. 15, 91 and 122; also p. 11.
385 Dagan, op. cit., pp. 4–5.
386 Drumont, *TA,* pp. 231–2; also pp. 383–93.
387 See Chapter X, pp. 294–7 above.
388 Lazare, *L'Antisémitisme,* pp. 385–6.
389 See Charles Gide in Dagan, op. cit., p. 57; also A. Hamon in Bournand, op. cit., p. 215; and Memmi, op. cit., pp. 52–3.
390 Suarez, op. cit., I, p. 160.
391 Report, Police agent, Paris, 18 February 1898. AN F7 12474.
392 Report, Commissaire spécial, Besançon, 7 February 1899. AN F7 12466.
393 Report, Commissaire spécial, Chalandray, 8 January 1900. AN F7 12453.
394 See Report, Commissaire spécial, Saint-Dié, 19 November 1900. AN F7 12457.
395 See Sorlin, *"La Croix" et les Juifs,* pp. 64 and 69.
396 See particularly Mayeur, "Les Congrès nationaux", pp. 203–6; Montuclard, *Conscience religieuse et démocratie,* pp. 121–38 and *passim;* and my "Catholic Populism in France at the time of the Dreyfus Affair", pp. 692–8; also chapter XIV, pp. 526 and ff. below.
397 See Rollet, op. cit., I, pp. 422–3.
398 See Police reports, 4 April 1905 and 11 August 1906. AN F7 12720, Dossier, "Union des Travailleurs Libres"; Daudet, *Au Temps de Judas,* pp. 213–15.
399 See Daudet, op. cit., pp. 215–16; Mosse, "The French Right and the Working Classes", pp. 201–2.
400 Leroy-Beaulieu, *L'Antisémitisme,* p. 42.
401 Dagan, op. cit., pp. 15–16; see also ibid., pp. 3–5, 40 (Reclus); and 64 (Henry Maret); also Verdès-Leroux, *Scandale financier,* p. 172; and Duroselle, "L'Antisémitisme en France", p. 67. This contrasts with findings from the United States and Britain more recently, which suggest that antisemitism is more prevalent among lower income-groups and those with least education. Is this a general post-Second World War phenomenon, or something peculiar to Anglo-Saxon countries?—see Glock and Stark, *Christian Beliefs and Anti-Semitism,* pp. 69–77; and Robb, *Working-Class Anti-Semite.* It is interesting here to note that Levasseur believed in 1899 that antisemitism in the United States was much more a working-class phenomenon than it was in France; see Dagan, op. cit., p. 10.
402 Blum, *Nouvelles Conversations, L'Oeuvre de Léon Blum 1891–1905,* p. 262.
403 Daily Report, Prefect of Police, 29 April 1898. APP Ba 106.
404 Dagan, op. cit., p. 24.
405 Sartre, op. cit., pp. 30–1. This view was also formulated by Julien Benda. On a visit to Memphis (Tennessee) in March 1936, he noted: " 'Waiting room for coloured.' J'évoque: 'Salles d'attente pour juifs; hôtels pour juifs; bains de mer pour juifs . . .' Je suis un blanc et par cela seul, sans que j'aie à faire l'ombre de preuve, fussé-je le pire des idiots ou des bandits, je suis un être supérieur. Je comprends l'antisémitisme." Benda, *Les Cahiers d'un clerc,* p. 25.
406 Drumont, *DB,* p. 17; also *TA,* pp. 29–30.

407 Mirbeau, *Le Journal d'une femme de chambre*, pp. 24, 103–5, 134–41, 146–7 and *passim.*
408 Ibid., p. 105.
409 See my "Catholic Populism in France at the time of the Dreyfus Affair", pp. 674–81. Montuclard argues that a similar paternalism was inherent in the whole Christian Democratic movement.
410 Drumont, *TA*, p. 88.
411 Drumont, *FM*, p. 122.
412 Viau, op. cit., pp. 13–14 and 291.
413 *La Croix Meusienne*, 13 February 1898.
414 See Silberner, "Proudhon's Judeophobia", pp. 62–3; Robert L. Hoffmann, *Revolutionary Justice, The Social and Political Theory of P.-J. Proudhon* (Urbana, Ill., 1972).
415 Drumont, *FJ*, I, pp. 407–8; also II, p. 255.
416 Drumont, *DB*, p. 455.
417 Ibid., p. 16.
418 Arnoulin, *M. Edouard Drumont*, pp. 5–7.
419 Bernanos, op. cit., p. 205.
420 Leroy-Beaulieu, *L'Antisémitisme*, pp. 58–9.
421 Zola, "Procès-Verbal", loc. cit., *L'Affaire Dreyfus, La Vérité en marche*, p. 86.
422 Daudet, *Au Temps de Judas*, pp. 189 and 261.
423 Viau, op. cit., p. 113.
424 See, for example, on the cult of popular bandits and Robin Hood figures: Nisard, *Histoire des Livres Populaires*, I, chapter VIII; E.J. Hobsbawm, *Primitive Rebels; Studies in Archaic Forms of Social Movement in the 19th and 20th Centuries* (New York, 1965, also Manchester, 1972), chapter 2; Articles by R.H. Hilton, J.C. Holt and Maurice Keen, *Past and Present*, nos 14, 18 and 19 (1958 and 1961); Chesneaux, "Critique sociale et thèmes anarchistes chez Jules Verne", pp. 44–50, (on Captain Nemo); and, on the vogue of Flash Gordon (1934), Le Fantôme (1936), Superman (1938), and Batman (1939) in France, see Blanchard, *Histoire de la bande dessinée*, pp. 218–19, 238–41 and 270–2.
425 Fore-Fauré, op. cit., pp. 297–306. The phrase "struggle for life" is in English.
426 It will be argued in chapter XIII, pp. 483–4 below, that racial antisemitism, in particular, was a response to, perhaps an outcome of, prevailing egalitarian norms, a view that derives from Louis Dumont, *Homo Hierarchicus, The Caste System and its Implications* (London, 1972), pp. 27–55 and *passim.*
427 Drumont, *DB*, p. 265
428 Ibid., pp. 38–9.
429 "La Révolution pour l'ordre". Henri Desprez, *L'Esprit conservateur* (Paris, no date), p. 12.

CHAPTER XII

NATIONALIST ANTISEMITISM: "FRANCE FOR THE FRENCH"

WE HAVE SEEN THAT ECONOMIC ANTISEMITISM IN LATER NINETEENTH-CENTURY France had a nationalist emphasis, being directed against foreign immigrants and naturalized French citizens, as well as against vaguer cosmopolitan Jewish financial powers that were supposed to control, or to be planning to take over, the French economy. Similarly, the "socialism" of antisemites was patriotic and nationalist in complexion; it was thoroughly opposed to any orthodox Socialism that had internationalist implications, and it branded Collectivism as something foreign, and alien to French traditions. We must now look more directly at the nationalist component of antisemitic ideology.[1] First, nationalism was one of the most important explicit themes in antisemitic writing and speeches. Secondly, the specifically antisemitic movement was closely connected with the various organizations which, in the 1890s and 1900s, put forward nationalism as their main platform, and these organizations, themselves, subscribed to antisemitism. Thirdly, it was claimed by antisemites that the Jews were indelibly foreign, and that they were involved in a more or less successful conspiracy with other forces to dominate and rule France to the detriment of its native citizens. The nationalism of the antisemites was thus directed, fourthly, against internal enemies primarily; its function had less to do with France's external policy than with dampening potential internal conflict, projecting a hierarchical conception of society, and providing its adherents with security in a world of complexity and change.

I

On the manifest level, and in terms of propaganda, nationalism was one of antisemitism's most important themes. Antisemites were, first of all, against the Jews, but, secondly, they were against the Jews, because they were for France and the French. The wider opposition movement, of which organized antisemitism formed a part, called itself and was known as the "Nationalist" movement.[2] The slogan of *La Libre Parole*, which was adopted by most antisemitic organizations, was "France for the French".[3] Several antisemitic groups used the word "nationalist" or "national" in their names, for example, the Union Nationale, the Jeunesse Antisémite et Nationaliste and the Groupe Antisémite-Nationaliste de Rennes.[4] Drumont dissociated himself from the "revanchisme" of Déroulède and the Boulangists, and even ridiculed the patriotic cult of Alsace-Lorraine, but only because he saw both as ultimately damaging to the national interest;[5] and of his own patriotic intentions there was no doubt. "In combating the harmful influence of the Jews," he proclaimed in February 1895, "in exposing their evil deeds, their exactions and their plunders . . . I have been fighting for the cause of the Nation, and for that cause alone . . ."[6] Similarly, Fore-Fauré stressed in 1891 that antisemites belonged to the "Opposition simply and solely out of concern for the Nation, for France".[7] "For the honour and the salvation of France", appealed the campaign to boycott Jewish shops, in the same vein, "buy nothing from the Jews." Again, Sorlin has pointed out that the revival of antisemitism in La Croix in the 1890s coincided with a conversion to a nationalism of a militarist and Catholic complexion, that antisemitism became for the newspaper a sign of ultra-patriotism[8]; and the same can be said of the Union Nationale and Le Peuple Français[9]. Millevoye, at a meeting in March 1898 of "the antisemites of Montmartre . . . lauded the French nation, the tricolour, the Republic of the French and the Russian alliance", and attacked "the gang of cosmopolitans" and Jews.[10] As a hostile pamphleteer wrote in 1898, "antisemitic propaganda wears a patriotic mask",[11] an observation made by other contemporaries. Leroy-Beaulieu wrote in 1902 that "antisemitism was able to become a political force . . . under the cover of an equivocal nationalism . . .";[12] while Clermont-Tonnerre commented later, with irony: "On the one side, were the Jews, the Protestants and the Freemasons; and, on the other, the upright French citizens, the honest patriots, who called themselves Nationalists."[13]

The meaning of this contrast between Nationalists and Jews becomes clearer in the more explicit and elaborate ideological statements of Barrès. He was an overt antisemite, as we have seen—he and Drumont expressed mutual admiration for each other's works[14]—;he was also one of the first writers, if not the first, in France to use the term "Nationalism" in the new way.[15] For Barrès, nationality was an existential and historical datum, which could only be acquired through many generations of residence in a country and belonging to it. The Jews, therefore, who were recently naturalized citizens, and who maintained their own particular communal ties, had not acquired, and could probably never acquire, French nationality. "The Jewish question is thus linked to the National question", Barrès wrote in his Nancy programme of 1898. "Assimilated to the French of French origin by the Revolution, the Jews have retained their distinctive characteristics; and, having been persecuted in the past, they have become dominant . . . by means of their habits of monopolization and speculation and their cosmopolitanism."[16] And again in 1900:[17]

> The Jews have no homeland, no nation in the sense in which we understand it. For us, the nation is the soil and our ancestors; it is the land of our dead. For them, it is simply the place where it is in their greatest interest, for the

moment, to live. Their "intellectuals" can thus arrive at their notorious definition: "The Nation is an idea." But what idea? That which is most useful to them, for example, the idea that all men are brothers, that nationality is a prejudice that must be destroyed, that military honour stinks of blood, that we should disarm (and leave nothing standing but the power of money) . . .

Some antisemites expressed the same general view by regarding the Jews as a distinct nationality. "They constitute a nation among the other nations, a state within the State . . .", wrote Paul Adam, for example, in 1890.[18] But this only emphasized the argument that Jews were different from and hostile towards the French, for Jewish national sentiment was unattached to French society or territory: "The nation of the Jews," declared one writer in 1901, is in Jerusalem; for them, other countries are only provisional dwelling-places, camping places."[19] Bainville even claimed, misusing a real insight, that "the city on which the affections and attachments of the Jews is centred is not an earthly state at all, but the ideal Zion, the heavenly Jerusalem."[20]

All of this reflected, to some extent, the fact that, as Memmi has written, "the Jew was frequently, *objectively* and legally, a man in breach of nationality or of fragile nationality, a foreigner or a naturalized citizen."[21] As such, Jews posed an ever-present threat to the whole Nationalist concept of the political world, and to the security which it provided. Lazare wrote in 1894 that the Jews "destroyed the idea of the Nation by their presence, that is to say any narrow and particular concept of the nation".[22] "The Jew", agreed Leroy-Beaulieu, "is said to be a foreign body, inassimilable, and denationalizing the peoples in whose midst he takes up his residence. This is a terrible reproach in a century like this, in which the different peoples are showing themselves to be so strongly . . . attached to their nationality."[23] Adopting the antisemites' analysis, although welcoming the consequences which they deplored, Romain Rolland declared in 1912:[24]

The Jews have obeyed their sacred mission, which is to remain, among the other races, the foreign people, the people, which weaves, from one end of the world to the other, the web of human unity. They break down the intellectual barriers of nations, to make a free field for the action of divine Reason. The worst corrupters, the ironical destroyers of our traditional beliefs, those who kill the memory of our beloved ancestors, they are all working without realizing it at a sacred task, they are all creating new life.

It should be pointed out here, however, that although some French Jewish intellectuals, as we have seen, did put forward the idea that the Jews embodied a universal revolutionary spirit that was inimical to nationalism, and although, largely as a result of the Dreyfus Affair and of the revival of antisemitism in the 1890s, some, including Lazare, became Zionists, most French Jews were anxious to make very explicit their attachment to France, and often did so in ultra-patriotic terms. As Mauriac has commented, one of the supreme ironies of the Affair was the fact that Dreyfus was himself intensely patriotic, precisely because he was an Alsatian Jew.[25]

The identification of nationalism and antisemitism was clearly expressed in organizational terms. Antisemitic organizations were nationalist in name and policy, and Nationalist organizations openly espoused antisemitism. Leroy-Beaulieu commented cynically:[26]

> The men and the parties who compete for power have not been ashamed to hold out their hands to antisemitism. Nationalists on the one hand, Royalists on the other, have not blushed to beg favours of it. How could men of ambition, indeed, fail to do just this, since in welcoming antisemitism, they earned themselves applause, at the same time, in the salons and in the street? If they did not always dare to adopt its colours openly, they willingly borrowed its jargon; they took over its specious slogan: "France for the French". They were not afraid to associate themselves with its vague social ideas, and they made much of its simplistic racial philosophy of history.

As this suggests, antisemitic and Nationalist groups were also rivals, and the whole movement was disparate, united only in opposition, torn by petty quarrels.[27]

> It is not a party with a doctrine, a method, a programme. [declared Louis Barthou in 1902] It is a loose coalition of disappointments and resentments, of ambitions and appetites. Its triumph would be the very signal for its downfall. The vehement apostle of graduated income tax rubs shoulders there with the die-hard partisans of social conservatism. Displaced Freemasons exchange smiles with rebellious monks. Such and such an ex-*communard* hob-nobs with a certain ex-Minister of War. Unconverted Jews there profess antisemitism. The French Academy descends into the street and mingles its smart green uniform with the white blouses of news-vendors. Even Boulangism never offered us so odd a mixture.

And partisans, by this time, made the same observation, with sadness rather than glee. Maurras wrote to Barrès in April 1901: "Everyone agrees on the general issue of nationalism. So: Long live the Nation, France, the army, etc. Slogans of this kind are the order of the day . . . But no one agrees on the means that are necessary to put nationalism into practice."[28] Disagreement and rivalry existed, in particular, between the "professional" antisemites and other Nationalists, who were more consciously "using" antisemitism. Guérin, for example, at a meeting of the Ligue Antisémitique Française in February 1898, expressed the fear "that the antisemitic movement might get merged in the purely Nationalist movement. This is why he required, from now on, of speakers, and particularly of Millevoye and Thiébaud, a clear declaration of antisemitism."[29] And, later, he pointed out that Drumont and Déroulède, leader of the Ligue des Patriotes, had attacked each other in print, and claimed that quarrels of this kind between antisemites and Nationalists had lost the opposition seats in the 1902 elections.[30]

But this in-fighting and political rivalry (which existed also within the antisemitic movement proper, as we have seen) overlaid a basic similarity in attitude, and should not disguise the fact that during the period of the Dreyfus Affair, Nationalists and antisemites were able to maintain a relatively common front, and, more important, presented a relatively homogeneous ideology.[31] The circumstances of the Affair and the hostile attitude of the government from 1899 helped to maintain this coherence in the opposition movement, and in public conception of it. Most obviously, when repressive action was taken against the anti-Dreyfusard opposition in 1899 and 1900, the leaders of the four most important component organizations of that opposition, the Ligue des Patriotes, the Ligue Antisémitique Française, the Jeunesse Antisémite and the Royalist L'Oeillet Blanc, were arrested and put on trial together.[32] Another factor to take account of in this context, and which lent the Nationalist movement consistency as well as earning it support, was the very general acceptance in France at the time of the legitimacy of patriotism. Patriotism and Nationalism can be distinguished by historians, and were distinguished by contemporaries, but the distinction was not at first easy to make. Even an intellectual and a political opponent of the Nationalists, like Jules Renard, could write in a letter in 1901: "But, my dear friend, are we not all, basically, unfortunate nationalists?".[33]

All the main Nationalist organizations in France in the period espoused antisemitism in varying degrees, as well as having relations with the specifically antisemitic movement and press. This is true of the oldest ultra-patriotic movement in France, Bonapartism, which seems in the late 1890s, in Paris particularly, to have sought to retrieve its dwindling fortunes through a partial reversion to its own democratic tradition, running parallel to an involvement in the popular campaign against the Jews.[34] Dubuc, the president of the Jeunesse Antisémite, was an active Bonapartist;[35] and antisemitism was frequently expressed in Bonapartist meetings in the capital in 1898, if only through combining the slogans: "Down with the Jews!" and "Long live the Emperor!"[36] The Bonapartist deputies Paul de Cassagnac and Lasies (from the Gers) were well known as antisemites, and belonged to the antisemitic parliamentary group.[37] Moreover, although he was personally involved in political competition with the Bonapartists, Drumont expressed sympathy for both the First and the Second Empires, and reminded readers of *La France juive* that Napoleon I had "controlled" the Jews with special legislation.[38]

Boulangism, which was in many ways a popular non-dynastic Bonapartism,[39] provided another link between Nationalism and antisemitism. The original Boulangist movement of the late 1880s, taking its cue from Boulanger himself, showed little interest in antisemitism,[40] though, as we have seen, some of the first antisemitic deputies, Laur, Delahaye, Barrès, were Boulangists.[41] However, the remnants of the Boulangist movement, which survived to play an important part in the Nationalist and anti-Dreyfusard movement a decade later, often adopted it wholeheartedly. Contemporaries pointed out that, in its aims and its style, the anti-Dreyfusard movement had all the characteristics of Boulangism, that it was, in effect, a "neo-Boulangism".[42] Léon Blum explained that many ex-Boulangists saw in the agitation of the Affair an opportunity to avenge the failure of their own movement: "The Boulangist cadres had, to a large extent, survived Boulanger. The most resolute and faithful of the Boulangist leaders were still there, closely linked and in touch with each other, despite the extreme diversity of their origins, and breathing vengeance."[43] Lanessan could even write, in *Le Rappel* in January 1898, that "Boulangism has become antisemitism . . ."[44] Drumont claimed in 1890 that Boulangism had been "launched by a Jewish syndicate",[45] and he continued to criticize the movement in the mid- and late 1890s.[46] But he had voted Boulangist in 1889,[47] and he then blamed Boulanger's failure on his Jewish entourage, rather than his own incompetence, and, in retrospect, bestowed praise on the Boulangists for their patriotic endeavour.[48] Moreover, despite this coolness on the part of the antisemitic leader, Boulangists had been prominent in the first Ligue Antisémitique de France of 1889, and Drumont acted as honorary president of a Ligue Radicale Antisémite, founded in 1892, according to the police, as an instrument of liaison between the antisemites and the Left-wing Boulangists.[49] Co-president with him was Morès, who was more openly pro-Boulangist.[50]

Simultaneously, and more positively, many ex-Boulangists combined an attachment to their former leader with declarations of nationalism and antisemitism. Déroulède, whose espousal of antisemitism was hesitant, but ultimately clear, as we shall see below, proclaimed in the mid-1890s: "How many times have I not shouted in public meetings at which I have been reproached with having been a Boulangist . . . "No, I have not been a Boulangist . . . I still am a Boulangist."[51] Millevoye, whom we have already encountered as an antisemitic orator, "saluted the memory of Boulanger" at a meeting organized at the Salle Wagram in Paris by the Ligue Antisémitique Française in March 1898; and, at another antisemitic meeting in the same month, after attacking the Jews, "he evoked Boulanger, who had not allowed the gang of cosmopolitans to carry on their work of dissolving French patriotism . . ."[52] Millevoye, who had been a Boulangist deputy, was elected on an antisemitic ticket in 1898, as we have seen; and at least two other candidates in the 1898 elections in Paris had made a similar switch: Vervoort, who stood as an "anti-Jewish patriot" in the 18th *arrondissement,* and the "Socialist" Roche, who stood in the same *arrondissement* and who boasted to a public meeting that he had been "a fervent Boulangist".[53] Barrès, too, of course, had been a Boulangist deputy, and, if he later acknowledged the shortcomings of the earlier movement, he maintained a commitment to its memory and to its populist patriotism, as he evolved later in a conservative direction. Most important, Barrès had been an antisemitic Boulangist. As Sternhell writes: "The Boulangist candidate at Nancy [in 1889] was one of the first, if not the first French politician, to exploit the revival of antisemitism in the 1880s."[54] Other Boulangists who were actively involved in the Nationalist and antisemitic movement of the 1890s included Susini, Paul Adam, Paulin-Méry, Chiché, André Castelin, Borie, Le Hérissé and Vacher; the last six were antisemitic deputies in 1898.[55] Nor should two more important figures be forgotten here: Rochefort, whom we discussed in the last chapter; and Georges Thiébaud. Thiébaud, a conservative ex-Bonapartist, had been Boulanger's electoral and fund-raising manager. He abandoned the cause after Boulanger's flight from France in 1889, and later joined the Ligue des Patriotes and the Ligue de la

Patrie Française. He was also a leading member of the first Ligue Antisémitique, and an occasional contributor to *La Libre Parole*. Bournand referred to him in 1898 in these terms: "In his speeches and his writings, M. Georges Thiébaud has always shown himself to be one of the *leaders* of antisemitism and one of the most ardent defenders of French Catholicism against what he calls the *Jewish-Protestant Invasion*."[56]

The Ligue des Patriotes was the oldest of the Nationalist leagues of the 1890s, and provided another direct link between the Nationalist movement and Boulangism, which it had vigorously supported.[57] Antisemitism was not one of its original characteristics, although there is some evidence that, by 1890, its leader, Paul Déroulède, was prepared to make public statements of an antisemitic kind. This is the more significant in that Déroulède enjoyed a popularity unequalled by the other Nationalist leaders;[58] and, more, that his patriotic poetry had been accorded a kind of official status, being recited on public occasions and learned by heart in state schools.[59] Déroulède attended the first major antisemitic rally in France, at Neuilly in January 1890, sitting on the platform alongside Drumont and Morès, and, according to Viau, he there declared himself to be "the enemy of the Jews."[60] In the Chamber of Deputies, to which he had been elected as deputy for Angoulême in 1890, he made similar pronouncements, accusing the Jews, for example, in October 1891 of wanting "to dechristianize France",[61] and objecting in December 1892 to the fact that Cornélius Herz had been made a *chévalier* of the Légion d'Honneur on the grounds that he was "a little German Jew".[62] However, Viau wrote also that, although Déroulède came frequently to the offices of *La Libre Parole* in the late 1890s, and had information and publicity about the activities of the Ligue des Patriotes inserted in the newspaper:[63]

> I don't believe that he much liked Drumont, who had at one time cruelly ridiculed him in his books, on the subject of his Boulangism. Déroulède claimed not to be an antisemite, and, for that reason, was not very fond of Guérin either; moreover, rightly or wrongly, he suspected Guérin of having some agreement with the Royalists. The members of his league never mixed with members of the Grand Occident or of the Jeunesse Antisémitique. To sum up, these different elements of the *active Opposition* were rivals, and, till 1899 at least, followed no common policy.

As we have seen, Guérin also indicated that serious differences existed between Drumont and Déroulède, and between Déroulède and himself.[64] Moreover, it was true, as Viau claimed, that Drumont had, in the past ridiculed Déroulède and his league. Déroulède was described in *La France juive* as "an imbecile", "a poseur", and "this dangerous and conceited braggart of patriotism";[65] and Drumont later pointed to the fact that Naquet, "this infamous Jew", was a vice-president of the Ligue des Patriotes.[66] Similarly, Léon Daudet and Maurras, while expressing a certain admiration for Déroulède, were highly critical of him as a politician; and Daudet, like Drumont, saw him as an essentially comic figure: "He was a hero of Corneille who had wandered into a farce by his uncle Emile Augier . . ."[67]

But although these rivalries, suspicions and hostile judgments existed between Déroulède and the antisemitic leaders, there is little doubt of Déroulède's serious commitment to antisemitism by the time of the Affair, nor that, by 1898, the Ligue des Patriotes was an overtly antisemitic organization.[68] As we have seen in an earlier chapter, the revival of the Ligue was directly linked with the development of anti-Dreyfusard agitation, but its antisemitism was frequently more directly expressed. Seven of the antisemitic deputies elected in May 1898 either belonged to the Ligue or publicly supported it, and three of them belonged to the antisemitic parliamentary group.[69] In June 1898 Marcel Habert, Déroulède's second-in-command, delivered "a long patriotic and anti-Jewish speech" at a public meeting in Paris.[70] According to the police again, the initiative for the reconstitution of the Ligue des Patriotes in Marseille in September and at Valenciennes in December 1898 was taken by local antisemitic groups;[71] and, in June 1899, the police referred to the Loge des Amis de Morès in Marseille as "a branch" of the Ligue des Patriotes.[72] In July 1899, speeches by Déroulède, Habert and Coppée at a Ligue meeting in Paris were greeted with shouts of "Death to the Jews!";[73] and the following month a police agent reported: "The Ligue des Patriotes has decided to support Guérin to the hilt . . ."[74] That the authorities took such a report of a community of interest, to say nothing of a conspiracy, between the two extremist organizations seriously is indicated, as we have already mentioned, by the simultaneous arrest of the leaders of both the Ligue des Patriotes and the Ligue Antisémitique Française shortly afterwards.

In the subsequent period of repression, and following the banishment of Déroulède and the imprisonment of Guérin, the Ligue des Patriotes seems to have made an even stronger affirmation of antisemitism. Shouts of "Down with the Jews!" appear to have been commonplace at Ligue meetings in Paris through 1900.[75] At Le Mans and Laval in late 1899 and 1900, stickers reading: "Down with the Jews!" and "Long live Déroulède!", and of the same format, were posted together.[76] A Ligue meeting in Paris in January 1901 attended by 3,000 people was addressed by Max Régis, former antisemitic mayor of Algiers, who associated "Guérin with Déroulède and Habert".[77] A regionalist and Nationalist congress held in Rouen the same month passed a resolution in support of Déroulède, Habert and Guérin, and broke up with shouts of "Down with the Jews!"[78] At this time, moreover, the organ of the Ligue, *Le Drapeau*, was being edited by Barrès.[79] Although Déroulède declined an invitation to the annual banquet of *La Libre Parole* in 1903,[80] the police reported that: "The new campaign, which the Nationalist party (and particularly the Ligue de Patriotes) is going to open on the subject of the revival of the Dreyfus Affair, will be mainly directed against the Freemasons and against the Jews";[81] and, in January 1904, Gaston Méry told a Ligue meeting at Saint-Cloud that "the division that in the past separated the two leaders Drumont and Déroulède no longer exists, since Déroulède's complete adhesion to antisemitism [in a New Year's message to his supporters] . . ."[82] The following year, at a meeting in Levallois-Perret, Habert similarly made a public declaration of his adhesion "to the authentic brand of antisemitism of which

. . . M. Drumont is the sole representative."[83] Although this change in attitude on the part of the leaders of the Ligue des Patriotes is in large part a function of the internal history of the Ligue and of its relations with other Nationalist organizations, and, as such, is not of enormous intrinsic importance, it has also to be explained as a move of desperation on their part in face of the declining fortunes of the Ligue and of the whole Nationalist movement after 1899; and here it does reflect a fundamental characteristic of the ideology which they reflected and formulated. Antisemitism and nationalism were the two sides of one coin, and when one side seemed to be losing its effect, it was natural to put more emphasis on the other. Thus, paradoxically, as antisemitism generally lost ground as a political force, the Ligue des Patriotes clung more anxiously to it; and this mechanism can be detected in the behaviour of the other leagues, too.

The same rivalries and jealousies that existed between the antisemitic movement and the Ligue des Patriotes existed also between that movement and the Ligue de la Patrie Française.[84] The rapprochement of Drumont and the Ligue des Patriotes from 1900, indeed, seems to have been directed against the more successful Patrie Française, which Drumont had initially supported.[85] Viau claimed that the success of the Nationalists in the 1900 municipal elections in Paris was primarily a victory for the Patrie Française, which Drumont very much resented, feeling that his own influence was on the wane. To counter what he regarded as "the attempt to take over Antisemitism by these last-minute converts", he founded a new organization, as we have seen, the Comité National Antijuif, to fight the 1902 elections, as well as moving closer to Déroulède.[86] At the same time, the Patrie Française seems to have made overtures to Guérin and to the remnants of the Ligue Antisémitique Française.[87] All of this indicates, as Leroy-Beaulieu pointed out, that antisemitism was still seen after 1900 as a potential vote-catcher, and a political platform that was worth squabbling over; moreover, as in the case of the Ligue des Patriotes, incidental differences between the antisemitic movement, or sections of it, and the Ligue de la Patrie Française overlay a clear commitment on the part of the latter to antisemitic ideology.

Like the Ligue des Patriotes, but more so, the Ligue de la Patrie Française, which was essentially a grouping of conservative intellectuals, Barthou's French Academy taking to the street, expressed some initial hesitations about adopting antisemitism. The literary critic Jules Lemaître, first president of the Ligue and one of its main speakers, made a pro-Jewish speech in January 1899, two months after the Ligue had been founded, pointing to "the great intellectual calibre of the children of Israel scattered over the globe", and lamenting that the Ligue did not have more Jewish members.[88] At this stage also, Brunetière, one of the founders of the Ligue, whose ambivalent attitude towards antisemitism we have already discussed, was reported as saying: "We most definitely reject antisemitism as a doctrine . . .", although he added: "This does not prevent us from welcoming the antisemites . . . among us." However, Barrès, another founder member of the Ligue, objected to this as a statement of Ligue policy, and, as we know, his own antisemitism was openly proclaimed. It seems probable that Barrès's influence was important in shifting the Ligue's attitude here,[89] in combination with general considerations of expediency and simple swimming with the tide. Léon Daudet wrote later that "antisemitism, which had become an impetuous national current of opinion, was amply represented among the leaders of the Patrie Française."[90] Certainly, from 1900, antisemitism, and not merely anti-Dreyfusism, occupied an important place in the Ligue's propaganda. A speaker from the Patrie Française, for example, made a speech attacking the Jews at Epernay in April 1900;[91] another told a working-class audience at Senones in November 1900 that the Jews were taking over France, and must be excluded from the army and the civil service.[92] In the same month, at Saint-Dié, a speaker at a Patrie Française meeting, attended by 1,000 people, said that the Ligue "is not antisemitic", which, he explained, meant that it was tolerant of Jewish religious beliefs; but, he went on: "What it will not put up with, is the intrusion of Jews into the internal or the external policy of France", adding that the Ligue was for "France for the French", and that the Jews were an alien race.[93] At another big Patrie Française meeting at Nancy in December 1901 addressed by Lemaître, Cavaignac and General Mercier, Charles Bernard, antisemitic deputy for Bordeaux, made a similar and more outright attack on the Jews.[94] Nor were such expressions of antisemitism on the part of the Ligue's speakers confined to the East, where they could be expected to earn special popular approval. At a Patrie Française conference at Joinville-le-Pont in April 1901, a speaker delivered an attack on the government and "the Jewish-Masonic sect";[95] while in February 1902 Lemaître gave a talk to La Jeunesse Catholique et Antijuive de Saint-Germain-en-Laye.[96] At Lille, moreover, the local section of the Patrie Française had been founded in August 1899 with the support of Dubuc, national president of the Jeunesse Antisémite.[97]

The antisemitism of the Action Française, the longest-lived of the anti-Dreyfusard leagues, was much more clear-cut, although this fact was obscured in retrospect by its leaders. Where the Ligue des Patriotes and the Ligue de la Patrie Française had been initially hesitant and had then adopted antisemitism openly from 1899 or 1900, the Action Française espoused and propagated a thorough-going antisemitism in this period, which, much later, it played down, specifically repudiating some of its violent and racialist implications.[98] However, Maurras was sufficiently honest in Au Signe de Flore (1931) to write: "Real, profound and moderate, our antisemitism cannot lose sight of the fact that it is not our business to revive 'those wars of race and religion', which the [Pretender's] San Remo Manifesto deprecates. 'Well-bred' Jews have thus been welcomed in our movement"; but to add: "But this does not in any way diminish the need to combat, to fight as hard as we can against their congenerates . . . suspicion of . . . the Jewish 'State' had top priority in our research and enquiries"; or, again, that "Shut up, you insolent Jew! Here comes the king!" could have been the slogan of the early Action Française.[99] As we have seen, Maurras, himself, was one of the leading antisemitic intellectuals of the turn of the century. Author of "Le Premier Sang", celebrating the patriotic martyrdom of Colonel Henry, he was also an occasional contributor to *La Libre Parole;* [100] and his antisemitism seems to have become even more marked in the decade before the First World War, if his letters to Barrès are any guide. [101] On the general level, it is certain that the Action Française kept organized antisemitism alive in France after the eclipse of most other movements around 1906. [102] In 1911, in reply to the assertion by Larègle and Judet that antisemitism could no longer be regarded as a serious political programme, Maurras riposted: "The time will come, one of these days, to demonstrate how, on the contrary, it is precisely via the antisemitic programme that all the rest of the nationalist and Royalist programme will be translated from theory to action, and put into execution." [103] This echoed the view of one of the founders of the movement, Henri Vaugeois, expressed in 1900: "One has to be an antisemite; this, we must get across to the Nationalists; for antisemitism is, in effect, the psychological root of all the ideas and sentiments which have brought the Nationalists together in the first place." [104]

The strength of this conviction is evident from the place accorded to antisemitism in the action and propaganda of the neo-Royalist movement. In May 1900, for example, Xavier de Magallon gave a speech in honour of Morès at an Action Française meeting. [105] In December 1901, the Action Française organized an antisemitic conference in the Eure, which was addressed by Gaston Méry, and by two antisemitic deputies, Firmin Faure and Charles Bernard; according to the Prefect: "The meeting, which was particularly antisemitic in orientation, ended with shouts of 'Down with the Jews' . . ." [106] A decade later, the Action Française organized demonstrations against the staging of Bernstein's *Après Moi* at the Comédie Française, and plastered the theatre and its environs with stickers that read: "The Jewish Deserter"—only one example of its continuation of minor antisemitic demonstrations in the decade before 1914. [107] Nor were such demonstrations confined to the capital. The Marseille group organized a demonstration in January 1909 on the occasion of the presentation at the Théâtre du Gymnase of *Le Foyer* by "the Anarchist Mirbeau" and "the Jew Natanson". [108] Moreover, as Paugam has recently indicated, the *Revue de l'Action Française* propagated in the decade after 1899, albeit to a restricted audience, an ideologically extreme type of antisemitism, such as Maurras and others later disclaimed. Bainville, for example, in March 1901, called for the expulsion of Jews from public employment in France, referring to "the eternal chimerical imagination of their race". Vaugeois wrote in August 1900 of his "almost physical sense of repulsion against the Jew and his skin, a 'primitive' sensation that most of the lofty souls of today regard with disdain . . ."; while Robert Launay remarked of the Jew in June 1901: "In creating this animal half-way between a monkey and a man, one can only think that the good Lord was playing a practical joke . . ." [109] Reaching a much wider audience were the contributions of Léon Daudet to *La Libre Parole,* for which he was a leader-writer from 1900 until 1908, [110] and his antisemitic novels, such as *Les Morticoles* (1894) and *Le Pays des parlementeurs* (1901). As we have seen, moreover, despite Drumont's hostility to political Royalism, Daudet was his consistent admirer and, in a sense, his disciple.

II

Having established the general involvement of the Nationalist movement in antisemitism, as well as the importance of nationalism as a theme of the organized antisemitic movement, it remains to examine the content and meaning of this interlocking nationalist antisemitism on the ideological level, and to suggest what its sociological functions may have been. The main charge laid against Jews here was that they were not French but foreign, and therefore, from a nationalist point of view, alien invaders of France and actual or potential traitors. Along with other alien forces, they represented a permanent international conspiracy aimed at dominating and ultimately destroying France.

"Can a Jew be French?", asked Jarzel's *Petit Catéchisme nationaliste* of 1901, and replied: "He can be so only by preferring the French nation to the Jewish race. In reality, the Jew belongs to a nationality that is scattered throughout the civilized world, and which does not mix with the other nations among whom it pitches camp."[111] In 1898 Bournand quoted the former Minister of Public Instruction, Alfred Rambaud, in the same general sense: "The Jews are like an Asiatic colony established in France. They live in our country as in a foreign land, a land that is foreign three times over, for they are neither French, nor Christian, nor even European."[112] As we have seen, antisemites disagreed as to whether the Jews did in fact constitute a nation. The Socialist Chirac, for example, wrote in 1888 that the Jews were a separate nation within the French nation.[113] Drumont, in *La France juive*, quoted Portalis: the Jewish people "exists among all the nations without being mixed with them; the Jews always feel that they are living in a foreign country . . . everywhere they form a nation within the nation; they are neither French, nor German, nor English, nor Prussian, they are Jewish."[114] But *La Croix* was less categorical, expressing doubts about Jewish claims to the dignity of nationhood;[115] while Dom Besse of the Action Française wrote that "the Jews are foreigners and foreigners of a special kind. There is no Jewish nation; and this lack of nationality makes resistance to Jewish penetration very difficult."[116] However, there was no doubt on the negative side: the Jews were not French. Abbé Garnier asserted in 1894: "the Jews are not and have never been French."[117] Léon Blum wrote that "the theoreticians of antisemitism presented the contribution of the Jews to a society as the introduction of a foreign body into it, a body that it was impossible to assimilate, and against which the parent organism opposed a natural defensive reflex."[118] Drumont made the common claim in 1892 that: "These people really do not have brains like ours; their evolution is different from ours; and everything to do with them is exceptional and odd . . . No one knows where they come from; their life is a mystery, and their deaths are obscure . . .",[119] an expression of a fundamental otherness, which we will examine further in the context of racial ideas.

But, from the idea, the feeling that Jews were different and foreign, "the foreigners of the interior", in the words of Barrès,[120] it followed, for antisemites, that Jews must be enemies in the midst, the equivalent, probably the ally, inside France's frontiers of the country's foreign enemies. "Despite all his protestations," wrote Fore-Fauré in 1891, "the Semite remains the foreigner *par excellence,* the enemy."[121] In the same year, Jacques de Biez asserted: "the peril within is more threatening than ever; and the peril within is the Jewish peril."[122] Léon Harmel referred in December 1897 to "the internal Triple Alliance, the coalition of Freemasons, Jews and Protestants",[123] a common idea in the antisemitic propaganda of the period, and, again, a way of casting the Jew as an enemy. The Prospectus of *La Croisade Française* declared in the same terms in 1898 that "Its programme of action was the struggle against the internal Triple Alliance of the enemies of the Nation: the Jews, Freemasonry and Protestantism";[124] while a pamphlet entitled *Le Complôt protestant* claimed in 1899: "There exists . . . a Triple Alliance inside France as well as outside. This alliance is as much the enemy of France as the alliance of Germany, Austria and Italy, to which, moreover, it is connected by many ramifications."[125] Simpler, and more familiar, was the claim that Jews were German. Many writers attached the epithet "German" to "Jew" almost without thinking, as a matter of course.[126] Drumont made a distinction between German and non-German Jews, an approximation to the distinction between Ashkenazim and Sephardim, but claimed that the German Jew was "the real Jew";[127] and, in political terms, that "Jewish influence corresponds with German hegemony in the world . . ."[128]

Since the Jews were foreigners and enemies living in France, it followed that they were spies[129] and traitors, thus expressing an eternal Jewish penchant, most obviously symbolized in the betrayal of Christ by Judas. The word "Judas" was used in common parlance to mean traitor;[130] and Judas the traitor was a traditional stereotype in popular literature,[131] and figured also in popular Easter rituals.[132] Hugo, whose prestige in France in the last third of the century equalled if it did not exceed that of Béranger in the 1830s and 1840s, referred to "the soul of black Judas".[133] Antisemites thus had a ready-made myth to exploit. Léon Bloy declared of the Jews in 1892: "Judas is their type, their prototype, their archetype, or, if one prefers, the definitive paradigm of the ignoble and sempiternal conjugations of their avarice . . ."[134] Drumont wrote in *La France juive:* "It is incontestable that every Jew betrays the person who employs him",[135] and cited a large number of examples, including Simon Deutz, who allegedly betrayed the Duchesse de Berry in 1832,[136] and Mme de Païva.[137] More generally, he claimed that French involvement and defeat in the Franco-Prussian War was the result of a grand Jewish betrayal.[138] Similarly, the Italian Jesuit organ, *La Civiltà Cattolica,* which was widely quoted in France, wrote in February 1898: "The Jew was created by God to serve as a spy, wherever treason was being prepared";[139] while a pamphlet, entitled *La Fin de la France: Le complôt juif,* produced at the time of the Rennes trial in 1899, referred to "the Jews, a people of traitors . . ."[140]

As these last two examples remind us, the Dreyfus Affair was, of course, both an instance on a monumental scale, and the occasion for the extensive development, of this theme of Jewish treason. Blum, again recalled:[141]

To appreciate "the Affair" correctly, one must remember that Dreyfus was a Jew, that once a Jew always a Jew, that the Jewish race is impervious to certain moral concepts, that it is marked by certain hereditary taints! And one of these ethnic traits, indefinitely inheritable, was it not precisely the innate predisposition to treason? Had not whole centuries shunned the Jewish race as the descendants of Judas? . . . the antisemites thus did not hesitate to . . . presume Dreyfus guilty, simply because he was a Jew. The race of the criminal provided them with an overriding explanation for the crime. As antisemitism, in other areas was able to affect the specious appearance of a movement of social protest, so the intervention of the army High Command allowed it here to take on the fine air of patriotism.

Thus Daudet called his memoirs of the period, *Au Temps de Judas;* Barrès entitled his account of the degradation of Dreyfus in January 1895: "La Parade de Judas"; and wrote during the Rennes trial: "That Dreyfus is capable of treason, I conclude from his race . . . Through these long hearings, I have watched the face of Dreyfus, sweating treason."[142] *La Croix* commented on the news of Dreyfus's original arrest: "It is the Jewish enemy betraying France";[143] and Drumont, in *La Libre Parole*, expressed the same knowing lack of surprise:[144]

> The affair of Captain Dreyfus . . . is simply another episode in Jewish history. Judas sold the God of mercy and love. Deutz gave up the heroic woman who had entrusted herself to his honour. Simon Mayer ripped the tricolour flag from the Vendôme column and threw it on a dungheap. Naquet and Arthur Meyer deceived poor General Boulanger and led him to his ruin . . . Captain Dreyfus has sold to Germany our mobilization plans and the names of our intelligence agents. This is all just a fatal running to type, the curse of the race. And it is ourselves and not the Jews who are really guilty; for they could quite rightly say to us: why have you broken with the tradition of your ancestors? Why do you entrust your secrets to those who have always betrayed you?

But Jews were not only occasional predestined and impenitent traitors; their presence in France represented a full-scale foreign invasion. In *La France juive*, Drumont traced the various phases of this invasion through the course of French history. Beginning before the Revolution, Jewish infiltration was only given its head with legal emancipation, and a position of dominance was only achieved by the time of the Third Republic:[145]

> In 1790, the Jew arrived; under the first Republic and under the first Empire, he came in, prowled about and looked for a place for himself; under the Restoration and the July Monarchy, he took a seat in the salon; under the Second Empire, he began to sleep in the beds; under the Third Republic, he began to drive out the French from their home or to force them to work for him.

This fear of invasion, of being turned out of house and home, graphically conveyed in Drumont's metaphor, became common in antisemitic writing at the end of the century. Barrès's Nancy Programme of 1898 announced:[146]

At the top of the social edifice as well as in the depths of the provinces, in the moral as well as the material order of things, in the commercial, the industrial and the agricultural worlds, and, even on the shop floor where he is competing with French workers, the foreigner, like a parasite, is taking away our strength. Any new policy for France must be based on the principle that French nationals must be protected against this invasion . . . The Jewish question is linked to the national question.

As we have seen, this sense of being invaded stemmed in part from experience of an objectively high incidence of immigration into France, and hostility to immigrants as such, whether Jewish or not, tended to blend with resistance to post-emancipation efforts to assimilate on the part of Jews.[147] Thus Barrès elsewhere referred to France's being "so brutally invaded", and to "the kingdom of Israel which has so marvellously developed in the course of our Third Republic".[148] Maurras, too, immediately assumed that foreign shop names in the 1880s in Paris were Jewish, and asked: "Are the French at home in their own country?"[149] The debating society, the Conférence Molé-Toqueville, invited the government in the spring of 1898 "to take the necessary measures to stop the dangerous invasion [of France] by the Jewish race".[150] And Drumont, again, had warned in 1889: "the Jewish tide is rising ceaselessly, and any Frenchman, who has not sufficiently recovered his wits to recognize where the enemy is, will have to give way to the invader. [Even then] how will the native be able to resist, since the police, the magistracy, authority in all its forms, influence in all its manifestations, now belong to the German Jew?"[151] Such, of course, was the message conveyed by the title of La France juive. Moreover, Drumont, like Barrès, pointed out that the Jewish invasion was a moral as well as a material phenomemon. "French souls had been invaded by the Semitic spirit", he wrote in 1890.[152] The persistence of such claims and of the fears that lay behind them is indicated by the fact that they were being reiterated in much the same terms twenty years later by Daudet. Over the last four decades, he asserted in L'Avant-Guerre (1913), "the Jew and the German have patiently and silently . . . accomplished their infiltration of our country"; they have worked in collusion, he wrote, to "treat us as a conquered country . . . to undermine our cultural heritage, and to threaten our property and even our lives . . ."[153]

As these last quotations demonstrate, the Jewish "invasion" did not merely represent, for antisemites, the presence in France of a strange and foreign community, but meant that France was under foreign occupation, under foreign rule. For abbé Chabauty, for example, the Jews were "our masters".[154] Drumont wrote, in La France juive, of "the Jewish army" that was taking over France, and referred to "the conquest of all Christian States by the Jew", citing Toussenel to the effect that: "Europe is now enfeoffed to the power of Israel".[155] Pursuing the military metaphor, he later evoked "the triumphal entry of the Jews into Parisian society";[156] and claimed that "the Jews have put France to pillage . . ."[157] Jacques de Biez, similarly, referred to France as "a conquered province";[158] and Bishop Meurin to "the state of subjection of Christian peoples . . . under Jewish domination";[159] while abbé Lemire told the Lyon Christian Democratic Congress of 1898 that France had been "delivered into the hands of the Protestants, the Jews and the Freemasons . . ."[160]

We saw, in the context of economic antisemitism, that the Jews were seen to be running or ruining the French economy, particularly via their financial manipulations, but, as these various statements indicate, this was only part of a wider picture of Jewish power and domination. "The history of the Jew, Picard told Bournand, "is made up of monopolies and of conquests . . ."[161] Guérin, for example, at an antisemitic meeting in Paris in March 1898, "described the economic situation, and showed the Jew introducing himself everywhere, in the world of finance, in the administration of justice, in the civil service."[162] Drumont, too, claimed that the Jews controlled not only the economy, but also high society, the political system, the Légion d'Honneur, the Academy, the magistracy and the press.[163] And such claims were commonplace in antisemitic propaganda. A speaker at a Union Nationale meeting in Vincennes in January 1898 said that "the Jews had got their hands on half France's wealth . . ."[164] Chirac told a Jeunesse Antisémite meeting in April 1898 that France was in danger of becoming another Poland, "the victim of Jewish usurers and cosmopolitans."[165] Maurras recalled that, at the time of the Affair:[166]

> Paris opened its eyes: Jewish salons had the upper hand. The newspapers it opened were Jewish newspapers. People thought that the Jews were just financiers, in control of Money. But Money had delivered everything else into their hands: an important sector of the University, an equivalent sector of the judicial administration, a sector, less important but appreciable, of the army, at its highest levels.

The same idea was conveyed in the title of a volume in Victor Joze's series of novels, *Les Rozenfeld: Histoire d'une famille juive sous la Troisième République*, published in 1904, *La Conquête de Paris.*[167] Similarly, a speaker at the Congrès Nationaliste des Ardennes, in March 1900, asserted: "The Jewish cabal is in control of everything . . ."[168]

In this perspective, antisemitism was conceived to be a legitimate movement of defence on the part of French people, a movement of resistance to the fact or the threat of foreign domination. Jacques de Biez explained that he was an antisemite, "because France is under the orders of the Jews and not of our own people . . ."[169] Georges Romain presented the struggle against "the masonic and Jewish perils", in 1895, as "an economic and patriotic war against invaders who claim to lord it in our country, and who want to monopolize all the positions of power and influence in France, as well as controlling its wealth."[170] The cartoonist Forain denied that he was "an antisemite, in the strict sense", and told Bournand that he had only founded the satirical anti-Dreyfusard (and antisemitic) periodical *Psst!* in reaction to "the odious manoeuvres of the [Jewish] Syndicate . . . I thought that the time had come for patriots to close ranks against these blackguards, against these foreigners . . ."[171] Royalist stickers posted in Lille in February 1898 quoted the Pretender, the

Duc d'Orléans as saying: "I would rather get my head broken than submit to Jewish domination!"[172] Barrès wrote in Le Journal in October 1898: "The moment that one realizes the enormous power of the Jewish nation, which threatens to overthrow the French State, any objections one might have to the antisemitic movement are removed."[173] The pamphlet, La Fin de la France: Le complôt juif (1899) sounded a shriller note of alarm: "It is with terror that I ask myself if we French people have at our disposal, to protect the very heart of our country, weapons that can in any way match those [used by the Jews] . . ."[174] Again, a speaker at an antisemitic meeting at Rennes about the same time "pointed to the role of the Jews in French society from the point of view of the monopolization of finance in all industries and in trade, and stressed the urgent need for real French people to band together so as to be able to banish from our soil all these cosmopolitan hordes."[175] The manifesto of a new antisemitic and nationalist group, formed in Belfort in 1901, called for a similar rallying of Frenchmen against the Jewish invader: "A gang of foreign Jews and anti-national Socialists are trying to lay down the law in our country . . . the Nation is in danger . . ."[176] As Maurras concluded in 1905: "antisemitism exists only because French people are reduced to asking themselves if they are still the masters in their own country."[177] We have encountered the same conception of antisemitism as a movement of legitimate defence in the self-characterization of antisemites as "victims", and also in its presentation by Drumont and others as a movement of social protest. But perhaps more significant is the fact that this same "defensive" conception enjoyed some currency even among those unsympathetic to antisemitism as such, mitigating or removing their initial hostility to it. Brunetière, for example, in an article in the Revue des Deux Mondes in March 1898, criticized the antisemites, but accepted their claims that Jews, Freemasons and Protestants shared a privileged position in the France of the Third Republic, and suggested that the antisemitic movement could be seen in part as a natural and democratic reaction on the part of the mass of the French population against this dominant and unrepresentative élite.[178]

Antisemites frequently attempted to provide evidence for their assertions of Jewish domination. An Indicateur des Juifs, published in Lyon in 1898, for example, gave a full list of "Jews in the French press, the army and the financial world of Paris";[179] and several local "indicateurs" of the same kind were published, as we have seen. La Libre Parole regaled its readers with specific examples of the occupation of places of influence by Jews, as did books, such as Drumont's La France juive and La Fin d'un monde, and Daudet's L'Avant-Guerre. Two things are of especial interest in this attempt to prove the assertion that France was dominated by the Jews. First, the indication of particular areas of Jewish domination provides an important clue to the motivation behind this kind of antisemitic propaganda. Second, the apparent rationality of this matter-of-fact demonstration went along with a totally irrational belief in an all-embracing Jewish plot to dominate, a Jewish conspiracy of terrestrial or even cosmic dimensions. This suggests very strongly that antisemites did not in fact proceed from the discovery that there was a higher proportion of Jews in positions of power and in some important professions than their numbers in the total population might lead one to expect, to the adoption of antisemitism, but that they used such examples of prominent Jews as they could find to back up and to illustrate a prior conviction that Jews were dominant or wished to be. This is not to say that the presence of Jews in prominent positions or leading professions (which seems, in fact, to have been very limited) is not relevant to the motivation of antisemites. But the presence of Jews was picked on as a "cause" or a "sign" of other difficulties experienced by antisemites that were not logically connected with Jewish presence at all. For this reason, although of interest in general terms, and particularly for the study of the French Jewish community itself,[180] to establish objectively what positions of influence Jews occupied in France would not be of much help in explaining antisemitism. What is relevant here primarily is not the objective situation, which antisemites probably more than other contemporaries could not and did not perceive, but the situation as antisemites saw it, which the historian must then try to interpret in the light of what he, from his unique vantage-point, knows of the objective situation.

First, then, as far as antisemites were concerned, it was mainly bourgeois society that was being taken over by the Jews. A speaker at a meeting organized by the Ligue de la Patrie Française at Epernay in April 1900 attacked the Jews, "pointing to their ceaselessly growing influence, principally in the ruling classes".[181] This reflected the mainly bourgeois complexion of antisemitism. Péguy commented that "the bourgeois antisemites only know about the Jews who are bourgeois . . ."[182] But it reflected more than just this. The Jews were accused of invading particular professions, notably the various branches of government employment, the civil service, the magistracy, the army and the University, also the press and journalism, politics and the liberal professions. In his Nancy Programme of 1898, Barrès claimed that:[183]

> In the army, in the magistracy, in the ministries, throughout the administration, the Jews infinitely exceed the normal proportion to which their numbers would entitle them. They have been appointed as prefects, treasurers of the fisc, officers, because they have the money to buy their way. Without even changing the law, simply by demanding more care from those who govern us, this dangerous disproportion must be destroyed, and more respect obtained for the rights of our true nationals, children of Gaul and not of Judah.

In the same vein, a Union Nationale broadsheet of November 1897 claimed that there were 49 Jewish prefects and sub-prefects in France, and 19 Jews in the Conseil d'Etat.[184] In January 1899, Maurras went further than simply pointing to the number of Jews in the administration, or calling for non-statutory restraint in this area, arguing in La Gazette de France that, since Jews were "foreigners and dangerous foreigners . . . they should be banned from public employment altogether";[185] and a Bill was put down in the same year in the Chamber of Deputies by Pontbriand, which demanded three generations of French citizenship as a prerequisite for entry into the civil service or the armed forces.[186] Cailly, in a speech at Lille in April 1900, showed the same concern, citing "the enormous numbers of Jews who are encumbering the ministries . . ."[187] Brunetière commented that the Third Republic had selected its political and administrative personnel "more than it ought to have done from among our Freemasons, our Protestants and our Jews . . . These groups have taken over politics, the administration, the education system, and now rule the roost there; and, if we want to be honest, we must recognize that antisemitism is just a label that is being used to cover up what is, in effect, a strong desire to oust them."[188]

The press was another area that was said to be dominated by the Jews. Proudhon had claimed in 1862 that the newspaper press in both France and Germany was owned by Jews.[189] And the claim was reiterated later by Maurras, Drumont and others. Drumont wrote in *La France juive* that "nearly all the newspapers and organs of publicity in France are in the hands of the Jews or depend indirectly on them", a charge which he repeated again and again in the same and other works.[190] As Maurras was to do later, Picard pointed to the crucial importance of this area of Jewish influence: "With money, one can control journalism, and journalism makes opinion . . . whoever controls money, controls the press; whoever controls money and the press, controls politics; and whoever controls politics determines the whole orientation of a country."[191] *La Croix* also alleged that the press was in the hands of the Jews,[192] and pointed again to the enormous danger that this represented. *Le Complôt juif*, a broadsheet put out by *La Croix* in 1898, quoted the Jews as saying: "If gold is the first power in this world, the second, without any doubt, is the press . . . The possession of gold . . . will make us the arbiters of public opinion and will give us control over the masses."[193] As this suggests, not only were Jews supposed to have financial control of the press, but they were seen to be directly involved in journalism in a decisive way. "The Jew excels in twisting facts and in flattering the passions of his readers", wrote Desprez of the Action Française; "by insinuating himself, and under the cover of pseudonyms, he manages to get his articles into the opposition papers, even those that are clearly Catholic . . ."[194] While attributing less grandiose motives to his stereotype of the Jewish press magnate, M. Walter, in *Bel-Ami*, Maupassant also presented Jewish journalism as both eclectic and effective. Walter's paper, which "had been founded only to further his Stock Exchange transactions and his other enterprises", was by turns "governmental, Catholic, liberal, Republican, Orleanist, upper-crust and penny press".[195] Drumont, similarly, claimed that even *L'Intransigeant* was dependent on Jewish finance;[196] and stressed the talent of the Jews in the field of publicity.[197]

As Byrnes and Sorlin have pointed out,[198] the claim on the part of antisemites that the French press was controlled by Jews was clearly related to a crisis of adaptation and development in the press, and was inspired by commercial considerations. As in the field of retail trading, the two decades around 1900 were a period of "concentration" for the press, in which the mass "information" press was tending to squeeze out the old "opinion" press, to which the antisemitic newspapers belonged. New technology meant that greater capital was required to found a newspaper, particularly a daily, and then to keep it running. Economic viability also required higher circulations.[199] The examples of La Croix founded in 1880, La Libre Parole founded in 1892, and L'Action Française founded in 1908, showed that there was a readership for an antisemitic daily or dailies in France, and also that the antisemitic press was by no means lacking in commercial acumen. But, nevertheless, the situation of all three remained chronically insecure, from a financial point of view, a situation that was exacerbated by their own mutual competition. It has been suggested with reason that the Dreyfus Affair was blown up by a press that was involved in a fundamental crisis and a circulation war,[200] and antisemitism was certainly used deliberately in an attempt to boost circulations. We have seen that both Picard and La Croix, for example, entertained a manipulative view of the role of the press, though attributing that view to the Jews. Drumont made the same oblique avowal when he wrote that: "One of the things that has done most to impede the antisemites in their work of salvation has been the resistance which they have encountered in a press, which, with rare exceptions, is sustained by Jewish subsidies."[201]

Moreover, journalists, threatened by increasing insecurity in an already insecure profession,[202] and sensitive to changes in their own status, could, at the same time, explain this phenomenon to themselves, and hope to mitigate it, by positing a tightening of Jewish control of the press. Drumont pointed, in La France juive, to the fact that "the press . . . has been almost totally transformed in the last few years . . .";[203] and, characteristically, he contrasted the present venality and commercialism of the press with the time when it had a function akin to that "a priesthood", and when the role of the journalist represented "a veritable public office".[204] "No one could have a higher standard of probity and disinterestedness that the journalist of French and Christian origin", he asserted with professional pride;[205] but it was virtually impossible for a journalist to succeed now, without being dishonest and selling himself. The Jews who controlled the press either dismissed such "honest" journalists, or forced them to abandon their standards by exploiting the fact that they had livings to make and families to feed. Moreover, a new type of journalist was in the ascendant, a "new generation to which the sentiments of the literary man are quite alien, in particular a certain respect for the written word, and the notion of freedom of speech and discussion, which any writer worthy of the name must adhere to."[206] Mention should also be made of two other branches of the media, where Jewish domination was alleged. Drumont claimed that the Jews controlled France's book market, instancing Hachette's monopoly of railway station bookstalls. As we have seen, this particular charge must have had something to do with the fact that Hachette refused to stock Drumont's works on their stalls.[207] More generally, it reflected a malaise in the French publishing industry, related to that of the newspaper press, and stemming from the same phenomena of "concentration" and adaptation to a new mass market; it seems that French publishers over-produced in the 1890s, anticipating demand that the general economic depression cut back.[208] Jews were also supposed to control the theatre. "The theatre . . . has taken on an abnormal, almost monstrous, importance", wrote Drumont again, in *La France juive,* "and this can be explained by the single fact that most theatre directors and nearly all the well-known actors and actresses are Jews. The profession of the actor is one that inevitably attracts the Jews: it pays well, . . . it satisfies a certain petty vanity and it demands no very great talent; thus Jews have rushed into this career with real fury. All the theatres of Paris are controlled by Jews."[209] This passage should be read in the light of the fact that writing for the theatre very often represented the height of a writer's ambition for prestige and fame in nineteenth-century France, as well as being potentially his most lucrative employment, as the unfortunate forays into drama by Balzac and Zola remind us. Drumont,[210] and doubtless many others, shared this ambition, and its disappointment could naturally be laid, like so much else, at the door of the Jews. The association of Jews with the theatre raises other interesting problems, too, which we will discuss in a later chapter.

In rather the same way, as Brunetière suggested, the idea that politics and the public administration in France were dominated by Jews served to express and to explain the fact that outsiders, and particularly Catholics and conservatives, found it hard to enter the political system of the Third Republic and thus obtain a share in its spoils. Thus, for Drumont, as we have seen, the Third Republic was "the Jewish Republic";[211] and he denounced its politics as a system wholly manipulated by patrons such as Gambetta in their own interest, using the grossest forms of corruption and fraud.[212] "All honest and decent people had [thus] been driven out of public functions."[213] In particular, Catholic and liberal magistrates had, for reasons of conscience, been unable to apply the early legislation of the Third Republic against the religious orders, and "Christian magistrates had been replaced by Jews", who were both partial and venal.[214] Drumont also claimed that the police was in the hands of the Jews, giving an antisemitic slant to a familiar complaint, particularly by opponents of the government and the régime, against the use of the police as a political instrument of surveillance.[215] As one of our important sources indicates, if the police were not, of course, in the hands of the Jews, they were vigilant observers and opponents of organized antisemitism.

More interesting, perhaps, because of its wider appeal, was the assertion that the Jews had invaded or taken over the liberal professions. As we have seen, Barrès protested that foreigners had invaded "all our occupations and even the liberal professions (including the Faculty of Medicine and the state school of civil engineering)".[216] *Le Complôt juif* declared: "The magistracy is for us an institution of the first importance"; and added that Jews should also seek to enter "the Bar . . . teaching", and medicine.[217] In *Les Morticoles* (1894), Léon Daudet depicted medicine as an area of Jewish dominance: "Among doctors, as everywhere else, the Jewish race forms a group apart, detested but powerful"; and he suggested that Jews succeeded in medicine through a mixture of string-pulling and sharp practice.[218] The Jewish doctor, moreover, was something of a stock-type in the antisemitic fiction of the period, with Daudet's own Wabanheim in *Les Morticoles,* and Dr Blumevin in *Ceux qui montent* (1912), and Dr Bax in Paul Adam's *Le Mystère des foules*

(1895), for example.[219] The choice of the doctor, with his quasi-magical prestige as the wielder of the power of life and death, a prestige greatly enhanced by advances in applied medical science in the last decades of the nineteenth century,[220] as the symbol of Jewish power, is understandable. For all its heavy irony, the title of *Les Morticoles* is significant here. *Le Complôt juif* explained also: "A doctor is initiated into the most intimate secrets of a family, and therefore has in his hands the health and the life of our mortal enemies, the Christians."[221] One must remember, too, the existence of a very ancient traditional association of Jews with the practice of medicine.[222]

However, the charge that the Jews were taking over the liberal professions, as well as the civil service, had, at the same time, a more mundane explanation, for, as we have noted, these were the two favoured careers of the French bourgeoisie, and careers, moreover, where competition in the 1890s was becoming more intense. Already in 1883, Zola, through the mouthpiece of the successful owner of a department store, Mouret, had referred to "the poor devils, who have picked up a bit of book learning and who encumber the liberal professions, without earning enough to eat decently . . ."[223] Such, just about, was the theme of Vallès's *Le Bachélier* (1879). The phenomenon is to be explained largely as the consequence of increased social mobility, specifically via the educational system, and of the related democratization of career and class structures, though neither should be exaggerated.[224] Charles-Louis Philippe represented, for example, in *La Mère et l'enfant* (1900), what was a common aspiration of more and more ordinary parents for their children, in this case a clog-maker's wife: "Your son will pass his *baccalauréat*, and those who do that become doctors, vets, clerks in the Bridges and Highways Department. They have an easy life . . ."[225] In practice, of course, even for those who obtained the coveted posts and practices, life was not always easy, and the gap between the meritocratic ethos propounded via the educational system and this reality needed to be explained. And the fact that a widening of this gap, and increasing competitiveness, coincided with the actual entry into the liberal professions and the civil service for the first time on an important scale of French Jews, provided such an explanation.

The legal emancipation of French Jews had been effected during the French Revolution and its aftermath. As we have seen, Jews were admitted to the ranks of active citizenship in 1791; and full civil rights were only temporarily denied them again by Napoleon. The Jewish religious establishment had been attached to the state budget in 1830, giving it equal status with the Catholic and the Protestant ones; while in 1839, with the abolition of the oath *more judaico*, the last vestige of legal discrimination against Jews in France disappeared.[226] However, it took one or two generations more for Jews to become sufficiently assimilated to aspire to careers in the liberal professions, the civil service or the armed forces.[227] When Jews did begin to succeed in the 1890s in these careers that had been formerly closed to them, the Jewish press took some pride in broadcasting the fact, as Marrus has pointed out,[228] though attitudes became more cautious later. Both Herzl and Léon Blum, himself one of the first Jews to enter the Conseil d'Etat, for example, laid stress in the late 1890s on the hostility which this influx seemed to have occasioned.[229] Blum explained later, as we have seen, that the low profile maintained during the Affair by many upper-class Jews was to be explained by the fact that they did not wish to put in jeopardy their new social and professional status.[230]

The plausibility of an antisemitic explanation of the difficulties experienced by those in or trying to enter such careers must have been considerable, in many cases overriding any professional commitment to a more orthodox rationality. We have certainly encountered, in previous chapters, much evidence of the importance of antisemitism among the liberal professions, in particular. Some leading antisemites played down this "bourgeois" element in their following in an attempt to foster "popular" support. Drumont, for example, claimed in 1891: "I have not met with any support among the ruling classes";[231] but most contemporaries took the opposite view, if the latter term is widely defined. Levasseur, for example, agreed with Dagan that "it is in the bourgeois classes that antisemitic passions are brewing . . ."[232] Reinach wrote of the Republican bourgeoisie: "In recent years particularly, it has not been exempt from antisemitism. The disease was widespread not only among businessmen and industrialists, small rentiers and shopkeepers . . . but also among the liberal professions."[233] Again, we have come across much evidence of the leading role played in the antisemitic movement by lawyers, doctors, journalists and intellectuals. (Intellectuals are something of a special case, and will be discussed separately in a later chapter.[234]) Prominent antisemites in this social category included Edmond Picard, an advocate at the Cour de Cassation de Belgique; Dr Pédébidou, deputy, then senator, for the Hautes-Pyrénées from 1893 to 1925, who opposed the practice of medicine in France by foreigners; the radiologist Paulin-Méry, deputy for the Seine from 1889 to 1902; the deputies Charles Bernard and Delmas, who were pharmacists; as well as the large number of antisemitic deputies who were lawyers.[235] Mention should also be made of Léon Daudet, who made an abortive entry into the medical career;[236] and of Charles Maurras, member of a declining class of Provençal notables.[237]

Both antisemites and their critics, moreover, were well aware of this professional motivation. Benoît Malon noted in *La Revue Socialiste* in 1886 that Jews were breaking out of their traditional confinement to the spheres of commerce and finance, and were invading "all the branches of politics and literature".[238] Daudet protested in 1911: "That there is hardly any avenue in any occupation or profession that is not occupied, controlled or blocked by one or more naturalized citizen."[239] Leroy-Beaulieu stressed this aspect of antisemitism, its function as a kind of professional protectionism:[240]

Abandoning business and the Stock Exchange, leaving the trading occupations in which they had been forced to specialize for so long, many Jews rushed towards other careers. They turned to the liberal professions, to the Bar, to medicine, to teaching, to literature and to science. And what became of this effort to open up new outlets for themselves? Having been reproached for their long-standing preference for finance and business, they were now accused of invading the liberal professions . . . Antisemitism, here, was the mask for a unique kind of protectionism. What it was attacking in the person of the Jew was a competitor, and a talented competitor.

Elisée Reclus similarly estimated that antisemitism was "almost entirely the expression of the base envy of candidates left behind in competitive examinations, of functionaries disappointed in the distribution of posts", a view that was shared by another contributor to Dagan's *Enquête*, Duclaux, who saw antisemitism as "above all a rivalry of interests, the envy of people who are disappointed, or unlucky. It is the old: 'Get out, you're in my place!' "[241] Among Jews, too, as we have see, such an interpretation of antisemitism was not uncommon, and Lacretelle's Silbermann explained "the explosion of antisemitism in France" at the time of the Affair in these terms:[242]

> It is a base expression of self-interest, the vilest envy. There have come to your country recently people who are more subtle, bolder, more persevering than some of you, and who have thus succeeded better in their undertakings; but instead of competing with them for the greater good of all, you gang up against them, and try to rid yourselves of them . . . The class that is most active against us is the bourgeoisie, the upper bourgeoisie, because, with us, it encounters rivals in the careers that until now it has monopolized.

It is relevant here to note that, under Vichy, a *numerus clausus* for Jews in the liberal professions was established.[243]

One element in Lacretelle's view should be stressed. The upper bourgeoisie believed that it had an exclusive right to certain careers. When the education system seemed to be acting to extend this right to others, rather than simply preserving it for them, members of this group became alarmed. But one is not dealing here purely with selfish class-interest, but also with a real and profound clash of attitudes. For a large section of the upper bourgeoisie at least, status and occupation were not things that one had to strive for; they were given, taken for granted; and to them the whole conception of competitiveness was alien. This is well brought out, in the context of antisemitism, in a speech by Yves Guyot:[244]

> Many people of Catholic origin, but now more or less agnostic, are too easy-going; they don't want to take the trouble to learn a foreign language; they don't want to submit themselves to the tedium of hard work; they don't want to strain themselves by mastering the complexities of high finance; they want jobs and positions to come to them without effort in the traditional way. They are thus very jealous of the Jews who demonstrate in these jobs and positions the qualities of perseverance and know-how that they lack; and, like good protectionists, they don't try to do better, to compete; they demand that their rivals be removed; they pretend that they are persecuted, while, in fact, it is they who want to persecute those whom they blame for their own lack of success!

Daudet typified another aspect of the same hierarchical attitude towards occupation when he wrote that "the Jew as merchant and banker, and confined to these occupations at which he excels . . . would be tolerable . . ."[245] Also involved here was a negative reaction to changing styles in the liberal professions themselves. As we have seen in the case of journalism, the theme of Jewish invasion or dominance could be the means by which new practices and standards were registered and explained, and their rejection rationalized. Daudet complained of "rigged examinations" at the Faculty of Medicine, and of the power of dictatorial "patrons".[246] Drumont pointed to the decline in the integrity of notaries, as well as to the increased difficulties of their obtaining practices.[247] He also, as we have seen, gave expression to the rancour of Catholic magistrates who resigned their functions in 1880 rather than administer the decrees against the religious orders.[248] At a lower social level, Maupassant's M. Caravan, "principal clerk at the Navy Ministry" is presented as "a man of Order, a reactionary, belonging to no particular party, but an enemy of all novelties . . ."; "when every evening he walked up the avenue des Champs-Elysées, he considered the surging crowd of other pedestrians and the rolling flood of carriages in the way that a foreign traveller might who was crossing a strange land . . ." His anomie exacerbated by the Right-wing newspaper that he read so credulously, would he not, a decade later have been an antisemite?[249]

The fears of the upper bourgeoisie, anxious to preserve their privileges, and the fears and hopes of those aspiring to bourgeois occupations, were perhaps both at their most acute at the crucial, and intensely competitive, preparatory stage, that is to say among students. Vallès saw students as essentially a-political around 1870, though he interpreted this as meaning that they were in a general sense conservative.[250] Drumont claimed in 1889 that students were apathetic and uninterested in nationalism and antisemitism, although earlier he had praised the attempt by students in 1883 to clear the Latin Quarter of prostitutes, and mentioned demonstrations by medical students in Paris in 1884–6 against the Opportunists.[251] And there is some evidence of more commitment by the early 1890s, if not the late 1880s. As a Boulangist, Barrès claimed that he represented "the youth of the universities".[252] Léon Daudet remembered that, when he was a medical student in the late 1880s, "students from all the Great Schools were devouring Drumont's book [La France juive], and discussing it with passion."[253] By 1891, Drumont, himself, suggested that "all virile energy" was not, after all, dead in "the youth of today", and claimed that "all the men of the young generation" read his books.[254] We have seen in previous chapters the large part played by students in the antisemitic movement of the late 1890s, and in the Affair. Some students, of course, were Dreyfusards, for example, most of those at the Ecole Normale Supérieure, but many more, it seems, were anti-Dreyfusards.[255] Nationalism and antisemitism, moreover, remained important among students in the decade before 1914. "I am shocked", declared Péguy in 1910, ". . . to see how far our young people have become strangers to all that Republican thought and the Republican mystique represented."[256] Sartre has indicated that the antisemitism of the students of the Great Schools persisted well into the inter-war period.[257]

As we have suggested, this enduring prevalence of antisemitism among French students can, to some degree, be explained by the supposed threat that Jews represented to their obtaining coveted jobs and places through the competitive examination system. General fears, stimulated by increased competitiveness and the prospect of unemployment,[258] were directed against the Jews in particular, since they were a convenient target. Benda wrote later that: "The triumph of the Reinachs at the General Examination of all *lycées* seems to me to have been one of the essential causes of the antisemitism that broke out fifteen years later [i.e. in the 1890s]. Whether the Jews realized it or not, such successes were regarded by other French people as an act of violence against them . . ."[259] A Dreyfusard pamphleteer also claimed in 1898 that the attack on the Jews arose from the competitive examination system, and particularly from the rivalry of candidates from state and Catholic schools for entry into the army: "The religious houses that prepared young Catholics for the military academies had every interest to eliminate rivals who were becoming increasingly numerous and formidable."[260] There is probably some truth in this, particularly since at this time upper-class Catholics and nobles felt, and to some extent were, excluded from most other employments, at least in the public sector, and regarded the army as their last important source of employment, their refuge.[261] But fear of Jewish competition was by no means confined to potential officers. Drumont and Daudet, as we have seen, provided evidence of its existence among Parisian medical students;[262] and anti-Dreyfusism was particularly marked at the Paris Law School.[263]

Another factor to take account of here is the élitist nature of the French conscription system. As Urbain Gohier mocked in 1899:[264]

"Long live the army!" shouts the so-called "youth of our colleges and universities". What are they on about? All these young men with special dispensations, who are working desperately to obtain no matter what diploma from no matter what school so as to avoid the full three years of military service, they are going a bit too far with their demonstrations of military fervour. They only do one year; they are never sent far from their homes; they are quite safe from colonial expeditions.

The 1889 conscription law, in effect, while abolishing the purchase of exemption from the full three-year period of service, maintained the privilege of a single year of service for those in higher education. As Messimy told the Senate in 1901 this helped to flood higher education with "innumerable postulants, eager for studies without a future, and all aspiring for membership in that fortunate intellectual élite which will exempt them from two years in the barracks."[265] Ralston links this incentive to the large rise in the number of those studying for the liberal professions, in particular, in the decade after 1889. The number of doctorates in medicine issued per annum, he points out, rose from a steady 500–600 through the 1880s to 1,200 in 1897; the number of doctorates in law from 100 in 1889 to 230 in 1900.[266] The conscription law thus contributed to the overcrowding of the liberal professions that we have already encountered, but it also suggests a further element in the make-up of student antisemitism: bad conscience. Those who were in higher education, at least in part to avoid the full rigours of military service, made an exaggerated display of their attachment to the army, as Gohier observed; and they projected their sense of guilt on to the Jews, their rivals, foreigners and potential traitors. The relative lack of antisemitism at the Ecole Normale Supérieure, which was primarily a centre for disinterested study, is probably significant here. Herriot recalled that a review produced by ENS students in the 1890s was sponsored by Jules Simon and financed "through the generosity of our comrade Henri de Rothschild . . ."[267] The Tharaud brothers mention certain acts or supposed acts of hostility against Jews at the Ecole in the same period, but suggest that they were always disapproved of and resisted, and conclude: "at the *lycée* and at the Ecole, we always had the same close relations with our Jewish comrades that we had with those who were Christians; we never dreamed that there could be any fundamental difference between us."[268]

However, as we have suggested, the Ecole Normale Supérieure was not typical in this, as in other respects, and there is considerable evidence that antisemitism was common in *lycées,* at least by the late 1890s. Herriot testified to the lack of antisemitism at the Collège Sainte-Barbe in the late 1880s;[269] and, as we have seen, the Tharaud brothers remembered none there or at the Lycée Louis-le-Grand in the early 1890s.[270] F. Gregh similarly recalled that there was no antisemitism among the pupils at the Lycée Michelet (Vanves) or the Lycée Condorcet until the outbreak of the Affair, though Jews and Protestants did form a distinct group known as "the dissidents".[271] However, Donnay mentions the merciless teasing of a converted Jewish boy at the Lycée de Vanves in the early 1870s;[272] and Léon Daudet's headmaster *(Proviseur)* at Louis-le-Grand was an antisemite and let the boys know it.[273] The Affair, in effect, seems to have legitimized and encouraged existing tendencies. André Maurois, for example, was persecuted at the *lycée* of Rouen at the start of the Affair, after a period of being tolerated.[274] This outburst of antisemitism in French secondary schools has, of course, received its classic treatment in Lacretelle's *Silbermann.* [275] What is particularly unpleasant about it is the way in which adults lent it their approval. "If there are little Jews in your classes, there is trouble, isn't there?" Gyp asked Bournand's son. "You, young people don't like them either, do you? . . . At Condorcet, I know very well, there are continual fights and disputes with Jewish pupils."[276]

Lacretelle suggested that this antisemitism was to some extent a reaction to the novelty of having Jewish boys in *lycées,* and said that it declined as they became more numerous and less remarked; but he also stressed that Silbermann was disliked, among other reasons, because he was the cleverest boy in his classes. And envy and fear of Jewish scholastic success does seem to have been important among parents and pupils, confirming our general argument. Already in 1856, Alfred de Vigny was writing, without hostility and to illustrate "the superior aptitudes" of the Jews: "they always win the first prizes in the *lycées.* Fourteen of them at the Ecole Normale have taken all the first places. It has been necessary to restrict the number of them who will be allowed, in future, to compete in public examinations."[277] Maurois related the hostility against him at the *lycée* of Rouen, to the Affair, but also to the fact that he had come top of his class in most subjects. Léon Blum was "one of the most redoubtable snatchers of prizes" in the history of the Lycée Charlemagne, according to one of his biographers; and having been head of his class for four years, he went on to complete his law studies with highest honours.[278] The novelist Julian Green, who was a pupil at the Lycée Janson in Paris around 1910, wrote later that:[279]

> Jewish boys topped the list [of grades]. They understood all the problems, handed in the best compositions, and collected most of the prizes at the end of the year. There was no vying with them; they were far ahead of us, and even offered to coach us during recreation hours. Mathematics, languages, literature, everything seemed to be their forte.

The equation of academic success, which was the entry to professional success, with being Jewish became so firmly established in the minds of some that Drieu La Rochelle, who was born in 1893, could put these words into the mouth of Carentan in *Gilles:* [The Jews jump straight out of the synagogue into the Sorbonne.] "For me, a provincial, a rural bourgeois, who, by instinct and by study, feel myself attached to an old and complex culture, the Jew at the Ecole Polytechnique or the Ecole Normale represents something horrible."[280] As we have seen, Maurras and others claimed that the University itself was dominated by Jews, in its faculty and administration. Drumont wrote in *La France juive:* "Before very long the whole of higher education will be in the hands of Jews".[281] And antisemites could point to the academic positions occupied by Emile Durkheim, Frederic Rauh and others.[282] Student antisemitism and the assertion that France's education system was in the hands of the Jews or their allies, should of course, be seen in the context of the whole conflict between the Third Republic and its opponents in the arena of education. During the period of the Dreyfus Affair and its aftermath, the government revived its campaign against Catholic schools, banning the religious orders from teaching altogether.[283] But, even before this, Drumont had attacked the University and its personnel, and had criticized the education policy of the Republic.[284] Barrès, in *Les Déracinés* (1897), laid the burden of his critique of France's political régime on its education system;[285] while the Action Française inveighed against the secular primary school and the godless German-influenced state University, which, it claimed, were responsible for France's decadence.[286]

Some further, psychological, aspects of student antisemitism should be noted here, though we will discuss them more fully in a later chapter. Erikson has argued persuasively that Nazism had many of the features of an adolescent revolt, and has seen its antisemitism as an expression of a fear of sexuality related to the prolonged and repressed adolescence of German youth at the start of this century and later.[287] The same fear of sexuality can be detected in French antisemitic imagery of the 1890s, and French adolescence was similarly prolonged and repressed.[288] It is significant that, at a later period, the rumour of Orléans began among adolescent girls, and was related again to fears of sexuality.[289] Another factor of relevance in this context is the special appeal to adolescents of a simple ideological view of the world that satisfies their need for identity,[290] though as we shall argue, this appeal and this need were not confined to adolescents.

To return then to the adult world, a further motivation behind middle- and upper-class assertions that the Jews were invading or that they dominated French society, was snobbery, resentment against the entry of newcomers into an exclusive social milieu to which antisemites belonged or would have liked to belong. Arthur Meyer wrote in 1911 that the Jew was "an invader in the social, literary and artistic domains, like all those to whom these domains had been for a long time closed . . ."[291] Blum, who, like Meyer, must, as a Jew, have experienced some measure of the hostility which he described, noted that the antisemitism of the 1890s "was born in certain restricted circles of Parisian society, both social and professional; its direct cause had been the indiscreet intrusion of enriched Jews or the penetration, judged to be too rapid, of educated Jews."[292] Proust also linked the rise of antisemitism in this period with "a more abundant movement towards the penetration of society by Israelites . . ."[293] Barrès remarked, from a slightly different perspective: "With the Jews . . . we can go to the salons of their wives, which are their sign of respectability, their façade; and, meanwhile, the husband will be engaged in intrigues to destroy our traditional ideals and our country, our moral and our material well-being."[294] We must be careful not to take these explanations too literally. Jews were objectively penetrating French society, in both senses, but so were many others, as Meyer observed; yet Jews were singled out for hostility and blame. Their "invasion" was chosen to explain and symbolize a more general process. The Jew was the butt for all hostility to the social upstart, the self-made man; and, as we saw in examining antisemitic attitudes towards the aristocracy, which still largely set the tone for "high society", the Jew represented money, the dissolver of rigid systems of status, and the rapid social mobility that threatened to destroy that society altogether.

In claiming that the Nation was in danger of being taken over by the Jews, bourgeois (and aristocratic) antisemites were thus saying in fact that their own jobs, places and privileges were threatened by more powerful or more skilful competitors, or else by the very institution of competition itself. They were explaining this phenomenon to themselves, and giving expression to the feeling of insecurity, the lack of confidence that it engendered. This lack of confidence is well conveyed in a passage in Vogüé's *Les Morts qui parlent*:

"You are sure to encounter, in any Parisian gathering, whether of men about town or scholars, of the very wealthy or the intellectually distinguished, a high proportion of Jews", [asserts one character]. "Indeed, it is just that that is held against them: their supremacy in every kind of activity, using all the means at their disposal", agreed Ferroz. "They have learned the great secret of mechanics: never waste energy, steam, that can be used . . . It is all very well your being numerically superior, all that escaping steam just makes a cloud of steam; but a little steam that is compressed and put

to work, that can accomplish something." "That is all very fine", interrupted the agriculturalist, "but can't you see that we are being eaten alive?"
—"Of course I see it", the pundit replied. "You are, it seems, eminently
edible . . . Is your world coming to an end, as people are saying? If so, then
the Jewish ferment will accomplish its historical function there, its function
as a decomposing agent, as the dissolver of societies that are worn
out . . ."[295]

Underlying this lack of confidence was a thoroughgoing social fear, which
we have encountered in another guise in connection with socialism. For the
bourgeois antisemite (and not necessarily only the bourgeois), the whole idea
of social mobility and particularly of assimilation was profoundly frightening,
for it assumed a society in flux, permeable, in which social identities were not
given, but could, or worse had to, be made, and in which they could be lost.
A speaker at a Union Nationale meeting in Vincennes in January 1898
complained that "In its generosity, France in 1789 welcomed the Jews by
declaring them equal to French people before the law; but the contract has
been broken by the Jews . . .", a common charge.[296] Paul Bollot referred in
1887 to "the arrogance of these Jews, emancipated yesterday, yet who want
to run everything today".[297] According to Jacques de Biez: "They trample
France under their fat gouty feet . . . These people whom we emancipated
cast us to the bottom of the social ladder, and pass judgment on us with the
true stupidity of parvenus."[298] But a contractual interpretation of emancipation was not enough of a safeguard against such a derogation. The threat posed
by the idea of assimilation, a threat to the whole concept of a hierarchical
society, was much more effectively countered not by claiming merely that
assimilation had proved a failure, and denouncing Jewish ingratitude, but by
asserting that it was impossible. Thus, according to the programme of the
Jeunesse de l'Union Nationale (1895), the Jew was "not open to any kind of
assimilation . . ."[299] This was the implication of the repeated claim that the
Jew was foreign, that he could never become French because he belonged to
a different nation, a different race or species; and, against the concept of a
society into which Jews might be assimilated, antisemites posited a counter-
concept of France as a nation, even a race, as we shall see,[300] that simply did
not allow assimilation. Although many antisemites did propose, in line with
this requirement that France be nationally or racially homogeneous, that the
Jews be expelled from France, others were quite happy to allow them to
remain so long as their special inferior status was officially recognized and
established. Maurras, for example, proposed in La Gazette de France in
January 1899 that the Jews should be treated in this way, as resident aliens:
"this was the precaution taken in the Middle Ages. This is the system that
we apply without worrying . . . to our colonial subjects. Personal status,
protection, a system of justice, this is all that we owe the Jews."[301] This
proposed revival of a special Jewish "order" was, in effect, a paradigm of the
total organization of society as a static hierarchy, without social mobility or
class conflict, that antisemites desired. But, before we explore the function of

this variety of nationalism further, we must turn to the conspiracy theory, with which the idea of Jewish invasion or domination was usually associated.

III

The domination of French society by the Jews was attributed to essential Jewish characteristics, as we have seen: "Jewish pride, the Jewish spirit of domination";[302] but these were, it was claimed, deliberately exercised through the medium of a planned conspiracy.[303] Norman Cohn has shown that the myth of the Jewish world-conspiracy, as presented in the *Protocols of the Elders of Zion*, derived in large part from nineteenth-century French sources: Maurice Joly's *Dialogue aux enfers* (1864); Gougenot des Mousseaux's *Le Juif, le Judaïsme et la Judaïsation des peuples chrétiens* (1869); and abbé Chabauty's *Les Francs-maçons et les Juifs: Sixième age de l'Eglise d'après l'Apocalypse* (1881), and *Les Juifs nos maîtres* (1882).[304] Another source of the *Protocols*, "the Rabbi's Speech" from Hermann Goedsche's novel *Biarritz*, published in Berlin in 1868, was also occasionally published in France as an alleged Jewish policy statement.[305] It appeared in *Le Contemporain* in 1881, in Bournand's *Les Juifs et nos contemporains*, and in several antisemitic newspapers in mid-1898, including *Le Nouvelliste de l'Ouest*.[306] "The Rabbi's Speech" was also published by *La Croix* as a pamphlet in April 1898, under the title *Le Complôt juif*, in which form we have already encountered it; the police collected copies in places as far apart as Perpignan, Avignon, Laval and Amiens. The speech was here said to represent "a premeditated plan, worked out a long time ago . . . the plan that cosmopolitan Jewry has been pursuing for centuries, in the version that applies particularly to France in this century . . ."[307]

In this particular form, however, the myth played little part in late nineteenth-century and early twentieth-century antisemitic propaganda in France, although the belief in a Jewish conspiracy was widespread. Drumont, taking his cue from Gougenot des Mousseaux and abbé Chabauty, claimed that a Jewish plot to rule the world existed.[308] He emphasized repeatedly that Jews believed that they had a right, an obligation, to rule and oppress non-Jews.[309]

> The dream of the Semite, [he wrote in *La France juive*] . . . his obsession, has always been to reduce the Aryan to servitude . . . The right of the Jew to oppress other peoples is part of his religion, it is for him an article of faith that is announced in each line of the Bible and of the Talmud [and, quoting an eighteenth-century document] the Jews wish only to arrive at a universal Empire; they regard all property as rightfully belonging to them . . . The Jews . . . are the secret enemies of the human race . . . since they propose one day to enslave it.

In *La Dernière Bataille*, he related this will to power more explicitly to the Jewish conviction that they were a chosen people: "There is a predestined people, blessed by Jehovah, to whom the conquest of the world has been promised, and outside this people there are the goyim, that is to say, the seed of cattle."[310] Nor did he neglect the problem of how will to power was translated into effective conspiracy, singling out in particular the role played by the Alliance Israélite Universelle: "One cannot imagine a more powerful instrument of domination, and one can see how it is that it rules the world."[311] Other antisemites shared Drumont's view of the Jews' sense of superiority and will to power. According to Picard: "The Jew . . . cannot resign himself to his inferiority. Not only does he believe himself to be intellectually the equal of the Aryan, he thinks that he is superior. He takes his low aptitude for accumulating money, and for succeeding in conflicts and intrigues . . . as a sign of election."[312] Picard also retailed an alleged confession made by a Jewish banker to the Goncourts, that "he enjoyed feeling the Christians under my boot"; and claimed that "the Rothschild dynasty is seeking to conquer and enslave us . . .", that the first Rothschild had told his sons on his death-bed: "The world will be yours".[313] Léon Daudet wrote, similarly, that "the Jews are already too disposed to believe that they are omnipotent . . ."[314]

Here, it is important to stress that the beliefs of antisemites were a distillation of beliefs that had a much wider currency, among Jews and among non-Jews. Julien Benda wrote that among the editors of *La Revue Blanche* "there were certain magnates, financiers rather than literary men, with whom the belief in the superiority of their race and in the natural subjection of those who did not belong to it, was visibly sovereign."[315] Gide claimed, just before the First World War, that Blum believed in a Jewish destiny to rule.[316] Most significant, and perhaps surprising, the same idea was propounded by Zola in *Paris* in 1898. When his daughter converts and marries a Christian, Justus Steinberger[317]

> with the stubborn hope of triumph peculiar to his race . . . doubtless considered that Eve would prove a powerful dissolving agent in the Christian family which she had entered, and thus help to make all wealth and power fall into the hands of the Jews . . . the old Jew banker . . . ceased all intercourse with his daughter . . . [but] took a keen interest in everything she was reported to do or say, as if he were more than ever convinced that she would prove an avenging and dissolving agent among those Christians, whose destruction was asserted to be the dream of his race . . . the extraordinary fortune to which his blood had attained, by mingling with that of the harsh, old-time masters of his race, to whose corruption it gave a finishing touch, therein perhaps lay that final Jewish conquest of the world, of which people sometimes talked.

It is relevant also that the conspiracy myth was used in France in the nineteenth century in other contexts and in other forms. Anticlericals, for example, posited a world-conspiracy of the Jesuits;[318] supporters of General Boulanger saw him as the victim of a conspiracy.[319]

The explicit theme of a Jewish conspiracy was, moreover, as Cohn's researches demonstrate, well established in nineteenth-century France, though the antisemites at the end of the century extended and elaborated it. Drumont, for example, referred in *La France juive* to Bécourt's *Conspiration universelle du Judaïsme, entièrement dévoilée,* published in 1835.[320] Proudhon believed that the Jews had plans to rule the world, which they were destined to realize.[321] As we have seen, the crash of the Union Générale was very generally blamed on a Jewish conspiracy, and Bontoux, the head of the unsuccessful Catholic finance house, later claimed that it "was brought down by the blows dealt to it by the Jewish and Masonic coalition . . ."[322] The title of a pamphlet published at Autun in 1887 referred to "the Grand Plot organized [by the Jews and others] to ruin France".[323] In Les Rois de la République (1888), Chirac made the familiar claim that the Jews "want to be masters of the world",[324] a view also propagated by La Croix in its columns.[325] The statutes of the first Ligue Antisémitique of 1889 referred, as we have seen, to "the Jewish-financial Oligarchy, whose occult and pitiless plot puts each day more in jeopardy the Prosperity, the Honour and the Security of France."[326] By the 1890s such a theme had become very common.[327] In 1894, for example, La Libre Parole denounced "the great Jewish plot that will deliver us into the hands of the enemy . . ."[328] In the same year, Morès asserted yet again that "the goal of the Jew is the conquest of the world";[329] and claimed that the Jews were preparing "an immense financial crash . . . a Franco-German blood-letting [and] . . . a series of ritual murders", in order to avenge the condemnation of Dreyfus.[330]

The Dreyfus Affair, in effect, provided the occasion for a special and very popular version of the Jewish conspiracy idea: the Syndicat Dreyfus that was alleged to be organizing the campaign for Dreyfus's retrial, and to be working more generally by this means to discredit the French army and to undermine France's national defence; as a character in Martin du Gard's Jean Barois put it: "The Dreyfus Affair is an immense plot hatched by the Jews."[331] As Sternhell has pointed out, the idea of a Jewish syndicate as the embodiment of the Jewish will to power was not a complete novelty, having been explicitly used by Barrès in the 1880s,[332] but it now took on unprecedented extension. The Dreyfusard publisher Stock wrote that: "despite all the evidence to the contrary . . . people believe in the famous syndicate; they believe in the millions sent in by all the Jews of the world to save their co-religionist who has betrayed his country . . ."[333] "The Syndicate", wrote Zola, in Le Figaro in December 1897, ". . . has ended up by becoming a powerful underground organization, a shameful conspiracy to glorify the traitor and flood France with ignominy."[334] A pamphlet entitled Le Complôt maçonnique and put out in 1898 or 1899 affirmed: "After the infamous campaign of the Dreyfus–Zola syndicate, no reasonable person can now deny the reality of a vast Jewish plot against France, prepared well in advance."[335] Gohier referred ironically about the same time to the "Phantom-Syndicate".[336]

However, the idea of the Syndicate was well established before the Dreyfus Affair came to a head in 1898 and 1899, which suggests, as we have said, that the ground was well prepared. A police agent reported in November 1896 that Dreyfus's brother-in-law was believed to be "at the centre of the famous syndicate organized to achieve the revision of the Dreyfus case";[337] and the police and their agents seem to have given credence to such ideas. A dossier, entitled Syndicat, contains reports from 1897 that the revisionist campaign in

Le Figaro, for example, was being financed by Jews, including the Roth-schilds;[338] and a report, dated November 1897, recounts a conversation with Levaillant, editor of *L'Univers Israélite:*[339]

> He does not conceal that there is now among the Jews a feeling that they must fight, for which the Dreyfus Affair is really only a pretext. They feel that what is at stake is no longer a private affair, the business of an officer and of his family, but a political struggle, engaged in by a great party, by a race, to preserve or to reassert its authority, and the prerogatives which it is losing.

Here, one senses, an authentic Jewish response to the Affair, is being cast into a semi-conspiratorial mould. More clear-cut is a note, headed "Section of National Security", from the same period, which refers to a Jewish banker as being "one of the leading members of the Dreyfus Syndicate".[340] Such reports continued into 1898. Police agents reported in January 1898 that *"Le Siècle* has gone over to the Dreyfus Syndicate, whose existence is so hotly denied by the Chief Rabbi M. Zadoc Kahn and his entourage"; and that the Anarchist *Le Libertaire* appeared to be getting funds for revisionist propaganda from the same source.[341] In February, the police at Montpellier referred to "all the machinations of the Dreyfus Syndicate";[342] and, in March, a police agent in Paris reported, more plausibly: "It appears that a group of Jewish financiers is now trying very actively to organize renewed agitation over the Dreyfus trial."[343]

The fact that police agents and some members of the police itself, which was in general hostile to the antisemites, believed in the existence of the Syndicate, for some considerable time, is an indication of the pervasiveness of such an idea; but it was, of course, propagated, encouraged and kept alive by the anti-Dreyfusard press and its supporters. The Catholic deputy for the Morbihan, the Comte de Mun, lent the belief the weight of his authority, declaring in the Chamber of Deputies on 4 December 1897: "We must know if there really is, in this country, a mysterious and occult power that is strong enough to cast suspicion, as it wishes, on those who lead our army . . . We must decide whether this occult power is really strong enough to turn the whole country upside down, as has happened in the last two weeks . . ."[344] Public meetings in Paris in the first half of 1898 leading up to the General Elections also reflected widespread belief in the Syndicate, and acted to spread that belief. Guérin and others founded a Comité de Protestation contre les Agissements du Syndicat Dreyfus in January 1898, which organized several public meetings.[345] At a Union Nationale meeting in the 18th *arrondissement* in February, abbé Garnier called on French citizens to "expose the activities of the Dreyfus Syndicate . . ."[346] At a "patriotic lecture" at Suresnes in the same month, organized by the Ligue Antisémitique Française, Millevoye claimed that the revisionist campaign in France was being mounted by an international Jewish "syndicate".[347] A public meeting organized by the Comité d'Union Socialiste des Batignolles-Epinettes, also in February, voted a resolution against "the syndicate of shame"; and a meeting of the Comité

Central Républicain Socialiste of the 18th *arrondissement* voted a similar resolution in March, attacking "the Dreyfus syndicate".[348] At a *"punch-concert"* organized in June by the Union des Républicains Patriotes Socialistes, Millevoye again attacked "the syndicate of treason".[349]

Le Journal de Chartres, in October 1898, repeated the familiar charge that the Jews controlled the French press, this time via the Syndicate: "The papers created, owned or simply financed by the Dreyfus Syndicate number seventeen or eighteen for Paris. Those that the Syndicate supports, more or less, in the provinces, number about sixty."[350] *L'Eclair* in February 1899 lent another common touch of spurious detail to the Syndicate myth, when it accused the Chief Rabbi of being the master-mind of the revisionist campaign, as well as organizing a Jewish infiltration of the army.[351] What is interesting in this and previous examples also is the way in which the myth was propagated by those well outside the antisemitic movement proper, something which was true, of course, of anti-Dreyfusism generally. Other examples of the Syndicate or Jewish plot idea in 1899, this time from specifically antisemitic propaganda and both already quoted, are the brochure *La Fin de la France: Le complôt juif* which was published on the occasion of the Rennes trial,[352] and a poster, "Appel aux Patriotes," which was put up in Lyon in August and which appealed: "If you believe in the danger of a cosmopolitan invasion; if the mysterious and frightening power of the masonic Lodges worries you; if the weakness of our foreign policy alarms you; if you believe in the need for energetic action against the anti-French tendencies of the Syndicate that is ruling the country, then GROUP TOGETHER, UNITE TO DEFEND YOURSELVES."[353] The relation of the idea of a conspiratorial Syndicate to a defensive nationalism could not be more clearly stated.

Having established the currency of the Jewish conspiracy idea, embodied in the Syndicate myth and in other forms, we must now examine its characteristics with a view to explaining its social meaning. One of its obvious features was the ascription to the Jews of power and influence out of all proportion to their actual strength and numbers. *La Fin de la France: Le complôt juif* stated that there were 30,000 Jews in France, but that their power was nearly equal to that of the rest of the French population of nearly 40 millions. Drumont asserted in *La France juive* that his antisemitism represented "the struggle of a single man against a united nation"; France was "at the mercy of a small band of Freemasons and Jews".[354] "The strength of the Jew", he wrote again, with particular but by no means exclusive reference to the eighteenth century, "lay in his apparent weakness"; and, quoting a document of that period: "To allow a single Jew to open just one business in a town, would be to open the doors to the whole nation."[355] A speaker at a Union Catholique meeting at Nancy in February 1900 claimed: "We are at the mercy of a handful of sharpers, cosmopolitans and foreigners . . ."[356] As we have seen, moreover, antisemites frequently cast themselves as powerless victims. "The Jews control everything", complained a Union Nationale broadsheet of 1897, ". . . and treat all French people like milch cows . . ."[357] "Since 1870, we have been completely at the mercy of the Jews", agreed Drumont, who entitled one of the books of *La France juive:* "The Jewish Persecution".[358] As Leroy-Beaulieu commented in 1897,[359] antisemites thus attributed to the Jews

> an importance out of all proportion to their numbers or their genius or the real influence of the Jewish element in our societies . . . Antisemitism magnifies and exalts the Jew beyond measure . . . [antisemites] make the meagre remnants of Israel into the arbiters of the modern world. They lend the Jew a superhuman force, mistakenly elevating him above all other nations and races . . . It is a kind of apotheosis in reverse . . .

Péguy explained this exaggeration as a kind of optical illusion. As white on black seems larger than black on white, so "every act, every operation, every square *Jew over Christian* seems to us, is actually seen by us as much greater than the same square *Christian over Jew.*"[360] But, as modern psychological studies of antisemitism have suggested, such an illusion requires powerful motivation. Antisemites were expressing a sense of powerlessness, a feeling of being overwhelmed, but they projected their "omnipotence fantasies" onto the Jews *because* they were objectively weak. Jewish omnipotence explained the whole drift of modern society which antisemites deplored, but it also gave them culprits to blame and to attack who would not be able to retaliate.[361] The French antisemites were not entirely unaware of these dimensions of their obsession. Drumont admitted, for example, that Jewish persecution could cause persecution mania among its victims.[362] Bishop Meurin concluded *La Franc-maçonnerie, Synagogue de Satan* on this optimistic and "rational" note:[363]

> But the crisis of our century, provoked by Freemasonry (in alliance with the Jews), is not at all as formidable as some people think. Once it has been unmasked, this secret society will be detested by everybody and abandoned by its honest members . . . This movement of exodus from the Lodges, once begun and well under way, will mark the beginning of the final overthrow of this power of darkness which had appeared invincible.

However, although they, too, believed in the effectiveness of exposing the conspiracy, most antisemites, on one level at least, held a more purely "manichean" view of the powers of darkness with which they contended. The Jews might be a minority, but they were nevertheless virtually omnipotent and omnipresent; their numbers were greater than it seemed, and they had many allies or auxiliaries. Antisemites may, here, have been countering rational objections to the paradox of an all-powerful minority, but they were more obviously following the demands of their own "paranoid" logic. This can be seen in their tendency to exaggerate the size of the Jewish population in France.[364] Drumont rejected the "official" figure of 45,000, preferring one of 500,000–600,000, but provided no evidence for the revised figure.[365] *La Gazette de France* in July 1894 claimed that the Jewish population of France was between 300,000 and 400,000, and that between 50 and 60 Jews were admitted annually to both the military school of Saint-Cyr and to the Ecole Polytechnique severally, whereas, as a Dreyfusard pamphleteer pointed out, the largest figure that available statistics and estimates of total Jewish population could yield was 75,000, and only 20 Jews at the most were admitted each year to the two establishments mentioned taken together.[366]

Significantly also, the apotheosis in reverse took the form, for some antisemites, of an identification of the Jews with the Devil, the survival of a traditional belief that we will discuss further in a later chapter.[367] In general however, though it could be argued that this is a transposition of the old belief, the powers of the Jewish minority were inflated by granting them secular allies. We have already come across various references to these allies, for the Jews were seen by antisemites as part, and usually the directing part, of a coalition which included the Freemasons, the Protestants and foreigners in general. Different antisemites stressed different elements in this conspiratorial pantheon. Sometimes all four received equal weight, as in Maurras's concept of the "four confederated states, masters of France".[368] "The Masonic order, the foreign colony, the Protestant association, the Jewish nation, these are the four elements which have increasingly gained ground in France since 1789", he wrote in 1905,". . . their oligarchies, held together by a natural interest . . . have taken over everything . . . Finance, the Conseil d'Etat, the universities, the administration, the academies."[369] Sometimes only three were evoked. Abbé Garnier, for example, as we have seen, claimed at a meeting in Troyes in February 1899 that the Third Republic was "the régime of the Jews, the Protestants and the Freemasons";[370] and a meeting in Dijon in February 1900 passed a resolution against "the combination of the Jews, the Huguenots and the Freemasons".[371] But, more often, each of the three was coupled singly with the Jews for the purposes of propaganda. We have dealt already with the campaign against foreign immigrants, and with the claim that the Jews themselves were foreign, but the hostility towards "metics" and foreigners was never pitched at the same ideological level as that directed against Protestants and Freemasons, whereas anti-Protestantism and anti-Masonry were developed in the 1890s as satellite ideologies around nationalist antisemitism.

There is no doubt of the strength of anti-Protestantism in France in the late 1890s, nor of its close association with antisemitism. Leroy-Beaulieu wrote that: "Anti-Protestantism was the twin of antisemitism . . ."[372] Senator Fabre of the Aveyron objected in the Senate in April 1897 to the Christian Democratic Congresses of Lyon, "which have . . . cast an anathema on all those French people who have been unfortunate enough to be born Jews or Protestants . . ."[373] Paléologue noted a conversation at the house of Henri Germain in December 1897: "Everyone agreed in foreseeing a violent revival of antisemitism in France, and, then, of anti-Protestantism."[374] An English visitor, Miss Betham-Edwards, referred to "a time when anti-Protestant feeling in France had almost attained the proportion of anti-Semitism".[375] Jules Isaac recalled, as we have seen, that, at the time of the Affair, "Jews and Protestants were associated, willy-nilly, in the conflagration . . ."[376] Like antisemitism, of course, anti-Protestantism was a prejudice of long standing, particularly in the South and in the East, where there were important Protestant communities;[377] but it was not entirely related to a tradition of coexistence. Jules Vallès remembered that when he was a boy in the Lot-et-Garonne in the 1830's and

1840's, he and his friends were very surprised when they actually saw some Protestants for the first time, and realized that they looked like everyone else and did not have balls and chains attached to them: "Protestants actually existed then! I had read about them in the library [of his uncle the *curé*] at Chaudeyrolles, and the Protestants who had been burned and sent to hell seemed to me to be a race of the damned."[378] Lecanuet suggested that, on the Protestant side, fears of persecution were still strong in the 1870s, fears shared by the Freemasons and by the Jews. Faced with the possibility of a Royalist restoration in 1873, he wrote: "In the Lodges, the Freemasons lost their heads and multiplied signs of alarm; the Jews tried in vain to reassure themselves; and the Protestants evoked with horror the *"Dragonnades"* and the Revocation of the Edict of Nantes."[379] Here it is probable that his assessment was coloured by the situation twenty-five years later, but, for our purposes, this makes it even more significant.

Like traditional anti-Protestantism, that of the time of the Affair was particularly, but not exclusively, a Catholic phenomenon. The Assumptionists who ran *La Croix* were a religious order founded in Languedoc in the middle of the century, with the reconversion of Protestants as one of its specific aims;[380] and *La Croix* maintained a special hostility towards Protestantism.[381] The Assumptionists were responsible for a pamphlet, *Le Complôt protestant,* distributed in 1899, which accused the Protestants of playing a large part in the revisionist campaign, and also claimed that a wider Protestant conspiracy existed. "There is a Protestant problem", it was asserted; and Protestants were said to play

> a preponderant role in the State . . . From the time of the Revolution until the end of the Second Empire, the Protestants prepared their weapons, waiting for the right moment to enter the city and chase out the Catholics. We find the Protestant element well represented in the Revolution of 4 September, as it is in all revolutionary movements . . . To achieve their aim of dominating France, the Protestants counted on its being seriously weakened, as the result of a war in which it would be defeated. The Franco-German war of 1870–1 thus filled them with joy. Some of them, moreover, were the most precious supporters of Bismarck.

Protestants, it was claimed, preferred Protestant Germany and England to Catholic France, which, however, through the medium of the Third Republic, they had come to control:[382]

> once they had the power in their hands, their first concern was to molest the Catholics and to combat the true Church . . . The most ferocious anticlericals and advocates of secularization were either Protestants, or came from Huguenot families . . . Moreover, the University has been Protestant for the last twenty years . . . and all public functions are reserved for Protestants; this invasion explains why Catholics . . . have been systematically excluded from all state employment.

The parallel with accusations made against the Jews is exact. *La Croix* also recommended to its readers Ernest Renauld's *Le Péril protestant* (1899), according to which: "It is certain that the Jews, the Freemasons and the Protestants have contracted an alliance against the Catholic nations, in order to assure their supremacy in the whole world . . . The main culprit is Protestantism. Protestants are the shock troops, who fired the first shot against the Church."[383] Renauld also provided a list of the names of all Protestants in the civil service, on the lines of the *Indicateurs des Juifs*. Moreover, a more official Catholic voice engaged in the same kind of anti-Protestant polemic. The Italian Jesuit organ, *La Civiltà Cattolica*, widely quoted in France, claimed in February 1898, that: "The Protestants have made common cause with the Jews to constitute a Syndicate. Most of the money for this comes from Germany . . ."[384]

However, anti-Protestantism was not confined to Catholics, or to the confessional press. Guillemin remarks on Zola's "intense aversion towards Protestants",[385] an indication that such hostility was not confined to the Nationalists and the antisemites. Among the latter, Drumont, like the Assumptionist Fathers, saw the Protestants as a dominating force in the Third Republic, and claimed that they abused their power to persecute the Catholics. He held the Protestants responsible, with the Jews, for the secularizing policies of the Republic;[386] and pointed to the Monod family as an example of Protestant influence in France,[387] a theme to be elaborated later by Maurras. Thus he wrote in *La France juive* that "the Protestants without going as far as the Jews . . . none the less worked vigorously to dishonour and to persecute the religion of the majority of French people";[388] and elsewhere in the same book, he suggested a closer alliance between Protestants and Jews: "From the start of the Republic, French Protestantism made an alliance with Jewry . . . The close connection that exists between the Jew and the Protestant has been established again and again . . . Protestantism . . . sealed its alliance with the Jew in a denial of the Cross . . .";[389] and he even wrote that "Every Protestant . . . is half-Jewish".[390] Anti-Protestantism was also a common theme in *La Libre Parole*, and among its contributors. Viau recounted that when Thiébaud joined the paper in 1896, "we were indebted to him for a series of virulent articles against the Protestants, whom he dubbed Traitors to France, of the same order as the Jews."[391] Bournand, who was also on the staff of *La Libre Parole*, wrote in 1898: "For some years now, the Protestants have formed a secret alliance with the Jews, have been taken in tow by them. There is nothing surprising in this, since the big banking houses are all Jewish or Protestant, and their interests are the same."[392] Gyp's *Chiffon* declared: "I detest Protestants . . . They are intriguers, dishonest, hypocritical . . . rats, if you like! . . . Naturally, there are a few exceptions . . . but I'm talking about the mass of Protestants . . ."[393]

Anti-Protestantism was also important among the younger generation of antisemites, whose attachment to the Catholic Church was often purely political. Barrès wrote, like Bournand, that "the financial oligarchy" that dominated France was made up of the Jews and "the Protestant banks";[394] he also claimed that "These Protestants do not belong to the Nation";[395] and, in reply to an enquiry, published in the *Revue de l'Action Française* in May

1900, coupled "Jews and Protestants" as anti-national forces at work in France.[396] Maurras was more anti-Protestant than Barrès. "The violence of M. Maurras against the Protestants", wrote Guy-Grand in 1911, "is only equalled by his violence against the Jews".[397] There is some truth, even, in Roudiez's contention that "he devoted more energy to attacking the Protestants" than he did to attacking the Jews,[398] although he presented the two as working together, as we have seen.

> The years 1789, 1790, 1791 and 1792, [he wrote in 1905[399]] were marked in France by a series of "liberations", whose effects have not been sufficiently noted: the Jewish nation was promoted to full civil existence; the Huguenots, proscribed or in emigration since 1685, had full civil rights again granted to them. Nationalist writers observe that our Jews, thus naturalized, have not ceased for this reason to form a community of their own, a state quite distinct from the French State: their practice of marrying, either among themselves, or with their kin from the North or the South of Europe, accentuates this difference between Jewish society and the rest of French society. A similar complaint . . . has been raised against the Huguenots who are counted among us. Though they were originally of irreproachable French blood, they are intellectual and moral dissidents, and have special affinities with our most redoubtable foreign rivals. It is to be regretted that such traits have not been corrected . . . [as it is] Protestant society has come to have a mentality quite different from the traditional French mentality; and between the two there has developed, more and more, a state of secret war, not a war of race, or even of religion, but, rather, of culture, of thought and of taste . . .

Maurras's most important contribution to anti-Protestant ideology was a series of articles, published in 1900 under the title *Les Monod peints par eux-mêmes: Histoire naturelle et politique d'une famille de protestants étrangers dans la France contemporaine,* and later appearing in book form. Here, through tracing the history of a single Protestant family, the Monods, symbol of Protestant domination in France, Maurras sought to show that, unless he reacted forcefully, "every Frenchmen is . . . destined to perish under the blows of the Monod tribe or those in league with them."[400] The Monod family constituted a state or "estate" within France. It was without attachments to the French or any other nation: "Born polyglot, they are hardly conscious of frontiers, and are always on the move . . . Capricious but demanding tenants of the countries which have received them, they are not French."[401] Moreover, like other immigrants, the Monods, in contrast to the French, were prolific, but of bad blood: "The Monods are peopling France with apes and lunatics."[402] Taking advantage of the weakening of France by the French Revolution and the democratic governments of the nineteenth century, the Monods had come to occupy a position of dominance, notably in the civil service and the University. Again the parallel with the role of the Jews in the ideology of Maurras and others is clear. Anti-Protestantism seems to have had more currency in the press and among intellectuals than in public meetings, although it did occasionally occur in the latter. For example, at an electoral meeting in Paris in April 1898, two candidates, supported by the Comités Nationalistes de la Rive Droite, "criticized the present government and attacked the Jews and the Protestants . . ."[403]

Much more popular than anti-Protestantism was anti-Freemasonry, which was frequently coupled with antisemitism, via the tandem concept of "Judeo-Masonry".[404] Gougenot des Mousseaux had claimed that the Jews used Freemasonry as a means of overthrowing Christianity.[405] Abbé Chabauty's *Les Francs-maçons et les Juifs: Sixième age de l'Eglise* (1881), a book praised by Drumont, made the same assertion.[406] Drumont, himself, popularized the association in *La France juive* and elsewhere, writing, for example: "The Jewish origin of Freemasonry is manifest . . . Governed by invisible masters, whose identity is not suspected, Freemasonry was a sort of open Judaism . . . Sheltering behind this war machine which hid him from view, the Jew was able to accomplish his evil work, without seeming responsible for it . . ."[407] By the 1890s, such ideas had become well-established clichés of antisemitic propaganda, particularly among Catholics. One of the first publications in France, together with that of Gougenot des Mousseaux's book, to posit the existence of a Judeo-Masonic conspiracy was Mgr Gaston de Ségur's *Les Francs-maçons* (1867); moreover, at least 20 books on the same theme, written by priests, were published between 1882 and 1886, in the wake of that of abbé Chabauty.[408] Catholic anti-masonry was encouraged by the fact that Freemasonry had been formally banned by the Church from 1738, and that it was officially blamed for the calamities that had befallen the Church since the French Revolution, for example in the encyclical *Quo Graviora* of 1826. Further encyclicals in 1873, 1884, 1890 and 1892 renewed the ban, and reiterated the claim that Freemasonry was a Satanic organization, whose aim was the Church's destruction.[409] It is not surprising, therefore, to find the intransigent Mgr Fava, bishop of Grenoble, sponsoring *La Revue de la Franc-maçonnerie Démasquée* in 1884, a publication that was taken over by the Assumptionist *Maison de la Bonne Presse* in 1894, and which survived until 1924.[410] The Jesuit Bishop Meurin of Port-Louis (Mauritius) asserted in 1893, in a book entitled *La Franc-maçonnerie, Synagogue de Satan,* that "everything in Freemasonry is fundamentally Jewish, exclusively Jewish, passionately Jewish, from the beginning to the end"; and that "it is by means of Freemasonry that the Jew will dominate the universe . . ."[411] *La Croix* stated that it was engaged in a war against "the Judeo-Masonic army";[412] and among the declared aims of the Assumptionist order was "a war on the secret societies".[413] As we have seen, it took over Fava's anti-Masonic review. The Assumptionists, moreover, put out a pamphlet in 1898 or 1899, in the same format as *Le Complôt juif* and *Le Complôt protestant,* entitled *Le Complôt maçonnique,* which accused the Freemasons of being the main allies of the Jews in a plot to take over France, and to destroy the Nation and the Catholic religion.[414] As Pierrard has shown, the anti-Masonic crusade continued unabated among the clergy until the First World War and beyond, producing pamphlets, books and more reviews.[415] The most extraordinary testimony to its appeal was the success of the anti-Masonic frauds of Léo Taxil, which we will discuss in a later chapter.[416]

The theme of the Judeo-Masonic conspiracy played a large part in antisemitic and Nationalist propaganda at the time of the Affair. So much so that Brunetière was reported to have claimed that "antisemitism was primarily a protest against Freemasonry",[417] a view that Daudet, to some extent, shared.[418] It was claimed, without justification, that Dreyfus was a Freemason. Reinach quoted *La Civiltà Cattolica*, which declared in February 1898 that the Jews "have taken hold of Freemasonry; Dreyfus is both a Jew and a Mason; and Masonry is, notoriously, the real master of the French State. Thus, the Jews control the Republic, which is less French than Hebrew . . ."[419] A deputy, the Comte de Lanjuinais, told a meeting of La Jeunesse Royaliste in Paris in January 1898 that "the country had been delivered into the hands of the Freemasons and the Jews."[420] A speaker told a meeting of the Comité Electoral Catholique of the 15th *arrondissement* in February that Catholics should support only those candidates pledged to fight "the Jewish and Masonic sectaries who have all the power".[421] Another speaker, at a Union Nationale meeting in the 11th *arrondissement* in April, declared: "We want no more of the Jews or the Freemasons . . ."[422] The Comte de Sabran-Pontevès, at another Jeunesse Royaliste meeting in Paris in April, "launched an attack on the Jews and the Freemasons . . ."[423] In the following years, the theme remained popular in Paris and the provinces. A big Union Nationale gathering in Paris in April 1900 featured various speeches against "Judeo-Masonry".[424] At a meeting organized by La Jeunesse Républicaine Nationaliste in Lyon in January 1901, a speaker called for the continuation of the struggle "against the Jew and the Freemason . . ."[425] Cavaignac was still denouncing the occult power of Freemasonry in French government and administration in 1902.[426] In Nantes, in August 1903, the local antisemitic press published lists of shops and businesses owned by both Jews and by Freemasons, with an appeal to boycott them, and declared: "All Jews are affiliated to Freemasonry."[427] At about this time, the Action Française offered for sale a similar *Répertoire maçonnique de 30,000 adresses de francs-maçons*, as well as various other books on Freemasonry by Gustave Bord, Copin-Albancelli and others;[428] only examples, as we have seen, of what was a flourishing genre. In Nantes, again, in October 1903, a Nationalist conference passed a resolution against "Judeo-Masonic power".[429] Maurras claimed in 1905 that Freemasonry was an organization used for nefarious purposes by foreigners and Protestants, as well as by Jews; it was "a secret society, originating in Germany, according to some, and, according to others, in England, and which seems to have acted as a liaison agency and an employment and recruiting office for recently naturalized citizens or those too much imbued with heterogeneous influences . . ."[430] The following year, a pamphlet put out by the Association des Catholiques de la Mayenne reiterated the more familiar claim that "Freemasonry has managed to gain power in France . . . Being the instrument of the Jews, it has sworn to destroy our religion."[431] Similarly,

Arthur Meyer, the editor of *Le Gaulois,* referred in 1911 to "the three forces hostile to the Catholics, the Jews, the Freethinkers and, above all, the Freemasons . . ."[432]

Leroy-Beaulieu wrote in 1902 that "the antisemites' insistence on confounding the Freemasons and the Jews in what they call Judeo-Masonry, only demonstrates their bad faith or their ignorance."[433] However, as in the case of the Protestants, there was some objective justification for seeing the Freemasons as a body hostile to the Catholic Church, and as a body that was or had been involved in the formulation and application of the anticlerical policies of the Third Republic, and particularly, in the drive to secularize primary education.[434] An anonymous article "La Franc-maçonnerie en France" based on transcripts of Masonic meetings, that Brunetière's *Revue des Deux Mondes* published in May 1899, provided considerable substantiation for Catholic suspicions here;[435] though, as Headings reasonably insists: "the Masons were not all-powerful; they formed a strong pressure-group, which worked in cooperation with other Leftist organizations."[436] Further "confirmation" of anti-Masonic claims was provided in 1904 by the revelation that the Masonic lodges had been used, apparently at the request of the Minister of War, General André, to collect information on the religious and political views of senior army officers.[437] However, although the deliberate use of the lodges in this case may have been a new departure, such surveillance itself was no novelty,[438] and the *"affaire des fiches"* simply showed that the lodges were a convenient network and not an agency capable of grand initiatives. The Nationalists, indeed, seem to have sensed this, since they used the affair to discredit General André and to force his resignation, thus implying that the responsibility for the whole matter was his. It must be said, too, in more general terms, that the secret society nature of Freemasonry aroused legitimate speculation about its activities and intentions. At a time also, when other associations, and particularly the religious orders, were the objects of official and legal harassment, the apparent immunity of the lodges gave grounds for grievance and suspicion, expressed most obviously in Guérin's decision to change the name of the Ligue Antisémitique Française to the Grand Occident de France. Also, as Leroy-Beaulieu pointed out in 1897, the Judeo-Masonic myth itself had some slender foundation in reality, since the Masonic Lodges were regarded by some Jews as "a means of 'arriving' . . . a way of forcing an entry into a society that was closed to them."[439]

However, none of this is sufficient to justify or to explain the whole conspiracy myth, to which Freemasonry was said to be party. Sorlin has pointed out that, in the constellation of enemies evoked by *La Croix,* foreign nationals and Protestants had some concrete being, while the Jew was purely abstract, referred to in the abstract singular as a disembodied spirit of evil.[440] This distinction may hold in so far as *La Croix* alone is concerned, but, in antisemitic nationalist ideology generally, Freemasonry and the Protestants were equally abstract entities. The Freemasons appeared, more often than not, in the form of the purely abstract concept of Judeo-Masonry, as we have seen. Barrès explicitly evoked "the Jews and the Protestants considered in the abstract";[441] while Maurras claimed in *La Gazette de France* in March 1898 that, whereas the Jews were a material force, "there is, by contrast, and without a doubt, *a Protestant spirit . . .* which threatens not only the French spirit, but . . . every spirit, every nation, every State, and reason itself . . . It dissolves societies; it constitutes, according to Auguste Comte's fine definition, *a sedition of the individual against the species."*[442] The conspiracy myth, in effect, did not proceed from the particular to the general, but operated the other way round. Objective enemies or threats were not proved, or even assumed, to be in collusion, but rather an abstract conspiracy was posited in the first place, and a group of enemies was then chosen to figure as its agent. Here the elasticity of the Syndicate concept is typical. Ostensibly anchored in reality as a way of referring to the Dreyfusard campaign, it immediately conferred an over-determination on its object, and allowed it, at the same time, to flow into a near-cosmic design. The Syndicate was also a means of expressing the conviction that all enemies were essentially the same, were essentially one. As a connoisseur of antisemitic ideology put it, with an awareness that French antisemites did not usually share: "It is part of the great leader's genius to let it always appear that even widely separated enemies belong to a single category only, since among weak and vacillating characters the awareness of different enemies leads all too easily to the beginning of a doubt of the justice of their own case."[443]

Relevant here is the concept of the *"judaïsant"*, the fellow-traveller or virtual Jew. Antisemites had inevitable difficulties in deciding who was or was not a Jew. Drumont argued, in *La France juive,* that there were three types of Jews: "The real Jews . . . who officially venerate Abraham and Jacob . . . the Jews disguised as freethinkers . . . who put their Jewishness into their pockets . . . [and] the conservative Jews who are Christian to all appearance, but who have the closest links with the first two categories and who provide their comrades with secrets that may be useful to them."[444] All Jews were Jews, in effect, but some Jews were more Jewish than others. Edmond Adam was described, for example, as "a Jewing Jew of Jewry".[445] The term *"judaïsant"*, with its vagueness, helped to overcome, or evade, these problems of definition, but it also allowed the category of Jewish to be infinitely extended. "We make no distinction", stated Boisandré's *Le Petit Catéchisme antijuif* (1900), "between the Jew and the *'judaïsant'*, that is to say, the businessman who behaves like a Jew."[446] Drumont exploited popular usage in the same way, writing of the Prussian Finance Minister in 1891: "if this Miquel is not a Jew, he is worthy of being one, since he is one of the worst pirates of German finance . . ."[447] But the term *"judaïsant"*, as used by the antisemites,[448] went far beyond popular usage, and served as another means by which enemies were confounded in a single "Jewish" bloc.

The same mechanism can be detected if attitudes towards the ostensible foreign enemies of France, particularly England and Germany, are examined. The Nationalists did pay a certain amount of attention to foreign policy, especially after 1905,[449] but it was never a primary consideration with them. Less emphasis was placed, in their ideology, on Germany as a foreign power outside France's frontiers, than on Germany as a foreign body working within France economically and through the medium of ideas. So, in *L'Avant-Guerre*, Léon Daudet exposed the German infiltration of France's vital industries with the aid of the Jews; and Maurras denounced "the intellectual annexation" of France by Germany in the later nineteenth century, and declared in 1905: "the process of *de-Germanization* has begun; a patient and definitive reaction has developed against foreign ideas and masters."[450] More generally, Wicart, in 1898, wrote that "his pride was particularly provoked by seeing the heavy hand of the Foreigner weighing on France, and stirring up confusion, demoralization and national collapse", and, by the Foreigner, he added, he meant "our avowed enemies, the English, the Germans and the Italians".[451] This conceptualization of a foreign power as an internal enemy can be seen particularly clearly in the treatment of England in antisemitic nationalist ideology. Colonial rivalry and the Fashoda crisis provided a rationale for Anglophobia (always mitigated by upper-class Anglomania),[452] but it was essentially a phobia. Wicart claimed, for example, that "the English are mainly to blame for our troubles, our defeats, our misfortunes and our revolutions, which they know how to provoke when they wish", and, as we have seen, he blamed the English for France's low birth-rate.[453] Here the English have attributed to them the same ubiquity, the same omnipotence as the abstract Jew. Drumont characterized the English in much the same terms;[454] while Léo Taxil, in the guise of "Dr Bataille", saw them as another people whom God had cursed: "The Englishman casts a blight on everything that he touches; it seems that this is an infirmity with which God has visited this heretical people, as a visible sign of his malediction."[455] *La Croix* presented England as France's hereditary enemy, but identified England with International Finance and Free Trade, and with the Jews and the Protestants, internal enemies.[456] At a meeting in Lille in April 1900, a speaker attacked England over the question of the Boer War, another opportune and much-used occasion for the expression of Anglophobia, but claimed also that the war was the responsibility of the Jews.[457] The identification of the English and the Jews was made more explicitly in Louis Martin's *L'Anglais est-il un Juif?* (1895) and Martin-Chagny's *La Sémitique Albion* (1898);[458] while the *Indicateur des Juifs* published in Lyon, also in 1898, claimed that ten of the twelve tribes of Israel were now English.[459]

Antisemites were here engaged in an essentialist and dualist exercise in classification, and, once an entity had been labelled evil rather than good, it became the equivalent of all the other entities placed under that heading. Thus Jew equalled Freemason equalled Protestant equalled England equalled Germany, and so on. Moreover, the equation went in that order. Nationalist antisemitism was a movement directed against internal enemies. Attacks were made on foreign powers or other nations, but in their manifestation as enemies within France, while the Jews, the Protestants and the Freemasons were said to be the agents of foreign powers largely to discredit them and to express their difference. Thus Millevoye, for example, claimed that "the Jews are the agents of Germany and England",[460] and accused "M. Clemenceau", at an antisemitic meeting, "of delivering us into the hands of England";[461] and Daudet denounced "Jewish-German espionage";[462] but, in each case, the internal enemy was primary, the Jews or Clemenceau, and the accusation of collusion with a foreign power was used as a pretext to denounce them and as a means of conveying their "alien" nature. Making the same point, with less emphasis, Leroy-Beaulieu wrote in 1902: "it is no longer just against the foreigner that Nationalism . . . excites the distrust and the aversion of the masses, it is against fellow-citizens, against other French people, against those whom it dares to call enemies of the interior."[463] Several critics pointed to an irony in this situation, suggesting that antisemitism's nationalistic denunciation of other French citizens was a way of masking its own foreign origins. "Antisemitism came to us from Russia, from Austria and from Germany", declared Charles Gide, for example, "and it is amusing to see this movement, which is itself a foreign import, taking as its slogan: 'France for the French'. . ."[464]

As we have seen, there is no doubt about the indigenous roots of French antisemitism, despite the encouragement that it may have received from external example,[465] and the exotic origin of the term *"antisémitisme"* itself. But antisemitism represented, nevertheless, a fundamental anxiety about nationality. It defined itself, characteristically, by exclusion. For the antisemitic Nationalists, Leroy-Beaulieu commented, "patriotism seems to consist of denying the quality of being French to others . . . This quality which belongs to all of us, whatever our opinions may be . . . they attribute to themselves as a privilege they seek to monopolize. If the most extreme of them are to be believed, the French, the real French, are a minority in France"; the Nationalist movement thus behaved like a church, or rather a sect, excommunicating "heretics, in the name of some kind of dogma, of an orthodoxy".[466] Leroy-Beaulieu saw nationalist antisemitism, therefore, as a socially divisive force, although in effect it was an attempt to provide social unity of a totalitarian kind, precisely by means of a classification of exclusion. As we have seen, again and again, Drumont and other antisemites made statements referring to "all" Jews, to "all" real Frenchmen, and the words, *"tout"*, *"toute"*, *"tous"*, recur endlessly in their speeches and writings. The appeal for national unity, moreover, was frequently made on a manifest level. Drumont wrote in *La France juive*, for example, that "the religious persecution [of the 1880s] has divided into two camps French people who ought to love each other and make a common front against the foreigner."[467] Maurras entitled a collection of his articles, "chronicling the national revival of 1895–1905": *Quand les Francais ne s'aimaient pas.*[468] At a meeting of the Comité de Protestation contre les Agissements du Syndicat Dreyfus in January 1898, Guérin called on all "men of good will to affirm the communion of ideas of all French people against the enemies of the nation . . ."[469]

But this unity operated in fact only on the level of the Nationalist-antisemitic movement itself. This movement, as we have seen, was a medley of groups with no unifying factor other than their common adhesion to the cause: "From monarchists to 'patriotic socialists', what a motley crew there was assembled under that banner!", commented Leroy-Beaulieu.[470] The Nationalist-antisemitic ideology provided precisely the only ideology that could pretend to hold such forces together, with its assertion that they all belonged to the nation, that they were really French, and that those who did not belong or who did not support them were not French. Guérin told a Ligue Antisémitique meeting in March 1898: "There are now but two parties in France . . . those who are for France and those who are against her. The antisemites are the first party . . ."[471] Antisemites, in effect, as Sartre observed later, defined themselves and found their identity by means of the excluding classification; they were French because they were not Jews or *"judaïsants"*.[472] The importance of this negative means of self-identification has been stressed by other students of antisemitism, and of belief-systems in general;[473] and it explains the crucial role played in Nationalist antisemitism by the conspiracy of abstract forces arrayed against France. In the words of Hans Toch, the conspiracy was the means by which "the person maintains his integrity and self-esteem only at the expense of others . . . The function of a conspiracy-oriented movement is not to do battle with conspiratorial forces, but to provide reassurance and security to its own members."[474] Security was obtained by negative self-identification, and by the definition of the forces of evil, the agents of misfortune, but the function of the myth does not end there. The enemy was deliberately lent an other-worldly Satanic grandeur and a unity, which tended to rule out taking practical steps against him, but, at the same time, the enemy was broken down; differentiations were made, within the single conspiracy, between Jews, Protestants, Freemasons, and so on. Both unity, and diversity within unity, were important.[475]

But, to return to the negative identification function of the myth, in so far as the conspiratorial forces were unreal, so also was the "nation" that was set against them. A passage from Drumont's *La Fin d'un monde* points to the mechanism by which an artificial nation was created by the Nationalists to match its artificial enemies.[476]

> The trouble is, [he wrote] that our France can no longer think for itself; it is like a balloon on a string; it is made to go up; the string is pulled, and it comes down again. There is not a nation, in effect, any more, and one cannot exist without a sense of the race, without fixed institutions, without traditions; what we have are simply atomized individuals, they float like impalpable dust in the atmosphere until the wind drops . . . then they fall to the ground; and when the rain falls, they become inert mud . . .

Here, Drumont was expressing a sense of social dislocation, of anomie, not uncommon in his day. He was also expressing a manipulative view of social organization, which antisemites frequently attributed to others, while, unconsciously, acting on it themselves. The reaction of the Nationalist and antisemitic movement to the social disorganization, which it diagnosed, was to create for itself the nation which its members needed, to provide its atomized units with precisely the fixed institutions, the sense of tradition and belonging which they desired. The actual national society, diverse and changing, could not, or could no longer, fulfil this function. It was therefore claimed that it had become the prey of, the vehicle for, alien forces, that it was no longer the real nation, which the Nationalists had to recreate by defining and excluding these forces. This scheme of things was made very plain in the contrast drawn by Maurras and others between "the legal country", which was the France of the Third Republic, and "the real country", which was the (imaginary) Nation of the Nationalists.[477]

But, with the Nationalist antisemitic movement, of course, we are not dealing with abstracted individuals who happened to join a movement for purely personal psychological reasons; we are dealing with individuals from particular social groups or classes, from particular professions, from particular parts of France, who joined a collective movement with a collective ideology, at a particular moment in time. In the main, as we have seen, they were bourgeois or petty bourgeois, and the antisemitic and Nationalist ideology performed certain particular functions for them. We have examined some of these from an economic and a professional point of view, and have begun to suggest what was perhaps a more general underlying social function for antisemites and Nationalists as members of a single "class". We must now take these suggestions further.

IV

What antisemitic nationalism sought to explain and come to terms with in a general way was suggested by Maurras, in his presentation of the idea of the conspiracy of the "four confederated states" in 1905:[478]

> It is very remarkable that the introduction, the return or the progress of these four elements has coincided: 1. with the fall of the national dynasty, axis of our State; 2. with the disorganization of the nobility and the clergy; 3. with the destruction of workers' corporations; 4. with the abolition of the special privileges of towns and provinces; 5. with the institution of departments, absolutely fictive territorial units, often quite opposed to local traditions, interests and customs; 6. with the persecution of Catholicism; 7. with the establishment of equal partible inheritance which limits paternal authority within families and leads to a low birth-rate; 8. with the achievement of centralization; 9. with the domestication of learning, by means of bureaucratic control over the Academies and the University. These nine coincidences explain the rise to power of the four intruders. In effect, with the royal State decapitated and the family broken up, with the professions disorganized, and local and provincial government paralysed or destroyed, what would one expect to happen to French society as a whole? It has been said again and again: it has become a swarm of individuals, a desert of atoms.

Here, along with an indication of the various particular functions of the Nationalist-antisemitic ideology that we have already discussed, we have the clue to its general function, expressed in terms reminiscent of Marx.[479] Nationalists and antisemites felt themselves to be individuals in a fictive society, a society lacking integration, without fixed structure or "natural" order, a *Gesellschaft* rather than a *Gemeinschaft*, in Tönnies's terminology;[480] and they sought, through their ideology, to explain and to overcome this uncomfortable state, returning, in their own perspective, to the stable rooted order of the past, but, in reality, creating their own artificial society of order and hierarchy in the face of the flux of social reality.[481] Of course, antisemites belonged to a society that was ordered and hierarchical enough by today's standards, but as bourgeois, often marginal bourgeois, they felt that this order and this hierarchy were unstable and under threat, both morally and materially. Martin du Gard's Jean Barois told young Nationalists that their movement expressed the fear and the instinct of self-defence of a privileged bourgeoisie: "you have sensed that the bold ideas of the nineteenth century will end by shaking up one by one all the bases upon which social harmony still rests."[482] The later nineteenth century was not only a period of unprecedentedly rapid social and economic change, but one in which changes in values were equally rapid and painfully acute. Moreover, bourgeois were presented with an analysis of their society and its transformation in terms of class conflict, an analysis which threatened them in their privileges and in their status. Nationalist antisemitism provided them, at once with a refuge, a community to belong to, the nation or the race, from which they could never, by definition, be ousted, and also explained that threat, that challenge to their status and well-being, not in terms of class conflict, a working-class or democratic movement aimed at setting up an egalitarian society, or of the simple levelling process of social change itself, but in terms, rather, of a mysterious world conspiracy of heterogeneous forces led by the Jews. L. Mirman thus characterized the antisemitic reaction in these terms: "It is not a question of competing political parties . . . Monarchists, Radicals, Socialists are irrelevant; what we have is simple Frenchmen, profoundly upset by the continuing spectacle of all these dark machinations, which will end up by breaking . . . the orderly pattern formed by the moral energies of the nation."[483]

Belief in this conspiracy, however, did not merely reflect a lack of social consciousness; it was not only an irrational social analysis; it was not simply, in Toch's words, "the frantic effort . . . the final rallying-cry of [an] overextended anachronism";[484] it was a social analysis that performed certain specific functions for those who adopted it. Like orthodox Socialist analysis, it explained the fact that society had changed and was still changing in a "capitalist" direction; it explained the change in social relationships, from the personal to the impersonal that seemed to have occurred as a result in the second half of the century, and also the development of bureaucracy; it explained the bourgeoisie's sense of having lost status, privilege and control, and of being threatened with the further loss of all three; but, unlike Socialist analysis, it relieved the bourgeoisie of responsibility for this change, it freed them from blame: they were not the real capitalists, the real exploiters, the real parasites, but rather the Jews. As Leroy-Beaulieu again commented, putting the question in a wider context, antisemitism "does not hesitate to affirm that the principle of evil is not in ourselves; it tells us again and again that the principle of evil comes from outside, that it is a virus foreign to our race, to our blood."[485]

Antisemitism, in the form of the conspiracy myth, moreover, was a mode of explanation that lacked the irreversibility of Socialist or progressive social analysis, which allowed that the conspiracy might be exposed and thus prevented, that the threat to the bourgeoisie might be removed, and that a stable, harmonious society of hierarchy and privilege might be restored. In the words of Edgar Morin: "The conspiracy, ultimate recourse of a delirious causality, is at the same time the first stage of a magical purification, a 'cure'."[486] That this solution was expressive rather than instrumental,[487] that it involved only a simulacrum of action, the joining in a purely ritual incantation of antisemitic formulae via reading newspapers, books and speeches, and writing them, and speaking or listening to speeches, did not lessen, but rather strengthened its escapist appeal.

Various aspects of this general function of antisemitic nationalism bear further examination. Take the sense of total crisis and particularly national decadence, expressed by so many writers in the second half of the nineteenth century, Taine, Renan, Durkheim, Zola, as well as the antisemites.[488]

> We must not be dazzled by the brilliant development of sciences, the arts and industry of which we are the witnesses. [wrote Durkheim, for example, in 1897[489]] This development is altogether certainly taking place in the midst of a morbid effervescence, the grievous repercussions of which each one of us feels . . . a pathological state [is] just now accompanying the march of civilization . . . a state of crisis and perturbation not to be prolonged with impunity . . . The abnormal development of suicide and the general unrest of contemporary societies spring from the same causes. The exceptionally high number of voluntary deaths manifests the state of deep disturbance from which civilized societies are suffering, and bears witness to its gravity.

In the next year, in his novel *Paris*, Zola evoked via his hero Pierre Froment, a conviction that French society was thoroughly corrupt and about to collapse in some violent catastrophe: "Every hour with frightful sadness he expected the collapse, Paris steeped in blood, Paris in flames."[490] He also evoked the conspiracy manias that developed out of such a sense of decadence, and were played up by the popular press, particularly in reaction to anarchism:[491]

> Some Anarchists, after carrying barrels of powder into a sewer near the Madeleine, were said to have undermined the whole district, planning a perfect volcano there, into which one half of Paris would sink. And at another time it was alleged that the police were on the track of a terrible plot which embraced all Europe . . . The signal for putting it into execution was to be given in France, and there would be a three days' massacre, with grapeshot sweeping everyone off the Boulevards, and the Seine running red, swollen by a torrent of blood.

Ironic or not in this particular case, such quotations indicate that the antisemites again were representing something more general in their own emphasis on French decadence, though their tone and their explanations were peculiar.

Drumont was obsessed by the themes of decadence, death and impending catastrophe. He referred, in *La France juive*, to "this epoch of decadence in which we live"; and evoked "that great day of reckoning, which must envelop in the shadow of death, and plunge into the silence of ruins, what will be left of France."[492] "Dear France!", he lamented in 1889, in the aptly-titled *La Fin d'un monde*,[493]

> to have mounted so high among the nations and to fall so low, to be the object of every insult and to be unable to respond, to lose each day another jewel from its shining crown, another remnant of its past glory! . . . Why such a fall? . . . What a noble flower! What a fine country! How loaded with talents by God, its people! What shame to finish thus! O Lord! spare us from this fate. Preserve us from the sophists, from the Freemasons and from the Jews.

His prayer unanswered, he prophesied, in *La Dernière Bataille:* "The destruction of France is imminent";[494] and declared a year later, in what he described as "his testament before the final catastrophe": "Human collectivities, societies, are like individuals in this respect; when they have become a prey to Sin, paralysis progressively invades them and Death wins control of their essential organs one by one." What his books illustrated was "the ultimate phase of a society in full dissolution, a world photographed in the spasms of its last agony".[495] In this scheme of things, the Jew was the agent of death, even represented Death itself: "Men . . . throw themselves on the Jew to die there . . . Each person once had his Death close by him. Each person now has close to him his Jew . . . he breaks down their vital parts, he decomposes them, he turns them to corpses, he puts them into the contortions of the final agony."[496]

Other antisemites shared Drumont's obsession, though they usually expressed it with less power. A leaflet presenting "the legislative programme of the Union Nationale" in July 1893 proclaimed: "France is threatened with catastrophe from four sides at once: 1. division; 2. ruin, unemployment and misery; 3. demoralization; and 4. the social question; all four are so many causes of death, which seem irremediable."[497] Much more prosaically, Bertillon referred in 1897 to "the effacement of France over the last two centuries", and to "the decline in its political and military effectiveness and its moral and intellectual influence . . ."[498] Wicart in 1898 announced his "ardent love for the Nation, for that France which was once so beautiful, so noble, so generous, whose history is an admirable poem", and regretted that "the régime of Cosmopolitanism has led our fine and glorious country to the edge of the abyss . . ."[499] A pamphlet, already mentioned, published at the time of the Rennes trial, echoed the title of Drumont's *La Fin d'un monde* in its own: *La Fin de la France: le complôt juif.*[500] So common had such harping on decadence become, even earlier, in such milieus that Maupassant could satirize it in *Bel-Ami.* When Duroy becomes a leader-writer for *La Vie Française*, "since he found it very hard to think of new ideas, he began to specialize in declamations on modern decadence, on the loss of moral fibre, on the lapse of patriotism and of French honour."[501] But this is to set down to a trivial opportunism, what was an authentic and profound conviction, particularly among intellectuals.

The insistence of a Jules Soury on "the decline of the West",[502] the meditations on death of both Maurras[503] and Barrès,[504] as well as Drumont, were witness to their sense that civilization, as they knew it, was doomed, that their values and their view of the world were losing their validity, as society changed. Theirs, in Stern's phrase, was a "politics of cultural despair".[505] Drumont and others denounced the moral depravity of the age, pointing, like Durkheim, to the increase in the crime-rate, in alcohol consumption, in prostitution and divorce.[506] Most decisive, the Bourgeoisie, the élite was "morally decadent";[507] "both the revolutionary Bourgeoisie . . . and the opportunist Bourgeoisie . . . are rotten to the core . . ."[508] Deriving from this moral decadence in some way was a failure of intelligence and of constructive artistic creativity. Drumont, again, like many others, lamented the decline in educational standards;[509] and accused the élites, bourgeois and noble of "complete intellectual degeneracy . . ."[510] Maurras inveighed against the ruinous and permanent influence of Romanticism in all spheres, and sought to uphold the threatened principles of classical order.[511] The Jews, of course, were to blame for this state of affairs, as they were the arch-representatives of the new "low" standards. Drumont dwelled on the alleged bad taste of the Rothschilds;[512] and wrote that, since the Jews controlled education and the arts in France, "there is nothing in the world of thought beyond the loves of Jewish actresses and works by Jews who are more or less Prussian."[513] According to Gaston Méry, writing in La Libre Parole in February 1897: "Edmond de Goncourt squarely accused the Jews of being, in great part, the cause of the decadence of our art and our literature."[514]

Méry introduced another element into the theme of decadence, which linked the cultural despair of intellectuals with what were older and perhaps more popular considerations. In the preface to a book by Baron de Novage, published in 1896 and called Ce qui va nous arriver: Guerre et révolution: d'après 45 prophéties anciennes et modernes, he evoked "the end of the century", in millenarian terms: "From the top to the bottom of the social scale, people are worried and ask what the new century will bring; they believe, from a thousand signs, that we are threatened by violent catastrophes."[515] Pointing to some of these signs, and ones that had social meaning, Mlle Verne, the priest's sister in Martin du Gard's Vieille France, declared: "The prophets have announced it: when vehicles begin to move by themselves, when men begin to fly in the air, and when women start wanting to live like men, the world will be condemned. And its end will be near!"[516] Michel de Certeau has written, in another context, that "the diabolical is . . . the index of an end of things [the end of an order, and the end of the world] . . .";[517] antisemitism, whose diabolical associations we shall later discuss, was another such index.

But the theme of decadence and of the end of things must be placed in its immediate socio-historical context, as well as in longer perspectives. Here, whatever its objective justification in details (and we have seen that it was linked to the experience of demographic stagnation, in particular), the harping on national decline and decadence can be seen as the means of expressing the sense of the decline of a certain form of society, with its attendant values, a form which had given undisputed pre-eminence to an educated bourgeois or noble élite. As Simone de Beauvoir has commented for a later period: "The death of Europe, the decline of the West, the end of a world, the end of the world: the Bourgeoisie lives in the imminence of the cataclysm that will destroy it."[518] As we have seen, this connection was explicitly made by late nineteenth-century antisemites. Drumont, for example, wrote in 1891: "You feel the demented fear of this world, of this country, which is on the eve of a terrible war, which hears on all sides the threatening signs of a social revolution . . ."[519] This view is confirmed by the fact that antisemites set their diagnosis of decline in a particular "historical" perspective. The decline of modern France was measured by the yardstick of an idealized "old France", in which, it was stressed, there had been a legal hierarchical ordering of society, and a privileged and hereditary ruling class. The aim of La France juive, according to Drumont, was to show how "France had been invaded, corrupted, made so stupid, that it could destroy with its own hands all that had made it powerful, respected and fortunate in the past."[520] Catastrophe, the day of reckoning, revolution, were symbolic, stylized representations of general social change.

The sense of decadence, and the conspiracy theory that went with it, reflected a loss of confidence on the part of the bourgeoisie. But rather than adopt an attitude of thorough-going social pessimism, like that of Gobineau,[521] most Nationalists and antisemites sought new grounds for confidence through their adoption of the Nationalist-antisemitic ideology itself. Drumont concluded La France juive by asking: "Have I drawn up our last will and testament? Or have I prepared our renaissance?";[522] and his expressions of despair were always offset by the hope that his propaganda might reverse the trends which he described. "Are we then a finished people, and ought we to die quietly [and] . . . make way for younger peoples, more energetic, better armed for the struggle?", asked Daudet, and replied emphatically in the negative;[523] while Maurras, in 1905, welcomed "the reaction of the classical spirit and of national sentiment", which, he claimed, had been brought about by the Nationalist movement.[524] But it was within the movement that the social insecurity of its adherents was essentially bolstered up and overcome. As we have noted repeatedly, antisemites and Nationalists continually expressed the need for security. The statutes of the first Ligue Antisémitique, for example, accused the Jews of compromising "the Security of France".[525] National security, however, symbolized social, professional, personal security. Barrès's Nationalist Nancy Programme of 1898 promised remedies for the "insecurity" suffered by workers, small traders, agriculturalists and bourgeois.[526] Concrete remedies of a kind were offered, but security was found essentially within the Nationalist-antisemitic ideology and its movement, in the contemplation of an ideal "Old France", a common heritage, in the sense of being rooted in that past, of being French vis-à-vis the Jews and other aliens. A young Nationalist in Martin du Gard's Jean Barois explained to Barois what he and his generation got out of Nationalism: "We find in it a security which you have always lacked!"[527] Drumont expressed the same feeling in symbolic form in 1892, when he contrasted the ephemeral mansions of Jewish financiers like Cornélius Herz "with the ancient dwellings of honest folk that remain standing!"[528] "Nationalism is made for nobodies", commented Benda. "This explains its eternal appeal. It allows them to claim solidarity with something great."[529]

This quest for vicarious prestige and security can be seen especially clearly in the cult of the army, that was so important a part of the ideology of nationalist antisemitism at the time of the Dreyfus Affair. So much so that an Allemaniste could claim in 1898 that "the incidents provoked by the Affair had only been stirred up to arouse patriotic feeling in the people, to polish up the glory of the army and to revive the prestige of the High Command."[530] As Girardet has shown, this cult of the army was something of a novelty. Until after 1871, the army was not generally popular in France, and its new popularity derived from the experience of the Franco-Prussian War itself, and from the switch from a professional to a conscript force.[531] However, Republican suspicions of the conservative officer corps remained lively,[532] and were aroused again by the experience of Boulangism and, more so, of the Affair itself. Opposition to the remaining professional element in the army was the burden of anti-Dreyfusard anti-militarism, if it can be called such. Gohier's *L'Armée contre la nation* (1899), an extreme example of its genre, was an attack, not on the army as such, but on military corruption, incompetence and wasting of public funds, and, above all, on the officer corps: "some imbeciles . . . have accused us of attacking the army," Gohier wrote in defence of himself and Dreyfusards as a whole. "They use this word to designate the military professionals, but they are not the army at all. The military professionals are functionaries, our salaried officials . . . and they number a mere 22,000. The army is the three million citizen soldiers who pay for the defence of the nation with their money and their blood."[533] Moreover, anti-Republican and opposition forces did not, before the end of the century, display a pronounced or a unanimous attitude in favour of the army. Déroulède and the Ligue des Patriotes did provide a direct link with post-1871 popular militarism;[534] but *La Croix,* until the time of the Affair, maintained the more common view that the army was a school of vice,[535] an opinion which the experience of the sons of the bourgeoisie, now obliged to do at least some military service, helped to strengthen and spread. "Military service, with the subjections which it entails, is a ferment for antimilitarism", declared Léon Daudet. "I did my 'volunteer' year . . . in 1887, at the time of the Boulangist 'fever', and there existed among the malcontents, even at that time, a latent hostility to the barracks and to military discipline."[536] This feeling found manifest expression in novels such as Abel Hermant's *Cavalier Miserey* (1887), Lucien Descaves's *Sous-offs* (1889) and Georges Darien's *Biribi* (1890), and in Georges Courteline's satirical pieces, *Les Gaîtés de l'escadron,* some of which were put on as a review in Paris in 1895.[537]

With the Affair, however, this hesitancy and distaste were completely dissipated, and the cult of the army became one of the main themes of opposition propaganda.[538] Generals and officers, like Mercier, Galliéni, and

Marchand became the fêted heroes of the Nationalist and antisemitic move-ment,[539] which looked, like Boulangism, for "the Providential Soldier", who would sweep away the Republican and parliamentary régime.[540] "If France had only possessed a [professional] army," mused Zola's General de Bozonnet, "one might have swept away that handful of bribe-taking parliamentarians who preyed upon the country and rotted it."[541] The function of this milita-rism can be directly related to the general function of nationalism, as already presented, particularly since the army was explicitly regarded as the symbol of the nation. "When one writes about the army", declared Drumont, as early as 1890, "one's pen falters and one pauses, for it conjures up the image of the flag of the Nation in mourning."[542] However, although there were real, historical reasons for this cult, and although antisemites and Nationalists expressed fears lest the Affair objectively endanger France's security vis-à-vis foreign powers, we have seen that their primary concern was with internal enemies; and the army was set in opposition, not so much to Germany or England, as to the Jews. In public meetings, shouts of "Long live the army!" and "Down with the Jews!" went together, like antiphonal responses in a liturgy.[543] The Prefect of the Mayenne reported in 1899: "People have been told that all those who call for the revision of the Dreyfus Affair are Jews and enemies of the army."[544] Drumont insisted, like others, that Jews were totally antipathetic to the army and the military life. "The Israelites have maintained . . . a sacred horror of the profession of arms", he wrote in *La France juive;* and he praised the German army for its refusal to accept Jews.[545]

This concern for the integrity of the army, this desire to preserve it from Jewish contamination, can be better understood if it is remembered that, beyond national defence, the French army had an important role as an internal police force, a role that had been conspicuously manifested in the repression of the Paris Commune in 1871. This role assumed new importance again at the end of the century, in the eyes of a bourgeoisie faced by a growing working-class movement, that was beginning to take more frequent and more effective strike action against employers,[546] and in whose ideology, in the 1890s, the general strike was becoming increasingly important.[547] Not only was the military relied on to quell or break strikes,[548] but it could be seen as the last protection against that "day of reckoning" that the idea of a general strike seemed to announce.[549] The espousal of militarism by the Right and its "populist" allies and of anti-militarism by the Extreme Left[550] was thus the reflection of a "class struggle", in which the army was the ultimate defence of the bourgeois social order. On another level, as we have seen in examining the Henry Subscription,[551] the army provided Nationalists and antisemites with a model of the hierarchical and stable society, which they wished to rescue from the social flux represented by Socialist, syndicalist and Jew. With its fixed ranks, its discipline, its faith, the army, like the Church, like the Old Régime, stood for order, permanence and security in a world of chaos and confusion. Already in 1872, introducing a new conscription law to the Na-tional Assembly, the Marquis de Chasseloup-Laubat had spoken of the army as "a social institution, upon which will be based, let us hope, important reforms in our morals, our customs and our laws", and, indicating the conservative intention behind such proposed "reforms", had stressed that the nation needed that "obedience to one's superiors which is military discipline".[552] Taking up the same theme twenty years later, Drumont claimed that the army and the Church were "the only two bodies in the State in which there still burns the flame of devotion to duty, in which there still lives the spirit of sacrifice . . ."[553] "There is one thing which a Frenchman must not insult," he wrote therefore in 1891, well before the outbreak of the Affair, "and that is the honour of the sword . . ."[554] And this imperative became even more crucial when the Affair was at its height. Thiébaud referred, at that time, to "the army to which we all belong and which remains our one and only belief";[555] while Paul de Cassagnac implored: "The army is our last refuge. Jews or judaised Christians, do not touch it!"[556]

As we have seen in the context of the Affair, the support given by antisemites to the army was reciprocated, at least by officers.[557] Drumont reported in 1890 on interviews with a number of senior army officers, who were overt antisemites, one a captain aged forty, decorated with the Tonkin medal, another "who had occupied a high position at the Ministry of War"; he also noted that the younger generation of the aristocracy was very hostile to the Jews, "the generation that had passed through the army . . ."[558] There is other evidence to suggest that antisemitism was strong among colonial officers, particularly in the African army;[559] and, as the Affair revealed, it influenced the judgment of the High Command and of successive Ministers of War. Drumont could claim, too, that he enjoyed the support of "retired officers".[560] Two retired generals, Baron Fririon and du Barail, gave public support to the antisemitic movement in interviews published by Bournand in 1898.[561] General Fririon testified to the long-standing hostility to Jews among officers: "Already, at that time [the time of his grandfather], army officers had a horror of the Jew. They could remember the scavengers who followed the army, and who belonged to the race of Israel—who grew fat on the detritus of war, like a flock of crows; [and later] in the army of the Second Empire, to which I belong, Jewish officers were rare and disliked."[562] Another retired general, Jacquey, was more actively involved in the antisemitic movement. Closely associated with the Ligue Antisémitique Française, he was elected as an antisemitic deputy for Mont-de-Marsan (Landes) in 1898, a seat that he represented until 1910.[563] Among officers on active service, according to Georges Renard in 1899, antisemitism was supported "in particular by those who had been educated in religious schools", a view which Zola and others shared.[564]

Antisemitism was thus traditional in the French officer corps, but it seems to have been exacerbated at the end of the nineteenth century[565] by a number of factors, similar to those operating in civilian professions, and to which antisemites often gave a voice, and antisemitism an explanation. Ralston has pointed out that peace meant inevitable promotion blocks in the army by the 1880s. Officers spent increasingly long periods of time in lower ranks. By 1900, a lieutenant had to wait eleven or twelve years before becoming a captain; a captain about the same before becoming a major. Young graduates of military schools entering the army in the late 1890s had even worse career prospects. Officers were also poorly paid by civilian standards, but had to keep up a social position on low salaries. Premature resignations from the officer corps were thus common even in the 1880s, and "all too justified by the inadequate pay and the disheartening slowness of promotion", as *Le Spectateur Militaire* commented in 1886.[566] There was also resentment among officers at the growing bureaucratization and politicization of the army, which was expressed by the officers interviewed by Drumont. A captain on active service complained that "colonels have become bureaucrats"; a second officer that "Senior officers are constantly moved about, and they command troops with whom they have been in contact perhaps once a year, from their desks by means of circulars and memoranda . . ."[567] The captain also objected to the fact that the army was under the direction of a Minister of War, who was essentially a politician: "We need as our chief a *soldier*, a man of action and a man of faith, an independent minister who would show his scorn for politics and for politicians, and who would fear God instead of quaking in his boots before deputies, Jewish financiers and Freemasons . . ."[568] The second officer made the same point, adding that the post of Chief of the General Staff had become one that required political and diplomatic, and not military, skills, so that the future generalissimo was badly prepared for his task of leading the army in war.[569] Both officers felt that this bureaucratization threatened to destroy the paternalist relationship between officers and men on which the fighting effectiveness of the army depended: without this, "how can you expect our three-year conscripts to love the noble profession of arms, and to form, around their leader, the little family, united, strong, valiant, brave, disciplined, trusting and enthusiastic . . . that will be able to endure with abnegation the hardships and fatigues, the misfortunes and the perils of war?"[570] Both officers also contrasted the real military qualities of officers and troops of the line with the lack of such qualities in the military bureaucrats and staff officers: the former "were now the only really active and living part of the army"; only there could be found still "the qualities of devotion to duty, of abnegation and enthusiasm which have been the basis of France's glory in the past . . ." But favours, decorations, promotions went, not to such "real" officers, but to those "clever enough to avoid active service".[571]

This helps to explain the peculiar hostility directed against Dreyfus, himself a staff officer as well as a Jew, and thus doubly a target for resentments. General Fririon told Bournand that Jewish officers were most numerous in the Commissariat, where they were, up to a point, accepted: "There they could exercise their special aptitude for trading and business."[572] But Jewish officers on the General Staff did not fit the traditional stereotype at all. As one of Dreyfus's examiners at the Ecole de Guerre commented: "We can't have Jews on the General Staff."[573] Dreyfus was thus regarded as an intruder by his colleagues when he did gain entry to their jealously guarded preserve; but, as an intruder, he was also convenient to them, and could be singled out by them as a target against which hostility towards staff officers as a whole could be deflected. This combination of factors would certainly explain what seems to have been the special intensity of antisemitism among officers of the General Staff.[574]

More generally, as Edgar Morin has pointed out, career officers, isolated from the general community in their barracks to a great extent, as well as through their special mode of life and by their tradition of political non-involvement and thus political naïveté, would be especially prone to the credulity and the conspiracy theories on which antisemitism thrived.[575] Staff officers in the Deuxième Bureau (or Intelligence Department) like du Paty de Clam and Henry, might have very particular proclivities in this direction. Account must also be taken of the feelings of threat experienced by officers from aristocratic and Catholic milieus, who, "excluded from other public employment by the triumph of democracy, had directed their sons into the military career."[576] By the 1890s, as we have already indicated, these groups saw their position in the army itself threatened by the new stress being laid on competitive entry and on academic training, and the threat could be symbolized in this, as in other careers, as a "Jewish invasion".

The antisemitism of army officers thus fitted into a more general pattern, as the cult of the army was part of a wider nationalism. We will discuss the social conservatism of antisemites, that took the army as a model, more fully in a later chapter, and will conclude here by mentioning one further general function of nationalism, that has often been emphasized in other contexts.[577] In his Nancy Programme, Barrès asserted that "nationalism necessarily engenders socialism",[578] a claim that we have examined in the previous chapter. Various historians have investigated French "National-Socialism" in the period,[579] and have stressed, rightly, that it represented an appeal for national unity against class conflict. The Anarchist Faure attacked the slogan "France for the French" on these grounds, at a meeting in Paris in February 1898: "He said that it was the most dangerous slogan because it misled the workers and encouraged them to believe in an economic and financial nationalism."[580] The strength of this belief among the population at large, and the good judgment of the Nationalists in their attempts to cultivate and exploit it, were demonstrated by the overwhelming unanimity of patriotic response, by the "Union Sacrée", when war came in 1914.[581]

But nationalism was not just a deliberate ideological counter to Socialism; it was an authentic substitute for, and alternative to it. Although, as we have argued, one of its intentions was to dampen class conflict at home on the pretext that national unity was necessary against external enemies, thus defending the class structure from attack, another function, equally if not more important, was to introduce the idea of an internal conflict of a different kind. This was not an objective conflict arising from real tensions or differences of interest in society, but an abstract scheme imposed on social reality. It used the terminology of externally-directed patriotism; it wished to avoid and to parry actual class conflict; but it was primarily a representation of the social world, rather than a policy for social action within that world. It was thus different in kind from orthodox Socialism, an explanation of reality, but an explanation that could only come to terms with the real world by trying to replace it with an artificial world of its own creation, rather than grappling with confused reality and trying to mould or change it, though the difference may be more one of degree than of kind. A voice from that real world interrupted Guérin's speech at the meeting of the Comité de Protestation contre les Agissements du Syndicat Dreyfus, already quoted: "Where is the nation of people like us, without a roof over our heads, and who are always under somebody's thumb?"[582]

NOTES

1 On the general association of antisemitism with nationalism, see Ginsberg, "Antisemitism", pp. 200–1; Loewenstein, *Christians and Jews*, pp. 48–9, 65 and 77; and Memmi, *Portrait d'un Juif*, pp. 185, 232–3, 254, and 276.

2 See, for example, Péguy, *Notre Jeunesse*, p. 123; also Rémond, *La Droite en France*, chapter VI; and Girardet, *Le Nationalisme français*, chapters III and IV.

3 "La France aux Français!". This slogan was still current at the time of Vichy; see Morin *et al.*, *La Rumeur d'Orléans*, p. 181.

4 See Police reports. AN F⁷ 12480; AN F⁷ 12720; and AN F⁷ 12464.

5 See Drumont, *La France juive*, I, pp. 329 and 389; *La Dernière Bataille*, pp. 524–7; and *Le Testament d'un antisémite*, p. 231.

6 Drumont, "Merci!", 5 February 1895, *De l'Or, de la boue, du sang*, p. 330.

7 Fore-Fauré, *Face aux Juifs!*, p. 310.

8 See Sorlin, *"La Croix" et les Juifs*, pp. 65–9 and 218–19.

9 See my "Catholic Populism in France at the time of the Dreyfus Affair", p. 692.

10 Daily Report, Prefect of Police, 31 March 1898. APP Ba 106. For another example of antisemitic enthusiasm for the Franco-Russian alliance, see Biez, *Les Rothschild et le péril juif*, pp. 6–9.

11 "L'Archiviste", *Drumont et Dreyfus*, p. 10.

12 Leroy-Beaulieu, *Les Doctrines de haine*, p. 10.

13 Clermont-Tonnerre, *Mémoires*, I, p. 240; see also Dagan, *Enquête sur l'antisémitisme*, p. 33; and Barrès-Maurras, *La République ou le roi*, pp. 228–31.

14 See Drumont, *TA*, pp. 126–7; and Barrès, *Mes Cahiers*, II, (1898–1902), p. 248; and, on Barrès's antisemitism generally, Barrès-Maurras, op. cit., p. 177; and Sternhell, *Maurice Barrès*, pp. 128–31 and *passim*.

15 See Barrès, *Scènes et doctrines*, II, p. 159 n., referring to an article in *Le Figaro* (1892); also Girardet, *Le Nationalisme français*, pp. 7–10 and *passim;* and Leroy-Beaulieu, *Les Doctrines de haine*, pp. 22–3, who stresses the novelty of the word "Nationalisme" as applied to France. Reinach claimed that the term "nationaliste", in the same sense, was first used by Thiébaud in 1897; Reinach, *Histoire de l'Affaire Dreyfus*, III, p. 577. The Barresian formulation of nationalism was not of course entirely novel, as this quotation from Veuillot, writing in 1870, indicates: "Moi, chrétien catholique de France, vieux en France comme les chênes et enraciné comme eux, je suis constitué, déconstitué, reconstitué, gouverné, régi, taillé par des vagabonds d'esprit et de moeurs. Rénégats ou étrangers, ils n'ont ni ma foi, ni ma prière, ni mes souvenirs, ni mes attentes." Louis Veuillot, *L'Univers*, 16 November 1870, cit. Pierrard, *Juifs et catholiques français*, p. 26.

16 Barrès, *Scènes et doctrines*, II, p. 161.

17 Barrès, Reply to an "enquête" of the Action Française, 15 May 1900, ibid., I, pp. 67–8. See also Benda, *Les Cahiers d'un clerc*, p. 11 (written 13 February 1936 in New York), for the impact of this concept: "J'ignore la civilisation française, m'offre en toute joie à celle que je découvre, goûte à plein ce qu'elle a d'unique, de grand. J'entends Barrès: 'Nous avions cru que notre culture avait mordé sur toi. Naïfs que nous étions. Tu n'es qu'un Juif sans patrie. Te voilà prêt à faire litière de notre France qui te nourrit depuis soixante ans, à accepter un monde tout autre . . .'"

18 Adam, *L'Essence du Soleil,* p. 195, cit. Randall, *The Jewish Character in the French Novel,* p. 75.
19 Jarzel, *Petit Catéchisme nationaliste,* p. 3.
20 Bainville, *Journal, 1901–1918,* p. 24 (14 August 1905); see also Drumont, *FJ,* I, p. 59.
21 Memmi, op. cit., p. 254.
22 Lazare, *L'Antisémitisme,* p. 302; also ibid., chapter XI, "Nationalisme et Antisémitisme".
23 Leroy-Beaulieu, *Les Doctrines de haine,* p. 111.
24 Romain Rolland, *Jean Christophe, La fin du voyage: La nouvelle journée* (Paris, 1912), p. 82, cit. Randall, op. cit., p. 159.
25 Mauriac, "L'Affaire Dreyfus", p. 17; and Dreyfus, *Cinq années de ma vie,* pp. 274–80 and *passim.* For other indications of Jewish patriotism at this time, see Benda, *La Jeunesse d'un clerc,* pp. 134–5 and *passim;* Maurois, *Mémoires,* I, pp. 12–22 and 99; and Marrus, *The Politics of Assimilation,* chapter 5. Jewish patriotism was again demonstrated during the First World War; see Pierrard, op. cit., p. 229; and Landau, "Aspects et problèmes de l'histoire des Juifs en France", p. 237. See also, generally, Memmi, op. cit., pp. 250–1; and chapter XIX, pp. 693–4 below.
26 Leroy-Beaulieu, *Les Doctrines de haine,* pp. 10–11.
27 Barthou, *Le Glaneur,* 6 April 1902, cit. Bousquet-Mélou, *Louis Barthou,* pp. 115–16. The ex-*communard* was Rochefort, and the ex-Minister of War Cavaignac. Cavaignac's ambition to lead the Nationalist movement conflicted with the rival ambitions of Rochefort, Déroulède and others; see Dardenne, *Godefroy Cavaignac,* p. 477 and *passim;* Piou, *Le Comte Albert de Mun,* p. 192; and Barrès-Maurras, op. cit., p. 666.
28 Barrès-Maurras, op. cit., p. 326; also pp. 291, 381 and 665–6.
29 Daily Report, Prefect of Police, 22 February 1898. APP Ba 106.
30 Guérin, *Les Trafiquants de l'antisémitisme,* pp. 272–6 and 282–3.
31 On the Nationalist movement in general see, in addition to the works cited in n. 2, Daudet, *Au Temps de Judas,* pp. 84–5, 162–5, 173–4 and 267–75; Clermont-Tonnerre, op. cit., pp. 240–3; Pierrard, op. cit., chapter 3; Sternhell, *Maurice Barrès,* pp. 61–3 and 337; and my "L'Action Française et le Mouvement Nationaliste français".
32 See Viau, *Vingt ans d'antisémitisme,* pp. 230–1; and Sorlin, *Waldeck-Rousseau,* pp. 415–18.
33 Renard, Letter to Maurice Pottecher, 22 July 1901, *Correspondance,* p. 244; see also ibid., p. 296; and Reinach, op. cit., III, p. 247.
34 On Bonapartism generally in this period, see J. Rothney, *Bonapartism after Sedan* (Ithaca, 1969).
35 See Daily Report, Prefect of Police, 14 February 1898. APP Ba 106; and AN F⁷ 12720, Dossier, "La Jeunesse Antisémite et Nationaliste".
36 See Daily Reports, Prefect of Police, 17 January, 18 February, 7 March, 3 April, 2 May, and 19 June 1898. APP Ba 106.
37 See Bournand, *Les Juifs et nos contemporains,* pp. 103–10; Reinach, op. cit., III, p. 17; Daudet, *Paris vécu,* Ier série, p. 30; Daudet, *Salons et journaux,* p. 283; and chapter VIII, pp. 215 and ff. above.
38 Drumont, *FJ,* I, pp. 300–29, 435 and 443; *DB,* pp. 223–6; and *TA,* pp. 389 and 400–3.
39 See Rémond, *La Droite en France,* pp. 22, 172 and 286; and Patrick H. Hutton, "Popular Boulangism and the Advent of Mass Politics in France, 1886–90", *Journal of Contemporary History,* 11 (1976), pp. 85–106.
40 See Elio Zorzi, *L'Avventura del Generale Boulanger: Storia di una Rivoluzione mancata (1886–1891)* (Milan, 1937), p. 209; Byrnes, *Antisemitism in Modern France,* pp. 234–5; Seager, *The Boulanger Affair,* pp. 174–81; Sternhell, *Maurice Barrès,* pp. 134 and 236.

41 See chapter VIII, p. 213 above.
42 See, for example, Report, Police agent, "Boulangisme et antisémitisme"; and Police report, 2 February 1898. AN F⁷ 12459; Report, Prefect, Calvados, 15 November 1898. AN F⁷ 12460; *Le Journal de Rouen*, 21 January 1898; Report, Prefect, Seine-Inférieure, 22 January 1898. AN F⁷ 12467; Daily Reports, Prefect of Police, 1 January, and 30 June 1898. APP Ba 106; Gohier, *L'Armée contre la nation*, p. 266; Reinach, op. cit., I, p. 471; and III, p. 578; Zévaès, *Au Temps du Boulangisme*, p. 242; Lauris, *Souvenirs d'une belle époque*, p. 94; and Halévy, *Degas parle*, pp. 121–2.
43 Blum, *Souvenirs sur l'Affaire*, pp. 65–6.
44 L.-J. de Lanessan, *Le Rappel*, January 1898, cit. Bournand, op. cit., p. 122.
45 Drumont, *DB*, p. 163.
46 Drumont's hostility to Boulangism at this time was motivated in great part by the fact that, in his unsuccessful bid to be elected as municipal councillor for the Gros Caillou *quartier* of the 7th *arrondissement* in 1890, he had been opposed by a Boulangist candidate; on this and generally, see Drumont, *DB*, pp. 137–138, 158–159, 164, 166, 176, 178–180, 183 and 188; and *TA*, pp. x, 11, 49, 98–101, 104, and Book V, "Une élection municipale en 1890"; also Viau, op. cit., p. 14.
47 According to Daudet, *Les Oeuvres dans les hommes*, p. 156; also Beau de Loménie, *Edouard Drumont*, pp. 92–4.
48 See Drumont, *La Fin d'un monde*, pp. 312–19; and "Sur l'escalier", *OBS*, pp. 41–2.
49 Police report, 13 August 1892. AN F⁷ 12459.
50 See Schwarzschild, "The Marquis de Morès", p. 15.
51 Cit. Camille Ducray, *Paul Déroulède 1846–1914* (Paris, no date), p. 180.
52 Daily Reports, Prefect of Police, 5 and 31 March 1898. APP Ba 106.
53 Daily Reports, Prefect of Police, 2 and 5 May 1898. APP Ba 106; see also Zévaès, *Au Temps du Boulangisme*, p. 177; and Sternhell, *Maurice Barrès*, p. 249.
54 Sternhell, *Maurice Barrès*, p. 232; see also Barrès, *Mes Cahiers*, I, pp. 174 and 250 (1897); and Sternhell, "Barrès et la Gauche".
55 See Barrès-Maurras, op. cit., p. 259; Zévaès, *Au Temps du Boulangisme*, pp. 90, 182–3, 210, 226 and 234–5; Sternhell, *Maurice Barrès*, pp. 234–5 and 249; and Chapter VIII, pp. 213 and ff. above.
56 Bournand, op. cit., p. 45; see also Zévaès, *Au Temps du Boulangisme*, pp. 97–8 and 160; Drumont, *DB*, pp. 167–71 and 176; Drault, *Drumont, La France juive et La Libre Parole*, p. 198; Daudet, *Salons et journaux*, pp. 80–4; Barrès-Maurras, op. cit., p. 151 n.; Sternhell, *Maurice Barrès*, pp. 104–5, 147 and 342.
57 See Girardet, "La Ligue des Patriotes", pp. 3–6; and chapter II, pp. 53–4 above.
58 See Maurras, *Au Signe de Flore*, p. 97.
59 See, for example, Thabault, *Education and Change in a Village Community*, pp. 184 and 223.
60 Viau, op. cit., p. 14; see also Drumont, *TA*, pp. 91–2.
61 Cit. "L'Archiviste", op. cit., p. 10.
62 Cit. Ducray, op. cit., p. 188.
63 Viau, op. cit., p. 196.
64 Guérin, op. cit., pp. 200–1 and 272–6.
65 Drumont, *FJ*, I, pp. 483, 485 and 487; also ibid., II, p. 212.
66 Drumont, *TA*, pp. 1 and 92–3; and *DB*, p. 138.
67 Daudet, *Au Temps de Judas*, p. 162; also ibid., p. 87; Daudet, *Salons et journaux*, pp. 122–4; Barrès-Maurras, op. cit., pp. 260–3, 316–17 and 475.
68 See Reinach, op. cit., III, pp. 386–7; Sternhell, "Paul Déroulède and the origins of French nationalism", p. 54; Sternhell, *Maurice Barrès*, p. 70; and Rutkoff, "The Ligue des Patriotes", pp. 590 and 601. Sternhell does, however, pass over Déroulède's earlier antisemitic statements; while Pierrard, op. cit., p. 134, plays down the antisemitism of Déroulède and the Ligue des Patriotes altogether; Drault paradoxically claimed that Déroulède was not an antisemite, but that he

had coined the nickname "Boule-de-Juif" for Reinach; see Chapter XI, n. 90; and Drault, op. cit., pp. 141, 252 and 274–5

69 They were Habert, Ferrette, Faure, Goussot, Gauthier de Clagny, Paulin-Méry and Cluseret.
70 Daily Report, Prefect of Police, 12 June 1898. APP Ba 106.
71 Report, Commissaire spécial, Marseille, 28 September 1898; and Telegram, Commissaire spécial, Valenciennes, 6 December 1898. AN F⁷ 12449.
72 Report, Commissaire spécial, Marseille, 6 June 1899. AN F⁷ 12449.
73 Report, Prefect of Police, 3 July 1899. AN F⁷ 12458.
74 Report, Police agent, 17 August 1899. AN F⁷ 12870.
75 See, for example, Report, Prefect of Police, 24 October 1900. AN F⁷ 12458.
76 Reports, Commissaire de police, Le Mans, 9 May 1900; and Prefect, Mayenne, 28 November 1899. AN F⁷ 12453–12454.
77 Report, Police agent, 19 January 1901. AN F⁷ 12870.
78 L'Intransigeant, 21 January 1901.
79 Sternhell, Maurice Barrès, p. 249 n.
80 See Viau, op. cit., pp. 318–19.
81 Report, Police agent, 7 December 1903. AN F⁷ 12870, Dossier No. 5, "Ligue des Patriotes, 1903".
82 Report, Police agent, 24 January 1904. AN F⁷ 12457.
83 Report, Police agent, Paris, 14 March 1905. AN F⁷ 12719.
84 See Chapter II, pp. 57–8; Chapter VII, pp. 200–1; and Chapter IX, p. 239 above.
85 See Daudet, Au Temps de Judas, p. 146.
86 Viau, op. cit., pp. 196, 270–2 and 287–9; see also, on Drumont's hostility to the Ligue de la Patrie Française: Bernanos, La Grande Peur des bien-pensants, p. 349; and on Nationalism in Parisian municipal politics, Watson, "The Nationalist Movement in Paris".
87 See Viau, op. cit., pp. 286–7; and Police report, 9 February 1904. AN F⁷ 12449.
88 Police report, 9 February 1904. AN F⁷ 12449.
89 Cit. Barrès, "La Ligue de la Patrie Française" (February 1899), Scènes et doctrines, I, p. 71; also pp. 69–101.
90 Daudet, Au Temps de Judas, p. 168; see also Pierrard, op. cit., pp. 134–6.
91 Report, Commissaire de police, Epernay, 29 April 1900. AN F⁷ 12456.
92 Report, Commissaire spécial, Saint-Dié, 19 November 1900. AN F⁷ 12457.
93 Report, Commissaire spécial, Saint-Dié, 18 November 1900. AN F⁷ 12457.
94 Report, Commissaire spécial, Nancy, 2 December 1901. AN F⁷ 12456.
95 Report, Prefect of Police, 29 April 1901. AN F⁷ 12458.
96 Report, Commissaire de police, Saint-Germain-en-Laye, 2 February 1902. AN F⁷ 12457.
97 See Pierrard, op. cit., pp. 134–6.
98 See, for example, Daudet, Paris vécu, Ier série, pp. 27–8 and 30–1; Pierre Dominique, Léon Daudet (Paris, 1964), pp. 59–60; and Le Procès de Charles Maurras, pp. 127–8; also Pierrard, op. cit., p. 306.
99 Maurras, Au Signe de Flore, pp xiv, 133 and 141.
100 See Drault, op. cit., p. 198; Barrès-Maurras, op. cit., pp. 396–7; and Jouveau, "L'Itinéraire félibréen de Charles Maurras", p. 86.
101 See particularly a letter dated 14 July 1906, Barrès-Maurras, op. cit., p. 473.
102 See Pierrard, op. cit., pp. 170 and 184; and my "L'Action Française et le Mouvement Nationaliste français".
103 L'Action Française, 4 January 1911, cit. Weber, The Nationalist Revival in France, p. 176.
104 Vaugeois, La Revue de l'Action Française, 15 August 1900, cit. Duroselle, "L'Antisémitisme en France", p. 69; and Pierrard, op. cit., p. 175.
105 Report, Prefect of Police, 22 May 1900. AN F⁷ 12458.
106 Report, Prefect, Eure, 2 December 1901. AN F⁷ 12455; and L'Antijuif, 7 December 1901.

107 Police reports. AN F⁷ 12854; Weber, *The Nationalist Revival in France*, p. 78; and Weber, *Action Française*, chapters 1–3.
108 See Gérard Gaudin, "Chez les Blancs du Midi: du légitimisme à l'Action Française", *Etudes Maurrassiennes*, 1 (1972), p. 66.
109 *La Revue de l'Action Française*, 15 August 1900; 15 March, and 15 June 1901, cit. Paugam, *L'Age d'or du Maurrassisme*, pp. 40–1.
110 See Daudet, *Paris vécu*, Ier série, p. 26; Daudet, *Au Temps de Judas*, pp. 169–70; Daudet, *Les Oeuvres dans les hommes*, pp. 161, 170–1 and 193; and Pierrard, op. cit., pp. 178–81.
111 Jarzel, op. cit., p. 3.
112 Alfred Rambaud, *Histoire de la civilisation française* (Paris, 1885), p. 417, cit. Bournand, op. cit., p. 172.
113 Auguste Chirac, *Les Brigandages historiques* (Paris, 1888), II, p. 139, cit. Silberner, "French Socialism and the Jewish Question", p. 9.
114 Drumont, *FJ*, I, p. 312.
115 See Sorlin, *"La Croix" et les Juifs*, pp. 154–8.
116 Cit. Pierrard, op. cit., p. 183.
117 Cit. "L'Archiviste", op. cit., pp. 19–20.
118 Blum, *Souvenirs sur l'Affaire*, p. 63.
119 Drumont, "Le Drame juif", *OBS*, p. 77.
120 Barrès, "Le Devoir des diverses ligues" (July–December 1899), *Scènes et doctrines*, I, p. 106.
121 Fore-Fauré, op. cit., p. 38.
122 Biez, *Les Rothschild et le péril juif*, p. 6.
123 *La France Libre*, Supplément, 10 December 1897, cit. Mayeur, "Les Congrès nationaux", p. 205.
124 AN F⁷ 12842, Dossier No. 24.
125 *Le Complôt protestant*. AN F⁷ 12463; see also Sorlin, *"La Croix" et les Juifs*, pp. 154–8.
126 E.g. Biez, op. cit., p. 7; and Daudet, *Au Temps de Judas*, p. 105; see also Verdès-Leroux, *Scandale financier*, pp. 123–4; and Blumenkranz, ed., *Histoire des Juifs en France*, p. 352. It is ironic to note that German antisemites made the quite opposite but parallel claim that Jews were *not* German; see, for example, Mosse, *The Crisis of German Ideology*, pp. 126–9.
127 Drumont, *FJ*, I, pp. 28–39.
128 Drumont, *DB*, p. 39; see also ibid., p. 321; *FJ*, I, pp. 4, 367, 372, 425–6 and 433; and II, pp. 214–16, 221, 364 and 424; and *TA*, pp. 15, 217, 317 and 360.
129 On the general preoccupation with espionage in France after the Franco-Prussian War, see Johnson, *France and the Dreyfus Affair*, pp. 49–51; and Gauthier, ed., *Dreyfusards!*, pp. 31–2; see also Gyp, *Le Mariage de Chiffon*, p. 193; and Edward Harrison Barker, *Two Summers in Guyenne* (London, 1894), p. 85. The author of the last was arrested as a spy at Martel by a zealous *garde-champêtre* in 1892 or 1893—apparently not an uncommon experience for tourists.
130 See, for example, Vallès, *L'Insurgé*, p. 217; Zévaès, *Au Temps du Boulangisme*, p. 205; and Memmi, op. cit., p. 150; also Littré, *Dictionnaire de la langue française* (1878).
131 See Bollême, *La Bibliothèque bleue*, pp. 156–7 and 224–5.
132 See, for example, Nicole Belmont, *Mythes et croyances dans l'ancienne France* (Paris, 1973), p. 78.
133 Victor Hugo, *Les Contemplations* (1856) (Paris, 1969), p. 442.
134 Bloy, *Le Salut par les Juifs*, p. 38.
135 Drumont, *FJ*, I, p. 66.
136 Ibid., I, pp. 61–6; Drumont *TA*, p. 98; Bournand, op. cit., p. 29; see also Hugo, *Les Contemplations*, p. 367; and Z. Szajkowski, "Simon Deutz: Traitor or French Patriot?", *Journal of Jewish Studies*, 16 (1965), pp. 53–65.
137 Drumont, *FJ*, I, pp. 109–11 and 197–8.

138 See ibid., I, p. 483; and II, pp. 12, 112, 115, 372, 379 and 389–94; *DB*, pp. 26–7, 39, 296 and 303–5; and *TA*, pp. 144–5; for the same view, see also, Fore-Fauré, op. cit., Chapter V.

139 Cit. Reinach, op. cit., III, p. 24; and Seignobos, *L'Evolution de la Troisième République*, p. 196.

140 *La Fin de la France: Le complôt Juif.* AN F⁷ 12465.

141 Blum, *Souvenirs sur l'Affaire*, pp. 64–5.

142 Barrès, *Scènes et doctrines*, I, pp. 142–5, 161 and 219.

143 *La Croix*, 3 November 1894, cit. Zévaès, *L'Affaire Dreyfus*, p. 30.

144 *La Libre Parole*, 3 November 1894, cit. ibid., p. 31. In fact, the espionage of which Dreyfus was accused was much less serious than is here suggested. For other examples of the exaggerated fear of being betrayed by the Jews, see Drumont, *FJ*, I, pp. 403–4; Barrès-Maurras, op. cit., p. 131; and Rouquier and Soumille, "La Notion de Race chez les Français d'Algérie", p. 5.

145 Drumont, *FJ*, I, p. 333; also ibid., I, pp. xvii, 8, 291, 336, 339 and 422; and II, pp. 51 and 59; *DB*, pp. 146 and 405; *TA*, pp. 19, 45, 359–60 and 383.

146 Barrès, *Scènes et doctrines*, II, p. 161.

147 See Lazare, *L'Antisémitisme*, pp. 222–3; and Marrus, *The Politics of Assimilation*.

148 Barrès, *Scènes et doctrines*, II, pp. 200 and 182–3; see also Barrès-Maurras, op. cit., pp. 477–8.

149 Maurras, *Au Signe de Flore*, p. 31.

150 Cit. Reinach, op. cit., III, p. 540.

151 Drumont, *FM*, p. 42.

152 Drumont, *DB*, pp. 129–30.

153 Daudet, *L'Avant-Guerre*, pp. vii and x.

154 Abbé Chabauty, *Les Juifs nos maîtres* (Paris, 1882); see Cohn, *Warrant for Genocide*, p. 45.

155 Drumont, *FJ*, I, pp. 52 and 346.

156 Drumont, *TA*, p. 181.

157 Drumont, *DB*, p. 321.

158 Cit. Drumont, *TA*, p. 155.

159 Mgr. Léon Meurin, *La Franc-maçonnerie, Synagogue de Satan* (Paris, 1893), p. 7.

160 Mayeur, "Les Congrès nationaux", p. 205; for similar charges, see Picard, *Synthèse de l'antisémitisme*, p. 83; Biez, op. cit., p. 8; and Daudet, *Les Oeuvres dans les hommes*, pp. 143 and 161–2.

161 Bournand, op. cit., p. 17.

162 Daily Report, Prefect of Police, 17 March 1898. APP Ba 106.

163 See particularly, Drumont, *FJ*, II, Book V; and *FM*, Books VII and VIII.

164 Daily Report, Prefect of Police, 30 January 1898. APP Ba 106.

165 Daily Report, Prefect of Police, 21 April 1898. APP Ba 106.

166 Maurras, *Au Signe de Flore*, p. 54.

167 See Randall, op. cit., pp. 114–22.

168 Report, Commissaire de police, Mézières, 19 March 1900. AN F⁷ 12455.

169 Biez, op. cit., p. 3.

170 Georges Romain, *Le Péril franc-maçon et le péril juif* (Paris, 1895), cit. Weber, *Satan franc-maçon*, p. 16.

171 Bournand, op. cit., pp. 139–42.

172 Report, Commissaire spécial, Lille, 13 February 1898. AN F⁷ 12854.

173 Barrès, *Le Journal*, 4 October 1898, *Scènes et doctrines*, I, p. 37.

174 Report, Commissaire spécial, Paris, 16 August 1899. AN F⁷ 12465.

175 Report, Police agent, Rennes, 25 July 1899. AN F⁷ 12464.

176 Report, Commissaire spécial, Belfort, 25 December 1901. AN F⁷ 12455.

177 Maurras, "De la Liberté suisse à l'Unité française" (November 1905), *Quand les Français*, p. 215.

178 Brunetière, "Après le Procès", loc. cit., p. 431.
179 AN F⁷ 12463.
180 See Marrus, op. cit., Chapter 3, for a description of the socio-professional structure of the French Jewish community.
181 Report, Commissaire de police, Epernay, 29 April 1900. AN F⁷ 12456.
182 Cit. Isaac, *Expériences de ma vie*, I, p. 360.
183 Barrès, *Scénes et doctrines*, II, p. 161.
184 "UN", November 1897. AN F⁷ 12480.
185 Maurras, *La Gazette de France*, 7 January 1899, cit. Roudiez, *Maurras jusqu'à l'Action Française*, p. 304.
186 See ibid..
187 Report, Commissaire spécial, Lille, 2 April 1900. AN F⁷ 12456.
188 Brunetière, "Après le Procès", p. 430.
189 See Silberner, "Proudhon's Judeophobia", p. 69.
190 Drumont, *FJ*, I, p. xv; also ibid., I, pp. 74, 258–9, 355–6, 451, 541–3; and II, pp. 57, 92, 200, 456 and 563; *FM*, pp. 147–8; *DB*, pp. vii, 26, 143, 338, 393, 398 and 405; and *TA*, pp. ix, 24, 31, 58–90, 319, 322 and 397.
191 Picard, op. cit., pp. 81 and 87.
192 See Sorlin, *"La Croix" et les Juifs*, pp. 175–80.
193 *Le Complôt juif*. AN F⁷ 12463.
194 Desprez, *L'Esprit conservateur*, p. 37.
195 Maupassant, *Bel-Ami*, p. 76; also pp. 32, 370–1 and *passim*.
196 Drumont, *TA*, pp. 82–4; see also Waleffe, *Quand Paris était un paradis*, p. 312.
197 Drumont, *FJ*, I, pp. 541–2. On Jews and the press generally, see also Bloy, *Le Pal*, pp. 55 and 60; abbé Gayraud, cit. Bournand, op. cit., p. 198; and Daudet, *Au Temps de Judas*, p. 29.
198 See Byrnes, *Antisemitism in Modern France*, pp. 140–8 and 280–90; and Sorlin, *"La Croix" et les Juifs*, pp. 175–80.
199 See E. Dubief, *Le Journalisme* (Paris, 1892); Manévy, *La Presse de la IIIe République*, Chapter 1 and *passim;* Jacques Kayser, *Le Quotidien français* (Paris, 1963), pp. 15–37; and Bellanger *et al* ed., *Histoire générale de la presse française*, III, pp. 61–103, 137–45, 165–74 and *passim*.
200 See Miquel, *L'Affaire Dreyfus*, pp. 7 and 119–20.
201 Drumont, *TA*, p. 58.
202 Maurras claimed that between a quarter and a third of Parisian journalists were out of work in 1896; Maurras, *L'Avenir de l'intelligence*, p. 91; see also Bernard Voyenne, "Les Journalistes", *Revue Française de la Science Politique*, 9 (1959), pp. 901–4; and Mitterand, *Zola journaliste*, pp. 82 and *passim*.
203 Drumont, *FJ*, II, p. 194.
204 Drumont, *DB*, pp. 317 and 273.
205 Drumont, *FJ*, II, p. 194.
206 Drumont, *TA*, p. 80; also ibid., p. 79; *FJ*, I, pp. 196–8; and *DB*, pp. 318, 400–2 and 406–8. On the undoubted venality of the French press, and particularly its subsidization by home and foreign governments, see Bellanger *et al* ed., op. cit., III, pp. 258–75; and ". . . L'Abominable Vénalité de la Presse . . ." d'après les documents des archives russes (1897–1917) (Paris, 1931).
207 See Drumont, *FJ*, II, pp. 218–19; *TA*, pp. 118–27; and *FM*, pp. 85–98.
208 See Byrnes, "The French Publishing Industry and its Crisis in the 1890s".
209 Drumont, *FJ*, II, p. 239; also pp. 240–1, 246–7 and 255.
210 See Byrnes, *Antisemitism in Modern France*, pp. 114–42.
211 Drumont, *FJ*, I, p. 275; and *DB*, p. viii.
212 Drumont, *FJ*, I, pp. 490–9, and Book III, pp. 529–73, "Gambetta et sa cour"; see also, in the same genre, Léon Daudet, *Le Pays des parlementeurs* (Paris, 1901).
213 Drumont, *FJ*, II, p. 466.
214 Ibid., II, p. 495; also ibid., I, p. 75; and II, pp. 370, 491–3 and 496; and *TA*, pp. 222–4; see also Paléologue, *Journal de l'Affaire Dreyfus*, pp. 159–61 and 180.

215 Drumont, *FJ*, I, pp. 69–70; and II, pp. 448 and 467; see also, for the later development of this theme, Léon Daudet, *L'Agonie du régime* (Paris, 1925), pp. 93–5; Daudet, *Le Palais de police* (Paris, 1931); Daniel Halévy, "Clio aux enfers, Notes sur la Police en France (1871–1930), *Décadence de la liberté* (Paris, 1931), pp. 141–93; and Maurras, *Dictionnaire politique et critique*, IV, p. 52.
216 See Chapter X, n. 439.
217 *Le Complôt juif.* AN F⁷ 12463.
218 Léon Daudet, *Les Morticoles* (Paris, 1894), pp. 253–4 and *passim*; see also Daudet, *Les Oeuvres dans les hommes*, pp. 203–4. The incidence of antisemitism in the medical profession is hard to assess for this period, but it seems to have been high in the inter-war period; see Loewenstein, op. cit., p. 87; and Morand, *Les Idées politiques de Louis-Ferdinand Céline*, p. 44. Céline, of course, was a medical man.
219 See Randall, op. cit., pp. 78–80 and 86. The Jewish doctor was a variant of a general stereotype of the doctor in fiction; see Balzac, *Le Médecin de campagne* (Paris, 1833); Ivan Turgenev, *Pères et enfants* (Paris, 1863); and Zola, *Le Docteur Pascal* (Paris, 1893), three examples from "high" fiction from three distinct generations, in which the doctor occupies a central role, in novels which their authors regarded as among their most important, as a symbol of "science" and "progress".
220 See William Ostler, *The Evolution of Modern Medicine* (New Haven, 1921), chapters V and VI; Richard Harrison Shryock, *The Development of Modern Medicine. An Interpretation of the Social and Scientific Factors Involved* (Philadelphia, 1936), particularly chapters XIV–XVIII; Shryock, "Medicine and Public Health", in Guy S. Métraux and François Crouzet, eds, *The Nineteenth-Century World* (New York, 1963), pp. 193–253; and Zeldin, *France 1848–1945*, I, chapter 2.
221 *Le Complôt juif.* AN F⁷ 12463.
222 See Chapter X, n. 254.
223 Zola, *Au Bonheur des Dames*, p. 79.
224 See Thabault, op. cit.; and Daumard, "L'Evolution des structures sociales en France à l'époque de l'industrialisation".
225 Charles-Louis Philippe, *La Mère et l'enfant* (Paris, 1971), p. 97; see also René Johannet, *Eloge du bourgeois français* (Paris, 1924), pp. 73 and 76: "En France, depuis toujours, l'étude mène à tout en fait de bourgeoisie."
226 See Lazare, *L'Antisémitisme*, pp. 192, 201 and *passim*; Howard M. Sachar, *The Course of Modern Jewish History* (London, 1958), chapter 3; and Blumenkranz, ed., op. cit., Part 3, chapters 1 and 2, by François Delpech.
227 See Benda, *La Jeunesse d'un clerc*, p. 30; Maurois, *Mémoires*, I, p. 20; and Blumenkranz, ed., op. cit., p. 325. The phenomenon was reflected in contemporary fiction, in which the Jewish lawyer or magistrate is a stock figure alongside the Jewish doctor; for example, Public Prosecutor Lehmann in Zola's *Paris*, "one of those shrewd Israelites who make their way in very honest fashion by invariably taking the part of the Government in office." (English edition, p. 234).
228 See Marrus, op. cit., pp. 40–5; also Byrnes, *Antisemitism in Modern France*, p. 97.
229 See Bournand, op. cit., p. 299; Stokes, *Léon Blum*, pp. 37–8; and Blum, *Nouvelles Conversations* (1901), *L'Oeuvre de Léon Blum 1891–1905*, pp. 263–4.
230 See chapter II, n. 216.
231 Drumont, *TA*, p. 40; see also Picard, op. cit., pp. 120–1; and Chapter X, pp. 358–63 above.
232 Dagan, op. cit., p. 10.
233 Reinach, op. cit., III, p. 261; see also Reclus in Dagan, op. cit., p. 40; Blum, *Souvenirs sur l'Affaire*, pp. 62–3; and Sartre, *Réflexions sur la question juive*, pp. 41–2.
234 See chapter XVI, pp. 606 and ff. below.

235 Jolly, ed., *Dictionnaire des parlementaires français.*
236 See Dresse, *Léon Daudet vivant,* pp. 58–77, "Le Médecin manqué"; and Dominique, *Léon Daudet,* pp. 20–43.
237 See Nguyen, "Problèmes de l'antisémitisme maurrassien", Paper given at Colloque sur l'Idée de Race, 1975.
238 Benoît Malon, "La Question Juive", *La Revue Socialiste,* 3 (1886), cit. Silberner, "French Socialism and the Jewish Question", p. 8.
239 Daudet, *L'Avant-Guerre,* p. 6.
240 Leroy-Beaulieu, *L'Antisémitisme,* p. 56; see also pp. 31–2.
241 Dagan, op. cit., pp. 39 and 52; see also Duroselle, "L'Antisémitisme en France", p. 54.
242 Lacretelle, *Silbermann,* pp. 134–5.
243 See Memmi, op. cit., pp. 192–3; and Poliakov, "Les Juifs à l'heure de Vichy", loc. cit., p. 168. On middle-class hostility to Jews in the liberal professions elsewhere, see Ginsberg, "Antisemitism", pp. 201–2.
244 Cit. Bournand, op. cit., pp. 113–14.
245 Cit. Dominique, op. cit., p. 59.
246 Daudet, "Le Professeur Charcot ou le Césarisme de Faculté", *Les Oeuvres dans les hommes,* pp. 203–4 and 197–243 *passim.*
247 Drumont, *DB,* pp. 79–80 and 223; and *TA,* p. 268.
248 See, for example, Drumont, *DB,* p. 498.
249 Guy de Maupassant, "En Famille", *La Maison Tellier* (1881) (Paris, 1961), pp. 127–9.
250 Vallès, *L'Insurgé,* pp. 214–15.
251 Drumont, *FM,* pp. 47–8; and *FJ,* II, pp. 275 and 546–7.
252 Sternhell, *Maurice Barrès,* p. 157.
253 Daudet, *Les Oeuvres dans les hommes,* pp. 154 and 168.
254 Drumont, *TA,* pp. 231 and 29.
255 See, for example, Reinach, op. cit., III, pp. 244 and 248–9; Tharaud, *Mes années chez Barrès,* pp. 25–6; Guillemin, *Zola légende et vérité,* pp. 161 and 163; Smith, "L'Atmosphère politique à l'Ecole Normale Supérieure", pp. 255–7; and chapter II, pp. 75–7 above.
256 Péguy, *NJ,* pp. 18–19; see also Martin du Gard, *Jean Barois,* pp. 429–40 and 452; and Agathon, *Les Jeunes Gens d'aujourd'hui.*
257 See Sartre, op. cit., pp. 198–9. Antisemitism and Nationalism seem also to have had a special appeal for youth in Germany and Austria in the later nineteenth century, see, for example, Mosse, *The Crisis of German Ideology,* pp. 5–6, 150, and chapter 7; and Walter Z. Laqueur, *Young Germany, A History of the German Youth Movement* (London, 1962), chapter 9 and *passim.*
258 Thabault, op. cit., p. 178, refers to "the fears of the bourgeoisie in the face of the rising tide of unemployed lads who had passed their *baccalauréat.*"
259 Benda, *La Jeunesse d'un clerc,* p. 43, cit. Blumenkranz, ed., op. cit., pp. 348–9.
260 "L'Archiviste", op. cit., p. 7.
261 See Girardet, *La Société militaire,* pp. 187–9 and 195–200.
262 Drumont, *FJ,* II, p. 546; and Daudet, *Les Oeuvres dans les hommes,* p. 168.
263 See, for example, Guillemin, *Zola légende et vérité,* pp. 160–1.
264 Gohier, *L'Armée contre la nation,* p. 4.
265 Cit. Ralston, *The Army of the Republic,* pp. 302–3; see also Gohier, op. cit., p. 5.
266 Ralston, op. cit., pp. 302–3.
267 Herriot, *Jadis,* I, p. 86.
268 Tharaud, *Notre cher Péguy,* I, pp. 134, 69–72 and 110.
269 Herriot, op. cit., pp. 42–3.
270 See n. 268; and Tharaud, *Petite Histoire des Juifs,* p. 235.
271 Gregh, *L'Âge d'or,* pp. 287–8; the same term was in use at the *lycées* of Elbeuf and Rouen; see Maurois, *Mémoires,* I, pp. 62–4.

272 Donnay, *Des Souvenirs*, p. 105.

273 Daudet, *Au Temps de Judas*, pp. 107–8.

274 Maurois, *Mémoires*, I, pp. 65–6.

275 Lacretelle, *Silbermann*, pp. 12–14, 23–6, 34–5, 41, 48–51 and *passim;* see also Mauriac, "L'Affaire Dreyfus". A similar hostility to Jewish schoolfellows could be found, apparently, in state primary schools at this time, as well as in private schools; see Bloch, *Lévy*, p. 38; and Maurice Sachs, *Le Sabbat: Souvenirs d'une jeunesse orageuse* (Paris, 1946), p. 40 and *passim*. The Collège de Luza attended by Sachs had a 10% quota for Jews.

276 Bournand, op. cit., p. 135.

277 Alfred de Vigny, *Journal d'un poète*, cit. Poliakov, "Racisme et Antisémitisme: Bilan provisoire de nos discussions et essai de description", Paper given at Colloque sur l'Idée de Race, 1975, p. 3. It would be interesting to know whether this quota system was really introduced.

278 Stokes, op. cit., pp. 32–3 and 37–8. France's most prominent radical Jewish politician of the next generation, Pierre Mendès-France, was the youngest boy to take the *baccalauréat* in his class, and then the youngest graduate of the Ecole des Sciences Politiques; Alexander Werth, *The Strange History of Pierre Mendès-France and the Great Conflict over French North Africa* (London, 1957), p. 5.

279 Julian Green, *Memories of Happy Days* (London, 1944), pp. 72–3.

280 P. E. Drieu La Rochelle, *Gilles* (1939–1942) (Paris, 1962), p. 112.

281 Drumont, *FJ*, II, p. 441.

282 See, for example, Maurras, *Quand les Français*, p. 100; also Lukes, *Emile Durkheim*, pp. 99–108 and 363–78; André Spire, Préface, Henri Franck, *Lettres à quelques amis* (Paris, 1926), pp. 18–27; and Marrus, op. cit., pp. 41–2.

283 See Mona Ozouf, *L'Ecole, l'Eglise et la République*, chapters VII and VIII, and *passim*.

284 See, for example, Drumont, *FM*, pp. 440–3; *DB*, pp. 509–10; and *TA*, p. 228.

285 Barrès, *Les Déracinés;* see chapter X, n. 507 above.

286 See my "A View of the Past: Action Française Historiography and its socio-political function", *Historical Journal*, 19 (1976), pp. 135–61.

287 See Erik Homburger Erikson, "Hitler's Imagery and German Youth", *Psychiatry*, 4 (1942), pp. 475–93.

288 See, for example, Jean-Louis Flandrin, *Les Amours paysannes (XVIe–XIXe siècle)* (Paris, 1975), pp. 191–200; and, more generally, R. P. Neuman, "Masturbation, Madness, and the Modern Concepts of Childhood and Adolescence", *Journal of Social History*, 8 (1975), pp. 1–27.

289 See Morin *et al.*, *La Rumeur d'Orléans*, pp. 65 and *passim.*

290 See Erikson, *Childhood and Society*, p. 254; and Bruno Bettelheim, *The Children of the Dream* (London, 1973), p. 222.

291 Meyer, *Ce que mes yeux ont vu*, p. 125.

292 Blum, *Souvenirs sur l'Affaire*, p. 63.

293 Proust, *A la Recherche du temps perdu* (English edition), XI, pp. 219–20.

294 Barrès, *Mes Cahiers*, I, p. 232 (1897).

295 Vogüé, *Les Morts qui parlent*, p. 423.

296 Daily Report, Prefect of Police, 30 January 1898. APP Ba 106; see also Drumont, *FJ*, I, pp. 339–40 and 353; and Verdès-Leroux, *Scandale financier*, p. 136.

297 Paul Bollot, "L'Invasion juive", *Revue du Monde Catholique*, 4e série, 9, no. 43, January 1887, cit. Verdès-Leroux, op. cit., pp. 130–1.

298 Biez, op. cit., p. 12.

299 Police report, no date. AN F⁷ 12480.

300 See Chapter XIII.

301 Maurras, *La Gazette de France*, 7 January 1899, cit. Roudiez, op. cit., p. 304. This is a rare example, for France at least, of a justification of antisemitism by reference to the colonies. A general thesis linking antisemitism with colonial imperialism has, of course, been propounded by Hannah Arendt, *The Origins of Totalitarianism*.

302 Maurras, *Au Signe de Flore*, pp. 58 and 115.
303 On the antiquity of the idea of a Jewish conspiracy, see Lovsky, *L'Antisémitisme chrétien*, pp. 307–16.
304 See Cohn, op. cit., pp. 25–31, 41–50, 60–5 and 71–6.
305 See ibid., pp. 34–40, and Appendix I.
306 See Bournand, op. cit., pp. 283–6; and P. N. Stearns, ed., *The Impact of the Industrial Revolution, Protest and Alienation* (Englewood Cliffs, N.J., 1972), pp. 57–9. Stearns seems to have been unaware of the significance and the provenance of the document which he reproduces.
307 *Le Complôt juif.* AN F⁷ 12463; see also Police reports. AN F⁷ 12480–12481.
308 See, for example, Drumont, *La France juive devant l'opinion* (Paris, 1886), pp. 26–30.
309 Drumont, *FJ*, I, pp. 7, 19–20, 232 and 234; also ibid., I, p. 293; and II, p. 251.
310 Drumont, *DB*, pp. 114–15; see also *TA*, p. 53.
311 Drumont, *FJ*, II, p. 54, and Book V.
312 Picard, op. cit., p. 101.
313 Ibid., pp. 40, 83 and 101–2.
314 Daudet, *Au Temps de Judas*, p. 23.
315 Benda, *La Jeunesse d'un clerc*, p. 210.
316 André Gide, *Journals 1889–1949* (Harmondsworth, 1967), pp. 194–5 (January 1914).
317 Zola, *Paris* (English edition), pp. 83 and 411.
318 See, for example, Sue, *The Wandering Jew*, Part I, pp. 47–50 and *passim*.
319 See, for example, Zévaès, *Au Temps du Boulangisme*, p. 56. For examples of conspiracy myths in other societies, see A. G. Dickens, *Reformation and Society in Sixteenth-Century Europe* (London, 1966), p. 137, on the Anabaptist conspiracy; Keith Thomas, *Religion and the Decline of Magic, Studies in Popular Beliefs in Sixteenth- and Seventeenth-Century England* (Harmondsworth, 1973), p. 647 n., on Popish plots; and Hofstadter, *The Paranoid Style*, pp. 5–9, 19–23, 29–30 and *passim*; Shils, "Authoritarianism: 'Right' and 'Left' ", in Christie and Jahoda, eds, *Studies in the Scope and Method of "The Authoritarian Personality"*, p. 38; Cohen and Young, *The Manufacture of News*, pp. 104–15 and 157; and Murray Edelman, *The Symbolic Uses of Politics* (Urbana, Ill., 1974), p. 8, on conspiracy theories in Western societies today.
320 Drumont, *FJ*, I, p. 355.
321 See Silberner, "Proudhon's Judeophobia", pp. 69–70.
322 Eugène Bontoux, *L'Union Générale, sa vie, sa mort, son programme* (Paris, 1888), p. 138, cit. Verdès, "La Presse devant le krach d'une banque catholique", p. 147.
323 Jean Brisecou, *La Grande Conjuration organisée pour la ruine de la France* (Autun, 1887); see Verdès-Leroux, *Scandale financier*, p. 128.
324 Cit. Silberner, "French Socialism and the Jewish Question", p. 10.
325 See Sorlin, *"La Croix" et les Juifs*, pp. 175–80.
326 See Chapter X, n. 9.
327 See Sternhell, *Maurice Barrès*, pp. 315–18.
328 Cit. Seignobos, op. cit., p. 193.
329 Morès, *Le Secret des changes* (Marseille, 1894), cit. Schwarzschild, "The Marquis de Morès", p. 22.
330 Cit. "L'Archiviste", op. cit., p. 22.
331 See chapter II, n. 222.
332 See Sternhell, *Maurice Barrès*, pp. 128–130.
333 Stock, *Mémorandum d'un éditeur*, Troisième série, p. 9; also pp. 166–93, "Le Syndicat".
334 Zola, "Le Syndicat", *Le Figaro*, 1 December 1897, *L'Affaire Dreyfus, La Vérité en marche*, p. 76.
335 *Le Complôt maçonnique.* AN F⁷ 12463.
336 "Syndicat-Fantôme". Gohier, op. cit., pp. 265–6; see also Vauthier, *La France et l'Affaire Dreyfus*, p. 28.

337 Reports, Police agent, 11 November 1896. AN F⁷ 12464; and AN F⁷ 12473.
338 Reports, Police agents, 8 October, and 5 November 1897. AN F⁷ 12473.
339 Report, Police agent, Paris, 20 November 1897. AN F⁷ 12473.
340 Note, Direction de la Sûreté Générale. AN F⁷ 12473.
341 Reports, Police agents, 10 and 11 January 1898. AN F⁷ 12473.
342 Report, Commissaire spécial, Montpellier, 27 February 1898. AN F⁷ 12474.
343 Report, Police agent, Paris, 28 March 1898. AN F⁷ 12473. This may be a reference to the activities of the clandestine Comité de Défense contre l'Antisémitisme; see chapter XIX, pp. 717–18 below.
344 Cit. Zévaès, *L'Affaire Dreyfus*, pp. 75–6. The revisionist campaign of Scheurer-Kestner and his associates had begun in the press, notably in *Le Figaro*, in mid-November. De Mun, himself an ex-army officer, was the main inspirer of the Catholic Oeuvre des Cercles d'Ouvriers, whose aim was to rechristianize the working classes and thus avert popular insurrections like the Paris Commune; see Piou, *Le Comte de Mun*, chapter 1; and Charles Molette, *Albert de Mun 1872–1890* (Paris, 1970).
345 See Daily Report, Prefect of Police, 24 January 1898. APP Ba 106.
346 Daily Report, Prefect of Police, 3 February 1898. APP Ba 106.
347 Daily Report, Prefect of Police, 10 February 1898. APP Ba 106.
348 Daily Reports, Prefect of Police, 17 February, and 15 March 1898. APP Ba 106.
349 Daily Report, Prefect of Police, 10 June 1898. APP Ba 106.
350 *Le Journal de Chartres*, 5 October 1898, cit. Stock, op. cit., p. 166. As a picture of the actual alignment of the press on the Affair at this time, this is, of course, very misleading; see chapter II, pp. 87–8 above.
351 *L'Éclair*, 2 February 1899.
352 See Report, Commissaire spécial, Paris, 16 August 1899. AN F⁷ 12465.
353 See chapter II, n. 265; for other indications of the widespread belief in the "Syndicat", see chapter II, n. 223.
354 Drumont, *FJ*, II, pp. 217 and 536.
355 Ibid., I, pp. 262 and 233.
356 Report, Commissaire spécial, Nancy, 5 February 1900. AN F⁷ 12456.
357 Broadsheet, "Union Nationale", Report, Police agent, 10 November 1897. AN F⁷ 12480.
358 Cit. Bournand, op. cit., p. 34; and Drumont, *FJ*, II, Book VI, "La Persécution Juive"; also *FJ*, I, p. 299; and II, pp. 144, 148 and 293.
359 Leroy-Beaulieu, *L'Antisémitisme*, p. 6.
360 Péguy, *NJ*, p. 187; also pp. 180–1.
361 See Daniel J. Levinson, "The Study of Antisemitic Ideology", in Adorno *et al.*, *The Authoritarian Personality*, chapter III, p. 98 and *passim;* Frenkel-Brunswik, ibid., chapter XIII, p. 485; and Adorno, ibid., chapter XVI, pp. 613 and 640–1; Ackerman and Jahoda, *Anti-Semitism and Emotional Disorder*, pp. 57–8; Hofstadter, *The Paranoid Style*, p. 32; and Hofstadter, in Ionescu and Gellner, eds, *Populism*, p. 21.
362 Drumont, *FJ*, II, p. 218.
363 Meurin, op. cit., p. 463.
364 The same tendency to exaggerate the numbers of their enemies is found among sixteenth- and seventeenth-century witch-hunters, and opponents of the Moriscos, as well as modern American opponents of Blacks, though only the last two, of course, were involved with real minorities; see, for example, Michel de Certeau, *L'Absent de l'histoire* (Paris, 1973), pp. 31–2; Braudel, *The Mediterranean*, II, pp. 793–4; and Rose, "The Roots of Prejudice", *Race and Science*, UNESCO, p. 416.
365 Drumont, *FJ*, I, pp. 97, 101 and 103; see also Pierrard, op. cit., pp. 25–6.
366 See "L'Archiviste", op. cit., p. 20. Marrus, op. cit., p. 31, agrees with the total Jewish population figure of around 75,000; see also Maurras, *Quand les Français*, p. 220; and Blumenkranz, ed., op. cit., pp. 347–8.
367 See chapter XIV, pp. 543–50 below.

368 See Maurras, "La Théorie des quatre Etats confédérés maîtres de la France", *De Démos à César* (Paris, 1930), II, pp. 33–7.
369 Maurras, "De la Liberté suisse à l'Unité française", loc. cit., pp. 217–19.
370 Report, Commissaire central, Troyes, 20 February 1899. AN F⁷ 12466.
371 Report, Commissaire spécial, Dijon, 25 February 1900. AN F⁷ 12455.
372 Leroy-Beaulieu, *Les Doctrines de haine*, p. 140; also ibid., chapter 3.
373 Cit. Mayeur, Les Congrès nationaux", p. 184.
374 Paléologue, op. cit., p. 84 (13 December 1897).
375 Miss Betham-Edwards, *Home Life in France* (London, 1905), p. 296.
376 See chapter III, n. 10; also Abbé de Saint-Poli, *L'Affaire Dreyfus et la mentalité catholique*, p. 25; and Mours and Robert, *Le Protestantisme en France*, pp. 311–12.
377 See Lacretelle, *Silbermann*, p. 66; Siegfried, *Géographie électorale de l'Ardèche sous la IIIe République*, pp. 54–66; Daniel P. Resnick, *The White Terror and the Political Reaction after Waterloo* (Cambridge, Mass., 1966), chapter III and *passim;* Mours and Robert, op. cit., pp. 330–3 and *passim;* Szajkowski, *Jews and the French Revolutions*, p. xxx; and chapter II, pp. 82–3 above.
378 Jules Vallès, *L'Enfant* (1884) (Paris, 1973), p. 180.
379 R. P. Lecanuet, *L'Eglise de France sous la Troisième République*, I (Paris, no date–1907?), p. 215.
380 *L'Assomption et ses oeuvres*, pp. 71–125 and 356; and Sorlin, *"La Croix" et les Juifs*, pp. 15–24.
381 See Sorlin, op. cit., pp. 117 and 131–2. A "réynion antiprotestante" in Paris in March 1901, organized by the Comité Justice-Egalité, an Assumptionist-inspired body, broke up "à un appel à l'insurrection contre les Huguenots, et aux cris enthousiastes de: 'Vive le Saint-Barthélémy!' ", according to a report in *Le Siècle*, 13 March 1901.
382 *Le Complôt protestant*. AN F⁷ 12463.
383 Cit. Zévaès, *L'Affaire Dreyfus*, p. 10.
384 Cit. Seignobos, op. cit., p. 196.
385 Guillemin, *Présentation des Rougon-Macquart*, pp. 187–8; see Zola, "Protestantisme"; and "Réponse aux Protestants" (1881–1882), *Oeuvres complètes*, XIV (Paris, 1970), pp. 597–608; also Guillemin, *Zola légende et vérité*, p. 73 n.
386 Drumont, *FJ*, II, pp. 351 and 373–6; and *TA*, p. 262.
387 Drumont, *FJ*, II, pp. 352 and 366.
388 Ibid., II, p. 364.
389 Ibid., II, pp. 360 and 377; also p. 311.
390 Ibid., I, p. 190.
391 Viau, op. cit., p. 123; see also Bournand, op. cit., pp. 47–8.
392 Bournand, op. cit., p. 207.
393 Gyp, *Le Mariage de Chiffon*, pp. 192–3.
394 Barrès, *Scènes et doctrines*, II, pp. 180–2.
395 Barrès, *Mes Cahiers*, II, p. 160 (1899).
396 Barrès, "Le Protestants par rapport à la France"; and "Des Juifs et des Protestants considérés 'in abstracto' ", (1899 and 1900), *Scènes et doctrines*, I, pp. 62–8; see also Sternhell, *Maurice Barrès*, pp. 310–13.
397 Guy-Grand, *La Philosophie nationaliste*, p. 33.
398 Roudiez, op. cit., p. 305.
399 Maurras, "De la Liberté suisse à l'Unité française", loc. cit., pp. 216–17.
400 Maurras, *Au Signe de Flore*, p. 165.
401 Ibid., pp. 174–6.
402 Ibid., p. 183.
403 Daily Report, Prefect of Police, 26 April 1898. APP Ba 106.
404 See, generally, Jacob Katz, *Jews and Freemasons in Europe 1723–1939* (Cambridge, Mass., 1970), chapters X and XI and *passim.*
405 Henri Gougenot des Mousseaux, *Le Juif, le Judaïsme et le Judaïsation des peuples*

chrétiens (1869); see Byrnes, *Antisemitism in Modern France*, p. 114; and Cohn, op. cit., pp. 41–5.

406 See Cohn, op. cit., pp. 45–7; and Drumont, *FJ*, II, p. 347.
407 Drumont, *FJ*, II, pp. 312 and 322; see also ibid., I, pp. 87, 174–7, 247, 260–9, 277–8, 490 and 562; and II, pp. 4, 64, 320–1, 347 and 425; *FM*, pp. xxviii, 17, 74 and 530; *DB*, pp. 22 and 67; and *TA*, pp. 335, 356–7, 406–7 and 438.
408 See Byrnes, op. cit., p. 56; Verdès-Leroux, *Scandale financier*, p. 138; and Pierrard, op. cit., pp. 28–9.
409 See Headings, *French Freemasonry under the Third Republic*, pp. 36–8; Weber, *Satan franc-maçon*, pp. 164–5 and 199–202; and Pierrard, op. cit., p. 210.
410 See Pierrard, op. cit., pp. 29, 108 and 209; and Barral, *L'Isère sous la Troisième République*, pp. 243–4 and 287–9.
411 Meurin, op. cit., pp. 101 and 260, cit. Cohn, op. cit., p. 48; also Meurin, op. cit., pp. 2, 7, 182 and 194–210 *passim*.
412 Cit. Sorlin, *"La Croix" et les Juifs*, p. 106; see also ibid., pp. 131–2 and 187–93.
413 *L'Assomption et ses oeuvres*, p. 20.
414 *Le Complôt maçonnique*. AN F⁷ 12463. This was only one of many anti-Masonic pamphlets produced by *La Maison de la Bonne Presse* in the period; see AN F⁷ 12480–12481, for a selection of these.
415 See Pierrard, op. cit., pp. 110–14, 121 and 151–60.
416 See chapter XIV, pp. 546–7 and ff. below.
417 Dagan, op. cit., p. 70.
418 See Daudet, *Au Temps de Judas*, pp. 208–12.
419 *La Civiltà Cattolica*, 5 February 1898, cit. Reinach, op. cit., III, p. 23.
420 Daily Report, Prefect of Police, 31 January 1898. APP Ba 106.
421 Daily Report, Prefect of Police, 8 February 1898. APP Ba 106.
422 Daily Report, Prefect of Police, 3 April 1898. APP Ba 106.
423 Daily Report, Prefect of Police, 14 April 1898; for other examples, see Daily Reports, Prefect of Police, 10 March, and 17 and 19 April 1898. APP Ba 106.
424 Report, Prefect of Police, 4 April 1900. AN F⁷ 12480; for further examples of Union Nationale propagation of this theme, see my "Catholic Populism in France at the time of the Dreyfus Affair", p. 695.
425 Report, Prefect, Rhône, 15 January 1901. AN F⁷ 12457.
426 See Dardenne, op. cit., pp. 662–3.
427 See Reports, Commissaire spécial, Nantes, 25 and 27 August 1903. AN F⁷ 12459.
428 See Desprez, *L'Esprit conservateur*, p. 96.
429 Report, Commissaire spécial, Nantes, 1 October 1903. AN F⁷ 12456.
430 Maurras, "De la Liberté suisse à l'Unité française", loc. cit., p. 217.
431 Cit. Denis, *L'Eglise et la République en Mayenne*, p. 226.
432 Meyer, op. cit., p. 128.
433 Leroy-Beaulieu, *Les Doctrines de haine*, p. 90.
434 See, for example, Mona Ozouf, op. cit., pp. 26–33; and Marcel Boivin, "Les Origines de la Ligue de l'Enseignement en Seine-Inférieure, 1866–1871", *Revue d'Histoire Economique et Sociale*, 46 (1968), pp. 203–31.
435 "La Franc-maçonnerie en France", *Revue des Deux Mondes*, 1 May 1899, vol. 153, pp. 80–124.
436 Headings, op. cit., p. 8.
437 See ibid., pp. 150–5; Daudet, *Au Temps de Judas*, pp. 134–7; Général André, "Cinq Ans de Ministère, Fragments de Mémoires", *Le Matin*, June 1906 (AN F⁷ 12924); and Emile Combes, *Mon Ministère, Mémoires 1902–1905* (Paris, 1956), pp. 242–8.
438 See, for example, François Bédarida, "L'Armée et la République; Les opinions politiques des officiers français en 1876–8", *Revue Historique*, 232 (1964), pp. 119–64.
439 Leroy-Beaulieu, *L'Antisémitisme*, p. 17; see also Katz, op. cit., pp. 16–18, who makes the same point.

440 Sorlin, *"La Croix" et les Juifs*, pp. 131–2.
441 See n. 396.
442 Maurras, "La Guerre religieuse", *La Gazette de France*, 23 March 1898, cit. Roudiez, op. cit., pp. 103–4.
443 Hitler, *Mein Kampf* (1943 edition, pp. 128–9), cit. Stern, *Hitler*, p. 81.
444 Drumont, *FJ*, I, p. 52.
445 "du Juif juivant de Juiverie . . .". Ibid., II, p. 227.
446 Boisandré, *Le Petit Catéchisme antijuif* (Paris, 1900), cit. Pierrard, op. cit., p. 72.
447 Drumont, *TA*, p. 144.
448 See, for example, Drumont, *FJ*, I, p. 50; and *DB*, pp. 16 and 520; and the use of the concept in *Le Monument Henry;* see chapter IV, p. 150 above.
449 See, for example, Léon Daudet, *La France en alarme* (Paris, no date–c. 1904); Charles Maurras, *Kiel et Tanger 1895–1905, La République française devant l'Europe* (Paris, 1910); and Jacques Bainville, *Le Coup d'Agadir et la Guerre d'Orient* (Paris, 1913).
450 Maurras, *Quand les Français*, pp. 27 and xiv-xv; see also ibid., Books I and II; Barrès-Maurras, op. cit., p. 260; and Digeon, *La Crise allemande de la pensée française (1870–1914)*, chapters VIII and IX.
451 Wicart, *Les Deux Causes de la décadence*, p. 4.
452 See, for example, Paléologue, op. cit., p. 141; Clermont-Tonnerre, op. cit., p. 189; Proust, *A la Recherche du temps perdu*, VIII, p. 202; Astier Loutfi, *Littérature et colonialisme*, pp. 89–93; and Christopher Andrew, *Théophile Delcassé and the Making of the Entente Cordiale* (London, 1968), particularly chapter 5.
453 Wicart, op. cit., p. 11.
454 See Drumont, *FJ*, I, pp. 449, 455 and 546; and II, pp. 108 and 249–53; and *TA*, pp. 111–12, 114, 146, 152 and 158–64.
455 Cit. Weber, *Satan franc-maçon*, p. 62.
456 See Sorlin, *"La Croix" et les Juifs*, pp. 114–17.
457 See Reports, Commissaire spécial, Lille, 2 April 1900. AN F⁷ 12456; and Prefect, Rhône, 28 December 1899. AN F⁷ 12457.
458 See Pierrard, op. cit., p. 91 n.
459 AN F⁷ 12463.
460 Cit. Bournand, op. cit., p. 110.
461 Daily Report, Prefect of Police, 31 March 1898. APP Ba 106.
462 Daudet, *L'Avant-Guerre, passim.*
463 Leroy-Beaulieu, *Les Doctrines de haine*, p. 26.
464 Cit. Dagan, op. cit., p. 56; for other examples, see ibid., p. 29; "L'Archiviste", op. cit., p. 9; Reinach, op. cit., VI, p. 457 ("plaidoirie" of Mornand, Cour de Cassation, July 1906); and Levaillant, "La Genèse de l'antisémitisme sous la Troisième République", p. lxxxiv.
465 Drumont referred admiringly to antisemitic leaders in other countries, including Lueger and Stöcker; see *FJ*, I, p. xvi; and *TA*, pp. 136, 141–2 and 148. Caran d'Ache apparently acquired his antisemitism in Russia; see Byrnes, "Jean-Louis Forain: Antisemitism in French Art", pp. 250–1; see also, generally, Biez, op. cit., p. 6; and Bournand, op. cit., pp. 257–65.
466 Leroy-Beaulieu, *Les Doctrines de haine*, pp. 24–5 and 27.
467 Drumont, *FJ*, II, Notes Rectificatives, p. 11.
468 See chapter XI, n. 280.
469 Daily Report, Prefect of Police, 24 January 1898. APP Ba 106. In this context, see Barthes, *Mythologies*, p. 138.
470 Leroy-Beaulieu, *Les Doctrines de haine*, p. 22.
471 Daily Report, Prefect of Police, 5 March 1898. APP Ba 106.
472 See Sartre, op. cit., pp. 29 and 100–1.
473 See, for example, Levinson, *The Authoritarian Personality*, Chapter III, p. 71; Erikson, *Childhood and Society*, p. 347; Max Gluckman, *Custom and Conflict*

in Africa (Oxford, 1956), chapter V; Le Roy Ladurie, *Les Paysans de Languedoc*, p. 244; Cohen and Young, op. cit., pp. 236–8 and 341; Ionescu and Gellner, eds, op. cit., pp. 3–4; Louis Dumont, *Homo Hierarchicus*, p. 15; Stern, *Hitler*, pp. 198–9; and Lucy Mair, *Witchcraft* (London, 1973), pp. 33–42, on the "nightmare witch".

474 Hans Toch, *The Social Psychology of Social Movements* (Indianapolis, 1965), pp. 56 and 69; also chapter 3, "The Benefit of Perceiving Conspiracies".

475 See the comments of Alan Macfarlane, *Witchcraft in Tudor and Stuart England* (London, 1970), p. 243, citing Nadel; also Erikson, *Childhood and Society*, p. 396; and Edelman, op. cit., pp. 8 and 71.

476 Drumont, *FM*, p. 251.

477 "le pays légal" and "le pays réel"; see, for example, Maurras, *Dictateur et Roi* (1928); and *Vingt-cinq ans de monarchisme* (1909–1928), *Oeuvres capitales*, II, pp. 390–9 and 459.

478 Maurras, *Quand les Français*, pp. 217–18.

479 See, for example, Karl Marx, *The Eighteenth Brumaire of Louis Bonaparte*, Karl Marx and Frederick Engels, *Selected Works* (Moscow, 1962), I, pp. 334–45.

480 See Ferdinand Tönnies, *Community and Society* (1887) (New York, 1957); also Durkheim's discussion of lack of social integration and "anomie" in *Suicide*, particularly pp. 386–92. It is, of course, very significant that Tönnies and Durkheim developed these concepts in the period.

481 For similar interpretations of Nationalism generally, see R. Rifflet, "Visions nouvelles de l'Histoire contemporaine", *Sentiment national en Allemagne et en Belgique (XIXe–XXe siècles)*, Colloque des 25 et 26 avril 1963, Centre National d'étude de problèmes de sociologie et d'économie européennes (Brussels, no date), pp. 149–77; and Anthony D. Smith, *Theories of Nationalism* (London, 1971), pp. 23, 33–5 and 53.

482 Martin du Gard, *Jean Barois*, pp. 442–3.

483 Cit. Bournand, op. cit., p. 111.

484 Toch, op. cit., p. 70.

485 Leroy-Beaulieu, *L'Antisémitisme*, p. 74. One of the characteristics of the "Fascist personality", according to Adorno and his colleagues, is "a tendency to shift responsibility from within the individual on to outside forces beyond one's control . . ." *The Authoritarian Personality*, chapter VII, p. 236.

486 Morin *et al.*, op. cit., p. 115; see also Hofstadter, *The Paranoid Style*, pp. 29–30; and Simone de Beauvoir, "La Pensée de Droite aujourd'hui", *Privilèges* (Paris, 1955), pp. 145–7.

487 For a discussion of this distinction, see Beattie, *Other Cultures*, chapter 12.

488 See Hippolyte Taine, *Les Origines de la France contemporaine* (Paris, 1875–1894) (*La France juive* was seen by Drumont and others as a work in the same genre as Taine's; see *FJ*, I, p. v; and Beau de Loménie, *Edouard Drumont*, pp. 67–8); and Ernest Renan, *La Réforme intellectuelle et morale* (1871), *Oeuvres complètes*, I (Paris, 1947); also *The Journal of Eugène Delacroix* (London, 1951), pp. 336–7 (1857); Gohier, op. cit., pp. v–xxxiii; and, generally, Konraed W. Swart, *The Sense of Decadence in Nineteenth-Century France* (The Hague, 1964); F. W. J. Hemmings, *Culture and Society in France, 1848–1898* (London, 1971), pp. 209–17; Sternhell, *Maurice Barrès*, pp. 38–43; and Revel, *Les Idées de notre temps*, p. 191.

489 Durkheim, op. cit., pp. 368–9 and 391; see also Jack D. Douglas, *The Social Meanings of Suicide* (Princeton, 1973), pp. 17–19.

490 Zola, *Paris*, pp. 9, 55–6, 80 and *passim;* see also Zola, Letter, December 1885, *Correspondance*, *Oeuvres complètes*, XIV, p. 1449, cit. Richard H. Zakarian, *Zola's "Germinal"*, *A Critical Study of its Primary Sources* (Geneva, 1972), p. 165; Mitterand, op. cit., p. 95; Guillemin, *Présentation des Rougon-Macquart*, p. 356; and Steenhuyse, "Quelques jalons dans l'étude du thème du 'Grand Soir' ".

491 Zola, *Paris*, pp. 134–5.

492 Drumont, *FJ*, II, pp. 121 and 562; also ibid., I, pp. 467–8, 495, 507, 516 and 524; and II, pp. 104, 151, 222, 228 and 305–6.
493 Drumont, *FM*, pp. 529–30.
494 Drumont, *DB*, p. 194; also pp. 236–7.
495 Drumont, *TA*, pp. 2, 206 and 220.
496 Drumont, *DB*, pp. 136–7 and 141; also *FJ*, I, pp. 452 and 510–11.
497 "Programme législatif de l'Union Nationale" (July 1893). AN F⁷ 12480.
498 Bertillon, *Le Problème de la dépopulation*, pp. 2 and 6.
499 Wicart, op. cit., pp. 4 and 14.
500 See Report, Commissaire spécial, Paris, 16 August 1899. AN F⁷ 12465.
501 Maupassant, *Bel-Ami*, p. 198.
502 Cit. Sternhell, "Le Déterminisme physiologique et racial à la base du nationalisme de Maurice Barrès et de Jules Soury", p. 5.
503 See Halévy, *Péguy and Les Cahiers de la Quinzaine*, pp. 105–7; my "History and Traditionalism: Maurras and the Action Française", *Journal of the History of Ideas*, 29 (1968), pp. 377–8; and Philippe Ariès, "Le Thème de la Mort dans 'Le Chemin de Paradis' ", *Etudes Maurrassiennes*, 1 (1972), pp. 27–32.
504 See Maurice Barrès, *Du Sang, de la volupté et de la mort* (Paris, 1910); Barrès-Maurras, op. cit., pp. iv and 17; and Sternhell, *Maurice Barrès*, pp. 257, 282–3 and 299–300.
505 See Fritz Stern, *The Politics of Cultural Despair, A Study in the Rise of the Germanic Ideology* (New York, 1965); also Mosse, *The Crisis of German Ideology*, p. 128; Swart, op. cit., p. 259 and *passim;* and Victor Nguyen, "Approche de la notion maurrassienne d'*héritage*", *Etudes Maurrassiennes*, 2 (1973), p. 164.
506 See, for example, Drumont, *FJ*, II, pp. 272–3 and 286–90; and "Programme législatif de l'Union Nationale" (July 1893).
507 Drumont, *TA*, p. 185.
508 Drumont, *OBS*, pp. 168–9.
509 See, for example, Drumont, *FJ*, II, p. 442.
510 Drumont, *OBS*, p. 226; also *FJ*, II, pp. 72–3, 77 and 79.
511 See particularly Maurras, *L'Avenir de l'intelligence;* and *Romantisme et révolution* (Paris, 1922).
512 See Drumont, *FJ*, II, pp. 108–16. In fact the Rothschilds were discriminating patrons of the arts in France, as Clermont-Tonnerre, op. cit., pp. 208–9, points out.
513 Drumont, *TA*, p. 317.
514 *La Libre Parole*, 7 February 1897, cit. Bournand, op. cit., p. 181.
515 Cit. Weber, *Satan franc-maçon*, p. 17.
516 Roger Martin du Gard, *Vieille France* (1933) (Paris, 1974), p. 149.
517 Certeau, *L'Absent de l'histoire*, p 29. On prophecies generally, see Keith Thomas, op. cit., chapter 13; and Bollême, *La Bibliothèque bleue*, chapter 2.
518 Beauvoir, *Privilèges*, p. 93; also ibid., pp. 131–9; Stern, *Hitler*, pp. 29, 33–4 and 78–9; and Guy Michelat and Jean-Pierre Hubert Thomas, *Dimensions du Nationalisme, Enquête par questionnaire (1962)* (Paris, 1966), p. 92.
519 Drumont, *TA*, p. 244.
520 Drumont, *FJ*, II, p. 565; see also my "A View of the Past"; and further discussion of this theme in chapter XVI, pp. 614–17 below.
521 See Alexis de Tocqueville, *"The European Revolution" and Correspondence with Gobineau* (New York, 1959), pp. 248 and 283–7; and Michael D. Biddiss, *Father of Racist Ideology, The Social and Political Thought of Count Gobineau* (London, 1970), Part 1, chapter 10 and *passim.*
522 Drumont, *FJ*, II, p. 565.
523 Daudet, *L'Avant-Guerre*, p. x. Besides referring to a common idea that there were decadent "old" nations and virile "young" ones, Daudet is probably alluding to a remark supposedly made by Renan to Déroulède: "Jeune homme, la France se meurt; ne troublez pas son agonie."; see Daniel Halévy, *Histoire d'une Histoire*

esquissée pour le troisième cinquanténaire de la Révolution Française (Paris, 1939), p. 46.

524 Maurras, *Quand les Français*, p. 229.

525 See Viau, op. cit., p. 8.

526 Barrès, *Scènes et doctrines*, II, pp. 162–5.

527 Martin du Gard, *Jean Barois*, p. 430.

528 Drumont, "La Suprême Entrevue", 21 November 1892, *OBS*, pp. 74–5.

529 Benda, *Les Cahiers d'un clerc*, p. 15 (13 February 1936).

530 Daily Report, Prefect of Police, 31 January 1898. APP Ba 106.

531 See Girardet, *La Société militaire;* see also Bernard Schnapper, *Le Remplacement militaire en France: Quelques aspects politiques, économiques et sociaux du récrutement au XIXe siècle* (Paris, 1968).

532 See Daudet, *Au Temps de Judas*, pp. 121–2; Bédarida, op. cit.; and Ralston, op. cit., *passim.*

533 Gohier, op. cit., p. 32; also pp. 40–2 and *passim.*

534 See Girardet, "La Ligue des Patriotes"; and Sternhell, *Maurice Barrès*, pp. 68–75.

535 See Sorlin, *"La Croix" et les Juifs*, pp. 65–6.

536 Daudet, *Au Temps de Judas*, p. 120. As we have seen, those in higher education could "volunteer" to do only 1 year's military service instead of the usual 3 or 2. There is some evidence that Jewish conscripts had a more enthusiastic attitude towards conscription than was normal; see n. 545 below.

537 See Girardet, *La Société militaire*, pp. 213–22; Drumont, *DB*, p. 469; and Courteline, *Les Gaîtés de l'escadron* (1884–1895), pp. 147, 169–87 and *passim.*

538 See Daudet, *Au Temps de Judas*, pp. 120–1; Ralston, op. cit., pp. 83 and *passim;* P. Dumont, *La Petite Bourgeoisie à travers les contes quotidiens du "Journal"*, pp. 55–66; Sternhell, *Maurice Barrès*, pp. 320–1; and chapter II, pp. 77–8 above.

539 See, for example, Barrès, "Marchand et les Parlementaires"; and "Le Général Galliéni", *Scènes et doctrines*, II, pp. 91–111; Barrès-Maurras, op. cit., pp. 186–97; Daudet, *Salons et journaux*, pp. 181–98; Daudet, *Au Temps de Judas*, pp. 133 and 163–4; Daudet, *Les Oeuvres dans les hommes*, pp. 178–9; and *Le Petit Journal*, Supplément Illustré, 30 January 1898, Frontispiece, "Vive l'Armée!", just one typical example of the iconography of the military cult.

540 Viau, op. cit., pp. 215–16.

541 Zola, *Paris*, pp. 273–4.

542 Drumont, *DB*, p. 469; see also Brunetière, "Après le Procès", pp. 433–42.

543 See, for example, Daily Report, Prefect of Police, 26 January 1898. APP Ba 106 (on a meeting of the Union Nationale in the 20th *arrondissement*).

544 Cit. Denis, op. cit., p. 59.

545 Drumont, *FJ*, II, p. 36; and I, pp. 9 and 421; see also ibid., II, pp. 25 and 232–6; *TA*, pp. 48 and 312; and Bournand, op. cit., p. 168. In fact, French Jews often showed unusual enthusiasm for the army, both as conscripts and professionals; see, for example, Benda, *La Jeunesse d'un clerc*, pp. 167–77; Maurois, *Mémoires*, I, pp. 110–17; and Dreyfus, *Cinq années de ma vie, passim.*

546 See Chapter XI, n. 341; and J. Néré, "Aspects du développement des grèves en France, 1883–9", *Revue d'Histoire Economique et Sociale*, 34 (1956), pp. 286–302; J. Julliard, *Clemenceau briseur de grèves, L'affaire de Draveil Villeneuve-St Georges (1908)* (Paris, 1965); P. N. Stearns, "Against the Strike Threat: Employer Policy towards Labor Agitation in France, 1900–1914", *Journal of Modern History*, 40 (1968), pp. 474–500; and Sorlin, *Waldeck-Rousseau*, pp. 463–9.

547 See Robert Brécy, *La Grève générale en France* (Paris, 1969).

548 See Karl Liebknecht, *Militarism and Anti-Militarism* (1907) (New York, 1972), pp. 65–7.

549 An idea popularized in intellectual circles by Georges Sorel's *Réflexions sur la violence* (Paris, 1908). Sorel was not, of course, directly representative of the militant labour movement.

550 See Liebknecht, op. cit., pp. 102–12; Maitron, *Histoire du mouvement anarchiste,*

pp. 346–56; Fiechter, *Le Socialisme français*, pp. 155–60; Jean-Jacques Becker and Annie Kriegel, "Les inscrits au 'Carnet B', Dimensions, composition, physionomie politique et limites du pacifisme ouvrier", *Le Mouvement Social*, no. 65 (1968), pp. 111–20; and Andréani, "L'Antimilitarisme en Languedoc".

551 See chapter IV, pp. 138 and 146–8 above.
552 Cit. Ralston, op. cit., p. 35.
553 Drumont, *DB*, p. 462; also *FJ*, II, pp. 418–19 and 447.
554 Drumont, *TA*, p. 48.
555 Cit. Bournand, op. cit., p. 47.
556 Ibid., p. 104.
557 For the parallel, but, it seems, more extreme, situation in the German officer corps, see M. Kitchen, *The German Officer Corps 1890–1914* (Oxford, 1968), pp. 37–48.
558 Drumont, *DB*, pp. 471, 479 and 41.
559 See, for example, Drumont, *FJ*, II, pp. 37–8; Barrès-Maurras, op. cit., p. 652 (Marchand); and Blumenkranz, ed., op. cit., p. 331.
560 Drumont, *TA*, p. 365; see also Mirbeau's portrait of the "typical" retired officer, Capitaine Mauger, in *Le Journal d'une femme de chambre*, pp. 190 and *passim*.
561 Bournand, op. cit., pp. 152–4 and 186–7.
562 Ibid., pp. 186–7. The charge that Jews scavenged on battlefields was also made by Drumont, quoting Mirbeau: "ces Juifs sordides qui, le soir des batailles . . . vont dépouiller les blessés et détrousser les cadavres." *FJ*, I, pp. 510–11.
563 See L'Hermite, *L'Anti-Pape*, pp. 234–5; Grenier, *Nos Députés 1898–1902*, p. 234; Grenier, *Nos Députés 1902–1906*, p. 239; and Jolly, ed., op. cit..
564 Cit. Dagan, op. cit., p. 24; also ibid., p. 21.
565 See also Reinach, op. cit., VI, pp. 458–60. Reinach was himself deprived of his rank in the territorials in 1898 by General Billot, then Minister of War, for having criticized his superior officers in print; see Reinach, op. cit., III, pp. 634–9. A Comte de Reinach, an officer in the hussars, wrote to Drumont as early as 1890 to dissociate himself from the Jewish Reinachs; see Drumont, *DB*, p. 131.
566 *Le Spectateur Militaire*, 1 August 1886, cit. Ralston, op. cit., p. 257; see also ibid., pp. 254–6.
567 Drumont, *DB*, pp. 470 and 480–1; also ibid., pp. 471–3.
568 Ibid., p. 478.
569 Ibid., pp. 481–6.
570 Ibid., pp. 477–8.
571 Ibid., pp. 480 and 478; also pp. 488–94.
572 Bournand, op. cit., p. 186.
573 Cit. Reinach, op. cit., VI, p. 457.
574 See Paléologue, op. cit., pp. 7, 35–6, 38 and *passim*; Blum, "Le Procès" (15 March 1898), *L'Oeuvre de Léon Blum 1891–1905*, p. 350; Martin du Gard, *Jean Barois*, p. 310; Duroselle, "L'Antisémitisme en France", p. 63; and Mauriac, "L'Affaire Dreyfus", p. 12; but see also Johnson, op. cit., p. 37.
575 See Morin *et al.*, op. cit., p. 80 n.
576 Reinach, op. cit., III, p. 555; see also Girardet, *La Société militaire*, pp. 195–200.
577 See my "Late Nineteenth-Century Nationalism".
578 Barrès, *Scènes et doctrines*, II, p. 162.
579 See, for example, Byrnes, *Antisemitism in Modern France*, chapter VI, "Morès, The First National Socialist"; Weber, "Nationalism, Socialism, and National-Socialism in France"; and Mosse, "The French Right and the Working Classes".
580 Daily Report, Prefect of Police, 13 February 1898. APP Ba 106.
581 See *Le Mouvement Social*, no. 49 (1964), Numero spécial, "1914: La Guerre et la Classe ouvrière européenne"; and Annie Kriegel, "Patrie ou Révolution: Le Mouvement ouvrier français devant la Guerre (juillet-août 1914)", *Revue d'Histoire Economique et Sociale*, 43 (1965), pp. 363–86.
582 Daily Report, Prefect of Police, 24 January 1898. APP Ba 106.

CHAPTER XIII
RACIAL ANTISEMITISM: "A RACE APART"

I

IN THE PREVIOUS CHAPTER WE SAW THAT ANTISEMITES WERE CONCERNED TO establish the otherness of the Jews, to stress "all that made them *different* from the rest of the nation",[1] in the words of Maurras; and we have seen in passing that this otherness, this difference, was expressed in racial terms. It was frequently claimed that the Jews were a race, with special and indelible qualities that distinguished them from the French, and marked their inferiority. They could not be assimilated; on the contrary, they represented a foreign body in French society, which, as we have seen, was believed to be suffering from their corrupting and dominating presence. We must now attempt to assess the significance and importance of this aspect of French antisemitism.

The racial colouring of French antisemitism at the end of the nineteenth century is reflected in the use of the term *"antisémitisme"*. "The importance attached by modern antisemitism to the idea of race is manifested in the name which the movement has given itself", wrote Leroy-Beaulieu.[2] The term made its appearance in France during the 1880s. The Supplement to Littré's *Dictionnaire de la langue française*, published in 1877, does not include the word,[3] and subsequent dictionaries provide the earliest literary examples of its use from around 1890.[4] However, the term was current in the newspaper press from the early 1880s, and a weekly called *L'Anti-Sémitique* was published in 1883.[5] The term was familiar enough, moreover, in 1889 to be applied to the first Ligue Antisémitique. By the mid- and late 1890s, it was well established, and predominated over the term *"anti-juif"*, which was still occasionally used, however, for example in the title of Guérin's weekly, *L'Antijuif*. It is probably significant here that Guérin and the Ligue Antisémitique Française had a special connection with the anti-Jewish movement in Algeria, for which, as Leroy-Beaulieu pointed out, the attempt to exploit Arab sentiment against the Jews, made the term *"antisémitisme"* problematic.[6] Making the same point, though insisting on the "scientific" terminology, Picard emphasized that the term "Semite" included both Arabs and Jews, and that antisemitism was directed against both.[7] In practice, however, the term *"antisémitisme"* was used to apply almost exclusively to the Jews. Contemporaries seem agreed that the term originated in Germany. Lazare referred here to Marr's *Der Sieg des Judentums über das Germanentum,* which was noticed in France in 1879;[8] Leroy-Beaulieu, more vaguely, to "this pedantic word, antisemitism, imported . . . from pedantic Germany".[9]

What were the connotations of the term *"antisémitisme"*? To what extent did it imply adherence to an allegedly "scientific" or biological racial theory? Certainly, a number of writers made explicit use of the categories "Aryan" and "Semite". Drumont was able to cite from *Les Sémites et le Sémitisme aux points de vue ethnographiques, religieux et politiques* (1882) by the Blanquiste Gellion-Danglar, a work made up of articles written in the late 1860s that proclaimed Aryan supremacy over the Semites and other inferior races.[10] Tridon's *Du Molochisme juif* (1884), also referred to by Drumont, posed an eternal opposition between two races, the Aryan and the Semitic, the first being the creator and sustainer of higher civilization, which the latter constantly undermined and threatened.[11] Drumont, himself, in *La France juive,* similarly presented the course of world history as an endless struggle between Aryans and Semites, or Jews. He specifically claimed to be going beyond popular clichés about Jews; he was engaged, he wrote, in

> a more thorough and a more serious examination . . . of the traits which differentiate the Jew from other men . . . We begin our work, therefore, with an ethnographical, physiological and psychological comparison of the Semite and the Aryan, these two personifications of races that are distinct and irremediably hostile to each other, whose antagonism has dominated the world in the past and will continue to trouble it even more in the future. [While] the generic name Aryan . . . designates, as everyone knows, the superior branch of the white race . . . which alone possesses the notion of justice, the feeling for liberty and the concept of beauty, the Semite, by contrast was "not made for civilization".

Each race, moreover, was characterized by opposite physical and psychological qualities that were interrelated and hereditary: "The Semite is greedy for money, grasping, scheming, clever, deceitful; the Aryan is enthusiastic, heroic, chivalrous, disinterested, open . . .".[12] According to Daudet, it was thanks to Drumont that "the Jewish question was posed as an ethnic question" in France.[13]

And it is true that the Aryan-Semitic terminology was increasingly used by antisemites from the late 1880s. Regnard, for example, attacked the Jews in a series of articles in *La Revue Socialiste* from 1887 to 1889 entitled "Aryans and Semites".[14] For some writers, the terms were merely fashionable labels, significant nevertheless as such; for others, they were the vocabulary of a more thoroughgoing and deliberate racialism. In the latter category was Jules Soury, the first writer in France, according to Sternhell, to elaborate "a racial theory of physiological determinism".[15] Soury wrote, for example, at the time of the Rennes trial:[16]

> We must fight for France and for the Aryans . . . Rennes is a sacred battlefield . . . what is involved is not the fate of a poor little Jewish captain, but the eternal struggle between Semitism and the Aryan. The world philosophy of Semitism is summed up in the words: *I believe;* while the Aryan proclaims: I know, and founds science. Semitism has always opposed science with a sterile negation, from the time of Chaldea and Babylon . . . I believe that the Jew is a race; or rather, a species . . . I really believe that the Jew is born of a special category of anthropoid like the black man, the yellow man, or the redskin . . . Read Renan's *Langues sémitiques.* There is no doubt about his scorn for this species. He says that the Jew represents an inferior type of human nature . . . the Semitic race compared with the Indo-European race really represents an inferior type . . . Morality itself has always been understood by this race in a very different way from ours. The Semite knows only self-interest. The pursuit of revenge, laying claim to what he believes he has a right to, both are a kind of obligation, in his eyes. By contrast, to ask him to keep his word, to administer justice in a disinterested manner, is to ask the impossible . . . Thus the Semitic race is marked almost exclusively by negative qualities. It has no mythology, no epics, no science, no philosophy, no literature, no art, no civil life. In everything, it appears to be deficient . . .

Soury is worth quoting at length for his inconsistent attempt to appear to be "scientific", a characteristic which he shared with Drumont and others. His claim that Aryans and Semites were biologically different, reacting differently to different diseases, displaying different physiological and even anatomical traits, and his racial explanation of psychological and cultural qualities,[17] were not uncommon either, though they were usually formulated by others in less esoteric terminology, as we shall see.

Sternhell has recently recalled that Soury had some influence on Barrès,[18] and particularly on the way in which the latter formulated his racial ideas from the later 1890s. Certainly, as we have seen, by the time of the Affair, Barrès expressed his antisemitism in racial terms. He wrote, for example, at the time of the Rennes trial, echoing Soury, and via Soury, Renan: "One can speak of an Indo-European race and of a Semitic race . . . Perhaps indeed they are two different species."[19] Again in May 1900, he declared: "I am, by every instinct of the tradition of Lorraine . . . My different blood fortifies me in my aversion to Judaism (a race opposed to mine) . . ."[20] Such antisemitism, moreover, was part of a wider racial philosophy. He wrote, in July 1899, to condemn mis-cegenation: "M. Forzinetti is said to have been born of a Frenchman and an African woman. This demi-Semitism, this cross-breeding perpetrated on the edges of the desert, produces misfits, a scum that is feared along all the shores of the Mediterranean."[21] In *Scènes et doctrines du nationalisme,* he quoted with approval a passage by the Socialist Léon Hennebicq[22] that had appeared in *Le Peuple* in February 1897:[23]

From now on it is puerile, save for the Radicals who still think that the universe is guided by the principles of the Rights of Man, to deny the existence of races, and of their wars and conflicts. Not only is the explanation of history impossible without taking account of them; not only is collective heredity in fact even the essential and durable element which gives events their continuity; but contemporary trends all make racial considerations more important. We cannot attach such influence to economic questions, when it is established that the economy of a people depends on its heredity, that is to say its race. All the great social forces, art, religion, law and morality derive from the historical and geological tradition of societies. *Each race and each piece of territory* has its own law, its own art, its own religion. A race, which is absorbed by another, is gangrened, enslaved, belittled. It is because I am aware of this racial conflict at the root of the transformations and the evolution of societies, that I am with the Edmond Picard, the Rochefort, the Drumont and the Barrès . . .

We have already encountered Picard, another Belgian, whose writings were published and often quoted in France,[24] and whose antisemitism was expressed in racial terminology of unusual consistency. Antisemitism arose, he explained in Dagan's *Enquête*,[25] as a result of

the presence among peoples of Aryan race of numerous individuals of Semitic race—who are not content with simply living among Aryans, but who proceed methodically to deprive their hosts of their property and who aim to exercise control privately and politically over the civilization that is especially Aryan . . . The psychologies of the two races differ in every respect, and in every order of thought, action and human feeling. They differ much more than the physical types which are easily distinguishable. The impression of similarity given by dress and by modern manners is superficial and of no account. Thus every Aryan institution, public or private, that is controlled by a Jew takes an abnormal turn which shocks, irritates and exasperates the Aryan, and appears to him irregular or unjust . . . [Antisemitism is] an ETHNIC reaction first and foremost . . . These individuals of foreign Jewish race must be removed from any involvement or interference in the government or direction of the Aryan race, which is endowed with a special "spirit", which has its unique destiny, and which must remain completely free to pursue it, without being hampered or diverted from its course, as it is all the time by a "spirit" which is ethnically different . . .

"Our people are obeying the ethnic law, the zoological law of the conservation of the species", agreed an antisemite in Vogüé's *Les Morts qui parlent.*[26] In his contribution to Dagan's *Enquête*, Picard was resuming the thesis of his book, *Synthèse de l'antisémitisme* (1892), which, like *La France juive*, presented the course of human history as an eternal conflict between Aryan and Semite. Picard, however, was more devoted than Drumont to strict racial theory. Each race, he maintained,[27] had

a solidarity and a perennial quality . . . Its singularity is the result of indestructible elements. Of race one can say that it is IRREVOCABLE . . . It is not altered by any change of milieu; it persists: it is always there, like one of those mineral poisons, which, once introduced into an organism, can never escape analysis . . . With whatever disguise a Semite living among us may masquerade, he will remain himself, in his body, and more so in his soul. Should he interbreed with one of us, his Semitic blood will affect all his issue; we know enough now about heredity for this point not to be insisted upon.

Insist upon it, nevertheless, Picard did, emphasizing again and again the dangers of miscegenation:[28]

One can affirm that, wherever the Semite has dominated the Aryan and wherever their bloods have been mixed, there has occurred a decline for the Aryan, from the point of view of his civilization and his destinies . . . Contact with the Semite is, thus, for the Aryan, dangerous, and cross-breeding with him is pernicious . . . A race must never . . . inter-breed with another.

Some antisemites, however, expressed doubts about employing such racialist arguments against the Jews. Racialism was, first of all, difficult to square with Catholic theology and the injunction to work for the conversion of the Jews. But that theology did embody, along with the concept of universal salvation, that of inherited guilt, not only in the doctrine of the Fall, but also, more particularly, in the idea that the Jews were collectively responsible for the death of Christ.[29] Racial arguments also provided a means by which Catholics could attack the Jews without ostensibly attacking Judaism or religion in general. "The religious issue", wrote Drumont, "plays only a secondary part beside the racial issue, which predominates over all the others."[30] Antisemitism was "definitely not a religious question," declared Le Télégramme d'Alger in January 1898, "but a racial one."[31] Catholic antisemites, therefore, either avoided racial terminology of the modern type, or sought to qualify it. Christian Democrats, on the whole, eschewed racial antisemitism. Abbé Gayraud, for example, a deputy who supported antisemitic measures, wrote in La Justice Sociale in July 1898: "Strictly speaking, there is no such thing as a Jewish race."[32] Sorlin has pointed out that racialism embarrassed the editors of La Croix. Apart from the universalist premise of the Christian religion, the Biblical idea that the Jews were God's chosen people was hardly compatible with the assertion that they were an inferior race, even if it could be argued that they had forfeited their privileged status by refusing to recognize Christ as the Messiah, or had earned God's curse for their role in the crucifixion. Moreover, the Assumptionist Fathers had to admit that conversion eradicated Jewishness. However, despite these theoretical reservations, and although racialism did remain a secondary feature of the newspaper's antisemitism, in practice La Croix did refer to the Jews as an inferior race, while evoking supposedly Jewish vices and pointing to Jewish physical characteristics. This effective racialism was accentuated during the time of the Dreyfus Affair, which was presented, as it was by Soury, as a struggle between two races, though in this instance between the Franks and the Jews. Jews were said to be a race apart or a "cursed race"; while the Jewish mentality and the Jewish physique were pilloried in words and in cartoons.[33] A further indication of the way in which effectively racial antisemitism could be cast in a Catholic mould, with only a token gesture of qualification, is provided by a passage from Mgr Jouin's *Le Péril judéo-maçonnique*. The Jew, he wrote, is "a being apart, who in every different ambience or milieu, in every latitude, in whatever situation, happy or otherwise, in which he finds himself, remains invariably a foreigner . . ." He belonged to[34]

> a fallen race; there is deep inside him an atavistic tendency, which means that at the crucial hour there rise from his heart to his brain all the heady eternal dreams of his fathers, scheming incessantly to conquer the world, and all the ancestral hatreds which, throughout twenty centuries, have repeated the clamour of Calvary: "Let his blood be on us and on our children." The Jew is always a Jew, his thought is Talmudic, his will despotic and his hand is the hand of a deicide. Until he falls on his knees at the foot of the Cross of Christ, he will remain the enemy of mankind.

The doubts or the ambivalence of Catholics vis-à-vis racial explanations were not unique among antisemites. There was a similar ambiguity, for example, in the attitude of a non-believer like Maurras. He declared in 1897, seeking an explanation for the continuity in style of Florentine architecture: "I ruled out any idea of an unchanging racial genius, since this type of explanation has been so abused in our time."[35] And his scepticism about the value of race as a cultural concept was matched by a stronger conviction that as a biological concept it was either dangerous or otiose.[36] Yet he could write in 1894: "I wonder whether there is not some biological law which condemns to death classes and castes which, having begun by neglecting the appeal of fame, become insensible finally to the most eminent dangers."[37] He also used the concept of "blood" in social explanations, presenting the course of history in *L'Avenir de l'intelligence* (1905) as a struggle between "Gold" and "Blood";[38] and writing of the Monod family: "It would indeed have been extraordinary, if the Monods had not received, in the course of their multiple fornications, at least a drop of our blood!"[39] Moreover, he used such terminology in the context of attacks on the Jews, writing again in *L'Avenir de l'intelligence*: "From the authority of princes of our own race, we have passed under the knout of the merchants of Gold, who are of a different flesh from us, that is to say of a different language and a different mentality."[40] And he also referred directly to the special characteristics of the Jewish race: "It is clear from the philosophy of Comte [and, he might have added, of the younger Renan] that the Jewish race is a race whose evolution has been stunted . . ."[41]

The attitude of other members of the Action Française, some of whom were Catholics, was similarly ambivalent. Léon Daudet, for example, who was a forceful exponent of the idea of an irremediable Jewish character of an inferior kind, as we have seen, and who was not loath to use racial terminology to express or to reinforce such an idea, contrasting the Jews with "those of French race",[42] was yet worried by some of the socially pessimistic implications of later neo-Gobinist racial theory. We saw that he rejected any idea of French decadence, expressed in ethnic terms, asserting in 1911: "The ardour, the courage, the initiative, the ingenuity displayed by our aviators furnish one proof, among a thousand others, that our race has lost none of its traditional qualities . . ."[43] We have seen also that various contributors to the *Revue de l'Action Française* expressed their antisemitism in racial terms, including Bainville, who wrote, however, in *La Gazette de France* in October 1905, that "Gobinism would lead straight to suicide any nation that became persuaded by it. Gobinism would cause France to be disgusted with itself, since its ethnic origins are so disparate . . ."[44] Maurras also vigorously rejected Gobinism.[45] Thus the Action Française writers, while repudiating certain racial theories and the specifically biological concept of race, nevertheless used the terminology of race, emptied ostensibly of its predestinarian and pessimistic implications, but in practice still an instrument for the hierarchical classification of peoples as distinct entities that were and ought to be kept separate.

A good example of this usage is provided by the concept of "Latin Race", employed by Algerian antisemites as we have seen,[46] and developed in France by Frédéric Amouretti and others.[47] "It would, in effect, be absurd", wrote Amouretti in *Le Soleil* in June 1898, "to maintain that the French and the Spaniards are of Latin blood. We know very well that they are not descended from a few Latin colonists who came over with Julius Caesar or with Scipio . . . But this does not mean that the Latin races do not exist, nor that they are not much more real than the Cro-Magnon race ever was . . ." The unity of the Latin race, he asserted, reverting to the philogical origins of racial theory, "is established above all by language . . . There is much more resemblance between a brown brachycephalic and a white dolichocephalic, of the same spiritual formation and speaking languages of the same family, than there is between two brown brachycephalics, one of whom speaks French and practices Catholicism, while the other speaks Bengali and practices Brahmanism."[48] Race here was a cultural and historical concept, and, as such, could be applied to the French specifically. Amouretti referred in 1909 to "France [and] . . . its fine race . . ."[49] But others, more inclined to biological racialism, were wary of this particular usage. Barrès lamented in 1899: "Alas! there is not a French race, but a French people, a French nation . . .",[50] a sentiment, whose formulation he had significantly qualified by 1902, writing then: "Let us make it clear once and for all: it is inexact to talk in the strict sense of a French race. We are not a race, but a nation . . ."[51] Barrès, like Maurras, characteristically preferred the vaguer term "blood" to that of "race" in this context. "Since I have no Greek blood in my veins," he wrote later, "I can hardly understand Socrates or Plato."[52] Drumont used the term "the French race",[53] and also such expressions as "of Gallic stock";[54] but they were not concepts which he explicitly developed. Significant here is the term "real Frenchmen" *("vrais Français")*, which was much more frequently employed by Drumont and others. This term enabled them, consciously or not, to avoid the difficulties raised by more precise formulations, and yet to distinguish absolutely between the French and the Jews. Its ideological function, in effect, was the same as more explicit racialism. A speaker, for example, at a Union Nationale meeting at Roanne in March 1899, called for "the union of all those who are really French against the Jewish people".[55]

"Race" was, in effect, a convenient term to use to categorize the Jews and to emphasize their otherness, but it was felt by antisemites to be innappropriate or even dangerous when applied too strictly to the French. The ambiguity of racial terminology in antisemitic usage, however, only reflected a much more widespread uncertainty and vagueness surrounding the whole idea of race. Leroy-Beaulieu represented this state of confusion well. He was a cogent critic of racialism and its implications, but, in his criticism of it, he continued to employ racial terminology. "If there is a Jewish race", he wrote, "it is— dare I say?—the artificial product of the Mosaic law and of our own laws of the Middle Ages, it is the work of the Torah and of the Ghetto, much more than the natural product of a soil or a climate, or the spontaneous fruit of the Semitic stem or of the blood of the Patriarchs. No race perhaps is so manifestly the creation of historical evolution."[56] He wrote also that antisemitism itself was "a case of atavism",[57] and he referred to himself as an "Aryan".[58] Several other critics of antisemitism showed the same uncertainty, the same inability to free themselves from thinking or writing in racial terms. Renard told Dagan: "From the ethnic point of view, the Jews suffer the consequences of not having known how or not having wished to be assimilated into the nation in which they lived, of having remained through their practice of endogamy a race having clearly distinguishable characteristics."[59] Levasseur commented:[60]

It is clear that if the Jews possess to a certain degree that clannishness with which they are so often reproached, this is the result of the situation which they occupied in the past, until the French Revolution. A legislation, discriminating against them in a particularly cruel way, kept them in a continual isolation. It is quite natural that a close solidarity should have been created in their race and that it should finally have become a hereditary quality fixed in their blood.

The socio-historical explanation, by implication anti-racial, had, it seems to be clinched by an appeal to race. Also among the contributors to Dagan's Enquête, Letourneau, a professor at the Ecole d'Anthropologie, asserted that "it is absolutely anti-scientific to say that the Jews are born with any special gifts for dealing in money", but he admitted that certain commercial aptitudes might have been able, over the years, "to fix themselves in the blood . . ."[61] Even Emile Durkheim, while elsewhere rejecting the general concept of race as a means of social explanation,[62] and though stressing that Jews were losing "their ethnic characteristics", allowed that such characteristics existed, "certain deficiencies of the Jewish race . . ."[63]

Durkheim, himself, was a Jew,[64] and Marrus has recently shown that French Jews, in the second half of the nineteenth century made extensive use of the concept of race in order to express their own sense of community in a way that did not appear to deny their French nationality, and in a situation where growing secularization made identification through attachment to the Judaic religion increasingly untenable.[65] J. Cohen, for example, as early as 1864, in a book refuting the charge of deicide, referred to "the vigorous religious race to which I belong."[66] The Radical politician Alfred Naquet, an anticlerical, used the term "race" to describe the Jews, and also employed the term "Aryan"; and he even admitted, in a speech in the Chamber of Deputies in May 1895, that he had once accepted that the Jews were racially inferior to the Aryans.[67] Daniel Halévy wrote apologetically in his diary in December 1898 of "the tainted idiosyncrasies of my race";[68] while Blum, in a very different tone, referred to Lazare as "a Jew of the great race, of the prophetic race . . ."[69] Blum was here echoing Péguy, who also referred to the Jews as "a race of prophets" and the "chosen race",[70] a mode employed by other non-Jewish philosemites in this loose way, but also more strictly. The anti-Drumontist Théodore Vibert presented the Jews as the model people, ancestors of the Europeans and authors of the principles of democracy, in a book entitled La Race Sémitique.[71] Some Jews, however, were aware of the danger that this use of racial terminology represented and realized that it could play into the hands of the antisemites. Reinach, for example, protested that the Jews were not a race in the strict sense, writing that there was hardly "a drop of the blood of the Semites of Palestine . . . in the veins of the Jews of Europe . . ."[72]

Both Jews and antisemites had, in effect, taken over, for very different reasons, what Leroy-Beaulieu called "a conventional ethnology",[73] with all its vagueness and potentiality to mislead. "People are so impressed by the word race that they think they have explained everything when they have uttered it", commented Manouvrier, another professor at the Ecole d'Anthropologie. "The influence of race! Everything is attributed to it, without any attempt at serious justification, and even those characteristics which are least likely to be hereditary."[74] We must now examine the force and the provenance of the idea of race in nineteenth-century France a little more carefully.

II

As we have begun to see, the term "race" was used in a great variety of ways, with a variety of implications. First, it could be used to describe mankind as a whole, "the human race".[75] Then it could be used to describe a people or a nation without necessarily having any ethnic or biological connotations. It was used in this sense by Péguy,[76] for example, and it was in this sense that Martin du Gard's Jean Barois, a Dreyfusard, referred to the French as "our race".[77] Similarly, Thiers explained in 1867 that the theory of nationalities meant that "most States should be made up of a single race, that is to say of peoples with the same origins and speaking the same language."[78] Again, it could be used to indicate local origin. The autobiographical hero of Vallès's Le Bachélier declared of a friend: "He belongs to my race, he was born in the same department, in the same town, almost in the same street."[79] Here the term was often used to express or to explain differences of regional type in a way that can be properly called racialist.[80] Delacroix, for example, wrote from

Strasbourg in 1857: "The inhabitants . . . positively seem to belong to a different race."[81] The Marquis de Castellane wrote that "M. de Falloux was Angevin by origin and had absorbed his sincere religiosity from his native soil . . . it had entered his veins like the natural sap that emanates from certain soils."[82] Alphonse Daudet claimed characteristically of the population of the Midi: "Among the people, urban and rural, drunkenness is almost unknown. As a race, they have an instinctive fear and horror of it. The Southern race is fiery by birth, and does not need to get drunk."[83] Such racial stereotyping of Southerners in particular, and usually hostile in intention, was common,[84] but the concept of race was also used by regionalists to express their sense of having a separate identity within the French nation, a usage parallel to that employed by the Jews.[85] Maurras, who was a fervent Provençal patriot, declared in his old age: "I can never forgive Alphonse Daudet for having helped to make the people of my race ridiculous."[86]

It is significant that the antisemites in the 1890s and 1900s, including Maurras, contributed to or joined in this pejorative regional racialism, and sometimes linked it with their hostility to the Jews. Drumont, for example, described Constans as "this Southerner, who belongs both to the exuberant and to the murderous species . . . There is in him a sly side and a sinister side, the remnant of the old Albigensian, who, centuries later, finds again his old accomplice the Jew, and plots with him again . . ."[87] In *Jean Révolte* (1892), Gaston Méry presented the Southern menace as a danger equalled only by the Jewish menace. In the political takeover of France, "it is the Jew who gives the orders and the Southerner who carries them out."[88] Maurras, himself, sought to disabuse Barrès of his preconceptions about the Southerner, but only by restricting the racial stereotype to a narrow area. He also associated it with the Jews, and the Protestants:[89]

> You persist in confusing one or two restricted cantons of the department of the Gard with the whole of the Midi. This is a mistake for which Alphonse Daudet is responsible. It is quite true that the population of Nîmes is a rag-bag of Protestants, Jews and dealers from Beaucaire. It is a coarse race, thick-blooded, immoderate in gestures and loud-mouthed. Also deceitful and treacherous, as well as very stupid . . . But you should know that these people are held in scorn by all the rest of the Midi.

Anti-Southern prejudice, here and generally, reflected in part the fact that the South was politically a stronghold of the Left and the Extreme Left, and was seen as the seedbed of powerful and dangerous tribunes of the people, like Gambetta and Jaurès.

By extension perhaps, race could also be used to describe social or psychological types of a general kind. Vallès, again, in *Le Bachélier*, referred to the café in a provincial town, "where all the young blades and daredevils congregated, young fellows devouring their inheritances. I did not know that this race of people existed in the district."[90] And, later, his hero commented: "By my origins, I had roots only in the earth and the fields—not in the race of the fortunate! . . . I mixed with people who did not have my education, and who did not belong to my race [meaning the peasantry or the lower classes] . . ."[91] Further, in *L'Insurgé*, Vallès evoked "the race of those who have just enough money to get by, the 'honest folk' of all classes and all countries . . ."[92] "Race" was commonly used in this way as a means of social differentiation, explicitly and implicitly, and particularly to mark the barrier between the upper and middle classes and the "dangerous" lower classes.[93] Here, it had moral connotations that could, however, be evoked separately. Maupassant, for example, in *Bel-Ami*, evoked the fellow-feeling between the careerist Duroy and a well-known courtesan in these terms: "He felt perhaps vaguely that they had something in common, that there was between them a natural link, that they were of the same race, had the same kind of soul . . ."[94] And, in a similar way, Lyautey wrote, in a letter to the Vicomte de Vogüé in 1899, of "our admirable race of explorers and soldiers".[95]

The moral and social connotations of the term race were perhaps most obviously blended when it was applied to the aristocracy. The idea of race was inherent in that of an aristocracy of birth, and had been made explicit by the defenders and the opponents of the hereditary privileged nobility from the eighteenth century.[96] Leroux declared, for example, in the *Revue Encyclopédique* in 1831: "Racial prejudice is abolished: nobility and hereditary privilege no longer exist, and all men are equal."[97] However, the idea that the aristocracy formed a distinct and superior, if not Frankish, race survived through the nineteenth and into the twentieth century. Vigny recalled that as a schoolboy during the Consulate, "I felt that I belonged to a cursed race"[98] Nobles of later generations had the same feeling of being racially different, but often took considerable pride in the fact. The Marquis de Castellane, for example, wrote in 1909 that "his mother exercised the art of conversation, as though she had it in her blood . . ."[99] Boni de Castellane, writing of his latter-day "poverty" in 1925, declared: "It has always seemed to me a sign of race not to be ashamed of the bitter moments that destiny reserves for us."[100] Gobineau's developed racial theories have been seen as a defence of "the threatened interest of the aristocratic caste of Europe against the rising tide of democracy . . ."[101] The aristocratic conception of race, moreover, was adopted and propagated by commoners. The aristocratic origin of the idiot beggar-girl, Stéphanie de Vandières, in Balzac's story "Adieu" (1830), is proclaimed in her white skin.[102] Maupassant's Duroy declares of the Comte de Vaudrec: "He is charming . . . You can feel his race."[103] Zola, like Balzac, presented a fallen aristocratic girl in *Au Bonheur des Dames:* Mlle de Fontenailles works as a shopgirl, and "only her fine white hands still proclaimed the distinction of her race".[104]

Two further uses of the term "race" were connected with or derived from this aristocratic concept. First, it was used to describe a family, usually in the sense of a line. Victor Hugo, for example, declaimed in 1839 against the cemetery of Père-Lachaise, "with its hideous little fussy edifices, with their compartments and their cubby-holes, where the good Parisian stows away his father, his mother, his wife, his children, and all his race, as if putting them in a chest of drawers".[105] Here the race was decidedly bourgeois, but "race" in this sense was usually employed of noble or royal families. Hugo, again, referred to the Orléans family as a "race",[106] and the Bourbons and the Bonapartes were described by others in the same way.[107] Perhaps the most curious use of the term race to designate a line was that of Sue in *Le Juif errant*. The "race" of the Rennepont in the novel includes French aristocrats, bourgeois and workers, as well as an Indian prince, and is descended in some mysterious way from the Wandering Jew.[108] By extension from its aristocratic use, and related also to its use to describe breeds of domestic animals and particularly thoroughbreds, "race" could also be employed as a synonym for "excellence", in the form of natural talent or goodness. Thus, according to Balzac, the terms, "horse of pure blood, woman with race", became fashionable among dandies of the later Restoration period.[109] Vigny referred in 1832 to "the two races of men that inhabit the earth—the noble and the ignoble",[110] meaning noble in the moral sense. "In that time of mediocre races", wrote Alphonse Daudet of his hero Numa Roumestan, the petty-bourgeois Southern politician, in the early 1870s, "men of pure blood were rare, and the new leader triumphed . . ."[111] In much the same vein, Drumont referred in 1890 to "those country priests, of a strong and valiant race . . ."[112] Martin du Gard's Jean Barois, similarly, referred to Brisson as "a Republican of the old race";[113] while Rosny *aîné* bestowed a common form of praise on Jean Lorrain by describing him as "a writer of race".[114] Fernand Gregh, finally, expressed his admiration for an old teacher by saying that "he was a man with a mind of real race . . ."[115]

These various uses of the term "race" are all examples of what one might call incidental usage, sometimes implying racialist assumptions, but rarely attaching them to any deliberate theories. However, at the same time, such theories were developed in France, reinforcing and depending on popular usage, at least for their propagation. As Poliakov has pointed out, the extent to which the idea of race was present in the thought of nineteenth-century intellectuals has been obscured: "It seems as though through shame or through fear of appearing racist, the West wants never to have been racist, and has chosen a few minor figures (Gobineau, H. Chamberlain, etc.) to act as scapegoats. As a result a vast chapter in the thought of the West has been conjured away, and this vanishing-trick represents a collective suppression of troubling memories and awkward truths."[116] All we can do here, for France, is to point to some of the obvious features of this submerged intellectual tradition.

Already in the eighteenth century, the idea of race was being developed by intellectuals in two contexts. It was used in the debate over the raison d'être and thus the origins of the nobility and of the Third Estate, the former being seen as Frankish and the latter as Celtic. This "two-races" theory of French origins was adopted by polemicists on both sides, and was carried into nineteenth-century French historiography, informing the work of Augustin Thierry and Guizot, for example.[117] Drumont was characteristically one of its last proponents.[118] Writers of the Enlightenment involved in this debate, such as Montesquieu and Voltaire, also used the concept of race more generally in order to classify human types and cultures.[119] By the mid-nineteenth

century, when the "two-races" theory was losing something of its vogue, this
more general function had received reinforcement from the field of philology.
In particular, Renan in his *Histoire générale et système comparé des langues
sémitiques* (1855) and Max Müller in his *History of Ancient Sanskrit Literature*
(1859) had inferred the existence of distinct Aryan and Semitic races from the
existence of Aryan and Semitic languages.[120] Also in the second half of the
nineteenth century, anthropologists, following eighteenth-century precedents
and encouraged by the work of such philologists, set about a systematic
classification of the various races and sub-races of mankind, two of the most
notable practitioners of this academic exercise in France being Paul Topinard
(1852–1918) and Joseph Deniker, whose *Les Races et les Peuples de la Terre*
was published in 1900.[121] Topinard, a Catholic academic, whose works were,
for this reason, particularly welcomed in conservative circles, wrote typically
in 1900, in a book aimed at a general audience:

> The black races of Africa and Oceania, which are physically the most ugly
> . . . are also the most inferior in civilization . . . The characteristic of all
> the black races is their inability to improve themselves on their own . . . The
> yellow races are certainly characterized by a certain basic intelligence, which
> allows them to satisfy the immediate needs of life and to render their
> existence agreeable; but they have little initiative, they do not know how
> to improve themselves, and they are condemned to remain at their present
> low level of civilization. This leaves the white races. They have nowhere
> been found at a low level of civilization. Even in the prehistoric period in
> Europe, they were relatively civilized . . . What characterizes the white races
> is their ability to evolve by their own efforts . . . their constant cerebral
> activity and their spirit of initiative . . .

Topinard distinguished four sub-categories within the white race, one of which
included the Semites, but he did not otherwise single out the Jews.[122]

Such ideas received a considerable boost from the experience, direct or
indirect, of colonization. Tocqueville, for example, wrote in 1855 to Gobineau,
with whose racial theory of history he profoundly disagreed: "The European
races are often the greatest rogues, but at least they are rogues to whom God
gave will and power and whom he seems to have destined for some time to
be at the head of mankind. Nothing on the entire globe will resist their
influence . . . Europe will, within a hundred years, have transformed the globe
and dominated the other races."[123] Colonial imperialism and racialism more
obviously reinforced each other when the liberal democratic colonial ideology
of assimilation became ousted in the 1890s and 1900s, on the official level, by
that of association, which more realistically abandoned the alleged policy of
assimilating colonial populations to French culture, which was ethnocentric
but vestigially universalist in its assumptions, and recognized the distinctness
of those populations and at the same time emphasized their inferiority.[124] As
Astier-Loutfi and others have pointed out, the general public in France remained indifferent to the colonial Empire until the 1880s; but, from then on,
an increasingly popular literature of fiction and travel made colonialism a part
of general culture in France, strengthening the conviction of French white

superiority and making available a range of non-European racial stereotypes of an almost exclusively pejorative kind.[125]

The contemporaneous emergence of racial antisemitism and of racial colonialism was not a coincidence, as Hannah Arendt has forcefully argued,[126] but in France the relation between the two developments was complex, and was mediated through the general body of ideas about race. There was a strong anti-colonial tradition in France which was never entirely eclipsed, and to which many Nationalists and antisemites subscribed. Drumont, for example, was an outspoken critic of colonial expeditions, which, he claimed, were inspired by the Jews: "It is to enrich the Jews that our soldiers, under this Republic of ours, are dying of typhoid fever in Tunisia or of cholera in Tonkin . . . ." Nor did he reserve his sympathy for the colonial troops; he also exposed what he saw as the hypocrisy of the colonial ideology:[127]

> It should be noted . . . that the tendency to slaughter and to dispossess fellow-humans varies in direct proportion with the facility with which the slogans of civilization and humanity are proclaimed . . . on the pretext of civilizing them, the so-called savage peoples have been cruelly exploited and held to ransom . . . French democracy and English liberalism have behaved towards the peoples whom they have enslaved, like the Arabs and the Indians, with a frightening lack of all justice and humanity . . .

Rochefort had been a merciless critic of the colonial policies of the Second Empire, and, like Drumont, he vigorously opposed the Tunisian expedition of 1881 and later expansion in Indo-China, contributing thereby to the fall from power of Ferry in 1885.[128] Maurras also declared in 1900 that he was "an old adversary of colonialism".[129] Anti-colonialism was a good stick with which to beat the government, and also a convenient vehicle for Anglophobia, but the authentic note in Drumont's condemnation, in particular, should not be ignored. As Gobineau's similar attack on European colonialism also reminds us,[130] racial ideologies are easier to condemn than to understand.

By the last decades of the nineteenth century, however, the idea of race was well established in a large body of academic work in different disciplines, and, although scholars were beginning to question its validity as a scientific concept, it had gained wide currency, as such, among the educated public in France, finding ready ground for acceptance in the more general usage, which we described earlier. Thus the *Dictionnaire de l'Académie Française* of 1878 provided this definition of "race":[131]

> Line, all those who come from the same family . . . RACE, refers by extension to a multitude of people who come from the same country, and who resemble each other by their facial traits and their outward appearance. *The Caucasian race. The Mongol race. The Jewish race* . . . It is used equally of a constant variety of the human species. *The white race. The black race. The yellow race* . . . RACE is used again of particular species of some domestic animals, like dogs, horses, etc. . . . .

Moreover, certain non-specialist writers helped to propagate the idea of race, in its more sophisticated forms, among the general public in the latter part of the century. Gobineau, whose *Essai sur l'inégalité des races humaines* was published in 1854, and who was so cultivated by later German antisemitism, was comparatively neglected in France during his lifetime, and in the three decades after his death in 1882 his complex racialist theory of history appealed to very few. As we have seen, the French antisemites of the 1890s rarely mentioned him, and, when they did, they were usually critical.[132] Much more influential were Renan, Taine and Zola. Renan and Taine were the intellectual mentors of two generations, that which came to maturity in the 1870s and that which came to maturity in the 1890s, while Zola was the best-selling serious novelist of his day.

"If he is not the first of French writers," Henry James wrote of Renan in 1876, "I don't know who may claim the title . . ."[133] The Catholic critic and novelist Paul Bourget referred to him in 1899 as "one of those famous writers (whose work was available) . . . to guide the imagination of young people who are seeking self-knowledge through reading books . . . He was a seductive and disturbing influence . . . to how many of us did he reveal the strange horizons of our own hearts!"[134] Henri Massis wrote in 1923 that "the whole of modern thought must recognize in Renan the man who gave it birth, who formed its traits, who modelled its inner being";[135] and such testimonies to Renan's enormous impact, in the 1880s and 1890s in particular, could be multiplied.[136] His contribution to racial thinking, and especially to the ideology of Aryanism versus Semitism, is thus very significant, and worth examining. We have mentioned his *Histoire générale et système comparé des langues sémitiques*, first published in 1855, and reissued in 1858 and 1863. In the book, like other philologists of the day, he inferred the existence of defined races from linguistic phenomena, and proclaimed the inherent inferiority of the Semitic race, which included the Jews.[137]

> I am . . . the first to recognize that the Semitic race, compared with the Indo-European race, represents an essentially inferior type of human nature. It has neither that high level of spirituality which India and Germany alone have produced, nor that sentiment of the just mean and of perfect beauty that Greece has passed on to the Latin nations, nor that delicate and profound sensibility which is the dominant characteristic of the Celtic peoples.

The Semites lacked a philosophic and scientific culture; their literature was poor; and they had no plastic arts. Moreover, they were unable to build a civilization in the Western sense, since they were deficient in the civic and military virtues. Their "morality" was purely egocentric; they were incapable of any discipline or subordination, of self-abnegation or of the sentiment of hierarchy. Their qualities, in effect, were all negative ones, and they were an "incomplete" and immature race.[138] Renan was here writing primarily about the ancient Semites, and he qualified his remarks in important ways. First, he insisted that "the unity of humanity is a sacred and scientifically incontestable truth",[139] and he reminded his readers that this unity, expressed in the form of equality before one God, was "the fundamental doctrine of the Semites, and their most precious legacy to mankind".[140] Second, he stressed that, although the Arabs and the Jews constituted recognizable physical types, "the Semitic and the Indo-European races display no essential difference from the point of view of physiology . . ."[141] He also pointed out that the physical and cultural differences within the Indo-European race, say between a Brahman and a Russian, could be greater than those between an Indo-European and a Semite. Third, he allowed that modern Semites had become assimilated to Western civilization. Some cultural differences remained, but in general, "the Semites and the Aryans now form a single race, the white race, and a single intellectual family, the family of civilization . . ."[142] The important racial division in the modern world was not, therefore, between Aryans and Semites, but between these two "noble races" and the "inferior races" outside Europe.[143]

Renan's characterization of the Semites, without his qualifications, was noted and reproduced by a succession of antisemites at the end of the nineteenth century, including Soury and Barrès, as we have seen, and also Drumont, Picard and Maurras.[144] Renan subsequently departed even further from his commitment to the Aryan-Semitic race theory and to racially-orientated explanations in general. In a famous lecture on the definition of a nation, delivered at the Sorbonne in 1882,[145] he declared:

> Ethnic factors . . . have counted for nothing in the constitution of the modern nations . . . The truth is that there is no such thing as a pure race, and to base political analysis on ethnic factors is to base it on a chimera. The noblest countries, England, France, Italy, are those whose blood is most mixed . . . Human history is essentially different from geology. Race is not a decisive factor there, as it is with the orders of rodents or carnivores. No one has the right to go about measuring people's skulls, so that he can then embrace them and say: You are of our blood; you belong to us! Beyond anthropological characteristics, there are the principles of reason, of justice, of truth and of beauty, and these are universal.

To the dismay of some antisemites, though they were able to discount it as a senile aberration,[146] Renan also, at this time, began to express openly philo-Semitic opinions. In a lecture given to the Société des Etudes Juives, for example, in 1883, he claimed that the West owed both Christianity and the concept of social justice to the Jews; and he castigated "the deplorable ingratitude of Christendom towards the Jews, whom it treats in the cruellest manner".[147] Nevertheless, racial concepts remained unrepudiated in the corpus of Renan's writings through the second half of the nineteenth century, for example in the *Essais de morale et de critique* (1859)[148] which included a study on "The Poetry of the Celtic races"; in the *Vie de Jésus* (1863); in *Caliban* (1878) and in the *Souvenirs d'enfance et de jeunesse* (1883). The Carthusian prior in *Caliban* puts forward the idea that "It is the aristocracy which has disciplined the inferior races, which . . . like the emancipated negroes, at first showed a monstruous ingratitude towards their civilizers . . ."[149] As Pierre Guiral has commented, "Renan . . . is a much more

intransigent racist than Gobineau . . ."[150] Renan, also, despite his latter-day
philo-Semitism, continued to refer to the Jews as though they were a distinct
and identifiable race, even in a lecture given to the Cercle Saint-Simon in
1883, in which he sought to show that the Jews were not a pure race, that
more than one Jewish type existed, and that Jewish physical types were the
product of social isolation.[151] Given Renan's enormous prestige in the period
under consideration, therefore, and the large sales of his many books, it can
be assumed that they served to popularize and legitimize the general idea that
there was a racial hierarchy, and, more specifically, that the Jews had a racial
identity of an inferior kind. Here, of course, it should be remembered that
Renan, the apostate and the agnostic, was anathema to Catholics, including
Catholic antisemites. The *Semaine Religieuse* of Grenoble, for example, in
1892 described Renan as the "new Judas", and claimed that his *Vie de Jésus*
had been commissioned by Rothschild.[152] Moreover, several leading Dreyfusards claimed that Renan would have supported their cause had he lived.[153]
But this anxiety to enlist his posthumous support is itself significant; and
Catholics, too, like Drumont, as we have seen, did not allow their general
hostility to Renan, in his lifetime and after, to prevent their citing him as an
authority for their racial antisemitism.

Taine's intellectual influence in France in the later nineteenth century was
only rivalled by that of Renan. Indeed the two were seen as coupled or
complementary. "Our two great intellectual providers at that time", wrote the
Tharauds of their time at the *lycée* Sainte-Barbe around 1890, "were Taine
and Renan."[154] "Taine, Renan, the ideas which they had lived, were not for
us inanimate beings, dead concepts, things to be learnt," agreed Massis. "They
were part of our destiny, they informed our most intimate discussions."[155]
And Maurras recalled, too, that Taine and Renan together were, for his
generation, "the two men who, in common, initiated us to the life of the mind:
they were listened to, rejected, taken up again, abandoned, but always present
within us, always discussed."[156] According to Brunetière in 1897, "few writers
of our time have exercised a greater influence than Taine"; while Victor
Guiraud wrote in 1908 that Taine was "the most fully representative and the
most universally admired writer of his generation . . ."[157] Taine never gave
the same direct support to antisemitism as did Renan, but his contribution
to popularizing the concept of race as a tool in socio-historical explanation was
probably greater. His use of the concept was certainly more systematic, and
it formed a deliberate and essential part of his general methodology.

This is set out most fully in the Introduction to the *Histoire de la littérature
anglaise* of 1863. The civilization of a people, he postulated, was conditioned
by three factors: *"race, milieu* and *moment".*[158] By "milieu" he meant cli-
matic and geographical conditions, and the conditions given by political and
social systems, what might now be called "structure"; by "moment" he meant
the specifically historical and temporal situation, what might now be called
"conjuncture". The third factor,

> what is called *race*, refers to those innate and hereditary dispositions which
> man is born with, and which are usually joined to marked differences in

temperament and in physical make-up . . . There are naturally different varieties of men, as there are different varieties of cattle and of horses, some brave and intelligent, others timid and unintelligent, some capable of superior conceptions and creations, others limited to rudimentary ideas and inventions . . . just as one sees that some breeds or races of dogs have a greater aptitude for racing, others for fighting, others for hunting, others still for guarding houses or flocks. Race is a distinct force, so distinct that despite the enormous variations that the two other forces have imprinted on it, one can still recognize it. So much so, that a race like the ancient Aryan people, scattered across the world from the Ganges to the Hebrides, established in every climate, existing at all levels of civilization, and transformed by thirty centuries of revolutions, yet manifests in its languages, its religions, its literatures and its philosophies, a community of blood and spirit which links all its parts together . . . Man is forced to achieve a balance with his multiple environment, and in so doing contracts a certain temperament and certain suitable characteristics. This temperament, these characteristics become virtually permanent acquisitions, since the external conditions which brought them about are repeated again and again and are passed on by heredity to his progeniture . . . Race is the first and richest source of those leading faculties from which historical events derive . . .

Although most commentators have pointed out that Taine's use of the term race had limited biological connotations and that it was used in good faith as an instrument for serious socio-historical enquiry;[159] and while it can be argued, further, that his methodology is an important precursor of that of Durkheim and the modern French historical school,[160] what we are concerned with here is its effect on his contemporary readers. We have stressed that Taine had enormous prestige and influence as a thinker, and there seems little doubt that he must have done a great deal to give the concept of race intellectual status and respectability. The *Histoire de la littérature anglaise,* in particular, had run through twelve editions by 1905; and Taine's nephew, André Chevrillon, wrote in 1932 that "that famous formula . . . *race, milieu, moment . . .* had become nearly proverbial . . ."[161] Moreover, as François Leger has recently emphasized, Taine's concept of race was in effect profoundly ambiguous, and had "a resonance which we would call ethnic . . ."[162] It is not surprising therefore that Taine's influence on the antisemitic nationalists of the 1880s and 1890s seems to have been considerable, nor that they were anxious to proclaim the fact, as in the case of Renan. Drumont, we have seen, sought to emulate *Les Origines de la France contemporaine* with *La France juive,* and he referred often to Taine in his works, usually with admiration and approval.[163] Barrès was another admiring reader of Taine,[164] and *Les Déracinés* includes a celebrated homage to him, supposedly modelled on a real encounter between Taine and Maurras.[165] The latter's debt and sense of debt, we have already recorded, and other names could be added. For example, Simone de Beauvoir attributed her father's antisemitism in part to his reading of Taine.[166]

The case of Zola is rather different, in that he was a leading Dreyfusard, and the object of extreme hostility on the part of antisemites and Nationalists. Where Renan and Taine were famous, Zola was notorious. He was accused of being a foreigner, a traitor, a coward and a careerist, and attacks were made on his antecedents, his private life, his mental stability and his personal habits. François Mauriac remembered that when he was a child at the height of the Affair, his parents taught him to call his chamber-pot a *"zola"*.[167] Waleffe recounted a visit that he made to Zola's apartment in the rue de Bruxelles at the same time: "we heard beneath the windows a procession of Nationalist students, chanting rhythmically: 'Down with Zola! Down with Zola!' "[168] Claude Roy concluded that Zola was "probably the most insulted writer of the century";[169] and Guillemin has written that "it is extremely difficult for us today to comprehend the unheard-of and demented violence of the hatred that Zola provoked in 1898."[170] Politically motivated hostility towards the author of *"J'accuse"* was mixed with the horror inspired in the respectable classes by the allegedly "pornographic" nature of his novels. The diplomat Jusserand wrote that Zola was "detested for his filth by men of taste . . ."[171] Léon Bloy, a former admirer, protested in 1900: "The author of *La Terre* and so many other obscene works, become the avenger of wronged Innocence! the champion of Justice!! the spokesman for Truth!!! This is the final ignominy, the insult to France to crown all insults!"[172] This notoriety, of course, was good publicity, and, as Guillemin has commented, the hostility towards Zola on the part of other writers was motivated to a large extent by professional jealousy; he was a "writer greatly envied by his colleagues for his enormous sales".[173] Moreover, his commercial success came only late in his career after years of hostile reception from the critics.[174] But, when it came, that success was unprecedented,[175] and gave Zola a huge potential influence, albeit at a lower social level than that of the more "serious" Renan and Taine.

Zola was a vigorous opponent of antisemitism, but he shared and helped to propagate and legitimize current ideas about race, and, as we have seen, he gave expression to conventional anti-Jewish stereotypes. The Rougon-Macquart cycle of novels was built on the idea of an inescapable heredity, which determined the life and destiny of individuals. Influenced by Taine, and apparently by Lucas's *Traité philosophique et physiologique de l'hérédité naturelle* (1847–50),[176] Zola wrote in the Preface to the cycle, in 1871:[177]

> The Rougon-Macquarts, the group, the family which I propose to study, is characterized by uncontrolled appetites . . . Physiologically, they represent the slow succession of those irregularities in the temperament and in the blood of a race that follow an original organic lesion, and which determine, depending on the milieu, the sentiments, the desires, the passions, all the thoughts and actions of each individual of that race . . .

Although "race" here refers to a family, its connotations are more directly physiological and determinist than with Taine or Renan. Guillemin has argued that Zola's "theory" was not terribly important in the fiction itself, being more in the nature of a publicity exercise, a bowing to current intellectual fashion.[178] But this in itself is most significant. Zola's theory of heredity was an up-dated version of one commonly used by nineteenth-century novelists in France,[179] and, moreover, it does appear to have influenced Drumont. Despite his later contribution to the campaign against Zola,[180] Drumont had, at one time, like Bloy, been an admirer. He wrote a favourable review of *Au Bonheur des Dames* in *La Liberté* in 1883, for example;[181] and he referred with approval, in *La France juive,* to the thesis of the Rougon–Macquart cycle on the heredity of psychological characteristics.[182]

Drumont could also have cited numerous examples of antisemitic stereotypes and prejudice in Zola's novels. M. Kahn, for example, in *Son Excellence Eugène Rougon* (1876), represents the type of the time-serving politician, though the portrait is not entirely hostile.[183] In *L'Argent* (1891), Zola, to some extent, accepted the antisemitic explanation of the crash of the Union Générale, and he allowed a character to inveigh against the racially-determined character of the Jews. Saccard feels against Gundermann "the ancient rancour of race . . . He drew up an indictment against the [Jewish] race, that cursed race that has no country, no ruler, that lives like a parasite among the other nations . . ."[184] In *La Débâcle* (1892), evoking the pillage of bodies after the battle of Sedan, Zola referred to "a whole crowd of low, preying Jews, following in the wake of the invasion . . .", echoing almost word for word similar charges made by Drumont in *La France juive.*[185] As we have seen, *Paris* (1898), written at a much more critical time, and which includes a satire on Drumont and *La Libre Parole,* is not free of hostile antisemitic stereotyping and reference to Jewish "racial" characteristics. Lehrmann, for example, is presented as an "Alsatian Israelite with cunning eyes", while Baroness Duvillard's "Jewish origin was revealed by her somewhat long and strangely charming face, with blue and softly voluptuous eyes. As indolent as an Oriental slave, . . . she seemed intended for a harem life . . ."; and her son Gérard "had inherited . . . her long face full of Oriental languour . . ."[186]

Many other names could be added to the list of writers who helped in France to popularize the "scientific" concept of race: for example, Michelet,[187] Vacher de La Pouge,[188] Gustave Le Bon[189] and, of course, indirectly, Darwin. Renard stressed in 1899 that "the theories of Darwin, by showing how the different races or species devour one another, have contributed to broadcasting the idea (which is, of course, quite false) that the same struggle for life must take place among men as among the animal and the vegetable orders."[190] It should be noted, however, that several antisemites rejected Social Darwinism.[191] Nevertheless, in general terms, it seems indisputable that racial antisemitism developed in a favourable intellectual climate, that it grew out of a context in which the concept of race, in all its variety and convenient ambiguity, was common intellectual currency. It should be added that various writers, not often possessing the same prestige as those that we have mentioned above, did raise objections to the idea of race. We have seen that Renan in his later years expressed a certain scepticism about the value of the concept, though continuing to employ the term. Lazare argued against any idea of racial inequality, and observed that all the so-called races, including the Jewish, were extremely heterogeneous in origin and makeup: "what is improperly called a race is not an ethnic unit", he concluded, "but a historical, intellectual and moral unit."[192] Several of the contributors to Dagan's *En-*

quête of 1899 made the same point, if not always so clearly. Albert Réville said
that the modern Jews were not the direct descendants of the ancient Jews;
rather, "the Jews of today are, like the French themselves, the result of the
mixing of several races . . ." Duclaux asked: "Have war and migrations not
profoundly altered the character of each race?"; and Manouvrier explained
that the term "Semitism" was vague in the extreme, and that to try to explain
Jewish characteristics or behaviour "by reference to racial influence was not
in the least scientific".[193] However, even those who thus rejected racial explanations were inevitably involved in a debate, whose terms of reference were
largely defined by their opponents and by the general conception which they
wished to criticize.

III

What were the influence and the function of such racial ideas in French
antisemitism of the period? Were strict racial concepts widely adhered to?
What did they, and more general concepts, express? In an article in the *Revue
des Deux Mondes* in March 1898, Brunetière gave it as his opinion that the
influence of scholarly concepts of race had been considerable:

> One must have the courage to admit, that, if antisemitism, which was
> perhaps to start with only a paradox of journalism and idle conversation,
> seems to have become, in the last few years, a public menace, we are all more
> or less responsible [i.e. writers and intellectuals] . . . "Science" has most to
> answer for here, or rather a pseudo-science, whose affirmations are in general
> the more arrogant as the assumptions or hypotheses on which they are based
> are the more arbitrary . . . It is scholars . . . who have posited the classifica-
> tion of the different races of men into "inferior" and "superior" races; and
> who have assured us, that just as it is a waste of time "to try to whiten a
> negro", so it is also a waste of time to try to make an Aryan of a Semite;
> and it is indubitably they who have thus promoted among men, in the name
> of their science, what are truly animal hatreds, physiological, founded on
> blood.

Moreover, students of language, and notably Renan, had also propagated the
idea of "the irreducibility of different ethnic mentalities . . . and we have seen
the historian and the critic, in their turn, proposing to explain, by this same
inequality of the races, the evolution of literature and the development of
civilization." It was not surprising, therefore, Brunetière argued, that racial
ideas should have percolated down into "the popular imagination", to stir up
or to justify hostility towards the Jews.[194] Leroy-Beaulieu also considered that
the ideas of Renan and other intellectuals were in some part responsible for
the development of antisemitism in France.[195] However, other contemporary
observers disagreed with this idealist interpretation. "How can you expect the
masses to be influenced by scientific hyptheses?," asked Letourneau. "How
many people, even among those with some education, understand those questions?"; while Yves Guyot asserted that "the ethnic aspect of antisemitism is
insignificant in France".[196]

Here a distinction needs to be made between the leaders of antisemitism and the rank and file, and between strict Aryan-Semitic racial theories, which appealed only to a section of the former, and the general concept of race, which had a much wider currency among both leaders and led. We have seen that several antisemitic publicists accepted and propagated the idea of Aryan superiority and Semitic inferiority, each being indelible and unalterable. To give a few further examples, Drumont praised the Blanquistes in 1889, we have seen, because "alone among the revolutionaries, they have had the courage to lay claim to membership of the Aryan race and to affirm the superiority of that race."[197] Barrès wrote, during the Rennes trial, that it was wrong to expect Dreyfus to be like a Frenchman: "We expect this child of Sem to display the fine qualities of the Indo-European race. But he can in no way be stimulated by the emotions which are excited in us by our country, our ancestors, our flag, and by the word 'honour'."[198] Ernest Judet, in an article in *L'Eclair* in June 1906, quoted a letter from Soury, which expressed a more extreme and biological version of the same racialism:[199]

> Bring up a Jew from birth in an Aryan family; give him a religious education, Catholic or Protestant; confer on him all the sacraments and all the orders of the Church; make him . . . a bishop, a cardinal, the Pope; call him, according to national circumstance, French, or German, or Russian; neither the profession or the non-profession of a religion, nor legal nationality, nor language, will have modified one atom of the germinal cells of this Jew; the structure and the hereditary texture of his tissues and of his organs will be unchanged.

Less explicitly, and with reference to the French, Henri Rouzaud referred, in a letter to René de Marans in 1905 to "our physical race".[200]

But, although explicitly "scientific" racialism was rare, even among intellectuals, it gave fashionable expression to a central feature of their antisemitism, the conviction that Jews were physically peculiar. Usually conveyed in popular terminology, this idea was nevertheless profoundly racialist. Drumont, for example, though he used the terminology of anthropological race, as we have seen, was much more at home with more vulgar stereotypes, though out of some kind of inconsequential intellectual snobbery he warned his readers against them.[201] In *La France juive*, he presented a classic formulation of the antisemite's Jewish physical type:[202]

> The main signs by which one can recognize the Jew are these: the famous hooked nose, the blinking eyes, the clenched teeth, the projecting ears, the finger-nails square instead of being almond-shaped, the torso too long, the flat feet, the round knees, the extraordinarily prominent ankles, the soft and slimy hands of the hypocrite and the traitor. They also often have one arm shorter than the other.

He claimed that there was a single Jewish type: "No type has a more strongly etched physiognomy [than the Jewish]; none has more faithfully retained its primeval mark . . . While the Aryan race includes an infinite variety of types and temperaments, the Jew always resembles another Jew . . ."[203] Illogically, he went on to draw a crucial distinction between the Southern and the

Northern Jew, and even claimed that each of the twelve tribes of Israel had maintained its own physical peculiarity.[204] However, he overcame this inconsistency to some extent by claiming that "the real Jew was the Northern Jew", and that "one can understand the civilized Jew only if one has the *natural* or original [Northern] Jew in view."[205] The Northern Jew, he described in these terms: "The rheumy eyes never look straight at you, the skin is yellowish, the hair like fish-glue in colour. The beard is nearly always vaguely reddish, but sometimes black with a disagreeable green tinge . . . He is the typical merchant of cannon fodder, the back-street usurer, the shady tavern-keeper."[206] Taking the idea of hereditary physical characteristics a stage further, Drumont even claimed that "many Jews are born circumcised".[207]

Such evocations of the Jewish physical type were commonplace, and seem to be faithful reflections of popular stereotypes, as we have suggested. A few examples must suffice to illustrate this point, examples chosen from writers unconnected with the antisemitic movement, and, in one case, overtly hostile to it. In an article in *L'Echo de Paris* in 1898, Huysmans described the Jews of Hamburg in these terms:[208]

> They were hideous with their skulls covered with astrakhans, their glassy eyes bulging as if on stalks, their mouths like unbandaged wounds, their beards like dirty yellow vegetation, their cheeks puffed-out and crimson, like the raw backsides of monkeys. They stank like animals; all the horror of immiscible tribes was there . . . a detailed map of all the vices; they seemed to me to represent, in their features, in the lines on their faces, the folds and crevasses of innumerable bankruptcies, a whole chart of the geography of greed and money-making.

Less studied, almost casual, is Mme Steinheil's description of a German Jew, who, she claimed, was blackmailing her husband; he was "a small man of about fifty with a long Jewish nose, with scanty hair and moustache that were dyed black, small beady eyes, sly and shifty, and a sallow complexion. His dress-suit was shabby and even greasy. The shirtfront was not clean and was adorned with two large paste-diamond studs. The man's ill-shaped hands wanted washing and were certainly not the hands of a gentleman. His whole figure inspired me with repulsion, even fear."[209] The association of Jews with dirt, so clear in both these passages, is a crucial element to which we will return. More significant than either, perhaps, is the emphasis on Jewish physical characteristics in Lacretelle's *Silbermann*, which is a specific attack on antisemitism. Silbermann himself was described as "a very obvious Semitic type . . . His face . . . was very strongly featured, but quite ugly, with prominent cheek-bones and a pointed chin. Its colour was pale, tending to yellow; his eyes and eyebrows were black, his lips thick and fresh in colour"; while his father had "lifeless eyes, a yellowish skin, an unkempt beard, a large nose, and fleshy lips . . ."[210]

Such descriptions could, of course, reflect real observations, though their repetitions suggest, as Memmi has commented more generally, that people had a preconceived idea of what Jews looked like, which conditioned the way in which they saw individual and actual Jews. They were not concerned with the complex variety of the latter, but with the reinforcement of the physical stereotype.[211] This view is confirmed by other features of that stereotype. Not only were Jews distinctive in appearance, but their internal physiology was peculiar, and they were subject to special diseases and immunities. Balzac wrote that "in Rome attention has been drawn to the absence of malaria in the unhealthy Ghetto, which is overcrowded with Jews."[212] Toussenel referred to the Jews as a "leprous people".[213] Drumont asserted that there was a special (unspecified) "Jewish disease", and that, as a result of this, Jews were immune from the plague: "It seems that the Jew carries inside him a sort of permanent plague, which guarantees him against the ordinary plague; he is his own vaccine, and, in some way, a living antidote."[214] He also claimed, more generally, that, "absolutely different from the Christian in his evolution as race and as individual, the Jew is also quite different as far as health is concerned. He is subject to all the maladies caused by the corruption of the blood: scrofula, scurvy, scabies, dysentery, plica ... and hereditary leprosy ..."; and the Rothschilds, in particular, were said to be "all more or less poorly and ailing. Some of them have their spinal cords infected, some have synovial effusions ... while others become prematurely blind ..."[215] It is true that the prolonged practice of endogamy has given Jews a heightened susceptibility to certain pathological conditions, for example of the eyes,[216] but antisemites were here again exploiting ill-digested data to reinforce their biological stereotype. No data at all was available to support the additional claim, made by Drumont and by Gyp, that Jews were physically incapable of pronouncing French correctly,[217] nor the more common charge, made, we have seen by Huysmans, that Jews were peculiarly odorous. "The Jew has a bad smell", declared Drumont in *La France Juive*. "Even the smartest of them have this odour, *fetor judaica* ... which is a sign of their race, and helps them to recognize each other."[218]

Most significant of all, as many of our quotations have indicated, nineteenth-century French antisemites saw the physical characteristics of the Jews as signs of hereditary psychological and cultural traits. This, according to Poliakov, is the essential mark of racism, "to apprehend the soul via the body."[219] So Drumont, while emphasizing the Jewish physical stereotype, asserted also that "the Jew's brain is not made like ours",[220] and that there was a distinct "Jewish soul"[221] to match the Jewish physique. Not only were Jewish qualities, their money-making aptitude, their perfidy, their musical and theatrical talents, for example, instinctive and hereditary, but they were passed on from generation to generation via the quasi-physical vehicle of "neurosis ... the implacable malady of the Jews ..."[222] Again, he referred to "the transmission by heredity of the religious hatreds and anti-social instincts" of the Jews;[223] and wrote that ritual murder was endemic in Eastern Europe, as if it were a physical entity: "the hereditary ferments, the seeds of this horrific monomania are present there in a state of constant incubation ..."[224] Similarly, Daudet could write of La Jeunesse that "his strange ugliness was the image of his soul ..."[225] As Memmi has commented, "the ugliness, the infirmities and the diseases of the Jew in fact reveal a hideous soul. His crooked fingers betray his avidity and his wickedness, while their dirtiness adds a moral offence to his physical disfavour. Biology signifies a particular psychology, and the one explains the other and vice versa."[226] We may note here a paradoxical implication of this racialism, brought out earlier in Barrès's remarks about Dreyfus, and a crucial element in the explanation of one possible avenue of antisemitic action. Since Jews were psychologically predetermined by heredity, they were properly beyond morality. Drumont claimed that the Jews bore the burden of "a second original sin" in addition to the first borne by all men;[227] but, though, or rather because, they were doubly guilty, essentially evil, they were not responsible for what they did. "It is not their fault", he wrote, for example of their attacks on the Church: "they are like that."[228] And if Jews were beyond morality, might not antisemites be so also, in their dealings with them?

Racialism could thus be expressed without recourse to the term "race", though, of course, the phrase, "the Jewish race" was very widely used, not only by overt antisemites like Proudhon, Drumont, Mgr Meurin or abbé Lémann.[229] Mme d'Agoult referred in the 1870s to the Princess of Sayn-Wittgenstein as "a woman of the Jewish race";[230] and the term was also used by Gide and by Paléologue among others.[231] Clemenceau again wrote in 1898: "The Jews are, without a doubt, a distinct race . . ."[232] As we have seen, the concept was used by Jews themselves, and also by their defenders. Camille Pelletan, for example demanded: "What is held against the Jews? that, after a century, they have not acquired all the qualities which their adversaries, themselves, claim to possess? . . . I am prepared to admit", he went on, "that the Jews have retained certain defects peculiar to their race . . .", but this, he explained, was the result of resistance to their full assimilation, on the part of French people.[233] One has the impression that, even at this very general level, the concept of race was more commonly expressed by intellectuals than by others; it occurs, for example, more often in intellectual antisemitic study groups than in general public meetings, though it does have some currency in the latter. This can be seen from the police reports of meetings in Paris in the first half of 1898. A Catholic speaker at a public meeting organized by Le Libertaire in February declared that Dreyfus belonged to "a race which oppresses the worker". In the same month, Jarre addressed a Jeunesse Antisémite group on the subject of "the Races"; while a speaker at a Union Nationale meeting referred more casually to "the Jewish race". In April, the Cercle Antisémitique d'Etudes Sociales held a discussion on "the Jewish race which forms a nation within the nation". In May, at a Ligue Antisémitique meeting in the 11th arrondissement, a speaker called for Jews to be deprived of their French nationality, on the grounds that they were really aliens: "the Jewish race is a constant danger to French security"; while a speaker at another Ligue Antisémitique meeting in June, in the 2nd arrondissement, "warned that to drive out this race, which has insinuated itself everywhere, will require long and patient efforts."[234]

Race, in effect, in its strict or its general sense, was an ideal instrument for expressing Jewish otherness. It enabled antisemites to establish a clear and absolute distinction between Jews and non-Jews, and to suggest, if not to demonstrate in their own view, that Jews were not only irremediably different, but also irremediably inferior, and, at the same time, eternally dangerous. As Lazare wrote: "For the antisemite, the Jew is an individual of a foreign race, incapable of adapting himself, hostile to Christian civilization and the Christian faith, immoral, anti-social, with an intellect different from the Aryan intellect, and, in addition, predatory and harmful."[235] Drumont referred, in *La France juive*, to "the Jew, that singular creature, so completely different from all others . . . other foreigners share with us certain ideas and principles that are common to all civilized peoples; but the Jews are not among these peoples: they are beyond the pale, utterly alien . . ."[236] A speaker at a Union Nationale meeting at Roanne in March 1899 "tried to demonstrate that the Jewish people could not be assimilated with any other".[237] Maupassant made the same point, in a different way, in *Mont-Oriol* (1887) by presenting William Andermatt and his non-Jewish wife as a couple who could neither understand nor communicate with each other, nor indeed produce children together: "They were doubtless too different, too far away from each other, of races that were too dissimilar."[238] Barrès, similarly, justified the possible miscarriage of justice against Dreyfus, on the grounds that "there can be justice only within the confines of the same species".[239] Absolute Jewish otherness was most graphically expressed perhaps by Léon Daudet in *Le Voyage de Shakespeare* (1896). Fischart there tells the English poet:[240]

> The Jew is a being apart. Love, hatred, joy and sorrow are, with him, warped, disordered, unrecognizable . . . The Jew has no pride, no delicate feelings, no sense of honour, no pity, no anger. He sets the Christians fighting among themselves, and insinuates himself amongst them. He regards them as so much pig's meat, and every contract with a Jew turns out to be as firm as the bone in a sausage. The Jew is cowardly because he has no idea what courage is. He is a traitor because he enjoys being in bad odour. He is cruel because he follows blindly the logic which pushes him to exalt his own nation at any price . . . The Jews are the vermin of the human race . . . All Jews have some sickness. Look at the hunchbacks, the pot-bellies, around us, the lame, the one-eyed, the ones with running sores. They are marked with special and disgusting blemishes . . . There is as great a distance between you and them as there is between a cow and an albatross, or a fox and an ant. What deceives you, is that in order to dupe you more easily, they assume an outward form that is identical to yours.

This racial antisemitism backed up and clinched the arguments of nationalist antisemitism. "Can a Jew be French?", asked Jarzel's *Petit Catéchisme nationaliste;* and replied, as we have seen: "He cannot unless he were to prefer the French nation to the Jewish race"; asking again: "Why cannot the Jew become French? Because of his mentality. The Jew does not think like a Frenchman; he does not have the same tastes, or the same customs and morals."[241] Drumont declared that "the Jew cannot be acclimatized in France. The most diverse races, Celts, Gauls, Gallo-Romans, Germans,

Franks, Normans, have been blended into that harmonious ensemble which is the French nation . . . The Jew alone has been unable to enter the amalgam . . . [as a result] of his special innassimilability . . ."[242] Similarly, a speaker at a Patrie Française meeting in Saint-Dié in November 1900 asserted that the Jews "are not part of what one might call the real heart of the nation. In a word, they are a race apart."[243] The programme of La Jeunesse de l'Union Nationale, in September 1895, defined its aim as "the struggle against the Jew, the foreigner of the interior, completely refractory to all assimilation, irreducibly opposed to our traditions, our customs, our mentality and our interests."[244] *Le Patriote de Neufchâteau* wrote of the Jews in February 1898: "They are a race, a dangerous race . . . they must always be treated with suspicion."[245] Abbé Gayraud, deputy for Finistère, concluded:[246]

> In my view, antisemitism consists today, for most people, in regarding the Jews . . . above all as a race, which forms in the midst of us, in our own country, a distinct nation, parasitical and evil-doing. From this it follows that the Jew must not be treated as the equal of the true sons of France, but rather as a foreigner, a man without a country, a real cosmopolitan, whose power to do harm must be prevented and whose hostility must be contained by close surveillance. This is the basis, the essence, of contemporary antisemitism.

This racial nationalism directed against the Jews was reinforced by the racial basis being given to nationalism positively. We have seen that there was a tendency on the part of some nationalists to refer to "the French race". Barrès explicitly based his nationalism on the cult of "the earth and the dead", and he, and others, explained national sentiment by evoking the concept of "blood".[247] Writing of his experience of the Franco-Prussian War, Maurice Donnay declared: "I am French, I love France . . . I love her; this is a feeling which cannot be explained; I have it in my blood."[248] Léon Daudet gave the same profession of national racialism a regional colouring, at the same time inverting the hostile stereotype of the Southerner: in 1897, he wrote, "I was already a Nationalist and a Clerical, thanks to my good old Nîmois blood, my blood of the Rey district, which was stronger than the precious education which I received, and the general political and literary ambience in which I lived."[249] And he refuted Reinach's charge that Drumont was a tool of the Jesuits by the same argument: "French blood, warm and clear, flowed in Drumont's veins, with noble vehemence, bearing the hereditary virtues of his peasant and bourgeois forebears, and these virtues harmonized with his sincere religious faith. But a Jew, spawned in the ghettoes of Frankfurt, . . . could understand nothing of that."[250]

Why did antisemites have recourse to this absolute mode of categorization? What were they thereby expressing? Perhaps most obviously, racial antisemitism expressed a sense of mystery and fear in the face of an alien culture. Though the term antisemitism was a novelty at the end of the century, as we have explained, hostility towards the Jews, of a racialist type, was not; rather it was, in some way, a traditional response.[251] And, in some cases, antisemitism was inspired, in our period, by the direct, but partial experience of the strangeness of Jewish culture. Mauriac, who came from a Catholic and antisemitic family, related that as a child in Bordeaux, the Jew was for him "a mysterious creature"; and he remembered that his grandmother let an apartment in her house to a Mme Léon:[252]

> I recall that on passing by her door, I imagined a world different from ours. I was told: "One of your uncles sets foot in there sometimes . . ." I heard tell, that when Mme Léon died, an odour of burnt aromatic herbs had invaded the storeys occupied by my grandmother, and this convinced me that her apartment must have been the scene for some unimaginable witches' sabbath.

The narrator of Lacretelle's *Silbermann* regarded his Jewish friend as having "a mysterious genie living inside him", as "the magician of some Oriental tale, who possessed the key to all the wonders of the world"; and, as we have seen, he recounted that, when his mother took him to see the Jew's House at Nîmes, he sensed in her the same sense of mystery and the same movement of suspicion that were aroused by the place, outside the town, where the gypsies camped.[253] The narrator of J.-R. Bloch's *Lévy* had the same sense of Jewish strangeness, relating that, when going to call on a Jew, he felt as though he were entering a brothel.[254] Many, perhaps most, "professional" antisemites lacked this direct experience of Jewish culture, but the appropriate response was widely diffused in French culture, and could be almost gratuitously distilled by them for other, more general, purposes.

For the sense of otherness had the profoundest psychological roots, stemming from the very process by which the individual personality is formed.[255] Potentially, for every member of one culture, "the Other is a scandal which threatens his essence", as Roland Barthes has put it,[256] and in Western culture, this scandal had traditionally been projected on to the Jew. The negative stereotype of the Jew, as we have argued, was an important way in which non-Jewish values were defined and sustained. Moreover, as Louis Dumont and others have argued, in a society with declared egalitarian values, like nineteenth-century France, there were special reasons for the expression of otherness and cultural difference in racial terms. George Sand proclaimed confidently in *La Filleule* (1853):[257]

> France is the country where, on this score, things are most equitable and where people are most free from barbarous prejudice, where Jews, negroes and gypsies are seen to be different from us in fact, but where they are equal under the law, where finally we have the justice and the intelligence to understand that the abasement and the corruption of the races that have been for so long oppressed are the fatal work of persecution, of shame and of misery.

But, as she herself betrays, cultural difference was not so easily conceived without recourse to the idea of race. Kenneth Little has pointed out that, in modern times, it is the "peoples . . . who have a traditional attachment to Christianity, democracy and egalitarianism, [who] are also those who have made the sharpest distinction between races." Racialism, he suggested, provided them "with an explanation of what is incongruous", and particularly helped ideologically to bridge the gap between democratic theory and colonial or post-colonial practice.[258] Dumont's perception of the same link between egalitarianism and "racism" is more directly relevant to the elucidation of racial antisemitism. The latter, he argues is "a serious and unexpected consequence" of the former.

> In a universe in which men are conceived no longer as hierarchically ranked in various social and cultural species, but as essentially equal and identical, the difference of nature and status between communities is sometimes reasserted in a disastrous way: it is then conceived as proceeding from somatic characteristics—which is racism . . . racism fulfils an old function under a new form. It is as if it were representing in an egalitarian society a resurgence of what was differently and more directly and naturally expressed in a hierarchical society.

Racism thus derived from the inability of Europeans to conceive of or accept cultural difference within the framework of their egalitarian ideology.[259] Dumont's interpretation is the more illuminating in that, as we have seen, Drumont and others combined a profound dislike of democratic politics with a thoroughgoing "democratic" populism, and that they sought via racial antisemitism to reconstruct a hierarchical society, though here one must point out that Dumont uses the term "hierarchy" in rather a special way. More simply perhaps one can relate the use of racial concepts to the fact of assimilation. As Jews became objectively assimilated, losing the traditional marks of their difference, the idea that they were different could only be maintained on essentialist racialist grounds. Thus paradoxically racial antisemitism was a response to the real decline of Jewish particularism and an attempt to preserve it on the ideological plane. From another angle, Max Weber emphasized another function of racialism in an egalitarian society, when he wrote that "the idea of a chosen people derives its popularity from the fact that it can be claimed to an equal degree by any and every member of the mutually despising groups . . .", an insight developed by Sartre.[260]

Certain features of racial antisemitism as a means of classification and as an ideology of exclusion deserve further illustration and analysis. First, as we saw in discussing the Henry Subscription in chapter IV,[261] and as several of the passages quoted earlier in this chapter have reminded us, the idea that Jews were other, a different "species", was often put across by directly denying their humanity, by depicting or describing them as animals. Veuillot complained in 1870: "I am the subject of the heretic, the Jew and the atheist, and of an amalgam of all these species, which resembles an animal more than anything else."[262] "Man, Jew, monkey . . . That puts the Semite in his proper place in the zoological order of things", declared Fore-Fauré.[263] Drumont reported, in La France juive, that in Algeria Arab women did not bother to cover themselves in the presence of a Jew: "For them, the Jew is not a man"; and he referred to the composer Hérold as a Jew, who had, unusually, been "humanized" by the Parisian environment.[264] Jews were identified by antisemites with an enormous variety of animals, birds, insects and other creatures: vultures, crows, apes, monkeys, hyenas, jackals, foxes, wolves, dogs, goats, pigs, rats, snakes, crocodiles, reptiles, toads, sharks, worms, locusts, fleas, spiders, slugs, wasps—to name but a few.[265] It will be seen at once that many of these are beasts or birds that have traditionally symbolized inestimable human qualities: rapaciousness, avidity, slyness, cowardice and so on. The preying and parasitic nature of the Jew could also be graphically conveyed in such terms. Drumont, for example, quoted Alphonse Daudet's evocation of the Jew as "the spider with long entangling arms, always alert, and ready to seize its prey"; and according to an eighteenth-century document, also quoted by Drumont, "one can compare the Jews to wasps who invade the hives to kill the bees, to open up their bellies and extract the honey from their entrails."[266] In *La Dernière Bataille*, Alphonse de Rothschild is described as "belonging to the rodent order; he looks like a rat, a colossal Leviathan of a rat"; while the Jews generally were compared to parasitical worms: "Planted in the most nutritious parts of the gut, there where the red blood flows, and the yellow fat, and the carefully distilled rich juices, these creatures, armed with monstrous hooks, . . . gorge themselves . . ."[267]

Three other features, or functions, of this antisemitic bestiary should be emphasized. First, as Fore-Fauré makes clear, Jews, on one level, posed a real classificatory problem. They were felt to be human, but not human, and to identify them as apes or monkeys was a way of expressing this. Thus abbé Desportes in his novel, *Le Juif—Franc-maçon* (1890), described the Jew Deutsch as being "as ugly as the picture of a monkey . . ."[268] The painter Degas recounted, also in 1890, what must have been a popular joke about the Rothschilds: two monkeys were lost in the Château de Ferrières, and, when the whole household was assembled, two extra heads were counted, but no one was sure which two heads did not belong to the Rothschild family.[269] A series of coloured posters, dating from 1898 or 1899, entitled "Le Musée d'Horreurs", showed leading Dreyfusards and prominent Jews as animals, Reinach as an ape.[270] Léon Daudet wrote of Joseph and Théodore Reinach: "When they entered a drawingroom, one after the other, the effect was prodigious. It was Orang leading Outang."[271] The same confusion of categories was expressed by describing Jews as mythical animals, hydras, or vampires, for example.[272] Second, Jews were associated with dirty creatures, with rodents and other vermin, and with pigs. A placard in Carpentras in January 1898, referred typically to "the Jewish vermin".[273] According to Toussenel, "the pig is the emblem of the Jew, who is not ashamed of wallowing in baseness."[274] Drumont described a member of the Rothschild family as having "a grotesque face, the face of a pig who had drunk champagne through its snub nose."[275] A song by André Sioul, called "Les Dreyfusards sont des cochons", recounted how, after Reinach had looked at a pregnant woman, "she gave birth to a little Jewish pig . . ."[276] This categorization of Jews as animals, harmful, domestic or vermin, thirdly, while being a convenient way of symbolizing their otherness and their threat, a device, moreover, that was applied to other out-groups and deviants,[277] also reflected or suggested how Jews should be treated. Conceptualization here was a justification for, or a spur to, behaviour and action. A poster put up in Rennes during Dreyfus's second trial, for example, entitled "Le Placard Antijuif", showed Frenchmen with canes driving a crowd of Jews in front of them like a flock of animals.[278] As Memmi commented: "Stripped of all human qualities, the Jew . . . becomes in effect a species of animal. One can understand then how periodically, at times of antisemitic paroxysm, crushing the Jew can appear as a duty. It is a kind of hunt against a dangerous animal . . ."[279] This echoes (unconsciously?) a passage from La France juive in which Drumont declared the Jew to be "the dangerous animal par excellence, and at the same time the one which it is most difficult to catch".[280]

The characterization of Jews as dirty animals brings us to a second important feature of antisemitism, that is closely linked to the concept of race, for this characterization is only one example of an emphasis in antisemitic propaganda on the polluting quality of the Jew. The term "dirty Jew" was a commonplace phrase in late nineteenth-century France, the adjective going with the noun without deliberate thought. In Maupassant's Bel-Ami, for example, Walter is referred to as "this dirty Jew".[281] Paléologue records that Nisard, head of the political section of the Foreign Ministry, called Dreyfus "a dirty Jew".[282] Lacretelle's Silbermann attempted fruitlessly to counter the cliché in a rational manner, asking his non-Jewish friend: "The Jews are dirty, are they? Where do you think that one can find more bathrooms, in those houses [the houses of the Parisian Jewish élite], or in the aristocratic hotels of the Faubourg Saint-Germain?"[283] The antisemites employed a whole repertoire of variations on this conventional theme, associating the Jews with vomit and excrement, with bad odours, with disease and germs, and with corruption generally.[284]

Drumont referred to Jewish "vomitings against the Church" and to "the Jews vomited on us from the ghettoes of Germany . . .";[285] and wrote in La France juive: "Now that they are the masters, they vomit on us all the excrement swallowed by Ezekiel . . ."[286] Again, he asserted that the Jews had "a real mania for the stercoraceous . . ."[287] It was thus natural that Léo Taxil's anticlerical propaganda should have been published by Jews: "It represents a real descent into the Jewish hell, into that hell of excrement described by Swedenborg, into that 'Jerusalem of filth, stinking of rats, in which Jews, covered in muck, scramble for pieces of gold' ".[288] In the same vein, Drumont recounted that "according to the Talmud, it is a presage of good luck to dream of faecal matter."[289] He gave one Jewish businessman the nickname "Dreyfus the Guano", and wrote of the Jewish politician, Camille Dreyfus: "Everyone knows on what dunghill this poisonous flower of the ghetto originally sprouted . . ."[290] The Duc d'Orléans, he noted, used the term "I am going to write to the Jews" to announce his visits to the lavatory.[291] Though particularly attracted by this genre, Drumont was not alone in using it. Picard, for example, described Rothschild as a "main sewer";[292] while Daudet indicated how objections to the allegedly scatological nature of Zola's writings were related to the association of the Jews with excrement. It was no coincidence, he wrote that Zola's collaborator Busnach was a Jew: "Busnach had a taste for what was filthy . . . He went to Zola, like a dung-beetle going after his food."[293] In the same context, as we have seen, Jews were supposed to have a special and unpleasant odour. A mark of uncleanness and a sign of racial inferiority, this was also an indicator of evil.[294]

We have referred also to the charge that Jews suffered from peculiar and hereditary diseases. Two features of this idea are relevant here. First, Jewish diseases were particularly unclean diseases, diseases of the gut, and diseases of corruption. Drumont wrote, for example, that Jews suffered "from horrible maladies, diseases known only to Jewish doctors: special neuroses, peculiar cancers of the stomach, decomposition of the blood, visceral disorders, rotting of the spinal cord . . ."[295] Germane also in this context is the traditional association of the Jews with leprosy. Miss Costello reported in 1843: "In some places in Brittany, the trade of cooper was looked upon with contempt, and the opprobrious names of *caqueux* was given to them because they were thought to belong to a *race of Jews* dispersed after the ruin of Jerusalem, and who were considered *leprous from father to son.*"[296] It is interesting that the name given to this vestigial "race" of lepers, of which other examples are found in France, should again be associated with excrement. This old association was picked up by the antisemites at the end of the century. Drumont, for example, referred to Marat as a leprous Jew.[297] Second, Jews were believed to be the carriers of disease, and particularly of epidemics, to non-Jews. Sue's Wandering Jew was the involuntary bearer of cholera;[298] Drumont claimed that the Jews were the bearers of cholera and plague.[299] Léo Taxil provided an up-dated version of the same idea with his fantasy of Masonic agents preparing for germ warfare on a world-wide scale in their laboratories under the Rock of Gibraltar, "cultivating a supply of microbes so as to be able, at will, to inflict one plague or another on any country they chose . . ."[300] Less literally, Drumont characterized the Jewish press as "a pestilential vapour emanating from the boulevard . . ."[301]

Such ideas were related to the old charge that Jews were poisoners, and particularly that they poisoned wells, a belief that was still alive in nineteenth-century France.[302] During the cholera epidemic of 1832 in Paris, according to Sue, the inception and spread of the disease were popularly attributed to well-poisoning.[303] Drumont repeated the general charge of well-poisoning in *La France juive,*[304] and extended it by claiming that the Jews and their allies were poisoning the non-Jewish population of France by stimulating alcohol consumption and by adulterating food.[305] Drumont, indeed, seems to have believed, on at least one occasion, that he was personally the victim of Jewish poisoning, for Goncourt recorded in his *Journal* in April 1890: "At dinner, Léon Daudet, who had just left Drumont, told us that he thought he had been poisoned by the Jews. He drank a glass of water three days ago at an electoral meeting, and has been vomiting ever since, and the Marquis de Morès is in the same condition."[306] Nor were such fears pure idiosyncrasy. When President Faure died in mysterious circumstances in 1899, Marcel Habert of the

Ligue des Patriotes apparently recommended to members of the league that they spread the rumour that the President had been poisoned by the Jews, and this suggestion was made in several newspapers.[307]

Related again to these charges that Jews were poisoners and the bearers of disease was the characterization of the Jews themselves as a "poison",[308] or as germs. We have encountered the latter image in the Henry Subscription, and it was not uncommon in France in the late nineteenth century and after.[309] Drumont deliberately compared[310] the Jews with

> those swarming multitudes, the microbes, the generators of putrefaction, which invade societies that are decomposing . . . infinite in number and moving infinitely fast, they colonize such societies, reproduce themselves there, instal themselves in force, and hasten their hosts' destruction; they create a seething mass where unity dies, they upset synthesis by analysis, and transform what is solid into liquid, what is liquid into gas . . .

This metaphor was used of other menaces; various characters, for example, in Zola's *Au Bonheur des Dames* refer to the big department store as a "cholera";[311] and antisemitism, itself, was described by one contemporary as "a cholera, a new epidemic",[312] an emotive and misleading mode of explication employed by some modern students of the subject.[313] But the image of germs was particularly apposite in antisemitic ideology, as we pointed out in an earlier chapter, for it conveyed in one vivid metaphor the idea that the Jews were an all-powerful, dangerous and omnipresent minority.

The uncleanness of the Jews generally, moreover, was not simply a sign of their inferiority; it represented a threat to non-Jews; as a mode of characterization, it expressed that threat. Antisemitic writing betrays again and again a fear of being polluted by the Jew. "Once the Jews have touched something", wrote Drumont, ". . . and they have an urge to touch everything, the question of money defiles the purest intentions."[314] Picard asked rhetorically: "Does not the Jew threaten the Aryan soul in its psychological independence and in its purity?"; and asserted: "Every affair that a Jew has anything to do with becomes infected . . ."[315] Drumont again measured the progress of urban squalor in Paris by the progress of Jewish influence. Referring to the "axiom" formulated by Maxime du Camp that "the closer men are to Judaism, the dirtier they are", he wrote: "The way in which the streets of Paris have become foul and evil-smelling since it has become a Jewish city provides a striking proof of this."[316] A political twist was given to the same theme in the familiar attribution of French national decadence to Jewish contamination or corruption. Dubuc, president of La Jeunesse Antisémite et Nationaliste reproached the Jews with "wishing to defile the national flag".[317] Barrès referred to the Jews as "the corrupters of our national spirit"; and to "the miasmas of Rennes that poison the blood . . ."[318] Drumont expressed much the same idea in 1894, writing of "the mud of Panama, real mud, black, sticky and clinging, which no brush can make disappear, whose ignominious traces the absence of legal proceedings cannot efface . . ."[319] This was only one example of the way in which unclean Jews made France, and particularly its Republican régime unclean. France, wrote Drumont in *La Dernière Bataille* was like "a sick man . . . wallowing in his excrement"; its régime was "this Republican rottenness . . . this heap of dung".[320]

> As for the grandeur of France, the Christian knows what has become of it. He has only to look out of his window to see the river of mud that flows without ceasing, bearing with it the course of contemporary history, as a sewer bears lumps of muck and dead dogs, carrying in its noisome depths, the peculations and special deals of ministers, the bribes of deputies, the sales of decorations, ignominies and robberies, scandals and treasons.[321]

This theme of Jewish political corruption was lent a special sexual, as well as religious, connotation in the claim that the secular education policy of the Republic represented a Jewish "desire to befoul the souls of children . . ."[322]

If the Jews were agents of pollution and corruption, then antisemitism was a cleansing operation. Drumont was working, he claimed in *La France juive*, "to purify us from these Jewish miasmas . . .";[323] and he quoted approvingly, in *Le Testament d'un antisémite*, words spoken by M. de Lamarzelle in the Chamber of Deputies: "I have not come to this rostrum to play politics, but to carry out a sanitary exercise . . ."[324] In August 1898 a member of the departmental council of the Côte d'Or, of which Reinach was a member "called on his colleagues to associate themselves with the great 'public health' movement that is taking place at this moment, and to demand the resignation of Joseph Reinach, who is unworthy to sit among us."[325] With a greater appearance of rationality, the antisemitic municipal council of Constantine voted in 1896 to exclude Jewish children from public primary schools on the grounds that they "brought to school all kinds of contagious diseases."[326] The same statement about the purifying function of antisemitism was made symbolically by *La Libre Parole* when it offered, as the prize for the best essay on the means to destroy Jewish power in France, a medal "in virgin gold, that is to say, untouched by Jewish hands".[327]

A final passage, evoking Jewish uncleanness, from Daudet's *Le Voyage de Shakespeare*, brings together many of the aspects of this conceptualization which we have discussed, particularly the links between uncleanness and race, and uncleanness and money. It also gives an important clue to the wider social meaning of the antisemites' obsession with pollution. Daudet describes the Jewish *quartier* of sixteenth-century Amsterdam as "littered with foul refuse, running with thick brown ooze, swarming with squabbling and shouting verminous brats. Filth sweated from the walls . . . The air was fetid." That this was not simply an evocation of the squalor of an early modern city, is indicated by the words which Daudet puts into the mouth of Fischart:[328]

> What a race! growled Fischart, holding his nose. The descendants of the goat give off the odour of their ancestor, and even their excrement is twisted. I sincerely believe that God created the Jew on a day of drunkenness and shame. He modelled him out of shit and vomit, with urine and spit for cement . . . This explains the Jew's ineffaceable character, the putrefaction of his soul and of his skin; his scurvy fingers are made to grind

gold . . . The Jew needs his idol, and fashions his symbol, his holy of holies, the mystery of money, like a termite. He is like a little insect, the worm that lives in a book of magic. He is the dismal remains of sorcery, of witchcraft.

This passage, equating gold and excrement, brings out very clearly the anal connotations of money in antisemitic ideology.[329] But of more significance here is the identification of the Jew with the "little insect" and with the witch, for, as Mary Douglas has argued, like the witch, the Jew was an object of suspicion and horror, he aroused fear and hostility, because he was a marginal and interstitial figure.[330] Neither fully French, nor yet, despite assertions to the contrary, completely foreign, astride two cultures, traditionally a middle-man, engaged in the impersonal traffic of money, that anonymous, floating, liquid, mysterious force, the Jew occupied an ambiguous social position; he was indefinable, difficult to pin down, to catch. Thus Drumont referred to Jews as "interlopers",[331] and stressed again and again their Protean nature. They were "this strange people which has changed its orientation so often, which had its warlike and patriotic phase in its defensive struggle against the Romans, its conspiratorial phase in the thirteenth and fourteenth centuries with the Templars, its dark and bloody phase after the failure of these attempts, its phase of quiescence in the sixteenth and seventeenth centuries, its Masonic phase in the eighteenth century, its Socialist, financial and cosmopolitan phase in the nineteenth century."[332] But even this evocation of their historical metamorphoses did not bring out the essential indefinability of the Jews and their works. "The latent action of the Jew is very difficult to analyse; there is a whole subterranean side of it, which it is almost impossible to seize hold of . . . the dangerous Jew is the vague Jew, the socialist . . . the agent provocateur, the spy . . . the elusive animal: he has poked his nose into so many things, that one does not know how to get hold of him."[333] Again Drumont quoted Blowitz as the incarnate modern Jew. Asked what country he belonged to, he replied: "I have no idea; I was born in Bohemia and I live in France, where I write in English . . ." Drumont added that "as a cosmopolitan, Wolff is even more complete: he has no country, he has no religion, he even has no sex. This *neuter* is a unique product, who fits into no existing category."[334] The same point was made by a character in Bourget's novel *Cosmopolis*, with reference to the Jewish Baron Justus Hafner and his daughter:[335]

They are the incarnation of the modern world . . . They have no country to start with . . . What is he, this Baron Justus Hafner, German, Austrian, Italian? Does anyone know? . . . They have no religion. Their name, their looks proclaim them to be Jews, yet they are Protestants, for the time being . . . until they become schismatics, Moslems or whatever . . . They have no family. Where was he brought up, this gentleman? What did his father do, or his mother, or his brothers and sisters? Where are his roots, his traditions? Where is his past, all that constitutes a man as a moral person? . . . You may look, but everything about them is shrouded in darkness . . .

Evoking Daudet's "little insect" ready to emerge from the cracks, and also the additional problems of definition presented by naturalization, Barrès insisted in his Nancy Programme, as we have seen, that: "We must above all put obstacles in the way of easy naturalization, for it is through this fissure that we have received the worst Jews . . ."[336]

Also referring to Jewish immigration, a passage from *La France juive* shows how indefinability became synonymous with uncleanness:[337]

> The Jew . . . does not constitute a fixed disease, a bog whose extent and whose foulness are more or less fixed. He is a kind of perpetual discharge, a flow that it is impossible to stop. The great reservoir of Semitism, Galicia and the neighbouring Russian provinces, pour forth incessantly their stinking hordes . . . who let fall vermin wherever they pass and create a constant danger to public health.

The identification of the Jew with dirt, filth and vermin, in effect, was an important way of overcoming the threat that Jewish indefinability and ambiguity posed. Paradoxically, because Jews were indefinable, they needed to be over-defined, and this negative over-definition allowed the antisemite to define himself and his own values. The antisemite wished society to be clear and ordered, and making an absolute distinction between what was clean and pure and what was dirty and polluting was a means of establishing that order. By defining the Jew as a polluting agent, the purity and health of the non-Jewish group, the French nation, could be proclaimed.[338] Or rather, if things were wrong with the French nation, if it was unhealthy, this was because it had been polluted by the Jews, whom, as we have seen, antisemites identified with disease, corruption and death as well as with dirt. France could thus be restored to health, things could be put "right", by controlling or by expelling the offending "vermin". In the words of a character in Vogüé's *Les Morts qui parlent:* "If these foreign elements become superabundant . . . our people instinctively eliminates them . . ."[339] But, as we have argued earlier, antisemitism as a purification, a cleansing exercise, was an ordering of society of a ritual rather than a practical kind. Antisemites were less concerned to eliminate an objective enemy, the Jew, than to use their ideology of exclusion to put forward a view of what society ought to be like, and would be like if only the Jew were excluded from it. As Sartre has put it: "The task of the antisemite is essentially negative: there can be no question of really constructing a new society, but only of purifying that which exists . . . As the Champion of Good, the antisemite is sacred; but the Jew also, in his fashion is sacred, too; sacred like the Untouchables, like those on whom there is a taboo."[340]

The theme of pollution here converges with that of race, for as Blum commented, "racial distinctions lead logically to a classification, to the establishment of a hierarchy".[341] The concept of race, like that of pollution, provided a way of ordering social reality in an absolute way. Race, in particular, was a means of postulating that society ought to be organized as a static hierarchy. This can be seen in the writings of Drumont. As we have seen, the ideal, model society for him was that of "old France", one of legal orders, governed by an aristocracy of birth, a racially selected and defined élite.[342] Although Drumont characterized the old "upper classes" as "finished races",[343] this judgment, and his lengthy attacks on the contemporary French aristocracy, were motivated by his view that its members had abandoned their traditional paternalist role in society, and he continued to pay tribute to the hereditary aristocratic virtues. In 1889, he wrote that, in contrast to the Bourgeoisie, the aristocracy still maintained a special delicacy of feeling and behaviour, a certain generosity, a sense of honour, "a savoir-faire in the face of certain awkward situations, which the Bourgeoisie would not have. Ancestral influences dating back ten centuries are there."[344] Again in 1894, he contrasted the fact that Louis-Philippe had, on the petition of Victor Hugo, granted a reprieve in 1839 to Barbès, with the refusal of President Carnot to do the same for Vaillant in 1894, despite similar representations, and commented: "You see, to be a real democrat and receive a poet in the middle of the night, you need to have six hundred years of nobility in your veins."[345] But, for Drumont, such hereditary qualities were not simply incidental, nor was the hereditary determination of an individual's place in society confined, or to be confined, to the nobility. He put forward the view that children should continue to exercise the same social functions, and even adhere to the same ideas and values as their parents and grandparents, objecting to the fact that "the descendants . . . of the bloody Bourgeoisie of 1793 . . . today well off and comfortably installed in the place of the Aristocracy whom their grandparents dispossessed, now put on the airs of good honest people and declaim against the Anarchists who are simply doing what the old Terrorists did."[346]

This use of racialism to support social immobility and to justify a kind of "caste" system,[347] was part and parcel of an "internal racialism"[348] that had much wider currency, as we have seen, and which was used not only to differentiate regional types, but also social classes. We have mentioned the idea that the nobility had a distinct racial origin, but an implicitly racial categorization of the lower classes, urban and rural was also present in nineteenth-century France. Maurice Choury, for example, points out that at the time of the Paris Commune, classes were actually distinguished by skin colour.[349] As well as acting as an obstacle to social mobility, the concept of race was also used by antisemites to support the idea that populations should remain geographically immobile. For example, Biétry contrasted "the rooted races" with "the wandering races, the races without a homeland, the Jews in a word";[350] and, of course, Barrès was a vigorous advocate of "rootedness".[351] Drumont wrote that "the Jewish race is a race of nomads and Bedouins. When it momentarily pitches camp somewhere, it destroys everything around it; it cuts the trees, dries up the springs, and one finds only ashes in the place where it pitched its tents."[352] And referring again to Jewish immigration, he quoted Le Nord in 1891: "Russia is suffering, like every where else one should add, from the invasion of the native Aryan by the Semite, who has settled in the country on the course of his migrations and peregrinations."[353] While the context of this complaint is evidently important, the casting of the Jews and the Jews alone as the wandering race can be seen also, as we have argued earlier, as a form of categorization that served to explain the general phenomenon of increased population movement, so marked in the period under discussion,[354] while simultaneously asserting its abnormality.

As we have suggested, too, racial classification performed the same kind of function on the more general level. Late nineteenth-century French society was one in which the hierarchical classification in terms of orders, which had obtained under the Ancien Régime, was obviously inoperative, even in its modified post-revolutionary form. A complex status system, of course, existed, but it was complex, and shifting, based as it was to an increasing degree on "merit" and wealth, as well as on the older criteria of birth, family and patronage. The Jews, recently assimilated and "invading" bourgeois society, and traditionally associated with money and money-making pure and simple, both objectively represented an obvious case of the resultant uncertainty about social categorizations and ranking, and could also be used to symbolize this uncertainty as a wider phenomenon. To repeat, the Jews were French, but not French, bourgeois, many of them, but not bourgeois; they were a social group in a state of manifest transition and in process of dissolution. In these circumstances, racial terminology provided an anti-solvent, a new form of absolute and binding classification. "A race, a nation", wrote Maurras, "are palpably immortal substances!"[355] "The instinct of race", declared Drumont, ". . . this sentiment persists in the depth of the soul, like granite at the bottom of the sea."[356] To define the Jew was in some way, by sympathetic magic, to exorcize the general threat of social flux or dissolution, a threat felt the more keenly by many antisemites, in that they were themselves socially or professionally marginal people.[357] At the same time the confusion represented by the Jew had to be recognized and explained. So alongside the strict racial conceptualization of the Jew, there coexisted his conceptualization as an amorphous uncleanness, and also the idea of a wider coalition of alien forces, Protean, "Legion",[358] categorized very often as "Jewry",[359] a floating and indefinable conspiracy of outsiders and enemies, against which the French nation or the French race could be firmly defined and asserted. Race was thus a dual-purpose concept, a principle for categorizing and excluding the ambiguous and interstitial enemy, and then for establishing one's own sense of belonging, for fulfilling the need for a sense of stability and security in a society of rapid change and inescapable contingency. In a world of anomie, race remained, when all else failed, the one value, the one social quality of which the individual could not be robbed. This was made clear by Barrès, writing of Dreyfus during the Rennes trial in 1899, with a strange kind of compassionate fellow-feeling:[360]

> his education and upbringing, if they did not manage to establish him in a new social milieu, certainly removed him from the traditional Jewish community and its customs; they left him without any social framework, completely exposed. All that this solitary man had left to him was his race, a quality of which no circumstance, no volition, can deprive a Semite any more than an Aryan . . .

Race and heredity, too, were the means of conquering change, of sacralizing the present, of eliminating from the future all contingency, all freedom of action and all responsibility. As Tocqueville told Gobineau in 1853: "Your doctrine is a sort of fatalism, of predestination . . .";[361] while Drumont referred to "the fatality of race . . ."[362] Race, in effect, was a kind of secular equivalent of Destiny or Providence and had the same functions.[363] André Chamson's Maître Dalbèze explained: "What is heredity? . . . Merely Destiny in modern guise, what the Ancients used to call Fate, which we now find in the blood and marrow of men . . . Heredity explains all . . . beauty and ugliness . . . crime and virtue . . . genius and insanity!"[364] This function of race is particularly relevant to the millenarianism of the antisemites, though, as we have seen, they did not consistently adhere to its logic.

Such were the complex functions of the concept of race in nineteenth-century French antisemitism. It is worth noting, in conclusion, that although the structural similarities with Nazi racialism are great, the emphasis was significantly different. Although "race" was a term of very wide currency, sophisticated racial theory was confined to limited intellectual circles. It was discussed in groups such as the Cercle Antisémitique d'Etudes Sociales; it was propagated by writers such as Picard, Soury and Barrès; it was retailed by Drumont, though it did not occupy a very important place in his work. Educated opinion had only a vague conception of current "scientific" racial theory, although in this form it did serve, as we have seen, as an arsenal for antisemitic propaganda, and as a means of expressing its central ideas. But it remained only one means among others, if a particularly suitable one; and it was not yet an imperative that dominated antisemitic ideology. Leroy-Beaulieu pointed out that the use of racial terminology was a way of giving antisemitism an allegedly "scientific" status. Concepts of race, he wrote, "have been important factors in its success . . . A name that appears to be technical is a precious asset at a time when science has become a religion, or rather a superstition . . ." Race allowed antisemites "to dress up their hatreds in the cloak of science."[365] In this context, Drumont referred to his "mission as a sociologist."[366] But, although French antisemitism at the end of the nineteenth century did mark an important stage in the intellectualization of anti-Jewish feeling, although it did represent the deliberate construction of an ideological system on the basis of popular fears and prejudices (a point to which we will return),[367] its scientific cloak was still rather thin, and its adoption of pseudo-scientific racialism, as such, was still rather tentative. There is no doubt that it was racialist, but in expression its racialism was more often latent than manifest.[368] The contrast with German antisemitism of the 1930s and 1940s can perhaps be illustrated from the testimony of the Tharaud brothers. They had been secretaries to Barrès and were well-acquainted with the French antisemitic movement of his time.[369] They were also the authors of various books on Jewish life of antisemitic tendency, published in France in the inter-war period.[370] In 1933, they visited Germany where the campaign against the Jews was then entering a new phase, and noted at once that this was something of a different kind:[371]

> For the antisemitism now in fashion, the evil is not in what is written in books, it is in the Jews themselves. No baptismal water, no denial of self, can ever efface the fact of race. "In the past", a Jew told me, "they burnt

us so as to take our property, for our welfare even, for paradise. At least the intention was sometimes good, if the means were bad. But, today, there is no means of escaping the fate that threatens us . . ."

If this ignores many of the features of earlier antisemitism, many of the features of late nineteenth-century antisemitism that we have discussed, it indicates that that antisemitism was only a prelude, and, up to a point, an unwitting prelude, to something much more terrible, something of another order.

NOTES

1 Maurras, *Quand les Français ne s'aimaient pas*, p. 219; see also Barrès, *Scènes et doctrines*, I, p. 68 (May 1900): "Mais vous nierez point que le Juif soit un être différent."
2 Leroy-Beaulieu, *L'Antisémitisme*, p. 68.
3 See Émile Littré, *Dictionnaire de la langue française* (1863–1872) (Paris, 1965 edition), which includes the *Supplément* of 1877; also the 1878 edition of Littré.
4 Paul Robert, *Dictionnaire alphabétique at analogique de la langue française* (Paris, 1965) gives Anatole France's *Le Lys rouge* (1894) as its example of the earliest use of the word "antisémitisme", although the *Supplément* (1970) gives a reference to *Larousse supérieure* (1890) for "antisémite". The *Grand Larousse de la langue française* (Paris, 1971) gives Lazare's *L'Antisémitisme* (1894) as its example of the earliest use of the word.
5 See Verdès-Leroux, *Scandale financier et antisémitisme catholique*, pp. 99–100; and Byrnes, *Antisemitism in Modern France*, p. 135.
6 See chapter IX, n. 30; also L'Hermite, *L'Anti-Pape*, p. iii. There was also an Algiers newspaper called *L'Antijuif*, as we have seen.
7 Picard, *Synthèse de l'antisémitisme*, pp. 16–17, 30–5 and 201–13.
8 See Lazare, *L'Antisémitisme*, pp. 240–1; and Verdès-Leroux, *Scandale financier*, pp. 99–100; also Mosse, *The Crisis of German Ideology*, p. 130; Ferdinand Deml, "Antisemitismus in German Encyclopedias", *Wiener Library Bulletin*, 21 (4) (1967), pp. 31–6; Pierre Sorlin, *L'Antisémitisme allemand* (Paris, 1969), p. 55; and Poliakov, "Racisme et Antisémitisme", p. 2.
9 Leroy-Beaulieu, *Les Doctrines de haine*, p. 11.
10 See Drumont, *La France juive*, I, p. 6; and Verdès-Leroux, *Scandale financier*, pp. 111–14.
11 See Silberner, "French Socialism and the Jewish Question", p. 5; and Drumont, *FJ*, I, p. 13; and II, p. 407.
12 Drumont, *FJ*, I, pp. 5–6 and 9; also ibid., I, pp. 10–31; *La Dernière Bataille*, pp. 129, 295 and *passim;* and *Le Testament d'un antisémite*, pp. 152–6, 324 and 364.
13 Daudet, *Les Oeuvres dans les hommes*, p. 168; see also Blumenkranz, ed., *Histoire des Juifs en France*, p. 341.
14 See Silberner, op. cit., pp. 6–7.
15 Sternhell, "Le Déterminisme physiologique et racial à la base du nationalisme de Maurice Barrès et de Jules Soury", pp. 3–4.
16 Cit. Barrès, *Mes Cahiers*, II, pp. 117–20 (1899). The last part, cited by Barrès in indirect speech, is in fact taken from Renan.
17 See Sternhell, "Le Déterminisme physiologique et racial", pp. 20–2 and *passim;* also Byrnes, *Antisemitism in Modern France*, p. 325; Reinach, *Histoire de l'Affaire Dreyfus*, IV, pp. 495–6; Sternhell, *Maurice Barrès*, pp. 254–8.
18 See both works by Sternhell cited above.
19 Barrès, *Mes Cahiers*, II, pp. 141–2.
20 Barrès, *Scènes et doctrines*, I, p. 67 (1900).

21 Ibid., I, p. 205; see also Barrès, Letter to Maurras, November 1907, Barrès-Maurras, *La République ou le roi,* pp. 479–80; Tharaud, *Mes années chez Barrès,* pp. 26–7; Sternhell, *Maurice Barrès,* pp. 261–9 and 308; and Sternhell, "Le Déterminisme physiologique et racial", pp. 2, 10, 22 and *passim.*

22 Léon Hennebicq was an advocate at the Belgian Court of Appeal and a professor at the New University of Brussels; see Bournand, *Les Juifs et nos contemporains,* pp. 273–4.

23 Léon Hennebicq, *Le Journal,* 4 February 1897, cit. Barrès, *Scènes et doctrines,* II, pp. 175–6.

24 See, for example, Barrès-Maurras, op. cit., p. 293 (June 1900).

25 Dagan, *Enquête sur l'antisémitisme,* pp. 1–4.

26 Vogüé, *Les Morts qui parlent,* p. 424.

27 Picard, op. cit., pp. 64–5; also p. 13.

28 Ibid., pp. 57–8, 64 and 95; also pp. 105–6.

29 On the general idea of the inheritance of guilt, see Thomas, *Religion and the Decline of Magic,* p. 113; and Christopher Hill, *The World Turned Upside Down: Radical Ideas during the English Revolution* (Harmondsworth, 1975), pp. 147–8 and 157–8; for a fuller discussion of the deicide charge, see chapter XIV, pp. 541–3 below.

30 Drumont, *FJ,* I, pp. 39–40.

31 *Le Télégramme d'Alger,* 17 January 1898, cit. Rouquier and Soumille, "La Notion de Race chez les Français d'Algérie", p. 8; see also abbé Gayraud, cit. Bournand, op. cit., p. 201; and chapter XIV, pp. 509–11 below, for similar protestations.

32 *La Justice Sociale,* 2 July 1898, cit. Mayeur, "Les Congrès nationaux", p. 205.

33 Sorlin, *"La Croix" et les Juifs,* pp. 147–53 and 158–64.

34 Mgr E. Jouin, *Le Péril judéo-maçonnique,* II, *La Judéo-maçonnerie et l'Eglise catholique* (Paris, 1921), Part I, pp. 67–8, cit. Lovsky, *L'Antisémitisme chrétien,* p. 153. The first volume of Jouin's work, published in 1920, is a translation of the *Protocols of the Elders of Zion.*

35 Maurras, *Anthinéa,* p. 178.

36 See Victor Nguyen, "Race et Civilisation chez Maurras" in *Missions et démarches de la critique: Mélanges offerts au Professeur J. A. Vier* (Paris, 1973), pp. 563–72.

37 Maurras, *La Gazette de France,* 9 April 1894, cit. Jouveau, "L'Itinéraire félibréen de Charles Maurras", p. 85.

38 Maurras, *L'Avenir de l'intelligence,* pp. 12–13.

39 Maurras, *Au Signe de Flore,* p. 233.

40 Maurras, *L'Avenir de l'intelligence,* p. 12.

41 Maurras, *La Gazette de France,* 17 January 1904, in *Dictionnaire politique et critique,* I, pp. 289–93.

42 Daudet, *L'Avant-Guerre,* p. xiii.

43 Ibid., pp. x–xi.

44 Bainville, *La Gazette de France,* 9 October 1905, cit. Janine Buenzod, *La Formation de la pensée de Gobineau* (Paris, 1967), p. 594.

45 See, for example, Maurras, "Le système de Gobineau", *Gaulois, Germains, Latins* (Paris, 1926), pp. 29–30; also D. W. Brogan, "National Doctrine of M. Charles Maurras", *French Personalities and Problems* (London, 1946), pp. 65–6; Nguyen, "Race et Civilisation chez Maurras", p. 569.

46 See chapter IX, p. 232 above.

47 See, for example, Frédéric Mistral, "A la raco latino" in *Isclo d'or,* cit. Rollet, *La Vie quotidienne en Provence au temps de Mistral,* p. 11; Pierre Guiral, "Montesquieu précurseur de l'idée d'inégalité des races", Paper given at Colloque sur l'idée de Race, 1975, p. 6, citing Jules Verne and Lefebvre de Béhaine; and Louis Bertrand, "Vers l'unité latine", *Revue des Deux Mondes,* 15 September 1916, pp. 314–38. For Amouretti's influence on Maurras and the Action Française, see my "Fustel de Coulanges and the Action Française", *Journal of the History of Ideas,* 34 (1973), pp. 124–5.

48 Frédéric Amouretti, "Race Latine", *Le Soleil*, 18 June 1898, cit. André Cottez, *Frédéric Amouretti (1863–1913)* (Paris, 1937), pp. 193–6; see also Cottez, op. cit., p. 69.

49 Maurras, *Enquête sur la monarchie*, p. 397.

50 Cit. Dupré, Introduction, Barrès-Maurras, op. cit., p. iii.

51 Barrès, *Scènes et doctrines*, I, p. 20.

52 Maurice Barrès, *Le Voyage de Sparte* (Paris, 1922), p. 79, cit. Sternhell, *Maurice Barrès*, pp. 261–2; see also Sternhell, op. cit., pp. 269 and 308.

53 Drumont, *FJ*, I, pp. 553–4; and II, p. 252; *DB*, p. 404; *TA*, pp. 172, 319, 321 and 373.

54 Drumont, *TA*, p. 365.

55 Reports, Police agent, 3 and 6 March 1899. AN F[7] 12480; see also Drumont, *FJ*, II, p. 25; and chapter IV, pp. 144–5 above.

56 Leroy-Beaulieu, *Les Doctrines de haine*, p. 116.

57 Ibid., p. 12.

58 Leroy-Beaulieu, *L'Antisémitisme*, p. 6.

59 Dagan, op. cit., p. 23.

60 Ibid., pp. 7–8.

61 Ibid., p. 14.

62 Durkheim, *Suicide*, pp. 82–5.

63 Dagan, op. cit., p. 61.

64 Durkheim was the son and grandson of rabbis, and was expected as a child to follow in this tradition; see Lukes, *Emile Durkheim*, p. 39.

65 Marrus, *The Politics of Assimilation*, chapter 2.

66 J. Cohen, *Les Déicides: Examen de la vie de Jésus et des développements de l'Eglise chrétienne dans leurs rapports avec le Judaïsme* (Paris, 1864), p. xiii.

67 See Lovsky, *L'Antisémitisme chrétien*, p. 362.

68 Daniel Halévy, Diary, 2 December 1898, cit. Silvera, *Daniel Halévy and his Times*, p. 91.

69 Blum, *Souvenirs sur l'Affaire*, p. 20; see also *L'Oeuvre de Léon Blum 1891–1905*, pp. 262 and 264–5.

70 Péguy, *Notre Jeunesse*, pp. 69 and 73; also ibid., pp. 104, 108 and 184; and Pierrard, *Juifs et catholiques français*, p. 222.

71 L'Hermite, op. cit., pp. 103–16; see also Clermont-Tonnerre, *Mémoires*, I, p. 209.

72 Reinach, op. cit., IV, p. 445; see also Sartre, *Réflexions sur la question juive*, p. 103; and Harry L. Shapiro, "The Jewish People, A Biological History", *Race and Science*, UNESCO, pp. 107–80.

73 Leroy-Beaulieu, *Les Doctrines de haine*, p. 11.

74 Dagan, op. cit., p. 74.

75 See, for example, Bollême, *La Bibliothèque bleue*, p. 265; and Alfred de Vigny, *Théâtre*, II, *Journal d'un poète* (Paris, no date-Nelson edition), p. 438.

76 E.g. Péguy, *NJ*, pp. 10–12, 15–17 and *passim*.

77 Martin du Gard, *Jean Barois*, p. 284.

78 Thiers, *Discours parlementaires*, XI (Paris, 1881), p. 37, cit. Jean Stengers, "Race et nationalité chez Emile de Laveleye", Paper given at Colloque sur l'Idée de Race, 1975, p. 16; see also the same usage à propos France by a more conservative contemporary, the Marquis de Castellane: Castellane, *Hommes et choses de mon temps*, pp. 123 and 231–2.

79 Vallès, *Le Bachélier*, p. 73.

80 See Bourguet, "Une Race d'administrés: Les Français de l'An IX vus par leurs préfets", pp. 9, 15–19 and *passim*; and Stendhal, *Mémoires d'un touriste*, I, pp. 25–7, 71 and 131–5, for the early nineteenth century.

81 *The Journal of Eugène Delacroix* (1951), p. 267 (3 August 1857).

82 Castellane, *Hommes et choses de mon temps*, p. 81. This mode of explanation was common in French literary criticism until very recently and still has a certain vogue.

83 Alphonse Daudet, *Numa Roumestan* (1880) (Paris, no date—Nelson edition), p. 310; see also Daudet's Tartarin novels.

84 See Bourguet, op. cit., p. 7; Guiral, "Montesquieu précurseur de l'idée d'inégalité des races", p. 6; Georges Liens, "Le stéréotype du Méridional vu par les Français du Nord de 1815 à 1914", Paper given at Colloque sur l'Idée de Race, 1975; and Nguyen, "Race et civilisation chez Maurras", pp. 565–7.

85 See F. Pomponi, "Stéréotypes et concept de Race aux origines du régionalisme corse (1870–1914)"; also Rouquier and Soumille, "La Notion de Race chez les Français d'Algérie", p. 2; and Lothe, "L'Idée de Race et Régionalisme chez les militants wallons avant 1914", pp. 5 and 20–1 (all papers given at Colloque sur l'Idée de Race, 1975).

86 Xavier Vallat, *Charles Maurras, numéro d'écrou 8321* (Paris, 1953), p. 254.

87 Drumont, *DB*, p. 62; see also *TA*, p. 13, on the Vendéens.

88 Gaston Méry, *Jean Révolte* (Paris, 1892), p. 167, cit. Nguyen, "Race et Civilisation chez Maurras", p. 567; see also Liens, op. cit., p. 9.

89 Maurras, Letter to Barrès, 9 June 1904. Barrès-Maurras, op. cit., p. 79.

90 Vallès, *Le Bachélier*, p. 151.

91 Ibid., pp. 222 and 233.

92 Vallès, *L'Insurgé*, p. 183.

93 See Chevalier, *Classes laborieuses et classes dangereuses*, pp. 519–31; also p. 492 below.

94 Maupassant, *Bel-Ami*, pp. 168–9.

95 Lyautey, Letter to Vogüé, 3 January 1899, *Choix de lettres*, p. 167.

96 For traditional ideas about an honourable and virtuous noble "race", see Bollême, op. cit., pp. 196 and 206; on the theory of the Frankish origins of the French nobility, see Marc Bloch, "Sur les Grandes Invasions: Quelques positions de problèmes" (1945), *Mélanges historiques* (Paris, 1963), I, pp. 90–109; Poliakov, "Le Mythe Aryen", *Les Juifs et notre histoire*, pp. 111–12; and Guiral, "Montesquieu précurseur de l'idée d'inégalité des races", pp. 4–5.

97 Cit. Viard, "L'*Encyclopédie nouvelle* de Pierre Leroux et l'idée de race", p. 5; see also Poliakov, "Racisme et Antisémitisme", pp. 14–15.

98 Vigny, op. cit., p. 408.

99 Castellane, *Hommes et choses de mon temps*, p. 85.

100 Boni de Castellane, *L'Art d'être pauvre*, p. v; also p. 60.

101 Michel Leiris, "Race and Culture", *Race and Science*, UNESCO, p. 215.

102 Balzac, *Christ in Flanders* (London, 1931), pp. 208 and 234; see also Balzac, *La Cousine Bette* (Lupton edition), p. 398.

103 Maupassant, *Bel-Ami*, p. 296.

104 Zola, *Au Bonheur des Dames*, p. 345.

105 Hugo, *Choses vues 1830–1846*, p. 163 (5 May 1839).

106 Ibid., p. 240 (21 July 1840).

107 E.g. Vigny, op. cit., p. 395 (1847); and Castellane, *Hommes et choses de mon temps*, pp. 171 and 231–2.

108 See Sue, *The Wandering Jew*, Part II, p. 97 and *passim*.

109 Balzac, *Le Père Goriot*, p. 389.

110 Vigny, op. cit., p. 252.

111 Alphonse Daudet, *Numa Roumestan*, p. 68.

112 Drumont, *DB*, p. 463.

113 Martin du Gard, *Jean Barois*, p. 288.

114 J.-H. Rosny aîné, *Portraits et souvenirs* (Paris, 1945), p. 61; see also *L'Oeuvre de Léon Blum 1891–1905*, p. 148, for the same usage.

115 Gregh, *L'Age d'or*, p. 103.

116 Poliakov, *Les Juifs et notre histoire*, pp. 93–4.

117 Ibid., pp. 102–25; see also Bloch, "Sur les Grandes Invasions"; and my "Fustel de Coulanges and the Action Française", p. 127.

118 See Drumont, *TA*, p. 12.

119 See Guiral, "Montesquieu précurseur de l'idée d'inégalité des races"; Poliakov, "Racisme et Antisémitisme", pp. 9–10, 13 and 15–16; René Duchac, "La Race à fleur de peau: remarques sur quelques thèmes de l'anthropologie du XVIIIe siècle", Paper given at same Colloque.

120 See Louis L. Snyder, *The Idea of Racialism* (New York, 1962), pp. 39–46; and Marrus, op. cit., pp. 10–11; see also pp. 470–2 below.

121 See Snyder, op. cit., pp. 11–12 and 108–11.

122 Paul Topinard, *L'Anthropologie et la science sociale* (Paris, 1900), pp. 226–8.

123 Tocqueville, Letter to Gobineau, 13 November 1855. Tocqueville, *The "European Revolution" and Correspondence with Gobineau*, p. 268; see also Jardin, "Alexis de Tocqueville, Gustave de Beaumont et le problème de l'inégalité des races", Paper given at Colloque sur l'Idée de Race, 1975.

124 See Hubert Deschamps, *Les Méthodes et les doctrines coloniales de la France* (Paris, 1953), pp. 142–50; Brunschwig, *Mythes et réalités de l'impérialisme colonial français*, pp. 173–7; M. D. Lewis, "One Hundred Million Frenchmen: The "Assimilation" Theory in French Colonial Policy", *Comparative Studies in Society and History*, 4 (1961–2), pp. 129–53; and William B. Cohen, *Rulers of Empire: The French Colonial Service in Africa* (Stanford, 1971), pp. 44–9 and 72–9.

125 See Astier Loutfi, *Littérature et colonialisme*, pp. 4, 44–5, 69–71, 80–5 and *passim;* Poliakov, "Racisme et Antisémitisme", pp. 5–8; and papers given at the Colloque sur l'Idée de Race, 1975, by Jean-Pierre Chrétien, Gérard Pio, Pierre J. Simon, Pierre Soumille and Mlle Valensi.

126 See Arendt, *The Origins of Totalitarianism*, Parts I and II.

127 Drumont, *FJ*, II, pp. 227 and 44–5; and I, pp. 476–7 and 494; see also ibid., I, pp. 465, 471, 475–6, 478–80, 495–98 and 503–7; and II, pp. 38–47.

128 Zévaès, *Henri Rochefort*, pp. 114–15 and 169–76.

129 Maurras, Letter to Barrès, January 1900. Barrès-Maurras, op. cit., p. 260; see also Girardet, *Le Nationalisme français*, pp. 107–15; Girardet, *L'Idée coloniale en France*, Part I; and Astier Loutfi, op. cit., pp. 22 and 136.

130 See, for example, Arthur de Gobineau, *Essai sur l'inégalité des races humaines*, I, pp. 44–9; and II, pp. 527–32, cit. Jean Boissel, *Gobineau polémiste* (Paris, 1967), pp. 82–8 and 150–5; and passages cited by Michael D. Biddiss, ed., *Gobineau: Selected Political Writings* (London, 1970), pp. 156–7.

131 *Dictionnaire de l'Académie Française* (Paris, 1878).

132 On Gobineau generally, see Biddiss, *Father of Racist Ideology*, an admirable "explication", but not concerned with Gobineau's influence in France. Gobineau wrote to Tocqueville in May 1856: "I am somewhat annoyed, though not really hurt, by the slowness with which knowledge about the existence of my book and its principal tenets spreads in France" (Tocqueville, op. cit., pp. 287–8). Gobineau claimed to have influenced Renan (ibid., pp. 331 and 334), but, according to Leger, his influence on Taine was nil (François Leger, "L'idée de race chez Taine", Paper given at Colloque sur l'Idée de Race, 1975, p. 1). For his neglect in France until the early decades of this century, see Louis Thomas, *Arthur de Gobineau, Inventeur du racisme (1816–1882)* (Paris, 1941), pp. 10–23; Boissel, Contribution to Colloque sur l'Idée de Race; John Lukacs, "A Note on Gobineau", in Tocqueville, op. cit., pp. 183–4; Verdès-Leroux, *Scandale financier*, pp. 111–13; Sternhell, *Maurice Barrès*, p. 13. Sternhell's claim that Gobineau did influence Taine, and also Drumont, is unsubstantiated (see Sternhell, "Le Déterminisme physiologique et racial", p. 3); Gobineau does not figure in the very full index to *La France juive;* and he was not, of course, an antisemite as such (see Lukacs, op. cit., p. 186, for example).

133 Henry James, *Parisian Sketches: Letters to the New York Tribune 1875–1876* (New York, 1961), p. 125 (27 May 1876).

134 Paul Bourget, "M.Ernest Renan" (1898), *Essais de psychologie contemporaine* (Paris, 1920), I, p. 38.

135 Henri Massis, *Jugements, Renan—France—Barrès* (Paris, 1923), p. 3.
136 For further testimony to Renan's influence in the 1890s in particular, see Herriot, *Jadis*, I, p. 80; and Halévy, *Apologie pour notre passé*, pp. 50–5.
137 Ernest Renan, *Histoire générale et système comparé des langues sémitiques, Oeuvres complètes*, VIII (Paris, 1958), pp. 145–6.
138 Ibid., pp. 149–56.
139 Ibid., p. 558.
140 Ibid., p. 563.
141 Ibid., p. 576.
142 Ibid., p. 577.
143 Ibid., pp. 580 and 585–6.
144 See Barrès, *Mes Cahiers*, I, p. 74; and II, pp. 117 and 142–3; Drumont, *FJ*, I, pp. 11–15 and 135; and *DB*, p. xvi; Picard, op. cit., pp. 77–8 and 105; and Mgr Anselme Tilloy, *Le Péril judéo-maçonnique: Le mal, le remède* (1897), cit. Pierrard, op. cit., p. 67. Maurras and other Nationalist writers were less attracted by Renan's ideas about race than by his cultural and political élitism; see Maurras, "Portrait de M. Renan" (1932); and "Notre Renan" (1923), *Oeuvres capitales* (Paris, 1954), III, pp. 499–504; Guiral, "Renan et Maurras", *Etudes Maurrassiennes*, 1 (1972), pp. 71–80; Paul Bourget, *Nouvelles Pages de critique et de doctrine* (Paris, 1922), II, p. 36; Jules Lemaître, *Les Contemporains*, huitième série (Paris, 1918), p. 214.
145 Renan, "Qu'est-ce qu'une nation?", Conférence faite en Sorbonne, (11 March 1882), *Oeuvres complètes*, I, pp. 896 and 898.
146 See, for example, Drumont, *FJ*, I, pp. 14–16; and II, pp. 381–2.
147 Renan, "Identité originelle et séparation graduelle du Judaïsme et du Christianisme", Conférence faite à la Société des Études Juives (26 May 1883), *Oeuvres complètes*, I, p. 919; see also ibid., pp. 912–13; and Ernest Renan, *Souvenirs d'enfance et de jeunesse* (1883) (Paris, 1904 ?), p. 190.
148 Renan, "La Poésie des Races Celtiques", *Essais de morale et de critique* (Paris, 1924), pp. 375–456.
149 Ernest Renan, *Caliban* (Paris, 1878), p. 91.
150 Guiral, "Renan et Maurras", p. 77; also ibid., pp. 72 and 79. This aspect of Renan's thought has not been emphasized by earlier critics, but see here Eugène Meyer, *La Philosophie politique de Renan* (Paris, no date), pp. 92 and 177; and Jean Pommier, *Renan* (Paris, 1923), pp. 60–1 and 91. H. W. Wardman, *Ernest Renan: A Critical Biography* (London, 1964), the most recent study of Renan in English, inexplicably omits all reference to Renan's ideas on race, and does not list the *Histoire générale et système comparé des langues sémitiques* in either index or bibliography.
151 See Renan, "Le Judaïsme comme Race et comme Religion", Conférence faite au Cercle Saint-Simon (27 January 1883), *Oeuvres complètes*, I, pp. 925–44; some contributors to Dagan's *Enquête* appear to have been influenced by this lecture. On Renan and antisemitism, see also Marrus, op. cit., p. 12.
152 *La Semaine Religieuse de Grenoble*, 15 December 1892, cit. Verdès-Leroux, *Scandale financier*, p. 206; see also Drumont, *DB*, pp. 267, 420 and 515.
153 See Dagan, op. cit., pp 21 and 53 (Zola and Duclaux). Renan died in 1892.
154 Tharaud, *Notre cher Péguy*, I, p. 39.
155 Henri Massis, *Evocations, 1905–1911* (Paris, 1931), p. 4.
156 Charles Maurras, *Poésie et Vérité* (Lyon, 1944), p. 165; see also, for Maurras, unpublished manuscript, cit. Leger, "Taine et Maurras", *Etudes Maurrassiennes*, 1 (1972), p. 98; and, generally, Albert Thibaudet, "Renan et Taine", *Réflexions sur la Littérature* (Paris, 1938), pp. 200–8.
157 Victor Guiraud, *Hippolyte Taine: Etudes et documents* (Paris, 1928), pp. 279 and 167; see also Henry James, op. cit., p. 47; Guiraud, *Essai sur Taine: Son oeuvre et son influence* (Paris, 1900), chapter IV; André Chevrillon, *Taine: Formation de sa pensée* (Paris, 1932), p. i; and Maxime Leroy, *Taine* (Paris, 1933), pp. 180–1.

158 Hippolyte Taine, *Histoire de la littérature anglaise* (1863) (Paris, 1905 edition), I, pp. xxii–xxiv.

159 See, for example, Guiraud, *Essai sur Taine*, pp. 122–3; Guiraud, "La Philosophie de Taine" (1891), *Hippolyte Taine*, p. 28; and Chevrillon, op. cit., pp. 325 and 335–9.

160 Taine has been curiously neglected by modern scholarship, leaving an important gap in nineteenth-century French intellectual history, and in the history of French historiography and sociology; see, however, a recent short study: Leo Weinstein, *Hippolyte Taine* (New York, 1972).

161 Chevrillon, op. cit., p. 325.

162 Leger, "L'idée de race chez Taine", p. 7.

163 See, for example, Drumont, *FJ*, I, pp. v and viii; and II, p. 516; *DB*, pp. 23, 154 and 511; *TA*, pp. 74 and 225.

164 See, for example, Barrès, *Mes Cahiers*, I, pp. 217–18, 220–1 and 225–8; Barrès, *Scènes et doctrines*, I, p. 83; and Sternhell, *Maurice Barrès*, pp. 259–60 and 290–9.

165 See Barrès, *Les Déracinés*, I, chapter 7; Maurras, *Dictionnaire politique et critique*, V, p. 320; Barrès and Maurras, op. cit., p. 320; Maurras, "Taine et les idées du XIXe siècle" (1900); and "Ce que nous devons à Taine" (1905), *Oeuvres capitales*, III, pp. 505–14; Leger, "Taine et Maurras"; and n. 156 above.

166 Beauvoir, *Memoirs of a Dutiful Daughter*, p. 36. For Taine's influence on other Nationalist writers, see Paul Bourget, "M. Taine" (1882); "M. Taine historien" (1884); and "Un élève de M. Taine" (1897), *Essais de psychologie contemporaine*, I, pp. 197–274; Bourget, "Réflexions sur l'art de l'histoire", *Etudes et Portraits* (Paris, 1889), pp. 281–97; Louis Dimier, *Les Maîtres de la Contre-Révolution au dix-neuvième siècle* (Paris, 1917), pp. 158–63; Henri Rouzaud, *Sous les Lauriers de Languedoc: L'oeuvre d'un enraciné* (Toulouse, 1926), pp. 63–4 and 83–4.

167 Mauriac, "L'Affaire Dreyfus", p. 15.

168 Waleffe, *Quand Paris était un paradis*, p. 80.

169 Claude Roy, "Le génie de l'amour sublime", *Zola*, Collection Génies et Réalités, chapter V, p. 154.

170 Guillemin, "L'Affaire", ibid., chapter VIII, p. 249; see also ibid., Illustrations, pp. 248 and 269; Mirbeau, *Le Journal d'une femme de chambre*, pp. 104–5; Léon Daudet, "Emile Zola ou le Romantisme de l'égout", *Les Oeuvres dans les hommes*, pp. 91–141; Daudet, *Au Temps de Judas*, pp. 54–61; Mitterand, *Zola journaliste*, p. 247; Guillemin, *Présentation des Rougon-Macquart*, pp. 304, 351 and 374; Guillemin, *Zola légende et vérité*, pp. 7–11 and 160–9; AN F⁷ 12474, "Procès Zola 1898–1899".

171 Jusserand, *What Me Befell*, p. 155.

172 Bloy, *Je m'accuse* (1900), *Oeuvres*, IV, p. 223. For Bloy's earlier favourable opinion of *La Terre*, see *Inédits de Leon Bloy*, pp. 135–51.

173 Guillemin, *Présentation des Rougon-Macquart*, p. 15.

174 See ibid., pp. 30–1, 35–8, 51–2 and *passim;* and Mitterand, op. cit., pp. 49, 167–9, 204–5 and *passim.*

175 By 1902, the year of Zola's death, *La Terre* (1887) had sold 129,000 copies; *Nana* (1880) 193,000; and *La Débâcle* (1892) over 200,000. Guillemin, *Présentation des Rougon-Macquart*, pp. 179, 289 and 371; see also ibid., pp. 15, 113, 283, 336 and 364; and Péguy, "Les Récentes Oeuvres de Zola" (4 December 1902), *Oeuvres en prose 1898–1908*, p. 557; and, on Zola's "fame" generally, Henry James, op. cit., p. 111; Maurras, *L'Avenir de l'intelligence*, p. 61; Donnay, *Des Souvenirs*, pp. 193–4; Mitterand, op. cit., p. 265; Guillemin, *Zola légende et vérité*, pp. 79 and *passim.*

176 See Blum, "En lisant", *L'Oeuvre de Léon Blum 1891–1905*, p. 91; Mitterand, op. cit., pp. 21–3, 34, 52 and 186, and F. W. J. Hemmings, *Emile Zola* (Oxford, 1966), pp. 55–7.

177 Emile Zola, *La Fortune des Rougon* (Paris, 1871), Préface, *Oeuvres complètes*, II (Paris, 1966), p. 19.
178 Guillemin, *Présentation des Rougon-Macquart*, pp. 149, 169, 245, 271, 322–3 and 400.
179 Novels based on the theme of a hereditary burden or curse include Sue's *Le Juif errant;* and George Sand's *Mauprat* (1846); see also Edmond and Jules de Goncourt, *Charles Demailly* (1868) (Paris, 1926), p. 139.
180 See Drumont, *DB*, pp. 7, 52 and 168; *TA*, pp. 31, 120–5, 129–30 and 311–13.
181 See Guillemin, *Présentation des Rougon-Macquart*, p. 216.
182 Drumont, *FJ*, II, p. 452.
183 Zola, *Son Excellence Eugène Rougon* (1876) (Paris, 1962), pp. 6 and 81–2.
184 Zola, *L'Argent* (Paris, 1891), *Oeuvres complètes*, VI, pp. 402–3; see also Bouvier, "Le Monde des Affaires", *Zola*, pp. 187–9; and the contrary view of Guillemin, *Présentation des Rougon-Macquart*, pp. 353 and 361.
185 Zola, *La Débâcle* (1892), cit. Lovsky, *L'Antisémitisme chrétien*, p. 39; also Drumont, *FJ*, I, p. 511, citing Mirbeau, perhaps a common source.
186 Zola, *Paris* (London, 1898 edition), pp. 353, 24 and 29; also pp. 46–7 and *passim*.
187 See, for example, Jules Michelet, *Tableau de la France* (1833) (Paris, 1949), pp. xvi and 38–9; Michelet, *La Femme* (Paris, 1860), pp. 133–52 and 241–2; Viard, "L'*Encyclopédie nouvelle* de Pierre Leroux et l'idée de race", pp. 6–7. Michelet, however, laid much less emphasis on race as a factor in historical explanation than did many of his contemporaries.
188 See Thuillier, "Un anarchiste positiviste: Georges Vacher de Lapouge".
189 See Marrus, op. cit., p. 14; Sternhell, *Maurice Barrès*, pp. 14–15; and Picard, op. cit., pp. 66 and 113.
190 Dagan, op. cit., p. 23; see also Sternhell, *Maurice Barrès*, pp. 11–12.
191 Fore-Fauré, *Face aux Juifs!*, pp. 298–306, for example, rejected what he called the Jewish "struggle for life" principle.
192 Lazare, *L'Antisémitisme*, pp. 269 and 272.
193 Dagan, op. cit., pp. 33–4, 52 and 74.
194 Brunetière, "Après le Procès", loc. cit., pp. 428–9. The reference to Taine seems clear here. Already, a decade earlier, Brunetière had rejected racial explanation of Jewish difference, and had asserted that "nos érudits", and particularly Renan, had proved that the Jews were a people of mixed ethnic origin; Brunetière, "Revue Littéraire, 'La France Juive' ", loc. cit., p. 695.
195 Leroy-Beaulieu, *Les Doctrines de haine*, p. 11. On the role of intellectuals generally in the elaboration of antisemitism in France, see chapter XVI, pp. 606 and ff. below.
196 Dagan, op. cit., pp. 12 and 30; also ibid., p. 53.
197 See chapter XI, n. 139.
198 Barrès, *Scènes et doctrines*, I, p. 153; see also Guinon, *Décadence*, pp. 112–13.
199 E. Judet, "Les Juifs et l'Antisémitisme", *L'Éclair*, 29 June 1906.
200 Henri Rouzaud, Letter to René de Marans, 12 May 1905. Rouzaud, op. cit., pp. 54–7.
201 See Drumont, *FJ*, I, p. 5.
202 Ibid., I, p. 34.
203 Ibid., I, pp. 3 and 23.
204 Ibid., I, pp. 34–6 and 38; also *TA*, p. 324.
205 Drumont, *FJ*, I, pp. 38 and 23.
206 Ibid., I, p. 36.
207 Ibid., II, p. 413.
208 Cit. Bournand, op. cit., pp. 148–9.
209 Steinheil, *My Memoirs*, pp. 143–4.
210 Lacretelle, *Silbermann*, pp. 51, 11 and 52.
211 See Memmi, *Portrait d'un Juif*, pp. 106–9, 115–16, 121–2 and 137.
212 Balzac, *Le Cousin Pons* (1847) (Paris, 1959), p. 115 *("mala aria")*.

213 Cit. Blumenkranz, ed., op. cit., p. 312.
214 Drumont, *FJ*, I, pp. 278 and 104.
215 Ibid., I, p. 103; and II, p. 107; see also, for similar claims, Raoul Berget, *L'Algérie telle qu'elle est* (1890), cit. Verdès-Leroux, *Scandale financier*, p. 126; Tharaud, *Petite Histoire des Juifs*, pp. 21–2; and Rouquier and Soumille, "La Notion de Race chez les Français d'Algérie", p. 7.
216 I am grateful for this information to Dr John Pyne, eye consultant at the Norfolk and Norwich Hospital.
217 See Drumont, *FJ*, I, p. 31; and Gyp, cit. Bournand, op. cit., p. 135.
218 Drumont, *FJ*, I, p. 104; see also Drumont, *DB*, p. 46; Bloy, *Le Salut par les Juifs*, p. 25; Daudet, *Au Temps de Judas*, pp. 18 and 92; and Adorno *et al.*, *The Authoritarian Personality*, chapter XVI, p. 610. For further discussion of this theme, see pp. 486–9 below.
219 Poliakov, "Racisme et Antisémitisme", p. 12.
220 Drumont, *DB*, p. xvi.
221 Drumont, *FJ*, I, p. 283.
222 Ibid., I, p. 105; and II, pp. 264, 423 and *passim*.
223 Ibid., II, p. 451; also p. 561.
224 Drumont, *TA*, p. 324.
225 Daudet, *Au Temps de Judas*, p. 110.
226 Memmi, op. cit., p. 202.
227 Drumont, *FJ*, II, p. 427, allegedly quoting Bourdaloue.
228 Drumont, *TA*, p. 35.
229 See, for example, ibid., pp. 150 and 235; Silberner, "Proudhon's Judeophobia", pp. 65–8 and 70–1; Meurin, *La Franc-maçonnerie, Synagogue de Satan*, p. 101; and Lémann, *La Préponderance juive*, I, pp. 147 and 174.
230 Comtesse d'Agoult, *Mémoires (1833–1854)* (Paris, 1927), p. 217.
231 See André Gide, *If It Die*, p. 192; and Paléologue, *Journal de l'Affaire Dreyfus*, pp. 71 and 224.
232 Cit. Bournand, op. cit., p. 102.
233 Cit. ibid., p. 119.
234 Daily Reports, Prefect of Police, 2, 10 and 13 February, 16 April, 25 May, and 28 June 1898. APP Ba 106.
235 Lazare, *L'Antisémitisme*, pp. 244–5; see also Sartre, op. cit., p. 44.
236 Drumont, *FJ*, I, pp. 3 and 231–2.
237 Report, Commissaire spécial, Roanne, 6 March 1899. AN F[7] 12480; see also Daudet, *Au Temps de Judas*, pp. 106–7; Guy-Grand, *La Philosophie nationaliste*, p. 53; and Lovsky, *L'Antisémitisme chrétien*, p. 277.
238 Maupassant, *Mont-Oriol* (1887), *Romans* (Paris, 1959), p. 814, cit. Schmidt, *Maupassant par lui-même*, pp. 119–20.
239 Barrès, *Scènes et doctrines*, I, p. 167.
240 Léon Daudet, *Le Voyage de Shakespeare* (1896) (Paris, 1929), p. 187, cit. Randall, *The Jewish Character in the French Novel*, p. 94.
241 Jarzel, *Petit Catéchisme nationaliste*, p. 3.
242 Drumont, *FJ*, I, pp. 185 and 31.
243 Report, Commissaire spécial, Saint-Dié, 18 November 1900. AN F[7] 12457.
244 AN F[7] 12480.
245 *Le Patriote de Neufchâteau*, 17 February 1898.
246 Abbé Gayraud, cit. Bournand, op. cit., p. 201.
247 See Soucy, *The Case of Maurice Barrès*, chapters 3 and 4.
248 Donnay, *Des Souvenirs*, p. 70.
249 Daudet, *Au Temps de Judas*, p. 124.
250 Daudet, "Edouard Drumont ou le Sens de la Race", *Les Oeuvres dans les hommes*, pp. 157–8; see also Daudet's more extended development of such themes in *L'Hérédo: Essai sur le drame intérieur* (Paris, 1916).
251 See, for example, Cecil Roth, "Marranos and Racial Antisemitism, A Study in

Parallels", *Jewish Social Studies*, 2 (1940), pp. 239–48; Poliakov, *Les Juifs et notre histoire*, pp. 23–4, 54–8 and 98–102; and Lovsky, *L'Antisémitisme chrétien*, pp. 354 and *passim*.

252 Mauriac, "L'Affaire Dreyfus", pp. 12–13.
253 Lacretelle, op. cit., pp. 26 and 67.
254 Bloch, *Lévy*, pp. 20–3; see also Gide, *Journals 1889–1949*, pp. 195–6; Tharaud, *Petite Histoire des Juifs*, pp. 20–1; and Wirth, *The Ghetto*, p. 30.
255 See Poliakov, "Racisme et Antisémitisme", pp. 16–17, referring to Freud and C. Guillaumin.
256 Barthes, *Mythologies*, pp. 151–2.
257 Cit. Viard, "L'*Encyclopédie nouvelle* de Pierre Leroux et l'idée de race", p. 4.
258 Kenneth L. Little, "Race and Society", *Race and Science*, UNESCO, pp. 101–2.
259 Louis Dumont, *Homo Hierarchicus*, pp. 51 and 303–6.
260 Max Weber, cit. Glock and Stark, *Christian Beliefs and Anti-Semitism*, p. 21; and Sartre, op. cit., pp. 28–38 and *passim*.
261 See Chapter IV, pp. 153–4 above.
262 Veuillot, *L'Univers*, 16 November 1870, cit. Pierrard, op. cit., p. 26.
263 Fore-Fauré, op. cit., pp. 25–6.
264 Drumont, *FJ*, II, pp. 14 and 426.
265 See, for example, ibid., I, pp. 232 and 326; and II, pp. 15 and 264; *DB*, pp. 108 and 467; *TA*, pp. 140 and 364; Picard, op. cit., p. 41; Bournand, op. cit., p. 138 (Gyp); Biez, *Les Rothschild et le péril juif*, p. 7; Daudet, *Les Oeuvres dans les hommes*, pp. 156–7; Martin du Gard, *Jean Barois*, p. 216; Lacretelle, op. cit., pp. 21, 29 and 75–6; Verdès-Leroux, *Scandale financier*, pp. 126–7; Pierrard, op. cit., pp. 68–9, 89 and 110; and Rouquier and Soumille, "La Notion de Race chez les Français d'Algérie", pp. 6–7.
266 Drumont, *FJ*, I, pp. 103 and 232.
267 Drumont, *DB*, pp. 30–1 and 192–3.
268 Cit. Pierrard, op. cit., p. 110.
269 Halévy, *Degas parle*, pp. 43–5 (14 December 1890).
270 AN F⁷ 12453–12454.
271 Daudet, *Au Temps de Judas*, p. 17.
272 E.g. Rouquier and Soumille, op. cit., pp. 6–7.
273 Telegram, Prefect, Vaucluse, 21 January 1898. AN F⁷ 12467.
274 Cit. Drumont, *FJ*, II, p. 455.
275 Drumont, *DB*, p. 102.
276 Cit. Pierrard, op. cit., p. 89.
277 Animal epithets were used in nineteenth-century France of Catholics, and partic-ularly the Jesuits, and of the *communards;* see Sue, *The Wandering Jew*, Part I, p. 47; Part II, pp. 105 and 137; Part III, pp. 45 and 144; Vallès, *Le Bachélier*, p. 65; and Lidsky, *Les Ecrivains contre la Commune*, pp. 40–9 and 154–8; see also, for a contemporary Anglo-Saxon example, Frank Pearce, "How to be im-moral and ill, pathetic and dangerous, all at the same time: mass media and the homosexual", in Cohen and Young, eds, *The Manufacture of News*, p. 290; and, generally, C. W. Bardsley, *English Surnames; Their Sources and Significations* (London, 1889), pp. 486–98, on animal names as nicknames; and Edmund Leach, "Anthropological Aspects of Language: Animal Categories and Verbal Abuse", in Pierre Maranda, ed., *Mythology* (Harmondsworth, 1972), pp. 39–67.
278 Police reports, Rennes, 5 July 1899. AN F⁷ 12464.
279 Memmi, op. cit., pp. 211–12. The characterization of Jews as animals was not, of course, peculiar to French antisemites; see, for example, Rosenberg, *From Shylock to Svengali*, p. 35; and Mosse, *The Crisis of German Ideology*, p. 193.
280 Drumont, *FJ*, I, p. 317; see also p. 322, where Lyon and the department of the Rhône are said to be "infestés" with Jews.
281 Maupassant, *Bel Ami*, p. 374.
282 Paléologue, op. cit., p. 62 (16 November 1897).

283 Lacretelle, op. cit., p. 137.
284 See, in addition to references below, Drumont, *FJ*, II, pp. 420–1 and 463; and *DB*, p. 108; Bloy, *Le Salut par les Juifs*, pp. 26–9; Verdès-Leroux, *Scandale financier*, p. 125; and Sternhell, *Maurice Barrès*, pp. 240–1; and, for the general association of Jews with dirt and pollution, Wirth, *The Ghetto*, pp. 30, 34 and 42; Levinson, "The Study of Anti-Semitic Ideology", Adorno *et al.*, op. cit., pp. 63 and 98; Ackerman and Jahoda, *Anti-Semitism and Emotional Disorder*, pp. 26, 28, 47, 67 and 72; Lovsky, *L'Antisémitisme chrétien*, pp. 231–5; and Thomas S. Szasz, *The Manufacture of Madness* (London, 1973), pp. 244 and 345. See also the discussion of this theme in the Henry Subscription in chapter IV, pp. 153–6 above.
285 Drumont, *TA*, pp. 35 and 19.
286 Drumont, *FJ*, I, p. 95.
287 Ibid., II, p. 422.
288 Drumont, *TA*, p. 419.
289 Ibid., p. 419; also *FJ*, II, p. 455.
290 Drumont, *FJ*, II, pp. 498 and 422.
291 Ibid., I, p. 556.
292 Picard, op. cit., p. 46.
293 Daudet, *Les Oeuvres dans les hommes*, p. 115; also ibid., pp. 113–17, 122 and 126; and see pp. 473–4 above.
294 See Certeau, *La Possession de Loudun*, pp. 51–3.
295 Drumont, *DB*, p. 109.
296 Miss Costello, *Béarn and the Pyrenees* (London, no date-c. 1845), II, p. 276; also p. 328.
297 Drumont, *FJ*, I, p. 292.
298 Sue, *The Wandering Jew*, Part I, p. 55; and Part III, pp. 3–4.
299 E.g. Drumont, *DB*, p. 204.
300 Cit. Weber, *Satan franc-maçon*, pp. 79–80; also p. 55.
301 Drumont, *FJ*, II, p. 192.
302 See Rosenberg, op. cit., p. 26; Szasz, op. cit., pp. 324 and 326; Baron, *A Social and Religious History of the Jews*, XI, pp. 158–64; Lovsky, *L'Antisémitisme chrétien*, pp. 265–9; Weber, *Satan Franc-maçon*, pp. 54–5. On the general theme of poisoning in popular mentality, see Charles Mackay, *Selections from Extraordinary Popular Delusions* and *The Madness of Crowds* (1841–1852) (London, 1973), pp. 41–68.
303 See Sue, op. cit., Part III, pp. 51 and 61–4.
304 Drumont, *FJ*, I, pp. 174–7.
305 Ibid., I, pp. 452–3 and 455; and II, pp. 286–96 and 365–6; *DB*, p. 136; and *La Libre Parole*, 20 April 1892, cit. Lovsky, *L'Antisémitisme chrétien*, p. 270; see also Meurin, op. cit., p. 159.
306 Edmond and Jules de Goncourt, *Mémoires de la vie littéraire, 1879–1890* (Paris, 1956), III, p. 1165 (27 April 1890). The family of Gougenot des Mousseaux believed apparently that he also had been poisoned by the Jews, this time with fatal results; see Byrnes, *Antisemitism in Modern France*, p. 155. Moreover, Fernisoun, in Apollinaire's "Le Juif Latin" (March 1903), *Oeuvres complètes*, I, p. 123, tries to poison the narrator.
307 See Reinach, op. cit., IV, p. 553; and Steinheil, op. cit., pp. 117–18.
308 Lémann, op. cit., I, p. 8; and Daudet, *Les Oeuvres dans les hommes*, p. 163.
309 For examples from the 1940s in France, see Pierrard, op. cit., pp. 290 and 302; and from the 1960s, Revel, "Le Juif à la Vichyssoise" (8 May 1967), *Les Idées de notre temps*, p. 369. The image was also used in Nazi propaganda, and recurs in recent Arab propaganda against Israel; see Erikson, "Hitler's Imagery and German Youth", pp. 487–8; Lovsky, *L'Antisémitisme chrétien*, p. 235; Stern, *Hitler*, pp. 50–1; and Poliakov, *Les Juifs et notre histoire*, pp. 88 and 73.

310 Drumont, *DB*, p. 193; see also Weber, *Satan franc-maçon*, p. 15, quoting Huysmans.

311 Zola, *Au Bonheur des Dames*, pp. 252 and 433; see also Vallès, *Le Bachélier*, p. 86.

312 Prolo, *La Caverne antisémite*, p. 3.

313 See, for example, Foreword by Max Horkheimer and Samuel H. Flowerman to Ackerman and Jahoda, op. cit., p. v, where antisemitism is referred to as "a social disease" with "periods of quiescence" and of "virulence", and "outbreaks" like an epidemic; and Introduction to the same book by Carl Binger, p. xi, who compares antisemitism with tuberculosis, rabies and yellow fever, and the endeavours of the authors with those of Koch, Pasteur and Reed. The authors themselves describe antisemitism as "a symptom of social pathology" (p. 2).

314 Drumont, *FJ*, II, p. 133; see also Guinon, op. cit., p. 114.

315 Picard, op. cit., pp. 56 and 44.

316 Drumont, *FJ*, II, p. 421; also ibid., I, pp. 212, 339 and 343.

317 Daily Report, Prefect of Police, 14 February 1898. APP Ba 106.

318 Barrès, *Scènes et doctrines*, II, p. 30; and I, p. 213.

319 Drumont, "De Reinach à Vaillant" (28 July 1894), *De l'Or, de la boue, du sang*, pp. 266–7.

320 Drumont, *DB*, pp. 84 and 91.

321 Ibid., p. 506; see also *FJ*, II, pp. 275–6.

322 Drumont, *FJ*, II, p. 456; also ibid., II, p. 522; *TA*, p. 45.

323 Drumont, *FJ*, II, p. 466.

324 Drumont, *TA*, p. 76.

325 Cit. Dardenne, *Godefroy de Cavaignac*, p. 786.

326 Cit. Pierrard, op. cit., pp. 144–5.

327 Cit. ibid., p. 65.

328 Daudet, *Le Voyage de Shakespeare*, pp. 185–7.

329 See S. Ferenczi, "The Ontogenesis of the Interest in Money", *Contributions to Psycho-Analysis* (London, 1916), pp. 269–79; and Norman O. Brown, *Life against Death; The Psychoanalytic Meaning of History* (London, 1959), pp. 234–304. For further consideration of this and other sexual aspects of antisemitism, see chapter XV. The magical significance of excrement should also be noted here, and its importance as a theme in popular literature; see Dmitry M. Segal, "The Connection between Semantics and the Formal Structure of a Text", in Maranda, *Mythology*, pp. 247–248; and Mikhail Bakhtin, *Rabelais and His World* (Cambridge, Mass., 1968), pp. 146–52 and *passim*. Daudet is deliberately writing in Rabelaisian idiom.

330 See Mary Douglas, *Purity and Danger* (Harmondsworth, 1970 edition), chapter 6, and particularly pp. 124–5: "Witches are social equivalents of beetles and spiders who live in the cracks of the walls and wainscoting. They attract the fears and dislikes which other ambiguities and contradictions attract in other thought structures, and the kind of powers attributed to them symbolize their ambiguous, inarticulate status . . . [Jews are similar] Belief in their sinister but indefinable advantages in commerce justifies discrimination against them-whereas their real offence is always to have been outside the formal structure of Christendom." On Jewish marginality generally, see Wirth, op. cit., pp. 14, 36, 42, 91, and 128; Loewenstein, *Christians and Jews*, pp. 23, 55–6, 140 and 147–53; Braudel, *The Mediterranean*, II, pp. 808, 811 and 814–17; Memmi, op. cit., pp. 253, 279 and 378–9; Landau, "Aspects et problèmes spécifiques de l'histoire des Juifs en France", p. 232; Morin *et al.*, *La Rumeur d' Orléans*, pp. 48–9; and Stanley Rothman and Philip Isenberg, "Freud and Jewish Marginality", *Encounter*, 43, no. 6 (December 1974), pp. 46–54. The association of the Jews with witchcraft and the Devil is discussed in chapter XIV, pp. 543–51 below.

331 Drumont, *FJ*, I, p. 374; see also ibid., II, pp. 50 and 141; and *TA*, pp. 152–3.

332 Drumont, *FJ*, II, p. 412.

333 Ibid., I, pp. xviii and 316–17; also II, p. 467.
334 Ibid., II, p. 213.
335 See chapter X, n. 276.
336 Barrès, *Scènes et doctrines*, II, p. 161.
337 Drumont, *FJ*, I, pp. 451–2.
338 On the "purificatory" function of antisemitism generally, see Levinson, "The Study of Anti-Semitic Ideology", p. 95; Ackerman and Jahoda, op. cit., p. 58; Shils, "Authoritarianism: 'Right' and 'Left'," pp. 41–2; and, for other examples of the same ideological mechanism, see Cohen and Young, eds., op. cit., p. 341; Edgar Morin, *L'Homme et la mort* (Paris, 1970), p. 115; Barthes, "Soap-powders and Detergents", *Mythologies*, pp. 36–8; Ophuls, *The Sorrow and the Pity*, pp. 52 and 54; MacFarlane, *Witchcraft*, p. 243.
339 Vogüé, *Les Morts qui parlent*, pp. 424–25.
340 Sartre, op. cit., p. 50.
341 Blum, *Souvenirs sur l'Affaire*, p. 64.
342. On racialism as a general argument or justification for social "élitism", see Beauvoir, *Privilèges*, pp. 122–9.
343 Drumont, *DB*, pp. 183–4; and *TA*, p. 20.
344 Drumont, *La Fin d'un monde*, p. 403.
345 Drumont, "Barbès et Vaillant" (26 January 1894), *OBS*, p. 160.
346 Drumont, "Un anarchiste d'autrefois" (11 December 1893), *OBS*, p. 110.
347 As Louis Dumont has insisted, the assimilation of the term "caste" to the concepts of "race" or "class" can be misleading (see Dumont, "Caste, Racism and Stratification; Reflections of a Social Anthropologist", *Homo Hierarchicus*, Appendix, pp. 287–307); its use here, in a very loose sense, seems justified by popular usage.
348 "racisme intérieur", a term coined by Robert Lafont, *La Révolution régionaliste* (Paris, 1967), p. 207; see Liens, "Le stéréotype du Méridional", p. 9.
349 Choury, *Les Poètes de la Commune*, pp. 22–3; see also Chevalier, op. cit., pp. 519–31 and *passim*; Lidsky, op. cit., pp. 13, 80–5, 103–5, 110 and *passim*; Guillemin, *Présentation des Rougon-Macquart*, p. 36; Little, "Race and Society", p. 104.
350 Biétry, *Le Socialisme et les Jaunes*, p. 42.
351 "enracinement". An investigation into the origins and development of this still very popular concept would be of great value. Barrès, of course, derived it, in large part, from Taine. For a recent discussion, idealist in orientation, of Barrès's use of the concept, see Soucy, op. cit., chapter 3.
352 Drumont, *DB*, p. xvi. Note the similarity to the Lacretelle passage quoted in chapter X, p. 299 (n. 518).
353 Cit. Drumont, *TA*, p. 152.
354 See, for example, Louis Chevalier, *La Formation de la population parisienne au XIXe siècle* (Paris, 1950); Armengaud, *La Population française au XIXe siècle*, chapter 5; and chapter X, pp. 297–8 above.
355 Maurras, *L'Avenir de l'intelligence*, p. 17.
356 Drumont, *TA*, p. 45; see, for this general line of argument, Comas, "Racial Myths", *Race and Science*, UNESCO, p. 18; and Sartre, op. cit.
357 See generally on the marginality of antisemites, Adorno *et al.*, op. cit., chapter XIII, p. 485; Morin *et al.*, op. cit., p. 81; and Angus Stewart, "The Social Roots", Ionescu and Gellner, eds, *Populism*, pp. 180–1.
358 Drumont, *FJ*, II, p. 467.
359 See, for example, R.P. de Pascal, *La Juiverie* (Paris, 1887); and Sorlin, *"La Croix" et les Juifs*, pp. 143–7; see also chapter XII, p. 422 above.
360 Barrès, *Scènes et doctrines*, I, p. 159
361 Tocqueville, Letter to Gobineau, 17 November 1853. Tocqueville, op. cit., p. 227.
362 Drumont, *DB*, p. 30; see also *TA*, pp. 141 and 149.

363 On the concept of "Providence" and its functions, see Thomas, *Religion and the Decline of Magic*, chapter 4.

364 Chamson, *A Time to Keep*, pp. 129–30.

365 Leroy-Beaulieu, *Les Doctrines de haine*, p. 11.

366 Drumont, *La France juive devant l'opinion*, p. 203.

367 See chapter XVI, pp. 602–6 below.

368 The concept of "latent" and "manifest" functions derives mainly from Freud (see Freud, *Introductory Lectures on Psycho-Analysis* (1916–17), English Standard Edition, XV (London, 1963), pp. 113–25); but owes its formulation as a sociological tool primarily to Robert K. Merton, "Manifest and Latent Functions" (1948), in Merton, *On Theoretical Sociology; Five Essays Old and New* (New York, 1967), pp. 73–138.

369 See Tharaud, *Mes années chez Barrès*.

370 For example, J. and J. Tharaud, *L'Ombre de la croix* (Paris, 1917); *Un Royaume de Dieu* (Paris, 1920); *Quand Israël est roi* (Paris, 1921); *L'An prochain à Jérusalem* (Paris, 1924); *La Rose de Sâron* (Paris, 1927); and *Petite Histoire des Juifs* (Paris, 1927).

371 J. and J. Tharaud, *Quand Israël n'est plus roi* (Paris, 1933), p. 17.

CHAPTER XIV
RELIGIOUS ANTISEMITISM: "AMONG FRENCH CATHOLICS"

I

CONTEMPORARIES DISAGREED ABOUT THE IMPORTANCE OF THE RELIGIOUS motive in antisemitism. The Catholic critic Brunetière wrote in 1898: "I do not believe that one can really say . . . that much religious fanaticism enters into antisemitism: France is not religious enough for that . . ."[1] Drumont denied that his hostility to the Jews was religious in inspiration, and maintained, disingenuously, that he had always shown a proper respect for Judaism.[2] "It seems perfectly useless", he wrote in 1890, ". . . to repeat yet again that we have never waged a religious campaign against the Jews . . . We have never written or pronounced a single word against the religion of Israel . . . The Jewish question has never been, at any time, in any country, a religious question, but always and everywhere an economic and social question."[3] And he referred, as if to make his protest irrefutable, to the existence of anti-Jewish hostility in Islamic societies.[4] Such protestations, made on a variety of other grounds, were common on the part of antisemites. *L'Anti-Youtre* proclaimed, for example, in April 1892 that antisemitism "is not a question of religion; the Jew is of a race that is different from and the enemy of ours."[5] *La Libre Parole* launched an essay competition in 1895 on the subject of "Practical means to arrive at the destruction of Jewish power in France, the Jewish peril being considered from the racial and not the religious point of view."[6] Abbé Gayraud also emphasized the racial element in antisemitism, and insisted that it did not derive "from regarding the Jews as people of a different religion from ours, and one that was the declared enemy of Christianity . . ."[7] The 1895 Programme of the Jeunesse de l'Union Nationale protested similarly that its antisemitism was "the consequence of its patriotism, and did not represent the religious struggle of the Catholic against the Israelite, of the Church against the Synagogue, but the struggle against the Jew as the internal foreigner who could not be assimilated . . ."[8] Picard repeated the refrain in 1898: "Antisemitism is not a religious question", adding the interesting explanation that the religious interpretation of antisemitism "is so much cultivated for the reason that it provides an ideal means of representing every antisemite as a narrow-minded diehard wishing himself back in the Middle Ages."[9] Certainly, Maurras, who was anxious to give his conservatism a modern tone, vigorously rebutted in 1905, the suggestion "that our antisemitism . . . is a confessional or a clerical movement . . .";[10] and the same motive may have inspired similar denials from more traditional and Catholic conservatives, like the Royalist leader Buffet, or abbé Delassus.[11] Other antisemites even claimed that the idea that antisemitism was a religious phenomenon was invented and disseminated by the Jews. "The great ruse of Israelism", wrote Rochefort in 1898," has always been to transform what is a racial question into a religious one."[12] "It is really clever of the Jews to present things in this false light", explained Paul de Cassagnac; "it is an admirable way of concealing the real reasons for the violent antipathy which they encounter wherever they go . . . [and] it is a well-chosen means of gaining the sympathies of liberals."[13]

As many of these protests explicitly suppose, the contrary view prevailed among "liberals", and on the Left generally. The Radical politician Brisson referred to antisemitism in February 1898 as "the campaign undertaken to provoke religious hatreds".[14] Levasseur believed that "religious passions are an important motive in this agitation . . ."[15] For Yves Guyot "antisemitism is one of the forms of religious intolerance . . .",[16] an opinion with which Molinari concurred: "I consider this social malady to have its origins in religious intolerance."[17] The Socialist historian Zévaès wrote similarly that the origins of antisemitism in France were "exclusively clerical and feudal . . .";[18] while Zola characterized the movement as "the preaching of a new holy war . . . , an attempt to instigate a religious war, to return to the wars of religion, and to revive religious persecution . . ."[19] Herzl's view that modern antisemitism was a mediaeval throw-back made the same point less directly.[20] Adding a further element of explanation the syndicalist Pelloutier maintained, as we have seen, in a speech given in Paris in June 1898 that antisemitism represented a deliberate attempt to revive support for religion in France "in the face of the rising tide of Socialism . . ."[21] In the same general perspective, though from the other side, Claude Janiot, the main Catholic economist of the day, also stressed the religious motivation of the antisemitic movement, as a means of playing down its anti-capitalist implications.[22] And other Catholics adopted the religious interpretation of antisemitism, though for different reasons. In a lecture on "L'Antisémitisme" given in August 1898, Père Hyacinthe Loyson put the "liberal" view, and incidentally met Brunetière's objection to it:[23]

> The war declared on the Jews is not a racial war; it is a religious war, a war of religious fanaticism, that men of my generaation would never have believed possible. We find what we read in the newspapers incredible. A *religious war?* people ask, in this age of scepticism and indifference to religion? Yes, a religious war, for hatred survives faith, and often indeed is exacerbated as faith evaporates, that faith which at first was its justification.

As we shall see, moreover, in more detail, the denials of antisemites on this score were disingenuous in the extreme. Drumont, for example, despite his protestations, made continual attacks on the Jewish religion. He claimed that the Jewish drive to world-domination derived from the religious teaching of Judaism, and his use of the term "Synagogue" to designate the Jews was symptomatic of the general Catholic tone of his antisemitism.[24] More openly, Biez proclaimed that "the war against the Jews is a Holy War . . ."[25]

These disagreements on the part of contemporaries about the importance of the religious element in antisemitism can thus be explained in terms of differences of viewpoint and intention, and must not obscure the fact that the involvement of French Catholics in the upsurge of anti-Jewish hostility was unequivocal. "There is no doubt", wrote Duroselle, "that the majority of French Catholics were influenced by the anti-Jewish movement";[26] and his view is shared by the other historians who have studied the problem, Sorlin, Verdès-Leroux and Pierrard. According to Pierrard, "one can say that all types of Catholic, before 1914, were impregnated with antisemitism";[27] while Verdès-Leroux has referred to "the decisive part played by Catholics in the elaboration and the diffusion of antisemitism in France."[28] As we have seen in a previous chapter, Catholics were prominent in the ranks of the anti-Dreyfusards. As abbé Brugerette testified in 1904, it was accepted as axiomatic by most Catholics that "a Catholic could only be an anti-Dreyfusard . . . The prisoner on Devil's Island encountered in the ranks of Catholic orthodoxy a nearly unanimous opposition . . . in the course of this unfortunate Dreyfus Affair, the passions aroused by antisemitic hatred have led the Christian conscience into the most deplorable derelictions."[29] And with pride, rather than Brugerette's mixture of sadness, disappointment and indignation, Maurras declared in 1906 that "the immense majority of French Catholics, people and élites, the parish clergy and the bishops as well as thinkers and teachers, took sides, in fact, against the Dreyfusard anarchy, which, in threatening the Nation, threatened, indirectly, but no less certainly, the security of the Church."[30] Catholic anti-Dreyfusism was, as we shall see, only one example of Catholic antisemitism in the period, or indeed in the nineteenth century as a whole. Catholics had opposed Emancipation, and antisemitism was present in Catholic literature and sermons of the early and middle as well as the later parts of the century. Leading Catholic ideologues such as Bonald and Veuillot were overtly, if occasionally, antisemitic, while Gougenot des Mousseaux, one of the first systematic and single-minded antisemitic propagandists in France, was a Catholic who had been publicly honoured by the Pope.[31]

Catholic antisemitism in France, of course, had much deeper roots than these. As Clemenceau put it in a newspaper article in 1898: "The Jewish question in France has been entirely created by the clerical party, which derived it from the traditions of the Church."[32] Lazare referred to a traditional "collusion of Christianity" with antisemitism;[33] and Drumont himself pointed out that the Church "had for centuries struggled against the Jew, had defended Christian society against the corrupting tyranny of money, had protected the labour of all from exploitation by parasites and usurers."[34] The emphasis of Drumont, and of Maurras, on the Church as an institution is a significant one, to which we will return, but account must also be taken of the doctrinal motivation or justification for the Church's traditional hostility to the Jews. As J. Cohen wrote in 1864, "the Jews were, in effect, for triumphant Christianity a living and eternal objection. Through all their beliefs and their affirmations, they told the religion of Christ: 'You are a lie.' "[35] According to Rochefort in 1898, the Jews claimed that "the Christians persecute us because we do not accept the divinity of Christ".[36] What, more precisely, was the nature of this "theological" antisemitism, and what influence did it have on nineteenth-century French Catholics?

Investigating antisemitism in the United States in the 1960s, Glock and Stark concluded: "historically it is clear that the heart and soul of anti-Semitism rested in Christianity . . . certain attributions of Christian theology and teachings strongly predispose church members to hold hostile religious images of the modern Jew."[37] Closer to the French situation, Memmi agreed: "For many Christians, as one knows, the Jew possesses above all a particular theological character: his is a special destiny, culpable of, and, of course, condemned for various grave crimes, of which the most terrible is the murder of Jesus Christ."[38] As these modern comments indicate, Christianity, from its origins, had been inextricably involved with the Jews and with Judaism. Christianity was originally, in the words of Poliakov, "a dissident Jewish sect",[39] but, if Christianity owed its very existence to Judaism, it was also a rival to the older religion. "It was necessary for the Christians to prove that ancient Israel had lost favour in the sight of God and that Christianity was the true Israel. This blend of attachment and obligation to Judaism, on the one hand, and of resentment and revolt, on the other . . . has been typical of the Church's attitude towards Judaism."[40] Concomitantly, as the remarks of Cohen, and, more recently of Memmi remind us, "for the Jew who has not ceased to believe in and to practice his own religion, Christianity is the greatest theological and metaphysical usurpation in his history: it is a blasphemy, a scandal and a subversion."[41] But more was involved in Christian–Jewish relations than simple religious rivalry. The Jews and Jewish sacred texts were given an important place in Christian theology, and a definite doctrine on the Jews was worked out by the Early Church. The Jews had rejected the true Messiah; they were collectively responsible for the Crucifixion (Matthew, chapter 27; John, chapter 19); and, related to this, they were the agents of the Devil. For this heresy, this blindness, for the crime of deicide, they were eternally punished; their dispersion, their status of pariahs in Christian society, were divine punishment.[42] But, at the same time, the Bible, "the sacred texts of the Jews, and, by extension, the Jews themselves" provided Christianity with "authentification of its own message".[43] They were, paradoxically, "witnesses of the true Christian faith: their very existence was proof of the Gospels and their abasement proof of the triumph of Christianity."[44] Even their role as deicides was seen by St. Paul as necessary to the wider divine plan for human salvation. Moreover, according to St. Paul again, the Second Coming of Christ would depend on the conversion of the Jews.[45] The Jews thus occupied an important, crucial and paradoxical place in Christian theology and eschatology. They were the enemies of Christianity, deicides, heretics, agents of Satan, and, as such, were the objects of suspicion, contempt and persecution on the part of the Early and the Mediaeval Church; but they had, at the same time, to be protected and preserved, since their "continued existence", their ultimate conversion, were "necessary for the salvation of the Christian world".[46]

This is not the place, even were it possible, to trace the way in which this theological anti-Judaism was handed down, preserved, and developed, in Catholic tradition. Suffice it to mention that, while remaining present in official texts and in the liturgy, it received new expression, in France, in the writings of Bossuet and Fleury in the seventeenth century, writings that remained influential over the next two centuries,[47] and to say that reference to it, implicit and explicit occurs fairly frequently in nineteenth-century texts. Bonald, for example, opposed the Emancipation of the Jews in 1806, in these terms:[48]

> Those who voluntarily close their eyes to the light, and refuse to see anything supernatural in the destiny of the Jews, attribute the vices with which they are reproached solely to the oppression under which they have suffered, and, these people, following their own logic, wish the benefit of emancipation to precede the reformation of Jewish vices. But those who, on the contrary, see the Jewish religion as the root-cause of the degradation of the Jewish people and of the hostility which exists between the Jews and all other peoples, and who consider the misfortunes and even the vices of the Jews as the punishment of a great crime and the accomplishment of a terrible anathema, these people believe that the correction of Jewish vices must precede any change in their political state.

Pierre Leroux retailed the old theology with a more friendly intention in 1846;[49] and, in a lecture in 1883 on "The Original Identity and Gradual Separation of Judaism and Christianity", Renan assumed that his audience were acquainted with an orthodoxy which he then turned inside out: "the world became Jewish when it was converted to the laws of gentleness and humanity preached by the disciples of Jesus."[50]

Catholic antisemitic writers of the latter half of the century too, like Bonald earlier, referred, with varieties of emphasis, to the theological basis of the Church's anti-Judaism. Occupying an important place, for example, in the work of Gougenot des Mousseaux in the 1860s,[51] it was more incidental to the argument of Bishop Meurin, who wrote in 1893: "How strange this people of Israel is, compared with the rest of humanity! How great and majestic in its history, so long as it remained obedient to the Lord! How great also, and above all terrible in its hatred of the Messiah, whom it refused to recognize and whom it killed on the cross!"[52] Important here is the acknowledgment of the Church's role as protector of the Jews, which was made by abbé Lemire and Mgr d'Hulst among others,[53] and by Drumont himself. Without, it seems, fully appreciating the theological implications of such an admission, he claimed in 1890 that "without the Church, there would no longer be any Jews; the Jews of Europe would have disappeared like the Redskins of America."[54]

It is significant also that a writer like Picard, who denied the religious element in antisemitism, should have nevertheless pointed specifically to the paradox of the Church's attitude to the Jews, a paradox that could only be explained by reference to its doctrine of salvation. "By an astonishing aberration", he wrote, "at the same time that Aryan Christianity appropriated the sacred books of these Semites, idealizing their barbarous and crude contents, making its own the cruel and primitive history of this uncivilized tribe, it treated their descendants as the scum of humanity, confining them in special insalubrious quarters where they were locked in at night like wild beasts, refusing them civic rights or proper status, and periodically persecuting them in a pitiless manner."[55] Theological anti-Judaism also survived, in some form, in the myths of ritual murder and of the Satanic Jew, as we shall see, and also in the myth of the Wandering Jew.

Very different in its explicitness and its sophistication was the restatement and elaboration of the traditional Catholic theology vis-à-vis the Jews by Léon Bloy in *Le Salut par les Juifs* (1892). This text was an exegesis of John 4:22, "For salvation is of the Jews"; but it was also a polemical pamphlet directed against Drumont and what Bloy regarded as secular antisemitism masquerading as an expression of Catholicism. For Bloy, the Jews were deicides, the great collective sinners, but for this reason they remained, as they had been before the coming of Christ, the People of God. As instruments of Evil, of Satan, they were also "the instruments of Redemption" and agents of the Holy Spirit.[56] They were indeed outcasts in Christian society, hideous and repulsive, but this was the sign of their divine mission. The antisemites' image of the Jew was thus correct, but they mistook its significance, its meaning. In the plan of Redemption, the Jews had to be evil, until the end of the world. Like Christians, but "in a totally different way", the Jews "were condemned to bear the burden of the Cross . . . in the emptiness of their devastated souls . . . "; and their state of spiritual void, of abjection, "their disgusting aspect", were more telling testimony of mankind's ultimate salvation than Christians themselves could produce.[57] However different in kind from the "untheological" journalism of Drumont, Bloy's pamphlet in some ways simply brought into sharp focus vague assumptions that most Catholic antisemites had been making, and, far from weakening the force of "vulgar" Catholic antisemitism, as Bloy perhaps hoped, it can only have strengthened it and lent it legitimation. As Eve Grosjean has said, whatever Bloy's ultimate intention, his pamphlet was profoundly antisemitic in effect: "It is impossible for a Jewish conscience not to be painfully wounded by the constant use of insult which in *Le Salut par les Juifs* is the necessary prelude to Israel's accession to glory, but which deeply offends any sense of justice."[58] It is fair to add that the pamphlet was the work of an eccentric and was little read, though it was republished in 1906; and that Bloy later revised, or tried to explain his position more carefully. He wrote, for example, in *Le Pèlerin de l'Absolu* (1910) that in their treatment of the Jews, "the Christians have again crucified the Redeemer"; and in *Le Vieux de la montagne* (1911) that "antisemitism, which is a wholly modern phenomenon [itself a condemnation in Bloy's eyes], is the most horrible blow which Our Lord has received in the course of his Passion which still endures; it is the most painful and the least pardonable blow because he receives it on the face of his Mother and from the hands of Christians."[59] A similar neo-traditionalist restatement of the role of the Jews in Catholic theology can be found in the work of Claudel. Though both Claudel and Bloy may ultimately have been opposed to vulgar antisemitism, they both, as Jacques Petit has pointed out, took a wholly Christianocentric view of Jewish history, and refused to accept the idea of Jewish assimilation, since it interfered with the crucial role that Jews had to play, as a separate, if not a cursed and punished people, in the Christian view of salvation.[60]

It was Bloy's contention that the antisemites of his day were ignorant of the Church's traditional teaching on the role of the Jews, and, though they were aware of it in a vague and general way, it is true that most of them lacked any thorough or detailed grasp of the doctrine, only one instance incidentally of the general theological "illiteracy" of the Catholic laity and clergy at this time in France.[61] A crude example of this ignorance is the claim made by several antisemites that Christ was not a Jew. According to Picard, "Jesus is the opposite of a Semite, he is the typical Aryan."[62] The Protestant H. Monnier wrote in *La Mission historique de Jésus* (1906), less forthrightly, that "Jesus was not properly speaking a Jew; he was a Galilean, which is not the same thing";[63] while Biez, a Catholic, claimed that Christ was a Celt.[64] That such views were widespread among Catholics is indicated by the emphatic rejection of them by Mgr Hulst[65] and by Bloy who insisted that Christ was "the Jew par excellence",[66] and who stressed the crucial importance of the Jewishness of Christ for Christians by referring to the Redemption as "the boldest speculation that a Jew ever conceived . . ."[67]

A similar misunderstanding or ignorance of traditional Catholic theology was evident in attitudes towards Jewish conversion. While expecting Jewish "blindness" to persist and while placing the conversion of all Jews at the end of time, the Church had always taught that Jews could and ought to be converted to Christianity, and had, in the past, put considerable pressure on them to do so. As Glock and Stark have pointed out, this assumed that Judaism was an inferior, not to say false, religion, but it indicated also a belief that, as individuals, Jews were not indelibly wicked or different.[68] That such a belief in the possibility and the desirability of conversion could coexist not only, as was traditional, with the view that the Jews were being collectively punished for deicide, but also with a more conventional modern antisemitism, is demonstrated by the example of abbé Lémann, whose book *La Prépondérance juive* we have quoted from, and who was himself a Jewish convert.[69] But many antisemites did not allow that conversion was possible, let alone desirable. Drumont accepted the possibility of Jewish conversion in theory, but claimed that in practice it was always a pretence, citing the examples of the Marranos, of abbé Bauer, chaplain to the Empress Eugénie, and of the Portuguese Jews of Bordeaux who "conformed scrupulously to all the external practices of the Catholic religion . . . but, who after having lived thus for nearly 150 years, had remained as faithful to their old beliefs as on the day that they arrived. As soon

as it became opportune . . . they returned openly to Judaism . . .".[70] He
maintained also that "the idea of the conversion of the Jews at the end of time
is a tradition in the Church, but is in no way an article of faith."[71] Picard
abandoned the idea of religious conversion even more deliberately. For him,
it was "a mirage"; "There is the Catholic solution [to the Jewish problem]:
religious conversion! As if changing the religious cult he attends could modify
the real nature of the convert. His brain would not be altered; it would simply
have inside it foreign ideas that would never be at home there."[72] As Picard
makes quite explicit, conversion could have no place in a thoroughgoing racial
version of antisemitism.[73] But such considerations did not apply only to
non-Catholics. We have seen in the last chapter, the extent to which race
concepts had entered the mentality of Catholics like everyone else. Abbé
Demnise, for example, referred to the Jews as "that cursed race" in a collection
of popular songs.[74] Even Bloy in his supposed reassertion of traditional doctrine wrote of "the Race that is anathema . . .";[75] while Lacretelle's Silbermann declared: "The words of the Gospel came back to me: Unbelieving and
perverse race . . ."[76] The point is that such adoption of racial terminology by
Catholics encouraged them also to doubt whether the genuine and real conversion of Jews to the Christian faith was possible. Marie Colombier, for example,
in her fictional attack on Sarah Bernhardt, *Sarah Barnum*, emphasized that
the actress had been baptized as a matter of form, since she attended a convent
school, and wrote that "baptism had not destroyed in her the commercial
instinct inherent in her race."[77] Of relevance here is the fact that very little
Jewish conversion to Catholicism actually took place in nineteenth-century
France, there being, particularly after the establishment of the anticlerical
Third Republic, small incentive to convert from considerations of professional
advancement or social acceptability.[78] Had there been more conversion, the
Church's traditional position on the subject might have been less eroded by
other more fashionable dogmas.

   So far we have considered only the opinions of individuals vis-à-vis the
Church's traditional teaching on the Jews, but that teaching was more directly
and officially represented in the Catholic liturgy itself. This stressed the
desirability of conversion, but singled out the Jews in an invidious and hostile
manner. The Proper of the Season for Good Friday called on the faithful "to
pray also for the perfidious Jews, that the Lord our God may remove the
blindness from their hearts and bring them to acknowledge with us our Lord
Jesus Christ"; and this exhortation was followed by the prayer: "All-powerful
and eternal God, whose mercy has not been refused even to the Jews after
their perfidy, grant our prayers for the blindness of this people, that recogniz-
ing the light of your truth, which is Jesus Christ, they may be saved from their
darkness." Whereas prayers for all other categories in this liturgy: Church,
Pope, clergy, people, the sick, prisoners, widows, and even heretics and schismatics, were followed by Amens and were read while the congregation knelt
or genuflected, the prayer for the Jews had neither accompaniment. Kneeling
was not introduced here until 1956, and the word "perfidious" was not
removed until 1959. The Improperia, sung on Good Friday, and the words

of the Fifth Station of the Cross, moreover, made more explicit reference to the deicide theme.[79] The impact of this liturgical consecration of antisemitism, despite its being shrouded in Latin, is testified to by Bloy and by Barrès,[80] among others, and by Pierrard who wrote:[81]

> Jules Isaac was so right to fight for the abolition of the Good Friday ritual relating to the Jews. I can still feel the shock which was provoked in the long, rather droning succession of the Good Friday prayers, the sudden break which the prayer *Pro perfidis Judaeis* represented. While the six prayers which had gone before and the eighth and last one [for the pagans] were preceded by the words "Oremus Flectamus genua. Levate" which accompanied a collective genuflexion, the prayer for the Jews was deprived of this ritual accompaniment, something which obviously struck our young sensibilities. When I wish to imagine what is meant by a "moral ghetto", it is to the distress which this experience caused me that I refer.

Antisemitism was also present in certain local and unofficial Catholic rituals. Barrès told Drumont, for example, that "when I was a boy, I used to 'kill the Jew' . . . Your slogan: 'Down with the Jews!' does not shock me. We used to 'kill' them on Good Friday." This was a reference to the custom at Charmes of ending the Good Friday liturgy with a symbolic killing of the Jews by the choirboys, though other witnesses did not give the ritual this antisemitic interpretation.[82] A similar custom was still extant in Tunisia in 1900, by which Jewish children were beaten by Christian children during Holy Week, and antisemitism was also an important feature in the Passion plays performed there.[83] Though the origin of such customs is not clear, it seems probable that they were brought over by French settlers.

We have stressed the negative aspect of the Church's traditional anti-Judaism, since it was this aspect that nineteenth-century Catholic antisemites themselves stressed, but the positive aspect was also, if more tenuously, present. This is clear from the testimony of Mauriac, who wrote, looking back: "Our provincial antisemitism . . . was profoundly rooted in Christianity . . . [but] the Old Testament, filtered and presented to us in a particular way, complicated our fundamental racism." Jewish characters, like Tobias, Joseph, Esther, were lent a heroic status, and "Israel was a name that had a special resonance in my inner life."[84] And the same is true for Bloy and for Claudel. What this brings out again is the ambiguity in the relationship between Catholicism and the Jews, and it is that basic ambiguity, rather than simple hostility, which does much to explain the scope and the peculiarly passionate nature of Catholic antisemitism.

II

Whatever the influence of traditional theology, there is no doubt of the prevalence of antisemitism among French Catholics at the end of the century. Not only did members of the laity and the clergy express antisemitic opinions and belong to antisemitic organizations, but Catholic organizations and the Catholic press played an active role in the propagation of such opinions and in the general campaign against the Jews. As Léo Taxil wrote in the supposed Memoirs of Diana Vaughan: "In France . . . nearly all the Catholic militants are antisemites."[85] As we have seen, this antisemitism very often had a non-religious orientation, economic, social, nationalist or racialist, but specifically religious elements were also present in it. In particular, the accusations of deicide and the practice of ritual murder, and the old identification of the Jews with the Devil were maintained; while the Jews, together with the Protestants, freethinkers and Freemasons, were held to be responsible for the dechristianization of France. Here antisemitism had an important function in explaining the declining status of the Church in France and its dwindling popular support.

We have already encountered a great deal of evidence of the support which antisemitism enjoyed among Catholics in the 1890s and 1900s in particular. Catholics were prominently involved in the riots of 1898.[86] Two hundred declared Catholics and about 350 members of the clergy contributed to the Henry Subscription.[87] And such direct, quantitative indications can be supplemented by the declarations of individual antisemites and the comments of observers. Biez, for example, denounced Rothschild "because I am a Frenchman and a Christian".[88] Henry de France, a candidate in the 1898 elections for the 2nd *arrondissement* of Paris, told a public meeting that he was a Catholic "and therefore an antisemite".[89] Albert Réville referred in 1899 to "the aid and encouragement that antisemitism has found in the clerical world";[90] while Caillaux wrote that Drumont's writings enjoyed "an enthusiastic reception in the clerical world . . ."[91] Leroy-Beaulieu, himself a liberal Catholic, lamented in 1902 that so few Catholics had openly opposed antisemitism: "Some did not understand what antisemitism was; others did not dare to resist it. The anti-Jewish and anti-Protestant press exercised a veritable reign of terror over certain classes of the population, and particularly over Catholics and members of the clergy."[92] This rightly emphasizes the influence of the press, and especially the Catholic press, but, as the other quotations suggest, Catholic support for antisemitism was more positive and more active than Leroy-Beaulieu allowed, and particularly among the clergy.

Hertzberg has pointed out that the *Cahiers* of the clergy in 1789 indicated that "the overwhelming majority of the clergy, even some of the most literate among them, continued to hold to mediaevalist, anti-Jewish opinions . . ."[93] The Catholic clergy instigated or encouraged the antisemitic riots of 1832 in Alsace, partly as an objection to the law of 1831 making rabbis salaried officials like the Catholic and Protestant clergy.[94] Moreover, antisemitism is very evident in many of the writings of the Catholic clergy in the early nineteenth century, for example in abbé Desgarets's *Le Monopole universitaire, destructeur de la religion et des lois*, published in Lyon in 1843.[95] The antisemitism of the clergy later in the century was thus not unprecedented, although as the volume of evidence suggests, it does seem to have reached new proportions and to have become much more explicit. Charles Brunellière wrote in March 1900 that "the country clergy [of the Nantes region] are out and out supporters of antisemitism",[96] and it is certain that this phenomenon was not confined to the West. Henry Maret, an anticlerical, claimed in 1899 that "the clergy en masse" supported antisemitism,[97] and several Catholics agreed with him. Bloy, for example, proclaimed in *Le Salut par les Juifs:*[98]

> One has seen more priests than one can count—many of them, without a doubt, sincere servants of God—become enflamed by the hope of some imminent violent reckoning in which the blood of Israel will be spilt on a scale to glut all the dogs in France . . . The movement has been so sudden, the impulse behind it so compelling that, even today, none of them seem to have paused to ask themselves whether there is not the gravest danger for the soul of a priest in thus petitioning for the extermination of a people whom the Apostolic Roman Church has protected for nineteen centuries . . . and from whom have come the Patriarchs, the Prophets, the Evangelists, the Apostles, the early Disciples, all the early Martyrs, and, one hardly dares to add, the Virgin-Mother and Our Lord himself . . .

Less dramatically, with less exaggeration, representing liberal Catholic rather than neo-traditionalist opinion, Léon Chaine made the same charge a decade later: "Never . . . has so important a section of the French clergy been to such a point imbued, saturated, with antisemitism."[99] And that such views were widely held is indicated in other ways. For example, though denying the truth of the opinion, Paul de Cassagnac admitted: "It is . . . frequently claimed . . . that the antisemitic movement in France derives from religious fanaticism and intolerance, and that it is instigated by the Catholic clergy . . ."[100] Moreover, the antisemitic priest was a stereotype in popular fiction.[101]

Direct evidence confirms such subjective assessments, as we have seen in the case of the Henry Subscription. Five hundred members of the clergy attended the Antisemitic Congress held in conjunction with the Congress of Christian Democracy at Lyon in 1896;[102] and about the same number attended the Ecclesiastical Congress at Reims the same year, which, if only incidentally antisemitic in complexion, yet had well-known antisemites among its organizers.[103] In 1896 also, 25,000 members of the clergy were estimated to be readers of *La Croix,* and a smaller number acted as the newspaper's local correspondents and distributors.[104] The clergy were also prominent among the readers and supporters of Drumont and *La Libre Parole,* as we shall see in more detail below;[105] and priests played an important role in other antisemitic organizations. Leadership of the Union Nationale was provided in large part by members of the clergy; for example, of the 23 directors of its regional committees in 1898, only 4 were not ecclesiastics, and its parish committees, formally under lay presidents, were frequently controlled in fact by the *curé* or one of his *vicaires.*[106] Even the allegedly anticlerical Ligue Antisémitique Française often had priests among its supporters and organizers in the provinces.[107] Members of the clergy also made an important contribution to the antisemitic literature of the period, which included works by the abbés Chabauty, Lémann, Henry Desportes, Paul Barbier and Delassus, to some of which we have already referred. In a more popular vein, antisemitic songs were composed by abbé Demnise, whose collection *Poésies patriotiques* appeared in 1896, and by abbé Bouland, founder around 1890 of L'Oeuvre de la

Chanson Chrétienne Populaire.[108] Moreover, four priests were among the
prize-winners of the antisemitic essay competition sponsored by *La Libre
Parole* in 1895.[109]

All of this refers to the lower clergy, and such overt expressions of antisemitism were usually avoided and sometimes deprecated by the upper clergy,
whose circumspection was shared, Bernanos suggested, by Catholic notables
generally.[110] Mgr Coullié, Archbishop of Lyon, refused to take part in the
1896 Congress of Christian Democracy "because of the part played in it by
antisemitism and leading antisemites". Although the Catholic deputy Jules
Delahaye thereupon accused the French episcopate as a whole of being hostile
to antisemitism, this was not the case, for Mgr Coullié's disapproval of the
1896 Congress was offset by the blessings which it received from the Archbishops of Aix and of Chambéry, and from the Bishops of Bayeux, Grenoble,
Montpellier, Périgueux, Verdun and Versailles.[111] Leroy-Beaulieu commented in 1902:[112]

> Too many Catholics, too many members of the clergy, too many so-called
> religious newspapers have allowed the cause of the Church to be identified
> with that of antisemitism. The upper clergy, it is true, and the episcopate
> in particular, has not gone so far; it is too careful for that. The bishops rather
> have kept quiet; their prudence has taken refuge in silence; but this silence
> itself, with which the antisemites have sometimes reproached them, has
> been taken by others as the sign of a tacit acquiescence in antisemitism.

And the same judgment was delivered in 1904 by another Catholic opponent
of antisemitism, abbé Brugerette, this time with special reference to the
attitude of the bishops towards the Dreyfus Affair in its later stages:[113]

> No authorized voice was raised in the Church of France against these
> judicial monstrosities [particularly the Rennes verdict], whose iniquity was
> loudly denounced by Vaughan, Ireland and other foreign prelates. The
> universal silence of the French episcopate appeared as a crime to those who
> could not understand its prudence. The great moral authority which the
> Church represents was dumb . . . it did not protest, it did not wax indignant,
> when forgery, collusion and perjury combined in broad daylight to mislead
> the conscience of Christians.

As Pierrard has pointed out,[114] the silence of the French bishops on the Affair
stemmed largely from their adherence to the convention that they should
refrain from any involvement in politics, a convention insisted upon by the
Republican administration, and backed up by the threat of sanctions, and also
from the fact that, under the concordatory régime, bishops were usually
selected for their ability to compromise. But this would not altogether explain
their similar silence vis-à-vis the extremism of their own subordinates and of
the Catholic press. No member of the episcopate, for example, publicly disa-
vowed the antisemitic campaigns of *La Croix*, although the Archbishop of
Bourges and the bishops of Beauvais and Arras apparently made known their
disapproval to the editors privately.[115] Moreover, though most bishops ignored antisemitism, some were not so prudent.

To cite one example from earlier in the century, the bishop of Luçon, in a pastoral letter of 1849, attacked the appointment of Isidore Cahen as philosophy teacher at the *lycée* of Bourbon-Vendée, on the grounds that he was a Jew, and placed the chapel of the *lycée* under an interdict.[116] In the period that properly concerns us, we have seen that Bishop Meurin of Port-Louis (Mauritius), albeit only a colonial bishop, published an extreme antisemitic diatribe in 1893.[117] Bishops in France itself did not go so far, but many of them sanctioned or supported the antisemitic publications of their clergy. On the publication of his *Les Francs-maçons et les Juifs* in 1881, abbé Chabauty received letters of congratulation from 20 bishops.[118] Abbé Lémann's *La Prépondérance juive* (1889) received the *imprimatur* of Cardinal Foulon, then Archbishop of Lyon. Mgr Trégaro, bishop of Séez, congratulated abbé Desportes on his *Le Mystère du sang chez les Juifs* (1890), which retailed the charge of ritual murder, although, according to Drumont who made much of this episcopal encouragement, Desportes's own bishop, Mgr Thomas of Rouen dismissed him from his post in the seminary of the diocese for having written the book.[119] More significant than these individual and mainly private manifestations of support for literary antisemitism on the part of bishops is the fact that, as Verdès-Leroux has shown, nearly all the official diocesan bulletins of France, the *Semaines Religieuses*, were more or less antisemitic in the early 1890s. Only 15 of the 75 bulletins studied did not publish anti-Jewish articles, while 19 used racial terminology or gave credence to stories of ritual murder.[120] Bishops also lent their patronage, often in an indirect manner, to the organized antisemitic movement. The Archbishop of Tunis, for example, officiated at the funeral of the Marquis de Morès in 1896;[121] and the Union Nationale, whose antisemitism was fairly blatant, enjoyed the official backing of the Archbishops of Paris, of Reims and of Lyon, and of several other bishops. Of these Mgr Fava of Grenoble was probably most enthusiastic in his support, which was financial as well as moral.[122] Nor were all French bishops necessarily as neutral in the Dreyfus Affair as even their critics supposed. It is hard to believe that Mgr Turinaz of Nancy was alone in the praise which he lavished on Catholic anti-Dreyfusards in his open letter to the Protestant Paul Sabatier in January 1906: "It will be to the eternal credit of French Catholics of this time that not a single one has been found . . . who has lent his support to the traitors and who has not been thoroughly opposed and shocked by those who have denigrated the army."[123] The tone is patriotic, but the antisemitic implications of the sentiment must have been as obvious to the bishop and his readers as they were to abbé Brugerette.

The attitude of the French bishops towards antisemitism seems, to some degree, to have reflected the ambivalent attitude of the Holy See itself. Successive Popes condemned antisemitism on the theological level, although they did so from the stand-point of the Church's traditional anti-Jewish doctrine. Moreover, a legalized ghetto had been maintained in Rome until 1885,[124] which gave some kind of encouragement to those like Drumont who expressed admiration for the old legal controls on Jews imposed and sanctioned by the mediaeval Church.[125] In addition, several periodicals published in Rome were overtly antisemitic, and gave the impression that antisemitism had at least tacit Vatican approval. These included the Jesuit fortnightly *La Civiltà Cattolica*, which we have mentioned in previous chapters and to which we will return, and the official *L'Osservatore Romano*, which declared in January 1898: "Jewry can no longer be excused or rehabilitated. The Jew possesses the largest share of all wealth, movable and immovable ... The credit of States is in the hands of a few Jews. One finds Jews in the ministries, the civil services, the armies and navies, the universities and in control of the press ...", adding: "If there is one nation that more than any other has the right to turn to antisemitism, it is France, which first gave their political rights to the Jews, and which was thus the first to prepare the way for its own servitude to them."[126] This was not a direct expression of papal opinion or policy, although, as far as France was concerned, the papal position vis-à-vis Catholic antisemitism was so equivocal that some might have imagined that it was.[127] Pope Leo XIII, for example, apparently wrote a letter to the Governor-General of Algeria in 1898 condemning the antisemitic movement there,[128] but the move received little or no publicity; and two years earlier the same Pope had sent his blessing to the Christian Democratic Congress of Lyon, and rather than express any view on the antisemitic part of that Congress, he had simply omitted all reference to it in his message.[129] Leo XIII also gave his official support to the Union Nationale, one of the organizations involved in the 1896 Congress. *Le Peuple Français* received a letter of support from Cardinal Rampolla, then Secretary of State, shortly after its foundation, and the papal blessing was extended to the movement as a whole on the occasion of its Annual Congress of 1895, a favour renewed in 1896. Abbé Garnier was a frequent visitor to Rome in the 1880s and the 1890s, and seems to have had a close personal relationship with Leo XIII. These visits and private meetings continued later with Pius X. Leo XIII's support in particular was clearly motivated by the fact that the Union Nationale was an organization that was working to implement in France the social policy outlined in the Encyclical *Rerum Novarum* as well as the policy of Catholic *"ralliement"* to the Republican régime, but that support also gave sanction to the movement's antisemitism.[130] Two further examples of Vatican insensitivity to the way in which an antisemitic interpretation could be put upon its actions by antisemites and others may be mentioned. *Le Matin* reported in 1906, on the occasion of the final exoneration of Dreyfus, that Mgr Montagnini, representative of the Vatican in Paris, had noted as an indication of the "wrong spirit" among seminarists in France, their sympathy for Loisy and "Modernism", for disarmament, and for Dreyfus.[131] And some French Catholics welcomed the placing of the works of Bergson on the Index in June 1914 as an action taken against Jewish influence.[132]

Antisemitism seems to have been as strong, if not stronger, among members of the regular clergy in France. Anatole France accused the Assumptionists, the Dominicans and the Jesuits, of particular involvement in antisemitism and anti-Dreyfusism,[133] and there is considerable evidence to support his view. *La Croix*, the most important mouthpiece of Catholic antisemitism, was founded and run by the Assumptionists, and their publishing house, La Maison de la Bonne Presse, also produced many antisemitic pamphlets and posters, to which we have referred. In addition, the Assumptionists lent support and gave financial backing to the anti-Dreyfusard cause generally[134] and to other antisemitic organizations. Abbé Garnier had worked for *La Croix,* and the connection between it and the Union Nationale was a close one. Editors of *La Croix* were prominent in the leadership of the movement, for example at Lyon, Roanne and Grenoble, and they attended its congresses. There was also co-operation in the sponsoring of candidates in the 1898 elections, and the Assumptionists provided Garnier and his organization with important subsidies.[135] With such activities in mind, and concurring with the opinion of Republican anticlericals, an opinion which inspired the legislation of Waldeck-Rousseau and Combes, directed against all the religious orders, Bloy declared in 1900: "Ordinary, human, words are quite inadequate to assess and appreciate the degradation of the priestly office represented by these terrible monks."[136]

The Assumptionists were a modern order, whereas the Mendicants had a tradition of hostility to the Jews dating back to the Middle Ages.[137] However, it would be silly to assume that nineteenth-century Franciscans and Dominicans were especially aware of or influenced by this tradition, and it seems, in fact, that antisemitism was much rarer and much less extreme among members of these orders than it was with the Assumptionists. It had nothing either of the collective and semi-official status lent to Assumptionist antisemitism by the existence of *La Croix* and other publications of La Maison de la Bonne Presse. Nevertheless, Pierrard has noted that many of the tracts written between 1905 and 1914 for L'Association Franciscaine by Père Hilaire de Barenton, and recommended by the Catholic press as a whole, were antisemitic. Among the Dominicans Père Vincent Maumus was one of the rare Catholic Dreyfusards,[138] but Père Didon was prominent on the other side of the conflict. Despite this, however, and although he associated the Jews with money and a cash-orientated society in the manner of the antisemites, Didon actually opposed the antisemitic movement.[139] Another celebrated Dominican preacher, Père Monsabré, who preached regularly at Notre-Dame de Paris from 1872 to 1890,[140] was more whole-heartedly antisemitic, as Bournand was pleased to advertise in 1898. He told the journalist that "the Jewish element is a danger", but rejected proscription or physical violence as a remedy, on the grounds that both had proved unsuccessful. Instead, combining a kind of fiscal eugenics with the more traditional imperative of conversion, he suggested that a tax should be levied on marriages between Jews, and a financial reward offered to Jewish men who would marry Catholics and bring up their children in the Christian faith.[141]

Anatole France was not the only opponent of the Jesuits to accuse them of being peculiarly antisemitic. Henry Maret, editor of *Le Radical,* declared in 1898: "Antisemitism is simply an *invention and the revenge of the Jesuit party.* The Jesuits, so unpopular, have tried very skilfully to deflect the wave of unpopularity aimed at them against the Jews."[142] Jacques Prolo announced similarly in 1902: "Today, the Jesuits are setting in motion their new weapon, antisemitism";[143] and Prolo, Arnoulin, Guérin and Reinach all claimed that Drumont was an agent or a stooge of the Society of Jesus.[144] As we shall see, this particular claim can almost certainly be discounted, but there is no doubt of Jesuit support for antisemitism in general. Drumont, himself, pointed out that "the Jesuits have always avoided the Jews like the plague" and that Jews were formally banned from entering the order,[145] a ban not lifted until 1946.[146] Arnoulin alleged that Gougenot des Mousseaux had been praised for his book by Père Voisin in 1869;[147] and Jesuits contributed to the antisemitic literature at the end of the century. Bishop Meurin was a Jesuit, as was Père Constant, author of Les Juifs devant l'Eglise et devant l'histoire (1897). Such individual contributions from members of so disciplined an order are significant, but even more weight attaches to the antisemitism of Jesuit periodicals. As we have seen, the order's Italian organ, La Civiltà Cattolica, gave voice to an extreme antisemitism;[148] and the French organ, Etudes, published admiring reviews of antisemitic works as well as antisemitic articles of its own.[149] On the level of action, Jesuits, according to Reinach and others, made an important contribution to the anti-Dreyfusard campaign;[150] and, more certainly, they gave support to the Union Nationale, for example in Paris and at Grenoble.[151]

Examples of antisemitism can also be found among other orders, not singled out by France. The Oratorians, and their supporters in the press, made much, in their dispute in 1890 with Cardinal Place, Archbishop of Rennes, of the charge that he was a Jew.[152] The Sub-prefect of Mayenne reported, in December 1897, that a Catholic procession in the town of Villaines-la-Juhel had stopped outside a house that was not decorated for the Christmas season, and that Père Thiriet of the Oblats de Marie-Immaculée, who was leading it, then declared to his followers: "That house must be inhabited by Jews . . ."[153] According to Mayeur, Père Dehon, Superior of the Prêtres du Sacré-Coeur, was an active antisemite;[154] while Pierrard has testified to the violent anti-Dreyfusism of the Frères des Ecoles Chrétiennes.[155] The probable reasons for the intensification of antisemitism among the clergy, and indeed among Catholics generally, at the end of the century will be discussed below, but some indication can be given here of the special factors that may help to explain the antisemitism of the religious orders. Drumont claimed that they were the main targets of the Jewish attack on the Church, in great part because they represented a type of social institution that was thoroughly "alien and opposed to the [Jewish] values of speculation and money-making".[156] This claim reflected the undoubted fact that the religious orders were the main targets, not of the Jews, but of the anticlerical legislation of the Third Republic, and that they thus represented the body in the Church most likely to feel persecuted, and to seek a comforting explanation for the hostility displayed towards them. They were also, like army officers but more so, a group removed from normal society, and prone therefore to irrational and conspiratorial modes of social explanation.

The antisemitism of the clergy is clearly the most important aspect of

Catholic antisemitism, since the clergy were the guides and mentors of the laity. Significant here is the fact that many Catholic organizations, national and local, were overtly and actively antisemitic, for such organizations were usually run by the clergy for the laity, though some had an independent lay leadership, like de Mun's Oeuvre des Cercles Catholiques d'Ouvriers.[157] A wide variety of organizations can be included under this heading, though they were not all involved in antisemitism to the same degree. The groups of La Jeunesse Catholique, for example, in the 4th *arrondissement* of Paris and at Saint-Germain-en-Laye, actually called themselves La Jeunesse Catholique Antijuive;[158] and, as we have seen, some of the antisemitic organizations of small-traders were formed under Catholic auspices; while some groups of Catholic workers were antisemitic.[159] Other, local, antisemitic organizations of Catholics included La Société Saint-Yves at Rennes,[160] France d'Abord at Armentières, founded in July 1900, and Les Chevaliers de La Croix at Valenciennes, one of several groups in the Nord, formed to distribute material put out by the Assumptionist Bonne Presse.[161]

Antisemitism thus appealed to groups that differed greatly in scope and importance, and in social complexion, and it was also a characteristic which was shared by Catholic organizations right across the spectrum of political and religious opinion, from Right to Left. Reinach commented that "the Catholic Right as a whole, impenitent monarchists and those who 'rallied' to the Republic, were more or less infected with antisemitism . . ."[162] We have seen the degree to which the Royalists were antisemitic,[163] and, as Reinach suggests, the *"ralliés"* were no less so. Firmin Faure, former antisemitic deputy for Oran, for example, became a member of Piou's Action Libérale; and the annual Congress of the movement was addressed in 1905 by Gaston Méry.[164] A police agent reported the same year that "the tactic of the antisemites just now . . . is to mark time behind the banner of the Action Libérale",[165] a tactic that could scarcely have been conceived had not that banner been in some way appropriate. And the indications are that the Action Libérale was not simply a refuge for militant antisemites after 1905, but that it shared and propagated their opinions. The diocesan Congress of Nevers, for example, in 1907, declared its support for the Alliance Libérale, which seems to have been an alternative label, and one speaker described it as "an organism that was marvellously suited to create, uphold and develop everywhere institutions destined to counter the deadly enterprises of the Jews, of Freemasonry and of Socialism, and to give France back to the French, and restore its ancient honour, together with prosperity and social peace."[166] Parallel on the political spectrum to extreme political conservatism, and usually overlapping with it, was Integral Catholicism, a somewhat inchoate movement of Catholics dedicated to resisting any change in the traditional attitudes and practices of the Church. As Pierrard and Emile Poulat have recently shown, this movement also was to a high degree antisemitic. Mgr Delassus, for example, the author of several antisemitic books and editor of *La Semaine Religieuse de Cambrai*, was also an ardent Integral Catholic.[167] Mgr Benigni, founder in 1909 of the Sodalitium Pianum or La Sapinière, an important "Integrist" secret society, was a convinced antisemite and a believer in ritual murder.[168] More significant than these important individual cases was the antisemitic tone of the many "Integrist" reviews, for example, *La Vigie* (1912–14), edited by abbé Paul Boulin; *L'Idéal* (1909–11), organ of the Ligue de la Communion Fréquente et Quotidienne; *L'Assaut,* founded in 1906 by Hervé de Ranville of *La Libre Parole* and a member of the Action Française; and *Le Bloc Catholique,* founded at Toulouse in 1902, and which had close links with both *La Croix* and the Action Française. According to Félix Lacointa, writing in *Le Bloc Catholique* in March 1906, Freemasonry was "inspired and directed by the Jewish race, that parasitical and vampire race, always and everywhere scorned and shunned, that wandering race, witness over the centuries of the curse which weighs upon it . . . The Church of Satan is incarnated in the Jewish race . . ."[169] This gives some idea of the way in which antisemitism fitted into the neo-traditionalist and "irrational" mode of Catholicism represented by the Integrist movement. Significant also is the close association of Integral Catholicism with the "Integral Nationalism" of the Action Française.[170] Antisemitism persisted in both movements after it had declined elsewhere.

Antisemitism was also evident in the related Social Catholic and Christian Democratic movements, which both emphasized the duty of Catholics to concern themselves with the "social question" and to try to alleviate the condition of the working classes. The conservative and paternalistic Social Catholic movement dated from the early nineteenth century. Christian Democracy, though it could claim Lamennais as a precursor, was essentially a movement of the 1890s, and was more directly inspired by the Encyclical *Rerum Novarum* of 1891.[171] Pierrard has written that "nearly all the Social Catholics were, at one time or another, either provisionally or definitely, antisemitic."[172] We have seen, for example, that the Comte de Mun was an active anti-Dreyfusard.[173] Another leader of the movement, Léon Harmel was, according to Rollet, "very hostile to the influence of the Jews", and the Cercle Saint-Rémi, a Catholic workers' club under his auspices, called in 1895 for Jews to be deprived of French citizenship.[174] Again, at the 15th Congrès des Jurisconsultes Catholiques, a body that was Social Catholic in orientation, held at Angers in 1889, resolutions were passed by which members promised not to marry Jews, never to read Jewish newspapers and to abstain from commercial relations with Jews. The General Assembly of the Catholiques du Nord et du Pas-de-Calais of 1895 and the Congrès National Catholique held in Paris in December 1898 both proposed a similar boycott of Jewish businesses.[175] Among Social Catholic writers who were overt antisemites, Pierrard cites the very influential La Tour du Pin, whose study "La Question Juive et la Révolution sociale" appeared in 1898 in *L'Association Catholique,* the organ of the Oeuvre des Cercles Catholiques d'Ouvriers, and which was republished in a book, *Vers un ordre social chrétien,* in 1907. La Tour du Pin not only attacked Judaism as a religion, but also alleged that the Jews dominated the world economically through the medium of liberalism, and thus called for the restoration of the corporative system and for the treatment of

Jews as foreigners.[176] Pierrard also quotes from an article by Paul Lapeyre, which appeared in *La Sociologie Catholique* in mid-1898, and which claimed[177] that

> the misfortunes of the Jews are simply the just punishment of their abominable actions. The repression of which they are victims, indeed, in no way matches the enormity and the number of their crimes. What is the massacre of a few thousand Jews in comparison with thousands of Christians reduced to dying of hunger or poverty, or *prevented from being born* by the usury, the exactions and the swindling of the Jews? If, for every Christian whom the Jews have prevented from living, a Jew had been put to death, the devilish knife of the Talmud would long ago have disappeared from the face of the earth.

This could hardly be more extreme, and we will return to some of the sentiments which it expresses. Among the clergy associated with Social Catholicism was Mgr Delamaire, Bishop of Périgueux and later Archbishop of Cambrai, who declared in 1902 that the Jews were particularly opposed to "the social influence of the Gospel . . . they want to be left alone to crush the poor with intolerable burdens."[178] One can see here, as in the case of La Tour du Pin, how antisemitism fitted into the Social Catholic critique of the laissez-faire economy, which was identified very generally, as we saw in chapter X, with the Jews. And the same consideration inspired the particular appeal of antisemitism for the Christian Democratic movement.

As we have seen, the Antisemitic Congress of Lyon in 1896 was organized by the Christian Democrats, and abbés Gayraud, Lemire and Garnier sat on the platform of the Congress alongside Drumont and Guérin, who made a speech advocating the expulsion of the Jews from France and the hanging of the Rothschilds.[179] Resolutions passed at the Congress called, more moderately, for the exclusion of Jews from the army, the magistrature and the civil service, and for the creation of an "antisemitic information agency".[180] Antisemitism was also a theme in the discussions at the subsequent 1897 and 1898 Lyon Congresses of Christian Democracy, though no separate antisemitic sessions took place. The "professional" antisemites were not invited in 1897, but Guérin, Lasies and Magallon attended in 1898.[181] Abbé Gayraud, an ex-Dominican, deputy for Finistère from 1897 to 1911, was the author of *L'Antisémitisme de Saint Thomas d'Aquin* (1896) and later a fervent anti-Dreyfusard like nearly all the Christian Democrats. He gave a paper at the 1896 Congress on "Christian Morality and the Jewish Preponderance", published in *Le XXe Siècle* in January 1897, in which he declared: "The Jew is the enemy of Christ; the Jew is the enemy of Christian France"; and in an earlier publication, *Le Devoir des Catholiques français au moment présent* (1892), he had denounced "the anticlericalism of the Jews and the Freemasons".[182] Abbé Lemire, deputy for Hazebrouck from 1893, later maintained that he was not involved in "the antisemitic agitation", although he claimed paradoxically to be fighting "what is commonly known as Jewry".[183] Other leading Christian Democrats of pronounced antisemitic tendency included

Père Dehon, abbé Desportes, abbé Six and, of course, abbé Garnier.

Père Dehon (1843–1925) was the Superior of the Prêtres du Sacré-Coeur, as we have seen, and attended all three Lyon Congresses.[184] He was also the author of two of the most successful statements of Christian Democratic ideas in book form, *Manuel social chrétien* (1894) and *Catéchisme social* (1898). Some quotations from the latter will indicate how antisemitism served the related concerns of Christian Democrats to reverse the trend of dechristianization and to redress the "injustices" of the capitalist economy.

> The Church has no hostility against Jews individually. She prays for them and desires their conversion, but she cannot mitigate her basic suspicion of them. The Jews have retained their hatred of Christ, and, as a result, they are inclined to combat the action of the Church everywhere. They give aid and encouragement to all the enemies of the Church; and it is not surprising to see them supporting the secret societies. The Church distrusts them particularly from the economic point of view: they are nearly all adherents of the Talmud, in which they find economic principles of a very particular kind . . .

"In the centuries of faith", Christian society had defended itself against Jewish influence by means of special laws; since these laws had been abolished, Christian society "had been invaded and was now dominated by the Jews, which is a proof among a thousand others of the interest that nations have in following the direction of the Church". The modern reaction against Jewish influence was therefore to be welcomed, though it had sometimes been too violent: "It is certain that the Jew and the Christian are not equally armed for the struggle, since the Talmud frees the Jews from moral restraints in their dealings with Christians. To restore the balance, it is thus necessary to impose certain restrictions on the liberty enjoyed by Jews."[185]

We have already encountered abbé Desportes as the author of *Le Mystère du sang chez les Juifs* (1889), a book which, in addition to earning the commendation of at least one French bishop, was also apparently well received by Cardinal Rampolla in the name of the Pope. With Charles Pontigny, abbé Desportes launched a monthly in 1890, called *L'Alliance Antijuive*, whose declared aim was to act as "an organ of publicity, a guide, a liaison agency and an arsenal for all those who consider the Jew to be the destroyer of our French society and the most implacable enemy of the Catholic religion." *L'Alliance Antijuive* disappeared in 1892, but Desportes replaced it in January 1893 with another monthly, *La Terre de France*, in which he defended rural interests and values, and lent his support to the newly-founded Ligue Française du Coin de Terre et du Foyer, whose aim was to stem the exodus of population from the countryside to the towns.[186] The programme of abbé Six and his periodical *La Démocratie Chrétienne* included: "The fight against Masonic and Jewish domination and the abrogation of the 1791 decree in favour of the Jews [i.e. the Emancipation decree]".[187] Some Christian Democratic leaders, as we have seen in the case of abbé Lemire, expressed reservations about the antisemitism on which others placed so much emphasis. Abbé Dabry, for example, criticized abbé Delassus in print for his extremism in this and other spheres, although Dabry himself was not free of antisemitism. The least antisemitic of the *abbés démocrates* was abbé Naudet, who attacked Drumont and Cassagnac in his periodical *La Justice Sociale*, and who tried to remain neutral in the Dreyfus Affair.[188]

We must now consider, in more detail, the case of abbé Garnier, editor of *Le Peuple Français* and founder of the most important politically-orientated "Christian Democratic" organization, the Union Nationale, though a good number of Christian Democrats did not recognize it as such.[189] The Union Nationale was founded in the early 1890s, and included a very wide variety of institutions, friendly societies, co-operatives, clubs, clinics, community centres, study groups, youth groups, as well as local sections engaged in political activity and electioneering, all co-ordinated by a central committee in Paris. By 1898, *comités* of the Union Nationale existed in 35 departments and in all but two *arrondissements* of Paris, and in 1900 their total number was put at 280. Total membership of the organization at this time was probably around 12,500. The general aim of the Union Nationale was to rechristianize France by preaching and implementing the social message of the Gospel, and by accepting and working within the framework of the Republican régime. It was thus responding directly to the Encyclical *Rerum Novarum* and to the papal policy of *"ralliement"*, but, in each case, as we have argued elsewhere, its aims were, to a considerable degree, offset and its efforts frustrated by the persistence inside and outside the movement of older attitudes. It proved very difficult to break with the Church's old association with the political Right, and, in the Catholic perspective, no really cogent analysis or thoroughgoing critique of "capitalist" society proved possible.[190] These contradictions help to explain the Union Nationale's very pronounced involvement in antisemitism.

This involvement dates from the movement's origins, before the Dreyfus Affair brought antisemitism into new vogue. As we have mentioned, between 1888 and 1893, abbé Garnier worked for *La Croix*, and he retained a close association with the Assumptionist daily. Friendly relations also existed with Drumont and *La Libre Parole*. A police agent reported of Garnier in 1893: "he willingly declares that he and M. Drumont are in complete agreement."[191] The Union Nationale's electoral programme for Paris in the same year had as its epigraph the slogan of Drumont's paper: "France for the French", and linked its opposition to divorce and to Socialism to the fact that both were allegedly the work of Jews.[192] *Le Peuple Français*, Garnier's daily founded in 1893, was also clearly antisemitic from the start, calling in one of its first issues for the reversal of the Emancipation of French Jews.[193] Dagan described the paper in 1899 as one of the principal organs of antisemitism in France, along with *La Libre Parole* and *La Croix*,[194] and it amalgamated with *La Libre Parole* in 1910.[195] Despite occasional disagreements, the Union Nationale maintained close links with Drumont and his newspaper through the 1890s and early 1900s.[196] Moreover, in 1898, the movement supported and collaborated with deputies belonging to the antisemitic parliamentary group.[197] A further indication of the Union Nationale's emphatic commitment to antisemitism was its very close association with the Ligue Antisémitique Française. The Ligue claimed at times to be anticlerical, and, as we have seen, it became a political ally or tool of the Royalists,[198] two things that might have been expected to repel rather than attract the ostensibly Catholic and Republican Union Nationale. However, the latter's central committee accepted in February 1898 that the Ligue and the Union Nationale had "many things in common", and authorized a delegate to attend the meetings of its fellow-organization.[199] This was followed up by close collaboration between the two groups in the May 1898 elections in Paris.[200] In September of the same year the *comité* of the Saint-Ambrose parish in Paris was said by the police to be "under the virtual control of the Ligue Antisémitique"; and a similar overlapping of the two organizations was also reported in the provinces, at Roanne, where the local section of the Ligue Antisémitique was founded by members of the Union Nationale, and at Grenoble, where "the Ligue Antisémite and the Union Nationale have amalgamated . . ."[201] In a speech at Troyes in February 1899, Garnier referred to the "entente" that existed between the Union Nationale and the Ligue; while a Paris meeting of the former in April 1900 concluded with shouts of: "Down with the Jews! Long live Guérin!"[202] Very close links existed also between Garnier's movement and La Jeunesse Antisémite, whose leader Dubuc was a member of the Union Nationale.[203] The Union Nationale, in effect, was largely "directed against the Jews", in the words of a police agent, or, as Garnier told the regional congress of Beaujeu in 1896, it was "a league against the Jews [and their allies]."[204]

This was reflected more directly, as the many examples cited in previous chapters indicate, in the propaganda put out by the Union Nationale, and, most obviously, in its calls for the exclusion of Jews from public employment in France, for the withdrawal of full rights of citizenship from them and their treatment as "suspect foreigners", and even for their expulsion from France.[205] The movement insisted that its motives here were not religious. The 1895 Programme of La Jeunesse de l'Union Nationale proclaimed, as we have seen, that "its antisemitism was not the religious struggle of the Catholic against the Israelite, of the Church against the Synagogue, but the struggle against the Jew as the internal foreigner . . ."[206] However, the Union Nationale's nationalism was inseparable from its conception of Catholicism, as its name suggested,[207] and there is considerable evidence, as one would expect, of a specifically Christian element in its hostility to Jews. "In its fight against Jewish influence", affirmed La Jeunesse de l'Union Nationale again in 1897, "the French people have everything to gain from having as their leaders a majority of Catholics . . .",[208] sentiments, we have seen, that Père Dehon also voiced. The same view was expressed by a Union Nationale speaker at Roanne in 1899: the Jews, he said, were "the irreconcilable enemies of Christians", and he concluded "by urging all true French people and particularly all Catholics to unite against the Jews."[209] This same association of Catholic interests with antisemitism was assumed by another speaker in Paris in 1898:

"De Massue said that it was essential this year for all Catholics to join with the Union Nationale in order to make the Joan of Arc demonstration as imposing as possible, and thus protest against this Jewish campaign which is dishonouring France [i.e. the campaign to reopen the Dreyfus case]."[210] Similarly, Turquet delivered a speech in Paris in March 1900, in which he recommended "religious principles and sentiments as the only basis for national dignity", and, in the next breath, denounced "the odious campaign of the Jews, the Protestants and the Freemasons, who are running the government . . .",[211] a reference to the legislation passed by the Waldeck-Rousseau government to control the religious orders. From another angle, Catholic antisemitism was given the ultimate legitimation by an abbé Couget, who claimed, at a meeting of *comité* presidents in May 1899, that Christ himself had been an antisemite, since "he had driven out the Jews of his time . . ."[212] The explicit motive for this confessional antisemitism was the conviction that the Third Republic's anticlerical legislation was mainly inspired by the Jews: "if Catholics have seen Parliament pass laws that are veritable declarations of war against them, whose fault is it?", asked Garnier. "Who was responsible for the abominable divorce law? A Jew, Naquet. Who was the first to throw the crucifix out into the street? Hérold the Jew. Who dreamed up *lycées* for girls? Sée the Jew."[213] Like other antisemites, members of the Union Nationale here saw the Jews as the ringleaders of a wider conspiracy, that included the Freemasons, the Protestants and Left-wing politicians generally, and these other elements were included in their attacks. An anti-Masonic petition was organized by the Union Nationale in 1899, for example, and accumulated 170,000 signatures.[214] Antisemitism thus served, in conjunction with other themes, to explain anticlericalism as an external conspiracy of hostile forces, thus playing down the implications of the diagnosis that saw it as a reaction to political stances taken by the Church, and an outcome of the Church's failure to meet the problems of modern society. The Union Nationale sought to make good Catholic shortcomings in both related areas, but, caught in the impasse of *Rerum Novarum,* and blocked by yet more traditional attitudes, it could not envisage fundamental change. Antisemitism provided an outlet for its frustration here, and an explanation for its failure. Indirectly, too, as we have already suggested, and as we shall argue on a wider front later, the Judeo-Masonic conspiracy accounted for the steady progress of dechristianization in a way that avoided thoroughgoing questioning and relieved the Church itself of responsibility.

On the secular level, similarly, the Union Nationale acknowledged the existence of a "social question", but could not provide or allow any radical solution to it. Here again, antisemitism furnished both an explanation for the existence of that "social question", and a means of meeting it, which headed off any more revolutionary outcome. Modern society was typically characterized as "capitalist", as dominated by money and material interests, and was thus inimical to the Christian religion. Christ, according to Garnier, "revolted against the adoration of the Golden Calf and the power of money . . ."[215] "Capitalism", moreover, was seen as a system that exploited the workers, and it was identified with the Jews, as we saw in an earlier chapter. Billiet, for example, in a speech delivered in Paris in 1898, denounced "the Jews and the capitalists", and pointed to "capital as the cause of the present misery of the worker . . .", words which "provoked applause and loud shouts of: Down with the Jews!"[216] But if antisemitism was the vehicle for an attack on the evils of "capitalism", it also had the equally important function of exposing Socialism as a fraud. From the early 1890s, Socialism was identified with the Jews in Union Nationale, as in other antisemitic, propaganda, and was thus shown up as an attempt to divide French society and to manipulate French workers in the interests of their worst exploiters.[217] The particular hostility which the Union Nationale displayed towards Socialism is doubly significant here. As a Catholic organization, it was doctrinally bound to defend the institution of private property, following the Church's teaching on the subject, recently restated in *Rerum Novarum;*[218] and anyway its main support came from small property owners. As a Christian Democratic or Social Catholic organization, that is a radical element in the Church, it had to make it especially plain to fellow-Catholics that it had no truck with a movement that was regarded as atheist and anti-Christian. This illustrates the general dilemma of the Union Nationale, and of the tendency which it represented, and helps to explain the appeal which antisemitism had for it. Committed to the existing social order, though anxious to alleviate its incidental brutalities, the Union Nationale was nevertheless convinced that that order was threatened, probably beyond help, by fundamental change or collapse at the hands of godless and revolutionary forces. Antisemitism provided some kind of explanation for this apparent state of affairs; it also complemented the call for a return to the faith and for an expansion and remodelling of charity with a theory and a plan of action that seemed to go beyond these remedies, that seemed to offer more direct and more total contact with the real social world, while at the same time keeping other-worldly options open.

But this is to anticipate the general discussion of the function of antisemitism for Catholics, and before embarking on that we must complete our survey of the scope and incidence of Catholic antisemitism. The general involvement of the Christian Democratic movement in antisemitism is already very clear from our examination of the attitude of its leading figures and of the Union Nationale, but it can be illustrated further in other ways. Confirming the impression that we have already gained from examples cited, Montuclard concluded from his study of the Christian Democratic press: "Periodicals, linked with the movement, like *Le Peuple Français, La Voix de la France, L'Observateur Français, La Terre de France, Le Peuple Ardennais* . . . campaigned fairly violently against the Jews, the race of Iscariot. A solid monthly like *La Sociologie Catholique* rejoiced, in April 1897, at the fact that antisemitism has finally emerged as a real force in France. *La Justice Sociale, La Démocratie Chrétienne, Le XXe Siècle,* among others, were not so carried away by the prevailing hysteria, but they did not escape its influence either . . ."[219] To these papers and reviews should be added the Lyon weekly, *La France Libre,* which ran from 1893 to 1899, and whose editor Mouthon was one of the main inspirers of the Lyon Congresses.[220] Again, well before the 1896 Congress, Drumont expressed solidarity with the Christian Democratic movement, praising abbé Lemire, for example, in 1893, as "the defender of the poor and the exploited".[221] Abbé Duvaux and Guérin appeared on the same platform at a meeting of the Union Démocratique de Charonne-Père-Lachaise in February 1898, and both delivered speeches against the Jews. In 1901, as we have seen, abbé Duvaux assumed the leadership of the Grand Occident de France.[222] The Cercle Démocrate Chrétien of Saint-Étienne was reported by the police in January 1898 to be actively anti-Dreyfusard and antisemitic.[223] There is some evidence, finally, that some members of the Sillon movement, closely related to the Christian Democratic movement of the turn of the century, were attracted by antisemitism,[224] although their leader Marc Sangnier was a Dreyfusard, and the Sillon was officially in clear opposition to and in conflict with organized antisemitic nationalism.[225] Antisemitism was thus a central feature of Christian Democracy, though, as both Montuclard and Mayeur have stressed, its tone was very often more secular than purely religious, more anti-capitalist than anti-Judaic.[226] It was, in the words of abbé Lemire's invitation to the Lyon Congress of 1896, "the negative side of the Christian Democratic programme",[227] and, as such, it characterized the French Christian Democratic movement as much as those of Germany and Austria.[228]

The antisemitism of the Christian Democratic press was only one example of a much more general phenomenon, as we have already begun to see. Referring to the intransigent editor of L'Univers, the journalist A. Servanine even claimed, in 1898, that antisemitism as "a movement of opinion did not exist before the appearance of a certain article by Veuillot, insulting in tone and with sinister implications, entitled: 'Beware of the Jews!' "[229] Among the provincial press, we have already encountered Le Nouvelliste de l'Ouest, which was, according to the police in 1900, "a Nationalist and Catholic rallié organ, whose great guide and mentor was Jules Guérin";[230] and it was not an isolated example.[231] In the 1880s and 1890s, much of the Parisian Catholic daily press was antisemitic too, Le Monde, L'Univers,[232] and, above all, of course, La Croix, which took the lead in terms of its circulation, the violence of its tone and its obsession with the subject. It boasted in August 1890 that it was "the most anti-Jewish newspaper in France";[233] and, with its many regional editions, its influence extended far beyond the capital. La Libre Parole, the other big circulation daily with an antisemitic emphasis, was not specifically Catholic, but its editors were often sympathetic towards Catholicism, and its readership seems to have been largely Catholic.[234] Viau, for instance, recounted that the newspaper was frequently approached by members of the clergy to give publicity to their charities.[235] But we will discuss the problem of Drumont's Catholicism and his relations with Catholics in detail in the next section. In addition to newspapers, a host of periodicals proclaimed a specifically Catholic hostility to the Jews. These included the weekly, Le Pèlerin, which had a circulation of 140,000 in 1897, and Les Questions Actuelles, founded in 1887, which were both run by the Assumptionist Bonne Presse; *Le Correspondant;* the Jesuit *Etudes,* which we have referred to; *Le Lillois,* an illustrated provincial weekly;[236] and, of course the various Christian Democratic reviews already mentioned. Antisemitism was also present in Catholic non-periodical literature, and not only in pseudo-scholarly treatises and the works of intellectuals,[237] but at the popular level. Jews were attacked and stereotyped in a hostile way in Catholic popular songs and popular fiction, that were both influential. Pierrard has written that he and his school-mates knew one example of the latter genre, *Le Franc-maçon de la Vierge,* published in 1888, by heart.[238] Another telling example of popular Catholic antisemitic propaganda was Henry Jarzel's *Petit Catéchisme nationaliste,* which we have already cited. Put out by the Librairie Antisémite in 1901, it followed the familiar pattern of the Catholic catechism. As Pierrard concluded, "between 1890 and 1900"—and the time-span could be considerably expanded—antisemitism characterized "the immense majority of Catholic writers and journalists".[239]

We have suggested in a previous chapter that antisemitic journalism had a commercial motive, and mention should be made here of another category of Catholics, who may have had a commercial interest in antisemitism. The manufacturers and retailers of church ornaments and other religious objects were not uncommonly members of antisemitic organizations, and Pierrard has suggested that their hostility to the Jews can be explained by the rivalry of Jewish business in this area.[240] Certainly, antisemites, and perhaps Catholics generally, seem to have believed that the trade was being or had been taken over by Jews. Drumont claimed in *La France juive* that "nearly all the traders in sacred objects and church ornaments are Jews", and that, as such, they acted as spies in "the ecclesiastical world".[241] He elaborated on the charge later, protesting that "the descendants of the Jewish merchants whom Jesus drove out of the Temple have installed themselves at Lourdes, the town of the Virgin. One sees there the same Jewish traders in religious objects who swarm all over the *quartier* of Saint-Sulpice." The same phenomenon was to be found, he averred, around the basilica of the Sacré-Coeur in Montmartre, and everywhere it was tolerated and even encouraged by the episcopate.[242] The last part of Drumont's claim can be discounted, for the diocesan bulletins of at least six dioceses in 1892 protested against the fact that Jews were trading in religious objects, including First Communion garments.[243] But this only confirms that his general charge represented a widespread Catholic belief. To give only one further example, in Francis Jammes's novel *M.le Curé d'Ozeron* (1918), the priest's servant and her friends buy "innumerable holy medals and rosaries . . . from a Jewish bazaar . . ."[244] It should be added that Drumont's allegations about Jewish trading in religious objects, was related to a much more general complaint that Catholics were failing to patronize Catholic small traders and were giving their custom instead to Jewish ones, which usually meant big department stores.[245] So the antisemitic campaign on behalf of small traders and against the big stores was given a confessional slant.

III

Further evidence of Catholic antisemitism is provided by the way in which Catholics approved of or were involved in organized antisemitism. We have already seen that Catholics frequently belonged to antisemitic groups. They were prominent in the membership of the first Ligue Nationale Antisémitique of 1889,[246] of the Comité National Antijuif of 1902,[247] and even of Guérin's Ligue Antisémitique Française. The Action Française, moreover, enjoyed the support, particularly in the decade before 1914, of a considerable section of the Catholic laity and clergy in France, and appears to have had powerful patrons in Rome.[248] On another level, many of the deputies of the Antisemitic Parliamentary group were militant Catholics, for example Delpech-Cantaloup and Massabuau, both members later of the Action Libérale; Paul de Cassagnac; Pontbriand; and Gervaize, candidate at Nancy of the "Parti Catholique Républicain". Catholic antisemitic deputies outside the group included Derrien, L'Estourbeillon, abbé Gayraud, La Ferronays, Lerolle and Largentaye.[249]

Here we must discuss the complex problem of the relationship between Drumont and Catholics. In 1898, and at other times as we have seen, Drumont denied that his antisemitism had religious motives or intentions,[250] or that it was

> directed or protected by the Ultramontanes, the Jesuits, or any dignitaries of the Catholic Church . . . I am a Christian and a Catholic, it is true. It is in my blood to be so, since I was born a Catholic and I am descended from a Catholic race. But what has that got to do, I ask you, with my antisemitic opinions . . . In our ranks, you can find men of the most diverse religious affiliations and beliefs, and also atheists and Freemasons. As to dignitaries of the Church or Jesuits showing an interest in our movement, I have absolutely no knowledge of any, and personally I am not the intimate of any cardinal, bishop or Jesuit . . . on the contrary, the members of the upper clergy are hostile rather than friendly towards our ideas. They are servants of the Jews like many of our magistrates and our politicians. If we have friends among the clergy, they are to be found in its lower ranks. The poor village priest—who receives a pittance from the government which treats him like a slave—he is close to the people, and understands its difficulties and needs, and he therefore wishes us well.

These various claims or rather disclaimers seem to be largely well founded, though it is very significant that Drumont felt it necessary to make them. He and his movement were very widely regarded as Catholic if not clerical. However, in countering the exaggerations of this view, he did here underestimate the support which he enjoyed in Catholic circles, high and low, partly because he tended to imagine that his own animosities were always reciprocated, which they were not.

Drumont, as he said, was a Catholic, though he did not have an orthodox Catholic education, and he only returned to the faith after a lapse of several years in adolescence and early manhood.[251] According to Léon Daudet, he was devout, and his faith was sincere and important to him.[252] Certainly, as Pierrard has noted, "it was as a Catholic that he presented himself to his readers",[253] and we have seen that, despite statements to the contrary, his antisemitism had a strong religious colouring. While some of his colleagues and assistants on *La Libre Parole* were "very lukewarm as far as religion was concerned", in the words of Viau,[254] others were Catholics, like Joseph Ménard, Gaston Méry and abbé Cantenot.[255] According to Drault, there was a crucifix in every one of the newspaper's offices.[256] Drault also confirms that the Catholic orientation of *La Libre Parole* and its editor was reflected in its readership. He quoted an unknown contemporary journalist who described it as "this curious paper which is read by *communards* and *curés*"; and he himself referred to "the Catholic conservative middle class among whom Drumont's most faithful readers were recruited from the start, and who later became the most ardent subscribers to *La Libre Parole.*"[257]

But Drumont's Catholicism was always of an independent, even an anti-clerical variety. It is here significant that he was so anxious to refute the charge made by Arnoulin and others that he was "the man of the Jesuits".[258] The claim itself seems to have had very little substance, though Drumont was apparently on friendly terms with Père du Lac.[259] The point is that this and any other connection that may have existed did not mean that the Jesuits escaped from Drumont's general attack on Catholics and on the Church.[260] This attack was an important facet of his populism, and provides some insight into the motives which lay behind at least one type of Catholic antisemitism. Drumont accused Catholics in general, but mainly upper-class Catholics, of lacking both charity and a sense of justice. *La France juive,* for example, pinned responsibility for the repression of the Paris Commune, which was called an act "of savage iniquity", on the Catholic majority of the National Assembly.[261] More generally, in the same work, the Catholic bourgeoisie were indicted for their callous enjoyment of comfortable and luxurious living at the expense of an exploited class of workers, and for their failure to defend the interests of the Church.[262] But the ultimate responsibility for this state of affairs lay with the clergy, who had failed to come to terms with the modern world and its problems: "The Church, in the past, constantly accompanied men in their everyday lives to enlighten and guide them . . . Today, preachers avoid current affairs and real burning issues . . . To listen to them, one would think that they were preaching to people who have been dead for three hundred years."[263] This critique had something in common with that of the Christian Democrats, with whom, as we have seen, Drumont expressed some sympathy, though he was extremely hostile towards what he regarded as the hypocrisy of Social Catholicism.[264] But it was no simple plea for an accommodation with modern society, whose values, of course, he utterly rejected. Rather, it represented an "Integrist" appeal for more militancy and for the total regulation of society along Christian lines. Drumont, for example, contrasted the conventional Catholicism of most upper-class Catholics with his own cult of St Michael, "the great national saint of the fifteenth century";[265] and what attracted him about the Middle Ages was that it was a period when the Church had maintained "the social reign of Christianity". In particular the Church had outlawed usury, the basis of modern capitalist society; and when the Church abandoned its traditional ban on usury, it effectively "adhered to the Jewish system". It is not surprising, therefore, to find that Drumont regarded *Rerum Novarum* with some scorn,[266] nor that abbé Cantenot was very much opposed to all Leo XIII's "progressive" policies.[267]

Drumont's critique of the Church of his day and its leadership was in some ways a kind of updated Richerism, a defence of the lower clergy and an attack on their superiors. In *La France juive,* he pointed out that the "persecution" of Catholics under the Third Republic fell on the poor rather than on the rich, on the lower rather than the upper clergy: "The bishop, disposing often of considerable resources, the *curé* of a large town, have been left alone. The blows have fallen with special force on the curate [*desservant*] and on the monk. Among the religious orders even, it has been the poorest who have suffered most."[268] If the upper clergy had been comparatively untouched by governmental anticlericalism, it was because they had compromised with it, and with its instigators, the Jews and the Freemasons. In 1891, Drumont castigated "this submission" of "the upper clergy" to the Jews; "there are evidently traitors in the upper levels of the Church, prelates affiliated to the inner Lodges of Masonry . . ."[269] The bishops generally were accused of being corrupt and in the pay of the Jews, and of failing for this reason to lead or defend the Church, and, in particular, Drumont launched a full-scale attack on Mgr Place, Archbishop of Rennes.[270] Nor were the religious orders excluded from this attack on the ecclesiastical establishment, although, as we have noted, Drumont expressed some sympathy for them as victims of official anticlericalism. The religious orders were accused of patronizing Jewish banks and traders;[271] and the Dominican Père Didon was singled out for special opprobrium for his alleged philosemitism.[272] Here again antisemitism was linked to a nostalgia for a Christianity on the "mediaeval" model, and Drumont contrasted the contemporary regular clergy with their more heroic predecessors, for example the Dominicans of the time of the Inquisition who "in order to save their country . . . did not hesitate to suppress all the Jews . . ."; "there does not exist . . . a religious order in which one can find support, which personifies, as did certain orders of the Middle Ages, the resistance of the Aryan genius against the Jewish invasion."[273]

By contrast, Drumont was a consistent champion of the lower clergy. These were "the honest clergy",[274] close to the people, as we have seen, and selflessly serving it. When workers were shot down at Fourmies, wrote Drumont in 1892, "it was the priest who rushed into the line of fire to save and to bless those whom the Jew had had gunned down, the poor priest towards whom the people, misled by the ghetto press, have been so unfair recently."[275] But Drumont did not only defend the parish clergy against anticlericals, he also opposed the "despotism" which the bishops exercised over the lower clergy, and in turn the "despotism" which the Pope exercised over French bishops.[276] The fact that the bulk of the lower clergy in France were *"desservants"* with no security of tenure, who could be disciplined arbitrarily and moved about at will by their bishops, was a very long standing grievance among them, and Drumont's voicing of it must have predisposed many of them in his favour. "The 'ecclesiastical proletariat' ", wrote Drault, "felt that it had in Drumont a defender who gave expression to its bitterness and its worries."[277] It is less certain that the lower clergy shared his Gallicanism, for Ultramontanism could be a means of opposing the power of the bishops.[278] But one can see here an additional reason for the antisemitism of the lower clergy. Open opposition to episcopal authority was virtually out of the question, but some satisfaction might be gained from imagining, with Drumont, that the bishops were tools of the Jews.

Drumont coupled his attacks on the Catholic bourgeoisie and the upper clergy with the claim that they gave no support to the antisemitic movement. "Christians", he wrote in 1890, "lend the smallest assistance to those who are defending their Nation against the Semitic invasion";[279] and he complained the following year that the clergy were not using their pulpits to denounce "the machinations of the Freemasons and the Jews . . ."[280] In particular, he claimed that, when he presented himself as an antisemitic candidate in the municipal elections in Paris in 1890, Catholic leaders had organized to oppose him: "all the Catholics [in the ward of Gros Caillou voted] . . . against a man who had defended the Church . . ."[281] Again, Drumont blamed his defeat at Algiers in the 1902 elections on the fact that the clergy had not supported him.[282] Whatever the truth of these particular claims, it is known that some Catholics made their hostility to Drumont very clear, from a variety of motives. An abbé Didiot of the Theological Faculty of Lille wrote to La Croix in 1890 to criticize Drumont not for his antisemitism, but for his "socialism".[283] We have seen that Bloy's Le Salut par les Juifs was in large part a pamphlet directed against Drumont, objecting to his ignorance of the theological basis of Catholic anti-Judaism, to his claim to represent Catholicism despite the secular tone of his antisemitism, and, above all, to his deliberate exploitation of popular prejudice for fame if not for money:[284]

> this copious journalist . . . the pamphleteer of La France juive can pride himself upon having found the goose that lays the golden eggs. Realizing, with the profound wisdom and the cool cunning of a clever leader that by far the easiest way to influence and to please people is to fill their bellies with their favourite swill, he directed against the Jews the consistent and explosive demand that they disgorge their cash . . . It should be added that this great man made this noble demand in the name of Catholicism.

Another opponent was abbé Frémont who criticized La France juive in a sermon at the fashionable church of Saint-Philippe-du-Roule in Paris shortly after its publication, which led to a storm of protests. He commented in 1892: "Hatred of the Republic and of the Jews is the daily bread of the French clergy, and Drumont is their prophet. Any attempt to remove this sustenance is dangerous; those who try are at once assailed by libels and calumnies."[285]

As this suggests, explicit disapproval of Drumont and opposition to his influence were rare among Catholics, at least in the 1880s and 1890s, while explicit approval and support were very common. This is true even where the upper clergy were concerned, despite the fact that Drumont openly criticized them as we have seen, and claimed that they opposed him precisely because he was defending the cause of the Church too vigorously.[286] According to Duroselle, the bishops became hostile after the publication in 1891 of *Le Testament d'un antisémite* and in reaction to its critique of their leadership and of the subservient status of the lower clergy.[287] But Verdès-Leroux's researches indicate continuing support for Drumont in a fair number of official diocesan bulletins after that date. "Drumont is not the only one to wax indignant at the insolence and the baseness [of those in power in France]", declared *La Semaine Religieuse du diocèse de Mende*, for example, in July 1892, "but it is around his name that the souls that have had enough of the yoke are rallying . . ." That of Valence was more cautious: "Without approving of all M. Drumont's conclusions, we are quite willing to recognize that his campaign is worthy of encouragement . . ."; while others were more enthusiastic. *La Semaine Religieuse de Périgueux et de Sarlat* reproduced the first editorial of *La Libre Parole* in its own columns in April 1892, and described Drumont as "the valiant writer who has declared so implacable and so legitimate a war on the Jews", adding: "We welcome the new paper with all our heart, and we hope most ardently that the patriotic campaign which it has undertaken will be crowned with success."[288]

Drumont also received similar support and encouragement in the Catholic press generally. According to Pierrard, "in general, the Catholic press received *La France juive* and Drumont's other books very sympathetically, and even with warmth and enthusiasm." Admiring reviews of *La France juive* appeared, for example, in *L'Univers, Le Monde, La Croix* and *La Revue du Monde Catholique;* while *La Dernière Bataille* and *Le Testament d'un antisémite* were praised in *La France Catholique* despite their attacks on the episcopate and on Catholics as a whole.[289] *La Croix*, a commercial rival, kept its distance from Drumont and *La Libre Parole* after 1892, and gave it as its opinion that Drumont was not "a completely devoted soldier of the Church".[290] However, *La Croix d'Alger* celebrated Drumont's electoral victory there in 1898 as a sign of divine intervention, and compared him with Joan of Arc, and even with Christ himself driving the money changers from the Temple.[291] Again, when Drumont presented himself as a candidate for election to the Academy in 1909, he had the support of *L'Autorité, La Croix, Le Peuple Français* and *L'Action Française*, which were all more or less Catholic papers.[292]

However, there is no doubt that Drumont's decisive support came not from the Catholic establishment, but from the ranks of the lower clergy. "It is through talking to the country clergy and through reading their letters", Drumont declared after the publication of *La France juive*, "that I discovered how useful my book had been . . .";[293] and, in 1914, he affirmed again: "The country priests . . . have always encouraged and supported me . . ."[294] And other evidence lends support to his claims. Members of the lower clergy formed an important proportion of the readership of *La Libre Parole*, and of those who supported its subscriptions.[295] In addition to many letters from the clergy, Drumont received gifts from them, and especially from those in the Paris region.[296] Various priests, moreover, were habitués of the *Libre Parole* offices, like abbé Cantenot, whom we have mentioned, and abbé Desportes and abbe Barbier were among the antisemitic authors of the time who acknowledged themselves to be Drumont's disciples.[297] There is some evidence, too, that this support might have been more widespread and more vocal had it not been tempered by fear of episcopal disapproval. "How many times, after the appearance of *La France juive*", Drumont wrote in 1891, "have priests come up and told me, when I was in Normandy: If you only knew, how we are itching to say something to our flocks about your work and your ideas, but the bishop would not like it . . ."[298] And Drault made the same point more generally later: "If we did not have the bishops on our side, we did have the country clergy. Nearly all of them read *La Libre Parole*, sometimes secretly, for if their bishops never forbade them to read it in any pastoral letter, they often let it be known semi-officially that the newspaper was personally disagreeable to them."[299] As we have suggested antisemitism here revealed and to some extent expressed a latent antagonism between the lower and the upper clergy. The special support of the rural clergy also points to another important aspect of Drumont's Catholicism, which may help to explain its easy assimilation to popular antisemitism, and this was the fact that it seems to have reflected an authentic popular Catholicism, untheological, though "manichean" in tendency, suspicious of all novelties, and to a great extent outside and beyond the debates and divisions which preoccupied the better-educated. Relevant here is the fact that Drumont was a great admirer of Henri Lasserre, whose *Notre-Dame de Lourdes* did so much to popularize the Lourdes cult.[300]

The support which Drumont enjoyed among the lower clergy and the laity as well as the failure of the hierarchy to dissociate itself very clearly from him and from his attacks on the Jews are further important indications of the strength of Catholic antisemitism in France. Negatively, indeed, the absence of Catholic opposition to antisemitism generally is striking. We have mentioned the criticism of Drumont by Bloy and by abbé Frémont. Drumont also claimed that an abbé Le Nordez had attacked him from the pulpit of Notre-Dame in Paris.[301] We have referred, too, to the very small number of Catholics and particularly of members of the clergy who joined the ranks of the Dreyfusards. Paul Viollet's Comité Catholique pour la Défense du Droit, founded in February 1899 to campaign for the revision of the Dreyfus Case, had only 120 members, of whom 15 were priests,[302] which is not much to set against the anti-Dreyfusard leagues. One of these priests, abbé Pichot, published a brochure, *La Conscience chrétienne et l'Affaire Dreyfus*, in which he called for revision and also attacked *La Croix;* he was shortly afterwards dismissed from his post as a teacher at the *petit séminaire* of Felletin in the diocese of Limoges.[303] Another priest who braved the anti-Dreyfusard orthodoxy was abbé J. Brugerette from Lyon, whom we have quoted. He took the precaution, however, of publishing *L'Affaire Dreyfus et la mentalité catholique* in 1904 under a pseudonym.[304] We have also encountered Mgr Coullié, who expressed his disapproval of antisemitism generally in 1896, and mention should be made, too, of Aynard the director of *L'Express de Lyon* and, of course, of Anatole Leroy-Beaulieu, who had to remind a hostile audience at the Institut Catholique de Paris in February 1897: "The blood which flowed in the veins of Christ, the blood, which, according to the Christian faith, redeemed the world was Semitic blood. The Virgin Mary, the Apostles, the first disciples of the Redeemer were also all of the Jewish race."[305] But such opponents of antisemitism were very rare, and they came from groups, they represented currents of opinion within Catholicism that were anyway small and without influence. Most were liberal Catholics, faithful to a minority view that had been in decline, if not eclipse, since 1870.[306] Others were even less orthodox, for example Père Hyacinthe Loyson, an ex-Carmelite of "modernist" inclinations, who seceded from the Church after the Vatican Council, married, and subsequently played a leading role in various breakaway or schismatic "Catholic churches" in France and in Switzerland;[307] or Péguy, a socialist who rejected the Church's traditional teaching on the Jews, with its assumption that Judaism was an inferior religion and that Jewish conversion from it was desirable.[308]

IV

Having established the importance of antisemitism among French Catholics, we must now examine the content of that antisemitism and try to explain further why it had such appeal. We have seen that it was theologically unsophisticated in the main, but a number of old religious themes still occupied some place in it. These were the accusation that the Jews had a collective responsibility for deicide, and, related to this, for the "betrayal" of Christ; the idea that, as a result of this crime, the Jews were under a divine curse; again, related to both these charges, the identification of the Jews with the Devil; and, last, the accusation that Jews engaged in the ritual murder of Christians.

J. Cohen had felt obliged in 1864 to write a scholarly refutation of the charge of deicide, "to combat energetically", in his words, "the prejudices which have been directed against the Jews for the last eighteen centuries as a result of the incomprehensible accusation of DEICIDE";[309] and it would be unlikely that he would have engaged upon this task, had the accusation been abandoned by Catholics. Though attaching less importance to it, Zola forty years later agreed that "the persisting anger of the Christian against the Jew who crucified his God" was probably an underlying factor in modern antisemitism.[310] Picard, who prided himself on his modern and "scientific" racial antisemitism, did indeed suggest that the deicide theme belonged to the past: "it is true that, in the past . . . the Jewish question was dressed up in religious form; it was connected with the crucifixion of Christ, with the betrayal of Judas . . . But these puerile justifications [for antisemitism] are only invoked now out of ignorance or prejudice . . ."[311] But antisemitism was precisely the sphere of "ignorance" and "prejudice"; and Picard admitted that the deicide theme was still current in the popular mentality: "Vulgarly, it is believed that antisemitism dates from the crucifixion of Jesus Christ . . ."[312] The belief was certainly an old and a widespread feature of popular Catholicism in France and elsewhere,[313] and survived in this and other milieus until very recently,[314] being specifically condemned by the Vatican only in 1965.[315] Many writers have thus seen it as an important element in the perpetuation of antisemitism in Christian societies. "Instinctively, our Christian detests the Jew", wrote the Tharauds, "since the Jew bears the ineffaceable taint of having put Jesus Christ on the Cross."[316]

And, as far as nineteenth-century France is concerned, there is much to support such a view, as we have already begun to indicate. The deicide theme does seem to have been a part of Catholic teaching and belief. The curé in Tillier's Mon Oncle Benjamin (1842) said that the Jews were accused of "the greatest crime that a people can commit, of a deicide."[317] Dom Guéranger declared in 1841: "The spectacle of an entire people placed under a curse for having crucified the Son of God gives Christians food for thought . . ."[318] At the end of the century, belief in Jewish responsibility for the Crucifixion was common among the Catholic populations of Tunisia and Algeria. Vibert was told, we have seen, while electioneering in Algiers in 1898: "How can you expect us not to hate the Jews? They put Jesus to death."[319] In France itself, an attack on Sarah Bernhardt published in the early 1880s referred to "the God, whom the Jews sent to Calvary!"[320] In a debate in the Chamber of Deputies in May 1895, a number of Catholic deputies, including abbé Lemire, interrupted a speech by Naquet to declare that the Jews had "voluntarily killed Jesus".[321] And André Gide recounted in his Journal in 1904 that the family of an acquaintance "tries to move him to pity Christ's sufferings on the Cross and to arouse indignation against the bad men who nailed him there", which seems to be a reference to the same belief.[322] Nor was the deicide charge confined to Catholics, perhaps because it was a belief inculcated in childhood which survived other changes of opinion about religion. It is interesting for example to find that Pierre Leroux assumed Jewish responsibility for the Crucifixion in an otherwise philosemitic article, published in 1846.[323]

"Deicide", too, was a not uncommon theme in antisemitic propaganda, whether written by members of the clergy or by laymen. Bishop Meurin referred to the Jews as "the deicide people" and to "their hatred of their Messiah, whom they refused to recognize and whom they killed on the Cross!"[324] La Croix also referred, in November 1890, to the Jews as "the deicide people";[325] and La Croisade Française alleged in February 1898 that the Jews had shouted: "To death with Jesus".[326] While claiming, like Picard, that "the memory of their deicide" was not "the determining cause of the public safety measures taken against the Jews in the past",[327] Drumont nevertheless retailed the old accusation. He referred, in La France juive, for example, to "this Christ whom the Jews still hate as much as on the day that they crucified him", and to "the Jews who crucified the true Messiah . . .";[328] and he presented the alleged contemporary persecution of the Church by the Jews as the continuation of their original deicide: "Christ insulted, covered with opprobrium, crowned with thorns, crucified. Nothing has changed in eighteen centuries. The Jews are the same, their wilful blindness, their hatred are the same . . . Paris is full of Jews as obstinate in their deicide as at the time of Caiaphas . . ."[329] And many other antisemites wrote or spoke in the same vein. Goncourt described the Jews as "a race bespattered with the blood of a God . . ."[330] Bourget was reported to have said in December 1897: "I hate the Jews because they crucified Jesus . . ."[331] La Tour du Pin referred about the same time to "the deicide nation",[332] a term that we have already encountered in a slightly different form. Of special significance here is the subscription to the same belief by Bloy, since he was a notable critic of Drumont and modern antisemitism, as we have seen, and claimed to be reaffirming a traditional doctrine. Not only are the Jews said, in *Le Salut par les Juifs*, to have "crucified the Son of God", but particular emphasis is laid on this theme: "I am not personally very much interested in what the Jews are reproached with by theologians and economists. It is enough for me to know that they have committed the supreme Crime, . . . the nameless and measureless sin against the very Integrity of God . . .".[333]

A theme related to that of Jewish responsibility for deicide was the identification of the Jews as a whole with Judas the man who betrayed Christ. We have seen in an earlier chapter that Judas remained a popular stereotype of the traitor,[334] and it is perhaps significant that the idea of Jewish treason was so frequently expressed through this religious image. Barrès, for example, as we have seen, entitled his account of Dreyfus's degradation in January 1895: "The Parade of Judas";[335] and he reported that Mme Henry shouted "Judas" at Dreyfus several times in the court-room at Rennes.[336]

The theme of deicide also implied that the Jews had been and were still being punished for this crime, and for their refusal to recognize Christ as the Messiah, that they lived, in effect, under a divine curse. "His blood be on us, and on our children", Pilate was told, according to St Matthew.[337] Perpetuated in the writings of Pascal, Bossuet and others, and, more popularly, in the myth of the Wandering Jew, this idea persisted among nineteenth-century French Catholics. *La Revue du Monde Catholique* explained in 1887: "The Jew had the Redeemer put to death, and ever since this heinous crime was committed, the curse of heaven has been upon the deicide people; they have been dispersed all over the earth, odious to all other people, cursed by all other people, always wandering, at home nowhere."[338] The same theme occurs in Bloy's *Le Salut par les Juifs;* he wrote that "the cursed fig tree [was] indisputably the symbol of the Jewish people"; and that the Jews were "these cursed people . . . condemned to bear the Cross nearly two thousand years ago . . ."[339] And the "professional" antisemites also made use of the idea. Drumont referred to "the cursèd Yids",[340] a term that was common in the antisemitic press of Algeria.[341] Attaching the idea more explicitly to Catholic belief, though lending it also a racial colouring was Biez, who wrote: "The Jews have been cursed for all Eternity . . . They are, as a people, in revolt against any idea of Redemption, being chained by their instinctive bestiality to the yoke of matter . . . The curse of Golgotha will fall on their shoulders . . . they will pay in a final reckoning for the vices of their race . . ."[342]

More popular and more developed was the identification of the Jews with the Devil, and their association with sorcery, magic and witchcraft. Deriving from a verse in the Gospel of St John, which refers to "the Devil" as the "father" of the Jews,[343] and developed by St John Chrystostom and other Fathers of the Church, this was, according to Poliakov, with that of deicide, one of "the two cardinal themes of Christian antisemitism . . ."[344] Léon Pinsker wrote in 1882 that "Judeophobia is a variety of demonopathy";[345] and Poliakov has argued that modern antisemitism was simply "a variation on the old demonological themes of the Middle Ages, adapted to the sensibility of the nineteenth-century man in the street."[346] It is undoubtedly helpful to see many of the features of modern antisemitism, as a system of beliefs, as analogous to, if not an adaptation or a secularization of, an older, more literal, anti-Judaic demonology, but this should not obscure the fact that "the old demonological themes" often survived into the nineteenth century with little or no adaptation, or, at least, that they appeared in more explicit form than Poliakov's remarks might lead one to suppose.

The association of the Jews with the Devil was alluded to by a number of writers through the century, and was an important theme in antisemitic propaganda at the end of the century in particular. Toussenel called the Jews "people of Satan".[347] Proudhon referred to "the evil principle, Satan, Ahriman, incarnated in the race of Sem."[348] Michelet retailed the ancient association of the Jews with the Devil and with witchcraft more deliberately, for example in *La Sorcière* (1862), and Drumont quoted him as an authority on the subject in *La France juive.*[349] The Devil, of course, was a common figure or theme in Romantic and post-Romantic literature in France,[350] which must have encouraged the survival or the revival of this antisemitic motif, which, as our references above indicate, was not confined to Catholics. But it must, nevertheless have had special appeal or relevance for them, particularly when it is remembered that literal belief in the reality of the Devil and in the agency of diabolical powers in the natural world was still common among the faithful; and that this belief existed not only at the level of folk-religion, but also among educated persons. The *curé* d'Ars, for example, who was the object of a popular, and later of an official, cult, was persistently tormented by devils, and this was taken to be a sign of his sanctity.[351] From a later period, the Tharauds recounted that, while a novice at Solesmes, a friend of theirs saw a devil making fellow-novices misbehave.[352] Bloy told a friend in a letter in March 1890 that he was oppressed by demons;[353] while Huysmans affirmed in the preface to Jules Bois's *Le Satanisme et la magie* (1895): "the reality of Satanism is undeniable."[354] Drumont himself like other members of the *Libre Parole* team, not only believed "in prophecies, in fortune-telling and in signs",[355] but also in the Devil. It was, indeed, he argued, one of the master-strokes of the "Demon" 's strategy "to remain for many years without manifesting himself",[356] thus inducing people to doubt his existence, but, he declared in 1891, "Satan, the father of lies, the king of darkness, now reveals himself clearly as the master of the hour."[357] In Huysmans, Drumont and others, folk-beliefs merged or were elaborated into a Romantic occultism. This process was paradigmatic of antisemitic ideology as a whole, as we shall argue in a later chapter.[358] Here it is enough to note that an element that can be called religious was thereby preserved, and that the partial change which it underwent may, as Poliakov suggests, have increased rather than reduced its force.

Moreover, Drumont explicitly attached his belief in the Devil and his power to the idea that the Jews were his agents with magical powers to do harm. In *La France juive*, he claimed that the Templars had been a sect of devil-worshipping Jews, and he made many references to the old association of the Jews with magic and witchcraft, astrology and alchemy, frequently citing Michelet as an authority as we have noted. "The real witch was the Jew", he quoted, for example; and he asserted that, with Emancipation, "the Jew ceased to be the cursed witch, that Michelet has shown us carrying out his evil magic under cover of darkness; he was transformed, and began to operate in the light of day"; but this only increased the scope and effectiveness of his evil powers and soon the "bewitching" of all Christian society by the Jew was accomplished.[359] In *La Fin d'un monde*, he evoked the Jewish celebration of the Black Mass, "the eternal parody . . . with its impious fooleries, the sign of the cross made with the left hand, the Gospel read backwards with the buttocks of a witch for a lectern".[360] Again, in *La Dernière Bataille*, he referred to Jewish powers of "sorcery"; and he described the *Exposition* of 1889, that "the Jew . . . has made in his own image", as "base Magic incarnate with its deceiving lights, its fantastic evocations, its phosphorescent effects in which objects are decomposed . . ."[361] More literally, he claimed in *Le Testament d'un antisémite* that "in Russia, Roumania and Galicia, the most violent antisemites never try to resist a Jew . . . who has been granted the right of 'Asaka' over them . . . [if they did] their harvests would wither in the fields or rot in their barns . . ."[362] Later, he referred to Cornélius Herz, a Jewish financier involved in the Panama scandal, as a kind of modern wizard; he was "this fantastic doctor . . . a strange mixture of Faust and Vautrin, an amalgam of Balsamo and Barnum, of Figaro and Nucingen; he is mysterious like an alchemist . . ."[363] In *La Fin d'un monde* again, he used the image of Satan tempting Christ in the wilderness to evoke the Jewish dominance of Paris: "the spirit of Semitism, with his long beard and his triumphant and lugubrious air, squats on the Arc de Triomphe, and watching all Paris go by, murmurs: 'All this belongs to me!' "[364] The same image was repeated in *De l'Or, de la boue, du sang* in an illustration showing the figure of a devil hovering over the Paris Stock Exchange.[365]

Other antisemites elaborated on the same general theme. Abbé Chabauty's *Les Francs-maçons et les Juifs* (1881) argued that the Jewish world conspiracy was the instrument of Satan.[366] Bloy referred in 1892 to the "infernal obstinacy" of the Jews, a term which he intended to be taken literally.[367] A song by abbé Demnise, published in *Poésies patriotiques* (1896), included the lines: "Here comes a dirty Jew . . . He comes straight from Hell, and rivals his own boss the Devil . . ."[368] The brochure, *La Fin de la France*, 2,000 copies of which were seized by the police in Paris in August 1899, referred to "the cruel God of the Jews";[369] while *Le Croisade Française* declared in February 1898 that the Jew resembled "the Devil".[370] A handwritten poster discovered by the police at Rennes in July 1899 alleged that Jews believed that the souls of non-Jews came from the Devil, an interesting reversal of the usual identification.[371] As we have seen for the earlier part of the century, even Socialist antisemitism drew on this Catholic tradition. Gustave Tridon in a book called, significantly, *Du Molochisme juif* (1884) claimed that the Jew was "the evil genius of the earth"; while Jaclard, in *La Revue Socialiste* in 1893, gave the Jew the Satanic epithet of "the King of Fraud".[372] Nor again was the theme confined to "professional" antisemites in this period. It was found for example, in the short stories published by *Le Journal* in the 1890s.[373] Silbermann, in Lacretelle's novel, explains his unusual erudition to a nun by saying: "I'm the devil, you see";[374] while in Albert Malaurié's *La Femme de Judas* (1924), Christ calls Judas "the Devil" and "Satan".[375]

Perhaps the most developed version of the Satanic theme was made in the context of attacks on Freemasonry, which, as we have seen, was generally regarded as a Jewish organization. The papal Epistle *Scite Profecto* (1873) and the Encyclical *Humanum Genus* (1884) both described Freemasonry as Satanic.[376] In France, the same thesis was propounded by abbé Chabauty in a work which we have already referred to, and it received further elaboration in Bishop Meurin's attack on Freemasonry, published in 1893, which was subtitled *Synagogue de Satan.* Masonry was there presented as a Satanic cult, with which the Jews and Judaism were closely associated.[377] In January 1894, in the same vein, *L'Echo de Rome* quoted this passage from *L'Osservatore Romano:* "Freemasonry is *Satanic* from every point of view . . . It is *Satanic,* making common cause today with Judaism. Freemasonry is, in effect, the main influence and the indispensable arm which Judaism uses *to banish from this world the reign of Jesus Christ and to substitute that of Satan.* "[378] But the most remarkable example of this genre was "Dr Bataille"'s *Le Diable au XIXe siècle,* published in monthly illustrated instalments between 1892 and 1894, and in book form in 1896. This "organ of combat against High Masonry and contemporary Satanism" made a series of preposterous "revelations" about Freemasonry, involving not only the claim that it was a sect of devil-worshippers, but also that its leaders maintained contact through a diabolic telephone system, that they had a germ-warfare department under the Rock of Gibraltar, and that devils in person assisted at their rites. These imaginative claims, in fact the work of a former anticlerical hack Léo Taxil, were reiterated and added to in "Diana Vaughan"'s *Mémoires d'une ex-palludiste* from 1895, and in other writings.[379] What is significant is that Taxil's fabrications proved extremely popular, and were taken to be authentic revelations by many Catholics, clergy and laity, including the Bishops of Grenoble, Montpellier and Coutances, Bishop Meurin, Père Monsabré, and the editors of *La Croix, L'Univers, La Civiltà Cattolica, La Revue Bénédictine* and many other Catholic periodicals.[380] A priest writing in *La Revue Catholique de Coutances* in June 1896, for example, commented on the latest publication of "Diana Vaughan": "The whole of contemporary history is here condensed, explained, and light is shed on its profoundest mysteries."[381] It is fair to add that other

Catholics were sceptical, and that several leading antisemites were among the sceptics. *La Croix* later reversed its early enthusiasm for Taxil; the Jesuit *Etudes* had never taken him seriously; and Drumont was extremely hostile; while in 1896 both Mouthon in *La France Libre* and abbé Garnier in *Le Peuple Français* denounced the whole Bataille–Diana Vaughan affair as a fraud.[382] However, the remarkable success of Taxil's fabrications—and they continued to be believed in even after Taxil had confessed to his fraud—indicates the great willingness of Catholics and others to believe in the intervention of the Devil in the natural world and to associate the enemies of the Church, Freemasons and Jews, with the Devil.

The same syndrome can be seen, in more literary and sophisticated form, in the writings of Barrès on the Dreyfus Affair.[383]

> The people of the Middle Ages, in order to express the inpenetrable mysteries of that unknown sea that extended to the South, called it the Dark Sea. The soul of Dreyfus is a dark sea, and I concur in the sentiments which the Church, in its prudence and mercy, makes manifest in this context. O Lord, dissipate the darkness of this perfidious Jew, so that I may see clear . . . How different he is from us, this miserable creature, half-dead, but whose arrogance feeds and is revived, like the petals of a Jerusalem rose, by the buckets of stinking muck that his lawyer throws at the leaders of our army! I suspect that on his prison rock he nourished his pride with all the many commentaries that his crime provoked. From this filth that stifled France, he took his strength, his evil joy, and his Satanic power.

And Barrès wrote similarly of Picquart at the Rennes trial: "In the midst, at the heart of the anti-French forces . . . the proud and bitter face of Picquart completed the sad and powerful scene with a final note, that of Lucifer."[384] But Dreyfus and Picquart did not only personify Satanic pride, as "soldiers stripped of their rank", they were like unfrocked priests, ministers of an inverted cult, of an anti-patriotism.[385] Léon Daudet, too, used the same imagery in the context of the Affair, writing that, at the salon of Gustave Dreyfus after the news of the traitor's pardon was known, "one would have thought that one was present at a witches' sabbath . . ."[386] Was it a coincidence that Dreyfus was imprisoned on Devil's Island?

Another literary version of the diabolization of the Jews is found in the fictional characterization of the Jewess as the "femme fatale", the she-devil, the witch. Mediaeval in origin,[387] the theme was common in the nineteenth century, and examples include Flaubert's *Hérodias* (1877), Séphora in Alphonse Daudet's *Les Rois en exil* (1879), and Edmond de Goncourt's *Manette Salomon* (1898), "who, like the devil, takes possession of the artist's soul."[388] Guy de Maupassant's fascination with the theme has been emphasized, too, by Schmidt. The woman in *L'Inconnue* (1885), for example, has a witch's mark; she is "one of those dangerous and perfidious beings whose mission is to lead men astray into unknown abysses"; and the narrator knows instinctively that she is Jewish. Schmidt comments generally, and with great insight:[389]

The almost nostalgic passion which drives Maupassant to set so high a value on the special qualities of the Jewish woman probably derives from an unfortunate tradition whose harmfulness one cannot too strongly denounce. According, unconsciously, to every Jewess a magical vocation, Maupassant experiences towards her the equivocal feeling, made up of sadistic desire and of sacred horror, which inspires the simple in their dealings with witches and their ideas about vampires. He thus believes that he is risking a great deal in soliciting her caresses. He thinks that, instructed by the demon which possesses her, she dispenses evil spells while satisfying sexual appetites.

We will return to the sexual aspect of this theme, which is related to that of pollution, in the next chapter,[390] though mention may be made here of a later example which, interestingly, explicitly rejects and reverses the old association of the Jewess with sexuality. Judas's wife Léa in Malaurié's *La Femme de Judas* represents "the great force of evil", and is ultimately responsible for her husband's betrayal of Christ, but she is the opposite of the temptress, disapproving of Mary Magdalene, a social climber, interested only in money, calculating, "sensible" and "respectable".[391]

The theme of the Jewess as the agent of the Devil was taken up by the "professional" antisemites, who sometimes had close links with its literary exponents.[392] According to an anonymous publication, *Joseph et Mardochée: Etude critique sur l'hégémonie sémitique* (1887), the Jewess was "an instrumental woman whose mission is to bring about ruin and death".[393] And a similar claim was made by Drumont in *La France juive:* "the representatives of old families, noble and bourgeois . . . give themselves up to pleasure, taking as mistresses Jewish girls who corrupt and ruin them . . ."[394] It is relevant here that *La Libre Parole* and other papers accused Mme Steinheil of being a Jewish Delilah, who had murdered her lover, President Faure.[395] But the most developed version of the theme was in Maurras's *L'Etang de Marthe et les hauteurs d'Aristarché* (1901). Marthe, the Semitic witch, was here presented as the symbol of the forces of evil and disorder in French history, in contrast to the classical order represented by Aristarché: "Marthe had great gifts, impudence, obstinacy, the talent for solemn religious utterance, much subtlety. All this is Jewish." Inhabiting the unhealthy marshes of the Provençal coast, "she gave forth prophecies, did harm by evil magic, withdrew her spells and cast them again, and the tragic solitude in which she dwelt was the apt setting for her oracle; the atmosphere of the place, the thick smoke of her lair, the pernicious fever present in the heavy air added to the effect of the incantations which she chanted from the depth of her throat. She agitated men's hearts. She isolated them and seduced them." Maurras went on to refer to "her sacred evil", and asked: "Does not even her shadow bring harm? . . . Every irrationality comes to us from her, the break with the highest traditions of the mind, the return to savagery . . . The great historical crises of the West can all be interpreted as deriving . . . from the same Jewish and Syrian miasma."[396] The way in which this intellectualized version of the diabolization myth relates to the general functions of antisemitism, discussed in previous chapters, will be clear. It also takes us back to Poliakov's point that antisemitism was an adaptation of the old anti-Judaic demonology to modern needs.

What were the functions of the identification of the Jews with the principle of evil, whether in traditional Christian or in secular form? First, one of the significant characteristics of the Jews in antisemitic ideology, which they shared with the Devil and his agents,[397] was the fact that they were at once omnipresent and invisible. Drumont emphasized the Jewish ability to disappear: "he disappears, vanishes in a fog, goes to ground to plot new schemes, and emerges again several centuries later."[398] But such disappearances were only apparent. Drumont wrote again with reference to the Regency period: "At that time, the Jew, who was admitted nowhere, was in reality everywhere."[399] An anonymous Catholic theologian told Bournand in 1898: "Today . . . without having a political existence anywhere, without an inch of territory which it can call its own, the Jewish people is everywhere, has taken root everywhere."[400] "All comes from the Jew; all returns to the Jew", affirmed Drumont more gnomically.[401] As we saw in discussing the conspiracy theory, the antisemites required not only a total principle of explanation, but they needed to show that the Jews, objectively a small minority, could be all-powerful. Lending them the demonic powers of invisibility and omnipresence did just this, as well as providing the rationale for their undeviating will to harm and destroy non-Jews.

On another level, the characterization of the Jews as demonic was a reflection of the strangeness, "the mystery" of Jewish culture for Christians or members of Christian society. "The essence of the drama in which the Jew is involved", wrote Drumont, "is that he is always mysterious."[402] The Tharauds explained the diabolization of the Jew in "the popular imagination" very much in these terms:[403]

> If the Jew keeps to himself, leads a secret life, it must be because he has things to hide. Frightful deformities, vices and crimes of all sorts, revolting customs, are thus attributed to him, of which one can read the horrifying descriptions in Jewish and Christian chronicles. If he never removes his hat, as his Law prescribes, it must be that he has horns on his brow like a goat. From this, it is only one step, as Bernard Lazare wittily remarked, to giving him a tail like a devil. And this step, of course, was taken.

We have seen from the testimony of Mauriac that this mechanism still operated in the late nineteenth century, although, of course, the stereotype was well established and did not have to be derived from direct experience. Another contributing element was economic, the association of the Jews with Finance, Money and Credit, regarded still in the nineteenth as in earlier centuries as "diabolical", because mysterious. Drumont, himself, claimed for example, in *La France juive*, that paper money was an invention of the Devil.[404]

Jewish strangeness was in itself a threat, a scandal, but Jews, of course, in Christian society were not simply strangers; they were enemies, the living

denial of Christian values that were meant to be absolute. As such they had
to be identified with the principle of evil, with the Devil, for no religious or
cultural pluralism could be contemplated.[405] Such considerations still had
force and meaning for nineteenth-century Catholics, particularly since pluralism had been specifically rejected by the *Syllabus of Errors* (1864) and later
papal pronouncements.[406] Thus *La Croix* identified the Jews with the Devil
very much in the traditional manner, claiming that Judaism was a Satanic
anti-Christianity, and, that before the End of the World, the Jews would
establish the reign of Anti-Christ.[407] And, as we have seen, Drumont associated Judaism and the Jews with the reversal of Christian ritual; the Jews
were "always haunted by the love of what was upside down, abnormal, distorted"; and their cult involved "the ancient sabbath of the witches, the mass
read backwards, the sign of the Cross made with the left hand".[408] By this
means also, as we have already argued, Christianity and Christian society
found and maintained their own identity by negatively defining and emphasizing what was not Christian. In this sense, as Loewenstein has put it, the Jews
"are the indispensable complement of Christian culture."[409] But Catholics in
the late nineteenth century had special reasons for reviving or re-emphasizing
this traditional response, which we will discuss more fully in the next part of
this chapter. Suffice it to point out here that manicheanism in the general
sense and demonology had always been a temptation for Christianity, resorted
to in circumstances of difficulty and attack, and that such circumstances
obtained at the end of the nineteenth century. It was not therefore surprising
that many Catholics imagined that the Church was being assailed by demonic
forces. Rambaud, editor of *Le Nouvelliste de Lyon*, referred to the contemporary struggle between "the sons of Darkness and the sons of Light."[410] Bloy
described the situation in which the Church found itself in 1878 as "Satanic";[411] and declared later: "Everything modern is the work of the
Devil."[412] In the same vein, since the antagonism between all that was
"modern" and the Church was accepted and proclaimed, abbé Lémann referred to "Satan . . . the grand maker of revolutions";[413] and the largely, if
not wholly, imaginary heresy of "Americanism" within the Church was frequently described as the work of Satan also.[414] More explicitly again, Bishop
Meurin claimed that the Church was being subjected to a special offensive on
the part of "Lucifer and his emissaries . . . Satan and the evil spirits that roam
the world . . ."[415] Modernity, of course, was frequently equated with the Jews,
and they were readily identified by such authors as the demonic agents in
question, both directly and indirectly. Guillemin remembered being told as a
child by a priest at Mâcon that "Zola was Satan".[416] Pierrard has written that
Catholics found it very easy to see the Church's struggle with the anticlerical
governments of the Third Republic, in particular, as "a manichean combat
between the Church of God and the forces of the Enemy, incarnated in the
Masonic Jew . . ."[417]

But, as Poliakov suggests, such manicheanism went beyond its original
Catholic framework, and satisfied socio-psychological needs that were perhaps
peculiarly modern, and related to the erosion of fixed and traditional values.

As Hofstadter has pointed out in a different context, the delineation of the enemy as demonic, "a kind of moral superman: sinister, ubiquitous, powerful, cruel, sensual, luxury-loving" is an evocation of a complete liberty, which is both attractive and extremely alarming.[418] Nineteenth-century French antisemites seem to have had some awareness of this. Bishop Meurin warned, for example: "Liberty of conscience, in masonic language, means licence to do evil."[419] The demonic Jew thus represented what the antisemite might be, what he might like to be, but what he did not dare to be. But, paradoxically, the characterization of the Jew "as an absolutely formidable being, as a power of extraordinary evil", in Memmi's words,[420] in short, as the Devil, also relieved the antisemite of his burden of freedom, for it reduced the course of events to a manichean struggle which he could in no way influence. It was thus, as Sartre has argued, a substitute for social and political action,[421] an ideology *per se*, which again gives it a purely religious dimension, an orientation away from the real world of contingency.[422]

Associated with the belief that Judaism was a Satanic religion was the idea that it required the sacrifice of Christian victims, particularly children. This old and widespread belief in ritual murder[423] was still alive among French antisemites at the end of the nineteenth century. "The fact that Jews murder Christian children is as evident as that the sun rises", wrote Drumont in 1891.[424] Although he admitted that such "ritual murder" was not prescribed by Mosaic law and that human sacrifice had been opposed by the Prophets, he yet insisted, in *La France juive*, that it represented "the accomplishment of a liturgical principle"; the Jews worshipped Moloch, "who required children and virgins as human sacrifices"; they believed "that, if Christ is really the Messiah, a drop of blood of a baptized Christian absorbed by a circumcised Jew will be enough to assure his salvation."[425] He claimed that ritual murder had been "a custom which the medieval Jews had habitually practised, and that, in countries where the Jew still exists in his savage state, these crimes are constantly renewed".[426] He retailed many historical accounts of "this bloody sacrifice, this charge proved a thousand times", from the Middle Ages to the seventeenth century;[427] and boasted of having "very many testimonies"[428] about ritual murders in contemporary Eastern Europe and the Near East, referring in particular to the well-publicized trials at Damascus in 1840 and at Smyrna in 1883, "which evidence it is impossible to deny, since the events occurred in the middle of the nineteenth century."[429] Moreover, Drumont suggested that spectacles showing ritual murder should be used in antisemitic propaganda.[430]

This suggestion does not seem to have been followed up, but the theme itself was certainly important in antisemitic propaganda. "Yes, mothers of France", announced *La Libre Parole* in December 1894, "to revenge themselves against your patriotism, the secret leaders of Judaism have decided that next year Israel will feed on unleavened bread soaked in that blood which the sacrificer draws from the poor Christian babies who disappear from time to time in a mysterious way. Only this time, it will be a hecatomb, and Christian children by the hundred will be bled dry for the next Passover."[431] The tone of this, its presentation as news, was perhaps unusual, but similar charges were very generally made in antisemitic writing. Earlier in the century both abbé Chiarini in *Théorie du Judaïsme* (1830) and Gougenot des Mousseaux retailed the myth as though it were fact.[432] At the time of the trial of a number of Jews at Tisza-Eszlar in Hungary in 1882–3 on the charge of ritual murder, most of the French press was incredulous, but *Le Pèlerin* and *L'Univers* expressed their belief in the charge.[433] In 1890, posters were put up in the *quartier des Halles* in Paris on 1 May, warning mothers not to let their children out, because the Jews needed their blood for the Passover rites. In March 1892, the *Journal de l'Indre-et-Loire* claimed to have discovered a ritual murder at Châtellerault, and this "discovery" was taken seriously by several important Catholic papers, including *La Croix*.[434] Qualified support to the general charge of ritual murder was given at the same time by both Bishop Meurin and abbé Lémann;[435] while Morès and *La Croix* endorsed it more whole-heartedly.[436] During the time of the Dreyfus Affair, according to Reinach,[437] the theme received even more support in antisemitic propaganda, and variations on it were produced. Abbé Puig, in a book published in 1897, claimed that Jewish newly-weds consumed ritual eggs in which Christian blood had been incorporated.[438] The Dominican, Père Constant, affirmed in *Les Juifs devant l'Eglise et devant l'histoire* (1897) that "The deicide race re-enacts, as far as it is able, the horrible crime of its ancestors, and subjects Christians, nearly always children, to the crucifixion of Calvary",[439] a claim that had also been made by Drumont in *La France juive*, and, in April 1892, by *La Semaine Religieuse de Luçon*.[440] Later, *La Libre Parole*, *La Croix* and *L'Univers* again gave full credence to the ritual murder charge in the Beilis trial at Kiev in 1913;[441] and Barrès apparently retained a belief in the general myth.[442]

Very significant in all this was the authority given to the idea of ritual murder by the ecclesiastical authorities. Drumont was able to point out that the Catholic Church had canonized several alleged victims of ritual murder;[443] he was also able to quote *La Civiltà Cattolica*,[444] whose championship of the myth has recently been examined by Charlotte Klein.[445] Moreover, Verdès-Leroux has shown that the myth was retailed by several official diocesan bulletins in France in the early 1890s. We have mentioned that of Luçon, and those of Auch, Le Puy, Montauban, Cambrai, Valence, Laval and Savoie should be added to it.[446] Some Catholic bishops outside France, notably Cardinals Manning and Bourne, had publicly rejected the idea of ritual murder, in response to Jewish objections,[447] but their voices found little echo among French bishops or at the Vatican, which allowed antisemites to ignore or ridicule what they said, and to uphold without gainsaying the idea that the reality of ritual murder was accepted by the Church.[448] As we have seen, Mgr Thomas, Archbishop of Rouen, did censure abbé Desportes in 1890 for publishing *Le Mystère du sang chez les Juifs*, which retailed the myth, but, as Drumont was able to note, the bishop of Séez, Mgr Trégaro, had congratulated the author for the same book, and Desportes had sent another pamphlet, *Tué par les Juifs*, to Rome in the same year, and had received the papal blessing.[449] In conclusion, it is interesting to see that this traditional

Catholic theme, like others, could be given a new modern meaning. Referring to the secular education policy of the Third Republic, Drumont wrote of the Jew in *La France juive:* "In the past, he attacked the body of children; today, it is their souls which he is after by teaching them atheism . . ."[450]

V

The characterization of Jews as agents of the Devil, in these various ways, was the means of expressing the feeling that they were the implacable enemies of the Catholic Church, as we have suggested, and only one means among others of indicating that it was the Jews who were mainly responsible for the dechristianization of France and for the Church's loss of support and status in the course of the nineteenth century. Lazare noted that the Jews were accused in his time of aiming at "the destruction of the religion of Christ".[451] Leroy-Beaulieu agreed that one of the most frequent accusations levelled by antisemites against the Jews was that they were "the great agents of the dechristianization and . . . secularization of modern societies".[452] Dagan observed that, despite the claim by some antisemites that their motives were not religious, "the Jews have nevertheless been accused of being the agents of dechristianization";[453] while Caillaux estimated that the success of antisemitic propaganda among Catholics derived in large part from its function as an explanation of anticlericalism; Catholics were easily persuaded that "the Jews, who were in the main Republicans, were stirring up the anticlerical movement, were seeking to persecute Catholics."[454] Such an interpretation of dechristianization on the part of Catholics was of course objectively mistaken—for one thing, it ignored the fact that secularization and the decline of religious practice affected Judaism as much as Catholicism—[455], but there is no doubt that it was a theme of overriding importance in antisemitic writings.

Gougenot des Mousseaux, in *Le Juif, le Judaïsme et la Judaïsation des peuples chrétiens,* first published in 1869, but reissued in 1886, presented a picture of the Catholic Church as the victim of a concerted attack by the forces of Freemasonry and Jewry.[456] Drumont took up the same theme in *La France juive,* accusing the Jews of having attacked and undermined the Catholic Church throughout French history, using the various guises of Albigensianism, Protestantism, Freemasonry and anticlericalism.[457] At first "silent and invisible", "the old hatred against Christianity" came into the open at the time of the French Revolution, when Jews took a leading part in the pillaging of churches and in the persecution of the clergy.[458] The anticlerical policy of the Third Republic was again inspired by the Jews, and was the latest reflection of their essential hatred of Christianity, of "the hatred of the Cross which is the Jew's dominant sentiment".[459] "Who are the instigators, the instruments and the accomplices of the persecution which began with the expulsion of our holy monks", asked Drumont, "which then attacked the souls of our children, and which deprived the poor, dying in hospitals, of their last hope and consolation . . . ?";[460] and the answer, of course, was the Protestants, the Freemasons and the Jews, with the Jews playing the leading role. "The persecution of religion takes on, with the Jews, an intensity that is quite peculiar to them. Nothing, for them, has changed: they hate Christ in 1886, as they hated him at the time of Tiberius Augustus, and they subject him to the same outrages."[461] And he claimed elsewhere later that "the whole priest-eating Republican world is run and controlled by the Jews", and that the anticlerical press was Jewish.[462] He could assert, therefore, in 1884 that the Jews "have destroyed the foundations of Christian society, if not of Christianity";[463] though he wrote, more optimistically in 1891 that "from the time that the antisemitic movement made its presence known, the attacks against the priests and the religious orders ceased almost completely",[464] thus demonstrating, to his own satisfaction, that anticlericalism was indeed a Jewish affair.

But Drumont's voice here was but one among many; yet again he was representative of a wide body of opinion. Père Pascal, for example, referred in 1887, to "the Jewish hatred of Christians . . ."[465] Déroulède, we have seen, accused the Jews, in the Chamber of Deputies in October 1891, of wanting "to dechristianize France".[466] La Croix claimed also that the Jews were active enemies of the Church, and those mainly responsible for dechristianization. In January 1899, the paper reiterated what was for it a familiar claim: God had allowed the French Church to suffer like Christ himself, "to be betrayed, sold, jeered at, beaten, covered with spittle, and crucified by the Jews."[467] A song published by L'Oeuvre de la Chanson Chrétienne Populaire in 1894 made more explicit reference to the secularizing policies of the Republic:

"Then, do you see / The anger of the Jews was loosed / Against the monk, the sister and the priest / Against the Lord our Master? . . . / Then, let's banish them / The Jews and the Masons / Who always want to harm the priest / And chase the Lord our Master / From school and hospital . . .".[468]

Bournand claimed in 1898 that it was the Jews who made antisemitism a religious question since "their hatred of the Christian" was nothing if not "religious", and he wrote also that Catholicism was being "attacked with particular venom in the Jewish press . . ."[469] And contributors to his volume made similar claims. Huysmans, for example, declared: "I am an antisemite, because I am convinced that it is the Jews who have turned France into the sad country, agitated by the lowest passions, the sad country without God, which we now see."[470] The pamphlet, Le Complôt juif, published about the same time, attributed these intentions to the Jews:[471]

Since the Christian Church is one of our most dangerous enemies, we must work with perseverance to lessen its influence; as far as possible, therefore, the ideas of free-thought, scepticism and schism must be grafted into the minds of those who profess the Christian religion, and religious disputes must be provoked among Christians so as to exacerbate their existing divisions. Logically, a start should be made by running down the ministers of that religion: let us declare an open war upon them, let us provoke suspicions about the genuineness of their piety, about their private lives, so that by ridicule and gossip we may undermine the prestige which is attached to their station and their cloth.

The same charge against the Jews occupied an important place in the propaganda of Christian Democracy. In the words of Mayeur, "it is common to see attributed to the Jews, allied to the Freemasons, liberated by the Revolution, a large share of the responsibility for the secularization policy [of the Republic], and, more generally, for all the misfortunes that the Church had suffered since 1789."[472] From another quarter, the convert Arthur Meyer, editor of the conservative daily, *Le Gaulois,* wrote in 1911: "In order to dechristianize France, Jules Ferry naturally relied on the support of three forces hostile to Catholics, the Jews, freethinkers and above all the Freemasons . . . The Republic governed for the Jews and against the Catholics, and antisemitism was born and developed as a pious protest against this state of affairs."[473] Léon Daudet pointed out that Eugène Mayer, editor of the anticlerical paper *La Lanterne* was a Jew, and wrote more generally of the same period: "Jewish clericalism, with its strong ethnic roots, went to war against the Catholic religion which is that of the majority of French people, and it placed its formidable financial resources at the disposition of the anticlericalism of Waldeck-Rousseau, the heir to the old anticlericalism of Gambetta."[474] Like many others, he saw what was allegedly a secular anticlericalism as a mask for Jewish anti-Christian religious fanaticism, a point made even more clearly in a remark about Zola's dramatic collaborator Busnach. "Anticlericalism", Daudet claimed, ". . . appealed to his fanatical Judaism, which he concealed under a conventional scepticism . . ."[475] The same theme could be used also in a political context. Jacques Piou, the Catholic *rallié* leader, asked, in his election campaign in the Lozère in 1913: "Do you want the Lozère to demand respect for its old religious beliefs . . . or do you want it to fall once again under Jewish and Masonic influence?"[476] All our examples so far have been from Catholics, but a non-Catholic like Séverine could also write in *La Libre Parole* in April 1895 that the Jews had brought antisemitism upon themselves by their attacks on the Catholic religion.[477]

As some of our quotations indicate, the coupling of antisemitism with anti-Freemasonry and with anti-Protestantism, which we have discussed in an earlier chapter,[478] and which was so common, itself implied that the Jews were hostile to the Catholic Church, and pointed to Jewish responsibility for dechristianization and anticlericalism. That antisemitism provided a crucial explanation of this phenomenon, which increasingly preoccupied Catholics is further underlined by the clergy's readiness to adopt it, for it was they who were most directly concerned with the decline in religious faith and practice. "When the French *Kulturkampf* began", commented Drumont, "the clergy did not know who their real enemies were, they could not explain to themselves the reasons for the relentless campaign directed against them. They had been told about the Freemasons, the unbelievers, the enemies of the Church, but no one had yet explained to them that it was the Jew who was behind it all", that is, not until the publication of *La France juive,* which then enlightened them.[479] It is certainly the case that a number of priests explicitly adopted the mode of explanation that antisemitism offered, and one can reasonably infer that in this they must have been fairly typical, as Drumont

suggests. Abbé Delassus, for example, wrote that the Alliance Israélite Universelle was "the headquarters of the anti-Christian conspiracy . . ."[480] Drumont,
again, quoted a letter from a country priest in 1891, which referred to "the
war being waged against the faith and the life of Christians by Jewish Freemasonry".[481] Among the upper clergy, Bishop Meurin expressed the same sense
of threat or persecution and singled out the same culprit against whom resistance must be directed,[482] evoking

> the humiliations inflicted by Freemasonry [and the Jews] on a harmless,
> pious and patient people . . . they attack the faith by means of atheistical
> education, the sanctity of marriage by divorce, moral purity by blasphemous
> plays and obscene literature, the freedom of worship by revolting prohibi-
> tions, property by inquitous and audacious robbery, the prestige of the
> clergy by incessant calumnies . . . The time has come to call a halt . . . We
> do not wish to be the slaves of the Jews, and we will never be.

Responsibility for the anticlerical policies of the Third Republic, moreover,
was pinned on the Jews by a considerable number of diocesan bulletins in the
early 1890s, including those of Quimper, Bourges, Pamiers, Perpignan, Sens,
Chartres and Aix.[483]

The idea of a Jewish conspiracy against the Church points to the profound
affinities which existed between antisemitism and late nineteenth-century
Catholicism. Both, in effect, were manifestations of the same mentality; both,
as we have suggested, were dualist or manichean, viewing the world and the
cosmos in terms of two distinct principles of Good and Evil, represented by
God and the Devil, by Christian and Jew. It is significant here that several
antisemites specifically criticized Judaism on the grounds that it was monotheistic. Jules Soury in Campagne nationaliste (1902) declared that "The greatest
harm done by Israel is to have infected our Western Aryan races with its
monotheism."[484] Probably echoing this, Barrès wrote in the same year: "Semitism and semitism alone is monotheistic. Christianity is quite different; it
represents a happy mean. The Aryans have always been polytheists . . .";[485]
while Maurras referred, in a letter to Barrès in 1905, to "my old objections
. . . to Hebrew unitarianism".[486] The function of this dualism was to construct
or to affirm the existence of an integrated society of the Good, by excluding
from it all that was evil, all that was impure. This was the reaction of the
antisemite in the face of a world of diversity, confusion and rapid social
change, and it was also the reaction, specifically, of the Catholic confronted
by a society which had rejected the totalitarian claims of the Church, and
changed that Church willy-nilly into a sect.[487] As we have seen, in another
context, Leroy-Beaulieu observed that the Nationalist movement behaved like
a sect, excommunicating French nationals from the "nation" in the name of
some arbitrary orthodoxy, which establishes another parallel.[488]

Three features of Catholic "sectarianism" in the later nineteenth century
are of special relevance in understanding this convergence with antisemitism.
First was the tendency of Catholicism, particularly on the popular level, to

retreat into "superstition" and irrationalism. As Weber has put it, "a new wave of popular fundamentalism engulfed the Church: miracles, prophecies, relics, visions, pilgrimages . . ."[489] This was the era of the Lourdes cult, of which Drumont we have seen was a devotee, of St Thérèse of Lisieux, of devotion to the Sacred Heart, and of pilgrimages to shrines old and new, with which the Assumptionists and abbé Garnier were closely associated. Some bishops were dismayed by these developments,[490] but they could not afford to dampen so welcome a sign that not all popular religiosity was dead. Many intellectuals, too, positively relished these manifestations of religious emotionalism, and were attracted back to the Church by them.[491] Antisemitism with its neo-mediaeval myths fitted well into this climate, while benefitting from the atmosphere of ready credulity which it encouraged.

A second "sectarian" trait of late nineteenth-century Catholicism, related to the first, was its tendency towards isolationism, towards cutting itself off from the rest of society. In 1897 Dr. Encausse explained the success of the frauds of Léo Taxil in these terms, but he could just as well have been explaining the success of antisemitism among Catholics: "Sheltered behind newspapers written especially for it in a special style, carefully avoiding any books not recommended by these papers, kept in near-total ignorance of the way in which modern society operates, the Catholic world as a whole was all set to be mystified, since it had been deprived of all means of protection against it."[492] As a closed world, too, Catholicism was all the more prone to see the outside world as necessarily hostile. Bloy, for example, made the typically exaggerated claim in 1878 that "the universally dominant sentiment in Europe, and above all in France is quite simply . . . the execration of Christianity."[493] What was mainly in objective terms a growing indifference towards religion, and only for a minority positive hostility, was seen as a total threat, as a deliberate and massive conspiracy. And, of course, as we have argued, no aspect of the Church, nothing within the confines of the faith, the faithful, the "pure", could explain this indifference or this hostility. The reasons for it had to be external, and antisemitism, together with anti-Masonry provided those reasons. Another feature of isolationism was a new stress on internal orthodoxy and discipline, reflected in the pronouncement of the doctrine of Papal Infallibility in 1870, and in subsequent papal denunciations of heresies, some of which, like "Americanism" condemned in 1899, seem to have existed mainly in the minds of those who condemned them.[494] Most significant here is the condemnation in the Encyclicals *Pascendi Gregis* and *Lamentabili Sane Exitu* of 1907 of Modernism, a heresy again which had more reality in those Encyclicals than in the writings of those whom they condemned, and which put an end to the attempt to reconcile the Church's traditional teaching with modern Biblical criticism.[495] At the same time Integrism, which stood for a policy of utter refusal to compromise with the outside modern world, and which, we have seen, was closely associated in France with the antisemitic Action Française, achieved a position of ideological dominance in the Church.[496] Antisemitic nationalism, as this association

suggests, represents a similar isolationism, a similar rigid orthodoxy, and antisemitism and Catholicism again converged here around an attachment to fixed
and absolute manichean categories.

Third, Catholicism in the later nineteenth century refused to come to terms
with a situation in which it was merely one of several competing denomina-
tions in a fundamentally secular society. Objectively, it became a sect, but it
still maintained its claims to be a universal religion. Indifferentism had been
formally condemned in the *Syllabus of Errors* of 1864, and, more recently, the
Encyclical *Immortale Dei* of 1885 had laid down that "the equal toleration
of all religions . . . is the same thing as atheism . . ."[497] But, much more was
concerned here than doctrinal intolerance, for the Church was assuming here
that its monopolistic status ought to be officially and legally recognized and
upheld. As Gadille has recently demonstrated, the Catholic hierarchy in
France, as late as the mid-1880s, maintained with near-unanimity that State
and society should be officially and legally Christian,[498] and there is little
evidence that attitudes fundamentally changed on this issue over the next two
decades. It is true that some Catholics favoured and others acquiesced in the
Separation of Church and State in 1905, but this was mainly because it freed
them from the surveillance and control which the Concordatory régime placed
in the hands of what was by then a decidedly anticlerical administration, and
the Pope, of course, refused to accept the Separation on or in the terms laid
down by the French government.[499] This refusal was in line with what was
a very general reaction of Catholics to the progress of secularization, and that
was a more exaggerated, and now inevitably sectarian, attachment to a total
Christian order. This, rather than some reconciliation with modern society,
was the aim of Social Catholicism, according to Rollet,[500] and, we have seen,
that it was the aim of the Union Nationale. And, here again, a fundamental
Catholic assumption converged with antisemitism. Michel Lévy had observed
in 1836 that "the emancipation of the Jews was an anti-Catholic event".[501]
Lazare argued in 1894 that "the Jew is the living testimony to the disappearance of that Christian state, which had its basis in certain theological principles, a state which the Christian antisemites dreamed of reconstituting. The
day that a Jew was appointed to a civic office, the Christian state was in peril
. . ."[502] Catholics and antisemites were both attached to a conception of an
old Christian France, which the Jew threatened not only as a religious anti-
Christian but also as a citizen. Thus, as Lovsky has noted, secularization itself
"feeds Christian antisemitism".[503] This can be seen from the writings of
Catholic antisemites. Biez, for example, asserted that France was in essence
"the country of the Gospel in action, the land blessed by Christ who loves the
Franks", and looked forward to the time, when, rid of its Jews, it "would again
become wholly Christian."[504] And similar views were expressed in the propaganda of the Union Nationale.[505] In his *Vers un ordre social chrétien*, La Tour
du Pin told his readers that they "must never lose sight of the fact that France
is a kingdom of Christ, and that if the deicide nation comes near it, it can
only be to give it the kiss of Judas."[506] More practically and apparently more
modestly, Bishop Meurin, in his attack on Jewish Freemasonry, stressed that

Catholics wanted "to take their legitimate share in the public administration of our country".[507] Relevant also are the views of the antisemitic Joseph in Mirbeau's *Le Journal d'une femme de chambre*. He is said to be "not a clerical, but just for religion", yet he declares: "So long as religion has not been restored in France as it was in the old days . . . so long as everyone is not obliged to go to mass and to confession . . . we won't have got anywhere . . ."[508] This overlap between antisemitism and a totalitarian conception of Catholicism is the more significant in that it is in line with the finding of Glock and Stark, for the United States, that antisemitism is most likely when traditional Christian beliefs about Jews are "combined with a particularistic conception of one's own religion".[509] A further consideration under this heading must be that Catholics combined isolationism, which involved distrust and ignorance of the outside social world, with the pretention to direct and order that world. Unaware of real social mechanisms, as Dr Encausse pointed out, they yet required a social doctrine, they needed some explanation of the social process; and this they could conveniently find in the simplistic formulae of antisemitism. Antisemitism, too, did not merely "explain" the modern world and the modern economy, it condemned them in the name of older higher values to which militant Catholics above all proclaimed their allegiance.

French anticlericalism was primarily a reaction against the Church's view that it had this social and political role to play. It was this view and the action that sprang from it that contemporaries called "clericalism". A number of anticlericals saw "clericalism" and antisemitism as going hand in hand, as we have just shown that they did, but, for anticlericals, there was a strong tendency to regard this coupling as a deliberate attempt to manipulate opinion. As we have seen, Georges Renard of *La Petite République* told Dagan in 1899: "The antisemitic agitation . . . seems to me to be an episode in the 'clerical' reaction which began in the early 1880s, and which seduced the rich bourgeoisie, terrified by the prospect of social reforms . . ."[510] Henry Maret declared similarly at about the same time that "antisemitism is the invention and the revenge of the Jesuit party";[511] while Prolo agreed, writing in 1902: "What we see is the revival of the clerical campaign, carried on under the cover of antisemitic nationalism."[512] Clemenceau explained in more detail in the late 1890s:[513]

> It was no good hoping to arouse the masses directly for the defence of religious beliefs, for those beliefs were not really threatened. It was much easier for the Church to lay claim to a monopoly of patriotism, to range itself with the cry of "France for the French" and denounce the Jews, the Protestants and the Freethinkers as unpatriotic. The Catholic party as a whole devoted itself to this enterprise with the greatest enthusiasm. And, as a result, the peril of clericalism was eclipsed by the Jewish peril.

This "diversionary", or even manipulative, dimension of Catholic antisemitism should not be ignored. Antisemitism was seen as a means of reviving the appeal of Catholicism, particularly, as we have seen, by providing it with a social and economic doctrine or message, and one that overlaid or disguised its essential conservatism. As such, antisemitism proved particularly attractive to both Social Catholics, and, more so, to Christian Democrats. This function of antisemitism has been made clear in our examination of the Union Nationale, and Drumont's "populist" denunciation of the Catholic hierarchy and Catholic notables must be seen in the same light. *La Croix,* too, saw antisemitism as a weapon in the campaign to rechristianize the masses, a campaign motivated by the totalitarian imperative that we have already discussed, and which could not distinguish between a society in which religious faith and practice were vigorous and a certain social order. As Père Picard of the Assumptionists put it in 1873:[514]

> The workers today form a caste that is the enemy of society . . . because they have lost the faith and closed their hearts to the hope of bliss in heaven, they have had to open them to the passion for material pleasures, and they have come to covet all the things of which they are deprived. To save society from their envy and their hatred, they must be converted again to the faith.

But one should be careful here to distinguish between function and motive, and to avoid attributing to Catholics and antisemites a greater degree of social awareness or social consciousness than they in fact possessed. Indeed, we have earlier stressed that Catholic antisemitism was an indication of the "alienation" of Catholics, of their lack of social awareness, of their bewilderment in the face of the Church's loss of influence and prestige. As Pataut has put it:[515]

> The clergy as a whole and the lay leadership were experiencing the decline, the regression of Catholicism . . . and they were all alarmed by the scale and the rapidity of the process. But, in seeking to fight against it, to safeguard existing positions, if not to reconquer those that had already been lost, they seem never to have appreciated either the real causes or the exact nature of that process.

They sought "moral" and political explanations for what was a social and cultural phenomenon. Hence the appeal of the antisemitic explanation of dechristianization, which had the added advantage of entirely relieving Catholics of any responsibility for the situation. It even allowed them, paradoxically, to deny that the movement away from, or against, the Church had any real popular backing. Drumont, for example, asserted, in *La France juive,* that "the unleashing of invective and insults against Christ, the Virgin, the Church and the Clergy, in no way reflects any real feeling among the people; it is absolutely artificial, being organized by the Jews with the skill which they habitually employ to create false currents of opinion through their newspapers about financial affairs."[516] If this is a striking testimony to the antisemites' belief that opinion could be manipulated, it also suggests that any effective implementation of this belief had a formidable barrier of misapprehension and sociological naïveté to overcome. If the antisemites were deliberately misleading people, it was a case of the blind misleading the blind.

Two further issues were involved in the manipulative interpretation of Catholic antisemitism made by anticlericals. The first we have touched on, and that is the association of Catholicism with a backward-looking hierarchical view of the social order. Here again antisemitism overlapped with the traditional Catholic view. Drumont claimed that, in the past, the Church "had been not only a gentle director of souls, but also a marvellous organizer of social life . . . She protected the Labour and the Savings of men against the covetous greed of the Jew";[517] and he celebrated "that ban on usury by means of which the Church, with maternal solicitude, protected the wealth of the hard-working and simple Aryan, for centuries, against the covetousness of the astute and greedy Semite."[518] There was a tendency, too, to regard the Church itself as a paradigm of the general social order which antisemites yearned for. Drumont again put forward the army and the Church as models; they were, as we have seen, "the two bodies in the State" in which "the flame of devotion to duty" still burned, in which "the spirit of sacrifice" still lived.[519] Moreover, as Renard suggested, many non-Catholics came to share Père Picard's conviction that Catholicism was a necessary bulwark of the social order. Barrès, for example, had been an anticlerical at the time of Boulangism, but arrived a decade later at the view that the Church was an essential "force for order", that was "useful to society . . ."[520] Maurras held this conviction even more strongly.[521]

The second point is that antisemitism was the means by which Catholics were able to proclaim their patriotism. This can be seen very clearly in the case of the Union Nationale. The title chosen for itself by this Catholic organization is itself significant, but it was only one indication of the chauvinistic mould in which it cast its Catholicism. It continually evoked the "divine vocation" of the French nation,[522] and it campaigned for the recognition of Joan of Arc as France's patron saint.[523] One motive of this exaggerated patriotism was the desire on the part of French Catholics to avoid and refute the charge that they were, in fact, as Catholics, less than patriotic, that they belonged to an international organization. One of abbé Garnier's speeches in 1894 was interrupted by a heckler, who said: "All Catholics are unworthy of the name of Frenchmen: they are under orders from the Pope."[524] Sorlin has concluded, à propos of La Croix, that "antisemitism served to prove that Catholics were members of the national community."[525] National identity was asserted here, as in other quarters, in contrast to the excluded Jew, but, with Catholics this mechanism had a parallel function, for it was the means also by which a threatened Catholicism asserted its own identity and unity, in sectarian and artificial fashion. While maintaining its totalitarian pretensions, the Church had also to draw a stricter line between itself and the secular forces which were, or which seemed to be, undermining it. And antisemitism again was a means of doing just this. Albert Réville, the historian of religions, argued, in this context, in 1899, that antisemitism was a campaign "directed systematically against non-Catholics . . . The slogan: 'France for the French' means, in the last analysis: 'France for the clericals' ".[526] And there is much in Catholic antisemitic propaganda to support his view. The president of the Comité Electoral Catholique of the 15th arrondissement of Paris, for example, in February 1898 "urged Catholics to unite . . . against 'the Jewish and Masonic heretics' . . ."[527] La Croisade Française, in the same year, coined the slogan: "Among French Catholics";[528] while a speaker at a Union Nationale meeting in Roanne, in March 1899, called for "the union of all Catholics against the Jewish people".[529] We have noted that this was a period in which new emphasis was placed on strict orthodoxy within the Church, and at least one observer claimed that antisemitism played a part in this movement to eliminate ideological dissidence. Lombroso remarked that it was used by the clergy and the Vatican, "who, under the pretext of avenging the good Lord . . . sought to suffocate those spirits in the Church who, to some degree, represented modernity and new ideas . . ."[530] The argument is a little obscure, though there is no doubt, as we have argued above, that anti-modernism in the Church, whatever its form, and antisemitism went together, and that they can both be seen as reflections of the same isolationist mentality.

In apparent opposition to the mainly Catholic nature of French antisemitism was the anticlerical strand, that we have already encountered in connection with the Ligue Antisémitique Française. As Hertzberg and Delpech have recalled, this strain in French anti-Jewish sentiment derived from the Enlightenment, and such anticlerical antisemitism was particularly pronounced in the work of Voltaire.[531] It occurred, too, among certain Jacobins, for example Rewbell, who was a deputy from Alsace;[532] and it was characteristic of a number of early nineteenth-century antisemites, notably Tridon, whose *Du Molochisme juif* was an attack on Christianity.[533] *La Libre Pensée*, a review which appeared in 1866–7, combined violent anticlericalism with racial antisemitism in a similar way.[534] At the end of the century, as we have seen, antisemitism lingered on in Left-wing, Socialist and Anarchist circles, and was frequently combined there again with attacks on religion and the Church. Paule Mink, for example, delivered an attack on religion and on "Jewry" at a meeting of "antisemites and freethinkers" of the 20th *arrondissement* of Paris in March 1898.[535] Armand Charpentier wrote in the anticlerical *L'Action* in July 1904: "Priests, pastors, rabbis, they are all the same: religious faith stifles reason and the critical faculty."[536] But anticlericalism was also present within the antisemitic movement itself. An early antisemitic periodical, *L'Anti-Youtre*, which appeared briefly in 1891–2, was anticlerical in tone, announcing in its first issue that "until now, only the clericals have attacked the Jews", a situation which it intended to remedy.[537] As we have seen, Barrès was an anticlerical at the start of his political career, and was defeated as such by Gervaize in the 1898 elections at Nancy.[538] A speaker at the Cercle Antisémitique d'Etudes Sociales, in March 1898, reproached Catholics for "their close relations with the Jews"; while another speaker at the Cercle, in April, stressed that antisemites should makes the masses understand "that they are absolutely independent of any religious confession."[539] Cantaloube, an antisemitic candidate in the 1898 elections in the 3rd *arrondissement* of Paris, called for the Separation of Church and State in his programme, which was at this time an anticlerical platform.[540] As we have seen, too, the Ligue Antisémitique Française, in its bid for popular support and its rivalry with Drumont and *La Libre Parole*, which were Catholic in orientation, also adopted an anticlerical stance. Although Guérin continued to express his "profound respect" for religious beliefs,[541] a speaker told a meeting of the Ligue in May 1898 that antisemites should be on their guard against "the intrusion of the clergy in their ranks. He warned also against the spirit of domination which characterizes the priest, and told members that they must, above all, avoid the reproach which was levelled against antisemites by their enemies, the reproach that they were, if not the defenders, at least the allies of clericalism."[542] The same considerations seem to have weighed also, though less heavily, with those Catholic antisemites, like Drumont, who protested, on occasions, that their antisemitism was not religious in complexion. Relevant here is the attitude of Picard, who was not a Catholic. He claimed that "antisemitism . . . appealed not only to faithful Catholics, but also to minds absolutely detached from its beliefs", and he was anxious to rid antisemitism of its Catholic and theological associations, which, he thought, made some anticlericals sympathetic towards the Jews.[543] Significant, finally, is the example of another prominent figure in the antisemitic movement, Max Régis. He was an anticlerical, but apparently enjoyed the support of Catholics in Algiers, despite this.[544] Anticlerical antisemitism was thus extremely complex, but it can be seen, among other things, as one more indication of the importance of the Christian and Catholic element in anti-Jewish ideas and attitudes. Ideologically, anticlericals were opposed to the Jews, in large part because they saw Christianity as deriving from Judaism; while, on the tactical and political level, it is telling that such care had to be taken by non-Catholic antisemites, on the one hand, to guard themselves against being dominated by Catholics or being associated willy-nilly in people's minds with clericalism, and, on the other hand, to avoid offending Catholic susceptibilities.

More generally, too, anticlerical and clerical antisemitism exemplified a common credulity, "an exaggerated, instinctive credulity, impervious to all rational arguments",[545] that, in its turn, expressed an overpowering need to believe. We have already come across many examples of this, but the point is worth underlining. Abbé Pichot, in a letter to the press in December 1898, drew attention to this phenomenon. The French clergy, he said, were not responsible for the anti-Dreyfusard hysteria, any more than for the Léo Taxil affair; they were simply dupes, believers: "The clergy has doubtless put its trust *a priori* in the High Command, in the military leaders, as it put its trust in Léo Taxil; its blind trust prevented it from asking questions, from studying the evidence. It believed in the 'Syndicate of Treason' as it believed in Diana Vaughan, but its good faith was unquestionable.[546]" *Le Temps* commented in April 1897 on the success of the Taxil frauds: "Today 'fideism' is more in favour than the intellectualism of St Thomas Aquinas. And this new tendency, by weakening the critical spirit, has probably contributed to encourage, among the faithful, this burgeoning of superstitions, all more or less occult, which recalls the great flourishing of magic, which accompanied . . . the agony of paganism."[547] Abbé Brugerette commented similarly that the Affair had revealed that there existed among Catholics, in particular, "a lamentable and seemingly boundless credulity"; and he, too, saw the links between the Dreyfus and the Taxil affairs: "Those who perpetrated the forgeries in the General

Staff were, in a way, carrying on the work of Taxil. Only the theme had changed." And on Catholic willingness to be taken in in both cases, he commented: "Not only have we made a spectacle of ourselves as people incapable of thinking for ourselves, but we have shown that we cannot even follow out own logic. Instead of checking, as was our duty, the testimony of those from whom we derived our convictions, we preferred to accept them blindly as authorities."[548] On another level, the Prefect of Mayenne reported in 1899: "It is said that all those who are calling for the revision [of the Dreyfus case] are Jews and enemies of the army. The people, who most readily accept ideas that are simple, have believed this."[549] With the Affair, to a certain extent, and with Taxil, we are dealing with deliberate and successful attempts to hoodwink people, and to manipulate opinion. And more extreme or more material examples of the same phenomenon can be adduced. The antisemitic and nationalist review, La Croisade Française, for example, founded in 1898, with Quesnay de Beaurepaire as its political director, issued mail-order catalogues to its readers, offering a wide range of products for sale. This side of its activities was revealed in 1905 to be a large-scale fraud.[550] In the same genre was the Oeuvre des Enfants Tuberculeux run by a "Sister Candide". This alleged Catholic charity, which raised considerable sums for its supposed cause, was again revealed in 1910 to be a fraud.[551] And we have seen that there was a money-making side to the activities of the professional antisemites.

But it would be a mistake to overemphasize this manipulative element, as some contemporaries were prone to do. Anatole France, for example, wrote in Voltairean fashion that "the credulity of the masses is infinite. Seduced and angry, they ran headlong into the trap set for them by the antisemites."[552] It is necessary, first, to make the obvious point that, if people are being duped and manipulated, they must be eminently open to being duped or manipulated, and this is not a quality that one can presume about any population or section of the population. Besides testifying to the existence of this credulity, the observations of contemporaries provide some explanations for it. Some, like the Prefect of Mayenne, saw it as the residue of an ancient lack of enlightenment. Referring to antisemitic beliefs generally, Duclaux wrote in La Petite République in December 1898 that "through lack of any critical spirit, the traditional hatred for the Jew has remained more or less rooted in people's minds."[553] Among Catholics especially, such traditional beliefs combined with an enormous respect for authority and with the sectarian tendencies, which we have already discussed. But traditionalism, a term which is anyway far too simplistic, is not a sufficient explanation. As we shall discuss in a later chapter, nineteenth-century antisemitism derived from traditional beliefs, but it was not the same as them. A more plausible suggestion, it would seem here, would be to relate the need to believe with the bewilderment or anomie associated with cultural change, that is, precisely with the weakening or the collapse of traditional values. Antisemitism can then be seen as an attempt to reconstruct those values, a neo-traditionalism, and as a creed, among others, which fills a "religious" and cosmological vacuum. There is certainly no doubt that antisemitism and the antisemitic movement had qualities that were religious, that they were a faith. Viau recounted that those working on *La Libre Parole* believed in "antisemitism, only redeemer of France in peril", in the same way that Christians believed in their Redeemer. The staff of the newspaper, he said, were not employees "but rather apostles of Drumont . . . every remark of M. Drumont was like the Gospel for us . . ."[554] An entry to the 1901–2 subscription of *La Libre Parole* declared: "If necessary, Drumont, we will be your martyrs."[555] A police agent commented in June 1900 on those who subscribed to the anti-Dreyfusard leagues that they were "simple patriots, for whom the Idea was all, and who really feared that Reinach and the Jews were selling France to Germany . . ."[556]

The evidence in this chapter supports those writers who have stressed the importance of the Christian roots of modern antisemitism. As Poliakov has put it, "the envies of 'economic antisemitism', or the phantasmagoria of 'racial antisemitism' derive . . . from the entirely distinctive passion which underlies religious antisemitism, and to which a sufficiently profound analysis nearly always reduces them, in one way or another."[557] But while admitting the enduring vitality of myths and images deriving from traditional Christianity, and while taking account of the fact that attitudes towards Jews were historically moulded by their position as an alien religious group in Christian society, one need not follow Poliakov's reductionism all the way. If economic and racial antisemitism had a Christian substratum, it remains true that late nineteenth-century antisemitism in France was, to a high degree, secular in formulation and in function, although it was strongest among Catholics or in "those milieus which claimed to be Catholic".[558] But Catholic antisemites were concerned mainly about the secular social and political status of the Church, and their contact with traditional theological stances vis-à-vis the Jews was, with few exceptions, extremely tenuous. Their ignorance of Jewish life and thought, of Judaism, was, moreover, nearly complete. Pierrard has written: "for me as for many children brought up in Catholic colleges [in the early years of the twentieth century], the synagogue was a strange and forbidden place . . . whose doors were perpetually closed to us, and whose walls, we knew, hid from us invisible mysteries . . ."[559] As Gamzon has commented, even a man like Claudel, who devoted considerable and serious attention to Judaism, totally neglected post-exilic thought and literature.[560] Even within the course of the nineteenth century, there seems to have been an important shift here. Early Catholic antisemites like abbé Chiarini or Gougenot des Mousseaux had concentrated their attention on the Talmud, and had taken the Fathers of the Church as an important point of reference.[561] Theirs was still essentially a religious anti-Judaism. Even Veuillot had claimed: "We are the enemies of Judaism . . . not of the Jews."[562] By contrast, Drumont and his contemporaries were engaged in a secular and racialist ideology, an antisemitism proper, which was still "religious", as we have stressed, but religious in a significantly different way. Ironically, what was a protest against the secularization of society, is itself an indicator of the progress of that secularization.

NOTES

1 Brunetière, "Après le Procès", p. 432; see also Durkheim, in Dagan, *Enquête sur l'antisémitisme*, pp. 61–2.

2 See Drumont, *La France juive*, I, pp. 37, 86, 145, 456–7; and II, pp. 64, 417 and 433; and Bournand, *Les Juifs et nos contemporains*, pp. 37–42.

3 Drumont, *La Dernière Bataille*, pp. ix–xiii; also Pierrard, *Juifs et catholiques français*, pp. 38–9.

4 See Drumont, *DB*, p. xv. Since both Islam and Christianity were religions indebted, in different degrees, to Judaism, Drumont's point has no force at all. One could argue, indeed, in contrary fashion, that the comparison of attitudes to and the treatment of Jews in Islamic and in Christian societies, highlights the religious factor. Islam, which had a more tenuous link with Judaism, treated Jews, on the whole more favourably than Christendom, whose faith was much more closely enmeshed with the older religion; see Poliakov, "La Condition juive dans l'Empire des Califes", *Les Juifs et notre histoire*, pp. 34–53; and Lovsky, *L'Antisémitisme chrétien*, pp. 123–5; but also Littmann, "Jews under Muslim Rule in the late Nineteenth Century", on the persecution of Jews in North Africa, persecution that was not, however, officially sanctioned at the highest level.

5 *L'Anti-Youtre*, 26 April 1892, cit. Verdès-Leroux, *Scandale financier*, p. 144; also ibid., p. 138; and Vaucelles, *"La Nouvelliste de Lyon" et la défense religieuse*, p. 219.

6 See Pierrard, op. cit., pp. 64–5.

7 Abbé Gayraud, cit. Bournand, op. cit., p. 201.

8 AN F7 12480.

9 Picard, in Bournand, op. cit., pp. 7 and 21.

10 Maurras, *Quand les Français*, p. 215.

11 See, for Buffet, Maurras, *Enquête sur la monarchie*, p. 43; and, for Delassus, Pierrard, op. cit., p. 114.

12 Rochefort, *L'Intransigeant*, 17 February 1898, cit. Bournand, op. cit., p. 54.

13 Cassagnac, cit. ibid., p. 105; also Drumont, in ibid., p. 37.

14 Daily Report, Prefect of Police, 24 February 1898. APP Ba 106.

15 Dagan, op. cit., p. 8.

16 Ibid., p. 30.

17 Ibid., p. 42.

18 Zévaès, *L'Affaire Dreyfus*, p. 211.

19 Zola, "Pour les Juifs" (1896); and "Procès-Verbal" (1897), *L'Affaire Dreyfus, La Vérité en marche*, pp. 59, 61, and 85.

20 See Bein, *Theodore Herzl*, p. 38.

21 See chapter XI, n. 365.

22 See Sorlin, *"La Croix" et les Juifs*, pp. 96–107.

23 Cit. Bournand, op. cit., p. 149. Loyson was, it should be added, highly unorthodox; see n. 307 below.

24 See Drumont, *FJ*, I, p. 293; and *Le Testament d'un antisémite*, p. x.

25 Biez, *Les Rothschild et le péril juif*, p. 12.

26 Duroselle, "L'Antisémitisme en France", p. 58.

27 Pierrard, op.cit., p. 116.

28 Verdès-Leroux, op. cit., p. 13; also p. 171.

29 Saint-Poli, *L'Affaire Dreyfus et la mentalité catholique*, pp. 11, 24–5 and 64.

30 Maurras, *La Gazette de France*, 28 January 1906, cit. Pierrard, op. cit., p. 209; see also ibid., pp. 81 and ff; Mauriac, "L'Affaire Dreyfus", pp. 11 and 15; and chapter II, pp. 81–2 above.

31 See Blumenkranz, ed., *Histoire des Juifs en France*, p. 267; and Pierrard, op. cit., pp. 21–2. Gougenot des Mousseaux was a Commander of the Order of Pius IX.

32 Clemenceau, *La Dépêche de Toulouse*, 12 March 1898, cit. Bournand, op. cit., p. 74.

33 Lazare, cit. Péguy, *Notre Jeunesse*, p. 129.
34 Drumont, *TA*, p. 345; also *DB*, p. 506.
35 Cohen, *Les Déicides*, p. 310.
36 Rochefort, *L'Intransigeant*, 17 February 1898.
37 Glock and Stark, *Christian Beliefs and Anti-Semitism*, pp. xvi and 99.
38 Memmi, *Portrait d'un Juif*, p. 196. See also, from widely differing epochs and societies, the declarations of Cervantes' Sancho Panza: "I've always believed in God and all the tenets of the Holy Roman Catholic Church . . . I am a mortal enemy to the Jews." (Cervantes, *Don Quixote* (Penguin edition), p. 516, cit. Szasz, *The Manufacture of Madness*, p. 203); and of Hitler: "I believe that I am acting in accordance with the will of the Almighty Creator: by defending myself against the Jew, I am fighting for the work of the Lord." (cit. Glock and Stock, op. cit., p. xv).
39 Poliakov, *Les Juifs et notre histoire*, p. 13; see also Cohen, *Les Déicides*, pp. lv–lvi and *passim;* Lovsky, *L'Antisémitisme chrétien*, p. 15; and Glock and Stark, op. cit., p. 65.
40 Loewenstein, *Christians and Jews*, p. 94; see also A, Lukyn Williams, *Adversos Judaeos, A Bird's Eye View of Christian Apologiae until the Renaissance* (Cambridge, 1935); Sigmund Freud, *Moses and Monotheism: Three Essays* (1939), Freud, English Standard Edition, XXIII (London, 1964) pp. 86, 88–91, 135–6 and *passim;* Marcel Simon, *Verus Israël* (Paris, 1948); Jules Isaac, *Genèse de l'antisémitisme, Essai historique* (Paris, 1956); Glock and Stark, op. cit., p. 44; and Poliakov, *Les Juifs et notre histoire*, p. 14.
41 Memmi, op. cit., p. 224.
42 See n. 40; and Poliakov, *The History of Antisemitism*, I, pp. 17–25, 50–6 and 123–37; Poliakov, *Les Juifs et notre histoire*, p. 13; Loewenstein, op. cit., p. 98; Lovsky, *L'Antisémitisme chrétien*, chapters II and III; Hertzberg, *The French Enlightenment and the Jews*, pp. 35–7; Glock and Stark, op. cit., p. 50; and Blumenkranz, ed., op. cit., p. 267.
43 Poliakov, *Les Juifs et notre histoire*, p. 14.
44 Loewenstein, op. cit., p. 98.
45 See particularly *The Epistle of Paul the Apostle to the Romans*, Chapter XI; also the comments of Jacques Maritain, *Antisemitism* (London, 1939), pp. 16–17.
46 Loewenstein, op. cit., p. 190; also ibid., pp. 24, 98, 101 and 193; Lovsky, *L'Antisémitisme chrétien*, chapter IV; Wirth, *The Ghetto*, pp. 58–60; Tharaud, *Petite Histoire des Juifs*, p. 23; Edmund Wilson, *A Piece of My Mind* (London, 1957), chapter VI; Prajs, "Péguy et le peuple juif", pp. 396–7; and Landau, "Aspects et problèmes spécifiques de l'histoire des Juifs en France", pp. 232–5.
47 See Lovsky, *L'Antisémitisme chrétien*, pp. 139–42 and 163–4; and Blumenkranz, ed., op. cit., pp. 267–8. Bossuet's *Discours sur l'histoire universelle* was republished many times in the eighteenth and nineteenth centuries; the *Oeuvres de l'abbé Fleury* were republished in Paris in 1837.
48 *Le Publiciste*, 1806, cit. Joseph Hours, "Un Précurseur oublié de l'antisémitisme français: le vicomte de Bonald", *Cahiers Sioniens*, III, no. 11 (1950), p. 168, and Lovsky, *L'Antisémitisme chrétien*, p. 285.
49 See Viard, "L'*Encyclopédie nouvelle* de Pierre Leroux et l'idée de race", p. 16.
50 Renan, *Oeuvres complètes*, I, p. 921 and *passim*.
51 See Byrnes, *Antisemitism in Modern France*, pp. 113–14, and Lovsky, *L'Antisémitisme chrétien*, pp. 119 and 245.
52 Meurin, *La Franc-maçonnerie, Synagogue de Satan*, p. 465; also pp. 192–4.
53 See L'Hermite, *L'Anti-Pape*, p. 229; and Bournand, op. cit., p. 193. Mgr d'Hulst (1841–1896), Rector of the Institut Catholique in Paris, and a liberal Catholic, was not an antisemite (see R. P. Lecanuet, *La Vie de l'Eglise sous Léon XIII* (Paris, 1930), pp. 314–15 and 350–4; and Alec R. Vidler, *A Variety of Catholic Modernists* (Cambridge, 1970), p. 65); the position of abbé Lemire, a leading Christian Democrat, was more equivocal (see pp. 527–8 and ff. below).

54 Drumont, *DB*, p. xiv; see also *FJ*, I, p. 306.
55 Picard, *Synthèse de l'antisémitisme*, p. 38.
56 Bloy, *Le Salut par les Juifs*, p. 33.
57 Ibid., pp. 56–8; also ibid., generally.
58 Eve Grosjean, "Le Juif d'Anvers", *Cahiers Paul Claudel*, 7, pp. 116–17.
59 Cit. Pierrard, op. cit., p. 220.
60 See Jacques Petit, "Claudel et Bloy", *Cahiers Paul Claudel*, 7, pp. 378–86; also Petit, *Bernanos, Bloy, Claudel, Péguy*, pp. 33–59 and *passim*; Denise R. Gamzon, "Claudel rencontre Israël"; and Charles Galpérine, "L'Exégète et le témoin", *Cahiers Paul Claudel*, 7, pp. 71–101 and 137–74.
61 See Pierrard, op. cit., pp. 20 and 52–3; Duroselle, op. cit., pp. 58–9; and C. Marcilhacy, *Le Diocèse d'Orléans sous l'épiscopat de Mgr Dupanloup* (Paris, 1962), pp. 21–47, 86–96, 134–52 and *passim*.
62 Picard, op. cit., pp. 134 and 153; see also Dagan, op. cit., p. 4.
63 Cit. Prajs, "Péguy et le peuple juif", p. 392.
64 See Drault, *Drumont, La France juive et La Libre Parole*, pp. 42–5.
65 See Bournand, op. cit., p. 195.
66 Bloy, *Le Vieux de la montagne* (1911), cit. Pierrard, op. cit., p. 220.
67 Bloy, *Le Salut par les Juifs*, p. 68.
68 Glock and Stark, op. cit., pp. 78–9; also Lovsky, *L'Antisémitisme chrétien*, pp. 201–11; and Hertzberg, op. cit., pp. 249–67 (on abbé Grégoire's advocacy of proselytism).
69 See Lémann, *La Prépondérance juive*, I, pp. 2–3 and *passim*.
70 Drumont, *FJ*, I, p. 225; also ibid., I, pp. 125, 216–17, 228 and 374; and Andrieux, *A travers la République*, pp. 314–15.
71 Drumont, *La France juive devant l'opinion*, pp. 32–3.
72 Picard, op. cit., pp. 98–9.
73 Ibid., pp. 38–9, 42 and *passim*.
74 Abbe Demnise, *Poésies patriotiques* (1896), cit. Pierrard, op. cit., p. 86.
75 Bloy, *Le Salut par les Juifs*, p. 52.
76 Lacretelle, *Silbermann*, p. 84.
77 Marie Colombier, *Les Mémoires de Sarah Barnum* (Paris, no date-c. 1885), p. 27; also p. 19.
78 See Pierrard, op. cit., pp. 22–4; Landau, op. cit., pp. 239–40; Tharaud, *Notre cher Péguy*, II, p. 60; Benda, *La Jeunesse d'un clerc*, p. 134; Blumenkranz ed., op. cit., p. 326; Marrus, *The Politics of Assimilation*, pp. 60–2; and Mirbeau, *Le Journal d'une femme de chambre*, p. 104. For the opposite view, see Anatole France, *L'Eglise et la République*, p. 126, where he claims that "des juifs riches" were among "les piliers de l'Eglise romaine". On the disincentive to convert provided by the humiliating ritual involved, see Sachs, *Le Sabbat*, pp. 162–4; and, for individual case histories of conversion, see Sachs, op. cit., pp. 21 and ff; Hirsch, *De Moïse à Jésus*; and René Schwob, *Moi Juif, Livre posthume* (Paris, 1928).
79 See Lovsky, *La Déchirure de l'absence*, pp. 270–9; André Chouraqui, "La Voix de Paul Claudel sur Israël", *Cahiers Paul Claudel*, 7, p. 182; Glock and Stark, op. cit., p. xix; Memmi, op. cit., pp. 370–1; and Louis Allen, "Jews in Popular Catholicism", *The Month*, November 1975, pp. 322–6. (I am grateful to Helen Sutton for this last reference).
80 See Bloy, *Le Salut par les Juifs*, p. 50; and Barrès, *Scènes et doctrines*, I, pp. 149 and 152, where the Good Friday liturgy is quoted at length.
81 Pierrard, op. cit., p. 298. Following other reforms of the liturgy mentioned above, the title of the prayer for the Jews was changed in 1963 from "Pour la conversion des Juifs" to "Pour les Juifs"; see Lovsky, *La Déchirure de l'absence*, pp. 273–8.
82 Barrès, *Mes Cahiers*, II (1898–1902), pp. 247–8, and 342–3, referring to the testimony of Louis Blaison. Barrès's remarks seem to come from the draft or the copy of a letter to Drumont, but may be a simple diary entry. Easter rituals of a similar kind were traditional elsewhere in France, for example in nineteenth-

century Languedoc and in Corsica; see Fabre and Lacroix, *La Vie quotidienne des paysans de Languedoc au XIXe siècle,* p. 156; and John Mitchel Chapman, *Corsica, An Island of Rest* (London, 1908), pp. 59–60.

83 See Soumille, "L'Idée de Race chez les Européens de Tunisie", p. 4.
84 Mauriac, "L'Affaire Dreyfus", p. 12. Similarly, Old Testament figures were heroes in French traditional popular literature; see, for example, Bollême, *La Bibliothèque bleue,* pp. 221–2.
85 Diana Vaughan, *Mémoires d'une ex-palludiste,* cit. Weber, *Satan franc-maçon,* p. 141.
86 See chapter III, pp. 111–13 above.
87 See Quillard, *Le Monument Henry,* pp. 94–104 and 216–31. Quillard lists 332 clergy plus 5 groups of uncertain size, which is certainly more than the 300 suggested by Mayeur in criticism of my earlier figure of 400, which may, however, be slightly inflated; see my "Le Monument Henry: La structure de l'antisemitisme en France 1898–1899", *Annales,* 32, (1977), pp. 265–91; and J. M. Mayeur, "Les catholiques dreyfusards", *Revue Historique,* 261 (1979), pp. 337–61.
88 Biez, op. cit., p. 10.
89 Daily Report, Prefect of Police, 21 June 1898. APP Ba 106.
90 Dagan, op. cit., p. 35.
91 Caillaux, *Mes Mémoires,* I, p. 131.
92 Leroy-Beaulieu, *Les Doctrines de haine,* pp. 276–7.
93 Hertzberg, op. cit., p. 249.
94 See Szajkowski, "French Jews during the Revolution of 1830 and the July Monarchy", pp. 116–20.
95 See Paul Viallaneix, Introduction, Michelet et Quinet, *Des Jésuites* (Paris, 1966), pp. 10–11.
96 Brunellière, Letter to Auguste Andrieux, 12 March 1900, Willard, ed., *La Correspondance de Charles Brunellière,* p. 172.
97 Dagan, op. cit., p. 64.
98 Bloy, *Le Salut par les Juifs,* pp. 24–5.
99 Léon Chaine, *Les Catholiques français et leurs difficultés actuelles* (Lyon, 1903), cit. Pierrard, op. cit., pp. 206–7.
100 Cit. Bournand, op. cit., p. 105; see also A. Latreille and R. Rémond, *Histoire du Catholicisme en France* (Paris, 1962), III, pp. 492–4.
101 See, for example, Dumont, *La Petite Bourgeoisie vue à travers les contes quotidiens du "Journal",* pp. 46–7.
102 See Mayeur, "Les Congrès nationaux", p. 180.
103 See Rémond, *Les Deux Congrès ecclésiastiques de Reims et de Bourges,* pp. 39 and *passim.*
104 See Sorlin, *"La Croix" et les Juifs,* pp. 40–6.
105 See pp. 535–40 below.
106 Report, Prefect of Police, 2 March 1898; and Miscellaneous police agent reports. AN F7 12480; Rollet, *L'Action sociale des catholiques en France,* I, p. 525.
107 See chapter VI, pp. 183 and 192 above.
108 See Lecanuet, op. cit., pp. 576–7; and Pierrard, op. cit., pp. 72–3 and 114. Abbé Barbier's main contribution was *Les Propagateurs de l'irréligion, Les Juifs* (1908).
109 Pierrard, op. cit., p. 66.
110 Bernanos, *La Grande Peur des bien-pensants,* p. 230.
111 *La France Libre,* 15 November 1896, cit. Mayeur, "Les Congrès nationaux", p. 178; also ibid., pp. 179–82.
112 Leroy-Beaulieu, *Les Doctrines de haine,* pp. 276–7. The "prudence" of the French episcopate vis-à-vis antisemitism was exhibited at a later date also. In contrast to the leaders of the Reformed Church, French bishops did not protest publicly against Vichy's *"statut des Juifs"* in 1940, though they did speak out publicly in 1942 against more direct persecution; see Poliakov, *Les Juifs et notre histoire,* pp. 169–70.

113 Saint-Poli, op. cit., pp. 137–8.
114 See Pierrard, op.cit.,p. 82.
115 Sorlin, *"La Croix" et les Juifs*, pp. 223–4.
116 See Gerbod, *La Condition universitaire en France au XIXe siècle*, pp. 210 and 217.
117 See Meurin, op. cit.; and Cohn, *Warrant for Genocide*, pp. 48–51.
118 Pierrard, op. cit., p. 28; and Cohn, op. cit., p. 50.
119 Drumont, *TA*, pp. 325–7.
120 Verdès-Leroux, op. cit., pp. 148–9 and 207–28.
121 See Soumille, op. cit., p. 8.
122 See Reports, Police agent, 29 December 1895; Prefect, Rhône, 22 August 1896; and Police agent, 30 April 1901. AN F⁷ 12480; Daily Reports, Prefect of Police, 17 January, and 18 June 1898. APP Ba 106; and Reports, Commissaire central, Grenoble, 10 and 12 September 1899. AN F⁷12453.
123 Cit. Zévaès, *L'Affaire Dreyfus*, p. 209; and Pierrard, op. cit., pp. 211–12. Zévaès thought that the letter was not published until 1916, though written before that date.
124 See Emmanuel Rodocanachi, *Le Saint-Siège et les Juifs: Le Ghetto à Rome* (Paris, 1891), pp. 58–9 and *passim;* Wirth, *The Ghetto*, p. 114; Glock and Stark, op. cit., p. 148.
125 See Drumont, *DB*, p. 505; also Tharaud, *Petite Histoire des Juifs*, pp. 24–5; and Lovsky, *L'Antisémitisme chrétien*, pp. 27 and 212–13.
126 Cit. Bournand, op. cit., p. 281.
127 Paléologue noted in March 1898 that the Vatican avoided direct comment on the Dreyfus Affair: "Mais, avec une insidieuse ténacité, on n'y perd aucune occasion de plaindre la pauvre France, qui mesure maintenant à quelles épreuves, à quels périls s'expose une nation lorsqu'elle se laisse gouverner par les francs-maçons, les protestants, les athées et les Juifs!" Paléologue, *Journal de l'Affaire Dreyfus*, p. 117 (5–20 March 1898).
128 L'Hermite, op. cit., pp. 228–9.
129 See Byrnes, *Antisemitism in Modern France*, p. 180; and Mayeur, "Les Congrès nationaux", pp. 178–9. Drumont commented on the equivocal attitude of Leo XIII towards antisemitism, in the context of a criticism of *Rerum Novarum;* Drumont, *TA*, p. 201.
130 See Report, Police agent, 25 August 1897; and Dossier, "Union Nationale" (December 1898). AN F⁷12480; Mayeur, "Les Congrès nationaux", pp. 178–80; Rollet, op. cit., I, p. 523; and Divry, *L'Abbé Garnier*, pp. 167–78.
131 See Zévaès, *L'Affaire Dreyfus*, p. 210.
132 See Tharaud, *Notre cher Péguy*, II, pp. 219–23. On the passive public attitude of the Vatican towards the persecution and massacre of French Jews, among others, at a later period, see Poliakov, "Pie XII, les Nazis et les Juifs", *Les Juifs et notre histoire*, pp. 195–210.
133 France, *L'Eglise et la République*, pp. 49–62.
134 See Reinach, *Histoire de l'Affaire Dreyfus*, IV, p. 50.
135 See my "Catholic Populism in France at the time of the Dreyfus Affair", pp. 668–9 and 688–90.
136 Bloy, *Je m'accuse, Oeuvres*, IV, p. 225
137 See Poliakov, *Les Juifs et notre histoire*, p. 21.
138 Pierrard, op. cit., pp. 87–8 and 190;, Saint-Poli, op. cit., p. 213.
139 See Bournand, op. cit., pp. 188–91; and Stanislas Reynaud, *Le Père Didon: Sa vie et son oeuvre (1840–1900)* (Paris, 1904), pp. 376–81 and *passim.*
140 See Lecanuet, *L'Eglise de France sous la Troisième République*, I, pp. 317–18; and III, *La Vie de l'Eglise sous Léon XIII*, pp. 173–8.
141 Bournand, op. cit., pp. 192–3.
142 Cit. ibid., p. 79.
143 Prolo, *La Caverne antisémite*, p. 34.

144 Ibid., pp. 5–12; Arnoulin, *M. Edouard Drumont et les Jésuites*, pp. 116–20; Guérin, *Les Trafiquants de l'antisémitisme*, pp. 2–3; Reinach, op. cit., I, pp. 216–17; and III, pp. 22–3. In assessing the significance of such subjective claims, it should be remembered that the Jesuits were the traditional bogeymen of the anticlericals, as the Freemasons and the Jews were of the Catholics.
145 Drumont, *FJ*, I, p. 50.
146 Poliakov, *Les Juifs et notre histoire*, p. 58.
147 Arnoulin, op. cit., p. 136.
148 See Reinach, op. cit., III, pp. 23–4; Isaac, *Expériences de ma vie*, I, p. 125; Webster, *Christian Democracy in Italy*, pp. 124–6; and chapter XII, p. 420 above; also p. 552 below.
149 See Pierrard, op. cit., p. 91.
150 Reinach, op. cit., III, pp. 22–3.
151 Reports, Police agent, 13 February 1898. AN F⁷12480; and Commissaire central, Grenoble, 10 September 1899. AN F⁷12453.
152 See Drumont, *TA*, pp. 268–82; and Lecanuet, *La Vie de l'Eglise sous Léon XIII*, pp. 26–32.
153 Report, Sub-prefect, Mayenne, 27 December 1897, cit. Denis, *L'Eglise et la République en Mayenne*, p. 42.
154 Mayeur, "Les Congrès nationaux", p. 199; see also Pierrard, op. cit., p. 127.
155 Pierrard, op. cit., p. 88.
156 Drumont, *DB*, pp. 541–2; also *FJ*, I, p. 134; and II, p. 414; and *TA*, pp. 25–6.
157 See Rollet, op. cit., I, p. 525; and Molette, *Albert de Mun*.
158 Report, Commissaire de police, Saint-Germain-en-Laye, 2 February 1902. AN F⁷ 12457; and Dossier, "La Jeunesse Catholique Antijuive du IVe arrondissement" (1904). AN F⁷ 12720.
159 See chapter X, pp. 282–5; and chapter XI, pp. 360–1 above.
160 Police report, 4 July 1899. AN F⁷ 12464.
161 See Pierrard, op. cit., pp. 142–3.
162 Reinach, op. cit., III, pp. 32–3.
163 See, for example, chapter II, p. 78; and chapter X, p. 272 above.
164 Reports, Police agents, Paris, 28 June, and 19 December 1905. AN F⁷ 12719; and Guérin, op. cit., pp. 282–3.
165 Report, Police agent, Paris, 3 April 1905. AN F⁷ 12457.
166 Cit. Jean Pataut, *Sociologie électorale de la Nièvre au XXe siècle (1902–1951)* (Paris, 1953), I, p. 72.
167 Pierrard, op. cit., pp. 114–15.
168 See Poulat, *Intégrisme et Catholicisme intégral*, pp. 362–4 and *passim*.
169 Cit. Pierrard, op. cit., pp. 167–9; also ibid., pp. 165–7.
170 See Weber, *Action Française*, chapter 12; and Lucien Thomas, *L'Action Française devant l'Eglise* (Paris, 1965), chapters 1 and 2.
171 On Social Catholicism, see J.-B. Duroselle, *Les Débuts du Catholicisme social en France (1822–1870)* (Paris, 1951); and Rollet, op. cit., I and II. Montuclard, *Conscience religieuse et démocratie*, has argued, fairly convincingly, as we have indicated above, that Christian Democracy shared the same basic assumptions as the older and more obviously conservative Social Catholic movement. On Lamennais, see Alec R. Vidler, *Prophecy and Papacy: A Study of Lamennais, the Church and the Revolution* (London, 1954); and J.-R. Derré, *Lamennais, ses amis et le mouvement des idées à l'époque romantique (1824–1834)* (Paris, 1962), particularly chapters VIII and IX.
172 Pierrard, op. cit., p. 119.
173 See chapter II, n. 223; and chapter XII, p. 412 above.
174 Rollet, op. cit., I, p. 423.
175 Pierrard, op. cit., pp. 116–18.
176 Ibid., pp. 119–21.
177 Cit. ibid., p. 117.

178 Cit. Rollet, op. cit., II, p. 69.
179 See Mayeur, "Les Congrès nationaux", pp. 175–85; and Rollet, op. cit., I, pp. 420–3.
180 Pierrard, op. cit., pp. 123–6.
181 Mayeur, op. cit., pp. 199 and 203–5.
182 Cit. Pierrard, op. cit., p. 128; also Mayeur, op. cit., p. 203; and "L'Affaire Dreyfus et le Clergé", *Le Siècle*, 25 December 1898.
183 Dagan, op. cit., pp. 27–9; also Pierrard, op. cit., p. 126; and Mayeur, *Un Prêtre démocrate, L'abbé Lemire*, pp. 77–8, 119, 154, 196–7 and *passim*.
184 Mayeur, "Les Congrès nationaux", p. 199.
185 Cit. Pierrard, op. cit., p. 127.
186 See ibid., pp. 128–31; and Rollet, op. cit., I, pp. 472–8; and II, pp. 105–15 and 347–8, for similar reactions.
187 Cit. Pierrard, op. cit., p. 122.
188 See Rollet, op. cit., I, pp. 443 and 526; Pierrard, op. cit., p. 122; and Montuclard, op. cit., p. 235.
189 See Rollet, op. cit., I, pp. 420–3; Mayeur, "Les Congrès nationaux", pp. 177, 188 and 193–5; Montuclard, op. cit., pp. 29–30; and my "Catholic Populism in France at the time of the Dreyfus Affair", pp. 690–1.
190 See my "Catholic Populism in France at the time of the Dreyfus Affair", pp. 669–76 and *passim*.
191 Report, Police agent, 20 July 1893. AN F⁷ 12480.
192 "Programme Social Législatif de l'Union Nationale pour Paris et le département de la Seine", 1893.
193 "L'Archiviste", *Drumont et Dreyfus*, pp. 19–20; L'Hermite, op. cit., p. 341; Divry, op. cit., pp. 129 and 140–1.
194 Dagan, op. cit., pp. 87–95.
195 See Bellanger *et al.*, eds., *Histoire générale de la presse française*, III, p. 331; and Poulat, op. cit., pp. 238–9.
196 See Daily Report, Prefect of Police, 25 March 1898. APP Ba 106; "Déclaration du comité central de la Jeunesse de l'Union Nationale", *L'Espérance*, October 1897; and Reports, Police agents, 3 and 6 March 1899. AN F⁷ 12480; and 6 September 1899. AN F⁷ 12923.
197 Paulin-Méry was sponsored by the Union Nationale in the 13th *arrondissement* of Paris; Daudé-Gleize and Massabuau were guests at a Union Nationale "fête" in honour of Joan of Arc at Aubervilliers in June 1898; see Daily Reports, Prefect of Police, 20 April, and 27 June 1898. APP Ba 106; and Report, Police agent, 25 February 1898. AN F⁷ 12480.
198 See Chapter VI, pp. 182 and ff. above.
199 Report, Police agent, 10 February 1898. AN F⁷ 12480.
200 See Daily Report, Prefect of Police, 13 April 1898. APP Ba 106.
201 Reports, Police agent, 1 September 1898; and Commissaire spécial, Roanne, 28 April 1899. AN F⁷ 12480; and Commissaire central, Grenoble, 12 September 1899. AN F⁷ 12453.
202 Reports, Commissaire central, Troyes, 20 February 1899. AN F⁷ 12466; and Prefect of Police, 4 April 1900. AN F⁷ 12480.
203 Daily Reports, Prefect of Police, 25 April, and 18 June 1898. APP Ba 106.
204 Reports, Police agent, 29 December 1895; and Prefect, Rhône, 22 August 1896. AN F⁷ 12480; see also the judgment of abbé Frémont quoted by Divry, op. cit., p. 78.
205 Speech, Mazodieu, Roanne. Reports, Police agents, 3 and 6 March 1899. AN F⁷ 12480; also Report, Police agent, 16 June 1902. AN F⁷ 12451; Resolution of the *comité* of Vincennes; and Speech, Dubuc. Daily Reports, Prefect of Police, 30 January, and 18 June 1898. APP Ba 106; and Song, "Les Trois Points", no date. The *Règlement Général* of 1897 simply proposed: "Le retrait du droit de cité français aux juifs qui en abusent."
206 See n. 8 above.

207 See my "Catholic Populism in France at the time of the Dreyfus Affair", pp. 691–2.
208 "Déclaration du comité central de la Jeunesse de l'Union Nationale" (1897).
209 Speech, Mazodieu. Reports, Police agents, 3 and 6 March 1899. AN F⁷ 12480.
210 Speech at meeting of *comité du centre*. Daily Report, Prefect of Police, 15 February 1898. APP Ba 106. The Union Nationale played a leading role in the annual demonstrations in honour of Joan of Arc which began in 1894, and in the movement to have her recognized as France's national patron saint; see Rosamonde Sanson, "La Fête de Jeanne d'Arc en 1894, Controverse et Célébration", *Revue d'Histoire Moderne et Contemporaine*, 20 (1973), pp. 444–63; and my "Catholic Populism in France at the time of the Dreyfus Affair", pp. 681 and 691.
211 Report, Prefect of Police, 14 March 1900. AN F⁷ 12458. It is significant that Turquet was an ex-Boulangist of previously anticlerical tendency.
212 Report, Police agent, 1 May 1899. AN F⁷ 12480.
213 Cit. Bournand, op. cit., p. 197.
214 Reports, Police agents, 28 April, 4 June, 1 July, and 30 November 1899. AN F⁷ 12480; and 6 September 1899. AN F⁷ 12923. For other examples of the Union Nationale's anti-Masonry, see my "Catholic Populism in France at the time of the Dreyfus Affair", pp. 695–6.
215 Cit. Divry, op. cit., p. 98.
216 Daily Reports, Prefect of Police, 21 and 26 January 1898. APP Ba 106.
217 See, for example, "Programme Social Législatif de l'Union Nationale pour Paris et le département de la Seine", 1893; and *Bulletin de l'Union Nationale*, March 1900, which denounced "l'alliance intime entre juifs, francs-maçons et socialistes"; see also my "Catholic Populism in France at the time of the Dreyfus Affair", pp. 676–8.
218 See *Rerum Novarum*, Sections 4 and 5, cit. Anne Fremantle, ed., *The Social Teachings of the Church* (New York, 1963), pp. 22–3. *Rerum Novarum* also explicitly condemned "Usury" and rejected Socialism. The Encyclical *Quod Apostolici* of 28 December 1878 had denounced Socialism in a more extreme and thoroughgoing way; see abbé André Deroo, ed., *Encycliques, Messages et Discours de Pie IX, Léon XIII, Pie X, Benoît XV, Pie XI, Pie XII et Jean XXIII sur les questions civiques et politiques* (Lille, 1961), pp. 31–6.
219 Montuclard, op. cit., p. 137.
220 Mayeur, "Les Congrès nationaux," pp. 173–5; and Pierrard, op. cit., p. 123.
221 Drumont, "La Bombe du Palais-Bourbon", 10 December 1893, *De l'Or, de la boue, du sang*, p. 104; see also Mayeur, *L'abbé Lemire*, pp. 77, 84, 154, 196 and 206–51 *passim*.
222 Daily Report, Prefect of Police, 25 February 1898. APP Ba 106; see also Rémond, *Les Deux Congrès ecclésiastiques*, p. 108; and chapter VI, p. 183 above.
223 Report, Commissaire spécial, Saint-Etienne, 8 January 1899. AN F⁷ 12466.
224 See Report, Prefect, Rhône, 9 June 1908. AN F⁷ 12487.
225 See Jeanne Caron, *Le Sillon et la démocratie chrétienne, 1894–1910* (Paris, 1967); and Vidler, *A Variety of Catholic Modernists*, chapter 8. Maurras and the "Integrists" were particularly vigorous opponents of the Sillon; see, for example, Charles Maurras, *Le Dilemme de Marc Sangnier: Essai sur la démocratie religieuse* (Paris, no date); Barrès-Maurras, *La République ou le roi*, p. 504; and Abbé Emmanuel Barbier, *Les Erreurs du Sillon: Histoire documentaire* (Paris and Poitiers, 1906); and their views prevailed when the movement was condemned by the Pope in 1910.
226 Montuclard, op. cit., pp. 136–8; Mayeur, "Les Congrès nationaux", pp. 203–6; also Rollet, op. cit., I, chapters XI and XII; Byrnes, *Antisemitism in Modern France*, pp. 205–12; and Molinari, in Dagan, op. cit., pp. 43–4.
227 Cit. Mayeur, "Les Congrès nationaux", p. 204.
228 See Pulzer, *The Rise of Political Anti-Semitism in Germany and Austria*, pp. 91–101, 162–75 and 181–205.
229 Cit. Bournand, op. cit., p. 124.

230 Report, Commissaire spécial, Nantes, 8 January 1900. AN F⁷ 12453; see also Report, ibid., 13 December 1898. AN F⁷ 12465.
231 See Montuclard, op. cit., pp. 257–61; and chapter VII, pp. 206–7 above.
232 See Montuclard, op. cit., pp. 136 and 257–61; Byrnes, op. cit., p. 201; Sorlin, *"La Croix" et les Juifs,* p. 197.
233 Sorlin, op. cit., pp. 95–6 and generally; see also Bloy's comments on "le scandale . . . le spectacle sans nom" of *La Croix's* gross antisemitism during the time of the Affair; Bloy, *Je m'accuse,* pp. 210–12 and 225.
234 See Quillard, op. cit., pp. 216–31; Caillaux, *Mes Mémoires,* I, p. 131; Byrnes, op. cit., pp. 324–37; and Latreille and Rémond, op. cit., III, p. 493.
235 Viau, *Vingt ans d'antisémitisme,* p. 363.
236 Pierrard, op. cit., pp. 89–91 and 129.
237 On the antisemitism of Catholic intellectuals, see Blumenkranz, ed., op. cit., p. 365; also Chapter XVI, pp. 606 and ff. below.
238 Pierrard, op. cit., pp. 84–6 and 108–9.
239 Ibid., p. 89; see also Verdès-Leroux, op. cit., p. 13.
240 Pierrard, op. cit., p. 147.
241 Drumont, *FJ,* I, p. 393.
242 Drumont, *TA,* pp. 296–8.
243 Cambrai, Le Puy, Rodez, Avignon, Séez, and Nevers. Verdès-Leroux, op. cit., p. 219.
244 Francis Jammes, *Monsieur le Curé d'Ozeron* (Paris, 1918), p. 128.
245 See, for example, Drumont, *TA,* pp. 333–6.
246 See Sorlin, *"La Croix" et les Juifs,* pp. 198–9.
247 Dossier: "Comité National Antijuif organisé pour les élections de 1902". AN F⁷ 12720.
248 See n. 170; and Communications, Cinquième Colloque Maurras, "La Condamnation de l'Action Française par l'Eglise Catholique", Aix-en-Provence, April 1976, to be published in *Etudes Maurrassiennes.*
249 See Jolly, ed., *Dictionnaire des parlementaires français.*
250 Cit. Bournand, op. cit., pp. 37–8.
251 See Drumont, *DB,* pp. 266–7 and 321; and Arnoulin, op. cit., pp. 17–23.
252 Daudet, *Les Oeuvres dans les hommes,* pp. 158 and 162.
253 Pierrard, op. cit., p. 18; see, for example, Drumont, "Un Dimanche à Sainte-Pélagie" (1892), *OBS,* pp. 61–6.
254 Viau, op. cit., p. 281.
255 Daudet, *Salons et journaux,* pp. 275–6 and 282; Drault, op. cit., pp. 180–9; Pierrard, op. cit., pp. 51–2.
256 Drault, op. cit., p. 88.
257 Ibid., pp. 88 and 11–12.
258 Arnoulin, op. cit., p. 199 and generally; "L'Archiviste", op. cit., p. 7; Pierrard, op. cit., pp. 59–60.
259 See Drault, op. cit., p. 27; Daudet, *Les Oeuvres dans les hommes,* p. 157; and *Au Temps de Judas,* p. 128.
260 See, for example, Drumont, *La Fin d'un monde,* pp. 413–15 and 437.
261 Drumont, *FJ,* I, pp. 406, 408 and 418–19.
262 Ibid., I, p. 525; and II, pp. 8, 161–8, 172–3, 279–80 and 526.
263 Ibid., II, pp. 170–1.
264 Drumont, *FM,* pp. 116–19, 125 and *passim.*
265 Drumont, *TA,* pp. 434–5; see also *DB,* pp. 519–20.
266 Drumont, *TA,* p. 201; also p. 345. However, *Rerum Novarum* could be read as a reaffirmation, in a modern context, of the Church's old ban on usury; see n. 218.
267 Drault, op. cit., pp. 180–9.
268 Drumont, *FJ,* II, p. 529.
269 Drumont, *TA,* pp. 333 and 336.

270 See ibid., pp. 268–82, 297–8, 312–13 and 340–42; also Verdès-Leroux, op. cit., p. 207.
271 Drumont, *DB*, pp. 539–40; *TA*, pp. 333–6.
272 Drumont, *TA*, pp. 23 and 321. Bloy also attacked Didon, referring to him in 1890 as "Le Révérend Père Judas". Bloy, *Les Dernières Colonnes de l'Eglise* (1903), *Oeuvres*, IV, pp. 239–46; also Bloy, *Lettres à René Martineau*, p. 193 (10 July 1903).
273 Drumont, *TA*, pp. 17 and 320–1.
274 Ibid., p. 370.
275 Drumont, *Le Secret de Fourmies* (1892), cit. Pierrard, op. cit., p. 46.
276 Drumont, *TA*, pp. 253–66 and 300–2; and Drault, op. cit., pp. 186–7.
277 Drault, op. cit., pp. 187–8. On the status and the grievances of the lower clergy, see, for example, Taine, *Les Origines de la France contemporaine*, XI, pp. 89–99; and Lecanuet, *L'Eglise de France sous la Troisième République*, I, p. 287.
278 See, for example, the situation in the diocese of Mayenne, described by Denis, op. cit.
279 Drumont, *DB*, p. 518; also *TA*, pp. 126–7.
280 Drumont, *TA*, p. vii.
281 Ibid., p. 439; also pp. 387 and 399–404.
282 See Viau, op. cit., p. 301.
283 Pierrard, op. cit., p. 129.
284 Bloy, *Le Salut par les Juifs*, pp. 21–3.
285 Cit. Verdès-Leroux, op. cit., p. 150; see also Drumont, *TA*, p. 343; Lecanuet, *La Vie de l'Eglise sous Léon XIII*, p. 198; and Pierrard, op. cit., pp. 187–9.
286 Drumont, *TA*, pp. 282–320.
287 Duroselle, "L'Antisémitisme en France", p. 60.
288 Cit. Verdès-Leroux, op. cit., pp. 146–8; also ibid., pp. 224–5.
289 Pierrard, op. cit., pp. 61–3; see also Verdès-Leroux, op. cit., p. 146.
290 Pierrard, op. cit., p. 52.
291 L'Hermite, op. cit., pp. 24–5.
292 Pierrard, op. cit., p. 64. Needless to say perhaps that he was not elected; see further chapter XVI, p. 609 and n. 73 below.
293 Drumont, *La France juive devant l'opinion*, cit. Pierrard, op. cit., p. 18; see also Drumont, *TA*, pp. 351 and 370; and Drault, op. cit., pp. 186–8.
294 Cit. Pierrard, op. cit., p. 53.
295 See ibid., pp. 54–6; p. 518 and n. 87 above; and Dossier: "Comité National Antijuif organisé pour les élections de 1902". AN F[7] 12720.
296 Viau, op. cit., p. 76.
297 Pierrard, op. cit., pp. 72–3.
298 Drumont, *TA*, pp. 342–3.
299 Drault, op. cit., p. 186.
300 Drumont, *TA*, p. 296.
301 Ibid., p. 344.
302 P. Dreyfus, *Dreyfus: His Life and Letters*, p. 211; and Pierrard, op. cit., p. 190.
303 P. Dreyfus, op. cit., p. 239; and Pierrard, op. cit., pp. 193–5.
304 Abbé Henri de Saint-Poli; see P. Dreyfus, op. cit., pp. 204–5; and Pierrard, op. cit., pp. 202–3; also chapter II, p. 82 and n. 182 above.
305 Leroy-Beaulieu, *L'Antisémitisme*, p. 30; see also Pierrard, op. cit., pp. 196–201.
306 See Marcel Prélot, *Le Libéralisme catholique* (Paris, 1969).
307 *Le Siècle*, 8 December 1898, published a letter from Loyson to Premier Dupuy, which urged: "A Paris comme à Alger . . . l'antisémitisme est un serpent qu'il faut savoir écraser non en lui marchant maladroitement sur la queue, mais en lui posant résolument le pied sur la tête." On Loyson's firm opposition to antisemitism, see also n. 23 above; and Letter to Alfred Dreyfus, 20 July 1899, cit. P. Dreyfus, op. cit., p. 205; and, on this and on his career generally, see Albert Houtin, *Le Père Hyacinthe* (Paris, 1920–1924), 3 vols, and particularly, III, pp. 64–8 and 126–32;

Michael de La Bédoyère, *The Life of Baron von Hügel* (London, 1951), p. 59; and L. V. Méjan, *La Séparation des Eglises et de l'Etat: L'oeuvre de Louis Méjan* (Paris, 1959), pp. 103 and 361. The modernist Marcel Hébert, who also left the Church, instructed that a Protestant pastor or a Jewish rabbi should give an address at his cremation; see Vidler, *A Variety of Catholic Modernists*, pp. 74–5.

308 Jules Isaac, "Israël dans l'oeuvre de Péguy", *Expériences de ma vie*, I, pp. 344–65; Prajs, "Péguy et le peuple juif"; Petit, *Bernanos, Bloy, Claudel, Péguy*, pp. 60–6.

309 Cohen, *Les Déicides*, p. xiii. On the psychological significance of the theme of deicide, see Charles Baudouin, *Psychanalyse du symbole religieux* (Paris, 1957), pp. 204–8.

310 Zola, "Pour les Juifs", *L'Affaire Dreyfus, La Vérité en marche*, p. 57.

311 Dagan, op. cit., p. 3; also Picard, op. cit., p. 38.

312 Cit. Bournand, op. cit., p. 7.

313 See, for example, Lovsky, *L'Antisémitisme chrétien*, pp. 168–73; Le Roy Ladurie, *Les Paysans de Languedoc*, p. 232; Bollême, op. cit., pp. 229–30; and Paul Friedrich, *Agrarian Revolt in a Mexican Village* (Englewood Cliffs, 1970), pp. 33–4.

314 See, for example, Stern, *Hitler*, p. 195; Glock and Stark, op. cit., p. 74; and Selznick and Steinberg, *The Tenacity of Prejudice*, p. 112.

315 See Lovsky, *L'Antisémitisme chrétien*, p. 167. As well as raising the problem of inherited responsibility, the old deicide charge lacks firm Scriptural basis, and the Gospel accounts must be interpreted in a particular way to support it.

316 Tharaud, *Petite Histoire des Juifs*, pp. 20–2; see also Sartre, *Réflexions sur la question juive*, pp. 81–2; Memmi, op. cit., pp. 68 and 196; Rose, "The Roots of Prejudice", *Race and Science*, UNESCO, pp. 409–10; Georges Friedmann, *Fin du peuple juif?* (Paris, 1971), pp. 240–6; and Poliakov, *Les Juifs et notre histoire*, p. 13. Freud, of course, explained the peculiar power of the deicide myth, by relating it to an "Oedipal" conflict between Christianity and Judaism; see Freud, *Moses and Monotheism*, pp. 86–92; also Freud, *Totem and Taboo* (1913) (London, 1965), pp. 154–5; Loewenstein, op. cit., pp. 37 and 40–2; and Poliakov, "Freud et Moïse", *Les Juifs et notre histoire*, pp. 235–36.

317 Tillier, *Mon Oncle Benjamin*, p. 79.

318 Cit. Szasz, *The Manufacture of Madness*, p. 336; see also Gelu, *Marseille au XIXe siècle*, p. 400.

319 See chapter IX, n. 28; also Soumille, "L'Idée de Race chez les Européens de Tunisie", p. 4.

320 Colombier, op. cit., p. 85.

321 Abbé Lemire, Debate, Chamber of Deputies, 27 May 1895—also interruptions by Marcel Habert and Vicomte d'Hugues, cit. Lovsky, *L'Antisémitisme chrétien*, pp. 362–3.

322 Gide, *Journals*, I, p. 119; see also Castellane, *Hommes et choses de mon temps*, p. 171, for another instance.

323 See Viard, "*L'Encyclopédie nouvelle* de Pierre Leroux et l'idée de race", p. 16.

324 Meurin, op. cit., pp. 188–91 and 465.

325 Sorlin, "*La Croix*" et les Juifs, pp. 104 and 132.

326 *La Croisade Française*, 20 February 1898; see also Pierrard, op. cit., p. 20.

327 Drumont, *DB*, p. xv.

328 Drumont, *FJ*, I, pp. 17 and 348.

329 Ibid., II, pp. 557–8; also p. 516; and *La France juive devant l'opinion*, pp. 32–3.

330 Cit. Drumont, *FJ*, II, p. 75.

331 See Paléologue, op. cit., p. 85 (13 December 1897).

332 La Tour du Pin, *Vers un ordre social chrétien* (1907), cit. Lovsky, *L'Antisémitisme chrétien*, p. 288.

333 Bloy, *Le Salut par les Juifs*, pp. 42 and 34; also pp. 47–9; and *Oeuvres*, IV, pp. 84–5.

334 See chapter XII, pp. 391–2 above.

335 Barrès, "La Parade de Judas", *Scènes et doctrines*, I, pp. 142–5.

336 Ibid., I, p. 205.

337 Matthew 27:25, though this Gospel, unlike that of St John, refers to "the people" rather than to "the Jews" explicitly; see also Loewenstein, op. cit., p. 183; Hertzberg, op. cit., pp. 35–7; Lovsky, *L'Antisémitisme chrétien*, chapters II and III; Blumenkranz, ed., op. cit., p. 267; and n. 315 above.

338 *La Revue du Monde Catholique*, 1 January 1887, cit. Verdès-Leroux, op. cit., p. 139.

339 Bloy, *Le Salut par les Juifs*, pp. 38, 48 and 56.

340 Drumont, *DB*, p. 504.

341 Rouquier and Soumille, "La Notion de Race chez les Français d'Algérie", p. 7.

342 Biez, op. cit., pp. 14–15.

343 John 8: 44.

344 Poliakov, *Les Juifs et notre histoire*, p. 13. On this theme generally, see, in addition to works cited in chapter IV, n. 136, Joshua Trachtenberg, *Jewish Magic and Superstition, A Study in Folk Religion* (1939) (New York, 1970), pp. 1–10; Poliakov, *The History of Anti-Semitism*, I, pp. 137–54; Baron, *A Social and Religious History of the Jews*, XI (1967), chapter XLIX; Lovsky, *L'Antisémitisme chrétien*, pp. 235–42; Rosenberg, *From Shylock to Svengali*, pp. 23–5; Thomas, *Religion and the Decline of Magic*, p. 668.

345 Cit. Loewenstein, op. cit., p. 15.

346 Poliakov, *Les Juifs et notre histoire*, p. 28; see also Otto Fenichel, "Psychoanalysis of Antisemitism", *American Imago*, I (1940), p. 35.

347 Cit. Blumenkranz, ed., op. cit., p. 312.

348 Proudhon, *Césarisme et Christianisme* (1883), I, p. 139, cit. Lovsky, *L'Antisémitisme chrétien*, p. 340; and Silberner, "Proudhon's Judeophobia", p. 67.

349 See, for example, Jules Michelet, *La Sorcière* (Paris, 1966), p. 85; and Drumont, *FJ*, I, pp. 168, 195 and 286.

350 See Mario Praz, *The Romantic Agony* (Oxford, 1933), chapter 2; Claudius Grillet, *Le Diable dans la littérature au XIXe siècle* (Lyon and Paris, 1935); Max Milner, *Le Diable dans la littérature française de Cazette à Baudelaire, 1772–1861* (Paris, 1960); and Weber, *Satan franc-maçon*, pp. 9–12. The identification of the Jew with the Devil and magic in "high" literature seems to have been more common in England than in France, though no systematic study exists. Launcelot Gobbo, for example, in Shakespeare's *The Merchant of Venice*, Act II, Scene II, refers to "the Jew, my master, who (God bless the mark!) is a kind of devil ... Certainly the Jew is the very devil incarnation." From the nineteenth century, Rosenberg instances Dickens's Fagin in *The Adventures of Oliver Twist;* Bulwer Lytton's *Zanoni;* and Svengali in Du Maurier's *Trilby;* Rosenberg, op. cit., pp. 116–29, 210–13 and 239–51. This raises the problem of how popular literary stereotypes relate to other expressions of antisemitism. The comparison of France and England in this respect suggests that there may be an inverse relation between the success of hostile stereotypes of the Jew in literature and the development of organized antisemitism. Where the literary stereotypes are strong and come to form part of the general culture, as in England, with Shylock and Fagin, organized antisemitism is of little importance. Where organized antisemitism is much more important, as in France, though literary stereotypes exist, they have not the same power or universality.

351 Abbé Alfred Monnin, *Life of the Blessed Curé d'Ars* (1861) (London, no date), particularly chapter VIII. The *curé* d'Ars died in 1859.

352 Tharaud, *Notre cher Péguy*, II, p. 68. Such a belief in devils or the Devil, accompanied by other magical beliefs, persisted in many rural areas among people and clergy; see, for example, La Varende, *Pays d'Ouche*, pp. 157–60 and *passim*, on rural Normandy; and Maurice Crubellier, *Histoire culturelle de la France, XIXe–XXe siècle* (Paris, 1974), pp. 66–8.

353 Bloy, Letter to Carton de Wiart, 21 March 1890. *Inédits de Léon Bloy*, p. 121.

354 Cit. Weber, *Satan franc-maçon*, p. 233.
355 Duroselle, "L'Antisémitisme en France", p. 60. Viau recounted that both Drumont and Gaston Méry consulted a clairvoyante, and that Méry took the exorcisms of abbé Schnorbelin very seriously; Viau, op. cit., pp. 109–11 and 147–53.
356 Drumont, *DB*, p. 508; also pp. 285, 293 and 513–14; see also Varende, op. cit., pp. 157–60, where the same point is made.
357 Drumont, *TA*, p. vii.
358 See chapter XVI, pp. 602–6 and ff. below. Barrès also had a special interest in the occult; see Robert Amadou, "Barrès et l'Occulte", *La Table Ronde*, March 1957, pp. 161–6.
359 Drumont, *FJ*, I, pp. 168–9, 173, 189, 193, 204, 207, 270 and 286–7; also ibid., II, pp. 405–51; and see n. 77 above.
360 Drumont, *FM*, pp. xv–xvi.
361 Drumont, *DB*, pp. 136, 503, 508 and 93.
362 Drumont, *TA*, p. 53.
363 Drumont, "La Suprême Entrevue" (1892), *OBS*, p. 68. The association: showman-wizard-Jew existed among English writers, too, as we have seen, and is related to the general association of Jews with the theatre. The title of Colombier's *Sarah Barnum* is significant here.
364 Drumont, *FM*, p. 511.
365 Drumont, *OBS*, p. 78.
366 See Cohn, op. cit., pp. 44–5.
367 Bloy, *Le Salut par les Juifs*, pp. 48 and 72.
368 Cit. Pierrard, op. cit., p. 86.
369 Report, Commissaire spécial, Paris, 16 August 1899. AN F[7] 12465.
370 *La Croisade Française*, 20 February 1898.
371 AN F[7] 12923.
372 Cit. Silberner, "French Socialism and the Jewish Question", pp. 5–6 and 10.
373 See Dumont, *La Petite Bourgeoisie vue à travers les contes quotidiens du "Journal"*, p. 46.
374 Lacretelle, *Silbermann*, p. 234; also p. 68.
375 Albert Malaurié, *La Femme de Judas* (Paris, 1924), pp. 68 and 104.
376 Weber, *Satan franc-maçon*, pp. 200–1. American Populists also believed that Freemasonry was Satanic; see Hofstadter, *The Paranoid Style*, pp. 16–18.
377 Meurin, op. cit., pp. 183, 211–29, 442–59 and *passim*.
378 *L'Echo de Rome*, 1 January 1894, cit. Weber, *Satan franc-maçon*, p. 98.
379 Weber, op. cit., pp. 22–5, 49–53, 62–84 and generally; also Bernanos, op. cit., pp. 230–43; Byrnes, op. cit., pp. 304–19; Montuclard, op. cit., pp. 246 and 259.
380 Taxil claimed to have the support of 17 members of the French hierarchy, and apparently received the papal blessing; see, for this, and generally, Weber, op. cit., pp. 110–13, 198 and 211–12; Meurin, op. cit., pp. 291–2; Daudet, *Au Temps de Judas*, pp. 211–12; Lecanuet, *La Vie de l'Eglise sous Léon XIII*, p. 578.
381 *La Revue Catholique de Coutances*, 12 June 1896, cit. Weber, op. cit., p. 110.
382 See Drumont, *TA*, pp. 404–37; and Weber, op. cit., pp. 112–13, 116 and 121–7.
383 Barrès, *Scènes et doctrines*, I, pp. 152 and 167.
384 Ibid., I, p. 195.
385 Ibid., I, pp. 200 and 204.
386 Daudet, *Au Temps de Judas*, p. 105.
387 See Lovsky, *L'Antisémitisme chrétien*, p. 242. The theme is, of course, a subvariant of that of the Demonic Woman, and has the profoundest resonance; see Praz, op. cit., chapter IV.
388 See Klein, *Portrait de la Juive dans la littérature française*, pp. 72–3 and 128; also Steinheil, *My Memoirs*, p. 130. Both Daudet and Goncourt were overt antisemites, and were associated with Drumont. Marpon and Flammarion only decided to publish *La France juive* in 1886 at the insistence of Alphonse Daudet; see Byrnes, op. cit., pp. 148–9; Beau de Loménie, *Edouard Drumont*, pp. 274–80 and 460–6; and Edmond et Jules de Goncourt, *Mémoires de la vie littéraire*, *passim*.

389 Schmidt, *Maupassant par lui-même*, pp. 115–16. "L'Inconnue" first appeared in *Le Gil Blas*, 27 January 1885, and was included in the collection of stories, *Monsieur Parent*, published in 1886.
390 See chapter XV, pp. 590–6 below.
391 Malaurié, op.cit., p. 25 and *passim*.
392 Maupassant was not a political antisemite, but both Alphonse Daudet and Goncourt were inclined in this direction, as we remarked in Note 388; Drumont, moreover, as we have seen, was a close friend of the Daudet family.
393 Cit. Verdès-Leroux, op. cit., pp. 133–4.
394 Drumont, *FJ*, I, p. 16.
395 *La Libre Parole*, 23 February 1899, cit. Zévaès, *L'Affaire Dreyfus*, p. 150; Reinach, op. cit., IV, p. 553; and Paléologue, op. cit., p. 174 (21 February 1899).
396 Maurras, *Anthinéa*, pp. 237–9 and 241–3. Interesting also here is the very obvious influence of Michelet on the "anti-Romantic" Maurras.
397 See, for example, Michelet, *La Sorcière*, pp. 159–60.
398 Drumont, *FJ*, I, p. 12; also p. 189.
399 Ibid., I, p. 259.
400 Cit. Bournand, op. cit., p. 205.
401 Drumont, *FJ*, I, p. vi. On Jewish omnipresence, see also Adorno *et al.*, *The Authoritarian Personality*, chapter XVI, p. 614.
402 Drumont, *FJ*, I, p. 122; also *DB*, p. 145.
403 Tharaud, *Petite Histoire des Juifs*, pp. 20–1.
404 Drumont, *FJ*, I, p. 371; see also Braudel, *The Mediterranean*, I, p. 321; and II, p. 696; and, for similar ideas among American Populists, Hofstadter, *The Paranoid Style*, chapter 7, "Free Silver and the Mind of 'Coin' Harvey".
405 See, for example, Braudel, op. cit., II, p. 825.
406 Among the doctrines condemned by the *Syllabus of Errors* was: "That in the present day, it is no longer necessary that the Catholic religion be held as the only religion of the State, to the exclusion of all other modes of worship . . ." Henry Bettenson, ed., *Documents of the Christian Church* (London, 1943), p. 381. This position was reaffirmed implicitly or explicitly in many later Encyclicals, for example, *Inscrutabili* (1878); *Diuturnum* (1881); *Nobilissima Gallorum Gens* (1884), addressed specifically to the French bishops; *Immortale Dei* (1884); and *Libertas Praestantissimum* (1888); see Deroo, ed., op. cit., pp. 29, 37–47, 53, 59–77 and 89–91.
407 Sorlin, *"La Croix" et les Juifs*, pp. 132–43 and 147–53.
408 Drumont, *DB*, p. 338.
409 Loewenstein, op. cit., p. 194.
410 Cit. Vaucelles, op. cit., p. 196.
411 Bloy, "Suprématie temporelle et universelle de l'Eglise" (1878), *Inédits de Léon Bloy*, pp. 32–3.
412 Cit. Weber, *Satan franc-maçon*, p. 14.
413 Lémann, *La Préponderance juive*, I, p. 31.
414 See Lecanuet, *La Vie de l'Eglise sous Léon XIII*, chapter XII; and Vidler, *A Variety of Catholic Modernists*, p. 208. Abbé Delassus characteristically also identified "Americanism" as the work of the Jews and the Freemasons.
415 Meurin, op. cit., pp. 468 and 462.
416 Guillemin, *Zola légende et vérité*, p. 7.
417 Pierrard, op. cit., p. 29. This view was encouraged by Papal pronouncements which referred to a "war" between the Church and anti-Christian forces, and to the latter as "plotting" against the Church; see, for example, *Diuturnum* (1881); and *Nobilissima Gallorum Gens* (1884), cit. Deroo, ed., op. cit., pp. 37 and 53.
418 Hofstadter, *The Paranoid Style*, pp. 31–2.
419 Meurin, op. cit., p. 351.
420 Memmi, op. cit., p. 197.
421 Sartre, op. cit., pp. 45–7.
422 This is not to say that it could not have social and political effects. Memmi,

indeed, argues that the characterization of the Jews as absolutely evil led logically to a policy of extermination. But, see Chapter XVII, pp. 684–5 below, for further discussion.

423 On ritual murder beliefs in the past, and in other parts of Europe in the modern period, see Baron, op. cit., XI, pp. 146–57; Poliakov, *History of Anti-Semitism*, I, pp. 57–64; Poliakov, *Les Juifs et notre histoire*, p. 19; Wirth, *The Ghetto*, p. 91; Lovsky, *L'Antisémitisme chrétien*, pp. 246–65; Landau, op. cit., p. 233; Memmi, op. cit., pp. 204–5; Arthur Nussbaum, "The 'Ritual-Murder' Trial of Polna", *Historia Judaica*, 9, (1947), pp. 57–79; and Mosse, *The Crisis of German Ideology*, p. 130.
424 Drumont, *TA*, p. 321.
425 Drumont, *FJ*, II, pp. 403, 405, 408, and 412.
426 Drumont, *TA*, p. 321.
427 Drumont, *FJ*, II, pp. 381–99.
428 Drumont, *TA*, pp. 322–3.
429 Drumont, *FJ*, II, pp. 399 and 400–3.
430 Ibid., II, p. 463.
431 *La Libre Parole*, December 1894, cit. Weber, *Satan franc-maçon*, pp. 15–16.
432 See Verdès-Leroux, op. cit., pp. 101–3.
433 Ibid., pp. 120–1; and Pierrard, op. cit., p. 26.
434 Verdès-Leroux, op. cit., p. 129.
435 Meurin, op. cit., p. 159; and Lémann, op. cit., I, p. 3.
436 See Sorlin, *"La Croix" et les Juifs*, pp. 142–3 and 152–3; also "L'Archiviste", op. cit., pp. 11 and 22; and Lazare, *L'Antisémitisme*, pp. 353–7.
437 Reinach, op. cit., III, p. 540.
438 Abbé Puig, *Solution de la question juive* (1897), cit. Pierrard, op. cit., p. 69.
439 Cit. ibid., p. 92.
440 Drumont, *FJ*, I, p. 158; and Verdès-Leroux, op. cit., p. 221.
441 Pierrard, op. cit., pp. 161–5.
442 See Thibaudet, *Les Princes lorrains*, p. 68.
443 Drumont, *TA*, pp. 322–9.
444 Drumont, *FJ*, II, p. 391.
445 Klein, "Damascus to Kiev: *Civiltà Cattolica* on Ritual Murder".
446 See Verdès-Leroux, op. cit., pp. 148–9, 217 and 221–2.
447 See Drumont, *TA*, pp. 328–30; and Poulat, op. cit., pp. 362–4.
448 Poulat, ibid.
449 Drumont, *TA*, pp. 325–7 and 330–1.
450 Drumont, *FJ*, II, p. 381; also ibid., I, p. 158.
451 Lazare, op. cit., pp. 350–1.
452 Leroy-Beaulieu, *L'Antisémitisme*, p. 9.
453 Dagan, op. cit., p. 81.
454 Caillaux, op. cit., I, p. 131. See also, for the same interpretation, Verdès-Leroux, op. cit., pp. 117 and 149; and Pierrard, op. cit., p. 29.
455 See Blumenkranz, ed., op. cit., pp. 349–51 and 364; and Marrus, op. cit., chapter IV.
456 See Byrnes, op. cit., pp. 113–14; and Cohn, op. cit., pp. 44–5.
457 Drumont, *FJ*, I, pp. 3, 17, 37–8, 125, 134, 154, 190–2, 201 and 218–19; see also *La France juive devant l'opinion*, p. 290; and *OBS*, p. 101.
458 Drumont, *FJ*, I, pp. 33, 220, 225, 227–8, 298 and 308–9.
459 Ibid., I, p. 183; also pp. 463, 516–17, 523, 530, 541 and 545; and II, p. 8.
460 Ibid., II, p. 309; also pp. 305, 311, 439, 443, 464, 467, 506 and 538–56.
461 Ibid., II, p. 381.
462 Drumont, *TA*, pp. 24 and 35; also *DB*, pp. x, 122–5, 293 and 519–20.
463 Cit. Byrnes, op. cit., p. 147; and Bernanos, op. cit., p. 199.
464 Drumont, *TA*, p. 21.
465 Pascal, *La Juiverie*, cit. Verdès-Leroux, op. cit., p. 129.

466 Cit. "L'Archiviste", op. cit., p. 10.
467 *La Croix*, 19 January 1899, cit. Larkin, *Church and State after the Dreyfus Affair*, p. 77; see also Sorlin, *"La Croix" et les Juifs*, pp. 132–43 and 147–8.
468 Cit. Pierrard, op. cit., p. 85.
469 Bournand, op.cit., pp. 39 and 194.
470 Cit. ibid., p. 148.
471 *Le Complôt juif*. AN F⁷ 12463.
472 Mayeur, "Les Congrès nationaux", p. 205.
473 Meyer, *Ce que mes yeux ont vu*, pp. 124 and 130.
474 Daudet, *Au Temps de Judas*, pp. 102 and 115.
475 Daudet, *Les Oeuvres dans les hommes*, p. 115.
476 Cit. Higonnet, *Pont-de-Montvert*, p. 129.
477 See Bournand, op. cit., p. 175.
478 See chapter XII, pp. 415–22 above.
479 Drumont, *TA*, p. 358.
480 Cit. Lecanuet, *La Vie de l'Eglise sous Léon XIII*, pp. 576–7.
481 Drumont, *TA*, p. 357.
482 Meurin, op. cit., p. 468.
483 See Verdès-Leroux, op. cit., p. 212.
484 Jules Soury, *Campagne nationaliste* (1902), p. 9, cit. Sternhell, "Le Déterminisme physiologique et racial", pp. 22–3.
485 Barrès, *Mes Cahiers*, II, pp. 274–5 (1902).
486 Maurras, Letter, December 1905. Barrès-Maurras, op. cit., p. 459. It is interesting that this view was shared by some Jewish writers, for example J. Cohen, who wrote that Jews regarded the Christian Trinity as "une transaction avec le polythéisme", and for whom Christianity was "la forme et l'instrument par lesquels l'ancienne société polythéiste a subi l'empire des idées juives." *Les Déicides*, pp. 332 and lv–lvi. See also the illuminating discussion of dualism by Mary Douglas, *Natural Symbols, Explorations in Cosmology* (Harmondsworth, 1973), chapter 7.
487 B. R. Wilson, *Patterns of Sectarianism, Organisation and Ideology in Social and Religious Movements* (London, 1967), pp. 23–4, lists the characteristics of a "sect" as including: "voluntary association . . . [;] membership by proof . . . of some claim to personal merit . . . [;] exclusiveness . . . [;] self-conception [as] . . . an elect, a gathered remnant . . . [;] and hostility or indifference) to the secular society and the state." Clearly late nineteenth-century Catholicism had only some of these characteristics, and "sectarian" tendencies were counter-balanced by its traditional ecclesiastical structure, but the term seems nevertheless applicable and of heuristic value.
488 Leroy-Beaulieu, *Les Doctrines de haine*, p. 27.
489 Weber, *Satan franc-maçon*, p. 12; see also Lecanuet, *La Vie de l'Eglise sous Léon XIII*, chapter III.
490 See, for example, Lecanuet, op. cit., pp. 154–8; and Denis, op. cit., p. 54.
491 See particularly Richard Griffiths, *The Reactionary Revolution, The Catholic Revival in French Literature 1870–1914* (London, 1966).
492 Papus (Dr Gérard Encausse), *Catholicisme, Satanisme et Occultisme* (Paris, 1897), p. 4, cit. Weber, *Satan franc-maçon*, p. 13; see also Pierrard, op. cit., p. 118.
493 *Inédits de Léon Bloy*, p. 35; see also, for the expression of a similar view by *Le Nouvelliste de Lyon*, Vaucelles, op. cit., pp. 187–8.
494 See n. 414 above.
495 See Dansette, *Histoire religieuse de la France contemporaine*, pp. 670–704; Latreille and Rémond, op. cit., III, pp. 516–19; Bernard M.G. Reardon, *Roman Catholic Modernism* (London, 1970), pp. 237–48 and *passim;* Vidler, *A Variety of Catholic Modernists.*
496 Latreille and Rémond, op. cit., III, pp. 519–22; Poulat, op. cit.; Vidler, op. cit., pp. 48–50, 103–4 and 212–18.

497 Cit. Glock and Stark, op. cit., p. 81; see also n. 406 above.
498 Gadille, *La Pensée et l'action politiques des évêques français au début de la IIIe République*, particularly I, chapter 2; see also *Inédits de Léon Bloy*, pp. 32–3.
499 See Dansette, op. cit., pp. 597–624; and J.-M. Mayeur, *La Séparation de l'Eglise et de l'Etat* (Paris, 1966).
500 Rollet, op. cit., I, p. 686.
501 Cit. Szajkowski, *Jews and the French Revolutions*, p. xxx.
502 Lazare, op. cit., p. 361.
503 Lovsky, *L'Antisémitisme chrétien*, p. 34.
504 Biez, op. cit., pp. 16 and 11.
505 See my "Catholic Populism in France", p. 692.
506 Cit. Lovsky, *L'Antisémitisme chrétien*, p. 288.
507 Meurin, op. cit., p. 468.
508 Mirbeau, *Le Journal d'une femme de chambre*, pp. 103–4.
509 Glock and Stark, op. cit., p. 74. This does not apply to Catholicism in the USA in the 1960s, and the explanation offered is that Catholics are, and always have been, a minority group there, and accept their denominational status.
510 See Chapter XI, n. 349.
511 Cit. Bournand, op. cit., p. 79.
512 Prolo, op. cit., p. 65. Much the same view was expressed by Huc, director of *La Dépêche de Toulouse*, and by Jean Ajalbert, of *Les Droits de l'Homme*; see Bournand, op. cit., pp. 82 and 176.
513 Clemenceau, cit. Bournand, op. cit., p. 75.
514 Cit. Sorlin, *"La Croix" et les Juifs*, pp. 23–4. This idea was very commonly expressed by bourgeois Catholics of the time; see, for example, Rambaud, director of *Le Nouvelliste de Lyon* (Vaucelles, op. cit., p. 82); and Mgr Delamaire, bishop of Périgueux (Rollet, op. cit., II, p. 69).
515 Pataut, op. cit., pp. 71–2; see also Vaucelles, op. cit., pp. 187–8 and 193–4.
516 Drumont, *FJ*, II, p. 413.
517 Drumont, *DB*, p. 506.
518 Drumont, *FJ*, I, p. 192.
519 See chapter XII, n. 553.
520 Barrès, *L'Appel au soldat*, p. 360; and *Mes Cahiers*, IX, p. 23, cit. Sternhell, *Maurice Barrès*, pp. 305–6.
521 See, for example, Maurras, *Quand les Français*, pp. 213 and 141: "l'Eglise catholique a été, vingt siècles durant, la vaisseau de l'ordre civilisé . . ."
522 For example, *Union Nationale de France, Règlement Général* (1897), p. 45: "Elle [France] a une vocation divine. Elle a fait, pour la cause de Dieu ce qu'aucune autre nation n'a jamais tenté."
523 See n. 210 above.
524 Cit. Divry, op. cit., p. 75.
525 Sorlin, *"La Croix" et les Juifs*, p. 218.
526 Dagan, op. cit., pp. 34–5.
527 Daily Report, Prefect of Police, 8 February 1898. APP Ba 106.
528 "Entre Français Catholiques". Dossier no 24, *"La Croisade Française"*. AN F⁷ 12842.
529 Report, Commissaire spécial, Roanne, 6 March 1899. AN F⁷ 12480.
530 Dagan, op. cit., p. 47.
531 See Hertzberg, op. cit., pp. 7–11, chapter IX and *passim;* and Blumenkranz, ed., op. cit., pp. 269–71.
532 Hertzberg, op. cit., pp. 354–7.
533 See, for example, Paz, "Idée de race chez Blanqui", p. 3.
534 See Georges Weill, *Histoire de l'idée laïque en France au XIXe siècle* (Paris, 1929), pp. 195–6.
535 Daily Report, Prefect of Police, 11 March 1898. APP Ba 106.
536 *L'Action*, 26 July 1904.

537 Cit. Verdès-Leroux, op. cit., p. 144.
538 Sternhell, *Maurice Barrès*, p. 231 and *passim*.
539 Daily Reports, Prefect of Police, 12 March, and 2 April 1898. APP Ba 106.
540 Daily Report, Prefect of Police, 3 May 1898. APP Ba 106.
541 Guérin, op. cit., p. 138.
542 Daily Report, Prefect of Police, 11 May 1898. APP Ba 106.
543 Picard, op. cit., p. 42.
544 L'Hermite, op. cit., p. 88.
545 Vauthier, *La France et l'Affaire Dreyfus*, p. 28.
546 Pichot's letter was published in *Le Figaro* and *Le Siècle* on 12 December 1898, and is quoted by L'Hermite, op. cit., pp. 310–13; and Pierrard, op. cit., p. 195.
547 *Le Temps*, 21 April 1897, cit. Weber, *Satan franc-maçon*, pp. 214–15. The distinction drawn here between "fideist" and Thomist tendencies is probably a false one, since both trends went together, and both can be seen as expressions of sectarianism, Thomism representing an attempt to provide Catholicism with a more coherent classificatory system, i.e. strengthening "grid" in Mary Douglas's terminology; see Douglas, *Natural Symbols*, chapter 4.
548 Saint-Poli, op. cit., pp. 116–17 and 47–8; also pp. 25–7 and 39–61. The same point was made by Père Hyacinthe in a letter to *Le Journal* in December 1898; see Houtin, op. cit., III, p. 68.
549 Cit. Denis, op. cit., p. 59.
550 AN F⁷ 12842, Dossier no. 24. As *procureur-général* attached to the Cour d'Appel de Paris, and newly-appointed to the post because his predecessor had resigned in protest against alleged political interference in the matter, Quesnay de Beaurepaire (1838–1923) had been the chief prosecutor of General Boulanger and his associates before the Haute-Cour in 1889, which had made him a much-hated figure in Boulangist circles. He later attracted attention again for his dilatory investigation into the Panama scandals, and was censured in the Chamber of Deputies in 1897–8 for his conduct in the prosecution of the Anarchists. In January 1899, he resigned as President of the Chambre Civile of the Cour de Cassation, claiming that the Chambre Criminelle, then considering whether the Dreyfus case should be reopened, was partial and had committed irregularities, and his resignation contributed to the Government's decision to pass the *loi de dessaisissement*. He then became an active anti-Dreyfusard; see Mermeix, *Les Coulisses du Boulangisme*, pp. 156–8; Zévaès, *Au Temps du Boulangisme*, pp. 157–9 and 171; Zévaès, *L'Affaire Dreyfus*, pp. 146–7; Guy Chapman, *The Dreyfus Case: A Reassessment* (London, 1963), pp. 245–6, 249 and 278; Johnson, *France and the Dreyfus Affair*, pp. 156–7.
551 AN F⁷ 12926, Dossier no. 7, "Affaire de la Soeur Candide, 1910".
552 France, op. cit., p. 50.
553 *La Petite République*, 7 December 1898.
554 Viau, op. cit., pp. 95–6 and 118–20.
555 Cit. Pierrard, op. cit., p. 56.
556 Report, Police agent, 8 June 1900. AN F⁷ 12719.
557 Poliakov, *Les Juifs et notre histoire*, p. 12; see also Loewenstein, op. cit., pp. 43, 192, 199 and *passim;* Glock and Stark, op. cit., pp. 130–8 and 146, and Uriel Tal, *Religious and Anti-Religious Roots of Modern Anti-Semitism*, Leo Baeck Memorial Lecture 14 (New York, 1971).
558 Verdès-Leroux, op. cit., p. 207.
559 Pierrard, op. cit., pp. 297–8; also pp. 20–1.
560 Gamzon, "Claudel rencontre Israël", pp. 100–1.
561 See Verdès-Leroux, op. cit., pp. 101–3; and Lovsky, *L'Antisémitisme chrétien*, pp. 40–1.
562 Cit. Bournand, op. cit., p. 172.

CHAPTER XV
SEXUAL ANTISEMITISM: "HORRIBLY SENSUAL"

THE SEXUAL CONNOTATIONS OF ANTISEMITISM HAVE INESCAPABLY PRE-
sented themselves in the course of previous chapters, in our discussion of the
Henry Subscription, in our discussion of the polluting quality of the Jew, in
the image of the demonic Jewess. In this chapter we shall consider this aspect
directly and in more detail. First, Jews were generally associated with sexuality
and with special sexual potency. Fear and hatred of Jews was a way of expressing fear and hatred of sexuality. Particular significance was attached by antisemites to the fact that male Jews were circumcised, and, perhaps more important, that they were circumcisers. An association was established here between
sexuality and physical violence, which also found expression in verbal sadism.
Related to this was the more ambiguous image of the erotic Jewess, seductress,
enchanter, prostitute and witch. Finally, in less explicit form, sexual elements
underlay antisemitic attitudes to money, to the nation and to the Jew as a
deicide. Discussion, particularly of these last aspects, must rely to a considerable extent on Freudian insights and assumptions, but it must be stressed that
we are not primarily concerned with antisemitism in the context of the
individual psyche, but again with antisemitism as a set of ideas and values,
publicly expressed, and with their social functions.

French antisemites characterized the Jews in sexual terms, both explicitly
and implicitly. *L'Antijuif d'Alger*, for example, in January 1898, referred to
"the libidinous instincts, the bestial passions, the lustful desires" of the Jew.[1]
Léon Daudet drew attention to Naquet's physical ugliness and wrote that his
nihilism "had a sexual power; it was like a libido." Similarly, he described
Catulle Mendès as "lyrical and salacious, a character out of the *Satyricon*";
and he commented on the sexual attractiveness of the "strangely ugly" La
Jeunesse.[2] The physical stereotyping of the Jew as a thick-lipped, odorous,
dirty, animal, also had clear sexual connotations, as Erikson and others have
pointed out.[3] The old association of Jews with red hair has sexual significance,
too.[4] The same pattern of attributing sexual characteristics to the enemy is
very evident in the ideology of witch-hunting[5] and in anti-Black white racial-

ism.[6] It is interesting here to note that a hairdresser, asked to uncurl the young Sarah Bernhardt's hair, commented that it was like that of "a white negress".[7] In all three cases it is possible to see the same externalization and projection of a sexuality that is for some reason repressed;[8] and the sexual mode in each case expresses sentiments that are profoundly ambiguous, and, for that reason, extremely powerful. Envy and admiration complement rejection and fear. As Sartre has written, "one of the components of the antisemite's hatred is a profound and sexual attraction to the Jews."[9]

Nevertheless, Jewish sexuality was nearly always manifestly expressed in negative ways. In general terms, it was evoked as something perverse, mercenary and predatory. Drumont, for example, wrote of Catulle Mendès: "The Venus which he celebrates is the Venus of perversion, the Venus of paroxysms, of neuroses, of hysterias, the Venus with circles beneath her eyes, with bloodless lips and icy hands, who only exchanges the caresses of the Marquis de Sade for those of Sappho."[10] Jews were also associated with prostitution, a point to which we will return. Drumont claimed that Naquet glorified prostitution, and wrote that "the ancient Germans, pure Aryans, never sent out prostitutes, as did the Semitic peoples, to seduce the generals of their enemies and to murder them, while making love . . ."[11] More generally, as we have seen, the narrator in J.-R. Bloch's Lévy said that he felt as if he were visiting a brothel when he went to call on a Jewish family;[12] and Pierrard recalled that young men of his generation regarded the synagogue as a kind of "maison close".[13]

As the quotation from Drumont makes clear, Jewish sexuality was felt as a threat, and again and again it was presented as a facet of the predatory nature of the Jews. Their aim here, as in other spheres, was to seduce, pervert and exploit. Drumont cited an eighteenth-century document on the Jews of Bordeaux: "The Jews employ as domestic servants pretty peasant girls, whom they make pregnant in order to have wet-nurses for their own children, while they send the offspring of the girls to the home for abandoned children."[14] In the same vein, he claimed that lycées for girls were set up in the 1880s by the Jews in order to provide themselves with mistresses, and commented: "Fodder for the fisc, cannon-fodder, flesh for sale, isn't this the destiny of the Christian, of his daughter and of his sisters?"[15] And he added, more generally, that "the essential thing", as far as the Jews were concerned, was "the perversion of youth . . ."[16] On another level, he expressed the idea, already present in the ritual murder myth, that the Jews (and also the Protestants and the Freemasons) captured Christian women and children for nefarious sexual purposes. He quoted an Austrian writer, for example, to the effect that, for the Jews, "to shed the blood of a non-Jewish virgin is the highest form of sacrifice . . ."[17] Such themes were common in antisemitic propaganda of the time. The antisemitic press in France and Algeria, for example, reported many stories of children being kidnapped for sexual purposes; Le Télégramme d'Alger declared in January 1898: "The Jews seek to deflower as many young virgins as possible"; and it was also suggested that it was dangerous for Gentile women to enter Jewish shops, where they might be sexually attacked.[18] Similar fears were being expressed in the sixteenth century,[19] and they were a central feature of the "Rumour of Orléans" in the middle of this century,[20] which makes their interpretation in socio-historical terms a delicate matter.

Certain comments in this direction may be made, however. First, as the ritual murder myth itself makes plain, antisemites tended to confuse or equate sexual intercourse with violent death. For Drumont, the shedding of blood signifies sexual intercourse, but also murder. The projection of fears of sexuality here has strong sadistic connotations, something to which we will return, and relates to the calls for the torture and extermination of Jews, which we encountered in chapter IV. Also involved were fears of pollution and miscegenation. Drumont wrote of his horror on hearing that the Comtesse de La Rochefoucauld had given her arm at a ball to Arthur Meyer: "the great name of La Rochefoucauld, which recalls centuries of heroism . . . all that soiled by promiscuous contact with a former secretary of Blanche d'Antigny [a high-class prostitute]."[21] Or again, he protested at the willingness of the daughters of the aristocracy not simply to touch, but to marry Jews:[22]

> This adorable young woman, this ravishing Aryan, with her proud, virginal figure, whom one would not even dare to look at too intensely for fear of harming the pure bloom on the maturing fruit, she gives herself to one of these frightful cosmopolitans, mangy, evil-smelling, a man who used to hawk oranges on the quays of Tunis or Alexandria, or who worked as a waiter in some Russian village inn . . . Everything falls to the Jew.

On one level, this was simple sexual jealousy, adolescent in tone, and also a reflection of the desire to prevent intermarriage. It is interesting here to note that Drumont related the danger most clearly to the maintenance of the aristocracy, that is of a racially-selected élite; elsewhere he referred to the Jews' usurping "the bed of others . . ."[23] Racial purity and endogamy are thus seen as the means of preserving social hierarchy, a mechanism that has also been detected in the case of pre-industrial societies and of modern racialist societies.[24] The horror inspired by the idea of sexual relations between Jews and non-Jews, of course, had other dimensions. Jewish blood was felt to be dominant, and intercourse or intermarriage would thus increase Jewish numbers.[25] It was also corrupting. Silbermann declared that non-Jews feared intermarriage, because it meant mixing their blood with "a new blood rich in sensuality . . ."[26] More materially, Jews were thought to transmit disease, and particularly venereal disease, to their sexual partners and their offspring. Drumont claimed, for example, that syphilis in Russia had been spread by the Jews.[27]

Fear of sexuality as symbolized by the Jews was thus closely related to racial antisemitism, but it also had connections with the other types which we have isolated for the purposes of analysis. The theme of Jewish takeover and invasion had connotations of rape; and Drumont used a more ambiguous sexual image in the same context, writing that, "around Wilna, that *Vagina of the Jews*, were organized those movements of exodus which have occupied Germany, crossed the Vosges and conquered France!"[28] Again the theme of

Jewish treason was evoked in terms of the traditional image of the kiss of Judas.[29]

The expression of sexual anxiety in antisemitic terms was paralleled in the case of Drumont and others by a general "puritanism" and hostility to "permissive" trends in late nineteenth-century French society. In an article entitled "L'Amour Libre" in 1894, for example, Drumont denounced the general promiscuity of Parisian élite society, and the whole idea of "Free Love", which, he claimed, was accepted, if not practised, universally.[30] He also denounced the "pornography" of writers like Zola and Catulle Mendès, "writers who have prostituted themselves and used their pens to corrupt the minds of French people and to demoralize the nation".[31] Pornography had also invaded the popular press, where it was used in particular in attacks against the Church. "Between 1880 and 1886", wrote Drumont in 1891, "Anus was king . . . It was the heyday of the excremental stories of La Lanterne and of the Semitic pornographies of the rue du Croissant."[32] At the same time, it was claimed, prostitution had increased, and, more important, attitudes towards it had changed. It was no longer shameful. The leading figures of the demi-monde were now accepted socially; they even stayed at the same hotels, ate in the same restaurants, as honest women; while at a lower social level, "the common prostitute" had come to be regarded as just another worker. All this, Drumont commented, was the sign of a profound social and moral decadence.[33] Moreover, it was a trend which was encouraged, if not engineered by the Republican authorities. Brothel-keepers in Paris, he claimed in La France juive, enjoyed official protection: "they serve the good cause . . . by corrupting the young generation, by destroying in the masses all the honest feelings that might help the nation to rise out of the mire."[34] As we have seen, the secular education provided by the State was supposed to have the same effect. Girls' lycées were breeding-grounds for prostitution and lesbianism;[35] while, more generally, education divorced from Catholicism could only be education in vice. Here, Drumont quoted Chevé to the effect that modern educational theory was a "leprous theory of debauchery and adultery", and that secular teachers were "preachers of incest, peddling a hellish science, teaching their pupils how to deflower all that is holy in the human spirit . . ."[36] One can see in all this how sexual promiscuity symbolized modernity, the abandonment of hierarchy, the confusion of traditional categories. It is significant that Drumont, ignoring its traditional origin, explicitly condemned the Mardi-Gras carnival of the Parisian students in just this perspective: "The scandalous scenes of Mardi-Gras . . . are one of the most characteristic events of our time. Can one conceive anything more terrible than an orgy in a hospital . . . [?]"[37] Modern students of the psychology of antisemitism have pointed out that it is frequently correlated with sexual puritanism in the way that we have described, and have also indicated that this puritanical crusade against sexuality is itself an expression of prurience and voyeurism.[38] And this pattern is very evident in the antisemitism of Drumont and his contemporaries. The "excremental" element condemned in anticlerical propaganda, for example, was an important feature of much antisemitic writing, as we have seen; and Drumont condemned sexual irregularities only after describing them with some relish.[39] This can be seen, in large part, as a trait inherent in popular journalism, then and since, which sought to attract readers by straying into forbidden territory, while ultimately reassuring them with a reassertion of traditional norms and values. Dumont's analysis of the stories published in *Le Journal* reveals the same catering for a taste in mild pornography (and sadism), coupled with an overt disapproval of both.[40]

The antisemites' preoccupation with the Jewish custom of circumcision is also expressive of sexual anxiety, but on a more ambiguous, profounder level. The old idea that circumcision was a sign of divine punishment, "the bodily mark which identifies the Satanic race of Jews", was still present,[41] and the tendency to perceive a cultural trait as a biological characteristic seems to have been accentuated.[42] We have seen that Drumont claimed that at least some Jews were born circumcised.[43] French antisemites also used the term *"circoncis"* very generally to refer to the Jews, and Maurras suggested the inspection of penises as a means of applying sanctions against Jews in France.[44] But circumcision was not only a sign of Jewishness and of Jewish inferiority. Marianne in Mirbeau's *Journal d'une femme de chambre* is "against the Jews . . . about whom she knew nothing however, save that they had something missing somewhere."[45] Circumcision here symbolized the mystery of the Jew, his secret sexual nature, which was felt to be different, odd and thus frightening, like the celibacy of a Catholic priest.[46] The quotation also indicates how circumcision might evoke fears of castration, as Freud and others have suggested that it did.[47] For Jews were not only circumcised, they were circumcisers. Paul Lapeyre referred in *La Sociologie Catholique* in mid-1898, as we have seen, to "the demon of the Talmud with his secateurs".[48] Drumont claimed that the Jews wished to "circumcise all Frenchmen".[49] Lapeyre also asserted that the Jews were preventing Christian children from being born, a reflection of the collective fears of depopulation, which we discussed in chapter X, but also possibly of a more personal fear of emasculation or impotence. Impotence was traditionally ascribed to witchcraft,[50] with which the Jews, we have seen, were associated. It was also related to a fear of female sexuality, which again was given an antisemitic interpretation, and it could be contrasted with the allegedly abnormal sexual potency of the Jew. This is speculative, but it is interesting to note that *Le Précurseur*, the weekly organ of the Parti National Antijuif, gave considerable space to advertisements for patent cures for impotence.[51] It should be noted in this general context that circumcision aroused such extreme fears and reactions in France, as it probably did in other Catholic countries, because it was a minority custom there, almost exclusively confined to the Jews. In societies where it was general practice, such as those of Islam,[52] or where it was much more common, as in Britain, it cannot have served as the focus for the same anxieties. Such ritual mutilation of the body bears an enormous weight of symbolic significance, and it is a pity that we do not know more about it, as far as European societies are concerned.

Circumcision, in the thinking of antisemites, was assimilated to ritual murder and grosser forms of mutilation; as we have seen, the term *"circoncire"* was used by subscribers to the Henry Subscription to mean, to exterminate.[53] Jews were supposed to have murderous intentions towards non-Jews, to carry out tortures and murders that had sexual sadistic implications—Bournand, for example, suggested that Jack the Ripper must be a Jew;[54] and these provided the rationalized justification for, while in fact mirroring, the sadistic desires that antisemites directed towards the Jews. This was well perceived by Octave Mirbeau, and expressed in his portrait of the antisemitic Joseph, who "hates the Jews, and constantly threatens to torture them, to kill them, to burn them alive", and who is also a sadist, who enjoys administering slow deaths to animals, and who is, it is hinted, a child-murderer too and the perpetrator of sex crimes.[55] We have already encountered many direct examples of antisemitic sadism in the Henry Subscription, and two further examples must suffice to illustrate the point, neither directed specifically against the Jews. In *Le Testament d'un antisémite,* Drumont described the Persian torture reported by Herodotus, in which the victim was coated with honey and left in the sun to be stung to death by insects.[56] In *L'Intransigeant,* in October 1898, Rochefort suggested how the magistrates of the Criminal Chamber of the Cour de Cassation, supposed to be favourable to the revision of the Dreyfus Case, should be treated:[57]

> A specially trained torturer should first of all cut off their eyelids with a pair of scissors . . . When it is thus quite impossible for them to close their eyes, poisonous spiders will be put in the half-shells of walnuts, which will be placed on their eyes, and these will be securely fixed by strings tied round their heads. The hungry spiders, which are not too choosy about what they eat, will then gnaw slowly through the cornea and into the eye, until nothing is left in the blind sockets.

Two things may be said about this horrifying product of the antisemitic imagination. First, the use of eye symbolism makes the sexual connotation of such verbal sadism clear.[58] Secondly, models for such evocations of torture and mutilation existed in traditional culture high and low. One thinks of the descriptions of dismemberment and violence in the work of Rabelais, of the detailed descriptions of the punishments suffered by sinners in Hell, of which Dante's is only the most sophisticated.[59] But in traditional culture such descriptions were part of a wider, coherent system of ideas and values; they had a meaning beyond themselves, which is only present in antisemitic writing as a pale unconscious reflection. They were also the product of a society, which practised the cruelty which they evoked. Antisemitic verbal sadism, by contrast, was divorced from social reality, and represents the projection of private phobias. But it was not, of course entirely private. At the level of the printed word it had a social existence and took a collective form. Once again antisemitism seems to be an attempt to recast elements already present in popular culture to suit new circumstances, and its verbal expression of sadism is perhaps an area where the frustrations of anomic egos and their desire to find or recreate a semblance of traditional values converged with the need, in a society which was becoming progressively less violent, for some kind of ritual outlet for aggression and violence. Here it should be set beside other contemporary phenomena, which could be interpreted in the same way: the interest of the popular press in crime and criminality,[60] for example, or the emphasis on violence and horror in popular literature and melodrama.[61]

We must now discuss what was probably the most important, the most compelling theme in sexual antisemitism, "the erotic, exciting and scandalous image of the Jewess".[62] As Sartre has pointed out, this was an expression of the sadism which we have just reviewed: "There is in the words *une belle Juive* [a beautiful Jewess] a very particular sexual significance, very different from that which is found in those of *belle Roumaine, belle Grecque* or *belle Américaine,* for example. They evoke rape and massacres. The *belle Juive* is she whom the Cossacks of the Tsar drag by the hair through the streets of her village in flames . . ."[63] But the image has many other related meanings and dimensions. It was, first, the expression in sexual terms of Jewish strangeness, and exoticism. Barrès commented in his *Cahiers:* "The synagogue, that representation of the feminine, has always inspired painters. They depict it in the image of Herodias. They feel, they sense the Orient there."[64] Here the representation of the exotic Jewess in terms of a special and excessive sexuality parallels representations of Black women in the White racialist mentality, and of "native" women generally in colonial attitudes and writing.[65] The image of the Jewess also conveys with exceptional clarity the ambiguity which the Jews represented and with which they were perceived; for, as Klein and Verdès-Leroux have recently emphasized, the image of the Jewess was a dual one. It was conceded that she was beautiful, but she was "shameless, lascivious and cold all at once, and venal; her beauty was restless, disturbing". In more extreme form, a "good" Jewess was presented in contrast to an "evil" one,[66] who, as we have seen, was lent the attributes of she-devil and witch.

This dual image of the Jewess was very generally present in French culture, and we must consider it in this wider context, before examining how it was used by the "professional" antisemites. The idea of the "good" or noble Jewess was espoused by a number of Romantic writers, who were often influenced by British models, notably Rebecca in Scott's *Ivanhoe.*[67] Chateaubriand, for example told Fontanes: "Jewesses have escaped the curse which rests upon their race. There were none of them in the crowd which insulted the Son of Man, which scourged him, crowned him with thorns, and made him suffer the ignominy and the agony of the cross. The women of Judaea believed in the Saviour, loved him, followed him and comforted him."[68] Stressing the physical rather than the moral qualities of the Jewess, and already sounding an ambivalent note, Stendhal, commenting on the beautiful women of Avignon in 1837, wrote: "As I was admiring the truly oriental eyes of one of these ladies who was shopping in the market-place, I was told that she was Jewish."[69] This favourable view survived into the later part of the century. Paléologue, for example, who cited the Chateaubriand quotation in his diary in 1899, remarked: "He was susceptible to the charm of Jewesses, like many a Catholic writer of our time."[70] The diplomat Jusserand, who was born in 1855, recalled the figure of Scott's Rebecca with affection in his autobiography.[71] But one has the impression that the complementary unfavourable image was by this time predominant; perhaps it always had been, for as Rosenberg has illustrated for Britain, hostile images of the Jew seem always to have had more power than their opposites, which were very often created by eccentric well-wishers specifically to counter the former. It should be noted, too, that the image of the "good" Jewess was nearly always in fictional representations a foil to her "evil" male counterpart.

In fiction and in life, in nineteenth-century France, as elsewhere,[72] the Jewess was associated with prostitution. From Balzac's Josepha Mirah, Sarah and Esther Gobseck and Mlle Coralie, through Maupassant's Rachel in *Mademoiselle Fifi*, to Proust's Rachel, Jewish prostitutes of different classes and categories appear again and again as literary stereotypes.[73] And this apparently reflected real attitudes. Zola recalled that, when he was a youth at Aix-en-Provence, "the officers of the garrison tried to outdo each other in gallantries to compete for the favours of the young Jewesses, who were, moreover, very beautiful", and boasted of their affairs with them.[74] Maupassant indicated that, in the institutional context, the Jewess was a necessary type in the repertoire of a brothel, to be played by a stand-in if need be. In *La Maison Tellier*, "Raphaële, from Marseille, a dockland tart, played the indispensable role of the 'Beautiful Jewess', thin, with her prominent cheek-bones well-rouged, her black hair . . . and her arched nose . . ."[75] In part, the association stemmed perhaps from an inability to fit what non-Jews knew of the social life of Jewish women into other categories. Alphonse Daudet in 1880 thus evoked a picture that might have been that of a brothel or a harem, though this does not seem to have been his express intention: "There was, among these Bordeaux Jewesses, a low and dirty rapacity, a love of expedients, which led them to stay at home for days on end, dressed in all kinds of odds and ends, in waistcoats over full skirts, their feet in old dancing slippers . . .", playing cards and shouting at each other.[76] But much more was involved than this. The Jewess, the Jewess as prostitute, was the symbol par excellence of Jewish sexuality in general.

Vallès, in *Le Bachélier*, described the appeal of "a girl with whom an entire literary set had fallen in love. She was, in effect, very pretty, this brunette with the Jewish looks, and no woman of the profession, no *grisette*, has ever given me a feeling that can compare with that which the rustling of her skirt produced."[77] And the same view that the Jewess had special sexual appeal and intense sexuality was expressed by very many writers; Zola equated the Jewess, Eve Steinberger, in *Paris*, with "voluptuousness";[78] Jean Barois discovers, in Martin du Gard's novel, that Julia Woldsmuth has an aspect to her character that is "sensual, horribly sensual . . .";[79] Marie Colombier's Sarah Barnum is "ten times a woman . . ." However, as we have seen, this heightened sexuality went along with a basic emotional coldness, with the will and the power to seduce and to exploit. Colombier again presents Sarah Barnum as a cold "female Don Juan . . . a being anaesthetized against love . . .", pursuing but never finding sexual pleasure; but she has "a strange power of seduction which puts an army of men at her feet . . ."[80] She is also wholly mercenary. And this theme, of course, is inherent in the whole idea of prostitution. Here it is interesting to note that not only prostitutes themselves, but also the organizers of prostitution, were frequently said to be Jewish, for example the procuress Mme Rebecca Ranvet in Mirbeau's *Journal d'une femme de chambre*.[81] According to *Le Nord*, the Russian Jew was, among other things, "the boss of the local brothels and the supplier of personnel to the harems and the brothels of the East . . ."[82] This suggests a more general convergence between ideas about Jews and about prostitution, which L'Hermite made explicit. "Are not all prostitutes 'Jews', usurers in their way", he asked, "since what they lend, they only lend for a large sum of money? Their flesh, whether it is in fact 'kosher' or not, like the synagogue meat, is it not always the cursed flesh of the pig?"[83]

A further illustration of the importance of the dual image of the Jewess in French culture is provided by the phenomenon of the "fame" of Rachel[84] and particularly of Sarah Bernhardt, each the most celebrated actress of her generation. "As for Mlle Sarah Bernhardt", wrote Henry James, "she is simply, at present, in Paris, one of the great figures of the day. It would be hard to imagine a more brilliant embodiment of feminine success";[85] while Waleffe wrote that she was "one of the glories of France, the only one perhaps, with Napoleon, who was known all over the world . . ."[86] In each case the quality of being a "star" was linked to the fact that they were Jewish and that they led scandalous private lives. Rachel had a strong attachment to her Jewishness, and resisted pressures on her to convert, even on her death-bed. She had a series of much-publicized liaisons with leading figures of the day, including Prince Napoleon and Emile de Girardin, and had an illegitimate son.[87] The case of Sarah Bernhardt is worth considering in more detail, since the period of her "fame" coincided with that of the rise of organized antisemitism. She was converted to Catholicism as a child, while attending a convent school, and seems to have been a genuine and devout Catholic as a young girl, if not later;[88] but members of her immediate family continued to be practising Jews, and her entourage was mainly Jewish.[89] Moreover, her enemies made much of the fact that she was of Jewish extraction. An anonymous letter, which she quotes in her *Memories,* told her in 1879: "You will do well not to show your horrible Jewish nose at the opening ceremony [of the Comédie Française] the day after tomorrow. I fear that it would serve as a target for all the potatoes that are now being cooked specially for you in your kind city of Paris."[90] At least two fictional attacks, Colombier's *Sarah Barnum,* to which we have referred, and Félicien Champsaur's *Dinah Samuel* (1882), also berated her as a Jewess.[91] On and off stage, too, she was seen as the epitome of the passionate woman. Hahn described her in *La Samaritaine* (1897) as "a creature of pleasure . . . saturated in perfumes".[92] Earlier, in 1885, Arsène Houssaye had written: "She has sought everything, known everything, the joys of pride and of passion. She has been queen, she has been woman. She has been all women . . ."[93] According to Clermont-Tonnerre, "this daughter of Jerusalem resembled a priestess who had abandoned the temple of Solomon for that of Baal

. . . She incarnated the feminine serpent in all her displays of voluptuousness across the universe, playing in turn a Byzantine princess, a Florentine adventuress, a courtesan dying of consumption . . .", and she referred to "the spell of Sarah Bernhardt . . ."[94] Colombier stressed this demonic, witch-like aspect writing that she was "Mephistophelean with the serpentine and fluid lines of her body . . . a slender witch . . . [who] put [her lovers] under a spell . . ."[95] Colombier also sought, as this suggests, to publicize her subject's scandalous private life, which was hardly necessary, since it seems to have been common knowledge.[96] The extent, indeed, to which Sarah Bernhardt had become a popular sex symbol is suggested by a story which Waleffe tells in his autobiography. At a hotel in Sofia some time in 1900, he had a room next door to a French honeymoon couple, and heard the girl say again and again to the man: "Make love to me as if I were Sarah Bernhardt!"[97]

How does one explain the fact that a society which was basically antisemitic bestowed "fame" on a Jewess? Two comments are relevant. First, "fame", itself a novel phenomenon related to the development of mass media, was usually bestowed on outsiders, marginal figures: Gambetta, de Lesseps, Victor Hugo; it was something outside and beyond the normal social structure. Second, as actress and courtesan, the Jewess conformed to the stereotype Jewess; as such she caused no threat, no alarm, but could be accepted, even celebrated. Not, however, by the professional antisemites. Both Picard and Drumont objected to the cult of Rachel and of Sarah Bernhardt. Drumont quoted Philarète Chasles to the effect that Rachel was "a little Bohemian tigress, a lascivious Jewess", and saw the success of Sarah Bernhardt as yet another example of the Jewish takeover of France.[98] But it is interesting that even here the strongest objection was voiced to the Jewish actress's going beyond what was regarded as her proper role. Drumont quoted an article in *La France Chrétienne* in December 1889 by Taxil, protesting against the casting of Sarah Bernhardt in Jules Barbier's *Jeanne d'Arc*, which was to open in the New Year:[99]

> To represent a sublimely Christian figure, the enemies of God have chosen a Jewish actress, whose scandalous adventures currently fill the gossip-columns of the press of the Boulevards. This Jewess will deliberately play the role of Joan of Arc in the wrong way; she will present her as a hysterical woman who has hallucinations; she will make her behave in the most extravagant way; she will turn the holy girl into a mad and grotesque virago.

This brings us to the general way in which the antisemites made use of the image of the Jewess. They did occasionally evoke the image of the "good" *belle Juive*, as a contrast to the evil male Jew. Writing of the Jews of Pressburg, for example, in *La France juive*, Drumont declared: "There are there old Jews of astonishing ugliness alongside young girls, dressed in rags, of an admirable beauty . . ."[100] Bourget is reported to have said: "I hate Jewish men because they crucified Jesus; I adore Jewish women because they wept for him."[101] But, on the whole, this image was rejected in favour of the hostile one which associated Jewesses with predatory sexuality and with prostitution. Picard wrote that "the legend of the *belle Juive* has done enormous harm", and declared that, from a racial perspective, all Jews, of both sexes, were bad.[102] Drumont asserted, in *La France juive*, that "it is the Jewesses who provide the largest contingent of prostitutes in all the great capitals". Moreover, Jewish prostitution was particularly mercenary and served Jewish plans for domination. Jewish parents, unlike Christian parents, sold their daughters into prostitution: "Jewesses prostitute themselves for money, but coldly, without the slightest sign of strong emotion . . . The prostitute, moreover, serves Israel in her fashion; she accomplishes a kind of mission, by dishonouring the sons of the aristocracy."[103] Later, he commented on the predominance of Jewish prostitution in Paris at the time of the 1889 *Exposition;*[104] and presented an image of the Jewish prostitute as ancient, death-like: "an old Jewess, all withered, painted like an Indian idol, like a corpse";[105] or "old Rebecca, with her knowledge gathered in all the harems of the East".[106] As well as evoking the association with witchcraft with this Sybilline figure, Drumont here makes sexuality equivalent to death, an extreme form of the rejection of sexuality which we have already encountered. In addition to identifying her with prostitution, Drumont also presented a more general picture of "that figure so essentially peculiar: *the Jewess.*"[107] According to this Jewish women were indolent, living the lives of Eastern women, but egotistical. In *La France juive*, he evoked "these African Jewesses, half-sprawling on cushions in a room in the depth of their dwelling, holding their hands, loaded with rings, over fat, flabby bellies . . . over-fat at thirty, their skins shiny with grease . . .";[108] but Jewesses in Paris were not much different:[109]

> The Jewish woman of the leisured class lives in the Eastern manner, even in Paris, takes a siesta in the afternoon, retains a certain closed-up and somnolent quality. She never experiences the violent passions that so often trouble the heart of the Christian woman . . . she is preserved from this precisely by that absence of any sense of the Ideal, which characterizes the Semites.

But, "behind their langourous attitudes, Jewesses hid cunning, egotism and hardness . . ."[110] From another quarter, *La Semaine Religieuse de Fréjus* declared in September 1892, in a review of Joseph Maurain's *L'Elu du Peuple*, a book recommended by various diocesan bulletins: "Héléna Cleuss, the Jewess, the actress, represents the Semitic character in all its revolting reality, steeped in pride, in vengefulness, in felony, insatiable for sensual pleasure, for fame, for money."[111]

We must now attempt to explain the appeal and the function of such images of the Jewess. First, as the last example above reminds us, the concept of the hyper-sexual Jewess is related to the general view of women propagated by the Catholic Church. It is interesting to see this view filtered through the writings of Zola, who presented female sexuality as evil and frightening on his own account, too, notably in *Nana* (1880). Abbé Faujus in *La Conquête de Plassans* (1874) tells Marthe Mouret: "You are the temptation from below, the great cowardice . . . The priest has no other enemy but you, and you women should be excluded from the churches, for you are cursed and impure."[112] Similarly, in *La Faute de l'abbé Mouret* (1875), Brother Archangias declares that women "stink of the devil . . . they stink in their legs, in their arms, in their bellies, everywhere . . . they have damnation in their skirts . . ."[113] Qualities attributed in a certain Catholic view to all women were thus projected selectively on to the Jewess. But there was another complementary view of womanhood, Catholic and bourgeois, to which the image of the Jewess formed a convenient contrast. Drumont presented this in *La Fin d'un monde.* In "Aryan civilization", he wrote, the role of women was to represent "grace and goodness", while men represented "courage"; and he quoted Chevé: "The function of the woman is like that of the priest; for she is destined to moralize and to sanctify man by her example, through the three ages of her life, as virgin, as wife and as mother. Her empire over the world will increase as she becomes more pure and more holy; and she will come to rule, because she forgets her self." Moreover, the woman's place, of course, was in the home; she should never go out to work in "those workshops of ignominy where monstrous governments give a license to prostitution".[114] Similarly, a speaker told a meeting of the Union Nationale in the 7th *arrondissement* of Paris in February 1898: "Our aim is to return women to the conjugal home and to obtain the total suppression of women's work . . .";[115] and Guérin and other antisemitic leaders subscribed to the same general view of women as homemakers and mothers.[116] There was some feeling, however, that the traditional position of women was under threat. Drumont wrote, evoking France's decadence,[117]

what is perhaps more worrying than all the rest, is this abasement of French women. In epochs of decadence, it has been observed that women rise whereas men fall; but this time there is no sign of this happening . . . "Courtesan or housewife", said Proudhon, "for woman there is nothing between." Sister of Charity or call-girl, such is the dilemma of the upper-class Frenchwoman of today. Many, rich, beautiful . . . leave everything to give themselves to Christ . . .; but, with few exceptions, one sees, among those who remain in the world, few of those strong and charming women . . . who have a sense of the honour of their race, of the social function which their privilege of wealth requires of them . . .

If women's traditional public roles were being abandoned, attempts to create new roles were doomed to failure. This was the meaning of the antisemites' attacks on girls' *lycées.* These, according to Drumont, produced "large numbers of unfortunate women, too irreligious to be admitted into honest homes, too well-educated to rest content with the miserable condition that is the lot of women in our disorganized society . . ."; emancipated and educated women, he added, quoting *L'Echo de Paris* for August 1884, were "nihilists vis-à-vis love and the family . . . beskirted Bohemians", and often lesbians as well.[118] Another factor which offended against the traditional concept of women, and which was seen as undermining it, was the institution of divorce, which, as we have noted, was regarded as a Jewish enterprise. "A Jew . . . , the apostle

of divorce, has been able to break the sacred links which once united couples
. . .", commented Drumont.[119]

In a number of ways, the Jewess stood in contrast to the woman of the
traditional image, and symbolized the new woman; and it is significant that
emancipated non-Jewish women were described in the same terms as the
Jewess. Houssaye, for example, compared George Sand to "a pythoness or a
demon", and wrote that "all the characters who came to life in her novels
loomed up around her like a witches' Sabbath . . ."[120] Moreover, Mme Curie's
election to the Academy of Sciences in 1911 was opposed on the grounds that
she was a woman, and because she was said to be Jewish.[121] As actress, the
Jewess also stood for feminine professional success, as James remarked of Sarah
Bernhardt. As such she was behaving like a man, and it is not surprising to
find Colombier describing Sarah Barnum as "the pseudo-woman", as an artificial woman, even as a gynaecological oddity. The charges of sexual perversion
reflected, too, the fear that a woman might no longer accept unquestioningly
her reproductive role; perversion meant sex for sex's sake. Also involved were
male anxieties about female sexuality, not new, but exacerbated perhaps by
changes in women's attitudes and behaviour. The Jewess was insatiable but
cold; she was promiscuous, the prostitute, unwilling to accept "a single
adorer".[122] But a married woman was expected to be the opposite of these
things, faithful and obedient to one man, warm, though perhaps sexually
passive.[123] She was also expected, on the whole, to confine herself to wifely
and motherly duties in the home, and Drumont's evocation of the home-life
of Jewish women can perhaps be related to anxiety about this ideal. In some
ways, Drumont's picture is a caricature of the ideal: Jewish women are too
closely confined to the house; they have too little to do and grow bored and
fat; and beneath their outward passivity lie a cunning and a concern for their
own interests. Is it too far-fetched to see this as the expression of some kind
of worry about a threat contained in the condition of bourgeois women, a
distant reaction to an embryonic feminism?[124]

This brings us to the problem of women's antisemitism. As we saw in
examining the Henry Subscription, antisemitism does seem to have had a
special attraction for women, though, of course, this cannot be measured.
L'Hermite, for example, reported that the enthusiasm for Max Régis and for
Drumont in Algiers came mainly from women.[125] At a "punch" held by the
Ligue Antisémitique Française in June 1898, Guérin "rendered homage to the
women of Algeria for their gracious support and to their proud and energetic
sentiments".[126] More generally, the antisemites certainly assumed that they
had, or would obtain, the backing of women, and the propaganda against the
big department stores was aimed mainly at women, though this was only one
example of such an orientation. In a lecture, organized by the Jeunesse Royaliste of the 1st and 2nd *arrondissements* of Paris in April 1898, the Comte de
Sabran-Pontevès, as we have seen, "launched an attack on the Jews and the
Freemasons, and called on the women in the audience to teach their children
to execrate them."[127] Interpretation of specifically female antisemitism is
hazardous, but three lines of approach may be suggested. First, there is some

evidence that antisemitism as an expression of fear of sexuality was particularly a female as well as an adolescent phenomenon. Second, the Jews were sometimes identified with feminity, and hostility to Jews may have been an expression of women's rejection of their gender and its disabilities. Some of the entries to the Henry Subscription are explicit about this, and it was a factor of some significance in a certain kind of antisemitism in the United States in the 1940s.[128] Third, women, like army officers and the clergy though in a different way, were socially isolated, excluded from public civic life, and thus very prone to "irrational" modes of social and political explanation. Though the context is different, the factors adduced by Edgar Morin to explain the fact that the "Rumour of Orleans" began among adolescent girls, and was then accepted by older women, but rarely by men, were probably equally if not more significant half a century earlier.[129]

In conclusion, some of the sexual implications of the more general charges made against the Jews by antisemites must be mentioned. Drumont and others frequently claimed that Jewish power and domination were achieved by "corruption", that the Jews were "the corrupters" of French society.[130] A connection was made, moreover, between their desire to lay their hands on everything, and their preoccupation with "dirty" money: "Once the Jews touch something . . . and they lust to touch everything, the question of money dirties the best intentions."[131] The sexual lust of the Jews, in effect, as George L. Mosse has observed, tended to be related in antisemitic thinking with their lust for money. As we have seen, Mme Steinheil recounted that an old admirer of the Jewish actress had told her: "Rachel loved love and loved gold."[132] Jewish money-making, too, was rejected like pure sexuality because it produced nothing, because it was sterile. The Jew, wrote Picard, "takes without producing. He sucks, he swells up like the leech. He absorbs without giving anything in compensation. Like a gambler, he shifts money about in a sterile manner."[133] Here the antisemite seems to be projecting his own anal characteristics on to the mythical Jew. Certainly, the antisemite's whole preoccupation with money can be seen as an anal characteristic, related to his general authoritarianism.[134] In this way, the sexual aspect of antisemitism is linked once again to its more obviously social functions.

NOTES

1 *L'Antijuif d'Alger'*, 30 January 1898, cit. Rouquier and Soumille, "La Notion de Race chez les Français d'Algérie", p. 6.
2 Daudet, *Au Temps de Judas*, pp. 90–2 and 110–11.
3 See Erikson, "Hitler's Imagery and German Youth", pp. 486–8; Fenichel, "Psychoanalysis of Antisemitism", pp. 30–1; Ackerman and Jahoda, *Anti-Semitism and Emotional Disorder*, pp. 105–6, 111–12, 118–19 and 128–9; Adorno *et al.*, *The Authoritarian Personality*, p. 642; Mosse, *The Crisis of German Ideology*, p. 303.
4 See Rabelais, *Gargantua*, Book I, chapter 25, cit. Bakhtin, *Rabelais and His World*, p. 430; Rosenberg, *From Shylock to Svengali*, pp. 22–3; Drumont, *La Dernière Bataille*, p. 102.
5 See, for example, Szasz, *The Manufacture of Madness*, p. 193.
6 See, for example, Dollard, *Caste and Class in a Southern Town* (3rd ed., New

York, 1957), chapter VII; Erikson, *Childhood and Society*, pp. 234–5; Rose, "The Roots of Prejudice", *Race and Science*, UNESCO, p. 398; Hernton, *Sex and Racism*.

7 Sarah Bernhardt, *Memories of My Life: Being my Personal, Professional and Social Recollections as Woman and Artist* (1908) (New York, 1968), pp. 83–4.
8 See Fenichel, op. cit., pp. 30–1.
9 Sartre, *Réflexions sur la question juive*, p. 54.
10 Drumont, *Le Testament d'un antisémite*, p. 119; see also Rose, op. cit., p. 398; and Sartre, op. cit., p. 56.
11 Drumont, *La Fin d'un monde*, pp. 111–12.
12 Bloch, *Lévy*, pp. 22–23.
13 See chapter XIV, n. 559.
14 Drumont, *La France juive*, I, p. 229. This is a muddled reference to two well-established customs of the Ancien Régime, still extant in the nineteenth century: the putting of babies out to nurse, and the practice of abandoning unwanted infants, or infants who could not be provided for, at public orphanages; both were fairly common, and not especially, if at all, Jewish customs; for some recent studies, see *Hommage à Marcel Reinhard* (1973); and *Annales de Démographie Historique* (1973), "Enfant et Sociétés".
15 Drumont, *FJ*, II, pp. 443–4.
16 Ibid., II, p. 446.
17 Ibid., II, pp. 403–4; also pp. 361 and 524–6.
18 *Le Télégramme d'Alger*, 17 January 1898, cit. Rouquier and Soumille, op. cit., p. 6.
19 See Braudel, *The Mediterranean*, II, p. 807.
20 Morin *et al.*, *La Rumeur d'Orléans*, pp. 39–52.
21 Drumont, *FJ*, II, pp. 185–6.
22 Ibid., II, p. 174.
23 Ibid., I, p. 333. This recalls the claim made in Britain today (1975–6) that "Reds" are in or under beds.
24 See Gene Brucker, ed., *The Society of Renaissance Florence: A Documentary Study* (New York, 1971), pp. 245–7; Le Roy Ladurie, *Les Paysans de Languedoc*, p. 229; *Race and Science*, UNESCO, pp. 23–4, 364 and 470–2; Dollard, op. cit.; Hernton, op. cit.
25 Père Monsabré was unusual in advocating intermarriage as a means of ensuring that all Jews would eventually become Catholics; see Bournand, *Les Juifs et nos contemporains*, p. 193; also Tharaud, *Petite Histoire des Juifs*, p. 162.
26 Lacretelle, *Silbermann*, p. 140.
27 Drumont, *TA*, pp. 150–1.
28 Drumont, *FJ*, I, p. 8. The Wandering Jew in Apollinaire's "Le Passant de Prague" is presented as having unusual sexual stamina; see n. 46 below.
29 See, for example, *The Confessions of Arsène Houssaye*, p. 75; and chapter XIV, p. 558 and n. 506 below.
30 Drumont, "L'Amour Libre", 16 January 1894, *De l'Or, de la boue, du sang*, pp. 145–53.
31 Drumont, *TA*, p. 318; also pp. 119–25; and *FM*, pp. 368–9.
32 Drumont, *TA*, p. 363; see also *FJ*, II, pp. 455–9 and 487–90; Biez, *Les Rothschild et le péril juif*, p. 4.
33 Drumont, *TA*, pp 182–6.
34 Drumont, *FJ*, II, p 276.
35 See, for example, ibid., II, p 443; and *FM*, pp 354–5.
36 Drumont, *FM*, pp. 113–14.
37 Drumont, *FJ*, II, p. 550.
38 See, for example, Shils, in Christie and Jahoda, eds, *Studies in the Scope and Method of "The Authoritarian Personality"*, p. 40; also Adorno *et al.*, *The Authoritarian Personality*, pp. 239–41 and 390–441.

39 See, for example, Drumont, *FM*, pp. 357–8.
40 Dumont, *La Petite Bourgeoisie vue à travers les contes quotidiens du "Journal"*, pp. 86–94.
41 Leschnitzer, cit. Szasz, op. cit., p. 136; see also Lovsky, *L'Antisémitisme chrétien*, pp. 153–5.
42 See Memmi, *Portrait d'un Juif*, pp. 137–41.
43 See chapter XIII, p. 478 and n. 207 above.
44 See Guy-Grand, *La Philosophie nationaliste*, pp. 53–4.
45 Mirbeau, *Le Journal d'une femme de chambre*, p. 105.
46 See Barrès, *Scènes et doctrines*, I, p. 204; Memmi, op. cit., pp. 137–41; and Baudouin, *Psychanalyse du symbole religieux*, p 206. Apollinaire, in "Le Passant de Prague" (p. 112), seems to have associated the Wandering Jew's unusual sexual powers with the fact that he was circumcised: "Son sexe circoncis évoquait un tronc noueux, ou ce poteau de couleurs des Peaux-Rouges, bariolé de terre de Sienne, d'écarlate et du violet sombre des ciels d'orage. Au bout d'un quart d'heure, ils revinrent. La fille lasse, amoureuse, mais effrayée, criait en allemand: —Il a marché tout le temps, il a marché tout le temps!"
47 For Freud, see chapter IV, n. 176; see also Fenichel, op. cit., pp. 36–7; and Ackerman and Jahoda, op. cit., pp. 2, 10, 15, 17–20 and 95–130.
48 Cit. Pierrard, *Juifs et catholiques français*, p. 117; see also ibid., p. 56.
49 Drumont, *DB*, pp. 130 and 133; see also Fenichel, op. cit., pp. 36–7.
50 See, for example, Oscar Lewis, *The Children of Sanchez: Autobiography of a Mexican Family* (Harmondsworth, 1964), pp. 143, 163, 176 and 499.
51 AN F⁷ 12843.
52 See Reuben Levy, *The Social Structure of Islam* (Cambridge, 1965), pp. 251–2.
53 See chapter IV, pp. 156–7 and nn. 194 and 197 above.
54 Jean de Ligneau (F. Bournand), *Juifs et antisémites en Europe* (Paris, 1891), cit. Lovsky, op. cit., p. 246; see also Apollinaire, "Le Juif Latin" (March 1903), *Oeuvres complètes*, I, pp. 119–27, a story about a Jewish mass-murderer; and Dickens' evocation of Fagin's attachment to his knife. Charles Dickens, *The Adventures of Oliver Twist* (1838), cit. Rosenberg, op. cit., pp. 25 and 266.
55 Mirbeau, op. cit., p. 157; also pp. 104, 146–7, 151–8 and *passim.*
56 Drumont, *TA*, p. 295.
57 *L'Intransigeant*, 18 October 1898, cit. Zévaès, *L'Affaire Dreyfus*, p. 145.
58 See, generally, Sartre, op. cit., p. 54; and Hofstadter, *The Paranoid Style*, p. 34; and, more particularly, Ferenczi, "On Eye Symbolism", *Contributions to Psycho-Analysis*, pp. 228–33. Both Oedipus and Samson suffered blinding for sexual offences.
59 See, for example, Bakhtin, op. cit., pp. 196–213; Bollême, *La Bibliothèque bleue*, pp. 247–64; and Michel Vovelle, *Mourir autrefois: Attitudes collectives devant la mort au XVIIe et XVIIIe siècles* (Paris, 1974), pp. 123–5 and 211–12.
60 See, for example, Michel Foucault, ed., *Moi, Pierre Rivière, ayant égorgé ma mère, ma soeur et mon frère . . . , Un cas de parricide au XIXe siècle* (Paris, 1973), citing *La Gazette des Tribunaux*, etc.; and Steinheil, *My Memoirs*, pp. 189–91, 230–3, 238–41, 268, 308–12 and *passim*, referring to the publicity given in the press to the crime of which she was accused, and to her being hounded by journalists before her arrest.
61 Study of this topic seems unfortunately not to have been undertaken for France, despite the initiative provided by Bollême and Mandrou's research on earlier popular literature. On the genre in English literature, see, for example, Margaret Dalziel, *Popular Fiction 100 Years Ago* (London, 1957), especially chapters I–IV; Montague Summers, *The Gothic Quest: A History of the Gothic Novel* (New York, 1964); William W. Watt, *Shilling Shockers of the Gothic School: A Study of Chapbook Gothic Romances* (New York, 1932 and 1967); Louis James, *Fiction for the Working Man, 1830–50* (Oxford, 1963).
62 Memmi, op. cit., p. 139.

63 Sartre, op. cit., pp. 56–7.
64 Barrès, *Mes Cahiers*, II, p. 129.
65 See Memmi, op. cit., p. 139; Dollard, op. cit., chapter VII; Hernton, op. cit., chapter 5; and Astier Loutfi, *Littérature et colonialisme*, pp. 36–7 and 60–1.
66 Verdès-Leroux, *Scandale financier*, pp. 131–2; see also Klein, *Portrait de la Juive dans la littérature française*, pp. 18–20 and *passim.*
67 See Rosenberg, op. cit., pp. 34–5, 75–6 and 85–92; Klein, op. cit., chapter III; and Sartre, op. cit., p. 57.
68 Cit. Paléologue, *Journal de l'Affaire Dreyfus*, p. 213.
69 Stendhal, *Mémoires d'un touriste*, I, p. 211.
70 Paléologue, op. cit., p. 213 (15 August 1899).
71 Jusserand, *What Me Befell*, p. 19.
72 See Wirth, *The Ghetto*, pp. 3–4 and 35.
73 See, for example, Balzac, *La Cousine Bette*, pp. 14–15 and *passim; Splendeurs et misères des courtisanes* (1848) (Paris, 1964), pp. 51–3 and *passim;* and *Illusions perdues* (1843); W. H. Van der Gun, *La Courtisane romantique et son rôle dans la 'Comédie Humaine' de Balzac* (Leiden, 1963), pp. 115, 125 and generally; Schmidt, *Maupassant par lui-même*, p. 37; and Proust, *A la Recherche du temps perdu*, particularly III, pp. 212–13, and V, *passim.*
74 Dagan, *Enquête sur l'antisémitisme*, p. 19.
75 Maupassant, *La Maison Tellier*, pp. 13–14.
76 Alphonse Daudet, *Numa Roumestan*, p. 355.
77 Vallès, *Le Bachélier*, p. 49.
78 Zola, *Paris*, p. 24.
79 Martin du Gard, *Jean Barois*, p. 253.
80 Colombier, *Sarah Barnum*, pp. 117, 37–8, 45, 192 and 195; also pp. 140, 272, 311 and 330.
81 Mirbeau, op. cit., p. 266.
82 Cit. Drumont, *TA*, p. 153; see also Apollinaire, "Le Passant de Prague", p. 112, where, in the Jewish quarter, "par nuit, chaque maison s'est transformée en lupanar."
83 L'Hermite, *L'Anti-Pape*, p. 90.
84 See Drumont, *FJ*, II, pp. 246–7; Steinheil, op. cit., p. 40; and Richardson, *Rachel*, pp. 38–44, 65–6, 74 and *passim.*
85 Cit. Richardson, *Sarah Bernhardt*, p. 59; see also ibid., pp. 11, 40, 59, 71, 82–93 and *passim.*
86 Waleffe, *Quand Paris était un paradis*, pp. 39–40; see also Donnay, *Des Souvenirs*, p. 120; Reynaldo Hahn, *La Grande Sarah, Souvenirs* (Paris, 1930), pp. 40–1, 46–7, 52, 137–8, 161 and *passim;* and Bernhardt, op. cit., pp. 239, 277–8, 294–300, 310, 341–2 and *passim.*
87 See Richardson, *Rachel*, pp. xi, 167, 187, 190–7, 201, 204–6 and *passim.*
88 See Bernhardt, op. cit., pp. 37–8, 46, 53–5, 93 and 117.
89 Ibid., p. 157 and *passim;* and Hahn, op. cit., pp. 131–2 and 175.
90 Bernhardt, op. cit., p. 341.
91 Richardson, *Sarah Bernhardt*, pp. 104–6.
92 Hahn, op. cit., p. 15; also p. 10.
93 Cit. Richardson, *Sarah Bernhardt*, p. 188; see also ibid., pp. 12, 74, 99, 108 and 112.
94 Clermont-Tonnerre, *Mémoires*, I, p. 183.
95 Colombier, op. cit., pp. 76 and 80.
96 See Richardson, *Sarah Bernhardt*, pp. 26, 29, 32, 94, 109–11, 123 and *passim;* and Louis Sapin, "La 'Scandaleuse' Sarah Bernhardt", in Gilbert Guilleminault, *La Jeunesse de Marianne* (Paris, 1958), pp. 113–49.
97 Waleffe, op. cit., p. 171.
98 Drumont, *FJ*, II, p. 246; see also Drumont, *DB*, p. 551; Picard, *Synthèse de l'antisémitisme*, p. 103.

99 *La France Chrétienne*, 18 December 1889, cit. Drumont, *TA*, p. 408; also Richardson, *Sarah Bernhardt*, p. 119.
100 Drumont, *FJ*, I, p. 24.
101 Cit. Paléologue, op. cit., p. 85 (13 December 1897).
102 Picard, op. cit., p. 121; see also Drumont, *FJ*, I, p. 218.
103 Drumont, *FJ*, I, pp. 88–9.
104 Drumont, *DB*, pp. 94–5, 507 and 551.
105 Ibid., pp. 136–7.
106 Drumont, *TA*, p. 420, citing Taxil.
107 Drumont, *FJ*, I, pp. 111–12.
108 Ibid., I, p. 471.
109 Ibid., I, pp. 89–90.
110 Ibid., II, p. 266.
111 Cit. Verdès-Leroux, op. cit., p. 213.
112 Cit. Guillemin, *Présentation des Rougon-Macquart*, p. 66.
113 Cit. ibid., p. 88; see also pp. 79, 167 and 171.
114 Drumont, *FM*, pp. 111 and 113.
115 Daily Report, Prefect of Police, 5 February 1898. APP Ba 106.
116 See, for example, Daily Reports, Prefect of Police, 14 April, and 1 June 1898. APP Ba 106.
117 Drumont, *FJ*, II, pp. 175–6.
118 Ibid., II, pp. 444–5; see also speech at Union Nationale meeting. Report, Commissaire spécial, Nancy, 5 February 1900. AN F[7] 12456.
119 Drumont, *FM*, p. 111.
120 *The Confessions of Arsène Houssaye*, p. 65.
121 Eve Curie, *Madame Curie* (London, 1938), p. 279.
122 Colombier, op. cit., pp. 192, 140, 272 and 195.
123 For a general discussion of different attitudes in this sphere, mainly for Britain and the United States, see Carl N. Degler, "What Ought To Be and What Was: Women's Sexuality in the Nineteenth Century", *American Historical Review*, 79 (1974), pp. 1467–90. No such study exists for France, but it is unlikely that attitudes were very different, or more liberal; see also chapter XVI, p. 624 below.
124 Feminism in France was less developed than in Britain or the United States; see Emile Faguet, *Le Féminisme* (Paris, 1910). There seems to be no modern study.
125 L'Hermite, op. cit., pp. 91–4 and 247–51.
126 Daily Report, Prefect of Police, 1 June 1898. APP Ba 106.
127 Daily Report, Prefect of Police, 14 April 1898. APP Ba 106.
128 See chapter IV, p. 154 above; and Ackerman and Jahoda, op. cit., pp. 42, 47–50, 70–1 and 92–3.
129 See Morin *et al.*, op. cit., pp. 23–7 and *passim*.
130 Drumont, *TA*, pp. 45, 58–90 and 137.
131 Drumont, *FJ*, II, p. 133.
132 Mosse, *The Crisis of German Ideology*, pp. 141–2; and Steinheil, op. cit., p. 40; see also Rosenberg, op. cit., pp. 27–33.
133 Picard, op. cit., p. 44.
134 See Freud, *Three Essays on the Theory of Sexuality* (1905), English Standard Edition, VII, pp. 123–43; Freud, *Character and Anal Eroticism* (1908), ESE, IX, pp. 167–75; Freud, *From the History of an Infantile Neurosis* (1918), ESE, XVII, pp. 72 and ff; Adorno *et al.*, *The Authoritarian Personality*; and works cited in chapter XIII, n. 329.

CHAPTER XVI
ANTISEMITISM AS AN IDEOLOGY AND ITS GENERAL FUNCTION

I

So far, in this part of the book, we have discussed various aspects and functions of antisemitism separately chapter by chapter, but it must be stressed now that, despite differences of emphasis on the part of different groups and writers, we are dealing with a single and relatively coherent ideology. This characteristic of antisemitism has not always been acknowledged or perceived by students trained to look for a particular kind of rationality in any system of thought. Dagan declared, for example, in 1899 that "Antisemitism cannot be considered, like Socialism or Anarchism, as a political system or as a social philosophy."[1] The brothers Tharaud recounted a meeting in 1933 with a French intellectual who lived in Berlin; even at that date he could not take Hitler's antisemitism seriously, explaining: "all that he writes or says is at once confused, banal and contradictory, when it is not simply absurd."[2] And even modern scholars of great acumen betray the same tendency. Delpech has written that *"La France juive* . . . is absolutely incoherent . . .", though he added that this incoherence was the reason for its success;[3] while Sorlin concluded that: "La Bonne Presse did not preach an antisemitic doctrine: it distilled an anti-Jewish sentiment . . ."[4] Against this view, we maintain that if it is compared not with modern political ideologies of which Socialism is the model, but with belief-systems that are more "popular", more common and more diffuse, with popular religion and mythology, antisemitism can be seen to have a certain unity and structural coherence. It can be seen, too, like witchcraft beliefs, to have its own "rationality", its own power of explanation, different from but as compelling as "scientific rationality". Two further factors lend force to this interpretation. First, as we have frequently pointed out and illustrated, antisemitism was not a private opinion, formulated by individuals for themselves, it was a social, cultural phenomenon, an already existing ideological system, to which they adhered with more or less conviction, or which they ignored or rejected. Second, in the last decades of the nineteenth century in France precisely this system achieved a new degree of coherence; a set of old beliefs and ideas about Jews was articulated and systematized by writers and journalists to serve new functions. Antisemitism was by origin and mode a "popular" ideology, but, in its modern shape, it was formulated by intellectuals.

Though offering very different explanations of it, a growing number of scholars, including Ginsberg, Levinson,[5] Sartre, Verdès-Leroux, and Selznick and Steinberg, have come to see antisemitism as a coherent ideology or set of beliefs. According to Sartre, "antisemitism is not a simple 'opinion' about the Jews . . . , it is, in its own right, a way of thought and a conception of the world."[6] Echoing this, Verdès-Leroux has described antisemitism as "a complete world-view";[7] while Selznick and Steinberg have declared "that anti-Semitism is not a haphazard conglomeration of beliefs but has a definite structure."[8] Contemporaries, whether critics or adherents, shared this view. "The Jew-haters of today", wrote Lazare, "want to explain their hatred . . . anti-Judaism thus becomes antisemitism. And how is this antisemitism manifested? It has to be manifested in the written word."[9] Bearing the same testimony, despite his dismissive tone, Albert Réville told Dagan:[10]

> Injustice and stupidity are always enchanted when they find a theory which seems to give their prejudice the outward appearance, the consecration of rational motivation; many people who detest the Jews without knowing why, simply "because they don't happen to like them", have lent a complaisant ear to the often slanderous utterances and the violent attacks made by the spokesmen of antisemitism.

And these spokesmen themselves certainly believed that they were promulgating more than a series of disconnected prejudices. With special reference to the writings of Drumont, Bernanos declared that antisemitism was "a grand political theory";[11] and Drumont regarded his antisemitic propaganda in ideological terms. "What is written cannot be unwritten", he declared sententiously in 1891, and he regretted that antisemitism had "momentarily been prevented from assuming in the realm of fact the place which it already occupied in the realm of ideas."[12] Similarly, and more optimistically, Maurras asserted in *La Gazette de France* in February 1901, as we have seen, that antisemitism was "the first organic and positive idea, the first counter-revolutionary and Nationalist idea to have enjoyed real and substantial popularity in France in the last hundred years."[13]

The ideological nature of antisemitism has been made clear in previous chapters. Its ideological unity, very apparent in the work of Drumont, can be illustrated here from *Le Complôt juif,* a short pamphlet, outlining an alleged Jewish plan for world-domination, put out by *La Croix* in April 1898. This pamphlet combines most of the aspects of antisemitism that we have discussed. The Jews are said to be engaged in a "war against the Church . . . For several centuries our scholars have struggled courageously and with indefatiguable perseverance against the Cross." The Jews are also engaged in "the conquest of the world by means of gold . . . They have become the masters of other nations via the Stock Exchange, state loans, public works, and taxation." Although "commerce and speculation" remain their main fields of operation, they have extended their influence into other spheres. They are making great efforts "to acquire land", and they "are taking over all public employments, the magistrature, and legislative functions." They are also very influential as doctors and in the world of the arts, and they control the press. They are anxious to corrupt Christians by fostering intermarriage, and they are working "to deprave Christian virgins" and "to destroy the family". They are also encouraging and directing Socialism and popular movements in order to precipitate the Revolution. In all this, the aim of the Jews was to ruin and to exploit Christians: "Our unique aim is to reign over the earth, as was promised to our ancestor Abraham."[14] Further evidence of unity and coherence is provided by the fact that pamphlets, entitled *Le Complôt protestant* and *Le Complôt maconnique* were issued by the same agency at the same time and in the same format.

The inherent rationality and explanatory function of antisemitism have also been repeatedly stressed in the course of this work. As Verdès-Leroux has commented, "at the heart of antisemitism, in effect, there is the wish to explain, to rationalize at any price."[15] Some earlier students of the subject have measured antisemitism by the criteria of scientific enquiry, and, finding it wanting, have dubbed it "irrational", but as Hyman and Sheatsley have pointed out, this is an unwarranted, or at least an unhelpful, procedure.[16] In its social and cultural context, antisemitism has both an internal logic and an explanatory power. Like witchcraft and other systems of belief, it explains the otherwise inexplicable, on the personal and on the social level.[17] If anything, it is over-rational rather than "irrational", as Adorno himself realized, writing in *The Authoritarian Personality:* "Anti-Semitic writers and agitators . . . have always maintained that the existence of the Jews is the *key* to everything . . . they speak as if they were in the know and had solved a riddle otherwise unsolved by mankind . . ."[18] And French antisemites certainly presented and regarded antisemitism in this way. "Things, which, at first sight, seemed beyond all probability, monstrous", wrote Drumont, "appear, in effect, almost simple and quite natural, once one realizes that the Jew is at the heart of Freemasonry . . .";[19] and he declared, more generally: "The day that you attack the Jew, you lay hold of Reality, you measure up against your real enemy."[20] Similarly, Bishop Meurin claimed that his book, *La Franc-maçonnerie, Synagogue de Satan,* "explains our tormented century";[21] while Wicart described the situation which antisemitism offered to meet in these terms: "Existence today is so complicated, our daily life is so full of details, our time and our means are so limited, that it is very difficult for most people to have any picture of the real situation of things and of people."[22] Lazare agreed that the appeal of antisemitism in such a situation was that it offered a simple and readily accessible explanation of social and economic processes that were otherwise mysterious to those who suffered them: "Simple minds did not look for the real causes of their distress; they saw only the efficient causes", that is, the Jews and their allies.[23]

As critics of the purely psychological approach to antisemitism have also emphasized, it is an autonomous set of attitudes and beliefs, with an independent existence as a "social fact". Selznick and Steinberg have written "that anti-Semites do not have to invent anti-Semitism; it is part of the cultural heritage and available to them in the same way as many other beliefs and attitudes." Like them, like other "prejudices", it is a "social grammar"; and "individuals acquire anti-Semitism through the normal processes of socialization."[24] Similarly, according to Memmi,[25]

the antisemitic phenomenon . . . lies beyond personal will or good-will; it is cruelly outside the control of individuals, Jews or non-Jews; we encounter it, almost as soon as we are born and throughout our lives, this mean and disturbing phenomenon, but indisputable and already familiar, already chronic. It is almost an institution; it is part of the collective way of life, of the culture, like certain ancient monuments, huge and ugly, but which no one dreams any more of destroying, since their age and their mass now seem to defy demolition, to require an effort beyond the strength of those who might dismantle them . . . One risks . . . failing to understand the misfortune of the Jews, one risks minimizing and distorting it, if one forgets that it is primarily a collective, a global phenomenon.

We have seen that antisemitism in nineteenth-century France was embedded in the culture in the way that Memmi describes. This is evident, for example, in the literature of the period, and, more significantly, in the theatre, a more popular and direct medium. Three of the plays most often performed on the Parisian stage in the second half of the century presented stereotypes of the Jew, mainly hostile. These were Erckmann-Chatrian's *Le Juif polonais*, first staged in 1869, and successfully revived in 1877, 1878, 1892 and 1895;[26] Sue's *Le Juif errant*, a popular success from the first half of the century, that was revived in 1877, 1894, 1895, 1898 and 1902;[27] and various versions of *The Merchant of Venice*, put on in 1876, 1889, 1890, 1902 and 1905.[28] Other plays staged in Paris with antisemitic themes—from the 1890s of a more sophisticated kind—included *Israël*, put on at the Théâtre du Château d'Eau in 1879; Lavedan's *Le Prince d'Aurec* (1892); a dramatization of Goncourt's *Manette Salomon* (1896); Donnay's *Le Retour de Jérusalem* (1903); Guinon's *Décadence* (1904); and Savoir and Nozière's *Le Baptême* (1907).[29] According to Drault, Donnay's play was intended "to be favourable to the Jews, but appeared on stage as an antisemitic polemic . . ."; it ran for over 400 performances at the Théâtre du Gymnase.[30] Both *Décadence* and *Le Baptême* were less successful, encountering opposition, it appears, from Jewish theatre managers and playgoers.[31] It is fair to add that the antisemitic tone of the French theatre was to some extent offset by the important place occupied by Jewish actors, of whom Sarah Bernhardt was only the most famous, and by the success of Jewish playwrights, such as Porto-Riche and Bernstein, in the pre-1914 period. But even they were influenced by the prevailing climate. Simone Le Bargy, though apparently opposed to antisemitism, played the leading role in *Le Retour de Jérusalem*, and the authors of *Le Baptême* were of Jewish extraction.[32]

But to establish that antisemitism in late nineteenth-century France was a cultural datum does not go far enough, for precisely in this period the nature of that cultural datum changed; it became more deliberate, more self-conscious, more coherent. In the last two decades of the century, as Verdès-Leroux has put it, "the old hostility to the Jews was transformed into a political ideology . . ."[33] Its components were not new, but their elaboration into a total system, a synthesis, was.[34] Antisemitism thus preserved elements from popular traditional culture, but recast them into forms that suited the modern context of literate and national democratic culture, while at the same time enormously enhancing their explanatory function. An analogy may perhaps be found with the way in which disparate folk-beliefs were elaborated in earlier centuries into an intellectualized demonology.[35] Again, contemporary critics and adherents were aware of this process. Lazare stressed, in 1894, that literate antisemitism was the articulation of latent popular attitudes: "If the antisemitic writers have provided the unconscious antisemites with reasons, the former have none the less been engendered by the latter; they have tried to explain what the rank-and-file felt . . ."[36] And Péguy was referring to the ideological aspect of antisemitism, when he wrote in *Notre Jeunesse* that "the antisemites . . . are much more modern than we are . . . they are much more modern than they think . . ."[37] Moreover, a number of leading antisemites were quite aware of their ideological role. Drumont wrote in 1891 that ordinary people "are unable to co-ordinate all these ideas; they cannot arrive by themselves at the realization that cosmopolitan Jewry is running everything. Newspapers have to assume the responsibility of explaining the situation to them . . ."[38] More tentatively, Forain explained that in drawing his antisemitic cartoons, "I was acting . . . quite simply, as the echo of the public;"[39] while Picard declared, more generally and with much greater self-consciousness, that antisemitism "began among the people . . . It was not caused by laws or by written propaganda . . . The men who preached antisemitism did not create it from nothing; and if they are listened to, it is because they speak a language that is already known, because they are formulating tendencies that already existed, but which needed to be elaborated and made explicit."[40]

A crucial aspect of this elaboration of antisemitism into an ideology was the active role of intellectuals in the process. As we have seen, the "new" antisemitism found expression primarily in newspapers, journals, pamphlets and books, and its proponents were writers and journalists. As Audiffred, president of L'Association Républicaine, lamented in a letter to Yves Guyot, the antisemites "had succeeded in reviving all the anti-Jewish hatreds, all the prejudices of race; and it is incontestable that men of intelligence are devoting themselves to this task."[41] And, from a very different point of view, Léon Daudet boasted of the leading part played in the development of antisemitism by "those in literary circles, who are the most intelligent, the most independent and the most lively [members of society]".[42] However, although leading writers of the day, like Alphonse Daudet,[43] Edmond de Goncourt,[44] Huysmans,[45] Gyp[46] and Coppée,[47] gave organized antisemitism their support, those who elaborated antisemitic ideology were writers of lesser prestige and status, but men with a sense of their status as writers none the less. It is also relevant that artists, including Forain and Caran d'Ache but also Degas, should have supported antisemitism,[48] as well as academics such as Alfred Rambaud, the historian and at one time Minister of Public Instruction,[49] and François Bournand, who was professor of History and of Art at the Ecole Professionnelle Catholique.[50] While articulating general grievances, in effect, the antisemitic intellectuals were also expressing grievances peculiar to intellectuals, and these are worth enquiring into.

On the most general level, antisemitism was the expression of a sense of cultural decadence, a "politics of cultural despair", in Stern's phrase. In pointing to the Jew as the author of modern society, a Maurras, for example, was seeking to explain his conviction that civilization itself was under threat, that classical and Catholic values were being destroyed by materialism and democracy.[51] Using a symbolic argument favoured by many conservative intellectuals today, Drumont expressed the same view by pointing to the perversion of language:[52]

> The Jew, in effect, has created a special vocabulary for the peculiar society that he has created; he has adulterated the dictionary like everything else; he has counterfeited words as well as money. *"Credo"* has become credit exploited by crooks at the expense of the naïve; the word *"action,"* which used to mean the effort of a man of action, now refers to an inert piece of paper (a share), belonging to a man who expects a reward without doing anything.

Underlying this concern was an anxiety about the role and status of the intellectual in a democratic society, for the traditional concept of civilization depended on a thoroughgoing cultural élitism. Here it is significant that the term "intellectual" was first used in France in the late 1890s, and, precisely, in the context of the Dreyfus Affair. The fact that it was primarily applied to and adopted by Dreyfusards must not obscure the general meaning of this development.[53] Intellectuals, in the objective sense, were involved in both sides in the controversy, and this represented, on their part, a new claim to a civic role. As Pierre Dreyfus commented, the Affair provoked a "ripening of civic spirit and social conscience. This was observable in every class, and particularly among the intellectuals, who up to that time had been indifferent to public affairs."[54] As it stands, this is slightly misleading; intellectuals had been involved in the Revolution of 1848; intellectuals led the debate into the fundamental reasons for France's defeat in 1870–1; but these had been unwonted departures from a normal quietism, from a cultivation of "art for art's sake", or learning for learning's sake, and they had not entailed any basic discussion of the social role of the intellectual.[55] In the 1890s, by contrast, it was felt that the social and political underpinning of the "high culture" of the intellectuals needed ideological defence, and the whole position and role of the intellectual had become problematical, threatened. This was evident even before the Affair highlighted and crystallized the issue. Drumont, for example, in *La France juive* in 1886, displayed a jealous concern over the status ac-

corded to intellectuals. He wrote indignantly that "M. de La Rochefoucauld
. . . receives Rothschild and Meyer, but he does not invite Hervilly to a *soirée*,
at which one of his plays is being performed."[56] We have seen that he felt
that the status of journalists had been degraded, and he made the same point
about the medical profession: "Medical schools . . . are only a shadow of what
they used to be before the Jews entered them. All the traditions of professional
honour are tending to disappear there too."[57] However, what interested him
most closely was the role of the "pure", as opposed to the practical intellectual.
The role of the writer, he declared in 1890, quoting Carlyle, was akin to that
of the priest; he had "a grand and fine mission" to fulfil.[58] In the same vein,
the young team of writers who edited *La Cocarde* in 1894–5, and who
included Barrès and Maurras, put forward the idea of "intellectual power",
and stressed the special role of the intellectual in society. Camille Mauclair,
referred, for example, in September 1894, to "the aristocracy of thought, the
only valuable and worthy aristocracy".[59]

Perhaps the most extended development of this theme was Maurras's
L'Avenir de l'intelligence, published in 1905. He claimed:

> Life is taking on a certain grossness. The moral situation of the educated
> Frenchmen in 1905 is no longer at all what it was in 1850. The reputation
> of the writer has been lost . . . the writer is . . . more than anyone else
> *déclassé* . . . The ancient predisposition in favour of a class of intellectual
> mandarins has retained its force in the obscure and profound mass of the
> reading public, but it cannot do so for long. The bourgeoisie, among whom
> the amateur flourishes almost to the same degree as among the aristocracy,
> has freed itself from any favourable illusions in this sphere and from all
> reverence. Its positivistic spirit observes that there are four or five thousand
> artists or writers wandering in the streets of Paris on the brink of starvation.

Maurras went on to point out that the intellectual was not wholly abandoned
to a philistine commercialism; he had acquired a new patron in the State; but
this patronage reduced him to a position of tutelage and dependence: "By
means of the education system which belongs to it, the State seeks to prolong
a situation in which the credit of Intelligence is maintained, but Intelligence
here becomes a thin façade hiding state power, and a device by which the
control of the State by Money is dissimulated. And if Intelligence thus continues to be painted in glowing colours, by the same token it loses status." State
patronage creates "an intellectual proletariat" as its clientèle, who compete for
places and favours.[60] Thus antisemitic intellectuals were complaining not only
about their economic insecurity and lack of recompense, but also about their
real or threatened loss of independence. As an example of the former, one can
cite Forain's complaint to Bournand: "We artists, like you writers, we live
from hand to mouth; we only earn just enough to stay alive and keep on
working, while the most insignificant little Jew who sets up in business is the
possessor of a fortune at the end of a year or two."[61] Similarly, a succession
of writers inveighed against Jewish printers, publishers, agents and newspaper
owners. Vallès declaimed in *Le Bachélier:* "The printing business today! Do

you know what its real name is? Its name is *Shylock*, Shylock the money-grubber, the miser, the Jew, only interested in his pound of flesh!"[62] Bloy, whose own books were commercial failures, expressed a bitter envy of success-ful writers like Zola, and claimed that his literary agent was a Jew.[63] Drumont, who harped on the familar theme that publishing and the press were con-trolled by the Jews, explained the failure of so many writers in these terms in *La France juive:* "Any writer who attacks the Jews . . . is met by a conspiracy of silence, on the orders of the Jewish press . . . a writer who, persists in causing trouble is reduced to despair by the Jews, and is pushed into alcoholism or madness."[64] Byrnes has suggested that the crisis in French publishing in the 1890s exacerbated the insecurity and the fears of writers that frequently found expression in antisemitism in this way.[65]

But Maurras's second point about official patronage was equally if not more important. As was often the case elsewhere,[66] French antisemitic intellectuals were outside the new intellectual establishment. Whether they were autodi-dacts like Proudhon, Drumont and the Assumptionists[67], or well-educated mandarins like Barrès and Maurras, they at the same time rejoiced in their beleaguered independence, and envied the official status of the rivals whom they professed to despise. In Drumont's case, this perhaps helps to explain his determination to make his work "scientific",[68] to give it the appearance of scholarship; he claimed that *La France juive* was "a work of rigorous analysis . . ."[69] The same considerations underlie the pejorative use of the term "intellectual" by the anti-Dreyfusard intellectuals; those whom they attacked were not only on the political Left, they were also mainly university and state school teachers.[70] More directly, of course, the antisemites and the National-ists attacked the state University and the state education system.[71] The intellectuals of the Ligue de la Patrie Française were sometimes, like Brune-tière and Lemaître, members of the French Academy, but Drumont was a vigorous critic of this conservative intellectual institution also, which he de-scribed in 1890 as "a consortium of pornographers, mountebanks, advertising men, Jews and their clients, all with only the remotest connection with literature, to which are affiliated a few parasitical writers in a menial capac-ity."[72] Something of the motivation behind such criticism is revealed by the fact that, as we have seen, Drumont later tried to enter the Academy, thus following a well-worn tradition of writers who denigrated the institution on which their ambitions were really set.[73]

A profounder paradox in the attitude of antisemitic intellectuals, the ideo-logical counterpart of their attack on "official" intellectuals, was their espousal, together with claims to represent "Intelligence" of an overt anti-intellectual-ism. Drumont, we have seen, laid claim to being scholarly and "scientific", but he also celebrated the "pure instinct . . . [of] the masses", and poured scorn on the habit of "analysis . . . [and] reasoning . . . [of] the upper classes", which inhibited them from action.[74] Père Didon declared, in July 1898, at the prizegiving at the Collège d'Arcueil, of which he was the principal, a ceremony presided over by General Jamont: "The enemy is intellectualism which pro-fesses to disdain force . . ."[75] This theme was much more developed in the work of Barrès, who rejected the rationalism and positivism of Taine and his generation in favour of intuition, and the cult of the unconscious, of action and force.[76] This trend can be seen as part of a much wider rejection of nineteenth-century rationalism, which was evident from the 1890s in France and elsewhere.[77] Its adoption by antisemites has peculiar features, but also throws light on the general phenomenon.

It was fairly common at the turn of the century in France to associate Jews with unusual intellectual powers. The narrator in Lacretelle's novel, for example, says of Silbermann that he had never met anyone who "had so pronounced a taste for intellectual matters . . . One word, which he seemed to adore, kept recurring in his conversation: Intelligence"; and Silbermann, himself, explained non-Jewish hostility towards Jews in these terms: "Your great grievance is the Jewish intellect, the famous Jewish intellect . . ."[78] Gide referred in his *Journal* in 1905 to "Copeau with a subtle mind like that of a Jew (at first I thought he was a Jew) . . ."[79] Thus, unsurprisingly, since the idea was commonplace, "for the antisemite, intelligence is Jewish", as Sartre put it later.[80] There was, of course, some objective justification for such a view. A very high premium had been set on religious learning in traditional Jewish culture, and after Emancipation this traditional bias, together with the remaining impediments to entry to or success in other fields, had frequently led Jews to take up secular intellectual pursuits and careers, in which they often excelled.[81] The high esteem in which such intellectual pursuits were held is testified to by many French Jewish writers, themselves examples of Jewish success in this sphere. Julien Benda, for example, recounted that his parents instilled in him "a respect for academic work, for disinterested knowledge, and an utter scorn for money and worldly honours"; as a boy, and thereafter, the academic life appeared to him as "something noble, the supreme mode of existence".[82] Emmanuel Berl had the same youthful ambition, later fulfilled like that of Benda, to become "a great mind". "A serious blot . . .", he recalled, "lay on the Berl family, in the eyes of the Lange family [his mother's family] and in my eyes. There were no professors or teachers among them. The Berls, by some aberration, which I found inexplicable, did not even seem to regret this." By contrast, the Langes revered the memory of his uncle Emmanuel, who had gone to the Ecole Normale, and had died of tuberculosis in his early twenties. Berl's mother wanted her son to follow in his uncle's footsteps: "For her, the Ecole Normale signified much more than the preparation for a certain career; it represented a special and superior way of life, an initiation into something like a religious order . . ."[83] More objectively, Durkheim observed that Jews had a much greater interest in education that Catholics or Protestants, and suggested that this was in order "to be better armed for the struggle . . . . a means of offsetting the unfavourable position imposed on [them] . . . by opinion and sometimes by law."[84]

Antisemitic criticism of Jewish intelligence was thus to some extent an expression of the jealousy of one set of intellectuals for another, parallel to the hostility shown towards the "official" intellectuals with their degrees and diplomas, and their positions in the state education system. As we have seen, moreover, from the autobiographies of Benda and Berl, Jewish intellectual ambitions naturally centred on the University. Thus the Action Française was able to combine an attack on the University and its "official doctrine" in 1912, with an attack on Durkheim and his Jewish influence.[85] Jews, like Durkheim, in effect, in the eyes of antisemitic intellectuals, had attained the role of an intellectual élite, to which they themselves aspired. As Benda wrote later: "I considered those who had had a grand literary education, and above all those who had read the serious books, which the vulgar crowd never reads, to be a superior caste, into which I was entering . . ."[86] But more was involved here than simple rivalry or professional jealousy. Jewish intelligence, Jewish thought, was endowed with special and alarming qualities. The narrator in Lacretelle's novel, again, described the effect made on his mother by the intellectual Silbermann: "I saw my mother looking at him with fear, as though in this rare intellectual activity, she had detected a diabolical principle."[87] The Jewish banker de Horn in Lavedan's *Le Prince d'Aurec* saw Jewish wealth and general intelligence as having essentially the same threatening quality. The aristocratic d'Aurecs, he told the novelist Montade, were frightened equally by each: "They feel that things are running away with them, and they are afraid of us as people are afraid of tomorrow and of the unknown. We alarm them each to the same degree, myself because of the millions which I own, you because of your intellectual faculties."[88] And Drumont wrote that "Europe had been profoundly upset by . . . Jewish ideas."[89] Drumont, himself, anxious not to allow the Jews any kind of superiority, claimed that "the intelligence of the Semite . . . is basically limited . . . [the Jew] lacks true cultural refinement and intellectual superfluity . . . one very rarely encounters brilliant and chimerical theories in a Jew . . ."[90] But other antisemites revealed their objections to Jewish thought more openly. Barrès, for example, in *L'Ennemi des lois*, wrote that Jewish "reasoning was too clear, impersonal, like a bank account . . ."[91] Bainville wrote in 1905 that the Jewish "cast of mind was one of perpetual abstraction, because Talmudic education has desiccated their intelligence . . ."[92] It seems indeed that Jewish thought was alarming, upsetting, for antisemites because, with its tendency towards abstraction and generalization, its relativism, it often flatly opposed the particularism and the absolutism which they cultivated. The emancipated Jewish intellectual was able, was perhaps forced, to view the society to which he did not properly belong in a critical and objective spirit. "That distance . . . which we sometimes have vis-à-vis events, persons and things", Memmi has written, "can on occasions be a strength, can allow us an ironic stance, a liberty . . . The two men who have done most to unveil how society actually functions have both been Jews: Marx and Freud . . . And this is not pure chance: it was probably necessary to be a Jew in order to observe society in this way, both from the inside and from the outside."[93] And to the names of Marx and Freud, he could have added that of Durkheim. Nothing of course could have been further from and more threatening to the antisemite's closed and unquestioning social view than such a critical universalism. As Simone de Beauvoir has argued in a more general context, "thought" in this sense, "Jewish thought" in the language of the antisemites, also more specifically undermined the concept of privilege, élitism and hierarchy.[94] The simultaneous anti-intellectualism of the antisemitic writers and their defence of the intellectual's mandarin role are thus intimately related to their more general attachment to a society of rigid order.

But before we go on to discuss this general function of antisemitic ideology in more detail, something should be said briefly about the broad relationship between antisemitism and levels of education. Selznick and Steinberg have recently drawn attention to this dimension of antisemitism, pointing out that: "Emphasis in the past has been on the emotive or expressive aspects of anti-Semitism. Largely ignored has been the sheerly cognitive dimension."[95] Their findings for the United States highlight this dimension, indicating a strong correlation between the adoption or acceptance of antisemitic beliefs and low levels of education, which they explain by suggesting that the poorly educated have acquired no moral or intellectual reasons for rejecting such beliefs. They also contend that "the construction and promulgation of anti-Semitic ideology is typically the work of the half-educated—those who are able to give some semblance of intellectual articulation to an essentially primitive and unsophisticated belief system."[96] We have no quantitative material to compare with their findings for the rank-and-file antisemites, but our information about militants suggests divergences from their picture, which, it seems, they would expect, given the very different context. First, though some French antisemitic leaders might be called "half educated", by the standards of the day most of them were better educated than average, and some were very highly educated. It seems that in this period, when antisemitism was being elaborated as a coherent ideology, it was very much more a phenomenon of the educated and of intellectuals than it subsequently became. Another implication here is that norms of "scientific rationality" were much less well-established among educated Frenchmen in the 1890s than they were among educated Americans in the 1960s. The other crucial difference lies in the field of general social norms. As we shall see in more detail, in nineteenth-century France prejudice against Jews was not officially disapproved of to the degree that it was in the United States after the Second World War, and its incidence was thus less strongly related to exposure or lack of exposure to official norms. It does seem to be true, however, in France, that adoption of official Republican values acted as a disincentive to involvement in extreme or organized antisemitism, though this reflected less a difference in levels of education than in religious and political options or values. Positively, one can conclude that in the nineteenth-century context the cognitive dimension of antisemitism was crucially important, but that this did not imply any correlation with relative lack of education. One needs to remember here that universal primary education was still a novelty in the 1890s, and that only a very small proportion of the population went beyond this educational stage.[97] It is possible in such circumstances that the "new" antisemitism appealed to the educated, while the relatively uneducated and mainly rural population were still at the stage of an unsophisticated anti-Judaism, Catholic in tone. This section of the population is certainly absent, on the whole, from the documentation of organized and overt antisemitism. As far as antisemitism among the educated is concerned, one should be careful too to avoid anachronistic surprise or disbelief.[98] Though separated from us by less than a century, the mentality of educated people of the 1880s and 1890s was very different from ours, and the problem of understanding their antisemitism is in some ways akin to that of understanding the belief in witchcraft of the great intellects of the sixteenth, seventeenth and earlier centuries.[99]

II

In preceding chapters we have discussed the particular functions of antisemitic ideology, but these were all aspects of something more general, and that was a rejection of modern society, as antisemites conceived and experienced it. Simone de Beauvoir's characterization of the Right-winger generally, here applies to the antisemite: "Dejected or arrogant, he stands for refusal; his real certainties are all negative. He says no to the 'modern world', no to the future . . ."[100] But, within antisemitic ideology this refusal was expressed via a number of polarities. The rejected modern world was contrasted with an imagined "Old France"; modern change and mobility were measured against a static view of past society; modern disorder, diversity and relativism were set against order, hierarchy and absolute values. In this perspective, antisemitism itself can be seen as an indicator of social change, like Durkheim's suicide-rate. Where social relationships were being loosened, it provided a new sense of belonging. Where status was uncertain, it offered a new means of social identification. If old values and norms were under threat, it reasserted them. If people were caught up in processes which they did not understand, it offered both mythical explanation and a scapegoat. It was in this sense that Bernanos wrote that Drumont's work was less "a positive doctrine" than "the expression of a movement of anguish, of a tragic experience . . ."[101]

That antisemitism in France at the end of the nineteenth century was, in some way, a rejection of modern society was noted by critics and more friendly observers. We have seen that it was regarded by Zola and others as a reversion to a mediaeval fanaticism. Brunetière, in his review of *La France juive* in 1886, wrote that "M. Drumont [is] discontented with the century in which he lives."[102] More generally, Jacques Piou declared that antisemitism was the expression of "a profound disgust for the present".[103] And such comments simply reflected what the antisemites themselves stated quite explicitly. In *La France juive,* for example, Drumont unfavourably contrasted "modern existence" with "the way that we used to live in the past", and criticized what he called "modernism."[104] The rejection of modernity, of course, was most obviously expressed by identifying it with the Jews, a common feature incidentally of antisemitism elsewhere, and in France at a later date.[105] Leroy-Beaulieu pointed out that "the Jewish spirit" in antisemitic writing usually meant "the modern spirit";[106] and Péguy wrote that, according to the antisemites: "The modern world is an invention, an artificial and counterfeit construction; it has been invented, put together from top to bottom by the Jews . . . It is a régime which they made with their own hands, which they impose on us, and by means of which they dominate us . . ."[107] In confirmation of such an interpretation, Drumont denounced "Judeo-modern civilization" in *La France juive;*[108] and described the Paris *Exposition* of 1889 as "a really Jewish celebration . . . the last word in Modernism . . ."[109] And, slightly outside our period, but none the less significant because written by a man who had links with the thinking of the 1890s and 1900s through the Action Française, is a remark in the same vein made by Carentan in Drieu La Rochelle's Gilles: "I cannot stand the Jews, because they more than anyone else represent the modern world which I abhor."[110]

We have already come across many of the particular features of modern society which antisemites abhorred. Some we can therefore refer to briefly, while others deserve more extended treatment. First, the modern world was loosely "capitalist", dominated by money and money-making. Drumont wrote for example of the time of the July Monarchy: "At that time, the [modern] Jewish spirit, cruel and mercantile, had not yet destroyed France's moral fibre."[111] Again, the modern world was identified with the city, and the supposed evils of urban life.[112] Within the city, hostility was directed against new buildings, redevelopment and all manifestations of modern technology. It is significant that both Drumont and Fore-Fauré selected the Eiffel Tower as a symbol of modernity, "the monument and symbol of industrialized France . . . of its imbecility, bad taste and stupid arrogance", according to Drumont, and that Drumont was an early sentimental conservationist.[113] Léon Bloy expressed the view in 1901 that automobiles were "invented and propagated by demons in order that the poor should be run down, and for the damnation of souls"; and, a little later, he declared his "horror of this modern phenomenon . . . the underground railway".[114] This was just one aspect of an identification of modern society with new technology and with science. Drumont, in 1890, declared his dislike for electric lighting, which, even after the First World War, Boni de Castellane associated with "dissipation".[115] Here it is relevant that the Ligue Antisémitique Française organized demonstrations at Nantes in August 1898 against the Congress of the Association pour l'Avancement des Sciences.[116] Another manifestation of "modernism", which we have already encountered, was linguistic change and alleged debasement. Drumont referred disparagingly in *La France juive,* for example, to "this boulevard slang which the Jews have made fashionable . . ."[117] Similarly, attacks on modern art were couched in antisemitic terms. In *L'Intransigeant* in March 1903, Rochefort described those who bought Impressionist paintings at the sale of Zola's estate as "Jews and Jew-lovers".[118] Other issues involved in the antisemitic hostility to modern society become clear if one turns to the antisemites' contrasting picture of "Old France" and the values associated with it.

The image of "Old France" occurs again and again in the work of Drumont and of other antisemitic writers. In 1890, for example, Drumont declared that the Comte de Paris was or ought to be "the standard-bearer of old France"; and, reflecting on the general apathy of his contemporaries, he commented: "The old France of the land and of the peasantry, so strong, which, in the past, produced such unusual individual initiatives in times of crisis, now seems to be absolutely dormant." By contrast, he claimed that "the French Canadians have remained faithful to the customs and beliefs of old France; they have preserved the faith of their ancestors, and they are prospering."[119] In *Le Testament d'un antisémite*, the French clergy were said to be recruited from "old peasant France", and the Royalists of the 7th *arrondissement* of Paris were described as being "faithful to the tradition of old France"; while, more generally, Drumont explained his failure to recruit general and electoral support at this time in these terms: "My fundamental mistake was to have believed that there still existed an old France, a body of good people, nobles, bourgeois, small proprietors, faithful to the sentiments of honour and to the traditions of their race, and who, having been led astray . . . would regain consciousness of themselves if one showed them the situation as it really was, and would rally round to try to save their country . . ."[120] Again, in less political and less pessimistic vein, he evoked in 1892 "an old forgotten France brought back by a childhood melody".[121] Reiterating the same theme, Paul Bourget declared in 1894: "We must search for what remains of old France and attach ourselves to it by every fibre in our being . . ."[122] And, of course, "old France", the France of tradition and of the past, could be celebrated in other ways, without employing the specific slogan itself. In *La France juive*, for example, Drumont referred to "the great and noble France of our ancestors";[123] and, in the Preface to *La Dernière Bataille*, addressed to the Marquis de Morès, he claimed some kind of special fellowship with the marquis via their common involvement in that historical France: "As descendants of the Crusaders, we belong to the same family . . ." Developing this idea further, elsewhere in the same work, he evoked "the great memories of the Past", and he contrasted the Hôtel des Invalides with the buildings put up on the Place des Invalides for the 1889 *Exposition:* "This great palace for old soldiers has many fine stories to tell after all, true stories of courage, such as little children like to hear in the evenings by the fire-side. The True France is there. The False France is here: in the ramshackle constructions on the Place des Invalides."[124] Similarly, a fair held in the Tuileries gardens was regarded by Drumont as an insult to historical France: "It was an outrage against the glories of France which had so often had this place for their setting . . . it showed a lack of respect for the illustrious dead . . ."[125] The well-known cult of Barrès for "the land and the dead" was another, more elaborate, version of the same attachment to a traditional France of the past.[126] The writers of the Action Française, too, expressed the same option via a complex historiographical mythology, which celebrated the virtues of the Ancien Régime and the Monarchy. Though it was mainly a phenomenon of the inter-war period, the ideological bases of this enterprise were laid in the decade after 1900 by Maurras and others.[127]

For antisemites, "Old France" was set in explicit opposition to the Jews. "If the France of M. Grévy, as everyone moreover agrees, hardly resembles that of Louis XIV and still less that of St Louis, the fault, or rather the crime, lies with the Jews. . .", commented Brunetière in his review of *La France juive* in the *Revue des Deux Mondes.* [128] And, indeed, Drumont repeatedly asserted

in his book that the Jews "hated all that was fine and glorious in our past
. . . old French society . . . the France of St Louis, of Henry IV, of Napoleon,
of Condé, of Bossuet and of Fénelon . . ."[129] Thus Drumont noted, for
example, that in a Jewish-owned restaurant the waitresses were dressed in the
costume of the queens of France, and observed: "We find here the overriding
need of the Jew to besmirch, to render vile or ridiculous all that was great in
the past . . ."[130] Concomitantly, "Old France" had preserved itself from the
Jews by means of strict legal controls, or by expelling them: "If ancient France
was happy and glorious for many centuries, it was because it carefully guarded
itself against the Jew."[131] Moreover, "Old France", the Ancien Régime, had
been ultimately destroyed by the Jews. In *La France juive*, Drumont wrote,
he had sought to show "how, little by little, through the action of the Jews,
old France was dissolved, decomposed, how a disinterested, happy, loving
people was replaced by a people full of hatred, hungry for gold and soon dying
of real hunger . . . how this France, the land of the royal lilies, the kingdom
of the azure blue, let itself become Jewish, let itself be rigged out in the yellow
garb of the Jews."[132] Again, using a different metaphor to make the same
point, Drumont wrote in 1894 of the Hôtel de l'Infantado, which stood near
the place where Marie-Antoinette had been guillotined: "It is yet another
symbol, this palace, so close to the fateful spot where the most generous, the
purest blood of old France flowed in torrents. It signifies that the Jew is king
. . ."[133] And, as we have seen, Drumont returned repeatedly to the disturbing
idea that the historical residences of France's kings, queens and great nobles
were, in his day, owned and occupied by rich Jews.[134] An extension of this
idea was the observation that the great vineyards of France were now in the
hands of the Jews, and, more particularly, of the Rothschilds: "Romanée
belongs to Alphonse; Château-Lafite to Gustave; Mouton was owned by James
. . . Our wine, in which the national spirit was steeped in the past, is the
property of the Jews like everything else."[135]

Sartre has suggested that antisemitic attachment to historical France can
be interpreted as a claim of "ownership" over it, and thereby to a status that
is impregnable because it is inherited and not achieved. In this perspective,
the antisemite is always superior to the Jew, who may own everything in the
legal and currently conventional sense, but to whom French history does not
belong, and who indeed has no real history of his own either.[136] One must
quarrel with Sartre's apparent endorsement of the last idea, a relic, it seems,
of the Hegelian philosophy of History,[137] but his main thesis fits our argument
and can be directly illustrated from *La France juive*. "In what corner of a
village or a town are their family tombs then?", Drumont asked of the Jews
of France. "In what old parish register can you find the name of these
newcomers, who, less than a century ago, did not even have the right to live
on the land from which they now wish to drive us? What links have they with
the traditions of our race?";[138] and again: "Ask yourself why a Reynal, a
Bischoffsheim, a Leven should be attached to the France of the Crusades, of
Bouvines, of Marignan, of Fontenoy, of St Louis, of Henry IV and of Louis
XIV. By its traditions, by its beliefs, by its memories, this France is the

absolute negation of the entire Jewish temperament. When it did not burn the Jew, this France obstinately closed its doors to him, covered him with scorn, and made his name the cruellest of insults." By contrast, even the most destitute Frenchman "owned" and belonged to France, because his ancestors had lived there. Drumont thus protested vigorously, as we have seen, against a proposed law on recidivists that would have led to the banishment from France "of men whose forefathers had lived on the land of France for centuries".[139] Attachment to "Old France" thus marked the dispossession of natives by the Jews,[140] proclaimed also in the slogan: "France for the French", but, at the same time, provided a compensating security, positing a criterion by which French people could never "really" lose their rightful inheritance.

In addition to providing this security, a point to which we will return, attachment to "Old France" implied attachment to certain traditional, or neo-traditional, values, which modern society had abandoned or held in scorn. "There is a world of difference between the France of the past and the France of today, degraded by opportunism, dead to all great thought, rotten to the core, preoccupied with dirty dealing, pornography and scandals", Drumont declared in La France juive.[141] "The man of the Past . . . had noble reasons for living", he wrote again later; "the man of today has only a few pretexts for not killing himself";[142] and: "French society of the past, being Christian, had as its motto: work, sacrifice, devotion to duty. Present-day society, being Jewish, has as its motto: living off others, idleness and egotism."[143]

This and earlier quotations give an indication of what these "old" values were. At the most abstract level, perhaps, was the cult of heroism and of honour. In La France juive, Drumont castigated his own epoch as one in which "all heroism has disappeared"; or not quite all, for he was able to write of the Lang-Son débâcle: "In the midst of all these shameful events all that stands out is the glorious and pure figure of Admiral Courbet . . . that heroic sailor . . . that Stoic, the slave of duty, who sacrificed his life in obedience to the orders of men for whom he had the profoundest scorn, and who seems the incarnation of military France . . ."[144] As we have seen, of course, the military was, with the Church, the last upholder of the old order and its values. Elsewhere, Drumont wrote of the men of the Middle Ages that they were "less soft, less flabby than the men of today";[145] and he celebrated the Chouans in these terms: "It had a truly wild grandeur, this Chouan movement; what an epic gesture it was, these Breton peasants and landed gentry defending . . . their faith as Christians and their Royalist convictions."[146] In the same year, 1894, he evoked also the heroism and grandeur of the Napoleonic epic, with particular reference to Waterloo: "Who spares a thought today for the heroic deeds of the men who fell on this piece of earth? What remains of the ideas for which they died? Rothschild, whose grandfather entered Paris behind Blücher's horse, is our king and master."[147] The cult of heroism was again related here to the cult of the army, and it can be seen more generally as a reaction to the routine and prosaic nature of modern urban life. It had another dimension, too, which Péguy brought out in an article in L'Essor in February 1898. Demagogic antisemitism succeeded, he wrote, because it directed popular resentments against a strictly defined minority, but its appeal also lay in the fact that it presented its attack on this minority as a courageous protest against an all-powerful élite:[148]

> the common man is naturally cowardly like everyone else; since he is also naturally stupid, he is only too pleased to attack minorities that are clearly designated; but his happiness is without bounds if, in addition, one can make it appear that in thus attacking a minority, he is nobly sacrificing himself for some great cause, that he is acting for the salvation of humanity; falling upon those who are weaker is a source of mixed pleasure only; but falling upon those who are weaker, and representing such an action to oneself as a great sacrifice, such a combination gives pure satisfaction.

The tone of several entries to the Henry Subscription[149] and of much antisemitic writing confirms the truth of this observation. Drumont claimed, for example, in the Preface to *Le Testament d'un antisémite,* that in attacking the Jews he "had faithfully accomplished his duty as a Frenchman . . ."[150]

As this indicates, heroism implied an attachment to a concept of honour, and to the related virtues of fidelity and honesty, all of which the antisemites held in high esteem. The first Ligue Antisémitique claimed to stand, among other things, for "the Honour . . . of France".[151] Drumont appealed for the support of "men of honour and faith";[152] and wrote in 1886 that the crash of the Union Générale "has just taken away from the French nobility what, in the past, was more precious to it than money, more precious than life itself: honour."[153] He also celebrated the memory of "my good parents . . . [who were] so honest",[154] and, more generally, "the honest folk of the old days . . ."[155] Again, combining the concepts of honour and honesty, he wrote of himself as a young man: "even when he was very poor, he lived very honorably; he paid his grocer and his coal merchant regularly, and the district where he lived was an old *quartier* of Paris whose inhabitants were for the most part honest folk . . .";[156] and, relating the concept of honour to the cult of the army, he claimed that most army officers shared his own disgust at the corruption and devaluation of the Légion d'Honneur.[157] In the same vein, abbé Garnier told a Union Nationale meeting at Courbevoie in June 1898: "All the efforts of honest folk must be directed against the Jews and the Freemasons . . ."; and the campaign against the Dreyfusards frequently invoked the claim that they were "dishonouring France."[158]

Like heroism, honour and honesty had become rare virtues in modern society: "The French character has been absolutely transformed and turned inside out in the last twenty years. A century ago, an artisan belonging to one of our ancient guilds, a farm worker, man or woman, from the Vendée, had, as far as honour, probity, and modesty are concerned, a refinement, a sensitivity, that most society people today lack entirely."[159] This change reflected the predominance of "Jewish" values in modern society, since, according to the antisemites, the Jews had no concept of honour and were systematically dishonest. "The Jew has never been able to attain that sense of honour . . . that native pride, which are characteristic of superior races", declared

Drumont in 1891. The Jewish view of society was thus one in which "every notion of modesty and honour has disappeared"; according to "Semitic ideas, Money is everything [and], in Semitic eyes, probity and honour are meaningless expressions."[160] It was thus characteristic that in his duel with Drumont, Arthur Meyer should have broken the rules, thereby offending against "the honour of the sword", sacred to all true Frenchmen.[161] Moreover, in commercial matters all Jews acted on "the theory of Rothschild that a promise given to a non-Jew never bound a Jew". This meant that "Jews had an enormous advantage: the honesty of their rivals, which prevented them from taking reprisals."[162] This reveals a significant inconsistency in antisemitic thinking. Honour and probity were said to have been generally abandoned, yet Jewish dishonesty and lack of honour were still contrasted with the honesty and sense of honour of non-Jews, or at least of antisemites. Reflected here, it seems, is a certain guilt over the abandonment of the old virtues, which is projected on to the Jews. Evoking the familiar polarity of Money and Honour, Brunetière commented: "if we very much prefer money to honour ... it is the Jews whom we blame ..."[163] And to confirm this interpretation, de Massue, cited above, who claimed that the Dreyfusards were "dishonouring" France, immediately added that their campaign "was also doing considerable damage to the commercial interests of the country".[164] The commercial interests, which antisemitism undoubtedly reflected, seem here to be engaged, via their intellectual spokesmen, in some kind of ideological vanishing trick, exaggerating their own "honesty" in the face of "unfair" and "dishonest" Jewish competition, almost to the extent of denying that they were involved in making money at all, but always with an underlying commercial aim in view. Thus Drumont lamented that "the entry into it of Jews has dishonoured French commerce, which used to enjoy such renown throughout the world."[165] Here, in the same way that it made bullying heroic, antisemitism gave the pursuit of commercial interest the most flattering self-image, placing it not under the aegis of Money at all, but under that of Honour; but, at the same time, it was made clear that honour very often meant commercial honesty and attachment to older commercial methods. One can see in this instance, as will be seen more generally later, how antisemitism was a neo-traditionalism, invoking and using "traditional" values in a thoroughly modern setting.

Another element in the attachment to honour and honesty was the designation of what might, at a later date, have been called the "silent majority" under these headings. Drumont referred in 1890 to "that grey mass of honest folk who represent what is best in France"; and asked: "What do they think, all those men of honour and faith scattered all over France and of whom no one speaks?"[166] Here again "anti-modern", "traditional" epithets are strangely bestowed upon the "grey mass", a thoroughly modern phenomenon or concept. Note should also be taken of the association of "honour" and "honesty" with "modesty" ("*pudeur*"), a word with clear sexual connotations. This links them with the themes discussed in the last chapter, but also with other "traditional" values to be considered below, and notably with the cult of the family. Abbé Garnier in the speech already quoted in which he opposed Jews and Freemasons to "honest folk", explained that the former "wished to do away with the nation, the family and property".[167]

A paradox similar to that involved in the concept of honour is present in the adoption by mainly urban antisemites of "rural" values, a phenomenon to which we have referred in an earlier chapter.[168] Drumont, for example, characteristically told his readers in December 1892 that, while in prison at this Christmas season, he dreamed of "beautiful meadows and the verdant countryside, of the old peasant dances and the adorable rustic refrains of the Morvan and of Berry . . ."[169] More generally, La Croix subscribed to the same conservative, "rustic" mythology, contrasting the "good" Christian country-side with the "wicked" God-less and Jewish city.[170] One can see here how the reassertion of rural, traditional values, to some degree still authentically pres-ent, was much more a reaction to the fact that urban, modern "capitalist" values were in the ascendant. Antisemitism was a movement in which genuine traditionalism was overshadowed by a neo-traditionalism, in which first-hand resistance to the impact of modernization had given way, though perhaps not entirely, to a second stage of nostalgic refusal within the urban context. By its tone, by its means of propaganda, it sought to maintain or to recreate traditional values artificially, and represented in effect a real movement of modernization itself on the cultural level. This is evident, as Sartre has empha-sized, in the antisemites' attachment to a certain "rural" concept of property. According to this conception, property was inherited and not bought, and was conceived of in social or moral rather than economic terms:[171]

> There is an incomprehension of the various forms of modern property: money, shares, etc.; these are abstractions, creations of a reason which is closely akin to the abstract intelligence of the Semite . . . The antisemite only understands a primitive and land-oriented type of appropriation, based on possession of a magical kind and in which the object possessed and its possessor are united by the bond of a mystical participation: he is the poet of landed property.

Such a concept has much in common with traditional peasant attitudes to-wards the land,[172] but what is significant, as Sartre points out, is that it was adopted by those who were not peasants or landowners: "It takes root ordinar-ily among the middle classes, precisely because they do not possess land, or country seats, or even a house, but only liquid cash and a few stocks and shares in the bank."[173]

A range of other themes are involved in this neo-traditionalism, and have similar implications. First, as the reference to La Croix makes clear, "rural" France, "Old France" was completely Christian, and, therefore, "those who have participated in the war waged against the beliefs of the majority of French people . . . have destroyed old France . . ."[174] Enemies of the Church and the Faith, the Jews were necessarily enemies of the France of tradition and history, and vice versa. And, symmetrically, the upholders of the old, heroic values were necessarily Christian. The Chouans were defending "their faith as Christians", and Admiral Courbet was both "the heroic sailor" and "this great Christian".[175] This reflects a very general tendency among modern French Catholics to assume that pre-Revolutionary France had been wholly Christian, and that subsequent dechristianization had been an urban phenomenon. Such assumptions were half-truths at best,[176] but, more important, they embodied a myth that was both comforting and despairing: the dream of a total Christian society had once been realized, but modern society was fundamentally antagonistic to religion. Drumont, moreover, spelled out the social meaning of these conceptions. The Ancien Régime had been a society in which charity had been universally practised: "For the Christians of the old days, the pauper was Jesus Christ in person . . .";[177] and it had been a society, therefore, in which social conflict and resentments were absent or muted: "Hatred and envy, which are everywhere today, were then rare in the noble country of France. Christianity had created among us such a wealth of faith, of devotion to duty, of abnegation . . . The people of that time, who had not yet been perverted, knew that it was Christianity which had changed the world, bringing to it fraternity and love."[178] This assumes that social relationships were firmly hierarchical, a point to which we will return, but, as this implies also, they operated within a framework that was both traditional and moral.

> The clearest result of the Revolution (which effectively brought "Old France" to an end), [Drumont wrote in 1891][179] was to make the situation of small people more difficult, and, in contrast, to strengthen the situation of the rich and powerful by freeing it of all moral responsibility . . . the old régime allowed everyone to resist injustice, assured everyone of rights which permitted them to defend themselves against arbitrary power. The modern régime . . . endeavours by every means to make it impossible for the humble to hold their own against the powerful.

And the last point was made with more emphasis elsewhere: "In old France, everything that wounded the sentiment of justice innate in the souls of our ancestors, everything which went against the interests of the natives, everything which simply threatened custom and tradition was the pretext for noisy demonstrations, for indignant protests, for songs and *charivaris* . . ."[180] Here was a historical precedent[181] for antisemitic populism, but, more important, a model that assimilated popular protest and social hierarchy under the aegis of Christian justice and traditional values. Paradoxically also, within such a framework local diversity could be celebrated, and from such a stance modern social uniformity could be condemned. We have seen that the antisemites attacked the modern State in the name of a certain regionalism. Bourget, for example, urged his readers to seek "the natural and hereditary unity of the province beneath the artificial divisions of the departments,"[182] thus appealing both to tradition and to that essentialism which also informed racial antisemitism.[183] And, in another context, Drumont regretted that "the police . . . had caused to disappear all those innocent eccentrics, all those freaks, all those strolling musicians who gave Paris such colour and variety",[184] an illustration also of another deviation of neo-traditionalism, this time not into essentialism, but into a purely nostalgic cultivation of the picturesque.

The concept of an "Old France" imbued with Christian values had a socio-economic dimension too. Drumont declared in the Preface to *La France juive:* "If the old society was able to live happily and in tranquillity without experiencing social wars, insurrections and strikes, it was because it was based on the principle: 'No profits without work.' The nobles had to fight for those who worked; every member of a guild had to work himself and he was forbidden to exploit other human beings just because he had some capital . . ." The concept of a hierarchy of reciprocity, to which we will return, was thus linked to a criticism of work in capitalist society and to a celebration of traditional work. The two were frequently contrasted in Drumont's writings. Thus, he described the worker of the Ancien Régime in these terms in *La France juive:*

> Worker in the fields or in the towns, he was content in a land where there were only Frenchmen like himself. If he was a peasant, he danced in the evening to the sound of the pipes, or sang the old songs passed down from his forebears . . . If he was an artisan, he had his fraternal associations . . . He loved his work which he had the leisure to do well and which he enhanced with that attractive craftsmanship which enchants us in the least relic from the past.

By contrast, the modern worker, "this pariah of our great industrial cities, weighed down by a labour which consumes him, worn out before his time to enrich his masters, brutalized by drink . . . is no better than was the slave of antiquity . . ." And a little later in the same work, Drumont asserted:[185]

> The poor fireman, who stands night and day on his locomotive, exposed to heat and cold . . . and who contracts one of those terrible diseases that science is powerless to cure, is far worse off, both physically and morally, than the good villager, living peacefully in some corner of old France, who never worked beyond his strength and who died calmly in the hope of enjoying eternal beatitude.

A number of comments may be made about this familiar contrast with a view to elucidating its meaning for antisemites.

First, the modern differentiation of work and leisure was highlighted, pointing to a trend that was real enough and a departure from the pre-industrial, pre-capitalist situation.[186] Related to this, the esthetic quality of the products of traditional work was characteristically singled out for praise by Drumont, a bourgeois intellectual. Here it perhaps worth recalling that Drumont was a contemporary of William Morris, and like him, an unorthodox "socialist".[187] Then, one of the functions of the religious setting of traditional work is made explicit. The artisans and peasants of the Ancien Régime lived and worked in the hope of a bliss in the afterlife, and, although, in the rosy picture given of their existence, this has little obvious significance, were the painting to be darker and more realistic, it would serve, as it does in other situations, as a sacred compensation for terrestrial misery, exploitation and injustice.[188] This is a reminder of the general function of religious and other-worldly perspectives in conservative ideology. Another underlying difference between modern and traditional work, stressed elsewhere by Drumont, was that in the latter employer and worker were personally related. Whereas "the partners of firms today, the owners of shares in factories or manufactures, live royally off the labour of workers whom they have sometimes never seen . . . the industrialists of the old days saw their workers and were seen by them, and could claim that they also worked."[189] This observation represents more than a simple option for personal rather than impersonal relations and a critique like that of Marx of the cash nexus; with his typical and repeated rejection of Speculation in favour of Work, with his insistence on the value of work and on the fact that members of the bourgeosie are workers, Drumont seems both to be urging on working people an imperative to work beyond considerations of remuneration, thus countering the opposite tendency of trade-unionism to correlate work with wages and to withhold labour unless it was adequately paid for, and to be insisting that, though a section of the Bourgeoisie was idle, living off the work of others and from financial manipulation, another section was contributing its full share of useful work to the community. Thus, in *La France juive*, he celebrated "the true France, honest, patriotic and hard-working";[190] and he wrote later of this book: "It was in an atmosphere of work, of virtue, of a life that was worthy and simple, that there germinated, almost without my wishing it, this work which expresses such a frank hatred of thieves and exploiters."[191] And, in *La Fin d'un monde*, he drew a sharp contrast between "the gilded Bourgeoisie which has entered into the Jewish system . . . which has become speculating in its turn" and "the other part of the Bourgeoisie, the worthiest and the most French, that which works for its living . . ." The general identification of the idle, speculating Bourgeoisie with the Jews makes the diversionary function of the argument very clear. However, the assertion of the value of work, in its traditional form, implied no divergence from social hierarchy, no assimilation of employer and employed. Quite the opposite, for Drumont lamented in the passage just cited that the working Bourgeoisie "is in process of being proletarianized".[192] This point was clearly perceived by Mirbeau, an opponent of organized antisemitism, in his *Journal d'une femme de chambre*. Joseph, the antisemite, is a model servant: "He was the typical old-style servant, the pre-Revolutionary retainer"; and he tells Celestine: "We must love our masters . . . the masters are the masters . . ."[193] In antisemitic ideology, in effect, close personal relations between employer and employed in an ambience of Christian love and charity were a means of legitimizing and thus upholding and preserving socio-economic inequality.

A final component of the neo-traditionalism of the antisemites, intimately related to previous themes, was a particular attitude towards the family. Like other conservatives,[194] they believed that in modern society the family was in decline or under some kind of threat. "The idea of the family . . . no longer means what it used to mean in the past", Drumont wrote in 1891. "Modern French people do not have towards their parents those sentiments of respect that were innate in earlier generations"; and he also expressed a general concern that French couples were having fewer children.[195] The Union Nationale was a champion of the Family, a pillar of the social order that, it was felt, required defence. The alleged threat to or decline of the family, moreover, was associated with or attributed to the Jews. The narrator's mother in Lacretelle's *Silbermann* contrasted his friendship with a Jew with his being "sensitive to the tradition of our family . . ."[196] *Le Complôt juif*, in more extreme fashion, asserted of the Jews that "they are changing existing notions of honour and virtue. They are destroying the family",[197] a claim very similar to one made by abbé Garnier and cited above. Expressive of the same syndrome was Drumont's accusation that Naquet had declared "that religion was at an end, that property was a crime and that the family must be suppressed . . ."[198] One apprehension behind such ideas was fear of the possible emancipation of women, to which we alluded in the previous chapter. Divorce, secondary education for girls, diversification of women's employment all seemed to threaten the family and its role in the traditional structure of society. The Comité Antisémite of Rennes, for example, heard a speech in July 1899 on "The Emancipation of Women, the danger of women going out to work, first as far as the home is concerned from which they are absent, and then as it tends to discourage the growth of the population."[199] It is interesting here to note that Morin saw the Orléans Rumour in the 1960s as a reaction to modernization and, more precisely, as "a myth of female emancipation."[200] An important element in the Rumour, anxiety about new fashions in female clothing (and especially the mini-skirt), also found expression in France at the turn of the century, though it was not directly related to antisemitism.[201]

Two conflicting concepts of the family seem to have been ambiguously thrown together in antisemitic thinking. First, there was the family as a *"ménage"*, a home centred on mother and children, which Coppée, for example, celebrated in an autobiographical piece quoted by Drumont. His mother, the widow of a "modest clerk" nevertheless brought up four children decently: "Thanks to the vigilant care and to the spirit of order and economy of the good mother, the three little girls always had dresses that were clean and smart and the little man was always cleanly dressed too . . . if the meals were sparse, the table with its white cloth was always neat and there were flowers on it to brighten it up and to make a nice scent."[202] Alongside this modern ideal[203] there was the concept of the family as a line, guardian of its honour and of a patrimony, passing on property, but also status, occupation and obligations from generation to generation. "Little concerned to found a family in the sense that the word had in the old days", wrote Drumont in 1891, showing some sense of the distinction, "the French of today have no notion either of the patrimony, which, born of work, takes on its sacred character . . . which is added to by honest means and which one passes on to one's descendants."[204] In a broader sense, the notion of inheritance, cultural, social, familial, was of capital importance in the work of Maurras.[205] Moreover, Drumont was in favour of professions and occupations following the same hereditary pattern of succession as property rights, pointing, for example, to the model provided by old military families.[206] He seems also to have attached the guilt for crimes and misdeeds to families rather than to individuals, or rather to have believed that the misdeeds of the individual involved other members of his family. In his attack on Mgr Place, for example, he made much of the allegation that his brother was a traitor;[207] and he asked, more generally, in *La France juive:*[208]

> Can the son of a convict be a saint?; [and provided this answer]: Yes, says the Church. But the sociologist, while accepting this affirmation, is obliged to recognize that, in order to remain on the path of virtue, such a man must make far greater efforts than others. If he has received some education, the man born in such a condition will avoid everything that is actually against the law . . . but basically he will remain the son of a convict.

This follows the general pattern of antisemitism which associated all Jews in the behaviour of any one of them, and which made each Jew responsible for the real or supposed anti-social actions of any other. The idea that modern Jews were still collectively responsible for the Crucifixion was here a paradigm.[209] But the notion of inherited and familial guilt was also related to that of ritual pollution, which was again directly involved in antisemitism,[210] and, on another level, reflected the ancient customary and legal assumption that the actions of an individual involved all his kin,[211] an assumption that was not completely extinct in nineteenth-century France in the sphere of social reality as opposed to that of ideology. This is illustrated by Balzac's story of the Tascheron family from the Limousin in *Le Curé de village* (1837–45).[212]

> As the law now stands, the father is no longer responsible for his son's crime and the father's guilt does not attach to his children, a condition of things in keeping with other emancipations which have weakened the paternal power, and contributed to the triumph of that individualism which is eating the heart of society in our days . . . [However] the old order still exists . . . in remote districts . . . where all the members of a family suffer for the crime of one, and the children for the sins of their fathers.

Half a century on the meaning of such a view had changed, if only because the social reality behind it had been largely effaced. The antisemitic concept of the family had become ambiguous, combining old and new, and its "traditional" element functioned in a mainly negative way, to express vague fears of tentative moves towards a new role in society for women, of demographic stagnation, and, of new relationships between parents and children brought about by social and economic change, by greater professional mobility and by greater state intervention, especially in the realm of education. A Union Nationale pamphlet of 1904 roundly condemned "those false egalitarian ideas that have such an unfortunate effect on the relations" not only "between workers and employers [*patrons*]" but also "between children and parents . . ."[213] The parallel drawn here and the connotations of the term *"patron"* point to another dimension of the ideological use of the family theme: the family was a model for the paternalistic organization of society at large. As far as relations between parents and children are concerned, one should remember that antisemitism had a special appeal for young people, perhaps expressing generational conflict from the other side, only one example incidentally, as we shall see, of the multi-purpose function of antisemitism. Positively, concern for the family patrimony can probably be related to concern to stem rural depopulation. Drumont claimed that "cosmopolitan Jewry" was the enemy of "the Patrimony, that is to say of all legitimate and durable property".[214] This was not only an assertion of the "archaic" conception of property that we have already encountered, but can also be linked, more particularly, to the conviction of antisemites and others that peasant families should be given encouragement to stay on the land by making the family property inalienable and fiscally immune.[215]

The contrast between the modern and the traditional in antisemitic ideology was linked to a number of other polarities, all of which implicitly or explicitly expressed anxiety about and rejection of social change. The dynamism of modern society was unfavourably contrasted with the static nature of traditional society; disorder and diversity with order and hierarchy; relative with absolute values; and, in each case, the first element in each pair was identified with the Jews. "The latest transformations of French society have been accomplished in effect with a frightening rapidity", wrote Drumont in 1890. "What would in the past have taken a century is today a matter of a few years. There was already an abyss between the state of mind, the ideas, the moral conceptions of the men of 1871 and the point of view of the men of 1848; the men of 1889 seem to belong to a different epoch from that of the men of 1871"; or again, emphasizing social and economic rather than cultural change, stressing less the rapidity than the totality of change, and pointing to Jewish responsibility: "One fact sums up this period of a hundred years [since 1789]: the triumph of the Jew, the absolute transformation of all the conditions of economic and social life under the influence of the Jew ..."[216] A further passage, from *La France juive,* spelled out the nature of this change in more detail and in terms that must by now be familiar:[217]

> People lost the taste for work; they looked for affairs which brought in big profits without much effort. The number of shops and taverns rose incredibly, even in the countryside. The peasants became impoverished and were forced to sell up; the artisans left their guilds, and deprived of this salutary protection, fell into want and misery. Too many people threw themselves all at once into speculative affairs, with the result that most were ruined and joined the ranks of an angry proletariat. Wealth increased rapidly for some, but the mass of the people became poorer.

Such change, such rapid change, moreover, could only end in disaster: "How can you expect a country to carry on living the good old life of the past ... with rogues of the stamp of Mayer about, always busy with some new deal? If nothing is done about them, within twenty years they will have blown up Paris, France and Europe."[218]

Geographical and social mobility were particularly deplored by antisemites. Writing of the 1889 *Exposition,* for example, Drumont combined the themes of uprooting and rural exodus, of "rustic" traditionalism, and of Jewish takeover:

Here, in his turn, there arrives on the excursion trains the peasant, whose stability has for so long exasperated the Jew, the peasant who seemed to be fixed for ever on the fields which his forebears had cultivated . . . When he returns home, he will take with him the disturbing impression of all these accumulated marvels; he will come back fully corrupted with the infection which they exhale, his eyes glinting with a new and unprecedented covetousness; from then on he will find mean and boring the village that used to be so dear to him . . . the land will lose him and he will become a victim for the Jew . . . he will have begun by being the dupe of the Jewish financier, he will end up by becoming the tool of the Jewish industrialist, and he will toil to make millions for factory-owners whom he will never see.

And, again, more generally, Drumont expressed the view that[219]

A human being . . . is made up of traditions which attach him to those who have lived before him, of sentiments which unite him with those who come from the same place as he does. Once he is stripped of all that, once he has placed himself outside his religion, outside his race, outside his country, he no longer has any support, any roots, any place of his own within the social organization; he is an outsider, a foreigner everywhere . . .

Not yet a sociological commonplace, this was, of course, the theme of Barrès's novel Les Déracinés; and, as we have seen, the rootless, migrant wanderer par excellence in antisemitic and Nationalist writing was the Jew.

The Jew also exemplified rapid social mobility. Drumont wrote of "German Jews . . . who entered the country in rags and who now display an insolent luxury",[220] and of "these big Yids in the capital cities whose fathers wallowed in the squalor of the ghettos and who are now the masters of the world . . ."[221] Similarly, he was offended by the idea that Camondo who, he alleged was once a second-hand clothes dealer in the slums of Istanbul, should have acquired "a palace on the Bosphorus, and a bank that is larger than a palace";[222] and that Arthur Meyer, supposedly the son of a rag-merchant, should have become the editor of a "society" newspaper.[223] He claimed here that there was an important contrast between the modes of social ascension among Aryans and among Semites. Among the former, "over many generations, the vital spirit, genius, are economized; then the tree whose roots plunged deep into the soil lifts to the top a man of distinction who sums up the qualities of his people. It sometimes takes a century for such a predestined being to develop"; and, on the more mundane level, a French family would take at least three generations to move up from the lower bourgeoisie into the aristocracy. But[224]

in the Semitic race things happen differently. In the East, a camel-driver, a water-carrier, a barber, is singled out by the sovereign. And at once he becomes a pasha, a vizier, the prince's confidant . . . It is the same with the Jew . . . he is born in the depths of a judengasse, he makes a bit of money in a first operation, he launches himself in Paris, he gets himself decorated through the offices of some Dreyfus or other; then he buys the title of baron, boldly seeks membership of one of the big clubs, and takes on the airs of someone who has always been rich. With him, the transformation is just about instantaneous . . .

What the Jew symbolizes here is not perhaps so much the spectacular individual ascension that is manifestly attacked, for Drumont seems prepared to accept this in the Aryan context so long as it remains rare, and elsewhere he commented favourably on the fact that a servant-girl from the block of flats where he was born had subsequently become a great lady,[225] though, of course, the social ascension of women is of less significance than that of men, in these circumstances. What is symbolized rather is a more general movement of social mobility that threatened the whole static social structure, which individual ascension in fact tended to legitimize, and a movement also that had democratic political connotations.

It is characteristic here that Drumont, despite his populism, expressed his thorough hostility towards the rise of the "new social strata" hailed by Gambetta in his famous Grenoble speech of 1872,[226] and identified them with the Jews.

> Following the events of 1870, [he wrote in *La France juive* [227]] a host of adventurers descended on France. A new world was born, or rather sprouted like a poisonous fungus on ground that had been profoundly shaken. Gambetta was quick to notice this filth that was erupting and the successive strata that rose from it; he realized that something could be done with it and pronounced at Grenoble, in 1872, his notorious harangue on the "new strata", which is the only speech of his which contains a real idea, the only one which corresponds to a real situation . . . The new stratum was made up of a lot of Jews with a number of supporting Freemasons . . ., of unscrupulous shopkeepers, Bohemians, and café-politicians, of doctors without patients, and of the débris of 1848 . . . It was, with the Semitic element thrown in, the eternal mob, shameless and consumed by greed . . .

Hostility to social mobility, and particularly to rapid social promotion, was apparent among other antisemites. Bourget wrote, for example, explaining the theme of his novel *L'Etape* (1902): "One does not change one's milieu and one's class without profound disorders becoming manifest in one's being . . ." "For this reason", added Léon de Montesquiou, who quoted Bourget in *Les Raisons du nationalisme*, "such a change should be made with great care, if it is not to be a source of the greatest misery for the person who experiences it."[228] Similarly, La Tour du Pin declared that[229]

> the popular classes were the natural reservoir for the upper classes, and both need to interpenetrate in order to exist. But this interpenetration must take the form of infiltration and not of frontal assault; in other words, it is better that social ascension, whether within one class or from one class to another, should have a familial and a gradual character, rather than being purely individual and sudden . . .

Anxiety about social ascension, moreover, was matched by worry about social derogation, as the quotations by Drumont referring to the actual or imminent proletarianization of artisans and petty bourgeois indicate. By reference to a fixed conception of the social hierarchy, indeed, the upward mobility of some could only mean the downward movement of others. Related to this was what has been called an "usurpation complex",[230] the feeling that Jews, in particular, had usurped places in the political and social structure that rightfully belonged to others. According to Drumont, "when he restructured the organization of Algeria so profoundly [i.e. by giving the Jewish community full civil and political rights], Crémieux committed . . . an usurpation within an usurpation", the Government of National Defence being already illegitimate.[231]

Geographical and social mobility were signs among others for the antisemites of social disorganization, of disorder, of "the disorganized condition of society", as Drumont wrote, quoting Carlyle.[232] France was "a country . . . for a long time deprived of that calm which is the basis for stable institutions and for principles that everyone accepts";[233] it was "a world that was upset, out of control and plunging to the abyss, like the old Roman Empire"; "every thinker, who has sought to analyse the phases through which this society that is fast decomposing has passed, has had this impression of chaos and of universal disorder . . . [of] the profound anarchy of this society in which no serious organization is still functioning and in which there appears to be no social authority." The Socialists were "witnesses to the frightening disorder that reigns everywhere today", and Drumont extended his sympathy to them because they wanted "to reorganize society on new bases . . ."[234] Making the same point with explicit symbolic reference to confusion of the social hierarchy, Drumont described French society again as "this unforgettable, unbelievable and fabulous procession, in which there march, arm in arm, pell-mell, duchesses and high-class tarts, dukes and pimps, members of the big clubs and guttersnipes, old parliamentarians and bully boys, with street-hawkers of every kind, déclassés of every colour, crooks of every kind, charlatans and wide boys of every category . . ."[235] And with the disorientation deriving from the mixing of social categories went "intellectual and moral disorder";[236]

> There has been too much striving over the last century, too much hectic effort, too much haste, [and, as a result], knowledge has become fragmentary, dispersed, illusory. We have lived as it were inside a kaleidoscope, and, obliged to take notice of social theories, scientific discoveries, as well as literary productions, all at the same time, our eyes have become tired, and our vision fitful and wavering.

This reflects an authentic "intellectual crisis", the collapse, or the much more complex recasting, of the "Positivist" view of the world, associated in France with the work of Durkheim and Bergson among others, but also with the absorption of German philosophical ideas.[237] The impact of this crisis can be measured in a large amount of autobiographical and semi-autobiographical material from the period, for example Martin du Gard's *Jean Barois*, and, of course, the early writings of Maurras and Barrès.[238] It was particularly felt by young men in the 1890s and 1900s, and one can see how antisemitism and Nationalism could provide an escape from the uncertainties which it engendered, particularly since the new disconcerting ideas could be described as Jewish and/or German. Guy-Grand wrote in 1911 that Nationalism was "a possible, and, in a sense, an expected reaction, to the state of moral and intellectual confusion in which every young man in his twenties, who had just assimilated the results of the critical thought of the nineteenth century, was almost necessarily bound to find himself."[239]

But the state of confusion was not simply intellectual or confined to intellectuals. French people, Drumont claimed in 1890,[240] were

> absolutely disorientated as far as politics are concerned ... In politics, the Jews have acted the same way; they have destroyed everything around them and created a void. Even a few years ago, there existed Royalists, Bonapartists, Republicans, Radicals ... a Socialist party ... All that has gone up in smoke, has been pulverized, atomized. And we are confronted with this strange spectacle: a country where all the citizens are divided, but where one can discern no parties, no party leaders. We have discord together with impotence ... Such a dissolution is characteristic of all countries where the Jews have come to have at their disposal the whole machinery of the State, and to dominate the economic situation completely.

It is interesting to note here that the object of Drumont's critique was the state of flux and of the blurring of options from which antisemitism itself benefited as a political movement. The same image of atomization, of reduction to dust was used by Drumont on the level of general values and beliefs, too. "In the last twenty years", he wrote in 1894, "Jewish Freemasonry has reduced to dust all that consoled and refreshed men's souls ... Dust, the old traditions and the ancient beliefs ... Dust, the noble sentiments of the old days: the cult of the flag, the integrity of magistrates, fidelity to principles, respect for a name honourably borne from father to son ..."[241] And, evoking or expressing anomie more directly, he wrote again, about the same time:[242]

> There is patently no longer any moral direction, no sense of where one is going in this country ... Perhaps, reading these pages, you will have the same feeling, and will be struck also by the strange, the pathetic, the startling nature of all these spectacles, by the utter senselessness of all these agitations, by the absence of any dénouement in these charades which begin but which never end. One can say of life today, in the words of Shakespeare: "It is a tale told by an idiot, full of sound and fury, signifying nothing."

Social and cultural disorder went with diversity and pluralism, as some of the quotations above indicate. Drumont wrote, for example, in 1891, of a Jewish old-clothes merchant: "he provides an ironic comment on the emptiness of life with the disparate conglomeration of incongruous articles that he has gathered together on his rounds; all mixed up, he has mourning veils and dancing slippers, a summer dress ... and military uniforms ..."; and he made the meaning of this symbolization clear:[243]

> The Jews have made a society for us in the image of their own soul, and that society, from which all notions of decency and honour have disappeared, is the society of today. One must be with us or with them ... From the moment that one lives with other people, it is necessary to accept their view of things, their mentality, their way of judging questions of conscience, otherwise social life becomes a hell.

Or, as he wrote in *La France juive:* "When a Jew or a Jewess is concerned
. . . the ordinary conditions of morality are changed."[244] As we have seen, the
Jew, for the antisemite, stood for the Other, for what was different, and thus
an offence and a scandal for orthodoxy, and through his expulsion from the
community, ritual or otherwise, difference and diversity could be overcome,
the threat to the established order and the established view of the world could
be overcome, and the ideal of cultural uniformity could be achieved or regained.[245] In another context, it is significant that Drumont praised Richelieu
retrospectively for getting rid of heretics and traitors, thus using the traditional
model of religious uniformity to express and reinforce his own programme.[246]
This is in line with the general adherence of Catholics to the idea of a total
Christian society, which, we have seen, many antisemites fully embraced. The
non-believing Maurras was thus a champion of the Catholic Church because
he saw it as providing a principle of social and cultural order as against Judaism
and Protestantism, which represented disorder and diversity.[247] This was only
one, if a crucial, expression of his fundamental hostility to radical cultural
diversity and of his desire for unity and uniformity as far as essentials were
concerned: "A united people is better than a divided people; a society animated by one faith is better than one which is in disagreement over the destiny
of man and of the world."[248] Guy-Grand pointed out that such a view was
representative of Nationalism as a whole, which was "a dream of political,
spiritual and moral unity . . ."[249]

On another level, against relative "Jewish" values, against Jewish relativ-
ity,[250] the antisemites posited a world of moral and cultural absolutes. Here
they typified what a number of writers have called the "essentialism" of the
Right, the "disease of thinking in essences, which is at the bottom of every
bourgeois mythology of man", as Barthes has put it. Such mythology, he
argues, turns history into nature, "it abolishes the complexity of human acts,
it gives them the simplicity of essences, it does away with all dialectics . . .
it organizes a world which is without contradictions because it is without depth
. . . it establishes a blissful clarity . . ."[251] Such essentialism was inherent in
the manicheanism of antisemitism and in its racialism, and can be seen as a
general principle of its ideology, though this should not lead one to reduce its
complexities too exclusively to this principle or to neglect the fact that it
expressed as well as explicitly rejecting contradiction, two temptations to
which its existential critics are prone. Essentialism was reflected also, and more
particularly, in the concept of the "true Frenchman", which we have already
discussed,[252] and in that of fate or "destiny". Destiny was frequently invoked
explicitly or implicitly as a principle of historical explanation. Drumont referred, for example, in 1890, to "the invincible force of things", and, inferring
that the course of historical change was totally determined, declared: "We will
follow the magnetic current . . ."[253] As we have seen, the essentialist imperative here contradicted the demands of political action, a dilemma that faced
all neo-traditionalists.[254] But the sense of helplessness expressed via the idea
of an inevitable Jewish takeover, had also a positive side. If the antisemite had
no control over the course of events, he was also absolved from responsibility

for their outcome and from blame.[255] A contradiction of a different order was involved in nationally or, particularly, racially, based moral absolutism. According to Picard, "transformations by passing from one race to another are fundamentally impossible, even if they appear to happen. For we are talking about entities that are absolutely irreducible to the same moral denominator."[256] But, as Sternhell has pointed out in the case of Barrès, such absolutism represented in effect an extreme moral relativism. There was a French justice, a French truth even, which did not apply to Dreyfus and the Jews, or to any other nation, people or race.[257] And the implication was that such particularist values could only achieve absolute status by excluding and then by destroying what threatened and contradicted them, unless they could all be accommodated in some over-arching hierarchy or scale of values.

We have moved from the negative to the positive pole of one of the sets of polarities present in antisemitic ideology, and we must follow suit for the others. The opposition of social change and social stability may be dealt with briefly, since we have already implicitly dealt with it, and since it is in large part subsumed under the discussion of hierarchy which follows. All the traditional values upheld by the antisemites, Catholicism, the family as line, honour, the idealization of the rural world, implied attachment to a stable society. More explicitly, Drumont typically opposed any tendency towards change within the Church, to which he held precisely because "it claims to be the depositary of the immutable Truth, and speaks in Time in the name of Eternity."[258] Similarly, as Sternhell has emphasized, Barrès was engaged in a search for "principles of stability".[259]

Social disorder and disorganization were opposed by the idea of social order or hierarchy. "Every antisemite . . .", wrote Sartre, "adores order, but *social* order. One could say that he provokes political disorder in order to restore social order . . ."[260] One can agree with both parts of this statement, although antisemites in late nineteenth-century France ostensibly claimed to be working for political order also. Drumont was a critic of the government of *"Ordre Moral"* of the early 1870s, but declared that its name was "the finest imaginable after that of government of *Christian order* . . ."[261] Sartre adds, however, that the ideal social order of the antisemite was "an egalitarian and primitive society",[262] and here one must disagree, for social order as far as our antisemites were concerned nearly always implied the concept of social hierarchy. Their aim, as Guy-Grand wrote of the Nationalists generally, was "to reconstitute social ranks . . ."[263] Thus Mme René Johannet, a supporter of the Action Française, declared in 1922: "France can only survive, if the sense of order and of hierarchy is reestablished among us . . .";[264] and Drumont made the same point again and again in a variety of ways. Attacking the anticlerical policy of the Third Republic, he complained in 1886 that, since the removal of nuns from hospitals, "there is no longer any discipline or control." He evoked the painful dilemma of Catholics anxious to resist governmental action and persecution, but naturally respectful of order and of "social conventions": "The misfortune of these honest victims of persecution is that they remain civilized people, believing that we are still living under the rule of law, that magistrates are real magistrates, and that the police, the administration, the courts are functioning normally." Again, he expressed his concern that, as a result of Jewish influence, the profession of actor had become one of excessively high status:[265]

> So long as actors remained simple Christians, the job of actor remained one that was not much esteemed in itself, though the great talent, the dignity of a particular artist could occasionally enhance it. It requires, in effect, the loss of all moral sense and of all common sense to admit that, in the social hierarchy, the buffoon . . . should be the equal of a soldier who exposes his life for his country, of a sailor who risks his in storms at sea, of a doctor who defies epidemics.

On a personal level, he recalled the unease which he felt as a boy as the inmate of an aristocratic school boarding-house, where "I was caught between two classes . . ." And he sought a model for his ideal of social hierarchy in the past, writing of the Crusades: "If the Vallombrosa, the de Luynes, the d'Uzès and the Kervéguen went there on horseback, the Buchon and the Drumont, of whose mettle there is no doubt, must also have gone; only they would have gone on foot and, as they were modest unassuming people like myself, they would have been lost in the crowd." He noted, too, that on the occasion of the visit of Pope Innocent II to Saint-Denis, "all the professional guilds, every social group figured in the royal procession, which was an image of a severely hierarchical society in which everyone had his rank."[266] In the same vein, Boni de Castellane criticized the practice of Jewish antique dealers of taking objects and fittings from their original settings: "I believe that decoration must be done according to an order, a hierarchy . . ."[267] Relating such a concept to other neo-traditional themes, Jules Soury wrote to Barrès: "One can only exist and endure in the world through discipline, respect for a hierarchy and the observation of an invariable set of rules. In effect, all that is left standing is the Army and the Church . . . What matters, is . . . the cult of the perpetual adoration of honour, of the honour of caste and of nation."[268]

The Jews were seen as the enemies of hierarchy. "To make money", wrote Drumont in La France juive, "to rule through the financier over this world [of the Ancien Régime] which believes only in the priest and in the soldier, in poverty and in heroism, this was always the policy of the Jews . . . What they needed to overthrow before they could accomplish anything, was the old hierarchy, the Church, the monasteries, the Papacy."[269] Thus the French Revolution, which emancipated the Jews and which was based on "Jewish" principles, spelled the end of the Ancien Régime: "The formidable Semitic invasion dates really from 1789 and from the reforms realized by the Revolution in the direction of equality and fraternity."[270] As this indicates, therefore, antisemites were, in general, opposed to the whole idea of an egalitarian society, even when they made much of their democratic sentiments. Drumont, the socialistic Republican, criticized the aristocracy of his day and lambasted the Royalists,[271] yet he celebrated the virtues of the "real" old aristocracy, which still carried out its paternal functions,[272] and he idealized the monarchs of the past.[273] And the more conservative Maurras, of course, led the Action Française into a thoroughgoing political neo-Royalism.[274] There is a parallel here with Populism in general, which, according to Wiles, "opposes social and economic inequality produced by the institutions it does not like . . . but . . . accepts the traditional inequalities due to the way of life of its own constituency",[275] though antisemites were attached to hierarchy in a much more positive way than this suggests, and their attitude was as much a reaction against as a reflection of their "way of life".

It is, moreover, on the social and the cultural rather than on the specifically political level, that the concept of heirarchy was most significant. First, it provided, in Szasz's words, an "image of an orderly universe",[276] in which every thing and every person had a place and was in its place. One remembers Maurras's complaint that the modern criterion of money could not serve "to *classify* a man . . ."[277] The Jew was disturbing precisely because one could not "place" him;[278] but even he might be accommodated, and his destructive power be neutralized, in a hierarchy as clear as that of the Middle Ages. Drumont pointed out that "the Jews had their place" in the mediaeval procession to Saint-Denis already referred to.[279] With a rather different emphasis, and raising other implications, Picard maintained that Jews in France had been "serfs" until the time of the Revolution.[280] As Sartre has argued, antisemitism itself created its own hierarchy, "a scale of petrified values", giving the antisemite a permanent sense of superiority over the Jew;[281] but this hierarchy was paradigmatic, almost a ritual representation, of something larger, of the total society for which it was a model. Drumont noted, in 1891, that, when they were frightened, Jews became polite and deferential, adding: "I tell myself then: Decidedly, society is beginning to reorganize itself; everyone is getting back in his place."[282]

But hierarchy did not simply imply a social ladder of ranks, an order *qua* order, though it had that function; it was an order with the supplement of meaning and justification. Drumont commented in 1891 on Léon Daudet's civil marriage:[283]

When the leading people, the authorities, the élite show this lack of care and principle in a matter of conscience, how can one expect the masses to be other than they are: without beliefs, detached from everything . . . angry only that they are without the necessities of life while a few privileged persons have more than they know what to do with, and telling themselves that before long their turn will come?

And he wrote a year earlier, with reference to corporate bodies rather than the leisure class, but significantly using the common term "authority": "Never have the social Authorities, to use an expression of Le Play, been in a position to exercise such influence; in this period of individualism and of general disintegration . . . anything resembling a corporate body has a collective moral power and takes on an importance, that are exceptional."[284] Durkheim was to express much the same sentiment a little later in the decade.[285] The point is that privileges meant duties; that social hierarchy was a system based on the division of labour and of social functions, but also on reciprocity; that an élite had to rule and protect, to lead, and not simply to enjoy itself. Thus Drumont could ask: "One wonders how this society still holds together, this society where one sees, at the top, only selfishness, vanity, the love of pleasure, the absence of all sense of duty and responsibility, all thought of sacrifice and, even, of all instinct of self-preservation, and, at the bottom, only hatred and envy."[286] The linking of "self-preservation" with "sense of duty", with reciprocity, is crucial. For it was only if the upper classes set an example, gave a lead, only if they provided moral guidance and preserved traditional beliefs and values, only if they fulfilled the paternalistic role of the old aristocracy, that the social hierarchy would be saved and maintained, that they would retain their authority and their position as an élite in the face of the rising claims of popular democracy, or the inchoate barbarism of the masses. So much was being said by very many conservatives in the nineteenth century. What the antisemitic version does is to highlight two features of the argument that were not always so explicit. First was the emphasis on the hereditary basis of the hierarchy, of children following parents in their social roles, occupations and property; such a system was ideally unchanging, and could be supported, up to a point, by an appeal to race. Second was the point that all groups in society benefited from the hierarchical system and thus had an equal interest in maintaining it, if they were not misled; populism here joined élitism via reciprocity. The model was the society of "orders" of the Ancien Régime,[287] but there is an analogy, albeit weak and partial, on the ideological level with an authentic caste system.[288]

All of this was a reaction to actual changes in French social structure, which the position of the Jews reflected and could symbolize. As the antisemites sensed, the Jews as a distinct and different community could be fitted fairly easily into the old society of "orders".[289] In the post-Revolutionary, democratic model of society, on the other hand, such a community was an anomaly. Its continued existence, in attenuated form, represented a fidelity to the past, to the old order, which the antisemites desired for themselves and society as a whole, and which they thus envied and resented. At the same time, Jews were becoming assimilated, and the post-Emancipation cultural and social insecurity of the Jews could stand for and symbolize the general insecurity felt by many people in the course of "modernization" and all it implied.[290] Antisemitism was thus an ideal mode for the expression of a social and cultural malaise that was very widely felt in the late nineteenth century. The structure and content of antisemitic ideology as so far expounded already suggests that it had this general function, that it registered and sought to explain, to contain and to exorcize the process of social change or disorganization. Durkheim described antisemitism in 1898 as "the superficial symptom of a state of social malaise";[291] and Ginsberg wrote later that: "The occurrence of antisemitic outbursts is a symptom of social disorganization."[292] Such observations support our argument, but, in an important sense, they do not go far enough.

Antisemitism was more than a symptom, it was, on the ideological or the mythical level, an expression of social change; and it was not, in this and other senses, superficial.

It is important to emphasize that antisemitism was part of a much wider movement of criticism and refusal of the modern industrial world and its values. As Simone de Beauvoir has put it, "the simple dignity of the humble, the abnegation of women and of faithful servants, accepted disciplines, burdens assumed, sons following fathers, soldiers obeying their leaders, marriage, the house and home, the family . . . a vast literature sings the praises of these bourgeois institutions and the great virtues which spring from them."[293] Beauvoir is here referring to Right-wing Catholic literature, which was often infected by antisemitism, but, more strikingly, the opponents of antisemitism often shared its general attitudes. Péguy, for example, like Drumont, opposed the modern world of change, banality and materialism to the old world imbued with Christian and heroic values:[294]

> The modern world, the world which knows all the answers, the world of the high-brows, of the *avant-garde,* of the knowledgeable, of those who will take no advice, of those who are never caught out . . . the modern world is not only the opposite of the French Ancien Régime, it is at odds with all old régimes taken together, with all ancient cultures, with all ancient civilizations, with all that a culture, with all that a civilization means.

Again, Péguy's Dreyfusism was above all a proclamation of heroic values: "We were heroes . . . the question which faced us . . . was not at all to know whether *in reality* Dreyfus was innocent . . . It was to know whether one would have the courage to recognize that he was and to declare his innocence . . ." Moreover, like others, Péguy maintained that his Dreyfusism was ultimately a defence of Order: "People always talk as though it was we who came to introduce disorder into a society of order . . . But one must acknowledge that there can be an order which is purely apparent and which conceals, which is, the worst kind of disorder . . ."[295] Similarly, as has been mentioned already, Durkheim, in his analysis of modern society in *Le Suicide* (1897), stressed the loosening of traditional social ties, the erosion of common values and the absence of a recognized system of social classification, and called for the reestablishment of corporations to recreate group solidarity;[296] while Leroy-Beaulieu believed that France was "in a state of moral civil war".[297]

But, if antisemitism was in some ways a typical reaction to modern society and to modernization, it had various special features. It was, first, an extreme reaction; and it offered both explanations and solutions. If much in antisemitic writing can be seen as a response to particular and real social phenomena: the high level of immigration, the rural exodus, the spread of department stores, for example, there was present also a much vaguer and more total sense of loss and of threat. Péguy characterized the antisemitic view of the world as one "in which the Jews are perfectly happy, and in which we are, in which they make us, perfectly unhappy".[298] Bernanos wrote that *La France juive* expressed "less the fear of a definite danger than the state of anxious anticipation of simple people, than a popular presentiment".[299] Images of "peril" and "danger" recur again and again in antisemitic writing,[300] merging with and culminating in apocalyptic fears of an imminent end of the world. As Adorno and others have seen, antisemitism was a mode for the expression of such fears, but it also at the same time served to allay them. The sense of threat related to an alienation from the social world, to a failure to understand either intuitively or intellectually the "social processes" in which antisemites were involved, which left them confused, uncertain and disorientated. What antisemitism did in such circumstances was to objectify the social processes in the form of the Jewish conspiracy, thus providing explanation, and, by penetrating "the darkness of reality like a searchlight", a kind of certainty.[301]

Antisemitism also offered its adherents other forms of security beyond the ontological. In a matter-of-fact way, Barrès announced in his Nancy Programme of 1898: "Over many centuries, the French nation has managed to give its members political security. It must now protect them against the economic insecurity from which they are suffering at all levels."[302] Such an approach was unusual in its concreteness, and could be misleading. The development of organized antisemitism in France did coincide with a period of economic depression, but what antisemitism seems to have expressed, and, to some degree, to have overcome, was a social malaise, as we have stressed, one that was highlighted, exacerbated perhaps by short-term economic crisis, but which was more basic, more far-reaching and related to longer-term structural change.

A number of students of antisemitism have suggested that there is a correlation between its incidence and the incidence of both upward and downward social mobility, and have thus seen it as an expression of "status anxiety".[303] The French antisemites' attacks on social mobility, and their ideal of a fixed social hierarchy, suggest that such an interpretation applies to them, particularly when these ideological features are set beside the "marginal" situation of many of the movement's supporters, which cannot unfortunately be quantified. It seems that, losing status themselves, they were obsessed by the rising status of others, and symbolically of the Jews; here it should be recalled that the criteria of status were themselves in question, both objectively, causing authentic disorientation, and also, to some degree, because antisemites deliberately refused to accept criteria which gave them low status. As has been argued for other cases, too,[304] antisemitism in France offered a compensation for this anxiety. Uncertain of their place in a real world that was changing, more or less unattached to it, antisemites "belonged" to "the nation", and, if they were militants, they "belonged" to the movement. "In the Ligue Antisémitique", Guérin told his members, "we have a solidarity in which the least of us fully shares . . ."[305] Related to this, antisemites also had the security provided by attachment to a fixed set of categories and beliefs, the security of ideological conformism.[306] As Leroy-Beaulieu pointed out, other "sectarian" movements and ideologies, and notably anticlericalism and Socialism, fulfilled some of the same functions,[307] which again indicates how general were the sentiments that antisemitism articulated, and the needs which it satisfied. But the comparison shows, too, how antisemitism was better equipped for the task than other movements more closely meshed with the real social and political world. This is particularly true as far as the overcoming of "status anxiety" is concerned, for, as several French writers have stressed, antisemitism gave the antisemite an instant and superior status vis-à-vis the Jews. " 'I am certainly not a Jew!', he tells himself," wrote the Tharauds. "And for him, that is a naïve reason to affirm that he is somebody."[308]

Many writers, from Péguy to Memmi, have pointed to the internal contradictions of antisemitism, which associated the Jews with capitalism and with Revolution, with individualism and with group solidarity, which claimed that they were racially inferior, yet that they were masters of the world, and so on.[309] "The sentiments, the passions and the ideas which shelter behind the name antisemitism are equivocal and thoroughly confused", concluded Dagan in 1899.[310] But this basic characteristic of antisemitic ideology should not be taken, as it often has been, as a purely negative quality. As earlier chapters in this part of the book have shown, different types of antisemitism, appealing to different social milieus, can be isolated. "Inside a single country," as Memmi has written, "all social groups are more or less involved in antisemitism, each in its own way . . . For there exists a hostility of traders and a hostility of the liberal professions, a hostility of military men and a hostility of churchmen . . . There exists also a hostility of the rich and a hostility of the poor, of small shopkeepers and wage-earners."[311] And the multifarious nature of antisemitism was noted also by contemporary observers like Lazare and Leroy-Beaulieu.

It is to this heterogeneous mixture of good and evil, of misplaced idealism and of practical materialism, of naïve protests against the cult of Mammon and of unavowed coveting of wealth, of indignant rejection of the predominance of money and of self-interested rancours or envious jealousies, [wrote the latter in 1902[312]] that antisemitism owes its popularity and its wide diffusion . . . there enter into it, at the same time, disgust at the evils of the day, conscientious revulsion against the corruption of politicians, against the provoking display of wealth, and also the resentments of competitors who have been ousted or of unsuccessful businessmen against more successful or abler rivals; the grudges of landowners and landed gentry, whose incomes are drying up, against the banker and the stock-broker, whose capital assets seem always to be growing; the irritation of aristocrats at new fortunes and new influences, and the resentment of people in the provinces and in rural areas against those living in big cities and against foreign immigrants; not forgetting the bitterness and the envy of the small shopkeeper and the petty bourgeois vis-à-vis the big stores, the upper bourgeoisie and the big capitalists; so that one can say that antisemitism is the coming-together of every envy and resentment, exacerbated further by the fear of secret influences and dark forces, high finance and cosmopolitan syndicates, vague spectres whose invisible hand the ignorant and silly crowd believes that it can detect everywhere.

But, if antisemitism was a multi-purpose ideology, as this indicates, with such disparate support, it was also a single and coherent ideology, as we have sought to show. A number of explanations have been offered of this paradox. Edgar Morin, with reference to a later period, has suggested that the inter-class nature of antisemitism is a symptom of the growing homogeneity of modern society and a reflection of the disappearance of traditional class struc-tures.[313] And such an interpretation fits the situation at the end of the nineteenth century in some respects. As the antisemites lamented, the tradi-tional social hierarchy was altering, and the main vehicle of antisemitism was the newspaper press, symbol, symptom and maker of a homogeneous national culture. Extending a Marxist view of the function of Nationalism,[314] Sartre saw antisemitism as "a passionate effort to achieve a national unity *against* the division of societies into classes".[315] In this perspective, it was a means of creating a national community by stressing what French people had in com-mon, their non-Jewishness, thus playing down or overcoming the class antago-nisms and conflict, which Socialist ideology expressed and emphasized, and thereby preserving the existing social and political order. A cruder version of this interpretation, espoused by some contemporaries, saw antisemitism as the means by which the ruling classes manipulated a potentially hostile popular opinion, turning hostility from themselves against the Jews. "One can do what one likes with a people, when one knows how to excite them against the Jews", declared Woldsmuth in Martin du Gard's *Jean Barois*.[316] This version de-pends upon an unacceptably simplistic view of the way in which attitudes are formed and changed,[317] although it is probable that the mass press had an unusual impact and influence when it was still a novelty; and, if one largely discounts the element of manipulation, there is no doubt that antisemitism did express a desire for community, a rejection of social conflict and a prefer-ence for regarding social structure in terms of hierarchy rather than class. But it did not simply wish for the maintenance of the status quo, as we have amply demonstrated, nor did it represent solely the interests of a ruling group or groups.

The paradox is perhaps better understood if antisemitism is regarded as a complex myth, whose function, like that of other myths,[318] was precisely to contain and express contradiction, to map out the social universe in terms of polarities, such as Money versus Honour, Stock Exchange versus Land, Gold versus Blood, Jew versus Christian or Aryan. In this way, it expressed the experience, the cultural dilemmas of those living in a society whose traditional structures and values were being altered by the process of modernization with unprecedented rapidity. So, on the individual and on the social level, it mani-fested both a traditional submission to order and authority and a rebellion against the new order and authority. It was, in the words of Morin, "a discourse . . . that was deeply ambivalent, in which revolutionary urges ran to ground and were frustrated . . . in which fears, spurts of the fantastic imagina-tion were now unloosed, now held in check by conservative forces."[319] And, in line with this, antisemitism expressed both a refusal of the modern world, and the desire to compete successfully in it. The manichean and apocalyptic orientation of antisemitic mythology can also be related to the experience of modernization. This, our analysis has indicated, was felt by antisemites (and others) to be destroying traditional values and hierarchies, to be reducing an orderly social and moral universe to meaningless chaos, to "dust". According to Mary Douglas, such weakening of "classification" is accompanied in many societies by "millennial fervour" and by the development of a "small group" mentality and of "witch-dominated cosmologies".[320] Antisemitism in late nineteenth-century France fits well into this scheme. Firm classification, moral and social, weakened in society at large in the post-Revolutionary century, a situation to which antisemites were explicitly reacting. And their reaction took the form of a negative millenarianism, a pessimistic prediction that the end of the world was imminent, and of a severe dualism, which attributed all evils to the machinations of the all-powerful Jews, while giving them group-identity vis-à-vis the enemy. From a slightly different angle, another parallel of heuristic value may be established with other movements reacting to radical social and cultural change, for example, with the cargo cults of Melanesia.[321] Both movements appear to share a distinctive neotraditionalism, in that they reassert traditional values, but, since the traditional context has changed, they must do so in ways that are novel if not revolutionary; also, while thus rejecting the modern, they, at the same time, express the desire to participate in the the benefits that modernization brings, though they do not understand the process which produces them and are limited to inappropriate ritual gestures.

Nearer home, appreciation of the function and the appeal of antisemitism as a myth of modernization is enhanced if it is set beside the present day reaction in the United States and in Western Europe against industrial society and its values. This, too, is a neo-traditionalism, nostalgic for the past and the rural world, scornful of "materialism" and bureaucracy, often associated with religious revival, engaged in ritual forms of protest, having special appeal for the young, and difficult to classify in terms of the old political spectrum.[322] Of course, serious comparison would expose many differences also, but the point is simply again to try to understand, by analogy and without yielding one's sympathy, what antisemitism meant and expressed for so many people in France at the turn of the century.

NOTES

1 Dagan, *Enquête sur l'antisémitisme*, p. 87; see also ibid., pp. 53–4 (Duclaux).
2 Tharaud, *Quand Israël n'est plus roi*, p. 164.
3 Blumenkranz, ed., *Histoire des Juifs en France*, p. 341.
4 Sorlin, *"La Croix" et les Juifs*, p. 223.
5 See Ginsberg, "Antisemitism", *Essays in Sociology and Social Philosophy*, p. 192; and Levinson, The Study of Anti-Semitic Ideology", Adorno *et al.*, *The Authoritarian Personality*, chapter III.
6 Sartre, *Réflexions sur la question juive*, pp. 38–9.
7 Verdès-Leroux, *Scandale financier et antisémitisme catholique*, p. 124.
8 Selznick and Steinberg, *The Tenacity of Prejudice*, p. 29.
9 Lazare, *L'Antisémitisme*, p. 227.
10 Dagan, op. cit., p. 36.

11 Bernanos, *La Grande Peur des bien-pensants*, p. 151.
12 Drumont, *Le Testament d'un antisémite*, pp. ix and 39.
13 See chapter XI, n. 378.
14 *Le Complôt juif.* AN F⁷ 12463.
15 Verdès-Leroux, op. cit., p. 99.
16 See Herbert H. Hyman and Paul B. Sheatsley, "The Authoritarian Personality" —A Methodological Critique", in Christie and Jahoda, eds, *Studies in the Scope and Method of "The Authoritarian Personality"*, pp. 107–11.
17 See Lucy Mair, *Witchcraft*, particularly chapter 1; Macfarlane, *Witchcraft in Tudor and Stuart England*, pp. 203–4; Jerry Palmer, "Mickey Spillane: a reading", Cohen and Young, eds., *The Manufacture of News*, p. 311 and *passim.*
18 Adorno, *The Authoritarian Personality*, p. 619.
19 Drumont, Préface, Vanki, *L'Antéchrist ou origines de la Franc-maçonnerie et son but expliqué par ses symboles*, cit. Weber, *Satan franc-maçon*, p. 16.
20 Drumont, *TA*, p. 15; see also Duroselle, "L'Antisémitisme en France", pp. 50 and 55.
21 Meurin, *La Franc-maçonnerie, Synagogue de Satan*, p. 462.
22 Wicart, *Les Deux Causes de la décadence*, p. 4.
23 Lazare, op. cit., p. 119.
24 Selznick and Steinberg, op. cit., pp. xv, 20, 169 and 189; see also Loewenstein, *Christians and Jews*, pp. 25 and 197; and Paul Hartmann and Charles Husband, "The mass media and racial conflict", Cohen and Young, eds., op. cit., pp. 270 and 273.
25 Memmi, *Portrait d'un Juif*, pp. 58–9; also pp. 61–2.
26 See Antoine, *Le Théâtre* (Paris, 1932), pp. 14, 75, 95, 268 and 316.
27 See ibid., pp. 73, 308, 322, 368 and 435; and Bernhardt, *Memories of My Life*, p. 125.
28 Antoine, op. cit., pp. 64, 225, 237, 434 and 476; and Herriot, *Jadis*, I, p. 93.
29 See Antoine, op. cit., pp. 112, 272, 332, 450–1 and 465; Lugné-Poe, *La Parade*, III, *Sous les Etoiles; Souvenirs de théâtre (1902–1912)* (Paris, 1933), pp. 225–7; and Blum, *Souvenirs sur l'Affaire*, pp. 62–3.
30 Drault, *Drumont, La France juive et La Libre Parole*, p. 287; also ibid., pp. 283–7; and Antoine, op. cit., p. 466. On Donnay's anti-Dreyfusism and generally reactionary opinions, see Jules Renard, *Correspondance*, pp. 197–8 and 389 (1898 and 1909).
31 See Drault, op. cit., pp. 287–8; and Lugné-Poe, op. cit., loc. cit. Guinon claimed in the Préface to *Décadence*, published in 1901, that the play had been banned by "l'Administration . . . dans l'intérêt de la tranquillité publique" (p. ix). The play, modelled fairly closely on Lavedan's earlier success, is, however, much more hostile to the Jews.
32 See Pierre Brisson, *Le Théâtre des années folles* (Geneva, 1943), pp. 13 and 15; and Drault, op. cit., p. 287.
33 Verdès-Leroux, op. cit., p. 12; also pp. 99, 101, 110 and 114–15.
34 See Ginsberg, op. cit., p. 190; Bein, *Theodore Herzl*, p. 38; and Sternhell, *Maurice Barrès*, pp. 232–3; also Selznick and Steinberg, op. cit., p. xiv.
35 See H. R. Trevor-Roper, *The European Witch-Craze of the 16th and 17th Centuries* (Harmondsworth, 1969), pp. 40–54 and 114–15.
36 Lazare, op. cit., p. 228.
37 Péguy, *Notre Jeunesse*, p. 179.
38 Drumont, *TA*, p. ix.
39 Cit. Bournand, *Les Juifs et nos contemporains*, p. 141.
40 Picard, *Synthèse de l'antisémitisme*, pp. 15–16.
41 Cit. Bournand, op. cit., p. 113.
42 Daudet, *Les Oeuvres dans les hommes*, p. 168.
43 See, for example, Léon Daudet, *Au Temps de Judas*, p. 51; and Byrnes, *Antisemitism in Modern France*, pp. 109 and 148–50; see also chapter XIV, n. 388 above.

44 See, for example, Goncourt, *Journal*, VII, pp. 7–8; and Bournand, op. cit., pp. 181–5.
45 See Bournand, op. cit., p. 148.
46 See ibid., pp. 131–5; and chapter X, p. 272 and n. 259 above.
47 See ibid., p. 173; and Gregh, *L'Age d'or*, pp. 288–9.
48 See Bournand, op. cit., pp. 139–42; Byrnes, "Jean-Louis Forain: "Antisemitism in French Art"; Gide, *Journals*, I, p. 161 (1896); and Halévy, *Degas parle*, pp. 43–5 and 127.
49 See Bournand, op. cit., p. 172; and Reinach, *Histoire de l'Affaire Dreyfus*, III, pp. 247–8.
50 In addition to Bournand's own works, see Byrnes, "Jean-Louis Forain: Antisemitism in French Art", p. 248. On the parallel involvement of intellectuals in antisemitism in Germany, see Mosse, *The Crisis of German Ideology*, p. 132 and *passim;* and Stern, *The Politics of Cultural Despair*, pp. 91–5 and generally.
51 See my "History and Traditionalism: Maurras and the Action Française", *Journal of the History of Ideas*, 29 (1968), pp. 376–8.
52 Drumont, *TA*, p. 69. Does this last idea account at all for the popularity of the concept of "action" in Right-wing thinking in the 1900s and later, as expressed, for example, in the name of the Action Française?
53 See Louis Bodin and Jean Touchard, "Les Intellectuels dans la société française contemporaine, Définitions, statistiques et problèmes", *Revue Française de Science Politique*, 9 (1959), pp. 836–9; and, more generally, Florian Znaniecki, *The Social Role of the Man of Knowledge* (New York, 1940 and 1968).
54 P. Dreyfus, *Dreyfus: His Life and Letters*, pp. 191–2; see also Zévaès, *L'Affaire Dreyfus*, pp. 117–19.
55 See, for example, Pierre de Lacretelle, *Vie politique de Victor Hugo* (Paris, 1928); Henri Guillemin, *Lamartine et la question sociale* (Paris, 1946); Jean Larnac, *George Sand révolutionnaire* (Paris, 1947); Cesar Graña, *Modernity and its Discontents, French Society and the French Man of Letters in the Nineteenth Century* (New York, 1967); and Lidsky, *Les Ecrivains contre la Commune*, particularly chapter I.
56 Drumont, *La France juive*, II, p. 187.
57 Ibid., II, p. 547.
58 Drumont, *La Dernière Bataille*, pp. 319–20.
59 Mauclair, *La Cocarde*, 24 September 1894, cit. Nguyen, "Un Essai de pouvoir intellectuel au début de la Troisième République: *La Cocarde* de Maurice Barrès", p. 153.
60 Maurras, *L'Avenir de l'intelligence*, pp. 90–2.
61 Bournand, op. cit., p. 141.
62 Vallès, *Le Bachélier*, p. 94.
63 See, for example, Bloy, *Lettres à René Martineau*, pp. 142–43 (25 July 1902) and 174 (23 April 1903).
64 Drumont, *FJ*, I, pp. 74 and 54.
65 See Byrnes, "The French Publishing Industry and its Crisis in the 1890s".
66 See Mosse, *The Crisis of German Ideology*, p. 150; Kornhauser, *The Politics of Mass Society*, chapter 10; and Selznick and Steinberg, op. cit., pp. 92–3.
67 For Proudhon, see Silberner, "Proudhon's Judeophobia", pp. 61–2; and, for the Assumptionists, Sorlin, *"La Croix" et les Juifs*, p. 215.
68 See Daudet, *Les Oeuvres dans les hommes*, p. 161.
69 Drumont, *FJ*, I, p. 53. Hofstadter has commented that the "paranoid" politician imitates his "intellectual" enemy, and "will outdo him in the apparatus of scholarship, even of pedantry." Hofstadter, *The Paranoid Style*, p. 32. Emphasis on the formalities of scholarship is certainly a feature of much antisemitic writing, and of the work of the Action Française writers, before and after the First World War.

70 See J. and M. Charlot, "Un Rassemblement d'Intellectuels, La Ligue des Droits de l'Homme", pp. 1003–4; Herriot, *Jadis*, I, pp. 134–5; and Sternhell, *Maurice Barrès*, pp. 274 and *passim*.

71 See my "A View of the Past", pp. 136–9; and chapter XII, p. 406 above.

72 Drumont, *DB*, pp. 286–7; also *FJ*, II, pp. 238–9 and 409; and *TA*, p. 325.

73 Flaubert's *Dictionnaire des idées reçues* includes this definition: "*Académie Française. La dénigrer, mais tâcher d'en faire partie si on peut.*" Gustave Flaubert, *Bouvard et Pécuchet* (1881) (Paris, 1959), p. 403. (I am grateful to Janine Dakyns for drawing my attention to this reference.) For details on Drumont's bid to get elected to the Academy in 1908–9, see Jules Clarétie, *Souvenirs d'un Académicien, Les Oeuvres Libres*, no. 151, (Paris, January 1934), pp. 109 and 115–16.

74 Drumont, *DB*, p. 184.

75 Cit. Herriot, op. cit., p. 135; and see also Reynaud, *Le Père Didon*, pp. 356–8. It is fair to add that Didon was also criticizing the tendency of French graduates to avoid "practical" careers, in the army, but also in industry and business, and to prefer "intellectual" careers, particularly in education.

76 See Sternhell, *Maurice Barrès*, pp. 259–60 and 269–89.

77 See H. Stuart Hughes, *Consciousness and Society; The Reorientation of European Social Thought 1890–1930* (London, 1967); and pp. 629–30 and n. 237 below.

78 Lacretelle, *Silbermann*, pp. 31–2, 46–7, 139–40 and *passim*.

79 Gide, *Journals*, I, p. 128 (1905); see also Waleffe, *Quand Paris était un paradis*, p. 308.

80 Sartre, *Réflexions sur la question juive*, p. 26; see also Loewenstein, op. cit., p. 23.

81 See, for example, Tharaud, *Petite Histoire des Juifs*, pp. 208–10; Wirth, *The Ghetto*, pp. 54, 76–7 and 80–2; Loewenstein, op. cit., pp. 124–5, 135, 166 and 168; Mark Zborowski, "The Place of Book-Learning in Traditional Jewish Culture", in Margaret Mead and Martha Wolfenstein, eds, *Childhood in Contemporary Cultures* (Chicago, 1966), pp. 118–41; Hutchins Hapgood, *The Spirit of the Ghetto* (with Preface and Notes by Harry Golden) (New York, 1966), pp. xii, xiv, 9, 29, 53–75 and *passim*; and Memmi, op. cit., p. 279.

82 Benda, *La Jeunesse d'un clerc*, pp. 52 and 69; also pp. 71 and *passim*.

83 Berl, *Sylvia*, pp. 35–6, 51, 31 and *passim*.

84 Durkheim, *Suicide*, pp. 167–8; see also Maurois, *Mémoires*, I, p. 20; Bloch, *Lévy*, p. 38; and Colette Audry, *Léon Blum ou la politique du Juste, Essai* (Paris, 1955), p. 22.

85 See Pierre Lasserre, *La Doctrine officielle de l'Université* (Paris, 1912).

86 Benda, *La Jeunesse d'un clerc*, p. 101.

87 Lacretelle, op. cit., p. 68.

88 Lavedan, *Le Prince d'Aurec*, pp. 31–2.

89 Drumont, *TA*, p. 141.

90 Drumont, *FJ*, I, pp. 12 and 23.

91 Cit. Bournand, op. cit., p. 179.

92 Bainville, *Journal*, I, p. 24 (14 August 1905).

93 Memmi, op. cit., pp. 378–9; see also Loewenstein, op. cit., pp. 56 and 140.

94 Beauvoir, *Privilèges*, p. 102.

95 Selznick and Steinberg, op. cit., p. 136; also ibid., pp. 80–3, 90–1, 180–2, and chapter 8.

96 Ibid., pp. 92–3.

97 See, for example, Thabault, *Education and Change in a Village Community;* and Antoine Prost, *Histoire de l'enseignement en France 1800–1967* (Paris, 1968), particularly Parts I–III.

98 See the general remarks of Lucien Febvre, *Le Problème de l'incroyance au 16e*

siècle: La Religion de Rabelais (1942) (Paris, 1968), pp. 12, 16–17, 99–100, 424 and *passim.*

  99 See Lucien Febvre, "Witchcraft: nonsense or a mental revolution?" (1948), Peter Burke, ed., *A New Kind of History from the writings of Lucien Febvre* (London, 1973), p. 189; Trevor-Roper, op. cit., p. 47 and *passim;* Thomas, *Religion and the Decline of Magic.*

100 Beauvoir, op. cit., p. 199; also p. 117.

101 Bernanos, op. cit., p. 120, cit. Petit, *Bernanos, Bloy, Claudel, Péguy,* p. 24. See also Morin, *La Rumeur d'Orléans,* p. 106: "la tendance naturelle de l'angoisse est de susciter des fantasmes, de chercher un réfuge archaïque, de susciter par là-même les mécanismes d'expulsion et de purification: l'immolation d'un bouc émissaire."

102 Brunetière, "Revue littéraire, La France juive", p. 694.

103 Piou, *Le Comte Albert de Mun,* p. 186.

104 Drumont, *FJ,* I, p. 119; II, pp. 46 and 561.

105 See Mosse, *The Crisis of German Ideology,* pp. 22–8 and 130; Loewenstein, op. cit., pp. 59, 61 and 111; Morin *et al;* op. cit., pp. 56–63 and *passim;* and Pierrard, *Juifs et catholiques français,* pp. 254–5, citing *La Revue Internationale des Sociétés Secrètes* for 1932: "Le nudisme, le freudisme, le cocktail, le jazz, le cubisme, l'internationalisme . . . sont l'oeuvre du juif."

106 Leroy-Beaulieu, *Les Doctrines de haine,* p. 101.

107 Péguy, *NJ,* pp. 179–80.

108 Drumont, *FJ,* II, p. 47.

109 Drumont, *DB,* pp. 92–3.

110 Drieu La Rochelle, *Gilles,* p. 111.

111 Drumont, *De l'Or, de la boue, du sang,* p. 156. Contrary claims, of course, were being made in the period to which Drumont was referring; see, for example, Gelu, *Marseille au XIXe siècle,* pp. 400–5, retailing Toussenel.

112 See, for example, Sorlin, *"La Croix" et les Juifs,* pp. 215–17.

113 Drumont, *La Fin d'un monde,* p. iv; also Fore-Fauré, *Face aux Juifs!,* pp. 142–5; Drumont, *Mon Vieux Paris* (Paris, 1878 and 1897); and Byrnes, *Antisemitism in Modern France,* p. 144.

114 Bloy, *Lettres à René Martineau,* pp. 37 (1901) and 199 (1903).

115 Drumont, *DB,* pp. 217–18; and Boni de Castellane, *Vingt ans de Paris,* p. 75.

116 Reports, Commissaire central, Nantes, 3–6 August 1898. AN F7 12459.

117 Drumont, *FJ,* II, p. 447.

118 "juifs et judaïsants". *L'Intransigeant,* 9 March 1903, cit. Guillemin, *Présentation des Rougon-Macquart,* p. 265; see also George Melly and J. R. Glaves Smith, *A Child of Six Could Do It! Cartoons about Modern Art* (London, 1973), pp. 13–14; and, on Zola's support and patronage of the Impressionists, Mitterand, *Zola journaliste,* pp. 58–79.

119 Drumont, *DB,* pp. 187, 498–9 and 549.

120 Drumont, *TA,* pp. 375, 388 and 4–5.

121 Drumont, *OBS,* p. 88.

122 Paul Bourget, *Outre-Mer* (1894), cit. Leger, "Taine et Maurras", p. 105.

123 Drumont, *FJ,* I, p. 341.

124 Drumont, *DB,* pp. viii, 237 and 203–4.

125 Ibid., pp. 226–7; see also *FJ,* II, pp. 81–2; and Daudet, *Les Oeuvres dans les hommes,* p. 162.

126 See, for example, Blum, *Nouvelles Conversations de Goethe avec Eckermann* (1897), *L'Oeuvre de Léon Blum 1891–1905,* p. 223; Sternhell, *Maurice Barrès,* pp. 240–2.

127 See my "A View of the Past". For the similar stress on roots in the Past in German "volkish" ideology, see Mosse, *The Crisis of German Ideology,* chapters 4 and 8, particularly p. 150.

128 Brunetière, op. cit., p. 693.

129 Drumont, *FJ*, I, pp. 30, 418 and 425.
130 Ibid., II, p. 422; also pp. 438–9; and *DB*, p. 22.
131 Drumont, *FM*, p. 37; also ibid., pp. 109–10; *FJ*, I, p. 209; and II, p. 440; and Picard, op. cit., p. 85.
132 Drumont, *FJ*, I, pp. xvi and xviii; also ibid., I, pp. 136 and 274–5; and II, p. 441.
133 Drumont, *OBS*, p. 192.
134 See Drumont, *FJ*, I, p. 147; and II, pp. 82 and 230; *DB*, pp. 11–14; *TA*, pp. 33–4; *OBS*, p. vii; and chapter X, p. 278 above.
135 Drumont, *FJ*, II, p. 104. On the mythology of wine in France, see Barthes, *Mythologies*, pp. 58–61.
136 See Sartre, op. cit., pp. 101–2 and *passim*.
137 For a discussion of the role of the Jews and of Judaism in Hegel's view of world history, see Emil L. Fackenheim, *The Religious Dimension in Hegel's Thought* (Bloomington, 1967), pp. 133–9; and, for further evidence of Hegel's Christian anti-Judaism, see Hegel, *On Christianity, Early Theological Writings* (Chicago, 1948), pp. 177–8 and *passim*.
138 Drumont, *FJ*, I, p. 29. It is hardly necessary to point out that many French Jews were not newcomers at all, and that Jewish cemeteries existed in France in the Middle Ages, and were re-established from the seventeenth century; see Blumenkranz, ed., op. cit., pp. 43, 47, 54, 103–5, 171, 211, 240, 250–2 and 285.
139 Drumont, *FJ*, I, p. 60; and II, p. 278.
140 For a parallel in the ideology of the American "New Right", see Hofstadter, *The Paranoid Style*, pp. 23–4.
141 Drumont, *FJ*, I, p. 442.
142 Drumont, *TA*, p. 174—an interesting anticipation, in crude form, of the thesis of Durkheim's *Suicide*.
143 Drumont, *La France juive devant l'opinion*, cit. Pierrard, op. cit., p. 45.
144 Drumont, *FJ*, I, pp. 438 and 512.
145 Drumont, *DB*, p. xiv.
146 Drumont, "Les Chouans" (16 April 1894), *OBS*, p. 193.
147 Drumont, "Waterloo" (15 November 1894), ibid., p. 305.
148 Cit. Isaac, *Expériences de ma vie*, I, pp. 347–8.
149 See chapter IV, pp. 144, 150–1 and 156 above.
150 Drumont, *TA*, p. xi.
151 Viau, *Vingt ans d'antisémitisme*, p. 8.
152 Drumont, *DB*, p. 462.
153 Drumont, *FJ*, II, p. 101.
154 Drumont, *DB*, pp. 219–20.
155 Drumont, *OBS*, p. 29 (1892); see also *DB*, pp. 496 and 498.
156 Drumont, *TA*, p. 438.
157 Drumont, *DB*, pp. 488–94; and *FM*, pp. 448–60; see also Memmi, op. cit., pp. 101–2.
158 Daily Reports, Prefect of Police, 7 June and 15 February. APP Ba 106.
159 Drumont, *TA*, p. 186.
160 Ibid., pp. 44, 49 and 181; see also *FM*, p. 172.
161 Drumont, *TA*, p. 48.
162 Drumont, *FJ*, I, p. 365; and II, p. 459.
163 Brunetière, op. cit., p. 693.
164 Daily Report, Prefect of Police, 15 February 1898. APP Ba 106; and see chapter III, pp. 117–8 above.
165 Drumont, *FM*, p. 41.
166 Drumont, *DB*, pp. 545 and 462. The term "honnêtes gens" was, of course, a conventional expression in common usage.
167 Daily Report, Prefect of Police, 7 June 1898. APP Ba 106.
168 See chapter X, pp. 277–8 above.
169 Drumont, *OBS*, pp. 86–7.

170 Sorlin, *"La Croix" et les Juifs,* pp. 215–17.
171 Sartre, op. cit., pp. 26–7; see also Verdès-Leroux, op. cit., p. 123.
172 See, for example, Henri Mendras et Yves Tavernier ed., *Terre, paysans et politique: Structures agraires, systèmes politiques et politiques agricoles* (Paris, 1969), pp. 122–3 and *passim;* Mendras, "Un Schéma d'analyse de la paysannerie française", in Marcel Jollivet, ed., *Sociétés paysannes ou lutte de classes au village?* (Paris, 1974), pp. 25–8; Gaston Lanneau, "L'Entraide et la coöpération au village", Fabre and Lacroix, eds., *Communautés du Sud* (Paris, 1975), II, pp. 465–6; and Mair, *An Introduction to Social Anthropology,* pp. 137–42.
173 Sartre, op. cit., p. 30.
174 Drumont, *FM,* p. 443.
175 Drumont, *FJ,* I, p. 438.
176 See, for example, Michel Vovelle, *Piété baroque et déchristianisation en Provence au XVIIIe siècle* (Paris, 1973); and Christiane Marcilhacy, *Le Diocèse d'Orléans au milieu du XIXe siècle: Les hommes et leurs mentalités* (Paris, 1964).
177 Drumont, *FJ,* II, p. 279.
178 Drumont, *FM,* pp. 109–10.
179 Drumont, *TA,* p. 252.
180 Drumont, *DB,* p. 34.
181 Drumont's picture of popular protest in pre-Revolutionary France is by no means a complete distortion, though he does play down the importance of real conflict; see, for example, Bakhtin, *Rabelais and His World,* particularly chapter 3; Le Roy Ladurie, *Les Paysans de Languedoc,* pp. 223–47 and 321–43; Mousnier, *Peasant Uprisings;* Bercé, *Croquants et nu-pieds;* Robert Mandrou, *Introduction à la France moderne (1500–1640): Essai de psychologie historique* (Paris, 1961).
182 Bourget, *Outre-Mer,* cit. Leger, op. cit., p. 105; see also chapter XI, p. 346 above.
183 See p. 631 below.
184 Drumont, *FJ,* II, p. 275.
185 Drumont, *FJ,* I, pp. xiii, 287–8 and 351.
186 See, for example, Lanneau, "L'Entraide et la coöpération au village", pp. 472–81.
187 See chapter X, n. 204.
188 See my "Religious and Social Attitudes in 'Hymns Ancient and Modern' (1889)", *Social Compass,* 22 (1975), pp. 222–4.
189 Drumont, *FM,* p. 109.
190 Drumont, *FJ,* I, p. 435.
191 Drumont, *DB,* p. 229.
192 Drumont, *FM,* pp. 39–40.
193 Mirbeau, *Le Journal d'une femme de chambre,* pp. 151–2 and 341. In the event, Mirbeau shows that this stance is fraudulent, and Joseph robs his employers, for whom he has little respect.
194 See Philippe Ariès, *Centuries of Childhood* (Harmondsworth, 1973), pp. 7–8 and *passim;* and David Hunt, *Parents and Children in History: The Psychology of Family Life in Early Modern France* (New York, 1972), pp. 27–37.
195 Drumont, *TA,* p. 186; and see chapter X, pp. 292–4 above.
196 Lacretelle, *Silbermann,* p. 126.
197 *Le Complôt juif.* AN F⁷ 12463.
198 Drumont, *TA,* p. 99.
199 Report, Police agent, Rennes, 25 July 1899. AN F⁷ 12464; see also Sorlin, *"La Croix" et les Juifs,* pp. 175–80; and my "Catholic Populism in France at the time of the Dreyfus Affair", p. 677.
200 Morin *et al.,* op. cit., pp. 56–9 and *passim.*
201 See, for example, Ardouin-Dumazet, *Voyage en France,* 18e série, p. 373, commenting on the clothes of girls at the market of Etaples: "La plupart des vendeuses sont des jeunes filles ou des jeunes femmes coiffées de chapeaux à fleurs et vêtues de robes de confection. On dirait des bonnes parisiennes endimanchées. Evidem-

ment, les toilettes des baigneuses de Paris-Plage, de Berck et des autres stations du littoral ont une influence désastreuse sur la population féminine, dans les campagnes voisines." Erotic concern and concern about status signified by dress are here implicit in the explicit concern about the disappearance of regional costume.

202 Cit. Drumont, *DB*, pp. 244–5.
203 See Ariès, op. cit., Part III. It is interesting to note that middle-class Jews seem to have been particularly attached to the family in this sense; see Dreyfus, *Cinq années de ma vie*, pp. 26 and *passim;* Lacretelle, op. cit., pp. 52–3; Benda, *La Jeunesse d'un clerc, passim;* Maurois, *Mémoires*, I, pp. 18–19; Gide, *Journals*, I, p. 283 (December 1910).
204 Drumont, *TA*, p. 191.
205 See Nguyen, "Approche de la notion maurrassienne d'*héritage.*"
206 Drumont, *DB*, p. 487; see also *FM*, Book I, "L'Héritier".
207 Drumont, *TA*, pp. 269–71.
208 Drumont, *FJ*, II, p. 451.
209 See Sartre, op. cit., pp. 17 and 82.
210 See Douglas, *Purity and Danger;* Le Roy Ladurie, "La Domus à Montaillou et en Haut-Ariège au XIVe siècle", Fabre and Lacroix, eds., op. cit., I, pp. 170, 178 and 192; and chapter XIII, pp. 486–9 above.
211 See, for example, Le Roy Ladurie, "La Domus à Montaillou", pp. 182 and 214–17; Marc Bloch, *Feudal Society* (London, 1965), Part III; and Mair, *An Introduction to Social Anthropology*, pp. 64–5, 105–6, 110, 133, 135 and 137.
212 Balzac, *Le Curé de village* (London, 1930—Everyman edition), pp. 106–7 and *passim.*
213 Pamphlet, "Union Nationale, Comité d'Action Sociale" (1904). AN F⁷ 12480.
214 Drumont, *TA*, pp. 261–2.
215 See chapter X, p. 293; and chapter XIV, p. 528 above.
216 Drumont, *DB*, pp. 53 and 520. 1889 was the centenary of the start of the French Revolution.
217 Drumont, *FJ*, I, pp. 192–3. Drumont was here quoting de Bréda on the sixteenth century, but claimed that what he said applied to the nineteenth century also— a good indication of his historical sense.
218 Drumont, *FJ*, II, p. 209.
219 Drumont, *DB*, pp. 93–4 and 142.
220 Ibid., p. 321.
221 Drumont, *TA*, p. 331.
222 Drumont, *DB*, pp. 100–1.
223 Drumont, *TA*, pp. 55–6.
224 Drumont, *FJ*, I, pp. 20–2.
225 Drumont, *DB*, pp. 214–20.
226 Gambetta actually used the phrase "une couche sociale nouvelle" at Grenoble in September 1872, and "ces nouvelles couches sociales" at Auxerre in June 1874; see Pierre Barral, *Les Fondateurs de la Troisième République* (Paris, 1968), pp. 228–34. Drumont simply refers to "les *nouvelles couches*".
227 Drumont, *FJ*, I, pp. 539–41.
228 Montesquiou, *Les Raisons du nationalisme*, p. 75.
229 Cit. ibid., p. 78.
230 See Adorno *et al.*, op. cit., pp. 685–9.
231 Drumont, *FJ*, II, p. 11.
232 Drumont, *DB*, p. 318; and *TA*, p. 57.
233 Drumont, "Vaillant devant le jury" (5 January 1894), *OBS*, p. 119.
234 Drumont, *FM*, pp. i–ii, 103 and 2.
235 Drumont, *TA*, p. 46.
236 Ibid., pp. 58 and 171–2.

237 See, for example, Georges Fonsegrive, *L'Evolution des idées dans la France contemporaine* (Paris, 1917); Digeon, *La Crise allemande de la pensée française*, particularly chapter VIII; Hughes, op. cit., chapters 2–4; and Kriegel, *Le Pain et les roses*, pp. 101–2.

238 See, for example, Roudiez, *Maurras jusqu'à l'Action Française;* and Soucy, *The Case of Maurice Barrès*, chapter 2.

239 Guy-Grand, *La Philosophie nationaliste*, p. 17.

240 Drumont, *DB*, pp. 502 and 191–2.

241 Drumont, *OBS*, p. 265.

242 Ibid., pp. 190 and ii. Drumont misquotes *Macbeth* here.

243 Drumont, *TA*, pp. 55 and 49.

244 Drumont, *FJ*, II, p. 247.

245 See Adorno *et al.*, op. cit., pp. 485–6; Ackerman and Jahoda, *Anti-Semitism and Emotional Disorder*, pp. 34–5; Loewenstein, op. cit., pp. 30–1; Memmi, op. cit., pp. 78, 83–4 and 372; and Szasz, *The Manufacture of Madness*, pp. 303–4; also, generally, Barthes, op. cit., pp. 151–2; Ariès, op. cit., p. 399; and Edelman, *The Symbolic Uses of Politics*, p. 31, which show that antisemitism was, in this respect as in others, a development or special articulation of a much more general tendency.

246 Drumont, *DB*, pp. 513–14.

247 See Pierrard, op. cit., p. 174; Roudiez, op. cit., chapter IV; Thomas, *L'Action Française devant l'Eglise;* and chapter XIV, pp. 526 and 535 above.

248 Cit. Guy-Grand, op. cit., p. 49. As a Provençal regionalist, Maurras did want to preserve a considerable amount of local difference, but within a firmly national cultural and political framework.

249 Ibid., p. 56.

250 See Erikson, "Hitler's Imagery and German Youth", pp. 487–8.

251 Barthes, op. cit., pp. 75 and 142–3; see also Beauvoir, *Privilèges*, pp. 105, 146 and 188–92; and Colette Capitan Peter, "Révolutions bourgeoises et Idéologie essentialiste", *L'Homme et la Société*, nos 37–8, (1975), pp. 171–9.

252 Gauthier de Clagny declared, for example, on learning of Dreyfus's arrest in 1894: "Nous avons pourtant une consolation. C'est que ce n'est pas *un vrai Français* qui a commis ce crime.", cit. Reinach, op. cit., I, p. 206 (his italics); see also chapter IV, p. 145 above.

253 Drumont, *DB*, pp. 51 and 549; also ibid., pp. vi, 182, 192, 194 and 285; Picard, op. cit., pp. 54–5; and Bournand, op. cit., p. 29.

254 See my "History and Traditionalism: Maurras and the Action Française".

255 See Ackerman and Jahoda, op. cit., p. 26; and Revel, *Les Idées de notre temps*, p. 410.

256 Picard, op. cit., p. 54.

257 Sternhell, "Le Déterminisme physiologique et racial", p. 13.

258 Drumont, *TA*, p. 331.

259 Sternhell, *Maurice Barrès*, p. 290.

260 Sartre, *Réflexions sur la question juive*, p. 37; see also Sartre, *Les Mots* (Paris, 1972), p. 99.

261 Drumont, *FJ*, I, p. 539.

262 Sartre, *Réflexions sur la question juive*, p. 37.

263 Guy-Grand, op. cit., p. 23.

264 Cit. Pierrard, op. cit., p. 177.

265 Drumont, *FJ*, II, pp. 545, 516–17 and 257–8.

266 Drumont, *DB*, pp. 265, viii and xii–xiii.

267 Boni de Castellane, *L'Art d'être pauvre*, p. 55.

268 Cit. Barrès-Maurras, *La République ou le roi*, p. 271 n.; see also Marlin, "La Droite à Besançon de 1870 à 1914", p. 234.

269 Drumont, *FJ*, I, p. 189.

270 Picard, op. cit., p. 85. It is interesting to see that the very ambiguous idea of

"fraternity" was both accepted and repudiated by antisemites. As J. M. Roberts suggested in a paper on "Liberté, Egalité, Fraternité: The Origins of a Famous Slogan", given at the European History Research seminar at the University of East Anglia in March 1976, the whole topic of the elaboration of the myth of the French Revolution, with its slogans, in the course of the nineteenth century requires investigation, particularly since it still guides or obfuscates the historiography on the period.

271 For Drumont's savage attack on the aristocracy of his day, see, for example, *FJ*, I, p. xi; and II, pp. 72–5, 97 and *passim;* and *TA*, pp. 36–7, 40–5 and 389; for his related attacks on the Royalists, see, for example, *FJ*, I, pp. 276, 341, and 435–8; II, pp. 119, 193–4 and 280; *DB*, pp. 10, 39, 149, 182, 186 and 231; see also, for further illustration and discussion of both, chapter X, pp. 278–9 and n. 269; and chapter XIII, pp. 491–2 above.

272 See, for example, Drumont, *OBS*, p. 110; and chapter X, pp. 278–9 above.

273 See, for example, Drumont, *FM*, pp. 321–2.

274 The Action Française was not originally Royalist, though it became so shortly after its foundation, and received the official support of the Pretender from 1911; and many traditional Royalists found its ideas and methods antipathetic; see Louis Dimier, *Vingt ans d'Action Française* (Paris, 1926), pp. 70 and 187; Osgood, *French Royalism under the Third and Fourth Republics;* and Gaudin, "Chez les Blancs du Midi: du Légitisme à l'Action Française". Although this evolution had much to do with the ideological influence of Maurras, account must be taken in explaining it of more material factors, which provided the framework for the adoption of that ideology. The Royalists, unlike other Right-wing groups, had social networks and important funds at their disposal, and had sought to use the funds in particular to influence or control new Right-wing movements from Boulangism to the Ligue Antisémitique. The conversion of the Action Française to Royalism was thus the culmination of of a structural development spanning more than a decade.

275 Ionescu and Gellner, eds, *Populism,* chapter 7, p. 170.

276 Szasz, op. cit., pp. 303–4.

277 Maurras, *L'Avenir de l'intelligence,* p. 55 (his italics).

278 Loewenstein, op. cit., pp. 23–4, cites a letter from a patient, which stated that Jews "didn't have a country where you could 'place' them like other people."

279 Drumont, *DB*, p. xiii.

280 Picard, op. cit., p. 85.

281 Sartre, *Réflexions sur la question juive,* p. 31.

282 Drumont, *TA,* p. 36.

283 Ibid., p. 236. It is ironic that Léon Daudet, who was later divorced, afterwards joined the staff of *La Libre Parole,* and then became one of the leaders of the Action Française, and one of those who did most to keep Drumont's memory and ideas alive in the inter-war period.

284 Drumont, *DB*, p. 418.

285 See Durkheim, *Suicide,* pp. 378–84.

286 Drumont, *FJ,* II, pp. 262–3.

287 See Mousnier, op. cit., chapter I.

288 But see Louis Dumont's cautionary remarks about the drawing of such analogies. *Homo Hierarchicus,* chapters 10 and 11.

289 See Wirth, *The Ghetto,* p. 15.

290 See Jahoda, "Race Relations and Mental Health, *Race and Science,* UNESCO, p. 480.

291 Cit. Dagan, op. cit., p. 60.

292 Ginsberg, op. cit., p. 208.

293 Beauvoir, op. cit., p. 181. Such institutions and values were not, of course, in fact exclusively "bourgeois", though one can agree that their elaboration into an ideology was a "bourgeois" phenomenon.

294 Péguy, *NJ*, pp. 14–15; and Tharaud, *Notre cher Péguy*, II, pp. 53, 77 and *passim;* see also, for example, *The Confessions of Arsène Houssaye*, p. 319, where the Eiffel Tower is attacked as a symbol of modernity; and Lauris, *Souvenirs d'une belle époque*, p. 282.

295 Péguy, *NJ*, pp. 163–4 and 203.

296 Durkheim, *Suicide*, pp. 286, 380–2 and *passim;* see also D. Parodi, *Traditionalisme et démocratie* (Paris, 1909).

297 Leroy-Beaulieu, *Les Doctrines de haine*, p. 9.

298 Péguy, *NJ*, p. 180.

299 Bernanos, op. cit., p. 49.

300 See, for example, Drumont, *FJ*, I, p. 156; and Rouquier and Soumille, "La Notion de Race chez les Français d'Algérie", pp. 1 and 3–4.

301 Adorno *et al.*, op. cit., pp. 618–19; see also Ackerman and Jahoda, op. cit., pp. 25–9; and Edelman, op. cit., pp. 167–8.

302 Barrès, *Scènes et doctrines*, II, pp. 162–5.

303 See Adorno *et al.*, op. cit., p. 385; Ackerman and Jahoda, op. cit., pp. 37, 40, 61, 75 and 88–9; Jahoda, "Race Relations and Mental Health", pp. 466–9; and Selznick and Steinberg, op. cit., pp. 77–9 and 91, who discount this factor in the United States of the 1960s; see also Durkheim, *Suicide*, p. 285; and Joseph A. Schumpeter, *Imperialism and Social Classes* (1919) (Oxford, 1951), pp. 88–9, for comments on "status anxiety" from the period.

304 See Ackerman and Jahoda, op. cit., pp. 65, 69 and 75; and Stern, *Hitler*, p. 90.

305 Report, Commissaire spécial, Nantes, 13 December 1898. AN F⁷ 12465; see also Sartre, *Réflexions sur la question juive*, pp. 25 and 33–5.

306 See Adorno *et al.*, op. cit., p. 485; and Rose, "The Roots of Prejudice", p. 418.

307 Leroy-Beaulieu, *Les Doctrines de haine*, pp. 7–8, 19–20, 46–6 and 184–273; see also Baudouin, *Psychanalyse du symbole religieux*, p. 206. As an example of the ideological convergence of anticlericalism and antisemitism, one can point to Combes's denunciation of the religious orders as "cosmopolitan" and his claim that they were seeking to "dominate" France; see, for example, Partin, *Waldeck-Rousseau, Combes and the Church*, pp. 163–6.

308 Tharaud, *Quand Israël n'est plus roi*, p. 1; see also Benda, *Les Cahiers d'un clerc*, p. 25 (1936), cited chapter XI, n. 405; Sartre, *Réflexions sur la question juive*, p. 26 and *passim;* and Memmi, op. cit., pp. 207–8.

309 See, for example, Péguy, *NJ*, pp. 186–7; Loewenstein, op. cit., pp. 62 and 110–11; and Memmi, op. cit., pp. 158 and 198–200.

310 Dagan, op. cit., p. v.

311 Memmi, op. cit., p. 52; see also Sorlin, *"La Croix" et les Juifs*, p. 86; Lovsky, *L'Antisémitisme chrétien*, p. 10; Beau de Loménie, *Edouard Drumont*, pp. 12–13; and Glock and Stark, *Christian Beliefs and Anti-Semitism*, pp. 112–20.

312 Leroy-Beaulieu, *Les Doctrines de haine*, pp. 14–15; see also Leroy-Beaulieu, *L'Antisémitisme*, pp. 2–3; and Lazare, op. cit., pp. 228–9.

313 Morin *et al.*, op. cit., p. 82.

314 See, for example, Rosa Luxemburg, *The Junius Pamphlet, The Crisis in the German Social Democracy* (1916) (London, 1967), p. 10 and *passim.*

315 Sartre, *Réflexions sur la question juive*, p. 180.

316 Martin du Gard, *Jean Barois*, p. 284; see also Dagan, op. cit., pp. 84 and 95.

317 For a recent general discussion of this topic, see J.A.C. Brown, *Techniques of Persuasion from Propaganda to Brainwashing* (Harmondsworth, 1963).

318 See, for example, the approaches of Lévi-Strauss and of Leach: Edmund Leach, ed., *The Structural Study of Myth and Totemism* (London, 1967); Leach, *Genesis as Myth and Other Essays* (London, 1969); and Leach, *Lévi-Strauss* (London, 1970), particularly chapter 4.

319 Morin *et al.*, op. cit., p. 82; also ibid., pp. 60–3; and Fenichel, "Psychoanalysis of Antisemitism", pp. 26–7.

320 Douglas, *Natural Symbols*, pp. 169, 184 and *passim.*

321 See Worsley, *The Trumpet Shall Sound;* and Kenelm Burridge, "Cargo", in Pierre Maranda, ed., *Mythology,* pp. 127–35.

322 Among the more perceptive attempts to analyse this development are Theodore Roszak, *The Making of a Counter-Culture: Reflections on the Technocratic Society and its Youthful Opposition* (London, 1970); and, taking a case-study, Wanda Holohan, "Jacquerie sur la Forteresse, Le Mouvement paysan du Larzac (octobre 1970-août 1973)", in Fabre and Lacroix, eds, op. cit., II, pp. 362–432. For an intelligent, if not entirely convincing, answer to the contemporary critique, see Raymond Ruyer, *Éloge de la société de consommation* (Paris, 1969).

PART FOUR
ANTISEMITISM AND THE JEWS

CHAPTER XVII
ANTISEMITISM AND JEWISH PRESENCE: THE GEOGRAPHY OF ANTISEMITISM

W̲E HAVE DISCUSSED ANTISEMITISM SO FAR ON THE ASSUMPTION THAT IT was not mainly a direct reaction to the presence or behaviour of French Jews. We have argued that it was a myth of modernization that selected the Jews as its enemy and as its target in a symbolic way. This it was able, it was impelled, to do because around the Jews was clustered a complex of deep-seated beliefs and attitudes, which can be related to the actual history of the Jews in Christian European society over many centuries, and, more particularly, to the Christian perception of that history. Does this mean that late-nineteenth century antisemitism in France was quite uninfluenced by experience of co-existence with Jews? We shall seek, in this chapter, to answer that question by examining the geography of antisemitism, by trying to discover whether the incidence of antisemitism was in any way correlated with the presence of Jews, and whether antisemitism in areas where there were Jews was in any way different from antisemitism in areas where there were not. Whatever the importance of Jewish presence in stimulating or determining the nature of antisemitism, it was directed against Jews, and, in the remaining chapters of Part Four, we shall assess the aims of antisemitism as far as Jews were concerned, the ways in which it proposed to solve the "Jewish question"; and then we shall discuss the ways in which French Jews reacted to the various kinds of hostility directed against them.

The maps in the first two parts of this book enable one to construct a "geography of antisemitism" in late nineteenth-century France. Map 12[1] shows the departments with a high incidence of antisemitism, taking together the various indicators used in Maps 3, 7, 8, 9 and 11, that is, anti-Dreyfusard meetings in the provinces, the antisemitic riots of 1898, subscriptions to the Monument Henry, local sections of the Ligue Antisémitique Française, and the election of antisemitic deputies. Scores have been allotted to each department on a scale of 0 to 3 for each of the original maps, and have then been added together to produce Score A. To this has been added the number of

MAP 12 DEPARTMENTS WITH HIGH INCIDENCE OF ANTI-SEMITISM BY COMBINED CRITERIA.

Scores of 5 to 9

Scores of 10 and over

times that a department figures in the whole series of five maps (Score B) to arrive at a total Score C. As will be seen from Table VI, most high-scoring departments are high-scoring by both criteria, which considerably increases the reliability of Score C.

We have already discussed the relationship between the incidence of antisemitism by department and the patterns of political opinion and of religious vitality, as established by Goguel, Gadille and others, and we have also suggested that there may have been a correlation with the incidence of agricultural crisis. A number of additional remarks, qualifications and amplifications are appropriate here, before we go on to consider the question of correlation with Jewish presence. First, all the maps indicate that antisemitism was important in a large number of departments in different parts of France. As Lasies told a meeting of the Jeunesse Antisémite in Paris in June 1898, "antisemitism is not only a social question for Paris, but for France as a whole . . ."[2] The value of Map 12, however, of course, is that it allows us to qualify such a remark. The map shows more clearly than the earlier individual maps that antisemitism was strongest, outside the Paris region, in the four corners of France, in the departments furthest from the centre of government and nearest to, if not on, the frontiers. This fits in with its association with nationalism and regionalism, and its hostility towards the State. Map 12 also highlights the political diversity or ambivalence of antisemitism. It was important both in the traditionally Right-wing West, but also in the South-East where the Extreme Left had growing support. But it was strongest in the South-West and in the North-East, including four departments in the Paris basin, both regions that Barral has dubbed "regions in political evolution", the former moving electorally from Right to Left under the Third Republic and the latter from Left to Right.[3] Was antisemitism in some sense an outcome of these shifts, either as a convenient half-way house encompassing both Right and Left, or as a special reaction to a situation of political flux? Map 12 adds, too, to our picture of Catholic antisemitism, confirming our view that antisemitism was not a religious phenomenon as such, but rather a politico-religious one. Fifteen, or one-third of the, high-scoring departments were departments of high religious vitality, but this leaves as many departments of high religious vitality where antisemitism was not important, and 8 high-scoring departments were ones of low religious vitality. Significant also is the fact that 6 high-scoring departments were ones in which there were strong contrasts of religious practice, for example the Pyrénées-Orientales, where practice was high in the West of the department and low in the East.[4] Such constrasts, underlying clerical–anticlerical conflict must have been much more widely present than the departmental map suggests.[5]

A number of other general correlations should be mentioned. 31 departments both experienced revisionist meetings in 1898–9 and had sections of the Ligue des Droits de l'Homme founded in 1899 or shortly after (see Maps 2 and 6); of these, 22 were departments with high antisemitic scores, which means that in half the departments with a high incidence of antisemitism, there was also a high incidence of opposition to antisemitism. This is not very

TABLE VI: Geography of antisemitism by department

Department	Score A	Score B	Score C
Seine	13	5	18
Ille-et-Vilaine	9	5	14
Meurthe-et-Moselle	7	5	12
Seine-Inférieure	8	4	12
Vienne	7	4	11
Loire-Inférieure	7	4	11
Vaucluse	6	4	10
Bouches-du-Rhône	6	4	10
Vosges	6	3	9
Meuse	6	3	9
Nord	5	4	9
Seine-et-Oise	5	4	9
Maine-et-Loire	5	4	9
Rhône	5	4	9
Gironde	5	4	9
Haute-Garonne	5	4	9
Hérault	5	3	8
Gard	5	3	8
Drôme	5	3	8
Marne	4	3	7
Manche	4	3	7
Côte d'Or	4	3	7
Pyrénées-Orientales	4	3	7
Doubs	4	2	6
Belfort	4	2	6
Alpes-Maritimes	4	2	6
Var	4	2	6
Gers	4	2	6
Loire	3	3	6
Charente	3	3	6
Haute-Vienne	3	3	6
Dordogne	3	3	6
Hautes-Pyrénées	3	3	6
Ardennes	3	3	6
Aube	3	3	6
Calvados	3	3	6
Yonne	3	2	5
Lot-et-Garonne	3	2	5
Côtes-du-Nord	3	2	5
Loiret	3	2	5
Savoie	3	2	5
Deux-Sèvres	3	2	5
Haute-Saône	3	2	5
Landes	3	2	5
Indre	3	2	5

surprising, but it does illustrate the localization of the debate about the Dreyfus Affair, as well as emphasizing again that antisemitism was associated with situations of conflict or threatened conflict. Another confirmation provided by the map is that the highest incidence of antisemitism was found in urban departments. Five of the eight departments with scores of 10 and over were among France's most urbanized and industrial departments; and in many rural departments antisemitism seems to have been a mainly urban phenomenon, for example at Toulouse in the Haute-Garonne, at Nantes in the Loire-Inférieure. Again, in relatively urbanized departments, big cities stand out, for example, Lyon in the Rhône, the venue of the 1896 Congress,[6] and Lille in the Nord, from where Drumont's paternal family came incidentally.[7] Nevertheless, this leaves a fair number of rural departments lower down the list of high-scoring antisemitic departments. Two general explanatory factors suggest themselves here. Whereas urban departments were experiencing the strains of immigration from the countryside and in some cases from abroad (five of the high-scoring departments doubled their population in the nineteenth century), many rural departments, such as the Vienne, were experiencing or starting to experience, rapid depopulation.[8] Antisemitism may have been some kind of response to this, as Poujadism was to be later,[9] particularly when rural emigrants were replaced by foreign agricultural labour, as they were in the South-East, for example.[10] It is also possible that there was a connection with concern over natural demographic deficits, that is low birth-rates. The Rhône and the Gironde, for example, were among France's least fertile departments on the eve of the First World War.[11] More evidently, rural depopulation was associated with the agricultural crisis, which hit cereal and wine growing areas much harder than areas specializing in stock-rearing or dairy produce, and tenant farmers more than independent peasants or share-croppers, and which coincided with the eclipse of viable production of a number of industrial crops, such as linen and madder.[12] The departmental unit is a very crude one for the discussion of the pattern of French agriculture, but antisemitism could well be related in the South-West and in the North-East, too, to crises in cereal and wine growing, as we have argued that it was in the South-East.

Looking at some of the high-scoring departments in detail, a few additional factors may be adduced. Antisemitism in the Vienne seems to have been Catholic in tone. A claim was made, we have seen, in 1892 that a case of ritual murder had occurred at Châtellerault. It also seems to have been centred on Poitiers, which had an active antisemitic press. Biez's *Les Rothschild et le péril juif* was published as a supplement to *Le Petit Poitevin* in 1891. Verdès-Leroux notes, moreover, that the diocesan bulletin of Auch (Gers) was extremely antisemitic, giving credence to ritual murder claims.[13] Also relevant perhaps is the fact that the Bishop of Dax in the Landes, in a pastoral letter in September 1885, referred to "the economic crisis which gets worse each day", compared "the unknown maladies" that the vines were suffering with "the plagues of Egypt", and asked: "When God is denied, is it surprising that He asserts himself? ... when His religion is treated as the enemy, is it surprising that He takes vengeance?"[14] This was the kind of "fundamentalist" and "superstitious" Catholicism that tended to go with antisemitism. In the Nord, too, antisemitism was particularly strong at Cambrai, centre of a diocese, whose bulletin was extremely antisemitic in the early 1890s. We have already discussed the South-East in a previous chapter, but some additional points may be made. The diocesan bulletin of Valence in the Drôme was antisemitic. Moreover, Catholic antisemitism in the Midi may have been related to the presence of important Protestant communities, notably in the Gard. However, Protestantism here was very well established,[15] and more resentment may have been caused by Protestant missionary activity in other areas, such as the Nord and the Ardennes.[16] In the South-East again, antisemitism seems to have been particularly strong in Marseille, which had a large immigrant population and direct links with Algeria. Emmanuel Gallian, editor of one of the first antisemitic periodicals in France, the weekly L'Anti-Youtre which appeared in 1891, came from Marseille.[17] In the West, the correlation between antisemitism and political conservatism and Catholicism was by no means comprehensive, since there was a high incidence of antisemitism in only half the Western departments. Peculiar factors are involved in the case of the two highest-scoring Breton departments: the Ille-et-Vilaine was the venue for the Rennes trial, and the Loire-Inférieure was relatively urbanized, and antisemitism there was particularly important in Nantes, although it was not confined to the chef-lieu (the Loire-Inférieure elected 5 antisemitic deputies in 1898, and chose General Mercier as one of its Senators in 1900).[18] In Normandy, a number of factors that we have already discussed generally seem to have been linked with the high incidence of antisemitism in the three coastal departments. First, there was a situation of local political instability. Conservative predominance remained, but was under some threat, particularly in the Seine-Inférieure, which led Maurois to go so far as to say: "Normandy was conservative until the time of the Dreyfus Affair. Then the Radicals took over . . . ",[19] an exaggeration, but a significant one. Then the Manche and the Calvados, as well as being departments of high religious vitality, were also ones of early depopulation. In the Manche, Cherbourg, a naval town, seems to have been particularly prone to antisemitism. Abbé Garnier, a native of the Calvados, stood as a parliamentary candidate there in a by-election in 1895, reaching the second ballot;[20] and it was to Cherbourg that Mirbeau's Joseph retired, to open a cafe called "A l'Armée Française!"[21] Nationalism was also important in the Charente, where Déroulède was elected deputy for Angoulême in 1889 and 1898, and where a Bonapartist, Cunéo d'Ornano, represented Cognac continuously from 1876 to 1898.[22]

But our main task in this chapter is to discover how far the incidence of antisemitism can be linked to the presence of Jews. Map 13 shows the distribution of Jewish population in France in 1866.[23] Some redistribution took place after 1871, but unfortunately no statistical analysis of this has been attempted. However, this may not be too important a gap for our purpose, since memories of past Jewish presence are as significant as present experience of it, and, as far as new Jewish settlement in France is concerned, one knows that, though

MAP 13 JEWISH POPULATION BY DEPARTMENT (1866).

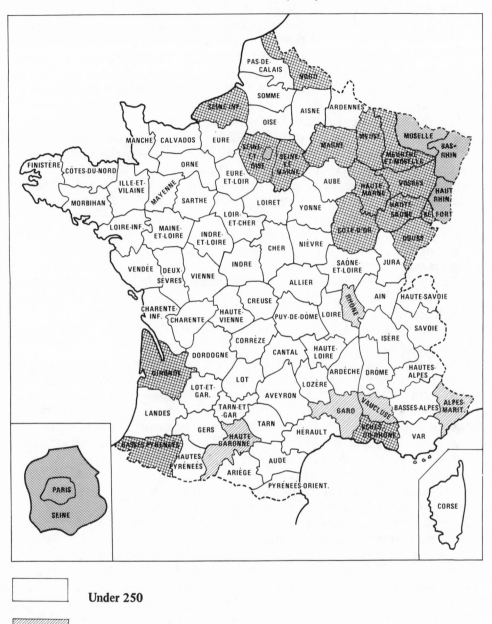

Under 250

250-1,000

1,000-5,000

Over 5,000

some immigrants ventured into new areas, for example, in the West, these were very few, and most went to Paris, or to existing centres of Jewish population.[24] At the end of the century, 60% of France's Jewish population of about 80,000 was concentrated in Paris, and communities of over 600 existed at Marseille (3,500), Bordeaux (2,110), Nancy (1,845), Lyon (1,370), Bayonne (865), Besançon (763), Lille (663) and Reims (640), according to the Consistoire Central. In 1914, there were 30,000 Jews in Alsace-Lorraine.[25] If Maps 12 and 13 are compared, it will be seen that 18, or two-fifths, of the departments with a high incidence of antisemitism were also ones with a relatively high Jewish population, though, in some cases, this meant only several hundred people. The other departments with a high incidence of antisemitism (three-fifths of the total number) had under 250 Jewish inhabitants, and, in at least one case, the Côtes-du-Nord, none at all. By contrast, only one department with a relatively high Jewish population, the Basses-Pyrénées, does not figure on the list of high-scoring departments. There is, therefore, for those 18 departments a strong presumption that antisemitism there was in some way and to some extent a reaction to the presence of Jews, though it should be remembered again that the number of Jews was often very small. The departments concerned fall into four groups: the Nord, the Seine-Inférieure, the Seine and the Seine-et-Oise; the Rhône and four other departments in the South-East; two departments in the South-West; and seven departments in the East. Is there any further evidence that can be adduced to suggest that antisemitism was indeed a reaction to Jewish presence, to the Jews as an actual minority, in the case of any group, or any single department?

We have already produced further statistical evidence which suggests a correlation between the distribution of Jewish population and of militant antisemitism within Paris. We have also referred to resentment at the acquisition by the Rothschilds and other wealthy Jewish families of landed estates in the Paris region.[26] More striking, but again only suggestive, is the very size of the Jewish community in the capital. Beyond this, there is little further direct evidence, for the Seine, the Seine-Inférieure or the Nord, that antisemitism was related there to the presence of Jews. At Lille, for example, Pierrard noted for a slightly later period, the Jewish community remained isolated and remote, outside the experience of most non-Jews.[27] In the Nord, too, as we have seen, other factors were clearly crucial in the generation of antisemitism: clericalism, and the nationalism and popular cult of the army which characterized this and other frontier departments.[28] In the South-East, there had long been Jewish communities, which had been the objects of hostility in the past,[29] and this may have provided a ground upon which modern antisemitism could build. Zola, for example, recalled in 1899 that "at Aix . . . where I spent part of my youth, a feeling of scorn for the Jews existed in a latent state among several families; by instinct, they detested the Jews";[30] and Drumont quoted Mistral in *La France juive* on the deeply-rooted popular antisemitism at Avignon.[31] But, on the other hand, there seems to be some truth in the idea that age-old coexistence had led to a certain tolerance in the Midi,[32] and we have argued that antisemitism in the South-East was the means for expressing grievances that had nothing to do with the local Jewish population, which was anyway small and declining. All of this applies with probably more force to the South-West, where, as we have seen, the presence of an ancient Jewish community in the Basses-Pyrénées provoked little or no demonstration of antisemitism in the period.

In the East, however, the situation does seem to have been different, and the situation there is somewhat better documented. Alsace and Lorraine had old and important Jewish communities, and hostility towards Jews there does seem to have been closely related to the economic functions which they actually fulfilled. Juillard has described their role in Basse-Alsace in the early and mid-nineteenth century in these terms:

> Cattle merchants, usurers, dealers of all kinds, they . . . lived in the small towns and in certain villages where they formed up to 20 or 30% of the population, but they were strictly excluded from the peasant community and were sometimes grouped in what amounted to ghettos. Their presence dispensed the villagers from almost all contact with the outside world. They were just about the obligatory intermediaries for the sale of livestock, of grain and of real estate, for buying cloth and various essential utensils, and even for arranging marriages between wealthy parties.

He pointed out that the Jews lost this dominant position in the last third of the century (after Alsace had become German), but that they retained control of the livestock market.[33] This supports Drumont's contention that "in Alsace, a peasant cannot sell his cow without having recourse to a Jew as a middleman."[34] The economic function of Jews in Lorraine, and perhaps elsewhere in the East, was similar; Jews acted as slaughterers, for example, in the Metz region in the 1870s.[35] Moreover, complaints against Jews from the East in the *Cahiers de Doléances* of 1789[36] as well as in the Enquête sur les Conditions du Travail Industriel et Agricole of 1848[37] were specifically directed against their activity as money-lenders and middlemen. This pattern seems to have continued later in the nineteenth century. "Who is exploiting the peasant?", asked a poster in Senones (Vosges), in February 1898; "The Jew!";[38] while stickers distributed by the Ligue Antisémitique Française at Vesoul in August 1898 were addressed to "farmers and peasants . . . ",[39] as we have seen. Referring simply to Jewish presence, *La Croix Meusienne* pointed out in February of the same year that Jews were more numerous in the Meuse than in most other departments in France.[40]

Antisemitism in the East thus seems to have been a long-standing response to Jewish presence and economic activity, an authentic popular tradition, as many witnesses testify. Durkheim, who was born at Epinal, and who was the son of the Chief Rabbi of the Vosges and the Haute-Marne, recalled in 1899 that the Jews had been blamed in the East for the French defeat in 1870, as they had been for the economic crisis of 1847–8.[41] Barrès, another Lorrainer, referred, also in 1899, to "the traditional antisemitism of Mulhouse", and claimed to have had direct experience of "Jewish life" in Lorraine and of the hostility which it provoked.[42] Stock, the son of a peasant from the Metz region, spent his childhood in Lorraine, and wrote after his conversion to Dreyfusism: "I don't think that I have ever rid myself completely from that antisemitism which was stuffed into my head as a child . . ."[43] Claudel's youthful antisemitism can probably be explained in the same way: he came from Bar-le-Duc, and both his father and his sister were antisemites.[44] Again, Gyp told Bournand in 1898: "I remember, when I was very small, I spent my holidays in the East, at Nancy,—where there was a Jewish quarter—people detested them there already at that time . . ."[45] We have seen, of course, too, that the riots and demonstrations of 1898 were particularly numerous and violent in the East, and the situation remained tense there afterwards. There was a further demonstration, for example, at Epinal in June 1899;[46] and troops were sent to a number of towns in the region in September 1899 as a precautionary measure on the eve of the announcement of the Rennes verdict.[47]

The context of antisemitism in the East obviously changed after the cession of Alsace and other territory to the German Empire, and with the movement of Jewish population away from the countryside and from the region, though many Jews from Alsace did not move too far from home. The nationalist element in antisemitism became more important. The Ligue Antisémitique stickers mentioned above appealed to "patriots" as well as to "peasants". The police reported in February 1898 from Epinal, where the antisemitic movement was said to be less important than elsewhere, that "persons worthy of esteem are critical of the tolerance that has been shown to the Jews up till now. Some of them believe that the Jews are capable of systematically serving the interests of a neighbouring power . . .";[48] and a local "Nationalist and antisemitic group" was formed at Belfort in 1901.[49] Clericalism, too, must have been a factor, particularly in the Vosges, a department of high religious vitality, though Verdès-Leroux points out that the diocesan bulletin of Saint-Dié was much more realistic in its attitude towards the Jews than some of its counterparts in Central and Western departments, where there were no Jews. It is safe to conclude therefore that antisemitism in the East was, to an important extent, though not exclusively, a response to Jewish presence.

What we have said applies to Lorraine, but can it be extended to other Eastern departments, to Champagne or the Franche-Comté? Almost certainly not to anything like the same degree, although the evidence is negative. Two pointers, however, exist, which suggest some link between antisemitism and Jewish presence there. Supposing that antisemitism acquired in childhood earlier in the century probably stems from popular attitudes vis-à-vis local Jewish communities, it may be significant that a number of prominent antisemites came from this part of France. Proudhon came from Besançon.[50] Colonel Henry was born at Pogny in the Marne.[51] The cartoonist Willette was born at Châlons-sur-Marne and educated at Dijon, while Forain came from Reims.[52] Less vague, but essentially short term, a number of Eastern departments had Jewish prefects in the early years of the Third Republic, as Drumont pointed out. Isaïe Levaillant was Prefect of the Doubs from 1883 to 1885, and Sée, was Prefect of the Haute-Saône at the same time.[53] Drumont also mentioned Hendlé in the Saône-et-Loire and an unnamed Jewish

Prefect of the Territory of Belfort.[54] However, objection to these men seems to have stemmed from the fact that they were militant Republicans and anticlericals rather than simply from the fact that they were Jews.

We must now turn to the more numerous high-scoring departments, where the Jewish population was very small or non-existent. The contrast with the situation in the East was obvious to contemporaries. Reinach noted, for example, that antisemitism was strong in Brittany:[55]

> There were without doubt very few Jews there, and thus no local cause of hostility against Dreyfus, caused by merchants or dealers in money of his race, who were either too successful or too rapacious, as would have been the case in Lorraine: but if antisemitism was unknown there in its economic form, in its religious form it was more deeply rooted than elsewhere; it was part and parcel of a Catholicism that was still intact, and at once mystical and savage . . .

Similarly, Siegfried wrote in 1913 of the West as a whole:[56]

> Jews were sometimes involved, not unsuccessfully, in urban electoral politics; but they were unknown in the countryside, and nowhere did they form, as in the East or in Alsace, those tightly-knit groups intimately associated with the rest of the population, which was economically dependent on them and which detested them. If antisemitism exists in the West, it has nothing in common with that of Alsace; instead of deriving, like the latter, from popular roots, it is purely theoretical: it is not a sentiment, it is a doctrine.

Moreover, Brunellière, as we have seen, wrote in March 1900 that the clergy and Catholics generally in the rural areas around Nantes were very antisemitic, "which is all the more curious in that there is not a single Jew in the countryside".[57] This assumption, itself significant, that antisemitism ought to be related to Jewish presence, was shared by some antisemites. A member who had spent several months in Brittany reported to the Jeunesse Antisémitique in Paris in June 1898 "that the antisemites are not organized in this province, since there are very few Jews there, save at Brest where they own some shops."[58] There is no doubt that antisemitism in the West was a Catholic and conservative phenomenon, but Reinach's interpretation requires some qualification, as we have suggested, for antisemitism was not evident to the same degree in all departments. The most antisemitic Breton department, the Loire-Inférieure, was also the most urban. Other factors to be considered are population movement, previously mentioned, local economic difficulties, and nationalism. Reinach also suggested that antisemitism in the West was linked with Anglophobia, which may indeed have been significant in the naval ports of Brest and Cherbourg, and possibly in fishing ports. All of this confirms that Jewish presence is of little or no significance in explaining antisemitism in this region, although it may have occasionally made some minor contribution. Philippe Robin tells the narrator in Lacretelle's *Silbermann* that at Houlgate in the Calvados, "there were too many Jews . . . You can't get away from them, on the beach, in the casino. My uncle Marc left after three days."[59] But this fictional example really proves the general point, for it does not refer to Jewish residents, and the antisemitism which it evokes was certainly not prompted by the experience which it recounts. In most South-Western departments, the absence of Jews was again striking. As Jacques Duclos recalled of his childhood in the Hautes-Pyrénées at the time of the Affair: "To hear people talking about a Jew was for me a novelty. I had never heard those in my village mention this variety of men about whom so much fuss was being made."[60] Here, once more, as we have argued before, antisemitism must be understood against a background of defensive Catholicism, political change, and, perhaps, nascent economic "backwardness".[61]

If one excepts the East and some quarters in Paris and perhaps other large cities, all of this supports the conclusion, arrived at by many students of antisemitism in other situations, that it does not arise primarily from direct experience of Jews or of coexistence with Jews. As Selznick and Steinberg put it, with reference to the United States, "people become prejudiced not by becoming acquainted with Jews, but by becoming acquainted with the prejudiced beliefs current in their environment."[62] Contemporary critics in France reached the same conclusion. Lazare wrote in 1894 that "the Jew is only one of the factors contributing to antisemitism; he provokes it by his presence, but that is not the only or determining factor."[63] More emphatically, and referring to France in particular, Péguy declared: "The antisemites talk about the Jews, but the awful truth must be told: THE ANTISEMITES KNOW NOTHING ABOUT THE JEWS. They talk about them, but they do not know them . . ."[64] And Duroselle, pointing to the small size of the total Jewish population in France, has suggested that antisemitism there was qualitatively different from antisemitism in Germany or in Russia at the same period.[65] This is probably too simple, but other aspects of antisemitism in France certainly reinforce the view that it did not arise from acquaintanceship with Jewish communities. Sorlin has pointed out that "the Bonne Presse was not concerned with the Jews, but with the Jew in the singular"; and over 60% of the editorials in La Croix referred to the Jew in the abstract, and not to the real Jewish communities in France;[66] and this lack of specificity is characteristic of French antisemitic propaganda in general. Moreover, as has been noted for the United States in this century,[67] prejudice or hostility against Jews in late nineteenth-century France was usually combined with prejudice and hostility against other groups, Protestants, Freemasons and foreigners in general, which does not suggest that such antisemitism was primarily a response to the Jews and their actual behaviour and activities. It has been pointed out, too, that Drumont was quite unacquainted with Jewish life and culture,[68] and such ignorance was indeed the rule among antisemites and others. Memmi wrote later that "one of my surprises on coming to Europe [from North Africa] was to hear the positive reality of the Jews so often denied."[69]

Furthermore, as has often been emphasized again in other contexts,[70] even when Jews were present, living in close proximity to them by no means implied real acquaintanceship with them or spontaneous reaction against them. They were perceived according to gross stereotypes, as Mauriac and Pierrard make clear. Many antisemites, of course, boasted of knowing the Jews collectively, or Jews individually,[71] but, though they might have Jewish friends, acquaintances or mistresses, this made no impact one way or the other on their antisemitism. Mirbeau made this point in *Le Journal d'une femme de chambre* by depicting both Marianne the cook and Célestine as antisemites, though the one "knew nothing about the Jews" and the other had worked for Jewish employers.[72] Similarly, Gregh recalled that, at the time of the Affair,[73]

> when I was dining one day with friends, they began to run down the Jews. I pointed out to them that they had no right to do this, since they were very close friends of the Strauses, and were the intimates of others who were one hundred per cent Jewish. They were charming and very intelligent people; but the old blind religious prejudice . . . was too strong to be gainsaid, even in the case of these agnostics.

One can conclude that there were two kinds of antisemitism in France, measured by antisemitism's relationship with the Jews: one a response to the Jews as a minority, the other a "doctrine" or an ideology, independent of direct Jewish presence. The former characterized the East, but by no means exclusively so; the latter predominated in the rest of France.[74] The former was a more traditional phenomenon and often expressed specific economic grievances; the generation and dissemination of the latter, building on the basis of the former, was a modern phenomenon, and expressed much wider and vaguer discontents. It was modern, both in the sense that it was a reaction to modernization, as we have argued in the previous chapter, and also because it depended on the existence of a literate national culture and a mass-medium as its vehicle. The religious element was strong in both, but its function was significantly different. In "traditional" antisemitism it represented an attitude of orthodoxy towards a real religious minority. In "modern" antisemitism, it expressed the fears of a Catholic minority in the face of a secularization symbolized by the Jews. Paradoxically, modern antisemitism in France not only lacked direct links with the Jews and with Jewish culture, but seems to have developed and become more ideologically extreme as these links were severed, through assimilation, on the one hand, and through the growing "compartmentalization" of modern social life, on the other.[75] Christian theology and coexistence in the past presented the Jews as scapegoats and targets; but the elaboration of antisemitism as a modern myth required the dilution of both, for its Jews were largely symbolic entities, rather than individual souls or actual inhabitants of social reality. This will become clearer if we turn to consider the professed aims of the antisemites vis-à-vis the Jews, and their proposed solutions of the "Jewish question".

NOTES

1 Our map differs in some respects from that of Sorlin, *"La Croix" et les Juifs*, p. 221. Departments of high incidence not included on his map are the Manche, the Calvados, the Indre, the Charente, the Dordogne, the Landes, the Lot-et-Garonne, the Gers, the Hautes-Pyrénées, the Gard, the Var, the Alpes-Maritimes, the

Yonne, the Seine-et-Oise, the Marne and the Ardennes. This is partly, but not entirely, to be explained by the fact that he uses as indicators only the existence of antisemitic groups and the occurrence of antisemitic demonstrations.

2 Daily Report, Prefect of Police, 9 June 1898. APP Ba 106.

3 Barral, "Géographie de l'opinion sous la Troisième République", pp. 151–3.

4 See Sorlin, *La Société française, 1840–1914*, Map VII, p. 219 (after Gadille).

5 See, for example, Theodore Zeldin, ed., *Conflicts in French Society: Anticlericalism, Education and Morals in the Nineteenth Century* (London, 1970). It is significant that 6 high-scoring departments experienced serious incidents during the Inventories crisis in 1906; see Mayeur, "Géographie de la résistance aux Inventaires", p. 1261.

6 See, for example, Drumont, *La France juive*, I, p. 322; and Mayeur, "Les Congrès nationaux", pp. 172–85.

7. See, for example, Drumont, *Le Testament d'un antisémite*, pp. 151–2; and *La Derniere Bataille*, pp. 229–30 and 258–9; and Pierrard, *Juifs et catholiques français*, pp. 94–5, 142 and *passim*.

8 See generally Sorlin, *La Société française*, Map VIII, p. 236; and, on the depopulation of the Vienne, which began in the 1890s, Jean Pitié, *Exode rural et migrations intérieures en France: L'exemple de la Vienne et du Poitou-Charentes* (Poitiers, 1971), p. 347 and *passim*. (I am grateful to Roger Price for this last reference.)

9 See Hoffmann, *Le Mouvement Poujade*, pp. 12–14; Kornhauser, *The Politics of Mass Society*, pp. 148–9.

10 See Merlin, *L'Exode rural*, p. 115.

11 Vaucelles, *"Le Nouvelliste de Lyon"*, p. 3.

12 See Zolla, *La Crise agricole*, pp. 71, 122 and *passim*; and Imbart de La Tour, *La Crise agricole*, pp. 27–9, 32–3, 108 and 122–6.

13 Verdès-Leroux, *Scandale financier et antisémitisme catholique*, pp. 120, 129 and 148–9. The diocesan bulletins of Luçon (Vendée), Laval (Mayenne) and Montauban (Tarn-et-Garonne), in this general area of France, also gave credence to ritual murder claims.

14 Mgr Delannoy, *Lettre pastorale portant communication du décret de la Sacrée Congrégation des Rites sur la dévotion au Saint Rosaire*, 22 September 1885, cit. Barral, *Les Agrariens français*, p. 82.

15 See Le Roy Ladurie, *Les Paysans de Languedoc*, p. 188 and *passim*; and Vovelle, *Piété baroque et déchristianisation*, p. 564.

16 See Mours et Robert, *Le Protestantisme en France*, pp. 109, 297 and 343. They also mention missionary activity in the Aisne, where Copin-Albancelli stood as an "anti-Masonic" candidate in the 1893 general elections; see Divry, *L'Abbé Garnier*, p. 57.

17 Drault, *Drumont, La France juive et La Libre Parole*, pp. 70 and 75.

18 Reinach, *Histoire de l'Affaire Dreyfus*, VI, pp. 57–8.

19 Maurois, *Mémoires*, I, p. 147; see also Barral, "Géographie de l'opinion", p. 149; and Goguel, *Géographie des élections françaises*, pp. 21–39 and 67–73. In fact, all deputies elected in the Seine-Inférieure in 1902 were conservative or Right-wing, and all but one in 1893 and 1898, but the Radical and the Socialist percentage of the vote was rising in the two decades before 1914.

20 Divry, op. cit., pp. 58–62.

21 Mirbeau, *Le Journal d'une femme de chambre*, pp. 164, 247, 330 and 345–7.

22 Grenier, *Nos Députés, 1898–1902*, pp. 84 and 86.

23 This map is based on that provided by Szajkowski, "The Growth of the Jewish Population of France", p. 317.

24 See Blumenkranz, ed., *Histoire des Juifs en France*, pp. 308–10 and 324–5; and Marrus, *The Politics of Assimilation*, pp. 30–5, who stresses the difficulty of obtaining reliable demographic data; see also Bloch, *Lévy*; and ... *Et Cie*, on Jews who moved to the West.

25 Blumenkranz, ed., op. cit., pp. 348 and 367.

26 See chapter IV, p. 132; and chapter VI, p. 189 above.
27 Pierrard, op. cit., pp. 297–8.
28 On the popular cult of the army in the Nord, see Ardouin-Dumazet, *Voyage en France*, 18e série, pp. 119–20.
29 See Szajkowski, "The Decline and Fall of Provençal Jewry"; Szajkowski, "The Jewish Community of Marseilles at the end of the 18th century", *Jews and the French Revolutions*, pp. 281–96; and Blumenkranz, ed., op. cit., p. 268 and *passim*.
30 Dagan, *Enquête sur l'antisémitisme*, p. 19.
31 Drumont, *FJ*, I, pp. 217–18.
32 See, for example, Landau, "Aspects et problèmes spécifiques de l'histoire des Juifs en France", pp. 238–9.
33 E. Juillard, *La Vie rurale dans la plaine de Basse-Alsace, Essai de géographie sociale* (Paris, 1953), pp. 447–8.
34 See chapter X, n. 225.
35 See Stock, *Mémorandum d'un éditeur*, III, p. 14.
36 See David Feuerwerker, "Les Juifs en France, Anatomie de 307 Cahiers de do-léances de 1789", *Annales*, 20 (1965), pp. 45–61, indicating also considerable support for positive measures to improve Jewish status; and Blumenkranz, ed., op. cit., pp. 274–6; see also Bourguet, "Une Race d'administrés", p. 17.
37 See, for example, Kahan-Rabecq, *Réponses du Département du Haut-Rhin à l'Enquête faite en 1848 par l'Assemblée Nationale sur les conditions du travail industriel et agricole* (no place, 1939), pp. 74–5.
38 See chapter X, n. 227.
39 Report, Commissaire spécial, Vesoul, 15 August 1898. AN F⁷12461.
40 *La Croix Meusienne*, 13 February 1898.
41 Dagan, op. cit., pp. 60–1; and Lukes, *Emile Durkheim*, pp. 39 and 41.
42 Barrès, *Scènes et doctrines du nationalisme*, I, pp. 158–9; *Mes Cahiers*, II, pp. 116–17, 247–8 and 342–3; Barrès-Maurras, *La République ou le roi*, p. 428.
43 Stock, op. cit., p. 15.
44 See Gamzon, "Claudel rencontre Israël"; and Galpérine, "L'Exégète et le témoin", *Cahiers Paul Claudel*, 7, pp. 73–81 and 152–3.
45 Bournand, *Les Juifs et nos contemporains*, p. 134; also pp. 136–7.
46 Telegram, Prefect, Vosges, 25 June 1899. AN F⁷12458.
47 See, for example, Report, Gendarmerie, Saint-Dié, 10 September 1899. AN F⁷12465.
48 Report, Commissaire spécial, Epinal, 19 February 1898. AN F⁷12474.
49 Report, Commissaire spécial, Belfort, 25 December 1901. AN F⁷12455.
50 See Silberner, "Proudhon's Judeophobia", p. 61.
51 Paléologue, *Journal de l'Affaire Dreyfus*, p. 34 (editor's note).
52 See Byrnes, "Jean-Louis Forain: Antisemitism in French Art", pp. 249 and 252–6.
53 Marlin, "La Droite à Besançon", p. 230.
54 Drumont, *FJ*, II, pp. 417–20; *TA*, p. 366.
55 Reinach, op. cit., V, p. 201.
56 Siegfried, *Tableau politique de la France de l'Ouest*, p. 391; see also Verdès-Leroux, op. cit., p. 123, virtually repeating Siegfried.
57 Brunellière, Letter, 12 March 1900. Willard, ed., *La Correspondance de Charles Brunellière*, p. 172.
58 Daily Report, Prefect of Police, 23 June 1898. APP Ba 106.
59 Lacretelle, *Silbermann*, p. 11.
60 Jacques Duclos, *Mémoires 1896–1924* (Paris, 1968), p. 49.
61 On the "backwardness" of the South-West, see, for example, André Armengaud, *Les Populations de l'Est-Aquitaine au début de l'époque contemporaine, Recherches sur une région moins développée (vers 1845–vers 1871)* (Paris and The Hague, 1961), pp. 463–7 and generally; and Fabre and Lacroix, *Communautés du Sud*, I, p. 30.
62 Selznick and Steinberg, *The Tenacity of Prejudice*, pp. 19–20; see also Fenichel,

"Psychoanalysis of Antisemitism", p. 32; Loewenstein, *Christians and Jews,* p. 23; Ackerman and Jahoda, *Anti-Semitism and Emotional Disorder,* pp. 82–4; Robb, *Working-Class Anti-Semite,* p. 159; and Glock and Stark, *Christian Beliefs and Anti-Semitism,* p. 186. Similar findings exist on attitudes towards coloured immigrants in Britain, where, according to a recent study, prejudiced views are more likely to be accepted from the media by those who lack real contact with immigrants; see Hartmann and Husband, "The mass media and racial conflict".

63 Lazare, *L'Antisémitisme,* p. 21; also p. vi.

64 Péguy, *Notre Jeunesse,* p. 183 (his capitals); see also p. 176.

65 Duroselle, "L'Antisémitisme en France", pp. 52–3. A thorough testing of such a comparative generalization would be of great interest, but it would have to encompass the peculiar case of the United States as well as Britain and Italy.

66 Sorlin, *"La Croix" et les Juifs,* p. 132.

67 See Levinson, *The Authoritarian Personality,* chapter IV, pp. 145–50, and chapter V, p. 207; and Christie and Jahoda, eds., *Studies in the Scope and Method of "The Authoritarian Personality",* p. 153.

68 See Prolo, *La Caverne antisémite,* pp. 23–4; and Pierrard, op. cit., pp. 38–9.

69 Memmi, *Portrait d'un Juif,* p. 306.

70 See, for example, Wirth, *The Ghetto,* p. 27; and Rose, "The Roots of Prejudice", pp. 398–9.

71 For example, Goncourt, *Journal,* 18, p. 47 (24 June 1891); Drumont, *DB,* pp. 114 and 137; Barrès, *Mes Cahiers,* I, p. 232; Barrès-Maurras, op. cit., p. 129; and Donnay, *Des Souvenirs,* pp. 302 and 304–5, who had his first sexual experience with a Jewish woman; see also Fenichel, op. cit., p. 32, generally.

72 Mirbeau, op. cit., p. 105.

73 Gregh, *L'Age d'or,* p. 258. There is evidence, however, that real and close friendship with Jews could occasionally overcome antisemitic prejudice, as it seems to have done in the case of Claudel; see Gamzon, op. cit., pp. 73–82.

74 There seems to be a parallel here with the distinction drawn by Selznick and Steinberg between Black antisemitism in the United States, which they see as a "hearsay" but also an "existential" phenomenon, and White antisemitism there, which they see as a purely "hearsay" phenomenon. Selznick and Steinberg, op. cit., pp. 128–9.

75 It may be relevant to note here that a Polish rural mayor observed that hostility towards Jews increased in his country as relations between Jews and Catholics became less close, less direct and less personal, as a result of Jewish migration from the countryside to the towns in the early decades of this century; see *From Serfdom to Self-Government: Memoirs of a Polish Village Mayor 1842–1927* (trans. William John Rose) (London, 1941), pp. 91 and 268–9.

CHAPTER XVIII
THE AIMS OF ANTISEMITISM

T HE FRENCH ANTISEMITES AT THE END OF THE NINETEENTH CENTURY proposed a wide range of solutions to the "Jewish question". These ranged from full assimilation through various legal controls to expulsion and extermination. Both the first and the last would, by very different means, have destroyed the Jews as a social entity, while legal controls would have maintained them as a distinct but inferior group. Generally speaking, one could identify the former as characteristic of "modern" antisemitism, antagonistic towards or oblivious of Jewish social reality and actual distinctiveness, and the latter as characteristic of "traditional" antisemitism, which was conscious of both and prepared to recognize them on its own terms. Nevertheless, traditional solutions were quite unrealistic in the modern French context, and we shall adopt a humanistic criterion, regarding assimilation as the least extreme solution and as one pole of a scale of increasing violence. Having discussed the various solutions, we shall consider how far they are to be seen as serious practical proposals, how far as ritual or rhetoric.

Assimilation was a very general aim or expectation, shared to a considerable extent by Jews themselves, as Marrus has indicated.[1] It was seen as a solution to the "Jewish question" by a number of "conventional", as against "professional", antisemites. Père Monsabré, as we have seen, hoped that the Jews would be absorbed completely into non-Jewish society through encouraging intermarriage by fiscal means, and through bringing up the children of mixed marriages as Catholics.[2] Arthur Meyer rejected the confiscation of property, exile or massacre as solutions, and regarded full assimilation as the only alternative. For this to come about, he added, it would be necessary to reassure Jews that "the ghettos are closed for ever".[3] A socialist variation on assimilationism was provided by Clovis Hughes, who considered "the Jewish question" to be an aspect of capitalism which "would find its natural solution in the realization of the idea of proletarian revolt."[4] But, as we have pointed out in a previous chapter, the "professional" antisemites were very hostile to the idea of assimilation, which they believed was impossible to implement, though fostered as a means of Jewish infiltration and ultimate domination. Their minimal solution, if one can put it that way, was to use their propaganda to put people on their guard against the Jews, and to frighten the latter into maintaining a low profile. Drumont wrote, for example, with reference to *La France juive,* that "the Semite was less bold, once he had been stripped naked, publicly whipped and exposed to the general regard in all his hideousness."[5] Drumont's writings were intended to unmask the largely secret power and influence of Jews collectively and individually, and thus to reduce their harmful potential. The same intention lay behind the disclosure in *La Croix* and *La Libre Parole* of the names of Jews occupying positions in the civil service and the army,[6] as well as the publication of departmental *Indicateurs des Juifs.* Praising Napoleon's policy of registering Jews, Drumont wrote, again, that "a Jew whom one can see, a Jew whom one knows is a Jew, is comparatively harmless . . ."[7]

This leads on to the antisemites' call for the imposition of legal controls on the Jewish population. First, there was a demand for a ban on Jewish immigration into France. The Conférence Molé–Tocqueville, for example, as we have seen, invited the government in 1898 "to take the necessary measures to stop the dangerous invasion [of France] by the Jewish race".[8] Going further, it was also proposed to reverse Jewish emancipation within France. In *La France juive,* Drumont urged that the Jews be returned to their pre-Emancipation status, thus losing their full rights as citizens: "One could do something for the Jew along the lines, for instance, of that wise Roman practice which distinguished between the full Roman citizen and the junior Latin inhabitant . . ." Other models suggested were the Jewish Statute of St Louis and, as we have noted above, the Jewish legislation of the First Empire, which imposed restrictions on economic activities and residence, as well as setting up a register of Jews.[9] Later, Drumont suggested that the American solution of "the Chinese question" might be a model for the solution of "the Jewish question" in France.[10] Such proposals were very generally supported and propagated by antisemites. Barrès, for example, in an article in *Le Courrier de l'Est* in 1889, called for "special legislation on the Jews . . ."[11] *La Croix,* in the early 1890s, proposed what it called a "Russian" solution to the "Jewish question", which meant the removal of civic rights, strict legal controls and surveillance.[12] Abbé Garnier, in *Le Peuple Français,* "demanded that the Emancipation of 1791 be reversed, because, he said, as so many others have done, the Jews are not, and never have been, French."[13] The Antisemitic Congress of Lyon in 1896 passed a resolution in the same vein: "The decree of 1791, which gave the rights of French citizens to the Jews, must be repealed, as well as the Crémieux decree on Algeria."[14] Again in 1897, Mgr Anselme Tilloy opposed the fusion of "the Jewish race with the French race through the medium of a common legal status."[15] Explicitly relating such proposals to the concept of hierarchy which we discussed in an earlier chapter, and ostensibly rejecting more extreme solutions, Léon Daudet declared later[16] that, kept under close surveillance by a power as clear-sighted as the monarchy, the Jew would be tolerable and almost acceptable . . . To persecute Israel would be unwise and odious. But to lay down guidelines limiting Jewish activity, particularly in the political sphere, would be a very good thing, and a benefit that Jews themselves would quickly appreciate . . . Many intelligent and prudent Jews are beginning themselves to feel the need for order, for an order which puts them, cordially but firmly, in their place.

Within the context of this "state antisemitism", as the Action Française leaders later called it,[17] certain emphases may be noted. The call to deprive Jews of full civil and political rights was invested with concreteness only as far as Algeria was concerned, where the aim was actual disenfranchisement and the reversal of recent naturalization. As far as metropolitan France was concerned, antisemitic proposals were much vaguer, save in the case of restricting the naturalization of immigrants.[18] It is characteristic that calls to recognize that Jews were not of French nationality were preferred to proposals for the removal of specific rights, reflecting the conviction of antisemites that nationality was not something that could simply be conferred by law.[19] Also relevant in explaining this vagueness is the fact that many antisemites were interested in more extreme solutions. There was, however, one area in which "legal" antisemitism was specific, and that was the very general call for the exclusion of Jews from the civil service and from the armed forces.

From the early 1890s, La Croix urged that Jews be banned from all government employment, including the field of education.[20] L'Indépendance de Franche-Comté declared in February 1895: "Let us leave the Jews alone and not persecute them as in the Middle Ages. But, at the same time, let us ensure that they are not placed in positions, in the army, in the magistrature, in the administration of finance, where they are in command of Christians."[21] The Antisemitic Congress of Lyon in 1896 resolved that, until Emancipation could be totally reversed, "Jews should be, at least, excluded from teaching in state schools, from the magistrature, from employment in public administration and from rising above the ranks in the army . . .";[22] and the same demands were reiterated in abbé Puig's Solution de la question juive in 1897,[23] and in much antisemitic propaganda in subsequent years. The Union Nationale section at Vincennes, for example, passed a resolution in January 1898 calling for "the exclusion of Jews from public office"; while the Ligue Antisémitique Française group of the 18th arrondissement of Paris heard a speech in March of the same year, in which preventing Jews "from entering the army or any branches of the civil service" was said to be a central part of the antisemitic programme.[24] Also in March 1898, as we have seen, the Agricultural Association of the Est declared, in an electoral programme, that it would only support "those candidates who pledged themselves to propose, support and pass a law depriving Jews of the franchise and banning them from positions in the civil service and the armed forces".[25] The proposal to disenfranchise the Jews was unusual, but the second part of the programme was not. In Paris again, in May 1898, Devos called on the antisemitic deputies, at a Ligue Antisémitique meeting in the 11th arrondissement, "to demand that Jews be banned from all public offices"; and, at another Ligue Antisémitique meeting in June, Gervaize, the deputy for Nancy, promised that he would heed this call and act on it in the Chamber of Deputies.[26] In *La Gazette de France* in January 1899, Maurras joined the chorus;[27] and, later that year, two of the contributors to Dagan's *Enquête* singled out the exclusion of the Jews from "public functions" as one of the main "policies" of the antisemites.[28] As a final example, Barrès, in a speech at a meeting of the Ligue de la Patrie Française at Saint-Dié in January 1900, "said, that, while the Jews should be tolerated, they should also be removed from all positions of public authority."[29]

Although most antisemites seem to have wanted a total ban on Jewish employment by the State, some proposed instead a *numerus clausus* or Jewish quota.[30] Many antisemites, too, looked for legislation to implement the ban, but others were opposed to this means, either because they had "democratic" scruples, or else because they thought it impracticable, or through a mixture of the two. Picard, for example, was in no doubt about the need to exclude Jews from public office. "The real solution", he told Dagan, "lies in the exclusion of Jews from all positions of political authority in Aryan countries";[31] and he wrote earlier of the need to maintain "a healthy suspicion vis-à-vis the Jews, and a reluctance to entrust governmental or pedagogic functions to them . . ." But, although he proposed "Draconian legislation" to prevent speculation on the Stock Exchange, he ruled out legislation directed exclusively against the Jews. This, he said, would represent an abandonment of the egalitarianism cherished by the modern Aryan; and thus "the Jew would have to be excluded from governmental functions by custom and convention rather than by law . . ."[32] Antisemites did not restrict their attention to Jews in public employment, although this preoccupied them particularly. Bishop Meurin, for example, wanted to ban Jews from the liberal professions, commerce and banking.[33] Other antisemites supported him in this, and proposed additional legal disabilities, including a ban on the ownership of land, and a special tax on trading by Jews.[34]

The idea of special Jewish legislation was taken a stage further with proposals for the restoration of legalized ghettos. This was implied in Maurras's plea in January 1899 that Jews should be treated "like foreigners and like dangerous foreigners: this was the precaution taken in the Middle Ages", though he went on to refer to the more recent precedent provided by colonial administrative practice.[35] Abbé Desportes, abbé Jacquet and Mgr Tilloy were more explicit on this subject,[36] as was an entry to the *Libre Parole* subscription of 1901–02, which expressed the wish: "Let's return the Jews to the ghetto."[37] Related to this, another mediaeval precedent was invoked by Drumont, who declared in *La France juive:* "We will make you wear the yellow robe again, my dear Sem"; and: "If Jews were obliged to wear a yellow badge, this would be of great service to many people who are easily deceived . . ."[38] Much the same proposal was made by Martinez in 1890, who suggested that "the authorities" should again require Jews to wear the yellow circlet of the Middle Ages "to protect the people against the legion of exploiters who are devouring them!"[39] In addition to affording economic protection to non-Jews, Drumont claimed that making Jews wear marks of identification would put on their guard those "who, hearing them declaim against our religion, imagine that they are upholding the cause of Progress . . ."[40] More directly, another entry to the *Libre Parole* subscription of 1901–2 called for "the disappearance of the synagogues".[41] On the whole, however, as we saw in chapter XIV, such open attacks on Judaism and advocacy of official religious intolerance were rare.

Legal controls and disabilities also included the expropriation of Jewish wealth. In *La France juive*, Drumont proposed in general terms that excess Jewish wealth should be confiscated, and, more particularly, that half the estate of Jews should be appropriated by the State when they died.[42] In *La Dernière Bataille*, he returned to the proposal and made its redistributive and radical implications clear: "It is clear that five hundred determined antisem- ites, allowing for those who might lose their lives in the operation, could become the masters of Paris within a year, and could then distribute to the people the money that the Jew has stolen."[43] Similarly, Fore-Fauré called for the total confiscation of the Rothschild fortune, and of all Jewish fortunes over the sum of 500,000 francs. This money was to be used, he proposed, to provide smallholdings of land and small shares in businesses for the poor: "In this way the Jewish millions, instead of fighting against us, would be made to work with us to improve the living standards of the worker and to increase the prosperity of France. In this way the civil war over cash would be brought to an end."[44] A number of conservative antisemites also proposed the confiscation of Jewish wealth, for example Bishop Meurin[45] and Paul de Cassagnac, who wrote in 1898 that "the Jews ought to be alarmed about the expropriation of their wealth which is imminent [and which] public opinion would regard as an act of legitimate reprisal."[46] Moreover, Père Bailly declared in *La Croix* in No- vember 1890: "We do not demand that the deicide people be massacred . . . But we do demand that they be bled of their gold, which is the blood of our people, for that gold is made of our sweat, since the Jew does no work, but only speculates."[47] Though *Le Pèlerin* continued to support this idea, it was, however, later abandoned by *La Croix*. As Sorlin explains, and as the proposals of Drumont and Fore-Fauré indicate, expropriation, even of Jews, was an attack on property rights, and evoked images of popular revolution and "communism" that did not generally commend it to conservatives.

So far we have dealt with solutions to the "Jewish question" which assumed that Jews would remain in France, though, as some commentators pointed out, antisemitic propaganda and harassment, as well as the proposals for special status and expropriation, were perhaps intended to induce them to leave the country. According to Molinari, for example, the aims of the antisem- ites, as expressed at the Lyon Congress of 1896, were to exclude Jews from public life, "then to draw up lists of Jewish traders and business-men and to organize local leagues in order to deprive them of their customers; in a word, to force them to emigrate."[48] And Elisée Reclus commented in 1899: "There is talk of killing, of exile, of internment, of expropriation . . . and, without waiting to be expelled, several Jews have already left France of their own accord in order to escape insult."[49] A few antisemites opposed the idea of forced Jewish emigration or expulsion. Bishop Meurin argued that it was not a real solution in that it simply shifted the problem to another country; it would also display "a lack of charity", and would be an indiscriminate measure "too hard on those among the Jews who are not guilty of the crimes committed by that audacious handful who exploit the nations by means of Freemasonry."[50] Barrès also opposed expulsion in 1889, though on different grounds; he argued that it would offend the principles of the French Revolution, and also endorsed the view that it would harm the French economy as the Revocation of the Edict of Nantes, effectively expelling the Huguenots, had done.[51] Picard, who, as a racialist, did not accept Meurin's view that one could make significant distinctions among Jews, was yet lukeward towards expulsion. In 1892 he conceded that it was a possible solution, but in 1899 he told Dagan that it was impractical. As in the area of public employment, he preferred voluntary to compulsory legal measures, and suggested that Jews should be positively encouraged to emigrate to their old homeland or elsewhere.[52] However, Léon Daudet argued later that voluntary emigration was a highly unlikely eventuality in the French case,[53] and most antisemites in the period seem to have supported the idea of expulsion.

In *La France juive* Drumont invoked historical precedents in its favour. In the past, he declared, when the Jews had infiltrated Christian societies, after a time, "there generally arises, in those countries which have not fallen into total decadence, a man of energy, who, armed with a vigorous broom, sweeps all those people beyond the frontiers." And he wrote of the expulsion of the Jews from France at the end of the fourteenth century:

> Thanks to the elimination of this poison, France, which was still plunged in the horrors of the Hundred Years War, was able to attain very rapidly an incredible degree of prosperity; she became the great European nation, predominant both militarily and in the fields of literature, the arts and of taste . . . Within France, everyone was if not rich, at least happy, for the Jew was no longer there to prey on the labour of others with his usury. In a word, from 1394, the date when she expelled the Jews, France rose continuously. From 1789, the date when she took back the Jews, France has been in continuous decline . . .

More generally, he boasted that France "has been the only European nation to extirpate the Jews completely from its midst".[54] In 1890, he wrote that people were saying: "If only someone would rid us of the Jews at any price! Send them back to Palestine and let's hear no more about them!";[55] and he declared in 1891 that the aim of the antisemitic movement was to put "the [Jewish] corrupters and invaders the other side of the frontier".[56] In the same vein, *La Croix* called in the early 1890s for pressure to be put on Jews to emigrate, as in Russia, and the newspaper also advocated direct expulsion.[57] Moves were also made at this time to implement such demands. In November 1891 Laur proposed the expulsion of Jews from France in the Chamber of Deputies; this and a similar proposal to expel the Rothschilds received the support of about 30 deputies. Again, in November 1894, Vicomte d'Hugues, deputy for the Basses-Alpes, called in the Chamber for an anti-Jewish "Revocation of the Edict of Nantes".[58]

Such demands were renewed with vigour at the height of the Dreyfus Affair. *La Croix*'s advocacy of expulsion became more urgent.[59] In 1897, Ernest Renault published a tract entitled *L'Expulsion des Juifs.*[60] Guérin and other leaders of the Ligue Antisémitique Française campaigned in 1898 for expulsion "after complete dispossession".[61] Gyp told Bournand the same year: "You ask what I want . . . *To see them leave France,* and hence to really scare them! I don't personally ask for them to be killed. I am not so ferocious as that. But let's drive them out, let's not do like the Russians who keep them and herd them into special areas. Let's drive them out!"[62] Such demands seem to have echoed or influenced popular opinion, for, again in 1898, 40 travelling salesmen from Brest sent an address to General Boisdeffre, which called for the expulsion of the Jews from France;[63] and a speaker at a Union Nationale meeting in Roanne in March 1899 made the same call,[64] which was also incorporated in a popular antisemitic song by Félix Sorlin, published that year: "They are a race of vermin,/They don't look very pretty,/They should be expelled/Or else have their brains bashed out."[65] As a final example of this general support for the expulsion of the Jews, the deputy Firmin Faure told an audience at a gala evening held at the headquarters of the Union Nationale in Paris in June 1902: "France will not be truly France until we have shown the Jews the door."[66]

As Gyp's remarks and Sorlin's song indicate, expulsion was sometimes, but not always and not unambiguously, seen as an alternative to more violent solutions, and it is to these that we must now turn, remembering that the solutions already discussed were regarded, more often than not, as means of intimidating the Jews. First, antisemites frequently intimated that some kind of spontaneous popular movement against the Jews was all but inevitable. Drumont declared, in *La France juive,* that the long-suffering Aryan had always eventually defended himself against the Semite: "Suddenly aroused, he . . . seizes again the sword that was lying in a corner, lays about him, and inflicts on the Semite who has been exploiting him, stealing from him, cheating him, one of those terrible punishments, whose effects the latter suffers for a period of centuries"; and he prophesied that "on the day that the Catholics become tired of defending a society that has become exclusively Jewish, and let the have-nots march on the finance houses and banks, as the convents and monasteries have been marched on, then these erstwhile beggars, become today's tyrants, will be crushed, though their blood will leave no more trace than the kosher meat which they eat."[67] In 1891, he wrote, again, that Jewish triumphs always ended in "a horrific catastrophe", and that, in the last twenty years, "the Jews have conquered Paris, piled up disasters and ruins and excited hatreds which are only waiting for an opportunity to manifest themselves in the most terrible way."[68] And, evoking governmental rather than popular action this time, he declared in 1890 that, were a Richelieu in power, "he would arrest the traitors, have them judged by a military tribunal and shot at Vincennes",[69] a perfect illustration of how the Dreyfus Affair was prepared for by existing antisemitic preconceptions. Barrès was making similar declarations at the same time. He wrote, for example, in an article in *Le Courrier de l'Est* in May 1889: "The excesses of certain Jews and the hatred which their adversaries bear towards them, could very soon lead to serious troubles"; and, in another in January 1890, he warned that, if the Semitic race persisted in "fighting the Gallic race", it could very well "disappear one of these days in a terrible upheaval".[70] A similar warning was issued by Bishop Meurin in 1893:[71]

> There is reason to believe that the public conscience will be aroused against the Jews . . . and it will not be the first time that popular indignation, held down for too long, has exploded and committed regrettable acts of violence against the Jews . . . Don't think, you Jews, that you will be able to escape the calamity which again threatens you! Your deicide nation has now arrived at one of those apogees of power and prosperity, which recur so often in your history, and which lead without fail to a great misfortune for your people.

And, in the same vein, at the end of the decade, *La Croix* proclaimed: "If the police and the government remain powerless, exasperated citizens must take the law into their own hands";[72] but here already warnings about imminent popular reaction were merging with the deliberate advocacy of violence against Jews.

The two, in effect, had always gone together. Drumont suggested in 1890 that the victims of Jewish speculation should gather outside the homes of the Rothschilds and throw stones;[73] and, in *La France juive*, he had gone further, writing approvingly of the burning of Jews in the past, and suggesting that a modern military leader should imitate the example of the seventeenth-century Vitry and use his sword against "the foreign Jews who are oppressing his country".[74] In *La Libre Parole* in March 1896, moreover, he advocated the execution of a few leading Jewish financiers as a kind of deterrent,[75] a course that *La Croix* had also recommended in the early 1890s.[76] Similarly, Morès called, at the Neuilly meeting of the first Ligue Antisémitique in 1890, for the "lynching" of Jews;[77] and Biez declared in 1891: "Since I respect the labour of the poor and hate the acquisition of wealth by foul means, I dare . . . to denounce the Rothschilds and to designate them as targets for the anger of the people . . ."[78] Again, in a speech at a gala organized by the Jeunesse Antisémite in January 1898, Jarre said that the war against the Jews should be waged without mercy, with revolvers if necessary, and drank "to the death of Reinach and B. Lazare". In June of the same year, at another Jeunesse Antisémite gathering, Firmin Faure declared that, if he did not succeed in getting the name of the rue d'Austerlitz, which, he claimed, was inappropriately inhabited entirely by Jews, altered, "he would have the place set on fire so as to burn the vermin which is swarming there"; and, in the same month, at a Ligue Antisémitique function attended by the Algerian deputies, Guérin praised the behaviour of Algerian antisemites and "hoped that French antisemites, too, would meet violence with violence".[79] In this context, one of the contributors to Dagan's *Enquête* also pointed to the importance of the Algerian example in encouraging the advocacy of violence among French antisemites, though he estimated that they knew the scope for violence in France to be strictly limited: "Drumont . . . has learned that, on African soil, one can effectively revive a massacre of Saint Bartholomew, which is impossible in France itself."[80] It should be noted also that the advocacy of violence against Jews does seem to have been genuinely popular, as the antisemitic leaders claimed. Our study of the Henry Subscription suggests this, as well as the use of the theme in public meetings, and the testimony of observers like Viau.[81]

One should add here that some antisemites were opposed to violent solutions, either on humane or on Christian grounds or as a result of more practical considerations. *La Croix,* for example, declared in August 1890: "As far as violent and above all bloody means are concerned, the Church, although it has the mission of combatting Anti-Christ and therefore of fighting against Judaism, has always condemned them"; and *Le Pèlerin* echoed this in 1892, pointing out that "the Church has always disapproved of acts of violence . . ."[82] However, as we have seen, the position of *La Croix* had become more ambiguous by the late 1890s, and the paper did then threaten the Jews with popular violence and selective executions. Barrès also declared against violent solutions in 1890, writing in *Le Figaro:* "If the antisemites simply confine themselves to their: 'Down with the Jews!', it is obvious that their movement will not last long. When the first Jew is killed, the movement will collapse. Parties based on passions are at the mercy of the smallest events that sway public opinion."[83] As we shall see, Barrès was soon to abandon this stance. Guided by the same "realism" as his friend, however, Maurras maintained his hostility to the extremes advocated by most leading antisemites in the late 1890s. He wrote in *La Gazette de France* in December 1898: "Care must be taken not to pass a law against the Jews which persecutes them, that is to say which injures them as human beings."[84] Again, he wrote to Barrès in March 1899 to inform him of a meeting which had been called "to mount an energetic antisemitic and nationalist propaganda campaign, but of a less violent kind than that of Drumont and Guérin. The leaded canes of the latter, the articles of the former arouse too much alarm. There is room to do something analagous to what they are doing and along the same lines, but in a lower key and aimed at a rather different section of the public";[85] and, much later, he declared: "We do not want the Jews to be hanged . . ."[86] Maurras was here echoing the Manifesto of San Remo, issued by the Duc d'Orléans in February 1899, which, in proclaiming the Pretender's support for antisemitism, also proclaimed his "firm opposition to persecution . . ."[87] But such scruples, principled or prudent, were not the rule among "professional" antisemites at least, and we must now discuss their advocacy of Jewish massacre or extermination.

First, the testimony of contemporary observers will be considered, and it will be seen that many, probably most, of those interested in the issue believed that this ultimate violence was the aim of antisemitism. In *Le Salut par les Juifs* in 1892, Bloy referred to the antisemites' "threats of extermination", and, as we have seen, he claimed that many of the clergy were "inflamed by the hope of some imminent violent reckoning in which the blood of Israel" would be spilt on a vast scale.[88] In 1898 Elisée Reclus declared that "the antisemites believe the Jews to be harmful and would like to see them massa-cred."[89] Jaurès agreed with this view, writing, in *La Dépêche de Toulouse* in December of the same year, that "extermination" or, at least, expulsion were the only serious solutions that antisemitism offered: "Beyond them, there is nothing and the barbaric policy of M. Max Régis is the only logical one. What then is the air of mildness that M. Drumont sometimes adopts all about? and whom is he trying to deceive? His policy is the policy of the wolf; and he can only soften it by denying it altogether."[90] This view was shared again by Arnoulin, who wrote in 1902 that "the final aim [of the antisemites] is the extermination and the plundering of the Jews and the destruction of the Republic";[91] and by Péguy, who told the antisemites in 1910: "Basically, what you want is that the Jews should not exist."[92] Observers also claimed that such aims were not confined to the antisemitic leadership but had real popular support. A French journalist writing in *Le Journal de Bruxelles* in February 1898, for example, claimed that "the idea of a Saint Bartholomew's massacre of the Jews has struck the French people like a flash of lightning." Were a war with Germany to break out, he declared, "I am sure, as sure as I am of anything, that, the next day, there would be no Jews still alive in France. They would all have their throats cut."[93] And this fear was, of course, echoed years later by Jules Isaac, who also referred to "a new Saint Bartholomew's massacre against the Jews and the Protestants" as a distinct possibility in 1898.[94] There were some dissenters from such dire assessments, notably Leroy-Beaulieu, who wrote that most antisemites in France did not advocate killing Jews: "they sense that, though it remains a practice in Eastern states, massacre no longer has a place in French politics";[95] but such reasonable optimism was not, as we have noted, the prevailing tone among observers of antisemitism at the height of the Dreyfus Affair.

Which view represented what antisemites were actually saying or propos-ing? We have seen that a number of prominent antisemites expressed their opposition to the use of violence against Jews, but this was often done in a highly ambiguous way. Maurras, for example, whom we saw deploring violent methods on tactical grounds in a private letter in March 1899, published an article in January of the same year, in which he stated: "Certainly, a bloody repression is inevitable."[96] Barrès, opposed to massacre in 1890, again it seems on tactical grounds, was writing, or proposing to write, to Drumont a decade later, as we have seen: "Your 'Down with the Jews!' does not shock me. [When I was a child], we used to 'kill' the Jews on Good Friday."[97] Again, Picard dismissed massacre as a solution to the "Jewish question" in these equivocal terms:[98]

> History offers us examples of more radical cleaning-up operations. Races that have stood in the way of the civilization of their superiors have been exterminated [like the Aztecs or the Incas] . . . But these ruthless practices

are impossible in Europe where the Aryan soul has reached such a high level of humanity. Only infrequently, does a popular explosion or a local massacre reveal anything of the old tendencies.

Even Déroulède apparently opposed Jewish extermination mainly on the grounds that it was impractical.[99]

The attitude of Drumont on this question is clearly crucial, but it is characteristically difficult to pin down. Léon Daudet, writing after the First World War and clearly anxious to show his old master in a favourable light, claimed: "Drumont was certainly not at all bloodthirsty. The very idea of a Russian pogrom inspired him with horror, and no one has spoken, with more scorn for the perpetrators and more pity for the victims, of the revolutionary September Massacres."[100] However, Arnoulin, a hostile critic, but writing at the time of the Affair, asserted that Drumont's policy was "to massacre the Jews, recover their wealth and distribute it to the people".[101] And, going further back, one of Drumont's early disciples, R. Lamilot, also claimed in 1887 that he "sentenced to death the Jew who is oppressing us".[102] The evidence of Drumont's own writings seems to bear out the view of Arnoulin and Lamilot rather than that of Daudet. As we have seen, vague catastrophes involving the Jews were frequently evoked there. Further, in *La Dernière Bataille*, Drumont referred to the "extermination" of the Jews and described them as being "condemned"; again, he wrote: "When the final crisis comes, when the atmosphere is charged with electricity, nothing will save the Rothschilds. The Jews will perhaps succeed in destroying France, but they will die in its ruins."[103] In *Le Testament d'un antisémite*, he protested: "I have never called for your rabbis to be shot", but he wrote elsewhere in the same work that the Dominicans of the Spanish Inquisition "were ardent patriots, *patriots like us . . .* to save their country, they did not hesitate to kill all the Jews . . ."[104] Finally, he wrote in *La Libre Parole* in November 1894, in a passage which seems to be related to the quotation from *Le Journal de Bruxelles* above: "Yes, our day will come . . . If France suffers some defeat, all that we have said . . . will come back to people's minds in waves of sudden anger. This cry: The Jews! It is the Jews! will recover the real meaning that it used to have for French people in the past . . . It will sum up every sort of indignation; it will justify every excess." To which he added: "A few innocent people may perhaps find themselves involved, mistaken for, mixed up with the guilty . . ."[105]

Other antisemites left fewer grounds for uncertainty about their views on this subject. "Only the gallows is sufficient to make the Jews pay for the evil which they have done us", declared Georges Meynié in 1888.[106] "Strike without hesitation and crush the vermin that is preying on you!", urged an article in *Le Courrier de l'Est* in April 1891, signed "The Anti-Yid".[107] By the late 1890s such exhortations seem to have become more common, and, as we have seen in examining the Henry Subscription, calls for the extermination of Jews were an important element in popular antisemitism during the Affair, when the slogan "Death to the Jews!" was commonly shouted at meetings and demonstrations. Millou, for example, wrote in *La Croix* in 1898 that the Jews were in danger of ending up like Judas "at the end of a rope in the potter's field";[108] and Bournand retailed an alleged statement by Max Nordau to the effect that "the extermination of the Jews has begun . . ."[109] A placard put up in Le Mans in February 1898 declared: "Worker, your only enemy is the Jew. Let's hang him on the nearest lamp-post";[110] while stickers appearing at Lille in the same month and claiming to speak for the Duc d'Orléans, promised: "when I am back in power, I will be damned if I will accept the domination of the Jews! Down with the Jews! Death to those who are sucking the blood of the French people!"[111] In mid-1898 again, as we have seen, Paul Lapeyre asked, in *La Sociologie Catholique:* "What is the massacre of a few thousand Jews, when set against the millions of Christians reduced to starvation or misery, or prevented from being born, by the usury, the exactions, the malpractices of the Jews?"; and he recommended that one Jew be put to death for every alleged victim of this Jewish persecution.[112] Less calculating, the president of the Ligue Antisémitique section in the 2nd *arrondissement* of Paris declared in June 1898 that the aim of the Ligue was "to do away with the Jews if that is possible";[113] and an antisemitic marching song published in the same year had this chorus: "Death to the Jews (Repeat)/They must be hanged/Without delay/Death to the Jews! (Repeat)".[114] On the more directly popular level, the testimony of a Perpignan newspaper is of interest. An editorial of *L'Indépendant des Pyrénées-Orientales* commented in January 1898, after the outbreak of disturbances in the town:[115]

> Young people who want to seem important went about the town shouting: "Down with the Jews!" Then someone happened to repeat the slogan: "Death to the Jews!" and then another yelled: "Let's kill the Jews." A witness tells me that the heard two workers, yesterday evening, agreeing on a proposal to go to the homes of our Jewish co-citizens and "do all the Jews" This is monstrous and provokes the most sombre reflections.

Another indication of such violent attitudes at the popular level is provided by Mirbeau's Joseph in *Le Journal d'une femme de chambre,* who averred: "Ah! if I was in Paris, my God! I'd kill . . . I'd burn . . . I'd take the guts out of some of these damned yids!"[116]

We must now attempt to assess the significance of these various proposals for the solution of the "Jewish question" and of the aims of antisemitism vis-à-vis the Jews. Did the former represent a realistic programme? Were they seriously intended? What support do they give to the idea that there is "a logic of destruction" inherent in antisemitism? What strikes one first about French antisemitic "aims" is their multiform and ambiguous nature. One can distinguish up to a point between those antisemites who preferred moderate and those who preferred extreme solutions, and there is a general chronological movement towards extremism from the early to the late 1890s, but, as we have seen, most antisemites proposed both moderate and extreme solutions at the same time, and there was no lack of extremism well before the Affair. It is characteristic, too, that solutions were often suggested or implied, notably by Drumont, rather than being directly and concretely presented. As Yves Guyot told Dagan in 1899, "the measures proposed by the antisemites . . . are vague. No one in France has dared to formulate an integrated piece of legislation on the matter."[117] Léon Daudet admitted later that Drumont had failed to provide a positive policy to overcome "the Jewish ascendancy": "the slogan 'France for the French' clearly represents a programme and a fine programme, but the master did not sufficiently indicate how it might be realized in practice, that is, in political terms."[118] Similarly, Leroy-Beaulieu described the antisemitic movement in 1902 as being composed of "vague groupings whose activities, in many ways, did not belong to the normal political arena".[119]

This would support the view, expressed by Sartre and others,[120] that antisemitism was not orientated towards political action or the implementation of a programme at all, resembling in this respect more recent "populist" movements, which, as Wiles has written, were "moralistic rather than programmatic" in function, and which, in MacRae's words, inhabited an "apocalyptic fantasy world, full of sadistic elements, holocausts, and retributive punishments on a cosmic scale",[121] but a world that remained one of fantasy. Although the advocacy of violence was taken at its face value by some contemporaries, as we have seen, others regarded it in this non-realistic light. A. Servanine, for example, declared in 1898:[122]

We are quite convinced that M. Drumont is not seriously contemplating the massacre of the Jews. If, by some extraordinary means, he were granted sovereign power, a man of his intelligence and moral stature would surely not give the signal for a series of bloody executions. And how many other antisemites, who shout: "Death to the Jews!" with conviction, are in effect much more harmless than they themselves believe, and would, if it came to it, be incapable of harming a fly, let alone a Jew! Many antisemites, ferocious in theory, but whose imaginary cruelty would recede if it were ever a question of putting it into practice, are really like Flaubert's Bouvard and Pécuchet, who loved simply to copy out from Machiavelli and other authors the most terrible maxims, brutal precepts and formulae of torture and violence.

In support of this interpretation, one can point to the fact that antisemitic sadism and evocation of death can be adequately explained as functions of sexual antisemitism and of a negative millenarianism respectively, as we have argued in previous chapters.[123] It is also significant that antisemites did not threaten violence against the Jews alone. Drumont, for example, regretted that a military *coup* had not been carried out after the Commune in 1871;[124] and he told Bournand in 1898: "I see no way out of the terrible situation in which we find ourselves, save by a general revolution which will sweep away our existing masters . . . ."[125] As we have seen, the idea of a *coup* was fairly generally supported by antisemites in the late 1890s.[126] Moreover, Drumont called on Catholics in 1891 to wage a new war of the Vendée against the government;[127] and, like others, he evoked another Massacre of Saint Bartholomew against the Protestants as well as against the Jews.[128] Similarly, Père Bailly of *La Croix* proclaimed in general terms in 1892: "Long live the violent!";[129] and the Ligue Antisémitique Française boasted of being a "revolutionary" as well as an antisemitic organization.[130] Again, it should be remembered that popular movements in France, as doubtless elsewhere, had a tradition of employing bloodthirsty rhetoric that rarely reflected their actual behaviour or real intentions,[131] a tradition that was maintained by late nineteenth-century Socialists and syndicalists.[132]

Nevertheless, it remains that the Jews were the focus of antisemitic threats, and that these threats, on the verbal level, tended to escalate towards the extreme of extermination. Does this support the argument, suggested by Jaurès in the passage cited above, and later elaborated by Sartre, Memmi and others, that what the antisemite "desires, what he is preparing is the *death of the Jew*";[133] that the identification of the Jew with "absolute evil . . . means quite specifically that his accuser requires that he suffer the penalty of death: in the end, negative identification can only lead to the reduction of the Jew to nothing, to the suppression of the Jew from the antisemite's world"?[134] To answer this question, we must examine some other aspects of the antisemites' "aims". First, there is the familiar idea that the Jews served as scapegoats, which was clearly put forward by Durkheim in 1899:[135]

When society undergoes suffering, it feels the need to find someone whom it can hold responsible for its sickness, on whom it can avenge its misfortunes; and those against whom public opinion already discriminates are naturally designated for this role. These are the pariahs who serve as expiatory victims. What confirms me in this interpretation is the way in which the result of Dreyfus' trial was greeted in 1894. There was a surge of joy on the boulevards. People celebrated as a triumph what should have been a cause of public mourning. At last they knew whom to blame for the economic troubles and moral distress in which they lived. The trouble came from the Jews. The charge had been officially proved. By this very fact alone, things already seemed to be getting better and people felt consoled.

Three points may be made about this theory of antisemitism, which has been very generally endorsed by previous chapters in this book. By the very analogy on which it is based, it underlines the ritual nature of antisemitism. Concomitantly, neither on the level of explanation nor on that of action, is antisemitism, by this theory, "realistic". Since the real issue is not the "Jewish question", but other grievances expressed through it, what happens to real Jews is, in a sense, irrelevant, and what the antisemite seeks via the Jews is "symbolic reassurance", to employ Edelman's term.[136] But, by the same token, as Sartre perceived, in order to provide reassurance for the antisemite, the Jew must always be there: "Unfortunately for the antisemite, he has a vital need of the enemy whom he wishes to destroy." Thus the destruction of the Jew must be renewable and his death symbolic.[137]

The same conclusion may be arrived at from another angle. French antisemites, as we have seen, saw themselves very often as "justiciars",[138] and violence against the Jews was frequently regarded as punishment. Drumont, for example, called in 1890 for "a necessary punishment" of the Jews;[139] and he told Bournand in 1898 that the Jews were laying themselves open to "just reprisals". Paul de Cassagnac wrote similarly that "the threat suspended today over the heads of the Jews" was "the inevitable, fatal punishment" for their crimes.[140] It has been argued in this connection by Memmi and Loewenstein that the extreme violence preached by modern antisemites against the Jews was the product of a spiral of guilt and self-justification. Since the Jews had been brutally persecuted in the past, it followed that they must have been guilty of terrible crimes; but the description of these (imaginary) crimes in its turn called for further persecution and punishment.[141] Drumont provided a minor example of this process at work in *La France juive*. He claimed that Reinach wanted "to drive out of the country, to exterminate" French recidivists, and this provided grounds in turn for a call to expel or to massacre the Jews.[142] This again illustrates the "non-pragmatic" nature of antisemitism. Punishment to some extent preceded the supposed crime, which was afterwards discovered to justify that punishment, and, again, the further punishment which was threatened in this ahistorical schema was a moral imperative, almost a divine ordinance, collective and symbolic payment for collective and symbolic guilt. It was "fatal", "inevitable", in the hands of destiny rather than of human actors. We are far indeed from "the normal political arena", from the realm of practical social or political action. Again, given the vagueness and the vastness of accusations against the Jews, only the direst apocalyptic outcome seemed appropriate. As Hofstadter has written of the "paranoid leader", he "does not see social conflict as something to be mediated and compromised, in the manner of the working politician. Since what is at stake is always a conflict between absolute good and absolute evil nothing but complete victory will do. Since the enemy is thought of as being totally evil and totally unappeasable, he must be totally eliminated." But, again, the context is metapolitical, metaphysical, and the solution sought is symbolic.[143]

But there is yet another consideration which suggests as strongly that antisemitic declarations of total war on the Jews require special interpretation. As we have many times insisted, the attitude of the antisemite towards the Jews, real or mythical, was profoundly ambiguous, and there entered into it, as Poliakov has said, "an element of implicit or even explicit admiration".[144] The Jews had endured centuries of persecution; the Jews had retained their collective identity and traditional values; the Jews had special qualities of intelligence, application and business acumen; the Jews had, from a position of weakness, come to dominate all the other peoples among whom they lived; so many themes by which nineteenth-century antisemites acknowledged and implicitly celebrated the superiority of their enemies. "The Jew is an aristocrat", declared Gougenot des Mousseaux in 1869, "whom poverty and hard times have overwhelmed, degraded, who suffers derogaticn in a thousand ways, but for whom the state of degradation is a mask, behind which he maintains the sense of having noble blood, a pride that is only waiting to revive."[145] *La France juive* is full of such tributes. Drumont referred, for example, to "the admirable solidarity practised by the Jews among themselves", and to "Jewish tenacity, their patience in enduring insults and their capacity even for pretending not to notice them"; and wrote: "Eighteen centuries of persecutions borne with an incredible endurance are witness to the fact that, if the Jew lacks pugnacity, he has that other kind of courage, resistance."[146] He also celebrated Jewish intelligence, will-power and audacity. He described Saint-Simonianism, which he saw as a mainly Jewish phenomenon, as "one of the most interesting schemes devised by the human mind", and he described Isaac Pereire as "a man of the highest value". He wrote that Eugène Mayer, the anticlerical journalist, possessed an "intellectual courage", which was lacking among his non-Jewish contemporaries:

> this man is very brave . . . At a time when one only lives by one's wits, he had the audacity which was required, mental audacity. Take a good look at this little yid from Cologne. He had everything against him; he had a name of ill repute; he had no literary talent; yet he managed to succeed in Paris, starting from the bottom; he found the means . . . to organize a big concern like *La Lanterne,* and to influence opinion.

By contrast, French Catholics, well-established and wealthy from the start "are impotent, in a state of collapse." And, more generally, Drumont asserted that "there is more intellectual energy, more will-power and perseverance in any Galician Jew than there is in the whole of the Jockey Club put together."[147] Drumont, too, could even admire Jewish boldness and ingenuity when it was used for criminal purposes. He wrote, with reference to the Jew who was able to sell fake Moabite pottery to the Berlin museum: "Among these Jewish dealers there are some who almost arouse our admiration. At a certain level of boldness, swindling comes close to genius; it appears as one of the manifestations of the intellectual superiority of one race over another . . . What a power of persuasion, what guile, what diplomacy, what skill in manipulating people it demonstrates!"[148] Here Drumont was expressing sentiments that seem to have been shared by many other antisemites. A letter published in *Le Courrier de l'Est* in May 1889, for example, declared that "the Jew is indispensable to our commerce and to our industry . . . he has at his service a special kind of intelligence and an absolutely remarkable capacity for hard work, which mean that he can adapt himself very well to any business or industrial affair. The Jew, moreover, has a tenacity that nothing can weaken or discourage, and since, for him, the end justifies the means, he achieves extraordinary results."[149] Similarly, but with different emphasis, *L'Antijuif Algérien* observed in December 1897: "This race could achieve great things because it is intelligent and it is able to adapt itself to all the different peoples among whom it finds a refuge."[150]

The Jews, in effect, were granted qualities that the antisemite admired, and which he resented only because they were possessed by Jews. The admiration involved self-denigration: non-Jews lacked what the Jew so eminently had, and thus the Jew was master. But this feeling stemmed, in the first place, from a sense of inadequacy and inferiority, which the device of building up and praising the Jew only served to make clear and to express. By this means the antisemite was again saying something about himself and about society as he perceived it via the medium of antisemitism; he was not primarily making an assessment of the Jews in any objective manner. Rather, the Jews were, in this sense, a screen on to which he projected his own predicament. If society was "sick" or "in decline", it was because people lacked certain qualities, and, particularly, traditional values. In a situation of general decadence, the Jews alone survived and thrived; they were the masters. They must, therefore, possess those qualities and values which everyone else lacked. The expression of admiration for the Jews, in this situation, led to envy and to the desire to "do down" or even to destroy the Jews.[151] But, what was the object of the resentment and hostility thus generated? Not the real Jews, but primarily the mythical Jew, which antisemitism had constructed to fulfil this and other functions. This brings us back to the general paradox of antisemitic aims and intentions vis-à-vis the Jews. The Jews of antisemitic ideology are largely mythical, not real, Jews, although the distinction is not, of course, absolute. This explains the vagueness, the floating and multiform nature of antisemitic solutions to the "Jewish question"; they represented a search for appropriate ways to attack and to destroy symbolic enemies who were at the same time a real social group in France, albeit a fluid one in process of assimilation. If we therefore stress the symbolic and ritual nature of antisemitic "aims" and insist that they are not to be taken literally, it remains that these "aims" did impinge on real Jews in France, and that, although the antisemitic movement was not orientated towards action in the real social and political world, it yet objectively occupied that world and necessarily made some mark on it.

Antisemitic manifestations of all kinds, though subjectively concerned with the mythical Jews (as the evidence on the geography of antisemitism in the last chapter confirms), was objectively an attack on real Jews. This is true of antisemitic propaganda, but, more obviously, of antisemitic action. The antisemitic movement did instigate physical attacks on real Jews, particularly in 1898. The gangs of the Ligue Antisémitique beat up Jews in the streets of Paris;[152] and, as we have seen in chapter III, in the riots of that year, the houses of Jews were placarded and stoned, while synagogues and Jewish shops were treated in the same way and broken into in some cases. An indication that even more extreme activity may have been contemplated by some is provided by the fact that the Ligue Antisémitique gave its members training in the use of guns, while Le Précurseur, the weekly organ of the Parti National Antijuif, carried advertisements for small arms. But this was the full extent of antisemitic action in pursuit of its extreme and violent "aims". Further action may have been possible on the psychological level, as Morin suggested it was in Orléans in the 1960s,[153] though even this remains doubtful; but, on the sociological level, further action was not possible; and French antisemitism reverted to its "proper" essentially ideological function.

NOTES

1 Marrus, *The Politics of Assimilation*, chapter V.
2 See Bournand, *Les Juifs et nos contemporains*, pp. 192–3.
3 Meyer, *Ce que mes yeux ont vu*, pp. 126–8.
4 Bournand, op. cit., p. 62; see also ibid., p. 220 (Reclus).
5 Drumont, *Le Testament d'un antisémite*, p. 364.

6 See Sorlin, *"La Croix" et les Juifs*, pp. 110–12; and "L'Archiviste", *Drumont et Dreyfus*, p. 15.
7 Drumont, *La France juive*, I, p. 316.
8 See chapter XII, n. 150.
9 Drumont, *FJ*, I, p. 311; also ibid., I, pp. 163, 312–21 and 333; and *La Dernière Bataille*, p. 505.
10 Bournand, op. cit., p. 36.
11 Barrès, *Le Courrier de l'Est*, 14 July 1889, cit. Sternhell, *Maurice Barrès*, p. 238.
12 Sorlin, op. cit., pp. 104–5.
13 "L'Archiviste", op. cit., pp. 19–20.
14 Cit. Lovsky, *L'Antisémitisme chrétien*, p. 305.
15 Mgr. Anselme Tilloy, *Le Péril judéo-maçonnique: le mal, le remède* (1897), cit. Pierrard, *Juifs et catholiques français*, p. 67.
16 Daudet, *Au Temps de Judas*, pp. 18–19; see also Fore-Fauré, *Face aux Juifs!*, pp. 288–9; and Viau, *Vingt ans d'antisémitisme*, p. 319, claiming that Déroulède supported a similar policy, barring the monarchism.
17 "antisémitisme d'Etat". See, for example, Dresse, *Léon Daudet vivant*, p. 104; and *Le Procès de Charles Maurras*, p. 128.
18 See, for example, Bournand, op. cit., pp. 139–42.
19 See, for example, abbé A.-J. Jacquet, *L'Anéantissement de la puissance juive* (1897), cit. Pierrard, op. cit., p. 66; R. P. Pascal, cit. Verdès-Leroux, *Scandale financier et antisémitisme catholique*, p. 141; and Daily Report, Prefect of Police, 25 May 1898 (on a meeting of the Ligue Antisémitique Française in the 11th *arrondissement*). APP Ba 106.
20 Sorlin, op. cit., p. 104.
21 *L'Indépéndance de Franche-Comté*, 16 February 1895, cit. Marlin, "La Droite à Besançon", p. 230.
22 Cit. Lovsky, op. cit., p. 305; see also Dagan, *Enquête sur l'antisémitisme*, p. 43 (Molinari); and Mayeur, "Les Congrès nationaux".
23 Pierrard, op. cit., p. 70.
24 Daily Reports, Prefect of Police, 30 January, and 22 March 1898. APP Ba 106.
25 See Chapter 1, Note 110.
26 Daily Reports, Prefect of Police, 25 May, and 1 June 1898. APP Ba 106.
27 Maurras, *La Gazette de France*, 7 January 1899, cit. Roudiez, *Maurras jusqu'à l'Action Française*, p. 304.
28 Dagan, op. cit., pp. 43 (Molinari) and 58 (Charles Gide).
29 Report, Commissaire de police, Saint-Dié, 28 January 1900. AN F7 12457.
30 For example, abbé Vial; see Pierrard, op. cit., p. 68.
31 Dagan, op. cit., p. 5.
32 Picard, *Synthèse de l'antisémitisme*, pp. 100 and 119–20.
33 Meurin, *La Franc-maçonnerie, Synagogue de Satan*, p. 464.
34 See, for example, Dagan, op. cit., p. 58 (Charles Gide); Fore-Fauré, op. cit., p. 292; and Verdès-Leroux, op. cit., p. 141.
35 Maurras, *La Gazette de France*, 7 January 1899. As we have pointed out, the analogy drawn between antisemitism and colonial imperialism lends support to Arendt's thesis, referred to elsewhere, though it should be stressed that such an explicit connection between the two phenomena was rarely made.
36 See abbé Desportes, *Le Mystère du sang chez les Juifs* (1889), cit. Verdès-Leroux, op. cit., p. 141; and Pierrard, op. cit., pp. 66–7.
37 Cit. Pierrard, op. cit., p. 55.
38 Drumont, *FJ*, I, pp. 18 and 157.
39 Martinez, *Le Juif, Voilà l'ennemi! Appel aux Catholiques* (Paris, 1890), p. 42, cit. Verdès-Leroux, op. cit., p. 125.
40 Drumont, *FJ*, I, p. 157.
41 Cit. Pierrard, op. cit., p. 56.
42 Drumont, *FJ*, I, pp. 311, 333 and 520–1.

43 Drumont, *DB*, pp. 468–9.
44 Fore-Fauré, op. cit., p. 291; also pp. 289–94 *passim*.
45 Meurin, op. cit., p. 464.
46 Paul de Cassagnac, "Les Biens des Juifs", *L'Express du Midi*, 12 August 1898, cit. Bournand, op. cit., pp. 108–9.
47 *La Croix*, 8 November 1890, cit. Sorlin, op. cit., p. 104.
48 Dagan, op. cit., pp. 43–4; see also ibid., pp. 38 (Albert Réville) and 58 (Charles Gide).
49 Ibid., pp. 40–1.
50 Meurin, op. cit., p. 464.
51 Barrès, *Le Courrier de l'Est*, 26 May, and 14 July 1889, cit. Sternhell, op. cit., p. 238.
52 Picard, op. cit., pp. 91–7; and Dagan, op. cit., p. 5.
53 Daudet, *Les Oeuvres dans les hommes*, p. 169.
54 Drumont, *FJ*, I, pp. 229 and 186; and II, p. 61.
55 Drumont, *DB*, p. 505.
56 Drumont, *Le Testament d'un antisémite*, p. 45.
57 Sorlin, op. cit., pp. 104–5.
58 See "L'Archiviste", op. cit., pp. 10 and 22; and Verdès-Leroux, op. cit., p. 141.
59 See Sorlin, op. cit., pp. 119–20.
60 See Pierrard, op. cit., p. 73.
61 Daily Reports, Prefect of Police, 1 and 10 June 1898. APP Ba 106.
62 Bournand, op. cit., p. 136. (their italics).
63 Reinach, *Histoire de l'Affaire Dreyfus*, III, p. 540.
64 Report, Commissaire spécial, Roanne, 6 March 1899. AN F⁷ 12480.
65 Félix Sorlin, *La Polka des Youpins* (Paris, 1899), cit. Pierrard, op. cit., pp. 88–9.
66 Report, Police agent, Paris, 16 June 1902. AN F⁷ 12451.
67 Drumont, *FJ*, I, pp. 12 and 123; see also II, p. 562.
68 Drumont, *TA*, pp. 369 and 82.
69 Drumont, *DB*, pp. 513–14.
70 Cit. Sternhell, op. cit., pp. 238 and 235.
71 Meurin, op. cit., pp. 464 and 466.
72 *La Croix*, 5 January 1898, cit. Sorlin, *"La Croix" et les Juifs*, p. 120.
73 Drumont, *DB*, p. 54.
74 Drumont, *FJ*, I, pp. 190–6.
75 Drumont, *La Libre Parole*, 18 March 1896, cit. Bournand, op. cit., pp. 163–7.
76 Sorlin, *"La Croix" et les Juifs*, p. 104.
77 Viau, op. cit., pp. 15–16.
78 Biez, *Les Rothschild et le péril juif*, p. 10.
79 Daily Reports, Prefect of Police, 21 January, and 9 and 1 June 1898. APP Ba 106.
80 Dagan, op. cit., p. 73 (N. Chmerkine).
81 See, for example, Viau, op. cit., p. 194.
82 *La Croix*, 12 August 1890; and *Le Pèlerin*, 18 December 1892, cit. Sorlin, *"La Croix" et les Juifs*, pp. 103 and 105.
83 Barrès, "La Formule anti-juive", *Le Figaro*, 22 February 1890, Barrès-Maurras, *La République ou le Roi*, p. 627.
84 Maurras, *La Gazette de France*, 23 December 1898, cit. Roudiez, op. cit., p. 304.
85 Maurras, Letter to Barrès, March 1899. Barrès-Maurras, op. cit., pp. 224–5.
86 Maurras, *Pour la Défense nationale* (Paris, 1931), I, p. 101.
87 Cit. Gérin-Ricard et Truc, *Histoire de l'Action Française*, pp. 35–6.
88 Bloy, *Le Salut par les Juifs*, pp. 41 and 24–5.
89 Cit. Bournand, op. cit., p. 220.
90 Jean Jaurès, "Le Combat", *La Dépêche de Toulouse*, 28 December 1898.
91 Arnoulin, *M. Edouard Drumont*, p. 180.
92 Péguy, *Notre Jeunesse*, p. 187.
93 *Le Journal de Bruxelles*, 17 February 1898, cit. Reinach, op. cit., III, pp. 441–2.

94 See chapter III, n. 10.
95 Leroy-Beaulieu, *Les Doctrines de haine*, pp. 135–6.
96 Maurras, "Les Solutions de la Question juive", *La Gazette de France*, 7 January 1899, cit. W. C. Buthmann, *The Rise of Integral Nationalism in France, with special reference to the ideas and activities of Charles Maurras* (New York, 1939), p. 232.
97 See chapter XIV, n. 82.
98 Picard, op. cit., p. 95.
99 Viau, op. cit., p. 319.
100 Daudet, *Les Oeuvres dans les hommes*, p. 169.
101 Arnoulin, op. cit., p. 115. Alexandre Weill, another critic of Drumont, shared this view, writing after the publication of *La France juive:* "M. Drumont . . . veut l'extermination des fils d'Israël . . .", cit. Pierrard, op. cit., pp. 58–9.
102 R. Lamilot, *La Fille de la France juive* (Perpignan, 1887), cit. Pierrard, op. cit., p. 71.
103 Drumont, *DB*, pp. 32, 130 and xix.
104 Drumont, *TA*, pp. 364 and 320–1. (my italics)
105 Drumont, *La Libre Parole*, 3 November 1894, cit. Zévaès, *L'Affaire Dreyfus*, p. 31.
106 Georges Meynié, *Les Juifs en Algérie* (1888), cit. Verdès-Leroux, op. cit., pp. 141–2.
107 "L'Anti-youtre", *Le Courrier de l'Est*, 4 April 1891, cit. Sternhell, op. cit., pp. 235–6.
108 Cit. Sorlin, *"La Croix" et les Juifs*, p. 120.
109 Cit. Bournand, op. cit., pp. 305–6. Nordau denied having made such a statement.
110 See chapter XI, n. 54.
111 Report, Commissaire spécial, Lille, 13 February 1898. AN F⁷ 12854.
112 See chapter XIV, n. 177.
113 Daily Report, Prefect of Police, 21 June 1898. APP Ba 106.
114 Cit. Pierrard, op. cit., p. 34.
115 "mata touts lous Jouéous". *L'Indépendant des Pyrénées-Orientales*, 20 January 1898.
116 Mirbeau, *Le Journal d'une femme de chambre*, p. 104; also p. 157.
117 Dagan, op. cit., p. 30.
118 Daudet, *Au Temps de Judas*, p. 168; and *Les Oeuvres dans les hommes*, p. 169.
119 Leroy-Beaulieu, *Les Doctrines de haine*, pp. 6–7.
120 See, for example, Sartre, *Réflexions sur la question juive*, p. 51; Ackerman and Jahoda, *Anti-Semitism and Emotional Disorder*, pp. 77–8; and Morin *et al.*, *La Rumeur d'Orléans*, pp. 115–16.
121 Wiles, in Ionescu and Gellner, eds, *Populism*, p. 167; and MacRae, ibid., pp. 157–8.
122 Bournand, op. cit., pp. 123–4.
123 See chapter XII, pp. 430–1; and chapter XV, pp. 588–90 above.
124 Drumont, *FJ*, I, pp. 441–9; and II, p. 79.
125 Bournand, op. cit., p. 37.
126 See chapter XI, p. 348; and chapter XII, p. 433 above.
127 Drumont, *TA*, pp. 13–14.
128 Drumont, *FJ*, II, pp. 358–60 and 376.
129 *La Croix*, 1 November 1892, cit. Sorlin, *"La Croix" et les Juifs*, p. 106.
130 See, for example, Police report, August 1899. AN F⁷ 12459.
131 See, for example, Le Roy Ladurie, *Les Paysans de Languedoc*, pp. 225–30; Bakhtin, *Rabelais and His World*, pp. 196–213; and Cobb, *The Police and the People*, pp. 87–8.
132 See, for example, Perrot and Kriegel, *Le Socialisme français et le pouvoir*, loc. cit.; and Henri Dubief, *Le Syndicalisme révolutionnaire* (Paris, 1969).
133 Sartre, op. cit., p. 58. (his italics).

134 Memmi, *Portrait d'un Juif*, pp. 203–4; also ibid., pp. 121–2, 205, and 308; and Ackerman and Jahoda, op. cit., pp. 76 and 78.
135 Durkheim, Dagan, op. cit., p. 61, cit. (and translated by) Lukes, *Emile Durkheim*, p. 345; see also, for other versions of this interpretation, Leroy-Beaulieu, *Les Doctrines de haine*, p. 16; Loewenstein, *Christians and Jews*, pp. 36 and 57; Rose, "The Roots of Prejudice", pp. 412–13; Memmi, op. cit., pp. 247–8 and 369; Szasz, *The Manufacture of Madness*, pp. 124–5 and 289–304.
136 Edelman, *The Symbolic Uses of Politics*, p. 168; also pp. 8 and 71.
137 Sartre, op. cit., pp. 33 and 58; see also Jahoda, "Race Relations and Mental Health", p. 481.
138 See chapter XI, p. 363 above.
139 Drumont, *DB*, p. xvii.
140 Cit. Bournand, op. cit., pp. 29 and 110.
141 Loewenstein, op. cit., p. 22; and Memmi, op. cit., pp. 204–9.
142 Drumont, *FJ*, II, p. 278 and *passim.*
143 Hofstadter, *The Paranoid Style*, pp. 29–31; see also Beauvoir, *Privilèges*, pp. 146–7.
144 Poliakov, "Racisme et Antisémitisme", p. 2; see also Leroy-Beaulieu, *L'Antisémitisme*, p. 6; and Memmi, op. cit., p. 78.
145 Cit. Poliakov, op. cit., p. 3.
146 Drumont, *FJ*, I, p. 425; II, p. 95; and I, p. 3; also ibid., II, pp. 247 and 251.
147 Ibid., I, pp. 346–9; and II, pp. 203, 208–9 and 77.
148 Ibid., II, p. 146.
149 "Lettre d'un antisémite", *Le Courrier de l'Est*, 26 May 1889, cit. Sternhell, op. cit., p. 238.
150 *L'Antijuif Algérien*, 30 December 1897, cit. Rouquier and Soumille, "La Notion de Race chez les Français d'Algérie", p. 8.
151 For further discussion of this mechanism, see the cases discussed by Ackerman and Jahoda, op. cit., pp. 42, 55–62 and 74–5.
152 See Viau, op. cit., pp. 157–63.
153 Morin *et al.*, op. cit., pp. 53–4.

CHAPTER XIX
ANTISEMITISM AND JEWISH RESPONSE

WHATEVER THE ANTISEMITE'S DISTANCE FROM REAL JEWS, AND DESPITE the degree to which antisemitism in France served functions that were only remotely, historically, and mythically related to the position and role of the Jews as an actual minority, it still represented, as we have just suggested, a set of attitudes and a pattern of behaviour that adversely affected and threatened them. Antisemitism was thus something with which French Jews had to come to terms. Some attention has been devoted in recent years to the problem of Jewish response to antisemitism, particularly in Germany, and research has indicated that this was often more active and positive than had been generally supposed.[1] The view that Jews in France at the time of the Dreyfus Affair reacted passively and even pusillanimously still has some currency,[2] but the evidence suggests that this view also requires qualification. The problem of Jewish response to antisemitism, moreover, is not simply of interest in its own right, still less an occasion for the expression of moral approval or disapproval; it provides another valuable indication of how antisemitism was experienced or perceived and a further guide to its social importance and its social meaning.

First, it is necessary to provide some idea of the general context within which Jews could and did react to antisemitism. This context, as Marrus has forcefully argued, was the still continuing process of assimilation. Attitudes, behaviour and lines of action were shaped and limited by this mould, shaped and limited, it could be argued, in a less conscious and thus in an even more decisive way than he allows. Assimilationism had become explicit Jewish orthodoxy on the political level, but it was a policy which contained inherent contradictions. Its implementation would imply the disappearance of the Jews as a distinct social entity, an eventuality which some contemporaries offered to them as ultimately the only cure for antisemitism. L. Andrieux appealed, for example, in *La République Française* in October 1896: "I draw the attention of Jews to the need for them to lose themselves more and more in the common melting pot, and to cease being a kind of Freemasonry within the nation, if they wish there to be no discrimination against them . . ."[3] From

this perspective, Jews could never defend themselves, as Jews, against antisemitism. Assimilationism, in effect, by denying Jewish particularity, by linking
antisemitism to that particularity, and by treating both as phenomena that
would simply fade away in the course of time, tended to negate the very idea
of a Jewish reaction to antisemitism. This contradiction on the level of Jewish
policy or ideology reflected the Jewish predicament on the level of experience.
The process or the prospect of assimilation blurred contrasts between the
Jewish and the non-Jewish, and transposed socio-psychological points of reference from the one to the other, or left them hanging in an uncomfortable
limbo between the two. Being Jewish was no longer something so total, so
exclusive, so coherent, so given as it had traditionally been; there entered into
it elements of degree, of choice, elements that were problematic, even pathological. Individuals were thus divided or disorientated, seeking but not always
finding secure social identity. Some might settle for an assertion of Frenchness; some for an assertion of Jewishness; most were probably caught somewhere between, torn in their loyalties, oscillating or uncertain in their attitudes, experiencing the existential tensions evoked by Sartre, Memmi and
others,[4] and which the development of antisemitism exacerbated.

Notable among those who took the first course was Arthur Meyer, a Catholic convert, who married into a French aristocratic family and became editor
of the fashionable Royalist daily Le Gaulois and a supporter of the Nationalist
movement.[5] Conversion to Catholicism here was a more decisive option than
adherence to Nationalism. For, not only was French culture even in its
secularized form still Christian in many ways—nearly all French people at this
time, for example, were baptized, married and buried according to Catholic
rites[6]—but Judaism, as many writers have emphasized, was much more than
a religion in the narrow denominational or doctrinal sense; it was a way of life,
perhaps the single factor above all others which had preserved and still preserved the Jews as a distinct people, and this function survived progressive
secularization.[7] A number of Jewish writers pointed to the way in which
Christianity provided a negative criterion of Jewishness. André Maurois, for
example, came to the realization that he was a Jew, while attending a Protestant Christmas service as a child, and he recalled that Jews and Protestants
were singled out at the Rouen lycée by being excluded from the mass which
opened the academic year.[8] Conversely, Julien Benda summed up his optimistic youthful view of things by saying: "In effect, I was Christian . . ."[9] More
explicitly telling of the significance of the adoption of Catholicism by a Jew
was the reason given for his conversion by René Schwob, who presented the
issue as a choice between the demands of community and family, and the
demands of the inner self: " 'Whoever does not abandon his father and his
mother cannot follow me.' That is precisely what Judaism never said to me.
That is the reason why I cannot be a Jew."[10]

However, as we have seen, conversion to Christianity was not common in
France, and French Jews generally asserted their Frenchness through the
medium of secular patriotism. Typical here was the attitude of Alfred Dreyfus,
an Alsatian Jew, whose father had opted for France in 1871, and whose choice

of a military career was a demonstration of his attachment to the nation.[11] His letters and memoirs abound in expressions of exaggerated patriotism. He wrote to his wife, for example, in December 1894: "Oh! my beloved France, whom I love with all my heart, and to whom I have dedicated all my strength, how could you accuse me of such a terrible crime?"; and in December 1898 again he still protested "his burning love for his country".[12] His writings also illustrate how very reluctant he was to abandon his passionate conviction that the French military and civil authorities were incapable of committing an act of injustice.[13] As Zola commented, Dreyfus was "an excellent officer . . . attaching too much importance even to discipline because he was an anxious Jew".[14] Another example of the ultra-patriotic Jew is provided by Pierre Hirsch's father, a trader from Lorraine, of whom he wrote: "He belonged . . . to various patriotic associations, and, when he went to their Sunday gatherings, his chest was covered with medals and insignia. He had fought in the war of 1870." And André Maurois has testified that his parents and uncles from Alsace made similar displays of French patriotism.[15] More generally, as we have noted earlier, it seems that Jews were much more enthusiastic about performing their military service than was the rule;[16] while attachment to the nation was demonstrated again in the pattern and scale of Jewish philanthropy.[17] But French patriotism on the part of Jews was most obviously manifested early in this century in their response to the First World War. Not only did Jews who were French citizens accept mobilization with some eagerness, but, as Rabi points out, a large proportion of the foreign Jewish colony, resident in Paris, volunteered to fight for France.[18] Moreover, among those of the older generation, Durkheim played a leading part in organizing and writing patriotic propaganda for the home front.[19] Jewish French patriotism, of course, requires special and careful interpretation, as Zola's remark reminds us. It was not necessarily a denial of Jewishness. A placard in French and Yiddish, carried in a procession in Paris in August 1914, read: "Brothers, the moment has come for us to pay our debt of gratitude to the country where we have found emancipation and material well-being."[20] But, more was involved than gratitude freely expressed. As Sartre and Memmi have stressed, Jews had to give proof of an unusual patriotic zeal in order to refute the charge, explicit or unspoken, that they were not fully French.[21] If they were thereby allaying an inner anxiety, they did so under external pressure. It should be remembered, too, that no amount of French patriotic display on the part of a Jew, no amount of conformity to French norms, could make him fully acceptable as a Frenchman and as a "true" patriot save to a minority of his fellow-citizens. For Léon Daudet, Meyer was always a "parasite of Nationalism . . . French patriotism is always mixed in this Jew . . . with a wary and cunning Jewishness.."[22] Again, for a later period, Werth pointed out that Mendès-France was still referred to as "a little Jew from the Sentier", although his paternal family had lived in France for over three centuries.[23]

It was the confrontation of this fact, the sense that assimilation was either a fraud or a threat to the existence of the Jews as a people, that prompted the opposite assertion of Jewish nationalism or Zionism,[24] but it is significant that

French Zionists, few in number anyway, were nearly all of non-French origin.[25] And Bernard Lazare, an interesting and notable exception to this rule, was influenced to some extent by the French nationalism of Barrès.[26] However, there is no doubt that Lazare's Zionism, like that of Lacretelle's Silbermann,[27] was a direct response to antisemitism in France and to the conviction that assimilationism represented a tantalizing delusion. Jewish response here complemented the view of antisemites, as expressed, for example, by Picard, both that assimilation, as so far accomplished was only superficial, and that, as assimilation proceeded, *"so antisemitism became more vibrant than ever before;* its resonance increased instead of diminishing."[28] As national allegiance became generally more important and more exclusive, the position of Jews became more uncomfortable, less tenable in terms of existing categories, and the problem of Jewish identity, the strains of what Joseph Jacobs called the "duplex culture" of the Jews,[29] of what Henry Bérenger, writing in January 1897 in *Le Mercure de France,* termed "the bi-laterality of the Jewish mind",[30] became more acute. As Memmi put it, "to be Jewish is not to have received naturally, as a gift, a birthright, those traditional presents bestowed by fairy godmothers: native land, nationality, insertion in a national history, and so on. As a Jew, these will be the objects of acrimonious discussion as far as you are concerned, conceded, taken back, put in doubt, so that you will almost never be able to share quite naturally in those conventional social dimensions which most people take for granted." In these circumstances, a Jew was willy-nilly to some degree "a being torn apart".[31] French nationalism and Zionism were apparent ways out of the Jewish dilemma, but neither could really escape it, and, as we have said, most French Jews avoided either extreme.

There is abundant evidence, biographical and autobiographical, of the different ways in which the problem of Jewish identity was experienced and expressed, on this middle ground, by articulate Jews. Julien Benda, for example, remarked, in his autobiography, on "my tranquil acceptance of myself . . . my lack of anxiety" as a youth; but he was aware, none the less, of having made a break with the cultural tradition of his forefathers, writing of his father: "Recalling his image, I see behind it, fading away into the depth of the past, across the ghettos of the East, a whole line of great Jews, with the same brow, the same eyes; ancestors of whom I know nothing, and who, doubtless, would not have liked me with the cast of mind, the form of soul, which the Latins have fashioned in me . . ."[32] Similarly, Emmanuel Berl declared: "Doubtless I am a Jew . . .",[33] explaining the element of doubt by the fact that his upbringing had been entirely secular:

> I belonged to one of those French families, which, at one and the same time, remained and were no longer Jewish. They rejected the idea of conversion, but no longer went to the synagogue. My uncle Alfred Berl, who worked for the Alliance Israélite and edited a Jewish paper, was incapable of reciting the Kaddish by his father's coffin, as I was myself incapable of reciting it by his. My father, who would have thought it dishonourable to have had me baptized, would have thought it stupid to have me fast at Yom Kippur. In our house, only my grandmother fasted; and she apologized for

doing so, saying that it was for old time's sake. So the word: Jew, the idea that I was a Jew, so loaded with meaning and with consequences, had for me a resonance that was sharp, but thin. For a long time, indeed, I did not register this important fact.

In Algiers, where he was taken on a holiday as a child at the time of the 1898 riots and heard the crowds yelling: "Death to the Jews", he recalled "that it was the word 'Death' which struck me and not the word 'Jews'."[34] But later he expressed a fundamental uncertainty about his own identity which can be related to this problematic Jewishness: "I cannot find myself either within myself or in my history . . .";[35] "My life bears no resemblance to my life. It never has. But I put up with this displacement between one self and another pretty well."[36] The dilemma was as acutely felt and perhaps more deliberately expressed and lived by Marcel Schwob (1867–1905). Léon Daudet, who knew him well, described him as "an authentic Jew";[37] and his father was the owner of Le Phare de la Loire, one of the few provincial papers to attack antisemitism; but Marcel, while contributing to the paper, also expressed his admiration for Drumont.[38] Moreover, Daudet, again, recalled that, while Schwob became a Dreyfusard, he was "without a doubt the gentleman of my acquaintance whom I heard speak in the most derogatory way of those whom he called the little Lévys, and who uttered the most threats against Jewish finance."[39] More interesting, Schwob's literary work, according to George Trembley, reflected an obsession with "his own duality", a quest to discover his identity, to bring together the different sides of his personality, the creative artist and the scholar, his social and his private self. Though this, of course, represents a very general and widespread dilemma, it is hard not to conclude that, as in the case of Berl, it must, to a degree, have reflected Schwob's particular dilemma as an assimilated Jew.[40] André Gide certainly related Schwob's fascination with masks and mirrors as literary symbols, and his actual habit of avoiding or covering over mirrors so that he could not see his own image, to the fact that he was an "educated Jew".[41]

Similar tensions, anxieties or contradictions were present in many other cases, either objectively or subjectively. Gamzon notes, for example, that André Suarès, who denied his Jewishness, declaring: "Living Jews are ghosts, insolent corpses . . . I invite Jews to cease being Jewish", was regarded by Claudel as one of "his Jewish friends".[42] Catulle Mendès, one of the most admired writers of his day, is reported to have said: "If I had not been a Jew, I would have had genius."[43] Durkheim, who broke with Judaism while a student, displayed a constant anxiety about his career, which drove him to work obsessively.[44] Léon Blum, who later claimed that he had always felt equally Jewish and French and that "I have never noticed the slightest contradiction, the slightest opposition between these two parts of my consciousness",[45] yet betrayed much less security on this score in fact in his early life, as we shall see.[46]

The uncertainty and the ambiguity of the Jewish condition were also evoked by contemporary French novelists of Jewish extraction, presumably a reflection of their own situations. Proust's Swann, for example, was apparently at ease and fully accepted in the highest aristocratic circles until the outbreak of the Dreyfus Affair, when, in the face of antisemitic hostility, he recalled and was drawn back to the community of his ancestors.[47] It is possible also to see the theme of homosexuality which pervades Proust's novel as paradigmatic of the pathological quality that Jewishness assumed for individuals, as it became divorced from a Jewish social context, and in the face of the conflict between the imperative of assimilationism and the new development of antisemitism, itself, in part, a reflection of alarm at the idea of unattached Jewishness. Proust's homosexuals belonged, like Jews, to a "community" by virtue of "given" qualities, which they sought paradoxically also to conceal, but which were eventually exposed.[48] It is relevant here that Maurice Sachs explicitly related his homosexuality to his Jewishness, and to the feeling that he was both "guilty" and unlike "normal" people.[49] Again, in J.-R. Bloch's . . . Et Cie, Joseph Simler's interest in French culture and his hopes of a Gentile marriage are ultimately overcome by the stronger pull of his own family and the interests of the family firm.[50] A similar conflict is present in Edmond Fleg's L'Enfant prophète (1926), which provides, too, a classic description of the childhood experience of discovering that one is a Jew, found also in several autobiographies.[51] The problem of Jewish identity, moreover, interested non-Jewish as well as Jewish writers. Lacretelle's Silbermann, as we have seen, attempted to reject his Frenchness and become simply a Jew, but admitted, after having emigrated to the United States: "When I tried to take another path, it was too late. I could not stop thinking of all that I had learned and loved in France, and that came between me and my life as a Jew"; and the conflict between the two influences finally destroyed him.[52] Again, with the characters of Sichel in Le Pain dur and Pensée in Le Père humilié (1916), Claudel, in Gamzon's words, "has analysed in a remarkable way the double movement of Jews in process of assimilation into the Christian world, of those Jews who want to obtain full access to Western Christian society, while maintaining their sombre pride in being children of Israel, children of a people at once cursed and blessed . . ."[53]

The circumstances of assimilation which conditioned the response of Jews also affect the way in which that response can be studied. The real problem of identity is reflected in a formal problem of definition. Enquiry into Jewish response to antisemitism does not simply involve a given minority and its reaction to discrimination against it, but raises the question: Who is a Jew?, as well as: What did antisemitism mean to Jews? "Can one say", asked the Tharauds, "that these Jews who have been settled among us for several generations, who have only a very vague idea of their ancestral customs, who have, for the most part, renounced all religious practice, have ceased to be Jews, and that they have no part in the history which occupies us?"[54] Different answers have been given to this question on different occasions and with different aims in view, ranging from the liberal's and the opportunist antisemite's assertion that the Jew is defined entirely and quite negatively by non-Jews and their hostility, to Memmi's rejoinder that: "The Jew is not only the person who is considered to be a Jew, nor even the person who responds to being considered in this way. He has another side: he lives a Jewishness, a Judaism, a sense of being a Jew, that are thoroughly positive."[55] Marrus has argued that one can reasonably speak of a Jewish community in France at the turn of the century, a community finding expression in formal religious institutions, but, more important, since these found comparatively little support, in a historically formed sense of community, maintained through adherence, however minimal, to customary practices, through a sense of tradition, and through family ties. Such a community was, nevertheless, tenuous, its solidarity uncertain and fluctuating, and its membership ill defined. Individuals were not exclusively and for all purposes in and of it; they were not distinguished by physical features, or even, increasingly, by dress or cultural traits. Concomitantly and perhaps paradoxically, as the social dimensions of Jewishness itself became less important with the progress of assimilation, so Jewishness tended to become both internalized within individuals and to be of social significance for individuals in a non-Jewish rather than a Jewish context. Jewish response to antisemitism, inevitably complicated and full of ambiguities in itself, is therefore inherently difficult to document and thus to measure and describe. The approach which we shall adopt is essentially empirical, accepting the definitions implicit in the documentation that is available. This not only allows a wide coverage of degrees of Jewishness and of types of response to antisemitism, but also places discussion of social attitudes and relations firmly in the concrete context of contemporaries' conception of them.

In order to discuss and assess Jewish response to antisemitism, it is also, of course, necessary, beyond having a general idea of what antisemitism implied in France in the 1890s and 1900s, to gauge how far it actually impinged on Jews and how seriously they had to regard it. Related to this, one must know, too, how antisemitism was generally interpreted and how non-Jews reacted to it. As we have seen, antisemitism in many parts of France was a relatively autonomous phenomenon unrelated to Jewish presence, but in the East and in Paris and other large urban centres it can be seen in part as a reaction to economic functions performed by resident Jews. Most of the 1898 riots occurred in towns where a Jewish community existed, and where their houses, shops and synagogues could serve as targets for attack. Organized antisemitism had its strongholds, too, in Paris, where over 60% of the French Jewish population was concentrated by the late 1890s, and in Algeria, which had a large and distinct community. So, alongside a "theoretical" antisemitism which did not derive from experience of coexistence with Jews and which might exist in areas where there were no Jews to experience it, there existed an antisemitism which was related to Jewish presence and directed against it. From somewhat haphazard evidence, it is possible to present some kind of picture of what this latter kind of antisemitism represented for Jews.

In general, the circumstances of the Dreyfus Affair, and especially the 1898 riots, do seem to have created an atmosphere of fear among Jews, that is testified to by Jules Isaac and others. One cannot measure, but one should probably not underestimate the impact made on Jews by the outpourings of the antisemitic press and of antisemitic orators, and of the election in 1898 again of a significant number of antisemitic deputies. More specifically, antisemitic activity affected individual Jews in five main ways. First, there was a certain amount of violence against persons, practised usually by members of antisemitic organizations. As we have seen, Guérin, like Morès before him, had a gang of men armed with clubs, who were used in street demonstrations, to break up rival meetings and also to beat up individual Jews.[56] The 1898 riots were also very violent in some places, and although no deaths occurred in metropolitan France, at least two Jews had been lynched in Algeria, a fact that was widely reported. Second, attacks were made directly on property owned by Jews. Again during the riots of 1898, attacks were made on synagogues or rabbi's houses in seven places in France, and Jewish shops were attacked and damaged in thirty places. Private houses belonging to Jews were also threatened or damaged on this and other occasions. During the Rennes trial, for example, the house of Victor Basch, a professor at the Faculté des Lettres, situated 3 kilometres from the town, was surrounded by a hostile crowd of young men who shouted slogans and threw stones.[57] During the night after the publication of the Rennes verdict, condemning Dreyfus for the second time, most of the windows in his brother's house at Belfort were smashed.[58]

Third, much more widespread but more difficult to document, were various forms of social discrimination or ostracism practised against Jews. We have already discussed some of these: exclusion from clubs, discouragement of intermarriage, special treatment and bullying of Jewish children in schools, for example.[59] There is some evidence that such discrimination had increased by the time of the Affair. Theodore Reinach noted already in 1894 that "the situation of Jews has become nearly everywhere painful and delicate; they feel themselves to be surrounded by an atmosphere of prejudice . . ."[60] Some indication of this can be gauged from the example of the Dreyfus family itself. According to Joseph Reinach, "after the degradation ceremony, a social void was made around the Dreyfus family. Only the Chief Rabbi and a few intimate friends brought them occasional consolation . . . they became pariahs."[61] The police, who kept a close watch on them after the condemnation, reported in December 1894: "On returning to Mulhouse on the day after the condemnation, the traitor's family . . . kept themselves virtually hidden from their fellow-citizens, but received a few close friends who were assured that Captain Dreyfus is innocent." The report added that the Dreyfus family were staying with relatives, afraid to be seen in the hotels of Belfort. A little later in January 1895, it was reported that Alfred's nephew had been expelled from the lycée at Belfort, for defending his uncle's reputation and making insulting remarks about French officers; the expulsion, it was said, "is generally approved in Belfort." At the same time another nephew abandoned a place at the Ecole Polytechnique to go instead into the family firm.[62] The following year, the police reported from Carpentras on Alfred's sister, married to a local textile merchant: "Since her brother's condemnation, Madame Joseph Valabrègue lives in virtual retirement at her country house a kilometre outside the town, and has broken off all social relations."[63] Obviously the case of the Dreyfus family was unusual in that its members were associated directly with a condemned traitor, but other Jews received similar treatment at this time. Proust evoked this at the highest levels of society with the example, already mentioned, of Swann who is repudiated by the Guermantes and their circle, and also that of Bloch, who is publicly insulted at Mme de Villeparisis's tea-party.[64] At Belfort again, in December 1897, Jews were openly insulted by army officers at one of the fashionable cafés in the town, a type of incident apparently fairly common in France during the Affair.[65] Viau wrote of organized antisemites in Paris: "Jews muttered as they passed, reading in their eyes the insult which their lips had not yet uttered."[66]

This social ostracism shaded off, fifthly, into economic boycott. At a Ligue Antisémitique meeting in February 1898, for example, "a travelling salesman, M. Boyeur, gave an account of the position into which Jewish salesmen were put by their colleagues. They were reduced to frequenting their own cafés and hotels";[67] and Viau noted the prejudice caused to the Jewish butchers of La Villette by the harassment of antisemites who were particularly numerous in the trade there.[68] Such discrimination was not simply the result of spontaneous hostile feeling, but the product, as we have seen, of a deliberate campaign mounted by antisemitic organizations. "Never buy from the Jews" was a constant theme of antisemitic propaganda, and lists were published of Jewish shops and businesses to be avoided. These were widely distributed, in some cases at church doors or through the post.[69] Their effect, in combination with other manifestations of antisemitism, seems to have been considerable. A gathering of Jewish notables in Paris at the house of Mme Léon Bloch was thrown into temporary panic in February 1898 when one of its habitués arrived to announce that "pillaging of shops belonging to Jews had begun and that Drumont and his bandits possessed lists indicating the private residences of leading Jews"; and many Jewish business men decided to close their shops and workshops at this time.[70] Such a reaction was not confined to Paris. At Lunéville, after serious antisemitic riots had broken out, the Sub-prefect reported that a Jewish industrialist, "who employs over 300 workers came to inform me this morning that he was preparing to close his workshops and to leave Lunéville."[71] In the context of the general economic *malaise* of 1898–9, the effects of such forced unemployment and halting of production and sales seem, in Paris at least, to have rebounded against the antisemites, and to have earned Jews some sympathies.[72] However, some cases of real and lasting economic hardship resulting from antisemitic campaigns were reported. For example, Léon Tabet, the representative in Algiers of a Montbéliard firm, was sacked in March 1898 on the grounds that, as a Jew, he could no longer carry out his functions effectively. Tabet sued the firm, but the Montbéliard Tribunal de Commerce dismissed his claim for damages, upholding the firm's right to terminate his employment, given "the ban imposed on traders of the Jewish race" in Algiers in 1898.[73]

In order to understand Jewish response to these various manifestations of antisemitism, it is necessary to place it in the context of the general response.

How important did contemporaries, in general, think antisemitism was, particularly in its organized form? How much of a threat to Jews or to anyone else? And how did they interpret it? The attitude of the French government and administration is of crucial importance here. If the authorities showed themselves hostile towards antisemitism, Jews could feel reassured that assimilation into French society remained a proper goal, and that, as French citizens, they had no serious cause for alarm. They could feel also that they could rely for protection on the regular forces of law and order, and had no need to organize their own defence. And such indeed seems generally to have been the case. As Bernard Lazare confidently affirmed in 1894, legalized governmental antisemitism on the pre-Revolutionary or the Russian model was out of the question in modern Republican France,[74] and Blum expressed a similar view in 1899.[75] When the 1898 riots showed that antisemitism was a threat to public order in France, the attitude of the government became quite clearly hostile to it, and more so from June 1899, when liquidation of the Dreyfus Affair became governmental policy and the anti-Dreyfusard leagues were prosecuted. However, although organized antisemitism found no sympathies at the apex of the state apparatus, it did make itself felt on occasion in the structure's lower levels. Most obviously, Algiers and some other Algerian towns were ruled for a period during 1898–9, before the metropolitan authorities stepped in, by municipalities which began to apply discriminatory legislation against Jews.[76] The military in Algeria had deliberately refrained from intervening in the 1898 riots, behaviour repeated in a less blatant form by some of their metropolitan counterparts; at Nantes, for example, the general commanding the regional army corps turned down the Prefect's request for more troops to deal with the riots there in January 1898.[77] The civil authorities, moreover, were sometimes engaged in minor harassment of Jews. During the Affair, the Dreyfus and Bernard Lazare were kept under police surveillance. Eugène Kahn, who sent a telegram at the end of 1897 mentioning the name Picquart, had his flat searched by the police; while official police enquiries into the case of an artillery officer who resigned his commission in 1896 because of his debts asked: "Is he a Jew?"[78] But, on the other hand, little or no sympathy for organized antisemitism is expressed in the many administrative and police reports on the subject, and no reports have been found of administrative discrimination against Jews in metropolitan France, with the possible exception of the secularization of Jewish schools in some *arrondissements* of Paris in 1900. The attitude of the courts was less reassuring. The Dreyfus Case itself, although strictly it involved only military justice, was a massive precedent for no confidence. Jews would have noticed, too, the failure of the Tabet suit at the Montbéliard Tribunal de Commerce to which we have referred and which was probably not unique; also that after the publication of Zola's "*J'accuse*", barristers from the bars of at least a dozen towns had sent public addresses of sympathy to the army.[79]

At the time of the Affair, therefore, Jews had some grounds for doubts about the firmness with which their basic civic rights might be upheld by the authorities in France, although the advent to power of the Waldeck-Rousseau government in mid-1899 seems to have reassured many of them. A police agent, who reported regularly on gatherings of Jewish notables in Paris, wrote at the end of June 1899: "In general, the fear felt recently by the Jewish colony is beginning to disappear and they are quite confident that Monsieur Waldeck has the will and the ability to put down with an iron hand all disorder and all attacks on the lives and property of the Jewish class"; and, again at the end of July 1899: "Generally speaking, all these gentlemen have complete confidence in Monsieur Waldeck and his subordinates . . ."[80] This confirmed the Republican assimilationist orthodoxy, but some at least must have felt, with some disillusion, that the government's tough line against antisemites could be explained more by the threat which the latter, in alliance with reactionary groups, represented to Republican institutions in France, rather than by any positive hostility to anti-Jewish prejudice as such.

The governmental view here seems to have reflected general political opinion. For both, organized antisemitism primarily represented a threat to public order, a pretext for violence and disturbance, which both had swung round to oppose by 1899. As already indicated, the economic *malaise* of the years 1898–9, associated by contemporaries with the political uncertainties generated by the Dreyfus Affair, was thought to have been exacerbated by the activities of the antisemites with their attacks on Jewish business, while the potentially dangerous role of antisemitism as a populist protest movement, providing some mass support and an organizational network for anti-Republican parties, was soon realized by the Republican authorities and their supporters, and was played up in order to disarm the movement. This political context coloured general interpretations of antisemitism. It was widely regarded, as we have seen, as something foreign to modern France, a throwback to mediaeval superstition, a phenomenon primarily religious in nature, a new guise adopted by reactionary clericalism, or a diversionary *ersatz* "socialism", all ways of explaining it away, of treating it as an aberration that would in the natural course of things simply disappear. The deeper roots of the movement, the positive reasons for its development and appeal at this particular point in French history were not often considered or debated, and the need for action against antisemitism, save on the police level, was rarely conceived of. To understand this, account must be taken of the very general presence in French society of latent antisemitism, to which we have many times alluded, and which inhibited objective appreciation of antisemitism in its more extreme forms. It must be remembered, too, that anti-Jewish prejudice in late nineteenth-century France was perceived by Jews and non-Jews without the sense of its potentialities given by present-day hindsight, and without the conceptual apparatus created in an attempt to explain its later enormities.[81] Antisemitism which was the fruit of a lack of social consciousness was thus felt, and viewed, very often, with the same lack of consciousness, even, one might say, with a kind of innocence.

Illustrative of this is the fact that many French writers were, by modern standards, quite inconsistent in their attitudes to antisemitism and the Jews. As Furth has pointed out,[82] the work of Erckmann-Chatrian, for example, includes books in which Jews are portrayed in conventional hostile fashion, but also *L'Ami Fritz* (1865), in which Rabbi Sichel is an important and an admirable character (which earned the book Drumont's express disapproval),[83] and *Le Blocus* (1867), which has a Jew, Moïse, and his family as its central characters and which celebrates their virtues. It may be true that the antisemitism of the former represented the views of Chatrian, more commercially-minded and more attuned to the prejudices of his readers than Erckmann, whose first-hand experience of and sympathy for the Alsatian Jewish community are reflected in the latter, but this does not entirely explain the contradiction or apparent contradiction, for all the books appeared as part of a coherent *oeuvre,* and the same contradiction is found in the work of those who did not write in collaboration. Maupassant, as we have seen, countered antisemitic prejudice in some of his writings, but exemplified it in others, referring, for example, to the Jews of Algeria, in the language of the antisemitic *colon,* as "these extortioners who are the scourge, the running sore of our colony . . ."[84] Similarly, Apollinaire's stories, "Le Passant de Prague" and "Le Juif latin," combine a sympathy with the Jewish condition and a rehearsal of antisemitic stereotypes; and the fact that the stories were published in the Jewish-run and Dreyfusard *La Revue Blanche* in 1902 and 1903, and were dedicated in book form to Thadée Natanson, further emphasizes that their antisemitism was not then so obvious or so clear cut as it has since become.[85]

It is not surprising therefore to find that, with few exceptions to which we shall return, responses to antisemitism by non-Jews rarely showed much empathy with Jews as Jews or took the form of defending Jews as Jews. As Léon Bloy, a passionate critic of Drumont, put it: "Sympathy for the Jews is a sign of turpitude, that goes without saying", and, of course, he adhered fully to the spirit of his own maxim.[86] Leroy-Beaulieu, to whose intelligent and courageous critique of antisemitism we have more often referred, declared in a lecture, given in 1897, admittedly before a hostile audience, that "antisemitism does not simply concern the Jews", and complained that "antisemitism magnifies the Jew, gives him a grandeur and an importance . . . that offend my pride as a Christian and as an Aryan."[87] The same combination of hostility to both antisemitism and Jews characterized the stance of other publicists, for example Urbain Gohier[88] and even Jaurès.[89] Socialists like Jaurès, as well as Anarchists like Sébastien Faure, generally interpreted and opposed antisemitism as an attempt to dupe the people and to divert them from effective struggle against the capitalist system;[90] as Memmi has commented, "Jewish reality was ignored by classical Socialist analysis."[91] More moderate Republicans opposed antisemitism on a variety of grounds all of which can be traced back to the egalitarian and assimilationist ethic, and which betrayed a similar difficulty in coming to terms with antisemitism as an ideology and a movement in its own right, that could be directed against real Jews. Reinach recalled that "many Republicans, even among the earliest Dreyfusards, were stupefied" by the sentiments expressed in the Henry Subscription.[92] The Radical Arthur Ranc, for example, wrote in *Le Matin* in September 1892 that antisemitism represented "a crazy campaign, because it runs counter to the conquests of the

Revolution, to the great principles of tolerance and freedom of thought",[93] a sentiment echoed later in the decade by Yves Guyot, Barthou and others.[94] According to Lanessan, writing in *Le Rappel* in January 1898, "public opinion today knows that the *war on the Jews*, and on the Protestants and the Freemasons, is only a mask behind which are hiding all the enemies of the Republic and of liberty";[95] while L'Hermite protested in May 1898, with reference to the actions of the municipal authorities in Algiers, that "true Republicans cannot admit or tolerate that workers should be persecuted and that those among them who are Jews or Protestants or Freemasons should be driven out, on the pretext that M. de Rothschild is rich."[96]

The Ligue des Droits de l'Homme, the most important organization to devote itself to opposing antisemitism, was inspired by the same principles. The Ligue was founded in direct response to the 1898 riots, and its first president Trarieux later emphasized its role in defending French Jews from persecution,[97] but, as its manifesto of July 1898 shows, it did not at the time interpret the riots or antisemitism in general primarily as an attack on Jews, but rather on egalitarian and Republican principles:[98]

> Antisemitism has succeeded in oppressing Algeria, thanks to the impunity with which it has been allowed to develop its threats and provocations; it must not be allowed to infiltrate metropolitan France and to turn its head also, gradually destroying there the principles of civil and political equality, which have opened up for us since 1789 that universal and humanitarian ideal, for which we are responsible in the eyes of the world! The unity of the Nation, which our fathers have bequeathed to us, is at stake.

At its most extreme, this attitude could actually deny that antisemitism or the Jews existed, albeit with the best of intentions. Henry Maret declared, for example, in 1898: "There is no Jewish question . . . I don't know what a Jew is."[99] Anticlericalism was an integral part of the Republican ethic, and antisemitism was also attacked as a clerical manoeuvre. Brisson, the President of the Chamber of Deputies, for example, delivered an attack on antisemitism at an electoral meeting in the 10th *arrondissement* of Paris in February 1898, in which he characterized it as "the campaign undertaken to provoke religious hatred."[100] Antisemitism was also opposed, from the late 1880s,[101] on the grounds that it represented a threat to public order, a motive that became perhaps predominant by the late 1890s, particularly on the part of the government, as we have seen.

However, not all non-Jewish response to antisemitism was of this kind, and, as the quotation from L'Hermite indicates, opposition from the stand-point of egalitarian Republican principles did not necessarily exclude empathy with Jews as a minority. Stressing one rather than the other was sometimes simply a question of emphasis, though this was not always so. We have seen that antisemitism was rightly associated by its critics with hostility to Protestantism, and there is evidence that traditional Protestant fellow-feeling with Jews was still alive at this time,[102] though it was by no means universal, as André Gide's hostile attitude towards Jews indicates.[103] André Maurois's father told him that Protestantism was "a fine religion, related to and deriving from our own", and he took his family to the Protestant church at Elbeuf.[104] The narrator in Lacretelle's *Silbermann* says of his mother that, "brought up in a district where Catholics and Protestants still confronted each other with some passion, she felt for the cause of the Jews the sympathy which generally unites minorities";[105] and it is significant that, both in this novel and in Fleg's *L'Enfant prophète*, the unpopular Jewish boy is befriended by a Protestant.[106] It is worth noting, too, that Stéphane Arnoulin, one of Drumont's most vigorous critics, was a Protestant.[107] Protestants were also, as we have seen, a noticeable element in the ranks of the Dreyfusards. Mme Dreyfus, for example, received a letter of support in August 1899 from Raoul Allier, professor at the Faculty of Protestant Theology in Paris.[108] More generally, Maurice Vernes, director of the Ecole des Hautes Etudes and a declared freethinker, delivered a forceful attack on antisemitism at a meeting of the Société des Etudes Juives in 1898, in which he significantly alluded to his Protestant upbringing.[109]

A number of other examples of sympathetic defence of Jews by non-Jews can be cited, some more deliberate and sustained than others. G. Valbert, for example, declared in an article on German antisemitism in *La Revue des Deux Mondes* in March 1882, "that the Jews of Bordeaux and of Paris have become excellent French citizens. This does not prevent them from remaining Jews, and sensible people will not complain about this. It is a good thing for a country to have influential minorities whose rights are respected; it is a good thing that their importance should be out of proportion to their numerical strength . . ."[110] Zola wrote his article "Pour les Juifs" in *Le Figaro* in May 1896.[111] Péguy wrote pieces attacking antisemitism from 1898 and, concomitantly, expressed a thoroughgoing philosemitism in a number of works published before 1914, for example *Notre Jeunesse*, from which we have quoted, and *Le Mystère de la Charité de Jeanne d'Arc* (1910). Moreover, *Les Cahiers de la Quinzaine* gave shelter and encouragement to several Jewish writers, including Fleg, Reinach, Benda and André Suarès.[112]

Nor was such expression of sympathy limited to intellectuals and to the printed word. At an antisemitic meeting held at Saint-Nicolas-du-Pont (Meurthe-et-Moselle) in July 1899, an uproar was caused, according to the police, when a Socialist worker called Hilaire stood up and protested: "Citizens, I am not Jewish, but in view of the harrying that Jews have been suffering for some time now, I would feel some pride could I say I were . . ."[113] Again, a speaker at a public meeting organized by the Fédération Socialiste Nantaise in June 1899 denounced the antisemitic movement in Algeria specifically on the grounds that it was engaged in active persecution of Jewish women and children and, perhaps ironically for a Socialist, in the destruction of Jewish property.[114] A year later, at Caudebec-les-Elbeuf in Normandy, a region where antisemitism had some following, vigorous popular opposition to it was once more demonstrated. A talk by Dubuc of La Jeunesse Antisémitique on "Socialism and Antisemitism" was brought to a premature end by the barracking of an audience of 600 workers. As the police explained:[115]

The inhabitants of Caudebec were quite keen to hear Dubuc expound his nationalism but, unfortunately, he had to go on to attack the Jews. Now, it must be noted that at Elbeuf nearly all the workers in the woollen mills are employed by Jewish firms; many of them were brought here from Alsace by their employers . . . And it is acknowledged by the workers themselves that they enjoy better conditions working for these firms than they would in many Catholic concerns.

A similar, if less calculating, devotion of non-Jewish workers to their Jewish employers is evoked in J.-R. Bloch's . . . *Et Cie.* [116] Moreover, in Paris in 1898, it was reported than non-Jewish employees laid off by their Jewish employers were "very worked up against Drumont and his gang", and were prepared to defend the former against antisemitic violence. [117] It is possible that the "movement of protest that is building up in the working-class population of Grenoble against the activities of the Ligue Antisémite of this town" in January 1899 had the same inspiration. [118] We have seen, too, that the 9th Congress of the Union of Railway Workers in Paris in April 1898 voted down a proposal from its Algiers branch to exclude Jews from membership. [119] One should also probably include under the heading of the expression of active sympathy for Jews the apparent decision of Hachette to refuse to sell *La France juive* from its railway kiosks. [120]

Nevertheless, on the whole, such sympathetic and active response was unusual, and Jewish response must be seen in a different general context, a context in which, despite continuing Socialist connections and pretensions, antisemitism was becoming associated more and more with clerical and reactionary politics, and in which anti-Jewish prejudice in organized form was seen less as discrimination directed against a particular minority, and more as part, and only part, of a much wider attack on democratic institutions and principles. In a sense, therefore, contemporary opinion was in line with our general interpretation of antisemitism, although contemporaries, of course, tended to take a narrowly political view of it, and usually failed to appreciate its broader and profounder functions. It must also be remembered that reaction in any form to antisemitism was not all that common, and that even those who were in some way aware of the threats which it posed were often content to do or to say nothing about it. Jean Renoir has written that his father feared the irruption "of anti-Semitism among the lower middle-class. He could envisage armies of grocers and similar tradesmen, wearing hoods and treating the Jews the way the Ku-Klux-Klan treated the Negroes. [But] his advice was to stay quiet and wait for the ferment to pass." [121] And Charles Gide told Dagan pessimistically: "It is probable that antisemitism will endure as long as the Jewish people endure, that is, for ever." [122]

Having discussed the general reaction to antisemitism, we are now in a position to discuss Jewish response itself, bearing in mind that, if the latter had its specific characteristics, its pattern and its limitations were to a large extent set by the former. Jews were Jews, but they were also citizens of the Third Republic. Jewish response can be ranged in a number of categories, running from active siding with or adoption of antisemitism, through masochistic acceptance of it, timidity, passivity or apparent indifference, to various kinds of positive opposition to it.

The adoption or expression of antisemitism by Jews has been a not uncommon way of denying or attempting to deny one's own Jewishness, either in an effort to resolve the internal conflict of personal identity which we have discussed above, or to escape "the stigma" which antisemitic prejudice attached to Jewishness, or both;[123] and some Jews took this course in France at the end of the nineteenth century. Péguy claimed in 1900 that "three-quarters of the Jewish upper bourgeoisie, half the Jewish middle bourgeoisie, and a third of the Jewish petty bourgeoisie" were antisemitic.[124] This is almost certainly an exaggeration, though, given Péguy's acquaintanceship with the Jewish community, notice should be taken of it. Other observers testified to the existence of the phenomenon, on a less extensive scale, and some examples can be quoted. Already in 1846, Victor Hugo recorded a conversation with Meyer, director of La Gaîté theatre, who was soliciting Hugo's support for his nomination to the post of director of Le Théâtre Français. "He came to see me", Hugo noted, "and brought me a memorandum. I told him: 'It is fine, M. Meyer, but if you are appointed, beware of the influence of Mlle Rachel and of all her family . . .'—'Rest assured!', he replied emphatically. 'I won't get mixed up with that bunch of Jews.' " To which Hugo added the comment: "M. Meyer is Jewish."[125] In our period again and more generally, Théodore Reinach wrote in La Grande Encyclopédie in 1894: "There are also antisemitic Jews . . ."[126] Daniel Halévy referred in his diary in December 1898, as we have seen, to "the tainted idiosyncrasies of my race . . ."[127] Proust made a number of Jews in his novel antisemitic, notably Bloch who changes his name to Jacques du Rozier.[128] Another fictional example is provided by Lacretelle's Silbermann, of whom the narrator says that, at one stage, he "developed a mania for telling me stories in which those of his race were the objects of ridicule . . ."[129] Again, Arthur Meyer, whom we have already encountered in this context, expressed his admiration for Drumont, and, writing in 1910, insisted: "When one has seen in France certain Jews . . . rushing to get places in the administration in order to collaborate with doctrinaire ministers in their odious campaign against Catholics, one can and one must become antisemitic."[130]

As this last example suggests, it seems that expressions of antisemitism were particularly common among converted Jews. L'Hermite asserted that "Jews who deny their religion are the most fanatical and shocking auxiliaries of Drumont . . ."[131] The Tharauds agreed, more generally, that, "whether converted in good faith or through hatred of their own milieu, Christianized Jews have always shown an incredible animosity against their former co-religionists . . . It is these converts who have drawn attention to and denounced everything in the Jewish scriptures that was capable of arousing the anger of the Church and its members.[132] "We are already familiar with the example of abbé Lémann, author of La Prépondérance juive,[133] and he was not unique. André Suarès declared, for example: "All my life I have felt a terrible partiality against the chosen race which has dared, wickedly, to reject its election. For me, the Jews effectively died on the first Christmas . . ."[134] Again, René Schwob, who converted to Catholicism in the 1920s, joined the Action Française shortly afterwards,[135] a course taken by a few other Jews both before and after the First World War.[136]

Such antisemitic response, often, to some degree, disguised, can be seen in the reaction of several Jews to the Dreyfus Affair. Mme Steinheil commented that "perhaps the strangest phenomenon of all in that strange time was the anti-Dreyfusard attitude of the Jewish élite . . ."[137] In January 1899, for example, a lieutenant Kahn wrote to the Chief Rabbi: "I have been profoundly upset, as a Jew, to see the Chief Rabbi, our religious leader, involving himself in such an active way in this unfortunate Dreyfus Affair."[138] Earlier, during the May 1898 election campaign, when grounds for believing Dreyfus the victim of a miscarriage of justice were, however, weaker, L.-L. Klotz, a Radical candidate at Montdidier (Somme), a constituency in which an antisemitic candidate was also standing, declared, in his electoral manifesto: "A patriot before everything else, I have not minced my words in condemning the odious campaign directed against the army, from the moment that it started . . . and I undertake to vote against revision of the Dreyfus case."[139] In 1903, in a letter to the Minister of War, a Russian immigrant Jew, Minkus, made an equally strong declaration of anti-Dreyfusism, and expressed a fundamental hostility to the rabbinate, which he accused of opposing modern civilization and perpetuating old superstitions and social divisions. He concluded his muddled plea for selective assimilation by deploring "the mass influx" into France from Eastern Europe "of Jewish workers without any education . . ."[140] Such hostility to recent immigrants or to further immigration by those already established in France was not rare, as Marrus has shown;[141] and could take the form of simply dissociating oneself from these unwelcome intruders who conformed too well to antisemitic stereotypes. Waleffe, for example, recorded that Catulle Mendès, who refused to take sides in the Dreyfus Affair, boasted: "Of course, I am a Jew, and I have never been baptized! But, please note!, a Portuguese Jew! These Jews have been, throughout the course of history, the intellectual branch of the race, a race of scholars and doctors, to whom making a profit from money has been quite alien . . ."[142] Jewish anticlerical antisemitism, motivated by hostility to the Judaic religion and the ghetto mentality which it helped to foster, was also not uncommon, especially among intellectuals such as Lazare and Herzl, who lived in France from 1891 to 1895 as Paris correspondent of the *Wiener Neue Freie Presse.*[143] But anti-Dreyfusism was not a monopoly of converted or anticlerical Jews, as the case of Rabbi Brauer of Tours indicates. Rabbi Brauer apparently expressed his complete acceptance of Dreyfus's second condemnation at Rennes in September 1899, in a private letter that was subsequently published. The hostile reaction of his congregation forced him to give up his post.[144]

Further examples of antisemitic response to antisemitism at the time of the Affair are provided by those Jews who contributed to the Henry Subscription.[145] Some Jews were also actively engaged in surveillance of fellow-Jews. Information about prominent Jews was furnished to the police during the

Affair, as we have seen. It seems likely that the informer who reported on Mme Léon Bloch's salon was Jewish; and information about Lazare was provided by a Jewish journalist, "Jacques Bahar (whose real name is Ben-Bahar) . . . and who claims to be a friend of M. Isaac [sic] Levaillant."[146] The motives here were probably pecuniary rather than ideological, and the same can be said of those Jews who were associated with the antisemitic press. For the first three years of its existence, up to 1895, *La Libre Parole* was run by a company, headed by a converted Jew, Wiallard, while *Le Petit Journal,* which gave instalments of *La France juive* away free to its readers in 1892, and was later firmly anti-Dreyfusard, had a Jewish administrator.[147] Clemenceau claimed, more generally, in 1898 that "when we are fighting against antisemitism in the name of universal tolerance, we find Jews ranged against us among our most eager adversaries: MM. Arthur Meyer of *Le Gaulois;* Pollonais of *Le Voltaire;* Klotz of *Le Soir* . . . Ellissen, manager of *Le Petit Journal,* and many others."[148] Arnoulin alleged, in addition, that the printer of *La France juive* had been a Jew.[149]

The line between reactions that can fairly be termed antisemitic, and those that can be called simply passive, cannot be drawn sharply, particularly since individuals did not consistently adhere to a single kind of response. Passive response, motivated by the desire not to attract attention, is also inherently difficult to document. The view that Jews reacted pusillanimously and negatively to antisemitism, however, was apparently widely held at the time. Drumont commented in *La France juive:* "The Jew is a coward, in the eyes of most ordinary people";[150] and later explained the attitude which gave rise to this idea: "The Jews . . . know deep down that the people detest them and they are thus anxious to avoid having attention directed towards them."[151] With greater understanding and sympathy, Péguy, in *Notre Jeunesse,* explained the same passive reaction of Jews to a tradition of persecution: "Now, obscurely, they would prefer that it did not start up again . . . the whole policy of Israel is not to make a noise in the world . . . to buy peace through a prudent silence . . . to be forgotten."[152] The Tharauds, more graphically, evoked the same context of adaptation to an unfriendly environment: "The Jews have become used to living with Christian society, as the sailor has become used to the sea, the mountain-dweller to the avalanche."[153]

Passive or negative response took various forms, some of which one can illustrate. First, there was a simple resignation in the face of antisemitism. "Each time that one of us has raised his head,/" wrote the poet André Spire, "The Gentile has marked our door-posts,/Has taken our first-born, and massacred our women."[154] On a different level, Benda wrote: "I have a horror of trouble-makers. This is perhaps a Jewish characteristic. Whether it is because we feel that we are weak and require protection, or because we have a particular feeling about the State, we always keep to the rules. *We would never dream of roughing up an agent of the law."*[155] Again, in Martin du Gard's *Jean Barois,* Woldsmuth alone of the editorial team of *Le Semeur* believed the first rumours that Dreyfus was innocent. In the face of his colleagues' disbelief, the author wrote, "Woldsmuth's eyes filled with little tears . . . He looked at them, one after the other, slowly, timidly. He felt quite alone, and smiled, with the resigned smile of the vanquished." Martin du Gard also evoked the sheer fear that could motivate such resignation, with the example of Woldsmuth's sister, Julia, terrified by the anti-Dreyfusard demonstration which took place outside the offices of the journal.[156] Resignation could also evolve into a kind of masochism. Lacretelle's Silbermann at first resisted his bullying at the *lycée;* then he adopted a more resigned attitude, enduring insults "with an adroit tenacity". Finally, he came to take a strange pleasure in his misfortune, giving way to "a tendency . . . hidden deep within him, like a grain of poison that could destroy everything: a secret admiration for the sufferings of his race". He wished to be "the unhappiest Jew of all", and he wrote antisemitic slogans on his bathroom mirror with soap, and contemplated "in a kind of ecstasy his image crowned with insults".[157]

Less extreme and more concrete manifestations of negative response were conversion to Catholicism, which we have already discussed (though not all conversion should be interpreted in this way), changing one's Jewish surname for a Christian one, and moving house or closing businesses in the face of antisemitic campaigns. Proust's instance of Bloch changing his name was probably based on the actual case of Franz Wiener, a Belgian Jew, who changed his name legally to Francis de Croisset when he came to Paris in the late 1890s. Though the adoption of pseudonyms by writers was not uncommon at this time in France, Wiener went a stage further than this, which supports the contention of some contemporaries that he was seeking to conceal his Jewishness by this means.[158] André Maurois, too, abandoned his family name, Herzog. We have seen that a number of Jewish businessmen were intimidated by the 1898 riots into temporary closures, and that some contemplated moving their businesses. At Bar-le-Duc, apparently, the rabbi and his family left the town after the riots there;[159] and, according to Elisée Reclus, as we have seen, several Jews left France altogether at the same time "to escape the campaign of insults."[160] There were also attempts to placate or to deflect antisemitic attacks. Drumont claimed that many Jews approached *La Libre Parole* through intermediaries, begging: "Don't mention this family! Keep quiet about this incident."[161]

Less abject, but still negative, was the response of those Jews who, from an assimilationist stance, played down the importance of antisemitism, or who chose to regard it primarily as an attack on Republican principles. Léon Blum took the first course, both in retrospect,[162] as we have seen, and at the time. His "Goethe" declared in April 1899:[163]

> I have heard some Jews in France complaining about being persecuted. Poor people! How is it that they have not learned that it depends entirely on an individual or on a race whether they are persecuted or not? For what constitutes persecution is not any vexatious measure, but the state of mind with which it is received and accepted. If the Jews are brave, if, far from emphasizing the effect of the discrimination against them, they absorb and attenuate it, if, instead of lamenting it, they smile about it, if they calmly trust, like their forefathers, that all injustice is precarious and that civiliza-

tion is irreversible, then no one will be able to say that they are persecuted
... I advise them, since, after all, their lives are secure and their existence
is on the whole tolerable, to cheerfully ignore these little affronts to their
pride or their interests. They are of such small importance in the life of an
individual, and of no importance at all in the life of a people. Above all,
no complaints!

And Blum followed his own precept in practice, reviewing Léon Daudet's *Le
Voyage de Shakespeare,* for example, in *La Revue Blanche* in May 1896,
without mentioning the book's blatant antisemitism.[164] Blum's over-optimis-
tic assessment of the implications of antisemitism may have been part of a
deliberate strategy, as he implied, but its effect was still to play down the
phenomenon. Again, Alphonse de Rothschild's dismissal of antisemitism as
"stupid and odious", in an interview published in *Le Figaro,* [165] had the same
effect. Such attitudes allowed Drumont to comment "on the blindness of the
Jews in the present crisis",[166] although elsewhere he indicated that this
apparent incomprehension was assumed. There is a great deal of evidence that
Jews often preferred to react to antisemitism as French citizens rather than
as Jews.[167] One example of this non-Jewish Jewish response, if one may put
it that way, was noted by Drumont. Various articles in *Les Archives Israélites*
in 1889 called for legislation to prevent antisemitism in the press, but for
legislation that would not be specifically in defence of Jews.[168]

According to Léon Blum again, as we noted in chapter II, the policy of not
attracting attention guided the general Jewish response to the Dreyfus Affair:
"A great misfortune had befallen Israel ... (but) The dominant feeling could
be expressed like this: 'It's something in which Jews should not get involved
... ' "[169] Similarly, Péguy noted that "it is among Jews that the Dreyfus
family, the emerging Dreyfus Affair, and emergent Dreyfusism encountered
at first the greatest resistance."[170] And considerable evidence can be found
to support this view, which was shared by others. Klotz reacted to the publication of Lazare's *Une Erreur judiciaire* in 1896, by regretting in *Le Voltaire*
that "our friend and former contributor" had so stuck his neck out, asking
rhetorically: "How ... can you let it be believed that in France, 'faced with
a Jew, people forgot about justice', and that if Dreyfus had not been a Jew,
he would not have been condemned?"[171] Another journalist recalled: "One
day one of the Bernheims told me: All that is sheer lunacy, and it is Bernard
Lazare who ought to be shot."[172] Police reports indicate, too, that presumably
studied indifference to the Affair was apparently widespread among French
Jewish communities. From the Pyrénées-Orientales, it was reported in February 1898 that the Jews of the region "have generally shown little interest in
this affair ... "[173] From Laon, it was reported in July 1898 that "the Jewish
element [remains] very reserved";[174] while, at Delle, after the news of the
Rennes verdict," the dozen Jewish families in the locality have acted as though
they had no interest in the matter ... "[175] Four years later in 1903, a police
report indicated that Jewish banking circles in Paris still feared the controversy
occasioned by the Affair, and wanted to delay a final revision for two or three
years longer, although "in principle, everyone in this milieu agrees that it

would be a good idea to resolve the Affair once and for all and to hear no more about it."[176] Even those who did become involved in Dreyfus's cause, some-times felt the need to stress that they had not become so simply because they were Jewish. Waleffe recalled that, at the height of the Affair, Sarah Bernhardt protested that, though her mother was Jewish: "By my father I am Christian. I have been baptized",[177] an interesting double precaution. And others easily lost heart. A police report from Paris in February 1898 indicated that some Jews were giving up hope in the Dreyfusard cause: "Many Jews are throwing in the sponge. They say that their clientèle is cooling off with this Zola affair, that has had such bad effects and has caused this business standstill that M. Méline has referred to in the Chamber. Meetings were taking place among certain Jewish businessmen and industrialists during the Zola affair. They have now ceased."[178]

The Dreyfus family itself, if less cautious than has often been supposed in its support for Alfred, was nevertheless conditioned by these defensive and deferential patterns of behaviour. A police agent reported, for example in June 1899 that, far from paying to send supporters to Rennes or Brest, "on the contrary the family of Captain Dreyfus will remain in the strict privacy of the family, avoiding all publicity or demonstrations which are quite alien to it, and to which it is opposed . . ."[179] It is well known that the publication of Lazare's *Une Erreur judicaire* was delayed a year, on the insistence of the Dreyfus family;[180] and in 1895 Mathieu Dreyfus turned down a plan to organize a petition on behalf of his brother.[181]

Writing this time as a Socialist leader and from the perspective of the thirties, Léon Blum interpreted this timid attitude towards the Affair harshly, particularly in the case of the Jewish bourgeoisie. Jews of Dreyfus' generation and class Blum claimed, who, like him, had managed to gain entry to the most sought-after branches of the civil service, were afraid that the Affair would damage their careers: "Rich Jews, middle-class Jews, Jews in the civil service were afraid of the struggle undertaken on behalf of Dreyfus . . . Their only thought was to lie low and to keep quiet. They imagined that the antisemitic fury would be deflected by their pusillanimous neutrality. They secretly cursed those among them who, in exposing themselves, made them also targets of the age-old hostility."[182] Such a judgment may, in large part, be true, but, unlike Péguy, Blum does not help to explain the attitude and behaviour which he condemned, and which, at one time, as we have seen, he came close to advocating himself. He underestimated the difficulties of overcoming what was a traditional Jewish defence mechanism,[183] and one common to most minority or oppressed groups.[184] Although he was referring to upper- and middle-class Jews only, he ignored, too, very probably, the extent to which outward "pusillanimity" and deference generally masked an acute and critical awareness of the opponent and his threat. As a police agent reported in June 1899: "The Jews are much better informed than we are about every move, every gesture that the Nationalists are proposing to make."[185] When the Nationalist leader Syveton struck General André in the Chamber of Deputies in 1904, Léon Daudet commented on Arthur Meyer's shocked reaction, despite his sympathy for the cause that Syveton represented; he remained, Daudet wrote, "an old Jew, for whom every blow, given or received, represented a threat to him personally".[186]

The actual context of possible protests must always be borne in mind, too. For example, if prominent Jews did not counter every journalistic insult and calumny, this had as much to do with their sheer volume, and with the traditional licence of the press of the Third Republic, as with an atavistic timidity. Press insults were directed against all persons in the public eye, and Jews were only following usual practice, if they ignored them. When the diplomat Jusserand was attacked in the press, not for the first time, in 1893, as he wrote later, "the Minister . . . highly approved of my intention to, just as before, say nothing, answer nothing."[187] Similarly, Mme Steinheil commented that when she was accused in the press of having poisoned President Faure, "the only policy was for me to ignore all insults and threats".[188] Again, President Loubet's *directeur de cabinet* explained that, although the Chief of State had his personal and political honour constantly impugned in the press, he made no riposte, for, "if he made one denial, he would have had to make new ones every morning."[189]

Turning now to those who did overcome these considerable inhibiting factors, a measure of positive Jewish response to antisemitism is provided, first, by the degree of Jewish involvement in the Dreyfusard campaign.[190] As Marrus has recently stressed,[191] official Jewish bodies and organizations in France, the consistories, the Jewish press, even the Alliance Israélite Universelle which had been founded in 1860 to fight "against injustice, prejudice and discrimination",[192] played little or no part in this campaign. However, Jewish bodies were in this instance, as more generally, unrepresentative, and the Dreyfusard cause in fact had a considerable amount of support from Jews, as we have already suggested in chapter II. The Affair, in the first place, evoked or revived a traditional Jewish solidarity,[193] as much a part of the instinctive defence mechanism of a minority under attack as the outward passivity which we have already discussed. It also created a new group-consciousness which was to lead some to Zionism.[194] The ex-Anarchist and future Zionist Bernard Lazare wrote to the moderate Republican politician Joseph Reinach in August 1896: "We are not in agreement in our political ideas and our views about society differ considerably . . . But we are both being attacked as Jews, Monsieur, and that is why we can forget our difference of opinion on economic matters and in general philosophy, and agree on the fight that must be fought against antisemitism";[195] and Reinach received several other letters of this kind during the Affair. J.-H. Lévy, an emancipated "non-Jewish" Jew, like Lazare, but an opponent of Zionism, reacted in a similar way. In an article entitled "Avis aux Israélites" in *Le Siècle* in February 1899, he proclaimed: "I have been completely separated from my Jewish co-religionists for a quarter of a century; but, when antisemitism developed and I was asked to join a Jewish association in order to oppose it, I said: Yes. I consider rabbinical theology to be ridiculous; but if the Jews are being persecuted, then I am a Jew."[196] Similarly, J.-R. Bloch's fictional Lévy declared later, voicing also a not uncommon concern about the too-effective assimilation of the younger generation: "Of course, I'm not a practising Jew myself any longer, but I still belong to the community . . . It is frightening how many of our young people are leaving us. Dare I say it? To revive the sentiment of our race among these young people, perhaps . . . we need another Affair . . ."[197] Again, more generally, both Théodore Reinach and Emile Durkheim made the same kind of observation about Jewish solidarity in the 1890s. Reinach wrote in 1894 that "the principal effect of antisemitism is to oblige the Jews to group together and to close ranks, and thus to revive Jewish particularism which was gradually breaking down";[198] and Durkheim explained the low suicide-rate among Jews by their strong sense of community: "Their need of resisting a general hostility . . . has forced them to strict union among themselves."[199] Among non-Jews, Leroy-Beaulieu observed in 1897 that "by declaring war on the Jews, by threatening to make them outlaws . . . antisemitism forces them again to group together";[200] while the liberal historian Levasseur commented in 1899: "I think that they were wrong to form a bloc to defend the cause of one of their fellows."[201] The antisemites, too, of course, pointed again and again to the phenomenon of Jewish solidarity: "the strength of the Jew is solidarity. All the Jews stand by each other . . .", Drumont declared, for example, in *La France juive.*[202] The fact that the movement of Jewish solidarity at the time of the Affair became inflated by antisemites into the famous Dreyfusard "syndicate", led, some claimed, by the Chief Rabbi himself,[203] yet another manifestation of the Jewish world conspiracy, has caused some historians, however, to ignore the real thing, which went well beyond the writings of intellectuals like Lazare or Lévy.

Lazare, himself, of course played a crucial role in initiating the revisionist campaign, and his contribution to it can only be compared with that of Zola. Daudet later referred to "Bernard Lazare, the Messianic Jew, who positively launched the Dreyfus Affair . . . like some wicked impresario . . ."[204] Reinach also played a leading part, with Mathieu Dreyfus,[205] and a long list could be made of individual Jews who quickly reacted in different ways to what they considered to be a gross act of discrimination against one of them: Marcel Proust,[206] Daniel Halévy,[207] Léon Blum,[208] Michel Bréal,[209] Salomon Reinach,[210] Victor Basch,[211] Paul Meyer,[212] Lucien Lévy-Bruhl,[213] Arthur Lévy,[214] Gustave Bloch, Albert Lévy,[215] Eugène Manuel,[216] Emile Durkheim,[217] Marcel Schwob,[218], Paul Grünebaum,[219] Ephraïm Mikhael,[220] the Natanson brothers,[221] Mme Emile Straus, whose salon became a kind of Dreyfusard headquarters,[222] and Elie Murmain, who helped to bring other Anarchists into the Dreyfusard cause,[223] to mention only the better-known. Their involvement took various forms, from individualistic gestures of support to signing petitions, joining organizations and publishing or writing Dreyfusard propaganda. The police reported, for example, in June 1899 that "a certain M.Worms, living at 8 rue de Florence [in Paris], on the fourth floor, has hung from his window a tricolour flag with the words: 'Vive Zola!' on it."[224] Daudet claimed that "the lists of [Dreyfusard] intellectuals published by *L'Aurore* were quickly filled up with a host of Jews . . ."[225] The Reinachs,

among others, wrote Dreyfusard pamphlets; and Léon Chaine's attack on
Catholic anti-Dreyfusism was published in 1903 by a Jewish publisher, Storck
of Lyon.[226] A number of French Jews, too, testified to the turning-point
which involvement in the Affair had represented in their lives, for example,
Julien Benda, Daniel Halévy and Pierre Hirsch, who wrote, explicitly that the
Affair had allowed him "to find an answer to my passionate self-interrogation"
about his real identity.[227]

These were mainly responses on the part of intellectuals and on the part
of individuals, albeit made with some general sense of Jewish solidarity, but
not all Jewish response fell exactly into these categories. Péguy stressed, as
Blum implied, that Dreyfusism was strongest among ordinary Jews, poor Jews,
Jews who were not well educated.[228] Moreover, although the process of
assimilation militated against collective response through the channel of Jewish organizations, there were collective manifestations of interest in and support for the Dreyfusard campaign that are all the more significant. In the
autumn of 1897, a police agent in Paris reported that "this Dreyfus Affair
remains a matter of passionate concern in Jewish circles generally"; and that
"one must foresee an extremely vigorous campaign on the part of Jews."[229]
After the riots of January and February 1898, expressions of Jewish support
of a general kind for the revisionist campaign were reported from Epinal,
Montbéliard, Belfort, Nice and elsewhere.[230] Sometimes the nature of this
support was specified. In January 1898, the rabbi of Nice and local Jewish
notables were said to be holding meetings to agree on measures to take in the
event of antisemitic demonstrations in the town.[231] In Paris, in February
1898, as we have seen, "meetings of certain businessmen and industrialists
took place during the Zola affair" with a similar intention. In March, a police
agent reported again from the capital that a group of Jewish financiers appeared to be very active in the organization of further Dreyfusard agitation;
and police agents also claimed about the same time that the revisionist press
was receiving Jewish financial backing.[232] In February 1898 also the members
of the Cercle Israélite of La Chaux-de-Fonds, just across the Swiss border,
formed a kind of local syndicate to support the Dreyfusard campaign, and in
April they sent to Zola "as an expression of gratitude, a magnificent chronome-
ter in gold, which will be paid for from the proceeds of a subscription that
has just been opened for this purpose . . ."[233] In November 1898 a similar
gift was despatched to Picquart.[234] Again, in Paris, in September 1899, a
group of Jewish Socialists held a meeting to protest against antisemitism.[235]

Jews played a notable part also in the main Dreyfusard organization, the
Ligue des Droits de l'Homme, as we have seen in chapter II. Joseph Reinach,
Paul Meyer and Isaac were on the national committee of the Ligue from the
start, Meyer becoming Vice-President, while Victor Basch was later President.[236] Durkheim was another founder-member.[237] The Marseille group in
1898–9 had two Jewish presidents, and Jews were reported to form its most
active and militant membership. At Nice, Jews were again prominent among
Ligue supporters, and, in August 1899, the president of the local section was
a Jew, Maxime Dreyfus. A police report from Paris in 1903 referred, as we

have seen, to "a fairly numerous Jewish group which constitutes the advanced wing of the Ligue des Droits de l'Homme".[238] This suggests that the Ligue may not have been as "assimilationist" as its manifesto suggests.

Jews seem to have acted collectively in the Affair through another kind of organization also: Alsace-Lorraine societies. These were by no means exclusively, if at all, "Nationalist" groups, but associations of those from the lost provinces who had opted for France in 1871, many of whom were Jews. The societies seem to have acted at the time of the Affair to give support to prominent Alsatian Dreyfusards, notably Scheurer-Kestner and Picquart, and also to express solidarity with Dreyfus himself as a fellow Alsatian Jew. One meeting of "Alsaciens-Lorrains" in Paris in December 1898 was addressed by Bernard Lazare; while another, which voted a resolution of support for Picquart was attended by "Alsatian Jews for the most part", according to the police, and was presided over by Arnold Netter, while speakers at it included Elie Murmain, Salomon Kahen, Hernani Cahen and Eugène Bloch.[239]

Although of crucial importance—we have seen that Levaillant regarded it as the necessary issue which crystallized for Jews the "political struggle . . . to preserve their rights"[240]—the Dreyfus Affair was by no means the sole occasion for Jewish resistance to antisemitism. Jews had countered antisemitism in a general way, from the 1880s and before, by means of the written word. *La France juive,* for example, had aroused a number of replies, notably the pamphlets of Alexandre Weill, published in 1886 and 1888.[241] The assumption that antisemitism could be met by rational argument was not, however, it seems, widely present, and more stress was laid in such literature on simply trying to make non-Jews more aware of the realities of Jewish life, religion and history, in the hope that such knowledge might dissipate prejudice. Whether such an intention was always present or not, it is no coincidence that the development of a Jewish literature in French coincided with the development of organized antisemitism; more or less consciously, a growing number of Jewish writers began, in the face of antisemitism, to assert their Jewishness in a positive way in their writing. The contrast between the attitude of an older writer like Catulle Mendès who died in 1909, and that of younger writers such as André Spire, Henri Franck, Edmond Fleg, Myriam Harry and J.-R. Bloch in the decade before the First World War is very striking; moreover, many of the latter were also more actively engaged in resisting antisemitism.[242]

Here they were following the precedent set some years earlier for a non-literary topical contestation of antisemitic claims and activity. In 1899, Durkheim had declared that it was necessary for "all men of good sense . . . to have the courage to proclaim aloud what they think, and to unite together in order to achieve victory in the struggle against public madness."[243] A lead in this kind of protest had been given by the Chief Rabbi, Zadoc Kahn. In a letter to *Le Temps* in January 1890, for example, he objected to the antisemitic rally held at Neuilly, albeit from a "democratic", assimilationist stance. Referring to the shouts of "War to the Jews!" that had been uttered there, he wrote: "France would cease to be France, that is to say a country with liberal traditions, if the words pronounced the other day can arouse the slightest echo."[244] The Chief Rabbi made a number of similar public protests against various manifestations of antisemitism in the early 1890s, but his "establishment" Republican approach proved much less effective in the context of the Affair. His attempt to set up a Comité de Défense contre l'Antisémitisme in 1894–5, made up of Jewish notables, led only to the establishment of a secret committee, whose existence did not become public knowledge until 1902.[245]

Jews also countered antisemites more systematically on their own favourite ground, the newspaper press. Marrus has pointed to a certain amount of positive, if cautious, reaction in the established Jewish press;[246] and there were some bolder attempts to combat the influence of La Libre Parole in particular. A bi-weekly, La Vraie Parole, edited by Isidore Singer, appeared for a short while in 1893, and a similar and equally unsuccessful paper L'Or et l'Argent, edited by Joseph Aron, in 1895.[247] According to Arnoulin, J.-B. Gérin, director of Le National, issued a special appeal for Jewish subscribers, a little earlier in 1890. "The Jews have been for some time the butt of odious calumnies which have proliferated in the columns of certain newspapers . . .", he wrote; Jewish leaders were therefore looking for a serious organ to defend Jewish interests; and Le National could fulfil this function. The appeal apparently failed, and Gérin became one of the chief financial backers of La Libre Parole. [248] Whatever the truth of all this, Jews were able to use the general press on occasion to attack antisemitism, as the quotation by J.-H. Lévy above indicates, and their reaction was not confined to specifically Jewish papers. In the provinces, for example, Le Petit Phare of Nantes, one of the main opponents and critics of antisemitism in the region, was owned and run by a Jew;[249] while, in the capital, L'Humanité, founded in 1904 very much as a Dreyfusard newspaper, had important backing from Jewish interests.[250] Mention should also be made here of the literary review, La Revue Blanche, run by the Natanson brothers, which had a number of Jewish contributors, including Blum and Muhlfeld, and which was staunchly Dreyfusard.[251] Early in 1898, the Revue severed its connection with Barrès, who retorted: "A Jewish review, which defends its own. What could be more natural?"[252]

On the practical level, a few cases are reported of Jews seeking legal redress against discrimination. As we have seen, the Jewish representative in Algiers of a Montbéliard firm sued it for damages, after he had been dismissed on the grounds that he was a Jew. The Jewish community of Lunéville sued a local Catholic priest, abbé Rohrbacher, for defamation in 1892—unsuccessfully since the abbé was able to show that his characterization of the Jew, in a sermon, as "a crook, a robber and a usurer" was in line with the definition provided by the Dictionnaire de l'Académie. [253] In 1893, La Libre Parole was sued for defamation by the rabbi of Vesoul and by two Jewish butchers, who won substantial damages. This was only the first of many such suits against the antisemitic newspaper; in 1900, for example, as we have seen, Henri de Rothschild sued Drumont and Viau after a series of defamatory articles had appeared in the paper, and was awarded 20,000 francs in damages.[254] Again, Joseph Reinach successfully sued Rochefort for publishing attacks on him in L'Intransigeant in 1898.[255] In January 1899, a Jewish business man from

Grenoble sued the leaders of the local Ligue Antisémitique after Jewish shops in the town had been daubed with paint, and on the grounds that its "Never buy from a Jew" campaign had been prejudicial to his commercial interests.[256] Guérin boasted that L'Antijuif had received over a thousand writs in the years 1897–1900 on behalf of Jews and others attacked in the newspaper.[257] Doubtless judicial records would reveal many more cases of this kind; and it is known that the secret Comité de Défense contre l'Antisémitisme did something to encourage them.[258] Whether such prosecutions were successful or not, and we have seen that some were, they indicate a determination on the part of many Jews to counter antisemitism when it affected their own interests, and a continuing belief that, despite the Affair, Jews could obtain justice in the courts. A similar determination to seek protection or redress through legal channels was displayed by the Jews of Algeria who sent formal petitions to both the Chamber of Deputies and the Senate in September 1898, complaining against the discriminatory measures imposed by local municipalities.[259]

Physical replies were also made to antisemitic violence and threats. A case was reported at Epinal, just before riots broke out in the town, of a Jew physically attacking a man who he mistakenly thought was putting up an antisemitic poster on a Jewish shop.[260] And such a case was not unique. Reinach wrote that, during the period of riots and demonstrations against Jews in Lorraine generally at this time, Jews often met violence with violence and even threw stones at antisemites.[261] Nor was physical resistance of this kind confined to the East. At a private meeting of the Ligue Antisémitique leaders in May 1898, for example, what seem to have been genuine fears were expressed that Drumont, on his return from Algiers after being elected deputy there, might be physically attacked by Jews.[262] Purely defensive measures of a physical kind were also not, it appears, unusual. For example, it was reported in January 1898 from Chalon-sur-Saône that the owner of a big store, which had been attacked by antisemites, had placed an armed guard on it.[263] A similar refusal to be intimidated was reported in September 1899 from Perpignan, where Jewish shops deliberately and unexpectedly stayed open immediately after the announcement of the Rennes verdict.[264]

Upper-class Jews frequently had recourse to the duel as a means of retaliation against insult. At the turn of this century, in Republican France as in Wilhelmine Germany and Habsburg Austria, the duel remained an important institution for settling affairs of "honour" among upper-class men. Although some French antisemites, like their German and Austrian counterparts, refused to fight duels with Jews, this was not the rule.[265] In May 1892, Captain Crémieu-Foa of the 8th Dragoon regiment wrote to Drumont, after La Libre Parole had published articles attacking Jewish officers: "In insulting the three hundred French officers on active service who belong to the Jewish faith, you are insulting me personally"; to which La Libre Parole replied: "If Jewish officers are wounded by our articles, let them choose by lot as many representatives as they wish and we will oppose them with an equal number of French swords. "In the following month, duels took place between Drumont and Crémieu-Foa and between Morès and a Captain Mayer, who was killed by his opponent, an outcome which led to a considerable outcry in the press, particularly on the part of fellow-Jews.[266] Later in the decade, in February 1898, a meeting of the Ligue Antisémitique discussed the question whether duels were permitted with Jews, and "Guérin expressed the view that one could fight with them, not as a matter of honour, but in order to get rid of them by legal means . . .",[267] a view which seems to have reflected current practice, and which meant that challenges issued by Jews were answered. Viau, who wrote articles attacking individual Jews in *La Libre Parole,* boasted that between 1892 and 1900 he had fought 12 duels as a result of these articles; and he indicated that at least 5 of these duels were fought as a result of challenges from Jews. He also mentioned other duels fought by leading antisemites in similar circumstances. Drumont, for example, was challenged, not only by Crémieu-Foa in 1892, but also by Arthur Meyer in 1886, by Camille Dreyfus in 1893, and by Bernard Lazare in 1896.[268] Other duels between Jews and non-Jews, which seem to have been most common at the time of the Affair itself, included those between Catulle Mendès and Paul Foucher, between Rochefort and Camille Dreyfus, between Déroulède and Reinach, between Léon Daudet and Henri Bernstein, and between Baron Robert de Rothschild and the Comte de Lubersac.[269] The famous Morès–Mayer duel was thus only one of a series of ripostes.

Three general points can be made in conclusion. First, despite the process of assimilation, Jews in France at the turn of this century retained many of the characteristics of an unassimilated minority, characteristics which antisemitism strengthened. One must therefore be extremely careful not to label as "passive" in any simple or pejorative sense, responses and attitudes which should be seen rather as natural modes of adaptation to a hostile social environment. Patterns of behaviour, outwardly "pusillanimous" could, and almost certainly usually did, serve as a mask for real hostility and resentment. In such circumstances the large amount of overt and active Jewish opposition to antisemitism, which our enquiry reveals, is all the more significant, and even surprising. This is especially so when one realizes that such opposition was mainly the option of individuals responding to some general sense of Jewish solidarity but lacking the support of established collective organizations, and that it frequently involved great personal sacrifice, as Péguy emphasized.[270] Second, although the element of individual courage in such behaviour cannot be overlooked, the main factor for its interpretation in socio-historical terms seems to be a confidence based on Jewish assessment of the strength and meaning of antisemitism in France. Most politically and socially conscious Jews seem to have sensed, correctly, that organized antisemitism was a minority movement, albeit one which depended on the existence of a much more widespread prejudice, and that it represented an important threat only in alliance with other forces, and as an attack on the democratic Republican régime. From a different perspective, governments of the Third Republic reached the same conclusion, and soon made clear their opposition to the antisemitic movement. The cause of assimilationism, which was seen by Jews in terms of assimilation into Republican France, was thus in many ways vindicated and strengthened by the antisemitic upsurge of the 1890s and its rapid collapse after 1900 in the face of governmental disapproval. Third, the often negative response of Jews to antisemitism must also be related to the nature of antisemitism as we have analysed it in previous chapters. If antisemitism was essentially an attempt to explain or to explain away "modernization" that only arbitrarily involved the Jews as mythical manipulators or polluters, what response by authentic Jews was appropriate or invested with meaning? Though the problem was rarely, if at all, posed in these terms, it is arguable that the difficulties which Jews experienced in coming to terms with antisemitism objectively reflected it. They were not simply the objects of explicit acts of discrimination or threats, to which they could react, or against which they could defend themselves. They were the central characters in someone else's mythical view of the world, which was, in important ways, a much less comfortable position to be in, if only because there was no clear way to extricate themselves from it.

NOTES

1 See, for example, Eleonore Sterling, "Jewish Reaction to Jew-Hatred in the First Half of the Nineteenth Century", *Leo Baeck Institute Year Book*, III (1958), pp. 103–21; Adolphe Asch and Johanna Philippson, "Self-Defence at the Turn of the Century: The Emergence of the K.C.", ibid., III, pp. 122–39; Margaret T. Edelheim-Muehsam, "Reactions of the Jewish Press to the Nazi Challenge", ibid., V (1960), pp. 308–29; Michael Meyer, "Great Debate on Antisemitism, Jewish Reaction to New Hostility in Germany 1879–1881", ibid., XI (1966), pp. 137–70; Henry Michel, "La Résistance juive dans la Résistance européenne", *Le Monde Juif*, 4 (1968), pp. 7–13; J. Presser, *Ashes in the Wind: The Destruction of Dutch Jewry* (London, 1968), pp. 278–84; Lucien Steinberg, *La Révolte des justes* (Paris, 1970); Ismar Schorsch, *Jewish Reactions to German Anti-Semitism, 1870–1914* (New York, 1972); Arnold Paucker, "Jewish Defence against Nazism in the Weimar Republic", *Wiener Library Bulletin*, 26, New Series, nos 26–7 (1972), pp. 21–31 and bibliography; Jacques Ravine, *La Résistance organisée des Juifs en France 1940–1944* (Paris, 1973); Kren and Rappoport, "Victims: the fallacy of innocence", *Societas* (1974).

2 See Arendt, *The Origins of Totalitarianism*, pp. 117–19; and, particularly, Marrus, *The Politics of Assimilation* (hereafter *PA*), chapter VI, pp. 141–58, and Chapter VIII. Amplifying Byrnes's slight but judicious account (*Antisemitism in Modern France*, pp. 97–104), Marrus provides a well-documented and sophisticated survey, and it is only his general emphasis which is at issue. Marrus has more recently returned to the problem in a more general setting in a paper: "European Jewry and the Politics of Assimilation: Assessment and Reassessment", *Journal of Modern History*, 1977.

3 *La République Française*, 19 October 1896, cit. Bournand, *Les Juifs et nos contemporains*, p. 121.

4 See Sartre, *Réflexions sur la question juive*, Part 3; Memmi, *Portrait d'un Juif*, Part I and generally; Felix Woltsch, "The Rise and Fall of the Jewish-German Symbiosis: The Case of Franz Kafka", *Leo Baeck Institute Year Book*, I, (1956), pp. 255–76; Isaac Deutscher, *The Non-Jewish Jew and other essays* (London, 1968).

5 See Arthur Meyer, *Ce que mes yeux ont vu;* Meyer, *Ce que je peux dire* (Paris, 1912); Daudet, *Salons et Journaux*, pp. 126–7 and 137–45; Daudet, *Au Temps de Judas*, pp. 104 and 148–9; Rémond, *La Droite en France*, p. 321; Beau de Loménie, *Édouard Drumont*, pp. 130–1. Daudet claimed, incidentally, that 9 members of the staff of *Le Gaulois* were Jewish.

6 See, for example, F. Boulard, *An Introduction to Religious Sociology, Pioneer Work in France* (London, 1960), p. 7; and François-André Isambert, *Christianisme et Classe ouvrière: Jalons pour une étude de sociologie historique* (Paris, 1961), p. 73; also Memmi, op. cit., pp. 219–30.

7 See, for example, Tharaud, *Petite Histoire des Juifs*, pp. 152–3; Wirth, *The Ghetto*, pp. 52–5 and *passim;* Moysheh Oyved, *Visions and Jewels, An Autobiography* (London, 1925), pp. 111–12; Ginsberg, "Antisemitism", p. 194; Loewenstein, *Christians and Jews*, p. 162; Shapiro, "The Jewish People: A Biological History", *Race and Science*, UNESCO, pp. 154–6; Memmi, op. cit., pp. 347–59; and, on Jewish secularization in France, René Schwob, *Moi, Juif*, p. xiii; Maurois, *Mémoires*, I, pp. 57–8; Emmanuel Berl, *Rachel et autres grâces* (Paris, 1965), pp. 20–1; Landau, "Aspects et problèmes spécifiques de l'histoire des Juifs en France", p. 235; Ziebura, *Léon Blum et le parti socialiste*, pp. 10 and *passim;* Dalby, *Léon Blum, Evolution of a Socialist*, pp. 25–6; Marrus, *PA*, chapter IV; Blumenkranz, ed., *Histoire des Juifs en France*, p. 367.

8 Maurois, op. cit., I, pp. 16 and 62–3; for an evocation of a similar experience, see the fictionalized autobiography of the Genevois Edmond Fleg, *L'Enfant prophète*, pp. 18–21, 29, 36–9 and 45–6.

9 Benda, *La Jeunesse d'un clerc*, pp. 107–8.

10 R. Schwob, op. cit., p. 52. The text quoted seems to be a paraphrase of two passages from the Gospels (Matthew, 10:7; Luke, 14:26). The same desire to escape the Jewish condition was present in the conversions of Maurice Sachs and Pierre Hirsch.

11 See Alfred Dreyfus, *Cinq années de ma vie*, pp. 25–6; and P. Dreyfus, *Dreyfus: His Life and Letters*, pp. 38–9.

12 Alfred Dreyfus, Letters, 6 December 1894, and 26 December 1898, cit. P. Dreyfus, op. cit., pp. 40 and 156; see also ibid., pp. 131 and 315.

13 See Alfred Dreyfus, op. cit., pp. 27–33 and *passim;* and P. Dreyfus, op. cit., pp. 41–2, 142, 146, 150, 160–2 and *passim.*

14 Cit. Guillemin, *Zola*, Collection Génies et Réalités, chapter 18, p. 249.

15 Pierre Hirsch, *De Moïse à Jésus*, p. 9; and Maurois, op. cit., I, pp. 15–22. See also Werth, *The Strange History of Pierre Mendès-France*, p. 4, for the similar case of Mendès-France's maternal grandfather; and Marrus, *PA*, pp. 97–100 and *passim*, on Jewish French patriotism generally.

16 See chapter XII, n. 545.

17 The list of benefactors of France's national museums, for example, includes a high proportion of Jewish names; and the Curie Foundation was created in 1920 on the initiative of Baron Henri de Rothschild, who also gave generous support to the French Radium Institute; see Eve Curie, *Madame Curie*, pp. 345 and 369.

18 Blumenkranz, ed., op. cit., pp. 363–6; also Landau, op. cit., p. 237; and Pierrard, *Juifs et catholiques français*, p. 229.

19 Lukes, *Emile Durkheim*, pp. 553–4.

20 Cit. Blumenkranz, ed., op. cit., p. 364.

21 See Sartre, op. cit., p. 104; Memmi, op. cit., pp. 250–1, 255 and 280–1; and also Loewenstein, op. cit., pp. 54–5.

22 Daudet, *Au Temps de Judas*, pp. 148–9.

23 Werth, op. cit., p. 4.

24 See Wirth, *The Ghetto*, pp. 102–6; Sartre, op. cit., pp. 133–42; Poliakov, "Le Sionisme", *Les Juifs et notre histoire*, chapter VII; Walter Laqueur, *A History of Zionism* (London, 1972); and David Vital, *The Origins of Zionism* (Oxford, 1975).

25 See Byrnes, op. cit., p. 99; Marrus, *PA*, chapter IX; and Blumenkranz, ed., op. cit., p. 367.

26 On Lazare, see Péguy, *Notre Jeunesse*, pp. 87–8, 108–10 and *passim;* Byrnes, op. cit., pp. 103–4; Nelly Jussem-Wilson, "Bernard Lazare's Jewish Journey; from

being an Israelite to being a Jew", *Jewish Social Studies*, 26 (1964), pp. 146–8; Marrus, *PA*, chapter VII.

27 See Lacretelle, *Silbermann*, pp. 47, 101, 138 and *passim*.

28 Cit. Bournand, op. cit., p. 19 (his italics).

29 See Wirth, *The Ghetto*, p. 128; and the development of the same idea by Loewenstein, op. cit., chapter V.

30 Cit. Jackson, *La Revue Blanche*, p. 115.

31 Memmi, op. cit., pp. 300 and 376; see also ibid., pp. 64–5, 233–8, 277, 301 and *passim;* Tharaud, *Petite Histoire*, pp. 144–5 and 277–82; Kafka, *Letters to Milena*, pp. 50–1, 147, and 219; Wirth, *The Ghetto*, pp. ix, 73, 110 and 261–7; Ginsberg, op. cit., p. 193; Sartre, op. cit., pp. 95–6, 106–7 and 161; Kazin, *A Walker in the City*, pp. 45–56 and *passim;* Shapiro, "The Jewish People", pp. 107–8; Poliakov, *Les Juifs et notre histoire*, pp. 67–70 and 232–4.

32 Benda, *La Jeunesse d'un clerc*, pp. 172–3 and 33; also pp. 12–22, 53, 81 and 107–8.

33 Berl, *Rachel*, p. 230.

34 Berl, *Sylvia*, pp. 9–10; see also ibid., pp. 10–11 and 247–8; and *Rachel*, p. 93.

35 Berl, *Rachel*, p. 43; also pp. 36–7.

36 Berl, *Sylvia*, p. 7.

37 Daudet, *Paris vécu*, Ier série, p. 27.

38 See Renard, *Correspondance*, pp. 114–15, 118 and 121; and Bellanger *et al.* ed., *Histoire générale de la presse française*, III, pp. 237 and 405.

39 Daudet, *Au Temps de Judas*, pp. 95–9. Gamzon, "Claudel rencontre Israël", p. 74, says, it seems wrongly, that Schwob was not interested in the Affair, but the uncertainty about his position is itself revealing.

40 George Trembley, *Marcel Schwob, Faussaire de la Nature* (Geneva, 1969), pp. 9–13, 20, 26, 30–42, 83–4 and *passim*. Trembley does not, however, offer this interpretation himself.

41 Gide, *Journals*, I, p. 110 (February 1902).

42 Gamzon, op. cit., pp. 74–5.

43 Gide, *Journals* (Penguin edition), p. 486.

44 Lukes, op. cit., pp. 44–5 and 100.

45 Cit. Audry, *Léon Blum*, p. 27.

46 See pp. 710–12 below; and Dalby, op. cit., chapter 4.

47 Proust, *A la Recherche du temps perdu* (English Uniform Edition), VII, pp. 125–6 and 145.

48 See my "Proust's *A la Recherche du temps perdu* as a Document of Social History", pp. 236–40; also Arendt, op. cit., pp. 80–5; Szasz, *The Manufacture of Madness*, pp. 268–9; and Sherban Sidéry, "Israel's Way", Peter Quennell, ed., *Marcel Proust 1871–1922: A Centenary Volume* (London, 1971), chapter 4.

49 Sachs, *Le Sabbat*, pp. 27, 32–3 and *passim*.

50 Bloch, . . . *Et Cie* (1918) (English edition, London, 1930). The book was written in 1911–14.

51 Fleg, op. cit., pp. 11–17 and *passim;* also Maurois, op. cit., I, p. 16; Berl, *Sylvia*, pp. 247–8.

52 Lacretelle, op. cit., pp. 243–4, 254–5 and generally.

53 Gamzon, op. cit., pp. 91–4; and Denise Goitein, "La Figure de Pensée", *Cahiers Paul Claudel*, 7, pp. 103–10. The passage in italics echoes a passage from Victor Hugo's *Les Contemplations* (1969 edition, p. 18): "la misère/Du peuple juif, maudit qu'il faut enfin bénir . . ."

54 Tharaud, *Petite Histoire*, p. 127.

55 "une judéite, un judaïsme et un judaïcité". Memmi, op. cit., p. 312. For various, and conflicting, approaches to the problem of definition, see ibid., pp. 96–7, 133–4, 306–8 and 312–15; Sartre, op. cit., pp. 69, 81, 84 and *passim;* Bernard Lazerwitz, "Some Factors in Jewish Identification", *Jewish Social Studies*, 15, (1953), pp. 3–24; "Forms and Expressions of Jewish Identification", Papers and

Proceedings of the Tercentenary Conference on American-Jewish Psychology, ibid., 17 (1955), pp. 205–37; Glock and Stark, *Christian Beliefs and Anti-Semitism*, p. 101; Landau, op. cit., pp. 236–8; Ralph Segalman, "Jewish Identity Scales: A Report", *Jewish Social Studies*, 29, (1967), pp. 92–111; Raul Hilberg, *The Destruction of the European Jews* (Chicago, 1967), pp. 43–53; and Deutscher, op. cit., chapter 2, "Who is a Jew?"

56 See Viau, *Vingt ans d'antisémitisme*, pp. 157–63; and chapter V, pp. 172–3; and chapter VI, pp. 183–5 above.

57 Report, Commissaire spécial, Rennes, 18 July 1899; Telegram, Prefect, Ille-et-Vilaine, 14 July 1899; and Report, Procureur de la République, Rennes, 27 July 1899. AN F⁷ 12464.

58 Havas telegram, Belfort, 10 September 1899. AN F⁷ 12465.

59 See chapter X, pp. 273–5; and chapter XII, pp. 405–6 above; and Pierre Moreau, "Tandis que Paul Claudel découvrait l'Israël moderne . . .", *Cahiers Paul Claudel*, 7, pp. 370–2.

60 Théodore Reinach, *La Grande Encyclopédie*, 1894, cit. Bournand, op. cit., p. 295.

61 Joseph Reinach, *Histoire de l'Affaire Dreyfus*, II, pp. 162–3.

62 Reports, Commissaire spécial, Belfort, 27 December 1894, and 7 January 1895. AN F⁷ 12473.

63 Report, Commissaire de police, Carpentras (Vaucluse), 11 November 1896. AN F⁷ 12464.

64 See Proust, op. cit., V, pp. 338–41; and VII, pp. 109, 111 and 204.

65 Report, Commissaire spécial, Belfort, 21–24 December 1897. AN F⁷ 12461.

66 Viau, op. cit., p. 161.

67 Daily Report, Prefect of Police, 20 February 1898. APP Ba 106.

68 Viau, op. cit., pp. 44–5.

69 In addition to discussion in previous chapters, see, for example, Reports, Prefect, Marne, 22 June 1896; Commissaire spécial, Toulouse, 30 March 1899; and Commissaire spécial, Nantes, 25 January 1898, and 25–27 August 1903. AN F⁷ 12460; and Prefect, Seine-Inférieure, 3 April 1898. AN F⁷ 12461.

70 Report, Police agent, Paris, 30 November 1897. AN F⁷ 12473; see also Dagan, *Enquête sur l'antisémitisme*, pp. 40–1 (Reclus).

71 Report, Sub-prefect, Lunéville, 23 January 1898. AN F⁷ 12467.

72 See Report, Police agent, 12 February 1898. AN F⁷ 12474; also Letter from Dufour to Prefect of Police, no date. APP Ba 1103.

73 *L'Aurore*, 8 December 1898.

74 Lazare, *L'Antisémitisme*, chapters VIII and IX.

75 See pp. 710–11 below.

76 See AN F⁸⁰ 1688–1689; and chapter IX, p. 233 above.

77 Telegrams, Prefect, Loire-Inférieure to Ministry of Interior, 20 January 1898; and *Général commandant* to Ministry of War, 21 January 1898. AN F⁷ 12467.

78 Police reports, 14 October, and 23 November 1896; and 20 November 1897; and Report, Prefect of Police, 23 November 1896. AN F⁷ 12473.

79 AN F⁷ 12474.

80 Reports, Police agent, 24 June 1899. AN F⁷ 12465; and 29 July 1899. AN F⁷ 12473.

81 The analyses of Lazare and Leroy-Beaulieu remain, nevertheless, very impressive, though weakest on their own time.

82 P.-P. Furth, "Le Personnage du Juif dans l'oeuvre d'Erckmann-Chatrian", *Europe*, 549–550, January–February 1975, pp. 106–13.

83 Drumont, *La France juive*, II, pp. 249–50.

84 Cit. Schmidt, *Maupassant par lui-même*, p. 118; see also Rouquier and Soumille, "La Notion de Race chez les Français d'Algérie".

85 Apollinaire, *L'Hérésiarque et cie, Oeuvres complètes*, I, pp. 33, 105–13 and 119–27.

86 Bloy, *Le Salut par les Juifs,* p. 34 and *passim;* see also chapter XIV, pp. 514–15 above.

87 Leroy-Beaulieu, *L'Antisémitisme,* pp. 2 and 6.

88 See, for example, Gohier, "Les Enjuivés", 17 June 1898, *L'Armée contre la nation,* pp. 263–8.

89 See, for example, Jaurès, "Le Combat", *La Dépêche de Toulouse,* 28 December 1898; Daily Report, Prefect of Police 8 June 1898. APP Ba 106; and chapter XI, pp. 337 and 357 above.

90 See, for example, Dagan, op. cit, p. 86; Sébastien Faure, *Le Libertaire,* 2 February 1898; and *Le Père Peinard,* February 1898, cit. Bournand, op. cit., pp. 227–33 and 238–40.

91 Memmi, op. cit., p. 262.

92 Joseph Reinach, op. cit., IV, p. 447.

93 *Le Matin,* 12 September 1892, cit. Bournand, op. cit., p. 114.

94 See Dagan, op. cit., p. 31 (Guyot); and Bousquet-Mélou, *Louis Barthou,* pp. 102 and 115, citing a speech made in May 1899.

95 Cit. Bournand, op. cit., p. 122; see also Arnoulin, *M. Edouard Drumont,* p. 180.

96 L'Hermite, *L'Anti-Pape,* p. 267.

97 See *Le Petit Méridional,* 7 April 1900, reporting on a speech made by Trarieux at Montpellier.

98 AN F⁷ 12487; see also Charlot, "Un Rassemblement d'Intellectuels, La Ligue des Droits de l'Homme", pp. 995–6.

99 Cit. Bournand, op. cit., p. 80. Maret did, however, recognize the existence of "israélites".

100 Daily Report, Prefect of Police, 24 February 1898. APP Ba 106.

101 See, for example, Verdès-Leroux, *Scandale financier et antisémitisme catholique,* pp. 162–8.

102 On traditional Protestant sympathies for Jews in France, see Poliakov, *Les Juifs et notre histoire,* pp. 22–3. At a later date, as we have seen, the French Reformed Church, unlike the Catholic hierarchy, protested against Vichy's Jewish Statute of 1940; see ibid., pp. 169–70.

103 In addition to other references cited earlier, see André Gide, *If It Die,* pp. 192 and 227.

104 Maurois, *Mémoires,* I, pp. 16–17.

105 Lacretelle, op. cit., p. 66. Lacretelle's mother actually came of a Southern Protestant family; see Douglas Alden, *Jacques de Lacretelle, An Intellectual Itinerary* (New Brunswick, 1958), p. 7.

106 Lacretelle, op. cit., pp. 28–35, 62–3 and *passim;* Fleg, op. cit., p. 58.

107 Pierrard, op. cit., p. 59.

108 P. Dreyfus, op. cit., pp. 207–8; see also, generally, chapter II, pp. 82–3 above.

109 See Bournand, op. cit., pp. 207–8.

110 G. Valbert, "Les Juifs allemands et leurs ennemis", *Revue des Deux Mondes,* 1 March 1882, 3e Période, LIIe Année, p. 225.

111 Reprinted in Zola, *L'Affaire Dreyfus,* pp. 55–62.

112 See Tharaud, *Notre cher Péguy,* I, pp. 248–51; Pierrard, op. cit., pp. 222–8; and chapter XIV, n. 308.

113 Report, Commissaire spécial, Saint-Nicolas-du-Port, 7 July 1899. AN F⁷ 12465.

114 Report, Commissaire central, Nantes, 30 June 1899. Ibid.

115 Report, Commissaire de police, Caudebec-les-Elbeuf, 29 July 1900. AN F⁷ 12457.

116 Bloch, . . . *Et Cie,* p. 379.

117 Report, Police agent, February 1898. AN F⁷ 12474.

118 Report, Commissaire central, Grenoble, 21 January 1899. AN F⁷ 12460.

119 Daily Report, Prefect of Police, 30 April 1898. APP Ba 106.

120 See Drumont, *La Dernière Bataille,* p. 263.

121 Jean Renoir, *Renoir My Father,* p. 242.

122 Dagan, op. cit., p. 59.

123 See, for example, Loewenstein, op. cit., pp. 145 and 147; Sartre, op. cit., pp. 125–6; Ginsberg, op. cit., p. 192; and Ackerman and Jahoda, *Anti-Semitism and Emotional Disorder*, pp. 46, 51–3 and 79–80.

124 Péguy, "Demi-réponse à M. Cyprien Lantier", November 1900, *Oeuvres en Prose, 1898–1908*, p. 290.

125 Victor Hugo, *Choses vues 1830–1846*, p. 474 (22 December 1846).

126 Cit. Bournand, op. cit., p. 295.

127 Cit. Silvera, *Daniel Halévy*, p. 91.

128 Proust, op. cit., IV, p. 49; and XII, p. 287.

129 Lacretelle, op. cit., pp. 102–3.

130 Meyer, *Ce que mes yeux ont vu*, pp. 134 and 124.

131 L'Hermite, op. cit., pp. 157–8.

132 Tharaud, *Petite Histoire*, p. 38.

133 See Lémann, *La Prépondérance juive*, I, p. 266 and *passim*; also Drumont, *DB*, p. 201.

134 Cit. Gamzon, op. cit., p. 75.

135 R. Schwob, op. cit., pp. 306–9 and *passim*.

136 See Barrès-Maurras, *La République ou le roi*, pp. 682–5.

137 Steinheil, *My Memoirs*, p. 103.

138 Cit. Barrès, *Scènes et doctrines*, I, p. 209. In fact Rabbi Kahn did not play a very active part in the Affair; see Marrus, *PA*, pp. 223–5.

139 Cit. Zévaès, *L'Affaire Dreyfus*, p. 122; also Grenier, *Nos Députés, 1898–1902*, p. 516.

140 Letter, 17 June 1903. AN F7 12925.

141 See Marrus, *PA*, pp. 158–62.

142 Waleffe, *Quand Paris était un paradis*, p. 42; see also Daudet, *Au Temps de Judas*, pp. 93–4.

143 See Bein, *Theodore Herzl*, pp. 35 and 49, and chapter IV. Henry J. Cohn, "Theodor Herzl's Conversion to Zionism", *Jewish Social Studies*, 32 (1970), pp. 101–10, has convincingly argued that this French experience was less decisive in Herzl's evolution than had been often supposed. Another, anti-Dreyfusard, Jewish intellectual who can probably be placed in the anticlerical category was La Jeunesse; see Daudet, *Au Temps de Judas*, p. 109.

144 Armand Charpentier, "L'Affaire du Rabbin Brauer", *L'Action*, 26 July 1904.

145 See Quillard, *Le Monument Henry*, pp. 3, 5, 410, 424, 476 and 631; and chapter IV, pp. 152–3 above.

146 Reports, Police agents, 27 October, and 30 November 1897; and 29 July 1899. AN F7 12473. Internal evidence and poor written French suggest that the first informer was a foreigner, possibly a woman. Bahar later became a Zionist, and Levaillant was editor of *L'Univers Israélite*; see Marrus, *PA*, pp. 260–1 and 137.

147 See Viau, op. cit., pp. 22, 36–7 and 96; Guérin, *Les Trafiquants de l'antisémitisme*, pp. 37–9; "L'Archiviste", *Drumont et Dreyfus*.

148 Cit. Bournand, op. cit., p. 103.

149 Arnoulin, op. cit., pp. 26 and 59.

150 Drumont, *FJ*, I, p. 3.

151 Drumont, *Le Testament d'un antisémite*, p. 368.

152 Péguy, *NJ*, p. 71; and pp. 67–72 *passim*.

153 Tharaud, *Petite Histoire*, p. 37.

154 André Spire, *Pogromes*, cit. Pierrard, op. cit., p. 328.

155 Benda, *La Jeunesse d'un clerc*, pp. 70–1 (his italics); see also Benda, *Les Cahiers d'un clerc*, pp. 25 and 214.

156 Martin du Gard, *Jean Barois*, pp. 210 and 253.

157 Lacretelle, op. cit., pp. 207, 247 and 253. On Jewish temptation to masochism generally, see Memmi, op. cit., p. 82.

158 See Waleffe, op. cit., pp. 14–16; and Arbellot, *La Fin du Boulevard*, pp. 27–8.

159 See Bournand, op. cit., pp. 136–7.

160 Dagan, op. cit., pp. 40–1.
161 Drumont, *De l'Or, de la boue, du sang*, p. 259.
162 Blum, *Souvenirs sur l'Affaire*, pp. 62–3; see Chapter III, p. 119 above.
163 Blum, *Nouvelles Conversations de Goethe avec Eckermann, L'Oeuvre de Léon Blum 1891–1905*, pp. 267–8; also p. 262.
164 Blum, "Les Livres", *La Revue Blanche*, May 1896, ibid., pp. 15–20.
165 Cit. Bournand, op. cit., p. 310.
166 Cit. ibid., p. 38.
167 See Marrus, *PA*, chapters V, VI and VIII.
168 Drumont, *DB*, pp. 125–7; see also Memmi, op. cit., p. 271, on this type of response generally.
169 See chapter II, n. 208.
170 Péguy, *NJ*, p. 73; also ibid., pp. 84–5 and 173; Mark Twain, "Concerning the Jews" (September 1899), *The Complete Essays of Mark Twain* (New York, 1963), p. 244; Daudet, *Au Temps de Judas*, p. 89; Blumenkranz ed., op. cit., pp 352–3.
171 *Le Voltaire*, 9 November 1896.
172 Jean Steens, "Souvenirs d'un Dreyfusard; Les Juifs", *La Patrie*, 7 April 1902.
173 Reports, Commissaire spécial, Perpignan, 24 February 1898. AN F7 12474; and 10 September 1899. AN F7 12465.
174 Report, Commissaire de police, Laon, 24 July 1898. AN F7 12467.
175 Report, Commissaire spécial, Delle, 12 September 1899. AN F7 12465.
176 Report, Police agent, 9 December 1903. AN F7 12470; see also Blumenkranz ed., op. cit., p. 364.
177 Waleffe, op. cit., p. 42.
178 Police report, 25 February 1898. AN F7 12474.
179 Report, Police agent, Paris, 24 June 1899. AN F7 12465.
180 See P. Dreyfus, op. cit., pp. 168–9; and Marrus, *PA*, p. 81; also Marrus, *PA*, pp. 214–17, more generally.
181 See Gauthier, ed, *"Dreyfusards!"*, p. 56. Mathieu Dreyfus was, nevertheless, in his own way, a tireless and courageous defender of his brother.
182 Blum, *Souvenirs sur l'Affaire*, pp. 25–7; see also Blum, *Nouvelles Conversations*, pp. 265–6; and chapter II, pp. 84–5 above.
183 On this, see, for example, Braudel, *The Mediterranean*, II, p. 803; Balzac, *Le Cousin Pons*, p. 14; Oyved, op. cit., p. 84; Loewenstein, op. cit., pp. 109 and 131–7; Sartre, op. cit., pp. 131, 142–3 and 157–8; Byrnes, op. cit., p. 98; Memmi, op. cit., pp. 282, 294–9, 309, 367 and 376–7; Morin *et al.*, *La Rumeur d'Orléans*, pp. 89–93 and 136.
184 "Prior to 1954 . . . Negroes found it necessary, in order to maintain whatever sanity they could, to remain somewhat aloof and detached from 'the problem'. We accepted indignities and the mechanics of the apparatus of oppression without reacting by sitting-in or holding mass demonstrations." Eldridge Cleaver, *Soul on Ice* (London, 1969), pp. 3–4. In addition to other studies of American Blacks, see the work of Fanon, Mannoni and Memmi on the socio-psychology of colonization; note also Beaumont's comments on the Irish in the nineteenth century: "l'Irlandais prend son parti de plier et saisant les seules armes qui soient à l'usage des faibles, il devient rusé, menteur, violent", cit. Jardin, "Alexis de Tocqueville, Gustave de Beaumont et le problème de l'inégalité des races", p. 12.
185 Report, Police agent, Paris, 24 June 1899. AN F7 12465.
186 Daudet, *Au Temps de Judas*, p. 222; see also Drumont, *TA*, p. 369; Paléologue, *Journal de l'Affaire Dreyfus*, pp. 239–40 (September 1899); and Memmi, op. cit., p. 46.
187 Jusserand, *What Me Befell*, p. 153; also pp. 59 and 69.
188 Steinheil, op. cit., p. 118.
189 Combarieu, *Sept Ans à l'Elysée avec le Président Emile Loubet*, p. 2; see also Paléologue, op. cit., p. 72, on the similar reaction of General Saussier, Military Governor of Paris, to attacks on him in *La Libre Parole* in 1897.

190 In addition to what follows, see chapter II, pp. 83–5 above.
191 Marrus, *PA*, Chapter VIII; also Byrnes, op. cit., p. 102.
192 Cit. Pierrard, op. cit., p. 24.
193 On Jewish solidarity and on the way in which antisemitism helped to revive or perpetuate it, see Tharaud, *Petite Histoire*, pp. 33–5; Wirth, *The Ghetto*, pp. 56, 109 and *passim;* Loewenstein, op. cit., pp. 179–80; Sartre, op. cit., pp. 14, 83–4, 111, 122 and 165; and Memmi, op. cit., pp. 149–50, 320–40, 344–6 and 361–6. Sartre, as Memmi has protested, grossly exaggerated the degree to which antisemitism itself "caused" or created Jewishness.
194 See Marrus, *PA*, chapter IX; see also nn. 24–26 above.
195 Letter, B. Lazare to J. Reinach, 28 August 1896. Bibliothèque Nationale, Papiers Reinach, Nouvelles Acquisitions Françaises 24897, pièce 180; see also Péguy, *NJ*, pp. 86–8, on Lazare's sense of solidarity with other Jews.
196 J.-H. Lévy, "Avis aux Israélites", *Le Siècle*, 2 February 1899.
197 Bloch, *Lévy*, p. 73.
198 Theodore Reinach, cit. Bournand, op. cit., p. 291.
199 Durkheim, *Suicide*, pp. 155 and 159–60; and, for other Jewish observations on the general phenomenon of solidarity at this time, see Herzl, cit. Bournand, op. cit., pp. 301–2; Blum, *Souvenirs sur l'Affaire*, p. 91; and Proust, op. cit., IV, pp. 40–1 and 99–100.
200 Leroy-Beaulieu, *L'Antisémitisme*, pp. 32–33; see also Leroy-Beaulieu, *Les Doctrines de haine*, p. 119.
201 Dagan, op. cit., p. 11.
202 Drumont, *FJ*, I, p. 53; also ibid., I, pp. 92, 335 and 425; II, p. 122; *DB*, pp. 189–90.
203 See, for example, *L'Eclair*, 2 February 1899. As we have seen, the police and their agents believed in the existence of the "Syndicate" for a while at least; a police agent reported on 11 November 1896, for example, that Dreyfus' brother-in-law, Hadamard was "l'âme du fameux syndicat organisé pour arriver à la révision du procès Dreyfus." AN F⁷12464; see also chapter II, p. 86; and chapter XII, pp. 411–13 above.
204 Daudet, *Au Temps de Judas*, p. 101; see also Péguy, *NJ*, pp. 74–7 and *passim;* Stock, *Mémorandum d'un éditeur*, III, pp. 28–32; and n. 26 above.
205 On Mathieu Dreyfus, see Gauthier, ed., op. cit.; and, on Reinach, in addition to his private correspondance and his *Histoire de l'Affaire Dreyfus*, see Barrès, *Scènes et doctrines*, I, pp. 33–4; and Stock, op. cit., pp. 196–8 and 242.
206 See George D. Painter, *Marcel Proust. A Biography* (London, 1959), I, pp. 221–55; also Proust's own work, particularly *Jean Santeuil* (London, 1955), Part V.
207 See Halévy, *Apologie pour notre passé;* and Silvera, op. cit., pp. 89–132.
208 See Police report, 22 May 1898, cit. Guillemin, *Zola légende et vérité*, p. 163; Blum, *Souvenirs sur l'Affaire*, pp. 96–8 and *passim;* Ziebura, op. cit., pp. 35–6 and 43; and Dalby, op. cit., p. 89.
209 See Blum, *Souvenirs*, pp. 18–19; and Zévaès, *L'Affaire Dreyfus*, p. 118.
210 See Zévaès, op. cit., p. 118; and Stock, op. cit., p. 236. As we have noted, Salomon Reinach wrote the pamphlet *Drumont et Dreyfus*, using the pseudonym "L'Archiviste"
211 See Zévaès, op. cit., p. 118; also p. 715 below.
212 See BN Papiers Paul Meyer; and Zévaès, op. cit., p. 118; see also chapter IV, pp. 139–40 above.
213 See Blum, *Souvenirs*, p. 28; and Zévaès, op. cit., p. 118.
214 See Gauthier, ed., op. cit., p. 56.
215 See Smith, "L'Atmosphère politique à l'École Normale Supérieure", pp. 249–51 and 258.
216 See Daudet, *Au Temps de Judas*, p. 107.
217 See Dagan, op. cit., pp. 62–3; and Lukes, op. cit., pp. 332–49.

218 See Blum, *Souvenirs*, pp. 96–8; and Daudet, *Au Temps de Judas*, pp. 95–8; also p. 696 above and n. 39 below.
219 See Blum, *Souvenirs*, pp. 96–8.
220 Ibid.
221 Ibid.; see also p. 717 below.
222 Lauris, *Souvenirs d'une belle époque*, pp. 152–6.
223 Daily Reports, Prefect of Police, 15 and 24 February 1898. APP Ba 106.
224 Cit. Guillemin, *Zola légende et vérité*, p. 169.
225 Daudet, *Au Temps de Judas*, p. 173.
226 See Pierrard, op. cit., p. 209.
227 Hirsch, op. cit., pp. 42–4 and 58–69; also Benda, *La Jeunesse d'un clerc*, pp. 191–200; Halévy, *Apologie*, pp. 56–60; and see Martin du Gard's fictional portrait of a Jewish Dreyfusard intellectual, Woldsmuth, in *Jean Barois*, pp. 217–31 and *passim*.
228 See Péguy, *NJ*, pp. 85, 176 and *passim*.
229 Reports, Police agents, 3 October, and 20 November 1897. AN F⁷ 12473.
230 Reports, Commissaire spécial, Epinal, 19 and 24 February 1898; Commissaire spécial, Montbéliard, 24 February 1898; and Commissaire spécial, Belfort, 25 February 1898. AN F⁷ 12474; and Telegram, Commissaire spécial, Nice, 11 December 1898. AN F⁷ 12465.
231 Report, Prefect, Alpes-Maritimes, 27 January 1898. AN F⁷ 12467.
232 See Chapter XII, n. 343; also Reports, Police agents, Paris, 8 October 1897, and 11 January 1898. AN F⁷ 12473.
233 Reports, Commissaire spécial, Morteau (Doubs), 15 February, and 17 April 1898. AN F⁷ 12474.
234 Telegram, Commissaire spécial, Bellegarde (Gard), November 1898. AN F⁷ 12465.
235 Blumenkranz, ed., op. cit., p. 349.
236 Daily Report, Prefect of Police, 5 June 1898. APP Ba 106; Press cuttings, AN F⁷ 12487; and Zévaès, *L'Affaire Dreyfus*, pp. 118 and 206.
237 Lukes, op. cit., pp. 347–8.
238 Reports, Commissaire spécial, Marseille, 29 December 1898, and 18 February, and 8 March 1899; and Police reports, Nice, 6 June 1899, 2 August 1899, and 5 March 1900; and Paris, 31 December 1903. AN F⁷ 12487. Further evidence of Jewish membership of and interest in the *Ligue* is provided by Fleg, op. cit., p. 85; and Marrus, *PA*, p. 227.
239 Reports in *L'Aurore*, 19 December 1898; and *Le Rappel*, 13 December 1898; and Report, Prefect of Police, 12 December 1898. AN F⁷ 12465; see also chapter II, n. 200 above; and Girardet, *Le Nationalisme français*, p. 237.
240 See Report, Police agent, 20 November 1897, cited in chapter XII, p. 412 and n. 339 above.
241 See Byrnes, op. cit., p. 99; Verdès-Leroux, op. cit., pp. 162–5; Pierrard, op. cit., pp. 58–9; Marrus, *PA*, p. 106.
242 On the high status enjoyed by Mendès as a writer, see Waleffe, op. cit., pp. 41–2; and, on the development of French Jewish literature in the two pre-1914 decades, see Gide, *Journals* (Penguin edition), p. 196 (January 1914); Moreau, "Tandis que Paul Claudel découvrait l'Israël moderne", *Cahiers Paul Claudel*, 7, pp. 364–70; Pierrard, op. cit., pp. 226–7; Blumenkranz, ed., op. cit., p. 365.
243 Dagan, op. cit., pp. 62–3, cit. Lukes, op. cit., pp. 346–7.
244 Cit. Pierrard, op. cit., p. 57; see also Viau, op. cit., pp. 17–18.
245 See Byrnes op. cit., pp. 101–2; Marrus, *PA*, pp. 223–5; and Marrus, "Le Comité de Défense contre l'Antisémitisme", *Michael*, IV, (1976), pp. 163–75.
246 That is, in *L'Archives Israélites* and *L'Univers Israélite*; see Marrus, *PA*, pp. 145–6, 205, and 219–38 *passim*.
247 Byrnes, op. cit., p. 103; and Marrus, *PA*, pp. 146–51.

248 Arnoulin, op. cit., pp. 163–5.
249 See Report, Commissaire spécial, Nantes, 13 December 1898. AN F⁷ 12460; and
n. 38 above. *Le Petit Phare* was the evening subsidiary of *Le Phare de la Loire*,
with a larger circulation than its parent-paper; both were owned by the Schwob
family.
250 See Sachs, *Le Sabbat*, p. 16; Andler, *Vie de Lucien Herr*, pp. 163–82; Goldberg,
The Life of Jean Jaurès, pp. 319–20; Henry Coston, *Partis, Journaux et Hommes
politiques d'hier et d'aujourd hui, Lectures Françaises*, December 1960, pp. 483–5;
and Bellanger *et al.*, eds., op. cit., III, p. 375.
251 See Daudet, *Au Temps de Judas*, pp. 111–12; Jackson, *La Revue Blanche*, p. 108
and *passim;* and Ziebura, op. cit., p. 37.
252 Barrès, Letter to Maurras, 15 February 1898, Barrès-Maurras, op. cit., p. 172; and
Tharaud, *Mes années chez Barrès*, p. 36.
253 See Verdès-Leroux, op. cit., p. 216.
254 Viau, op. cit., pp. 57–8 and 273–4.
255 Zévaès, *Rochefort*, pp. 239–40.
256 Reports, Commissaire central, Grenoble, 12 and 14 January 1899. AN F⁷
12460.
257 Guérin, op. cit., pp. 141–4.
258 See Public Letter of Le Comité de Défense contre l'Antisémitisme, 14 November
1902, cit. Marrus, "Le Comité de Défense", pp. 171–2. The Comité also appears
to have subsidized some press opposition to antisemitism.
259 See Paul Vibert, Préface, L'Hermite, op. cit., pp. viii–ix.
260 Report, Commissaire spécial Epinal, 20 January 1898. AN F⁷ 12474.
261 Joseph Reinach, op. cit., III, p. 276.
262 Daily Report, Prefect of Police, 25 May 1898. APP Ba 106. According to Viau,
Drumont was struck in the street in Paris in June 1902 by M. Dreyfus-Gonzalès,
whose wife had been insulted in *La Libre Parole;* and Viau himself was attacked
in the office of the newspaper in June 1899 by a Belgian called Bischoffsheim,
protesting against having been called a Jew by the journalist; see Viau, op. cit.,
pp. 305–6 and 200.
263 Report, Sub-Prefect, Chalon-sur-Saône, 20 January 1898. AN F⁷ 12467.
264 Report, Commissaire spécial, Perpignan, 10 September 1899. AN F⁷ 12465.
265 A notice distributed in Lunéville proclaimed: "Ni par le poing! Ni par l'épée! Les
Etudiants Français refusent de se commettre avec les Juifs . . .". Report, Prefect,
Meurthe-et-Moselle, 24 January 1898. AN F⁷ 12467; see also Marrus, *PA*, p. 197;
and Pulzer, *The Rise of Political Anti-Semitism in Germany and Austria*, p. 253.
Bruneau de Laborie, *Les Lois du duel* (Paris, 1906 and 1912) says nothing about
duels with Jews, although he does say that "le duel n'est raisonnable, et même
admissible, qu' entre égaux" (p. 13). On duels generally in France at this time,
which seem to have been especially common among journalists, see, for example,
Waleffe, op. cit., p. 277; Steinheil, op. cit., p. 88; and Arbellot, op. cit., pp.
101–22. It is also worth noting that, in addition to Jews and non-Jews meeting
as principals in duels, Jews acted as seconds for non-Jews and vice versa; see, for
example, Zévaès, *Au Temps du Boulangisme*, p. 206; and Arbellot, op. cit., p. 113,
for instances.
266 Joseph Reinach, op. cit., II, pp. 53–60; see also Viau, op. cit., pp. 25–6; Verdès-
Leroux, op. cit., p. 223; and Marrus, *PA*, pp. 197–201.
267 Daily Report, Prefect of Police, 10 February 1898. APP Ba 106. Though the
authorities in general turned a blind eye to them, duels were not of course legal
in France.
268 Viau, op. cit., pp. 60–1, 79–80, 102–7, 134, 182–3, 221–2 and 270; Waleffe, op.
cit., pp. 275–6; Arbellot, op. cit., pp. 104–5; Byrnes, op. cit., p. 151; Pierrard, op.
cit., pp. 32–3; Léon Daudet, *Souvenirs politiques* (réunis par René Wittmann)
(Paris, 1974), pp. 20–3. Accounts of the Meyer–Drumont duel, in which Meyer
is supposed to have laid his hand on Drumont's weapon, thus breaking the rules,

are conflicting as to its date and circumstances. Daudet's version has been taken as the most reliable.

269 Zévaès, *Au Temps du Boulangisme*, p. 207; Zévaès, *L'Affaire Dreyfus*, p. 161; Stock, op. cit., pp. 50–1; Arbellot, op. cit., pp. 105–6 and 111–14.

270 Péguy, *NJ*, pp. 174–6: "Ce que nos adversaires . . . ne peuvent savoir . . . c'est combien de Juifs ont été irrévocablement envéloppés dans le désastre de l'affaire Dreyfus, combien de Juifs ont été les victimes . . . Combien de carrières, combien de vies juives ont été irréparablement ruineés, brisées, cela, nous le savons, combien de misères juives, nous le savons . . . combien en sont restés marqués de misère pour leur vie entière; sans compter . . . ceux qui sont morts . . ."

PART FIVE
CONCLUSION

CHAPTER XX
CONCLUSION

I N THIS FINAL CHAPTER WE SHALL ATTEMPT TO SUMMARIZE THE FINDINGS OF this study and to draw some specific and general conclusions. If we accept Shlomo Bergman's distinction between two kinds of attitude that are covered by the term, antisemitism, the one a traditional dislike of Jews "rooted in the mores of the community", and the other an attitude emanating from "a definite centre of propaganda" and involving the elaboration of a set of anti-Jewish myths by "intellectuals",[1] we can say that France at the end of the nineteenth century saw the emergence and establishment of the second type of antisemitism. This depended on the first, and had deep historical roots, but developed it in a novel way into an ideology which provided a total explanation of history and society, while creating a specifically antisemitic movement as the vehicle for that ideology. This second type of antisemitism developed, of course, in many European societies at this time, and the French example suggests that it was a reaction to the crisis of "modernization" rather than a direct reaction to the presence or the behaviour of Jews or Jewish communities. And what it offered in this crisis was not so much a policy, as explanation and reassurance of a quasi-religious kind.

Odd examples of antisemitic ideology of the modern kind were produced in France earlier in the century, for example the work of Toussenel and of Gougenot des Mousseaux, but the ideology did not achieve real consistency and importance until the 1880s. As Verdès-Leroux has shown, the crash of the Catholic Union Générale bank in 1882 occasioned a significant antisemitic campaign in the newspaper press. The Catholic daily, La Croix, founded by the Assumptionist fathers in 1883, and their weekly, Le Pèlerin, developed an often virulent brand of antisemitism from the early and mid-1880's. But the real break-through came in 1886 with the publication of Edouard Drumont's La France juive, which was an immediate best-seller. In 1892, Drumont founded an antisemitic daily, La Libre Parole, which quickly achieved a circulation of 200,000, which was considerable by the standards of the day. Meanwhile, formal antisemitic organizations were created. Drumont, Morès and others founded La Ligue Nationale Antisémitique de France in September 1889, and Morès formed his own body, known as Morès et ses Amis, about the same time. The former, rather amorphous, body broke up after a year, but the latter, a smaller, tighter organization, paramilitary in style, survived and merged with the Ligue Antisémitique Française, formed by Jules Guérin in 1897. This was an altogether more important organization, operating on the national level. Two other antisemitic organizations that were national in scope also emerged at the end of the century: La Jeunesse Antisémite et Nationaliste, and La Fédération Nationale Antijuive, founded by Drumont and others in 1901–2. By the late 1890s, of course, the Dreyfus Affair had provided French antisemitism (which had, according to Byrnes,[2] suffered a slight setback in the middle of the decade) with an issue around which it could crystallize, and which enormously increased its appeal and support. A flood of antisemitic propaganda was produced in all forms, and all the anti-Dreyfusard Leagues were more or less antisemitic.

The Affair itself, while not of universal interest as has sometimes been supposed, yet preoccupied public opinion in Paris and the provinces, particularly in the years 1898 and 1899, and was an important issue in the 1898 elections. Groups particularly involved, on the anti-Dreyfusard side, were students, the military, many of whom departed thereby from their well-established apoliticism, and Catholics, and, on the Dreyfusard side, Protestants and Jews; and their views were articulated in a novel way by journalists and intellectuals. As the existence of the Leagues demonstrates, existing political organizations were slow to become involved, though the Leagues had the backing of the parties of the dynastic Right, and the Anarchists and then the Socialists eventually led the Left into supporting the cause of revision.

The considerable importance of organized antisemitism in the period can be gauged in a number of ways. Antisemitic books, particularly those of Drumont, and antisemitic newspapers enjoyed a large readership even before the Affair swelled the audience for both. The number of those who joined antisemitic organizations was naturally smaller, but none the less substantial by the standards of the time. The Ligue Antisémitique Française had between 5,000 and 10,000 members. Eighty delegates from Paris and the provinces attended a congress of the Jeunesse Antisémite in 1901. The Union Nationale had about 12,500 members in the late 1890s; while the Ligue de la Patrie Française claimed 40,000 in 1899. Two further indications of the impact of the "new" antisemitism at this time are provided by the 1898 riots and demonstrations, and by the election of antisemitic deputies in the same year. Riots and violent demonstrations, many to some extent orchestrated by antisemitic groups, took place in nearly 70 towns in France in the first two months of 1898, and troops had to be called in to restore order in at least five places, while in Algeria more serious pogroms occurred. Also in 1898, 22 declared antisemitic deputies were elected (4 from Algeria), who formed an official group in the Chamber. In addition, about 40 more deputies showed that they were willing to support antisemitic proposals in parliament, notably the move to repeal the Crémieux decree of 1870. The years 1898–9, however, marked the high-point of the antisemitic movement in France in this period. The Dreyfus Affair was effectively resolved by the Waldeck-Rousseau government which came to power in mid-1899. The disturbances brought about or encouraged by the antisemitic movement evoked firm and hostile reaction from the authorities, who played up the threat which they posed to the Republican régime. The divisions within the movement, moreover, and its lack of a clear policy disappointed many supporters and rendered it ineffective. Following Guérin's imprisonment in 1900, the Ligue Antisémitique fell apart; and the Jeunesse Antisémite and the big anti-Dreyfusard leagues suffered a similar, if less sudden, eclipse. Nine of the antisemitic deputies lost their seats in 1902, and, after further losses, the antisemitic parliamentary group was wound up. Organized antisemitism as an ideology and a movement did not disappear, being carried on in both forms into the pre-war decade and after by the Action Française in particular, but it had suffered a serious decline and lost the kind of mass support which it had for a time enjoyed.

The social complexion of that support can be measured in various ways. First, one has some idea of who belonged to antisemitic organizations, in terms of social class and occupation. Ligue Antisémitique militants seem to have been overwhelmingly bourgeois or lower middle class, with small businessmen, members of the liberal professions, ex-army officers and journalists well represented among them. The same pattern is evident among members of the Union Nationale, though members of the clergy were naturally more in evidence in this Catholic body. Students were important in both, and seem to have formed the bulk of the membership of the Jeunesse Antisémite. One then has the more impressionistic evidence of the readership of antisemitic newspapers, and particularly of *La Croix* and of *La Libre Parole*. In each case, it seems to have been similar in complexion to the membership of organizations, though both papers were especially popular among the lower clergy, and both tried to reach working-class readers, apparently without much success. The social complexion of antisemitic voters can only be gauged indirectly, and here it seems there was a wide variety. Antisemitic deputies were elected in rural constituencies as well as in big cities like Paris, Bordeaux and Nancy. However, the active support of the peasantry can probably be discounted in many rural constituencies, particularly in the West and the South-West, since these were often "pocket boroughs", where voters voted as the notables indicated. Nevertheless, it remains significant that a number of notables felt it suitable to adopt an antisemitic stance, and there is evidence that in the South-East rural voters were expressing a more positive option for antisemitism. The evidence of participation in antisemitic riots and disturbances is more concrete but more random. Demonstrators seem very often to have been students, but older men from the middle and working classes were also involved. Finally we have the evidence of the grievances expressed by antisemitic propaganda.

Probably the most coherent and sustained campaign mounted by the antisemites was that which called on the public to boycott Jewish shops and businesses, and which attacked the allegedly Jewish department stores. This clearly reflected the interests of small traders, whose business was threatened by new retailing methods; and the campaign was often sponsored or encouraged by local associations of traders and shopkeepers. Other economic grievances that found antisemitic expression, and which can be attached to particular social groups, were the general complaints about the agricultural depression, attacks on speculative finance, attacks on immigrant workers, and suggestions that the liberal professions were becoming overcrowded and difficult to enter. The fall in the price of agricultural products was blamed on the supposed domination of the market by Jews, while the "rural exodus" and the decline of large estates were also related to Jewish influence. This was perhaps a motive for peasant antisemitism where it existed, and more certainly for that of aristocratic landlords, whose rents were declining or who were forced to sell up in these years. The familiar identification of speculation and banking with the Jews expressed a general "anti-capitalism", but had particular appeal for rentiers, large and small, who had injudiciously invested in such concerns as the Union Générale or the Panama Company. Antisemites also called for severe controls over the influx of immigrant labour into France. Here no claim was made that all such immigrants were Jews, but the platform did offer some means of attracting French workers, who were not notably interested in antisemitism as such, but who did show some hostility towards foreign workers. The emphasis laid on France's dependence on an alien work-force also pointed to her sluggish birth-rate, a phenomenon which concerned both Catholics and Nationalists. Bourgeois feeling that access to the liberal professions and the civil service, their preferred occupations, was becoming more difficult, as numbers of potential applicants grew and entry by competitive examination replaced the old patronage system, was more directly expressed via the idea that Jewish competition was to blame. This anxiety was most directly felt by the young, and was probably an important underlying motive for student antisemitism.

Frequently overlapping with those that we have mentioned, two other kinds of grievance found expression in antisemitism: the grievances of Catholics, and those, less easily defined, of heterogeneous opponents of the social and political establishment, who could identify with the "populist" tone of a Drumont. We have seen abundant evidence that antisemitism in France was an overwhelmingly Catholic phenomenon. Catholic writers and journalists contributed fully in the elaboration of antisemitic ideology; Catholics were important in the ranks of antisemitic organizations; and Catholic organizations themselves propagated antisemitism. Most bishops prudently refrained from either supporting or condemning it, but the lower clergy, secular and regular, were frequently unrestrained supporters of the antisemitic movement. Such antisemitism was common to nearly all shades of Catholic opinion, to "Integrists" as well as to Christian Democrats; and only a few liberals, like Anatole Leroy-Beaulieu or abbé Brugerette spoke out against the dominant trend. Catholic antisemites maintained traditional religious charges against the Jews, notably those of deicide and ritual murder, but it seems, as Léon Bloy passionately complained, that their concerns were primarily non-theological. Catholicism in France as elsewhere was faced in the late nineteenth century with two related threats to its traditionally dominant position in society. The first was the rapid progress in urban, but also in rural, areas of dechristianization; the second was the coming to power of anticlerical governments determined to destroy the political power of the Church and to secularize the State, and notably to rid public education of its confessional character. Few Catholics could interpret these phenomena in dispassionate sociological or socio-historical terms, and most regarded them as an assault upon the Church by external unholy forces. If the Church was losing ground, they felt, it was through no fault of its own, but because it was being deliberately attacked and undermined, and the culprits, for many of them, were thought to be the Jews in alliance with the Freemasons and the Protestants. Antisemitism thus provided them with a reassuring explanation of the straits in which they found themselves.

Antisemitism was also the vehicle for anti-establishment protest. Drumont and others castigated the Republican régime and its beneficiaries not simply because they were anticlerical, but, with more emphasis, because they were venal and self-interested. This critique had a social dimension, too, for invective was also directed against the upper-classes in general, aristocracy and bourgeoisie, both allegedly corrupted by the Jews. In contrast, antisemites claimed to be the champions and defenders of the "people", a term which included the poor, the workers and the honest middle class. The importance accorded to this theme in antisemitic writings confirms the view that antisemitism did have special appeal for the politically and socially marginal, whose sense of alienation it in some way articulated. The extreme nationalism which nearly always accompanied antisemitism can be interpreted in the same light: it gave a sense of belonging to those who were socially adrift or insecure.

This leads us on to the political complexion of antisemitism. Was it a movement of the Left or of the Right, radical or conservative? The answer must be that it was politically heterogeneous and ambiguous. The antisemitic deputies, for example, came from all bands in the political spectrum, and included an ex-communard as well as Bonapartists and Royalists. There was a strong socialistic or "populist" element in antisemitism, well represented by Drumont. Here one must remember that antisemitism in the early nineteenth century in France had been preeminently a theme in the "Utopian" Socialists' critique of capitalism, of which the Jew, and in particular Rothschild, became a convenient and popular symbol. In the 1880s and 1890s, "orthodox" Socialists had not entirely abandoned this tradition. However, although a number of antisemites in this later period regarded themselves, and were regarded, as socialists, their attack was on Jewish capital and not on capitalism as such, and they envisaged no fundamental structural change of an economic kind, unless it was a supposed return to a vague corporatism. They were, moreover, thoroughly hostile to any extension of the power of the bureaucratic State. Politically too, a man like Drumont, while affirming his Republicanism and his love of the people, favoured authoritarian forms of government and was opposed to parliamentary democracy; and a large number of antisemites were overt political conservatives. Here it is significant that the antisemitic movement received financial backing from the political Right and made electoral bargains with it. There is some truth, indeed, in the claim, made by contemporary critics of antisemitism, that, in its "populist" guise, it was acting or being used as an instrument to divert popular support away from genuine Socialism towards a substitute that posed no real threat to the existing order. In all this, it must be remembered that the antisemitic movement, though involved in politics, was not primarily a political organization. It had no clear programme in the conventional sense, and had little interest in the realities of party politics. Its structure, moreover, of loosely related and competing groups engaged in internecine strife, rendered it practically ineffective.

This does not mean, however, that antisemitism lacked all coherence. On one level, the ideological, it had real consistency and unity, a characteristic that has been obscured by those who have approached it as if it were a "rational" system of political thought. It was rather a system of belief that provided a total explanation of a supposed state of cosmic and social decadence by identifying the Jews as the evil agents of that dislocation and decay. Like many others at the end of the nineteenth century, antisemites were upset and disorientated by fundamental changes, social, economic and political and by changing values, and their antisemitism explained these changes for them. More, antisemitic ideology presented them, too, with an ideal unchanging social world, where the old values were preserved, and to which they might in magical fashion return, if the power of the Jews could only be broken. It is the formulation of this ideology, we have suggested, which is the novelty of late nineteenth-century antisemitism, and this ideology was the creation of intellectuals. Antisemitism had its organizations as we have seen, but it was primarily located in the press and in books, in the written and the spoken word. Here it is characteristic that "the recognized leader of antisemitism"[3] in France was Drumont, a writer and a journalist, who had no talent at all as an organizer or a politician. What Drumont did have was great skill as a propagandist and an uncanny rapport with his public. He was a genuinely popular writer in both senses, boasting significantly that his only merit as a writer was to have "committed to print what everyone was thinking".[4]

One aspect of the new antisemitic ideology was its racial tone, which is reflected in the term *"antisémitisme"* itself. Imported from Germany, it seems, in the early 1880s, this term was quickly and almost universally adopted, and its adoption marks a qualitative leap from the old anti-Judaism. It announced the entry of Jew-hatred into the sphere of ideology. However, although it involved also the use of the terminology of Aryan and Semite, derived from philology, and of the concept of race, which was a commonplace of late nineteenth-century thinking, the new antisemitism in France at this time was not rigorously racialist in the formal sense. Jewish otherness and inability to become French were conveyed through the metaphor of physical stereotypes and animal analogies; the danger which Jews represented was expressed through the idea that they were dirty and polluting; but only a few would-be scholarly writers like Soury or Picard elaborated such ideas in biological or genetic terms. Racial concepts, in effect, reinforced the view that Jews were inherently different, and lent antisemitic ideology a modern and scientific air, but they were not themselves a determining factor in it. Behind them stood profound religious and socio-psychological urges, which had in the past, for example, found expression in the identification of the Jews with the Devil. However, the racial mode of the new antisemitism is of great significance, above all because it enabled antisemites to maintain in the face of progressive assimilation that Jews were none the less indelibly different from non-Jews and fundamentally unchanging. This function, more than anything else probably, explains why in later years this mode was emphasized even more.

If the new antisemitism is to be explained primarily as a negative reaction to modern secular and "capitalist" society and to social change, it remains to be explained why the Jews should have been selected to symbolize modernity, capitalism and change. Here general reference only can be made to the historical role of the Jews in European societies as outsiders and intermediaries, and to the traditional stereotypes in European culture of the Jew as deicide or denier of Christ, as usurer and financier, and as wanderer. Such stereotypes were still widely current in modern France, providing the basic ingredients from which antisemitic ideology was fashioned, and there is much evidence that a general hostility towards Jews prevailed in most quarters. Although French literature, for example, never produced single stereotypes of the power and popularity of Shylock or Fagin, fiction and drama at the "high" and popular levels did keep alive hostile images of Jews in a more diffuse way. The other point can perhaps be best illustrated by the fact that most critics and opponents of antisemitism in France at the end of the nineteenth century were by no means friendly to the Jews, and were rarely motivated by sympathy with them. This is true in varying degrees of Bloy, André Gide, Leroy-Beaulieu, Clemenceau, Jaurès and Zola, men of very different backgrounds and persuasions. By contrast the philosemitism of a Péguy was an isolated and peculiar phenomenon.

But if the Jews were cast historically for the central role which they occupied in antisemitic ideology, they were not directly or immediately the "cause" of its development. In general terms, the French Jewish community was small, about 0.2% of the total population in the 1890s. Nor is there evidence that French Jews were disproportionately represented in positions of power and influence, though like all minorities they had an atypical socio-professional structure. The geographical incidence of antisemitism, moreover, indicates that there was little or no connection very often between the presence of Jewish communities and the emergence and development of ideological hostility towards Jews. Paris, where the bulk of French Jews lived, was also the centre of French antisemitism, but this had as much to do with the fact that it was France's capital. In the East, there was a correlation between Jewish presence and antisemitic manifestations, and there existed there a popular tradition of hostility related to the economic role of local Jews; but elsewhere in France, for example in the West and the South-West, antisemitism flourished among populations who had little or no contact with Jews. More generally, it is evident again and again that antisemitic writers were profoundly ignorant of both Judaism and Jewish life.

We have already suggested that antisemitic ideology was not aimed at the real world of politics, and its proposed solutions of the "Jewish question" bear this out. These involved a whole range of measures from restricting Jewish immigration and the naturalization of Jewish immigrants, through the banning of Jews from all forms of public employment and the withdrawal of full citizenship from them, to the revival of the ghetto and the wearing of badges of identity, and then expulsion or extermination. But such measures never formed a coherent programme. Less and more extreme solutions were put forward at the same time by the same people, and there was a general reluctance to envisage concrete legislation. At the same time, most antisemites showed some enthusiasm for violence against the Jews, at least on the verbal level. All of this suggests that there was a large element of fantasy in antisemitic "policy", and that its function was expressive rather than instrumental, itself providing psychological satisfaction without having to impinge further on the real world. Nevertheless, as such, it was an affront to Jewish consciousness, and it was accompanied by actual, if sporadic, violence against real Jews, who responded in many cases, if not always, with suitable vigour.

It must be recalled, in this context, too, that forty years later France did experience a period of active antisemitic persecution, not only in the German Occupied Zone, but also in that controlled by the Vichy régime. Vichy's Statute of 3 October 1940 excluded Jews, defined on religious and racial grounds, from all political positions, from positions in the magistrature and the civil service, including education at all levels, and from the armed forces, and from posts in the media; and provided for quotas to be laid down for the liberal professions. A law of 2 June 1941 extended the range of professions from which Jews were banned to include banking, finance, property-dealing and advertising. A census of Jewish persons and property was ordered at the same time. In October 1940 the Crémieux decree of 1871, relating to the Jews of Algeria, was repealed; while in March 1941 a Commissariat Général aux Questions Juives was set up to administer Jewish affairs in France. It was headed first by Xavier Vallat, then by Darquier de Pellepoix, and finally by Charles Mercier du Paty de Clam, the son of Dreyfus's interrogator. In July 1941, the forced sale of Jewish property, already under way in the Occupied Zone, began in the Vichy Zone also, and a large number of Jewish enterprises were taken over by the State, some of them being resold to non-Jews. All of this was in line with policies advocated by French antisemites in the pre-1914 and inter-war periods, and the initiative behind such measures cannot be attributed to German pressure or example to any great degree. Vichy's antisemitic measures were passed and implemented, indeed, under the aegis of the familiar slogan of "France for the French", thus harking back quite explicitly to Drumont and his brand of nationalism.

But, if certain aspects of the persecution of Jews in Vichy France can be seen as part of a French tradition, albeit as the adoption of extremist measures by an authoritarian régime, such as no normal government would have contemplated, other aspects were the result of external force or pressure. The obligation laid on Jews to wear a yellow star was resisted by Vichy, and was never implemented in its zone, even after November 1942, when its autonomy was virtually ended. Similarly, in mid-1943, Laval refused to issue a law depriving French Jews of French citizenship. Both examples of resistance to German pressure must be seen in the wider context of Vichy's opposition to the deportation of French Jews to the extermination camps. Vichy's aim here seems to have been to prevent the deportation of French Jews by sacrificing foreign Jews resident in France to German demands. In all, about 65,000 Jews were deported from France to be exterminated, of whom about 6,000 were French. However, as Paxton points out, though Vichy's own antisemitic policy stopped short of genocide, its Jewish census and its internment of about 20,000 Jews did aid the implementation of a policy of genocide by the German authorities. It must also be remembered here that many Frenchmen in the Occupied Zone gave active support to the Germans in their task; and that, although Jews did receive help and protection from French people, particularly from 1943, there was probably more passive acceptance of their persecution than passive or active resistance to it from non-Jews.[5] But, if the Vichy episode underlines the strength of latent antisemitism in French society, it also affirms, as we have argued, that extraordinary circumstances were required to translate antisemitism from the realms of ideology and fantasy to those of law and action, and that the wholesale slaughter of Jews, while it may have been generally acquiesced in through fear, was rarely advocated by French antisemites in concrete terms.

What general conclusions can we draw from our study of antisemitism in France at the end of the nineteenth century? First, both the chronology of its fortunes as a movement as well as the content of its ideology indicate that it was a reaction to a period of crisis experienced by France as by other industrializing societies; but, although antisemitism was the vehicle for the expression of economic grievances on the part of certain groups, it should not be interpreted too exclusively in economic terms. It reflected a fundamental social and religious crisis, which can be seen in the conviction of antisemites that the end of a world, if not of the world, was upon them. In this context it is relevant that, if antisemitism was couched less and less in traditional religious terms, it was still mainly a Catholic phenomenon. Second, related to this, it was an ideology that not only asserted or recognized that the world was in crisis and under threat of dissolution, but that also provided an explanation for this state of affairs in the form of the Jewish conspiracy. Third, although the Jews as a mythical entity were central to it, antisemitism had very little to do with real Jews and their objective problems in the post-Emancipation era. The process of Jewish assimilation, however, could serve as a paradigm of a much more general transformation of social relationships and of the breakdown of a traditional hierarchy. For all these reasons antisemitism was puzzling to contemporaries, and remains puzzling in many ways to historians and sociologists. "Irrational", it had its own rationality; unrealistic, it reflected a real social crisis, and had a real impact on Jews. The way towards understanding it more fully, both as far as France is concerned and more generally, seems to lie in going beyond the approaches which have regarded it either as a psychological or as a political phenomenon, thus playing down its social and its ideological dimensions. Rather, as has been attempted in this book, the content and structure of its ideology should be analysed and related to its social complexion as a movement, and both should be placed and interpreted in the fullest possible socio-historical context. In all this, the closest and most helpful analogy would seem to be with religious movements of a sectarian kind, which have also operated in the world on the basis of unshakeable faith, which have frequently seen the world in terms of a manichean struggle, which have at times sought to exterminate their enemies, and which, while appealing to the highest values, have yet not avoided, too, a certain squalid opportunism.

NOTES

1 Bergman, "Some Methodological Errors in the Study of Antisemitism", loc. cit., p. 57.
2 Byrnes, *Antisemitism in Modern France*, pp. 337–9.
3 Daudet, *Les Oeuvres dans les hommes*, p. 178.
4 Drumont, *La France juive*, II, Nouvelles Notes Rectificatifs (no pagination).
5 In addition to works cited in chapter IX, n. 102 see Robert O. Paxton, *Vichy France, Old Guard and New Order, 1940–1944* (New York, 1972), pp. 173–85; and J. Lubetzki, *La Condition des Juifs en France sous l'Occupation allemande: La législation raciale* (Paris, 1945), CDJC, which provides a full discussion of the Vichy Statute and other laws. The actual texts of the laws can be most conveniently studied in *Les Juifs sous l'Occupation* (1945). The chapter in *France during the German Occupation 1940–1944: A Collection of 292 Statements on the Government of Maréchal Pétain and Pierre Laval*, Hoover Institution Documentary Series (Stanford, 1959), II, chapter XII, pp. 618–60, should be read with caution; J. Billig, op. cit., has pointed to the bias in the testimonies and to general lacunae in the picture presented.

GUIDE TO FURTHER READING

AMONG GENERAL STUDIES OF ANTISEMITISM, JEAN-PAUL SARTRE'S *REFLEX-ions sur la question juive* (Paris, 1946, and various later editions) (English translation, New York, 1948 and 1965, under title *Anti-Semite and Jew*) stands out for its insight and sheer intelligence. Albert Memmi's *Portrait d'un Juif* (Paris, 1962 and 1969) (English translation, London, 1963, under title *Portrait of a Jew*) should be read as a corrective to Sartre, as well as an unrivalled evocation and analysis of the Jewish condition. Of the various studies of antisemitism by more orthodox psychologists, Rudolph M. Loewenstein's *Christians and Jews: A psychoanalytic study* (New York, 1963) (a translation of *Psychanalyse de l'antisémitisme*, Paris, 1951 and 1958) is probably the most approachable and the most aware of the general social context. Morris Ginsberg's brief essay, "Antisemitism" (1943), reprinted in *Essays in Sociology and Social Philosophy* (Harmondsworth, 1968), provides a sociological approach, while two recent American studies: Charles Y. Glock and Rodney Stark, *Christian Beliefs and Anti-Semitism* (New York, 1966), and Gertrude J. Selznick and Stephen Steinberg, *The Tenacity of Prejudice: Anti-Semitism in Contemporary America* (New York, 1969), are of general interest for their methodology and their attempt to break away from the "psychological" emphasis which dominated the study of antisemitism immediately after the Second World War. Representative of that trend is T.W. Adorno, E. Frenkel-Brunswik, D.J. Levinson and R.N. Sanford, *The Authoritarian Personality* (New York, 1950). Edgar Morin *et al.*, *La Rumeur d'Orléans* (Paris, 1969) (English translation, London, 1971, under title *Rumour in Orléans*) is a pioneering study of the psychology of antisemitism on the collective rather than the individual level. Much can be learned also, in this area, from studies of "Populist" and Right-wing movements and ideologies in general. Two particularly interesting books here are: Richard Hofstadter, *The Paranoid Style in American Politics and other essays* (London, 1966); and Hans Toch, *The Social Psychology of Social Movements* (Indianapolis, 1965; London, 1966). On modern French Right-wing ideology, Simone de Beauvoir's essay, "La

Pensée de Droite aujourd'hui", in *Privilèges* ((Paris, 1955), offers a provocative explanatory analysis, while no student of modern ideologies and mythologies can ignore Roland Barthes, *Mythologies* (Paris, 1957; London, 1972).

For the general history of antisemitism, Léon Poliakov's *The History of Anti-Semitism*, 3 vols (London, 1966–75) can be recommended, and also his volume of essays, *Les Juifs et notre histoire* (Paris, 1973). F. Lovsky, *L'Antisémitisme chrétien* (Paris, 1970) provides a documentary survey of one of the main strands in this history.

For the general social and political history of France in the later nineteenth century, two recent studies may serve as an introduction: Pierre Sorlin, *La Société française 1840–1914* (Paris, 1969); and Jean-Marie Mayeur, *Les Débuts de la IIIe République 1871–1898* (Paris, 1973).

On antisemitism itself in France in the period, the best introduction is the pioneering general work by Robert F. Byrnes, *Antisemitism in Modern France*, I (New Brunswick, 1950), unhappily without a sequel, which was reprinted in 1969 (New York). In addition, there are now a number of valuable monographs on different aspects of French antisemitism in the late nineteenth and early twentieth centuries. On the impact of the crash of the Union Générale, and on Catholic antisemitism more generally in the 1880s and 1890s, see Jeannine Verdès-Leroux, *Scandale financier et antisémitisme catholique: Le krach de l'Union Générale* (Paris, 1969). The antisemitism of *La Croix* has been studied by Pierre Sorlin, *"La Croix" et les Juifs (1880–1899): Contribution à l'histoire de l'antisémitisme contemporain* (Paris, 1967); while Pierre Pierrard, *Juifs et Catholiques français: De Drumont à Jules Isaac (1886–1945)* (Paris, 1970) provides a more general account of Catholic antisemitism. Among leading antisemitic propagandists only Maurice Barrès has been adequately studied; see Zeev Sternhell, *Maurice Barrès et le nationalisme français* (Paris, 1972); but a full-length study of Charles Maurras is being prepared by Victor Nguyen, while Carol Iancu is working on Edouard Drumont. E. Beau de Loménie's *Edouard Drumont ou l'anticapitalisme national* (Paris, 1968) provides an interesting collection of texts, not readily available, but his commentary is slight and tendentious. The latter epithet must also be applied to Georges Bernanos's *La Grande Peur des bien-pensants: Edouard Drumont* (Paris, 1931), though the book does convey the kind of enthusiasm that Drumont's writings evoked.

On the Dreyfus Affair, Joseph Reinach's account, *Histoire de l'Affaire Dreyfus*, 6 vols (Paris, 1901–8), remains definitive. Among shorter general accounts, those of Alexandre Zévaès, *L'Affaire Dreyfus* (Paris, 1931) and Pierre Miquel, *L'Affaire Dreyfus* (Paris, 1961) may be particularly recommended. Zévaès, a Socialist, who lived through the time of the Affair, is alert to its wider social dimensions, while Miquel provides an admirably clear and concise up-to-date account. The most recent account in English is Douglas Johnson, *France and the Dreyfus Affair* (London, 1966). Emile Zola's journalism on the Affair has recently been republished: *L'Affaire Dreyfus, La Vérité en marche* (Paris, 1969). Other documents of special interest in print are: Alfred Dreyfus, *Cinq années de ma vie (1894–1899)*, Edition définitive (Paris,

1962), which includes François Mauriac's "L'Affaire Dreyfus vue par un enfant" as a preface; and *"Dreyfusards!": Souvenirs de Mathieu Dreyfus et autres inédits,* présentés par Robert Gauthier (Paris, 1965).

Among analyses of antisemitism from the period, Bernard Lazare's *L'Antisémitisme: Son histoire et ses causes* (Paris, 1894); and Anatole Leroy-Beaulieu's *L'Antisémitisme* (Paris, 1897) stand out. Two collections of views are also invaluable: Henri Dagan, *Enquête sur l'antisémitisme* (Paris, 1899); and François Bournand, *Les Juifs et nos contemporains: L'Antisémitisme et la question juive* (Paris, 1898). An insight into the ambience of organized antisemitism is provided by Raphaël Viau, *Vingt ans d'antisémitisme 1889–1909* (Paris, 1910).

On the French Jewish community and its history, see Michael R. Marrus, *The Politics of Assimilation: A Study of the French Jewish Community at the time of the Dreyfus Affair* (Oxford, 1971) and Bernhard Blumenkranz, ed., *Histoire des Juifs en France* (Toulouse, 1972). Of the various autobiographies by French Jews, Julien Benda, *La Jeunesse d'un clerc* (Paris, 1936); and Jules Isaac, *Expériences de ma vie,* I, *Péguy* (Paris, 1960) are among the more interesting. Jewish life and its problems are also evoked in the fiction of the period by Jews and non-Jews, Here special mention should be made of the work of Marcel Proust and J.-R. Bloch, and of Jacques de Lacretelle's *Silbermann* (Paris, 1922).

SELECT BIBLIOGRAPHY

(Dates are those of editions used and cited in the notes, and not necessarily of first publication)

PRIMARY WORKS

"Agathon" [Henri Massis and Alfred de Tarde], *Les Jeunes Gens d'aujourd-'hui* (Paris, 1913)

Almanach de Gotha (Gotha, 1913)

Andrieux, Louis, *A travers la République: Mémoires* (Paris, 1926)

Apollinaire, Guillaume, *Oeuvres complètes*, I (Paris, 1965)

"Archiviste, L'" [S. Reinach], *Drumont et Dreyfus: Études sur La Libre Parole de 1894 à 1895* (Paris, 1898)

Ardouin-Dumazet, *Voyage en France*, 18e série, *Région du Nord*, I, *Flandre et littoral du Nord* (Paris and Nancy, 1899)

Arnoulin, Stéphane, *M. Edouard Drumont et les Jésuites* (Paris, 1902)

Assomption et ses oeuvres, L', (Paris, no date—c. 1895)

Bainville, Jacques, *Journal 1901–1918* (Paris, 1948)

Balzac, H. de, *Le Père Goriot* (1834) (Paris, 1948)

Balzac, H. de, *La Cousine Bette* (1846) (New York, no date, Lupton edition)

Balzac, H. de, *Le Cousin Pons* (1847) (Paris, 1959)

Barrès, Maurice, *Les Déracinés* (Paris, 1897)

Barrès, Maurice, *Leurs Figures* (Paris, 1911)

Barrès, Maurice, *Mes Cahiers* (Paris, 1929–1938), 11 vols

Barrès, Maurice, *Scènes et doctrines du nationalisme* (Paris, 1925), 2 vols

Barrès, Maurice—Maurras, Charles, *La République ou le roi: Correspondance inédite (1888–1923)* (Paris, 1970)

Baudrillart, Henri, *Les Populations agricoles de la France*, 3e série, *Les Populations du Midi* (Paris, 1893)

Bazin, René, *La Terre qui meurt* (Paris, 1899)

Beauvoir, Simone de, *Memoirs of a Dutiful Daughter* (Harmondsworth, 1973)

Benda, Julien, *La Jeunesse d'un clerc* (Paris, 1936)

Benda, Julien, *Les Cahiers d'un clerc (1936–1949)* (Paris, 1949)

Berl, Emmanuel, *Sylvia* (Paris, 1952)

Berl, Emmanuel, *Rachel et autres grâces* (Paris, 1965)

Bernanos, Georges, *La Grande Peur des bien-pensants: Edouard Drumont* (Paris, 1931)

Bernhardt, Sarah, *Memories of My Life, Being My Personal, Professional and Social Recollections as Woman and Artist* (New York, 1968)

Bertillon, Jacques, *Le Problème de la dépopulation* (Paris, 1897)

Biétry, Pierre, *Le Socialisme et les Jaunes* (Paris, 1906)

Biez, Jacques de, *Les Rothschild et le péril juif: Réponse à M. le Commandant Blanc, Rédacteur-en-chef du "Petit Caporal"* (Paris, 1891)

Bloch, J.-R., . . . *Et Cie* (Paris, 1918) (London, 1930)

Bloch, J.-R., *Lévy: Premier livre de contes* (Paris, 1925)

Bloy, Léon, *Lettres à René Martineau 1901–1917* (Paris, 1933)

Bloy, Léon, *Inédits de Léon Bloy* (Montreal, 1945)

Bloy, Léon, *Je m'accuse* (1900), *Oeuvres*, IV (Paris, 1965)

Bloy, Léon, *Le Salut par les Juifs* (1892), *Oeuvres*, IX (Paris, 1969)

Blum, Léon, *Souvenirs sur l'Affaire* (Paris, 1935)

Blum, Léon, *L'Oeuvre de Léon Blum 1891–1905* (Paris, 1954)

Bournand, François, *Les Juifs et nos contemporains (L'Antisémitisme et la question juive)* (Paris, 1898)

Brunetière, Ferdinand, "Revue Littéraire, *La France juive*", *Revue des Deux Mondes*, 1 June 1886

Brunetière, Ferdinand, "Après le Procès", *Revue des Deux Mondes*, 15 March 1898

Caillaux, Joseph, *Mes Mémoires* (Paris, 1942–1947), 3 vols

Castellane, Boni de, *Vingt ans de Paris*, *Les Oeuvres Libres*, 52 (Paris, 1925)

Castellane, Boni de, *L'Art d'être pauvre* (Paris, 1926)

Castellane, Marquis de, *Hommes et choses de mon temps* (Paris, 1909)

Chamson, André, *A Time to Keep* (London, 1957)

Clermont-Tonnerre, E. de, *Mémoires*, I, *Au temps des équipages* (Paris, 1928)

Cohen, J., *Les Déicides: Examen de la vie de Jésus et des développements de l'Eglise chrétienne dans leurs rapports avec le Judaïsme* (Paris, 1864)

Cohen-Hadria, E., "Souvenirs: Les milieux juifs de Tunisie avant 1914 vus par un témoin", *Le Mouvement Social*, no. 60 (1967)

Colombier, Marie, *Les Mémoires de Sarah Barnum* (Paris, no date—c. 1885)

Combarieu, Abel, *Sept Ans à l'Elysée avec le Président Emile Loubet* (Paris, 1932)

Dagan, Henri, *Enquête sur l'antisémitisme* (Paris, 1899)

Daudet, Alphonse, *Numa Roumestan* (1880) (Paris, no date—Nelson)

Daudet, Léon, *Le Voyage de Shakespeare* (Paris, 1896 and 1929)

Daudet, Léon, *L'Avant-Guerre: Etudes et documents sur l'espionnage juif-allemand en France depuis l'affaire Dreyfus* (Paris, 1911)

Daudet, Léon, *Salons et journaux: Souvenirs des milieux littéraires, politiques, artistiques et médicaux de 1880 à 1908*, quatrième série (Paris, 1917)

Daudet, Léon, *Les Oeuvres dans les hommes* (Paris, 1922)

Daudet, Léon, *Paris vécu*, Ier série (Paris, 1929)

Daudet, Léon, *Au Temps de Judas* (Paris, 1933)

Delacroix, Eugène, *The Journal of Eugène Delacroix* (London, 1951)

Deroo, abbé André (ed.), *Encycliques, messages et discours de Pie IX, Léon XIII, Pie X, Benoît XV, Pie XI, Pie XII et Jean XXIII sur les questions civiques et politiques* (Lille, 1961)

Desprez, Henri, *L'Esprit conservateur* (Paris, no date)

Donnay, Maurice, *Des Souvenirs . . .* (Paris, 1933)

Drault, Jean, *Drumont, La France juive et La Libre Parole* (Paris, 1935)

Dreyfus, Alfred, *Cinq années de ma vie (1894–1899)* (Paris, 1962)

Dreyfus, Pierre, *Dreyfus: His Life and Letters* (London, 1937)

Drieu La Rochelle, P.E., *Gilles* (Paris, 1962)

Drumont, Edouard, *La France juive: Essai d'histoire contemporaine* (Paris, 1886 and no date), 2 vols

Drumont, Edouard, *La France juive devant l'opinion* (Paris, 1886)

Drumont, Edouard, *La Fin d'un monde: Etude psychologique et sociale* (Paris, 1889)

Drumont, Edouard, *La Dernière Bataille: Nouvelle étude psychologique et sociale* (Paris, 1890)

Drumont, Edouard, *Le Testament d'un antisémite* (Paris, 1891)

Drumont, Edouard, *De l'Or, de la boue, du sang: du Panama à l'anarchie* (Paris, 1896)

Durkheim, Emile, *Le Suicide: Etude de sociologie* (Paris, 1897 and London, 1970)

Erckmann-Chatrian, *L'Ami Fritz* (Paris, 1865)

Fleg, Edmond, *L'Enfant prophète* (Paris, 1928)

Fore-Fauré, *Face aux Juifs! (Essai de psychologie sociale contemporaine)* (Paris, 1891)

France, Anatole, *L'Eglise et la République* (1904) (Paris, 1964)

Gauthier, Robert (ed.), *"Dreyfusards!": Souvenirs de Mathieu Dreyfus et autres inédits* (Paris, 1965)

Gelu, Victor, *Marseille au XIXe siècle* (ed. Pierre Guiral) (Paris, 1971)

Gide, André, *The Journals of André Gide*, vol. 1: *1889–1913* (New York, 1955)

Gide, André, *If it Die . . .* (Harmondsworth, 1957)

Gide, André, *Journals 1889–1949* (Harmondsworth, 1967)

Gohier, Urbain, *L'Armée contre la nation* (Paris, 1899)

Goncourt, Edmond and Jules de, *Mémoires de la vie littéraire* (Paris, 1956–9), 4 vols

Gregh, Fernand, *L'Age d'or* (Paris, 1947)

Grenier, A.S., *Nos Députés, 1898–1902* (Paris, no date)

Grenier, A.S., *Nos Députés, 1902–1906* (Paris, no date)

Guérin, Jules, *Les Trafiquants de l'antisémitisme: La Maison Drumond and Co.* (Paris, 1905)

Guinon, Albert, *Décadence: Comédie en quatre actes* (Paris, 1901)

Gyp (Comtesse de Martel), *Le Mariage de Chiffon* (1894) (Paris, no date—Nelson)

Halévy, Daniel, *Apologie pour notre passé* (1907–1910), *Luttes et problèmes* (Paris, 1911)

Halévy, Daniel, *Visites aux paysans du Centre* (Paris, 1921)

Halévy, Daniel, *Péguy and Les Cahiers de la Quinzaine* (London, 1946)

Halévy, Daniel, *Degas parle . . .* (Paris, 1960)

Herriot, Edouard, *Jadis, Avant la première guerre mondiale* (Paris, 1948)

Hirsch, Pierre, *De Moïse à Jésus: Confessions d'un Juif* (Paris, 1929)

Houssaye, Arsène, *The Confessions of Arsène Houssaye, Man about Paris* (London, 1972)

Hugo, Victor, *Les Contemplations* (1856) (Paris, 1969)

Hugo, Victor, *Choses vues, Souvenirs, journaux, cahiers 1830–1846* (Paris, 1972)

Imbart de La Tour, Comte J., *La Crise agricole en France et à l'étranger: Etude de causes techniques, économiques, politiques et sociales et de leurs remèdes* (Nevers(?), 1900)

Isaac, Jules, *Expériences de ma vie*, I, *Péguy* (Paris, 1960)

James, Henry, *Parisian Sketches: Letters to the "New York Tribune" 1875–1876* (New York, 1961)

Jarzel, Henry, *Petit Catéchisme nationaliste* (Paris, 1901)

Jeanneney, J.-M. and Perrot, Marguerite, *Textes de Droit économique et social français 1789–1957* (Paris, 1957)

Jusserand, J.J., *What me Befell: The Reminiscences of J.J. Jusserand* (London, 1933)

Kafka, Franz, *Letters to Milena* (New York, 1953)

Kazin, Alfred, *A Walker in the City* (New York, 1951)

Lacretelle, Jacques de, *Silbermann* (Paris, 1950)

Lauris, Georges de, *Souvenirs d'une belle époque* (Paris, 1948)

La Varende, Jean de, *Pays d'Ouche, 1740–1933* (Paris, 1965)

Lavedan, Henri, *Le Prince d'Aurec: Comédie en trois actes* (Paris, 1894)

Lazare, Bernard, *L'Antisémitisme: Son histoire et ses causes* (Paris, 1894)

Lémann, abbé Joseph, *La Prépondérance juive*, I, *Ses origines (1789–1791)* (Paris, 1889)

Leroy-Beaulieu, Anatole, *L'Antisémitisme* (Paris, 1897)

Leroy-Beaulieu, Anatole, *Les Doctrines de haine: L'antisémitisme, l'anti-protestantisme, l'anticléricalisme* (Paris, 1902)

L'Hermite, *L'Anti-Pape: Drumont-Démon* (Issoudun, 1899)

Littré, Emile, *Dictionnaire de la langue française* (Paris, 1878 and 1965)

Lovsky, F. (ed.), *L'Antisémitisme chrétien* (Paris, 1970)

Lyautey, Hubert, *Choix de lettres 1882–1919* (Paris, 1947)

Martin du Gard, Roger, *Jean Barois* (Paris, 1965)

Maupassant, Guy de, *La Maison Tellier* (Paris, 1961)

Maupassant, Guy de, *Bel-Ami* (Paris, 1973)

Mauriac, François, "L'Affaire Dreyfus vue par un enfant", in Dreyfus, *Cinq années de ma vie* (Paris, 1962)

Maurois, André, *Mémoires*, I, *Les Années d'apprentissage* (New York, 1942)

Maurras, Charles, *L'Avenir de l'intelligence* (Paris, 1905)

Maurras, Charles, *Enquête sur la monarchie* (Paris, 1909)

Maurras, Charles, *Anthinéa* (Paris, 1920)

Maurras, Charles, *Quand les Français ne s'aimaient pas: Chronique d'une renaissance, 1895–1905* (Paris, 1926)

Maurras, Charles, *Au Signe de Flore: Souvenirs de vie politique, L'Affaire Dreyfus, la fondation de l'Action Française 1898–1900* (Paris, 1931)

Maurras, Charles, *Dictionnaire politique et critique* (Paris, 1932–4), 4 vols

Maurras, Charles, *Vingt-cinq ans de monarchisme* (1924), *Oeuvres capitales*, II (Paris, 1954)

Mermeix, *Les Coulisses du Boulangisme* (Paris, 1890)

Meurin, Mgr. Léon, *La Franc-maçonnerie, Synagogue de Satan* (Paris, 1893)

Meyer, Arthur, *Ce que mes yeux ont vu* (Paris, 1912)

Michelet, Jules, *La Sorcière* (Paris, 1966)

Mirbeau, Octave, *Le Journal d'une femme de chambre* (Paris, 1964)

Montesquiou, Léon de, *Les Raisons du nationalisme* (Paris, 1905)

Ophuls, Marcel, *The Sorrow and the Pity* (London, 1975)

Paléologue, Maurice, *Journal de l'Affaire Dreyfus, 1894–1899, L'Affaire Dreyfus et le Quai d'Orsay* (Paris, 1955)

Péguy, Charles, *Notre Jeunesse* (1910) (Paris, 1933)

Péguy, Charles, *Souvenirs* (Paris, 1939)

Péguy, Charles, *Oeuvres en prose 1898–1908* (Paris, 1959)

Picard, Edmond, *Synthèse de l'antisémitisme* (Paris and Brussels, 1892)

Procès de Charles Maurras, Compte rendu sténographique, Le (Paris, 1946)

Proust, Marcel, *A la Recherche du temps perdu*, English Uniform Edition (London, 1957), 12 vols

Quillard, Pierre, *Le Monument Henry: Listes des souscripteurs classés méthodiquement et selon l'ordre alphabétique* (Paris, 1899)

Reinach, Joseph, *Histoire de l'Affaire Dreyfus* (Paris, 1901–8), 6 vols

Renan, Ernest, *Oeuvres complètes* (Paris, 1947–61), 10 vols

Renard, Jules, *Correspondance* (Paris, 1953)

Renoir, Jean, *Renoir My Father* (London, 1965)

Rouzaud, Henri, *Sous les lauriers de Languedoc: L'oeuvre d'un enraciné* (Toulouse, 1926)

Sachs, Maurice, *Le Sabbat: Souvenirs d'une jeunesse orageuse* (Paris, 1946)

Saint-Poli, abbé Henri de (abbé J. Brugerette), *L'Affaire Dreyfus et la mentalité catholique en France* (Paris, 1904)

Schwob, René, *Moi Juif: Livre posthume* (Paris, 1928)

Sombart, Werner, *The Jews and Modern Capitalism* (New York, 1962)

Steinheil, Marguerite, *My Memoirs* (London, 1912)

Stendhal, *Mémoires d'un touriste* (Paris, 1953), 2 vols

Stock, P.-V., *Mémorandum d'un éditeur, troisième série, L'Affaire Dreyfus anecdotique* (Paris, 1938)

Sue, Eugène, *The Wandering Jew* (London, no date—Routledge edition)

Taine, Hippolyte, *Les Origines de la France contemporaine* (Paris, 1947), 11 vols

Thabault, Roger, *Education and Change in a Village Community: Mazières-en-Gâtine, 1848–1914)* (London, 1971)

Tharaud, J. and J., *Notre cher Péguy* (Paris, 1926), 2 vols

Tharaud, J. and J., *Petite Histoire des Juifs* (Paris, 1927)

Tharaud, J. and J., *Mes années chez Barrès* (Paris, 1928)

Tharaud, J. and J., *Quand Israël n'est plus roi* (Paris, 1933)

Tillier, Claude, *Mon Oncle Benjamin* (Paris, 1963)

Union Nationale de France, Règlement Général (Paris, 1897)

Vallès, Jules, *L'Insurgé* (Paris, 1962)

Vallès, Jules, *Oeuvres complètes, La Rue* (Paris, 1969)

Vallès, Jules, *Le Bachélier* (Paris, 1972)

Vauthier, Maurice, *La France et l'Affaire Dreyfus* (Paris, 1899)

Viau, Raphaël, *Vingt ans d'antisémitisme 1889–1899* (Paris, 1910)

Vigny, Alfred de, *Théâtre*, II, *Journal d'un poète* (Paris, no date—Nelson)

Vogüé, E.-M. de, *Les Morts qui parlent* (Paris, no date—Nelson)

Waleffe, Maurice de, *Quand Paris était un paradis: Mémoires 1900–1939* (Paris, 1947)

Wicart, E., *Les Deux Causes de la décadence du pays* (Roubaix, 1898)

Willard, Claude (ed.), *La Correspondance de Charles Brunellière (1880–1917)* (Paris, 1968)

Zévaès, Alexandre, *Au Temps du Boulangisme* (Paris, 1930)

Zévaès, Alexandre, *L'Affaire Dreyfus* (Paris, 1931)
Zévaès, Alexandre, *Henri Rochefort: Le Pamphlétaire* (Paris, 1946)
Zola, Émile, *L'Argent* (Paris, 1891)
Zola, Émile, *Paris* (Paris and London, 1898)
Zola, Émile, *Au Bonheur des Dames* (Paris, 1968)
Zola, Émile, *L'Affaire Dreyfus, La Vérité en marche* (Paris, 1969)
Zola, Émile, *Correspondance, Oeuvres complètes*, 14 (Paris, 1970)

SECONDARY WORKS

BOOKS

Ackerman, Nathan W. and Jahoda, Marie, *Anti-Semitism and Emotional Disorder: A Psychoanalytical Interpretation* (New York, 1950)
Adorno, T.W. et al., *The Authoritarian Personality* (New York, 1950)
Ageron, C.-R., *Les Algériens musulmanes et la France (1871–1919)* (Paris, 1968), 2 vols
Andler, Charles, *Vie de Lucien Herr (1864–1926)* (Paris, 1932)
Arbellot, Simon, *La Fin du boulevard* (Paris, 1965)
Arendt, Hannah, *The Origins of Totalitarianism* (Cleveland, 1962)
Armengaud, André, *La Population française au XIXe siècle* (Paris, 1971)
Astier Loutfi, Martine, *Littérature et colonialisme: L'expansion coloniale vue dans la littérature romanesque française 1871–1914* (Paris and The Hague, 1971)
Audry, Colette, *Léon Blum ou la politique du Juste: Essai* (Paris, 1955)
Augé-Laribé, Michel, *La Politique agricole de la France de 1880 à 1940* (Paris, 1950)
Avenel, Vicomte G.d', *Le Mécanisme de la vie moderne,* 1er série (Paris, 1898 and 1902)
Bakhtin, Mikhail, *Rabelais and His World* (Cambridge, Mass., 1968)
Banton, Michael (ed.), *The Social Anthropology of Complex Societies* (London, 1966)
Baron, Salo Wittmayer, *A Social and Religious History of the Jews* (New York and London, 1937–67), 12 vols
Barral, Pierre, *Les Agrariens français de Méline à Pisani* (Paris, 1968)
Barral, Pierre, *Le Département de l'Isère sous la Troisième République: Histoire sociale et politique* (Paris, 1962)
Barthes, Roland, *Mythologies* (London, 1973)
Baudouin, Charles, *Psychanalyse du symbole religieux* (Paris, 1957)
Beattie, John, *Other Cultures: Aims, Methods and Achievements of Social Anthropology* (London, 1964)
Beau de Loménie, E. de, *Edouard Drumont ou l'anticapitalisme national* (Paris, 1968)
Beauvoir, Simone de, *Privilèges* (Paris, 1955)
Bellanger, Claude, Godechot, Jacques, Guiral, Pierre and Terrou, Fernand (eds.), *Histoire générale de la presse française* (Paris, 1969–76), 5 vols
Bercé, Yves-Marie, *Croquants et nu-pieds: Les soulèvements paysans en France du XVIe au XIXe siècle* (Paris, 1974)
Biddiss, Michael D., *Father of Racist Ideology: The Social and Political Thought of Count Gobineau* (London, 1970)
Blanchard, Gérard, *Histoire de la bande dessinée* (Paris, 1974)

Blumenkranz, Bernhard (ed.), *Histoire des Juifs en France* (Toulouse, 1972)

Bollême, Geneviève, *La Bibliothèque bleue: La littérature populaire en France du XVIe au XIXe siècle* (Paris, 1971)

Bousquet-Mélou, Jean, *Louis Barthou et la circonscription d'Oloron (1889–1914)* (Paris, 1972)

Boussel, P., *L'Affaire Dreyfus et la presse* (Paris, 1966)

Bouvier, Jean, *Le Krach de l'Union Générale (1878–1885)* (Paris, 1960)

Bouvier, Jean, *Le Crédit Lyonnais de 1863 à 1882: Les années de formation d'une banque de dépôts* (Paris, 1961)

Bouvier, Jean, *Les Deux Scandales de Panama* (Paris, 1964)

Bramsted, Ernest K., *Aristocracy and the Middle Classes in Germany: Social Types in German Literature 1830–1900* (Chicago, 1964)

Braudel, Fernand, *The Mediterranean and the Mediterranean World in the Age of Philip II* (London, 1972–3), 2 vols

Brunschwig, Henri, *Mythes et réalités de l'impérialisme colonial français 1871–1914* (Paris, 1960)

Byrnes, Robert F., *Antisemitism in Modern France* (New Brunswick, 1950)

Certeau, Michel de, *La Possession de Loudun* (Paris, 1970)

Certeau, Michel de, *L'Absent de l'histoire* (Paris, 1973)

Chalmin, Pierre, *L'Officier français de 1815 à 1870* (Paris, 1957)

Chastenet, Jacques, *Histoire de la Troisième République*, III, *La République Triomphante 1893–1906* (Paris, 1955)

Chevalier, Louis, *Classes laborieuses et classes dangereuses à Paris pendant la première moitié du XIXe siècle* (Paris, 1958); also *Labouring Classes and Dangerous Classes* (London, 1973)

Choury, Maurice (ed.), *Les Poètes de la Commune* (Paris, 1970)

Cobb, Richard, *The Police and the People: French Popular Protest 1789–1820* (London, 1972)

Cohen, Stanley and Young, Jock (eds.), *The Manufacture of News: Deviance, Social Problems and the Mass Media* (London, 1973)

Cohn, Norman, *Warrant for Genocide: The Myth of the Jewish World-Conspiracy and the Protocols of the Elders of Zion* (London, 1967)

Curie, Ève, *Madame Curie* (London, 1938)

Dansette, Adrien, *Les Affaires de Panama* (Paris, 1934)

Dansette, Adrien, *Histoire religieuse de la France contemporaine* (Paris, 1965)

Dardenne, Henriette, *Godefroy Cavaignac: Un républicain du progrès aux débuts de la 3e République* (Paris, 1969)

Denis, Michel, *L'Eglise et la République en Mayenne, 1896–1906* (Paris, 1967)

Dictionnaire de biographie française (Paris, 1933–)

Digeon, Claude, *La Crise allemande de la pensée française (1870–1914)* (Paris, 1959)

Divry, Louis (abbé Rosat), *L'Abbé Garnier aux temps héroïques de l'apostolat des classes ouvrières* (Paris, 1936)

Dollard, John, *Caste and Class in a Southern Town* (New York, 1937 and 1957)

Dominique, Pierre, *Léon Daudet* (Paris, 1964)

Donnard, J.-H., *Les Réalités économiques et sociales dans La Comédie Humaine* (Paris, 1961)

Douglas, Mary, *Purity and Danger: An Analysis of Concepts of Pollution and Taboo* (London, 1966 and Harmondsworth, 1970)

Douglas, Mary, *Natural Symbols: Explorations in Cosmology* (Harmondsworth, 1973)

Dresse, Paul, *Léon Daudet vivant* (Paris, 1947)

Ducray, Camille, *Paul Déroulède 1846–1914* (Paris, no date)

Dumont, Louis, *Homo Hierarchicus: The Caste System and its Implications* (London, 1972)

Dumont, Patrick, *La Petite Bourgeoisie vue à travers les contes quotidiens du "Journal" (1894–1895): Etude de mentalité* (Paris, 1973)

Dupeux, Georges, *La Société française 1789–1970* (Paris, 1972)

Edelman, Murray, *The Symbolic Uses of Politics* (Urbana, Ill., 1974)

Erikson, Erik H., *Childhood and Society* (Harmondsworth, 1974)

Fabre, Daniel and Lacroix, Jacques, *La Vie quotidienne des paysans de Languedoc au XIXe siècle* (Paris, 1973)

Fabre, Daniel and Lacroix, Jacques (eds.), *Communautés du Sud: Contribution à l'anthropologie des collectivités rurales occitanes* (Paris, 1975), 2 vols

Ferenczi, S., *Contributions to Psycho-Analysis* (London, 1916)

Fiechter, J.-J., *Le Socialisme français: De l'Affaire Dreyfus à la Grande Guerre* (Geneva, 1965)

Foville, A. de, *La France économique, Statistique raisonnée et comparative* (Paris, 1890)

Freud, Sigmund, *Analysis of a Phobia in a Four-Year-Old Boy*, English Standard Edition, X (London, 1955)

Freud, Sigmund, *Leonardo da Vinci and a Memory of His Childhood*, English Standard Edition, XI (London, 1964)

Freud, Sigmund, *Moses and Monotheism: Three Essays*, English Standard Edition, XXIII (London, 1964)

Gadille, Jacques, *La Pensée et l'action politiques des évêques français au début de la IIIe République 1870–1883* (Paris, 1967), 2 vols

Gerbod, Paul, *La Condition universitaire en France au XIXe siècle* (Paris, 1965)

Gérin-Ricard, L. de and Truc, L., *Histoire de l'Action Française* (Paris, 1949)

Ginsberg, Morris, *Essays in Sociology and Social Philosophy* (Harmondsworth, 1968)

Girardet, Raoul, *La Société militaire dans la France contemporaine (1815–1939)* (Paris, 1953)

Girardet, Raoul, *Le Nationalisme français 1871–1914* (Paris, 1966)

Girardet, Raoul, *L'Idée coloniale en France de 1871 à 1962* (Paris, 1972)

Glock, Charles Y. and Stark, Rodney, *Christian Beliefs and Anti-Semitism* (New York, 1966)

Goguel, François, *La Politique des partis sous la Troisième République* (Paris, 1958)

Goguel, François, *Géographie des élections françaises sous la Troisième et la Quatrième République* (Paris, 1970)

Goldberg, Harvey, *The Life of Jean Jaurès* (Madison, 1962)

Guerrand, Roger-H., *Les Origines du logement social en France* (Paris, 1967)

Guillemin, Henri, *Présentation des Rougon-Macquart* (Paris, 1964)

Guillemin, Henri, *Zola légende et vérité* (Paris, 1971)

Guy-Grand, Georges, *La Philosophie nationaliste* (Paris, 1911)

Headings, Mildred J., *French Freemasonry under the Third Republic* (Baltimore, 1949)

Hernton, Calvin C., *Sex and Racism* (London, 1969)

Hertzberg, Arthur, *The French Enlightenment and the Jews* (New York, 1968)

Higonnet, Patrice L.-R., *Pont-de-Montvert: Social Structure and Politics in a French Village, 1700–1914* (Cambridge, Mass., 1971)

Hoffmann, Stanley, *Le Mouvement Poujade* (Paris, 1956)

Hofstadter, Richard, *The Paranoid Style in American Politics and other essays* (London, 1966)

Hommage à Marcel Reinhard: Sur la population française au XVIIIe et au XIXe siècles (Paris, 1973)

Hosmer, James K., *The Jews in Ancient, Mediaeval and Modern Times* (London, 1886)

Ionescu, Ghita and Gellner, Ernest (eds.), *Populism, Its Meanings and National Characteristics* (London, 1969)

Jackson, A.B., *La Revue Blanche (1889–1903): Origine, influence, bibliographie* (Paris, 1960)

Johnson, Douglas, *France and the Dreyfus Affair* (London, 1966)

Jolly, Jean (ed.), *Dictionnaire des parlementaires français: Notices biographiques sur les ministres, députés et sénateurs français de 1889 à 1940* (Paris, 1960–)

Juifs sous l'Occupation, Les, Centre de Documentation juive contemporaine (Paris, 1945)

Katz, Jacob, *Jews and Freemasons in Europe 1723–1939* (Cambridge, Mass., 1970)

Kayser, Jacques, *Les Grandes Batailles du radicalisme des origines aux portes du pouvoir, 1820–1901* (Paris, 1962)

Klein, Luce A., *Portrait de la Juive dans la littérature française* (Paris, 1970)

Kornhauser, William, *The Politics of Mass Society* (London, 1960)

Kriegel, Annie, *Le Pain et les roses: Jalons pour une histoire des socialismes* (Paris, 1973)

Larkin, Maurice, *Church and State after the Dreyfus Affair: The Separation Issue in France* (London, 1974)

Latreille, A. and Rémond, R., *Histoire du Catholicisme en France,* III (Paris, 1964)

Lecanuet, R.P., *L'Eglise de France sous la Troisième République,* I (Paris, no date [1907?])

Lecanuet, R.P., *La Vie de l'Eglise sous Léon XIII* (Paris, 1930)

Lefranc, Georges, *Le Mouvement socialiste sous la Troisième République (1875–1940)* (Paris, 1963)

Lehrmann, C., *L'Elément juif dans la littérature française* (Paris, 1960), 2 vols

Le Roy Ladurie, Emmanuel, *Les Paysans de Languedoc* (Paris, 1969)

Leuilliot, Paul, *L'Alsace au début du XIXe siècle: Essais d'histoire politique, économique et religieuse (1815–1830)* (Paris, 1960), 3 vols

Levasseur, E., *Questions ouvrières et industrielles en France sous la Troisième République* (Paris, 1907)

Lidsky, Paul, *Les Ecrivains contre la Commune* (Paris, 1970)

Ligou, Daniel, *Histoire du socialisme en France (1871–1961)* (Paris, 1962)

Loewenstein, Rudolph M., *Christians and Jews: A psychoanalytical study* (New York, 1951)

Lovsky, F., *La Déchirure de l'absence: Essai sur les rapports entre l'Eglise du Christ et le peuple d'Israël* (Paris, 1971)

Lukes, Steven, *Emile Durkheim: His Life and Work: A Historical and Critical Study* (London, 1973)

Madaule, Jacques, *Le Nationalisme de Maurice Barrès* (Marseille, 1943)

Mair, Lucy, *An Introduction to Social Anthropology* (Oxford, 1965)

Mair, Lucy, *Witchcraft* (London, 1973)

Maitron, Jean, *Histoire du Mouvement anarchiste en France (1880–1914)* (Paris, 1955)

Manévy, Raymond, *La Presse de la IIIe République* (Paris, 1955)

Maranda, Pierre (ed.), *Mythology* (Harmondsworth, 1972)

Marrus, Michael R., *The Politics of Assimilation: A Study of the French Jewish Community at the time of the Dreyfus Affair* (London, 1971)

Mayeur, J.-M., *Un Prêtre démocrate: L'abbé Lemire, 1853–1928* (Paris, 1968)

Memmi, Albert, *Portrait d'un Juif* (Paris, 1969)

Merlin, Pierre, *L'Exode rural*, Institut National d'Etudes Démographiques, Travaux et documents, Cahier no. 59 (Paris, 1971)

Miquel, Pierre, *L'Affaire Dreyfus* (Paris, 1968)

Mitterand, Henri, *Zola journaliste de l'Affaire Manet à l'Affaire Dreyfus* (Paris, 1962)

Molette, Charles, *Albert de Mun 1872–1890* (Paris, 1970)

Montuclard, Maurice, *Conscience religieuse et démocratie: La deuxième démocratie chrétienne en France 1891–1902* (Paris, 1965)

Morand, Jacqueline, *Les Idées politiques de Louis-Ferdinand Céline* (Paris, 1972)

Morin, Edgar *et al.*, *La Rumeur d'Orléans* (Paris, 1969)

Mosse, George L., *The Crisis of German Ideology: Intellectual Origins of the Third Reich* (London, 1966)

Mours, Samuel and Robert, Daniel, *Le Protestantisme en France du XVIIIe siècle à nos jours (1685–1970)* (Paris, 1972)

Mousnier, Roland, *Peasant Uprisings in Seventeenth-Century France, Russia and China* (London, 1971)

Néré, Jacques, *Le Boulangisme et la presse* (Paris, 1964)

Nisard, Charles, *Histoire des livres populaires ou de la littérature du colportage* (Paris, 1864)

Osgood, Samuel M., *French Royalism under the Third and Fourth Republics* (The Hague, 1960)

Ozouf, Mona, *L'Ecole, l'Eglise et la République 1871–1914* (Paris, 1963)

Partin, Malcolm O., *Waldeck-Rousseau, Combes and the Church: The Politics of Anticlericalism* (Durham, N.C., 1969)

Pataut, Jean, *Sociologie électorale de la Nièvre au XXe siècle (1902–1951)* (Paris, 1953)

Paugam, Jacques, *L'Age d'or du Maurrassisme* (Paris, 1971)

Perrot, Michelle, *Les Ouvriers en grève, France 1871–1890* (Paris and The Hague, 1974)

Perrot, M. and Kriegel, A., *Le Socialisme français et le pouvoir* (Paris, 1966)

Petit, Jacques, *Bernanos, Bloy, Claudel, Péguy: Quatre écrivains catholiques face à Israël. Images et mythes* (Paris, 1972)

Pierrard, Pierre, *Juifs et catholiques français: De Drumont à Jules Isaac (1886–1945)* (Paris, 1970)

Piou, Jacques, *Le Comte Albert de Mun: Sa vie publique* (Paris, no date [1919?])

Poliakov, Léon, *The History of Anti-Semitism* (London, 1966–75), 3 vols

Poliakov, Léon, *Les Juifs et notre histoire* (Paris, 1973)

Poulat, Emile, *Intégrisme et catholicisme intégral, Un réseau secret international antimoderniste: La Sapinière (1909–1921)* (Paris, 1969)

Prinet, Jean and Dilasser, Antoinette, *Nadar* (Paris, 1966)

Pulzer, P.G.L., *The Rise of Political Anti-Semitism in Germany and Austria* (New York, 1964)

Ralston, David B., *The Army of the Republic: The Place of the Military in the Political Evolution of France, 1871–1914* (Cambridge, Mass., 1967)

Randall, Earle Stanley, *The Jewish Character in the French Novel, 1870–1914* (Evanston, Ill., 1941)

Rémond, René, *La Droite en France de la première restauration à la Ve République* (Paris, 1963)

Rémond, René, *Les Deux Congrès ecclésiastiques de Reims et de Bourges 1896–1900: Un témoignage sur l'Eglise de France* (Paris, 1964)

Revel, Jean-François, *Les Idées de notre temps: Chroniques de "L'Express", 1966–1971* (Paris, 1972)

Reynaud, Stanlislas, *Le Père Didon: Sa vie et son oeuvre (1840–1900)* (Paris, 1904)

Richardson, Joanna, *Rachel* (London, 1956)

Richardson, Joanna, *Sarah Bernhardt* (London, 1959)

Robb, James H., *Working-Class Anti-Semite: A Psychological Study in a London Borough* (London, 1954)

Rollet, Henri, *L'Action sociale des Catholiques en France, 1871–1914* (Paris, 1948–58), 2 vols

Rollet, Pierre, *La Vie quotidienne en Provence au temps de Mistral* (Paris, 1972)

Rosenberg, Edgar, *From Shylock to Svengali: Jewish Stereotypes in English Fiction* (London, 1961)

Roudiez, Léon S., *Maurras jusqu'à l'Action Française* (Paris, 1957)

Rougerie, Jacques, *Paris libre 1871* (Paris, 1971)

Sartre, Jean-Paul, *Réflexions sur la question juive* (Paris, 1946 and 1954)

Schmidt, A.-M., *Maupassant par lui-même* (Paris, 1965)

Seager, Frederic H., *The Boulanger Affair: Political Crossroad of France 1886–1889* (Ithaca, 1969)

Seignobos, Charles, *L'Evolution de la IIIe République (1875–1914)* (Paris, 1921)

Selznick, Gertrude J. and Steinberg, Stephen, *The Tenacity of Prejudice: Anti-Semitism in Contemporary America* (New York, 1969)

Siegfried, André, *Tableau politique de la France de l'Ouest sous la Troisième République* (Paris, 1913 and 1964)

Siegfried, André, *Géographie électorale de l'Ardèche sous la Troisième République* (Paris, 1949)

Sorlin, Pierre, *Waldeck-Rousseau* (Paris, 1966)

Sorlin, Pierre, *"La Croix" et les Juifs (1880–1899): Contribution à l'histoire de l'antisémitisme contemporain* (Paris, 1967)

Sorlin, Pierre, *La Société française, 1840–1914* (Paris, 1969)

Soucy, Robert, *French Fascism: The Case of Maurice Barrès* (Berkeley, 1972)

Snyder, Louis L., *The Idea of Racialism* (New York, 1962)

Stern, Fritz, *The Politics of Cultural Despair: A Study in the Rise of the Germanic Ideology* (New York, 1965)

Stern, J.P., *Hitler, The Führer and the People* (London, 1975)

Sternhell, Zeev, *Maurice Barrès et le nationalisme français* (Paris, 1972)

Stokes, Richard L., *Léon Blum: From Poet to Premier* (London, 1937)

Szajkowski, Zosa, *Jews and the French Revolutions of 1789, 1830 and 1848* (New York, 1970)

Szasz, Thomas S., *The Manufacture of Madness: A Comparative Study of the Inquisition and the Mental Health Movement* (London, 1973)

Thibaudet, Albert, *Les Princes lorrains* (Paris, 1924)

Thomas, Keith, *Religion and the Decline of Magic: Studies in Popular Beliefs in Sixteenth- and Seventeenth-Century England* (Harmondsworth, 1973)

Thomas, Lucien, *L'Action Française devant l'Eglise* (Paris, 1965)

Toutain, J.-C., *La Population de la France de 1700 à 1959, Cahiers de l'Institut de Science Economique Appliquée,* Supplément no. 133 (Série AF, no. 3) (Paris, 1963)

Vaucelles, Louis de, *"Le Nouvelliste de Lyon" et la défense religieuse (1879–1889)* (Paris, 1971)

Verdès-Leroux, Jeannine, *Scandale financier et antisémitisme catholique: Le krach de l'Union Générale* (Paris, 1969)

Vidler, Alec R., *A Variety of Catholic Modernists* (Cambridge, 1970)

Weber, Eugen, *The Nationalist Revival in France, 1905–1914* (Berkeley, 1959)

Weber, Eugen, *Action Française, Royalism and Reaction in Twentieth-Century France* (Stanford, 1962)

Weber, Eugen, *Satan franc-maçon: La mystification de Léo Taxil* (Paris, 1964)

Webster, Richard A., *Christian Democracy in Italy 1860–1960* (London, 1961)

Werth, Alexander, *The Strange History of Pierre Mendès-France and the Great Conflict over French North Africa* (London, 1957)

Willard, Claude, *Le Mouvement socialiste en France (1893–1905): Les Guesdistes* (Paris, 1965)

Wirth, Louis, *The Ghetto* (Chicago, 1969)

Worsley, Peter, *The Trumpet Shall Sound: A Study of "Cargo" Cults in Melanesia* (London, 1957)

Zeldin, Theodore, *France 1848–1945*, I, *Ambition, Love and Politics* (Oxford, 1973)

Ziebura, Gilbert, *Léon Blum et le parti socialiste 1872–1934* (Paris, 1967)

Zola, Collection Génies et Réalités (Paris, 1969)

Zolla, D., *La Crise agricole dans ses rapports avec la baisse des prix et la question monétaire* (Paris, 1903)

ARTICLES AND PAPERS

Andréani, Roland, "L'Antimilitarisme en Languedoc méditerranéen avant la Première Guerre Mondiale", *Revue d'Histoire Moderne et Contemporain,* 20 (1973)

Barral, Pierre, "Géographie de l'opinion sous la Troisième République", *Information Historique* (1962)

Bédarida, François, "L'Armée et la République: Les opinions politiques des officiers français en 1876–8", *Revue Historique*, 232 (1964)

Bergman, Shlomo, "Some Methodological Errors in the Study of Antisemitism", *Jewish Social Studies*, 5 (1943)

Billig, J., "La Question juive", in *La France sous l'Occupation* (Paris, 1959)

Bordes, Maurice, "L'évolution politique du Gers sous la IIIe République", *Information Historique* (1961)

Bourguet, M.N., "Une race d'administrés: Les Français de l'An IX vus par leurs préfets", Paper given at Colloque sur l'Idée de Race dans la Pensée politique française (XVIIIème et XIXème siècles), Aix-en-Provence and Marseille, March 1975

Byrnes, Robert F., "Jean-Louis Forain: Antisemitism in French Art", *Jewish Social Studies*, 12 (1950)

Byrnes, Robert F., "The French Publishing Industry and its Crisis in the 1890s", *Journal of Modern History*, 23 (1951)

Charlot, Jean and Monica, "Un rassemblement d'intellectuels: La Ligue des Droits de l'Homme", *Revue Française de Science Politique*, 12 (1959)

Comas, Juan, "Racial Myths", in *Race and Science*, UNESCO (New York, 1969)

Dagen, François, "Courrier d'Algérie: Considérations sur les causes de la grandeur et de la décadence de l'antisémitisme en Algérie", *Cahiers de la Quinzaine*, 13ème cahier, 4ème série, February 1903

Daumard, A., "L'évolution des structures sociales en France à l'époque de l'industrialisation (1815–1914)", *Revue Historique*, 247 (1972)

Durieu, Louis, "Le prolétariat juif en Algérie", *Revue Socialiste*, 29 (1899)

Duroselle, J.-B., "L'Antisémitisme en France de 1886 à 1914", *Cahiers Paul Claudel*, 7, *La Figure d'Israël* (Paris, 1968)

Erikson, Erik H., "Hitler's Imagery and German Youth", *Psychiatry*, 4 (1942)

Fenichel, Otto, "Psychoanalysis of Antisemitism", *American Imago*, (1940)

Gamzon, Denise R., "Claudel rencontre Israel (1905–1920)", *Cahiers Paul Claudel*, 7 (1968)

Gaudin, Gérard, "Chez les Blancs du Midi: du légitimisme à l'Action Française", *Etudes Maurrassiennes*, 1 (1972)

Girardet, Raoul, "La Ligue des Patriotes dans l'histoire du nationalisme français, 1882–1888", *Bulletin de la Société d'Histoire Moderne*, douzième série, no. 6 (1958)

Guiral, Pierre, "Renan et Maurras", *Etudes Maurrassiennes*, 1 (1972)

Guiral, Pierre, "Montesquieu précurseur de l'idée d'inégalité des races", Paper given at Colloque sur l'Idée de Race, 1975

Jardin, "Alexis de Tocqueville, Gustave de Beaumont et le problème de l'inégalité des races", Paper given at Colloque sur l'Idée de Race, 1975

Jouveau, René, "L'itinéraire félibréen de Charles Maurras avant l'Action Française", *Etudes Maurrassiennes*, 1, (1972)

Klein, Charlotte, "Damascus to Kiev: *Civiltá Cattolica* on Ritual Murder", *Wiener Library Bulletin*, 27, New Series, no. 32 (1974)

Kren, George M. and Rappoport, Leon, "Victims: the fallacy of innocence", *Societas*, 4 (1974)

Landau, Lazare, "Aspects et problèmes spécifiques de l'histoire des Juifs en France", *Revue de l'Histoire de l'Eglise de France*, 59 (1973)

Leger, François, "Taine et Maurras", *Etudes Maurrassiennes*, 1 (1972)

Leger, François, "L'idée de race chez Taine", Paper given at Colloque sur l'Idée de Race, 1975

Levaillant, I., "La Genèse de l'antisémitisme sous la Troisième République", *Revue des Etudes Juives*, 53 (1907)

Lévy, Claude, "La presse de la Meuse devant les attentats anarchistes et les lois de répression (décembre 1893—juin-août 1894", in *Recherches sur les forces politiques de la France de l'Est*, Journées d'étude de Strasbourg organisées sous les auspices de l'Association Interuniversitaire de l'Est par l'Institut d'Etudes Politiques et la Faculté des Lettres et Sciences Humaines de Strasbourg, 1964 (Strasbourg, no date [1966?])

Lévy, Jean-Louis, "La vie du capitaine Dreyfus", in Dreyfus, *Cinq années de ma vie (1894–1899)* (Paris, 1962)

Marlin, R., "La Droite à Besançon", in *Recherches sur les forces politiques de la France de l'Est* (Strasbourg, no date)

Mayeur, J.-M., "Les Congrès nationaux de la 'Démocratie Chrétienne' à Lyon (1896–1897–1898)", *Revue d'Histoire Moderne et Contemporaine*, 9 (1962)

Mosse, George L., "The French Right and the Working Classes: Les Jaunes", *Journal of Contemporary History*, 7, nos 3–4 (1972)

Nguyen, Victor, "Un essai de pouvoir intellectuel au début de la Troisième République, *La Cocarde* de Maurice Barrès (5 septembre 1894–7 mars 1895)", *Etudes Maurrassiennes*, 1 (1972)

Nguyen, Victor, "Approche de la notion maurrassienne d'*héritage*", *Etudes Maurrassiennes*, 2 (1973)

Nguyen, Victor, "Race et civilisation chez Maurras", in *Missions et démarches de la critique: Mélanges offerts au Professeur J.A. Vier* (Paris, 1973)

Paz, Maurice, "La notion de race chez Blanqui et les révolutionnaires de son temps", Paper given at Colloque sur l'Idée de Race, 1975

Peter, J.-P., "Dimensions de l'Affaire Dreyfus", *Annales*, 16 (1961)

Pinsot, Jacques, "Quelques problèmes du socialisme en France vers 1900", *Revue d'Histoire Economique et Sociale*, 36 (1958)

Ponty, Janine, "La presse quotidienne et l'Affaire Dreyfus en 1898–1899: Essai de typologie", *Revue d'Histoire Moderne et Contemporaine*, 21 (1974)

Prajs, Lazare, "Péguy et le peuple juif", *Cahiers Paul Claudel*, 7 (1968)

Rose, Arnold, "The Roots of Prejudice" in *Race and Science*, UNESCO (New York, 1969)

Rouquier, Annie and Soumille, Pierre, "La Notion de Race chez les Français d'Algérie à la fin du 19e siècle", Paper given at Colloque sur l'Idée de Race, 1975

Schwarzschild, Steven S., "The Marquis de Morès: The Story of a Failure", *Jewish Social Studies*, 22 (1960)

Shapiro, Harry L., "The Jewish People: A Biological History", in *Race and Science*, UNESCO (New York, 1969)

Silberner, Edmund, "Charles Fourier on the Jewish Question", *Jewish Social Studies*, 8 (1946)

Silberner, Edmund, "Proudhon's Judeophobia", *Historia Judaica*, 10 (1948)

Silberner, Edmund, "French Socialism and the Jewish Question 1865–1914", *Historia Judaica*, 16 (1954)

Smith, Robert J., "L'atmosphère politique à l'Ecole Normale Supérieure à la fin du XIXe siècle", *Revue d'Histoire Moderne et Contemporaine,* 20 (1973)

Soumille, Pierre, "L'idée de race chez les Européens de Tunisie dans les années 1890–1910", Paper given at Colloque sur l'Idée de Race, 1975

Steenhuyse, D., "Quelques jalons pour l'étude du thème du 'Grand Soir' jusqu'en 1900", *Le Mouvement Social,* no. 75 (1971)

Sternhell, Zeev, "Barrès et la Gauche: du Boulangisme à *La Cocarde* (1889–1895)", *Le Mouvement Social,* no. 75 (1971)

Sternhell, Zeev, "Paul Déroulède and the Origins of Modern French Nationalism", *Journal of Contemporary History,* 6, no. 4 (1971)

Sternhell, Zeev, "Le déterminisme physiologique et racial à la base du nationalisme de Maurice Barrès et de Jules Soury", Paper given at Colloque sur l'Idée de Race, 1975

Szajkowski, Zosa, "The Decline and Fall of Provençal Jewry", *Jewish Social Studies,* 6 (1944)

Szajkowski, Zosa, "The Growth of the Jewish Population of France", *Jewish Social Studies,* 8 (1946)

Szajkowski, Zosa, "The Jewish Saint-Simonians and Socialist Antisemites in France", *Jewish Social Studies,* 9 (1947)

Szajkowski, Zosa, "Socialists and Radicals in the Development of Antisemitism in Algeria (1884–1900)", *Jewish Social Studies,* 10 (1948)

Szajkowski, Zosa, "French Jews during the Revolution of 1830 and the July Monarchy", *Historia Judaica,* 12 (1961)

Thuillier, Guy, "Un anarchiste positiviste: Georges Vacher de Lapouge", Paper given at Colloque sur l'Idée de Race, 1975

Verdès, Jeannine, "La presse devant le krach d'une banque catholique: l'Union Générale—1882", *Archives de Sociologie des Religions,* 19 (1965)

Viard, Jacques, "L'*Encyclopédie nouvelle* de Pierre Leroux et l'idée de race", Paper given at Colloque sur l'Idée de Race, 1975

Watson, D.R., "The Nationalist Movement in Paris, 1900–1906", in David Shapiro (ed.), *The Right in France 1890–1919,* St Antony's Papers, no. 13 (London, 1962)

Wilson, Stephen, "History and Traditionalism: Maurras and the Action Française", *Journal of the History of Ideas,* 29 (1968)

Wilson, Stephen, "The 'Action Française' in French Intellectual Life", *Historical Journal,* 12 (1969), and in John C. Cairns (ed.), *Contemporary France, Illusion, Conflict and Regeneration* (New York and London, 1978)

Wilson, Stephen, "Proust's *A la Recherche du temps perdu* as a Document of Social History", *Journal of European Studies,* 1 (1971)

Wilson, Stephen, "Fustel de Coulanges and the Action Française", *Journal of the History of Ideas,* 34 (1973)

Wilson, Stephen, "L'Action Française et le mouvement nationaliste français des années 1890 et 1900", Paper given at 4th Colloque Maurras, Aix-en-Provence, March 1974, in *Études Maurrassiennes,* 4 (1980)

Wilson, Stephen, "Catholic Populism in France at the time of the Dreyfus Affair: the *Union Nationale*", *Journal of Contemporary History,* 10 (1975)

Wilson, Stephen, "A View of the Past: Action Française Historiography and its socio-political function", *Historical Journal,* 19 (1976)

Wilson, Stephen, "Late Nineteenth-Century Nationalism and Imperialism in Europe: A Critique of the Manipulative Model", forthcoming

INDEX

Abel-Bernard, Emile (deputy), 217, 225, 227, 328
Absolute categories, 145, 146, 148, 149, 158, 261, 263, 482, 493, 558, 611, 613, 626, 631, 632, 634. *See also* Essentialism
Académie des Sciences, 295, 596
Académie Française, 57, 207, 382, 394, 539, 609, 643 n.73
"Accapareurs où sont-ils?, Les," 265
Action, 607, 609, 631, 642 n.52
Action, L', 562
Action Française (organization), 36, 37, 58, 210 n.71, 239, 240, 267, 272, 277, 284, 312 n.347, 328, 350, 364, 388–90, 397, 406, 420, 461, 526, 535, 557, 611, 614, 615, 632, 634, 642 n.52, 649 nn.274 and 283, 708, 735
Action Française, L' (newspaper), 95 n.28, 205, 210 n.71, 239, 398, 539
Action Libérale, 58, 525, 535
Actors and actresses. *See* Bernhardt, Sarah; Le Bargy, Simone; Rachel; Theatre
Adam, Edmond, 422
Adam, Paul, 257, 264, 381, 384, 399
Adorno, T. W., 604, 637, 743. *See also* Psychological and psychoanalytical approaches to the study of antisemitism
African Army, 138, 144, 434. *See also* Army; Officer Corps and army officers
Agen, 26, 32, 113, 121 n.16, 126
Agence Havas, 114

Agoult, Comtesse d', 480
Agricultural Association (of the Est), 19, 270, 673
Agricultural Commission, Chamber of Deputies, 270
Agricultural crisis and depression, 132, 133, 248, 269–71, 275, 277, 335, 342, 659, 736. *See also* Peasantry, and antisemitism; Rural antisemitism
Agricultural interests, 19, 267, 268, 270, 272, 308 n.246, 408, 431. *See also* Aristocracy; Landed estates; Landowners and landed interests
Ahasuerus, 298. *See also* Wandering Jew, myth of
Aims of antisemites, 157–9, 183, 185, 192, 193, 201–3, 491, 528, 671–87, 740. *See also* Assimilation; Boycott of Jewish shops and businesses; Civil rights and citizenship of Jews, and threats to; Discrimination exercised against Jews; Disenfranchisement of Jews, proposed; Emigration of Jews, forced; Exclusion from state service; Exemplary executions of Jews; Expropriation of Jews; Expulsion of Jews; Extermination of Jews; Ghetto; Jews in army; Legal discrimination against Jews, proposed; Sumptuary rules; Synagogues, attacks on; Verbal violence; Violence, antisemitic
Ain, 21, 22, 36, 130
Aisne, 10, 35, 128, 223, 224, 228, 668 n.16
Aix-en-Provence, 106, 120 n.6, 520, 556, 591, 662

Capitalism (*cont'd*)
the Jews, 208, 253–4, 260–3, 331–2.
See also Anti-capitalism; Banking
and banks; Cash nexus; Finance and
financiers; Money; Monopolies and
monopolization; Speculation, and
hostility towards; Wealth
Caran d'Ache, 208, 451 n.465, 607
Carentan, 144
Cargo cults, 158, 640
Carlyle, Thomas, 608, 629
Carmaux, 16
Carnot, President Sadi, 26, 295, 338,
492
Carpentras, 485, 699
Cash nexus, 252–4, 623. *See also*
Capitalism and capital; Money;
Social relations
Casimir-Périer, Jean, 65, 96 n.64, 320
Cassagnac, Paul de, 207, 215, 217, 223,
227, 383, 434, 510, 519, 529, 535,
675, 684
Castelin, André (deputy), 17, 213–14,
224, 228, 308 n.246, 384;
interpellation by, 11
Castellane, 132, 276
Castellane, Boni de, 132, 186, 228, 229
n.27, 272–4, 276–7, 309 n.282, 466,
614, 633
Castellane, Comte Jean de, 138
Castellane, Maréchal de, 276
Castellane, Marquis de, 305 n.180,
465–6
Castelnaudary, 228
Castration complex, 154, 164 n.176
Castres, 94 n.1
Catholic Church and Catholicism, 148,
154, 325, 400, 594–5, 632; attack on,
36, 419–20, 426, 480, 486, 511, 524,
528, 531, 542, 550, 553–7, 559–61,
562, 587, 603, 620, 624, 633, 659,
677, 707, 737; official attitude
towards Jews and antisemitism, 169,
511–12, 514–17, 519, 528, 547, 552,
561, 679; and politics, 83, 224, 225,
231, 277, 362, 525, 529; and social
order, 558–61, 620–2, 631, 632–3.
See also Anticlericalism; Bishops;
Christianity and Christians;
Clericalism; Concordat and
concordatory régime; Holy See;
Liturgy (Catholic); Ralliement and
Ralliés; Separation of Church and
State; Theological antisemitism
Catholic clergy, 135, 141, 148, 182,
190, 192, 219, 419, 588, 594, 597,

Catholic clergy (*cont'd*)
615; regular, 82, 112, 202, 265–6,
287, 347, 382, 399, 403, 406, 421,
522–4, 531, 537, 541, 553–4, 650
n.307, 736; secular, 28, 82, 130, 143,
145, 157, 511, 515, 519–20, 533,
535–40, 736. *See also* Bishops
Catholic clergy and antisemitism, 148,
517–18, 524–5, 555, 560, 569 n.87,
638, 665, 674, 680, 717, 735
Catholic Faculties, 75–6, 112, 607
Catholic opposition to antisemitism,
540–1
Catholic organizations and
antisemitism, 192, 517, 525 and ff.
Catholic press, 9, 82, 192, 207, 276,
397–8, 517–18, 519–20, 526, 532–3,
534, 539, 546, 557
Catholic schools, 58, 80, 82, 112, 147,
151, 404, 434, 565
Catholics, 9, 56, 57, 152, 253, 287,
288, 292, 293, 294, 347, 399, 403,
412, 436, 460, 462, 470, 482–3,
509–10, 514–15, 550, 556–7, 558–9,
563, 582 n.509, 587, 590, 595, 610,
617, 636, 686, 693, 706, 736; and
antisemitism, 102 n.182, 111–12,
115–16, 134, 138, 140, 148, 149,
171–3, 177 n.48, 182–3, 190, 192,
197, 198, 200, 202, 206, 207, 217,
219, 224, 226, 231–2, 234, 249, 252,
255, 265, 270–1, 285, 287, 289,
323–4, 350, 355, 357, 359, 385,
419–20, 460, 461, 472, 480, 510–11,
514, 517–18, 520 and ff., 532–3,
534–6, 541, 544, 556, 559–62, 565,
593, 612, 657, 659–60, 662, 664–7,
677, 736, 741; and army, 78; and
Dreyfus Affair, 9, 28, 56–7, 58, 78,
81–2, 91, 102 n.182 and 189, 107,
111–12, 115, 116, 120, 134, 138,
511, 520–4, 526–7, 533, 540, 563–4,
570 n.127, 715, 734; and
nationalism, 380, 530–1, 559, 561,
582 n.522; and race, 460, 461, 463,
468, 477. *See also* Assumptionists;
Bishops; Bourgeois and bourgeoisie,
Catholic; Christian Democracy;
Croix, La; Dechristianization;
Dominicans; Ecclesiastical Congress
of Reims; Franciscans; Integrism and
Integral Catholicism; Jesuits; Liberal
Catholics; Oratorians; Popular
Catholicism; Religious vitality, and
geography of; Social Catholicism;
Union Nationale